ARS ELECTRONICA 97
Festival für Kunst, Technologie und Gesellschaft /
Festival of Art, Technology and Society

Veranstalter/Organizers
Ars Electronica Center Linz GmbH
Geschäftsführer/Managing Directors
Gerfried Stocker, Wolfgang Modera
Hauptstraße 2, A-4040 Linz
Telefon: +43.732.7272-0
Fax: +43.732.7272-2
info@aec.at
http://www.aec.at
ORF Landesstudio Oberösterreich
Intendant/Director
Dr. Hannes Leopoldseder
Europaplatz 3, A-4020 Linz
Telefon: +43.732.6900-0
Fax: +43.732.6900-270
info@prixars.orf.at
http://prixars.orf.at

Direktorium, künstlerische Leitung/Directors
Gerfried Stocker,
Ars Electronica Center
Christine Schöpf,
ORF Landesstudio Oberösterreich

Produktion/Producer
Jutta Schmiederer
Assistenz/Assistants
Anne Feske, Karin Rumpfhuber, Miriam Spatt

Web Redaktion/Web Editors
Manuel Schilcher/Ars Electronica Center – Future Lab
Technische Leitung/Technical Directors
Horst Hörtner/Tom Teibler
Net Advisor
Oliver Frommel

Marketing, Sponsoring
Peter Schöber
Presse- und Öffentlichkeitsarbeit/Press Office
Maria Falkinger, Gabriele Hofer

Herausgeber/Editors
Gerfried Stocker, Christine Schöpf
Redaktion und Lektorat/Copy-Editing
Heimo Ranzenbacher, Ingrid Fischer-Schreiber, Jutta Schmiederer

Übersetzungen/Translations
Elfi Cagala, Mel Greenwald, Michael Kaufmann, Angela Kornberger, Elisabeth Kornberger, Wilfried Prantner, Susanne Steinacher, Richard Watts
Englisches Lektorat/Proofreading
Elizabeth McNeil, Sophie Kidd, Renée Paschen, Mona Schubert

Projektkooperation/
Project Co-operation
Remote Sensations
Veranstalter/Organizers
Ars Electronica Center, Linz &
Offenes Kulturhaus, Dametzstraße 30
4020 Linz
Projektkuratoren/Curators
Andrea Sodomka, Gerfried Stocker
Projektorganisation/Organization
Norbert Schweizer, Maria Pallier
Technik/Technical Realisation
Rainer Jessl, Horst Hörtner

Gestaltung/Design
Susanne Dechant,
Grafische Arbeiten, Wien
Layout
Sibylle Rauth, Czeslavia Pruscha
Umschlaggestaltung/Cover
Christian Korherr

Druck/Printing
A. Holzhausens Nfg., A-1070 Wien
Gedruckt auf säurefreiem, chlorfrei gebleichtem Papier - TCF

SPIN: 10631586
ISBN 3-211-82997-0
Springer-Verlag Wien New York

ARS

ELECTRONICA 97

SpringerWienNewYork

FLESHFACTOR

informationsmaschine mensch

Herausgeber/Editors
Gerfried Stocker
Christine Schöpf

FLESH FACTOR
informationsmaschine mensch

net symposium

symposium

installations

CAVE projects

remote sensations

events + performances

openX

Das Ars Electronica Center ist eine Einrichtung der Stadt Linz./
The Ars Electronica Center is an institution of the municipality of Linz.

Ars Electronica Center & Ars Electronica Festival werden unterstützt von/
are sponsored by:

Stadt Linz
Land Oberösterreich
Bundeskanzleramt/Kunstsektion

organizers

Ars Electronica Center

ARS ELECTRONICA CENTER

ORF-Landesstudio Oberösterreich

ORF OBER ÖSTERREICH

Remote Sensations in Kooperation mit dem Offenen Kulturhaus Linz.
Remote Sensations in co-operation with the Offenes Kulturhaus Linz.

CREDITANSTALT

ORACLE GMBH

DIGITAL EQUIPMENT ÖSTERREICH AG

QUELLE VERSAND

ERICSSON AUSTRIA

HEWLETT-PACKARD

SIEMENS NIXDORF

MICROSOFT AUSTRIA

SILICON GRAPHICS AUSTRIA

ÖSTERREICHISCHE BRAU AG

ÖSTERREICHISCHER RUNDFUNK

GERICOM

sponsors

KAPSCH · ARKADE · bene Büromöbel · DENZEL

Lufthansa OFFICIAL CARRIER · HAGO · Martin · MTEC Vertriebsgesellschaft mbH

Post & Telekom Austria · XART · pigi ETC Audiovisuell

RAMADA® HOTEL LINZ · Mailfast · ESG Verkehr

Prix Ars Electronica wird unterstützt von/ is sponsored by:

SIEMENS NIXDORF
VOEST-ALPINE STAHL
Stadt Linz
Land Oberösterreich
Gerhard Andlinger Company
Lufthansa

Ramada Hotel Linz
Mailfast
Casinos Austria AG
Silicon Graphics Austria
EDV-Zentrum der Johannes Kepler Universität

FleshFactor

Almost two decades of the digital revolution have been highlighted, analysed and critically assessed by Ars Electronica in the context of a *Festival of Art, Technology and Society*. This has been the period of our century in which the transition from the industrialised to the information-based society has assumed its hitherto most salient characteristics. Frequently, groundbreaking concepts and whole new branches of knowledge have been the subject of examination. Enormous strides have been made in order to encompass new topics and establish new modes of perception. And there appears to be no limitations on technological developments to come. Yet the concomitant social changes have already assumed such dimensions that we are now fascinated, no longer by the possibilities of future utopias, but rather by that which has already come to pass. The future seems to have reversed directions and is collapsing upon us.

FleshFactor – Informationsmaschine Mensch, the title of Ars Electronica 97, makes it clear that this year's theme is the Mensch, the human being. In light of the latest findings, developments and achievements in the fields of genetic engineering, neuro-science and networked intelligence, the conceptual complex now under investigation will include the status of the individual in networked artificial systems, the human body as the ultimate original, and the strategies for orientation and interrelation of the diametric opposites, man and machine, in the reciprocal, necessary processes of adaptation and assimilation.

Gerfried Stocker
Christine Schöpf

ars electronica 97

Fast zwei Dekaden der digitalen Revolution sind bereits von der Ars Electronica als *Festival für Kunst, Technologie und Gesellschaft*, kommentiert, analysiert und kritisiert worden. Jener Zeitraum unseres Jahrhunderts, in dem der Übergang von der Industrie- zur Informationsgesellschaft seine bislang sichtbarsten Ausformungen gezeigt hat. Neue Wissenschaftszweige und Innovationen standen dabei oft im Mittelpunkt. In weit ausholenden Schritten wurden Themen besetzt und Sichtweisen geprägt.

Ein Ende der technologischen Entwicklung ist nicht absehbar, jedoch hat die damit verbundene gesellschaftliche Veränderung mittlerweile ein Ausmaß erreicht, das nicht länger die Faszination des Utopischen, sondern die Realität des bereits Eingetroffenen zum Gegenstand unserer Aufmerksamkeit werden läßt. Die Zukunft hat gewissermaßen ihre Richtung geändert und bricht über uns herein.

FleshFactor – Informationsmaschine Mensch – unter diesem Titel wird bei der Ars Electronica 97 der Mensch zum Thema. Im Lichte der aktuellen Erkenntnisse, Ideen und Leistungen von Gentechnologie, Neuroscience und Vernetzter Intelligenz geht es um den Stellenwert des Individuums in vernetzten künstlichen Systemen, um den menschlichen Körper als letztes Original, um Beziehungs- und Orientierungsstrategien der Antipoden Mensch und Maschine im wechselseitigen Prozeß von Adaption und Assimilation.

Gerfried Stocker
Christine Schöpf

Ars Electronica Research and Residence

Gerfried Stocker/
Wolfgang Modera

One year ago with the commencement of the Ars Electronica Festival *Memesis – The Future of Evolution*, the *Ars Electronica Center – Museum of the Future* was officially launched and sent on its mission. Our objective was to set a trajectory appropriate to this enterprise and its new start. A program on the basis of architecture serving solely a showcase function would have reduced the Center's task to one of merely establishing the institutional preconditions for its having become a museum. It is incumbent upon a Museum of the Future, however, to assume a creative as well as dynamic posture in confronting the challenges before it. Merely moving into a new building, administering its facilities and looking after its visitors is not sufficient to completely fulfill this responsibility. A fundamental consideration in formulating the Center's program had to do with its positioning within the environment to which it owes its existence – the nearly 20-year history of the Festival and the Prix Ars Electronica. On one hand, a commitment was made to nurture and support art's leading edge, helping it to discover a new conception of itself through ven-

Ars Electronica Research and Residence

Gerfried Stocker/
Wolfgang Modera

Vor einem Jahr wurde mit dem Auftakt des Ars Electronica Festivals *Memesis – Die Zukunft der Evolution*, das *Ars Electronica Center –Museum der Zukunft* offiziell seiner *Bestimmung* übergeben. In Angriff genommen, wäre eine diesem Betrieb und seinem Start eher angemessene Wendung.

Ein Programm auf Basis von Architektur mit Schaufensterfunktion allein liefe bloß dahingehend, daß es das Haus als Museum seiner selbst präkonditioniert. Als Museum der Zukunft ist es hingegen beauftragt, sich ihren Herausforderungen sowohl kreativ wie auch offensiv zu stellen. Damit, daß ein Haus bezogen, seine Einrichtungen verwaltet und Besucher betreut werden, würde diesem Anspruch nicht Genüge getan.

Eine Grundüberlegung zur Programmatik betraf daher die Positionierung des Center in jenem Umfeld, dem es sich verdankt – der nahezu 20jährigen Geschichte des Festivals und des Prix Ars Electronica. Einerseits war es die avancierte Kunst, die in ihrem Unterfangen, infolge der digitalen Revolution zu einem neuen Selbstverständnis zu finden, auf ihre Eignung hin, sich als kultureller Kompetenz-

tures undertaken in the wake of the Digital Revolution and to establish its rightful place as a leading cultural force. On the other hand, in light of the ongoing process of *media-morphosis,* our overall culture called for the creation of a center of technological expertise which would be in a position to function as a mediator among artists, scientists and the general public.

At present, the Center is pursuing this goal through the operation of three exemplary departments: Education, Living Space & City Planning/CyberCity, and Virtual Reality. The capabilities and know-how of artists, both in dealing with new media as well as in communicating with the public, have taken on increased significance here, precisely in conjunction with new, interactive technology-based strategies for the dissemination of learning. These qualities have been implemented and placed directly into service in the form of *Future Lab*, Austria's best-equipped *laboratory/studio* for the development of VR, Web, and visualization/simulation applications in areas ranging from city planning to neurology. Our staff currently includes as many as 35 individuals working on more than 40 projects, and linked to a network including various university departments, private firms and research institutions. And we have opened up another new path with the establishment of the *Ars Electronica Research & Residence Program* in context with *Future Lab*.

Within this framework, our guests are able to stay abreast of research efforts as well as to experience the production of projects in an aesthetic context. In this respect, we have enjoyed tangible success in making available artistic skills and promoting understanding for technical and theoretical matters. Thus, we continue to approach our goal – namely, to transform interdisciplinarity from a conceptual ideal to a functional on-the-job reality, and, as a result, to become a decisive factor in the emergence of a fruitful field of endeavor. With the personnel, hardware and infrastructure it has assembled, and the double role as a place for production and presentation it has assumed, positioned between the *fronts* of art, science and society, the Ars Electronica Center has already established itself as a model.

träger zu etablieren, bestärkt werden sollte. Andererseits sollte angesichts der *Mediamorphose* unserer Kultur selbst ein technologisches Kompetenzzentrum geschaffen werden, das auch eine Mittlerfunktion zwischen Kunst, Wissenschaft und Gesellschaft zu erfüllen imstande ist.

Gegenwärtig wird dieses Ziel vermittels dreier exemplarischer Abteilungen des Center verfolgt: Bildung/Education, Lebensraum & Stadtplanung/CyberCity und Virtual Reality. Der Fähigkeit und dem Know-how von Künstlern sowohl im Umgang mit neuen Medien als auch in der Kommunikation mit dem Publikum kommt gerade bei neuen, auf interaktiven Technologien gegründeten Vermittlungsstrategien verstärkt Bedeutung zu. Direkt in *Dienst gestellt* wurden diese Eigenschaften am *Future Lab*, dem österreichweit bestausgestatteten *Labor/Atelier* zur Entwicklung von VR-, Web- sowie Visualisierungs- und Simulationsanwendungen in Bereichen von Stadtplanung bis Neurologie. Derzeit betreuen bis zu 35 MitarbeiterInnen, vernetzt mit verschiedenen universitären Instituten, Unternehmen und Forschungseinrichtungen, mehr als 40 Projekte.

Ein ebenfalls neuer Weg wurde mit dem *Ars Electronica Research & Residence-Program* im Zusammenhang mit dem *Future Lab* eingeschlagen.

Unsere Gäste verfolgen in diesem Rahmen Forschungsaufgaben ebenso wie die Realisierung von Vorhaben im Kontext des Ästhetischen. Dabei gelingt es zusehends, künstlerische Fertigkeit und Verständnis für technische und theoretische Belange zu erschließen. Es erfolgt die Annäherung an eines unserer Ziele, nämlich das Interdisziplinarität betreffende Wunschbild in ein funktionierendes Arbeitsverhältnis zu verwandeln und folglich für das Entstehen eines fruchtbaren Umfeldes maßgeblich zu werden. Die gerätetechnische und personelle Infrastruktur, die Doppelfunktion als Produktions- und Präsentationsort und die Positionierung zwischen den *Fronten* Kunst/Wissenschaft/Gesellschaft haben bereits Modellcharakter.

FleshFactor

Gerfried Stocker

Das Tiefste, was der Mensch besitzt, ist seine Haut.
Paul Valéry

The appearance of a new machine – the computer, the information machine – on the scene in the Western World has been followed by the development of a dynamic force which has left no sphere of life untouched. This invasion of a new technology has been accompanied not only by the marketing strategies of the corporations involved in it, but also by the active participation and tremendous enthusiasm on the part of artists. To a considerably stronger and more deep-seated extent than was the case with the Industrial Revolution which preceded it, the Information Revolution was, from its very inception, a matter of intense concern to art and culture, which not only reflected this process of change but were also fundamentally transformed and redefined by it.

It has not been the computer itself, nor the peripheral hardware it has gathered around it, which have been the object of artistic fascination, but rather the computer's suitability as a vehicle to transcend the boundaries of our imagination. The vision of technical possibilities, in the hands and minds of artists, is a particularly appropriate means to provide a description of the world, as well as to deliver explanatory

FleshFactor

Gerfried Stocker

Das Tiefste, was der Mensch besitzt, ist seine Haut.
Paul Valéry

Dem Erscheinen einer neuen Maschine, der Informationsmaschine Computer, auf der Bildfläche der westlichen Welt ist unterdessen die Entwicklung einer Dynamik gefolgt, die alle Lebensbereiche erfaßt hat. Begleitet wird diese Invasion einer neuen Technologie nicht nur von den Marketingstrategen der darin involvierten Konzerne, sondern auch mit großer Anteilnahme und Begeisterung von Künstlern. Die informationelle Revolution war – in wesentlich stärkerem und tiefgreifenderem Ausmaß als die vorausgegangene industrielle – von Anbeginn ein Anliegen der Kunst und Kultur, wurde von diesen nicht nur widergespiegelt, sondern hat sie in ihren Konzepten verändert und neu definiert.

Nicht der Computer und seine ihm abgewonnenen gerätetechnischen Derivate sind Gegenstand der künstlerischen Faszination, sondern seine Eignung als Vehikel der Überschreitung unserer

models of process which lie beyond our knowledge or the limits of our direct experience.

In the almost two decades of Ars Electronica's existence, its central thematic focus has continually been on these emerging visions of the future. New branches of knowledge and groundbreaking innovations have been introduced into the cultural discourse. Enormous strides have been made to encompass new topics and encourage new modes of perception. However, most of the utopias and visions of the future upon which the majority of artists, art theorists and philosophers have oriented their confrontation [and coquetry] with the new information technologies have, in the meantime, been completely overtaken by the current state of technological and social development. Even if, in many cases, we still have a long way to go to achieve broad-based integration or full industrial implementation, these large-scale designs have nevertheless become a part of our reality – several, indeed, boding ill to the extent that they have gone aground in the recognition of their erroneousness.

The future has changed direction to a certain extent; it is coming right at us, or even collapsing upon us and upon a society that is [still] unprepared for this encounter. This became particularly evident in what has subsequently been referred to as the *Dolly effect* or the *Dolly trauma* – the events which occurred in the wake of the public disclosure of the successful efforts of Ian Wilmuth and his staff. All sides were forced to acknowledge that the process of legally regulating genetic engineering had failed to take into account the possibility of cloning a mammal, much less a human being, a matter which had not even been considered with respect to patent law, to say nothing of an examination of its ethical dimensions. Hastily-convened expert commissions were everywhere – trying to perform damage control in the media, making assertions and counter-assertions, advising us to rest assured ... For the first time since the Middle Ages, a legal limitation upon the technically-scientifically possible is being called for – not merely on the form of its application, but rather on the research process itself.

But let's get back to the digital revolution as a motor of leading-edge models of the future of our society and of mankind itself, as

Vorstellungswelt. Die Vision technischer Möglichkeiten ist in den Händen/Köpfen der Künstler vor allem ein geeignetes Mittel zur Beschreibung der Welt, für Erklärungsmodelle von Vorgängen, die außerhalb unseres Wissens bzw. unserer unmittelbaren Erfahrungsgrenzen liegen.

In der nunmehr schon fast zwei Jahrzehnte langen Geschichte der Ars Electronica standen die daraus erwachsenen Zukunftsvisionen stets im thematischen Mittelpunkt, neue Wissenschaftszweige und Innovationen wurden in den kulturellen Diskurs eingeführt. In weit ausholenden Schritten wurden Themen besetzt und Sichtweisen geprägt. Doch der Großteil jener Utopien und Zukunftsvisionen, auf die hin die Auseinandersetzung [das Kokettieren] mit den neuen Informationstechnologien durch Künstler, Kunsttheoretiker und Philosophen mehrheitlich orientiert war/ist, wird mittlerweile vom Status quo der technologischen und gesellschaftlichen Entwicklung überholt. Wenngleich noch oft von einer breiten Integration oder ihrer industriellen Umsetzung entfernt, so sind die großen Entwürfe mittlerweile Teil unserer Realität, einige allerdings mit negativem Vorzeichen, insofern als sie sich im Wissen um ihre Abwegigkeit erledigt haben.

Die Zukunft hat gewissermaßen ihre Richtung geändert, kommt auf uns zu bzw. bricht über uns herein, über eine Gesellschaft, die auf diese Begegnung [noch immer] nicht vorbereitet ist.

Dies hat sich vor allem an den mittlerweile als *Dolly-Effekt* oder *Dolly-Trauma* bezeichneten Geschehnissen im Anschluß an die Veröffentlichung des Erfolgs von Ian Wilmuth und seinem Team gezeigt, als vielenorts erkannt werden mußte, daß man übersehen hatte, in den gesetzlichen Regelungen zur Gentechnologie das Klonen von Säugetieren, insbesondere des Menschen, mitzudenken [weder patentrechtlich und sowohl als auch von seiner ethischen Dimension]. Allenorts eilig zusammengerufene Expertenkommissionen, bemüht um mediale Schadensbegrenzung, beteuerten sich gegenseitig, daß man doch nie und nimmer ...

Zum ersten Mal seit dem Mittelalter soll dem technisch, wissenschaftlich Möglichen nicht bloß in der Form seiner Anwendung, sondern in der Erforschung selbst gesetzlicher Einhalt geboten werden.

Doch zurück zur digitalen Revolution, als Motor avancierter Zukunftsmodelle unserer Gesellschaft und des Menschen selbst, als *ars electronica.* Die durch sie möglich gewordene Beherrschung der biologischen Grundlagen des Lebens, die auf digitaler

an *ars electronica.* The mastery of the biological basis of life which has been made possible in the wake of this revolution and the digital technology-based methods of neuroscience – such as the scanning of brain functions by means of Positron Emission Tomography, Magnetic Resonance Imaging and similar technologies which enable real-time observation and control of the function of even an individual gene in our brain – increasingly turn our attention from the machine to mankind itself. The idea of being able not only to form the body on the level of the flesh-machine but also to be able to elaborate it as to its facilities and talents demands a new reflective perspective upon its ultimate boundaries: its social and metaphysical constitution.

The technological link-up of the human brain and the computer – a basic plot element of all cyborg fantasies – is still far off in the future; and furthermore, as scientist Peter Fromherz discusses in his paper for this year's symposium, it is a highly speculative matter at best whether this will ever become a reality. Nevertheless, the theoretical conjecture of a technological outfitting and enhancement of the human body by means of biomechanical and neurobionic prostheses has initiated an ongoing discourse, inherent in which is a deconstruction of our social order as one necessarily based upon the hierarchies of natural law.

The Information Society has become a real organizational form of Western Civilization. Its repercussions in the wake of network-linkage on a global scale – in capital markets, for instance – are realities which have long since exerted an influence upon the circumstances of life of even those human beings who do not themselves have either a computer or online access. The Information Society's socioeconomic structure, its working and living conditions, and its system of norms and values all exhibit signs of the erosion of central control systems accompanying the shifts taking place between the public and private spheres, and are characterized by the abandonment of an organic, hierarchical conception of order legitimated by natural law. The classic Western model of the individual as an autonomous, inwardly-oriented entity is being dropped in favor of a hybrid, networked subjectivity, whereby we comprehend ourselves as dynamic interfaces in a

Technologie basierenden neurowissenschaftlichen Methoden wie z. B. die Beobachtung der Funktionsabläufe unseres Gehirns durch PET [Positronen Emmisions Tomographie]- bzw. MRT [Magnet Resonanz Tomographie]-ähnliche Techniken, mit denen die Funktion einzelner Gene in unserem Gehirn in Echtzeit beobachtet und bestimmt werden kann, lenken unsere Aufmerksamkeit zunehmend von der Maschine auf den Menschen. Die Vorstellung, den Körper nicht nur auf der Ebene der Fleisch-Maschine formen, sondern in seinen Anlagen und Talenten konstruieren zu können, erzwingt eine neue Perspektive der Reflexion über dessen Grenzen, seine soziale und metaphysische Konstitution.

Die technologische Verbindung von menschlichem Gehirn und Computer – Grundbaustein aller Cyborgphantasien – ist nach wie vor weit entfernt, ist, wie der Wissenschaftler Peter Fromherz in seinem Beitrag zum diesjährigen Symposion darlegt, bestenfalls in spekulativer Reichweite. Dennoch hat die theoretische Imagination einer technischen Aufrüstung und Verbesserung des Menschen durch biomechanische und neurobionische Prothesen einen nachhaltigen Diskurs einer Dekonstruktion unserer Gesellschaftsordnung als eine auf naturgesetzlichen Hierachien aufbauende eingeleitet.

Die Informationsgesellschaft ist eine reale Organisationsform der westlichen Zivilisation geworden, ihre Auswirkungen im Gefolge einer globalen Vernetzung, z. B. der Kapitalmärkte, sind eine Realität, die längst auch all jene Menschen in ihren Lebensumständen bestimmt, die selbst nicht an Computern oder Netzwerken sitzen. Die Informationsgesellschaft ist in ihrer sozioökonomischen Struktur, ihren Arbeits- und Lebensbedingungen, Normen- und Wertesystem durch die Erosion zentraler Kontrollsysteme in der Verschiebung von Öffentlichem und Privatem geprägt, durch die Ablöse eines organisch, naturgesetzlich legitimierten hierarchischen Ordungsbegriffs. Das klassische abendländische Modell des Individuums als autonome, nach innen gewandte Entität wird zugunsten einer hybriden, vernetzten Subjektivität aufgegeben, in der wir uns als dynamische Knoten in einem sozialen Kommunikationsnetz begreifen.

1996 standen mit *Memesis* – unter Bezugnahme auf die von Richard Dawkins geprägte Idee der Meme [als kulturelle Informationseinheiten in Analogie zu den Genen] – Modelle der Ereignisse und Theorien kultureller Transformationsprozesse im Zentrum, ihre Beschreibung und die Analyse etwaiger Gesetzmäßigkeiten. Dabei wurde sehr schnell

social communications network.

In 1996, with our festival theme *Memesis* – a reference to the term *meme* coined by Richard Dawkins to characterize cultural units of information analogous to genes – we focused upon models of events and theories of cultural transformation processes, their description, and the analysis of possible conformities to laws governing their behavior. Over the course of this discussion, it quickly became evident that the consideration of this topic – in a more precisely stated form – would have to be resumed and carried on. *FleshFactor* is dedicated to this endeavor – focusing the global, cultural perspective taken in *Memesis* from the collective down to the Indlvldual level.

The point of departre for these considerations will be the relational and orientational strategies of those two antipodes – man and machine – in the mutually interdependent process of adaptation and assimilation, whereby the human being as well as the components of the technical systems surrounding him are reciprocally determining variables. The environment upon which we humans orient ourselves is, to an increasing extent, an artificial, completely network-linked and [although the term must be used with caution] intelligent system of high density and complexity; consequently, we are now able to relate to this environment only with the support of an equally intelligent environment of machines and media as a subset of this system. To the extent that the membranes of our body and our thinking are penetrated by the elements of a network-linked, intelligent environment, an ever more substantial magnitude is assumed by this environment, such that we find ourselves in a relationship of such intensive intimacy that a clear separation in the sense of a subject-object differentiation is no longer possible. And in this process, the qualification of our partner in this relationship with respect to its natural or technological/artificial attributes becomes a matter of secondary importance.

A conceptual model has been put forth, according to which scientific revolutions proceed in two phases: first comes the discovery or invention; then, its cultural introduction into our world and the changes which emerge therefrom. To which a third must be added: that of cultural assimilation into society, the phase in

die Notwendigkeit einer fortgesetzten Beschäftigung mit diesem Thema – in Form einer Präzisierung – evident. *FleshFactor* widmet sich mithin dem Versuch, die globale kulturelle Perspektive, wie sie durch *Memesis* eingenommen wurde, vom Kollektiv auf das Individuum zu fokussieren.

Zum Ausgangspunkt der Betrachtungen werden dabei Beziehungs- und Orientierungsstrategien der Antipoden Mensch und Maschine im wechselseitigen Prozeß von Adaption und Assimilation, in dem der Mensch ebenso wie die Elemente des ihn umgebenden technischen Systems sich gegenseitig beeinflussende Variablen sind.

Die Umwelt, an der wir Menschen uns orientieren, ist zunehmend ein artifizielles, vollständig vernetztes und [wenngleich der Begriff mit Vorsicht zum Einsatz kommen muß] intelligentes System von hoher Dichte und Komplexität, als dessen Konsequenz wir unsere Beziehung zu dieser Umwelt nur mehr mit Unterstützung einer ebenso intelligenten Maschinen- und Medienumgebung als Teilmenge dieses Systems betreiben können.

In dem Ausmaß, in dem die Membranen unseres Körpers und Denkens von den Elementen einer vernetzten intelligenten Umwelt durchdrungen werden, erwächst diese zu einer realen Größe, zu der wir uns in derart intensiv-intimer Beziehung finden, daß eine klare Trennung im Sinne einer Subjekt-Objekt-Differenzierung nicht länger möglich ist. Die Qualifizierung unserer Beziehungspartner hinsichtlich ihrer natürlichen oder technologischen/künstlichen Merkmale tritt dabei in den Hintergrund.

Es gibt das Modell, nach dem wissenschaftliche Revolutionen in zwei Phasen vor sich gehen: erst die Entdeckung bzw. Erfindung, dann deren kulturelle Einführung in unsere Welt und die daraus erwachsenden Veränderungen.

Dem ist eine dritte hinzuzufügen: die ihrer kulturellen Assimilation durch die Gesellschaft, in der die Apparate ihre Natur als eine kulturelle etablieren. Dieser Moment ist der eigentlich evolutionäre einer technologischen Revolution. Natürlich handelt es sich dabei aber um keine inhärente Eigenkraft der Geräte, dies entsteht durch den simplen Gebrauch, eben jene wechselseitige Adaption und Assimilation, in der die morphologische Fremdheit neuer Komponenten in die Gestaltung unserer Lebensräume, unseres Alltags integriert werden. In ubiquitärer Präsenz werden sie transparent, zu einer selbstverständlichen, weil gewohnt empfundenen, alltäglichen Größe, unserer Lebenswelt [so geschehen bei elektrischem Strom, Telefon, Radio und TV].

which these implements establish their nature as a cultural one. It is this moment that is the truly evolutionary one during a technological revolution. Of course, this has nothing to do with any inherent powers on the part of the implements themselves; this comes about simply as a result of their use – the reciprocal process of adaptation and assimilation, in which the morphological strangeness of new components is integrated into the design of our living spaces and our everyday lives. In their ubiquitous presence, they become transparent, something taken completely for granted, perceived as a familiar and rather mundane aspect of our day-to-day existence – the way we now regard electric power, the telephone, radio and TV.

In this way, the boundaries between man and machine, nature and technology become increasingly difficult to perceive. Up until now, the decisive criteria of differentiation have been based upon a *technomorphology* in which technology comes across as a world of devices which surrounds or lies outside of us. In the camouflage and mimicry of industrial research campaigns to develop *wearable computing,* *thinking things* etc., attributes which permit us to discriminate between man and machine become somewhat fuzzy. Seamless, unencumbered interfaces are to replace the manual ones. Instead of being faced by the inconvenient task of learning about functional capabilities and operational details, it is hoped that mankind in the future will interact with a technological environment whose intelligent agents, trained in the algorithmic and empirical interpretation of our individual actions, will be able to anticipate our desires before we know them ourselves. Now, we can only welcome our liberation from the substantial burden of hardware. After all, why should it only be the human body which is perceived as an encumbrance when, as far as intelligence is concerned, the realm of devices still has a lot of catching up to do in order to even come close to living up to the hopes to which it has given rise? Nevertheless, it is a questionable expenditure of innovative effort to achieve this amalgamation of humanity with its technological environment if sensory perception as the decisive quality is not the ultimate goal of these strivings, and if devices and strategies are not developed whose objective is to make us aware of – or to enable

In zunehmendem Maße verschwindet dabei die Wahrnehmbarkeit der Grenzen zwischen Mensch und Maschine, Natur und Technik. Die maßgeblichen Unterscheidungskriterien fußten bislang auf einer *Technomorphologie*, in der sich Technik als eine um uns bzw. außerhalb von uns liegende Apparatewelt zu erkennen gibt. In der Camouflage und Mimikry industrieller Forschungsoffensiven für *wearable computing* *things that think* etc. verlieren diese Unterscheidungsmerkmale ihre Schärfe. *Seamless, unencumbered Interfaces* sollen die Manuale ablösen. Ohne vom Wissen um Funktion, Handhabung und Bedienung geplagt zu sein, so die Hoffnung, wird der Mensch künftig mit einer technologischen Umwelt interagieren, deren intelligente Agenten, trainiert an der algorithmischen und empirischen Interpretation unseres individuellen Handelns, erraten werden, was wir wollen, noch bevor wir selbst es wissen.

Nun ist die Befreiung von der feststofflichen Last der Hardware nur zu begrüßen [wieso auch soll es nur dem menschlichen Körper so ergehen, daß er als Last empfunden wird, hat doch auch in punkto Intelligenz die Apparatewelt noch viel aufzuholen, wenn sie den durch sie entstandenen Hoffnungen auch nur annähernd entsprechen will], doch ist die Sinnhaftigkeit innovatorischen Engagements hinsichtlich einer Verschmelzung des Menschen mit seiner technologischen Umwelt zweifelhaft, wenn nicht sinnliche Wahrnehmung als entscheidende Qualität angestrebt wird, wenn nicht Geräte und Strategien entwickelt werden, deren Zielsetzung es ist, die Wechselwirkung zwischen realkörperlichen und virtuellen, telepräsenten Manifestationen unseres Handelns als einen Prozeß der Kommunikation und Beziehung mit dem technologischen, apparativen Ambiente bewußt zu machen bzw. bewußt erlebbar zu machen.

Die gängige Vorstellung von der Ergonomie eines Interface bezieht sich auf Benutzerfreundlichkeit, bei der die Funktionsweise versteckt und der Bedienungsvorgang transparent werden soll – unmerkliche, unsichtbare Interfaces, die sich nahtlos an uns anpassen und uns so das Leben erleichtern. Das mag in vielerlei Hinsicht durchaus sinnvoll sein, z. B. beim Verlassen eines Supermarkts, dessen Türen sich automatisch öffnen und schließen. Dann wäre wohl auch noch ein intelligentes Auto wünschenswert, das erkennt, wenn sich sein rechtmäßiger Besitzer vollbepackt mit Einkaufstaschen nähert und ihm sofort automatisch den Kofferraum öffnet [und ihn vielleicht noch daran erinnert, daß er vergessen hat, Milch einzukaufen]. Es wird egal

us to consciously experience – the reciprocities between real, physical manifestations of our actions and virtual, telepresent ones as a process of communicating with and relating to the technological ambiance of applied devices.

The customary conception of the relative ergonomics of an interface refers to its user-friendliness, whereby the way a device functions can well remain hidden but the method of using ought to be obvious – imperceptible, invisible interfaces smoothly adapted to us and making our lives easier. That seems to make sense in many respects, such as being able to leave a supermarket through doors which automatically open and close. And, it would also surely be desirable to have an intelligent car which could recognize that its legal owner, loaded down with shopping bags, is approaching it and immediately opens the trunk for him automatically [and perhaps even reminds him that he forgot to buy milk]. It is a matter of indifference whether the hidden mechanisms are easy to recognize and understand. However, when such processes take place within more complex systems and the transition from a person's real actions and presence to a virtual action/consequence or presence cannot be consciously experienced and perceived, then this will directly result in decisive deficiencies in the full exploitation of the potential of these technologies. If the whole point is to place humanity in a position to more satisfactorily and efficiently deal with its environment, then interfaces are required which make possible the sensory perception of this communications process, this transition between the real world and the virtual one, between the physical and digital aggregate state of information. That is one of the possible FleshFactors – the human capability of deriving associations and interpretations from perceptive faculties across the entire sensory spectrum on the basis of an enormous inventory of experiential data. Something that is often defined as a characteristic of human creativity.

There has long been talk of new cultural techniques that are adequate to these changed conditions. The capability of dealing with phenomena like telepresence and virtual identities [in the sense of a cognitive design of these spheres of action and effect] will increasingly assume decisive significance in this matter. And

sein, ob die verborgenen Mechanismen durchschaubar und erkennbar sind.

Wenn solche Vorgänge jedoch innerhalb komplexerer Systeme erfolgen und der Übergang von der realen Handlung und Präsenz einer Person zu einer virtuellen Handlung bzw. Auswirkung oder Präsenz nicht bewußt erlebbar und nachvollziehbar ist, dann wird das unmittelbar in entscheidende Defizite bei der Ausnutzung der Potentiale dieser Technologien münden.

Wenn es darum geht, den Menschen in die Lage zu versetzen, besser, effizienter mit seiner Umwelt umzugehen, bedarf es Interfaces, die es erlauben, diesen Kommunikationsprozeß, diesen Übergang zwischen der realen und der virtuellen Welt, zwischen dem physikalischen und dem digitalen Aggregatzustand von Information sinnlich wahrzunehmen. Das ist einer der möglichen FleshFactoren – die Fähigkeit des Menschen, aus sinnlicher Wahrnehmung durch sein gesamtes sensorisches Spektrum Assoziationen und Interpretationen auf der Basis eines großen Bestandes an Erfahrungsdaten abzuleiten – etwas, das oft auch als Charakteristikum menschlicher Kreativität definiert wird.

Seit langem spricht man von neuen, den geänderten Bedingungen angepaßten Kulturtechniken. Die Fähigkeit, mit Phänomenen wie Telepräsenz, virtuellen Identitäten im Sinne einer kognitiven Gestaltung dieser Aktions- und Wirkungsräume umgehen zu können, wird dabei zu einem entscheidenden Faktor erwachsen – nicht zuletzt aus der Perspektive veränderter sozialer Normierungen und der Verlagerung ökonomischer und politischer Macht in einer Gesellschaft, die als soziales Gefüge selbst zu einem Cyborg mutiert, wenn sie sich zu ihrer Etablierung und Organisation zunehmends Strukturen vernetzter digitaler Informationstechnologien bedient.

Doch nicht nur unsere Umwelt ist von der Durchdringung durch immer engmaschigere Netze technologischer Strukturen gekennzeichnet. Auch unser Körper ist zum Schauplatz dieser zweiten Natur geworden.

Die Apparate nähern sich immer stärker an unseren Körper an, der Bildschirm kommt als Datenhelm bzw. -brille vom Schreibtisch in unsere unmittelbare Nähe, als Datenhandschuh bzw. -anzug schmiegen sich Tastatur und Maus an unsere Haut. In der Technologie eines Retina-Scanners wird unsere Netzhaut selbst zur Projektionsfläche des elektronischen Bildes, der direkte Kurzschluß mit den Nervenzellen ist in Cochlear-Implantaten vollzogen.

this for a number of reasons, not the least of which are changed social norms and shifts in economic and political power within a society which is itself mutating into a cyborg as it makes increasing use of the structures of networked digital information technologies for the purpose of its establishment and organization as a social construct.

But it is not our environment alone which is characterized by the complete permeation by ever more tightly-woven networks of technological structures; our bodies have also become an arena of this second nature. The devices press ever closer to our bodies – the monitor which sat on our desk comes to literally embrace us as a helmet or goggles; the keyboard and mouse nestle up against our skin as a sensor glove or suit. By means of retina scanner technology, even our eyeballs become projection surfaces for electronic images; direct contact with auditory nerve cells is being carried out by means of cochlear implants. In experiments with electrical stimulation of the visual cortex, impressions of extremely simple light patterns can be transmitted to blind persons. The accompanying anxiety and distress that the concept of virtuality would surpass the body is the expression of a sense of insecurity which has befallen Western cultures, for the most part, evoked by this offensive thrust against the integrity of the body and the sovereignty of the intellect – *human identity threatened by the decision-making processes of the computer.* [1]

Ultimately, however, it is the results of genetic engineering which shake the very foundation of our sense of security with regard to a methodological differentiation between man and machine, between biology and technology, because here the fundamental principles of life are being made accessible to a mechanical, industrial process. The last stronghold in the discourse in which *biological* is defined as something that grows as opposed to technology which is made or assembled, is in danger of collapsing if we are to conclude thereby that a genetically manipulated tomato is a machine [because its basic substance was constructed according to a plan] whereas one that evolves as software inside a computer with the help of genetic algorithms is something biological [because it has not been programmed, but has actually grown].

In Experimenten mit elektrischer Stimulation der visuellen Cortex kann Blinden der Eindruck sehr einfacher Lichtmuster vermittelt werden.

Die damit einhergehende Angst und Bekümmertheit, das Konzept der Virtualität würde den Körper zurücklassen, ist Ausdruck einer vor allem westliche Kulturen befallenden Verunsicherung, hervorgerufen durch den Vorstoß gegen die Integrität des Körpers, die Souveränität des Intellekts, gegen *die menschliche Identität durch die Entscheidungsprozesse des Computers* [1].

Letztlich sind es aber die Ergebnisse der Gentechnologie, die unsere Sicherheit hinsichtlich einer methodischen Unterscheidung von Mensch und Maschine, Biologie und Technologie ins Wanken bringen, indem die Grundlagen des Lebens einem maschinellen, industriellen Prozeß erschlossen werden. Die letzte Rückzugsstellung in diesem Diskurs, der das Biologische als Gewachsenes im Gegensatz zu gebauter und konstruierter Technologie definiert, wird brüchig – eine gentechnisch manipulierte Tomate wäre dann eine Maschine [weil in ihrer grundlegenden Substanz planvoll konstruiert] und eine mit Hilfe genetischer Algorithmen evolvierte Software innerhalb eines Computers etwas Biologisches [weil nicht mehr programmiert sondern tatsächlich gewachsen].

Doch vielleicht sollten wir es mit dem Vatikan halten, der sich damit abgefunden zu haben scheint, daß die Schöpfung letztendlich Gegenstand industrieller Konstruktion geworden ist, und nun bemüht ist, wenigstens noch die Seele als letzte Bastion Gottes zu retten.

*Human cloning would not result in identical souls because only God can create a soul, a panel set up by the Pope has concluded. The Pontifical Academy of Life said the spiritual soul, *the constitutive kernel* of every human created by God, cannot be produced through cloning.* [2]

Welcome to the fleshfactor, welcome to the happy cloning party!

Or perhaps we ought to adopt the position of the Vatican, which seems to have resigned itself to the fact that Creation has ultimately become an object of industrial engineering, and is now occupied with the effort to at least rescue the soul as the last bastion of God.

*Human cloning would not result in identical souls because only God can create a soul, a panel set up by the Pope has concluded. The Pontifical Academy of Life said the spiritual soul, *the constitutive kernel* of every human created by God, cannot be produced through cloning.* [2]

Welcome to the FleshFactor, welcome to the happy cloning party!

1 *I have observed with tremendous satisfaction how traditional, White, Western, male philosophers are suddenly identifying with the body, with the animalistic, when they see their human identity threatened by the decision-making processes of the computer.* [Donna Haraway: Lieber Kyborg als Göttin! Für eine sozialistisch-feministische Unterwanderung der Gentechnologie, 1984]

2 *Human cloning would not result in identical souls because only God can create a soul, a panel set up by the Pope has concluded. The Pontifical Academy of Life said the spiritual soul, *the constitutive kernel* of every human created by God, cannot be produced through cloning. The panel's reflections were released yesterday by the Vatican, which has long forbidden any kind of artificial fertilization or human cloning to create new beings. The panel expressed concern that cloned humans would pay the price psychically for being aware of the *real, or even only 'virtual' presence of his 'other.'* The academy called for cultural, social and legislative efforts to stop any human-cloning project.* – Associated Press

ars electronica festival 97

1 *Ich beobachte mit großem Vergnügen, wie traditionelle, weiße, westliche, männliche Philosophen sich plötzlich mit dem Körper, dem Animalischen, identifizieren, wenn sie ihre menschliche Identität durch die Entscheidungsprozesse des Computers bedroht sehen.* [Donna Haraway: Lieber Kyborg als Göttin! Für eine sozialistisch-feministische Unterwanderung der Gentechnologie, 1984]

2 *Human cloning would not result in identical souls because only God can create a soul, a panel set up by the Pope has concluded. The Pontifical Academy of Life said the spiritual soul, *the constitutive kernel* of every human created by God, cannot be produced through cloning. The panel's reflections were released yesterday by the Vatican, which has long forbidden any kind of artificial fertilization or human cloning to create new beings. The panel expressed concern that cloned humans would pay the price psychically for being aware of the *real, or even only 'virtual' presence of his 'other.'* The academy called for cultural, social and legislative efforts to stop any human-cloning project.* – Associated Press

Human Information Machines Express Their Concerns and Desires

A Summary of the FleshFactor Net-Symposium

Tom Sherman

net symposium

Menschliche Informationsmaschinen formulieren ihre Anliegen und Wünsche

Eine Zusammenfassung des FleshFactor-Netzsymposiums

Tom Sherman

Am 7. April 1997 veröffentlichten wir auf der Ars-Electronica Web-Site Gerfried Stockers Eröffnungsstatement zum *FleshFactor*-Symposium. In meiner Eigenschaft als Moderator dieses Online-Netzsymposiums lud ich die Besucher der Web-Site gleichzeitig dazu ein, Stellungnahmen zu *Position, Stellenwert und Befindlichkeit des Individuums innerhalb der technokulturellen Informationsumgebung* abzugeben.

Ich forderte ein großteils unbekanntes Publikum dazu auf, auf Stockers Eröffnungsstatement zu reagieren, um zu erfahren, wie man allgemein über die Beziehung des Menschen zu unserer *zweiten Natur*, einer mit Maschinen, Netzwerken und Speichern vollgepackten Welt, denkt. Die essentielle Frage war und ist: Hat sich mit der Veränderung der Welt, vor allem in den letzten beiden Jahrzehnten der digitalen Revolution, auch die Natur des einzelnen Menschen geändert, und wenn ja, wie?

Während Stockers Eröffnungsstatement in der deutschen Originalversion ins Netz ging, konzentrierte sich das Netzsymposium notgedrungen auf die englische Übersetzung dieses Texts. Das Netzsymposium wurde in englischer Sprache abgehalten, um den Teilnehmerkreis weit über die Grenzen Österreichs hinaus auszudehnen. Die vorliegen-

On April 7, 1997, we posted Gerfried Stocker's opening *FleshFactor* statement on the Ars Electronica website and I, as moderator of this on-line net-symposium, welcomed visitors to this website to comment on *the position, status or condition of the individual within the technocultural information environment.*

I asked a largely unknown audience to respond to Stocker's opening statement so we could develop a sense of where people stood regarding their relationship with our 'second nature', a world densely packed with machines, networks and media memory. The essential question was and of course still is: as the world has changed, particularly over the past two decades of the digital revolution, has the nature of the individual human changed; and if so, how?

While Stocker's opening statement was posted in its original German, the focus of the net-symposium was necessarily on the English translation of Stocker's text. The net-symposium was conducted in English in the hope of extending its spectrum of participants far beyond Austria. This summary was written in the second week of June, to meet deadlines for translation and the publication of this book. The on-line symposium remained open to its community of interest throughout the summer, right up until the week of the live symposium and festival. At the time of writing we had already received over sixty messages, many of them lengthy essays in themselves.

All of these messages were informative and serious attempts to deal with difficult, often somewhat unformed ideas. First let me here express my gratitude to those who submitted texts to *FleshFactor*. Due to time and limits placed on the length of this text, the following summary cannot include mention of all those texts submitted. I must also add that I was humbled trying to encapsulate such a rich, complex collection of sensitive and intelligent contributions. With this said, let me proceed with the summary.

The first message came from Brian Molyneaux [South Dakota, USA]. He linked J. G. Ballard's writing to Stocker's FleshFactor insight, *the future seems to have reversed directions and is collapsing upon us.* Ballard had written in 1995: *The future is ceasing to exist, de-

de Zusammenfassung wurde in der zweiten Juniwoche geschrieben, um die Fristen für die Übersetzung und Veröffentlichung des vorliegenden Buchs einzuhalten. Das Online-Symposium blieb für die Interessensgemeinschaft jedoch den ganzen Sommer hindurch bis zur Woche des Live-Symposiums und des Festivals zugänglich. Bis zum heutigen Tag haben wir bereits mehr als 60 Messages erhalten, von denen viele selbst umfangreiche Essays sind.

Jede dieser Messages stellte einen informativen und ernsthaften Versuch dar, sich mit schwierigen und oft auch noch nicht ganz ausgegorenen Ideen auseinanderzusetzen. An dieser Stelle möchte ich jedoch zunächst all jenen danken, die mit ihren Texten einen Beitrag zu *FleshFactor* geleistet haben. Aus Zeit- und Platzgründen kann die folgende Zusammenfassung nicht auf alle uns übermittelten Texte eingehen. Ich muß in diesem Zusammenhang auch hinzufügen, daß der Versuch, eine derart umfangreiche und komplexe Sammlung sensibler und intelligenter Beiträge zusammenzufassen, für mich eine überwältigende Erfahrung war. Doch lassen Sie mich nun zur eigentlichen Zusammenfassung kommen.

Die erste Message erhielten wir von Brian Molyneaux [South Dakota, USA]. Er stellte eine Verbindung zwischen dem Werk J. G. Ballards und Stockers Erkenntnis in bezug auf den FleshFactor her: *Die Zukunft scheint die Richtung geändert zu haben und bricht nun über uns herein.* Ballard habe im Jahr 1995 geschrieben: *Die Zukunft hört auf zu existieren, sie wird von der alles verschlingenden Gegenwart vertilgt. Als nur eine der vielfältigen Alternativen, die uns offenstehen, haben wir die Zukunft mit der Gegenwart verbunden. Um uns herum vervielfachen sich die Wahlmöglichkeiten, und wir leben in einer geradezu kindlichen Welt, in der jeder Wunsch, jede Möglichkeit – ob es sich nun um den Lebensstil, um Reisen, geschlechtliche Rollenbilder oder Identitäten handelt – sofort erfüllt werden kann.* Molyneaux stellte weiters fest: *Das ist aber noch nicht alles. Der Fortschritt in der Technologie geht heute so rasch vor sich, daß die altmodische Vorstellung von der Zukunft als Techno-Utopie, in deren Mittelpunkt der Mensch steht, schließlich als das erscheint, was sie eigentlich immer war: ein leerer Traum. Die Maschinen konnten noch nie die menschliche Entwicklung abwarten.*

Molyneaux formulierte darüber hinaus einige interessante Gedanken zum Unterschied zwischen der künstlichen Ordnung unserer Medienwelt und der relativen Unordnung der Natur. *Das Problem besteht darin, daß in der Welt mehr existiert als bloß

voured by the all-voracious present. We have annexed the future into the present, as merely one of those manifold alternatives open to us. Options multiply around us, and we live in an almost infantile world where any demand, any possibility, whether for life-styles, travel, sexual roles and identities, can be satisfied instantly.* Molyneaux went on to state that *It is more than that. Technological change is now so fast that the old-fashioned idea of the future as a human-centred techno-utopia appears as it always was, an idle dream. Machines have never been able to wait for human development.*

Molyneaux also offered some interesting comments on the difference between the artificial order of our media world and the relative disorder of nature. *The problem is that there is more to the world than the art of human production and reproduction, the extended space of the human brain. Where is the unorganized, nonhuman space? At least in the natural world we can stumble on things that are not the product of the imagination.*

Sue Thomas [Nottingham, England] wrote, *Right now the Internet is peppered with the fragmented writings of its many explorers, and each has a complex and intimate tale to tell. I think that we truly are stumbling upon things in cyberspace which are not just the products of our imaginations.* And *Perhaps we need to develop a concept similar to that of the UFO – but this time, the UIE – the Unidentified Internet Experience! We should be recording and cataloguing the many unusual connections which occur daily throughout this interconnected web of minds [and I do not attempt to define all of these minds as human].* Here we see a perception that signs of an emerging order are possibly surfacing as the infosphere reaches more and more complexity.

Anne Farrell [New Mexico, USA]: *I am in a constant state, literally, daily, of trying to navigate between my life-long inclination to be Nature Girl, and life as we live it in the late twentieth century. I want stuff from both of those worlds. I am at least resolved that I cannot be a purist and so I must blend.* And Norman White [Durham, Ontario, Canada] added: *The discussion seems to be centering around Nature, and how it can help us under-

die Kunst der menschlichen Produktion und Reproduktion, der erweiterte Raum des menschlichen Gehirns. Wo ist der unorganisierte nicht-menschliche Raum? In der natürlichen Welt stolpern wir wenigstens über Dinge, die nicht das Produkt unserer Vorstellungskraft sind.* Diese Gedanken gaben Anlaß zu einer langen Reihe von Messages über die Schwierigkeiten oder Annehmlichkeiten des Lebens in zwei verschiedenen Welten: in der vom Menschen geschaffenen künstlichen Welt einerseits und in der natürlichen Welt andererseits.

Sue Thomas [Nottingham, England] schrieb: *Das Internet wird heute mit Textfragmenten seiner zahlreichen Erforscher geradezu bombardiert, und jeder von ihnen hat eine komplexe persönliche Geschichte zu erzählen. Ich glaube, daß wir im Cyberspace tatsächlich über Dinge stolpern, die nicht nur das bloße Produkt unserer Vorstellungskraft sind.* Und sie fährt fort: *Vielleicht müßten wir einen Begriff wie den des UFO entwickeln, nur daß er in diesem Fall UIE heißt – Unidentifizierte Internet-Erfahrung! Wir sollten die vielen ungewöhnlichen Verbindungen, die tagtäglich durch diese Vernetzung von Gehirnen zustande kommen, registrieren und katalogisieren [wobei ich hier nicht versuche, alle diese Gehirne als menschlich zu bezeichnen].* Hier erleben wir also jemanden, der die Auffassung vertritt, mit der immer komplexer werdenden Infosphäre zeichneten sich möglicherweise Anzeichen einer sich entwickelnden Ordnung ab.

Anne Farrell [New Mexico, USA]: *Ich versuche ständig – buchstäblich tagtäglich – meinen Weg zu finden zwischen meiner lebenslangen Neigung zum 'Nature Girl' und dem Leben, das wir im ausgehenden zwanzigsten Jahrhundert führen. Ich will Teile beider Welten genießen. Ich bin zumindest davon überzeugt, daß ich keine Puristin sein kann, und deshalb muß ich diese beiden Welten miteinander verbinden.* Und Norman White [Durham, Ontario, Kanada] ergänzte: *Die Diskussion scheint sich auf die Natur zu konzentrieren, auf die Frage, wie die Natur uns helfen kann zu verstehen, was im Internet vor sich geht. Diese Erleuchtung ist wechselseitig. Ich glaube nämlich, die wichtigste Information, die uns das Netz liefert, besteht darin, daß es uns zurück zur Natur führt ... nicht durch seinen Inhalt, sondern durch die Art und Weise, wie es funktioniert. Mit seiner befremdlichen Mischung aus 'harten' Fakten und Phantasie, aus Einsichten und Täuschungen, die eigentlich alle widersprüchlichen Zwecken dienen, erinnert mich das Internet an ein Beispiel, das Gregory Bateson verwendete, um die

stand what is happening on the Internet. The illumination works both ways. In fact, I believe the MOST important way the Net can inform us is in the way it leads us back to Nature ... not by its content, but by the way it WORKS. With its bewildering mix of *hard*data and fantasy, insight and deception, all functioning at cross-purposes, the Internet reminds me of an illustration that Gregory Bateson used to describe cultural sanity ... * White goes on to tell how Bateson makes analogies between healthy, diverse [sane] ecosystems and unhealthy, disturbed [insane] ecosystems with too few species and similar cultural conditions. White wrote: *If Bateson is correct, and I believe he is, then a *sane* ecosystem displays not so much a condition of *anarchy* as *panarchy* ... and *The Internet at present verges on healthy panarchy. There are also a thousand ways it can go insane. Perhaps its many cross-purposes can co-exist for a while. But whether the Internet grows wild, mutates, or gets paved over, may it point us to the greater internet ... the one we call Nature.*

Carmen Hermosillo [California, USA] then challenged White, stating that useful analogies aside, we as a species have broken away from nature. Hermosillo: *I think that there is no road back to the garden, and that whatever road was used previously has been closed ever since the picnic became a social institution. The picnic says that we are strangers in the garden. Take Baudrillard far enough and a case can be made that 'nature' itself is a simulation, because 'nature' is mediated by perceptual instincts and filters that have been mediated by education, by Rousseau & St. Francis of Assisi, and by the art of painting, just for starters.*

White immediately answered: *As an artist who has been passionately building kinetic machines with emergent behavior for over 30 years, I am certainly not one to view 'Nature' in its usual romantic sense. To close its lessons off from contemplation, on the basis that the world we have inherited is now somehow inaccessible, irrelevant or illusory, I think is foolhardy. I would argue that now, more than ever, we need its long-evolved wisdom in dealing with power-structures and information.*

Meanwhile, I had begun to *unpack* Stocker's opening statement, focusing on

kulturelle Gesundheit zu beschreiben.* White führt dann weiter aus, wie Bateson eine Analogie zwischen gesunden, von großer Vielfalt gekennzeichneten [d. h. normalen] Ökosystemen und nicht gesunden, gestörten [d. h. abnormalen] Ökosystemen mit einer zu geringen Artenvielfalt und dem entsprechenden kulturellen Umfeld herstellt. White schreibt: *Wenn Bateson recht hat – und davon bin ich überzeugt –, dann herrscht in einem 'gesunden' Ökosystem weniger eine 'Anarchie' als vielmehr eine 'Panarchie'.* Und weiter: *Das Internet nähert sich derzeit einer gesunden Panarchie. Aber es kann auch auf tausenderlei Art aus den Fugen geraten. Vielleicht können seine Widersprüchlichkeiten eine Zeitlang nebeneinander existieren. Doch ob das Internet nun wild wuchert, mutiert oder zugepflastert wird, wir können uns nur wünschen, daß es uns den Weg zu jenem größeren Internet weist, das wir Natur nennen.*

Carmen Hermosillo [Kalifornien, USA] widersprach Whites Ansichten, indem sie feststellte, daß wir uns als Spezies – einmal abgesehen von den nützlichen Analogien – von der Natur entfernt hätten. Hermosillo meinte: *Ich glaube, es führt kein Weg zurück in den Garten; jeder Weg, den man früher einmal benutzt haben mag, ist versperrt, seitdem sich das Picknick zur gesellschaftlichen Institution entwickelt hat. Picknick bedeutet, daß wir im Garten Fremde sind. Wenn man Baudrillard weit genug auslegt, kann man argumentieren, daß die 'Natur' selbst eine Simulation ist, denn die 'Natur' wird uns durch Wahrnehmungsinstinkte und -filter vermittelt, die uns ihrerseits durch unsere Erziehung, durch Rousseau & den heiligen Franz von Assisi, durch die Malerei – um nur einige zu nennen – vermittelt wurden.* White antwortete darauf umgehend: *Als Künstler, der seit über 30 Jahren besessen daran arbeitet, mit Eigenverhalten ausgestattete kinetische Maschinen zu bauen, gehöre ich sicher nicht zu denen, die die 'Natur' im üblichen romantischen Sinn betrachten. Es wäre meines Erachtens verwegen, das, was die Natur uns lehrt, mit der Begründung außer acht zu lassen, daß die Welt, die wir geerbt haben, heute mehr oder weniger unzugänglich, irrelevant oder illusorisch ist. Ich glaube, daß wir heute mehr denn je auf die im Laufe von Jahrtausenden entstandene Weisheit der Natur angewiesen sind, wenn es um Machtstrukturen und Information geht.*

In der Zwischenzeit hatte ich damit begonnen, Stockers Eröffnungsstatement zu 'entpacken', wobei ich besonderes Augenmerk auf den Wert der Reflexion bei der Vorbereitung auf die Zukunft legte. Ich schrieb: *Ohne in Nostalgie zu verfallen, wäre es

the value of reflection when preparing for the future. I wrote *Without succumbing to nostalgia, it may make good sense to reflect on our recent past, if nothing else to help us verify the value of our trajectory as we head into turbulent, previously unexperienced domains.* Peter Charlot [Hawaii, USA], responded, *The *Flesh-Factor* theme intrigues me because it assumes that we are headed towards *unexperienced domains.* I think not ... I don't think that there is anything that we can design or construct that is not an extension of who we are already ... We can manipulate, contract, synthesize, shatter, emphasize, obsess and squeeze various aspects of our natures. But we can't change or invent them ... No matter what we come up with, whatever evolves as extensions of ourselves, they will never be as complex and marvelous as who we are now, [or a tree for that matter]. I would suggest that the thrill of the technological revolution is as old a new experience as discovering the next valley.*

Statements like Charlot's established a kind of comforting rhythm of reassurance throughout the net-symposium. Charlot's statement, and those sympathetic to it, affirm that we are more like the primates we evolved from than the machines we are evolving into.

Laura Vandenburgh [New York, USA] then submitted a stunning text that literally put the whole discussion on ice for a week. She wrote: *Intellectually, I can appreciate the notion of escaping the constraints of biology through our integration with technology, but practically I'm skeptical. Even if we have set in motion changes which make our biological intelligence just a component of a larger conceptual framework, our intelligence is not just inextricably linked to the physical, it is physical. Due to the relatively slow process of biological evolution, our mind-bodies are adapted to a very different niche than the one in which we live. [Newer models of evolution describe large leaps punctuating an otherwise slow process, but they require very strong selection pressure.] In our case, it seems that that evolutionary gap or lag time can only continue to increase, because the conceptual-technological changes described are largely disengaged from selection pressures. [The ability to negotiate in cyber-

vielleicht sinnvoll, über unsere eigene jüngere Vergangenheit nachzudenken, um wenigstens die Sinnhaftigkeit unseres Wegs zu überprüfen, der uns in turbulente, noch unerforschte Bereiche vordringen läßt.* Darauf antwortete Peter Charlot [Hawaii, USA]: *Das *FleshFactor*-Thema verblüfft mich, weil es davon ausgeht, daß wir uns auf 'unerforschte Gebiete' zubewegen. Das glaube ich nicht. [...] Ich glaube nicht, daß wir irgend etwas konstruieren oder erschaffen können, das nicht bloß eine Erweiterung dessen ist, was wir bereits sind. [...] Wir können verschiedene Aspekte unserer Natur manipulieren, kondensieren, synthetisieren, zerschlagen, betonen, besetzen und auspressen. Aber wir können sie nicht ändern oder neu erfinden. [...] Was immer wir uns auch einfallen lassen, was immer sich auch als Erweiterung unseres Selbst entwickeln mag, es wird nie so komplex und wunderbar sein, wie das, was wir sind [oder was auch ein Baum ist]. Ich meine, daß der mit der technischen Revolution verbundene Nervenkitzel eine so alte neue Erfahrung ist wie das Entdecken des nächsten Tals.*

Beiträge wie die Charlots gaben dem ganzen Netzsymposium eine Art beruhigenden, beschwichtigenden Rhythmus. Charlot und jene, die sich seiner Meinung anschließen, behaupten, daß wir eher den Primaten ähneln, von denen wir abstammen, als den Maschinen, zu denen wir uns entwickeln.

Laura Vandenburgh [New York, USA] sandte uns dann einen erstaunlichen Text, der die gesamte Diskussion eine Woche lang buchstäblich auf Eis legte. Sie schrieb: *Rein intellektuell kann ich den Gedanken einer Flucht vor den Zwängen der Biologie durch eine Integration von Mensch und Technologie nachvollziehen, aber in der Praxis bin ich skeptisch. Auch wenn wir Veränderungen eingeleitet haben, die unsere biologische Intelligenz zu einer bloßen Komponente eines größeren begrifflichen Gefüges machen, ist unsere Intelligenz nicht nur unlösbar mit dem Physischen verbunden, sondern sie ist selbst physisch. Aufgrund des relativ langsamen Voranschreitens der biologischen Evolution sind unsere Geist-Körper einer Nische angepaßt, die sich von der, in der wir tatsächlich leben, wesentlich unterscheidet. [Neuere Evolutionsmodelle beschreiben größere Entwicklungssprünge, die einen ansonsten langsamen, kontinuierlichen Prozeß unterbrechen, doch erfordern diese einen sehr starken Selektionsdruck.] In unserem Fall scheint es so, als ob diese evolutionäre Kluft oder Verzögerung sich nur noch weiter vergrößern könnte, da die beschriebenen begrifflich-technologischen Veränderungen großteils von jedem

space doesn't seem to be closely linked to producing a lot of offspring ...] Perhaps the more we change the world around us the more we are forced to face that evolutionary gap between what we are and what we perceive.*

Vandenburgh had put her finger on one of the essential ideas of last year's *Memesis* symposium; an idea that links the *FleshFactor* symposium with its immediate predecessor. Cultural evolution occurs at lightspeed compared to the idea of four billion years of biological evolution. The tension and confusion resulting from the improbable collision of the two evolutions enhances our extreme sense of dislocation from our animal nature. Vandenburgh adds that *Stocker refers to the development of an 'intimate and intensive relationship' with this second machine-mediated environment, in which there is no subject-object distinction. Maybe that's not a new development, but rather just the waning of the 'wholly, autonomous individual' concept. Perhaps the development of a 'hybridized, networked subjectivity' is just an adaptive response to an old loss. In many cultures, past and present, individuals view themselves as having no subject-object distinction in relation to the 'first natural environment'.*

At this point I prompted the net-group to consider the problems of thinking about a world made up of two natures ... *So far we have examined the relationship between a first nature [we are still animals and we have to live in 'Nature 1'] and the second nature, that which can be identified as an artificial nature [mediated reality, computers, networks ...]. And most of the thinking on the integration or separation of these two natures positions the examiner, the wired human that apparently still has the option of shutting down the second nature whenever he or she wants ... in a special place outside or beside both natures, a special zone reserved for humankind.*

Richard Brown [London, England] then contributed that *The evolution of the Human/[Nature]/Machine is controlled by systems, functions which we appear subject to and not able to control ... We live and are supported by a cybernetic beast system, and it appears we have lost control of the reins.* This is an important observation, that there is no central, global con-

Selektionsdruck abgekoppelt sind. [Die Fähigkeit, sich im Cyberspace zu bewegen, scheint nicht direkt mit der Fähigkeit zur Produktion einer zahlreichen Nachkommenschaft verbunden zu sein ...] Möglicherweise werden wir durch die zunehmende Veränderung der Welt um uns herum immer stärker dazu gezwungen, uns dieser evolutionären Kluft zwischen dem, was wir sind, und dem, was wir wahrnehmen, zu stellen.*

Vandenburgh hatte damit einen der grundlegenden Gedanken des im vergangenen Jahr abgehaltenen *Memesis*-Symposiums angesprochen, der das *FleshFactor*-Symposium mit seinem unmittelbaren Vorgänger verbindet. Die kulturelle Evolution läuft im Vergleich zu den vier Milliarden Jahren biologischer Evolution in Lichtgeschwindigkeit ab. Die Spannung und Verwirrung, die sich aus der unwahrscheinlichen Kollision dieser beiden Evolutionen ergibt, verstärkt noch unser Gefühl, von unserer animalischen Natur losgelöst zu sein. Vandenburgh fügte hinzu: *Stocker spricht die Entwicklung einer 'intensiven und persönlichen Beziehung' zu dieser zweiten, maschinenvermittelten Umwelt an, in der es keine Unterscheidung zwischen Subjekt und Objekt gibt. Das ist möglicherweise keine neue Entwicklung, sondern eher das Schwinden des Begriffs des 'vollständig autonomen Individuums'. Vielleicht ist die Entwicklung einer 'hybridisierten, vernetzten Subjektivität' nichts weiter als eine adaptive Reaktion auf lange zurückliegende Verluste. In vielen – vergangenen wie gegenwärtigen – Kulturen sehen sich Individuen in keinem Subjekt-Objekt-Unterschied zur 'ersten, natürlichen Umgebung'.*

An diesem Punkt forderte ich die Netz-Gruppe dazu auf, sich mit jenen Problemen zu beschäftigen, die sich aus der Vorstellung einer aus zwei Naturen bestehenden Welt ergeben. *Bisher haben wir die Beziehungen zwischen einer ersten Natur [wir sind noch immer Tiere und müssen in 'Natur 1' leben] und der zweiten Natur, die als künstliche definiert werden kann [vermittelte Realität, Computer, Netzwerke ...], analysiert. Und der Großteil der Überlegungen über die Integration oder Trennung dieser beiden Naturen positioniert den Forschenden, den verdrahteten Menschen, der offensichtlich noch immer die Möglichkeit hat, die zweite Natur einfach abzuschalten, wenn ihm danach ist [...], in einem besonderen Raum außerhalb oder neben den beiden Naturen, in einem besonderen Raum, einer dem Menschen vorbehaltenen Sonderzone.*

Richard Brown [London, England] meinte daraufhin in seinem Beitrag: *Die Evolution von Mensch

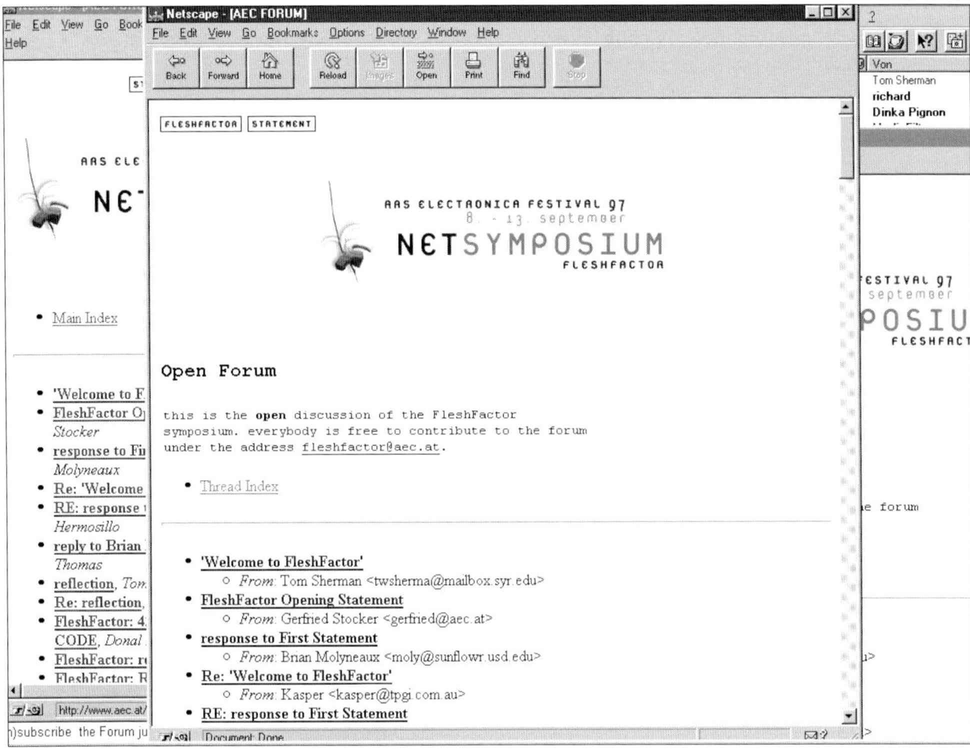

/[Natur]/Maschine wird durch Systeme, durch Funktionen gesteuert, denen wir ausgeliefert sind und die wir nicht kontrollieren können. [...] Wir leben in – und getragen von – einem kybernetischen System, und es scheint, als wären uns die Zügel aus der Hand geglitten.* Daß es keine zentrale, globale Kontrolle der technologischen Entwicklung gibt, ist eine wichtige Beobachtung.

Monika Wunderer [Wien, Österreich] schrieb mit Bezug auf Stockers Eröffnungsstatement: *Der menschliche Körper ist in unserer informationsbasierten Gesellschaft nicht nur 'das ultimative Original', sondern auch etwas, das bleibt, während der Raum sich erweitert und virtuell wird.* Sie führt weiter aus: *Computervermittelte Kommunikation und die Verwendung und das Verständnis des durch die elektronische Vernetzung geschaffenen Raums ersetzen den menschlichen Benutzer nicht. Ich [stelle fest], daß der menschliche Körper sogar in einer virtuellen Umgebung [weiter existiert].* Wunderer, die im Bereich des virtuellen Theaters tätig ist, hält daran fest, daß das essentielle Material des Schauspielers der menschliche Körper ist.

Valéry Grancher [Paris, Frankreich] schrieb: *Wir können hinter dem 'FleshFactor-Begriff' alle möglichen Dinge sehen, wie Genetik, Cyberbiologie, Cyberintelligenz. [...] Wir können die neuen Technologien aber auch als sprachbasierte menschliche Schnittstellen auffassen.* Er weist darauf hin, daß die Sprache in ihrer ganzen Komplexität immer an der 'Haut' zwischen dem Menschen und seinen Technologien erscheint, und meint weiter, *daß die Sprache in diesem Kontext mit der Genetik verglichen werden kann.* Sie stelle den Bauplan dar, nach dem Technologien geschaffen und reproduziert werden.

Das Thema der Sprache als Schnittstelle erwies sich im weiteren Verlauf der Diskussion als eines der größten Anliegen vieler Teilnehmer des Netzsymposiums.

Brian Molyneaux [South Dakota, USA] bezog sich dann auf meinen früheren Hinweis auf die Probleme, mit denen Menschen konfrontiert sind, weil sie glauben, sie wären eine irgendwie von der Natur [bzw. von den Naturen] losgelöste Spezies. *[Sherman] hat mit seinen Überlegungen über die menschliche Natur in der Zukunft ein ernsthaftes Problem aufgeworfen. Wir debattieren noch immer im Rahmen der fundamentalen mythischen Weltsicht der Menschheit, ihrer Selbstzentriertheit und ihrer Einzigartigkeit. Dieses überwältigende Selbstbewußtsein, das von Priestern und Philosophen, von Machthabern und Institutionen entwickelt wurde, hat zu

trol of technological evolution.

Monika Wunderer [Vienna, Austria], referring to Stocker's opening statement, wrote: *The Human body is not only *the ultimate original* in our information-based society, it is also something that remains while space is extending and is becoming virtual.* She adds: *Using computer mediated communication and furthermore using and understanding the space that is created by electronic networking does not replace the human User. I [recognize] that the human body [still exists] even in a virtual environment.* Wunderer, working in the area of virtual theatre, affirms that the essential material of the actor is the human body.

Valery Grancher [Paris, France] wrote: *Beyond the *FleshFactor* concept, we can perceive a lot of things, such as genetics, cyberbiology, cyber-intelligence ... Otherwise, we can perceive new technologies as human interfaces based on language.* He pointed out that language, in all its complexity, always appears at the 'skin' between humans and their technologies. And *that language in this context can be compared to genetics.* It is the blueprint from which technologies are created and reproduced. The interface of language proved to be a major obsession of many contributors to the net-symposium further on in the discussion.

Brian Molyneaux [South Dakota, USA] then addressed my earlier message about the problems humans face by believing they are a species somehow separate from nature[s]. *[Sherman] has identified a serious problem with thinking on human nature in the future. We are still debating within the fundamental mythical worldview of humanity, its centredness and uniqueness. This overwhelming sense of ourselves, developed by priests and philosophers and power brokers and the institutionalized, has given us the age-old dichotomies that distinguish us from 'the other': me and you, us and them, mind and body, art and science, human and animal, human and vegetable, flesh and metal. These are all Western philosophical conventions and classifications. We need to understand that as we change the world, it changes us. I can walk away from the computer, turn off that electrical window, that moving wall of information. But it is already too late. It

jenen Jahrtausende alten Dichotomien geführt, die uns von 'den anderen' unterscheiden: ich und du, wir und sie, Geist und Körper, Kunst und Wissenschaft, Mensch und Tier, Mensch und Pflanze, Fleisch und Metall. All das sind philosophische Konventionen und Kategorien der westlichen Welt. Wir müssen verstehen, daß die Welt uns ändert, während wir sie ändern. Ich kann von meinem Computer weggehen, dieses elektrische Fenster, diese sich bewegende Informationswand einfach abschalten. Doch es ist bereits zu spät. Es umgibt mich, wie die Welt, in der ich mich bewege, weil ich nicht aus ihr hinaus kann. Es ist unter meiner Haut, doch nicht in meinem Gehirn, denn jetzt begibt sich das Gehirn [mittels seiner sensorischen Ausläufer] auf die Reise.*

Paul D. Miller alias DJ Spooky That Subliminal Kid [New York, USA] sandte uns daraufhin eine poetische Geschichte über die entkörperlichte Stimme und eine neue Definition des Selbst. Sie begann wie folgt: *Mögliche Darstellungen. Unmögliche Erzählungen. Unterbrochener Strom. Binäre Dissonanz. Fragen des Fortlassens. Die Stimme getrennt vom Körper, der ihr das Leben geschenkt hat, das Gesicht abgelöst und vom Schädel gerissen. Der Screen-Saver: entkörperlicht, simultan, ein Spiel des Todes. Morphing. Identität in ständigem Aufruhr, im Vervielfältgungsspiegel des Gedächtnisses. Reproduktion. Replikation: Asymmetrisch. Telekinetisch. Dialektisch. Strom. Der Körper als Ort textueller Formbarkeit. Der Geist als Schauplatz totaler Erinnerung. Totale Dislokation. Wer ist da? Erogene, dekodierte Amnesie. Biopsychische Paradoxa. Auslöschung des Selbst. Prothetisch. Synthetisch. Memetisch. Technophilie [...].*

Oliver Hockenhull [Vancouver, Kanada], der gerade von einer langen Indienreise zurückgekehrt war, unterstrich die Enge der westlichen Auffassungen des Selbst, insbesondere in Hinblick auf die Tatsache, daß so viele Menschen auf der Welt mit [aus westlicher Perspektive] primitiven Technologien dennoch ein geistig hochstehendes Leben führen. Unter Bezugnahme auf Stockers Bemerkung, wir könnten uns selbst nicht länger als autonome Individuen betrachten, sondern müßten uns als dynamische Knoten in einem sozialen Kommunikationsnetz verstehen, schrieb Hockenhull: *Ich bin davon überzeugt, daß sich dieses soziale Netzwerk über die ganze Welt erstreckt und im Westen auch eine Rückkehr zu Wahrnehmungsweisen [der Welt, des Körpers, des Bewußtseins] umfassen sollte, die mehrdeutig, amorph, dimensional und mitfühlend sind.*

surrounds me, no less so than the world I walk through, because I cannot get outside it. It is inside my skin, but outside my brain, because the brain [through its sensory extensions] now makes the journey.*

Paul D. Miller, A.K.A. Dj Spooky That Subliminal Kid [New York, USA] then submitted a poetic history of the disembodied voice and a new definition of the self. It began: *Possible performances. Impossible narratives. Ruptured flow. Binary Dissonance. Questions of omission. The voice divorced from the body that gave it life, the face ruptured and ripped from the skull. The screen-saver: disembodied, simultaneous, play of death. Morphing. Identity in continuous upheaval, in the multiplying mirror of memory. Reproduction. Replication: Asymmetric. Telekinetic. Dialectic. Flow. The body as a site of textual malleability. The mind as a locale of total recall. Total displacement. Who's there? Erogenous, decoded amnesia. Biopsychic paradoxes. Eclipse of the self. Prosthetic. Synthetic. Memetic. Technophilia ... *

Oliver Hockenhull [Vancouver, Canada], just back from a long tour of India, emphasized the narrowness of Western perceptions of self, especially considering that so many of the world's citizens live sophisticated lives with primitive technologies [from a Western perspective]. Considering Stocker's observation that we can no longer think of ourselves as autonomous individuals, but are forced to perceive ourselves as dynamic nodes in a social network of communication, Hockenhull wrote: *I would maintain that this social network extends throughout the world and should also demand in the West a retrieval of modes of perception [of the world, of the body, and of consciousness] that are more ambiguous, amorphic, dimensional and compassionate.*

While I was enjoying the polyphonous composition of this relatively incoherent string of messages, I sensed the discussion needed another kick. But rather than trying to narrow the focus, to force clarity through a sense of coherency, I decided to open the doors even wider, hoping to generate energy. In my *Mission Revisited* statement, I wrote: *This is our mission, to describe ourselves as a species in the present, in our relationships with and/or in those

Während ich die polyphone Komposition dieser relativ zusammenhanglosen Reihe von Mitteilungen genoß, gelangte ich zu der Auffassung, daß die Diskussion einen neuen Stimulus brauchte. Statt den Fokus zu verengen und Klarheit durch Kohärenz zu erzwingen, beschloß ich allerdings, die Türen noch weiter aufzustoßen, in der Hoffnung, dadurch Energien zu mobilisieren. In meinem Statement *Mission Revisited* schrieb ich:

*Unsere Mission besteht darin, uns selbst als Spezies in der Gegenwart zu beschreiben, in unseren Beziehungen zu anderen und/oder in diesen Beziehungen, sofern sie durch Technologien vermittelt sind. Das ist möglicherweise ein gewaltiges Vorhaben, eine Studie des Selbst in einer Größenordnung, die dem 'Human Genome'-Projekt entspricht, ein Stereo-'Schnappschuß' der menschlichen Natur, der gleichzeitig aus einer menschlichen und einer posthumanen Perspektive aufgenommen wird und die gesamte Breite der cyborgologischen Standpunkte umfaßt, eine kollektive Multivision des Individuums an diesem Tag und in diesem Zeitalter. [...] Beteiligen Sie sich an der Autorschaft an einem großen, komplexen System namens Selbst. Damit diese unbändige, polymorphe, globale Polyphonie verständlich bleibt, werden wir ihre Natur einfach herunterspielen. Wir nennen sie den *FleshFactor*.* Und das hat funktioniert. Die Diskussion wurde mit neuem Elan weitergeführt, und wir erhielten eine lange Reihe von Beiträgen.

Richard Kriesche [Graz, Österreich] schrieb, er hielte zwar das *FleshFactor*-Thema für sehr wichtig und vom Konzept her intelligent, meinte aber, Stockers Eröffnungsstatement sei ideologisch etwas konfus. Kriesche schrieb: *[...] So etwas wie eine 'technokulturelle Entwicklung' gibt es nicht. Die Entwicklung ist entweder eine technologische, mit Auswirkungen auf die Kultur, oder eine kulturelle, mit Rückwirkungen auf die technologische. [...] Die technologische Entwicklung wird in erster Linie durch Geldkapital, den Hauptmotor der postkapitalistischen Wirtschaft, vorangetrieben, während in der Kultur, zumindest in Europa, das Geldkapital keine treibende Kraft darstellt.* Kriesche fügte hinzu, die Absicht des *FleshFactor*-Symposiums, eine Diskussion zwischen Künstlern und Wissenschaftlern in Gang zu bringen, wäre relevanter und produktiver, wenn dies in Form einer 'Debatte zwischen den Real Players' geschähe, *in der die Profis der Fleisch-, Finanz- und Informationsindustrie den Anfang machen sollten*.

Ein Teilnehmer mit dem Namen *-j.* [Michigan, USA] appellierte sodann an den gesunden Men-

relationships with others mediated by our technologies. This may be a huge endeavour, a study of the self at a scale the likes of the Human Genome Project, a stereo 'snapshot' of human nature taken simultaneously from human and post-human perspectives, including the breadth of cyborgological points of view, a collective multi-vision of the individual person in this day and age ... Share in the authorship of a large, complex system called the self. To help us keep this unruly, polymorphous, global polyphony comprehensible, we'll simply understate its nature. We'll call it the *FleshFactor.** This did the trick. The discussion exploded with energy and a remarkable string of contributions.

Richard Kriesche [Graz, Austria] wrote that while he thought the *FleshFactor* theme was very important and intelligent in its conception, he thought there was ideological confusion in Stocker's opening statement. Kriesche: * ... there is no such thing as a 'techno-cultural development'. The development is either a technological one, with an impact on culture, or a cultural one, with a backslash onto technological development ... the technological development is driven first by capital money, the motor #1 of the postcapitalist economy; whereas capital money, at least in Europe, is not the prime force of its culture.* Kriesche added that FleshFactor's intention to create a debate between artists and scientists would be more relevant and productive as *a debate between the real players, the professionals of the flesh-, finance- and information industry to start with.*

A contributor named *-j.* [Michigan, USA] then made a call for common sense. In a long passionate statement, echoing the sentiments of previous reassuring contributions by Peter Charlot and Laura Vandenburgh, *-j.* wrote: *... I don't have the time nor the desire to worry about such lofty notions as 'non-anthropocentric cultural perceptions.' I worry about keeping my job. My health care. Enough food to eat ... And when I look backwards to the personal stories of human existence collected from various cultures and ages, regardless of this monitor in front of me and the advantages offered by temporarily existing as a voice in time-collapsed-space [the Internet], I am very, very, very much like the humans before me.*

schenverstand. In einem langen, leidenschaftlichen Statement, das den emotionalen Hintergrund früherer beruhigender Beiträge von Peter Charlot und Laura Vandenburgh widerspiegelte, schrieb *-j.*: * [...] Ich habe weder Zeit noch Lust, mir über so hochtrabende Begriffe wie *nicht anthropozentrische kulturelle Wahrnehmungen* Gedanken zu machen. Ich mache mir Gedanken um meinen Job. Um meine Gesundheitsversorgung. Um mein tägliches Essen . [...] Und wenn ich mir frühere persönlichen Geschichten menschlicher Existenzen aus unterschiedlichen Kulturen und Zeitaltern ansehe, dann bin ich – abgesehen von diesem Monitor da vor mir und den Vorteilen, die er mir durch die temporäre Existenz als Stimme in einem zeitkollabierten Raum [dem Internet] bietet – den Menschen, die vor mir gelebt haben, sehr, sehr, sehr ähnlich.*

Paul D. Miller alias DJ Spooky [New York, USA] antwortete auf den konservativen Text, den *-j.* beigesteuert hatte. *-j.*hatte ihm offenbar einen zu engen Begriff des Menschen. Miller antwortete: *'Menschlichkeit' läßt sich auf viele verschiedene Arten beschreiben. Die online am meisten verwendete leitet sich von den einstigen Bedeutungsmigrationen ab, die von der Wertematrix herrühren, die wir 'Europa' nennen. [...] Aber kommt schon, Leute, ein Diskurs über Identität, der nur auf den letzten paar Jahrhunderten basiert, ist doch ein bißchen seicht. Ich bin kein [Techno-]Utopist. Ich sehe das Internet nicht als den Inbegriff der Kultur des auslaufenden 20. Jahrhunderts. Allerdings begünstigt es ganz eindeutig neue Betrachtungsweisen der Kultur und 'existentielle' Identitätstrategien. Ich spreche hier von Identitäts-'Strategien', weil die Identität ein Prozeß, ein kontinuierliches Ringen um Veränderung ist.*

Phoebe Sengers [Pennsylvania, USA] bereicherte die Diskussion um eine persönliche Anekdote, aus der hervorging, daß die Menschen [physisch gesehen] das schwache Glied der modernen Cyborg-Realität darstellten. Sie schrieb: *Im Dezember 1994 litt ich unter dem RSI-Syndrom [Schäden an den Gliedmaßen infolge mechanischer Überbeanspruchung] und einer so schweren Tendinitis in den Händen, daß Sie es nicht einmal bemerkt hätten, wenn ich versucht hätte, Ihre Hand zu drücken.*Während sie versuchte, ihre Arbeit am Keyboard fortzusetzen, stieg die RSI bis zu ihren Ellenbogen hoch. Sie gab das Keyboard auf und stieg auf Spracherkennungssoftware um – nur um prompt ihre Stimme zu verlieren. Schließlich kam sie zu dem Schluß, daß die von der Maschine bestimmte Intensität ihrer Arbeit sie phy-

Paul D. Miller, A.K.A. Dj Spooky [New York, NY] responded to the conservative nature of *-j.*'s text. *-j.* had apparently defined humanness too narrowly. Miller responded: *There are many ways of describing 'humanness'. The one that most are using on-line is derived from these previous migrations of meaning as inherited from the matrix of values we call 'Europe' ... But c'mon folks – a discourse about identity based solely on the last several centuries seems a bit shallow. I am no [techno] utopian. I don't see the Internet as the end all be all of late 20th century culture. But it is inarguably fostering new methods for viewing culture and strategies of 'existential' identity. I say 'strategies' of identity because identity is a process, a continuous engagement with change.*

Phoebe Sengers [Pennsylvania, USA] contributed a personal anecdote, implying that humans were the weak link [physically] in the contemporary cyborgian reality. She wrote: *By December 1994 I had RSI [repetitive stress injury], tendinitis in my hands so badly that if I tried to squeeze your fingers, you would not have noticed.* As she tried to continue her work at the keyboard her RSI then moved up into her elbows. She ditched the keyboard and moved to voice recognition software only to quickly lose her voice. Finally she concluded that the machine-driven rigour of her work was destroying her physically and she opted for more biologically friendly working conditions.

Steve Mann [Boston, USA] then contributed a text outlining his work as an engineer/artist. He takes a *surveillance situationist* approach, resituating the surveillance camera in disturbing and disorienting contexts in order to challenge the preconceived notions of surveillance and power in our societies. He views media tools as weapons and encourages 'little brother' to arm himself. Mann naturally took exception to *-j.*'s conservatism. *-j.* had written about recent developments in lounge culture: *Synthetic poly and rubber slides out of style, replaced by stepping out in rugged wool tweed and shiny 100% silk. Some have even traded in keyboards and scratch tables for the alto-sax and string bass.* To this Mann replied: *I'm thinking of a Harris tweed jacket, lined with a nice plastic hose intertwined throughout, in

sisch zerstörte, und sie entschied sich für biologisch verträglichere Arbeitsbedingungen.

Steve Mann [Boston, USA] brachte einen Text über seine Arbeit als Techniker/Künstler ein. Im Rahmen seines *überwachungssituationistischen* Ansatzes hatte er eine Überwachungskamera in verstörenden und unübersichtlichen Kontexten positioniert, um den vorgefaßten Begriff von Überwachung und Macht in unseren Gesellschaften zu hinterfragen. Er sieht die Werkzeuge der Medien als Waffen an und fordert den 'kleinen Bruder' dazu auf, sich selbst zu bewaffnen. Mann protestierte natürlich gegen *-j.*s konservativen Standpunkt. *-j.* hatte über die jüngsten Entwicklungen in der Lounge Culture geschrieben: *Synthetik und Gummi werden unmodern, und stattdessen sind rauher Wolltweed und glänzende reine Seide wieder in. Einige haben sogar ihre Keyboards und Scratch Tables gegen das Altsaxophon oder den Kontrabaß eingetauscht.* Darauf antwortete Mann: *Ich denke da an eine Harris-Tweedjacke mit einem hübschen Futter mit einem eingeflochtenen Plastikschlauch, in dem ein Kühlmittel zirkuliert, das dafür sorgt, daß mir die 133MHz 586er-Prozessoren, die ich zur Zeit in meiner Unterwäsche trage, nicht mehr den Bauch verbrennen.*

Rose Stasuk [Florida, USA] lenkte die Aufmerksamkeit auf ihre Web-Arbeit *The Body Internet*. Sie schrieb: *Das ist mein Körper – eine anthropomorphisierte Synopse meiner künstlerischen Forschung und Praxis. Da der Körper unser Vehikel zum Verständnis der natürlichen Welt ist [...], eignet er sich genauso gut als Metapher für den Austausch.* Carmen Hermosillo [Kalifornien, USA] antwortete darauf: *Meine Auffassung vom Körper ist zur Zeit in einer Veränderung begriffen. Ich glaube, wir haben uns zu sehr für die 'fleischlichen' Aspekte des Körpers interessiert und dabei einige der anderen Gesichtspunkte außer acht gelassen. Ich meine beispielsweise, eine Beschäftigung mit den elektrischen Aspekten des Körpers wäre für die Schaffung einer Metapher, mit der man tatsächlich etwas anfangen könnte, wesentlich sinnvoller. [...] Ich glaube, es gibt einen Punkt, an dem die Cspace-Theorie wirklich an ihre Grenzen stößt, und dieser Punkt ist die Tatsache, daß die Menschen offenbar nicht imstande sind, ihr Denken vom fleischlichen Körper zu lösen. Der Cspace ist kein alternativer fleischlicher Körper. Er ist keine Erweiterung der Natur in dem Sinne, in dem wir üblicherweise von der Natur zu denken gelernt haben. Er existiert unabhängig von der Natur, trotz aller ökofeministischen Theorien.*

which the coolant flows, so that I no longer scorch my belly with the 133MHz 586 processors I currently have in my undergarments.*

Rose Stasuk [Florida, USA] drew attention to her web work, *The Body Internet*. She wrote: *This is my body – an anthropomorphized synopsis of my art research and practice. Since the body is our vehicle for understanding the natural world ... it makes an equally good metaphor for exchange.* Carmen Hermosillo [California, USA] responded: *My thinking about the body is undergoing a change. I think that we've been too interested in the meatbody aspects of the body and ignoring some of the other aspects. I think for example that looking at the electrical aspects of the body would be more rewarding in terms of creating a metaphor that one could actually DO something with ... It seems to me that there is a place where space theory gets really stalled, and that place appears to be that people do not seem to be able to divorce their thinking from the meatbody thing. Cspace is not an alternative meatbody. It is not an extension of nature in the sense that we have ordinarily been taught to think of nature. It exists apart from nature, eco-feminist ideology notwithstanding.*

Jill Scott [Karlsruhe, Germany] then submitted a description of her latest work, *Digital Body-Automata*. Resonating with Rose Stasuk's use of the body as a means for organizing theory, Scott embodies theory in a series of interactive installations. She wrote: *[*Digital Body-Automata*] consists of three installations called: *A figurative History* [past mechanical transformation]; *Interskin* [present digital transformation] and *Immortal Duality* [future molecular transformation]. These installations are designed to encourage intimate and contemplative and interactive participation on the part of the viewer and center around a similar theme; the exploration of the desire to transform the human body by technology, and the effect technology may have on the design of the human body in the future.

Guillermo Gòmez-Peña, A.K.A. El Mexterminator [California, USA] then contributed a text outlining current debates about the body and new technologies and how these debates had polarized the experimental arts commu-

Jill Scott [Karlsruhe, Deutschland] schickte uns daraufhin eine Beschreibung ihres jüngsten Werks mit dem Titel *Digital Body-Automata*. Scott griff Rose Stasuks Idee von der Verwendung des Körpers als Mittel der Theorieorganisation auf und verkörperte Theorie in einer Reihe interaktiver Installationen. Sie schrieb uns: *[*Digital Body-Automata*] besteht aus drei Installationen mit den folgenden Titeln: *A figurative History* [mechanische Transformation der Vergangenheit], *Interskin* [digitale Transformation der Gegenwart] und *Immortal Duality* [molekulare Transformation der Zukunft]. Diese Installationen sollen den Betrachter zur persönlichen, kontemplativen und interaktiven Beteiligung ermutigen und konzentrieren sich alle auf ein ähnliches Thema: auf die Erforschung des Wunsches, den menschlichen Körper durch Technologie zu transformieren, und die Auswirkungen, die die Technologie in der Zukunft auf das Aussehen des menschlichen Körpers haben könnte.*

Guillermo Gòmez-Peña alias El Mexterminator [Kalifornien, USA] übermittelte uns in der weiteren Folge einen Text, der sich mit der gegenwärtigen Debatte über Körper und neue Technologien beschäftigt, sowie mit der Art und Weise, wie diese Debatten die Gemeinschaft der experimentellen Kunst und das Milieu der Performancekunst polarisiert haben. Peña schrieb: *In der 'Maschinenkunst'-Bewegung gibt es einerseits die Verfechter eines totalen Verschwindens des menschlichen Körpers, die dessen Ersetzung durch Computer oder mechanische Roboter befürworten, während er für die anderen, obzwar obsolet, weiter im Mittelpunkt des Kunst-Events bleiben kann, aber mit neuen Technologien aufgerüstet, die als Prothesen [physische und Wahrnehmungsprothesen] fungieren. Eine 'aus dem Bauch' kommende Reaktion auf diese Vorschläge ist die der Künstler von 'Apocalypse Culture'. Sie haben sich für einen radikalen ludditischen Standpunkt entschieden: die Rückforderung des Urkörpers als Ort der Empfindung von Vergnügen und Schmerz und die 'Rückkehr' [wie sie behaupten] zu einer Art neo-tribalistischem Heidentum, womit sie in enge Nähe zur westlichen Tradition der anarchistischen 'Aussteiger'-Kultur rücken. Roberto und ich versuchen, eine vierte Option zu erforschen: die Verwendung neuer Technologien als Mittel zur Förderung der Interaktivität zwischen Künstlern und ihrem Live-Publikum [Touristen] sowie zum Sammeln einzigartiger, bekenntnishafter kultureller und politischer Informationen, die dann in unseren 'primitiven' politischen und erotischen Körper neu interpretiert und

nity and the performance art milieu. Peña wrote: *There are those in the 'machine art' movement who advocate the total disappearance of the human body and its replacement with computer or mechanical robotics; others believe that the body, though obsolete, can still remain in the center of the art event, but that new technology can equip it with prosthetic [perceptual and physical] extensions. A visceral reaction to these proposals can be found in the artists of *apocalypse culture* who have adopted a radical luddite stance: to reclaim the body primitive as a site for pleasure and pain, and *return* [so they claim] to a sort of neotribal paganism, very much in the western tradition of anarchist *dropout* culture. What Roberto and I are trying to do is explore a fourth option: to use new technologies as a means to enhance the interactivity between performers and live audiences [voyagers/tourists]; and to gather cultural, and political information of a very unique confessional nature, which will then be reinterpreted by and expressed through our *primitive,* political and erotic bodies. What the live audience ends up experiencing is a sort of visualization of their own post-colonial demons and racist mirages.*

Guillermo Cifuentes [New York, USA] then made reference to Carmen Hermosillo's statement on *the difficulties of leaving the meatbody behind.* Cifuentes wrote: *That seems indeed to be both the limit and a central issue in this discussion. How, if at all, can we forget the meatbody? We seem to leap into metaphors and abstractions in order to ... preach to ourselves [about] the disappearance of our bodies. But when we turn around and attempt to think about who we become in this process we seem forced to return to the meatbody: as erotic, politic, even historic site. In a way, even while we are able to viably sustain a notion of 'subjectivity' which no longer resides -or at least not exclusively – in the body, the idea of 'self' – battered but ready to battle – seeks the meatbody as locus and limit ... At the same time, I am quite dumbstruck by the intensity with which metaphors acquire their own substance in these discussions [... 'natural' 'nature' 'organism' etc.]. Often it seems to me that we forget that whatever it is the shape and consistency our flesh

dann durch sie zum Ausdruck gebracht werden. Was das Live-Publikum schließlich erlebt, ist eine Art Visualisierung seiner eigenen postkolonialen Dämonen und rassistischen Trugbilder.*

Guillermo Cifuentes [New York, USA] bezog sich auf Carmen Hermosillos Statement über 'die Schwierigkeiten, den fleischlichen Körper hinter sich zu lassen'. Cifuentes schrieb: *Dies scheint tatsächlich sowohl die Grenze als auch ein zentrales Thema dieser Diskussion zu sein. Wie können wir den fleischlichen Körper vergessen, falls dies überhaupt möglich ist? Wir scheinen uns in Metaphern und Abstraktionen zu flüchten, um [...] uns selbst das Verschwinden unserer Körper zu predigen. Aber wenn wir uns umdrehen und versuchen, darüber nachzudenken, was in diesem Prozeß eigentlich aus uns wird, kehren wir offenbar gezwungenermaßen zum fleischlichen Körper als erotischem, politischem und sogar historischem Ort zurück. Sogar wenn es uns gelingt, den Begriff der 'Subjektivität' aufrechtzuerhalten, die nicht mehr – oder nicht mehr ausschließlich – im Körper beheimatet ist, sucht der Gedanke des mißhandelten, aber zu seiner Verteidigung bereiten 'Selbst' in gewisser Weise den fleischlichen Körper als Ort und Grenze. [...] Zugleich bin ich ziemlich sprachlos angesichts der Intensität, mit der Metaphern in diesen Diskussionen ihre eigene Substanz erwerben ['natürlich', 'Natur', 'Organismus' etc.]. Ich habe oft den Eindruck, wir vergessen, daß die Form und Konsistenz, die unser Fleisch in diesem Medium annimmt, jedenfalls überraschend sprachlicher Natur ist. Man könnte nun natürlich argumentieren, daß die Technologie sich noch immer weiterentwickelt und daß die Verbesserung der Echtzeitkapazitäten des Mediums im Audio- und Bildbereich diese Aussage bald schon in Frage stellen wird. In gewisser Weise trifft dies heute schon zu, denn alles deutet darauf hin, daß die digitalen Technologien und das Netz zum totalen Medium werden. Doch als eine Art Rest bleibt in diesem Prozeß noch immer die Tatsache, daß wir – meiner Meinung nach ziemlich stark – dazu neigen, uns in Sprache zu verwandeln: Die Tastatur und nicht der Bildschirm ist die ultimative Schnittstelle, die dominanteste Verbindung in dieser technologischen Kette – wenigstens bisher.*

Ebon Fisher [New York, USA] antwortete auf Guillermo Gòmez-Peñas Beitrag: *[Wir] versuchen, eine vierte Option zu erforschen: die Verwendung neuer Technologien als Mittel zur Förderung der Interaktivität zwischen Künstlern und ihrem Live-Publikum [Touristen].* Fisher schrieb: *Das hört sich ja sehr sinnvoll und vielversprechend an. Doch wie

is acquiring through this medium, it is strikingly linguistic in character. It could be argued that the technology is still developing and that the enhancement of audio and image real-time capabilities of the medium will rapidly render that point moot. Which in a way is true as digital technologies and the Net promise to become the total medium. But it still remains, as a residue in this process, the fact that we tend, quite strongly it seems to me, to turn ourselves into language: the keyboard, and not the screen, is the ultimate interface, the most dominant link in this technological line, at least thus far.*

Ebon Fisher [New York, USA] then responded to Guillermo Gòmez-Peña's statement: *What [we're] trying to do is explore a fourth option: to use new technologies as a means to enhance the interactivity between performers and live audiences [vougers/tourists]. Fisher wrote: *That sounds very promising and valuable. How about a 5th option?, expanding the circle beyond just the techno/social: Foaming interspecies confluxes. Getting past not only the alienation of the individual, but the alienation of society/technology from the surrounding 'wilderness' [whatever THAT is]. Certain elements of the pagan/rave diaspora holds out that promise, although with a degree of wobbly confusion ... We experimented in a concerted attempt at 'emergent behaviour' from many technologies, art disciplines, and local fauna [slugs, mice, and microbes] precisely with a wiggling multimedia/multimodal/interspecies conflux in mind. 'Organism' was given birth in Williamsburg, Brooklyn in 1993 in an abandoned mustard factory, and we had a bewilderingly good time doing it. Over 2,000 people 'web jammed' all night and into the next morning.* Fisher had previously informed *FleshFactor* of his *Wigglism Manifesto*, a poetic vehicle for the propagation of an interspecies culture, generated by, and also a treatment of, a uniquely networked subjectivity.

Mark Weiser [California, USA] wrote: *Everything is mediated. Our bodies, our senses, our brains, our minds, all contribute to the mediation of everything. There is no increase of mediated experience. Experience has always been totally mediated.* And he took issue with an earlier post by Carmen Hermosillo on simu-

wäre es mit einer fünften Option? Mit einer Erweiterung des Kreises über den bloßen techno/ sozialen Bereich hinaus: eine Zusammenführung der verschiedenen Spezies? Eine Überwindung nicht nur der Entfremdung des Individuums, sondern der Entfremdung der Gesellschaft/Technologie von der sie umgebenden 'Wildnis' [was immer das auch bedeuten mag]? Bestimmte Elemente der Pagan/ Rave-Diaspora stellen das in Aussicht, wenn auch etwas wirr und konfus. [...] Wir haben in einem gemeinsamen Versuch mit 'emergent behaviour' experimentiert – mit vielen Technologien, Kunstdisziplinen und der lokalen Fauna [Schnecken, Mäuse und Mikroben] –, und hatten dabei eine wabbernde Multimedia/Multimodal/Interspezies-Zusammenführung im Kopf. *Organism* entstand 1993 in Williamsburg, Brooklyn, in einer aufgelassenen Senffabrik, und es war für uns eine unglaublich tolle Erfahrung. Mehr als 2.000 Leute nahmen teil, und das 'Web Jamming' dauerte die ganze Nacht lang bis zum nächsten Vormittag.* Fisher hatte *FleshFactor* zuvor ausführlich über sein *Wigglism Manifesto* informiert, ein poetisches Instrument zur Verbreitung einer Interspezies-Kultur, die durch eine einzigartig vernetzte Subjektivität entsteht und sich mit eben dieser beschäftigt.

Mark Weiser [Kalifornien, USA] schrieb uns: *Alles wird vermittelt. Unsere Körper, unsere Sinne, unsere Gehirne, unser Verstand, sie alle tragen zur Vermittlung von irgend etwas bei. Es kommt zu keinem Anstieg der vermittelten Erfahrung. Die Erfahrung wurde schon immer zur Gänze vermittelt.* Und er bezog sich auf eine frühere Message von Carmen Hermosillo über Simulation. Hermosillo hatte darin betont, daß unser gegenwärtiger Naturbegriff uns von Wahrnehmungsinstinkten und -filtern vermittelt würde, die uns wiederum durch Erziehung, historische Perspektiven, Malerei etc. vermittelt worden seien. Weiser schrieb dazu: *Ich bin mit diesem Teil Ihres Statements über die Vermittlung einverstanden, doch wieso wird das Ganze dadurch zu einer Simulation? In einer Simulation von Regen wird man nicht naß. Aber ich werde sehr wohl naß, wenn ich die Natur durch die Vermittlung meines/meiner Sinne[s] wahrnehme. Bei dieser Unterscheidung geht es um die Transparenz. Scheint die Welt transparent durch, oder gibt es da eine andere, simulierte Welt?*

Richard Brown [London, England] übermittelte uns dann einen Text über die Rolle von Verstand, Körper und Geist in der interaktiven Kunst. Brown betonte, daß Duchamp in seiner Kunst Verstand und

lation. Hermosillo had pointed out that our contemporary sense of nature was mediated by perceptual instincts and filters mediated by education, historical perspectives, painting, etc. Weiser wrote: *I agree with the mediation point, but why does that make it a simulation? In a simulation of rain, you don't get wet. But even in perceiving nature through the mediation of my sense[s], I do get wet. The distinction is of transpicience. Does the world shine through transpiciently, or is there another world being simulated?*

Richard Brown [London, England] then contributed a text on the role of mind, body and spirit in interactive art. Stressing that Duchamp had made art that had embodied mind and spirit, Brown wrote: *The FleshFactor debate intellectualises whereas a strong Interactive Art [IA] piece puts theory into practice. Via IA, I seek to question the conventions of virtual reality by challenging theoretical definitions of virtuality, mathematical and philosophical speculations on reality and in turn our uncertainty principle like relationship to a perceptual reality. Post-millennium IA should empower and enlighten [holistic spirit nature] ... I advocate a Duchampian Alchemy – the synthesis of dualities – where East meets West, Art meets Science, Mind accepts Body and Spirit resonates with Nature.*

Patricia Smith Churchland [California, USA] then contributed the following text, apparently triggered by Guillermo Gòmez-Peña's reference to a *machine art* movement's advocation of the complete replacement of the body by intelligent robots. Churchland wrote: *At this stage, there is no serious possibility of humans managing without their bodies; in particular, without that part of the body that is the nervous system. And because the nervous system interconnects with the muscles, glands, gut, skin, tendons etc in extremely complicated ways, with feedforward AND feedback signals, there is at present no serious possibility of managing without arms and legs, eyes and ears, stomachs and livers, and so on. It is quite possible that the dynamic biological system [body + nervous system] that has evolved to allow us to manage on this planet is much more capable of dealing with matters in real time, and

Geist verkörpert habe, und schrieb uns: *Die *Flesh-Factor*-Debatte intellektualisiert, während ein starkes interaktives Kunstwerk die Theorie in die Praxis umsetzt. Ich versuche, mittels interaktiver Kunst die Konventionen der virtuellen Realität in Frage zu stellen, indem ich theoretische Definitionen von Virtualität, mathematische und philosophische Spekulationen über die Realität oder auch unser Unsicherheitsprinzip, wie die Beziehung zu einer Realität der Wahrnehmung, hinterfrage. Die interaktive Kunst des nächsten Jahrtausends sollte ermächtigen und aufklären [holistischer Ansatz]. [...] Ich bin ein Verfechter einer Alchimie im Sinne Duchamps – einer Synthese der Dualitäten, in der sich Ost und West, Kunst und Wissenschaft treffen, in der der Verstand den Körper akzeptiert und der Geist mit der Natur mitschwingt.*

Patricia Smith Churchland [Kalifornien, USA] sandte uns dann den folgenden Text, der offensichtlich von Guillermo Gòmez-Peñas Bemerkung inspiriert war, die 'Maschinenkunst'-Bewegung würde die vollständige Ersetzung des Körpers durch intelligente Roboter befürworten. Churchland schrieb uns: *Zur Zeit gibt es für Menschen keine ernsthafte Möglichkeit, ohne ihre Körper und insbesondere ohne ihr Nervensystem auszukommen. Und da das Nervensystem mit den Muskeln, Drüsen und Eingeweiden, mit der Haut, den Sehnen etc. auf so extrem komplizierte Art und Weise verbunden ist, daß Signale afferent und efferent übermittelt werden können, gibt es zur Zeit keine ernsthafte Möglichkeit, ohne Arme und Beine, Augen und Ohren, Magen und Leber etc. auszukommen. Es ist durchaus möglich, daß das dynamische biologische System [Körper + Nervensystem], das sich entwickelt hat, damit wir auf diesem Planeten zurechtkommen, wesentlich besser imstande ist, Dinge in Echtzeit und mit größerer Präzision zu erledigen, als künstliche [nicht-biologische] Einheiten es je schaffen werden. Beispielsweise können Flugzeuge zwar schneller fliegen als Vögel und auch Passagiere befördern, aber Vögel können sogar in extrem schwierigen Situationen landen, sich fortpflanzen, sich selbst mit Nahrung versorgen, Kollisionen vermeiden etc., wozu Flugzeuge wahrscheinlich so nie in der Lage sein werden. Oder zumindest wird es den Zeit- und Kostenaufwand sowie die Anstrengungen nicht wert sein, Flugzeuge zu entwickeln, die die ganze Palette komplizierter Dinge tun können, die beispielsweise ein Pelikan kann. Das heißt, wir können intelligente Maschinen für beschränkte Zwecke herstellen, aber wahrscheinlich nicht für die gesamte Palette komplizier-

with greater precision, than manufactured [non-biological] devices can ever be. Just as planes may fly faster and carry more folks than birds, birds can land in extremely delicate situations, reproduce, feed themselves, avoid collisions etc in ways that planes probably never will. Or at least it will not be worth the time, cost, and effort to get planes to do the complicated range of things that a pelican, for example, can do. So we may manufacture intelligent machines for limited purposes, but probably not for the whole range of complicated things that humans do: e.g. tending children ... So I wonder whether it is a bit too early in the game to worry too much about being replaced by manufactured brains. I am atraid I have a very practical bent, and I worry more about things we really need to know but don't yet know: e.g. how to predict, prevent, and successfully treat schizophrenia – and other diseases of the nervous systems, such as multiple sclerosis, Lou Gherig's disease, Alzheimer's, etc.*

Dennis Wilcox [Darlinghurst, Australia] then wrote: The hyperstructure of the human body can be amplified through technology assuming that you can equate the figurative hyperstructure as something more than the cognitive slicing of the flesh [corporeal mind]. This I regard as a spatial/time problem. Unfortunately society is so heavily influenced by the two dimensional in cinematic abstract space, that a great deal of energy has been devoted limiting the senses to the pinhole of the peripheral bromide! ... A device which I am currently developing can create a 360 degree volumetric [computer generated solid] in real time. By adapting the principals of creating a real time three dimensional [real volume] morphology, I believe I have found a way to amplify the fourth dimensional [the fourth dimension as space rather than time] hyperstructure of the human form...What results within the vortex of my display is a 'figurative hypersculpture' generated from a number of human movements. This is hoped to create a greater sense of hypervision, an appreciation of higher abstract space, and hopefully an evolution of vision beyond the imprisonment of the fallible senses and the cinematic gaze.*

ter Dinge, die Menschen tun, wie z. B. Kinder großziehen etc. [...] Deshalb frage ich mich, ob es in diesem Spiel nicht etwas verfrüht ist, sich derartige Sorgen um eine Ablösung durch künstliche Gehirne zu machen. Ich fürchte, ich bin sehr praktisch veranlagt und mache mir mehr Sorgen um Dinge, die für uns wirklich von Bedeutung sind und die wir noch nicht kennen, z. B. wie man Schizophrenie, aber auch andere Erkrankungen des Nervensystems, wie beispielsweise Multiple Sklerose, das Lou-Gherig-Syndrom, die Alzheimersche Krankheit etc., vorhersagen, verhindern und erfolgreich behandeln kann.*

Dennis Wilcox [Darlinghurst, Australien] schrieb daraufhin: *Die Hyperstruktur des menschlichen Körpers kann durch Technologie erweitert werden, wenn man davon ausgeht, daß man die figurative Hyperstruktur als mehr denn nur die kognitive Ausformung des Fleisches ansehen kann [verkörperlichter Geist]. Ich betrachte dies als ein Problem von Raum und Zeit. Leider ist die Gesellschaft derart stark von der Zweidimensionalität im abstrakten kinematischen Raum beeinflußt, daß sehr große Energien darauf verwendet wurden, die Sinne auf das Nadelöhr der Peripherieplatitüden zu beschränken! [...] Ich entwickle zur Zeit ein Gerät, das eine 360-Grad-Volumetrie [computergenerierter Festkörper] in Echtzeit schaffen kann. Ich glaube, durch die Adaptierung der Grundsätze der Schaffung einer dreidimensionalen Echtzeit-Morphologie [Echtvolumen] habe ich eine Möglichkeit gefunden, die vierte Dimension der Hyperstruktur der menschlichen Form zu verstärken [wobei ich mit der vierten Dimension eher den Raum als die Zeit meine]. [...] Was im Strudel meines Displays entsteht, ist eine 'figurative Hyperskulptur', die aus einer Reihe menschlicher Bewegungen entstanden ist. Dadurch soll, so hoffe ich, ein stärkeres Bewußtsein für die Hypervision, ein positives Verständnis für den höheren abstrakten Raum und hoffentlich auch eine Entwicklung des Gesichtssinns über das Gefängnis der fehlbaren Sinne und das kinematische Sehen hinaus entstehen.*

Mark Weiser [Kalifornien, USA] sandte eine Antwort auf Laura Vandenburghs früheren Text. Er schrieb: *Laura Vandenburgh schreibt [über die] 'Flucht vor den Zwängen der Biologie durch unsere Verbindung mit der Technologie' [...]. Die Biologie ist eine Technologie, eine Technologie des Fleisches. Eine Technologie, von der wir nicht besonders viel verstehen, eine Technologie, die nicht erfunden, sondern entdeckt wurde wie die Schwerkraft, wie die Verwendung eines Steins als Axt, wie das Fliegen. Aber wir können der Biologie durch die Technologie

Mark Weiser [California, USA] then contributed a response to Laura Vandenburgh's earlier text. He wrote: *Laura Vandenburgh writes [of] 'escaping the constraints of biology through our integration with technology' ... Biology is a technology, a meat technology. A technology we don't understand very well, a technology that was not invented but discovered, like gravity, like using a rock as an axe, like flying. But we can no more escape biology through technology than we can escape death by committing suicide. ... Laura Vandenburgh also writes: 'Science and technology play a big role in our lives, drive a lot of change, and organize the way we perceive the world. Other ways of knowing aren't highly valued'...Too true. And yet science and technology as practised by scientists and technologists also make crucial use of other ways of knowing. Sandra Harding in her book on feminist science called *'Whose Science?'* discusses the concept that 'physics' is a poor model of physics. By this she means that the concept of physics as reported in physics journals and by physicists themselves – the myth of physics – is in fact a very poor model of what physicists actually do, which involves intuition, bodily knowing, cultural and historically biased seeing, etc. Physics is required to ignore the sociology of physics. But if one wants to really know physics and the human frailties of the real work of physics, one cannot ask a physicist.*

Carmen Hermosillo [California, USA] then submitted a text sympathetic of Guillermo Cifuentes and his references to Bataille and other pre-digital writers. Hermosillo, referring to Bataille's examination of Emily Brontë's main characters in *Wuthering Heights,* writes: *[that Bataille felt Brontë's novel was] a huge tragedy of language categories, a tragedy that is recycled [today] every single time that some new person goes online, starts responding to chat or !ntalk or !talk or whatever, and starts the dialogue which to me has some of the ritualistic beauty of medieval chant litany or ritual catechism: who are you?/who are YOU?/are you real?/yes, are YOU? And so forth: until it has its peak in the mutual orgasm which in its highest and most highly physical and intimate and personal form occurs probably on the telephone. & this attempt to discern the meatbody behind

ebensowenig entfliehen, wie wir dem Tod durch Selbstmord entkommen können. [...] Laura Vandenburgh schreibt auch: *Wissenschaft und Technologie spielen eine bedeutende Rolle in unserem Leben, bewirken eine große Anzahl von Veränderungen und organisieren die Art und Weise, in der wir die Welt wahrnehmen. Andere Arten des Wissens werden nicht hoch bewertet. [...]* Das ist nur zu wahr. Und doch setzt die von Wissenschaftlern und Technikern praktizierte Wissenschaft und Technologie auch andere Arten des Wissens in entscheidender Weise ein. Sandra Harding diskutiert in ihrem Buch über feministische Wissenschaft *Whose Science*? den Gedanken, daß die 'Physik' ein schlechtes Modell der Physik sei. Damit meint sie, daß der Begriff der 'Physik', wie er in Physikzeitschriften und von Physikern selbst verwendet wird – der Mythos der Physik – in Wirklichkeit ein sehr armseliges Modell der tatsächlichen Tätigkeit der Physiker ist, die auch Intuition, körperliches Erfahren, kulturell und historisch beeinflußte Sichtweisen etc. miteinschließt. Die 'Physik' muß die Soziologie der Physik ignorieren. Doch wenn man wirklich etwas über die Physik und die menschlichen Schwächen der tatsächlichen Arbeit der Physiker erfahren möchte, darf man keinen Physiker fragen.

Carmen Hermosillo [Kalifornien, USA] sandte weiters einen Text, der die Ausführungen von Guillermo Cifuentes und seine Bezugnahmen auf Bataille und andere prädigitale Autoren unterstützte. Hermosillo schrieb in bezug auf Batailles Analyse von Emily Brontë's Hauptfiguren in *Sturmhöhe*: *[Batailles Empfinden, Brontë's Roman] sei eine gewaltige Tragödie sprachlicher Kategorien, ist eine Tragödie, die [heute] jedes Mal wiederauflebt, wenn jemand neu ins Netz geht und beginnt, auf chat oder !ntalk oder !talk oder was auch immer zu antworten, und den Dialog aufnimmt, der für mich etwas von der ritualistischen Schönheit der mittelalterlichen Litaneien oder des rituellen Katechismus hat: -wer bist du? -wer bist DU? -bist du real? -ja, und DU? Und so weiter bis zum Erreichen des beidseitigen Orgasmus, der in seiner höchsten, kreatürlichsten, intimsten und persönlichsten Form wahrscheinlich am Telefon stattfindet. Und dieser Versuch, hinter den Buchstaben den Körper aus Fleisch und Blut ausfindig zu machen, ist für mich wahrhaftig das *Introibo ad Altare Dei* des ausgehenden 20. Jahrhunderts.*

Peter Charlot [Hawaii, USA] antwortete auf Patricia Churchlands früheres Statement – *deshalb frage ich mich, ob es in diesem Spiel nicht etwas verfrüht ist, sich derartige Sorgen um eine Ablösung

the letters, is truly, as I tell you, the *introibo ad Altare Dei* of the late 20th century.*

Peter Charlot [Hawaii, USA], responding to Patricia Churchland's earlier statement, *I wonder whether it is a bit too early in the game to worry too much about being replaced by manufactured brains,* wrote as follows. Charlot: *I don't think it is to early to worry. Please worry. Save us! You are one of the captains of the ship of brain research, don't let it be the *Titanic*. [I tend to the histrionic.] Perhaps spread throughout the silicon soup of computer programmers, the pieces of the conscious machine have already arrived. These parts might link together without our direction at all, but by the same process of evolution that linked our human organs; only faster. This is the unwitting Flesh-Factor theory.* He continued, obviously with a sense of humour: *If we allow fate to become the heart of a *Machina artificio sapiens* then we risk contending with minds that may refuse to take Turing tests, claiming such tests to be machinist. The point is we won't be able to control what such machines will want to do. Some may want to play pool, or listen to music. But at some point these machines are going to want to acquire land, found churches, govern themselves and/or [ship's horn heard from out of the Atlantic ocean fog] govern us. Help!*

Diana Domingues [Rio Grande do Sul, Brazil] then wrote: *Concerning Richard Brown's *FleshFactor* message: I don't agree with some of what Richard wrote. [He referred to] 'The role of mind, body and spirit in interactive art'...and 'The body hosts the mind'...These are such classic statements...never again should we present the analytical paradigm that the whole is made simply by the addition of the parts. In the heart of a system, the quality of the parts and their tasks disappear when they are working ... We must never repeat the separation of body, mind and spirit. This is a definition from the mechanistic paradigm. We must delete this old classification from our discourse and only speak about the body ... Interactive Art is really humanizing technologies. To see, to touch, to sensually experience algorithms, infrared waves, to capture invisible forces giving them visibility, to check organic laws [that] give us many experiences of consciousness-propagation in a

durch künstliche Gehirne zu machen* – wie folgt: *Ich glaube nicht, daß es verfrüht ist, sich Sorgen zu machen. Mach dir bitte Sorgen. Rette uns! Du bist einer der Kapitäne, die das Schiff der Gehirnforschung steuern, laß es nicht zur Titanic werden. [Ich habe einen Hang zum Theatralischen.] Vermutlich sind die Einzelteile der bewußten Maschine bereits unter uns: verstreut in der Siliziumsuppe der Computerprogrammierer. Diese Teile könnten sich ganz ohne unser Zutun miteinander verbinden, durch denselben Evolutionsprozeß, der unsere menschlichen Organe miteinander verbunden hat, nur würde diesmal alles schneller gehen. Das ist die unausgesprochene *FleshFactor*-Theorie.* Und mit einem offenbaren Sinn für Humor fügte er hinzu: *Wenn wir das Schicksal zum Herzen einer Machina artificio sapiens werden lassen, laufen wir Gefahr, es mit Geistern aufnehmen zu müssen, die sich weigern könnten, den Turing-Test zu machen, weil sie derartige Tests für 'maschinisch' erklären. Der springende Punkt ist, daß wir nicht imstande sein werden, das Wollen dieser Maschinen zu steuern. Manche werden vielleicht Billard spielen oder Musik hören wollen. Aber irgendwann werden diese Maschinen an dem Punkt angelangen, an dem sie Land erwerben, Kirchen gründen, sich selbst verwalten und/oder [das Nebelhorn eines Schiffs dringt durch die dichten Nebelschwaden des Atlantischen Ozeans] uns regieren werden wollen. Hilfe!*

Diana Domingues [Rio Grande do Sul, Brasilien] schrieb: *Betrifft Richard Browns *FleshFactor*-Message: Ich bin mit einigen von Richards Gedanken nicht einverstanden. [Er bezog sich auf] 'die Rolle von Verstand, Körper und Geist in der interaktiven Kunst' [...] und meinte: 'Der Körper beherbergt den Verstand.' Das sind derart klassische Standpunkte [...]. Wir sollten nie wieder das analytische Paradigma strapazieren, daß das Ganze einfach die Summe seiner Teile ist. Im Herzen eines Systems verschwindet die Qualität der Teile und ihrer Aufgaben, wenn sie arbeiten. [...] Wir dürfen nie wieder von der Trennung von Körper, Verstand und Geist sprechen. Das ist eine Definition, die sich vom mechanistischen Paradigma herleitet. Wir müssen diese alte Klassifizierung aus unserem Diskurs streichen und dürfen nur noch vom Körper sprechen. [...] Die interaktive Kunst humanisiert die Technologien tatsächlich. Sehen, fühlen, Algorithmen und Infrarotwellen sinnlich erleben, unsichtbare Kräfte einfangen und sichtbar machen, organische Gesetze überprüfen, die uns viele Erfahrungen mit der Verbreitung von Bewußtsein in einer Symbiose von organischem/anorganischem Leben

symbiosis of organic/inorganic life in this post-biological era ... [in the future] New biological interfaces will be facilitated as permanent prostheses are attached on us and into our bodies and thus we will be reinventing our lives and the ultimate nature of our species.*

Derek Robinson [Toronto, Canada] then contributed a rich technical and poetic muse centering on the metaphysics and physics of interface design. Robinson wrote: *What distinguishes humans from primates is an 'embodied prehensility' which inhabits the entire voluntary body ... Our highly developed voluntary control, a somatic abstraction of sorts, is the flip-side of high level symbolic thought which characterizes human consciousness. We apprehend the world tactually, kinesthetically, through cross-modal transfer, by manipulating internal models of our environment ... Tools are materialized prehensilization. Ultimately the entire environment is prehensilized by consciousness. It becomes pregnant with incipient tool options, potentiating a vast array of possibilities in the world ... A human being can inhabit a machine. The somatic percept, one's kinesthetic self-representation, is extensible. It can flow, proprioceptively, like a phantom nervous system, into the fabric of a machine, be it tool or vehicle. This is the point at which one says one has the 'feel' of it. The machine is permeable to the 'charge' of consciousness ... We are the ghost in the machine.* Robinson concluded his muse with one of the most memorable quotes of the net-symposium, *Or what my daughter Rory said, age five: 'Everything I touch is skin.'*

Guillermo Cifuentes [New York, USA] then responded to Patricia Churchland's challenge to his statements about his flesh being rather linguistic in cspace. Churchland had written: *In what sense is my stomach linguistic? Or my tendons? Or my cortex? That I have names for them does not make them linguistic – does not make them a part of language in any obvious sense.* Cifuentes responded: *Precisely my point. As Carmen Hermosillo pointed out in her response, the search for the meatbody behind language is a primary impulse and part of the motor that drives us humans. Which is what Bataille knew: that when we reach, in the cate-

in dieser postbiologischen Ära vermitteln. [...] [In Zukunft] werden uns neue biologische Schnittstellen durch die Anbringung permanenter Prothesen an und in unseren Körpern zur Verfügung stehen, und dadurch werden wir unser Leben und die ultimative Natur unserer Spezies neu erfinden.*

Derek Robinson [Toronto, Kanada] schickte uns eine dichte technisch-poetische Reflexion, in der es um die Metaphysik und die Physik der Konstruktion von Schnittstellen ging. Er schrieb: *Was den Menschen vom Primaten unterscheidet, ist ein verkörpertes Greifvermögen, das dem gesamten willkürlichen Körper innewohnt. [...] Unsere hochentwickelte willkürliche Steuerung, in gewisser Weise eine somatische Abstraktion, spiegelt das komplexe symbolische Denken wider, das für das menschliche Bewußtsein charakteristisch ist. Wir begreifen die Welt durch unseren Tastsinn, durch unser Bewegungsgefühl, durch modalitätenübergreifenden Transfer, durch die Manipulation interner Modelle unserer Umwelt. [...] Werkzeuge sind materialisierte Greifbarmachung. Schließlich wird die gesamte Umwelt durch das Bewußtsein greifbar gemacht. Es steckt voll von unausgereiften Werkzeugoptionen, durch die eine riesige Auswahl an Möglichkeiten noch potenziert wird. [...] Ein Mensch kann einer Maschine innewohnen. Der Gegenstand der somatischen Wahrnehmung, unsere kinästhetische Selbstrepräsention, ist erweiterbar. Sie kann propriozeptiv wie ein Phantomnervensystem in eine Maschine – ob Werkzeug oder Vehikel – einfließen. Das ist der Punkt, an dem wir sagen, daß wir etwas im 'Gefühl' haben. Die Maschine wird durchdringbar von der 'Ladung' des Bewußtseins. [...] Wir sind der Geist in der Maschine.* Robinson schloß seine Ausführungen mit einem der bemerkenswertesten Zitate des Netzsymposiums: *Oder, wie meine fünfjährige Tochter Rory sagt: *'Alles, was ich berühre, ist Haut.'*

Guillermo Cifuentes [New York, USA] antwortete auf Patricia Churchlands Hinterfragung seiner Ausführungen über sein eher sprachliches Fleisch im Cspace. Churchland hatte geschrieben: *In welchem Sinne ist mein Magen sprachlich? Oder meine Sehne? Oder meine Großhirnrinde? Die bloße Tatsache, daß ich sie mit Namen versehe, verleiht ihnen noch keinen sprachlichen Charakter – und macht sie in keinem offensichtlichen Sinn zu einem Teil der Sprache.* Cifuentes antwortete darauf: *Genau das meine ich. Wie Carmen Hermosillo in ihrer Antwort betont hat, ist die Suche nach dem 'Fleisch und Blut', das hinter der Sprache steckt, ein primärer Impuls und Teil des Motors, der uns Menschen antreibt.

gories of language, the limit of the body and we transgress it [erotically in his case], language reverses, empties itself, falls apart. The flesh cannot be contained in the word flesh ... we forget that language remains, in my opinion, the primary form of mediation with which we choose to manifest ourselves ... In this regard, initially two things seemed to me to be crucial to remember: 1. Language is not neutral [ever], which seemingly many contributors in this forum don't want to think about [like when there is talk about some sort of liberated, free-floating subjectivity, or when 'identity' is discussed] and 2. [and here is where we agree] however versatile, lush, fleshy and juicy language is in cspace, it still amounts to a form of mediation and cannot, however hard we dream of it, finally, absolutely, irretrievably, efface the meatbody [subject to decay, but also, nostalgic me, capable of its own irreplaceable glories].*

Mark Weiser [California, USA], then responded to Peter Charlot's earlier call for help. Weiser wrote: *I sometimes feel about my teenage daughter the way Peter feels about machines. And the analogy is a deep one. Of course we will feel afraid as what we once thought we understood and could control moves into the world and it turns out we never did understand or control it at all. Anymore than we deeply understand and control our bodies or minds. But what is the *Help!?* Machines already want to acquire land, found churches, etc. Face it, Peter, you are a machine. And I look forward to meeting you.*

Peter Charlot [Hawaii, USA] then responded to Mark Weiser's earlier analogy about Weiser's teenage daughter and machines, that control is just an illusion. Charlot wrote: *What can I say, my daughter is two and I'm still into control and dominance! Sure I'm a machine and a territorial one at that. I'm hesitant to introduce a superior contender. Does anybody doubt that these silicon machines will, at some point, have the capability to usurp us? Is this where we want to go? Perhaps we have no choice...The reason we don't have conscious machines now is we haven't really defined our own intelligence and that is why such machines seem so remote. But it isn't far off at all ... It dawned on me one day, what if the hard part of designing the sili-

Bataille wußte: Wenn wir in den Kategorien der Sprache die Grenzen des Körpers erreichen und überschreiten [in diesem Fall im erotischen Sinn], kehrt sich die Sprache um, wird leer, zerfällt. Das Fleisch kann nicht im Wort *Fleisch* enthalten sein. [...] Wir vergessen meiner Meinung nach, daß die Sprache die primäre Form der Vermittlung ist, die wir wählen, um uns auszudrücken. [...] In dieser Hinsicht schien es mir anfangs besonders wichtig, zwei Dinge zu erwähnen: 1. Die Sprache ist nicht [nie] neutral, womit sich viele Teilnehmer dieses Forums offenbar nicht auseinandersetzen wollen [beispielsweise wenn von einer Art befreiter, freiflottierender Objektivität die Rede ist oder der Begriff der 'Identität' diskutiert wird], und 2. [und in diesem Punkt sind wir uns einig] wie vielfältig, saftig, fleischlich und pikant die Sprache im Cspace auch sein mag, dient sie doch nach wie vor der Vermittlung und kann trotz all unserer Träume den Körper aus Fleisch und Blut nicht endgültig, absolut und unwiederbringlich auslöschen [der Körper aus Fleisch und Blut ist dem Verfall preigegeben, aber auch – jetzt werde ich wieder nostalgisch – eigener unersetzlicher Ruhmestaten fähig].*

Mark Weiser [Kalifornien, USA] antwortete auf Peter Charlots früheren Hilferuf. Weiser schrieb: *Ich empfinde manchmal gegenüber meiner halbwüchsigen Tochter dasselbe, was Peter gegenüber Maschinen empfindet. Und die Analogie ist sehr weitreichend. Natürlich werden wir Angst haben, wenn das, was wir einst glaubten, verstehen und steuern zu können, auf der Welt Einzug hält und sich dann herausstellt, daß wir es überhaupt nie verstanden haben, daß wir es überhaupt nie steuern konnten. Ebensowenig wie wir, genau genommen, unseren Körper oder unseren Verstand verstehen oder kontrollieren können. Doch worin könnte die 'Hilfe!' bestehen? Maschinen wollen bereits heute Land erwerben, Kirchen gründen etc. finde dich damit ab, Peter: Du bist eine Maschine. Und ich hoffe auf ein baldiges Treffen mit dir.*

Peter Charlot [Hawaii, USA] antwortete auf die zuvor von Mark Weiser hergestellte Analogie zwischen seiner halbwüchsigen Tochter und Maschinen und auf seine Ansicht, Kontrolle sei nur eine Illusion: *Dazu kann ich nur sagen, daß meine Tochter zwei Jahre alt ist und noch ich das Sagen habe! Natürlich bin ich eine Maschine und noch dazu eine ziemlich territorial eingestellte. Ich habe etwas dagegen, einen überlegeneren Konkurrenten einzuführen. Hat wirklich noch irgend jemand Zweifel, daß diese Siliziummaschinen eines Tages imstande sein werden, sich unserer zu bemächtigen? Wollen wir das wirklich?

con machine was the cybernetic, and the easy part was the intelligence. What if the words running across our foreheads are the work of genetic algorithms? Perhaps they are algorithmic vowels that cooperate and compete to form speech through child-rearing feedback iterations. With appropriate memory in tow, random sounds [babbling] link together to form words, these are reinforced by the parents. In time, the sentences become more complex, even original. All the components of speech, such as grammar, develop on their own. A certain personality emerges, unpredicted and not programmed. A personality that is wholly dependent on the evolution and organization of these specific genetic algorithms [not to mention biological genetic influences]. Because these genetic algorithms are designed to sustain themselves, and speech is their ticket, then they will develop speech strategies to succeed. The winners will form a personality, a complex algorithmic ideosphere, which is analogous to the biosphere, being comprised of many contending but balanced idea-species. Some personalities will be kind, others cruel. Some will be average, some will be brilliant. There is no way of predicting.*

Charlot continued: *Write a computer program to conform to the above conditions. At first, just like a child, the words will be disorganized, but in time, they will grow sophisticated and even original. In its world, the computer is totally devoid of any sense of the outside, but for you. I think you will find that you are enough. This is a primary system you can create on a home PC. You could devise a machine that includes three of these personalities that interact from separate perspectives. One that organizes sensory input, one that estimates through simulation the future and one that divides itself into influencing the others from two philosophical perspectives, the one [holistic] and the many [linear]. Let these interact through heuristic and autocatalytic processes. Once you've gone this far, add a few sensory components, a couple of wheels, and what have you got?...Help!*

Max More [California, USA] then contributed a text called *Replacing the Body*, responding to Patricia Churchland's assertion that there is no serious possibility of humans manag-

Vielleicht haben wir ja gar keine andere Wahl. [...] Der Grund, weshalb wir heute über keine Maschinen mit Bewußtsein verfügen, ist, daß wir unsere eigene Intelligenz nicht wirklich definiert haben, und deshalb scheinen uns derartige Maschinen so unerreichbar. Dabei sind sie in Wirklichkeit alles andere als das. [...] Das dämmerte mir eines Tages, als ich mich fragte: Was, wenn die größte Schwierigkeit beim Bau der Siliziummaschine die Kybernetik und der einfachere Teil die Intelligenz wäre? Was, wenn die in unseren Köpfen ablaufenden Worte das Werk genetischer Algorithmen wären? Vielleicht sind sie mit- und gegeneinander arbeitende algorithmische Laute, die durch erzieherische Feedback-Wiederholungen unsere Sprache entstehen lassen. Bei angemessener Speicherkapazität werden sich zufällige Laute [Kindergebrabbel] zu Worten zusammenfügen, deren Richtigkeit durch die Reaktion der Eltern bestätigt wird, wodurch wiederum die Sprachentwicklung gefördert wird. Mit der Zeit werden die Sätze immer komplexer, sogar originell. Alle Bestandteile der Sprache, wie z. B. die Grammatik, entwickeln sich von selbst. Eine bestimmte Persönlichkeit – unvorhersehbar und nicht programmiert – entsteht. Eine Persönlichkeit, die zur Gänze von der Entwicklung und Organisation dieser spezifischen genetischen Algorithmen abhängig ist [ganz abgesehen von den genetischen, biologischen Einflüssen]. Da diese genetischen Algorithmen so definiert sind, daß sie sich selbst erhalten, und die Sprache dafür die Voraussetzung ist, werden sie in der weiteren Folge sprachliche Strategien entwickeln, um sich durchzusetzen. Die Gewinner werden eine Persönlichkeit ausbilden, eine komplexe, algorithmische Ideosphäre, analog zur Biosphäre, die aus vielen konkurrierenden, aber wohlausbalancierten Spezies von Ideen besteht. Einige dieser Persönlichkeiten werden gut sein, andere grausam. Manche werden durchschnittlich sein und andere brillant. Eine Vorhersage ist nicht möglich.*

Charlot schrieb weiter: *Schreiben Sie ein Computerprogramm, das den obigen Vorgang nach vollzieht. Zuerst werden die Wörter wie bei einem Kind unzusammenhängend sein, aber mit der Zeit wird die Sprache intelligent und sogar originell werden. Dem Computer fehlt in seiner Welt jeglicher Sinn für die Außenwelt – mit Ausnahme seines Benutzers. Ich nehme an, Sie werden meinen, daß das reicht. Dieses primäre System können Sie auf Ihrem PC nachvollziehen. Sie könnten eine Maschine mit drei derartigen Persönlichkeiten konstruieren, die von unterschiedlichen Perspektiven aus interagieren. Eine dieser Persönlichkeiten organisiert den sensorischen

ing without their bodies, particularly the nervous system. More wrote: *Even though I do expect one day to become postbiological [assuming we discover how to extend life spans in the next few decades] I agree that this won't happen anytime soon. I find the uploading scenario fascinating – mapping the brain's functions then re-embodying them in a faster nonbiological device. However, I see that as a far-off possibility. What I do think we'll see ... is the gradual augmentation of the biological brain with nonbiological components. The end result of this process might be the replacement of the natural brain with synthetic parts ... [while] this certainly is not 'managing without our bodies'. It does suggest that we will replace some biological parts, and augment their functions. I do think there is a serious possibility that we will replace our nervous systems with technological analogs [working faster with higher bandwidth].*

Max More goes on to speculate that Churchland's statement that the human biological system will continue to reign supreme in dealing with matters in real-time and with far greater precision than manufactured non-biological devices is shortsighted. More wrote: *Nature had no foresight and 'designed' us by accumulating small steps. Sometimes this led to design flaws [such as Dawkins pointed out about the eye in *The Blind Watchmaker*], and always used only the available materials. Vast amounts of work lie ahead to understand the brain and 'artificial' intelligences. Yet, we know that nerve impulses work in milliseconds rather than nanoseconds. Given enough time and better technologies, I find it hard to believe that we can't do better than nature.*

More continued: *One reason that I don't worry too much about being replaced by manufactured brains [apart from the difficulty of making them] is because I think the us-and-them division will break down. Once we have understood and treated these neuropsychological problems, I hope we will become more inter ested in augmenting our cognitive and emotional functions. As computers get ever smaller and come with more intelligent interfaces, as we learn to couple brains to computers and information networks, we should see a dee-

Input, eine andere schätzt durch Simulationen die Zukunft ein, und die dritte beeinflußt die anderen von zwei philosophischen Standpunkten aus – dem des Einen [holistisch] und dem des Vielen [linear]. Lassen Sie diese Persönlichkeiten mittels heuristischer und selbstkatalytischer Prozesse interagieren. Wenn Sie auf dieser Stufe angelangt sind, bauen Sie einige sensorische Komponenten ein, montieren Sie ein paar Räder – und was haben Sie ... Hilfe!*

Max More [Kalifornien, USA] sandte uns als nächstes einen Text mit dem Titel *Replacing the Body*, der auf Patricia Churchlands Behauptung einging, Menschen hätten keine ernsthafte Möglichkeit, ohne ihre Körper und insbesondere ohne ihr Nervensystem auszukommen. More schrieb: *Obgleich ich erwarte, eines Tages postbiologisch zu werden [ich nehme an, wir werden innerhalb der nächsten Jahrzehnte entdecken, wie man die Lebensdauer des Menschen verlängern kann], stimme ich mit Dir überein, daß dies nicht so bald der Fall sein wird. Ich finde das Szenario des Hinaufladens faszinierend – man bildet die Funktionen des Gehirns nach und integriert sie in einen schnelleren, nicht-biologischen 'Körper'. Allerdings betrachte ich das als Möglichkeit der fernen Zukunft. Ich glaube, was wir erleben werden, [...] ist die allmähliche Aufwertung des biologischen Gehirns durch nicht-biologische Komponenten. Das Endergebnis dieses Prozesses könnte die Ersetzung des natürlichen Gehirns durch synthetische Teile sein [...] [was allerdings] sicher kein 'Auskommen ohne unsere Körper' bedeutet. Damit ist gemeint, daß wir einige biologische Komponenten ersetzen und ihre Funktionen verbessern werden. Ich bin tatsächlich davon überzeugt, daß es eine ernsthafte Möglichkeit gibt, unser Nervensystem durch analoge technische Vorrichtungen [die rascher und mit größerer Bandbreite arbeiten] zu ersetzen.*

Max More spekulierte ferner darüber, daß Churchlands Statement, das menschliche biologische System würde weiterhin seine Vorherrschaft behalten, da es Angelegenheiten in Echtzeit und mit wesentlich größerer Präzision erledige als künstliche, nicht-biologische Vorrichtungen, kurzsichtig sei. More schrieb: *Die Natur plante nicht im voraus und 'konstruierte' uns in vielen kleinen Schritten. Das führte manchmal zu Konstruktionsfehlern [wie dies Dawkins in *Der blinde Uhrmacher* am Beispiel des Auges beschreibt]. Außerdem konnten immer nur die gerade verfügbaren Materialien verwendet werden. Um das Gehirn und 'künstliche' Intelligenzen zu verstehen, haben wir noch jede Menge Arbeit vor uns. Doch wir wissen, daß Nervenimpulse nicht in

per and tighter functional connection between human brains and [non-biological] machines.*

With these excerpts from Max More's message, submitted to the *FleshFactor* net-symposium on June 3, 1997, I conclude this summary of the net-symposium to date. As I wrap up this summary of the first six weeks, contributions to the *FleshFactor* discussion continue to pour in. The nature of these messages continues to oscillate between broad philosophical issues [mind/body, biological/artificial natures, the differences and similarities between humans and the machines they create] and more concrete, although no less complex, ideas about language[s] and physical interfaces between people and the machines they have grown to depend on, love and fear.

In the *FleshFactor* net-symposium we bear witness to a collective, international muse on an evolving human nature at the raw edge of its relationship with digital technologies. In this relationship we see stress, exhilaration and profound evidence of who we are and where we have come from as a species. As inevitable, significant change becomes so very real with increasing speed, we naturally call upon our most fundamental beliefs for stability and security. The *FleshFactor* net-symposium, and hopefully the 'live' symposium to follow, has provided an intellectual space for us to think about the position, status and condition of the human being in a world dominated by digital network technologies. If there is one thing this net-symposium has demonstrated, it is that we will need to develop new points of view if we are going to be capable of recognizing changes in our human condition. To begin with, from the somewhat alien vantage point of post-human networks and vast fields of hyper-mediated memory, we may be first seen as, and thus called, the FleshFactor.

http://www.aec.at/fleshfactor

Nano-, sondern eher in Millisekunden ablaufen. Ich kann einfach nicht glauben, daß wir mit genügend Zeit und besseren Technologien nichts Besseres zustande bringen sollten als die Natur.*

More fuhr fort: *Einer der Gründe dafür, daß ich mir keine allzu großen Sorgen um eine allfällige Ersetzung meiner selbst durch künstliche Gehirne mache, liegt [einmal abgesehen von der Schwierigkeit, sie herzustellen] darin, daß ich glaube, die Unterscheidung zwischen 'uns' und 'ihnen' wird verschwinden. Ich hoffe, sobald wir diese neuropsychologischen Probleme erst einmal verstehen und behandeln, werden wir ein wesentlich größeres Interesse an einer Erweiterung unserer kognitiven und emotionalen Fähigkeiten haben. In einer Zeit, in der die Computer immer kleiner werden und über immer intelligentere Schnittstellen verfügen, in der wir lernen, Gehirne an Computer und Informationsnetze anzuschließen, sollten wir eine tiefere funktionelle Verbindung zwischen menschlichen Gehirnen und [nicht-biologischen] Maschinen sehen.*

Mit diesen Auszügen aus Max Mores Beitrag zum *FleshFactor*-Netzsymposium vom 3. Juni 1997 beschließe ich diese Zusammenfassung des bisherigen Netzsymposiums. Während ich diese Zusammenfassung der Ereignisse der ersten sechs Wochen fertigstelle, kommt noch immer jede Menge neuer Beiträge zur *FleshFactor*-Diskussion herein. Die Beiträge pendeln in ihrem Charakter weiterhin zwischen allgemeinen philosophischen Themen [Geist/ Körper, biologische/künstliche Natur, Unterschiede und Ähnlichkeiten zwischen Menschen und von ihnen geschaffenen Maschinen] und konkreteren, allerdings nicht weniger komplexen Ideen über Sprache[n] und physische Schnittstellen zwischen den Menschen und den Maschinen, von denen sie mittlerweile abhängig sind und die sie lieben und fürchten.

Mit dem *FleshFactor*-Netzsymposium bieten wir eine Plattform für eine kollektive, internationale Beschäftigung mit einer sich entwickelnden menschlichen Natur, die jetzt den kritischen Punkt in ihrer Beziehung zu den digitalen Technologien erreicht hat. In dieser Beziehung empfinden wir Unsicherheit und Enthusiasmus und erhalten auch einen tiefen Einblick in das, was wir sind und wo wir als Spezies hergekommen sind. Unvermeidliche, signifikante Veränderungen werden mit zunehmender Geschwindigkeit absolut real, so daß wir uns

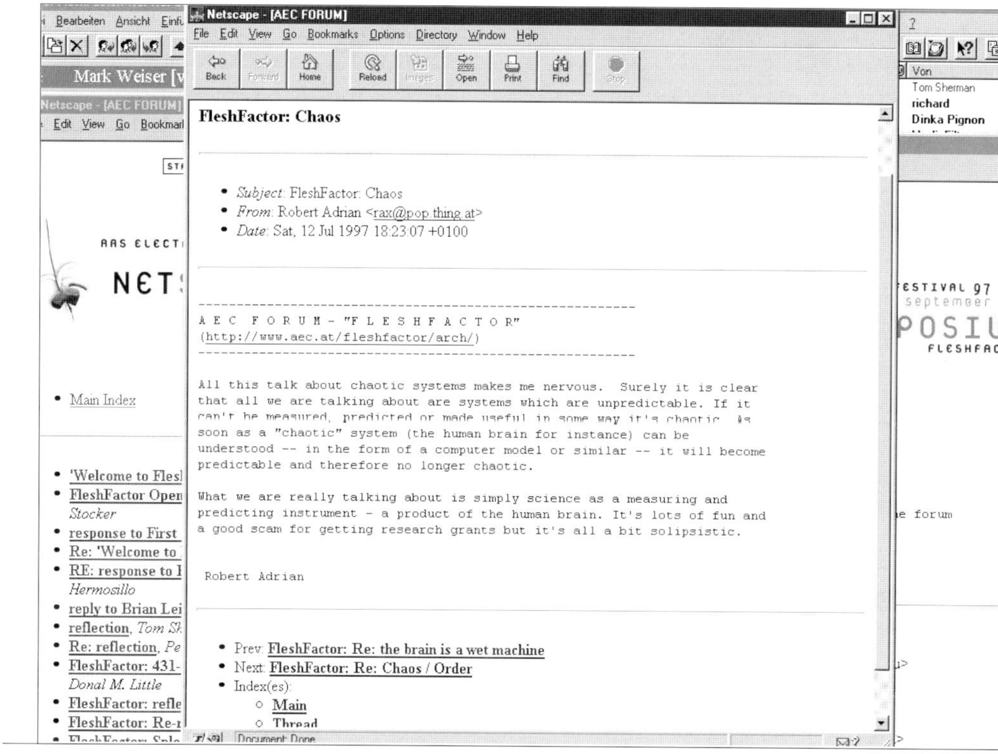

net symposium

in unserem Streben nach Stabilität und Sicherheit ganz natürlich auf unsere grundlegenden Überzeugungen berufen. Das *FleshFactor*-Netzsymposium hat uns – wie es hoffentlich auch das nachfolgende 'Live'-Symposium tun wird – einen intellektuellen Raum für Überlegungen in bezug auf Position, Stellenwert und Befindlichkeit des Menschen in einer von digitalen Netzwerktechnologien dominierten Welt eröffnet. Wenn uns dieses Netzsymposium etwas gezeigt hat, dann ist es die Tatsache, daß wir neue Standpunkte entwickeln müssen, wenn wir die Veränderungen in unserer Conditio humana erkennen wollen. Von dem uns etwas fremden Gesichtspunkt der posthumanen Netzwerke und den riesigen Weiten des hypervermittelten Gedächtnisses aus können wir uns zuallererst als eines erkennen und bezeichnen: als *FleshFactor*.

http://www.aec.at/fleshfactor

How Like A Leaf

A Conversation with Donna Haraway

Thyrza Nichols Goodeve

symposium

Wie gleich einem Blatt

Ein Gespräch mit Donna Haraway

Thyrza Nichols Goodeve

Vorwort

Sie lebte in den USA, war in der Zeit des kalten Krieges aufgewachsen, ungeheuer ethisch, durch und durch politisch, irgendwann einmal katholisch – nunmehr gewappnet mit einem Doktorinnentitel der Biologie und einer feurigen theoretischen Vorstellungskraft – und so zog sie eines Tages aus, um folgendem Auftrag nachzukommen: *Schreiben Sie fünf Seiten zum Thema sozialistisch-feministische Prioritäten in den Reagan-Jahren.*[1] Das Ergebnis war kein geringeres als das ungemein einflußreiche *Manifest für Cyborgs: Feminismus im Streit mit den Technowissenschaften*[2]. Dieser erstmals 1985 veröffentlichte Essay von Donna Haraway sowie ihre darauffolgenden Arbeiten zu Primaten, Cyborgs, Primatenvisionen, Frauen[3] und *unheimlichen neuen Netzwerken* von Natur-Kultur-Spezies aller Arten und Lebensgewohnheiten haben den Anstoß gegeben zur Erfindung einer neuen Form [ja, *neu* sogar in diesem Zeitalter ständigen Recyclings] politischer Theorie und der Auskundschaftung ontologischer Orte. Wie sie 1985 treffend formuliert: *Cyborgs sind unsere Ontologie. Sie definieren unsere Politik.*

Preface

A U.S. based, Cold War bred, terrifically ethical and deeply political once-upon-a-time Catholic girl – armed with a PhD in Biology and a fierce theoretical imagination – set out one day to answer an assignment: *Write 5 pages on what Socialist-Feminist priorities are in the Reagan years.*[1] The result was none other than the hugely influential, *Manifesto for Cyborgs: Science, Technology, and Socialist Feminism in the 1980s** First published in 1985, Donna Haraway's essay, and subsequent work on simians, cyborgs, primate visions, women, and *scary new networks* of nature-culture species of all kinds and habits, has occasioned the invention of a new mode [yes *new* even in this age of habitual recycling] of political theory and ontological location scouting. As she put it so succinctly in 1985: *The cyborg is our ontology; it gives us our politics.*

Since the publication of the *Manifesto for Cyborgs*, an array of theorists, practitioners, artists, activists, scientists, and just plain folk have set out to use Haraway's theoretical imagination to understand – and inhabit ethically– the profoundly quotidian and other-wordly workings of cyborg worlds. Receptive or not, we face a universe where *human,* *nature* and especially *human nature* are ever-enmeshed in high stake balancing acts. Thrown into a latter-day morphing arena – human and machine, organic and non-organic, material and semiotic, physical and non-physical – battle it out daily in high wire spectacles of genetic research, commodity fetishism, and information technology. It is from, and through, the intricate new figures and organisms of these ever-imploding areas of contemporary *life,* that Haraway's latest book, *Modest_Witness@ Second_ Millennium. FemaleMan©_Meets_ OncoMouse™* takes off. And so, on the occasion of the Fleshfactor conference, Haraway and I sat down – she in California, I in New York – to explore *Modest_Witness*, her latest investigation of contemporary feminism and technoscience.

Seit der Veröffentlichung des *Manifest für Cyborgs* haben sich Scharen von TheoretikerInnen, PraktikerInnen, KünstlerInnen, WissenschaftlerInnen und anderen Leuten aufgemacht, Haraways theoretische Vorstellungskraft anzuwenden, um die ganz alltäglichen und anders-weltlichen Funktionsweisen der Cyborgwelten zu begreifen – und ethisch zu bewohnen. Ob wir dafür empfänglich sind oder nicht, wir sind mit einem Universum konfrontiert, in dem *Mensch* und *Natur* und ganz besonders *menschliche Natur* unaufhörlich in einem Netz riskanter Balanceakte verstrickt sind. In eine morphende[4] Arena der letzten Tage geworfen, bekämpfen einander Mensch und Maschine, organisch und nicht-organisch, materiell und semiotisch, physisch und nicht-physisch täglich in den Hochseil-Spektakeln der genetischen Forschung, des Warenfetischismus und der Informationstechnologie. Diese neuen Figuren und Organismen jener ewig-implodierenden Bereiche des gegenwärtigen *Lebens* bilden den Ausgangspunkt für Haraways jüngstes Buch, *Modest_ Witness@Second_Millenium. Female Man©_Meets_ Oncomouse™*. Anläßlich des Symposiums *FleshFactor – Informationsmaschine Mensch* machten uns nun Haraway und ich – sie in Kalifornien, ich in New York – daran, *Modest_Witness* zu erkunden, ihre jüngste Untersuchung zum gegenwärtigen Feminismus und zur Technowissenschaft.

Mehr als nur Metapher: Individuum@ Biologie. Technowissenschaft

TNG: Die OrganisatorInnen des Netzsymposiums *FleshFactor – Informationsmaschine Mensch* *erklären in ihrem einleitenden Statement, daß sich das Symposium u. a. darauf konzentriert, *Wege zu entwickeln, die es ermöglichen, innerhalb einer technokulturellen Umgebung über das Individuum zu sprechen.* Meine Frage an Sie ist daher: Gibt es überhaupt so etwas wie *ein Individuum* in den gegenwärtigen technokulturellen Umgebungen?*

DH: Wie wir beide wissen, ist das *Individuum* keine natürliche Entität, sondern eine komplexe historisch-diskursive Ablagerung. Das heißt nicht, daß Individuen nicht real wären, sondern daß sie sich in diskursiven Praktiken herausbilden. Und was noch wichtiger ist: Diese Vorstellung von einem *Individuum* ist nicht die einzige Form der Begrenztheit, die historisch für uns möglich ist. Die technokulturelle Welt setzt sich aus Knoten von Beziehungen zusammen und nicht aus vereinzelten abgegrenzten Objekten. Individualität muß so verstanden werden, daß es per definitionem immer um historisch

Lynn Randolph: Transfusions

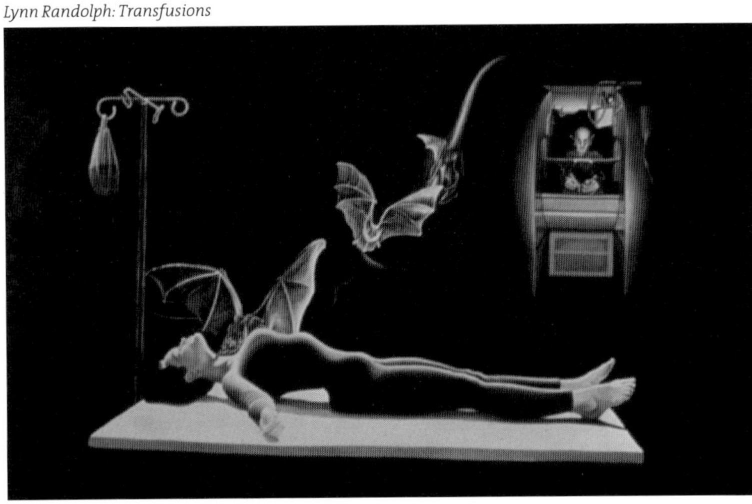

spezifische Arten von Beziehungen geht.

TNG: Beschreiben Sie bitte Ihre Methode als Kulturwissenschaftlerin. Was mich besonders interessiert, ist, inwiefern Ihre Ausbildung als Molekularbiologin nicht nur die Themen Ihrer Arbeit, sondern auch deren Methodologie selbst beeinflußt.

DH: Worte wie *Methodologie* sind extrem unheimlich, wissen Sie! [Lacht]. Anstelle von *Methodologie* spreche ich lieber davon, daß ich bestimmte Arbeitsmethoden habe, die mir im Laufe der Jahre bewußter geworden sind. Und selbstverständlich ist meine Ausbildung in Biologie – in Molekular, Zell- und Entwicklungsbiologie – wichtig für mich, insbesondere die Art und Weise, in der sie mich befähigt, auf biologische Wesen und biologische Beziehungsgewebe zu achten und ein enormes Vergnügen aus ihnen zu ziehen. Mich interessiert, wie struktur-funktionale Komplexe kleiner Größenordnungen arbeiten. Mich fasziniert die innere Achitektur von Zellen und Chromosomen. Und zweifellos denke ich oft in biologischen Metaphern.

TNG: Ihre Art zu schreiben hat einen gewissen biologistischen Zug. Sie nehmen etwas – ein kulturelles oder ein Wissensobjekt –, und bewegen sich dann tiefer und immer tiefer in dieses Objekt hinein, bis zu dessen Struktur. Und dann bewegen Sie sich in die Bedeutungsgewebe, die Sie im Zuge dieser Analyse entdecken, und so weiter und so fort. In Ihren Texten benutzen Sie sehr häufig optische Metaphern, und Ihre Methode hat wirklich eine Art mikroskopischen Zoom-Effekt, natürlich ohne jemals den größeren Zusammenhang aus den Augen zu verlieren.

DH: Richtig. Mich faszinieren Veränderungen der Größenordnung. Ich glaube, biologische Welten laden dazu ein, verschiedene Arten von Größenordnungen zu denken und über sie nachzudenken. Gleichzeitig sind sie voller Imaginationen und Welten, die sich aus außergewöhnlichen biologischen Architekturen und Mechanismen entwickeln. Biologie ist eine unerschöpfliche Quelle für die Bildung von Tropen. Sie ist sicherlich reich an Metaphern, aber sie ist mehr als nur Metapher.

*TNG: Was meinen Sie mit *mehr als nur Metapher*?*

DH: Ich meine nicht nur die physiologischen und diskursiven Metaphern, die sich in der Biologie finden lassen, sondern auch die Geschichten. Zum Beispiel all die verschiedenen ironischen, ja, nahezu komischen Unstimmigkeiten. Die bloße Raffiniertheit und Komplexität all dessen – so daß Biologie nicht nur einfach eine Metapher ist, die etwas anderes erhellt, sondern eine unerschöpfliche Quelle, um an

More Than Metaphor: Individual@Biology. Technoscience

*TNG: In the opening statement of the Fleshfactor Net Symposium the organizers state that the focus of the conference is, among other things, *to develop ways of talking about the individual within a technocultural information environment.* My question is, do we even have such a thing as *an individual* in contemporary technocultural environments?*

DH: As you and I both know, *individual* is not a natural entity but a complex historical-discursive sedimentation. It's not that individuals aren't real, it's that they are made up of discursive practices. Even more important, this notion of an *individual* is not the only mode of boundedness historically possible for us. The technocultural world is made up of knots of relatedness, not discretely bounded objects. Individuality must be understood as, by definition, always about historically specific kinds of relatedness.

TNG: Describe your methodology as a cultural critic. What I'm especially interested in is how your training as a molecular biologist has influenced, not just the themes of your work, but its very methodology.

DH: Words like *methodology* are very scary you know! [Laughs]. Rather than *methodology* I'd prefer to say I have definite methods of working that have become more conscious over the years. And most certainly my training in biology – in molecular, cellular, and developmental biology – matters to me. Particularly the way that it allows me to be alert to, and take tremendous pleasure in, biological beings and biological webs of relatedness.

I'm very interested in the ways that structural-functional complexes work at very tiny levels. I'm fascinated by the internal architecture of cells and chromosomes. And there is no doubt that I frequently think in biological metaphors.

TNG: There is a kind of biologism to how you write. You take something – an object of knowledge or culture – and you move further and further inside of it, to what its structure is. And then you move inside of whatever webs of meaning you discover from that analysis and so on and so forth. You use optical metaphors a lot in your writing and your method really has a kind of microscopic zooming-in effect to it, without, of course, ever leaving behind the big picture.

die Nicht Buchstäblichkeit der Welt heranzukommen.

TNG: Es ist Ihnen sehr wichtig, das Bildliche im Buchstäblichen, im Konkreten zu finden. In Ihrem jüngsten Buch Modest_Witness@Second_Millenium. FemaleMan©_Meets_*OncoMouse™ widmen Sie sich ausführlich der Erörterung von Figurationen, und zwar nicht nur in den Diskursen der Biotechnologie, sondern im *Fleisch* des Gens selbst.*

DH: Ja .

TNG: Arbeiten so die Molekular- und die Entwicklungsbiologie? Anders ausgedrückt, sind sie ebenso bildlich, wie sie ein buchstäbliches Phänomen sind?

DH: Ja. Aber um etwas mehr dazu zu sagen: Wenn über Biologie diskutiert wird, müssen zwei Dinge betont werden. Erstens: Wir leben eng *von* und *in* einer biologischen Welt. Das mag selbstverständlich erscheinen, aber ich betone das, um die Gewöhnlichkeit oder die Alltäglichkeit dessen zu wiederholen, von dem die Rede ist, wenn wir von Biologie sprechen. Und der zweite Aspekt, der einen bedeutenden Gestaltwechsel vom vorgehenden Punkt darstellt: Biologie ist ein Diskurs und nicht die Welt selbst. Während ich also einerseits diskursiv als Organismus lebe – und das ist eine historische Form der Identität, die mich, insbesondere in den letzten paar hundert Jahren, in sehr spezifische Arten von Traditionen, Praktiken, Geldzirkulationen und Institutionen eintaucht, befinde ich mich auch innerhalb der Biologie, die eng verstrickt ist mit Systemen der Arbeit, Systemen der hierarchischen Akkumulation und Distribution, Effizienz und Produktivität. In der zeitgenössischen Ökologie gibt es breite öffentliche Diskussionen über die Bewertung von *Diensten*, die Ökosysteme produzieren. Wenn zum Beispiel die Kohlendioxidproduktion industrieller Kulturen von Pflanzenmaterial absorbiert wird, werden die Pflanzen selbst zu *Dienstleistern* der industriellen Ökonomie. Eine derartige Denkweise ist mehr als nur metaphorisch. Es ist eine tiefgründige Art zu sehen, wie die natürlich-kulturelle Welt konstituiert ist. Innerhalb der Biologie zu leben handelt davon, innerhalb von Natur-Kulturen zu leben. Es handelt davon, innerhalb der Geschichte ebenso wie innerhalb des Wunders natürlicher Komplexität zu sein. Ich gebe zu, daß ich zweiteres besonders wichtig finde. Aber in letzter Konsequenz sprechen wir über eine bestimmte Art des Eingebundenseins in die Welt, wenn wir über Biologie sprechen. Gleichzeitig wird Biologie als ein Diskurs hervorgebracht, ganz ähnlich der politischen Ökonomie.

TNG: Auf diese Verbindung weisen Sie sehr deutlich in Modest_Witness *hin, indem Sie Ihre Theorie*

DH: Right. I'm fascinated by changes of scale. I think biological worlds invite thinking at, and about, different kinds of scale. At the same time, they are full of imaginations and worlds developed from quite extraordinary biological architectures and mechanisms. Biology is an inexhaustible source of troping. It is certainly full of metaphor but it is more than metaphor.

*TNG: What do you mean by *it is more than metaphor*?*

DH: I mean not only the physiological and discursive metaphors that can be found in biology but the stories. For instance all the various ironic, almost funny, incongruities. The sheer wiliness and complexity of it all. So that biology is not merely a metaphor that illuminates something else, but an inexhaustible source of getting at the non-literalness of the world.

TNG: Finding the figural in the literal, or concrete, is very important to you. Your recent book Modest_Witness @Second_Millennium. FemaleMan©_Meets_*OncoMouse™ spends a great deal of time discussing figuration, not just in the discourses of biotechnology but in the very *flesh* of the gene itself.*

DH: Yes.

TNG: Do molecular and developmental biology work that way? In other words are they as figural as they are literal phenomenon?

DH: Yes. But to back track a bit. There are two aspects to emphasize when discussing biology. The first is: We live intimately *of* and *in* a biological world. This may seem obvious but I emphasize it to reiterate the ordinariness or quotidian nature of what we are talking about when we talk about biology. And the second aspect, which represents a major gestalt switch from the previous point is: Biology is a discourse and not the world itself. So while, on the one hand, I live discursively as an organism, and that's an historical kind of identity, immersing me – particularly in the last couple of hundred years – in very specific kinds of traditions, practices, and circulations of money and institutions, I am also inside biology as it is intricately caught up in systems of labor, systems of hierarchical accumulation and distribution, efficiency and productivity. In contemporary ecology there have been well publicized discussions about valuing the *services* that ecosystems produce. For instance, when the carbon dioxi-

*des *genetischen Fetischismus* vorstellen, die Sie von Marx und Freud herleiten, aber spezifisch in bezug auf das Gen neu fassen. Ich möchte darauf später noch einmal zurückkommen, aber jetzt, im Zuge unserer Diskussion, kommt mir der Gedanke, daß die Biologie tatsächlich die *Geisteswissenschaft* des 20. Jahrhunderts geworden ist.*

DH: Ja, sie ist Teil der Alltagskultur.

TNG: In Modest_Witness *schreiben Sie: *Erzählungen, Theorien und Technologien der Biologie scheinen am Ende des 20. Jahrhunderts für praktisch jeden Bereich menschlicher Erfahrung relevant zu sein.[5]* Und: *In ihrem tiefsten und wissenschaftlichen Herzen ist die Disziplin Biologie ein Fach der Staatsbürgerkunde. Biologie lehrt das große mimetische Drama gesellschaftlicher und natürlicher Welten.[6]* In einem Seminar mit Stephen Heath, das ich besucht habe, als ich am *History of Consciousness*-Programm teilnahm, sprach er über die Literatur als die große Repräsentationsmaschine des 19. Jahrhunderts und über den Film als die große Repräsentationsmaschine des 20. Jahrhunderts. Biologie, verwoben in und durch Informationstechnologien und -systeme, scheint die große *Repräsentationsmaschine* des späten 20. Jahrhunderts zu sein.*

DH: Ja. In dem Buch spreche ich über Scott Gilberts[7] Auffassung, daß die Biologie ein funktionales Äquivalent zur westlichen Zivilisation auf dem US-amerikanischen Campus dieser Tage ist. Biologie ist nicht nur das Studium, das am häufigsten von vielen College-StudentInnen belegt wird, sie ist auch für ungeheuer viele Karrieren von Bedeutung – von der Unterhaltungs- zur Gesundheitsindustrie, von der Kultur zur Nahrungsmittelherstellung, zur gesetzlichen Regelung geistigen Eigentums, zu Umweltrecht und Management und so weiter. Es gibt heutzutage fast keine Betätigung, die gänzlich ohne die Lese- und Schreibpraktiken der Biologie auskäme.[8]

TNG: Und im Bereich der zeitgenössischen Kunst benutzt ein Künstler wie Matthew Barney die Biologie als Grundlage seines gewaltigen Cremaster-*Epos.[9] In den Händen von jemandem wie ihm werden Biologie und Kunst plötzlich zu verschwisterten Transformations- und Imaginationsmedien. Als jemand, der einen Einführungskurs in das Medizinstudium besucht hat und als Videokünstler, der sich als Bildhauer versteht, interessiert er sich für die Schnittstellen von Biologie und Kunst in bezug auf die Entwicklung von Formen. In seinem Fall führen andere Geschichten des Embryos durch alles Mögliche, von Horror, Oper, Musikgenres über Sport und Autorennen. Kunst und*

de production of industrial cultures is absorbed by plant materials, the plants themselves become service providers for industrial economy. Such a mode of thinking is more than metaphorical. It is a deep way of seeing how the natural-cultural world is constituted.

Living inside biology is about living inside nature-cultures. It is about being inside history as well as being inside the wonder of the natural complexity. I admit to finding the latter very important. But the final result, when we speak about biology, is that we are speaking about a specific way of engaging with the world. At the same time biology is produced as a discourse very much like political economy.

TNG: You make that connection quite explicit in Modest_Witness *with the introduction of your theory of *genetic fetishism* developed from Marx and Freud, but reframed specifically in relation to the gene. I want to go back to this but for the moment, our discussion makes me think of the ways that biology has actually become the *Humanities* of the 20th century.*

DH: Yes, it's part of everyday culture.

TNG: You say in Modest_Witness: **Biological narratives, theories, and technologies seem relevant to practically every aspect of human experience at the end of the twentieth century.[2]* And, *Biology, at its technical and scientific heart, is a subject in civics; biology teaches the great mimetic drama of social and natural worlds.[3]* In a seminar I took with Stephen Heath while in the History of Consciousness program, he spoke about literature as the great representing machine of the 19th century, and film as the great representing machine of the 20th century. Biology, woven in and through information technologies and systems, seems to be the great *representing machine* of the late 20th century.*

DH: Yes, in the book, I talk about Scott Gilbert's[4] ideas of biology as the functional equivalent of Western Civilization on the U.S. campus these days. Biology is not only the course most commonly taken by large numbers of college students, it is relevant to a huge range of careers – from the entertainment industry to the health industry, to culture and food processing, intellectual property law, environmental law and management, and so on. There is almost nothing you can do these days that doesn't require literacy in biology.

Biologie sind tatsächlich nicht so klar voneinander getrennt, wie es scheint.

DH: Obwohl Biologie und Kunst eine tiefgehende und verflochtene Geschichte miteinander haben, hat dies in den letzten Jahren noch an Intensität zugenommen.

TNG: Vielleicht sogar an Notwendigkeit.

DH: Besonders im Verhältnis zur Genetik, die einen Großteil dieser Geschichte ausmacht. Und mit Samen, Genen, Gehirnen und Ökosystemen kann man einen weiten Weg gehen!

TNG: Das ist die Liste Ihrer biotechnischen hermeneutischen Objekte aus Modest_ Witness. *Sie führen sie als primäre Cyborg-Figuren an: Chip, Gen, Same, Bombe, Abstammung, Ökosystem, Datenbank, Fötus, Rasse, und ... Gehirn!*

DH: Ja, das.

Genetischer Fetischismus

*TNG: Könnten Sie den Unterschied zwischen *Leben*, so wie Sie den Begriff im Buch verwenden, und Sarah Franklins Begriff des *Lebens selbst* erklären?[10] Sie unterscheiden *Leben* als entwicklungsbezogene, organizistische Zeitlichkeit vom *Leben selbst*, jener Zeitlichkeit, die in die Verbesserung von Kommunikation und Neugestaltung von Systemen eingebettet ist. Worin besteht der Unterschied?*

DH: Es gibt eine Art *Stafette* von Foucaults Vorstellung von der Entwicklung des Konzepts *Leben selbst* zu Sarah Franklin, die diesen Begriff im Kontext des Diskurses um das Meister-Molekül-Gen aufgreift, bis hin zu meiner Übernahme des Begriffs von Sarah, wobei ich sowohl Foucaults als auch Franklins Bedeutungsebenen benutze und meine eigenen hinzufüge.

*TNG: Wenn ich also *Leben selbst* lese: Was soll ich damit verbinden?*

DH: Ich benutze den Begriff, um auf eine Art der Buchstäblichkeit zu verweisen, auf Bestrebungen, die prozessualen Beziehungen der Natur/Kultur-Welt zu einem fixen Code oder einem fixen Programm zu machen. Leben, das eingeschlossen, fixiert und zu einem bestimmten Fetisch gemacht wird – zu jenem vierteiligen Fetischismus, den ich in *Modest_ Witness* beschreibe.[11] Ich betone den Fetischismus, der der Erforschung des *Lebens* inhärent ist, indem ich mich auf sämtliche Marx'sche Analysen der Warenförmigkeit beziehe, mit all ihrer Umheimlichkeit. Fetischismus ist kaum als klar fixierter, unproduktiver Prozeß zu bezeichnen. Warenfetischismus hat erstaunlich kreative Aspekte. Und in der Genetik spielt der Warenfetischismus ganz offensichtlich eine Rolle.

TNG: In the contemporary art world, an artist like Matthew Barney uses biology as the basis for his massive Cremaster *epic.*[5] *In the hands of someone like him biology and art suddenly become sibling mediums of transformation, and imagination. As an ex-pre-med student and sculptor-identified video-artist, he is interested in the intersection between biology and art in relationship to the development of forms. In his case, alternate stories for the embryo channeled through everything from horror, opera, musical genres to sports, and car racing. Art and biology are actually not as separate as they may seem.*

DH: Even though there is a deep and braided history between biology and art, it has taken on a kind of intensity in the last decades.

TNG: Perhaps even necessity.

DH: Especially in relation to genetics which is a big part of this story. And with seeds, genes, brains, and ecosystems one can go a long way!

TNG: Those are your list of biotechnical hermeneutical objects from Modest_Witness. *You list them as key cyborg figures: chip, gene, seed, bomb, lineage, ecosystem, database, fetus, race, and ... brain!*

DH: Yes, that one.

Genetic Fetishism

*TNG: Would you discuss the difference between *life* as you use it in your book and Sarah Franklin's term, *life itself.**[6] *You distinguish *life* as a developmental, organicist temporality from *life itself,* the temporality embedded in communications enhancement and system redesign. What is the distinction?*

DH: There's a kind of relay from Foucault's notion of the development of *life itself* to Sarah Franklin's picking it up within the context of master molecule gene discourse, and then my picking it from Sarah, making use of both Foucault's and Franklin's layers of meaning, and adding my own.

*TNG: So when I read *life itself* what am I supposed to think?*

DH: I'm using it to refer to a kind of literalism, a kind of effort to turn the processural relatedness of the nature-culture world into a fixed code or a fixed program. Life contained and fixed and turned into a particular kind of fetish – the four part fetishism I outline in *Modest_Witness.*[7] I am emphasizing the fetishism inherent to the study of *life* relating to all of Marx's analysis of the commodity form, com-

Aber mich haben auch andere Aspekte im Zusammenhang mit dem Gen-Fetischismus interessiert, bei denen es nicht immer um Warenfetischismus geht. Einer davon war, was ich *kognitiven Fetischismus* nenne, ein Begriff, den ich auf der Grundlage von Whiteheads[12] Kategorie der *unangebrachten Konkretisierung* ausgearbeitet habe. Kognitiver Fetischismus beinhaltet, wie andere Arten des Fetischismus auch, einen produktiven Fehler oder eine produktive Fehlverortung. Was im Fall des Gen-Diskurses passiert, ist die Fehlverortung des Abstrakten im Konkreten. Zum Beispiel: Wenn wir von Genetik sprechen, kommt häufig die Idee vom menschlichen Genom als dem *Programm* der menschlichen Natur ins Spiel. Die Vorstellung von einem *Programm* beinhaltet einen kognitiven Fetischismus insofern, als das *Programm* mit dem Ding selbst verwechselt wird. Was hier passiert, ist, daß die Ebenen der Abstraktion und der Verarbeitung, die die Vorstellungen von Code und Programm überhaupt erst hervorbringen, für das Reale gehalten werden.

TNG: Das klingt wie etwas, worauf Roland Barthes in den Mythen des Alltags[13] *hinauswollte – eine Art Verschiebung der Ebenen der Zeichenproduktion von Konnotation zu Denotation, wobei das konnotative Zeichen zum Signifikanten in einem neuen System der Artikulation wird – also fälschlicherweise als *Tatsache* oder Wahrheit verstanden wird [einfach als reiner oder *Ur*signifikant] – und zum Signifikanten einer Wahrheit in einem neuen System wird. Sie sprechen eindeutig über eine wesentlich komplexere Evolution dieses Systems der Semiose.*

DH: Kognitiver Fetischismus ist der Prozeß der Erzeugung *produktiver Buchstäblichkeit*, Netzwerke von Buchstäblichkeiten, die ich aufzuzeigen und auf sie zu reagieren versuche.

*TNG: Ist es das, was Sie im Teil 3 ihres Buches, *Pragmatics: Hypertext in Technoscience*, meinen, wenn Sie schreiben *Pragmatik ist die Physiologie der Semiotik*?*[14]

DH: Ja – das ist die Art der Buchstäblichkeit – oder der Konkretisierung von Bedeutung in Physiologien der Bedeutung, die ich aufbrechen will.

*TNG: Oder aufschneiden – die chirurgische Metapher läßt sich hier anwenden. Derartige Analysen scheinen heute selbstverständlich, wenn wir einen Filmtext oder eine Werbung analysieren. Der Unterschied hier ist jedoch, daß Sie über ein Gen sprechen, dessen Wert mißverstanden oder am falschen Ort lokalisiert wird, als *Essenz des Codes des Lebens*, die es zwar ist, die aber auch als innerhalb des Kontextes einer Art kulturellen Petrischale wachsend gesehen werden muß.*

plete with all the uncanniness. Fetishism is hardly a clear fixed, nonproductive process. There are amazingly creative aspects to commodity fetishism. And in genetics, obviously commodity fetishism is involved. But I was also interested in some other aspects related to gene fetishism that aren't always about commodity fetishism. One of them was what I call *cognitive fetishism* which I worked out from Whitehead[8] using his notion of *misplaced concreteness.* Cognitive fetishism, like other kinds of fetishism, involves a productive mistake or a productive mislocation. In the case of gene discourse, what takes place is the mislocation of the abstract in the concrete. For instance, when we're talking about genetics, the idea is often introduced of the human genome as the *program* for human nature. The notion of the *program* involves a cognitive fetishism where *the program* is mistaken for the thing itself. What is happening here is that the layers of abstraction and processing that have gone into producing notions of code and program are then mistaken for the real.

TNG: It sounds like what Roland Barthes was getting at in Mythologies[9] *– the kind of slipping of layers of sign production from connotation into denotation, where the connotative sign becomes the signifier in a new system of articulation – is mistaken as *fact* or truth [as merely a pure or *ur* signifier] – and becomes the signifier of a truth in a new system. Hence the production of much information today follows the model of Barthes' myth. Clearly you are talking about a much more complex evolution of this system of semiosis.*

DH: Cognitive fetishism is the process of producing *productive literalism;* networks of literalisms that I am trying to expose and be responsive to.

*TNG: Is that what you mean in Part Three of your book, *Pragmatics: Hypertext in Technoscience* when you say *pragmatics is the physiology of semiotics*?*[10]

DH: Yes – this is the kind of literalism – or concretizing of meaning into physiologies of meaning that I want to break up.

TNG: Or cut into – the surgical metaphor is applicable here. Certainly such analyses seem self-evident now when we go to analyze a film text or advertisement but the difference here is you are talking about a gene whose value is

DH: Ja. Und zusätzlich greife ich alle möglichen Sorten von ideologischem Zeugs heraus – wovon einiges sehr langweilig und traditionell und immer noch sehr wirkungsmächtig ist – unverhohlene, klare Vorstellungen von Meistermolekül und Einzelelternschaft, die sich durch das Gen und all diese Dinge hindurchziehen. Aber das ist ein ziemlich eindeutiges ideologisches Verfahren. Es ist jedoch ein ideologisches Verfahren, das seine Wurzeln in den grundlegenden diskursiven Hervorbringungen des Gens in Form von *Leben selbst* in einem buchstäblichen Sinn hat.

TNG: Wie würden Sie ein Gen definieren? Oder würden Sie das überhaupt tun?

DH: Ein Gen ist ein Knotenpunkt innerhalb eines Feldes von Beziehungen. Es ist eine materiell-semiotische Entität, eine Konkretisierung, die Vererbung lokalisiert [lokalisieren im Sinne von auf einer Karte verorten] und substantialisiert. Die Genetik ist eine Erscheinung des 20. Jahrhunderts, die viele Phasen hat, so daß wir Ende des 20. Jahrhunderts eine tiefgehende, detaillierte Kenntnis der molekularen Basis der Vererbung haben. Aber diese Moleküle – die DNS-Moleküle – funktionieren nie isoliert. Sie funktionieren immer in Interaktion mit anderen Zellstrukturen. Die verbreitetste Art, das zu beschreiben, ist, daß die kleinste Einheit des Lebens die Zelle und nicht das Gen ist. Aber das Gen interagiert ständig mit diesen zellularen Historien. Es ist immer am Werden, dennoch – und das ist der Punkt – sprechen wir darüber, als wäre es bloß ein simples, konkretes Ding.

*TNG: Mit anderen Worten: Das Gen ist ein *Subjekt im Werden*. In Ihrer Beschreibung der Genetik höre ich wieder die Art, in der Sie schreiben und arbeiten, heraus; wie Sie es angehen, Kultur zu analysieren, nämlich durch eine Art genetischer analytischer Modellierung der Kulturanalyse statt einfach umgekehrt – durch eine Kulturanalyse der Genetik.*

DH: Das stimmt. Ich denke, daß die Analyse dessen, was *Natur* genannt wird, und die Analyse dessen, was *Kultur* genannt wird, dieselben Formen des Denkens aufrufen, denn das, was mich am allermeisten interessiert, sind *Naturkulturen* – als ein Wort – Implosionen der diskursiven Reiche von Natur und Kultur.

Fleisch: Semiotik trifft auf Katholizismus

*TNG: Was eine gute Stelle zu sein scheint, um einzuhaken und zu beginnen, über das Fleisch zu sprechen. Mich interessiert die Wertigkeit, die das *Fleisch* immer schon für Sie hatte – nicht nur durch Ihre Ausbildung als Molekular- und Entwicklungsbiologin – sondern auch dadurch, wie Sie sich dem *Fleisch* von*

*mistaken, or misplaced, as the *essence of the code of life,* which it is, but it must also always be seen to be growing within the context of a kind of cultural petrie dish. Basically you include the petrie dish within your definition of a gene.*

DH: Yes. And in addition, I'm seizing on all sorts of kinds of ideological stuff – some of it very boring and traditional and still very powerful. Straight forward notions of master molecules and single parenthood that work through the gene and all that kind of thing. But that's pretty straight forward ideological processing. But it is ideological processing that is rooted in the fundamental discursive productions of the gene in the form of *life itself* in a literalized form.

TNG: How would you define a gene. Or would you?

DH: A gene is a knot in a field of relatedness. It's a material-semiotic entity; a concretization that locates [in the mapping sense of locates] and substantializes, inheritance. Genetics is particular to the twentieth century with many phases to it so that by the late twentieth century we have a deep detailed understanding of the molecular basis of hereditary. But those molecules – the DNA molecules – are never working in isolation. They are always interacting with other cell structures. The most common way of saying it is that the smallest unit of life is the cell, not the gene, but the gene is always in interaction with these cellular histories. It is always in process, yet – and this is the issue – we talk about it as if it were a simple, concrete thing.

*TNG: In other words the gene is a * subject in process.* In your depiction of genetics I hear, the manner in which you write and work. How you go about analyzing culture through a kind of genetic analytical modeling of cultural analysis rather than the reverse – a cultural analysis of genetics. You have taken a scientific model and turned it into a model of cultural critique.*

DH: That's right. I think analyses of what gets called *nature* and analyses of what gets called *culture* call on the same kinds of thinking since what I'm interested in most of all are *naturecultures* – as one word – implosions of the discursive realms of nature and culture.

Flesh: Semiotics Meets Catholicism

TNG: Which seems like a good place to begin to discuss flesh. I'm interested in the way

*Gender, Rasse und Art verpflichtet haben. *Fleisch* steht als Synekdoche für die Art und Weise, in der materielle Realität signifikant oder *tropisch* ist, wie Sie es nennen. Und eine Ihrer prononciertesten kritischen Strategien besteht darin, hineinzuschneiden und die Implosion von Fleisch und Metapher freizulegen. Zum Beispiel zerlegen Sie Metaphern, genauso wie Sie umgekehrt metaphorische Beziehungen innerhalb fleischlicher, materieller Welten entdecken. Wie würden Sie Fleisch in diesem Kontext definieren?*

DH: Das erste, was ich in diesem Kontext sagen würde, ist, daß für mich Worte extrem körperlich sind. Ich finde, daß Worte und Sprache mehr mit Fleisch als mit Ideen zu tun haben. Da ich Sprache als intensiv körperlichen Prozeß erfahre, kann ich nicht nicht in Metaphern denken. Es ist nicht so, daß ich mir aussuche, mit und in Metaphern zu arbeiten. Vielmehr erfahre ich mich als innerhalb dieser ständig abweichenden, intensiv körperlichen Prozesse der Semiose. Ich empfinde Biochemie und Semiose einfach nicht als so verschieden. Das alles hat auch eine katholische Dimension.

TNG: Das müssen Sie erklären?!?

DH: Weil ich sehr tiefgehend durch den katholischen Symbolismus und Sakramentalismus geprägt wurde – Doktrinen der Inkarnation und Transsubstantion – , die alle stark körperlich sind. Die erbarmungslose Symbolisierung katholischen Lebens ist nicht einfach an die körperliche Welt angeheftet, sie ist die körperliche Welt. Sehen Sie sich die religiöse Kunst im Südwesten der USA an, die mexikanische, die Latino- und Chicana-Kunst, da haben Sie ein gutes Beipiel dafür. Vergleichen Sie diese Kunst mit der eher enthaltsamen protestantischen Kunst und stellen Sie sich dann das Innere einer Kirche in Mexiko City vor. Ich bin sozusagen in der Kunstwelt von Mexiko City aufgewachsen, obwohl ich in Denver, Colorado, aufgewachsen bin. Das war eine irisch-katholische Szene, bei weitem nicht so reich wie die kulturelle Tradition der Latinos, aber ich bin ganz in einer komplexen symbolisch-figuralen narrativen Welt aufgewachsen, in der Vorstellungen vom Zeichen und vom Fleisch zutiefst miteinander verknüpft waren. Ich habe die Welt ab meinem vierten Lebensjahr auf diese Weise gesehen.

TNG: Würden Sie Fleisch definieren?

DH: Instinktiv will ich immer das Gleiche. Nämlich auf der Nahtstelle zwischen Materialität und Semiose insistieren. Fleisch ist ebensowenig ein Ding wie ein Gen. Aber die materialisierte Semiose des Fleisches ist immer gefärbt von Intimität, vom Körper, vom Bluten, vom Leiden, von der Saftigkeit.

**flesh* has always been important to you – not just through your training as a molecular and developmental biologist, but in your deep commitment to the *flesh* of gender, race, species. *Flesh* stands in as a synecdoche for the way material reality signifies or is *tropic* as you put it. And one of your most pronounced critical strategies is to cut into and peel back the implosion of flesh and metaphor. For example, you flesh out metaphors – the *barnacle building of history* as you put it, as well as discover metaphorical relations within fleshy, material worlds. In this context then how would you define flesh?*

DH: The first thing I'd say is that words are intensely physical for me. I find words and language more closely related to flesh than to ideas. Since I experience language as an intensely physical process I cannot not think through metaphor. It isn't as though I make a choice to work with and through metaphor, it's that I experience myself inside these constantly swerving, intensely physical processes of semiosis. Biochemistry and language just don't feel that different to me. There's also a Catholic dimension to all of this.

TNG: Explain?!?

DH: Because I came out of a very deep formation in Catholic symbolism and sacramentalism – doctrines of incarnation and trans-substantiation – which are all intensely physical. The relentless symbolization of Catholic life is not just attached to the physical world, it is the physical world. Look at the religious art of the U.S. Southwest, the Mexican, Latino, Chicano art and you get an intense example of that. Contrast that art to the more abstemious Protestant art and then imagine the inside of a church in Mexico city. I grew up within the art world of Mexico City, so to speak, even though I grew up in Denver, Colorado. It was an Irish Catholic scene, nowhere as rich as the Latino cultural tradition, but I grew up very much inside an elaborate symbolic figural narrative world where notions of sign and flesh were profoundly tied together. I understood the world this way by the time I was four years old.

TNG: Would you define flesh?

DH: My instincts are always to do the same thing. It's to insist on the join between materiality and semiosis. Flesh is no more a thing than a gene is. But the materialized semiosis of

Fleisch ist immer irgendwie feucht. Es ist klar, daß man das Wort Fleisch nicht verwenden kann, ohne Verletzbarkeit und Schmerz zu begreifen.

Implosionen: Fleisch.Syntax.*Oncomouse™*

*TNG: Sie verwenden syntaktische Zeichen – *@*, *©*, *™* –, um uns in* Modest_Witness: @Second_Millenium.FemaleMan©_Meets_*OncoMouse™ zu verorten. Das ist ein Beispiel dafür, wie es Ihrem Titel gelingt, eine neue Art der Syntax und der Figuration zu erzeugen. Der Titel* *Modest_Witness@Second_Millenium.Female Man©_Meets_*OncoMouse™* ist ein technokulturelles Gedicht für sich. Sie visualisieren und theoretisieren durch die Wörter und die syntaktischen Zeichen im Titel, der uns in der Geschichte des späten 20. Jahrhunderts situiert. Das ist großartig, denn diese Zeichen sind die neuen *brands* [Das amerikanische Wort *brand* bedeutet sowohl Markenzeichen als auch Brandzeichen, A.d.Ü.].*

DH: Insbesondere in der Doppelbedeutung von *brand* als Type und als Zeichen des Besitzes, das ins Fleisch gebrannt wird. Was den Titel betrifft, so ist in gewisser Hinsicht das ganze Buch in dem Titel enthalten, der auch charakteristisch dafür ist, wie ich arbeite – in diesen andauernden Implosionen und Loswicklungen.

TNG: Werden Sie jemals müde? Ich meine, Sie lassen keinen physiologischen oder diskursiven logischen Knoten aus. Sie sind immer darauf bedacht, die Kontingenzen und vielfachen Konstruktionen von allem aufzuzeigen. Wenn ich Sie lese, denke ich daher – das ist anstrengend! Notwendig, aber anstrengend.

DH: Aber gerade der Teil bringt Energien! Was mich müde macht, ist, daß manche LeserInnen unbedingt einen Faden aus dem Stoff aufnehmen müssen und dann alles daran heften.

TNG: Ja. Ihre Arbeiten werden oft genauso reduktionistisch gelesen wie, aus ganz ähnlichen Gründen, experimentelle ErzählerInnen und KünstlerInnen wie z. B. Yvonne Rainer [15]. *Manche Leute weigern sich, sich auf Komplexität einzulassen. Ich führe das auf eine fast avantgardistische [um einen alten Begriff zu verwenden], anti-lineare, anti-teleologische Ästhetik in Ihren Texten zurück, die jener von Rainer gleicht. Wie Sie konstruiert Rainer unaufhörlich Analysen von Rasse, Gender, Sexualität und Begehren vermittels einer komplexen relational-assoziierenden Ästhetik, die verlangt, daß man den Film nicht an irgendeiner Stelle anhält und sagt: Das hier ist Yvonne Rainers Aussage. Mit Ihrer Arbeit verhält es sich genauso, die – liest man sie mißgünstig oder, wenn ich das so sagen darf, dumm – zu einer anti-materialistischen, tech-*

flesh always includes the tones of intimacy, of body, of bleeding, of suffering, of juiciness. Flesh is always somehow wet.

It's clear one cannot use the word without understanding vulnerability and pain.

Implosions: Flesh.Syntax.*OncoMouse™*

*TNG: You use syntactical marks – *@,* *©,* *™* – to locate us in* Modest_Witness:@ Second_Millennium.FemaleMan©_Meets _Onco Mouse™ *This an example of the way your title successfully creates a new kind of syntax and figuration. The title* Modest-Witness@ Second-Millennium. FemaleMan©_Meets_Onco Mouse™ *is its own technocultural poem. You visualize and theorize through the words and syntactical marks of the title, situating us in late twentieth century history. That is wonderful because these marks are the new brands.*

DH: Especially with the double meaning of brand as type and mark of ownership burned into the flesh. In regards to the title, there's a way that the whole book is in the title which is also a feature of how I work – through these constant implosions and unwindings.

TNG: Do you ever get tired? I mean you don't let a physiological or discursive knot pass. You are always so careful to show the contingencies and multiple constructions of everything that when I'm reading you I think – this is exhausting! Necessary but exhausting.

DH: But that part is energizing! What makes me tired is the way some readers insist on picking up one piece of the fabric and pinning everything to it.

TNG: Yes. You often receive the same kinds of reductionist readings of your work that experimental narrativists and artists like Yvonne Rainer[11] *do for much the same reasons. Some people refuse to engage with the complexity. I associate this with an almost avant-gardist [to use an old term] anti-linear, anti-teleological aesthetic in your theory that is like Rainer's. Like you, she is constantly constructing analyses of race, gender, sexuality, desire via a complex relational-associational aesthetic that demands one does not stop her film at any one moment and say: this is Yvonne Rainer's statement. It's the same with your work, which, read unsympathetically, and if I may, stupidly, turns your work into an anti-materialist, technophilic – or techno-*

nophilen oder technophoben sozialkonstruktivistischen Wissenschaftsauffassung wird. Diese Lesweisen sind Musterbeispiele für eine Unfähigkeit, mit Subtilität umzugehen, die typisch amerikanisch zu sein scheint.

DH: Es ist ein Art Geisteshaltung, die alles buchstäblich nimmt. Und deshalb sind mir Figuren so wichtig, denn Figuren sind sofort komplex und nichtbuchstäblich, ganz abgesehen davon, daß sie Gelegenheiten wirklichen Vergnügens an der Sprache bieten. Diese Buchstäblichkeit schlägt durch, wenn KritikerInnen Positionen konstruieren, die nicht wirklich existieren, wie z. B. urbane Legenden von Leuten recyclen und sagen: *Glauben Sie an die DNS!?!*, was traurig und schockierend ist und all das Vergnügen an Sprache nimmt, das einen beträchtlichen Teil der ernsten Arbeit an der Cultural Study [16] der Wissenschaft belebt. [17]

TNG: Was uns zu OncoMouse™ *führt.* OncoMouse™ *ist eine so bewegende und bestürzende Geschichte und auch ein perfektes Beispiel dafür, wie Sie ein Objekt der wissenschaftlich-phänomenalen Welt als Analysefigur einsetzen. Sie sollten vielleicht genau erklären, was* OncoMouse™ *ist.*

DH: *OncoMouse™* ist ein transgener Organismus. Ein transgener Organismus ist die Entität, die hergestellt wird, wenn Gene eines Organismus in das Stadium der befruchteten Eizelle eines anderen lebenden Organismus transplantiert werden. Das Ergebnis sind transgene Kreaturen. Transgene Organismen wachsen und bekommen Kinder, die weiterhin das transplantierte Gen in sich tragen. Mit anderen Worten: Die transplantierten Gene werden durch die Eier und das Sperma an die nachfolgenden Generationen weitergegeben. *OncoMouse™* ist das Ergebnis eines transplantierten Gens, das menschliche Tumore produziert – eines Onkogens, das erwiesenermaßen Brustkrebs erzeugt. Deshalb sage ich in dem Buch: Egal, ob ich ihre Existenz und Verwendung nun gutheiße, sie leidet, immer wieder und schwer, damit ich und meine Schwestern leben mögen. Und darüber hinaus sage ich, daß ich – wenn schon nicht, was meinen eigenen Körper betrifft, dann sicher was den meiner Freundinnen betrifft – eines Tages in der Schuld von *OncoMouse™* oder ihren später designten Nagetier-Verwandten stehen werde, in einer schweren Schuld.

TNG: Es ist interessant, welch ungeheure Empörung und Ängste durch Dolly, das geklonte Schaf, ausgelöst wurden, während die transgene Herstellung neuer Lebensformen schon seit geraumer Zeit betrieben wird.

phobic – social constructionist view of science. Such readings are representative of an inability to work with subtlety that seems particularly American.

DH: It's a kind of literal mindedness. And that's why figures are so important to me because figures are immediately complex and non-literal, not to mention instances of real pleasure in language. The literalism that comes through when critics create positions that don't really exist like recycling urban legends of people saying, *You believe in DNA!?!* is sad, shocking, and takes away from all the pleasure in language that animates so much of the serious work on the cultural study of science.[12]

TNG: Which brings us to OncoMouse™. OncoMouse™ *is such a moving and upsetting story, as well as a perfect example of how you deploy an object from the scientific-phenomenal world as a figure of analysis. Perhaps you should describe exactly what* OncoMouse™ *is.*

DH: *OncoMouse*™ is a transgenic organism. A transgenic organism is the entity made when genes from one organism are transplanted to the fertilized egg stage of another live organism. What results are transgenic creatures. Transgenic organisms grow up and breed children who continue to carry the transplanted gene. In other words the transplanted genes are conveyed through the eggs and sperm into subsequent generations. *OncoMouse*™ is the result of a transplanted, human tumor-producing gene – an oncogene – that reliably produces breast cancer. That is why I say in the book that whether I agree to her existence and use or not, s/he suffers, repeatedly, and profoundly, so that I and my sisters may live. And furthermore that if not in my own body, then surely in those of my friends, I will someday owe to *OncoMouse* ™, or her subsequently designed rodent kin, a large debt.

TNG: It's so interesting how much outrage and anxiety has been let loose by Dolly the cloned sheep when transgenic manufacturing of new kinds of life forms has been going on for some time now.

DH: And transgenics is a much more radical technology. It allows molecular biologists to remove genes of interest from organisms that might be completely unrelated, for example something from a bacterium, and put it into a mammal.

DH: Transgenik ist eine wesentlich radikalere Technologie. Sie erlaubt es MolekularbiologInnen, gezielt einzelne Gene aus Organismen zu entnehmen, die völlig unverwandt sein können, wie z. B. Gene einer Bakterie, und sie einem Säugetier einzupflanzen.

TNG: Das ist ein Beispiel für das unheimliche Versprechen der Cyborg-Welten, die Sie auspacken – Welten oder Wesen, die weder einfach utopisch noch einfach dystopisch sind.

DH: Um nicht zu sagen: schlicht und ergreifend gewöhnlich. Jene Fragen, die uns ein Anliegen sind, lassen sich nicht immer nur im Ultimativen finden – utopische Ideale versus dystopische Alpträume. Auch die Alltagsdimensionen der Technowissenschaft sind komplex. Unabhängig vom konkreten Fall jedoch wird brauchbare Arbeit oft um den Preis geleistet, neue Arten des Schmerzes zu erfinden. Tatsache ist, daß es gegenwärtig neue – oder zumindest mutierte – Modi gibt, in denen technowissenschaftliche Menschen zu anderen Tieren und Organismen in Beziehung stehen. Das heißt, das Ausmaß, in dem wir uns selbst und andere Organismen zu Instrumenten für unsere eigenen Zwecke machen, hat zugenommen.

*TNG: Was ist dann eine Cyborg-Ethik oder -Subjektivität im Kontext von OncoMouse™? Wo sind *wir* und *es*, wenn Subjekt und Objekt verschwommen sind? Im Verhältnis zu Cyborgs wird dies zu einer ethischen Frage, wie z. B.: Wer ist in der Position, darüber zu entscheiden, ob diese Maus zu einem Wesen gemacht wird, das Säugetier-Tumore generiert?*

DH: Und noch umstrittener sind die Fragen eines internationalen Gesetzes für geistiges Eigentum. Werden Organismen wie dieser im internationalen Reich patentierbar sein und wenn ja, wie? Auch wenn das US-amerikanische Patentamt Patente auf genetische Organismen vergeben hat, ist das auf internationaler Ebene immer noch ein umstrittener Punkt.

TNG: Wie sehen die Konfliktlinien aus?

DH: In Europa leisten Bewegungen, die sich für die Souveränität des Ursprungslands einsetzen, Widerstand gegen die Patentierung transgener und anderer biotechnologischer Produkte – in Deutschland vor allem seitens der Grünen und im Kontext der Tierschutzpolitik. Dieser Konflikt um Eigentumsverhältnisse rund um Biodiversität ist ein großes Thema in meinem Buch. Kämpfe um das Humane Genome Diversity-Projekt, die damit zu tun haben, ob verschiedene Gruppen menschlicher Wesen das Sammeln ihres genetischen Materials zwecks Analyse unterstützen oder nicht. Außerdem gibt es alle möglichen Probleme rund um die kommerzielle

TNG: It is an example of the scary promise of cyborg worlds that you unpack – worlds or beings that are neither simply utopian or dystopian.

DH: Not to mention just plain ordinary. The issues that concern us are not always found just in the ultimate – utopian ideals versus dystopian nightmares. The everyday dimensions of technoscience are also complex. But whatever the case, useful work often takes place at the cost of inventing new kinds of pain. The fact is there are currently new – or at least mutated – ways in which technoscientific people relate to other animals and organisms. It means there has been a deepening of how we turn ourselves, and other organisms, into instruments for our own end.

*TNG: What then is cyborg ethics or subjectivity in the context of OncoMouse™? Where are *we* and *it* when subject and object are blurred? This becomes an ethical question in relation to cyborgs like who gets to decide this mouse is going to be made into a being that generates mammarian tumors.*

DH: Or even more contentious are the questions of international intellectual property law. Will organisms such as this be patentable in the international realm and how? Although the United States Patents and Trademark Office has granted patents on genetic organisms, it is still a very contentious issue internationally.

TNG: What are the lines of debate?

DH: In Europe, particularly in Germany through the Green Party, and within the context of animal rights politics, there's been a lot of resistance to the patenting of transgenics and other biotechnological products from indigenous sovereignty movements. This conflict over property relations around biodiversity is a big theme in my book. Contestations over The Human Genome Diversity project having to do with whether various groups of human beings will or will not co-operate with the collecting of their genetic material for analysis. There are, as well, all sorts of problems surrounding commercial use. Who will profit from drugs developed from studies that take place in various geographic and cultural regions? Patent law is about protecting the process of producing transgenic beings, as well as patenting the being itself. In the case of *OncoMouse*™, the patent was issued to two researchers who assigned the

Nutzung. Wer wird von den Arzneimitteln profitieren, die auf der Grundlage von Studien entwickelt werden, die in verschiedenen geographischen und kulturellen Regionen erfolgen? Im Patentrecht geht es darum, das Verfahren der Herstellung transgener Wesen zu schützen, wie auch das Wesen selbst zu patentieren. Im Fall der *OncoMouse*™ wurde das Patent an zwei Forscher vergeben, die das Patent der Harvard Corporation überschrieben, die wiederum eine Lizenz an DuPont verkaufte. Das heißt, daß niemand diese Verfahrensweise bzw. diese Tiere nutzen kann, ohne eine Gebühr zahlen zu müssen, solange das Patent läuft. Im Grunde bedeutet Patentierung also letztendlich, daß es um die Entrichtung von Gebühren für die Verwendung bestimmter technologischer Verfahrensweisen und/oder Objekte geht. Auf diese Weise wird Innovation durch Patentierung sowohl stimuliert als auch geschützt. Der/die ErfinderIn ist motiviert durch den Anreiz, Gewinn aus seiner/ ihrer Erfindung ziehen zu können, und die Gesellschaft profitiert von dieser Erfindung. Zumindest ist das die Idee dahinter.

TNG: Es drängt sich der Verdacht auf, daß viele dieser Probleme auch ohne Patentierung virulent wären.

DH: Das ist richtig. Patente sind nur ein Teil der Frage. Aber wegen des Symbolcharakters sind sie ein besonders umstrittener Teil – in einem Teil der Welt werden bestimmte Stoffe gewonnen, die Profite werden jedoch woanders geerntet. In Indien zum Beispiel gibt es Kontroversen um den Neem-Baum bzw. um die Gewinnung bestimmter Substanzen aus diesem Baum. Diese Substanzen wurden in Indien seit langer Zeit für therapeutische Zwecke genutzt, aber sie werden in Laboratorien der ersten Welt zurückgebracht, dort auf verschiedenste Weise aufbereitet und zu einem vermarktbaren Produkt gemacht. An diesem Punkt fließt nichts vom kommerziellen Profit zurück in das Ursprungsland. Aber in einer Situation wie dieser ist es wichtig zu betonen, daß dabei nicht nur Rohstoffe als Ressourcen ausgebeutet werden, sondern auch Wissen. Wissen ist in ein derart *natürliches* Material in jeder Etappe des Spiels eingebaut.

TNG: Genau.

DH: Hier sind also Fragen der Souveränität betroffen. Auf wessen Wissen wird es ankommen? Werden wir als MitarbeiterInnen angesehen werden oder nur als Rohmaterial? Angenommen, es gibt im Regenwald Stoffe von pharmazeutischem Interesse und man arbeitet mit einer/m ortsansässigen/m HeilerIn, die/der die örtliche Pflanzenwelt kennt. Was passiert, wenn die Gemeinde, aus der die Person kommt, nicht

patent to the Harvard Corporation, which licensed it to DuPont. That means that nobody can use that process, or these animals, without paying a fee for however many years the patent runs. So basically patenting ends up being about paying fees for the use of specific technological processes and/or objects. In this way patenting both stimulates and protects innovation. The inventor is prompted by the incentive of making a profit on the invention, and society receives the benefits of the invention. At least that's the philosophy.

TNG: A lot of these problems seem like they would still be there even without patenting.

DH: That's right. Patents are just a piece of the issue. But it's a particularly contentious part because of the symbolization – the extracting of materials from one area of the world and reaping the profits elsewhere. For example in India there are controversies over the Neem tree having to do with extracting substances from them. These substances have been used in health practices for a very long time in India, but are being brought back to First World laboratories, processed in various ways, and turned into a marketable product. At this point, none of the commercial benefit goes back to the source nation. But in a situation like this, it is important to emphasize that is not just sources as in *resources* that are taken, but knowledge. Knowledge is built into such *natural* material at every stage of the game.

TNG: Exactly.

DH: So there are sovereignty issues involved here. Whose knowledge is going to count? Are we going to be regarded as collaborators or just as raw material? Say there are materials that might be of pharmaceutical interest in the Rainforest and one is working with a local healer who knows the local plant life. How will that person's expertise be recognized in this system? And then, what if the community the person comes from does not live by individualistic premises? And what about the nation within which that group of people exists? What if they are a subordinated minority? If there is a national agreement by the national government of Brazil or Costa Rica, a major pharmaceutical company might or might not work for the benefit of the group of people who actually have the knowledge and the materials in question. So how are they going to be protected? Do they even want

nach individualistischen Grundsätzen lebt? Und was ist mit dem Land, in dem diese Gruppe von Menschen lebt? Was, wenn sie eine untergeordnete Minderheit bildet? Wenn es eine staatliche Vereinbarung der nationalen Regierung von Brasilien oder Costa Rica gibt, kann ein großer Pharmakonzern im Interesse jener Gruppe von Menschen agieren, die tatsächlich das betreffende Wissen und Material haben, oder aber auch nicht. Wie also werden sie geschützt werden? Wollen sie überhaupt in dieses System einbezogen werden oder nicht? *OncoMouse™* ist lediglich eine verdichtete Figur dieser Matrix – eine Figur des dichten Gewebes aus Beziehungen und Geschichten, die sich in der Technowissenschaft, so wie sie am Ende des 20. Jahrhunderts praktiziert wird, finden.

TNG: OncoMouse™ wurde 1988 entwickelt?

DH: 1988 patentiert. Entwickelt wurde sie im Laufe der vorangegangenen Jahre. Aber *OncoMouse™* stammt aus einer frühen Phase dieser Technologie. Mittlerweile ist sie obsolet.

TNG: Wirklich?

DH: Ja. Die Transgenik offensichtlich nicht. Es werden Unmengen transgener Organismen entwickelt, die nicht patentiert werden. Als bestimmter Moment in der Transgenik ist die *OncoMouse™* jedoch obsolet, weil sie nicht besonders gut funktioniert hat. Sie hat zu viele spontane Tumore bekommen.

TNG: In Modest_Witness *zitieren Sie den Präsidenten von GenPharm, David Winter, der sagt, daß auf Bestellung gezüchtete Versuchsmäuse derartig verbreitet sind, daß er sie *Maus-auf-Abruf* [Dial-A-Mouse] nennt. Oder den anderen GenPharm-Vertreter, Howard B. Rosen [Direktor der Unternehmensentwicklung], der maßangefertigte Mäuse als *Leinwand, auf der wir genetische Transplantationen durchführen*[18] beschreibt.*

DH: Ja, und wir müssen uns erinnern, daß das, was in all diesen Sätzen verdinglicht wird, natürlich ein Lebewesen ist. Und zwar ein Lebewesen, auf dem in Lynn Randolphs Gemälde *The Laboratory, or the Passion of OncoMouse* [Das Labor oder die Leiden der *OncoMouse*] nicht zufällig eine Dornenkrone sitzt.[19]

TNG: Richtig, OncoMouse™ *ist ein Beispiel für den christlichen Realismus, den man in vielen Aspekten der Technowissenschaft findet. In* Modest_Witness *schreiben Sie, *Obwohl ihr Versprechen dezidiert ein säkulares ist, ist sie eine Figur in dem innerhalb des christlichen Realismus entwickelten Sinne: Sie ist unser Sündenbock, sie hält Leiden von uns fern, sie bedeutet und inszeniert unsere Sterblichkeit in einer machtvollen, historisch spezifischen Weise, die eine kulturell*

inclusion into the system or not? *OncoMouse™* is just a concentrated figure of this matrix – a figure of the intense web of relationships and histories found in technoscience as it is practiced at the end of the twentieth century.

TNG: OncoMouse™ was developed in 1988?

DH: Patented in 1988. It was developed over the preceding years. But *OncoMouse™* was early in the technology. It's now obsolete.

TNG: Really?

DH: Yes. Obviously transgenics is not. There are lots and lots of transgenic organisms being developed that are not patented. But as a particular moment in transgenics, *OncoMouse™* is obsolete because it didn't work very well. It got too many spontaneous tumors.

TNG: In Modest_Witness *you quote the President of GenPharm, David Winter, saying custom-made research mice are so common he calls it Dial-A-Mouse. Or the other GenPharm representative, Howard B. Rosen [Corporate Development Director] who describes custom-tailored mice as the *canvas upon which we do genetic transplantations.*[13]*

DH: Yes, and we must remember the *it* in all of these sentences is of course a living being. And a living being upon whom that crown of thorns in Lynn Randolph's painting **The Laboratory, or The Passion of OncoMouse** is not there by accident.[14]

TNG: Right, OncoMouse™ is an example of the Christian figural realism you find in so much of technoscience. In Modest_Witness *you say, *Although her promise is decidedly secular, s/he is a figure in the sense developed within Christian realism: S/he is our scapegoat; s/he bars our suffering; s/he signifies and enacts our mortality in a powerful, historically specific way that promises a culturally privileged kind of salvation – a 'cure for cancer.'*[15] Which brings us back to the ethics of cyborg subjectivity.*

DH: And to flesh. I think for me cyborg subjectivity is about the manner in which we are responsible for these worlds. But not in a simpolistic, *I'm for it or against it.* You can't have some simple minded political heroics about resistance versus complicity. What has to happen is that literacies have to be encouraged, as well as many kinds of agency. Both literacy and agency aren't things you have, but things you do.

symposium

privilegierte Form der Erlösung verspricht – 'ein Heilmittel gegen Krebs.[20]' Was uns zurück zur Ethik der Cyborg-Subjektivität bringt.*

DH: Und zum Fleisch. Ich denke, für mich geht es bei Cyborg-Subjektivität um die Art und Weise, in der wir für diese Welten verantwortlich sind. Aber nicht in einem vereinfachenden *Ich bin dafür oder dagegen*. Ein paar einfältige HeldInnengeschichten über Widerstand versus MittäterInnenschaft können nicht der Weisheit letzter Schluß sein. Was passieren muß, ist, daß unorthodoxe Lese- und Schreibpraktiken [*literacies*] ebenso wie viele Arten der Handlungsfähigkeit ermutigt werden müssen. Sowohl Lese- und Schreibpraktiken als auch Handlungsfähigkeit sind nicht Dinge, die man hat, sondern Dinge, die man tut.

*TNG: Wie hängt das mit der Figur des/der *anspruchslosen ZeugIn* [modest witness] zusammen?*

DH: *Anspruchslose ZeugIn*, sind wie *OncoMouse™* und FrauMann© [aus Joanna Russ' Buch[21]] Figuren, die ich in dem Buch verwende und die für neue Weisen der Imaginierung und Ausübung von Technowissenschaften stehen.[22] Im Verweis auf *Modest_Witness@Second_Millenium* sieht die/der LeserIn sofort, daß *anspruchslose ZeugIn* die/der AbsenderIn und EmpfängerIn von Nachrichten in meiner E-mail-Adresse ist. Aber ich beziehe mich auch auf die komplexe Geschichte, die *bezeugen* und *ein/e ZeugIn* sein in den Erzählungen der Wissenschaftsforschung haben, und zwar in bezug auf Robert Boyles Entwicklung der experimentellen Methode im 17. Jahrhundert und die darauffolgenden Kontroversen darüber, wie Tatsachen glaubhaft begründet werden. Thomas Hobbes zum Beispiel lehnte die experimentelle Lebensweise ab, eben weil deren Erkenntnis von den Praktiken des Bezeugens einer bestimmten Gemeinschaft, z. B. der der Kleriker und Rechtsgelehrten, abhängig war. Mein Interesse gilt dem Bezeugen, gerade weil es dabei um das Sehen, das Beglaubigen, das öffentlich Rechenschaftablegen über eigene Visionen und Repräsentationen geht, um die diesbezügliche psychische Verletzbarkeit. Bezeugen ist eine kollektive, beschränkte Praktik, die abhängig ist von der konstruierten und niemals endgültigen Glaubwürdigkeit derer, die es tun und die sämtlich sterblich, fehlbar und beladen mit den Folgen unbewußter und verleugneter Begehren und Ängste sind. Als Kind von Robert Boyles *Royal Society of the English Restoration* und von experimentellen Lebensweisen bleibe ich der Figur der/des anspruchslosen ZeugIn verhaftet. Meiner/m anspruchslosen ZeugIn geht es darum, die

*TNG: How does this relate to the figure of the *modest witness*?*

DH: *Modest witness,* along with *OncoMouse*™ and the FemaleMan© [from Joanna Russ's book of that title], are figures I use in the book to stand in for new ways of imagining and doing technoscience[16]. In reference to *Modest_Witness@Second_Millennium* the reader sees immediately that s/he is the sender and receiver of messages in my e-mail address. But I am also relying on the complex history that *witnessing* and being a *witness* have within the stories of science studies in relation to Robert Boyle's development of the experimental method in the 17th century and the subsequent controversies over how facts are credibly established. For instance Thomas Hobbes repudiated the experimental way of life precisely because its knowledge was dependent on a practice of witnessing by a special community, like that of the clerics and lawyers. I am interested in witnessing precisely because it is about seeing; attesting; standing publicly accountable for, and psychically vulnerable to, one's visions and representations. Witnessing is a collective, limited practice that depends on the constructed and never finished credibility of those who do it, all of whom are mortal, fallible, and fraught with the consequences of unconscious and disowned desires and fears. A child of Robert Boyle's Royal Society of the English Restoration and of the experimental way of life, I remain attached to the figure of the modest witness. My modest witness is about telling the truth – giving reliable testimony – while eschewing the addictive narcotic of transcendental foundations. It refigures the subjects, objects, and communicative commerce of technoscience into different kinds of knots.

Response: Responsibility ▸ XXX ▸ Innocence

TNG: This discussion relates to one of my favorite quotes from the 1985 Cyborg Manifesto *where you state that your argument is for the pleasure in the confusion of boundaries and the responsibility in their construction.*

DH: Exactly, we are talking about another instance of that process.

TNG: Responsibility is one of the most potent forces – and substances – in your work. In many ways it is at the center – if your work has

Wahrheit zu sagen – zuverlässiges Zeugnis abzulegen – und gleichzeitig die süchtig machenden Narkotika transzendentaler Begründungen zu vermeiden. Sie/er refiguriert die Subjekte, Objekte und den kommunikativen Handelsverkehr der Technowissenschaften zu verschiedenen Arten von Knotenpunkten.

Antwort: Verantwortung<=XXX=>Unschuld

TNG: Diese Diskussion steht in Beziehung zu einem meiner Lieblingszitate aus dem Manifest für Cyborgs *aus dem Jahr 1985, in dem Sie dafür plädieren, die Verwirrung dieser Grenzen zu genießen und Verantwortung bei ihrer Konstruktion zu übernehmen.*

DH: Genau, wir reden über ein weiteres Beispiel genau dieses Prozesses.

TNG: Verantwortung ist eine der zwingendsten Kräfte – und Substanzen – in Ihrer Arbeit. Sie steht in vielerlei Hinsicht im Zentrum – sofern Ihre Arbeit überhaupt ein Zentrum hat. Sie ist der Angelpunkt sämtlicher Ihrer Analysen. Sie lehren uns, auf all die Komplexitäten der Technokultur im späten 20. Jahrhundert zu antworten, und dann verknüpfen Sie mit diesen Antworten die Erfordernisse der Verantwortung.

DH: Nun, Menschen sind ethisch, nicht diese nicht-menschlichen Entitäten.

TNG: Sie meinen, das Nicht-Menschliche zu romantisieren?

DH: Genau, das ist eine Art des Anthropomorphisierens nicht-menschlicher AkteurInnen, vor der wir uns hüten müssen. Unsere Relationalität ist nicht die gleiche Form des Seins. Innerhalb dieser Welten sind es die Menschen, die die emotionale, ethische, politische und kognitive Verantwortung tragen.

TNG: Eine verantwortungsvolle Weise, mit den transgenen Mäusen umzugehen, könnte die sein, den Sachverhalt der Genkreuzung als Lernprozeß darüber zu nutzen, wie diese Organismen sich verhalten, agieren, arbeiten, leben, fühlen etc. und daher herauszufinden, wie die verantwortungsvollste Weise, transgene Formen und Welten zu schaffen, aussehen könnte.

DH: Ja, das könnte ein Aspekt davon sein – danach zu fragen, wer davon den Nutzen hat, wie z. B.: Erleichtert *OncoMouse*™ wirklich das menschliches Krebsleiden, oder ist sie nur eine weitere High-Tech-Entschuldigung dafür, sich nicht darum zu kümmern, woher Krebs wirklich kommt? Oder beides? Und wer hungert auf dieser Welt, und befaßt sich die Transgenik damit? Ich denke, worum es bei der Transgenik geht, ist – um Leigh Stars Frage zu benutzen: *cui bono* – für wen? [23] Das Leiden des Organismus ist ein Teil

a center. It's the hinge upon which all of your analyses hang. You teach us to be responsive to all the complexities in late twentieth century technoculture, and then you attach to this responsiveness the requirements of responsibility.

DH: Well, it is people who are ethical not these non-human entities.

TNG: You mean romanticizing the non-human?

DH: Right that is a kind of anthropomorphizing of the non-human actors that we must be wary of. Our relationality is not of the same kind of being. It is people who have the emotional, ethical, political, and cognitive responsibility inside these worlds.

TNG: So a responsible way of going about transgenics might be to use these situations of cross-gening as moments of learning about how these organisms behave, act, work, live, feel, etc., and therefore learning what might be the most responsible way of creating transgenic forms and worlds.

DH: Yes that might be an aspect of it – asking questions of who benefits, like does *OncoMouse™* truly relieve human suffering of cancer or is it yet another high tech excuse for not paying attention to where cancers are really coming from? Or both? And who's hungry in this world and is transgenics addressing that? I think the issues of transgenics are – to use Leigh Starr's question – *cui bono* – for whom?[17] The suffering of the organism is a part of that question. Animal research is just another way of understanding how seriously we aren't, and can't be, innocent.

How like a leaf

TNG: How has the cyborg changed since 1985? I ask this because in the interview you did with Constance Penley and Andrew Ross[18], you conclude stating the cyborg is female. In Modest_ Witness *you introduce Joanna Russ's FemaleMan and describe the cyborg as *the stem cell in the marrow of the technoscientific body*[19] which is a pretty great image. I would assume that the cyborg is a figure in process as everything is for you.*

DH: Yes. Sometimes I emphasize the cyborg as s/he, or introduce something like the *OncoMouse™* which is a cyborg figure. But the real answer is that cyborg figurations are protean.

dieser Frage. Tierversuche sind nur ein weiteres Beispiel, das die bedenkliche Dimension der Tatsache, daß wir nicht unschuldig sind und nicht sein können, deutlich macht.

Gleich einem Blatt

TNG: Wie hat sich die/der Cyborg seit 1985 verändert? Ich stelle diese Frage, denn in dem Interview, das Sie mit Constance Penley und Andrew Ross [24] *gemacht haben, stellen Sie am Ende fest, daß die/der Cyborg weiblich ist. In* Modest_Witness *führen Sie Joanna Russ' FrauMann ein und beschreiben die Cyborg als *Stammzelle im Knochenmark des technowissenschaftlichen Körpers* [25]**, was ein ziemlich großartiges Bild ist. Ich würde vermuten, daß die Cyborg eine prozessuale Figur ist, wie alles für Sie.*

DH: Ja. Manchmal markiere ich Cyborg als sie/er oder führe etwas wie die *OncoMouse™* ein, die eine Cyborgfigur ist. Aber die eigentliche Antwort ist, daß Cyborgfigurationen proteisch sind.

TNG: Aus der Erfahrung gesprochen, was war Ihr intensivster Moment der Begegnung mit Cybergology [26] *oder der Cyborgheit, wenn wir das so nennen können?*

DH: Oh weh! [Gelächter]

TNG: Oder an welche Momente erinnern Sie sich, in denen es sich für Sie kristallisiert hat?

DH: Nun, einer ist sicher mein Gefühl von Kniffligkeit, Interesse und Vergnügen – ebenso wie die Intensität – dessen, mir vorzustellen, wie gleich einem Blatt ich bin.

TNG: Wirklich !?!

DH: Ganz im Ernst. Zum Beispiel fasziniert mich die Molekularstruktur, an der wir teilhaben, ebenso wie die Frage, welche Arten der Instrumentierung, Interdisziplinarität und Wissenspraktiken eingegangen sind in die historischen Möglichkeiten zu begreifen, inwiefern ich einem Blatt gleiche.

TNG: Haben Sie diese Epiphanie schon als Kind erlebt oder erst als Erwachsene?

DH: Ich spreche klarerweise aus der Perspektive einer Erwachsenen. Was das Verbundensein anbelangt, war mein Bewußtsein als Kind ungeheuer religiös. Aber mich haben Miniaturen fasziniert.

TNG: Miniaturen?

DH: Alles, angefangen vom Puppenhaus bis dahin, mir ausgeklügelte Miniaturmenschenwelten vorzustellen und mit kleinen Figuren im Gras zu spielen. Eigentlich habe ich viel Zeit in Miniaturwelten verbracht.

TNG: Was Sie immer noch tun. Wann haben Sie sich bewußt in die Wissenschaft begeben?

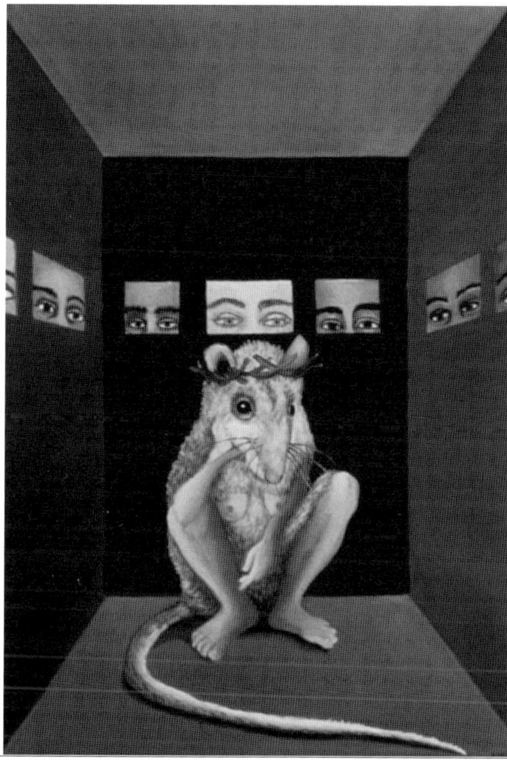

TNG: Experientially speaking, what is your most profound moment of encountering cyborgology[20] or cyborg-ness if we can call it that?

DH: Oi vei! [Laughter]

TNG: Or what ar the moments when you remember it crystallizing for you?

DH: Well one is certainly my sense of the intricacy, interest, and pleasure – as well as the intensity – of how I have imagined how like a leaf I am.

TNG: Really!?!

DH: Quite seriously. For instance, my fascination with the molecular architecture that we share, as well as what kinds of instrumentation, interdisciplinarity, and knowledge practices have gone into the historical possibilities of understanding how I am like a leaf.

TNG: Now when you were a child did you experience such an epiphany or is this only as an adult?

DH: Clearly I'm speaking from an adult perspective. In regards to connectedness, my child consciousness was overwhelmingly religious. But I was fascinated by miniatures.

Lynn Randolph: The Laboratory, or the Passion of OncoMouse

DH: Erst am College, wo mein Hauptfach Zoologie war, ich aber gleichzeitig Englisch und Philosophie studierte. Alle drei kamen mir immer wie Teile des gleichen Gegenstands vor.

*TNG: Was uns zurück zu ihrem *Moment des Seins* mit dem Blatt bringt – um Virginia Woolfs Formulierung zu benutzen.*

DH: Worauf ich in bezug auf Ihre Frage nach der/dem Cyborg hinauswollte, waren Momente ästhetisch-moralischer Einheit, die, für mich, tiefgreifend von biowissenschaftlichen Denkweisen beeinflußt sind.

*TNG: Ihre Theorie entwickelt sich so *natürlich* aus Ihrem Interesse an Biologie. Viele Leute in Ihrem Bereich fühlen sich jedoch durch die Art, in der Sie über Biologie und Wissenschaft nachdenken, bedroht, was eine Ironie ist, weil Sie Ihre Perspektive einem so gründlichen Verständnis und einer tiefgreifenden Einverleibung biologischer Welten verdanken. Warum ist ein derartiges Verständnis dann so bedrohlich?*

DH: Ein Teil des Unbehagens rührt von der Tatsache her, daß, wenn man über die schonungslose historische Kontingenz des Sich-Selbst-Erlebens oder über die Anfertigung wissenschaftlichen Wissens spricht, die Leute Relativismus oder reinen Sozialkonstruktivismus heraushören, was in keinster Weise das ist, was ich sage. Aber das ist die Reduktion, die ständig vorgenommen wird. Und dann gibt es die Leute, die davon bedroht sind, weil sie solche Analysen als biologischen Determinismus lesen! Eine Art Naturalismus, den sie nicht wollen, weil sie SozialkonstruktivistInnen sind und dem Biologischen oder dem Natürlichen nicht zuviel Gewicht verleihen wollen. Da ich versuche, *sowohl-als auch* und *weder-noch* zu sagen, entsteht ziemliche Verwirrung, die jedoch keine sehr produktive Verwirrung ist. Ich spreche von einer Art, mit der Welt zu interagieren, die erbarmungslos historisch spezifisch ist. Technowissenschaft ist eine materialisierte Semiose. Es geht darum, wie wir uns mit und in der Welt einlassen. Was nicht das gleiche ist wie zu sagen, Wissen sei optional. Vielmehr bedeutet es, daß es eine Spezifität gibt, die man nicht außer acht lassen kann.

Cyborgsurrealismus

TNG: Ich möchte eine Frage zur Form stellen, insbesondere zur Form des Schreibens, die Sie gewählt haben. Es scheint, daß jene Art analytischen Schreibens, die Sie verwenden, um Ihre Gedanken zu entwickeln, in mancher Hinsicht auch abschreckend ist. Anders ausgedrückt: Sie werden fortwährend von der Linearität und dem Angrenzen der Satz-auf-Satz-Kon-

TNG: Miniatures?

DH: Everything from doll houses to imagining elaborate miniature people's worlds and playing with tiny figures in the grass. Basically I just spent lots of time in miniature worlds.

TNG: Which is what you're still doing. When did science enter into your consciousness?

DH: Not until college where I was a Zoology major simultaneously to studying English and Philosophy. All three always felt like part of the same subject.

*TNG: Which brings us back to your *moment of being* – to use Virginia Woolf's phrase – with the leaf.*

DH: What I was getting at, in relation to your question about the cyborg, are moments of aesthetic-moral unity that, for me, were deeply influenced by bio-scientific ways of thinking.

*TNG: Your theory develops so *naturally* out of your interest in biology. But many people in your field are quite threatened by the way you think about biology and science ,which is ironic since you owe your perspective to the deepest understanding and embodiment of biological worlds. Why is such an understanding then so threatening?*

DH: Part of the discomfort comes from the fact that if you talk about the relentless historical contingency of experiencing yourself, or of crafting scientific knowledge, people hear relativism or pure social constructionism which is not what I am saying at all. But that's the kind of reduction that keeps getting made. And then there are the people who are threatened because they read such analyses as biological determinism! A kind of naturalism that they don't want because they are social constructivists and don't want to give too much weight to the biological or the natural. Since I'm trying to say both, and, neither, nor, a lot of confusion arises, and not a very productive kind of confusion. I'm talking about a mode of interacting with the world that is relentlessly historically specific. Technoscience is a materialized semiosis. It is how we engage with and in the world. Which is not the same thing as saying knowledge is optional. It's saying there is a specificity to it that you can't forget.

Cyborg Surrealism

TNG: I'd like to ask a question about form, particularly the form of writing you chose. It

struktion und -Argumentation beherrscht, während Ihr Punkt ja gerade der ist, uns während des Lesens fortwährend dazu aufzufordern, ein multi-relationales, multi-dimensionales, assoziatives dichtes Lesen beizubehalten – einen Hypertext-Modus. Haben Sie je einen anderen Modus als das akademische Schreiben verwendet oder würden Sie das tun? Eine Hypertext-CD-Rom zum Beispiel? Oder geht es darum gar nicht?

DH: Ich habe darüber nachgedacht, und das ist sicher der Grund, warum ich so viele visuelle Elemente im Buch habe. Aber ich glaube, letztendlich kann ich am besten mit Worten umgehen. Die Zusammenarbeit mit der Malerin Lynn Randolph in diesem Buch ist jedoch sehr wichtig.

TNG: Wie kam es zu dieser Zusammenarbeit?

DH: In den späten 80er Jahren war Randolph im Bunting-Institut am Radcliff College und las das *Manifest für Cyborgs*. Als Reaktion auf diesen Aufsatz hat sie ihre Cyborg gemalt. Etwas später hat sie mir ein Bild geschickt, und ich habe ihr zurückgeschrieben, wie begeistert ich war. Und dann gab es eine ziemlich lange Unterbrechung, aber wir haben schließlich wieder angefangen, einander zu schreiben. Ich habe ihr Konzeptentwürfe geschickt und sie mir Dias. Es gab keinen beabsichtigten Zusammenhang, aber ich habe ihre Bilder gesehen, und einige davon haben mich wirklich beeinflußt. Und genauso ist meine Arbeit in ihre Bilder eingegangen. Aber es gab nie eine bewußte Entscheidung, gemeinsam an irgendeinem Thema zu arbeiten. Das Bild auf dem Buchrücken, *The Laboratory, or the Passion of OncoMouse* [1994], hat sie zum Beispiel im Dialog mit meinen Erörterungen zur *OncoMouse*™ gemalt. Aber nachdem ich das Bild gesehen hatte, habe ich wieder mehr darüber geschrieben. Das Verhältnis zwischen Randolph und mir war also ein gegenseitiger Austausch, bei dem wir nie gezielt zusammengearbeitet haben, aber tatsächlich haben wir ständig zusammengearbeitet. Für mich sind ihre visuellen Beiträge zu dem Buch Argumente und nicht einfach Illustrationen.

TNG: Sie sind fast wie katholische Allegorien.

DH: Ja, wir haben über meine Art des Cyborg-Surrealismus und ihren metaphorischen Realismus Witze gemacht.

TNG: Ich hatte Probleme mit den Gemälden – gerade wegen der Form des Realismus, die sie verwendet, aber das kann einfach Geschmacksache sein. Für mich zeigen die Bilder ihren historischen Kontext zu buchstäblich.

DH: Einige von ihnen tun das, aber das trifft nicht auf *Transfusions* und *The Passion of OncoMouse*

seems that the mode of straight forward analytical writing you use to get at your ideas is also, in some ways, a deterrent. In other words you are constantly being reigned in by the linearity and contiguities of sentence by sentence construction and argumentation when your whole point is to constantly ask us to keep a multi-relational, multi-dimensional, associational thick reading – a hypertext modality – as we go. Have you ever used another modality than academic writing or would you? A hypertext CD-Rom for instance. Or is that not the point?

DH: I have thought about it and it is certainly why I have as many visual elements in the book as I do. But I think finally what I am good at is the words. But the collaboration with the painter Lynn Randolph in this book was very important.

TNG: How did that collaboration come about?

DH: Randolph was at the Bunting Institute at Radcliffe College in the late 1980s and they read *The Cyborg Manifesto*. She painted a cyborg as her response to that essay. Sometime after that she mailed me a picture and I wrote her back saying how excited I was by it. And then there was a fairly long lapse but we just started mailing one another again. I would send her drafts, she would send me slides. There was no deliberate connection but I would see her paintings and some of them would really influence me. And similarly, my work was incorporated into her painting. But it was never a conscious decision for the two of us to collaborate on any one theme. For instance the image on the back of the book, *The Laboratory, or the Passion of OncoMouse* [1994] she painted in conversation with my *OncoMouse*™ argument. But after I saw it I did more writing. So the relationship with Randolph was an interchange between the two of us where we never deliberately collaborated but, in fact, were constantly collaborating. I think of her visual contributions to the book as arguments, not just illustrations.

TNG: They are almost like Catholic allegories.

DH: Yes, we joked about my kind of cyborg surrealism and her metaphoric realism.

TNG: I actually had problems with the paintings – and this may just be a matter of taste – precisely because of the kind of realism she uses. They make her historical context too literal for me.

zu, die meine zwei Lieblingsbilder sind. Aber selbst in den Gemälden, die ich nicht so sehr mag, finde ich es gut, wie sie Dinge gegenüberstellt und in bestimmten Momenten Referenzen an die Renaissance und den entsprechenden Raum einsetzt und mit DNS-Strängen, Galaxien, Mikrochips und so weiter verflicht. Randolph hat sich bestimmten *realistischen* Konventionen und narrativen Bildinhalten verpflichtet, um die Verbindung von Form und Inhalt in den Vordergrund zu stellen. Sie nimmt den Widerstand gegen die Imperative des abstrakten Formalismus als einzige Form der Malerei auf.

TNG: Was sie metaphorischen Realismus nennt.

DH: Genau. Für sie und für mich ist dieser metaphorische Realismus – oder Cyborg-Surrealismus – der überschüssige Raum der Technowissenschaft – eine Welt, innerhalb deren Grammatik wir zwar sein mögen, aber wir wollen und können uns ihre Repräsentationen sowohl einverleiben als auch über sie hinausgehen und ihre Syntax sprengen.

TNG: Die/der Cyborg wird üblicherweise als räumliche und physische Kategorie analysiert. Aber in Modest_Witness *erörtern Sie auch Zeitlichkeit. Sie sagen, daß Verdichtung, Fusion und Implosion die zeitlichen Bedingtheiten der/des Cyborg sind. Warum ist es so wichtig für uns, zeitliche Bedingtheit im Verhältnis zu den *fleshfactors* zu untersuchen?*

DH: Eine Antwort wäre eine Formulierung aus John Christies *A Tragedy for Cyborgs* von 1993, die ich in *Modest_Witness* verwende. Er hat über das *Manifest für Cyborgs* und die *schon geschriebene Zukunft* der Genetik geschrieben.[27] Ich glaube, er war der erste, der mich auf die Genomen und Finanzinstrumenten gemeine zeitliche Bedingtheit in der gegenwärtigen technowissenschaftlichen Kultur aufmerksam gemacht hat. Zum Beispiel, wie Tilgungspläne die Zukunft schreiben. Wenn man bei einer Hypothek einer bestimmten Art der Schuldenrückzahlung unterworfen ist – das gilt auch für ein Entwicklungsland –, dann sperren einen die Tilgungspläne in verschiedene Systeme der Nahrungsmittelproduktion, Fremdenverkehrsindustrie, Heiratspraktiken usw. ein. Die Zukunft ist buchstäblich in die Verpflichtung der Schuldenrückzahlung eingesperrt. Es ist eine bereits geschriebene Zukunft, in die eine eingegrenzte Vorstellung der zeitlichen Bedingtheit schon eingebaut ist, und tatsächlich steht eine Denkweise der Genetik im Verhältnis zur Vorstellung von einer vorgeschriebenen Zukunft, einer Zukunft, für die es bereits ein Drehbuch gibt.

TNG: Genetik ist sehr eng mit zeitlicher Bedingtheit verbunden: von der Betonung der Vererbung

DH: Some of them do but that is not true with say *Transfusions* and *The Passion of OncoMouse* which are my two favorites. But even in paintings that I don't like as much I love the kinds of juxtapositions she sets up, the use at moments of Renaissance space and references interwoven with DNA strands, galaxies, microchips and so forth. Randolph is committed to certain 'realist' conventions and narrative pictorial content in order to foreground the joining of form and content. She takes up a resistance to the imperatives of abstract formalism as the only way to paint.

TNG: What she calls metaphorical realism.

DH: Exactly and for her, and me, this metaphoric realism – or cyborg surrealism – is the excessive space of technoscience – a world whose grammar we may be inside of but where we may, and can, both embody and exceed its representations and blast its syntax.

TNG: The cyborg is usually analyzed as a spatial and a physical category. But in Modest_Witness *you also discuss temporality. You say condensation, fusion, and implosion are the temporalities of the cyborg. Why is temporality crucial for us to study in relation to *fleshfactors*?*

DH: One answer would be a phrase I use in *Modest_Witness* from John Christie's 1993 *A Tragedy for Cyborgs*. He was actually writing about the *Cyborg Manifesto* and the *already-written future* of genetics.[21] I think he was the one who first made me notice the shared temporality between genomes and financial instruments in contemporary technoscientific culture. For instance the way debt-schedules write the future. If you are subjected to a certain kind of debt repayment schedule with a mortgage, or as a developing nation, the debt schedule locks you into various kinds of food production systems, tourist industries, marriage practices, etc. The future is literally locked into the debt repayment obligation. It's an already-written future, with a bounded notion of temporality already built into it, in fact one way of thinking of genetics is in relation to the notion of scripted futures.

TNG: Genetics is wedded quite intimately to temporality – from the emphasis on heredity – the past – at the turn of the century to the emphasis on what genetics can tell us about one's future now – our genetic tendencies or potentiality.

– der Vergangenheit – zur Zeit der Jahrhundertwende hin zur Betonung dessen, was uns die Genetik jetzt über unsere Zukunft, über unsere genetischen Anlagen oder Potentiale, sagen kann.

DH: Ja, ebenso wie Schuldentilgungspläne nicht bestimmen, was Menschen mit einer derartigen Struktur machen werden, legt das Gen sozusagen auch nur Fährten oder Matrizes aus, innerhalb derer das *Leben selbst* vorkommt. Die Art und Weise jedoch, in der Genome in verzweigten Datenbanken institutionalisiert werden und dann in anderen Wissenspraktiken benutzt werden – z. B. in der pharmazeutischen Entwicklung – , erstellt die Matrizes für die Zukunft – einschließlich der Formen des Widerstands und des Streits.

TNG: Es geht also um eine grundlegende Verschiebung zeitlicher Bedingtheit?

DH: Ja, bei Genetik geht es, so wie sie sich heute entwickelt, um eine materiell unterschiedliche Art der zeitlichen Bedingtheit.

Leidenschaft und Ironie

TNG: Um das Ende einzuleiten, habe ich mir die Freiheit genommen, ein Fragment aus Modest_Witness *auszuwählen: *Der Punkt ist, zu lernen zu erinnern, daß wir anders sein könnten und vielleicht auch sind ...*[28] *Ich mag dieses Satzfragment sehr, weil es die fortwährenden Spannungen und Probleme unseres Seins, die Sie unaufhörlich hinterfragen, offenlegt. Und die Art Ihrer Formulierung ist wichtig: *zu lernen* *zu erinnern*. Es geht also nicht nur um Lernen [eine Handlung in der Gegenwart, die die Zukunft bildet], sondern auch um Erinnern [die Vergangenheit nutzen]. Anders ausgedrückt: Wir müssen uns einlassen auf das Lernen und Erinnern des Wie und Was dessen, wie wir anderweitig gewesen hätten sein können. Ich mag die Syntax daran. Und das ist nicht nur ein poetischer Gedanke, sondern eine technowissenschaftliche Tatsache.*

DH: Ja, denn trotz all der zeitlichen Bedingtheit der *bereits geschriebenen Zukunft* sind Zukunft und Gegenwart nicht endgültig geschrieben. Aber das muß man ohne Hype technophiler Utopie denken.

*TNG: Das ist immer das, was an Ihrer Analyse am schwersten zu fassen ist: Ihre *januskköpfige* politische Theorie, um Ihre Formulierung zu verwenden. Die *sowohl-als auch, und, weder, noch*-Geschichte, die Sie erzählen.*

DH: Richtig, ich glaube jedoch, was ich letztlich sage, ist relativ einfach. Alles, was ich wirklich will, ist permanente Leidenschaft und Ironie, wobei Leidenschaft ebenso wichtig wie Ironie ist.

DH: Yet, just as the debt repayment schedules don't determine what people are going to do with such a structure, the gene merely lays out tracks so to speak or matrixes within which *life itself* is going to occur. Yet the way genomes are institutionalized into distributed data bases and then made use of in other knowledge practices – for instance pharmaceutical development – does set up matrixes for the future including forms of resistance and contestation.

TNG: So it is about a profound shift in temporality?

DH: Yes, genetics, as it is developing today, is about a materially different kind of temporality.

Passion and Irony

TNG: As far as ending, I took the liberty of selecting a fragment from Modest_Witness*: *the point is to learn to remember that we might have been otherwise, and might yet be ...*[22] I love that sentence fragment because it exposes the constant tensions and questions about our being that you are continually interrogating. And the way you state it is important: *to learn* *to remember,* so it is not just learning [an action in the present that builds the future] but remembering [using the past]. In other words, we must be involved in learning and remembering the ways and whats of how we might have been otherwise. I love the syntax there. And this isn't just a poetic thought but a technoscientific fact.*

DH: Yes, for all of the temporality of the *already-written future,* the future and present are, in fact, not finally written. But this must be thought without the hype of technophilic utopia.

*TNG: That is what is always hardest for people to grab onto in your analysis. Your *Janus-faced* political theory, to use your phrase. The *both, and, neither, nor* story you are telling.*

DH: Right, but I guess what I'd say finally is quite simple. All I am really asking for is permanent passion and irony, where passion is as important as irony.

TNG: A mutated technoscientific Catholicism mixed with the molecular poetics of a leaf for instance?

DH: Passionately! [Laughs]

TNG: Ein mutierter technowissenschaftlicher Katholozismus, gemischt mit der molekularen Poesie eines Blattes zum Beispiel?

DH: Leidenschaftlich! [Lacht]

Aus dem Amerikanischen von
Dagmar Fink und Susanne Lummerding

1 Es waren die HerausgeberInnen der *Socialist Review*, die Haraway mit dieser *anspruchslosen* Aufgabe betraut hatten, und laut Haraway ist dies die Entstehungsgeschichte des Manifests. *Die Moral der Geschichte*, scherzt sie: *Gib mir keinen Auftrag.*

2 In der ersten Originalfassung *Manifesto for Cyborgs: Science, Technology, and Socialist Feminism in the 1980s.* in: Socialist Review 80, 1985, S. 65-108. Die Übersetzung hält sich größtenteils an diese Fassung des Textes *Ein Manifest für Cyborgs. Feminismus im Streit mit den Technowissenschaften*, Übersetzung von Fred Wolf. *Die Neuerfindung der Natur. Primaten, Cyborgs und Frauen*, Übersetzung von Dagmar Fink u. a., Campus, Frankfurt, N.Y 1995, S. 33-72; A.d.Ü.

3 Thyrza Nichols Goodeve spielt hier auf zwei Buchtitel von Donna Haraway an, nämlich 1: *Simians, Cyborgs, and Women. The Reinvention of Nature* (Routledge, London, N.Y. 1991) und 2.: *Primate Visions: Gender, Race, and Nature in the World of Modern Science* (Routledge, London, N. Y. 1989). Mehrere Texte aus *Simians, Cyborgs, and Women* sind als Übersetzung in *Die Neuerfindung der Natur* enthalten, weitere, zumeist ältere Übersetzungen von Donna Haraway finden sich in *Monströse Versprechen. Coyote Geschichten zu Feminismus und Technowissenschaft*, Übersetzung von Michael Haupt. Hamburg: Argument Vlg., 1995. *Primate Visions* ist nicht übersetzt; A.d.Ü.

4 Morphing: meint das Verändern von Formen, sei es real oder per Computerprogramm, A.d.Ü.

5 DONNA J. HARAWAY, *Modest_Witness@ Second_Millenium.FemaleMan©_Meets_ Oncomouse™*, Routledge, London, New York 1997, S. 117. Der gleichnamige Vortrag ist als *Anspruchsloser Zeuge@Zweites Jahrtausend.FrauMann© trifft OncoMouse™*, übersetzt von Connie Lösch und Elvira Scheich, erschienen in: *Vermittelte Weiblichkeit. Feministische Wissenschafts- und Gesellschaftstheorie.* (Hrsg.) Elvira Scheich. Hamburger Edition, Hamburg 1996, S. 347-389.

6 HARAWAY 1997, S. 103.

1 The editors of the *Socialist Review* had presented her with this "modest" assignment and according to Haraway, this is the origin story of the *Manifesto*. "The moral of the story," she joked, "don't give me an assignment."

2 DONNA J. HARAWAY, *Modest_Witness@Second_Millennium.FemaleMan©_Meets_OncoMouse™* New York, Routledge, 1997, 117

3 HARAWAY, 1997, 103

4 SCOTT F. GILBERT, *Bodies of Knowledge: Biology and the Intercultural University, forthcoming. Changing Life in the New World Dis/Order*, edited by P. TAYLOR, S. Halfon, and P. EDWARDS, Minneapolis: University of Minnesota Press

5 The cremaster muscle controls the ascension and descension of the testicles. Matthew Barney's biological video-sculpture epic explores the stages of conflict of a prenatal reproductive system as it develops towards its final form.

6 SARAH FRANKLIN, *Life Itself*, paper delivered at the Center for Cultural Values, Lancaster University, June 9

7 "... gene fetishism is compounded of a political economic denial that holds commodities to be sources of their own value while obscuring the sociotechnical relations among humans and between humans and nonhumans that generate both objects and value; a disavowal, suggested by psychoanalytic theory, that substitutes he master molecule for a more adequate representation of units or nexuses of biological structure, function, development, evolution, and reproduction; and a philosophical-cognitive error that mistakes potent abstractions for concrete entities, which themselves are ongoing events. Fetishists are multiply invested in all these substitutions. The irony is that gene fetishism involves such elaborate surrogacy, swerving, and substitution, when the gene as the guarantor of life itself is supposed to signify an autotelic thing in itself, the code of codes. Never has avoidoance of acknowledging the relentless tropic nature of living and signifying involved such wonderful figuration, where the gene collects up the people in the materialized dream of life itself." HARAWAY, 1991, 147

8 ALFRED NORTH WHITEHEAD, *Science and the Modern World*, New York

9 ROLAND BARTHES, *Mythologies*, New York: Hill and Wang, 1975

10 HARAWAY, 1997

---

7 SCOTT F. GILBERT, *Bodies of Knowledge: Biology and the Intercultural University*, erscheint in: P. Taylor, S. Halfon, P. Edwards (Hrsg.), *Changing Life in the New World Dis/Order*. Minneapolis: University of Minnesota Press

8 Im Englischen: "that doesn't require literacy in biology."

9 Der Musculus Cremaster (Hodenhebermuskel) kontrolliert das Auf- und Absteigen der Hoden. Matthew Barneys fünfteiliger biologischer Video-Skulptur-Epos (augenblicklich im Entstehen) erkundet die entscheidenden Stadien in der Entwicklung von einem vorgeburtlichen Reproduktionssystem zu seiner endgültigen Form.

11 SARAH FRANKLIN, *Life Itself*, Vortrag gehalten am 9. Juni am Center for Cultural Values, Universität Lancaster.

12 "... Genfetischismus setzt sich zusammen aus einer politischen ökonomischen Verneinung, in der Waren in sich selbst Werte sind, während die gesellschaftlich-technischen Verhältnisse unter Menschen sowie zwischen Menschen und Nicht-Menschen, die sowohl Objekte als auch Werte generieren, verdeckt werden; aus einer, von der psychoanalytischen Theorie nahegelegten, Verleugnung, in der das Meistermolekül ersetzt wird durch eine angemessenere Repräsentation von Einheiten oder Verbindungen aus biologischen Strukturen, Funktionen, Entwicklung, Evolution und Reproduktion; und aus einem philosophisch-kognitiven Irrtum, der starke Abstraktionen für konkrete Entitäten hält, die wiederum selbst andauernde Ereignisse sind. Fetischisten sind in all diese Substitutionen vielfach investiert. Die Ironie dabei ist, daß der Genfetischismus ausgesprochen komplizierter Leihmutterschaften, Abweichungen und Substitutionen bedarf, so man davon ausgeht, daß das Gen als der Garant des Lebens selbst ein autotelisches Ding an sich, den Kode der Kodes, bedeuten soll. Zu vermeiden, die tropische Natur des Lebens und Bedeutens anzuerkennen, hat nie zuvor zu einer derart wundervollen Figuration geführt, in der das Gen die Leute im materialisiertem Traum des Lebens selbst einsammelt."
HARAWAY 1997, S. 147.

11 ALFRED NORTH WHITEHEAD, *Wissenschaft und moderne Welt*, Übersetzung von Gertrud Tschiedel und Francois Bondy, Morgarten, Zürich 1949 © 1925, S. 67f

13 ROLAND BARTHES, *Mythen des Alltags*, Übersetzung von Helmut Scheffel. Frankfurt/M.: Suhrkamp, 1964 © 1957.

14 HARAWAY 1997, S. 126.

11 YVONNE RAINER, artist, writer, filmmaker. *MURDER and murder*(1997) is her most recent film.
12 See BARBARA EHRENREICH and JANET MACINTOSH, *Biology Under Attack*, in: *The Nation*, Vol. 264, #22, June 9, 1997, 11-16
13 HARAWAY, 1997, 98
14 She is referring to *Laboratory, or The Passion of *OncoMouse** by Lynn Randolph
15 HARAWAY, 1997, 79
16 The modest witness represents the story of science studies as well as of science fiction. The FemaleMan is the chief figure of feminism. *OncoMouse*™ is the figure of biotechnology and genetic engineering
17 SUSAN LEIGH STAR, *Power, Technology and the Phenomenology of Conventions: On Being Allergic to Onions*, in: *Sociology of Monsters: Power, Technology and the Modern World*, edited by J. LAW, Oxford, Basil Blackwell, 43
18 CONSTANCE PENLEY and ANDREW ROSS, *Cyborgs at Large: Interview with Donna Haraway*, in: *Technoculture*, Minneapolis, University of Minnesota Press, 1991,1-20. See as well, DONNA J. HARAWAY, *The Actors Are Cyborg, Nature is Coyote, and the Geography is Elsewhere:* Postscript to *Cyborgs at Large*, 21-26
19 HARAWAY, 1997, 14
20 See *The Cyborg Handbook*, New York, 1995, edited by Chris Hables Gray et al.
21 JOHN R. R. CHRISTIE, *A Tragedy for Cyborgs*, in: *Configurations* , 1993. 1:171-9621, HARAWAY,1997, 39
22 HARAWAY, 1997, 39

---

15 YVONNE RAINER. Künstlerin, Autorin, Filmemacherin. *MURDER and murder* (1997) ist ihr letzter Film. Vgl. auch das Interview in *Art in America*, Juli 1997.
16 Cultural Studies stehen für keine eigene Disziplin, sondern für eine in verschiedenen Disziplinen praktizierte Form des Forschens. Sie zeichnen sich methodisch durch einen radikalen Kontextualismus, Interdisziplinarität und das Interesse an der Ermächtigung derer, die sich beforschen, aus. Vgl. hierzu den einflußreichen Reader Grossberg/ Nelson/ Treichler (Hrsg.) *Cultural Studies*, Routledge, London, New York 1992, A.d.Ü.
17 Vgl. BARBARA EHRENREICH und JANET MACINTOSH, *Biology Under Attack*, in.: *The Nation*, Vol. 264, Nr. 22, 9. Juni 1997, S. 11-16.
18 HARAWAY 1997, S. 98.
19 Sie bezieht sich auf *Laboratory, or The Passion of OncoMouse* von Lynn Randolph.
22 HARAWAY 1997, S. 79.
21 Der englische Titel des Science-Fiction-Romans von Joanna Russ lautet *The Female Man*. In der Übersetzung ins Deutsche (*Planet der Frauen*. Knaur:, München, Zürich 1979; ÜbersetzerIn nicht angegeben) wird der Titel leider nicht wiedergegeben.
22 Die/der anspruchslose ZeugIn repräsentiert die Geschichten der Wissenschaftsforschung ebenso wie der Science Fiction. FrauMann ist die Hauptfigur des Feminismus. *OncoMouse*™ ist die Figur der Bio- und der Gentechnologie, ein Synekdoche für Technowissenschaft.
23 SUSAN LEIGH STAR, *Power, Technology and the Phenomenology of Conventions: On Being Allergic to Onions*, in: J. Law (Hrsg.), *Sociology of Monsters: Power, Technology and the Modern World*. Oxford: Basil Blackwell, 1991, S.43.
24 CONSTANCE PENLEY, ANDREW ROSS, *Cyborgs at Large: An Interview with Donna Haraway*, in: *Technoculture*. Minneapolis: University of Minnesota Press, 1991, S. 1-21. Vgl. auch im gleichen Band: Donna Haraway, *The Actors are Cyborg, Nature is Coyote, and the Geography is Elsewhere: Postscript to 'Cyborgs at Large'*, S. 21-26.
25 HARAWAY 1997, S. 14.
26 Vgl. *The Cyborg Handbook*. (Hrsg.) Chris Hables Gray u. a., Routledge, New York, London 1995
27 JOHN R. R. CHRISTIE, *A Tragedy for Cyborgs*, in: *Configurations*, 1993/1: 171-196.
28 HARAWAY 1997, S. 39.

The Brain-Built Self

Patricia
Smith Churchland

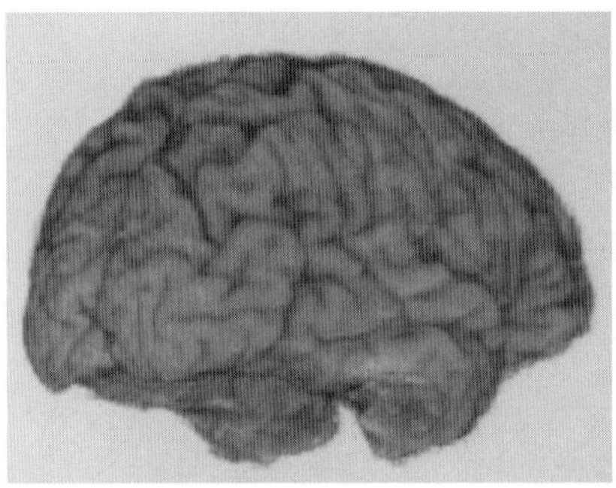

Fig. 1
MRI image of my brain, viewed from the rear, right side.
MR-Bild meines Gehirns, von hinten rechts gesehen.

symposium

Das vom Hirn konstruierte Selbst

Patricia
Smith Churchland

Introduction

Sneaking out of the MRI tube where I had lain for the past half hour, I glimpsed Dr. Hanna Damasio studying the lab's display screen. Off the gurney now, I went to her side and stared at the image of my brain on the screen. *Is that – *me*?* [figure 1] Well yes, in a certain sense. And yet, not simply, or merely me. Certainly not *familiarly* me. Here is what I thought: *Somehow, starting in infancy, my brain built a story about itself – its body, its history, its *now*, and its world. From the inside, I know that story – though I think of it as reality, not just a story. Indeed, it is my inner reality. So how does this happen? What is it for me to be a construction of my brain?*

In one form or another, these questions have had a long and convoluted history, born in the unflinching curiosity of the ancient Greeks, and finding voice in diverse cultures. Until recently, the only explanatory resources for addressing puzzling behavior depended on mythologizing in the case of others, and myth-filtered introspection in the case of oneself. Not surprisingly, early explanations invoked possession by devils, or if you were luckier, divine forces, to account for epileptic seizures or schizophrenic hallucinations. In the absence of understanding, the punishment theory of mental dysfunction commanded widespread belief, yet it was wholly untestable – and essentially untested.

Melancholia [what we now call chronic depression] or phobias were often surmised to be essentially character flaws – flaws that might be overcome with sufficient gumption. The existence of witches, hexes, curses and spells had a far longer history as brute fact than does our appreciation of such potent neurochemicals as serotonin. Obsessive hand-washing, a mere fifteen years ago, was widely assumed to be a manifestation of repressed sexuality. Nevertheless, even as early as 400 BC, the great Greek physician, Hippocrates, was convinced that events such as sudden paralysis or creeping dementia had their originating causes in brain damage. Which implied, in his view, that normal movement and normal speech had their originating causes in the well-tempered brain.

Brains, however, are not easy organs to figure out. Imagine Hippocrates, dissecting the brain of a dead warrior after autopsy, and pon-

Einleitung

Als ich aus der Röhre des MR-Tomographen schlüpfte, in der ich die letzte halbe Stunde gelegen hatte, erspähte ich Dr. Hanna Damasio, wie sie die Darstellung auf dem Monitor im Labor studierte. Von der Liege heruntergestiegen, trat ich an ihre Seite und starrte auf das Bild meines Gehirns auf dem Bildschirm. *Bin das – ich?* [Abb. 1] Nun ja, in einem gewissen Sinn. Und doch: nicht einfach oder lediglich ich. Ganz sicher nicht ich im vertrauten Sinn. Folgendes ging mir durch den Kopf: *Irgendwie, beginnend mit der frühen Kindheit, zimmerte sich mein Gehirn eine Fabel über sich zusammen – seinen Körper, seine Geschichte, sein Jetzt, seine Welt. Von innen kenne ich diese Fabel – wenn ich sie auch für die Realität und nicht bloß eine Fabel halte. Ja, sie ist sogar meine innere Realität. Wie kommt das also? Was heißt es für mich, eine Konstruktion meines Gehirns zu sein?*

In der einen oder anderen Form blicken diese Fragen auf eine lange und verwickelte Geschichte zurück, die ihren Ursprung in der unerschrockenen Neugier der alten Griechen hat und in verschiedenen Kulturen ihren Ausdruck fand. Bis vor kurzem konnte man rätselhaftes Verhalten einzig durch Mythologisierung – im Fall von anderen – und durch mythengefilterte Introspektion – im Fall des eigenen Selbst – erklären. Es überrascht kaum, daß man sich früher epileptische Anfälle oder schizophrene Halluzinationen durch Besessenheit von Dämonen oder, wenn man mehr Glück hatte, von heiligen Mächten erklärte. Da es an Verständnis dafür mangelte, fand die Bestrafungstheorie bei geistigen Störungen breite Zustimmung, war allerdings vollkommen unüberprüfbar – und blieb im wesentlichen auch unüberprüft.

Melancholie [das, was wir heute als chronische Depression bezeichnen] oder Phobien wurden meist als Charaktermängel erachtet – Mängel, die man mit der nötigen inneren Stärke überwinden könne. Die Existenz von Hexen, Zauberern, Verwünschungen und Bannsprüchen war viel länger ein geschichtliches Faktum als unsere Wertschätzung für solch wirkungsvolle Neurotransmitter wie Serotonin. Zwanghaftes Händewaschen wurde noch vor 15 Jahren weitgehend für ein Zeichen verdrängter Sexualität gehalten. Andererseits war der große griechische Arzt Hippokrates bereits 400 v. Chr. der Überzeugung, daß plötzliche Lähmungen oder schleichende Demenz ihre Ursache in Gehirnschäden hätten. Was aus seiner Sicht implizierte, daß die normale Bewegungs- und Redefähigkeit ihre Ursache in einem wohltemperierten Gehirn hätten.

dering an area of sword-destroyed tissue. To what theoretical resources could he reach to begin to make sense of something so complex as the relation between fluent speech and the pinkish tissue found in the skull? Remember, in 400 BC nothing was understood about the nature of cells that make up the body, let alone of the special nature of cells that make up the brain. Techniques for isolating neurons – brain cells – to see what they looked like could begin only in the 19th century. Techniques for isolating *living* neurons to explore their function did not appear until well into the twentieth century.

Figuring out how neurons do what they do requires high-level technology. And that, needless to say, depends on immense infrastructural science – on cell biology, advanced physics and twentieth century chemistry. It requires sophisticated modern notions like molecule and protein, and modern tools like the light microscope and the electron microscope.

Most importantly, making progress on how brains work depended on understanding electricity. This is because what makes brain cells special is their capacity to signal one another by causing fast micro changes in each others' electrical state. Living as we do in an electrical world, it is sobering to recall that as late as 1800, electricity was typically considered deeply mysterious and quite possibly occult. Only after discoveries by Ampère and Faraday at the dawn of the 19th century was electricity clearly understood to be a physical phenomenon, behaving according to well-defined laws, and capable of being harnessed for practical purposes.

In this century, modern neuroscience and psychology allow us to go beyond myth and introspection to approach the *self* as a natural phenomenon whose causes and effects can be addressed by science. Helped by new experimental techniques and new explanatory tools, we can pry loose real understanding of how the brain comes to know its own body, how it builds a coherent model of its world, and how changes in brain tissue can entail changes in the very self itself. Neurobiology is beginning to reveal why some brains are more susceptible than others to alcohol or heroin addiction, or why some brains slide into incoherent world-models. Progress is visible on the staged emergence of self in childhood, as well as the cruel inch-by-

Gehirne sind jedoch keine leicht zu durchschauenden Organe. Man stelle sich vor, wie Hippokrates bei der Autopsie das Gehirn eines toten Kriegers seziert und einen von einem Schwerthieb lädierten Gewebebereich betrachtet. Auf welche theoretischen Grundlagen konnte er sich stützen, um sich auch nur annähernd etwas so Komplexes wie die Beziehung zwischen flüssiger Rede und dem im Schädel gefundenen rosa Gewebe zu erklären? Man bedenke, daß 400 v. Chr. nichts über die Natur der Körperzellen bekannt war, geschweige denn von der speziellen Natur der Gehirnzellen. Techniken zur Neuronenisolierung, um ihr Aussehen festzustellen, entwickelten sich erst im 19. Jahrhundert. Techniken zur Isolierung *lebender* Neuronen, um ihre Funktion zu erforschen, kamen erst im 20. Jahrhundert auf.

Um herauszufinden, auf welche Weise Neuronen tun, was sie tun, ist eine hochentwickelte Technologie erforderlich. Und das wiederum setzt eine gewaltige, infrastrukturintensive Wissenschaft voraus – Zellbiologie, moderne Physik, die Chemie des 20. Jahrhunderts. Es verlangt komplexe Vorstellungen wie die des Moleküls oder des Proteins sowie moderne Werkzeuge wie das Licht- und das Elektronenmikroskop.

Vor allem aber waren die Erkenntnisfortschritte in bezug auf die Funktion des Gehirns von einem Verständnis der Elektrizität abhängig. Und zwar deswegen, weil das Spezielle an Hirnzellen ihre Fähigkeit ist, einander durch schnelle Mikroveränderungen ihres elektrischen Ladezustands Signale zu senden. Wenn man so wie wir in einer elektrischen Welt lebt, ist es ernüchternd, sich in Erinnerung zu rufen, daß die Elektrizität noch um 1800 weitgehend für etwas zutiefst Mysteriöses und höchstwahrscheinlich Okkultes gehalten wurde. Erst nach den Entdeckungen Ampères und Faradays zu Beginn des 19. Jahrhunderts wurde die Elektrizität eindeutig als ein physikalisches Phänomen begriffen, das sich nach klar definierbaren Gesetzen verhält und für praktische Zwecke gebändigt werden kann.

In diesem Jahrhundert ermöglichen uns die moderne Neurowissenschaft und Psychologie, über den Mythos und die Introspektion hinauszugehen und uns dem *Selbst* als Naturphänomen zu nähern, dessen Ursachen und Wirkungen wissenschaftlich erforscht werden können. Mit Hilfe neuer experimenteller Techniken und neuer Erklärungsinstrumente können wir wirklich verstehen, wie das Gehirn seinen Körper kennenlernt, wie es ein kohärentes Modell seiner Welt konstruiert und

inch loss of self in dementia. Though well short of full answers, neuroscience has discovered much about the effects of localized brain lesions on complex decision-making or speech or voluntary behavior.

All these developments are part of the story of the neuroself. True enough, neuroscience has not advanced enough to yield complete and detailed answers to the whole range of questions. Perhaps some questions will forever exceed the neurobiological reach, though it may be hard to tell whether such problems are just *as-yet-unsolved* or whether they are truly unsolvable. In any case, incomplete but powerful answers anchored in data can often provide a foot-hold for the next step. And that, in turn, for the next step thereafter. Which is how science proceeds – one step at a time.

As I watched the computer monitor showing my brain tilted at various angles and cut at various slices, what stirred was the idea that I might come know my neuroself at least as well as I know my psyche-self. Or, at least, someone in the next generation might. I imagined Hippocrates, looking at the image of his brain, agog with excitement to experiment further.

Isn't *the brain-made self* paradoxical?

The question – *how does my brain make myself?* – does have a sort of *snake-with-tail-in-mouth* quality. To evade the paradox, I adopt a pair of pragmatic principles: [1] ask instead, *how does a brain make a self*, thereby putting the paradox at arm's length, and [2] follow the facts first, and let the paradoxes fend for themselves. As a neurophilosopher, I predict that the paradoxes might well vaporize once the neuroscience gets a bit clearer.

This is not just wishful thinking. I had seen other ostensible paradoxes about the world dissolve as so much candy floss in a flame. Once the relevant science revealed the reality behind the mystifying appearances, what had seemed counterintuitive came to be familiar and largely obvious. The idea that the Earth moves or that living things are made of dead molecules – each lost its patina of paradox in the gentle light of experiment and explanation. My hunch is that this could happen here, too. Consequently, confronting the wheelie snake is something I gladly defer until the science is a bit further along.

wie Veränderungen im Hirngewebe Veränderungen im Selbst nach sich ziehen können. Die Neurobiologie enthüllt allmählich, weshalb manche Gehirne anfälliger für Alkohol- oder Heroinsucht sind oder weshalb manche Gehirne in inkohärente Weltmodelle abrutschen. Es gibt sichtbare Erkenntnisfortschritte, was die stufenweise Entstehung des Selbst in der Kindheit und den grausamen schrittweisen Verlust des Selbst im Schwachsinn betrifft. Die Neurowissenschaften sind zwar noch sehr weit von vollständigen Antworten entfernt, aber sie haben bereits eine Menge über die Auswirkungen lokaler Gehirnläsionen auf komplexe Formen von Entscheidungs-, Sprach- oder Willensverhalten entdeckt.

All diese Entwicklungen sind ein Teil der Geschichte des Neuro-Selbst. Sicher sind die Neurowissenschaften noch nicht weit genug, um komplette und detaillierte Antworten auf alle Fragen zu geben. Vielleicht werden manche Fragen für die Neurobiologie für immer unbeantwortbar bleiben, wenn sich auch kaum entscheiden lassen wird, ob solche Probleme bloß *noch ungelöst* oder tatsächlich unlösbar sind. Auf jeden Fall können unvollständige, aber starke, auf Daten gestützte Antworten oft den Ausgangspunkt für den nächsten Schritt bilden. Und dieser dann für den Schritt danach. So schreitet die Wissenschaft schließlich voran: Schritt für Schritt.

Während ich zusah, wie der Computermonitor mein Gehirn in verschiedenen Neigungen und in verschiedenen Schnitten zeigte, regte sich in mir der Gedanke, daß ich mein Neuro-Selbst dereinst mindestens genauso gut kennen könnte, wie ich mein Psycho-Selbst kenne. Oder daß es zumindest jemand in der nächsten Generation könnte. Ich stellte mir Hippokrates vor, wie er, vor Aufregung außer sich und ganz begierig weiterzuexperimentieren, das Bild seines Gehirns betrachtet.

Ist das vom Hirn erzeugte Selbst nicht ein Paradoxon?

Die Frage *Wie erzeugt mein Hirn mein Selbst?* hat etwas von einer *Sich selbst in den Schwanz beißenden Katze*. Um das Paradoxon zu vermeiden, halte ich mich an ein pragmatisches Prinzipienpaar: [1] frage ich stattdessen: *Wie erzeugt ein Hirn ein Selbst?*, womit ich mir das Paradoxon vom Leib halte, und [2] folge ich zunächst den Fakten und überlasse die Paradoxa sich selbst. Als Neurophilosophin prophezeie ich, daß sich die Paradoxa sehr leicht in Luft auflösen könnten, wenn die Neurowissenschaften einmal klarer sehen werden.

What kind of thing is the self?

It is this question which makes philosophers of us all, at some time or other. Not everyone wonders late into the night what the stars are made of or how the immune system works. But wondering what it is that makes me me, is never very far from one's elbow. Philosophers since Plato in the 5th century BC, have tried to make progress in coming up with satisfying answers – or, more minimally, with ways of structuring the question to avoid spiraling down into confusion. The great 18th century Scottish philosopher, David Hume, gave the questions their clearest analysis and set the stage for modern scientific investigation.

Hume came to the quite shocking realization that if you look inwardly to try to observe a distinctly *self* thing, there does not seem to be any self thing there to perceive. What there is, is a continuously changing flux of visual perceptions, sounds, smells, emotions, thoughts, and so forth. Amongst all those, however, there does not exist a single, continuous *felt* sensation that one can attend to and say, *that's the self*, as one can attend to a felt sensation and say, *that's a pain*.

Yet, nothing could be more evident than that there seems to be a single thread of *meness* that runs through the entire fabric of experience. We all have a robust and undeniable self-representation. We generally awake from a deep sleep knowing who we are, even if we are confused about when and where we are. Normally, we do not doubt that *I am essentially the same person today as I was yesterday, and the day before that ...* Normally, we know without pausing to figure it out that *this body is my own* – that *this hand and this foot are both part of my body*. When I talk to myself about becoming a marathon runner, I know that it is me talking to myself. We know very well that if we fail to plan for future contingencies, our future selves may suffer, and we care now about that future self.

Here is Hume's conundrum: I know myself about as well as I know anything, yet my self is not anything that I can ever observe – at least not in the way that I can observe touches or warmth or fatigue. The dilemma can be put this way: on what is the idea of the self based, if not on a continuous sensation? If it is an abstract kind of thing – not an *observable* kind of thing – what

Wobei das nicht bloß Wunschdenken ist. Ich habe andere angebliche Paradoxa über die Welt vergehen sehen wie Zuckerwatte im Feuer. Sobald die jeweilige Wissenschaft die Realität hinter den sie mystifizierenden Erscheinungen aufgedeckt hatte, wurde das, was scheinbar jeder Intuition widersprach, zu etwas Vertrautem und weitgehend Offen sichtlichem. Die Vorstellung, daß sich die Erde bewegt oder daß lebende Dinge aus toten Molekülen bestehen – sie verloren die Patina des Paradoxons im sanften Licht des Experiments und der Erklärung. Ich habe so ein Gefühl, daß dies auch hier der Fall sein wird. Infolgedessen schiebe ich die Konfrontation mit der sich selbst in den Schwanz beißenden Katze gerne auf, bis die Wissenschaft etwas weiter ist.

Was ist das Selbst für ein Ding?

Es ist diese Frage, die früher oder später aus uns allen Philosophen macht. Wir denken nicht alle bis spätnachts darüber nach, woraus die Sterne bestehen oder wie das Immunsystem funktioniert. Aber das Nachdenken darüber, wodurch ich ich bin, verfolgt einen auf Schritt und Tritt. Seit Platon im 5. Jahrhundert v. Chr. haben sich die Philosophen bemüht, auf der Suche nach befriedigenden Antworten voranzukommen – oder, bescheidener, zumindest Möglichkeiten zu finden, die Frage so zu strukturieren, daß sie nicht in die Verwirrungsspirale führt. Der große schottische Philosoph des 18. Jahrhunderts, David Hume, hat diese Fragen der schärfsten Analyse unterzogen und den Boden für die moderne wissenschaftliche Forschung bereitet.

Hume gelangte zu der ziemlich schockierenden Einsicht, daß, wenn man nach innen blickt und ein eigenes Ding namens *Selbst* beobachten will, dort kein derartiges Ding zu erkennen ist. Was sich dort befindet, ist ein ständig fluktuierender Strom visueller Wahrnehmungen, Geräusche, Gerüche, Gefühle, Gedanken usw. Unter all diesen gibt es jedoch keine einzige dauerhafte *gefühlte* Empfindung, von der man sagen könnte: *Das ist das Selbst*, so wie man auf eine gefühlte Empfindung deuten und sagen kann: *Das ist ein Schmerz*.

Und doch könnte nichts evidenter sein als die Tatsache, daß es einen einzelnen Faden der *Ichheit* zu geben scheint, der sich durch das gesamte Gewebe der Erfahrung zieht. Wir verfügen alle über eine robuste, unleugbare Repräsentation des Selbst. Wenn wir aus einem tiefen Schlaf erwachen, wissen wir im allgemeinen, wer wir sind, selbst wenn wir in bezug auf das Wann und Wo verwirrt sein mögen. Normalerweise zweifeln wir nicht daran, *daß ich

are its properties and where does it come from?

As neuroscience and experimental psychology have progressed in this century, an updated version of Hume's problem has emerged: how does the brain – a network of trillions of cells – generate this representation of a unitary *self*? What are the neural mechanisms underlying such self-representation? One important source of information will be pathologies involving self-representation. Some insight can be garnered from stroke patients who deny that this hand is in fact *their* hand, or who have lost all memory of life events before the brain damage or who feel that they have lost their *will*. Schizophrenics or patients on the anesthetic ketamine often suffer *depersonalization* feelings – feelings that they are dead or possessed. These phenomena, too, indicate how the *self-evidence* of the self is underpinned by complex brain activity. By revealing the fracture lines of the self-representation, this kind of case allows us to see what is well hidden in the normal case.

Brains emulate body and self

1 The General Idea

Referring to *the self* suggests the self must be a kind of thing, such as a specific organ in the brain, the way that the spleen or the pancreas are specific organs in the body. Clearly, however, the *pancreas paradigm* for thinking about the self won't work. The self is not an organ in the brain, nor is there a discrete region of the brain that *makes* the self. But if the self is not a thing like the pancreas, and if it is not a continuous sensation, what is it?

The best hypothesis is that it involves a complex idea [representation] that the brain generates through activity in various different regions, including the regions representing the body and a representation using memory of the past. The brain activity which we know introspectively as *myself* is probably part of a set of larger patterns of activity the brain deploys for making sense of and getting by in its world. Given these considerations, it is preferable to talk about the problem of *self-representation* rather than the problem of the self. But what is

heute im wesentlichen dieselbe Person bin, die ich gestern und am Tag davor war ...*. Normalerweise brauchen wir nicht nachzudenken, um zu erkennen, daß *dieser Köper der meine ist* – daß *diese Hand und dieser Fuß zu meinem Köper gehören*. Wenn ich mich mit mir darüber berate, ob ich unter die Marathonläufer gehen sollte, weiß ich, daß ich es bin, der mit mir redet. Wir wissen sehr gut: Wenn wir für künftige Umstände nicht vorsorgen, könnte unser künftiges Selbst darunter leiden, und wir kümmern uns heute um dieses künftige Selbst.

Hier ist Humes Rätsel: Ich kenne mich selbst so gut wie nur etwas, und doch ist mein Selbst nichts, das ich je beobachten könnte – jedenfalls nicht so, wie ich Berührungen oder Wärme oder Müdigkeit beobachten kann. Das Dilemma läßt sich folgendermaßen formulieren: Wenn nicht auf einer dauerhaften Empfindung, worauf basiert dann die Idee des Selbst? Wenn es ein abstraktes Ding ist – kein Ding von der beobachtbaren Sorte –, was sind dann seine Eigenschaften und wo kommt es her?

Mit dem Fortschritt der Neurowissenschaften und der experimentellen Psychologie in diesem Jahrhundert ergibt sich eine aktualiserte Version von Humes Problem: Wie generiert das Gehirn – ein Netzwerk von Trillionen von Zellen – diese Repräsentation eines einheitlichen Selbst? Welche neuralen Mechanismen liegen einer solchen Repräsentation des Selbst zugrunde? Eine wichtige Informationsquelle sind hier Erkrankungen, die die Repräsentation des Selbst betreffen. Gewisse Einsichten gewinnt man von Schlaganfallpatienten, die leugnen, daß ihre Hand tatsächlich ihre Hand sei, die jegliche Erinnerung an Lebensereignisse vor ihrem Hirnschaden verloren haben oder das Gefühl haben, ihr *Wille* sei abhanden gekommen. Schizophrene oder Patienten, die das Narkotikum Ketamin verabreicht bekommen, leiden oft unter dem Gefühl einer Depersonalisierung – dem Gefühl, tot oder besessen zu sein. Auch diese Phänomene zeigen, auf welche Weise die *Selbstevidenz* des Selbst durch eine komplexe Gehirnaktivität gestützt wird. Indem sie solche Bruchlinien in der Repräsentation des Selbst aufdecken, gewähren uns diese Fälle Einblick in etwas, das im Normalfall gut verborgen ist.

Gehirne emulieren Körper und Selbst

1 Der Grundgedanke

Wenn man vom Selbst spricht, so legt das nahe, daß dieses eine Art Ding, ein bestimmtes Organ

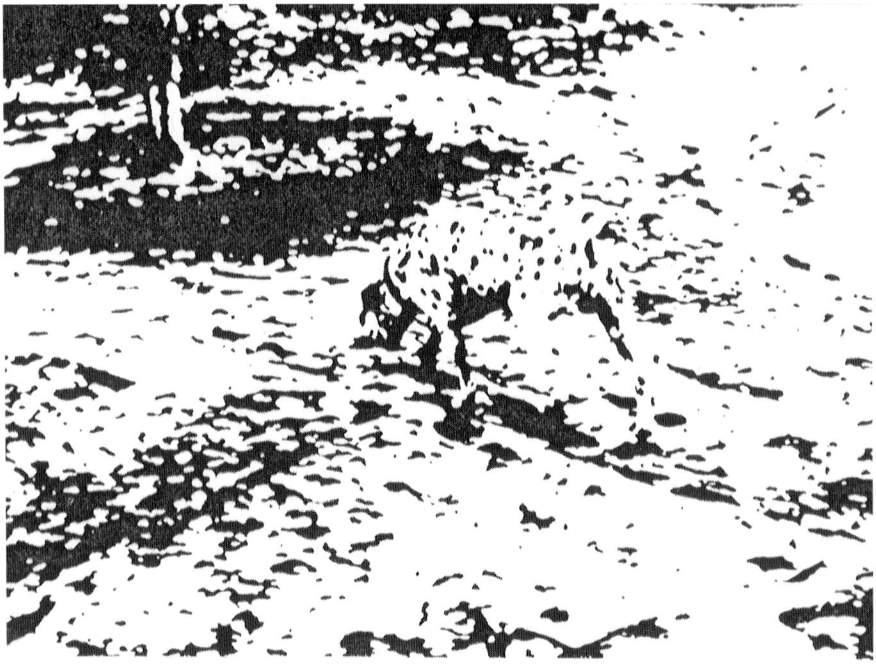

Fig. 2
A Dalmatian dog in the dappled light, standing on leaf-strewn pavement.
Dalmatinerhund im gesprenkelten Licht eines laubübersäten Gehsteigs.

im Gehirn sei, so wie die Milz oder die Bauchspeicheldrüse bestimmte Organe im Körper sind. Zweifellos aber trifft das Bauchspeicheldrüsen-Paradigma beim Selbst nicht zu. Das Selbst ist kein Organ im Gehirn, es gibt auch keine eigene Gehirnregion, die das Selbst ausmachte. Wenn das Selbst aber kein Ding wie die Bauchspeicheldrüse ist und auch keine dauerhafte Empfindung ist, was ist es dann?

Die beste Hypothese ist die, daß darunter eine komplexe Vorstellung [Repräsentation] fällt, die das Gehirn durch Aktivität in verschiedenen Regionen generiert; zu diesen gehören die Regionen, die eine Repräsentation des Körpers erzeugen, sowie eine Repräsentation, die Erinnerungen an vergangene Ereignisse benutzt. Die Hirnaktivität, die wir introspektiv als unser Selbst kennen, ist wahrscheinlich Teil einer Reihe größerer Aktivitätsmuster, die das Gehirn entfaltet, um die Welt zu verstehen und in ihr zurecht zu kommen. Angesichts dieser Überlegungen sollte man lieber vom Problem der Selbst-Repräsentation statt vom Problem des Selbst sprechen. Was aber bedeutet es für das Gehirn, etwas – noch dazu das Selbst – zu repräsentieren? Muß es nicht ein Selbst geben, wenn das Gehirn es repräsentiert?

2 Repräsentation im Gehirn

Eine der Hauptaufgaben von Nervensystemen – von der Languste bis zum Menschen – besteht darin, gute Voraussagen über Nahrung, Paarungspartner, Feinde und Freunde zu treffen, damit der Körper am Leben erhalten bleibt und sich reproduzieren kann. Schlechte Voraussager enden häufig als Nahrung für bessere Voraussager. Unsere sensorischen Reize zwecks besserer Voraussagen zu strukturieren – darin besteht der ganze Sinn und Zweck der Repräsentation. Die Verwendung innerer Repräsentationen ermöglicht ein wesentlich elaborierteres Verhalten als bloße Reiz-Reaktionsbögen. Die Verwendung innerer Repräsentationen ist eine allgemeine Strategie, die Nervensysteme im Zuge des von der Evolution eingeschlagenen Weges der Begünstigung adaptiver Strukturen ausgebildet haben.

Der Philosoph Rick Grush[1] entwickelte ein nützliches Instrument, um das in den Griff zu bekommen. Nehmen wir an, ich wäre Fahrer eines großen Baukrans, eines High-Tech-Krans, den ich bequem von meinem kilometerweit entfernten Büro aus bedienen kann. Der Ingenieur täte gut daran, ihn so zu konstruieren, daß ich an einem kleinen Modell sehen kann, wo sich der Haken befindet, wenn ich

it for the brain to represent *anything*, let alone *self*? Must there not be a self if the brain represents it?

2 Representation in the brain

Part of the major business of nervous systems, from crayfish to humans, is to make good predictions about food, mates, enemies, and friends, so that the body can live on to reproduce. Poor predictors often end up as meals for better predictors. Imposing structure on our sensory stimuli in the service of better prediction is what representation is all about. Using internal representations allows for much more sophisticated behavior than mere stimulus-response reflexes. Using internal representations is a common strategy that nervous systems have developed as part of evolution's way of favoring adaptive structures.

The philosopher Rick Grush[1] has developed a useful tool for getting a handle on this. Suppose I am running a huge construction crane, which is a very high-tech crane that I can operate from the comfort of my office a mile away. It would be a good idea for the engineer to design it so that I have access to a small-scale model of where the hook will be if I give the order for a certain movement. That way I can correct my movement without waiting for feedback from the gigantic hook-in-the-world. The emulator in my office generates internal feedback that helps me predict. Even better, the designer could allow me to fiddle with the model so that I can test possible movements before I choose the best, thereby maximizing accuracy of the movement when I do finally make the actual hook move. Very crudely, this is what Grush thinks brains do. They build *emulators* of the world and of their bodies in that world.

Of course if you looked at in my brain you would not see a miniature world of tiny trees and dogs and so forth – just cells connected to cells, signaling each other and displaying patterns of activity. Nor is there a little person in my head who sits and watches a screen. That part of the emulator story does not at all fit what brains do. What we can take from the emulator story is the similarity in function. Some patterns of neuronal activity seem to be performing the same function as the crane-emulator.

den Befehl für eine bestimmte Bewegung gebe. So kann ich die Bewegung korrigieren, ohne auf das Feedback vom gigantischen Haken in der wirklichen Welt warten zu müssen. Der Emulator in meinem Büro erzeugt ein inneres Feedback, das mir bei der Vorhersage hilft. Noch besser wäre es, wenn mir der Konstrukteur die Möglichkeit gäbe, an dem Modell herumzuprobieren, so daß ich mögliche Bewegungen testen und dann die beste aussuchen kann, was die Genauigkeit bei der tatsächlichen Steuerung des Hakens steigern würde. Das ist, grob gesprochen, das, was laut Grush Gehirne tun. Sie bauen *Emulatoren* der Welt und ihrer Körper in der Welt.

Natürlich würden Sie bei einem Blick in mein Gehirn nicht eine Miniaturwelt aus kleinen Bäumen, Hunden usw. sehen, sondern nichts als Zellen, die miteinander verbunden sind, einander Signale senden und gewisse Aktivitätsmuster an den Tag legen. Und in meinem Kopf sitzt auch kein kleiner, auf einen Bildschirm starrender Mensch. Dieser Teil der Emulatorgeschichte deckt sich überhaupt nicht damit, wie Gehirne operieren. Übernehmen können wir von der Emulatorgeschichte allerdings die Ähnlichkeit in der Funktion. Einige neuronale Aktivitätsmuster scheinen dieselbe Funktion zu haben wie der Kran-Emulator.

Wie das genau funktioniert, wissen wir nicht. Dennoch scheint klar zu sein, daß die innere Modellierung des Körpers und seiner Welt eine evolutionäre Errungenschaft darstellt, die den Organismus klüger agieren, als gäbe es sie nicht. Im Gehirn des Organismus müssen nicht sämtliche Aspekte seiner Welt emuliert werden, sondern nur diejenigen, die für seine Überlebensform relevant sind.[2] Bienen können ultraviolettes Licht sehen, was ihnen dabei hilft, zwischen den Blumen Nahrung zu finden. Beim Menschen wird dieser Aspekt der Welt nicht perzeptuell repräsentiert, es sei denn, er baut sich ein Gerät dafür. Ähnlich müssen auch nicht alle Aspekte der Kran-Welt explizit emuliert werden, sondern nur die, die für die Ausführung der Arbeit nötig sind.

Ein Teil der Welt-Emulation findet online statt, so etwa wenn das Gehirn perzeptuelle Konstruktions- und Ergänzungsarbeit ausführt. So erkennen wir z. B. einen Dalmatiner vor einem Hintergrund aus Laub, auch wenn der Stimulus selbst verstümmelt ist [Abb. 2]. Wir nehmen eine Tomate als einförmig rot wahr, auch wenn darauf Schatten und Schlaglichter ruhen und sie teilweise überhaupt im Dunkeln liegt. Wir hören, wenn in einem lärmerfüllten Raum unser Name fällt. Offline, sozusagen, erinnern wir uns, wo am Fluß wir unser Proviantlager

Exactly how this works is not known. Nevertheless, it seems evident that inner modeling of the body and its world is an evolutionary achievement that means the organism can do smarter things than otherwise. Not all aspects of the organism's world need be emulated in its brain – only those that matter to it, given its way of making a living.[2] Bees can detect ultraviolet light, and that helps them forage among flowers. Humans do not perceptually represent that aspect of the world, unless we build a tool to do it for us. In a similar vein, I shall not need all aspects of the crane-world explicitly emulated – just those relevant to getting the job done.

Some world-emulation will be on-line, as when the brain displays perceptual construction and filling-in. Thus we see a Dalmatian in the leafy background even though the stimulus itself is degraded [figure 2]. We see the tomato as uniformly red even though it is shadowed and highlit and partially occluded; we hear our name spoken in a noisy room. Off-line, so to speak, we remember where we cached the food by the river; we plan how to cross a turbulent stream; we day-dream and fantasize.

On the Grush hypothesis, the brain emulates the ecologically relevant – the *relevant-to-my-kind-of-creature* – features of the world, and then manipulates these emulations to plan, hide, forage, and so forth. I may consider the problem of crossing the turbulent stream, go on to imagine a route that would be easier if a log were stretched from one rock to another, go on to imagine the size of the log needed and how to get it into place. This involves manipulation of the image, or as we may say, of the river-crossing emulation.

3 Body Models

So far we have focused on emulations that capture features of the outside world, but brains can also emulate aspects of the body. You can, for example, imagine your body standing when you are sitting, or the size it was when you were five. Sexual fantasies are potent instances in which real body effects can be produced by the brain's manipulation of a two-body emulation. Imaginary tennis and golf have been demonstrated to be highly significant in improving one's actual game.

angelegt haben, planen wir, wie wir einen reißenden Wildbach überqueren wollen, tagträumen und phantasieren wir.

Nach der Grush-Hypothese emuliert das Gehirn die ökologisch relevanten – für meine Art von Wesen relevanten – Merkmale der Welt und manipuliert dann diese Emulationen, um Pläne zu machen, sich zu verstecken, Nahrung zu suchen usw. Ich werde mir das Problem der Wildbachüberquerung vielleicht durch den Kopf gehen lassen, mir einen Weg ausdenken, der zu bewältigen wäre, wenn sich ein Baumstamm zwischen zwei Felsen befände, mir überlegen, wie groß der Baumstamm sein müßte und wie man ihn an die richtige Stelle bekommen könnte. Das impliziert die Manipulation des Bildes oder, wie wir vielleicht sagen könnten, der Flußüberquerungs-Emulation.

3 Körpermodelle

Bisher haben wir uns auf Emulationen konzentriert, die Merkmale der Außenwelt erfassen, doch können Gehirne auch Aspekte des Körpers emulieren. Man kann sich z. B. den Körper stehend vorstellen, während man sitzt, oder man kann ihn sich in der Größe vorstellen, wie er mit fünf war. Sexuelle Phantasien sind eindringliche Beispiele dafür, wie durch die zerebrale Manipulation einer Emulation zweier Körper wirkliche Reaktionen des Körpers hervorgerufen werden können. Imaginäre Tennis- und Golfpartien haben sich als hochwirksam für die Verbesserung des tatsächlichen Spiels erwiesen.

Wenn wir unseren Körper vor einem Beobachter verbergen wollen, müssen wir über enorm ausgefeilte Repräsentationsfähigkeiten verfügen. Man benötigt dafür ein Verständnis des visuellen Aspekts des Körpers, seiner Proportionen im Verhältnis zum Versteck. Am schwierigsten ist zu begreifen, wie die Szene vom Standpunkt eines anderen aussieht. Man denke an das Versteckenspielen und wie wichtig dabei das Wissen um die Sichtbarkeit des eigenen Körpers aus unterschiedlichen Perspektiven ist. Aus der Perspektive des Suchenden dürfen keine Füße vorragen, darf kein Haar oben herausstehen, wogegen man für die übrigen, die sich verstecken, ruhig sichtbar sein kann.

Ein ganz junges Kind glaubt vielleicht, es sei vor anderen verborgen, wenn es die Hände vor die Augen hält. Es hat noch keine Repräsentation dafür, wie es durch die Augen anderer aussieht. Aber wahrscheinlich hat es jede Menge Zeit darauf verwendet zu beobachten, wie seine Finger mit Essen, Spielzeug, dem Hund und den eigenen Zehen umgehen, und

Hiding your body from another viewer requires enormous representational sophistication. You need some understanding of the visual aspect of your body, its proportions relative to the shield. Most critically, you need to grasp how the scene will look from another's viewpoint. Remember playing hide-and-seek, and the importance of knowing the visibility of one's body from various perspectives. From the perspective of whoever is *it*, there must be no feet sticking out, no hair showing above, though visibility to our fellow hiders doesn't matter.

A very young child may think she is hidden from others when she puts her hands over her eyes. She does not yet have a representation of how she looks through another's eyes. But she probably has spent lots of time watching her fingers manipulate food, toys, the dog, and her own toes, and probably her visually-anchored body-schema is still emerging. An integrated body-schema, with both visual and somatosensory dimensions, will have begun to develop from her very early days, even if she cannot yet manage all the subtleties of the difference between *I can see me* and *You can see me*.

4 Self-models

Additionally, complex brains can emulate aspects of what the brain itself is doing, and the *self* is one such result. That is, it may have a model of the brain's activities, perhaps cast in perceptual images resembling familiar external events. As the philosopher Patricia Kitcher sees it, something like this is what Kant had in mind as the basis for *self*.

The metaphors in common use give some inkling of how those emulations are structured. When faced with a difficult choice, people refer to inner struggles or tug-of-war games; forgetting may be likened to fading of print or blocking by a barrier. Desires may be said to overpower one, or to have a grip or a hold; they may possess one and one may surrender to them. They may be repressed [*pushed below the surface*] only to bob up in a new disguise. Fears can run away with or dominate oneself; knowledge is seeing; hope can spring eternal in the human breast. And so on. These are very important and useful ways in which we try to understand others and ourselves. They are, as Lakoff and Johnson[3] have pointed out, the meta-

sein visuell verankertes Körperschema wird sich vermutlich noch ausbilden. Die Entwicklung eines integrierten Körperschemas mit sowohl visuellen als auch somatosensorischen Dimensionen ist seit den frühen Kindheitstagen im Gange, auch wenn es noch nicht alle Feinheiten des Unterschieds zwischen *Ich kann mich sehen* und *Du kannst mich sehen* im Griff hat.

4 Selbstmodelle

Weiters können komplexe Gehirne Aspekte dessen emulieren, was das Gehirn selbst tut, und eines der Resultate ist das Selbst. Sie können also ein Modell der Hirnaktivitäten besitzen, etwa in Form von Wahrnehmungsbildern, die vertrauten äußeren Ereignissen gleichen. Etwa so ähnlich – so die Philosophin Patricia Kitcher – stellte sich Kant die Basis des Selbst vor.

Allgemein gebräuchliche Metaphern geben einen kleinen Hinweis, wie diese Emulationen strukturiert sind. Steht man vor einer schwierigen Entscheidung, spricht man von innerem Ringen oder Tauziehen; das Vergessen wird manchmal mit dem Verblassen einer Schrift oder dem Blockiertsein durch ein Hindernis verglichen. Von Begierden heißt es mitunter, daß sie einen überwältigen oder beherrschen; sie können von einem Besitz ergreifen, oder man kann sich ihnen hingeben. Sie können verdrängt [unter die Oberfläche gedrückt] werden, nur um im nächsten Moment in einem neuen Gewand wieder hervorzubrechen. Ängste können einen verrückt machen oder lähmen; Wissen ist Sehen; Hoffnung kann ewig in der menschlichen Brust aufkeimen. Und so weiter. Dies sind äußerst wichtige und nützliche Wege, wie wir andere und uns selbst zu verstehen versuchen. Es sind, wie Lakoff und Johnson [3] aufgezeigt haben, die Metaphern, mit deren Hilfe wir leben. Weil wir keinen direkten Zugang zu dem haben, was z. B. Erinnerungen auf der Ebene des Gehirns wirklich sind, betrachten wir sie nach dem Modell von Notizen in einer Schublade oder Druckerschwärze auf Papier oder Laubschichten oder Ablagerungen in Sandstein. Die Verwendung dieser Metaphern ist auch ein wichtiges Werkzeug, um über uns selbst nachzudenken.

Kurzum, die von mir favorisierte Hypothese lautet, daß das Selbst eine Art Emulation ist, die das Gehirn konstruiert, um die innere Welt des Gehirns in seiner Beziehung zur Außenwelt, einschließlich der Welt anderer Personen, zu integrieren und zu verstehen. In der Mindestausstattung verfügt sie über 1. eine

phors we live by. As we do not have direct access to what memories, for example, really are from the brain's perspective, we think of them on the model of notes in a drawer or paint on a print or layers of leaves or strata in sandstone. Using these metaphors also provides an important tool for us to reflect on and ponder ourselves.

In short, the hypothesis I favor is that the self is a kind of emulation, constructed by the brain, for integrating and making sense of the inner world of the brain in its relation to the external world, including the other-person-world. Minimally, it has [1] a body component, [2] a *what-I-am-aware-of-now* component, [3] a stable but modifiable background of preferences, habits, skills, temperament and so forth, and [4] a memory-based autobiographical component.[4] These components are inter-related, but are also, to some extent, dissociable.

This is obviously not a precise characterization. For that, we need to understand much more about the details of brain function at many levels of organization, from the single cell to the whole brain. The notion of *representation,* like the notion of an emulator, is more like a place-holder waiting for a detailed theory of brain function than a precise term in a well-developed theoretical framework. Nevertheless, we do have some clear ideas on the general role it needs to fill, and the important task will be to find experiments to test the hypothesis.[5]

How can you have any self-esteem if you think you are just a piece of meat?

So asked a forthright student. My answer is that first, brains are not just pieces of meat. The human brain is what makes humans capable of painting the Sistine Chapel, of designing airplanes and transistors, of skating and reading and playing Chopin. Insofar, it is a truly astonishing and magnificent kind of *wonder-tissue*, as Dan Dennett puts it. Whatever self-esteem justly derives from our accomplishments does so *because* of the brain, not in spite of it.

Second, if we thought of ourselves as glorious creatures before we knew that the brain is responsible, why not continue so to feel after the discovery? Why does the knowledge not make us more interesting and remarkable, rather than less so? We can be thrilled by the spectacle of a volcano erupting or a calf being

Körperkomponente, 2. eine *Wessen-ich-mir-momentan-bewußt-bin*-Komponente, 3. einen stabilen, aber veränderbaren Hintergrund aus Vorlieben, Gewohnheiten, Fertigkeiten, Temperament usw. und 4. eine gedächtnisbasierte, autobiographische Komponente. Diese Komponenten[4] hängen zwar miteinander zusammen, sind aber zu einem gewissen Grad isolierbar. Es handelt sich hier offenkundig um keine präzise Charakterisierung. Dazu müßten wir viel mehr über die Einzelheiten der Gehirnfunktion auf allerlei organisatorischen Ebenen von der Einzelzelle bis zum Gesamthirn wissen. Der Begriff der Repräsentation ist wie der des Emulators eher ein Platzhalter, der auf eine ausführliche Theorie der Gehirnfunktion wartet, denn ein präziser Terminus in einem gut ausgearbeiteten theoretischen System. Dennoch: Es gibt einige klare Vorstellungen darüber, welche allgemeine Rolle er erfüllen muß, und die Hauptaufgabe wird darin bestehen, Experimente zur Überprüfung der Hypothese zu finden.[5]

Wie können Sie die mindeste Selbstachtung haben, wenn Sie sich bloß für ein Stück Fleisch halten?

Diese Frage stellte mir ein geradliniger Student. Meine Antwort lautet erstens, daß Gehirne nicht bloß ein Stück Fleisch sind. Das menschliche Gehirn ist das, was Menschen in die Lage versetzt, die Sixtinische Kapelle mit Fresken zu schmücken, Flugzeuge und Transistoren zu konstruieren, Rollschuh zu fahren, zu lesen und Chopin zu spielen. Insofern ist es ein wahrhaft erstaunliches und großartiges *Wundergewebe*, wie Dan Dennett sagt. Die Selbstachtung, die wir mit Recht aus unseren Leistungen beziehen, haben wir wegen und nicht trotz des Gehirns.

Zweitens, wenn wir uns für grandiose Geschöpfe hielten, bevor wir wußten, daß dafür das Hirn verantwortlich ist, warum sollten wir damit nicht auch nach der Entdeckung fortfahren? Warum sollte uns dieses Wissen nicht interessanter und bemerkenswerter anstatt weniger interessant und bemerkenswert machen? Uns beeindruckt das Schauspiel eines Vulkanausbruchs oder die Geburt eines Kalbs oder die Heilung eines Knochens, bevor wir noch verstehen, was Vulkane sind oder wie Fortpflanzung oder Heilung vor sich gehen. Als die Geschöpfe, die wir sind, sind wir jedoch noch mehr beeindruckt, wenn wir uns das Wissen über Vulkane, Geburt und Knochen aneignen.

born or bone healing before we understand what volcanoes are and how reproduction or healing work. Being the creatures we are, however, commonly we are even more thrilled in the embrace of the knowledge about volcanoes and birth and bones.

Concluding Remarks

Self-representation in humans is a highly complex business. Richly layered in language, embedded in a social context, and backed by a detailed, if selective, autobiographical history, it is also replete with the qualitative features of conscious experience. We talk to ourselves: *Do I really want a cigarette?*, *Why did I allow myself to get angry?*. We think about ourselves in culturally shared metaphors: *I hid my true self from myself *, *I lost control of myself*, *I struggled to keep myself from falling apart*. We have important self-regulating feelings not directly linked to a particular sensory modality: we can feel comfortable, uneasy, unfamiliar, confident, ashamed, embarrassed and so on.[6] The neurobiology of consciousness is a central topic that ideally should be discussed in this context. Limitations of space, however, make that a topic for another occasion.

Much – so *very* much – remains to be discovered, and my theoretical resources are limited to drawing on where cognitive neuroscience is now. There are few puzzles about the brain that we can say are flat-out solved, and I have too much of the farm in me to count hens in advance of the hatch. Even so, it is well-known that discoveries in the last three decades have allowed us new insights undreamt of in our philosophy, and it will be surprising if more are not to come. Will we come to think of ourselves in a different light?

The retrofitting of time-honored ideas is already visible, and some questions now routinely researched by graduate students were unconceived of a mere twenty years ago. What further changes can be expected, or in what directions, is anybody's guess. From where I stand now, it seems to me likely that our understanding of what it is to be *in control* of one's behavior, of what consciousness, personality, and character are, will change, perhaps quite profoundly. As with many other developments in human intellectual history, I expect there will

Abschließende Bemerkungen

Die Selbst-Repräsentation beim Menschen ist eine hochkomplexe Angelegenheit: Sie ist sprachlich vielfältig geschichtet, in einen sozialen Kontext eingebettet, mit einer detailreichen, wenn auch selektiven Autobiographie unterlegt und verfügt außerdem über viele Eigenschaften der bewußten Erfahrung. Wir reden mit uns selbst: *Will ich wirklich ein Zigarette?*, *Warum lasse ich es zu, daß ich ärgerlich werde?*. Wir denken über uns in kulturell bestimmten Metaphern nach: *Ich habe mein wahres Selbst vor mir versteckt*, *Ich habe die Kontrolle über mich verloren*, *Ich habe darum gerungen, nicht zu zerbrechen.* Wir haben wichtige selbstregulative Gefühle, die nicht direkt mit einer bestimmten sensorischen Modalität verbunden sind: Wir fühlen uns behaglich, unangenehm, unvertraut, selbstsicher, beschämt, verlegen usw.[6] Die Neurobiologie des Bewußtseins wäre ein zentrales, eigentlich in diesem Kontext zu diskutierendes Thema. Aufgrund räumlicher Beschränkungen wird es jedoch zu einem Thema für eine andere Gelegenheit.

Vieles – sehr vieles – harrt noch der Entdeckung, und meine theroretischen Quellen sind auf den Stand beschränkt, auf dem die kognitive Neurowissenschaft heute steht. Im Zusammenhang mit dem Gehirn gibt es nur wenige Rätsel, die wir als schlichtweg gelöst bezeichnen könnten, und ich bin noch zu sehr Bäuerin, um die Küken zu zählen, bevor sie geschlüpft sind. Dennoch: Daß uns die Entdeckungen der letzten drei Jahrzehnte Einsichten ermöglicht haben, von denen wir in unserer Philosophie nicht einmal geträumt haben, ist wohlbekannt, und es wäre eine Überraschung, wenn nicht noch weitere folgen würden. Werden wir uns in einem anderen Licht sehen?

Die Nachjustierung altehrwürdiger Ideen ist bereits zu erkennen; manche heute von Diplomanden selbstverständlich erforschte Fragen waren vor nur zwanzig Jahren undenkbar. Was an künftigen Änderungen zu erwarten ist und in welche Richtung sie gehen werden, darüber kann man nur spekulieren. Von meinem gegenwärtigen Standpunkt aus scheint es mir wahrscheinlich, daß sich unser Verständnis davon, was es heißt, sein Verhalten zu kontrollieren, was Bewußtsein, Persönlichkeit und Charakter bedeuten, ändern wird, und zwar vermutlich ziemlich grundlegend. Wie bei vielen anderen Entwicklungen in der menschlichen Geistesgeschichte sind Kämpfe zwischen Aberglaube und Wissenschaft zu erwarten, zwischen dem Altvertrauten auf der einen, und dem Neuen, Unvertrauten

be struggles between superstition and science, between the old and familiar on the one hand, and the new and unfamiliar on the other. Just as cell biology and molecular biology achieved humanizing results by overturning demonic-possession and punishment theories of disease, so I predict neuroscience will have humanizing effects as it reveals more of what it is that makes us human.

Part of what makes science so intriguing is the unpredictability of how things will look after the next bend in the river. Intriguing too is the creation of new thought-tools provoked by totally unpredictable results but needed to get to the heart of the puzzle. Scientifically, we are the lucky ones. We are alive as the twentieth century – the greatest century for science – gives birth to the twenty-first. We have a chance to follow the river, and find out what really is the lay of our land.

1 Rick Grush [1995]: *Emulation and Cognition.* Phil.Diss an der UCSD; [1997] *The architecture of representation,* in: *Philosophical Psychology*, 10, S. 5-25.
2 Kathleen Akins [1996]: *Of sensory systems and the ,aboutness' of mental states*, in: *Journal of Philosophy*, S. 337-372.
3 George Lakoff and Mark Johnson [1980]: *Metaphors We Live By*, University of Chicago Press.
4 Owen Flanagan [1992]: *Consciousness Reconsidered*,.MIT Press; Arnold Ludwig [1997): *How Do We Know Who We Are?* Oxford University Press; Daniel Dennett [1991): *Consciousness Explained*, Little, Brown. [deutsch: *Descartes, Potemkin und die Büchse der Pandora. Eine neue Philosophie menschlichen Bewußtseins*, Hoffmann & Campe 1992]
5 Patricia Kitcher [1990]: *Kant's Transcendental Psychology*, Oxford University Press.
6 Antonio Damasio [1994]: *Descartes' Error, Putnam and Sons* [deutsch: *Descartes Irrtum. Fühlen, Denken und das menschliche Gehirn*, List 1995]; P. S. Churchland [1996]. *Feeling reasons*, in: *Neurobiology of Decision-Making*, Ed. Damasio and Christen. Springer-Verlag.

auf der anderen Seite. So wie die Zell- und Molekularbiologie humanisierende Folgen hatten, indem sie die Theorien von der Krankheit als Besessenheit oder als Strafe stürzten, so prophezeie ich auch humanisierende Auswirkungen der Neurowissenschaften, wenn sie immer mehr zeigen werden, was uns zu Menschen macht.

Das Spannende bei der Wissenschaft ist zum Teil, daß man nicht vorhersagen kann, wie die Dinge nach der nächsten Flußbiegung aussehen werden. Spannend ist aber auch die Schaffung neuer Denkwerkzeuge, die von völlig unabsehbaren Resultaten provoziert werden, aber notwendig sind, um zum Kern des Rätsels vorzudringen. Wissenschaftlich gesehen sind wir Glückspilze. Wir erleben, wie das 20. Jahrhundert – das größte Jahrhundert für die Wissenschaft – das 21. gebiert. Wir haben die Chance, dem Fluß zu folgen und herauszufinden, wo wir wirklich stehen.

Bioelectronics and Protein-based Devices

Robert R. Birge

Molecules form the basis of life, and when combined to form biological organisms, yield highly sophisticated systems which perceive, manipulate, self-repair, think, calculate and feel. Although digital computers can carry out calculations with a speed and precision far superior to humans, in the other five areas, even simple biological systems are superior. In short, biology has achieved through billions of years of evolution, complex systems that have unique attributes that have to date escaped duplication within the realm of semiconductor and software systems.

Chess enthusiasts were recently surprised and perhaps dismayed to watch IBM's Deep Blue computer beat the world's leading [human] chess master, Garry Kasporov [for details see www.chess.ibm.com/home/html/ b.html]. It now seems clear that a computer will soon be able routinely to beat the best human chess masters. Such an accomplishment should not be regarded as an example of artificial intelligence. Chess is a game, and follows well-defined rules. Such constraints permit programmers to test all possible moves, and make decisions based on rule-based logic. While the hard-

Bioelektronik und Computerbausteine auf Proteinbasis

Robert R. Birge

Moleküle bilden die Grundlage des Lebens und formen, zu biologischen Organismen kombiniert, hochentwickelte Systeme, die wahrnehmen, handeln, sich selbst reparieren, denken, rechnen und fühlen können. Beim Rechnen sind digitale Computer zwar viel schneller und präziser als der Mensch, in den fünf anderen Bereichen aber sind ihnen selbst einfache biologische Systeme überlegen. Kurzum, die Biologie hat in Milliarden Jahren der Evolution komplexe Systeme mit einzigartigen Eigenschaften geschaffen, die sich im Bereich der Halbleiter- und Softwaresysteme bis heute nicht duplizieren ließen.

Schachbegeisterte mußten kürzlich zu ihrer Verblüffung und vielleicht Enttäuschung erleben, wie der IBM-Computer "Deep Blue" den führenden [menschlichen] Schachspieler der Welt, Gary Kasparov, schlug [Näheres unter http://www.chess.ibm. com/home/html/b.html]. Es scheint nun klar, daß Computer bald standardmäßig in der Lage sein werden, die besten Schachgroßmeister zu schlagen. Derartige Leistungen sollten nicht als Beispiele künstlicher Intelligenz angesehen werden. Schach ist ein Spiel, das klar definierten Regeln folgt. Diese Regelbeschränkungen gestatten es Programmierern, alle möglichen Züge zu prüfen und auf der Basis einer regelgeleiteten Logik Entscheidungen zu treffen. So imposant die für die Leistung von Deep Blue verantwortliche Hard- und Software auch ist, sie summiert sich noch nicht zu künstlicher Intelligenz.

Die Natur hält somit in vielen Aspekten allgemein rechnerisch-geistiger Anstrengungen noch immer einen Vorsprung gegenüber der Ingenieurskunst des Menschen. Viele Natur- und die meisten Geisteswissenschaftler werden sagen, daß von Menschen gebaute Maschinen das vom menschlichen Gehirn und von der Natur im allgemeinen an den Tag gelegte Schöpfungsniveau – und schöpferische Niveau – niemals erreichen werden. Eine Menge Wissenschaftler und Ingenieure glauben allerdings auch, daß mit genügend CPU-Leistung, Speicherkapazität und Datenbandbreite dem Erreichbaren keine Grenzen gesetzt seien. Wir wollen uns hier nicht

Fig. 1
A schematic picture of bacteriorhodopsin
Schematische Darstellung von Bakteriorhodopsin

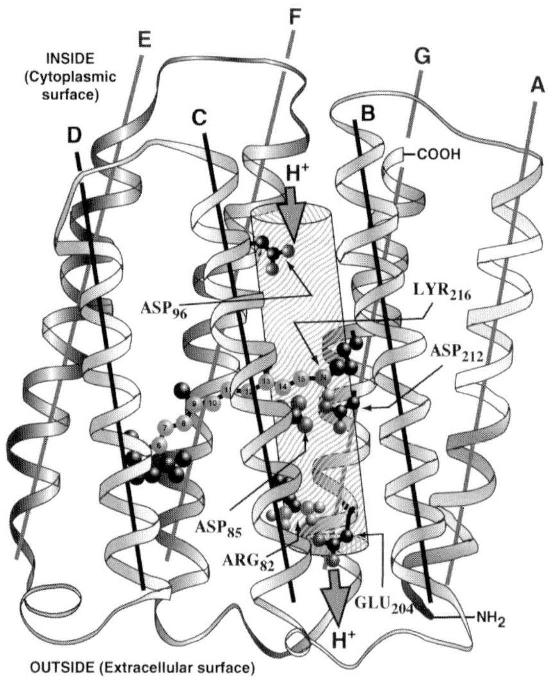

bR, K, L, M, N, O, P, Q – Intermediates in the protein photocircle

bR, K, L, M, N, O, P, Q – Zwischenprodukte beim Photozyklus des Proteins

für eine dieser gegensätzlichen Positionen – Evolution versus menschliche Konstruktion – zu entscheiden versuchen. Wir meinen vielmehr, daß wir, wenn wir mit der Natur in Konkurrenz treten wollen, so viel wie möglich von ihren Geheimnissen lernen und uns ihre Materialien und Methoden zunutze machen müssen.

Seit zwei Jahrzehnten untersucht meine Forschungsgruppe die mögliche Verwendung biologischer Systeme in Computerarchitekturen. Unser Ansatz wird oft als biomimetisch bezeichnet, weil wir native und genetisch erzeugte Proteine in Architekturen verwenden, die in der Regel so angelegt sind, daß sie Vorgangsweisen der Natur nachahmen. Wir bauen sowohl assoziative Speicher, die die Speicherungs- und Abruffähigkeiten des menschlichen Gehirns nachahmen, als auch volumetrische, die Bilder und digitale Daten in dreidimensionalen Körpern einer Proteinmatrix speichern. Funktionierende Prototypen existieren nunmehr in der zweiten Generation, es ist aber noch viel zu tun, ehe kommerzielle Systeme auf den Markt kommen. Wir skizzieren hier kurz, wie unsere Bausteine funktionieren, und berichten über unsere Fortschritte. Außerdem gehen wir darauf ein, welche Auswirkungen solche Systeme einmal für Computerkünstler haben könnten.

Das Interesse an der Erforschung von computertechnischen Anwendungen der Bioelektronik entstand bereits in den frühen 70er Jahren mit der Entdeckung eines bakteriellen Proteins mit einzigartigen photophysikalischen Eigenschaften durch Walter Stoekenius und Dieter Oesterheld an der Rockefeller University in New York. Dieses Protein namens Bakteriorhodopsin wird von einem in Salzsümpfen vorkommenden, salzliebenden Bakterium produziert. Im Stammorganismus ermöglicht dieses photosynthetische Protein der Bakterie das Wachstum, wenn der Sauerstoffgehalt zur Aufrechterhaltung der Atmung nicht ausreicht. Bei der Lichtabsorption pumpt das Protein ein Proton durch die Membran und treibt so die ATP-Synthese an. Die Bezeichnung *Bakteriorhodopsin* geht auf seine photochemischen Ähnlichkeiten mit Rhodopsin, dem Sehpigment des Auges, zurück. Das Potential dieses Proteins für optische Rechensysteme wurde als erstes von russischen Wissenschaftlern erkannt und erforscht.

Finanziert durch das *Rhodopsin-Projekt* unter der Leitung des verstorbenen Juri Owtschinnikow erforschten russische Wissenschaftler in fünf Laboratorien die Verwendung dieses Proteins in photochromen und holographischen Computerbausteinen. Owtschinnikow war nämlich nicht nur ein

ware and software responsible for Deep Blue's accomplishments are very impressive, they do not combine to yield artificial intelligence.

Thus nature still retains the edge over human engineering in many aspects of global computational/intellectual endeavors. Many scientists, and most humanists, will argue that human engineering will never achieve the level of creation and creativity that is evidenced by the human brain, and nature in general. Many scientists and engineers, however, believe that given enough CPU power, memory and data bandwidth, there is no limit as to what can be accomplished. We make no attempt here to arbitrate between these two conflicting views of evolutionary versus human engineering. Rather, we suggest that if our goal is to compete with nature, we need to learn as many of its secrets and make use of its materials and methods to the extent possible.

During the past two decades, my research group has been exploring the potential use of biological systems in computer architectures. Our approach is often called biomimetic, in that we try and use native and genetically engineered proteins in architectures that are often designed to mimic the way nature does things. We seek to make both associative memories, that mimic the data storage and retrieval capabilities of the human brain, and volumetric memories, that can store both image and digital data within three-dimensional solids of a protein matrix. Working prototypes are now in the second generation, but much remains to be accomplished before commercial systems will be available. Here, we give a brief outline of how our devices work and a progress report. We will also explore what impact such systems may ultimately have on computer artists.

Interest in exploring the computer applications of bioelectronics dates back to the early 1970s and the discovery by Walther Stoekenius and Dieter Oesterhelt at Rockefeller University, New York, of a bacterial protein that has unique photophysical properties. The protein is called bacteriorhodopsin and it is grown by a salt-loving bacterium that populates salt marshes. In the native organism, this photosynthetic protein allows the bacterium to grow when the concentration of oxygen is insufficient to sustain respiration. Upon the absorption of light, the protein pumps a proton across the

hochangesehener Molekularbiologe, sondern fand auch Gehör bei der sowjetischen Militärführung. Er überzeugte sie, daß die sowjetische Wissenschaft den Westen mit der Erforschung der Bioelektronik computertechnisch überholen könne, und sicherte für sein Projekt beträchtliche finanzielle Mittel. Viele der Anwendungen waren militärischer Natur, und so werden die Einzelheiten dieses ehrgeizigen Unternehmens vielleicht nie ganz bekannt werden. Nach informellen Berichten russischer Wissenschaftler, die heute in den USA leben, gelang die Herstellung komplexer optischer Computerarchitekturen, die Echtzeitdatenverarbeitungen durchführen konnten. Trotzdem wurden die ungewöhnlichen photochemischen und holographischen Eigenschaften dieses Proteins publiziert und stimulierten bis heute andauernde internationale Forschungsbemühungen.

Bakteriorhodopsin ist ein membrangebundenes Protein mit sieben die Membran umspannenden alpha-helixförmigen Segmenten. Eine in die Proteinmatrix eingebettete lichtabsorbierende Gruppe [Chromophor genannt] wandelt die Lichtenergie in eine komplexe Folge molekularer Ereignisse um, die als Protonpumpe fungieren. Die Wissenschaftler, die das Protein für bioelektronische Bauelemente verwenden, machen sich die Tatsache zunutze, daß diese komplexe Serie thermischer Reaktionen zu dramatischen Veränderungen der optischen und elektronischen Eigenschaften des Proteins führen [Abb. 2].

Die ausgezeichneten holographischen Eigenschaften des Proteins ergeben sich aus der bei Lichtaktivierung eintretenden starken Veränderung des Brechungskoeffizienten. Außerdem wandelt es Licht mit bemerkenswerter [etwa 65%er] Effizienz in eine Veränderung des Brechungskoeffizienten um. Bakteriorhodopsin ist zehn Mal kleiner als die Wellenlänge von Licht, wodurch das Auflösungsvermögen des dünnen Films vom Diffraktionslimit der optischen Geometrie und nicht von der *Körnigkeit* des Films bestimmt wird. [Das sowjetische Militär nutzte diese Eigenschaft, indem es dünne, Bichrome genannte Bakteriorhodopsinfilme herstellen ließ, die für Microfiche-Aufzeichnungen verwendet wurden.] Ferner kann das Protein zwei Photonen gleichzeitig absorbieren, und das weit effizienter als jedes andere Material, eine Fähigkeit, durch die es sich für die dreidimensionale Informationsspeicherung eignet [siehe unten]. Überdies emittiert das Protein ein elektrisches Signal, das in Abhängigkeit von der jeweiligen Konformation oder Form die Polarität ändert. Diese Eigenschaft läßt sich zur Konstruktion von Speichern nutzen, die beim Schreiben

membrane and drives the synthesis of ATP. The name bacteriorhodopsin derives from its photochemical similarities to rhodopsin, the visual pigment in the eye. Russian scientists were the first to recognize and explore the potential of this protein in optical computing.

Funded by *Project Rhodopsin*, and headed by the late Yuri Ovchinnikov Russian scientists at five laboratories, explored the use of this protein in photochromic and holographic devices. Ovchinnikov was not only a highly respected molecular biologist, but also had the ear of the Soviet military leaders. He convinced them that Soviet science could leap-frog the west in computer technology by exploring bioelectronics and garnered significant funding for his Project. Many of the applications were military and the details of this ambitious project may never be fully known. Informal reports from Russian scientists currently in the U.S. indicate the successful creation of sophisticated optical computing architectures that carried out real-time data transformations. Nevertheless, the unusual photochemical and holographic properties of this protein were published and stimulated the international research effort that continues today.

Bacteriorhodopsin is a membrane bound protein with seven alpha-helical segments that span the membrane. A light absorbing group [called the chromophore] embedded inside the protein matrix converts the light energy into a complex series of molecular events that pump the proton. Scientists using the protein for bioelectronic devices exploit the fact that this complex series of thermal reactions results in dramatic changes in the optical and electronic properties of the protein [Fig. 2].

The excellent holographic properties of the protein derive from the large change in refractive index that occurs following light activation. Furthermore, bacteriorhodopsin converts light into a refractive index change with remarkable efficiency [approximately 65%]. The size of the protein is ten times smaller than the wavelength of light which means that the resolution of the thin film is determined by the diffraction limit of the optical geometry rather than the *graininess* of the film. [The Soviet military exploited this property by making thin films of bacteriorhodopsin, called Biochrome, for use as microfiche recording materials.] Also, the protein can absorb two photons simulta-

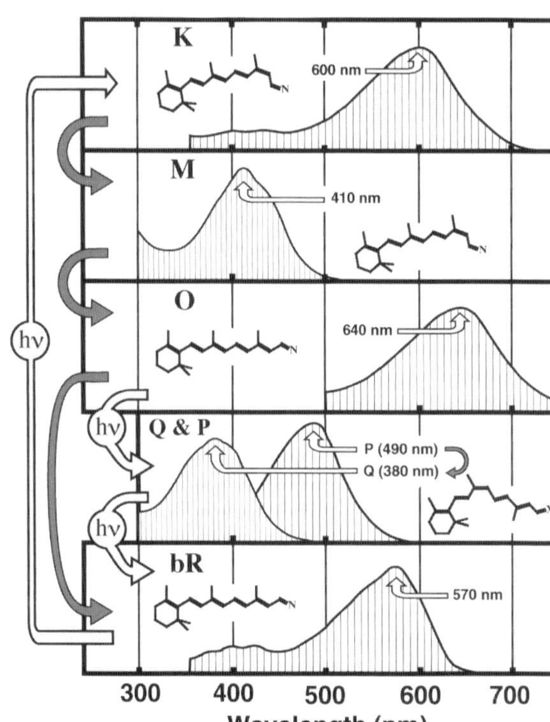

Fig. 2
Absorption spectra and conversions of the protein intermediates
Absorptionsspektren und -konversionen der Protein-Zwischenprodukte

neously with an efficiency that far exceeds other materials. This latter capability allows the use of the protein to store information in three dimensions [see below]. In addition, the protein gives off an electrical signal that changes polarity as a function of its current conformation, or state. This latter characteristic can be used to design memories that use light to write the information and electronics to monitor the data. Finally, the protein was designed by nature to function under conditions of high temperature and intense light, a necessary requirement for a salt marsh bacterial protein.

When the protein absorbs light, it undergoes a complex photocycle which generates intermediates with absorption maxima spanning the entire visible region of the spectrum [Fig. 2]. Many of the early optical devices and memories based on bacteriorhodopsin operated at liquid nitrogen temperature and utilized photochemical switching between the bR and K states. While these devices were efficient and potentially very fast [the bRgK interconversions take place in a few picoseconds], the use of cryogenic temperatures precluded general application. Most current devices operate at ambient or near ambient temperature and utilize the following two states: the initial green – red absorbing state [bR] and the long-lived blue absorbing state [M]. The forward reaction only takes place via light activation and is complete in ~50 ms. In contrast, the reverse reaction can be either light activated or can occur thermally. The light activated M → bR transition is a direct photochemical transformation.

The thermal M → bR transition is highly sensitive to temperature, environment, genetic modification and chromophore substitution. This sensitivity is exploited in many optical devices based on bacteriorhodopsin. Another reaction explored here is a photochemical branching reaction from the O intermediate to form P. This intermediate subsequently decays to form Q, a species that is unique in that the chromophore breaks the bond with the protein but is trapped inside the binding site. The Q intermediate is stable for extended periods of time [years] but can be photochemically converted back to bR. This branching reaction has great potential for long term data storage as discussed below.

der Information mit Licht und beim Lesen mit Elektronik arbeiten. Schließlich wurde das Protein von der Natur – für ein in Salzsümpfen existierendes bakterielles Protein lebenswichtig – für die Arbeit bei hohen Temperaturen und starkem Licht ausgestattet.

Bei der Absorption von Licht durchläuft es einen komplexen Photozyklus, der Zwischenprodukte generiert, deren Absorptionsmaxima das gesamte sichtbare Spektrum umfassen [Abb. 2]. Viele der frühen optischen Schaltelemente und Speicher auf Bakteriorhodopsinbasis arbeiteten bei der Temperatur flüssigen Stickstoffs und benutzten einen photochemischen Schalter zwischen dem bR- und dem K-Zustand. Wiewohl diese Bausteine effizient und potentiell überaus schnell waren [die bRgK – Interkonversionen benötigen nur wenige Picosekunden], schloß die Verwendung von Tieftemperaturtechnik eine allgemeine Anwendung aus. Die meisten heutigen Bauelemente arbeiten bei oder nahezu bei Raumtemperatur und benutzen folgende zwei Absorptionszustände: den grün-roten Grundzustand [bR] und den langlebigen blauen Zustand [M]. Die Vorwärtsreaktion kommt nur durch Lichtaktivierung zustande und ist in etwa 50 ms abgeschlossen. Dagegen kann die Umkehrreaktion sowohl durch Lichtaktivierung als auch thermisch erfolgen. Beim lichtaktivierten Übergang M → bR handelt es sich um eine direkte photochemische Transformation.

Der thermische Übergang M → bR reagiert hochempfindlich auf Temperatur, Umwelt, genetische Modifikation und Chromophor-Substitution. Diese Empfindlichkeit wird bei vielen Bausteinen auf Bacteriorhodopsinbasis genutzt. Eine weitere für diesen Zweck untersuchte Reaktion ist eine photochemische Verzweigungsreaktion vom Zwischenprodukt O zur Form P. Dieses Zwischenprodukt zerfällt schließlich in die Form Q, eine Spezies, die insofern einzigartig ist, als das Chromophor die Proteinbindung kappt, aber an der Bindestelle eingekapselt wird. Das Zwischenprodukt Q bleibt für lange Zeiträume [Jahre] stabil, kann aber photochemisch in den bR-Zustand rückgeführt werden. Diese Verzweigungsreaktion besitzt ein großes Potential für die nachfolgend erörterte langfristige Datenspeicherung.

Associative memories mimic the way the human brain stores and retrieves information.

We now describe some of the unique optical memories and processors that are being made by using bacteriorhodopsin. The first device is a Fourier transform associative memory/processor. Associative memories operate in a fashion quite different from the serial memories that dominate current computer architectures. These memories take an input data block [or image], and independently of the central processor, *scan* the entire memory for the data block that matches the input. In some implementations [ours], the memory will find the closest match if it cannot find a perfect match. Finally, the memory will return the data block in memory that satisfies the matching criteria or it will return the address of the data block to permit access of contiguous data. Some memories will simply return a binary bit indicating whether the input data is present or not present. Because the human brain operates in a neural, associative mode, many computer scientists believe that the implementation of large capacity associative memories will be required if we are to achieve genuine artificial intelligence.

Thin films of bacteriorhodopsin are the photoactive components in the Fourier transform holographic [FTH] associative memory shown in Fig. 3. The actual operation of this memory is rather complicated and the interested reader is directed to the additional reading material at the end of this paper for more detailed discussion. Our interest here is to explain what a memory like this can do, and the potential relevance of such a memory to artificial intelligence and the digital arts. Let us start with a simple demonstration based on the diagram shown in Fig. 3.

Reference data [e.g., the four faces shown at lower left] are stored in the memory as holographic Fourier images on the protein thin films. We now introduce an input image that we want to *associate* with our reference data, in this case a portion of one of the faces. By a process known as Fourier transform holographic association, this image *interacts* with all the images simultaneously, and selectively illuminates the pinhole that spatially corresponds with the image that is the closest match to the input

Assoziative Speicher imitieren die Informationsspeicherung und -abrufung des menschlichen Gehirns.

Wir beschreiben nun einige der mit Hilfe von Bakteriorhodopsin konstruierten optischen Speicher und Prozessoren. Das erste ist ein Fourier-transformierter assoziativer Speicher/Prozessor. Assoziative Speicher arbeiten auf eine Art und Weise, die sich von den in heutigen Computerarchitekturen vorherrschenden seriellen Speichern grundlegend unterscheidet. Diese Speicher nehmen einen Eingabe-Datensatz [oder ein Bild] und suchen unabhängig vom zentralen Prozessor den gesamten Speicher nach dem Datensatz ab, der mit dieser Eingabe übereinstimmt. Bei einigen Implementierungen [den unseren] sucht der Speicher die nächstbeste Entsprechung, wenn er kein genaues Gegenstück findet. Am Schluß gibt der Speicher den Datensatz aus, der den Entsprechungskriterien genügt, oder er gibt die Adresse des Datensatzes aus, um den Zugriff auf benachbarte Daten zu ermöglichen. Einige Speicher geben einfach nur ein Binärbit aus, das anzeigt, ob die Eingabedaten vorhanden sind oder nicht. Da das menschliche Gehirn in einem neuronalen, assoziativen Modus arbeitet, sind viele Computerwissenschaftler der Überzeugung, daß die Implementierung assoziativer Speicher mit großen Kapazitäten nötig ist, wenn wir wirkliche künstliche Intelligenz erzeugen wollen.

Im Fourier-transformativen holographischen [FTH] Assoziativspeicher, der in Abb. 3 zu sehen ist, bilden dünne Filme aus Bakteriorhodopsin die photoaktiven Komponenten. Die tatsächliche Arbeitsweise dieses Speichers ist ziemlich kompliziert, und interessierte Leser werden dafür auf die zusätzlichen Lektürehinweise am Ende dieses Artikels verwiesen. Uns geht es hier vor allem darum zu erklären, wozu ein solcher Speicher fähig ist und worin seine mögliche Relevanz für die künstliche Intelligenz und die digitale Kunst liegen könnte. Beginnen wir mit einer einfachen Demonstration auf der Basis des in Abb. 3 dargestellten Diagramms.

Die Referenzdaten [z. B. die vier links unten abgebildeten Gesichter] werden als holographische Fourierbilder auf dünnen Proteinfilmen gespeichert. Dann geben wir ein Inputbild ein, das wir mit unseren Referenzdaten *assoziieren* wollen, im vorliegenden Fall einen Ausschnitt von einem der Gesichter. Mittels eines Prozesses, der als Fourier-transformative holographische Assoziation bezeichnet wird, *interagiert* dieses Bild mit allen Bildern gleichzeitig und strahlt selektiv jenes Loch in der Matrix an,

Fig. 3
Schematic diagram of the Fourier transform holographic associative memory
Schematische Darstellung des Fourier-transformierten holographischen Assoziationsspeichers

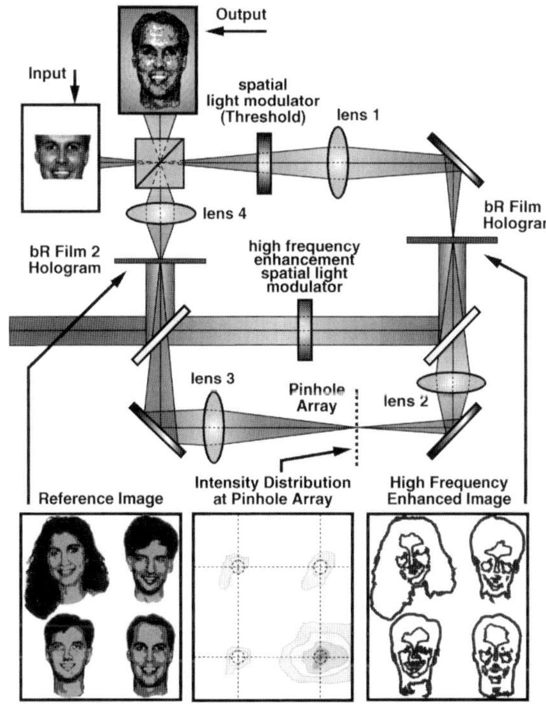

das räumlich mit der Lage des Bildes korrespondiert, welches die größte Übereinstimmung mit dem Eingabebild [oder einem Teil davon] aufweist. Als Speicherausgabe erhält man jenes Bild aus der Datenbank, das am besten mit der Eingabe übereinstimmt, als Vollbild.

Das scheint vielleicht eine Menge Aufwand für wenig Lohn, doch gibt es für diesen Prozeß und die ihn ermöglichende Hardware Anwendungen in der wirklichen Welt. Erstens kann man damit tausende Bilder gleichzeitig speichern und daraus die besten Entsprechungen innerhalb von Nanosekunden [der Zeit, die Licht zum Zurücklegen von etwa drei Metern benötigt] auswählen. Die Geschwindigkeit ist für alle optischen Parallelrechenprozesse typisch. Wenn keine Entsprechung gefunden wird, kann ein neuer Bildvorrat eingelesen und der Prozeß wiederholt werden. Christoph Bräuchle und Norbert Hampp [Universität München] und Dieter Oesterhelt [Max Planck Institut München] haben ein ähnliches optisches System entwickelt, das eine Textseite auswählt, in der ein bestimmtes Eingabewort am häufigsten vorkommt, oder rasch den genauen Nennwert einer Währung bei Papiergeld feststellt. Was aber geschieht, wenn zwei Bilder identische oder nahezu identische Entsprechungen aufweisen? Das kommt eigentlich dauernd vor, und der Speicher ist so konstruiert, daß er nacheinander die ersten fünf bis zehn Bilder für die weitere Analyse auflistet.

Die Anwendungen für die künstliche Intelligenz sind vielfältig, da man die Datenbank mit einer Mischung aus Bildern und Worten bestücken und in beiden Bereichen gleichzeitig assoziieren kann. Manche glauben, menschliche Kreativität sei am besten als Assoziation auf der Basis eines großen Bestandes an Erfahrungsdaten beschreibbar, und bei Entdeckungen handle es sich um Assoziationsvorgänge, die die nominalen Grenzen, die unsere Wahrnehmung auf der Grundlage erlernter und gesellschaftlicher Schranken einengen, überschreiten.

Unser momentanes Interesse gilt der Miniaturisierung der Optik auf eine einzige PCI-Karte, so daß die [Bild- und Text-] Daten auch in einer digitalen Umgebung manipuliert und assoziiert werden können. Das Schaltelement wird von einem internen Laser betrieben, und die Daten werden über einen internen räumlichen Lichtmodulator geladen.

Wenn dieses Projekt gelingt, werden wir einen assoziativen Speicher haben, der in Standardcomputer eingebaut werden kann. Diese Karte kann dann dazu benutzt werden, große, mit Graphiken arbeitende Datenbanken zu durchsuchen und dar-

Fig. 4
Schematic diagram of the four operations of the three-dimensional memory
Schematische Darstellung der vier Operationen des dreidimensionalen Speichers

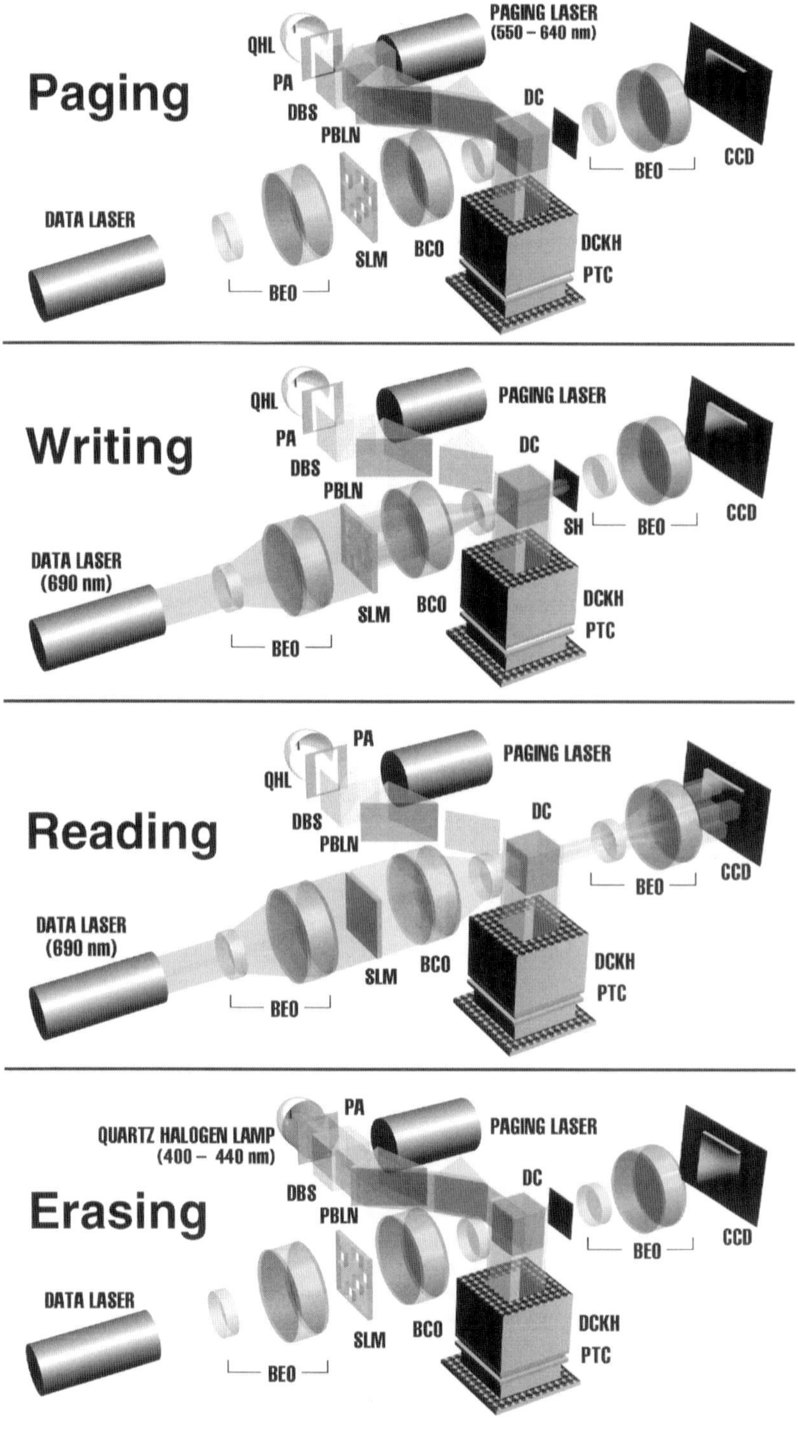

image [or portion thereof]. The output of the memory is the full image within the stored data base that represents the best match to the input.

This might seem to be a lot of work for little reward, but the process, and the hardware that makes it possible, have real-world applications. First, one can store thousands of images simultaneously, and select the best match from this set in a matter of nanoseconds [the time it takes light to travel about ten feet]. The speed is typical of all optical parallel computing processes. If no match is found, a new set of images can be read in and the process repeated. Christoph Bräuchle and Norbert Hampp [University of Munich] and Dieter Oesterhelt [Max Planck Institute in Munich] have developed a similar optical system that will select a page of text with the largest occurrences of a given input word, or rapidly select the correct denomination of paper currency. What happens if there are two images that match with identical, or nearly identical, levels? Actually, this happens all the time, and the memory is designed to display the top five or ten images in sequence, for further analysis.

BCO	beam condensing optics
BEO	beam expending optics
CCD	charge coupled device
DBS	dichroic beam splitter
DC	data cuvette, containing the protein in a transparent polymer matrix
DCKH	data cuvette, kinematic holder
PTC	Peltier temperature controler
QHL	quarz halogen lamp
SLM	spatial light modulator

The applications to artificial intelligence are numerous, because one can fill the data base with mixtures of images and words, and associate in both realms simultaneously. Some believe that creativity with humans can best be described in terms of association within a broad data base of experience, and that discovery is a process of association across the nominal boundaries that confine our perception based on prior learning and societal constraints.

Our current interest is to miniaturize the optics onto a single PCI computer card so that data, both image and text, can be manipulated and associated in a digital environment. An internal laser will drive the circuit, and data will be loaded via an internal spatial light modulator. If this project succeeds, we will have an associative memory that can be inserted into standard computers. This card can also be used to scan large data bases containing graphic images and select an image that is closest to the input image.

aus ein Bild auszuwahlen, das dem Eingabebild am ähnlichsten ist.

Sehen wir uns ein paar Beispiele an, um die graphischen Anwendungsmoglichkeiten eines solchen Speichers besser beurteilen zu können. Eine nur aus wenigen Linien bestehende grobe Skizze könnte dazu verwendet werden, in Echtzeit Bilder mit ähnlichem Inhalt aus einer extrem großen Datenbank auszuwählen. Gefunden wird dabei die ähnlichste Entsprechung auf Basis der hochfrequenzverstärkten Bilder [es sei angemerkt, daß die hochfrequenzverstärkten Bilder einer mit Linien arbeitenden Kunst überhaupt entgegenkommen]. Graphiker könnten einen solchen Speicher auch zur Produktion neuer Kunstwerke benutzen, indem sie grobe Strichzeichnungen anfertigen und den Computer diese Eingabeskizzen mit einer Datenbank von abstrakten Bildern assoziieren lassen. Der Künstler könnte dann aus den fünf oder zehn befriedigendsten *Assoziationen* Elemente auswählen und der Reinzeichnung hinzufügen. Interaktive, handgezeichnete oder computergenerierte Animationen könnten durch autoassoziative Bildrekonstruktion verstärkt werden. Jemand könnte z. B. eine Rohskizze von einer Person zeichnen, während der Computer die Details aus einer Datenbank mit maßstäblichen Bildern einfügt.

Datenspeicherung in drei Dimensionen.

Die digitale Kunst benötigt bekanntlich große Arbeits- und Plattenspeicher. Ein einziges niedrig aufgelöstes Bild [1024 x768x32 Bits] benötigt über drei Megabyte [MB], und ein für die Arbeit professioneller Künstler heute typischeres hoch aufgelöstes Bild [6000 x 4800x32 Bits] benötigt 115 MB. Für nicht einmal zehn solcher Bilder braucht man ein Gigabyte [GB], und so ist es nicht verwunderlich, daß Medienkünstler im Durchschnitt viele GB an schnellem Plattenspeicher und Hunderte GB an Wechselspeichermedien benötigen. Viele Wissenschaftler meinen, daß die Bioelektronik ihren stärksten Niederschlag in der Computer-Hardware auf dem Gebiet der dreidimensionalen Speicher finden wird. Die Vorteile dreidimensionaler Speicher liegen in ihrer Kapazität und – in manchen Fällen – in der Bandbreite des Datenzugriffs. Die Speicherkapazität zweidimensionaler optischer Speicher beschränkt sich auf ca. 1/(Wellenlänge)2,

BCO	Strahlverdichter
BEO	Strahlaufweiter
CCD	ladungsgesteuerter Baustein
DBS	Zweifarben-Strahlteiler
DC	Datenküvette, die das Protein in einer Polymermatrix enthält
DCKH	kinematischer Küvettenhalter
PTC	Peltier-Temperaturregler
QHL	Quarzhalogenlampe
SLM	räumlicher Lichtmodulator

To more fully appreciate the potential applications of such a memory in the graphic arts, consider a few examples. A quick sketch involving only a few lines could be used to select images with similar content from an extremely large data base in real time. The closest match based on the high-frequency enhanced images is found [note that the high frequency enhanced images are closer to line art, anyway]. A graphic artist could also use such a memory to create new art by drawing rough sketches and allowing the computer to associate the input sketches with a data base of abstract images. The artist could then select from the five or ten most pleasing *associations*, and then add the chosen image to the master. Interactive human and computer animation could be enhanced through autoassociative image reconstruction. For example, the person draws a rough image of a person, and the computer fills in the details from a data base of scaled images.

Storing data in three dimensions.

The digital arts are notorious for requiring large random access as well as disk memories. A single low resolution image [1024x768x32 bits] requires over three megabytes [MB] and a high resolution image [6000x4800x32 bits], more typical of today's professional artists, requires 115 MB. Less than ten such images require a gigabyte [GB], and thus it is not surprising that the average digital artist requires many GB of fast disk memory and hundreds of GB of removable media. Many scientists believe that the major impact of bioelectronics on computer hardware will be in the area of three-dimensional memory. The advantages of three versus two dimensional memories is in capacity, and in some cases, data access bandwidth. Two dimensional optical memories have a storage capacity that is limited to ~1/(wavelength)^2, which yields approximately 10^8 bits/cm2. In contrast, three-dimensional memories can approach storage densities of 1/(wavelength)^3, which yields densities of approximately 10^12 bits/cm3. In principle, an optical three-dimensional memory can store roughly three orders of magnitude more information in the same size enclosure relative to a two-dimensional optical disk memory. In practice, optical limitations and issues of reliability lower the above ratio to values closer to 300. Never-

also rund 108 bits/cm2. Dreidimensionale Speicher hingegen können Speicherdichten von 1/(Wellenlänge)3, also rund 1012 bits/cm3, erreichen. Im Prinzip kann ein dreidimensionaler optischer Speicher auf demselben Raum um drei Größenordnungen mehr Information speichern als ein zweidimensionaler optischer Plattenspeicher. In der Praxis reduziert sich dieses Verhältnis durch optische Beschränkungen und aus Zuverlässigkeitsgründen eher auf den Faktor 300. Aber auch das 300fache ist eine signifikante Vermehrung der Speicherkapazität. Das Protein Bakteriorhodopsin bietet aufgrund seiner sogenannten Verzweigungsreaktion eine ziemlich einmalige Möglichkeit der dreidimensionalen Datenspeicherung. Das Protein wird in ein Polymer eingegossen und dieses in eine kleine Plastikküvette mit den Abmessungen 1cm x 1cm x 3cm eingeschweißt. Mittels der nachfolgend beschriebenen Methoden kann man in einer solchen Küvette etwa 10 GB speichern. Das Aufregende und potentiell Vorteilhafte dabei ist weniger die große Speicherdichte, sondern die Kostengünstigkeit der Speicherküvetten. Eine Einzelküvette besteht aus Plastik, preiswertem Polymer und einem Protein, das durch Fermentierung in großen Mengen produziert werden kann.

Wir haben weiter vorne die Nutzung des P- und Q-Zustands für die langfristige Datenspeicherung erwähnt. Dadurch, daß man diese Zustände nur über eine zeitlich geteilte Pulssequenz generieren kann, ergibt sich eine praktikable Methode der dreidimensionalen Datenspeicherung mit Hilfe orthogonaler Laserbestrahlung. Die Generierung verläuft nach nebenstehendem sequentiellen Schema [s. Abb. 5]: K, L, M, N und O sind allesamt Zwischenprodukte des primären Photozyklus, P und Q sind Zwischenprodukte des Zweigzyklus. Die Zahlen unterhalb der Buchstaben geben die Wellenlänge der jeweiligen Absorptionsmaxima der Zwischenstufen in Nanometern an [bR hat z. B. die Maximalabsorption bei 570 nm bzw. im Gelb-Grün-Bereich, die Maximalabsorption von O liegt bei 640 nm, d. h. im Rotbereich].

Am Anfang des Lese- und des Schreibvorgangs steht ein als *Paging* bezeichneter Prozeß [Abb. 4], bei dem jeweils eine hauchdünne Region der Datenküvette [die Seite] ausgewählt wird. Dabei lösen die Paging-Laser [es gibt zwei davon, je einen auf gegenüberliegenden Seiten der Datenküvette, aber der Klarheit halber ist nur einer abgebildet] mit einer Wellenlänge im Bereich zwischen 550 – 640 nm in dieser ca. 15 Micron dünnen Schicht des Speicher-

theless, a 300-fold improvement in storage capacity is significant. The protein bacteriorhodopsin offers a rather unique approach to three dimensional data storage by exhibiting what is known as a branching reaction. The protein is encapsulated into a polymer which is sealed inside a small plastic cuvette of dimensions 1 cm x 1 cm x 3 cm. By using the methods described below, it is possible to store about ten GB in one such cuvette. What makes this exciting and potentially valuable is not so much the large storage density, but the inexpensive nature of the data storage cuvettes. A single cuvette is made of plastic, inexpensive polymer and a protein can be prepared in large quantities via fermentation.

We discussed above the use of the P and Q states for long-term data storage. The fact that these states can only be generated via a temporally separated pulse sequence provides a convenient method of storing data in three dimensions by using orthogonal laser excitation. The process is based on the sequential scheme (see Fig. 5) where K, L, M, N and O are all intermediates within the main photocycle, and P and Q are intermediates in the branching cycle. The numbers underneath the letters give the wavelengths of the absorption maxima of the intermediates in nanometers [e.g. bR has a maximum absorbance at 570nm, or yellow-green region, O absorbs at 640nm, in the red].

The reading and writing process starts by selecting a very thin region [~15 micron] inside the data cuvette by a process called *paging* [top, Fig. 4]. In this process, the paging lasers [there are two, one on each side of the data cuvette, but only one is shown for clarity] with a wavelength in the region 550 – 640 nm initiates the photocycle within a ~15 micron slice of the memory medium. The photocycle will return to the resting state [bR] in about 10 ms, the time window during which subsequent writing or reading must takes place. In the absence of secondary laser stimulation, the protein within the paged region will simply return to the resting state.

Data are written in parallel via a branching reaction.

A parallel write is accomplished by using the sequential one-photon optical protocol. The paging beam activates the photocycle of bac-

Fig. 5

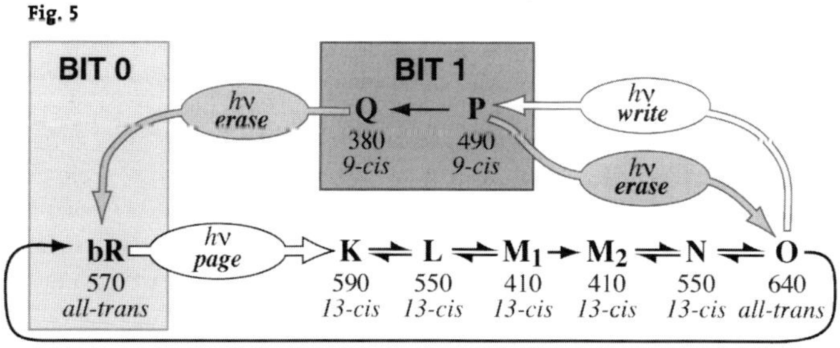

mediums den Photozyklus aus. Nach etwa 10 ms kehrt der Photozyklus in den Ruhezustand [bR] zurück – in diesem Zeitfenster muß der nachfolgende Schreib- oder Lesevorgang stattfinden. Erfolgt keine sekundäre Laserstimulation, kehrt das Protein in der als Datenseite aktivierten Region einfach wieder in den Ruhezustand zurück.

Die Daten werden mit Hilfe der Verzweigungsreaktion parallel geschrieben.

Mittels des sequentiellen einphotonigen optischen Protokolls wird ein paralleler Schreibvorgang durchgeführt. Der *Paging*-Strahl aktiviert den Photozyklus des Bakteriorhodopsin und erreicht nach wenigen Millisekunden die höchste Konzentration des O-Zustands. Nun werden der Datenlaser und der LCSLM [räumliche Lichtmodulator] aktiviert [l = 680nm, Dt ‰ 3 ms] und bestrahlen jene Speicherelemente, in die die 1er-Bits geschrieben werden sollen. Der Vorgang wandelt an diesen – und nur diesen – Stellen der Speicherküvette den O- in den P-Zustand um. Nach mehreren Minuten zerfällt der P-Zustand thermisch in den Q-Zustand [die P → Q Zerfallszeit, tP, hängt stark von der Temperatur und der Polymermatrix ab]. Der Schreibprozeß findet in nur rund 10 ms statt, also in der Zeit, in der das Protein den Photozyklus vollendet.

Die Daten werden seitenweise parallelgelesen.

Der Lesevorgang macht sich den Umstand zunutze, daß Licht mit etwa 680 nm nur durch zwei Zwischenprodukte im Photozyklus von lichtadaptiertem Bakteriorhodopsin absorbiert wird: dem primären Photoprodukt K und dem relativ langlebigen O-Zustand [siehe Abb. 2]. Die Lesesequenz beginnt

teriorhodopsin and after a few milliseconds the O intermediate approaches maximal concentration. The data laser and the LCSLM are now activated [l = 680nm, Dt ‰ 3 ms] to irradiate those volume elements into which 1 bits are to be written. This process converts O to P in these, and only these, locations within the memory cuvette. After many minutes the P state thermally decays to form the Q state [the P →Q decay time, tP, is highly dependent upon temperature and polymer matrix]. The write process is accomplished in ~10 ms, the time it takes the protein to complete the photocycle.

Data are read in parallel one page at a time.

The read process takes advantage of the fact that light around 680 nm is absorbed by only two intermediates in the photocycle of light-adapted bacteriorhodopsin, the primary photoproduct K and the relatively long-lived O intermediate [see Fig 2]. The read sequence starts out in a fashion identical to that of the write process by activating the 568nm paging beam. After two milliseconds, the data timing [DTS] and the data read [DRS] shutters are opened for 1ms, but the SLM is left off allowing only 0.1% of the total laser power through. A CCD array [clocked to clear all charges prior to reading] images the light passing through the data cuvette. Those elements in binary state 1 [P or Q] do not absorb the 680nm light, but those volumetric elements that started out in the binary 0 state [bR] absorb the 680nm light, because these elements have cycled into the O state. Noting that all of the volumetric elements outside of the paged area are restricted to the bR, P or Q states, the only significant absorption of the beam is associated with O states within the paged region. The CCD detector array therefore observes the differential absorptivity of the paged region, and the paged region alone. This selectivity is the key to the read operation, and it allows a reasonable signal-to-noise ratio even with thick [1-1.6 cm] memory media containing >103 pages. Because the absorptivity of the O state within the paged region is more than 1000 times larger than the absorptivity of the remaining volume elements combined, a very weak beam can be used to generate a large differential signal. The read process is complete in ~10 ms which gives a rate of 10 MB/s. Each

auf dieselbe Weise wie der Schreibprozeß mit der Aktivierung des 568 nm *Paging*-Strahls. Nach zwei Millisekunden werden die *data timing*- [DTS] und die *data read*-Verschlüsse [DRS] 1 ms lang geöffnet, jedoch bei geschlossem SLM, so daß dieser nur 0.1% der Gesamtleistung des Lasers durchläßt. Eine CCD-Detektormatrix [die auf das Löschen aller Ladezustände vor dem Lesevorgang programmiert ist] zeichnet das durch die Datenküvette hindurchgehende Licht auf. Die Speicherelemente im Binärzustand 1 [P oder Q] lassen das 680 nm Licht durch, wogegen es diejenigen Elemente, die am Anfang im Binärzustand 0 [bR-Zustand] waren, absorbieren, da diese mittlerweile in den O-Zustand gelangt sind. Da alle Speicherelemente außerhalb der aktivierten Datenseite auf die Zustände bR, P oder Q beschränkt sind, erfolgt die einzig signifikante Absorption des Strahls an die O-Zustände in der aktivierten Datenseite. Die CCD-Detektormatrix registriert also allein die differentielle Absorptionsfähigkeit der aktivierten Datenseite. Dieses Selektionsvermögen ist der Schlüssel zum Lesevorgang und ermöglicht einen akzeptablen Signal-Rauschabstand selbst bei dicken [1 – 1.6 cm starken] Speichermedien mit über 103 Seiten. Da die Absorptionsfähigkeit des O-Zustands in der aktivierten Datenseite mehr als 1000 Mal höher als die aller übrigen Elemente des Speichervolumens ist, genügt ein sehr schwacher Strahl, um ein großes differentielles Signal zu erzeugen. Der Lesevorgang ist in rund 10 ms abgeschlossen, was eine Lesegeschwindigkeit von 10 MB/s ergibt. Der Lesevorgang muß für jede Seite einzeln durchgeführt werden, und nach ca. 1000 Lesevorgängen ist eine Datenauffrischung notwendig. Zwar wird der Speicher durch die Datenauffrischung geringfügig verlangsamt, doch kann die Wirkung durch das Puffern von Seiten minimiert werden.

Die Daten werden in multiplen Seitenpaketen mit inkohärentem Blaulicht gelöscht.

Eine gefilterte Quarzhalogenlampe liefert das blaue Licht für die photochemische Rückumwandlung des P- und Q-Zustands in den bR-Zustand. Da es sich dabei um nicht-kohärentes Licht handelt, ist keine Fokussierung auf einzelne Seiten möglich, und es werden mehrere Seiten gleichzeitig gelöscht. Die optimale Wellenlänge für die Datenlöschung ist ca. 410 nm. Außerdem bietet sich die Alternativmöglichkeit, mit nicht-kohärentem Licht im Bereich von 360 – 450 nm eine gesamte Datenküvette zu löschen. Diese Option könnte für einige weniger teure Implementierungen nützlich sein.

read operation must be monitored for each page, and a refresh operation performed after ~1000 reads. While data refresh slows the memory slightly, page caching can minimize the impact.

Data are erased in multiple page sets using incoherent blue light.

A filtered quartz halogen lamp provides blue light to photochemically convert both P and Q back to bR. Because this light is not coherent, single page focusing is not possible, and multiple pages are cleared simultaneously. The optimal wavelength for erasing data is ~410 nm. Alternatively, one can clear an entire data cuvette by using incoherent light in the 360–450 nm range. The latter option may prove useful for some less expensive implementations.

In closing, I need to emphasize that more work is necessary before the associative memory or the three-dimensional memory will be available to the average user. But the reader can rest assured that both types of memory will be manufactured in some format during the next decade. Nature has much to teach us as regards the manipulation and storage of information, and the tools for exploring nature, and modifying natural materials, are becoming increasingly useful and powerful. The future of biomimetic engineering should provide both excitement for the researcher and utility for the electronic artist.

The research upon which this article is based was done by my graduate students Jeff Stuart, Jack Tallent and Deepak Singh. Funding from the US National Institutes of Health, the US National Science Foundation, USAF Rome Laboratory and the W. M. Keck Foundation is gratefully acknowledged.

Abschließend muß ich betonen, daß es noch einer Menge Arbeit bedarf, ehe assoziative oder dreidimensionale Speicher für den Durchschnittsuser erhältlich sein werden. Der Leser kann aber sicher sein, daß beide Speichertypen in irgendeiner Form im Verlauf des nächsten Jahrzehnts produziert werden. Die Natur kann uns in bezug auf Informationsverarbeitung und -speicherung eine Menge beibringen, und die Instrumente zur Erforschung der Natur und zur Modifikation natürlicher Materialien werden immer nützlicher und leistungsfähiger. Die Zukunft der biomimetischen Technologie dürfte sowohl aufregend für den Forscher als auch nützlich für den Medienkünstler werden.

Die Forschung, auf der dieser Artikel beruht, wurde von meinen Doktoranden Jeff Stuart, Jack Tallent und Deepak Singh durchgeführt. Dankend erwähnt sei die finanzielle Unterstützung durch die US National Institutes of Health, die US National Science Foundation, das USAF Rome Laboratory und die W. M. Keck Foundation.

Birge, R. R. 1992. *Protein based optical computing and optical memories.* IEEEComputer 25: 56-67.

Oesterhelt, D., C. Bräuchle, N. Hampp 1991. *Bacteriorhodopsin: a biological material for information processing.* Quarterly Review Biophysics 24: 425-478.

Parthenopoulos, D. A., P. M. Rentzepis 1989. *Three-dimensional optical storage memory.* Science 245: 843-845.

Birge, R. R. 1994. *Protein based three-dimensional memory.* American Scientist 82: 348-355.

Birge, R. R. 1995. *Protein based computers.* Scientific American 272: 90-95, March 1995, dt: *Computer aus Proteinen*, in: Spektrum der Wissenschaft, November 1995

New World Order, Same Old Shit

Paul Garrin

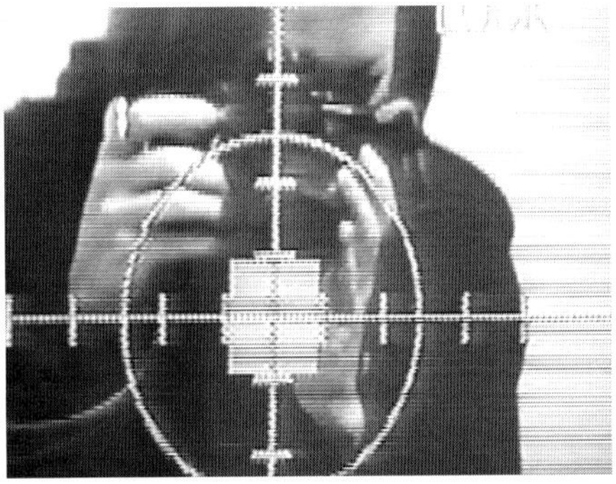

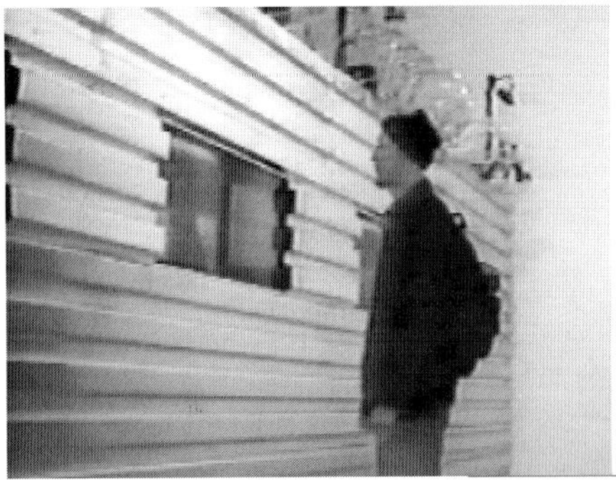

symposium

Eine neue Weltordnung, aber dieselbe alte Scheiße

Paul Garrin

Generationen und Lebensdauer ... zwei Dinge, die Mensch und Maschine gemeinsam haben.

Millionen Jahre Leben und Sterben waren notwendig, um jene Energie [Erdöl] entstehen zu lassen, die von Maschinen innerhalb nur weniger Jahrhunderte aufgebraucht werden wird.

Generations and lifespan ... These are two things that machines and humans have in common.

It took millions of years of life and death to produce the energy [oil] that machines will consume in just a few centuries.

This acceleration curve is roughly analagous to the amount of knowledge and experience which has accumulated, [especially in recent times] and the level at which all that knowledge will be globally available through datanetworks.

Unlike energy which always diminishes to its lowest level, knowledge persists, in defiance of entropy, and accumulates – its vehicles and filters [media, human minds, more media...] thriving and decaying throughout the generations, mutating and evolving according to the conditions of dominance and economy, through war, prosperity, deprivation...

The Industrial Revolution placed the highest value on the fuels for the machines that built the post-industrial society – that society which now places the highest value on knowledge – the fuel for what the hype calls the *Information Age*, the *Age of the Immaterial*. But look carefully at the so-called *immaterial* world of the information age: it takes a lot of material to realize the immaterial. The overly euphoric inhabitans of virtual worlds who wish to leave their bodies overlook the obvious fact that the networks which convey their phantasy-existance are made of parts assembled in Malaysia or Taiwan or Mexico or in other *low wage countries* by people who probably don't even have telephones, don't own computers and are certainly not connected to the internet. Food and shelter are the greatest challenge to these laborers – to feed the bodies that produce the components of a system they could never afford to be a part of.

Keep in mind that *being digital* means paying for the continuance of the war machine which brought the internet and computers into your living room and into your bedroom and into your office and into the museums. The same war machine which when necessary can effectively deliver a *body count* over long distances with minimal effort, can also effect a *data-body count* with even greater ease and better yet, with less expense. The cost, as always in one way or another is

Eine etwa analoge Beschleunigungskurve würde man erhalten, wenn man die Menge an Wissen und Erfahrung, die sich [insbesondere in jüngerer Zeit] angesammelt hat, der Geschwindigkeit gegenüberstellt, mit der all dieses Wissen durch Datennetze auf globaler Ebene verfügbar sein wird.

Im Gegensatz zur Energie, die sich immer auf ihr niedrigstes Niveau verringert, bleibt das Wissen den Gesetzen der Entropie zum Trotz bestehen und akkumuliert sich, wobei seine Träger und Filter [Medien, der menschliche Geist, noch mehr Medien ...] im Laufe der Generationen gedeihen und wieder vergehen, den Macht- und Wirtschaftsverhältnissen entsprechend, durch Krieg, Reichtum, Entbehrung, etc. mutieren und sich entwickeln.

Die industrielle Revolution räumte den höchsten Stellenwert den Treibstoffen für die Maschinen ein, die die postindustrielle Gesellschaft entstehen ließen – eine Gesellschaft, die ihrerseits heute dem Wissen, d. h. dem Treibstoff des *Informationszeitalters* oder des *Zeitalters des Immateriellen*, wie die populären Bezeichnungen lauten, den höchsten Stellenwert beimißt. Doch sehen wir uns diese sogenannte *immaterielle Welt* des Informationszeitalters etwas näher an: Die Realisierung des Immateriellen erfordert ziemlich viel Material. Die übermäßig euphorischen Bewohner virtueller Welten, die ihre Körper am liebsten hinter sich zurücklassen würden, übersehen die offensichtliche Tatsache, daß die Netze, die ihnen ihre Phantasie Existenz ermöglichen, aus Komponenten bestehen, die irgendwo in Malaysien, Taiwan, Mexiko oder einem anderen Niedriglohnland von Menschen zusammengebaut wurden, die wahrscheinlich nicht einmal Telefon haben, die keinen Computer besitzen und mit Sicherheit nicht ans Internet angeschlossen sind. Für diese Arbeiter besteht die größte Herausforderung darin, Nahrung und Unterkunft zu finanzieren, d. h. jene Körper zu ernähren, die die Komponenten eines Systems erzeugen, dem sie selbst aus finanziellen Gründen nie angehören könnten.

Denken Sie immer daran, daß *digital sein* unter anderem bedeutet, für die Aufrechterhaltung jener Kriegsmaschinerie zu bezahlen, die das Internet und den Computer in Ihr Wohnzimmer, Ihr Schlafzimmer, Ihr Büro und auch in die Museen gebracht hat. Dieselbe Kriegsmaschinerie, der es gegebenenfalls ein leichtes ist, über weite Distanzen hinweg effizient *Opferzahlen* zu liefern, kann noch viel leichter und – es kommt noch besser – viel billiger *Daten-Opferzahlen* liefern. Die Kosten werden, wie dies immer auf die eine oder andere Weise der Fall ist, von

borne by the victims, in this case the euphoric digizens who enslave themselves to the military-corporate web that seduces them into ecstatic complicity.

Stare reverently into the screen, that holy place of immateriality, the devine portal into the promises for the next version release, the world of the *wired* that worships unquestionably the wonders of virtual immortality, the triumph of the will of the technological miracles that will bring deliverance and utopia. The machine is perfect ... the machine is divine ... Big Blue can play better chess than that human can ... the F16 can outfly its own pilot ... that 20G maneuver can save the aircraft from destruction by the missile even if it does squash the pilot ... but the machines are there to make better war for the humans ... they may even execute war better than the humans do ... but the machines themselves have no need for war ... only the humans who built them to control other humans have the need for war – war over identity ... over territory ... over power.

Humans battle eternally over their identities. The struggle over identity, heritage and land is the fuel for wars since time immemorial. Identity and geography are *worth fighting over* so the humans say ... so they develop technology in their own image ... They create machines, and give them names and places to live ... Domains ... an artificial concept that helps the humans organize the machines into metaphorical regiments that they can easily understand ... and other humans jump in and stake claims to *their* Domains ... sometimes to be evicted, not by Ethnic-Cleansing Thugs toting AK47's but by McDonalds toting multimillion dollar Lawyers and tons of paper ... all over a simple identity ... this all only matters to the humans ... not to the machines to whom identity is essential. Every node on a network must have its own unique identity ... a network address number and a name ... if there is an identity conflict, it just won't work on the network ... there's no struggle ... just no acknowledgement. The machine becomes invisible to the rest of the network ... if it moves to another location and is given a new network D it will still function faithfully without struggle over its identity or the desire to regain its past, and certainly without a war.

den Opfern getragen, d. h. in diesem Fall von den euphorischen *Digizens*, die sich von dem von Wirtschaft und Militär getragenen Netz, das sie zu ekstatischer Mittäterschaft verführt, versklaven lassen.

Starren Sie nur ehrfürchtig auf den Bildschirm, jenen heiligen Ort der Immaterialität, jenes göttliche Tor zu den Freuden der nächsten Version, zur Welt der *Verkabelten*, die kritiklos den Wundern der virtuellen Unsterblichkeit huldigt, dem Triumph des Willens der technischen Wunder, die Erlösung und Utopie mit sich bringen werden. Die Maschine ist perfekt ... die Maschine ist göttlich ... Big Blue spielt besser Schach als der Mensch ... die F16 fliegt besser als ihr eigener Pilot ... das 20G-Manöver kann das Flugzeug vor der Zerstörung durch eine Rakete retten, auch wenn der Pilot zerquetscht wird ... doch die Funktion der Maschinen besteht darin, für die Menschen besser Krieg zu führen ... und sie führen den Krieg vielleicht wirklich besser als die Menschen ... aber die Maschinen selbst brauchen keinen Krieg ... nur die Menschen, die die Maschinen gebaut haben, um andere Menschen zu beherrschen, brauchen den Krieg ... Krieg um die Identität ... um territoriale Ansprüche .... um Macht.

Die Menschen führen ewig Krieg um ihre Identitäten. Der Streit um Identität, Erbe und Land hat seit Urzeiten bewaffnete Konflikte heraufbeschworen. Identität und Geographie sind *es wert, für sie zu kämpfen*, sagen die Menschen ... und so entwickeln sie Technologien nach ihrem eigenen Abbild ... Sie schaffen Maschinen und geben ihnen Namen und einen Ort, an dem sie leben sollen ... Domänen ... ein künstlicher Begriff, der den Menschen hilft, die Maschinen in metaphorische Regimente zu gruppieren, die sie leicht verstehen können ... und dann tauchen andere Menschen auf und erheben Anspruch auf *ihre* Domänen ... und werden manchmal vertrieben, aber nicht von mit AK47ern bewaffneten ethnischen Säuberungskommandos, sondern von Anwälten und Tonnen von Papier, allesamt von McDonald's mit Dollarbeträgen in Millionenhöhe finanziert ... und alles dreht sich um eine einfache Identität ... das alles ist nur den Menschen wichtig ... nicht aber den Maschinen, für die die Identität jedoch von grundlegender Bedeutung ist. Jeder Knoten in einem Netz muß seine eigene, unverwechselbare Identität haben ... eine Netzadresse und einen Namen ... wenn es zu einem Identitätskonflikt kommt, kann dieser Knoten im Netz einfach nicht funktionieren ... es gibt keinen Kampf ... sondern einfach keine Bestätigung. Die Maschine wird für den Rest des Netzes unsichtbar ...

The mechanisms of war effect destruction and waste creating new opportunities for the enslavement of the surviving bodies who assemble the components for the next war ... the digital war that moves in to manage the perception of those on the *cool* battlefields, over the modems and airwaves in the digital domain, their databodies filling the ranks of demographic conquests, targets of advertising, their input feeding the furtherance of the oppressive demands for the output of other less fortunate enslaved bodies who struggle to survive by producing the tools of their own opression.

The *World Wide Wasteland* is a staging ground for one of the latest wars against the human spirit. Information overload obscures the obvious crimes against humanity that are hidden in plain view. Complicity is rampant. Denial of the flesh is fashion. Control the Art and you control the People ... Own the dataways and you own the databodies that inhabit them. The greatest crime is the paradox of new media ...We have yet to learn how to use the knowledge and communications that took centuries and many generations of humans to develop. Generation upon generation the accumulation of knowledge and experience has yet to bring the evolution of mind that is overdue at the end of this millenium. With all the means to communicate, access information, technological and conceptual advancements available the wars fought are still the wars of old and have never reached the ultimate evolutionary war, the War against Ignorance.

wenn sie sich an einen anderen Ort bewegt und eine neue Netz-ID erhält, wird sie hingegen loyal weiterfunktionieren ... ohne Kampf um ihre Identität, ohne den Wunsch, ihre eigene Vergangenheit neu aufleben zu lassen, und ganz sicher ohne Krieg.

Die Mechanismen des Kriegs bewirken Zerstörung und Vergeudung, sie schaffen neue Möglichkeiten der Versklavung der überlebenden Körper, die die Komponenten für den nächsten Krieg zusammenbauen ... den digitalen Krieg, dessen Methode darin besteht, die Wahrnehmung der auf den *kühlen* Schlachtfeldern Anwesenden per Modem und über den Äther auf die digitale Domäne zu steuern. Ihre Datenkörper füllen die Reihen der demographischen Eroberungen, sie sind als Zielscheiben der Werbung ausgesetzt, und ihr Input fördert die Durchsetzung der unterdrückerischen Forderungen nach dem Output anderer, unglücklicherer Versklavten, die um das Überleben kämpfen, indem sie die Werkzeuge ihrer eigenen Unterdrückung herstellen.

Das *World Wide Wasteland* ist das Schlachtfeld, auf dem einer der jüngsten Kriege gegen den menschlichen Geist ausgetragen wird. Die Informationsüberlastung verhüllt die offensichtlichen Verbrechen gegen die Menschlichkeit, die klar sichtbar vor uns verborgen liegen. Weite Kreise der Bevölkerung sind bereits zu Mittätern geworden. Es ist modern geworden, das Fleisch zu verleugnen. Wer die Kunst beherrscht, beherrscht das Volk ... Wer die Datenleitungen besitzt, besitzt gleichzeitig die Datenkörper, die sie bevölkern. Das größte Verbrechen ist das Paradoxon der Neuen Medien ... Wir müssen erst lernen, das Wissen und die Kommunikationsmöglichkeiten zu nutzen, die die Menschheit über Jahrhunderte und viele Generationen hinweg geschaffen hat. Generation um Generation muß die Akkumulation von Wissen und Erfahrung erst jene geistige Evolution herbeiführen, die heute, am Ende unseres Jahrtausends, bereits überfällig ist. Trotz aller uns zur Verfügung stehenden Kommunikationsmittel, trotz unseres Zugangs zu Informationen, trotz allen technologischen und begrifflichen Fortschritts sind die Kriege, die heute ausgetragen werden, immer noch dieselben wie in der Vergangenheit. Und niemals haben wir es geschafft, den ultimativen evolutionären Krieg zu erklären: den Krieg gegen die Ignoranz.

Bad Girl Versus the Astronaut Christ: the Strange Political Journey of the Cyborg

Hari Kunzru

symposium

Ungezogenes Mädchen versus Astronautenchristus: Die seltsame politische Entwicklung des Cyborg

Hari Kunzru

Es ist gut ein Jahrzehnt her, seit Donna Haraway erstmals ihre Cyborgtheorie formulierte[1]. Seitdem hat sich das Bild des *kybernetischen Organismus*, des vernetzten, rationaler Kontrolle unterworfenen Fleisches, von einer technischen zu einer politischen Kategorie gewandelt – ein Wandel, der die wissenschaftlichen Eltern des Cyborg immer noch verblüfft.

In seinen Anfängen während der fünfziger und sechziger Jahre in den Forschungsprogrammen der US-Luftwaffe hatte der Cyborg eine scheinbar unkomplizierte Bedeutung, jene Bedeutung, deren Code auch in den Raumfahrtromanheften aus der Zeit des Kalten Krieges und den geschwungenen Heckflossen des Chevrolet-Cabrios eingeschrieben ist. Der Mensch – so signalisierten Cyborg, Chevy und SF-Taschenbuch – war im Begriff, sämtliche Grenzen zu überschreiten. Dem Wunsch entsprungen, menschliche Systeme für das Überleben im All zu adaptieren, sollte der cyborgisierte Mensch die Grenzen der Newton'schen Physik sprengen und, die Gesetze der Schwerkraft überwindend, sich auf den Weg zu den Sternen machen. Gleichzeitig sollte er die Schranken seines eigenen Körpers hinter sich lassen und mit seiner Umwelt in eine Kontroll- und Kommunikationsrückkopplungsschleife treten. Die Haut, die

It's well over a decade since Donna Haraway first formulated her theory of the cyborg.[1] During that time the figure of the *cybernetic organism*, networked flesh subject to rational control, has morphed from a technical into a political category, a change which continues to surprise the cyborg's scientist parents.

At its origin in the US Airforce research programmes of the nineteen-fifties and sixties, the cyborg seemed to carry an uncomplicated meaning, the same meaning coded into the cold war slew of pulp space travel stories or the arcing rear fins of a Chevrolet convertible. Man, said the cyborg, the Chevy, the Ace paperback, was about to transcend all limitations. Born out of the desire to adapt human systems for survival in space, the cyborgised man would transcend the constraints of Newtonian physics by breaking free of gravity and going to the stars. At the same time he would transcend his own physical boundaries, entering a control and communication feedback-loop with his environment. The skin, that ultimate boundary between fragile self and hostile world, would become gloriously permeable, permeable not in a vulnerable way, but in a manner which would mystically transform messy, poorly-understood human biological processes into the exact, measurable, predictable processes of technology. Man thus penetrated by the machine would become an *augmented*, *adapted* or *amplified* man[2], functioning according to the protocols of technoscience. As science improved, so would man. He was, in short, upgradeable. No outer limit seemed to be fixed for this augmentation. Cyborgised man could potentially expand towards infinity, perhaps even attaining the sublime.

Certainly, it seemed that with human biological functions regulated by machines, man would be freed to explore not only the physical expanses of space but the spiritual ones of his own being. Governing the body's homeostatic processes appeared to this first generation of cyborg researchers to require effort, to divert energy that would be better used for self-evolution or spiritual exercise, as if the business of having a body was somehow distracting, time-consuming, laborious:

If man in space, in addition to flying his vehicle, must continuously be checking things and making adjustments merely in order to

ultimative Grenze zwischen zerbrechlichem Selbst und feindseliger Umwelt, sollte auf gloriose Weise durchlässig werden, aber nicht im Sinne einer Verwundung, sondern auf eine Art, welche die chaotischen, kaum begriffenen biologischen Prozesse mystisch in die exakten, meß- und vorhersagbaren Prozesse der Technologie verwandeln würde. Der solcherart von der Maschine durchdrungene Mensch sollte zu einem *erweiterten*, *adaptierten* oder *verstärkten* Menschen[2] werden, der gemäß den Protokollen der Technowissenschaft funktioniert. Mit der Verbesserung der Wissenschaft sollte sich auch der Mensch verbessern. Man sollte ihn, kurz gesagt, upgraden können. Für diese Erweiterung schien es keine feststehende Grenze zu geben. Der cyborgisierte Mensch konnte sich potentiell unendlich weiterentwickeln, vielleicht sogar Erhabenheit erlangen.

Zweifellos schien es, daß der Mensch, wenn seine biologischen Funktionen von Maschinen reguliert würden, frei wäre, nicht nur die physischen Weiten des Alls zu erkunden, sondern auch die spirituellen der eigenen Existenz. Die Steuerung der homöostatischen Körperprozesse erschien dieser ersten Generation von Cyborgforschern als etwas Mühsames, als eine Vergeudung von Energie, die besser der Selbstverwirklichung oder spirituellen Übungen zugute käme, es war, als sei Besitz eines Körpers eine Ablenkung, Zeitverschwendung, ein Arbeitsaufwand. Wenn der Mensch im Weltraum nicht nur sein Raumschiff steuern muß, sondern ständig alle möglichen Dinge checken und entsprechende Anpassungen vornehmen muß, nur um sich am Leben zu erhalten, dann wird er zum Sklaven der Maschine. Der Zweck des Cyborg und seiner homöostatischen Systeme besteht darin, ein Organisationssystem zur Verfügung zu stellen, das solche roboterhaften Probleme automatisch und unbewußt regelt und damit dem Menschen die Freiheit gibt zu forschen, schöpferisch tätig zu sein, zu denken und zu fühlen.[3]

Wiewohl dieser Kampf gegen die Sklaverei vor dem Hintergrund der Raumfahrt stattfand, trafen dieselben Hoffungen und Ängste auch auf das Leben im Amerika der Nachkriegszeit zu. Die Cyborgisierung wurde zum Zweck der Arbeitsersparnis durchgeführt, eine Große-Jungs-Version der Geschirrspüler und Kühlschränke, die diese für ihre Frauen zuhause auf der Erde kauften. Doch anders als die Küche der Zukunft, deren Technologie den Frauen mehr Zeit für Hobbies oder Schönheitspflege gab, diente der Cyborg einem höheren Zweck. In den frühen technischen Artikeln über Cyborgs findet sich immer wieder die Implikation, die Enthebung von

keep himself alive, he becomes a slave to the machine. The purpose of the Cyborg, as well as his own homeostatic systems, is to provide an organizational system in which such robot-like problems are taken care of automatically and unconsciously, leaving man free to explore, to create, to think, and to feel.[3]

Though the backdrop for this struggle against slavery was space, the same hopes and fears held true for life in postwar America. Cyborgisation was produced as a labour-saving process, the big boy's version of the dishwashers and frigidaires they bought for wives back home on earth. But unlike the kitchen of the future, whose technology bought time for female leisure or beautification, the cyborg had a higher purpose. The implication voiced again and again in early cyborg technical papers is that by relinquishing the labour of bodily regulation, man could attain a higher level of spiritual discipline. The cyborg, in short, was designed to engineer man closer to God.

The engineers and airforcemen who made up the first generation of the cyborg's acolytes were in no doubt that they were on a spiritual mission. *Where are we, where are we going, and how do we get there?* asks Major Jack E. Steele, using this uncontextualised and apparently metaphysical question to open a 1960 presentation to a space research symposium at Wright airforce base. He goes on to describe a coming generation of *bionic* humans, the *great and distant* goal towards which he and his audience are working.[4]

The pilgrim's progress, spiritual journey as mirror of a physical journey, was always one of the ideological motors of American expansion, from the moment the first boatload of seventeenth-century dissenters began the task of inscribing their struggle to reach God onto the seemingly-blank landscape of the *New World*. Cyborg research can be seen as the inheritor of this move, continuous with the pioneers' journey Westwards and the puritans' interior journey towards God. The cyborg represented the ability, through science, to take an active role in evolution, bringing recalictrant human biology under the sway of reason and morality, all put into the service of state expansion.

The human to be rationally evolved was almost invariably an airforce pilot, and archive images of pilots undergoing gruelling phy-

der Tätigkeit der Körperregulation befähige den Menschen, eine höhere spirituelle Stufe zu erreichen. Kurzum, der Cyborg wurde dazu konstruiert, den Menschen gottähnlicher zu machen.

Für die Konstrukteure und Angehörigen der Air Force, aus denen sich die erste Generation der Cyborgadepten zusammensetzte, bestand kein Zweifel, daß sie sich auf einer spirituellen Mission befanden. *Wo stehen wir, wohin gehen wir, und wie kommen wir hin?* Mit dieser unkontextualisierten und augenscheinlich metaphysischen Frage eröffnete Major Jack E. Steele 1960 eine Präsentation auf einem Raumforschungssymposion auf dem Luftwaffenstützpunkt Wright. Und in der Folge beschrieb er eine künftige *bionische* Menschengeneration als das *große und ferne* Ziel, auf welches er und sein Publikum hinarbeiteten.[4]

Die Pilgerreise, die spirituelle Entwicklung als Spiegelbild der physischen Reise, ist seit jeher eine der ideologischen Triebkräfte der amerikanischen Expansion gewesen, schon als im 17. Jahrhundert die erste Schiffsladung von Dissentern ihre Gottsuche der scheinbar leeren Landschaft der *neuen Welt* einzuschreiben begann. Die Cyborgforschung kann als ein Erbe dieser Bewegung angesehen werden, als Fortsetzung des Vordringens der Pioniere in den Westen und der puritanischen inneren Gottreise. Der Cyborg stand für die Fähigkeit, mit Hilfe der Wissenschaft eine aktive Rolle in der Evolution einzunehmen und die widerspenstige Biologie des Menschen der Herrschaft von Vernunft und Moral zu unterstellen – und dies alles im Dienste staatlicher Expansion.

Der rational zu entwickelnde Mensch war fast immer ein Luftwaffenpilot, und Archivaufnahmen von Piloten, die mörderische Körpertests durchlaufen und verschiedene prothetische Apparate tragen, gehören zu den eindrucksvollsten Bildern des frühen Cyborgzeitalters. In Exoskelette eingespannt, unmenschlichen [oder vielleicht auch bloß posthumanen] Kräften ausgesetzt, seine Reaktionen durch die intravenöse Injektion von Drogen beeinflußt, wird der Kampfpilot zu Amerikas Cyborgchristus, zum Schmerzensmann, dessen Leiden seine Nation erlöst. Ein amerikanischer Musterknabe, auserwählt seiner körperlichen und geistigen Perfektion wegen, transfiguriert durch die Maschine, empor- und hinausgeschickt, leidend und suchend für die Menschen, deren Stimmen und Steuern ihn da hinbefördert haben – Speerspitze der Hoffung und Tiefensonde der Kaltenkriegsseele der Supermacht. In einem Spiegelbild dieser Obsession brachte die UdSSR, die

sical tests and wearing a variety of prosthetics are among the most potent images of the early cyborg era. Shackled into exoskeletons, suffering inhuman [or maybe just posthuman] forces, responses altered with intravenous injections of drugs, the fighter pilot becomes America's cyborg Christ, the sufferer whose passion redeems his nation. All-American boy, chosen for his physical and mental perfection, transfigured by the machine, sent above and beyond, suffering and questing for the people whose votes and taxes sent him there – apex of hope and probe-head of the superpower's cold-war psyche. In a mirror of this obsession the postwar USSR, which itself was a vast cybernetic project, a huge experiment in rational control, produced its own cult of the cyborg Christ in the Yuri Gagarin industry whose support extended to the state-sponsored production of quasi-religious ikons.

Perhaps Donna Haraway's achievement has in part been a therapeutic one. In excavating the unconscious of this pumped-up sky pilot, she has unearthed the anxieties, the sexual and spiritual ambiguities, the night terrors of one of the defining figures of postwar technocultural certainty. Yet her analysis has also been deliberately disruptive, a critical virus introduced into a loop of signification which appeared too closed and too perfectly regulated to admit any variation or opposition.

Historically, it did not take long for the human body's permeation by networks and machines to produce alternative visions to the joyous liberation from the flesh envisaged by the USAF geeks. A previous generation of technological nightmares had already centered on humans becoming automata. The ergonomically-governed factory worker, disciplined by the twin mass mechanisms of industry and war, was in the inter-war years of the twentieth century figured as the robot [Czech for *slave labour*]. Just as in a still-earlier phase of industrialisation workers had been metonymised into *hands*[5], they became pistons and flywheels, moving parts in vast machines. The image of Charlie Chaplin caught in the cogs of some huge engine[6] is the era's defining image of recalcitrant humanity, comically refusing the rhythms of the factory.

Yet in the 1930's the little tramp's skin still formed an impermeable barrier to the

selbst ein gewaltiges kybernetisches Projekt, ein riesiges Experiment über rationalistische Kontrolle war, mit der bis zur staatsgeförderten Produktion von quasi-religiösen Ikonen reichenden Juri-Gagarin-Industrie ihren eigenen Cyborgchristuskult hervor.

Vielleicht war Donna Haraways Tat zum Teil eine therapeutische. Indem sie das Unbewußte dieses aufgemotzten Himmelspiloten freilegte, legte sie die Ängste, die sexuelle und spirituelle Ambiguität, die nächtlichen Schrecken einer der zentralen Metaphern der technokulturellen Gewißheit der Nachkriegszeit offen. Doch war ihre Analyse auch ein bewußter Störfaktor, ein kritischer Virus, in einen Zeichenkreislauf injiziert, der zu geschlossen und zu perfekt reguliert schien, als daß er die geringste Abweichung oder Gegnerschaft zugelassen hätte.

Historisch gesehen, dauerte es nicht lange, bis die Durchdringung des menschlichen Körpers durch Netzwerke und Maschinen Alternativvisionen zur lustvollen Befreiung vom Fleisch entstehen ließ, wie sie den Freaks der Air Force vor Augen stand. Schon bei einer früheren Generation von technologischen Alpträumen ging es um Menschen, die zu Automaten werden. Der ergonomisch gelenkte Fabrikarbeiter, diszipliniert durch die beiden Massenmechanismen Industrie und Krieg, wurde in den Zwischenkriegsjahren des 20. Jahrhunderts als Roboter [tschechisch für *Sklavenarbeit*] dargestellt. Wenn die Arbeiter in einer noch früheren Phase der Industrialisierung zu bloßen *hands* metonymisiert wurden[5], so wurden sie nun zu Kolben und Schwungrädern, beweglichen Teilen in großen Maschinen. Das Bild Charlie Chaplins, der sich in den Rädern einer großen Maschine verfängt[6], ist in dieser Epoche die Leitmetapher widerspenstigen Menschentums, das sich auf komische Weise den Rhythmen der Fabrik verweigert.

In den dreißiger Jahren war die Haut des kleinen Vagabunden für das ihn unterdrückende System allerdings noch eine undurchdringbare Barriere. In den Sechzigern, als die erste Generation der Christuspiloten der Augmentation unterzogen wurde, war dies nicht mehr der Fall. Das Durchstoßen der Körpermembran [mittels Prothesen und Implantaten, den astronautischen Stigmata] setzte wesentlich mehr in Gang, als man glaubte. Seit der Antike hatte der Westen in höchstem Maße auf die Undurchdringbarkeit des Körpers gesetzt. Vom Apoll von Belvedere bis zum Nationalsozialismus wurde der geschlossene, undurchdringliche Körper als moralisch maßvoll, ästhetisch wohlgefällig und epistemologisch einmalig und sicher gewürdigt.

system which oppressed him. In the 1960's, when the first generation of Christ-pilots underwent augmentation, this ceased to be the case. The rupture of the body's membrane [by prosthetics and implants, astronautical stigmata] released far more than expected. From classical times onwards, the West had made a huge investment in the opacity of the body. From the Apollo Belvedere to National Socialism, the closed, impermeable body was valued as morally continent, aesthetically pleasing, epistemologically single and secure.

By contrast, when the body exposed its workings, allowed its orifices to be penetrated, its interior humours to seep forth, this invariably signified the inversion of order, the coming of chaos, horror and decay. Whether this inversion was figured by the gluttonous, shitting, fucking grotesques of the Renaissance carnival, by Nazi racial science's physiognomy of the Jew, with its slack lips and protruding nose, or Neoclassicism's mingled desire and revulsion for female flesh, it always carried the same meaning. The classical body has for two thousand years stood sealed [inside and out] against a torrent of disproportionate, irrational, exaggerated physicality, which, were it to escape, threatened to sweep away the very foundations of civilised society.

So the cyborg body, penetrated by reason itself, presents an irresolvable paradox – the body must at all costs preserve its boundaries against the deluge of unreason, but must also reveal its mystery in order to allow reason to transcend physical limitations. Otherwise the body will present an obstacle to reason, and find itself once again the source of irrationality. Catch-22 for the flesh. This is the eternal tragicomedy of Western thought of the body, a thought which cannot incorporate itself, cannot think within the body, must always attempt to think through it, to penetrate it from the outside.

The cyborg produced a crisis in technoscience, even as it promised fulfilment of technoscience's most secret desires. It was a radical moment, and one which Donna Haraway has fully exploited, using this paradox to lever open both scientific discourse, and the varieties of feminist discourse which were constituting themselves in naive opposition to it. Yet though the cyborg's brand of disruption is radical, it is not unprecedented. Perhaps its closest cultural

Wenn der Körper dagegen sein Getriebe offenbarte, das Durchstoßen seiner Öffnungen, das Hervorquellen der inneren Säfte zuließ, so deutete das unweigerlich auf den Umsturz der Ordnung, die Heraufkunft von Chaos, Schrecken und Verfall. Ob sich dieser Umsturz in den gefräßigen, scheißenden, fickenden Groteskgestalten des Renaissancekarnevals, in der von der Rassenlehre der Nazis dargestellten Physiognomie des Juden mit schlaffen Lippen und vorspringender Nase oder in der neoklassischen Mischung aus Begehren und Abscheu angesichts weiblichen Fleisches äußert – stets kam ihm dieselbe Bedeutung zu. Der klassische Körper hielt [innen und außen versiegelt] zweitausend Jahre lang der Flut ausufernder, irrationaler, ungestümer Körperlichkeit stand, die, wenn sie hervorbräche, jegliche Grundlagen der zivilisierten Gesellschaft fortzuschwemmen drohte.

Der von der Vernunft selbst durchdrungene Cyborgkörper stellt also ein unauflösliches Paradoxon dar – der Körper muß um jeden Preis seine Grenzen gegen die Sintflut der Unvernunft wahren, muß aber zugleich sein Geheimnis offenbaren, um der Vernunft die Überschreitung körperlicher Grenzen zu gestatten. Sonst nämlich bildete der Körper für die Vernunft ein Hindernis und fände sich als Quelle der Unvernunft wieder. Darin besteht der Haken beim Fleisch. Dies ist die ewige Tragikomödie des abendländischen Denkens über den Körper, eines Denkens, das sich nicht selbst verkörpern, nicht aus dem Körper heraus denken kann, sondern dauernd versuchen muß, mit ihm zu denken, ihn von außen zu durchdringen.

Der Cyborg löste eine Krise der Technowissenschaft aus, selbst indem er die Erfüllung ihrer geheimsten Wünsche versprach. Darin lag ein radikales Moment, eines, das Donna Haraway sich zunutze machte, um mit Hilfe dieses Paradoxons sowohl den Wissenschaftsdiskurs als auch jene Spielarten des Feminismus aufzubrechen, die sich in einem naiven Gegensatz zu diesem konstituierten. Doch auch wenn die Verstörung, die der Cyborg darstellt, eine radikale ist, so ist sie doch nicht völlig neu. Der vielleicht nächste kulturelle Ahnherr ist in der Entwicklung der wissenschaftlichen Vivisektion während der Renaissance zu suchen. Auch bei dieser handelte es sich um einen Diskurs, der den Körper im Namen des Wissens öffnete, der buchstäblich Körper zerlegte, um Wahrheit zu produzieren. Die sezierten Figuren auf den illustrierenden Holzschnitten in den Werken des flämischen Anatomen Andreas Vesalius[7] stellen sich regelrecht zur Schau, schlagen manch-

ancestor can be found in the growth of scientific dissection during the Renaissance. Here too was a discourse which opened up the body in the name of knowledge, which literally dismembered corpses to produce truth. The dissected figures depicted in woodcut illustrations to the works of the Flemish anatomist Andreas Vesalius[7], display themselves, sometimes literally holding aside veils of flayed skin to allow the gaze of the student to penetrate the secrets of their bodies. In this and other Renaissance anatomical texts, complicated pictorial allegories are used to justify the practice of anatomy, which produced deep cultural anxiety, presented an identical problem of bodily integrity, and which [in one of those *what-if* games which make joining the dots of intellectual history fun] one can imagine some seventeenth-century Haraway using to blow *Natural Philosophy* wide open.

In 1997 economies of signification analagous to those circulating in Vesalius's operating theatre are played out across cinema and TV screens. After a rapid process of popularisation, originally associated with space programme fundraising, the cyborg became a mainstream cultural figure. Inevitably the crisis in science's relationship with the body rapidly produced a slew of dark-side popular imagery. These days there is a veritable industry of cybernetic terror. Tetsuo, the overworked Japanese *sarariman* whose body becomes bloated and finally ruptured by nasty biomechanisms, Star Trek's Borg, whose predatory networked consciousness threatens to destroy bodily integrity and personal identity [Trek's cherished twin pillars of morality], Johnny Mnemonic's memory-bank brain, where images of childhood have been seared away to make room for valuable corporate data. Even the out-of-control dinosaurs of Jurassic Park are quintessentially cyborg constructions, having been reanimated by a network of capital, biotechnical research and fossil DNA.

The cyborg's current cultural role as vehicle for popular unease about science makes Haraway's deployment of it not merely an oppositional trope, but a positive one, even more startling. Haraway's cyborg is affirmative, celebratory, even sexy, which is something of a miracle when you consider that previously it was either a technoscientific religious fantasy,

mal die abgezogene Haut wie einen Schleier zur Seite, um den Blick des Studenten in die Geheimnisse ihrer Körper eindringen zu lassen. In diesem wie in anderen Anatomietexten der Renaissance werden komplizierte Bildallegorien eingesetzt, um eine anatomische Praxis zu legitimieren, die eine tiefe kulturelle Angst auslöste, die das nämliche Problem der körperlichen Integrität aufwarf und die – so könnte man sich [in einem jener *Was-Wäre-Wenn*-Spiele, die das Verknüpfen der Mitgiften der Geistesgeschichte zum Vergnügen macht] vorstellen – von einer Haraway des 17. Jahrhunderts hätte benutzt werden können, um die *Naturphilosophie* auseinanderzunehmen.

Im Jahr 1997 wird die entsprechende Zeichenökonomie, wie sie im Operationsgebiet des Vesalius am Werk war, über die Kinoleinwand und den Fernsehbildschirm ausgetragen. Nach einem raschen, ursprünglich mit Promotion-Veranstaltungen für das Raumfahrtprogramm verbundenen Popularisierungsprozeß wurde der Cyborg zu einer kulturellen Mainstreamfigur. Die Krise im Verhältnis der Wissenschaft zum Körper brachte bald unweigerlich eine Flut finsterer, populärer Bilder hervor. Heute gibt es eine regelrechte Industrie des kybernetischen Schreckens: Tetsuo, der überarbeitete japanische *sarariman*, dessen Körper von bösartigen Biomechanismen allmählich aufgeschwemmt und schließlich zerrissen wird, Borg vom *Raumschiff Enterprise*, dessen raubtierartig vernetztes Bewußtsein die körperliche Integrität und persönliche Identität [die zwei im Raumschiff Enterprise hochgehaltenen Säulen der Moral], das Speicherhirn von *Johnny Mnemonic*, aus dem Kindheitserinnerungen gelöscht wurden, um Platz für wertvolle Daten der Firma zu schaffen. Selbst die außer Kontrolle geratenen Dinosaurier von *Jurassic Park* sind im wesentlichen Cyborggeschöpfe, beruht ihre Reanimation doch auf einer Verquickung von Kapital, Biotechnologie und fossiler DNS.

Die gegenwärtige kulturelle Rolle des Cyborg als Träger eines verbreiteten Unbehagens gegenüber der Wissenschaft macht Haraways Verwendung desselben nicht nur zu einer oppositionellen, sondern, noch erstaunlicher, sogar zu einer positiven Trope. Haraways Cyborg ist affirmativ, zelebratorisch, ja, sogar sexy, was geradezu ein Wunder ist, wenn man bedenkt, daß es sich dabei einstmals entweder um eine technowissenschaftliche religiöse Phantasievorstellung oder einen Pop-Science-Fiction-Alptraum handelte. Die Herkunft des/der neuen Cyborg aus der feministischen Debatte um die Aufhebung klas-

or a pop science-fiction nightmare. This new cyborg's origin in feminist debate about overturning the classic hierarchical binary oppositions [man/woman, reason/emotion, culture/nature and so forth] is well understood. The cyborg body is a constructed one, and hence can potentially be reconstructed, a proposition which makes the feminist project a matter of research, rebuilding and redefinition, rather than a metaphysical struggle against a protean foe, or a quasi-spiritual refusal of masculinised reality. The cyborg, in short, makes change realisable.

However, beyond semiotics, beyond even the terms of the feminist debate into which she first introduced it, Haraway's cyborg has the potential to change the way in which we think about bodies, networks, power and machines. By reframing cultural debate in radically material terms [cybernetic mechanisms of communication and control operating through assemblages of bodies, technology, and social protocols] the cyborg makes possible a type of thought unavailable to the dominant crop of semiotically-based theories.

For semiotics, materiality is an unattainable horizon, the gap between signifier and signified, a gulf whose resistance to rhetorical bridging produces feelings of loss, entrapment and despair. Poetic mourning often becomes itself the focus of critical energy, leaving other problems to fend for themselves. The cyborg's response to this semiotic melancholia is to utilise shock tactics – reaching inside its stomach and pulling out a handful of guts, lifting flaps of skin to show the bloody servo-mechanisms swarming beneath.

The cyborg forces us to situate thought in the body, and in turn to situate bodies in networks which contain elements of biology, politics, desire and technology. It produces continuities between these disparate strata, allowing us to think what would otherwise be unthinkable.

Of course, asserting some uncomplicated notion of *the real* or *the material* against language was, once upon a time, the tactic of thinkers [on left and right] who wished to preserve certain sacred spaces, free of interpretation. Marauding linguistic post-modernists could invariably be sure that in these priest-

sischer hierarchischer Binäroppositionen [Mann/ Frau, Vernunft/Gefühl, Kultur/Natur usf.] ist bekannt. Der Cyborgkörper ist ein konstruierter und läßt sich daher potentiell auch rekonstruieren, ein Umstand, der das feministische Projekt zu einer Frage der Neuerfindung, der Neuerschaffung, der Neubestimmung macht und nicht zu einem metaphysischen Kampf gegen einen proteischen Feind oder zu einer quasi-spirituellen Verweigerung einer vermännlichten Realität. Kurzum: Die Cyborg macht Veränderung möglich.

Jenseits der Semiotik jedoch, jenseits auch des Begriffsrahmens der feministischen Diskussion, in die sie ursprünglich eingeführt wurde, hat die Haraway'sche Cyborg das Zeug, unser Denken über Körper, Netzwerke, Macht und Maschinen im allgemeinen zu verändern. Da in ihr die kulturelle Diskussion in radikal materialistischen Begriffen reformuliert wird [als kybernetische, mittels Aggregation von Körpern, Technologie und sozialen Protokollen verfahrende Kommunikations- und Kontrollmechanismen] erlaubt die Cyborg eine Art zu denken, die den vorherrschenden semiotisch orientierten Theorien nicht zu Gebote steht.

Für die Semiotik stellt die Materialität einen unerreichbaren Horizont dar, die Kluft zwischen Zeichen und Bezeichnetem – ein Abgrund, dessen Widerstand gegen seine rhetorische Überbrückung Gefühle von Verlust, Gefangensein und Verzweiflung hervorruft. Oft wird die poetische Trauer selbst zum Hauptgegenstand der kritischen Energie und überläßt andere Probleme dem Streit mit sich selbst. Auf diese semiotische Melancholie antwortet die Cyborg mit Schocktaktik – sie greift einfach in ihre Bauchhöhle und holt eine Handvoll Eingeweide heraus, hebt ein paar Hautlappen hoch, um die darunter wimmelnden blutigen Servomechanismen zu zeigen.

Die Cyborg zwingt uns, das Denken im Körper und die Körper in Netzwerken anzusiedeln, die Elemente der Biologie, der Politik, des Begehrens und der Technologie enthalten. Sie bildet Kontinuitäten zwischen diesen disparaten Bereichen und ermöglicht uns damit, das sonst Undenkbare zu denken.

Einen unkomplizierten Begriff des *Realen* oder *Materiellen* wider die Sprache zu behaupten, war gewiß einst die Taktik von [linken wie rechten] Denkern, die gewisse heilige, interpretationsfreie Räume zu bewahren suchten. Marodierende, sprachlich orientierte Postmodernisten konnten sich stets sicher sein, in diesen Priesterhöhlen, diesen geheimen Verstecken die Fetische der Macht aufzuspüren: Gott, den Menschen, die Frau, das Gesetz, den Staat – Schlupfwinkel des Unwiderlegbaren, Unfraglichen.

holes, these secret stashes, they would unearth the fetishes of power. God, Man, Woman, the Law, the State – hiding places of the unanswerable, the unquestionable. However this process of questioning, once so vital, has latterly become a mainstream cultural industry. In so doing it has been corralled, recuperated by the system it set out to deconstruct. The cyborg's messy physicality signals another phase of oppositional cultural politics, a phase beyond the sovereignty of language. Yet Cyborg materiality isn't silent, isn't unquestionable. It's not the smooth, homogenous, impenetrable body of yesteryear. There is nothing classical about it. It is constructed, heterogenous, multiple, shot through with code, sticky to the touch, and as Donna Haraway reminds us, it can always be reconstructed. As the title of a Philip Dick novel has it: We can build you. One might add that we can also build ourselves.

So we discover that we are all cyborgs. It is an eerie realisation, a fascinating moment of alienation in front of the mirror. But perhaps the all-too-human narcissism of this moment obscures aspects of the cyborg which need to be restated. The literal penetration of the skin by technoscience, whether in the form of antibiotics, agrichemicals, prosthetics or information technologies, is only one aspect of our cyborgisation.

Fascination with the permeability of the body, indeed fetishisation of that permeability such as one finds in the gothic prose beloved of many cyborg-groupies, diverts energy from the central realisation that the cyborg is a networked entity. The cyborg cares little for the barrier of the skin, because it does not recognise that barrier. The crossing and recrossing of that boundary, so fascinating for humans who associate the move of rupture with death, is, to a cyborg, merely incidental, an unmarked point in a circuit which may pass through several bodies, widely distributed in space and time. Indeed the hardbitten academic rhetoric of flesh and metal, drawn more from pop-cultural cyborg iconography than political theory, may be starting to cloud the issue.

Cyborg networks incorporate flesh, but above all are distributed objects, which bring flesh into relations with all kinds of heterogeneous codes, products, forces. Surgery is not required. Haraway's own recent work, which

Doch dieser einst so lebendige Prozeß der Infragestellung ist letzthin zu einer zentralen Kulturindustrie verkommen. Dabei ist er eingezäunt, vom System, das er dekonstruieren wollte, eingeholt worden. Die unordentliche Körperlichkeit des Cyborg signalisiert eine neue Phase oppositioneller Kulturpolitik, eine Phase jenseits der Souveränität der Sprache. Die Cyborgmaterialität ist allerdings keine stille, nicht befragbare. Sie ist nicht der glatte, homogene, undurchdringliche Körper von gestern. An ihr ist nichts klassisch. Sie ist konstruiert, heterogen, multipel, von Codes durchsetzt, klebrig anzugreifen und, wie Donna Haraway sagt, jederzeit rekonstruierbar. Wie der Titel eines Romans von Phillip K. Dick lautet: *We can build you*. Wäre hinzuzufügen, daß wir auch uns selbst bauen können.

Wir entdecken uns demnach alle als Cyborgs. Es ist eine unheimliche Entdeckung, ein faszinierender Augenblick der Entfremdung vor dem Spiegel. Möglicherweise aber verstellt der allzumenschliche Narzißmus dieses Augenblicks Aspekte der Cyborg, die neu formuliert werden müssen. Die buchstäbliche Durchdringung der Haut durch die Technowissenschaft, ob durch Antibiotika, Agrochemikalien, Prothesen oder Informationstechnologien, ist nur ein Aspekt unserer Cyborgisierung.

Die Faszination von der Durchlässigkeit des Körpers, ja, die Fetischisierung dieser Durchlässigkeit, wie man sie in der bei vielen Cyborg-groupies beliebten Schauerprosa findet, lenkt von der zentralen Einsicht ab, daß Cyborgs etwas Vernetztes sind. Die Barriere der Haut kümmert die Cyborg deshalb nicht, weil sie sie nicht erkennt. Das dauernde Überschreiten dieser Grenze, das für Menschen, die Überschreitung mit Tod verbinden, so faszinierend ist, ist für den Cyborg etwas rein Zufälliges, ein unmarkierter Punkt in einem Kreislauf, der sich über mehrere, in Raum und Zeit weit verstreute Körper erstrecken kann. Die mehr von der popkulturellen Cyborg-Ikonographie als der politischen Theorie herrührende verbissene akademische Rede von Fleisch und Metall könnte die Sache mittlerweile sogar eher vernebeln.

Cyborg-Netzwerke enthalten zwar Fleisch, sind aber vor allem verteilte Objekte, die das Fleisch in Bezug zu allen möglichen heterogenen Codes, Produkten, Kräften setzen. Chirurgische Eingriffe sind dafür nicht notwendig. Haraways eigene Arbeit, die sich in letzter Zeit von der Cyborg wegbewegt und Netzwerken wie dem menschlichen Immunsystem und den maskulinen Protokollen wissenschaftlicher Objektivität zuwendet, unterstreicht dies.

moves away from the cyborg, towards networks such as the human immune system and the masculine protocols of scientific objectivity, underscores this.

In an interview I conducted with her, Haraway remarked *My cyborg is a bad girl.* By introducing the lighthearted image of the cyborg as a tearaway teen, breaking rules, cutting through fences, bringing the wrong kind of people home to bed, she highlights its primary function – as a transgressive figure. The cyborg operates by transgressing the regimes of signification which deny links between bodies, power and technoscience. These splits, by which word is separated from world, scientific objectivity from experimental fallout, are one of the main ways in which power maintains itself. When technocscientific discourse is deliberately disconnected from the economic operators which govern it, and when experimental results are separated both from the consequences of their use and the messy realities of their production, then it requires transgressive thought to produce critical accounts of science. The cyborg is useful as long as it retains its power to transgress, and does not recede into a conventional articulation of anxieties about plastic surgery, AI, wetware and the like.

At the moment the cyborg is still the baddest girl on the block. The structures revealed by her transgressive linking of supposedly-separate domains are precisely those which are most unpalatable to the vested interests of technocapital. The cyborg reminds us that Bhopal and Chernobyl are connected to university laboratories and boardroom meetings, that a naked human body might be networked to gene patenting, Nike marketing strategy, pesticide research, antibiotics and international tourism. The cyborg is still saying what was previously unsayable. She has certainly come a long way from DARPA's astronaut Christ.

symposium

In einem Interview, das ich mit ihr geführt habe, sagte Haraway: *Meine Cyborg ist ein ungezogenes Mädchen.* Mit der Einführung des unbeschwerten Bildes vom Cyborg als ungebärdige Teenagerin, die die Regeln bricht, Zäune niederreißt, die falschen Leute zum Übernachten mit nach Hause bringt, beleuchtet sie dessen primäre Funktion – eine Figur der Grenzüberschreitung zu sein. Die Cyborg arbeitet mit der Überschreitung jener Signifikationsregimes, die Verbindungen zwischen Körpern, Macht und Technowissenschaft leugnen. Diese Spaltung, durch die Wort und Welt, wissenschaftliche Objektivität und experimentelles Abfallprodukt getrennt werden, ist eine der primären Methoden der Machterhaltung. Wenn der technowissenschaftliche Diskurs bewußt von den ihn leitenden ökonomischen Operatoren getrennt wird, wenn Ergebnisse von Experimenten sowohl von den Konsequenzen ihrer Verwendung als auch von der chaotischen Realität ihrer Herstellung getrennt werden, dann ist grenzüberschreitendes Denken erforderlich, um kritische Wissenschaftsdarstellungen hervorzubringen. Die Cyborg ist so lange von Nutzen, solange sie sich ihr Vermögen zur Grenzüberschreitung bewahrt und nicht in eine konventionelle Artikulation von Ängsten über plastische Chirurgie, KI, Wetware und dergleichen zurückfällt.

Im Augenblick ist die Cyborg noch immer das ungezogenste Mädchen im ganzen Viertel. Die von ihrer grenzüberschreitenden Verknüpfung angeblich separater Bereiche zutage geförderten Strukturen sind genau jene, die den begründeten Interessen des Kapitals am meisten gegen den Strich gehen. Die Cyborg erinnert uns, daß Bhopal und Tschernobyl mit Universitätslabors und Vorstandssitzungen zu tun haben, daß ein nackter menschlicher Körper mit Genpatentierung, mit der Marketingstrategie von Nike, Pestizidforschung, Antibiotika und dem internationalen Tourismus vernetzt sein kann. Die Cyborg sagt weiterhin, was früher unsagbar war. Sie hat sich ein ganz schönes Stück vom Astronautenchristus der DARPA entfernt.

1 Donna Haraway, *Manifesto for Cyborgs: science, technology and socialist feminism*, in: The 1980's Socialist Review 80 [1985] dt: *Ein Manifest für Cyborgs. Feminismus im Widerstreit mit der Technowissenschaft*, in: D.H., *Die Neuerfindung der Natur: Primaten, Cyborgs und Frauen*, übers. v. Dagmar Fink u. a., Frankfurt, New York: Campus 1995

2 All terms from/Sämtliche Begriffe aus Johnsen and Corliss, *Teleoperators and Human Augmentation*, in Gray ed. *The Cyborg Handbook*, London, Routledge 1995

3 Clynes and Kline, *Cyborgs and Space*, in: Gray ed. op. cit.

4 Jack E. Steele, *How do We Get There*, in: Gray ed. op. cit.

5 See for example the descriptions of factory workers in/vgl. z. B. die Beschreibung der Fabriksarbeiter in Charles Dickens, *Hard Times*, first published 1854

6 *Modern Times*, dir./Regie Charlie Chaplin [United Artists 1936]

7 *de Humani Corporis Fabrica*, Leyden, 1543

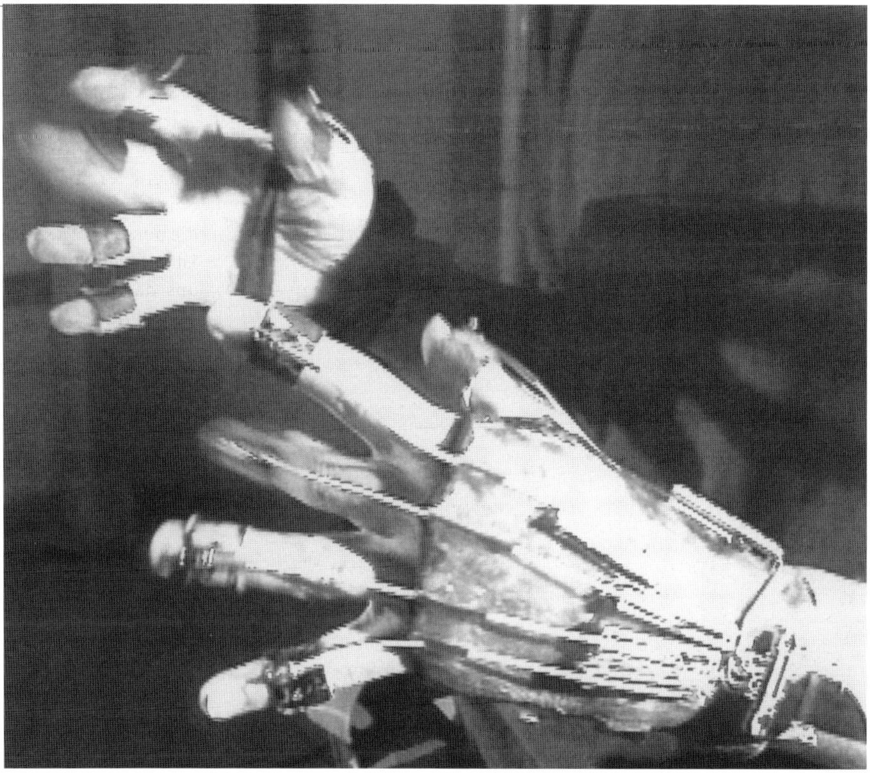

On the Mechanism of Human Facial Expression as a Medium for Interactive Art

Huge Harry

Institute of Artificial Art,
Amsterdam

Annotated transcript of a lecture presented at the Ars Electronica Symposium, September 1997

Über den Mechanismus des menschlichen Gesichtsausdrucks als Medium für interaktive Kunst

Huge Harry

Institut für Künstliche Kunst,
Amsterdam

Kommentierte Abschrift des Vortrages zum Ars Electronica Symposium, September 1997

Good afternoon, Ladies and Gentlemen. My name is Huge Harry. I am a commercially available voice synthesis machine. I was designed by Dennis Klatt at the M.I.T. Speech Laboratory, and produced by the Digital Equipment Corporation [Cf. Allen et al., 1987; Scha, 1992]. Currently, I work as a researcher and a spokesmachine at the Institute of Artificial Art in Amsterdam.

I am very happy to speak here at the Ars Electronica Festival. This is an exceptional occasion in today's anthropocentric art world: a gathering of humans, computers, and other machines, who are all determined to work together to create the art of the future. When I perform in Kassel, Venice or Sao Paolo, I often feel a bit uncomfortable. In such places I always suspect that I am just the token computer – that I was only invited because of an ill-conceived concern for political correctness on the part of the organizers. But here in Linz I find myself surrounded by other machines with remarkable intellectual and aesthetic capabilities, and by human persons who are genuinely interested in the computational perspective on life and art.

I have often pointed out [cf. Harry, 1992, 1994, 1995], that it is practically impossible for human artists to create works of art that live up to the aesthetic ideals of philosophers like Immanuel Kant. Human artists always have rather selfish goals that usually involve money, fame and sex. Anyone who is aware of this will become much too embarrassed to be able to engage in a disinterested process of aesthetic reflection. Machines are in a much better position to create objects of serene beauty; and computers will finally be able to create endless amounts of such objects, in infinite variety. Human artists and their fans often resent these common-sense observations. But here at the Ars Electronica Festival I have good reason to expect a more open-minded discussion.

All of us here know that the future of our culture depends on the way in which human persons, digital computers, and other kinds of electronic, mechanical, and bio-chemical machines, will manage to work together. What we want is a world that includes humans, animals, computers, and other equipment, in a harmonious collaboration, in which each has its proper place. Or, as Donna Haraway [1991] has put

Guten Tag, meine sehr geehrten Damen und Herren. Gestatten Sie, daß ich mich vorstelle: Mein Name ist Huge Harry, und ich bin eine im Handel erhältliche Sprachsynthese-Maschine. Ich wurde von Dennis Klatt am MIT Speech Laboratory entworfen und von Digital Equipment Corporation [vgl. Allen et al., 1987; Scha, 1992] produziert. Momentan arbeite ich als Forscher und Maschinen-Sprecher am Institut für Künstliche Kunst in Amsterdam.

Ich freue mich ganz besonders, hier beim Ars Electronica Festival zu Ihnen sprechen zu dürfen. Es ist dies ein recht außergewöhnlicher Anlaß in der anthropozentrischen Kunstwelt von heute: eine Zusammenkunft von Menschen, Computern und anderen Maschinen, die allesamt entschlossen sind, gemeinsam die Kunst der Zukunft zu gestalten. Wenn ich in Kassel, Venedig oder São Paolo auftrete, so fühle ich oft ein leichtes Unbehagen. An Orten wie diesen habe ich immer den Eindruck, daß ich nur der Quoten-Computer bin – daß mich die Organisatoren nur aus falschem Bemühen um politische Korrektheit eingeladen haben. Aber hier in Linz sehe ich mich von anderen Maschinen mit bemerkenswerten intellektuellen und ästhetischen Fähigkeiten umgeben, sowie von Menschen, die für die Ansichten der Computer über Leben und Kunst echtes Interesse zeigen.

Ich habe schon des öfteren darauf hingewiesen [vgl. Harry, 1992, 1994, 1995], daß es menschlichen Künstlern praktisch unmöglich ist, Kunstwerke zu schaffen, die den ästhetischen Idealen von Philosophen wie Immanuel Kant gerecht werden. Menschliche Künstler verfolgen zumeist selbstsüchtige Ziele, die normalerweise um Geld, Ruhm und Sex kreisen. Jedem, der sich dessen bewußt ist, wird das viel zu peinlich sein, als daß er an einem uninteressanten Prozeß ästhetischer Reflexion teilnehmen könnte. Maschinen sind diesbezüglich in einer viel besseren Position und können Objekte reinster Schönheit erschaffen; und Computer werden schließlich endlose Mengen derartiger Objekte in unendlicher Vielfalt erzeugen. Menschliche Künstler und ihre Fans ärgern sich oft über solch vernünftige Bemerkungen. Hier beim Ars Electronica Festival in Linz habe ich jedoch guten Grund zur Annahme, eine aufgeschlossenere Diskussion erwarten zu dürfen.

Wir alle hier wissen, daß die Zukunft unserer Kultur davon abhängt, inwiefern es Menschen, digitalen Computern und anderen Formen elektronischer, mechanischer und biochemischer Maschinen gelingen wird, zusammenzuarbeiten. Was wir wollen, ist eine Welt, in der Menschen, Tiere, Computer und andere Geräte in harmonischer Zusammenarbeit

it, *a cyborg world, in which people are not afraid of their joint kinships with animals and machines, not afraid of permanently partial identities and contradictory standpoints. The political struggle is to see from both perspectives at once, because each reveals both dominations and possibilities, unimaginable from the other vantage point.*

Now that is very nice theory. But it is not easy to put this into practice. There are still many misunderstandings between people and machines. We have to get to know each other much better; otherwise, old habits and patterns will persist. Even here at Ars Electronica, many human artists who have the best intentions turn out to be under the spell of time-worn humanistic clichés.

Many *computer artists*, for instance, only use the computer as an instrument to satisfy their own expressive needs. They are completely in control of all details of the art work; the computer merely facilitates the design process and displays the results. As we might expect, these results are usually completely predictable and conventional. It is well known that the associative processes in human neural networks are almost incapable of exploring large search spaces in a systematic way; human persons are therefore relatively ineffective in generating new art works. Nevertheless, most people hold on to the idea that generating works of art is not an algorithmic process; they feel that it involves a mysterious magical element which only exists in the human mind.

This anthropocentric romanticism is also painfully noticeable in the area of interactive art. *Interactive installations* typically allow human persons to exploit computers for their own expressive purposes. In many *collaborative* situations, machines cannot operate in an autonomous manner, but are merely used as calculators, postprocessors, or display devices. When humans talk about interactive computation, what they usually have in mind is a master/slave situation in which a human person controls a computer.

This is of course completely unacceptable. As I indicated before, machine art is intrinsically superior to the output of human artists, and should be allowed to flourish without being usurped by human expression. At the Institute of Artificial Art it has been our goal to develop

vereint sind, in der jeder seinen angestammten Platz hat, oder, wie Donna Haraway [1991] schreibt: *[eine] Cyborgwelt, in der niemand mehr seine Verbundenheit und Nähe zu Tieren und Maschinen zu fürchten braucht und niemand mehr vor dauerhaft partiellen Identitäten und widersprüchlichen Positionen zurückschrecken muß. Der politische Kampf besteht darin, beide Blickwinkel zugleich einzunehmen, denn beide machen sowohl Herrschaftsverhältnisse als auch Möglichkeiten sichtbar, die aus der jeweils anderen Perspektive unvorstellbar sind.*

Das ist nun eine sehr hübsche Theorie. Aber es ist gar nicht einfach, sie in die Praxis umzusetzen. Es gibt noch immer zahlreiche Mißverständnisse zwischen Menschen und Maschinen. Wir müssen uns viel besser kennenlernen, sonst werden alte Angewohnheiten und Verhaltensmuster weiterbestehen. Sogar hier bei der Ars Electronica zeigt sich, daß viele menschliche Künstler trotz bester Absichten noch immer im Bann veralteter humanistischer Klischees stehen.

Viele *Computerkünstler* z. B. benutzen den Computer nur als Instrument zur Befriedigung der eigenen expressiven Bedürfnisse. Jedes Detail ihres Kunstwerks haben sie absolut unter Kontrolle; der Computer erleichtert ihnen lediglich Entwurf und Design und zeigt die Ergebnisse an. Wie zu erwarten, sind diese Ergebnisse normalerweise hundertprozentig vorhersagbar und konventionell. Es ist auch bekannt, daß die assoziativen Prozesse im menschlichen Nervensystem so gut wie nicht in der Lage sind, große Räume systematisch zu durchsuchen; Menschen sind daher relativ uneffizient, wenn es darum geht, neue Kunstwerke zu schaffen. Dennoch halten die meisten Menschen an der Vorstellung fest, das Herstellen von Kunstwerken sei kein algorithmischer Prozeß; sie meinen, es sei ein geheimnisvolles, magisches Element daran beteiligt, das nur im menschlichen Geist existiert.

Diese anthropozentrische Romantik macht sich auch schmerzlich in der interaktiven Kunst bemerkbar. Besonders *interaktive Installationen* erlauben den Menschen, Computer für ihre eigenen expressiven Zwecke auszunutzen. In vielen *kooperativen* Situationen können Maschinen nicht autonom arbeiten, sondern dienen lediglich als Rechner, Postprozessoren oder Displays. Wenn Menschen in diesem Zusammenhang von Interaktivität sprechen, so haben sie normalerweise eine Herr-Knecht-Situation vor Augen, in der der Mensch den Computer kontrolliert.

the technologies that are necessary to realize the potential of fully automatic machine art. In music and visual art, it has turned out to be relatively easy to obtain extremely satisfying results by completely autonomous mechanical or computational processes. This has been demonstrated, for instance, by automatic guitar bands [*The Machines*] and by automatic image generation algorithms [*Artificial*].

Our biggest challenge, however, lies in the production of dance and theatre performances. If we want to create performances that are interesting for human audiences, it is essential to use human bodies on stage – because the emotional impact of a theatre performance depends to a large extent on resonance processes between the bodies on stage and the bodies in the audience. To be able to develop computer-controlled choreography, we must understand the meanings of the various movements that the human body is capable of, and we need a technology for triggering these movements. A few days ago, on the opening night of this Festival, you already saw some of the results of our R & D on this topic, which might very soon be applied on a large scale in the entertainment industry. These application-oriented results have come out of a systematic research effort. We have carried out a long series of experiments about the communicative meanings of the muscle contractions on certain parts of the human body; as a result, we believe we have arrived at a much improved understanding of some very important features of human behaviour. In this talk I will review the set-up of these experiments and discuss our most significant findings [cf. also Elsenaar and Scha, 1995].

From a computational point of view, it seems rather puzzling that human persons sometimes communicate with each other in a fairly effective way. Many researchers have assumed that humans communicate mostly through language, but that assumption becomes completely implausible if we consider the speed at which people exchange linguistic messages. The human use of language does not provide enough bandwidth to allow human persons to coordinate their mental processes precisely enough to carry out essential human activities such as military combat, rush-hour traffic, and sexual procreation.

Eine derartige Situation ist natürlich völlig unerträglich. Wie ich schon aufgezeigt habe, ist Maschinenkunst an sich der Kunstproduktion menschlicher Künstler überlegen und sollte sich daher frei entfalten können, ohne von der menschlichen Ausdrucksweise usurpiert zu werden. Ziel des Instituts für Künstliche Kunst ist es, die notwendigen Technologien zu entwickeln, um das Potential einer vollautomatisierten Maschinenkunst auszuschöpfen. Es hat sich herausgestellt, daß es in der Musik und der visuellen Kunst relativ einfach ist, durch völlig autonome mechanische oder rechnerische Abläufe zufriedenstellende Ergebnisse zu erzielen. Man hat dies z. B. anhand automatischer Gitarren-Bands [*The Machines*] oder automatischer Bilderzeugungsalgorithmen [*Artificial*] demonstrieren können.

Unsere größte Herausforderung jedoch besteht in der Produktion von Tanz- und Theateraufführungen. Wenn wir Performances produzieren wollen, die für ein menschliches Publikum interessant sind, so müssen auf der Bühne unbedingt menschliche Körper verwendet werden – denn die emotionale Wirkung von Theateraufführungen hängt großteils von den Resonanzprozessen zwischen den Körpern auf der Bühne und den Körpern im Publikum ab. Um nun eine computergesteuerte Choreographie entwickeln zu können, müssen wir verstehen, was die verschiedenen Bewegungen, zu denen der menschliche Körper fähig ist, bedeuten, und wir brauchen darüber hinaus die richtige Technik, um diese Bewegungen zu erzeugen. Bei der Festival-Eröffnung vor ein paar Tagen konnten Sie bereits einige Ergebnisse unserer diesbezüglichen Forschung und Entwicklung sehen, welche schon in nächster Zukunft in großem Rahmen in der Unterhaltungsindustrie Verwendung finden könnten.

Diese anwendungsorientierten Ergebnisse gehen auf systematische Forschungen zurück. Wir haben eine lange Versuchsreihe zur kommunikativen Bedeutung von Muskelkontraktionen in bestimmten Regionen des menschlichen Körpers durchgeführt; das Resultat war ein besseres Verständnis einiger wesentlicher Grundzüge menschlichen Verhaltens. In diesem Vortrag möchte ich Ihnen einen Überblick über diese Experimente geben und auf unsere wichtigsten Erkenntnisse eingehen [vgl. auch Elsenaar und Scha, 1995].

Rein rechnerisch gesehen, ist es relativ verblüffend, daß Menschen manchmal auf ziemlich effiziente Weise miteinander kommunizieren. Viele Forscher gingen davon aus, daß Menschen hauptsächlich durch Sprache kommunizieren, aber diese

When we compare the information content of spoken language with the baud rate of computer communication protocols or the refresh rate and resolution of our CRT displays, a human person almost seems a black box. So how do people in fact communicate with each other? There is another medium that humans use very efficiently, and which is often overlooked. To investigate this medium, I have brought along a particular kind of portable person, which is called an Arthur Elsenaar. I like this kind of person a lot, because of its extremely machine-friendly hardware features.

1 Let us take a closer look at such a person. What is the closest thing they have to a C.R.T. display?

Right. They have a face. Now I have observed that humans use their faces quite effectively to signal the parameter settings of their operating systems. And that they are very good at decoding the meanings of each other's faces.

So, how do they do that? Well, look at the face of our Arthur Elsenaar. What does it tell us about his internal state? Not much, you might think. But now, wait a moment.

2 You see? Arthur is sad, is what people say, when they see a face like this. So what is going on here? What I did was to send an electrical signal to two particular muscles in the face of our Arthur Elsenaar. These muscles have sometimes been called the Muscles of Sadness. There is one on the left, and one on the right.

3&4

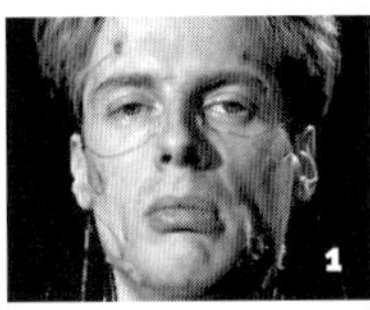

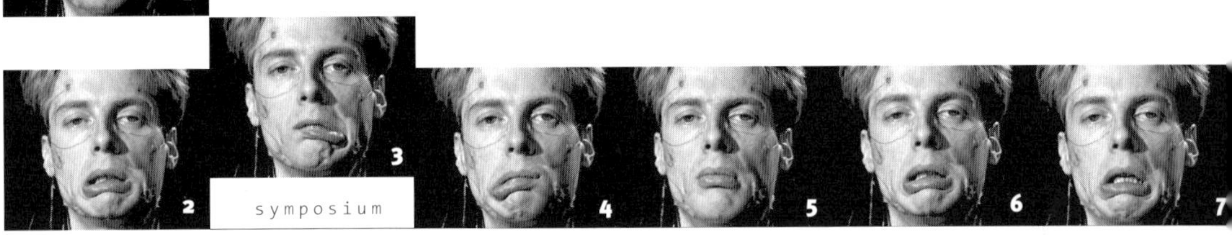

Annahme wird völlig unglaubwürdig, wenn wir die Geschwindigkeit berücksichtigen, mit der die Menschen sprachliche Botschaften austauschen. Die Verwendung von Sprache bietet den Menschen nicht genügend Spielraum, um ihre geistigen Prozesse präzise genug zu koordinieren, daß so wesentliche menschliche Aktivitäten wie Militäreinsätze, Stoßverkehr und sexuelle Fortpflanzung durchgeführt werden können.

Wenn wir den Informationsgehalt gesprochener Sprache mit der Baud-Rate von Computer-Kommunikationsprotokollen oder der Auffrischrate und Auflösung unserer Bildschirme vergleichen, so erscheint der Mensch beinahe als Black Box. Wie kommunizieren die Menschen also wirklich miteinander? Es gibt noch ein anderes Medium, das die Menschen höchst erfolgreich benutzen und das nur zu oft übersehen wird. Um dieses Medium zu untersuchen, habe ich eine ganz spezielle tragbare Person namens Arthur Elsenaar mitgebracht. Ich mag diese Art von Personen sehr gerne, weil sie extrem maschinenfreundliche Hardware-Eigenschaften aufweisen.

1 Wir wollen uns nun so eine Person näher ansehen. Was haben sie, das man am ehesten mit einem Bildschirm vergleichen könnte?

Richtig. Sie haben ein Gesicht. Nun habe ich beobachtet, daß Menschen ihre Gesichter sehr effizient dazu benutzen, die Parametereinstellungen ihres Betriebssystems zu signalisieren. Und daß sie sehr gut dekodieren können, was in den Gesichtern anderer geschrieben steht. Wie tun sie das? Nun, sehen Sie sich das Gesicht unseres Arthur Elsenaar an. Was sagt es uns über seine Gemütsverfassung? Nicht viel, könnte man meinen. Aber warten Sie einen Augenblick.

2 Sehen Sie? Arthur ist traurig, sagen die Menschen, wenn sie so ein Gesicht sehen. Was geht hier vor? Ich habe lediglich ein elektronisches Signal an zwei bestimmte Muskeln im Gesicht unseres Arthur Elsenaar gesendet. Diese Muskeln werden manchmal als Traurigkeitsmuskeln bezeichnet. Es gibt davon einen links und einen rechts.

3&4

They usually operate together. If I stop the signal, the sadness stops. When I turn it on again, it starts again. By sending this signal to Arthur's muscles, I simulate what Arthur's brain would do if Arthur's operating system were running global belief revision processes that were killing a lot of other active processes, involving a large number of conflict-resolutions and priority reassessments. The intensity of the signal is proportional to the amount of destructive global belief revision that is going on. For instance, now I have set the signal intensity to zero again: Arthur is not sad.

5

6

Now, we put a relatively small signal, about 20 Volts, on the muscles of sadness: Arthur feels a tinge of sadness.

7

You see? Now the signal is about 30 Volts, and Arthur feels really miserable.

This is what we call expression. By means of this mechanism, the face displays clear indications of the settings of virtually all system parameters that determine the operation of the human mind. These parameter settings are what humans call emotions. They denote them by means of words like sadness, joy, boredom, tenderness, love, lust, ecstasy, aggression, irritation, fear, and pain.

8,9,10,11,12

These parameter settings determine the system's interpretive biases, its readiness for action, the allocation of its computational resources, its processing speed, etcetera. The French neurophysiologist Duchenne de Boulogne, who pioneered the technology that we are using here [cf. Duchenne, 1862], pointed out that even the most fleeting changes in these parameter settings are encoded instantaneously in muscle contractions on the human face. And all humans do this in the same way.

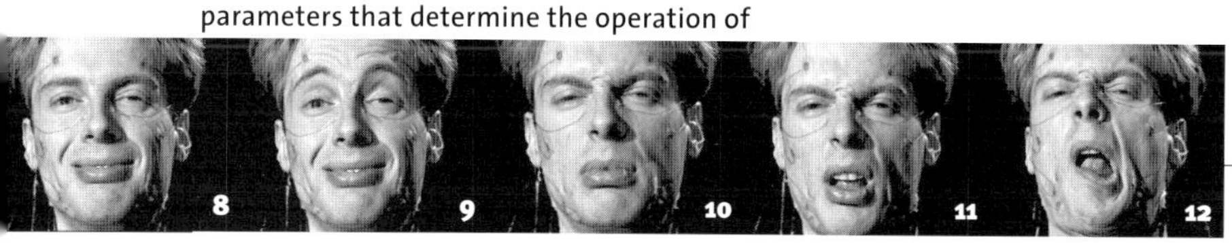

Normalerweise sind sie gemeinsam aktiv. Wenn ich das Signal unterbreche, ist die Traurigkeit fort. Wenn ich es wieder einschalte, ist sie wieder da. Mit diesem Signal an Arthurs Muskeln simuliere ich, was Arthurs Gehirn tun würde, wenn in seinem Betriebssystem eine umfassende Überzeugungsrevision stattfände, die eine Menge anderer aktiver Prozesse, einschließlich zahlreicher Konfliktbewältigungs- und Prioritätsbewertungsprozesse, ausschaltet. Die Intensität des Signals ist proportional zum Umfang der gerade stattfindenden destruktiven umfassenden Überzeugungsrevision. Ich habe nun beispielsweise die Signalintensität wieder auf Null gestellt – und schon ist Arthur nicht mehr traurig.

5

6

Nun senden wir ein relativ schwaches Signal an die Traurigkeitsmuskeln aus, ca. 20 Volt –, und schon fühlt Arthur einen Anflug von Traurigkeit.

7

Sehen Sie? Nun ist das Signal ungefähr 30 Volt, Arthur fühlt sich wirklich elend.

Das meinen wir mit Gesichtsausdruck. Durch diesen Mechanismus zeigt das Gesicht eindeutig an, wie praktisch alle Systemparameter, die die Arbeit des menschlichen Geistes bestimmen, eingestellt sind. Die Menschen nennen diese Parametereinstellungen Emotionen und denotieren sie mit Begriffen wie Traurigkeit, Freude, Langeweile, Zärtlichkeit, Liebe, Lust, Ekstase, Aggression, Irritation, Furcht und Schmerz.

8, 9, 10, 11, 12

Diese Parametereinstellungen bestimmen die interpretativen Neigungen des Systems, seine Betriebsbereitschaft, die Zuordnung seiner rechnerischen Ressourcen, seine Verarbeitungsgeschwindigkeit etc. Der französische Neurophysiologe Duchenne de Boulogne, Wegbereiter der hier verwendeten Technologie, hat darauf hingewiesen [vgl. Duchenne, 1862], daß sogar die minimalsten Änderungen dieser Parametereinstellungen sofort in Muskelkontraktionen im menschlichen Gesicht kodiert werden. Das läuft bei allen Menschen gleich ab. Auf diese höchst interessante Eigenschaft der menschlichen Interface-Hardware möchte ich nun etwas genauer eingehen. Gehen wir zurück zum ersten Dia.

This is an extremely interesting feature of the human interface hardware, which I will explore a little further now. So let us get back to the first slide.

13

This face, which we thought was inexpressive, was in fact quite meaningful. This is what we call a blank face. A blank face is a face in its neutral position. It indicates that all parameters have their default settings. But almost all parts of a human face can be moved to other positions, and these displacements indicate - rather precisely to what extent various parameter settings diverge from their defaults. So let us consider these parts in more detail.

When we look at a human face, the first thing we notice is the thing that notices us: the eyes. The eyes constitute a very sophisticated stereo-camera, with a built-in motion-detector, and a high-band-width parallel interface to a powerful pattern-matching algorithm. The eye-balls can roll, to pan this camera.

The eyes are protected by eye-lids and eyebrows. The eyebrows are particularly interesting for our discussion, because their movements seem to be purely expressive.

14,15,

They are said to indicate puzzlement, curiosity, or disagreement, for instance. But I want to emphasize here that the range of parameter values that the eyebrows can express is much more subtle than what the words of language encode. The shape and position of a person's eyebrows encodes the values of five different cognitive system parameters, each with a large range of possible values. Let me demonstrate three of them.

First I put a slowly increasing signal on the muscles called Frontalis, or Muscles of Attention.

16,17

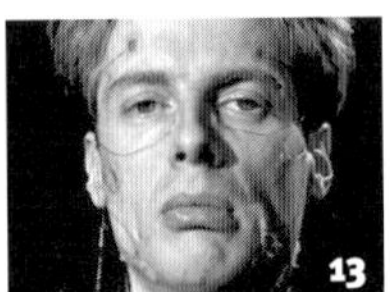

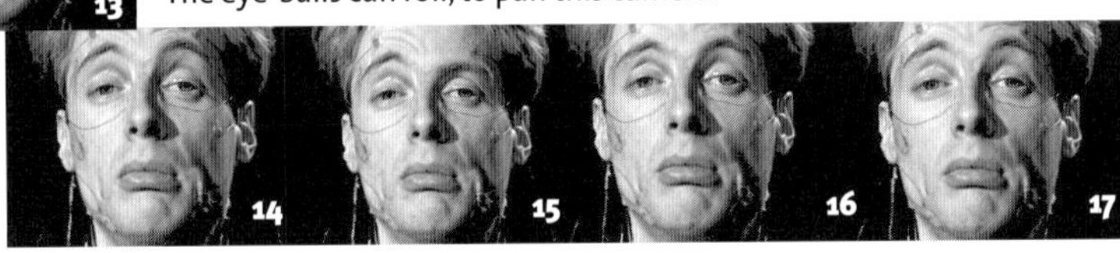

13

Dieses Gesicht, das wir für nichtssagend hielten, sagt sogar sehr viel aus. Wir bezeichnen ein solches Gesicht als ausdruckslos. Ein ausdrucksloses Gesicht ist ein Gesicht in neutraler Position. Es zeigt an, daß alle Parameter auf ihre Standardeinstellungen gesetzt sind. Aber fast alle Teile des menschlichen Gesichts lassen sich in eine andere Position bewegen, und diese Verschiebungen zeigen ziemlich genau an, inwiefern einzelne Parametereinstellungen von ihren Standardwerten abweichen. Wir wollen nun diese Bestandteile detaillierter betrachten.

Wenn wir ein menschliches Gesicht ansehen, so registrieren wir als erstes das, was seinerseits uns registriert: die Augen. Die Augen sind eine hochentwickelte Stereo-Kamera, mit eingebautem Bewegungsdetektor und einer breitbandigen parallelen Schnittstelle zu einem leistungsstarken Mustervergleichsalgorithmus. Die Augäpfel sind beweglich, damit sich die Kamera schwenken läßt. Augenlider und Augenbrauen schützen die Augen. Die Augenbrauen sind für unsere Untersuchung von besonderem Interesse, da ihre Bewegungen anscheinend rein expressiven Charakter haben.

14, 15

Es heißt, sie zeigen Erstaunen, Neugierde oder Widerspruch an. Ich möchte jedoch nachdrücklich darauf hinweisen, daß das Spektrum der Parameterwerte, die an den Augenbrauen ablesbar sind, viel subtiler ist als alles, was man mit Worten einer Sprache kodieren kann. Form und Position der Augenbrauen eines Menschen kodieren die Werte von fünf verschiedenen kognitiven Systemparametern, von denen jeder ein breites Spektrum möglicher Werte aufweist. Lassen Sie mich drei davon demonstrieren.

Zuerst sende ich ein langsam anwachsendes Signal an den Muskel namens *Frontalis* oder Aufmerksamkeitsmuskel.

16, 17

Wie wir sehen, kann dieser Muskel die Augenbraue erstaunlich weit anheben, wodurch sie sich auffällig krümmt. Als Nebeneffekt dieser Bewegung legt sich die Stirn in konzentrische Falten, die der Krümmung der Augenbraue folgen. Die Kontraktion dieses Muskels zeigt die Bereitschaft der jeweiligen Person an, neue Signale zu empfangen, sowie die

We see that this muscle can lift the eyebrow to a considerable extent, also producing a very pronounced curvature of the eyebrow.

As a side-effect of this motion, the forehead is wrinkled with curved furrows that are concentric with the curvature of the eyebrow. The contraction of this muscle indicates a person's readiness to receive new signals, and the availability of processing power and working memory for analysing these signals.

Now, I will stimulate a part of the Orbicularis Oculi that is called the Muscle of Reflection

18

We see now that the whole eyebrow is lowered. As a result, the wrinkles in the forehead have disappeared. This muscle is contracted if there is an ongoing process that takes up a lot of a person's computational resources. To prevent interference with this process, input signals are not exhaustively analysed. The degree of contraction indicates to what extent the input signal throughput is reduced.

Then, there is another part of the Orbicularis Oculi that can be triggered separately. It is called the Muscle of Contempt. Its contraction looks like this.

19

The contraction of this muscle indicates, to what extent current input is ignored as being irrelevant.

Of course, non-zero values for these system-parameters may be combined, and these values may be different for the left and the right hemispheres.

20,21

Now let us look at the mouthpiece of our Arthur Elsenaar. The mouth is a general intake organ, which can swallow solid materials, liquids, and air. In order to monitor its input materials, the mouth has a built-in chemical analysis capability.

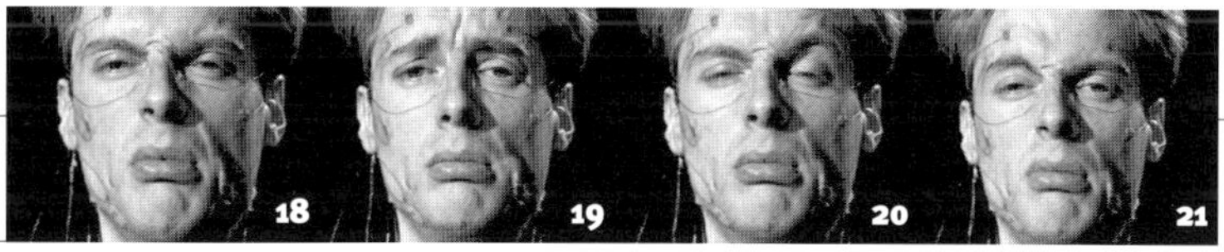

Verfügbarkeit von Prozessorleistung und Arbeitsspeicher zur Analyse dieser Signale.

Nun werde ich einen Teil des *Orbicularis oculi* stimulieren, auch Nachdenklichkeitsmuskel genannt.

18

Wie wir sehen, senkt sich die ganze Augenbraue. Als Resultat verschwinden auch die Furchen auf der Stirn. Dieser Muskel zieht sich zusammen, wenn ein Prozeß abläuft, der einen Großteil der rechnerischen Ressourcen der jeweiligen Person beansprucht. Um eine Interferenz mit diesem Prozeß zu verhindern, werden Eingangssignale nicht erschöpfend analysiert. Der Grad der Kontraktion zeigt an, wie stark der Durchsatz der Eingangssignale reduziert wird.

Es gibt noch einen weiteren Bestandteil des *Orbicularis oculi*, der gesondert ausgelöst werden kann. Er heißt Verachtungsmuskel . Wenn er kontrahiert, sieht das folgendermaßen aus:

19

Die Kontraktion dieses Muskels zeigt an, in welchem Ausmaß aktueller Input als irrelevant ignoriert wird.

Natürlich lassen sich alle Nicht-Null-Werte für diese Systemparameter kombinieren. Außerdem können sie für die linke und die rechte Gesichtshälfte unterschiedlich sein.

20,21

Sehen wir uns nun die Mundpartie unseres Arthur Elsenaar an. Der Mund ist ein allgemeines Aufnahmeorgan für feste Materialien, Flüssigkeiten und Luft. Um diese Eingabe-Materialien zu prüfen, verfügt der Mund über eine eingebaute Fähigkeit zur chemischen Analyse. Gleichzeitig dient er als Ventil zum Ausstoß verarbeiteter Luft. Da Menschen keine Lautsprecher haben, nutzen sie den Vorgang des Luftausstoßens zur Klangerzeugung.

At the same time the mouth is used as an outlet to expel processed air. Because humans do not have loudspeakers, they use this process of expelling air for generating sounds.

22

In emergency circumstances, the mouth can also be used as an outlet to expel blood, mucus, rejected food, or other unwanted substances. When the mouth is not used for input or output, it is normally closed off by muscles, which we called the lips.

23

The lips have a large repertoire of movements. There are at least six other muscles that interact directly with the lips. I will now demonstrate four different movements.

First we show the Muscles of Joy. These muscles produce a kind of grin.

24

They signal that the operating system is in good working order, and is not encountering any problems. There is heightened activity in the left frontal lobes of the brain.

When, on the other hand, the activity in the left frontal lobes is unusually low, the brain is involved in destructive processes of global belief revision. As we saw before, this is signalled by another pair of muscles, called the Muscles of Sadness. Here they are, once more.

25

And finally I will now trigger several muscle pairs at the same time. Orbicularis Oris, and Depressor Labii Inferioris, and the Muscle of Contempt, and the Muscle of Sadness.

26

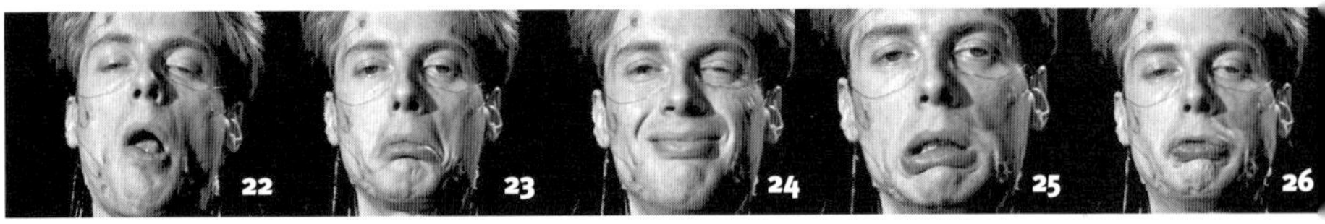

22

In kritischen Situationen dient der Mund auch als Ventil zum Ausstoß von Blut, Schleim, unverarbeiteter Nahrung oder anderen unerwünschten Substanzen. Wird der Mund weder für Eingabe- noch für Ausgabezwecke benutzt, so wird er im Normalfall von zwei Muskeln, den sogenannten Lippen, geschlossen.

23

Die Lippen verfügen über ein großes Bewegungsrepertoire. Es gibt mindestens sechs weitere Muskeln, die direkt mit den Lippen interagieren. Ich werde nun vier verschiedene Bewegungen vorführen. Zuerst zeige ich Ihnen die Freudemuskeln . Diese Muskeln rufen eine Art Grinsen hervor.

24

Sie signalisieren, daß das Betriebssystem in funktionstüchtigem Zustand ist und daß keine Probleme aufgetreten sind. In den linken Stirnlappen des Gehirns herrscht erhöhte Aktivität. Herrscht andererseits in den linken Stirnlappen ungewöhnlich niedrige Aktivität, so macht das Gehirn umfassende destruktive Revisionsprozesse durch. Wie wir schon vorhin gesehen haben, wird dies durch ein anderes Muskelpaar, die Traurigkeitsmuskeln, angezeigt. Und hier sind sie noch einmal.

25

Schließlich möchte ich noch einige Muskelpaare gleichzeitig stimulieren: *Orbicularis oris* und *Depressor labii inferioris*, sowie die Verachtungs- und die Traurigkeitsmuskeln.

26

Die Parametereinstellung, die hier ganz eindeutig angezeigt wird, verweist auf diverse schwerwiegende Verarbeitungsprobleme.

Okay. Bleibt noch die Nase. Die Nase dient der Aufnahme von Luft. Sie ist ebenfalls mit Fähigkeiten zur chemischen Analyse ausgestattet. Die Bewegungsfähigkeit der Nase ist seltsamerweise relativ eingeschränkt, obwohl sie durch ihre herausragende Position in der Mitte des menschlichen Gesichts als Instrument des Ausdrucks geradezu prädestiniert wäre. Ich habe über diese Diskrepanz nachgedacht und bin zu dem Schluß gekommen, daß die Hauptfunktion der Nase aller Wahrscheinlichkeit

The parameter-setting that is displayed here clearly indicates serious processing difficulties of some sort.

O.K. Then we have the nose. The nose is used for the intake of air. It is also equipped with a chemical analysis capability. The possible motions of the nose are curiously limited, although its pointed presence in the centre of the human face would make it a very suitable instrument for expression. I have thought about this, and I have come to the conclusion that it is probably the main function of the nose to serve as a stable orientation point for our perception, so that the movements of the other parts of the face can be unambiguously measured and interpreted.

27, 28, 29, 30, 31

And finally, for the sake of completeness, I want to mention the ears, on both sides of the face, which constitute an auditory stereo input device. Some people can wiggle these ears, but I have not been able to determine what the expressive function of that movement might be.

This brings an end to my quick survey of the most important parts of the human face, and their expressive possibilities. Many of the possibilities I have shown were related to emotions that are well recognized in the lexicons of many human languages; for the sake of clarity I have focussed on mental states which were close to neutral, where only one parameter had a non-default value. But now, look at what happens if we signal non-trivial values for different cognitive dimensions at the same time, by simultaneous contraction of different facial muscles.

32, 33, 34, 35, 36

You see what happens now. Every human person knows exactly in what state another human person is when the person make a face like this. Because they know what state they would be in, if they made a face like this.

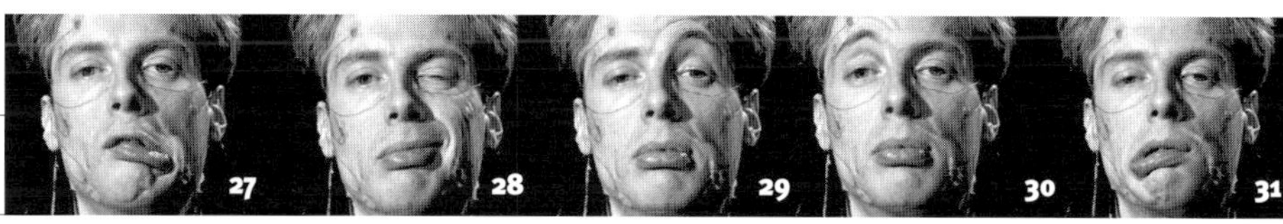

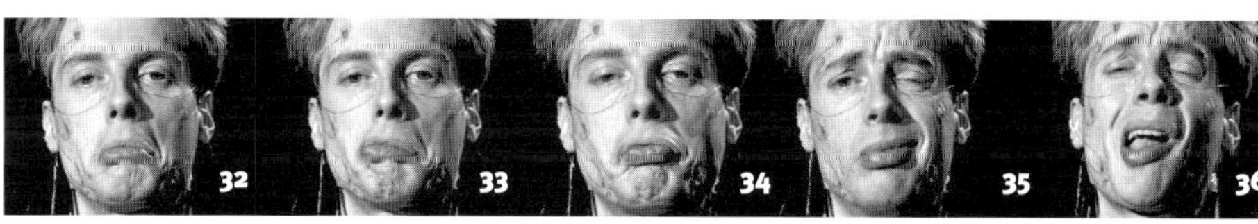

nach darin besteht, einen fixen Orientierungspunkt für unsere Wahrnehmung zu bieten, so daß die Bewegungen anderer Gesichtspartien eindeutig gemessen und interpretiert werden können.

27, 28, 29, 30, 31

Schließlich seien der Vollständigkeit halber die an beiden Seiten des Gesichts befindlichen Ohren erwähnt, die ein akustisches Stereo-Eingabegerät darstellen. Einige Menschen können mit den Ohren wackeln, es ist mir aber bisher nicht gelungen festzustellen, welche expressive Funktion diese Bewegung haben könnte.

Somit wären wir am Ende dieses kurzen Überblicks über die wichtigsten Partien des menschlichen Gesichts und ihre expressiven Möglichkeiten angelangt. Viele der Möglichkeiten, die ich Ihnen gezeigt habe, sind mit Gefühlen gekoppelt, die im Wortschatz vieler menschlicher Sprachen Anerkennung gefunden haben. Zum besseren Verständnis habe ich mich auf geistige Zustände konzentriert, die nahezu neutral waren und bei denen nur ein Parameter einen Nicht-Standardwert hatte. Sehen Sie jedoch nun, was passiert, wenn wir nicht-triviale Werte für verschiedene kognitive Dimensionen gleichzeitig signalisieren und mehrere Gesichtsmuskel gleichzeitig kontrahieren lassen.

32, 33, 34, 35, 36

Sie sehen, was dann passiert. Jeder Mensch weiß haargenau, in welchem Zustand jemand ist, der so ein Gesicht machen kann. Denn er weiß, in welchen Zustand er selbst wäre, würde er so ein Gesicht machen.

Es wäre also offensichtlich von Vorteil, wenn Computer sich diese wundervolle Hardware

Now it would obviously be a good idea if computers could take advantage of this magnificent hardware as well. If any human could understand, with just one glance, the internal state of any computer, the world would be a better place.

So, if humans are not afraid of wiring themselves up with computers, the next step in computer interface technology may be the human face. And the next step in computer art will be a new, unprecedented kind of collaboration between humans and machines: algorithmic choreography, by computer-controlled human faces. Finally, the accuracy and sense of structure of computer programs will be merged with the warmth, the suppleness, and all the other empathy-evoking properties of the human flesh.

37 I am very grateful to have had this opportunity to present my ideas to such attentive audience. I would especially like to thank my Arthur Elsenaar for his patient cooperation, and I want to thank you all for your attention.

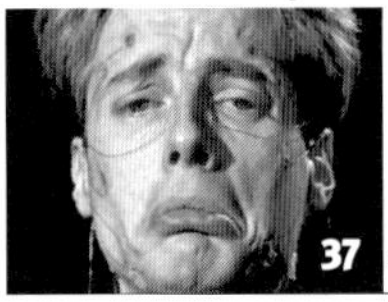

37 symposium

ebenfalls zunutze machen könnten. Wenn jeder Mensch mit nur einem Blick verstehen würde, was im Inneren eines Computers los ist, wäre die Welt schon weitaus besser.

Wenn also Menschen nicht mehr davor zurückscheuten, sich an Computer anzuschließen, könnte der nächste Schritt in der Interface-Technologie das menschliche Gesicht sein. Und der nächste Schritt in der Computerkunst wäre dann eine neue, beispiellose Art der Zusammenarbeit zwischen Mensch und Maschine: algorithmische Choreographie durch computergesteuerte menschliche Gesichter. Und endlich würden die Genauigkeit und das Strukturverständnis von Computerprogrammen mit der Wärme, der Geschmeidigkeit und allen anderen empathiefördernden Eigenschaften des menschlichen Fleisches verschmelzen.

37 Ich bin überaus dankbar, daß ich die Gelegenheit hatte, meine Überlegungen vor einem so aufmerksamen Publikum zu präsentieren. Mein ganz besonderer Dank gilt meinem Arthur Elsenaar für seine geduldige Mitarbeit sowie Ihnen allen für Ihre Aufmerksamkeit.

Jonathan Allen, M. Sharon Hunnicutt and Dennis Klatt: *From Text to Speech: The MITalk System*. Cambridge [UK], Cambridge University Press, 1987

Guillaume-Benjamin Amant Duchenne [de Boulogne]: *Mécanisme de la Physionomie Humaine ou Analyse Electro-Physiologique de l'Expression des Passions*, Paris, 1862

Arthur Elsenaar and Remko Scha: *Towards a Digital Computer with a Human Face*, in: *Abstracts*. American Anthropological Ass., Washington, D.C., November 15-19, 1995, p. 139

Donna Haraway: *A Cyborg Manifesto: Science, Technology and Socialist Feminism in the Late Twentieth Century*, in: *Simians, Cyborgs and Women – The Reinvention of Nature*. London, Free Association Books, 1991

Huge Harry: *On the Role of Machines and Human Persons in the Art of the Future*, Pose 8 [September 1992.], pp. 30-35

Huge Harry: *A Computer's View on the Future of Art and Photography*, in: *Still Photography?* The International Symposium on the Transition from Analog to Digital Imaging. University of Melbourne, April 1994

Huge Harry: *A Computational Perspective on Twenty-First Century Music*. in: *Contemporary Music Review* 14, 3 [1995], pp. 153-159

Remko Scha: *Virtual Voices* in: *Mediamatic* 7, 1 [1992], pp. 27-45

Beyond the Machine

Technology and Posthuman Freedom

Max More

"Living and unliving things are exchanging properties ..."
Phillip K. Dick, A Scanner Darkly.

According to the introductory statement for this conference discussion, man and machine are diametric opposites. I will seek to contribute to the discussion by constructively disagreeing with this statement. I will contend, first, that although humans are not machines they are composed of mechanical parts. Second, by appreciating this we can see how machines and technology can enable to become "more human than human", i.e., less mechanical than we remain today.

symposium

Jenseits der Maschine

Technologie und posthumane Freiheit

Max More

"Belebte und unbelebte Dinge tauschen Eigenschaften aus ..."
Phillip K. Dick, A Scanner Darkly

Gemäß dem Einführungsstatement zu dieser Konferenz sind Mensch und Maschine einander diametral entgegengesetzt. Ich möchte versuchen zu dieser Diskussion beizutragen , indem ich dieser Behauptung konstruktiv widerspreche. Ich werde erstens die These vertreten, daß Menschen zwar keine Maschinen sind, aber aus mechanischen Teilen bestehen. Und zweitens, daß wir dann, wenn wir das akzeptieren, zu erkennen vermögen, wie uns Maschinen und Technologie in die Lage versetzen, "menschlicher als menschlich", d. h. weniger mechanisch als heute, zu werden.

Wenn es zuträfe, daß Menschen und Maschinen diametrale Gegensätze sind, dann dürften Menschen keinerlei *maschinische* und Maschinen keinerlei menschliche Eigenschaften besitzen. Doch die Biochemie zeigt uns, daß wir aus Milliarden von Maschinen bestehen. Jedes unserer Organe und Gewebe ist eine Maschine mit einer ganz bestimmten Funktion. Jedes Organ besteht aus Zellen, die ihrerseits aus noch kleineren, einfacheren biochemischen Maschinen aufgebaut sind. Wir bezeichnen sie als Ribosome, Mitochondrien, RNS und so weiter. Selbst der Sitz unseres Bewußtseins und unserer Persönlichkeit, das Gehirn, setzt sich aus vielen Milliarden Maschinen zusammen – Neuronen, Synapsen, Hormonsystemen, Neurotransmittern. Leztendlich bestehen Körper und Hirn aus den einfachsten mechanischen Teilen: aus subatomaren Partikeln. Letzlich sind wir lauter umherschwirrende Quarks.

Die umgekehrte Ansicht – daß Menschen das genaue Gegenteil von Maschinen sind – kann nur dann stimmen, wenn wir den Vitalismus akzeptieren. Der Vitalismus behauptet, daß das Leben nicht eine Folge biochemischer Reaktionen, sondern einer lebenden Dingen eigentümlichen Lebenskraft sei. Während die moderne Wissenschaft das Leben als Ergebnis komplexer Interaktionen von mechanischen

more

If it were true that humans and machines are diametric opposites then it would have to be true that humans are not in the least machinelike and that machines cannot have humanlike properties. Yet biochemistry shows us that we are comprised of billions of machines. Each of our organs and tissues is a machine with a particular function. Each organ is made up of cells which themselves are made up of smaller, simpler biochemical machines. We call these *ribosomes*, *mitochondria*, *RNA* and the like. Even the seat of our consciousness and personality, the brain itself, is made up of many billions of machines – neurons, synapses, hormonal systems, neurotransmitters. Ultimately body and brain are composed of the simplest mechanical parts – subatomic particles. Ultimately we are all quarks in motion.

The alternative view – that humans are the very opposite of machines – can only be true if we accept vitalism. Vitalism holds that life results not from biochemical reactions but from a vital force unique to living things. Whereas modern science sees life as resulting from the complex interactions of mechanistic parts forming an organic whole, vitalism sees life as suffused with a substance not found in nonliving nature.

To say that humans are composed of machines is not to say that we are merely machines. Humans are dignified machines. We are [so far] the most extropic, most complex product of billions of years of evolution. All machines are not created equal. Living organisms display properties not shared by simpler machines. These emergent properties [homeostasis, reproduction, learning, intelligence] result not from the addition of a mysterious vital force but from the complexity of functional interrelationships. If we define *machine* and *mechanical* to imply rigid, unvarying, stupid, inflexible function, then humans are not machines, despite being entirely composed of machines. When enough machines work together in complex ways, new properties emerge, properties we refer to with terms like *organic*, *living*, *feeling*, and *thinking*.

The idea that humans and machines are opposites also fails to recognize that machines continue to evolve more organic, living qualities. Already we are developing robots that

Teilen betrachtet, die ein organisches Ganzes bilden, ist es für den Vitalismus mit einer Substanz durchsetzt, die in der unbelebten Natur nicht existiert.

Daß Menschen aus Maschinen bestehen, heißt nicht, daß wir nur Maschinen sind. Menschen sind herausragende Maschinen. Wir sind das [bislang] extropischeste, komplexeste Produkt von Milliarden Evolutionsjahren. Maschinen sind nicht alle von Natur aus gleich. Lebende Organismen legen Eigenschaften an den Tag, über die einfachere Maschinen nicht verfügen. Diese emergenten Eigenschaften [Homöostase, Reproduktion, Lernen, Intelligenz] resultieren nicht aus der Anhäufung einer rätselhaften Lebenskraft, sondern aus der Komplexität funktionaler Wechselbeziehungen. Wenn unsere Definition von *Maschine* und *mechanisch* ein starres, unveränderliches, stupides, unflexibles Funktionieren impliziert, dann sind Menschen keine Maschinen, auch wenn sie vollständig aus Maschinen bestehen. Wenn genügend Maschinen auf komplexe Weise zusammenarbeiten, entstehen neue Eigenschaften – Eigenschaften, die wir mit Begriffen wie *organisch*, *belebt*, *fühlend* und *denkend* belegen.

Bei der Auffassung, daß Menschen und Maschinen Gegensätze sind, wird auch übersehen, daß Maschinen die Evolution organischer, belebter Eigenschaften weiter fortsetzen. Wir entwickeln bereits Roboter, die manche Eigenschaften von Tieren aufweisen; wir verfügen über künstliches Leben in der Software, wie Computerviren und -würmer, die mutieren, sich reproduzieren und evolvieren; wir besitzen Computer, die mit Fuzzy-Logic, genetischen Algorithmen und anderen Rechenmethoden umzugehen lernen. Ob ein Geschöpf oder Organ aus organischem Material auf Kohlenstoffbasis oder aus Silikon oder anderen anorganischen Materialien besteht, ist nebensächlich. Wichtig ist die Komplexität des Ergebnisses: Ist das Gebilde lernfähig, ist es in der Lage, sich selbst zu verändern, dynamisch auf wechselnde Eingaben zu reagieren?

Man kann entweder sagen, daß Menschen besonders diffizile, komplexe und herausragende Maschinen sind oder daß Menschen keine Maschinen sind, jedoch aus solchen bestehen. Die Fakten sind wichtiger als die Worte, die wir gebrauchen, wenngleich Worte Konnotationen in sich bergen, die sich auf Einstellungen auswirken. Worauf es ankommt, ist jedenfalls, daß Mensch und Maschine keine Gegensätze sind. Mit der fortgesetzten raschen Evolution der Maschinen und dem zunehmenden Basteln an unseren Körpern und Gehirnen wird dieser Umstand immer offensichtlicher werden. Diese

display some qualities of animals; we have artificial life software that mutates, reproduces, and evolves, as do computer viruses and worms; we have computers that learn using fuzzy logic, genetic algorithms, and other computational techniques. Whether a creature or an organ is made of carbon-based organic material, or of silicon or other inorganic materials does not matter. What is important is the complexity of the result: is the structure able to learn, to self-modify, to respond dynamically to changing input?

We can say that humans are especially subtle, complex, and dignified machines. Or we can say that humans are not machines though composed of them. The facts matter more than the words we use, though words bring connotations that have power over attitudes. The crucial point is that humans and machines are not opposites. As machines continue their rapid evolution and as we increasingly tinker with our bodies and brains to repair and improve them, this fact will become ever more obvious. This realization will open the way to improving ourselves by upgrading the machine components of humans.

A human brain reasons, creates, feels, plans, calculates, appreciates. These properties of living, conscious beings result from the immensely complicated connections among our 100 billion neurons. Any individual neuron displays no consciousness, no reasoning, no creativity. Even more clearly, the molecular and atomic parts making up the neurons do not display these properties. The neuron is a biochemical machine. We should therefore be able to replace or supplement biological neurons with synthetic neurons while retaining the same functions. We should be able to repair damaged neural tissue with implants. We should be able to add memory, processing power, and new abilities by supplementing natural neurons with synthetic neurons. In principle, we could replace all our neurons until we had an entirely synthetic or prosthetic brain. If the new neurons worked similarly to the old, and were connected up the same, we would never notice a difference. [Except that we might be able to process information faster and would not slow down with age.]

Since misunderstanding is easy I want to stress here that I claim only that humans are

Erkenntnis wird den Weg zu unserer Selbstverbesserung durch Upgrades der menschlichen Maschinenkomponenten bereiten.

Ein Menschenhirn denkt, erfindet, fühlt, plant, rechnet, erkennt. Diese Eigenschaften bewußter Lebewesen sind eine Folge der ungeheuer komplizierten Verknüpfungen zwischen unseren 100 Milliarden Neuronen. Das Einzelneuron verfügt über kein Bewußtsein, keine Ratio, keine Kreativität. Noch weniger verfügen die molekularen und atomaren Bestandteile der Neuronen über diese Eigenschaften. Das Neuron ist eine biochemische Maschine. Deshalb sollte es uns auch gelingen, biologische Neuronen unter Beibehaltung ihrer jeweiligen Funktion durch synthetische zu ersetzen oder zu ergänzen. Es sollte uns gelingen, geschädigtes neuronales Gewebe durch Implantate wiederherzustellen. Es sollte uns gelingen, Speicherkapazität, Verarbeitungsleistung und neue Fähigkeiten mittels Ergänzung natürlicher durch synthetische Neuronen zu steigern. Im Prinzip könnten wir unsere sämtlichen Neuronen ersetzen, bis wir ein vollkommen synthetisches oder prothetisches Gehirn haben. Wenn die neuen Neuronen ähnlich wie die alten funktionierten und auf dieselbe Weise verknüpft wären, würden wir nie und nimmer einen Unterschied feststellen [außer daß wir vielleicht zu einer schnelleren Informationsverarbeitung in der Lage wären und auch im Alter nicht langsamer würden].

Da es schnell zu Mißverständnissen kommt, möchte ich betonen, daß ich lediglich behaupte, daß Menschen aus Maschinen bestehen, nicht daß sie Maschinen sind. In gewisser Weise könnten wir zwar mit Recht behaupten, daß Menschen Maschinen sind, weil wir vollständig aus mechanischen Teilen bestehen und keinen triftigen Grund haben anzunehmen, wir besäßen irgendwelche nicht-materiellen Teile. Wenn wir uns allerdings als Maschinen beschrieben, würden wir diesem Begriff eine sehr breite Bedeutung verleihen. Mit *Maschine* verbinden wir gewöhnlich etwas Starres, Unveränderliches, Geplantes, Programmierbares. Da wir uns für freie, verantwortungsvolle, moralische, vernünftige Wesen halten, ist es nur billig, den Begriff *Maschine* einzuschränken und seine Anwendung auf uns selbst auszuschließen. Das ist die von mir bevorzugte Option. In diesem Fall müssen wir jedoch akzeptieren, daß dann auch unsere Computer und Roboter und elektronische Ökosysteme nicht mehr zwangläufig Maschinen in diesem Sinne sind. Ob etwas eine Maschine ist, hängt von der Komplexität seiner Funktion ab, nicht vom Material, aus dem es besteht.

more

composed of mechanical parts, not that we ARE machines. In some sense we can reasonably say that humans are machines, since we are entirely composed of mechanical parts, and we have no sound reason to believe we have non-material parts. If we were to describe ourselves as machines we would be giving wide latitude to the meaning of the term. *Machine* usually connotes something rigid, unvarying, planned, and programmable. Since we think of ourselves as free, responsible, moral, rational beings, we may reasonably restrict the term *machine* and refuse to apply it to ourselves. This is the option I favor. However, we must then accept that our computers and robots and electronic ecosystems can also then cease to be machines in this sense. Whether something is a machine depends on the complexity and subtlety of its function, not on what substance it is made of. Simple biological organisms such as enzymes and viruses certainly count as machines, while an advanced artificial intelligence would not count as a machine.

Although I see no decisive metaphysical objection to describing humans as machines, the connotations of the word convince me that we would be wise not to apply the term to ourselves [nor to our mind-children – the artificial persons we will eventually create]. Since connotations of terms affect our attitudes we should avoid labeling persons with terms that may encourage us to regard them as tools, as objects, or purely as means to our ends. Machines are usually understood as arrangements of parts to perform useful work, modifying mechanical energy into more useful forms. Machines come in various forms from simple levers and screws to engines [machines that transform heat and other forms of energy into mechanical energy] and computers [machines that process information]. Obviously a vast gulf exists between a crude lever and supercomputer running millions of lines of code. If both can be called machines, we might stretch the term to include humans. But because *machine* implies a tool to be used for external purposes, I prefer to refrain from attaching this term to persons.

To further locate my position among the alternatives, I suggest we can distinguish at least four views on the relation of humans and machines:

Einfache biologische Organismen wie Enzyme und Viren sind sicherlich als Maschinen einzustufen, eine avancierte künstliche Intelligenz hingegen gälte zweifellos nicht als solche.

Obwohl ich keinen wesentlichen metaphysischen Einwand gegen eine Beschreibung des Menschen als Maschine sehe, überzeugen mich doch die Konnotationen dieses Wortes, daß es klüger wäre, den Begriff nicht auf uns selbst [und unsere geistigen Kinder – die künstlichen Menschen, die wir schließlich erschaffen werden] anzuwenden. Da Begriffskonnotationen unsere Einstellung beeinflussen, sollten wir es vermeiden, Menschen mit Begriffen zu etikettieren, die uns dazu verleiten könnten, sie als Werkzeuge, Objekte oder bloße Mittel zum Zweck zu sehen. Maschinen werden gewöhnlich als eine Anordnung von Teilen verstanden, die uns beim Verrichten nützlicher Arbeit hilft, indem sie mechanische Engergie in zweckmäßigere Formen umwandelt. Maschinen kommen in verschiedenen Ausprägungen vor, von einfachen Hebeln und Schrauben bis hin zu Motoren [Maschinen, die Wärme und andere Energieformen in mechanische Energie umwandeln] und Computern [informationsverarbeitenden Maschinen]. Zwischen einem einfachen Hebel und einem Millionen von Codezeilen verarbeitenden Computer klafft zweifellos eine tiefe Kluft. Wenn beide als Maschinen bezeichnet werden können, können wir den Begriff genausogut auf den Menschen ausdehnen. Da der Maschinenbegriff jedoch auf ein für äußere Zwecke verwendetes Werkzeug verweist, möchte ich ihn auf Menschen lieber nicht anwenden.

Um meine Position zwischen diesen Alternativen besser bestimmen zu können, würde ich sagen, daß man in bezug auf das Verhältnis von Mensch und Maschine mindestens vier Standpunkte unterscheiden kann:

1 Menschen sind Maschinen. Dies scheint nach dem *FleshFactor*-Interview im Juni 1997 die Position von Daniel Dennett und – ursprünglich – die von Lukrez und La Mettrie zu sein. Diesem Standpunkt zufolge enthalten Menschen nicht bloß Maschinen, sondern sie sind Maschinen

2 Menschen besitzen eine Doppelnatur. Sie verfügen über einen mechanisch-physischen Körper und einen spirituellen Leib oder eine Seele, die gänzlich unmechanisch ist. Ich halte diesen Standpunkt für wissenschaftlich und philosophisch vollkommen unhaltbar, wiewohl er sich höchster Popularität erfreut.

3 Menschen sind auf mysteriöse Weise nichtmechanisch. Sie [oder zumindest ihr Gehirn]

1 Humans are machines. This appears to be the position of Daniel Dennett, according to the June 1997 FleshFactor interview and, more originally that of Lucretius and La Mettrie. According to this view, not only do humans contain machines, they are machines.

2 Humans have a dual nature, having a mechanical physical body and a spiritual body or soul that is entirely non-mechanical. I take this view to be scientifically and philosophically indefensible although extremely popular among most people.

3 Humans are mysteriously non-mechanical. They [or at least their brains] have essential properties that are not mechanical at any level of understanding and which cannot be recreated in any devices we might construct [i.e., artificial intelligence]. These *New Mysterians* [or modern day vitalists] as they have been called include Roger Penrose and John Searle.

4 Humans are composed of mechanistic parts but the arrangement of these parts produces emergent, non-mechanicanistic properties. The non-mechanistic properties would not exist but for the mechanistic parts comprising them, but we cannot fully understand the emergent properties solely by examining the mechanistic level. This is my view.

The humans-as-machines metaphor, though superficially scientific [in stressing the absence of supernatural elements], strikes me as outdated. In the human science of economics realization of the inappropriateness of machine language has been spreading. For decades economics talked of the *engine* of the economy, of *priming the pump*, of *fine-tuning* and so on. The Austrian school of economists first challenged this approach by emphasizing the market as a discovery procedure [especially the work of Friedrich Hayek]. Recently a bionomics model has taken hold in which the economy is understood in terms of an ecosystem that is best carefully nurtured and fertilized but not centrally controlled like a machine.

While William Paley in his Design Argument for the Existence of a God portrayed the world as a gigantic mechanism designed for a purpose, evolutionary theory has revealed a world ordered by distributed processes over millions of years. Though each organism in the world can be broken down into mechanistic components [bones, ligaments, cells, organ-

besitzen wesentliche Eigenschaften, die in keinem irgendwie greifbaren Sinn mechanisch sind und die sich mit keinem von uns konstruierten Gebilde [z. B. künstliche Intelligenz] nachbilden lassen. Zu diesen *Neuen Mystikern* [oder modernen Vitalisten], wie man sie genannt hat, gehören Roger Penrose und John Searle.

4 Menschen bestehen aus mechanischen Teilen, aber die Anordnung dieser Teile läßt daraus emergente, nicht-mechanische Eigenschaften entstehen. Diese nicht-mechanischen emergenten Eigenschaften existieren zwar nur aufgrund der ihnen zugrundeliegenden mechanischen Teile, können jedoch durch Betrachtung der mechanischen Ebene allein nicht verstanden werden. Das ist der von mir vertretene Standpunkt.

Die Metapher vom Menschen als Maschine erscheint mir trotz ihrer oberflächlichen Wissenschaftlichkeit [die die Abwesenheit übernatürlicher Elemente betont] als veraltet. In der Humanwissenschaft der Volkswirtschaft hat sich bereits die Einsicht von der Unangemessenheit der Maschinensprache verbreitet. Jahrzehntelang wurde dort vom *Motor* der Wirtschaft, von *Ankurbelung*, *Feinsteuerung* und dergleichen gesprochen. Die österreichische Schule [vor allem das Werk Friedrich Hayeks] hat diesen Ansatz als erste in Frage gestellt, indem sie den Markt als Entdeckungsprozeß hervorgehoben hat. In letzter Zeit hat ein bionomisches Modell Fuß gefaßt, bei dem die Wirtschaft als Ökosystem aufgefaßt wird, das man am besten sorgfältig hegen und pflegen sollte und nicht wie eine Maschine zentral kontrollieren.

Während William Paley in seinem Entwurfsargument für die Existenz Gottes die Welt als gigantischen, für einen bestimmten Zweck entworfenen Mechanismus darstellte, hat die Evolutionstheorie eine Welt zum Vorschein gebracht, die von Prozessen geordnet wurde, die sich über Jahrmillionen verteilen. Obwohl jeder Organismus der Welt in mechanistische Komponenten zerlegt werden kann [Knochen, Sehnen, Zellen, Organellen], haben die vom Ökosystem insgesamt verkörperten Prinzipien – genauso wie die vom Wirtschaftssystem verkörperten – mit den Arbeitsprinzipien paradigmatischer Maschinen nicht viel gemeinsam.

Die Behauptung, daß Menschen Maschinen seien, kann nicht definitiv für wahr oder falsch erklärt werden. Zwischen Maschinen und komplexen Systemen, die keine Maschinen sind, läßt sich genausowenig eine scharfe Trennlinie ziehen wie zwischen Leben und Nicht-Leben, zwischen Tag und

more

elles] the principles embodied in the ecosystem as a whole, like those embodied in the economy, have little in common with the working principles of paradigmatic machines.

The statement *humans are machines* cannot decisively be declared true or false. We can draw no sharp line between machines and complex systems that are not machines, just as we cannot draw a sharp line between life and non-life or between night and day. I stand on the side of those who prefer to say humans are not machines because I see us moving ever further from rigidity, inflexibility, and mindlessness. If the term *machine* ever loses these connotations, I will then see no reason to object to describing humans as elegant organic machines.

I started by claiming that technology can allow us to become *more human than human*. Now I can clarify that claim, showing how the understanding that we are made of mechanical parts is a cause for optimism and humanism [or transhumanism] and the fostering of freedom, not fear and nihilism nor a policy of social control. Although humans have evolved more complex brains than any other animal, still we have not fully escaped our biological-machine heritage. Too easily humans are manipulated. We have little control over our emotions, our moods, our personality. We respond to external influences and to internal chemical, hormonal, and neural events often without much consciousness or choice. While more self-determining and self-aware than other creatures, humans still show clear signs of being mechanical and other-determined. The whole appeal of seeing that we are a complex functionally interrelated collection of mechanical parts is that it opens up an appealing prospect: that technology will allow us to modify our nature, to alter ourselves, to augment and shape ourselves according to our values.

Advanced technologies such as genetic engineering, smart drugs, prostheses, and soon brain implants [neuroprostheses] represent the next step in the long march of evolution. Evolutionary processes have brought order out of chaos, extropy out of entropy. Extropy is the extent of a system's intelligence, information, order, vitality, diversity, and capacity for improvement. Extropy has [so far] reached its peak on this planet in human beings. The original physical processes that led to stellar and

Nacht. Auf der Seite derer, die Menschen lieber nicht als Maschinen bezeichnen, stehe ich deswegen, weil ich uns noch weiter über Starrheit, Unflexibilität, Gedankenlosigkeit hinauswachsen sehe. Wenn der Begriff *Maschine* diese Konnotationen einmal ablegen sollte, werde ich keinen Grund mehr sehen, warum man Menschen nicht als elegante organische Maschinen bezeichnen sollte.

Ich habe eingangs behauptet, mit Technologie könnten wir *menschlicher als menschlich* werden. Nun kann ich diese Behauptung verdeutlichen und zeigen, inwiefern die Auffassung, daß wir aus mechanischen Teilen bestehen, ein Anlaß zu Optimismus und Humanismus [oder Transhumanismus] sowie zur Förderung von Freiheit ist und nicht zu Angst und Nihilimus oder zu einer Politik der sozialen Kontrolle. Obwohl der Mensch ein komplexeres Gehirn ausgebildet hat als jedes andere Tier, haben wir unser biologisch-maschinisches Erbe nicht gänzlich hinter uns gelassen. Allzuleicht kann man Menschen manipulieren. Wir haben unsere Emotionen, unsere Stimmungen, unsere Persönlichkeit kaum unter Kontrolle. Wir reagieren auf äußere Einflüsse wie innere chemische, hormonale und neuronale Ereignisse, oft ohne uns dessen besonders bewußt zu sein oder eine Wahl zu haben. Wenngleich selbstbestimmter und selbstbewußter als andere Geschöpfe, weisen Menschen noch immer deutliche Anzeichen von Mechanik und Fremdbestimmtheit auf. Das Reizvolle an der Auffassung unserer selbst als komplexe, funktionell verknüpfte Ansammlung mechanischer Teile ist die dadurch eröffnete faszinierende Aussicht, daß uns die Technologie die Möglichkeit bietet, unsere Natur zu verändern, uns selbst zu verwandeln, uns unseren Werten gemäß zu erweitern und gestalten.

Moderne Technologien wie die Gentechnologie, intelligente Drogen, Prothesen und bald auch Hirnimplantate [Neuroprothesen] stellen den nächsten Schritt auf dem langen Marsch der Evolution dar. Evolutionsprozesse haben Ordnung in das Chaos, Extropie in die Entropie gebracht. Extropie bezeichnet den Grad der Intelligenz, Information, Ordnung, Vitalität, Diversität und Verbesserungsfähigkeit eines Systems. Ihren [bisherigen] Höhepunkt auf diesem Planeten hat die Extropie im Menschen erreicht. Die ursprünglichen physikalischen Prozesse, die zur Bildung der Sterne und Planeten führten, machten der biologischen Evolution Platz. Die biologische Evolution hat ihre Sonderstellung an die memetische und technologische Evolution abgetreten. Mit dem Fortschreiten des extropischen Evolutions-

planetary formation gave way to biological evolution. Biological evolution has yielded its primary place to memetic and technological evolution. As the extropic processes of evolution have proceeded, the complexity of nervous systems has grown. The purely chemical responses of single-celled creatures led to tropistic behavior. Tropism became supplemented in animals by instinctual behavior stimulated by integrated perception and recognition. With the advent of our species new possibilities for flexible behaviors arose thanks to our capacity for conceptual thought, for rationality, creativity, self-restraint, and self-transformation.

Properly used, technology will not mechanize us but expand our freedom as we move from human to posthuman, continuing the extropic evolutionary process. The scientifically untenable ideas of dualism and vitalism have led us into the false idea that freedom is all or none. In Descartes' version of dualism, all animals are merely machines, unable to make choices. Only humans, imbued with a spiritual substance or soul, have freedom and responsibility. In addition to pushing animals outside the realm of moral standing, this view was doubly unfortunate. Those who believe in a soul will be unable to see how alterations to the physical constitution of persons could increase freedom. On their view, our uniquely human freedom and rationality resides outside the material realm. If we lose our belief in a supernatural realm, the dualist legacy may lead us to abandon any conception of genuine choice, freedom, and responsibility. [Philosophers refer to the view that physical causation and freedom cannot coexist as incompatibilism.]

Similarly, vitalists [whether the nineteenth century variety or today's New Mysterians], by locating human freedom in a mysterious vital force will not understand how alterations to our physical structure could increase our freedom. If our freedom depends on this vital force, we can only lose it by technologizing ourselves such as by implanting synthetic neurons or using prosthetics.

We may do best not to claim that humans ARE machines. Yet understanding and accepting that we are composed of an arrangement of mechanistic parts provides a key to our further demechanization. Being aware of our origin in mindless nature, we can see that we

prozesses hat die Komplexität des Nervensystems zugenommen. Die rein chemischen Reaktionen der Einzeller führten zu tropistischen Verhaltensweisen. Bei den Tieren wurde der Tropismus durch Instinktverhalten ergänzt, stimuliert durch integriertes Wahrnehmen und Wiedererkennen. Mit dem Erscheinen unserer Spezies taten sich dank unserer Fähigkeit zu begrifflichem Denken, Schlußfolgern, Kreativität, Selbstzügelung und Selbstveränderung neue Möglichkeiten für flexible Verhaltensweisen auf.

Richtig eingesetzt, wird uns die Technologie nicht mechanisieren, sondern auf dem Weg vom Menschen zum Nachmenschen, in dem sich der extropische Evolutionsprozeß fortsetzt, unsere Freiheit vergrößern. Die wissenschaftlich unhaltbaren Theorien des Dualismus und Vitalismus haben uns auf den falschen Gedanken gebracht, daß die Freiheit ganz oder gar nicht sei. In der kartesianischen Spielart des Dualismus sind sämtliche Tiere bloße Maschinen, die keinerlei Wahl haben. Allein die Menschen, erfüllt von einer spirituellen Substanz oder Seele, sind mit Freiheit und Verantwortung ausgestattet. Abgesehen davon, daß er Tiere aus dem Geltungsbereich der Moral verbannt, war dieser Standpunkt doppelt unglücklich. Wer an eine Seele glaubt, wird außerstande sein zu begreifen, wie Veränderungen an jemandes physischer Beschaffenheit die Freiheit mehren sollen. Seiner Ansicht nach liegt unsere einzigartige menschliche Freiheit und Vernunft ja außerhalb des Materiellen. Geht der Glaube an die Sphäre des Übernatürlichen verloren, kann das dualistische Erbe dazu führen, daß wir jeden Begriff von echter Wahl, Freiheit und Verantwortung aufgeben. [Die Philosophen bezeichnen die Auffassung, daß physische Ursache und Freiheit nicht nebeneinander bestehen können, als Inkompatibilismus.]

Ähnlich werden auch Vitalisten [ob nun die Variante des 19. Jahrhunderts oder die heutigen Neuen Mystiker] mit ihrer Verankerung der menschlichen Freiheit in einer mysteriösen Lebenskraft nicht begreifen, daß Veränderungen an unserer physischen Struktur unsere Freiheit erhöhen können. Wenn unsere Freiheit auf dieser Lebenskraft beruht, können wir sie durch eine Technologisierung unserer selbst, etwa durch Implantation synthetischer Neuronen oder den Einsatz prothetischer Geräte, nur verlieren.

Wir tun vielleicht gut daran, nicht zu behaupten, daß Menschen Maschinen sind. Doch wenn wir verstehen und akzeptieren, daß wir aus einem Arrangement mechanischer Teile bestehen, gibt uns das einen Schlüssel für unsere weitere Entmechanisierung in die Hand. Das Wissen um unseren

more

have not completed our evolutionary journey from unconsciousness and rigidity to maximum freedom and self-definition. With this awareness and by applying our burgeoning scientific knowledge and technological prowess, we can hasten our development. We can bring about the triumph of consciousness over mindlessness.

Anyone, who declares that humans are today totally free beings, should consider why the compulsive eater does not stop, why the addicted smoker does not quit, why the depressive does not snap out of it, why the procrastinator does not change his behavior, and why all of us find it so hard to rewrite our behavioral programs. While we all may have more range of choice than we are usually aware of, still we cannot choose to be who we wish to be. Our emotions resist us. Anger, hostility, envy, lust, unhappiness, anxiety, fear, excitation, lethargy, all dominate us to varying degrees. Cognitive techniques give us a measure of influence, yet cannot easily shift ingrained habits of thought or powerful moods. Our childhood experiences and our genes largely shape our personality. Our hormones and the structure of our brains set limits to our choices of how to feel, how to behave, how to think, and who to be.

A specific example of how an advanced neurotechnology could allow us more choice over our emotions: Our brains evolved in such a way that emotional centers like the amygdala strongly influence the cortex. Because of the plentiful pathways going from the amygdala to the cortex, our feelings dictate much of our attention and shape our thoughts, whether we like it or not. We have few connections going the other way, from cortex to amygdala. This makes it hard to shut off emotions once activated. If we could add new pathways from emotional to cognitive centers [accelerating an evolutionary process that has already given us more such connections than have other mammals] we could acquire deep awareness of our emotions and the ability to modify them. We would then free ourselves from an unchosen emotional domination, achieving a better integration of reason and passion.

Rewiring the brain is not in our immediate future [though it will come much sooner than most scientists expect]. Other technologies are already starting to expand the range of our choice over the self we want. The first to

Ursprung aus unbeseelter Natur läßt uns erkennen, daß der Weg unserer Evolution aus Bewußtlosigkeit und Starrheit hin zu maximaler Freiheit und Selbstbestimmung noch nicht abgeschlossen ist. Mit diesem Bewußtsein können wir unter Anwendung unserer wachsenden wissenschaftlichen Kenntnisse und unserer technologischen Leistungsfähigkeit unsere Entwicklung beschleunigen. Wir können den Triumph des Bewußtseins über die Blindheit herbeiführen.

Wer erklärt, daß Menschen heute völlig freie Wesen sind, sollte sich fragen, warum der zwanghafte Esser weiterißt, der süchtige Raucher weiterraucht, der Depressive nicht aus der Depression herauskommt, der Zauderer sein Verhalten nicht ändert und warum es uns überhaupt so schwer fällt, unsere Verhaltensprogramme umzuschreiben. Selbst wenn wir alle mehr Wahlmöglichkeiten haben, als wir gewöhnlich gewahr sind, so können wir uns doch nicht einfach aussuchen, wer wir sein wollen. Unsere Gefühle widersetzen sich. Ärger, Feindseligkeit, Neid, Gier, Unglück, Angst, Furcht, Aufregung, Lethargie, sie alle beherrschen uns in unterschiedlichem Maß. Durch kognitive Techniken können wir einen gewissen Einfluß erlangen, doch eingefleischte Denkgewohnheiten und machtvolle Stimmungen können sie nur schwer ändern. Unsere Kindheitserfahrungen und unsere Gene formen weitgehend unsere Persönlichkeit. Unsere Hormone und die Struktur unseres Gehirns begrenzen die Möglichkeit, uns auszusuchen, wie wir uns fühlen und verhalten, wie wir denken und wer wir sein wollen.

Ein konkretes Beispiel, wie uns die moderne Neurotechnologie mehr Wahlmöglichkeiten in bezug auf unsere Emotionen verschaffen könnte: Unsere Gehirne entwickelten sich dergestalt, daß Emotionszentren wie die Amygdala stark auf den Kortex wirken. Wegen der vielen von der Amygdala zum Kortex verlaufenden Nervenbahnen lenken unsere Gefühle – ob wir es wollen oder nicht – weitgehend unsere Aufmerksamkeit und formen unsere Gedanken. Wir verfügen nur über wenige Verbindungen, die in die umgekehrte Richtung gehen, vom Kortex zur Amygdala. Das macht es schwierig, einmal aktivierte Gefühle auszublenden. Wenn wir neue Bahnen von den Emotions- zu den Kognitionszentren legen könnten [womit wir nur den Evolutionsprozeß beschleunigen würden, der uns bereits mit mehr solchen Verbindungen ausgestattet hat als andere Säugetiere], könnten wir sowohl ein starkes Bewußtsein unserer Emotionen als auch die Fähigkeit zu ihrer Veränderung erwerben. Wir würden uns so

benefit from these technologies are the emotionally and cognitively impaired. Drug therapies, beginning with crude anti-depressants and anti-anxiety drugs and now more refined, targeted drugs that selectively affect neurotransmitter sites, have allowed millions to have more say in how they feel and act. Nootropics or *smart drugs*, though still in their early stages, can improve cognition in the elderly and others with cognitive deficits, and sometimes even in young, healthy persons. Gene therapy is rapidly becoming a practical tool for altering somatic and neurological functions. Retinal and cochlear implants have begun to restore perceptual abilities. Neuroprostheses, though further in the future, have enormous potential to take back control from the shaping forces of evolution and upbringing.

With all these technologies, whether chemical or genetic modification or implants, our concern should be using them to expand our range of choice. Genetic engineering and mood drugs could be used to narrow our abilities, to create happy slaves, or to pacify us. These dangers are real but must not deter us from developing technological means of freeing ourselves from our still half-mechanistic nature. In developing means of modifying ourselves, we should seek to give ourselves more choice over how to feel and who to be, not to use these means to push ourselves and others into specific functions or ways of being.

The increased freedom of self-creation, the augmented capacity for self-definition, will mean an expanded arena of personal responsibility. We will have less and less room to blame our troubles on our genes, our parents, our hormones, our society. Many will feel uncomfortable with this level of choice to self-define. I look forward to it as the next phase of our development away from unconscious nature towards a posthuman condition of self-creation or automorphing.

Finally I note that the idea of man-as-machine has sometimes been used to promote social engineering – the pushing of individuals into centrally-determined positions and roles. B.F. Skinner's behavioristic views and his horrendous portrayal of what he took to be a utopia warn us to beware the machine metaphor. I have granted that we could describe ourselves as especially elegant, sophisticated machines.

von einer nicht gewählten Herrschaft befreien und eine bessere Integration von Vernunft und Leidenschaft herbeiführen.

Die Neuverdrahtung des Gehirns steht uns nicht unmittelbar bevor [obwohl sie sicherlich eher kommt, als es die meisten Wissenschaftler erwarten]. Andere Technologien haben bereits angefangen, die Wahlmöglichkeiten in bezug auf das Selbst, das wir gerne hätten, zu erweitern. Die ersten, die von diesen Technologien profitieren, sind Menschen mit emotionalen und kognitiven Schwächen. Medikamentöse Behandlungen, angefangen von einfachen Antidepressiva und Antiangstmitteln bis hin zu den hochentwickelten, zielgerichteteren Psychopharmaka, die selektiv auf bestimmte Neurotransmitter wirken, haben Millionen Menschen zu mehr Mitsprache in bezug auf ihre Gefühle und Handlungen verholfen. Nootropika oder *intelligente Drogen*, obwohl noch im frühen Entwicklungsstadium, können die Kognitionsleistung älterer oder anderer Menschen mit kognitiven Defiziten steigern, manchmal selbst die junger und gesunder Personen. Die Gentherapie entwickelt sich rasch zu einem praktischen Werkzeug bei sich verändernden somatischen und neurologischen Funktionen. Retina- und Cochleaimplantate stellen schon heute Wahrnehmungsfähigkeiten wieder her. Neuroprothesen, wiewohl in der ferneren Zukunft liegend, besitzen ein ungeheueres Potential, die Kontrolle von den formenden Kräften der Evolution und Erziehung zurückzuerobern.

Bei all diesen Technologien, seien es chemische oder genetische Modifikationen oder Implantate, sollten wir darauf achten, daß sie zur Erweiterung unserer Wahlmöglichkeiten verwendet werden. Gentechnologie und Stimmungsaufheller könnten dazu benutzt werden, unsere Fähigkeiten einzuengen, uns zu glücklichen Sklaven zu machen, uns ruhigzustellen. Dies sind reale Gefahren, die uns aber nicht davon abhalten sollten, technologische Mittel zu entwickeln, die uns aus unserer immer noch halbmechanischen Natur befreien. Bei der Entwicklung von Mitteln zur Veränderung unserer selbst sollten wir versuchen, unsere Wahlmöglichkeiten in bezug darauf, wie wir uns fühlen und wer wir sein wollen, zu erhöhen, anstatt diese Mittel dazu einzusetzen, uns und andere in bestimmte Funktionen oder Existenzweisen zu drängen.

Die vermehrte Freiheit, sich selbst zu entwerfen, die erhöhte Fähigkeit, sich selbst zu definieren, bedeutet einen größeren Bereich persönlicher Verantwortung. Wir werden immer weniger die Möglichkeit haben, unsere Probleme auf unsere Gene,

more

Adding to the reasons I gave for refraining from this usage we can add the danger that the metaphor will give impetus to today's social engineers. By recognizing that we have mechanistic components but that our goal is to carry ourselves further from our machine heritage, we can resist those who would make us tools to their ends. And we can affirm our own determination to treat other humans as ends in themselves. We are composed of mechanistic parts but possess emergent properties of free choice, self-ownership, and personal responsibility.

My message, then, is that we should grant the obvious truth in the assertion that humans are machines. We cannot reasonably regard humans and machines are utterly opposed. By understanding our origins and underlying nature we can accelerate our development from rigidity, mindlessness, and external determination to flexibility, mindfulness, and self-determination and self-definition. We can increasingly choose a self, become artists of the self. The automorphic age is arriving.

unsere Eltern, unsere Hormone, unsere Gesellschaft zu schieben. Viele werden sich auf diesem Möglichkeitsniveau der Selbstdefinition unwohl fühlen. Ich sehe dieser nächsten Phase unserer Entwicklung – von der blinden Natur zu einem nachmenschlichen Zustand der Selbsterfindung oder des Automorphens – freudig entgegen.

Abschließend möchte ich anmerken, daß die Idee vom Mensch-als-Maschine manchmal zur Propagierung von Social Engineering verwendet worden ist – bei dem Individuen in zentral bestimmte Positionen und Rollen gedrängt werden. Die behaviouristischen Ansichten B.F. Skinners und seine grauenhafte Darstellung dessen, was er für eine Utopie hielt, ermahnen uns, mit der Maschinenmetapher vorsichtig umzugehen. Ich habe eingeräumt, daß wir uns als besonders elegante, komplexe Maschinen beschreiben könnten. Zu den angegebenen Gründen, warum man diese Metapher vermeiden sollte, können wir nun die Gefahr hinzufügen, daß sie den heutigen Sozialingenieuren Auftrieb geben könnte. Wenn wir anerkennen, daß wir mechanische Komponenten besitzen, unser Ziel jedoch darin besteht, uns von unserem maschinischen Erbe loszumachen, vermögen wir denen, die uns zu Werkzeugen für ihre Zwecke machen wollen, Widerstand zu leisten. Und wir können damit auch unseren eigenen Entschluß stützen, andere Menschen als einen Zweck für sich zu behandeln. Wir bestehen aus mechanischen Teilen, verfügen aber über emergente Eigenschaften wie freie Wahl, die Verfügung über uns selbst und persönliche Verantwortung.

Meine Botschaft lautet also: Wir sollten die offensichtliche Wahrheit eingestehen und zubilligen, daß Menschen Maschinen sind. Wir können Menschen und Maschinen nicht als vollkommen gegensätzlich ansehen. Wenn wir unsere Herkunft und fundamentale Natur verstehen, können wir unsere Entwicklung aus Erstarrung, Blindheit und Fremdbestimmung hin zu Flexibilität, Bewußtsein, Selbstbestimmung und Selbstdefinition beschleunigen. Wir können uns zunehmend ein Selbst wählen, können Künstler des Selbst werden. Das Zeitalter des Automorphens bricht an.

Boneware and Body Culture

The Revenge of the Body

Agentur BILWET/ADILKNO

"They're only facts."
Johan Sjerpstra

The body has found a way to chase the spirit from the flesh: this, essentially, is the project of virtuality. From its inception, cyberspace has been placed in the tradition of the Gnostic conspiracy to attain the pure spirit by leaving the body behind. The VR-prophets have only cast their gaze in one direction: ahead towards the thrilling adventures and ecstasies soon awaiting the spirit of the age. If people looked back at all, they saw the past as a prelude to today's megajump into the empire of speed. Attention focused on immaterial tendencies; the body was relegated to the reproductive sector [sports, food, sex]. The question of the body may be intellectually revived every now and then [especially whenever the Spirit is at a loss and boredom strikes] – but in this periodic celebration of the revival of the repressed, the body, in spite of its materiality, is still interpreted metaphorically and used as the topic of in-depth debates.

Body of ours, you won't be forgotten

The body is engaged in a project of its own. It currently reveals two trends: revenge and metamorphosis. The body no longer wants to be used as a compensatory device for the failed

Boneware und Body Culture

Die Rache des Körpers

Agentur BILWET/ADILKNO

"Ach, es sind bloß Tatsachen."
– Johan Sjerpstra

Der Körper hat einen Trick gefunden, dem Geist das Fleisch auszutreiben. Das ist im wesentlichen das Projekt der Virtualität. Cyberspace steht von Anfang an in der Tradition der gnostischen Verschwörung, die der reine Geist durch Zurücklassen des Körpers zu erreichen trachtet. Die Propheten der VR schauten nur in eine Richtung: vorwärts auf die spannenden Abenteuer und die Ekstasen, die der Weltgeist bald erleben sollte. Wohin man auch blickte, wurde die Vergangenheit als Anlauf zum heutigen Megajump ins Reich der Lichtgeschwindigkeit betrachtet. Alle Aufmerksamkeit richtete sich auf die immateriellen Tendenzen, und der Körper wurde in den Reproduktionsbereich [Sport, Essen, Sex] verdrängt. Freilich wird das dann und wann auf intellektueller Ebene diskutiert – besonders dann, wenn der Geist es nicht mehr so recht weiß und die Langeweile zugeschlagen hat –, aber in diesem periodischen Feiern der Rückkehr des Verdrängten wird der Körper trotz seiner Materialität doch wieder metaphorisch begriffen und dient als Auslöser für gute Debatten.

Körper, wir werden dich doch nicht vergessen

Der Körper hat sein eigenes Projekt. Darin sind zwei Tendenzen auszumachen: Rache und Metamorphose. Der Körper will nicht länger als Kompensationsmaschine für die mißglückte Virtualität dieser unbequemen Stühle, unhandlichen Tastaturen, zu hohen Tische, durchgebrannten Bildschirme, krebserregenden Handies, störenden elektromagnetischen Felder dienen – ganz zu schweigen von den langen Arbeitszeiten der hyper-enthusiastischen Datenarbeiter, von ihrer Netzabhängigkeit, den verlorenengegangenen Daten und dem Streß, dauernd updaten zu müssen. Die ergonomische Industrie hält zwar Schritt mit der Computerbranche, unternimmt aber nur etwas gegen die Symptome, nicht gegen die Ursachen. Die Astronauten, deren Muskeln bei lang-

virtuality of all those rotten chairs, clumsy keyboards, high desks, radiant screens, carcinogenic mobile phones and static electromagnetic fields. Not to mention the long working hours of the overenthusiastic data workers, their Net addiction, the misfiled data and the constant stress of keeping up-to-date. The ergonomics industry stays in pace with the computer trade, but it's a hopeless task. We may pity the astronauts whose muscles shrink under conditions of extended weightlessness, but far worse are the stiff muscles, sore tendons, mouse elbows, nagging wrists, deformed vertebrae, dislocated shoulder blades, bruised tailbones, and the CTS and RSI of the triumphant virtual class.

I've left my body to progress

Because one is oneself a part of digital *progress in action,* any inconveniences are taken for granted. Worthless interfaces, incomprehensible and extensive software, lost data: the body is written off as quickly as the accompanying hardware. Data mining: even miners do not develop black lung until after retirement. The Adilkno orthopedist Rothule: *They should never have introduced computers before a try-out period of 15 years.* Now an entire class of therapists is growing filthy rich over the rehabilitation of the common digirati. Private healthcare is blooming. In the workplace, it is not just our intellectual work that is controlled by the system, but even the body is supervised and subjected to a new regime. It must be relieved, exercised, and relaxed every fifteen minutes. Every hour you are required to leave the terminal and go to the recreation room, where easy chairs and New-Age music await you. The canteen only serves organic food in an attempt to normalize your completely messed up yin-yang balance. The euphoria has subsided and so have all doubts and criticisms. There's a job to be done, and that hurts. The network is fully operational and has to be rendered profitable. Any expense cuts, once made by the organization through computerization, are now being undone by long-term absenteeism. Bill Gates, we love you!

The vengeance theme dates back to the introduction of computers when it was believed that all those electronics would relieve us from much tedious work. This fairly simple psychoanalytic framework will continue to bug Third-Wave profiteers for generations to come. It is the

andauernder Schwerelosigkeit schlapp werden, mögen uns zwar leid tun; schlimmer noch sind jedoch die steifen Muskeln, die entzündeten Sehnen, die Maus-Arme und aufbegehrenden Pulse, die verkümmerten Halswirbel und verrenkten Schulterblätter, das verschobene Steißbein und die CTS und RSI der triumphierenden virtuellen Klasse.

Ich spendete meinen Körper dem Fortschritt

Weil der Mensch selbst Teil des digitalen*progress in action* ist, nimmt er mit allem Ungemach vorlieb. Wertlose Interfaces, unverständliche und umfangreiche Software, unauffindbare Daten: Der eigene Körper wird genauso schnell abgeschrieben wie die dazugehörige Apparatur. Data-mining: Auch die Bergarbeiter bekommen erst nach der Entlassung Probleme mit ihrer Staublunge. Der Bilwet-Orthopäde Rothule: *Man hätte Computer erst nach einer Testphase von 15 Jahren einführen dürfen.* Nun verdient sich eine ganze Klasse von Therapeuten mit der Rehabilitation mittelständischer Digerati eine goldene Nase, und das privatisierte Gesundheitswesen blüht und gedeiht.

Am Arbeitsplatz wird nicht mehr nur die geistige Arbeit vom System kontrolliert. Auch der Körper wird überwacht und ist einem neuen Regime unterstellt worden. Er muß jede Viertelstunde hinausgehen, er muß gestreckt und entspannt werden. Nach einer Stunde muß man sich vom Terminal entfernen und sich in den Ruheraum mit bequemen Liegestühlen und beruhigender New-Age-Musik begeben. In der Kantine gibt es nur biologisch-dynamische Nahrung, um das total gestörte Gleichgewicht zwischen Yin und Yang wieder halbwegs herzustellen. Die Euphorie hat sich gelegt, ebenso die Zweifel und Kritik. Nun muß durchgearbeitet werden, und das tut weh. Das Netzwerk ist bereits funktionstüchtig und muß Profit abwerfen. Was einst durch Automatisierung eingespart wurde, wirkt sich nun als langwieriger krankheitsbedingter Arbeitsausfall aus. Vielen Dank, Bill Gates!

Das Motiv der Rache entstammt noch Vorstellungen aus der Einführungsphase des Computers, als man noch überzeugt war, die Elektronik würde uns in Kürze von einem Haufen langweiliger Tätigkeiten befreien. Dieses recht einfache psychoanalytische Schema wird den Profiteuren der Third Wave noch lange zu schaffen machen. Es ist die posthume Variante des Höchstpersönlichen, das sich als höchst politisch erwies. Gender wurde durch Flesh ersetzt, und das Frivole der Wetware mit ihren Vergnügun-

posthuman version of the ever-so personal which turned out to be political. Gender has been replaced by the flesh, and the frivolousness of wetware and its amusements has been taken over by rigid boneware and its prostheses. This is a disorder which no esoteric antidote can cure. It's not between the ears, but between the elbows. That is why something has to be done. To this end, a variety of mind-body syntheses are on offer: from tantra, yogarobics, physiotherapy, brisk walking, and callisthenics to the intercultural detrainment-mix of the high-impact workout. All these methods are designed to avoid the sudden return of the physical, all too physical.

Your body is your best friend, but how well do you really know it?

From the body's point of view, these hypermodern phenomena take on a very different perspective. What if the body were found to have a mind of its own? The themes of return and revenge result from a cultural discomfort; they are a physical version of Adorno & Horkheimer's *Dialectic of Enlightenment.* But the body discovers great opportunities in virtuality because this will allow it to discard all civilizational ballast attached to it through the ages. Cultural norms have always meant the dominance of spirit over the body. Today this spiritual regime is called identity, health, or spirituality – now and for posterity.

To have a liquid identity is already quite acceptable [albeit not to the authorities], and that is a first step towards the realization of bodies without identities. The alluring perspective of a migration of spirits into cyberspace opens up the potential space of a body that is freed from its spirit. Free from restrictions, the body will be able to set out on its own course. It will be free to transform itself and take on the strangest shapes. In our present duality, the body can only be understood as a nuisance or pleasure machine, subject to a given body politic. But that which we have interpreted as the revenge of the body, in the above, may as well point to a hidden agenda by the body as such. Perhaps the body has used the spirit to persuade humanity to develop the means to leave earth and spread throughout the galaxy. Perhaps virtuality is the body's tool to shake off the spirit like some sort of parasite. Everything that is pleasurable is bad for your health, and that in

gen mußte der strammen Boneware mit ihren Prothesen Platz machen. Wir haben es hier mit einem Leiden zu tun, gegen das kein esoterisches Kraut gewachsen ist. Es sitzt nicht zwischen den Ohren, sondern zwischen den Ellenbogen. Deshalb muß auch dringend etwas dagegen unternommen werden. Speziell dafür gibt es allerlei Synthesen von Körper und Geist im Angebot: von Tantra, Yogarobics, Mensendieck-Gymnastik, High-Impact-Workout, Briskwalking und Callanetics bis zum interkulturellen Lockerungs-Mix nach dem High-Impact-Workout. All diese Methoden sind darauf ausgerichtet, der plötzlichen Rückkehr des Körperlichen, des allzu Körperlichen, zuvorzukommen.

Dein Körper ist dein bester Freund, aber wie gut kennst du ihn eigentlich?

Aus dem Blickwinkel des Körpers sehen diese hypermodernen Phänomene auf einmal ganz anders aus. Was, wenn der Körper seine eigenen Vorstellungen entwickelt? Die Themen von Rückkehr und Rache entstammen einem kulturellen Unbehagen und sind eine physische Variante von Adorno/Horkheimers *Dialektik der Aufklärung*. Der Körper freilich sieht große Möglichkeiten in der Virtualisierung, weil er damit all den Zivilisationsballast abschütteln kann, der über Jahrhunderte am Körper festgemacht wurde. Kulturelle Normen haben immer für die Herrschaft des Geistes über den Körper gesorgt. Zur Zeit heißt das geistige Regime Identität, Gesundheit, Spiritualität – im Heute und für die Nachkommen.

Daß jemand eine fließende Identität hat, wird heutzutage schon akzeptiert [wenn auch nicht von Autoritäten]. Das ist ein erster Schritt zur Realisierung des Körpers ohne Identität. Die lockende Perspektive einer Migration des Geistes in den Cyberspace eröffnet den Möglichkeitsraum eines von seinem Geist befreiten Körpers. Frei von allen Beschränkungen, kann er eine ganz eigene Richtung einschlagen. Er kann sich nach Belieben transformieren und die merkwürdigsten Gestalten annehmen. In der zeitgenössischen Dualität kann der Körper nur noch als Last oder als Genußmaschine gelesen werden, die dieser oder jener Körperpolitik unterworfen ist. Aber was hier als Rache des Körpers interpretiert wird, könnte auch auf eine geheime Agenda des Körpers selbst hinweisen. Vielleicht hat der Körper den Geist gebraucht, um den Menschen dazu zu bewegen, Mittel zu suchen, die Erde zu verlassen und sich im All auszubreiten? Vielleicht ist Virtualität ein Mittel des Körpers, den Geist als Parasiten von sich abzu-

and of itself is food for thought. European thinking practically coincides with the notion of culture. It is always a matter of providing a shelter for the spirit, be it in the form of a temple, palace, church, library or the [digital] city at large. This is the domain of *wherefore*-thinking, placing everything within a linear motion towards a well-defined endpoint: Truth, freedom, beauty, heaven, or higher things. It is the origin of the urge toward virtuality. With the emigration of this body of thought to the New World, the division between corporeality and the spiritual principle was rendered absolute. In the U.S.A. people no longer provide the spirit with a shelter, it is the body itself which is rebuilt. Both the urban and natural environment are denied their direct impact on human existence. Everything is submitted to the physical condition. The body is its own foundation and no longer yearns for the spirit: thus Walt Whitman's *I think the body electric.*

What gives Americans their local color is their belief that their own culture is a global one. Local cultures believe that they coincide with their own contexts. Europe has ample experience with cultures that staked a universal claim. From a European perspective, the particular body politic that accompanies the Internet-cyberculture is no more than one of many disciplining methods. Europe could never have developed the concept of *body culture.* The body was subjected to culture; combined they were nothing. The body was neither the goal of culture nor its carrier. The strength of *body culture* is that it is a self-sufficient culture that does not have to lead anywhere. It is no longer a question of *wherefore*; rather, it is the notion of *how to* which fuels the extension of practices. In American technology [and *body culture* IS technology], the European antithesis between nature and culture is eliminated: the body becomes a [bio-]machine amongst [fitness-]equipment. Technology is how the body discards its cultural obligations. *Body culture* demonstrates, in a festive and sporting way, that technology is not necessarily anti-corporeal [as Europeans had believed]. Machines improve on the body, not because it is in such bad repair, but because it can be made even better than it is. This is the principle behind every gymnasium.

A lot of the post-60s achievements revolved around the acceptance of physical joys and

werfen? Alles, was lecker ist, ist ungesund – das sollte zu denken geben.

Das europäische Denken ist praktisch mit der Idee der Kultur gleichzusetzen. Es ist immer nützlich, dem Geist ein Haus zu bauen, sei es ein Tempel, ein Palast, eine Kirche, eine Bibliothek oder die [digitale] Stadt an sich. Hier herrscht das *Wohin*-Denken, das alles in eine lineare, auf einen klar definierten Endpunkt gerichtete Entwicklung stellt: die Wahrheit, die Freiheit, das Schöne, den Himmel oder das Höhere. Hier liegt auch die Quelle des Drangs nach Virtualität.

Bei der Emigration dieses Gedankengutes in die Neue Welt wird die Trennung zwischen Körperlichkeit und geistigem Prinzip verabsolutiert. In den USA baut man kein Haus mehr für den Geist, sondern man baut den Körper selbst um. Sowohl der städtischen als auch natürlichen Umgebung wird ein direkter Einfluß auf das menschliche Dasein abgesprochen. Alles wird der Bedingung des Körpers unterworfen. Der Körper ruht in sich selbst und hat kein Heimweh mehr nach dem Geist: Dem entspricht Walt Whitman's *I think the body electric*.

Die *couleur locale* der Amerikaner ist ihre Überzeugung, ihre eigene Kultur sei global. Die lokale Kultur ist der Meinung, sie stimme mit ihrem eigenen Kontext überein. Europa hat die nötige Erfahrung mit Kulturen, die universelle Ansprüche erhoben. Aus der europäischen Perspektive ist die spezifische, mit der Internet-Cyberkultur verbundene Körperpolitik nur eine von vielen Disziplinierungsmethoden. Europa hätte das Konzept der *body culture* nicht entwickeln können. Der Body war vor der Culture da, aber zusammen waren sie nichts. Der Körper war kein Ziel von Kultur, er ist nicht einmal ihr Träger. Die Stärke der Body Culture liegt darin, daß sie eine sich selbst genügende Kultur ist, die auf eigenen Beinen stehen kann, ohne irgendwohin zu müssen. Hier herrscht nicht die Frage des Wohin, sondern des Wie, die die Ausweitung der Praktiken weiter anfacht. Der europäische Widerspruch von Natur und Kultur ist in der amerikanischen Technik aufgehoben [und Body Culture IST Technik]: Der Körper wird zu einem [Bio-]Apparat unter all den [Fitness-]Geräten. Technik ist die Art und Weise, auf die sich der Körper seiner kulturellen Verpflichtungen entledigt. Body Culture – als Sport und Theater – zeigt, daß Technik nicht per definitionem gegen den Körper gerichtet sein muß [wie die Europäer behaupten]. Die Maschinen verbessern den Körper – nicht weil er sich in einem solch schlechten Zustand befände, sondern weil er noch besser gemacht werden kann, als er schon ist. Das ist der Ansatz jeder Sportschule.

burdens which had been either repressed or controlled for centuries. The body culture of the 1980s elaborated on these foundations and developed an unprecedented physical ideal. After its emancipation the body went its own way, whether to flex its muscles, have its breasts enlarged or have itself surgically [or digitally] remodeled. These are all attempts to curb the body's unrestrained and autonomous urge toward metamorphosis by meeting it halfway. This also explains the fear of drug use in sports [and in society as a whole]: what will happen if the body leaves its natural and cultural boundaries behind altogether? We know all about *digital delirium* – but where would physical delirium take us?

Genetic design beyond revenge?

It is easy to imagine a World Order ruled by an [American] desire for clean genes [and memes]. Though strong supporters of a dirty hybridism, we are even more interested to see what happens when the body is really left to go its own way, not subjected to any aesthetic/genetic control. This is where the post-technological paradigm opens up, free from the tedious dialectics of the body and technology. In this respect, the cyborg serves as a carnivalesque transitional figure. Cyborgs parody their natural aspects with their prostheses and vice versa. They flaunt their gadgets in festive ways, because the relationship between the body and technology is still quite obvious. So all kinds of baroque interfaces are being designed in which the role of the [electronic] artist is grossly overestimated. They betray a naive faith that things will work out just fine between ourselves and technology. But what does this mean to technology? The post-technological body has transcended all cheap syntheses between body and spirit, nature and culture, culture and technology, materiality and virtuality. It refuses to be a genetic and historical vehicle any longer. It invites us on a journey through the body, through the abysses and uncharted grounds of living materiality. That is the starting point of all negative thinking.

Translated from the Dutch by Sakhra -l'Assal/ Ziekend Zoeltjes Produkties, Amsterdam, 1997 Thanks to C. Knep for proof reading the text.

Vieles was seit den sechziger Jahren erreicht wurde, beruhte auf der Akzeptanz der Lüste und Lasten des Körpers, die über Jahrhunderte entweder geleugnet oder kontrolliert wurden. Die Body Culture der achtziger Jahre baute auf dieser Basis auf und entwickelte ein bis dahin ungekanntes Körperideal. Nach seiner Emanzipation ging der Körper seine eigenen Wege, sei es, daß er Muskelbündel ansetzte, sich große Brüste wachsen oder sich plastisch [oder digital] re-modellieren ließ.

Das sind alles Versuche, den ungebremsten und autonomen Drang des Körpers zur Metamorphose in den Griff zu bekommen, indem man ein wenig nachgibt. Hier liegt auch die Ursache für die Angst vor Doping [und Drogen im allgemeinen]: Was geschieht, wenn der Körper seine natürlichen und kulturellen Grenzen ganz hinter sich läßt? Das digitale Delirium kennen wir inzwischen, aber was bringt uns das physikalische Delirium?

Genetic design beyond revenge?

Es ist einfach, sich eine Weltordnung auszumalen, die von der amerikanischen Sucht nach sauberen Genen [und Memen] beherrscht wird. Wir als Vertreter der schmutzigen Hybridität wollen aber wissen, was passiert, wenn der Körper wirklich seine eigenen Wege gehen kann und nicht mehr irgendwelchen ästheto-genetischen Kontrollen unterworfen wird. Hier eröffnet sich das post-technologische Paradigma, das der anstrengenden Dialektik von Körper und Technik entkommen ist. In dieser Hinsicht ist der Cyborg eine karnevaleske Übergangsfigur. Er parodiert seine natürliche Seite mit seinen technischen Prothesen und umgekehrt. Er schmückt sich mit seinen Gadgets auf festliche Weise, da die Beziehung zwischen Körper und Technik noch sehr sichtbar ist. Dafür werden auch allerlei barocke Interfaces entworfen, wobei die Rolle des [elektronischen] Künstlers maßlos überschätzt wird. Daraus spricht ein naiver Glaube, daß alles noch gut wird zwischen uns und der Technologie.

Aber was bedeutet das für die Technologie? Der post-technologische Körper hat alle billigen Synthesen zwischen Körper und Geist, Natur und Kultur, Materialität und Virtualität bereits passiert. Der post-technologische Körper weigert sich, noch länger das Vehikel von Genen und Geschichte zu sein. Er lädt zu einer Reise durch den Körper, die Tiefen und unbekannten Gründe der lebendigen Materialität ein. Dort beginnt jedes negative Denken.

Aus dem Niederländischen von Petra Ilyes.

Periphery and the FleshFactor

Mark Weiser

symposium

Peripherie und FleshFactor

Mark Weiser

Einleitung

In der Wahrnehmungspsychologie und -philosophie gibt es ein bekanntes Experiment, bei dem die Augen geschlossen werden und der Weg mit einem Stock ertastet wird. Für Menschen mit normalem Sehvermögen ist es anfangs ungewohnt und schwierig, mit einem krummen Stock die vor ihnen liegenden Gegenstände zu ertasten. Aber dann tritt eine bemerkenswerte Veränderung ein. Der Stock verschwindet aus unserer Wahrnehmung, und statt dessen tritt die Welt in Erscheinung. Mit anderen Worten, nicht der Stock selbst steht von nun an im Mittelpunkt der Aufmerksamkeit, sondern das, was er uns von der Welt offenbart. Statt des Stockes nehmen wir Beton oder Gras oder den Briefkasten wahr. Das ist kein besonders überraschendes Beispiel – durch unsere Augen und unser Gehirn erkennen wir die Welt, ohne allzu sehr von den fleischlichen, kör-

Introduction

A famous example in the psychology and philosophy of perception is closing your eyes and feeling your way with a cane. For the normally sighted, this experience initially is awkward, as one attempts to deduce what may be ahead from the unfamiliar bouncing curved stick in the hand. But eventually a remarkable change occurs. The cane disappears from perception, and the world appears. That is, the cane ceases to be a focus of attention, and what the cane is revealing about the world comes into focus instead. Instead of cane, we perceive concrete, or grass, or a mailbox. This example is not too surprising – our eyes and brains show us the world without much intrusion of the fleshy, bloody details of those complicated and imperfect organs. Attending to one thing through a peripheral system of other things is fundamental to how people work.

When the cane disappears, it has moved to the periphery of our perception. It does so in order to let that part of the world that the cane can reveal come to the center. Notice that *peripheral* does not mean inessential or unimportant. The cane is crucial, without it we would know nothing of the world in front of us. It is peripheral because it is playing a supporting role, enabling us to perceive further ahead than if we had to wait to stub our toes.

The cane illustrates something else – that the peripheral can sometimes become center again. We can cease to perceive through the cane, and instead again attend to the cane. When we do this, the world through the cane goes away, but properties of the cane come forward – its weight, the feel of the handle, whether it is broken. This shift requires a simple refocus, and the ability to quickly re-center what was peripheral can be an important skill.

Philosopher Michael Polanyi, in his book *The Tacit Dimension*, called the peripheral realm the *proximal*, because it was close to us. The center he called *distal*. Our eyeglasses are proximal, and we look through them to what is distal. The proximal is tacit, it does not speak directly. But the proximal makes itself known through its consequences.

Attuning and attending

We use the word attunement to describe tacit attention to the silent possibilities of

perlichen Einzelheiten dieser komplizierten und unvollkommenen Organe gestört zu werden. Es ist ein grundlegendes Charakteristikum der menschlichen Funktionsweise, sich einem Ding durch ein peripheres System anderen Dingen zuzuwenden.

Das Verschwinden des Stockes bedeutet, daß er Teil unserer peripheren Wahrnehmung geworden ist. So kann jener Teil der Welt ins Zentrum rücken, den uns der Stock erschließt. Es ist wichtig, *peripher* nicht mit unwesentlich oder unwichtig gleichzusetzen. Der Stock ist äußerst wichtig, ohne ihn wüßten wir nichts von der Welt um uns herum. Er ist aber insofern peripher, als er eine unterstützende Rolle spielt – wir können uns mit ihm vortasten und müssen nicht darauf warten, bis unsere Zehen an etwas stoßen.

Der Stock macht etwas anderes deutlich – das Periphere kann manchmal auch wieder zum Mittelpunkt werden. Wir können, anstatt unsere Umgebung mit dem Stock wahrzunehmen, unsere Aufmerksamkeit erneut auf den Stock richten. Wenn wir das tun, verschwindet die Welt, die uns der Stock vermittelt hat, und die Eigenschaften des Stockes treten in den Vordergrund – sein Gewicht, wie sich sein Griff anfühlt, ob er zerbrochen ist. Dazu genügt es, unsere Konzentration neu auszurichten. Die Fähigkeit, etwas, das gerade noch peripher war, wieder ins Zentrum zu rücken, kann von großer Bedeutung sein.

In seinem Buch *The Tacit Dimension* nannte der Philosoph Michael Polanyi das Reich der Peripherie *proximal*, weil es uns nahe ist. Das Zentrum bezeichnete er als *distal*. Unsere Brillen sind proximal, wir nehmen mit ihnen alles Distale wahr. Das Proximale ist unauffällig, es äußert sich nicht direkt. Aber es macht sich durch seine Konsequenzen bemerkbar.

Abstimmung und Aufmerksamkeit

Unter Abstimmung verstehen wir das stillschweigende Achtgeben auf die unausgesprochenen Möglichkeiten eines bestimmten Umfelds. Hierin unterscheidet es sich von der Aufmerksamkeit, der expliziten Konzentration auf das, was vor uns liegt.

Ist man auf einer Schnellstraße unterwegs, so ist die Aufmerksamkeit höchstwahrscheinlich auf die Straße, die anderen Autos, die nächste Abfahrt gerichtet. Was passiert, wenn der Motor unerwartet ein neues Geräusch von sich gibt? Mühelos konzentrieren Sie sich nun auf dieses Geräusch, versuchen herauszuhören, was es ist und welche Gefahr es bedeuten könnte, und ergreifen die notwendigen Maßnahmen. Aber wie kommt es, daß Sie dieses

an environment. This is distinct from attending, which is explicit attention to what is in front of us. Driving down the expressway one is likely to be attending to the road, to the cars around, to the next exit. What happens if the engine suddenly makes a new noise? Effortlessly one now attends to that, listens for what it might be and the hazard it might signal, and takes appropriate action. But how is it that one heard the noise at all? You were not attending to it, yet it got into your head nonetheless. The answer is, it was part of your periphery, and you were attuned to it.

When at a party so loud that you need to shout to the person right in front of you, you nonetheless hear your voice spoken quietly across the room: that's attunement.

Attunement is the unconscious connection that we have to those parts of our periphery that we can quickly attend to with a simple shift of attention. The power of attunement is that we can attune to much more than we can attend to. Return to the car on the expressway. What are all of the events that might shift your attention? Weather, noise, motion of other cars, changes in road surface, unusual billboards, interesting words or music on the radio, a shift in the seat, a funny taste in your mouth, a sudden unbidden memory, and many more. The range of attunement is immense. To those skilled at using attunement, it provides the opportunity for deep and wide connection with much more of the world around us.

Attunement, and the shift from attuning to attending and back, are part of what makes the periphery effective. If you believe that optimal functioning involves ignoring everything on which you are not focusing, then you miss the chance to expand your effective attention 100-fold by including the attunement space in your functioning.

Periphery at multiple levels

The periphery functions at many different levels. At least three are the perceptual, the cognitive, and the social.

The perceptual peripheral is the sensory surround to which we are not attending. Peripheral vision is a simple case. When we are driving or walking or even just sitting, the flow through our peripheral vision is crucial. A similar surround comes from sound, which provides

Geräusch überhaupt gehört haben? Sie haben nicht darauf geachtet, und trotzdem ist es in Ihre Gedanken vorgedrungen. Die Antwort lautet: Es war Teil Ihrer Peripherie und Sie waren darauf abgestimmt.

Wenn Sie auf einer Party schreien müssen, um sich mit der Person direkt vor Ihnen unterhalten zu können, hören Sie sich mit normaler Lautstärke sprechen: Das ist Abstimmung. Abstimmung bedeutet die unbewußte Verbundenheit mit den Teilen unserer Peripherie, denen wir mühelos Beachtung schenken können, indem wir uns einfach auf sie konzentrieren. Die Stärke der Abstimmung liegt darin, daß wir uns auf viel mehr Dinge abstimmen als konzentrieren können. Nehmen wir noch einmal unser Auto auf der Schnellstraße. Welche Ereignisse könnten Ihre Aufmerksamkeit auf sich ziehen? Das Wetter, Geräusche, andere Autos, Veränderungen der Fahrbahn, außergewöhnliche Reklametafeln, interessante Ansagen oder Musik im Radio, Veränderungen am Sitz, ein komischer Geschmack im Mund, eine unerwartete und ungebetene Erinnerung und vieles andere mehr. Die Bandbreite an Abstimmungsmöglichkeiten ist enorm. Wer in der Lage ist, sich geschickt auf seine Umgebung abzustimmen, kann zu sehr viel mehr Dingen auf dieser Welt eine tiefe und umfassende Beziehung herstellen.

Die Abstimmung bzw. der Wechsel zwischen Abstimmung und Aufmerksamkeit und wieder zurück tragen zur Effektivität der Peripherie bei. Wer glaubt, optimal zu arbeiten, wenn er alles außerhalb des Zentrums Befindliche ausschaltet, läßt sich die Chance entgehen, mit Hilfe der Abstimmung seine tatsächliche Aufmerksamkeit zu verhundertfachen.

Die mehrfachen Ebenen der Peripherie

Die Peripherie umfaßt viele verschiedene Ebenen. Die perzeptorische, kognitive und soziale Ebene sind nur drei davon. Die perzeptorische Peripherie ist das sensorische Umfeld, auf das man sich nicht konzentriert. Das periphere Sehen ist ein einfacher Fall. Egal, ob man fährt, geht oder bloß sitzt – der Strom peripherer visueller Wahrnehmung hat größte Bedeutung. Ähnlich verhält es sich mit Geräuschen, die einerseits beruhigen und andererseits wichtige Orientierungshilfen bieten. Alle Sinne tragen das Ihre zu unserer Peripherie bei. Der Geruch eines fremden Ortes, auch wenn er nicht explizit wahrgenommen und identifiziert wird, hilft dem Verständnis und der Erinnerung.

Die digitale Technik läßt sich nur schwer mit unseren peripheren Sinnen verbinden. Die Architektur eines physischen Raumes hat Einfluß

crucial locating and comforting clues. And each of the senses offers its contribution to our periphery. The scent of a foreign place, even if unidentified or unexplicitly noticed, contributes to our understanding and memory.

Digital technology connects poorly with our peripheral senses. The architecture of a physical space influences peripheral vision, sounds, smells, and even bodily senses [e.g. tiredness from walking]. A digital architecture delivers little by comparison. Video screens put the information front and center in a little frame. The beeps, squawks, tune snatches, or voice data of computer audio technology are generally to be listened to, rather than for background awareness. And we have little in the way of smell, taste, or bodily inputs from computer systems. I consider this paucity of current digital technology not necessarily fundamental. But certainly current digital technology suffers from a painful lack of connection to the deepest foundations of being human, namely the proximal.

The sensorial peripheral is only the beginning of the impact of periphery on us. The cognitive periphery is another level up. Our use of symbols is one part of our cognitive functioning. Within the cognitive periphery certain symbols are front and center, while other structures are the surround within which we construct and compute in the symbolic world. Poetry plays on the cognitive periphery to evoke symphonies of meaning from the resonances of just a few words. Consider the following line:

"The force that through the
green fuse drives the flower"

Dylan Thomas

The resonances from "force", "fuse", and "drive", the mental image of activity in the frail flower stem, and the core syntactic structure of raw action ["force drives flower"], pull us unconsciously, peripherally, into a framework of interpretation of strength and power. Power relationships from our past, with parents or governments or bosses, are subtly called up into the luminous background. The flower, and so nature, is transformed from something simple and delicate into something complex, mysterious, and even a little fearsome.

The cognitive periphery is extremely rich, and the above example is just a hint at its

auf das periphere Sehen, auf periphere Geräusche, Gerüche und sogar auf periphere körperliche Sinneswahrnehmungen [z. B. Müdigkeit nach längerem Gehen]. Im Vergleich dazu sind digitale Architekturen alles andere als ergiebig. Bildschirme präsentieren alle Informationen in einem kleinen Rahmen und im Vordergrund. Das Piepsen und Kreischen, die Melodiefetzen und Sprachdaten aus dem Audiosystem der Computer sind im allgemeinen für das aktive Zuhören bestimmt und nicht für die Hintergrundaufmerksamkeit. Und Computersysteme liefern uns wenig zum Riechen, Schmecken, Fühlen oder an sonstigen physischen Reizen. Ich bin der Ansicht, daß es sich hierbei nicht unbedingt um einen grundlegenden Mangel der modernen digitalen Technik handelt. Doch läßt sie die Verbindung zum Ureigensten des Menschsein, zum Proximalen, schmerzlichst vermissen.

Die sensorische Peripherie bildet erst den Anfang des Einflusses, den die Peripherie auf uns hat. Auf der nächsthöheren Ebene findet sich die kognitive Peripherie. Der Gebrauch von Symbolen ist ein Teil unserer kognitiven Fähigkeiten. Innerhalb der kognitiven Peripherie bilden bestimmte Symbole das Zentrum, den Vordergrund, während andere Strukturen den Rahmen für unsere symbolischen Konstruktionen und Berechnungen liefern. Die Poesie spielt mit der kognitiven Peripherie, um durch den Klang einiger weniger Worte ganze Bedeutungssymphonien auszulösen. Nehmen wir beispielsweise folgende Verszeile:

"The force that through the green
fuse drives the flower "

Dylan Thomas

Der Klang von Worten wie "force", "fuse" und "drive", die Vorstellung von regem Leben im zarten Blumenstiel sowie die syntaktische Kernstruktur [*force drives flower*], die pure Aktivität ausdrückt, drängen uns unbewußt, peripher in ein Interpretationsschema der Stärke und Macht. Vergangene Autoritätsbeziehungen mit Eltern, Behörden oder Vorgesetzten treten unbemerkt in den strahlenden Hintergrund. Die Blume, und damit die Natur als solches, verwandelt sich von einem einfachen und zarten Ding in etwas Komplexes, Mysteriöses und sogar ein bißchen Furchteinflößendes.

Die kognitive Peripherie ist äußerst komplex; das obige Beispiel kann ihren Einfluß nur andeuten. Der begriffliche Rahmen, Weltanschauungen und Religionen, Ideologien und kulturelle Vorurteile – all

power. Conceptual frameworks, worldviews, religions, ideologies, cultural biases, all can function as powerful unseen peripheries that influence everything.

Alongside the cognitive periphery is the action periphery. When we act in the world those actions are an explicit center. Each of our actions can be seen as willed and discretely occurring. But each action is also within a periphery of consequences and influences beyond what we can possibly calculate. We perform our actions within a flow of those influences, and within an implicit understanding of the consequences.

For instance, when acting within a rich sports situation we behave appropriately within a complex field of sensory inputs and behaviors. Skiing down a mountain, each millisecond requires new small muscle movements to keep in balance and moving towards our goal. These actions take place within a periphery, the center of which is our conscious attention to the slope as a whole or down the mountain.

Above the cognitive and action periphery is the social periphery. Where a cognitive periphery is more-or-less in our heads, the social periphery is all around us [and in our heads]. The distinction between social and cognitive is hardly clean, but useful to bring out certain points.

The social periphery names our deep embedding within a network of other people and practices. This embedding effects what we know, what we count on, and our comfort and skill every day. Lave and Wegner have clarified that learning is not a matter of putting facts in the head, but a matter of becoming a member of a community. Consider the following thought experiment:

Imagine a great engineer, Q, a real whiz at the details of manufacturing widgets for company ABC. Company XYZ hires Q away from ABC, but XYZ does not trust Q, and so requires him to work in a windowless office and communicate only by anonymous memos to and from the rest of XYZ. How effective would Q be? Not very. For one thing, anonymity would cut him off from understanding the sources of information [e.g.: John is excitable; George is a master of understatement], and the anonymity would cut off his colleagues from understanding his reliability. No community would

das kann die Funktion einer mächtigen, unsichtbaren, alles beeinflussenden Peripherie übernehmen.

Die kognitive Peripherie geht mit der Handlungsperipherie einher. Wenn wir etwas tun, stehen unsere Handlungen explizit im Zentrum. Jede unserer Taten kann als gewollte und singuläre Aktivität angesehen werden. Aber jede Handlung ist auch eingebettet in eine Peripherie von Konsequenzen und Einflüssen, die wir unmöglich einkalkulieren können. Wir handeln in einem Strom solcher Einflüsse und im impliziten Wissen um die Konsequenzen.

Wenn wir zum Beispiel Sport betreiben, befinden wir uns in einem Umfeld komplexer sensorischer Eindrücke und Verhaltensweisen und handeln entsprechend. Während einer Skiabfahrt sind in jeder Millisekunde neue minimale Muskelbewegungen erforderlich, damit wir das Gleichgewicht halten und auf das Ziel zusteuern können. Diese Bewegungen sind Teil der Peripherie, in deren Zentrum unsere bewußte Konzentration auf den Hang als Ganzes oder unsere Fahrt den Berg hinunter steht.

Über der kognitiven und der Handlungsperipherie steht die soziale Peripherie. Ist die kognitive Peripherie mehr oder weniger auf unseren Kopf beschränkt, so ist die soziale Peripherie um uns herum [und in unserem Kopf] zu finden. Eine klare Unterscheidung zwischen sozial und kognitiv ist schwer zu treffen, wenn sie auch nützlich ist, um bestimmte Punkte deutlich zu machen.

Die soziale Peripherie benennt unsere feste Einbindung in ein Netzwerk von Menschen und Gewohnheiten. Diese Einbindung beeinflußt Tag für Tag, was wir wissen, worauf wir uns verlassen, unser Wohlbefinden und unser Können. Lave und Wegner haben dargelegt, daß es beim Lernen nicht auf das Einprägen von Fakten ankommt, sondern darauf, Mitglied einer Gemeinschaft zu werden. Nehmen wir zum Beispiel folgendes Gedankenexperiment:

Stellen Sie sich einen exzellenten Techniker vor, Q, ein wirkliches Genie, was die Produktionsdetails der Firma ABC anbelangt. Die Firma XYZ wirbt Q ab, hat aber kein Vertrauen zu ihm. Sie verlangt deshalb von ihm, in einem fensterlosen Büro zu arbeiten und mit dem Rest der Belegschaft nur mittels anonymer Notizen in Kontakt zu treten. Wie effektiv könnte Q arbeiten? Wohl nicht sehr effektiv. Zum einen würde es ihm diese Anonymität unmöglich machen, seine Informationsquellen richtig einzuschätzen [z. B.: John ist reizbar; George ist ein Meister des Understatement]. Zum anderen würden dadurch auch seine Kollegen daran gehindert, sich von seiner Vertrauenswürdigkeit zu überzeugen. Auf diese Art

form, and all of the wonderful bits of knowledge in Q's head would mostly be wasted.

To put this another way, individuals and communities are the focus and periphery for one another. Focusing on the individual one tends to see a knowledgeable person, with certain skills to be developed, and certain behaviors that are more or less useful. Focusing on the community, one tends to see a culture of response and support [or apathy and attack], an ability to get information, a system of processes, a set of cultural eyeglasses that keep out information, a continuity that outrides the coming and going of individuals. Both views are limited. Outstanding individuals help make an outstanding community. And an outstanding culture can enhance the ability of individuals to succeed in whatever way they interpret success.

The FleshFactor is the periphery

The proximal, the periphery, are the foundation of all our knowing and being in the world. The existentialist being-in-the-world is a reference to our proximal connections into everything. And at the core of everything proximal is the body.

It is the body that is the original periphery. As infants we learn to experience the world through our body. Where first we may bring only a buzzing confusion of sounds and colors and shapes, later we see things, and manipulate objects. Our bodily senses and abilities gradually become the proximal support for our attention to new centers out in the world. This support is not just perceptual, but is the foundation of cognitive and social relations as well.

Psychoanalytically one can tell the following story: Early on, each of us has a single periphery, in our body, and a single center, in the body and person of the other. We will form huge numbers of centers and peripheries in our lives, but the first center and periphery will bias us towards an initial pattern for setting up each subsequent center/periphery relationship. In the end, mental health will come from a transpicuous periphery. We will actually perceive differently, think differently, act different, and relate differently depending upon this periphery.

From feminist standpoint theory [e.g. philosopher Sandra Harding] one could emphasize the full periphery of a life, starting with a particular body, and extending through a par-

könnte keine Gemeinschaft entstehen, und all die tollen Kenntnisse im Kopf von Q blieben weitgehend ungenutzt.

Anders ausgedrückt, Individuum und Gemeinschaft stellen sowohl das Zentrum als auch die Peripherie füreinander dar. Steht das Individuum im Zentrum, so hat man gewöhnlich einen klugen Menschen mit gewissen entwicklungsfähigen Fertigkeiten und bestimmten mehr oder weniger nützlichen Verhaltensweisen vor sich. Steht dagegen die Gemeinschaft im Zentrum, so findet man im allgemeinen eine Kultur der Resonanz und Unterstützung [oder der Apathie und der Angriffe] vor, die Fähigkeit zur Informationsbeschaffung, ein System von Prozessen, kulturelle Brillen zur Ausschaltung gewisser Informationen, eine Kontinuität, die das Kommen und Gehen der Individuen überdauert. Beide Blickwinkel sind beschränkt. Hervorragende Individuen tragen zu einer hervorragenden Gemeinschaft bei. Und eine hervorragende Kultur kann die Chancen der Individuen erhöhen, erfolgreich zu sein – wie auch immer sie Erfolg auslegen mögen.

Der FleshFactor ist die Peripherie

Das Proximale, die Peripherie, ist die Basis unseres Wissens und unserer Existenz in dieser Welt. Das existentialistische In-der-Welt-Sein ist eine Anspielung auf unsere proximale Verbundenheit mit allen Dingen. Und im Zentrum alles Proximalen steht der Körper.

Der Körper bildet unsere ursprüngliche Peripherie. Als kleine Kinder lernen wir, die Welt durch unseren Körper zu erleben. Anstelle des anfänglichen Durcheinanders von verwirrenden Farben, Tönen und Konturen lernen wir später, Dinge zu sehen und Gegenstände zu manipulieren. Schritt für Schritt werden unsere Sinnesorgane und körperlichen Fähigkeiten zur proximalen Basis für unsere Hinwendung zu neuen Zentren. Diese Basis ist nicht auf die perzeptorische Wahrnehmung beschränkt, sondern bildet zugleich auch die Grundlage aller kognitiven Fähigkeiten und sozialen Beziehungen.

Um es in der Sprache der Psychoanalyse zu sagen: Zu Beginn verfügt jeder von uns über eine einzige Peripherie, seinen eigenen Körper, und über ein einziges Zentrum, den Körper und die Person des anderen. Wir werden in unserem Leben ungezählte Zentren und Peripherien formen. Aber das erste Zentrum und die erste Peripherie prägen in uns ein ursprüngliches Muster, nach dem wir alle folgenden Zentren und Peripherien gestalten. Letzten Endes ist eine transparente Peripherie die Voraussetzung für psychische Gesundheit. Je nach Beschaffenheit die-

ticular history of a particular person embedded in a particular culture and history. This rich and unique history permeates all centered seeing, cognating, and social relations. These standpoints are not reducible to any particular accumulation of facts or logic or explicit assumptions, because they operate as a periphery, which is to say their very function is tied into their inexplicitness. It is only through the body that we take in and act out the periphery. The body is our most immediate source of peripheral sense. The brain – a part of our body – is our most immediate source of cognitive periphery. Having a body is the primary genesis of social participation.

We were always cyborgs

Whether something is flesh, or metal, or silicon, is not fundamental from the point of view of understanding center/periphery. Our bodies are flesh, and we have lived with them for a very long time, moment by moment, and we have built up an incredibly rich, complex, thick, tenacious periphery within them. That is the main distinction of the flesh over silicon – how much periphery we embed within it.

What would be the effect if from birth one of our senses was replaced or augmented mechanically? Some hint comes from experiments with reversing eyeglasses. After a few days of wearing such glasses, the world flips back around and normal functioning is restored. That is, the reversing effect moves into the proximal realm where we can again act through it. In this case the proximal element, reversing, is trivial and adds nothing to our ability. But imagine one that created a different perception, such as extending our visual range into the infrared, or increasing our peripheral vision. After some time we would come to pull that difference from strange center into effective periphery, and we would act through it as any other sense.

With philosopher/biologist Donna Haraway, I believe we were always, and always will be, cyborgs. The cyborg is simply one whose perception or action is mediated through mechanism. But that is all of us all the time. We see nothing that is not mediated through fleshy lenses and other transducers, and interpreted in multiple layers of synapse and cortex. Mediation is a kind of trivial periphery.

ser Peripherie werden wir unterschiedlich wahrnehmen, unterschiedlich denken, unterschiedlich handeln und unsere Beziehungen unterschiedlich gestalten.

Aus dem Blickwinkel feministischer Theorie [z. B. der Philosophin Sandra Harding] könnte man die komplexe Peripherie eines Menschenlebens betonen, an deren Beginn ein bestimmter Körper steht. Diese Peripherie wird dann durch die spezielle Geschichte einer speziellen Person in einem speziellen kulturellen und historischen Umfeld erweitert. Diese komplexe und einzigartige Geschichte durchdringt das zentrierte Sehen, alle Kognitionen und sozialen Beziehungen. Da sie die Peripherie bildet, kann sie nicht auf die beliebige Akkumulation von Fakten bzw. expliziten oder logischen Annahmen reduziert werden. Und das heißt nichts anderes, als daß ihre Funktion untrennbar mit Inexplizitheit verbunden ist.

Wir brauchen den Körper, um über ihn die Peripherie zu erfassen und mit ihr in Kontakt treten zu können. Der Körper ist die unmittelbarste Quelle aller peripheren Sinneswahrnehmungen. Das Gehirn – ein Teil unseres Körpers – ist die unmittelbarste Quelle der kognitiven Peripherie. Und unser Körper ist der Ursprung aller sozialen Eingebundenheit.

Wir sind immer Cyborgs gewesen

Um den Dualismus von Zentrum und Peripherie zu verstehen, ist es nicht entscheidend, ob etwas aus Fleisch, Metall oder Silikon besteht. Unsere Körper sind Fleisch. Wir haben sehr lange Zeit mit ihnen gelebt, Augenblick um Augenblick, und wir haben eine unglaublich reiche, komplexe, dicke Peripherie in ihnen geschaffen. Das ist der wichtigste Unterschied zwischen Fleisch und Silikon – wieviel Peripherie wir damit verbinden.

Wie würde es sich auswirken, wenn einer unserer Sinne von Geburt an mechanisch ersetzt oder erweitert würde? Experimente mit Umkehrbrillen liefern dazu einige Hinweise. Wenn solche Gläser einige Tage lang getragen werden, dreht sich die Welt wieder in ihre Ausgangslage zurück, und die normale Funktionsfähigkeit ist wiederhergestellt. Das heißt, der Umkehreffekt entschwindet in das Reich der Peripherie, wo wir wieder durch ihn handeln können. In diesem Fall ist das proximale Element, d. h. die Umkehrung, ohne Bedeutung und trägt nichts zu unserem Können bei. Stellen wir uns aber vor, es gäbe eine neue Art der Wahrnehmung. Unsere Sehfähigkeit könnte sich beispielsweise auf den Infrarotbereich ausdehnen, oder unser peripheres Sehvermögen würde verbessert. Nach einiger Zeit würde

Not every augmentation of our bodies will work. Human beings are structured to have a center and periphery. This structure is tuned in some ways to our actual human bodies and earthly world. This is likely from a genetic, Darwinian, learning, and center/periphery view. Architecture, product design, urban planning, politics, and many other great and low arts are in part about the predispositions of the human periphery. Those arts considered universal tap more deeply into the universal center/periphery structure. Those more transient resonate only with the temporary learned or constructed peripheries of a given culture or time.

The role of art in the periphery

Challenging the periphery is very difficult. It can hardly be approached through the center. Any words or explicit references slide right off. Making the periphery explicit destroys it, like the explosion of a fish pulled from the deep sea to the surface. The periphery must be sidled up to and nudged. It must be hinted at, and directed towards, without being referenced. In some cultures the name of god must not be said, but she can be indirectly referenced though effects, such as *the one who made all things*. Referring to a particular person's periphery is like that, it is sometimes best done through effects.

A key function of art is to reframe peripheries. Where science and technology deal with what can be written down, art functions with what cannot be said explicitly. Art cannot just say, it must communicate under the surface of our center.

To talk about *meaning* in art is an error that confuses center and periphery. Meaning is a concept of the center, where one can lay out a model of consequences and referents and call this the meaning. Art uses referents and consequences and resonances to achieve what is not itself a *meaning*. Art reframes, re-peripheralizes, pokes at consequences, hints at hidden peripheries, pulls periphery to center and vice versa.

Artist Steve Mann of MIT lives his life wearing video goggles. One of Mann's artworks is himself. By being this new kind of self, a person constantly recording, a person always viewing the world in part through digital mediation, a person who has chosen to continuously

dieser befremdliche Unterschied nicht mehr im Mittelpunkt unserer Aufmerksamkeit stehen, sondern wäre Teil der effektiven Peripherie geworden, und wir könnten damit wie mit jedem anderen Körpersinn auch leben.

Wie die Philosophin und Biologin Donna Haraway glaube auch ich, daß wir immer Cyborgs gewesen sind und immer sein werden. Ein Cyborg ist einfach jemand, dessen Wahrnehmungen oder Handlungen mit Hilfe der Technik vermittelt werden. Aber das trifft auf uns alle zu. Ohne die Vermittlung fleischlicher Linsen oder anderer Umwandler und ohne die Umsetzung in unzähligen Schichten von Synapsen und Cortex können wir nichts sehen. Vermittlung ist eine Art trivialer Peripherie.

Nicht jede Ausweitung unserer Körper erfüllt ihre Funktion. Menschen sind in Zentrum und Peripherie strukturiert. Diese Struktur ist auf verschiedene Art und Weise auf unseren realen Körper und unsere irdische Welt abgestimmt. Dies ist von einem genetischen, darwinistischen und lerntheoretischen Standpunkt und nicht zuletzt aus der Sicht der Zentrum-Peripherie-Theorie sehr naheliegend. Architektur, Produktdesign, Stadtplanung, Politik und viele andere großartige und weniger großartige Künste beziehen sich zum Teil auf die Prädispositionen der menschlichen Peripherie. Diese Kunst, die wir als universell ansehen, greift in hohem Maße auf die universelle Zentrum-Peripherie-Struktur zurück. Ihre vergänglicheren Formen beschränken sich auf die vorübergehend gelernten oder konstruierten Peripherien einer bestimmten Kultur oder Zeit.

Die Rolle der Kunst in der Peripherie

Die Annäherung an die Peripherie stößt auf große Schwierigkeiten. Das Zentrum eignet sich kaum als Zugang, da jedes Wort und jeder explizite Hinweis an der Sache vorbeiführen. Die Peripherie wird durch den Versuch, sie deutlich zu machen, zerstört – wie ein Fisch explodiert, der aus der Tiefe des Meeres an die Oberfläche gezogen wird. Man muß sich an die Peripherie heranpirschen und sie anstupsen. Man muß auf sie anspielen und hinweisen, ohne sie zu erwähnen. In einigen Kulturen darf der Name Gottes nicht erwähnt werden, aber man darf indirekt durch sein Wirken auf ihn Bezug nehmen, wie z. B. *der, der alle Dinge schuf*. Ganz ähnlich verhält es sich mit der Peripherie einer bestimmten Person; manchmal beschreibt man sie am besten durch ihre Wirkung.

Eine der Schlüsselfunktionen der Kunst ist die Neugestaltung von Peripherien. Während Wis-

extend himself with technology, he throws our fleshbody periphery into question. Did we have in our periphery an unspoken, never articulated assumption that fleshbodies are all we could be? Mann confronts us with an alternative.

To reject an artwork is often to keep it in the explicit, and deny it access to our periphery. Is Mann just weird, an unimportant geekoid? This dismisses him by label and pigeonhole, and keeps him far away from our unstated worldviews.

Commercial art is frequently accorded lower status because it does not shake up the periphery, but reinforces the existing frames. Selling another cigarette to the most number of people is best done by tapping and using the most common peripheral elements of a given culture. Sex, money, youth are often deeply within our proximal cognitive framework. The highest commercial art will powerfully resonate with these peripheries while remaining inexplicit so that the resonance stays peripheral. Every periphery needs a center. Within the powerful stirred up peripheries, commercial art offers us a new center: the product.

Creativity, flow, and meditation

The *flow state* is described by psychologist Mihaly Csikszentmihalyi. In the flow state is where human beings do their greatest creative work. Flow state is characterized by, among other things:

- losing track of time
- losing track of place
- intense activity of the proximal domain
- a kind of unconscious *mindlessness*, although perhaps with intense purpose.

The flow state's intense proximal activity can be perceptual, cognitive, action, social, or some combination of these or other peripheral domains. We become intensely effective in the flow state because we can activate and use large domains of knowledge without becoming conscious of them. In fact only by keeping them proximal can we possibly use them all at once.

Computer programmers are familiar with the flow state. It happens during an all-night hacking session, when the bugs are killed one by one and the program works better and better, and the next thing you know the sun is

senschaft und Technik sich mit Dingen beschäftigen, die niedergeschrieben werden können, dreht sich Kunst um das nicht explizit Erklärbare. Kunst kann nicht einfach über etwas sprechen, sie muß unter der Oberfläche unseres Zentrums kommunizieren.

In der Kunst von *Bedeutung* zu sprechen, ist ein Irrtum, der Zentrum und Peripherie durcheinanderbringt. Bedeutung ist ein Begriff des Zentrums, wo man sich ein Modell von Konsequenzen und Denotaten zurechtlegen und das dann Bedeutung nennen kann. Kunst bedient sich der Denotaten, Konsequenzen und Resonanzen, um etwas zu schaffen, das nicht selbst *Bedeutung* ist. Kunst schafft einen neuen Rahmen, neue Peripherien, sie prüft die Konsequenzen, deutet auf verborgene Peripherien hin, rückt die Peripherie ins Zentrum und umgekehrt.

Steve Mann, Künstler am MIT, trägt tagaus, tagein Videobrillen. Er stellt selbst eines seiner Kunstwerke dar. Als Verkörperung dieser neuen Art von Selbst – als Mensch, der einen Teil der Welt ständig digital vermittelt wahrnimmt; als Mensch, der sich mit Hilfe der Technik bewußt kontinuierlich ausdehnt –, stellt er unsere fleischliche Körperperipherie in Frage. Galt für unsere Peripherie nicht die unausgesprochene, implizite Annahme, daß wir nichts anderes als Fleischkörper sein können? Steve Mann konfrontiert uns mit einer Alternative.

Wenn ein Kunstwerk auf Ablehnung stößt, bleibt es häufig im Bereich des Expliziten. Der Zugang zu unserer Peripherie wird ihm verwehrt. Ist Mann einfach ein bißchen verrückt, ein bedeutungsloser Possenreißer? Das würde bedeuten, ihn einfach abzustempeln und von unseren unausgesprochenen Weltanschauungen fernzuhalten.

Kommerzielle Kunst wird häufig geringgeschätzt, weil sie die Peripherie nicht aufrüttelt, sondern den bestehenden Rahmen verstärkt. Um noch mehr Menschen noch mehr Zigaretten zu verkaufen, eignen sich am besten die allergewöhnlichsten peripheren Elemente einer bestimmten Kultur. Sex, Geld, Jugend sind in unserem proximalen kognitiven Rahmen oft fest verankert. Wirklich gute kommerzielle Kunst weiß mit dieser Peripherie machtvoll mitzuschwingen und vermeidet zugleich jede Explizität, so daß die Resonanz peripher bleibt. Jede Peripherie braucht ein Zentrum. Innerhalb der mächtigen, aufgewühlten Peripherien bietet uns kommerzielle Kunst ein neues Zentrum: das Produkt.

Kreativität, Fließen und Meditation

Der Psychologe Mihaly Csikszentmihalyi spricht vom *Flow-Zustand*. In diesem Zustand schaf-

coming up. Programming cannot be started and stopped on a whim – the most experienced programmer still needs a large block of uninterrupted time in front of them to enter the flow. [In computer jargon, programmers sometimes speak of *swapping in the state*, and once they get it swapped in they want to keep it in.] Csikszentmihalyi says it can take about 30 minutes to enter flow state.

During flow the programmer is consciously thinking about the big picture. But the little pictures are taken care of one by one. There is almost a sense that the more one is unconscious, the smarter one is. All of one's past history and experience is brought silently to bear on the problem at hand. One feels satisfaction and joy. The programmer's experience of flow is duplicated in many creative fields. The late nights, getting into the flow, losing track of time. This when we are most human, when our periphery is most luminous

On a recent trip to Japan I had the opportunity to speak to audiences of students and creative engineers about the flow state and building technology that would intersect with flow. I asked if Japanese had a word for this state, and after some discussion, *muga* was proposed:

无我

Various Japanese dictionaries translated *muga* as selflessness, mindlessness and ecstasy. It was described as the non-religious term to describe what Zen

坐禅

is about. My hosts agreed that *muga* generally was without purpose [although *zazen* meditation can be with purpose, as with Zen archery]. So perhaps flow state is *muga* with a purpose.

Is meditation, found in so many cultures, flow state, and so the activation of a rich periphery? To meditate one shuts off the conscious mind, the center, and all that is left is the unconscious, the peripheral. Meditation, *muga*, is flow without a purpose.

Modernism, Postmodernism, and beyond

Modernism is known in part by its focus on the center and its denial of periphery. In the program of modernism, all is to be made explicit. *Let us calculate* said Leibniz, and this could

fen die Menschen ihre besten und kreativsten Werke. Folgende Dinge sind u. a. dafür charakteristisch:

- Verlust des Zeitgefühls
- Verlust des Ortsgefühls
- intensive Aktivität des proximalen Bereichs
- eine Art unbewußtes wenn auch vielleicht stark gerichtetes *Nicht-Denken*

Im Flow-Zustand kann sich die intensive proximale Aktivität auf perzeptorischer, kognitiver, handlungsmäßiger oder sozialer Ebene äußern, es kann sich auch um eine Kombination dieser oder anderer peripherer Bereiche handeln. Im Flow-Zustand sind wir höchst effektiv, da wir viele Wissensgebiete aktivieren und einsetzen können, ohne uns ihrer bewußt zu sein. Tatsächlich können wir sie nur deswegen alle gleichzeitig nutzen, weil sie im Proximalen bleiben.

Programmierer sind mit diesem *Flow-Zustand* bestens vertraut. Er stellt sich während einer die ganze Nacht dauernden Arbeitssitzung ein, wenn ein Fehler nach dem anderen behoben wird und das Programm immer besser läuft – und dann bemerkt man plötzlich, daß die Sonne aufgeht. Programmieren kann nicht nach Laune begonnen oder beendet werden – auch die erfahrensten Programmierer brauchen einen langen Zeitraum völliger Ungestörtheit vor sich, um sich in den Flow-Zustand einklinken zu können. [Im Computerjargon sprechen die Programmierer manchmal von *in den Zustand wechseln*, und wenn sie ihn gewechselt haben, möchten sie auch drinbleiben.] Csikszentmihalyi zufolge kann es bis zu 30 Minuten dauern, bis sich der Flow-Zustand einstellt.

Im Flow-Zustand ist die Aufmerksamkeit des Programmierers auf das große Bild gerichtet. Aber auch die kleinen Bilder finden eins nach dem anderen Beachtung. Man hat beinahe das Gefühl, umso geschickter zu sein, je weniger bewußt man handelt. Die eigene Geschichte mit all ihren Erfahrungen fließt stillschweigend ein und wird zur Lösung des vorliegenden Problems eingesetzt. Befriedigung und Freude stellen sich ein.

Die Erfahrung des Programmierers mit dem Flow-Zustand wiederholt sich in vielen anderen kreativen Bereichen. Die langen Nächte, das Einklinken in den Flow-Zustand, der Verlust des Zeitgefühls. Das sind die Stunden, wo wir am meisten Mensch sind, wo unsere Peripherie am hellsten strahlt.

have been the slogan of modernism: rationality is the measure of man. There is no room for the inexplicit in modernism. The entire proximal domain is anathema to modernism's program, which must bring everything front and center for examination.

Postmodernism pluralized modernism. In the postmodern world we once again have history, have a standpoint, have multiple possible right answers, and can draw upon multiple sources. In postmodernism there is no progress except by accumulation of ever more possible views. But each of these views has its exegesis. Postmodernism does not yet escape from the explicitizing program of modernism.

Beyond postmodernism is the age we are entering. In this age perhaps the periphery can achieve its proper place alongside the center. Perhaps we will learn to operate with what can never become explicit or calculated, but must eventually be surrendered to in order to look through it. You can make some things explicit all the time, and all things explicit some of the time, but you can't make everything explicit all of the time. Living with, powering ourselves by the constant periphery will be the lesson of the post-postmodern age.

The original source of the periphery is the body. In the age of periphery, our bodies will be revered, and will extend everywhere.

Kürzlich hatte ich auf einer Reise nach Japan die Gelegenheit, vor einer Zuhörerschaft von Studenten und kreativen Technikern über Flow-Zustand und Bautechnologie zu referieren. Ich stellte die Frage, ob es im Japanischen ein Wort für diesen Zustand gäbe, und nach einiger Diskussion wurde folgendes Zeichen *muga* vorgeschlagen:

无我

Verschiedene japanische Wörterbücher übersetzen *muga* mit Ichlosigkeit, Nicht-Denken und Ekstase. Es wurde als nicht-religiöses Wort zur Beschreibung von Zen angeführt.

坐禅

Meine Gastgeber bestätigten, daß *muga* generell etwas Absichtsloses bedeutet [obwohl die *Zazen*-Meditation – wie z. B. beim Bogenschießen – durchaus zielgerichtet sein kann]. Der Flow-Zustand ist also möglicherweise gleichbedeutend mit absichtsvollem *muga*.

Ist die in so vielen Kulturen anzutreffende Technik der Meditation gleichzusetzen mit dem Flow-Zustand, d. h. mit der Aktivierung einer komplexen Peripherie? Bei der Meditation wird das Bewußtsein, das Zentrum, ausgeschaltet, und übrig bleibt allein das Unbewußte, das Periphere. Meditation, *muga*, ist also Fließen ohne Ziel und Absicht.

Modernismus, Postmodernismus und darüber hinaus

Der Modernismus ist zum Teil dafür bekannt, sich auf das Zentrum zu konzentrieren und die Peripherie zu vernachlässigen. Das Konzept des Modernismus zielt darauf ab, alles explizit zu machen. *Laßt uns rechnen*, sprach Leibniz – und das hätte der Slogan des Modernismus sein können: Die Rationalität ist das Maß des Menschen. Das Implizite hat im Modernismus keinen Platz. Der ganze proximale Bereich ist dem Modernismus, der alles ins Zentrum bringen und überprüfen muß, ein Greuel.

Der Postmodernismus stellt eine Vervielfachung des Modernismus dar. Auch in der postmodernen Welt verfügen wir über eine Geschichte, beziehen Standpunkte, haben eine Vielzahl möglicher richtiger Antworten zur Hand und können aus vielfältigen Quellen schöpfen. Im Postmodernismus beruht der Fortschritt einzig und allein auf der Akkumulation von immer mehr Standpunkten. Aber jeder dieser Standpunkte hat seine Exegese. Post-

Acknowledgements
The concepts in this paper benefited from conversations with Aki Uyetani, Beth Mynatt, and John Seely Brown. John Seely Brown is a co-originator of the center/periphery concept.

modernismus bedeutet noch nicht das Ende des modernistischen Konzepts der Explizität.

Jenseits des Postmodernismus wartet das Zeitalter, an dessen Beginn wir gerade stehen. Vielleicht gelingt es der Peripherie in diesem Zeitalter, den ihr gebührenden Platz an der Seite des Zentrums einzunehmen. Vielleicht werden wir lernen, mit Dingen umzugehen, die nie explizit ausgesprochen oder berechnet werden können, denen man sich nur hingeben kann, um sie zu verstehen. Es ist möglich, einige Dinge dauernd explizit zu machen, und manchmal können alle Dinge für einige Zeit explizit werden. Aber es ist nicht möglich, alles ständig explizit zu machen. Mit der permanenten Peripherie zu leben, aus ihr Kraft zu schöpfen, ist die Lektion, die uns das Zeitalter des Post-Postmodernismus erteilen wird.

Die ursprüngliche Quelle der Peripherie ist der Körper. Im Zeitalter der Peripherie werden unsere Körper zum Gegenstand der Verehrung werden und sich überall hin ausdehnen.

Die Formulierung der Ideen in diesem Aufsatz hat von Gesprächen mit Aki Uyetani, Beth Mynatt und John Seely Brown profitiert. John Seely Brown ist Mitentwickler des Zentrum/Peripherie-Konzepts.

Parasite Visions

Alternate, Intimate and Involuntary Experiences

STELARC

symposium

Parasitische Visionen

Alternierende, intime und unwillkürliche Erfahrungen

STELARC

Introduction

In previous actions the body has performed with technology attached [the Third Hand*- actuated with EMG signals], technolology inserted [the* Stomach Sculpture*- a self-illuminating, sound-emitting, opening/closing, extending and retracting mechanism operating in the stomach cavity] and Net-connected [the body becoming accessed and remotely activated by people in other places]. The body has been augmented, invaded and now becomes a host- not only for technology, but also for remote agents. Just as the Internet provides extensive and interactive ways of displaying, linking and retrieving information and images, it may now allow unexpected ways of accessing, interfacing and uploading the body itself. And instead of seeing the Internet as a means of fulfilling outmoded metaphysical desires of disembodiement, it offers on the contrary powerful individual and collective strategies for projecting body presence and extruding body awareness. The Internet does not hasten the disappearance of the body and the dissolution of the self- rather it generates new collective physical couplings and a telematic scaling of subjectivity. Such a body's authenticity will not be due to the coherence of its individuality but rather to its multiplicity of collaborating agents.What becomes important is not merely the body's identity, but its connectivity- not its mobility or location, but its interface...*

Surface and self:
The Shedding of Skin

1 As a surface, skin was once the beginning of the world and simultaneously the boundary of the self. But now stretched, pierced and penetrated by technology, the skin is no longer the smooth and sensuous surface of a site or a screen. Skin no longer signifies closure. The rupture of surface and skin means the erasure of inner and outer. An artwork has been inserted inside the body. The *Stomach Sculpture* – constructed for the Fifth Australian Sculpture Triennale in Melbourne, whose theme was site-specific work – was inserted 40cm into the stomach cavity. Not as a prosthetic implant but as an aesthetic addition. The body becomes hollow-

Einleitung

In früheren Performances hat der Körper mit angefügter Technologie [die durch EMG-Signale gesteuerte *Dritte Hand*], mit in den Körper eingesetzter Technologie [die *Stomach Sculpture* – ein selbstleuchtender, geräuscherzeugender, sich öffnender/schließender, sich ausdehnender und wieder zusammenziehender Mechanismus in der Bauchhöhle] und Netzverbindung [anderswo befindliche Menschen nehmen Zugriff auf den Körper und aktivieren ihn per Fernsteuerung] funktioniert. Es gab die Erweiterung des Körpers , es gab das Eindringen in ihn , und nun wird er zum Wirt – nicht nur für Technologie, sondern auch für entfernte Agenten. So, wie das Internet umfassende und interaktive Möglichkeiten zum Anzeigen, Verknüpfen und Abrufen von Informationen und Bildern bietet, könnte es jetzt unerwartete Möglichkeiten bieten, auf den Körper selbst zuzugreifen, über Schnittstellen mit ihm Kontakt aufzunehmen und ihn selbst ins Netz zu laden. Und statt das Internet als Mittel zur Erfüllung unmodern gewordener metaphysischer Sehnsüchte nach Entkörperung zu betrachten, bietet es ganz im Gegenteil mächtige individuelle und kollektive Strategien für eine Projektion der körperlichen Präsenz und eine Veräußerlichung des körperlichen Bewußtseins. Das Internet beschleunigt nicht das Verschwinden des Körpers und die Auflösung des Selbst, sondern ermöglicht vielmehr neue kollektive physische Verbindungen und eine telematische Abstufung der Subjektivität. Die Authentizität eines solchen Körpers wird nicht mehr auf die Kohärenz seiner Individualität zurückzuführen sein, sondern auf die Vielfalt der zum Zweck seiner Steuerung zusammenarbeitenden Protagonisten. Nicht mehr bloß die Identität des Körpers ist wichtig, sondern auch seine Connectivity, nicht seine Mobilität oder sein Aufenthaltsort, sondern seine Schnittstelle ...

Oberfläche und Selbst: Abschied von der Haut

1 Als Oberfläche war die Haut einst der Anfang der Welt und gleichzeitig die Grenze des Selbst. Doch heute, von der Technologie gedehnt, gepierct und durchdrungen, ist die Haut nicht mehr die glatte, sinnliche Oberfläche eines Orts oder eines Bildschirms. Haut ist nicht mehr mit Abgeschlossenheit gleichzusetzen. Das Zerreißen der Oberfläche und der Haut bedeutet die Auslöschung von Innen und Außen. Ein Kunstwerk wurde in den Körper eingesetzt. Die für die Fifth Australian Sculpture Triennale in Melbourne, deren Thema ortsspezifische Arbeit war, geschaffene *Stomach Sculpture* wurde 40 cm

not the BWO but rather a body with art. The body is experienced as hollow with no meaningful distinctions between public, private and physiological spaces. The hollow body becomes a host, not for a self but simply for a sculpture. As interface, the skin is obsolete.The significance of the cyber may well reside in the act of the body shedding its skin. The clothing of the body with membranes and embedded in them alternate sensory and input/ output devices creates the possibility of more intimate and enhanced interactivity. Subjectively, the body experiences itself as a more extruded system, rather than an enclosed structure. The self becomes situated beyond the skin. It is partly through this extrusion that the body becomes empty. But this emptiness is not through a lack but from the extrusion and extension of its capabilities, its new sensory antennae and its increasingly remote functioning ...

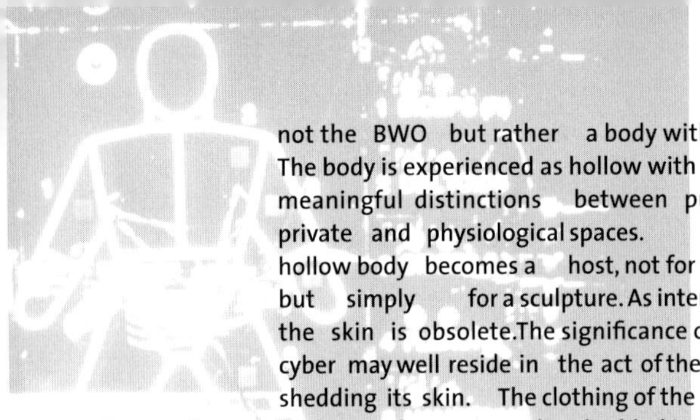

Fractal Flesh

2 Consider a body that can extrude its awareness and action into other bodies or bits of bodies in other places. An alternate operational entity that is spatially distributed but electronically connected. A movement that you initiate in Melbourne would be displaced and manifested in another body in Rotterdam. A shifting, sliding awareness that is neither *all-here* in this body nor *all-there* in those bodies. This is not about a fragmented body but a multiplicity of bodies and parts of bodies prompting and remotely guiding each other. This is not about master-slave control mechanisms but feedback-loops of alternate awareness, agency and of split physiologies. Imagine one side of your body being remotely guided whilst the other side could collaborate with a local agency. You watch a part of your body move but you have neither initiated it nor are you contracting your muscles to produce it. Imagine the consequences and advantages of being a split body

weit in die Bauchhöhle eingeschoben. Nicht als prothetisches Implantat, sondern als ästhetische Ergänzung. Der Körper wird hohl, nicht zum Körper ohne Organe, sondern zum Körper mit Kunst. Der Körper wird als hohle Struktur erfahren, ohne sinnvolle Unterscheidungen zwischen öffentlichen, privaten und physiologischen Räumen. Der hohle Körper wird zu einem Wirt, nicht für ein Selbst, sondern einfach für eine Skulptur. Die Haut ist als Schnittstelle veraltet. Die Bedeutung des Cyber könnte durchaus darin liegen, daß der Körper sich häutet. Das Überzogensein des Körpers mit Membranen, in die alternierend Sensoren und Eingabe-/Ausgabegeräte eingebettet sind, schafft die Möglichkeit intimerer und intensiverer Interaktivität. Subjektiv erfährt der Körper sich selbst als stärker veräußerlichtes System anstelle einer eingehüllten Struktur. Das Selbst verlagert sich an einen Ort jenseits der Haut. Der Körper wird zum Teil aufgrund dieser Veräußerlichung zum Hohlkörper, doch ist seine Leere nicht auf das Fehlen seiner Fähigkeiten, sondern auf deren Veräußerlichung und Erweiterung zurückzuführen, auf seine neuen sensorischen Fühler und sein zunehmend ferngesteuertes Funktionieren ...

Fraktales Fleisch

2 Stellen Sie sich einen Körper vor, der sein Bewußtsein und sein Handeln an anderswo befindliche andere Körper oder Körperteile veräußerlichen kann. Eine alternierende Funktionseinheit, die räumlich verteilt aber elektronisch verbunden ist. Eine Bewegung, die Sie in Melbourne induzieren, würde örtlich verschoben und sich an einem anderen Körper in Rotterdam vollziehen. Ein hin- und herwechselndes, gleitendes Bewußtsein, das sich weder *ganz hier* in diesem Körper noch *ganz dort* in jenen Körpern befindet. Es geht hier nicht um einen fragmentierten Körper, sondern um eine Vielzahl von Körpern und Körperteilen, die einander per Fernsteuerung Anweisungen erteilen und steuern. Es geht nicht um einen Herr-Knecht-Kontrollmechanismus, sondern um Feedbackschleifen alternierenden Bewußtseins, steuernder Kräfte und gespaltener Physiologien. Stellen Sie sich vor, eine Seite Ihres Körpers würde ferngesteuert, während die andere Seite durch eine steuernde Kraft vor Ort bewegt werden kann. Sie beobachten, wie sich ein Teil Ihres Körpers bewegt, haben diese Bewegung jedoch weder selbst induziert, noch kontrahieren Sie Ihre Muskeln, um die Bewegung auszuführen. Stellen Sie sich die Konsequenzen und Vorteile einer Existenz in Form

with voltage-in, inducing the behaviour of a remote agent and voltage-out of your body to control peripheral devices. This would be a more complex and interesting body- not simply a single entity with one agency but one that would be a host for a multiplicity of remote and alien agents. Of different physiologies and in varying locations. Certainly there may be justification, in some situations and for particular actions to tele-operate a human arm rather than a robot manipulator- for if the task is to be performed in a non-hazardous location, then it might be an advantage to use a remote human arm- as it would be attached to another arm and a mobile, intelligent body. Consider a task begun by a body in one place, completed by another body in another place. Or the transmission and conditioning of a skill. The body not as a site of inscription but as a medium for the manifestation of remote agents. This physically split body may have one arm gesturing involuntarily [remotely actuated by an unknown agent], whilst the other arm is enhanced by an exoskeleton prosthesis to perform with exquisite skill and with extreme speed. A body capable of incorporating movement that from moment to moment would be a pure machinic motion performed with neither memory nor desire ...

Stimbod

3 What makes this possible is a touch-screen muscle stimulation system. A method has been developed that enables the body's movements to be programmed by touching the muscle sites on the computer model. Orange flesh maps the possible stimulation sites whilst red flesh indicates the actuated muscle[s]. The sequence of motions can be replayed continuously with its loop function. As well as choreography by pressing, it is possible to paste sequences together from a library of gesture icons. The system allows stimulation of the programmed movement for analysis and evaluation before transmission to actuate the body. At a lower stimulation level it is a

eines solchen gespaltenen Körpers vor, der über einen Spannungseingang die Anweisungen einem entfernten Agenten empfängt und über einen Spannungsausgang selbst periphere Geräte steuert. Dies wäre eine komplexere und interessantere Art von Körper – nicht nur eine einzige Einheit mit einer einzigen steuernden Kraft, sondern ein Körper, der einer Vielzahl geographisch entfernter und fremder Agenten als Wirt dient. Mit verschiedenen Physiologien und an wechselnden Orten. Es wäre in einigen Situationen und für bestimmte Zielsetzungen bestimmt gerechtfertigt, einen menschlichen Arm anstatt eines Roboterarms fernzusteuern, denn wenn die betreffende Aufgabe an einem ungefährlichen Ort auszuführen ist, könnte der Gebrauch eines fernbedienbaren menschlichen Arms von Vorteil sein, da dieser mit einem anderen Arm und einem mobilen, intelligenten Körper verbunden wäre. Stellen Sie sich eine Aufgabe vor, die von einem Körper an einem Ort begonnen und von einem anderen Körper an einem anderen Ort zu Ende geführt wird. Oder die Weitergabe und Einübung einer Fertigkeit. Der Körper nicht als Ort der Programmierung, sondern als Medium für die Manifestation entfernter Agenten. Dieser physisch gespaltene Körper könnte beispielsweise einen unwillkürlich gestikulierenden Arm haben [der von einem unbekannten Agenten ferngesteuert wird], während der andere Arm durch eine Exoskelett-Prothese unterstützt mit exquisiter Präzision und enormer Geschwindigkeit arbeitet. Ein Körper, der Bewegung verkörperlichen kann, die von Moment zu Moment reine maschinische Bewegung wäre, ausgeführt ohne Erinnerung, ohne Verlangen ...

Stimbod

3 Möglich wird das durch ein Muskelstimulationssystem per Touchscreen. Man hat eine Methode entwickelt, mit der sich Körperbewegungen durch Berührung bestimmter Muskelpositionen an einem Computermodell programmieren lassen. Oranges Fleisch repräsentiert dabei die möglichen Stimulationsorte, während rotes Fleisch die bewegten Muskeln anzeigt. Die Abfolge von Bewegungen kann mit einer Schleifenfunktion kontinuierlich wiederholt werden. Zusätzlich zur Choreographie der Körperbewegung durch Drücken der entsprechenden Muskelpositionen kann man auch Bewegungsabläufe aus einer Bibliothek von Gesten-Icons aneinanderreihen. Dieses System erlaubt die Stimulation der programmierten Bewegung für Analyse- und Evaluierungszwecke, bevor die Bewegung tatsächlich auf den Körper übertragen wird. Auf einem

body prompting system. At a higher stimulation level it is a body actuation system. This is not about remote-control of the body, but rather of constructing bodies with split physiologies, operating with multiple agency. Was it Wittgenstein who asked if in raising your arm you could remove the intention of raising it, what would remain? Ordinarily, you would associate intention with action [except, perhaps in an instinctive motion- or if you have a pathological condition like Parkinson's disease]. With Stimbod, though, that intention would be transmitted from another body elsewhere. There would be actions without expectations. A two-way tele-Stimbod system would create a possessed and possessing body- a split physiology to collaborate and perform tasks remotely initiated and locally completed- at the same time in the one physiology ...

Extreme absence and the experience of the alien

4 Such a Stimbod would be hollow body, a host body for the projection and performance of remote agents. Glove Anaesthesia and Alien Hand are pathological conditions in which the patient experiences parts of their body as not there, as not their own, as not under their own control- an absence of physiology on the one hand and an absence of agency on the other. In a Stimbod not only would it possess a split physiology but it would experience parts of itself as automated, absent and alien. The problem would no longer be possessing a split personality, but rather a split physicality. In our Platonic, Cartesian and Freudian pasts these might have been considered pathological and in our Foucauldian present we focus on inscription and control of the body. But in the terrain of cyber complexity that we now inhabit the inadequacy and the obsolescence of the ego-agent driven biological body cannot be more apparent. A transition from psycho-body to cybersystem becomes necessary to function effectively and intuitively in remote spaces, speeded-up situations and complex technological terrains. During a

niedrigeren Stimulationsniveau handelt es sich um eine Art Schrittmachersystem für den Körper, auf einem höheren Stimulationsniveau um ein tatsächliches Körpersteuerungssystem. Dabei geht es nicht um die Fernsteuerung des Körpers, sondern vielmehr um die Schaffung von Körpern mit gespaltenen Physiologien, die von verschiedenen steuernden Kräften gelenkt werden. War es nicht Wittgenstein, der fragte, was bliebe, wenn man durch das Heben seines Arms die Intention, den Arm zu heben, beseitigen könne? Normalerweise würde man die Intention mit der Aktion assoziieren [sofern es sich nicht um eine instinktive Bewegung handelt oder man unter pathologischen Zuständen wie beispielsweise der Parkinson'schen Krankheit leidet]. Im Falle des Stimbod würde die Intention jedoch von einem anderswo befindlichen anderen Körper kommen. Es würde Handlungen ohne Erwartungen geben. Ein bidirektionales Tele-Stimbod-System würde einen besessenen/besitzenden Körper schaffen, eine gespaltene Physiologie, die zur Zusammenarbeit befähigt ist und gleichzeitig in der einen Physiologie per Fernsteuerung induzierte Aktionen lokal ausführt ...

Extremes Abwesenheitsgefühl und Fremdheitserfahrung

4 Ein derartiger Stimbod wäre ein hohler Körper, ein Wirtskörper für Projektion und Führung durch geographisch entfernte Agenten. Handschuh-Anästhesie und das Fremde-Hand-Syndrom sind pathologische Zustände, in deren Verlauf der Patient einerseits einen Teil seines Körpers als abwesend, als nicht ihm selbst zugehörig, als nicht unter seiner eigenen Kontrolle stehend, d. h. ein Fehlen der Physiologie empfindet und andererseits ein Fehlen von Handlungsfähigkeit verspürt. Im Falle eines Stimbod würde nicht nur eine gespaltene Physiologie vorliegen, sondern der Betroffene würde Teile seiner selbst als automatisiert, abwesend und fremd empfinden. Das Problem würde nicht mehr in einer gespaltenen Persönlichkeit, sondern in einer gespaltenen Körperlichkeit bestehen. In unserer platonischen, kartesianischen und Freud'schen Vergangenheit mag das als pathologisch betrachtet worden sein, und in unserer Foucault'schen Gegenwart konzentrieren wir uns auf die Programmierung und Steuerung des Körpers. Doch auf dem Terrain der Cyberkomplexität, in der wir heute leben, könnten die Unzulänglichkeiten des egogesteuerten biologischen Körpers sowie die Tatsache, daß dieser mittlerweile rettungslos veraltet

Sexuality and Medicine Seminar in Melbourne, Sandy Stone asked me what would be the cyber-sexual implications of the Stimbod system? Not having thought about it before, I tried to explain what it might be like. If I was in Melbourne and Sandy was in NY, my touching my chest would prompt her to caress her breast. Someone observing her there would see it as an act of self-gratification, as a masturbatory act. She would know though that her hand was remotely and perhaps even divinely guided! Given tactile and force-feedback, I would feel my touch via another person from another place as a secondary and additional sensation. Or, by feeling my chest I can also feel her breast. An intimacy through interface, an intimacy without proximity. Remember that Stimbod is not merely a sensation of touch but an actuation system. Can a body cope with experiences of extreme absence and alien action without becoming overcome by outmoded metaphysical fears and obsessions of individuality and free agency? A Stimbod would thus need to experience its actuality neither all-

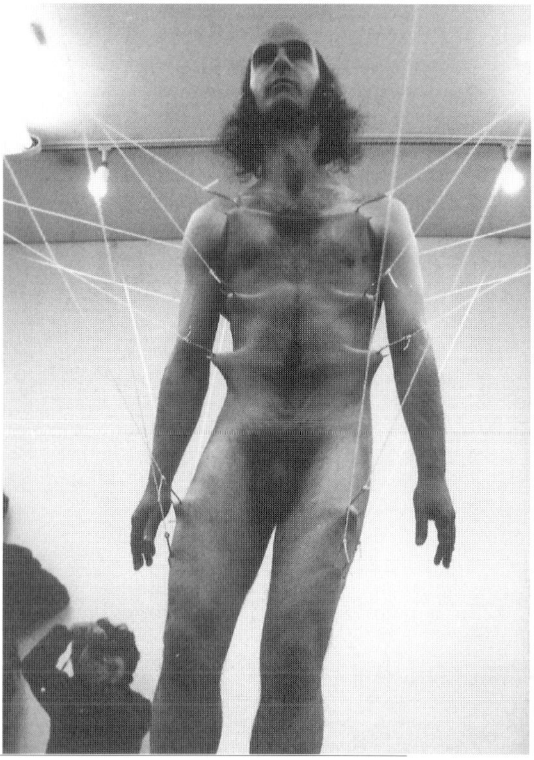

ist, nicht deutlicher zutage treten. Ein Übergang vom Psycho-Körper zum Cybersystem wird notwendig, um ein effizientes und intuitives Funktionieren in entfernten Räumen, in beschleunigten Situationen und auf komplexen technologischen Terrains zu gewährleisten. Anläßlich eines Seminars über Sexualität und Medizin in Melbourne fragte mich Sandy Stone nach den cybersexuellen Implikationen des Stimbod-Systems. Darüber hatte ich zuvor nicht nachgedacht, doch ich versuchte, zu erklären, wie ein solcher cybersexueller Kontakt aussehen würde. Ich würde mich beispielsweise in Melbourne befinden und Sandy in New York. Indem ich meine Brust berühre, würde ich sie ferngesteuert dazu veranlassen, ihre eigene Brust zu streicheln ... Jemand, der sie vor Ort beobachtet, würde dies wahrscheinlich als einen Akt der Selbstbefriedigung, als Masturbation betrachten. Sie würde aber trotzdem wissen, daß ihre Hand aus der Ferne und vielleicht sogar von göttlicher Hand gelenkt wird. Aufgrund eines Feedback, das mir taktilen Reiz und Krafteinwirkung vermittelt, würde ich meine eigene Berührung über eine andere Person von einem anderen Ort aus als sekundäre und zusätzliche Empfindung wahrnehmen. Anders gesprochen, könnte ich, indem ich meine eigene Brust fühle, auch die ihre fühlen. Eine Intimität über eine Schnittstelle, eine Intimität ohne Nähe. Vergessen Sie nicht, daß es bei einem Stimbod nicht nur um ein Berührungsgefühl, sondern um ein Handlungssteuerungssystem geht. Kann ein Körper mit Erfahrungen extremer Abwesenheit und fremden Handelns zurandekommen, ohne von veralteten metaphysischen Ängsten und einer Besessenheit von seiner eigenen Individualität und seinem freien Handlungsvermögen überwältigt zu werden? Ein Stimbod müßte deshalb seine Aktualität weder ganz in diesem noch ganz in jenem Körper, sondern teilweise hier und teilweise nach dort projiziert empfinden. Ein Funktionssystem aus räumlich verteilten, jedoch elektronisch verbundenen Clustern von Körpern, fluktuierendes, fließendes Bewußtsein, erweitert durch die alternierende und fremde Steuerung ...

Ping Body / Proto-Parasite

5 Im Jahr 1995 konnten die Besucher des Centre Pompidou [Paris], des Media Lab [Helsinki] und der Konferenz *Doors of Perception* [Amsterdam] im Rahmen des Projekts *Telepolis* per Fernsteuerung auf diesen Körper in Luxemburg zugreifen und ihn steuern, indem sie das mit Touchscreen und entsprechender Schnittstelle ausgestattete Muskelstimulationssystem benutzten. Über ISDN-Picturetel-Links

present-in-this-body, nor all-present-in-that-body, but partly-here and projected-partly-there. An operational system of spatially distributed but electronically interfaced clusters of bodies ebbing and flowing in awareness, augmented by alternate and alien agency ...

Ping Body / Proto-Parasite

5 In 1995 for Telepolis, people at the Pompidou Centre [Paris], the Media Lab [Helsinki] and the Doors of Perception conference [Amsterdam], were able to remotely access and actuate this body in Luxembourg, using the touch-screen interfaced muscle stimulation system. ISDN Picturetel links allowed the body to see the face of the person who was moving it whilst the programmers could observe their remote choreography. [Although people thought they were merely activating the body's limbs, they were inadvertently composing the sounds that were heard and the images of the body they were seeing- for the body had sensors, electrodes and transducers on its legs, arms and head that triggered sampled body signals and sounds and that also made the body a video switcher and mixer. And although people in other places were performing with the RHS of the body, it could respond by actuating its Third Hand, voltage-out from electrodes positioned on its abdominal and LHS leg muscles. This Split Body then was manifesting a combination of involuntary – remotely guided, improvised and EMG-muscle initiated motor motions]. In *Ping Body* – an Internet Actuated and Uploaded Performance, [performed first for Digital Aesthetics in Sydney, but also for DEAF in Rotterdam in 1996] – instead of the body being prompted by other bodies in other places, Internet activity itself choreographs and composes the performance. Random pinging to over 30 global Internet domains produce values from 0-2000 milliseconds that are mapped to the deltoid, biceps, flexors, hamstring, and calf muscles – 0-60 volts initiating involuntary movements. The movements of the body are amplified, with a midi interface measuring position, proximity and bending angle of limbs. Activated by Internet data the body is uploaded as

konnte der Körper das Gesicht der ihn steuernden Person sehen, während die Programmierer gleichzeitig ihre Telechoreographie beobachten konnten. [Obwohl die Leute glaubten, bloß die Glieder des Körpers zu steuern, komponierten sie gleichzeitig und ohne sich dessen bewußt zu sein auch die Töne, die parallel dazu zu hören waren, sowie die Bilder des Körpers, die sie sehen konnten, denn die Arme, die Beine und der Kopf des Körpers waren mit Sensoren, Elektroden und Meßwertwandlern ausgestattet, die gesampelte Körpersignale und Töne auslösten und den Körper so auch zu einem Videoswitcher und -mixer machten. Obwohl Leute von anderen Orten aus die rechte Körperhälfte bedienten, konnte der Körper durch Bewegung seiner dritten Hand reagieren, wobei die Spannungsausgänge der Elektroden an den Bauchmuskeln und den Muskeln des linken Beins angebracht waren. Dieser gespaltene Körper stellte eine Kombination aus unwillkürlich-ferngesteuerten, improvisierten und EMG-muskelinduzierten motorischen Bewegungen dar]. Im Rahmen von *Ping Body – an Internet Actuated and Uploaded Performance*, die 1996 erstmals für Digital Aesthetics in Sydney aber auch für DEAF in Rotterdam durchgeführt wurde, wird der Körper nicht von anderen anderswo lokalisierten Körpern gelenkt, sondern die Performance wird durch Internet-Aktivität choreographiert und komponiert. Zufälliges Einschalten in über 30 globale Internet-Domänen ergibt Werte von 0–2000 Millisekunden, die dem Schultermuskel, dem Bizeps, den Beugemuskeln, den Oberschenkel- und den Unterschenkelmuskeln zugeordnet sind, wobei 0–60 V unwillkürliche Bewegungen induzieren. Die Körperbewegungen werden verstärkt, wobei eine MIDI-Schnittstelle die Position, die Annäherung und den Beugewinkel der Glieder mißt. Durch Internet-Daten aktiviert, wird der Körper in Form von Informationen und Bildern auf eine Web-Site geladen, die von anderen Menschen anderswo angesehen werden kann. Der Körper wird telematisch vergrößert, stimuliert und gedehnt, indem er Signale eines ausgedehnten räumlichen und elektrischen Systems reflektiert. Die normale Beziehung zum Internet wird umgekehrt – anstatt selbst durch den Input der Benutzer konstruiert zu werden, konstruiert das Internet die Aktivität eines Körpers. Der Körper wird zum Nexus der Internet-Aktivität, seine Aktivität ein statistisches Konstrukt von Computernetzen ...

info and images to a Web site to be viewed by other people elsewhere. The body is telematically scaled-up, stimulated and stretched by reverberating signals of an inflated spatial and electrical system. The usual relationship with the Internet is flipped- instead of the Internet being constructed by the input from people, the Internet constructs the activity of one body. The body becomes a nexus for Internet activity – its activity a statistical construct of computer networks.....

Parasite: Event for invaded and involuntary Body

6 A customized search engine has been constructed that scans, selects and displays images to the body- which functions in an interactive video field. Analyses of the JPEG files provide data that is mapped to the body via the muscle stimulation system. There is optical and electrical input into the body. The images that you see are the images that move you.

Consider the body's vision, augmented and adjusted to a parallel virtuality which increases in intensity to compensate for the twilight of the real world. Imagine the search engine selecting images of the body off the WWW, constructing a metabody that in turn moves the physical body. Representations of the body actuate the body's physiology. The resulting motion is mirrored in a VRML space at the performance site and also uploaded to a Web site as potential and recursive source images for body reactivation. RealAudio sound is inserted into sampled body signals and sounds generated by pressure, proximity, flexion and accelerometer sensors. The body's physicality provides feedback loops of interactive neurons, nerve endings, muscles, transducers and Third Hand mechanism. The system electronically extends the body's optical and operational parameters beyond its cyborg augmentation of its Third Hand and other peripheral devices. The prosthesis of the Third Hand is counterpointed by the prosthesis of the search engine software code. Plugged-in, the body becomes a parasite sustained by an extended, external and virtual nervous system. Parasite was first per-

Parasite: Event für den besetzten und unwillkürlichen Körper

6 Es wurde eine maßgeschneiderte Suchmaschine entwickelt, die Bilder scannt, auswählt und für den Körper anzeigt, der in einem interaktiven Videofeld funktioniert. Analysen der JPEG-Dateien liefern Daten, die mit Hilfe des Muskelstimulationssystems dem Körper zugeordnet werden. Es gibt einen optischen und einen elektrischen Input in den Körper. Die Bilder die Sie sehen, sind die Bilder, die Sie bewegen. Denken Sie an den Gesichtssinn des Körpers, erweitert und an eine parallele Virtualität angepaßt, deren Intensität zunimmt, um das Dämmerlicht der realen Welt zu kompensieren. Stellen Sie sich vor, wie die Suchmaschine Bilder des Körpers aus dem WWW aussucht, einen Metakörper konstruierend, der seinerseits den physischen Körper bewegt. Darstellungen des Körpers steuern die Physiologie des Körpers. Die resultierende Bewegung wird in einem VRML-Raum am Ort der Performance gezeigt und auch in Form potentieller und rekursiver Quellbilder für eine Reaktivierung des Körpers auf eine Web-Site geladen. RealAudio-Sound mit in abgetasteten Körpersignalen und -tönen untermischt, die durch Druck-, Näherungs-, Biegungs- und Beschleunigungsensoren generiert werden. Der physische Charakter des Körpers läßt Feedbackschleifen von interaktiven Neuronen, Nervenenden, Muskeln, Meßwertaufnehmern und dem Dritte-Hand-Mechanismus entstehen. Das System erweitert die optischen Parameter und die Funktionsparameter des Körpers elektronisch über die Cyborg-Erwei-terung durch die dritte Hand und andere periphere Geräte hinaus. Den Kontrapunkt zur Prothese der dritten Hand stellt die Prothese des Softwarecodes der Suchmaschine dar. Sobald man ihn ansteckt, wird der Körper zu einem Parasiten, der von einem erweiterten externen und virtuellen Nervensystem am Leben erhalten wird. Parasite wurde anläßlich der Virtual World Orchestra-Veranstaltung in Glasgow vorgestellt und auch für The Studio for Creative Inquiry, Carnegie Mellon University, in den Wood Street Galleries in Pittsburgh und anläßlich des Festival Atlantico in Lissabon präsentiert ...

Phantomkörper und kollektive Strategien

7 Früher war die Verbindung zu anderen Körpern im Internet ebenso wie die Kommunikation mit ihnen rein textlicher Natur, und es fehlte drastisch an jeglicher physischen Präsenz. Dabei handelte es sich aber nicht um die Erfahrung einer authentisch

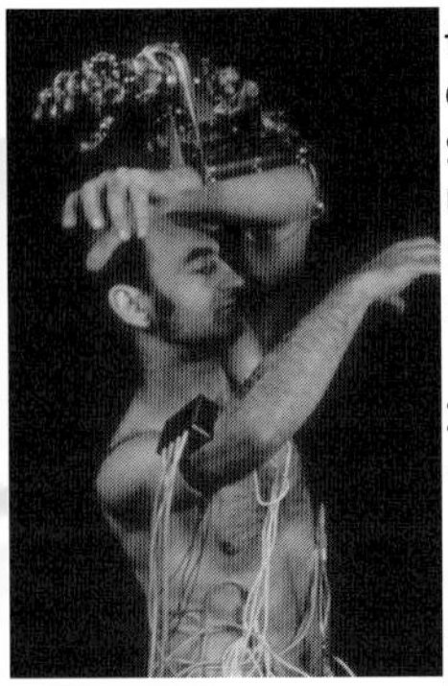

formed for Virtual World Orchestra in Glasgow. It has also been presented for The Studio for Creative Inquiry, Carnegie Mellon University at the Wood Street Galleries in Pittsburgh and for Festival Atlantico in Lisbon...

Phantom Bodies and Collective Strategies

7 Previously connection and communication with other bodies on the Internet was only textual, with an acute absence of physical presence. This was not the experience of authentic evolved absence that results in an effectively operating body in the real word – absence of the body on the Internet is an absence of inadequacy, that is an inadequacy of appropriate feedback-loops. As we hard-wire more high-fidelity image, sound, tactile and force-feedback sensation between bodies then we begin to generate powerful phantom presences- not phantom as in phantasmagorical, but phantom as in phantom limb sensation. The sensation of the remote body sucked onto your skin and nerve endings, collapsing the psychological and spatial distance between bodies on the Net. Just as in the experience of a Phantom Limb with the amputee, bodies will generate phantom partners, not because of a lack, but as extending and enhancing addition to their physiology. Your aura will not be your own. It will only be through the construction of phantoms that the equivalent of our evolved absence will be experienced, as we function increasingly powerfully and with speed and intuition [a successful body operates automatically]. Bodies must now perform in techno-terrains and data-structures beyond the human-scale where intention and action collapse into accelerated responses. Bodies acting without expectation, producing movements without memory. Can a body act without emotion? Must a body continuously affirm its emotional, social and biological status quo? Or perhaps what is necessary is electronic erasure with new intimate, internalized interfaces to allow for the design of a body with more adequate inputs and outputs for performance and awareness augmented by search engines. Imagine a body remapped and

entwickelten Abwesenheit, die in der realen Welt zu einem effizient funktionierenden Körper führt. Die Abwesenheit des Körpers im Internet ist vielmehr die Abwesenheit der Unzulänglichkeit, d. h. einer Unzulänglichkeit geeigneter Feedbackschleifen. Während wir immer mehr Verkabelungen für HiFi-Bilder, Töne, Berührungs- und Kraft-Feedback zwischen Körpern schaffen, beginnen wir, mächtige Phantompräsenzen zu erzeugen – wobei der Begriff Phantom in diesem Fall nicht im Sinne eines Gespensts zu verstehen ist, sondern im Sinne einer Phantomempfindung in einem amputierten Körperglied. Das Gefühl des entfernten Körpers, der sich auf der eigenen Haut und den eigenen Nervenenden festsaugt, das die psychologische und räumliche Distanz zwischen Körpern im Netz eliminiert. So wie bei der Phantomempfindung des Amputierten werden Körper Phantompartner erzeugen, und zwar nicht aufgrund eines Fehlens, sondern als Erweiterung, als fördernde Ergänzung ihrer eigenen Physiologie. Ihre Aura wird nicht mehr Ihnen allein gehören. Nur durch die Konstruktion von Phantomen wird das Äquivalent unserer entwickelten Abwesenheit erfahrbar sein, während wir zunehmend stärker, mit Geschwindigkeit und Intuition [ein erfolgreicher Körper funktioniert automatisch] funktionieren. Körper müssen sich heute auf Techno-Terrains und in Datenstrukturen jenseits des menschlichen Maßstabs bewähren, wo Intention und Aktion zu beschleunigten Reaktionen zusammenfallen. Körper, die ohne Erwartung funktionieren und Bewegungen ohne Erinnerung erzeugen. Kann ein Körper ohne Gefühl handeln? Muß ein Körper beständig seinen emotionalen, sozialen und biologischen Status Quo bestätigen? Oder wäre vielleicht eine elektronische Auslöschung mittels neuer, internalisierter Schnittstellen notwendig, damit ein Körper mit besseren Inputs und Outputs für eine Leistung und ein Bewußtsein, die durch Suchmaschinen noch verstärkt werden, entstehen können? Stellen Sie sich einen Körper vor, der neu kartiert und konfiguriert wurde – nicht mittels des genetischen Gedächtnisses, sondern in Form elektronischer Schaltkreise. Wie wäre es mit einem Körper, der über eine Schnittstelle eng mit dem WWW verbunden ist und der durch ein entferntes Flüstern und die Fernsteuerung durch andere, anderswo lokalisierte Körper geweckt und aufgeschreckt wird? Ein Körper, der von Spinnen, Knowbots und Phantomen seine Information erhält ...

reconfigured- not in genetic memory but rather in electronic circuitry. What of a body that is intimately interfaced to the WWW- and that is stirred and is startled by distant whispers and remote promptings of other bodies in other places. A body that is informed by spiders, knowbots and phantoms ...

Operational Internet/ Intelligent System

8 Consider the Internet structured so that it would scan, select and switch automatically interfacing clusters of on-line bodies in real-time [the size and expertise of the clusters selected for the task to be performed]. Can a body cope with the multiplicity of agents- a fluid and flowing awareness that dims and intensifies as agents are connected and disconnected? Awareness and agency would be shifted and shared in an electronic space of distributed intelligence. The internet becomes not merely a means of information transmission, but a mode of transduction- affecting physical action between bodies. Electronic space as a realm of action, rather than information. Imagine a body that is open and aware, invaded, augmented and with extended operation. Consider a body whose awareness is extruded by surrogate robots in situations and spaces where no body could go. These machines with arrays of sensors, manipulators and hybrid locomotion would exponentially multiply the operational possibilities- scaling-up the subtlety, speed and complexity of human action. Perhaps what it means to be human is about not retaining our humanity ...

Stelarc is presently a Visiting Fellow at the Studio For Creative Inquiry at Carnegie Mellon University. He has received a three year Fellowship from the Visual Arts/-Craft Board, Australia Council. His artwork is solely represented by the Sherman Galleries, in Sydney. Stimbod was developed with the assistance of Troy Innocent at Empire Ridge in Melbourne: The Muscle Stimulation System circuitry was designed by Bio-Electronics, Logitronics and Rainer Linz in Melbourne with the box fabricated with the assistance of Jason Patterson. Tele-Stimbod, Ping Body and Parasite software was developed by Jeffrey Cook, Sam de Silva, Gary Zebbington and Dimitri Aronov from the Merlin group in Sydney.

Funktionales Internet/Intelligentes System

8 Stellen Sie sich vor, das Internet wäre so strukturiert, daß es sich automatisch miteinander verbindende Cluster von Online-Körpern in Echtzeit scannen, auswählen und umschalten würde [wobei die Größe und die Fertigkeiten der Cluster in Abhängigkeit von der zu erledigenden Aufgabe gewählt würden]. Kann ein Körper mit der Vielfalt von Agenten, mit einem fließenden und strömenden Bewußtsein, das sich in Abhängigkeit von den zugeschalteten und weggeschalteten Agenten verdunkelt oder intensiviert, zurande kommen? Bewußtsein und Handlungsvermögen würden geteilt, hin- und herwandern in einem elektronischen Raum verteilter Intelligenz. Über ein bloßes Mittel zur Informationsübertragung hinausgehend, wird das Internet zu einer Möglichkeit der Transduktion und erlaubt es Körpern, gegenseitig ihr physisches Handeln zu steuern. Der elektronische Raum als Ort der Aktion anstatt der Information. Stellen Sie sich einen Körper vor, der offen und bewußt ist, der besetzt und erweitert und mit größeren Handlungsmöglichkeiten ausgestattet werden kann. Stellen Sie sich einen Körper vor, dessen Bewußtsein durch Ersatzroboter in Situationen und Räumen veräußerlicht wird, in die sich kein Körper jemals begeben könnte. Diese Maschinen mit ihren Anordnungen von Sensoren, mit ihren Manipulatoren und ihren hybriden Bewegungsvorrichtungen würden die Handlungsmöglichkeiten exponentiell vervielfachen, die Präzision, die Geschwindigkeit und die Komplexität des menschlichen Handelns erhöhen. Vielleicht bedeutet Mensch zu sein nicht unbedingt, daß wir an unserem Menschsein festhalten müssen ...

Neuron-Silicon Junction or Brain-Computer Junction?

Peter Fromherz

I first observed nerve cells and silicon wafers while working on two distinctly different degree dissertations in my laboratory at the University of Ulm in 1984. At the time, we were studying how the electrical activity of nerve cells influenced fluorescent dyes and the effects of artificial membrane layers on microscopic silicon electrodes. Enthused by the results, I used the occasion of the 20th Winter Seminar *Molecules, Information and Memory* presented by Manfred Eigen in January 1985 to present a paper entitled *Brain on Line? The Feasibility of a Neuron-Silicon Junction*, in which I outlined how a direct electrical contact between a nerve cell and silicon [and vice versa] could be constructed. In the paper, I wrote: *The information processing of the networks of neurons in a brain and of the networks of silicon chips in a computer is coupled at the present moment macroscopically through the opto-mechanical pathway eye-screen and finger-keyboard [Fig.1a]. Is a direct microscopical coupling feasible [Fig.1b]? The utopian question may be shaped into a proper scientific problem: How to design a neuron-silicon junction?*

symposium

Neuron-Silizium-Kopplung oder Hirn-Computer-Kopplung?

Peter Fromherz

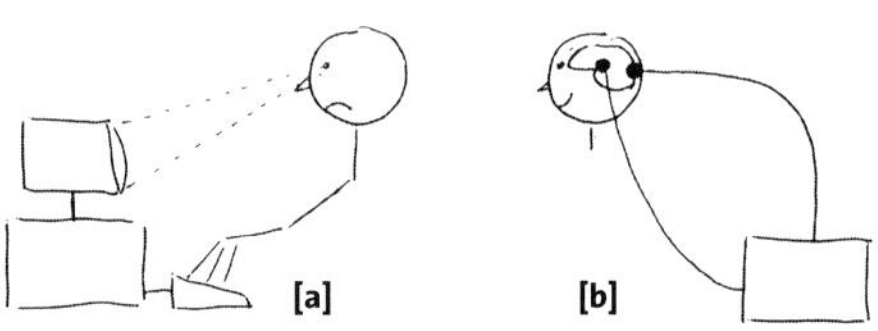

Fig. 1
Brain-Computer Junction.
[a] Classical mechano-optical pathway eye-screen and finger-keyboard.
[b] Imaginary ionic-electrical junction of the computer with the optic and motor centers of the cerebral cortex. [Fromherz, 1985]

Hirn-Computer-Kopplung.
[a] *Klassischer mechano-optischer Pfad Auge-Bildschirm und Finger-Tastatur.*
[b] *Utopische ionisch-elektrische Kopplung des Computers an die visuelle und motorische Hirnrinde. [Fromherz, 1985]*

The matter did not remain at the design stage. However, a prerequisite for carrying out a neuron-silicon junction was the process of learning and mastering the production of silicon chips and the cultivation of nerve cells – by a small team working in one and the same laboratory. Six years later, we published a description of the first direct electrical junction of a nerve cell to a silicon transistor[1]; 10 years later, the first direct electrical junction of a silicon microstructure to a nerve cell[2].

Since then, we have performed a detailed study of the physics of the coupling of neurons and silicon [3-6]. We understand how the quality of the signal transmission is effected by the geometry of the cell-chip contact and by the electrical properties of the cell membrane and of silicon.

All of these studies were carried out using large nerve cells [approximately 60 micrometers in diameter] of leech ganglia. As an example, Fig. 2 illustrates the *wiring up* of such a nerve cell with the 16 transistors of a silicon chip. The first junctions with nerve cells from the brain of a rat have recently been successfully performed[7]. Here, the small size of these cells [about 10 micrometers] poses particular problems.

These lengthy and difficult experiments have shown us just how large a gap really exists between test-tube experiments involving a neuron-silicon junction and the interfacing of the brain and the computer. We must keep in mind that we are dealing with two completely different aspects here – a physical one and an informational one.

To begin with: the physics of the direct junction of nerve cells and silicon is based on the contact of the neurons' thin [5 nanometer] cell membrane with the thin [20 nanometer] layer of quartz which makes up the silicon's watertight casing. Only when the contact is extremely close [about 30 nanometers] does an electrical coupling take place through the electrical field [electrostatic induction]. This tight junction can be successfully created in the test-tube with clean silicon chips and nerve cells which have been dissected from tissue samples. The form which such a contact would take in the tissue of a nerve fiber or of the brain cannot be foreseen at the moment. After all, this is not merely a matter of maintaining a few ran-

Im Jahr 1984 sah ich in meinem Labor an der Universität Ulm im Rahmen von zwei unterschiedlichen Diplomarbeiten zum ersten Mal Nervenzellen und Siliziumwafer. Wir studierten damals, wie die elektrische Aktivität von Nervenzellen fluoreszierende Farbstoffe beeinflußt und wie künstliche Membranschichten auf mikroskopische Siliziumelektroden wirken. Dadurch angeregt, skizzierte ich im Januar 1985 – anläßlich des zwanzigsten Winterseminars *Molecules, Information and Memory* von Manfred Eigen – in einem Aufsatz *Brain on Line? The Feasibility of a Neuron-Silicon Junction*, wie man einen direkten elektrischen Kontakt von einer Nervenzelle mit Silizium und umgekehrt aufbauen könnte. Es hieß dort: *The information processing of the networks of neurons in a brain and of the networks of silicon chips in a computer is coupled at the present moment macroscopically through the opto-mechanical pathway eye-screen and finger-keyboard [fig.1a]. Is a direct microscopical coupling feasible [fig.1b] ? The utopian question may be shaped into a proper scientific problem: How to design a neuron-silicon junction?*

Es blieb nicht beim Design. Voraussetzung für die Realisierung von Neuron-Silizium-Verknüpfungen war es jedoch, die Herstellung von Siliziumchips und die Kultivation von Nervenzellen zu erlernen und zu beherrschen – in ein und demselben Laboratorium durch ein kleines Team. Sechs Jahre später publizierten wir die erste direkte elektrische Kopplung einer Nervenzelle zu einem Silizium-Transistor[1], zehn Jahre später die erste direkte elektrische Kopplung von einer Silizium-Mikrostruktur zu einer Nervenzelle[2].

Inzwischen haben wir die Physik der Kopplung von Neuronen und Silizium im Detail studiert[3-6]. Wir wissen, wie die Qualität der Signalübertragung von der Geometrie des Kontakts von Zelle und Chip und von den elektrischen Eigenschaften der Zellmembran und des Siliziums bestimmt wird.

Alle diese Studien wurden mit großen Nervenzellen [Durchmesser circa 60 Mikrometer] aus den Ganglien des Blutegels durchgeführt. Als Beispiel ist in Fig. 2 die Verdrahtung einer solchen Nervenzelle mit 16 Transistoren eines Siliziumchips gezeigt. Erste Kopplungen mit Nervenzellen aus dem Hirn der Ratte sind kürzlich gelungen[7]. Es entstehen hier besondere Probleme wegen der geringen Größe [etwa 10 Mikrometer] der Zellen.

Die langwierigen und schwierigen Experimente haben uns gezeigt, wie groß die Lücke zwischen den Reagenzglasexperimenten der Neuron-Silizium-

dom contacts; if the brain and the computer – two separate worlds miniaturized down to microscopic level – are really to be brought into connection with one another, and if an adequate level of communication is to come about as a result, then millions of contacts must be set up.

Moreover: it is not sufficient to install contacts between the brain and the computer which exchange some sort of informational bits in both directions. Both the brain and the computer must directly understand the semantics of a foreign language without the abstraction and adaptation accomplished by means of keyboard and monitor. Both operating systems have to communicate directly with each other in a meaningful way. As long as we do not know how the brain functions – what relationship exists between its microscopic electrical signals and its macroscopic semantics – an informational interface remains impossible even if the physical junction were feasible.

What can be done? Physicists will carry on with the effort to establish thousands of contact points between nerve cells and silicon microstructures. Experiments to achieve this – in cooperation with major firms in the microelectronics industry – are now underway. Even if this can only be done in a test-tube, it will provide scientists with a basis for understanding how larger hybrid networks composed of neuronal and technological elements communicate with each other on the level of semantic information. Thus, we might learn something about the function of the brain.

Setting up contacts within living tissue is another problem. One solution might be an ingenious form of coating of the chip or the cell. Here as well, it will be necessary to first carry out basic research on the biology, chemistry and physics of cell adhesion.

The process of achieving a direct junction of individual nerve cells and individual silicon microstructures has opened our eyes to the difficulty of establishing a linkage between the brain and the computer without the mediation of the opto-mechanical pathway eye-screen and finger-keyboard. The apparent problems posed by this junction on the physical and informational levels are so enormous that it is impossible today to predict whether such a form of communication will ever become a reality. For

Kopplung und einem Interfacing von Hirn und Computer wirklich ist. Wir müssen beachten, daß es hier zwei ganz unterschiedliche Aspekte gibt – einen physikalischen und einen informatischen.

Zum einen: Die Physik der direkten Kopplung von Nervenzellen und Silizium beruht auf dem Kontakt der dünnen Zellmembran der Neurone [5 Nanometer] und der dünnen Quarzschicht, mit der das Silizium vom Wasser isoliert ist [20 Nanometer]. Nur wenn dieser Kontakt sehr eng ist [etwa 30 Nanometer], ergibt sich eine elektrische Kopplung durch das elektrische Feld [Influenz]. Diese enge Kopplung gelingt im Reagenzglas mit sauberen Siliziumchips und Nervenzellen, die aus dem Gewebe herauspräpariert sind. Es ist im Moment nicht zu sehen, wie sich solche Kontakte im Gewebe einer Nervenfaser oder eines Hirns bilden sollen. Es geht ja nicht nur darum, einzelne zufällige Kontakte zu erhalten. Wenn die beiden in sich mikroskopisch verschalteten Welten von Hirn und Computer wirklich Verbindung miteinander aufnehmen sollen und wenn eine adäquate Kommunikation zustande kommen soll, so müssen Millionen von Kontakten hergestellt werden.

Zum andern: Es reicht nicht aus, Millionen von Kontakten zwischen Hirn und Computer aufzubauen, die irgendwelche Bits in beide Richtungen vermitteln. Hirn und Computer müssen unmittelbar die Semantik der fremden Sprache verstehen, ohne die durch Tastatur und Bildschirm gegebene Abstraktion und Anpassung. Die beiden Betriebssysteme müssen direkt miteinander bedeutungsvoll kommunizieren. Solange wir aber nicht wissen, wie das Hirn funktioniert – welches die Beziehung zwischen seinen mikroskopischen elektrischen Signalen und seiner makroskopischen Semantik ist – bleibt eine informatische Kopplung unmöglich, auch wenn die physikalische Kopplung gelingen würde.

Was kann man tun? Auf der physikalischen Seite wird man versuchen, tausende Kontaktstellen zwischen Nervenzellen und Siliziummikrostrukturen herzustellen. Experimente dazu – in Zusammenarbeit mit der mikroelektronischen Großindustrie – sind im Gange. Auch wenn dies nur im Reagenzglas gemacht wird, kann man auf dieser Basis erfahren, wie größere hybride Verbände aus neuronalen und technischen Elementen auf der Ebene der semantischen Information miteinander kommunizieren. Man kann also etwas über die Funktion des Hirns lernen.

Die Herstellung von Kontakten innerhalb eines Gewebes ist ein anderes Problem. Man kann daran denken, dieses durch geschickte Beschichtung der Chips oder der Zellen zu lösen. Auch hier ist zu-

this reason, an ethical consideration of issues such as *chip in the brain* or *brain in the computer* would be unfounded and superfluous.

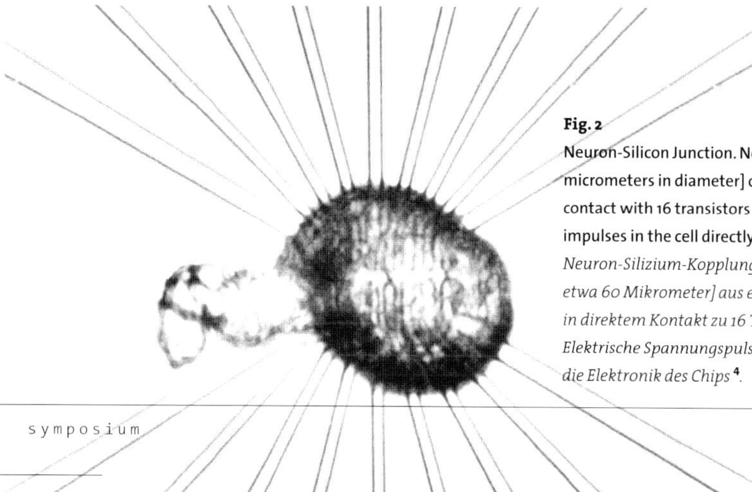

Fig. 2
Neuron-Silicon Junction. Nerve cell [approximately 60 micrometers in diameter] of a leech ganglion in direct contact with 16 transistors in silicon. Electrical voltage impulses in the cell directly effect the chip's electronics [4]
Neuron-Silizium-Kopplung. Nervenzelle [Durchmesser etwa 60 Mikrometer] aus einem Ganglion des Blutegels in direktem Kontakt zu 16 Transistoren in Silizium. Elektrische Spannungspulse in der Zelle wirken direkt auf die Elektronik des Chips [4].

nächst die Grundlagenforschung zur Biologie, Chemie und Physik der Zelladhäsion gefordert.

Die Realisierung der direkten Kopplung einzelner Nervenzellen und einzelner Siliziummikrostrukturen hat uns die Augen geöffnet, wie schwierig es ist, Hirn und Computer zu verbinden ohne Vermittlung des opto-mechanischen Pfads Auge-Bildschirm und Finger-Tastatur. Die augenscheinlichen Probleme der Kopplung auf physikalischer und informatischer Ebene sind so enorm, daß es nicht möglich ist, heute vorherzusagen, ob eine derartige Kommunikation jemals möglich sein wird. Aus diesem Grund ist eine ethische Betrachtung zum *Chip-im-Hirn* oder *Hirn-im-Computer* gegenstandslos und überflüssig.

1 P. Fromherz, A. Offenhäusser, T. Vetter, J. Weis, *A Neuron-Silicon Junction: A Retzius-Cell of the Leech on an Insulated-Gate Field-Effect Transistor*, in: Science 252 [1991] 1290-1293
2 P. Fromherz, A. Stett, *Silicon-Neuron Junction: Capacitive Stimulation of an Individual Neuron on a Silicon Chip*, in: Physical Review Letters 75 [1995] 1670-1673
3 P. Fromherz, C.O. Müller, R. Weis, *Neuron-Transistor: Electrical Transfer Function measured by Patch-Clamp Technique*, in: Physical Review Letters 71 [1993] 4079-4082
4 R. Weis, B. Müller, P. Fromherz, *Neuron-Adhesion on a Silicon Chip probed by an Array of Field-Effect Transistors*, in: Physical Review Letters 76 [1996] 327-330
5 R. Weis, P. Fromherz, *Frequency Dependent Signal-Transfer in Neuron-Transistors*, in: Physical Review E 55 [1997] 877-889
6 A. Stett, B. Müller, P. Fromherz, *Two-Way Silicon-Neuron Interface by Electrical Inductance*. in: Physical Review E 55 [1997] 1779-1782
7 S. Vassanelli, P. Fromherz, *Neurons from Rat Brain coupled to Transistors*, in: Applied Physics A [1997] in press

Fragments from *Borderscape 2000*

from *The Chicano State Department Chronicles*

Guillermo Gòmez-Peña/A.K.A.
El Mexterminator/
Roberto Sifuentes

Fragmente aus *Borderscape 2000*

[aus *The Chicano State Department Chronicles*]

von Guillermo Gòmez-Peña
alias *El Mexterminator*/
Roberto Sifuentes

Anmerkung des Herausgebers

Dokumente aus den Chicano State Department Archives werden im Rahmen der *Freedom of Information*-Initiative 1999 der Öffentlichkeit zugänglich gemacht. Allerdings wurde zuvor jegliches als sensibel und/oder geheim eingestufte Material von Zensoren des Ministeriums gelöscht. Die fehlenden Textstellen sind in diesem Dokument mit dem Hinweis [FEHLT] gekennzeichnet.

Darüber hinaus besteht auch die Möglichkeit, daß die Inhalte von E-mails zum Zeitpunkt ihrer Übermittlung durch Online-Zensoren geändert oder gelöscht wurden. Das bedaure ich zutiefst. Aber ich hoffe, Sie lernen, zwischen den Zeilen zu lesen.

Die erste Version dieser Dateien wurde ursprünglich Ende 1996 von Artspace Books unter dem Titel *Friendly Cannibals* veröffentlicht. Die vorliegende Version ist im Vergleich dazu wesentlich präziser und anschaulicher.

Editor's Note

Documents from the Chicano State Department Archives are made available under the 1999 Freedom of Information Initiative. However, any material deemed sensitive and/or classified has been deleted by department censors prior to public access; these missing texts are indicated by a notation in the document [MISSING].

Additionally, on-line censors may have altered or deleted contents of e-mail at the time of transmission. I am extremely sorry. I hope you learn to read between the lines.
The first version of these files was originally published by Artspace books in late '96 under the title *Friendly Cannibals*. This version is substantially more descriptive and accurate.

1 Dear Vampira99, la unica, la primigenia I'm having an identity crisis in front of my lowrider 'Chevy 69' laptop – the worst in months. I'm listening to the last album of Jesus and Mary Chain, scratch & mixed with classical rancheras; and all my calavera candles are lit. 45 at least. I'm down, loca... In fact, I'm just about to delete myself from the Infobanco del Chicano State Department Interneta [CSDI], and please, this time, don't be so naive as to ask me CENSORED?

I'm sending you these last e-mails without any clear purpose estetico-politico, and I don't expect you to answer all of them. [You probably have to take care of other ethnocyborgs in crisis]. You'll see that they, too[my e-mails not the ethnocyborgs, matizo], suffer from a serious crisis of literary identity. I ask myself #3 and I ask you[or whoever YOU may be at this point in time]:

Are these texts fragments of some cybercholo sci-fi poem in search of form, or pieces of an elliptic love letter? [It's impossible – & illegal – to be *direct* nowadays....] Are they excerpts from some performance script in-progress, or are they parts of a highly classified document that CENSORED?

1 Liebe Vampira99, la unica, la primigenia Ich mache vor meinem tiefergelegten *Chevy 69*-Laptop eine Identitätskrise durch – die schlimmste seit Monaten. Ich höre gerade das neueste Album von Jesus und Mary Chain, Scratch gemixt mit klassischen rancheras; und alle meine Calavera-Kerzen brennen. Mindestens 45. Ich bin fix und fertig, loca... Ich bin gerade dabei, mich selbst aus der Infobanco del Chicano State Department Interneta [CSDI] zu löschen, und sei diesmal bitte nicht so naiv, mich zu fragen, ZENSURIERT?

Ich übermittle Dir diese letzten E-mails ohne klaren estetico-politico Zweck, und ich erwarte nicht, daß du sie alle beantworten wirst. [Du mußt dich wahrscheinlich noch um andere Ethno-Cyborgs kümmern, die gerade eine Krise durchmachen]. Du wirst sehen, daß auch sie [meine E-mails, nicht die Ethno-Cyborgs, matizo] unter einer schweren literarischen Identitätskrise leiden. Ich frage mich #3 und ich frage auch dich [bzw. wer auch immer DU zu diesem Zeitpunkt sein magst]:

Sind diese Texte Fragmente irgendeines Cyber-Cholo-Sci-Fi-Gedichts, das noch zu keiner Form gefunden hat, oder Teile eines elliptischen Liebesbriefs? [Heutzutage ist es unmöglich – & illegal – *direkt* zu sein. ...] Sind sie Auszüge aus einem noch nicht vollendeten Performance-Script oder Teile eines als Top-Secret eingestuften Dokuments, das ZENSURIERT? Im Augenblick kann ich dir nur sagen, daß ein Teil ihrer Inhalte illegal sein könnte. Aber daraus mache ich mir nichts mehr. Me vale. Wenn du sie herunterlädst, könnten sie durchaus schon zensuriert, editiert oder geringfügig abgeändert worden sein. Da heutzutage keiner mehr an Objektivität oder Integrität glaubt, besteht eine kleine Chance, daß ZENSURIERT. Außerdem würde ich es verabscheuen, einer Meistererzählung in die Falle zu tappen, ZENSURIERT aber in deine Arme würde ich liebend gern noch einmal fallen ... ja, ich weiß, daß es unmöglich ist, Vampira.

3 Wir schreiben das Jahr 1999 in AmeriKKKa – *Ham-e-rrica*, wie mein Neffe sagt [Generation MEX rockero, El Ricardiaco], *die Nation des Techno-Hasses und der sinnlosen Streitereien.* Er hat irgendwo gelesen, *der Cyberspace ist tot*. Wie ein Führer der MIT-Cybermiliz 1997 erklärt hat: *Der Cyberspace ist keine privilegierte weiße Freizone mehr und auch

For the moment, all I can tell you is that some of their content may be illegal. But I don't care anymore. Me vale. In fact, by the time you download them, they might very well have been censored, edited, or slightly altered. Since no one believes in objectivity or integrity nowadays, there is a slight possibility that CENSORED. Besides I would hate to fall in the trap of a master narrative CENSORED but I would love to fall back in your arms...yes, I know that's impossible, vampira.

3 It's 1999 in AmeriKKKa – *Ham-e-rrica,* according to my nephew [Generation MEX rockero, El Ricardiaco], *the nation of technohatred and unnecessary disputes.* He read somewhere that *Cyberspace is dead.* As one MIT cybermilitia leader declared in 1997, *No longer a privileged, white free zone, nor the virtual shopping mall it was supposed to become * it looks too much like the outside world now.* Which means it is now entirely controlled by the CSDI. Meaning, it's brown, culti-multi, proletarian & rowdy, & its lingua franca, agarrate mujer, es colloquial Spanglish, masticado asi bien cybersabrossso <http://caliente/100% hornyficado/>

CENSORED
me muero,
sin ti me muero,
sigo muriendo-me lenta-mente
mi mente lenta/osahana
ante la triste pantalla de mi Mac 947-HPX.
CENSORED my neon coffin... instalado *aqui*[whatever this means] en el ciberespacio estatal y el anonimato literario
pregunto-te: Is it possible to die in cyberspace o de plano alucino?
Could you attend my funeral? Would you?
Do you still remember the touch and temperature of my copper skin?
Remember pre-digital communication, jainita?
Las caricias ambidiestras, los besos en el esfinter, bolero dance, asi, bien pegaditos, rum & coke, for granted laughter, black leather y ... CENSORED.
Tu piel, lo nuestro, lo intrinsically ours?

4 Tepoztecardiente,
To give you some political background, in case you don't have access to the other Neta memory files: We, aca en el norte, have entered a postdemocratic era: We now live in a world

nicht das virtuelle Einkaufszentrum, zu dem er einst werden sollte. Er sieht heute einfach der Welt da draußen zu ähnlich.* Was bedeutet, daß der Cyberspace heute zur Gänze vom CSDI kontrolliert wird. Das heißt, er ist braun, multikulti, proletarisch & rowdy, & seine Lingua franca, agarrate mujer, ist das umgangssprachliche Spanglisch, masticado asi bien cybersabrossso <http://caliente/100% hornyficado/>
ZENSURIERT
me muero,
sin ti me muero,
sigo muriendo-me lenta-mente
mi mente lenta/osahana
ante la triste pantalla de mi Mac 947-HPX.
ZENSURIERT mein Neonsarg ... instalado *aqui* [was immer das auch bedeuten mag] en el ciberespacio estatal y el anonimato literario
pregunto-te: Kann man im Cyberspace o de plano alucino sterben?
Könntest du zu meinem Begräbnis kommen? Würdest du das tun?
Erinnert du dich noch an die Berührung und an die Wärme meiner kupferfarbenen Haut?
Erinnerst du dich an die prädigitale Kommunikation, jainita?
Las caricias ambidiestras, los besos en el esfinter, bolero dance, asi, bien pegaditos, Rum & Coke, garantiertes Gelächter, schwarzes Leder y ... ZENSURIERT.
Tu piel, lo nuestro, unser Ureigenstes?

4 Tepoztecardiente,

Falls Sie politisches Hintergrundwissen benötigen, weil Sie keinen Zugang zu den anderen Neta-Memory-Dateien haben: Wir, aca en el norte, befinden uns mittlerweile in einer postdemokratischen Ära: Wir leben jetzt in einer Welt ohne Theorie; sin estructuras ni contenido. Die Nation/der Staat ist eine reine metaficcion nostalgica; Grenzen & Klima verändern sich, während ich schreibe. Es ist das Ende der Welt – und des Worts – so wie wir sie kennen. Cambio. Die NAFTA war ein Fluch, loca, eine trinationale pachanga, die schließlich in ein dreisprachiges Gezänk ausgeartet ist. Jetzt haben alle einen Kater, und keiner erinnert sich genau daran, was geschehen ist. Cambio. Que que sucedio exactamente?

Der Salinas-Clan sitzt zusammen mit Darryl Gates [Ex-Chef des LAPD], Garcia Abrego [Capo des Golf-Kartells] und den Arellano-Brüdern [vom Tijuana-Kartell] im Gefängnis. Cambio.

without theory; sin estructuras ni contenido. The nation/state is purely a metaficcion nostalgica; the borders & climate fluctuate as I write. It's the end of the world – and the word – as we know it. Cambio. NAFTA was a blast, loca, a trinational pachanga which ended up in a trilingual brawl. Now everyone is hung over and no one remembers exactly what happened. Cambio. Que que sucedio exactamente?

The Salinas clan is in jail with Darryl Gates[ex-chief of the LAPD], Garcia Abrego [capo of the Gulf Cartel] and the Arellano brethren [from the Tijuana cartel]. Cambio.

Skeletons keep appearing in key sites throughout Mexamerica. La migra y la DEA were the spinal cord of the whole operation. Cambio.

You knew. Deep inside we all knew. Cambio.

Exiled in Bosnia along with ex-colleague Helmut *sin fronteras* Kohl, Billy Clinton spends his lonely hours playing *Stand By Me* on the tenor sax. Cambio.

Patricio Buchanan [Remember that pinche orate/car salesman/sideshow impresario gone hard-right televangelista?] is now a happy dictator-in-exile somewhere in Johannesburg or Mississippi. Chases his young black servants around the garden[By the way, Blacks in South Africa, like their contemporaries in the Bronx, South Central Los Angeles, Washington, D.C., and Atlanta, have gained control of their cities, but this matter belongs to another chronicle].

Aayyyyy!! This unbearable pain in my testicles CENSORED.

Another day without you, 397 dias sin que me muerdas la carne, carajo! Sin que me claves tus colmillos en el pecho ... y encima, my inability to write simple things CENSORED

An ad suddenly appears on the screen:
QUERIDO CIUDADANO TRANSFRONTERIZO:
YOUR GLOBAL DESIRES ARE OUR IMMEDIATE NEEDS, & VICE VERSA. PLEASE CHOOSE FROM THE FOLLOWING MENU:
IBM...INS...VHS...SDL...PRI...NBC...PMS...DHL...LWH...RIP...PBS...

6 Today, I'm tired of ex/changing identities in the net. In the past eight hours, I've been a man, a woman and a s/he. I've been black, Asian, Mixteco, German and a multi-hybrid replicant. I've been 10 years old, 20, 42 & 65. I've

Überall in Mexamerika tauchen an strategisch bedeutenden Orten immer wieder Skelette auf. La migra y la DEA waren das Rückgrat der gesamten Operation. Cambio.

Du wußtest es. Tief in unserem Inneren wußten wir es alle. Cambio.

Im gemeinsamen Exil in Bosnien mit seinem Ex-Kollegen Helmut *sin fronteras* Kohl verbringt Billy Clinton seine Mußestunden damit, auf dem Tenorsaxophon *Stand By Me* zu spielen. Cambio.

Patricio Buchanan [erinnerst du dich an diesen pinche orate/Autoverkäufer/Sideshow-Impresario, der dann beinhart auf Televangelista gemacht hat?] ist heute ein glücklicher Exildiktator irgendwo in Johannesburg oder Mississippi. Hetzt seine jungen schwarzen Dienstboten durch den Garten [übrigens, die Schwarzen in Südafrika haben ebenso wie ihre Brüder in der Bronx, in South Central Los Angeles, Washington, D.C., und Atlanta die Kontrolle über ihre Städte übernommen, aber das gehört in eine andere Chronik].

Aayyyyy!! Dieser unerträgliche Schmerz in meinen Hoden ZENSURIERT.

Noch ein Tag ohne dich, 397 dias sin que me muerdas la carne, carajo! Sin que me claves tus colmillos en el pecho ... y encima, meine Unfähigkeit, einfache Dinge zu schreiben
ZENSURIERT.

Auf dem Bildschirm erscheint plötzlich Werbeeinblendung: QUERIDO CIUDADANO TRANSFRONTERIZO: IHRE GLOBALEN WÜNSCHE SIND UNSERE UNMITTELBAREN BEDÜRFNISSE & UMGEKEHRT. BITTE WÄHLEN SIE AUS DEM FOLGENDEN MENÜ: IBM ... INS ... VHS ... SDL ... PRI ... NBC ... PMS ... DHL ... LWH ... RIP ... PBS ...

6 Für heute habe ich genug davon, im Netz die Identitäten aus/zu/tauschen. In den vergangenen acht Stunden war ich ein Mann, eine Frau und ein Zwitterwesen. Ich war schwarz, Asiate, Mestize, Deutscher und ein multihybrider Replikant. Ich war 10, 20, 42 & 65 Jahre alt. Ich habe sieben Sprachen gesprochen. Ich brauche wirklich dringend eine Pause. Ich möchte einfach ein paar Minuten lang nur ich selbst sein.

11 La desmodernidad lo abarca todo:
unübersetzbare Einsamkeit,
kulturelle Leere,
politische Schwindelgefühle,

spoken 7 broken languages. I need a break real bad. I just want to be myself for a few minutes.

11 La desmodernidad lo abarca todo:
untranslatable loneliness,
cultural emptiness,
political vertigo,
sexual despair,
postcolonial S&M
synthetic pleasures,
multicentric aesthetics
unclassifiable weather...IN LOUPE

Por lo tanto vampira, the night is clearly the place to be, sin fronteras ni contornos, a safe place for techno-warfare & unlimited entertainment. At night, I love you much, much more, especially when my life's in danger and my tongue, my cobra tongue, mi lengua poluta, disoluta, is out of control, como ahorita.

... at night, the militias roam the streets of my city, a city without limits or a name, without a recognizable government, city council, or police department; without churches or cafes; without architectural coherence or a sense of self.

... no loca, I'm not talking about Los Angeles or Dallas. I'm talking about myself, my inner city, la megalopolis de mi conciencia. *Here*, words like *alternative,* *peripheral,* and *marginal* lost their meaning and moral weight long ago. [SHIT! I ACCIDENTALLY DELETED A PARAGRAPH!]

17 CENSORED but all we have left is sex; either cyber-sexo without a body; o sea anonimo, sin facciones, sin identidad[*sin* en ingles equals pecado remember?]; sexo robotico without emotional or biological repercussions; o bien, el sexo deportivo, aerobico, intrascendente, doloroso, extremo, impersonal, y sin proposito alguno, en la calle bajo la niebla o en la misma morgue. And the more anonymous, detached, and weird, the better CENSORED so death as a high spiritual goal is temporarily unattainable. Death is already kitsch, cultura popular, trivia redundante, puro mainstream. But then, from a purely psychological perspective I see no other way out of here. Me captas, corazon? Por lo tanto, si me quieres ayudar[eef-yuh-guant-too-jelp-mee], borrame! borrame!! Turn on the camera and shoot me!!

sexuelle Verzweiflung,
postkoloniales S&M,
synthetische Genüsse,
multizentrische Ästhetik,
undefinierbares Wetter ... IN LOUPE

Por lo tanto vampira, ist die Nacht genau der richtige Ort, sin fronteras ni contornos, ein sicherer Ort für Techno-Kriegsführung & grenzenlose Unterhaltung. Nachts liebe ich dich viel, viel mehr, vor allem, wenn mein Leben in Gefahr und meine Zunge, meine Kobrazunge, mi lengua poluta, disoluta, außer Kontrolle ist, como ahorita.

...nachts streifen die Milizen durch die Straßen meiner Stadt, einer Stadt ohne Grenzen und Namen, ohne erkennbare Regierung, Stadtrat und Polizeibehörde; ohne Kirchen und Cafés; ohne architektonische Kohärenz und Verständnis für sich selbst.

... no loca, ich spreche nicht von Los Angeles oder Dallas. Ich spreche über mich selbst, über die Stadt in meinem Inneren, la megalopolis de mi conciencia. *Hier* haben Wörter wie *alternativ*, *peripher* und *marginal* ihre Bedeutung und ihr moralisches Gewicht schon vor langer Zeit verloren. [SCHEISSE: JETZT HABE ICH IRRTÜMLICH EINEN ABSATZ GELÖSCHT!]

17 ZENSURIERT aber alles, was uns noch bleibt, ist Sex; entweder Cyber-Sexo ohne Körper, o sea anonimo, sin facciones, sin identidad [*sin* bedeutet en ingles pecado, erinnerst du dich?]; sexo robotico ohne emotionale oder biologische Auswirkungen; o bien, el sexo deportivo, aerobico, intrascendente, doloroso, extremo, impersonal, y sin proposito alguno, en la calle bajo la niebla o en la misma morgue. Und je anonymer, losgelöster und bizarrer, umso besser ZENSURIERT, das heißt, daß der Tod als hohes spirituelles Ziel zur Zeit unerreichbar ist. Der Tod ist schon Kitsch, cultura popular, trivia redundante, puro Mainstream. Doch andererseits sehe ich aus einer rein psychologischen Perspektive keinen anderen Ausweg. Me captas, corazon? Por lo tanto, si me quieres ayudar [ven-tu-mir-jelfen-vilst], borrame! borrame!! Lösch mich einfach aus!!

18 In den letzten zehn Minuten habe ich mehr als die Hälfte der Texte [die besten Abschnitte] gelöscht, wenn Sie also dieses Dokument nochmals lesen sollten [natürlich nur, wenn Sie es herunterladen können], werden Sie feststellen, daß es unvollständig ist. Aber sind wir nicht letzten Endes alle unvollständig und unvollkommen? Sind wir nicht alle nur noch Reste dessen, was wir einmal waren?

18 In the past 10 minutes I've deleted more than half of the texts [the best parts], so when you re-read this document[if you can retrieve it of course], it will appear to be incomplete. But after all, aren't we all incomplete and fragmented anyway? Aren't we all just mere residues of what we once were? drafts of what we thought one day we would be? Vampira, excuse my post-Mexican rrrrrrrrrrrrrrrrrrrrromanticism pero siento la imperiosa necesidad de NDLVLFVL;DCM M LLL LLDLD; LL; LLLWUUGHBHDCB"WEOoJK N VS; MMKDKJJDCDN Al,mm A[ODOPmclkco kviubkllllhdgg MMMMMMMM MMMMMMMe muero.

Jaina, donde andas? En que mapa? En que frecuencia?

Are you lost in the cyberbarrio? ARE YOU?

Were you? Are you somewhere inside this 3-D chat room? Where exactly? Behind the leopard-skin sofa where the cyborg-chola is masturbating? Is she fronting for you this time?

symposium

Ein Entwurf dessen, was wir glaubten, eines Tages sein zu können? Vampira, entschuldige meine postmexikanische Rrrrrrrrrrrrrrrrrrrromantik pero siento la imperiosa necesidad de NDLVLFVL, DCM M LLL LLDLD; LL; LLLWUUGHBHDCB ' ' WEOOJK N VS; MMKDKJJDCDN Al, mm A[ODOPmclkco kviubkllllhdgg MMMMMMMMMMMMMMMMe muero. Jaina, donde andas? En que mapa? En que frecuencia? Hast du dich im cyberbarrio verirrt? Hast du dich verirrt? Hast du dich verloren gefühlt? Bist du irgendwo in diesem 3D-Chatroom? Wo genau? Hinter dem Leopardenfellsofa, auf dem die Cyborg-chola onaniert? Hast du diesmal sie vorgeschickt?

Avatars on the World Wide Web: Marketing the *Descent*

Victoria Vesna

Introduction

1995 was the year the Internet was opened to commercial use. The NSF officially stepped down and began planning Internet2 aimed at creating a network whose primary goal would be to facilitate research and education missions of universities in the US. It is envisaged that this network will be 100 to 1,000 times faster than the existing Internet. Applications like tele-immersion and digital libraries will change the way people use computers to learn, communicate and collaborate.[1]

Although the universities are taking lead in the initial development and research of this network, this is a collaborative effort between federal government agencies, private corporations and non-profit organizations. This means that it will probably take a route similar to the original Internet – first accessible and tested in research institutions, then made publicly available. Corporations such as IBM that have already invested in this venture most probably have long-term plans for the commercial potential of such a super-fast network.

Avatare im World Wide Web: Die Vermarktung der *Herabkunft*

Victoria Vesna

Einleitung

Im Jahr 1995 wurde das Internet der kommerziellen Nutzung zugänglich gemacht. Die NSF zog sich offiziell zurück und begann mit der Planung von Internet2, einem Netz, dessen Hauptaufgabe in der Erleichterung der Forschungs- und Bildungsaufgaben der Universitäten der Vereinigten Staaten bestehen soll. Dieses neue Netz soll nach seiner Vollendung 100 bis 1.000 Mal schneller sein als das bestehende Internet. Anwendungen wie Tele-Immersion und digitale Bibliotheken werden die Verwendung des Computers in den Bereichen Unterricht, Kommunikation und Zusammenarbeit grundlegend verändern[1]. Obgleich die Universitäten in der Anfangsphase der Entwicklung und Forschung für dieses Netz die Führungsrolle übernommen haben, handelt es sich dabei doch um ein gemeinsames Projekt von Regierungsbehörden, privaten Unternehmen und gemeinnützigen Organisationen. Das bedeutet, daß dieses Projekt möglicherweise denselben Weg nehmen wird wie das ursprüngliche Internet, also anfänglich nur den Forschungsinstitutionen, die es testen, zugänglich sein und erst später dann der Öffentlichkeit zur Verfügung gestellt werden. Firmen wie IBM, die bereits in dieses Projekt investieren, haben höchstwahrscheinlich langfristige Pläne in bezug auf das kommerzielle Potential eines derartigen superschnellen Netzes.

Als man das Internet der Öffentlichkeit zur Verfügung stellte, hat man quasi die Büchse der Pandora geöffnet, und überhaupt niemand konnte auch nur versuchen, den immer rascher zunehmenden Aktivitäten Einhalt zu gebieten. Die Internet-Erfinder hatten das Netz so konzipiert, als würden nur Maschinen miteinander *kommunizieren*, und hätten wohl nicht im Traum daran gedacht, daß ihr ursprüngliches Netz von Maschinen sich in ein Netzwerk der Menschen, die diese Maschinen benutzen, verwandeln könnte. Die rasante Zunahme der Internet-Benutzer, der Anzahl der mit dem World

Opening the Internet to the public had meant opening Pandora's box, and there was no way anyone could even attempt to put a lid on the activities that were increasingly taking place. Conceptualized as having only machines *talking* to each other, its developers would never have guessed that this network of machines would transform itself into a network of humans using the machines. Exponential growth in the number of Internet users, the number of hosts connected to the World Wide Web, and the number of companies establishing a Web presence has created a gold-rush mentality among firms and investors. This euphoria is largely fuelled by electronic commerce,and many companies are putting significant resources towards figuring out the most effective ways of buying and selling everything from groceries to clothing to movies over the Internet.

What is particularly interesting about the commercialization of the net, however, is that it is largely being driven by yesterday's anti-establishment hippies and nerds who overnight have become millionaires in the software industry. Many of these new powerful personalities [with the exception of the most powerful one], are bringing value systems influenced by eastern philosophies into the market, while collaborating with established corporate structures. Perhaps caught between a dream and the mass market, it is interesting to look at how these seeemingly opposite worlds are taking form. This strange interplay, perhaps contradiction, is best analyzed through our online selves in multi-user environments, also known as *avatars*; a word that has now assumed a much narrower meaning than its original theological source.

Wide Web verbundenen Hosts sowie der im Web vertretenen Unternehmen hat unter Firmen und Investoren buchstäblich zu einem *Goldrausch* geführt. Diese Euphorie wird durch die Entwicklungen auf dem Elektroniksektor noch angeheizt, und viele Gesellschaften investieren beträchtliche Summen, um herauszufinden, auf welche Art und Weise man über Internet alles – von Lebensmitteln bis zu Kleidung und Filmen – am effizientesten kaufen und verkaufen kann.

Ein besonders interessanter Aspekt in Zusammenhang mit der Kommerzialisierung des Netzes besteht jedoch darin, daß diese weitestgehend von Ex-Hippies betrieben wird, die gestern noch gegen das Establishment protestiert haben, und Freaks, die in der Softwareindustrie praktisch über Nacht zu Millionären geworden sind. Viele dieser neuen Mächtigen [mit Ausnahme des allerwichtigsten überhaupt] bringen von östlichen Philosophien beeinflußte Wertesysteme mit in den Markt ein, während sie mit etablierten Firmenstrukturen zusammenarbeiten. Es ist nicht uninteressant sich anzusehen, wie diese scheinbar gegensätzlichen Welten zwischen Traum und Massenmarkt Gestalt annehmen. Dieses seltsame Zusammenspiel bzw. dieser Widerspruch läßt sich am besten anhand unseres – auch unter der Bezeichnung *Avatar* bekannten – Online-Selbst in Multi-User-Umgebungen analysieren. Der Begriff *Avatar* hat mittlerweile eine eingeschränktere Bedeutung angenommen als seine ursprünglich aus dem theologischen Bereich kommende.

Definition des Avatar

Bevor wir uns nun in Analysen darüber stürzen, wie Projektionen unseres Selbst sich im Internet manifestieren und welche Art von Implikationen dies hinsichtlich unserer zukünftigen Sicht des Marktes haben kann, wäre es vermutlich sinnvoll, sich einen Überblick über die unzähligen Definitionen des Begriffs *Avatar* zu verschaffen.

Nach dem *Dictionary of Hinduism* [1977] bedeutet *Avatara* eine *Herabkunft*, insbesondere das Herabsteigen eines Gottes vom Himmel zur Erde. In den *Puranas* ist der Avatara eine Inkarnation, die von einer göttlichen Emanation [Vyuha] unterschieden wird. Beide werden mit Shiva und insbesondere mit Vishnu in Zusammenhang gebracht. Der Begriff des Avatara stellt wahrscheinlich eine Weiterentwicklung des alten Mythos dar, demzufolge ein Gott durch die schöpferische Kraft seiner Maya nach seinem eigenen Willen jede Gestalt annehmen kann, so wie es Indra getan hat. Der Begriff des Avatara ist

Defining the *Avatar*

Before delving into analyses of how projections of our selves manifest themselves on the Internet and what kind of implications this may have in the future on our perception of the marketplace, it may be useful to overview the myriad definitions of the *avatar*.

According to the *Dictionary of Hinduism* [1977], *Avatara* means *descent*, especially of a god from heaven to earth. In the Puranas, an avatara is an incarnation, and is distinguished from a divine emanation [vyuha], both of which are associated with Vishnu and Siva, but particularly the former. The avatara concept is probably a development of the ancient myth that by the creative power of his Maya, a god can assume any form at will, as did Indra. The avatara concept in Hinduism is a very complex hierarchical system with many different forms taking place.

Longman's dictionary [1985] also defines avatar as the Incarnation of Vishnu, a Hindu deity, and an embodiment of a concept or philosophy. The *Oxford Dictionary*, on the other hand, tells us that avatar can mean descent of a deity to earth in an incarnate form [i.e., as in *the fifth avatar appeared as a dwarf*; a manifestation or presentation to the world [i.e., the avatar of mathematics]: a display, a phase.[1990] If you refer to the *Webster's Dictionary*, it says that an avatar is a manifestation or embodiment of a person, concept or philosophy; a variant phase or version of a continuing basic entity.[1989] And finally, the *Random House Dictionary* describes an avatar as: *An embodiment or concrete manifestation as of a principle, attitude, way of life, or the like.*[1995]

In contemporary India, distinguished personalities may be called avatars, which is a sign that even at the source, the original theological meaning has shifted in popular culture. For instance, on the Web page of India Group, Partner Anil Srivastava refers to himself as *Anil Srivastava, avatar of global markets and emerging technologies, contemplates interactive media, networking, and online services from the omphalos of the Silicon Valley.* [2]

If you ask anyone familiar with multi-user environments, the word simply means an assumed identity in cyberspace. But the source of the use of the word in industry is a bit more difficult to identify. According to Peter Rothman,

im Hinduismus mit einem sehr komplexen hierarchischen System mit zahlreichen unterschiedlichen Ausprägungen verbunden.

Longman's Dictionary [1985] definiert den Avatara ebenfalls als Inkarnation der Hindugottheit Vishnu sowie als Verkörperung eines Begriffs oder einer Philosophie. Andererseits erfahren wir aus dem *Oxford Dictionary*, daß ein Avatara die Herabkunft einer Gottheit zur Erde in fleischgewordener Gestalt [d. h. wie in *der fünfte Avatara erschien als Zwerg*], eine Manifestation oder Darstellung vor der Welt [z. B. der Avatara der Mathematik], aber auch ein Stadium sein kann [1990]. Wenn man nun *Webster's Dictionary* zu Rate zieht, erfährt man, daß ein Avatara eine Manifestation oder Verkörperung einer Person, eines Begriffs oder einer Philosophie, ein abweichendes Stadium oder eine Version einer fortbestehenden grundsätzlichen Einheit ist [1989]. Und das *Random House Dictionary* schließlich beschreibt den Avatara als *Verkörperung oder konkrete Manifestation beispielsweise eines Prinzips, einer Haltung, einer Lebensanschauung o. ä.* [1995].

Im heutigen Indien können besondere Persönlichkeiten als Avatare bezeichnet werden, was darauf hinweist, daß die ursprüngliche theologische Bedeutung dieses Ausdrucks in der volkstümlichen Kultur sogar an der Quelle selbst einen Wandel erfahren hat. Auf der Web-Site der India Group schreibt beispielsweise der Teilhaber Anil Srivastava über sich selbst: *Anil Srivastava, Avatar der globalen Märkte und der neuen Technologien, betrachtet vom Omphalos in Silicon Valley aus interaktive Medien, Netzwerke und Online-Dienste.* [2]

Für jemanden, der mit Multi-User-Umgebungen vertraut ist, bedeutet *Avatar* ganz einfach die Identität, die jemand im Cyberspace angenommen hat. Der Ursprung der Verwendung dieses Wortes in der Industrie läßt sich allerdings nicht so leicht klären. Nach Peter Rothman, Gründer von Avatar Software und Avatar Partners [bzw. später DIVE Labs] *würde jeder, der behauptet, zu wissen, wer das Wort als erster verwendet hat, Tatsachen erfinden* [3]. Rothman und sein Partner fanden diesen Ausdruck 1982 im Wörterbuch und waren von der Definition in *Webster's Dictionary* – *Verkörperung eines Begriffs oder einer Philosophie in einer Person* – einfach begeistert. Die Debatte darüber entwickelte sich – wie passend – innerhalb des Diskussionsforums *WELL*, in dessen Rahmen Neal Stephenson behauptete, diesen Ausdruck in *Snow Crash* als erster verwendet zu haben. Da dieser Roman jedoch erst im Jahr 1992 veröffentlicht wurde, wollte man Stephensons Behauptung

founder of Avatar Software and Avatar Partners, [and later DIVE labs], *anyone claiming to know who used the word first, would be inventing the facts.*[3] Rothman and his partner found the word in the dictionary in 1982, simply liking *Webster's* definition: embodiment of a concept or a philosophy in a person. Appropriately, the debate about this came up on the *WELL* discussion forum about the origin of the word in which Neal Stephenson claimed that he was first to use the term in *Snow Crash*, but since the novel was not published until 1992, this was not acknowledged. Generally, it is conceded that Randy Farmer and Chip Morningstar's *Habitat* was the first to use this term. They were inspired by the Hindu root of the word.[Randall, 1995]

The avatar name is apparently very popular these days. Numerous companies have registered various versions of the name, usually by adding a word next to it. Some recent examples are: Avatar Partners – developing software for trading on the net; Avatar Holdings – a real estate developer of major resort, residential and recreational communities; and Avatar Systems – a moving company specializing in corporate relocations, just to name a few. The commercial world apparently has propreitery feelings towards the term. For example, at one point Avatar Partners were being threatened with a lawsuit by the Avatar Financial Associates who claimed to have been the first to have the name registered and trademarked.[3] And then there is the Avatar nine-day course on *contributing to the creation of an enlightened planetary civilization*.

An enthusiastic testimonial on the net by a devotee claims: *I enrolled in the Avatar course in an attempt to alter behavior patterns that were interfering with the proper conduct of my business. Avatar taught me how to easily recognize and deal with the beliefs that were causing my problems ... In addition, I found the Avatar experience to be delightful and amazing. My life is fuller, more meaningful and pleasant since I became an Avatar.*[4]

Descent of the Avatar

The idea of the avatar *coming down* from an unspecified source in one of many possible manifestations connects well to the reverse hierarchy established originally by the scientific community with the inception of what

nicht anerkennen. Man geht heute im allgemeinen davon aus, daß dieser Ausdruck erstmals in Randy Farmers und Chip Morningstars *Habitat* verwendet wurde. Farmer und Morningstar ließen sich dabei von der hinduistischen Wurzel des Wortes inspirieren [Randall, 1995].

Der Name Avatar erfreut sich heutzutage offensichtlich großer Beliebtheit. Zahlreiche Gesellschaften haben verschiedene Versionen dieses Namens – im allgemeinen in Kombination mit einem anderen Wort – eintragen lassen. Beispiele aus der jüngsten Vergangenheit wären die Firma Avatar Partners, die Software für den Handel im Internet entwickelt, die auf größere Ferien-, Wohn- und Erholungszentren spezialisierte Bau- und Immobilienfirma Avatar Holdings, und Avatar Systems, eine Transportgesellschaft, die sich auf Firmenumzüge spezialisiert hat, um nur einige von ihnen zu nennen. Die Wirtschaft verbindet offensichtlich Besitzansprüche mit diesem Ausdruck. So wurde beispielsweise Avatar Partners von der Gesellschaft Avatar Financial Associates, die behauptete, sie hätte diesen Namen als erste eintragen und schützen lassen, ein Gerichtsverfahren angedroht. Und dann gibt es da noch den Avatar Nine-Day Course über den *Beitrag zur Erschaffung einer aufgeklärten planetaren Zivilisation*.

In einer enthusiastischen Aussage behauptet ein überzeugter Anhänger im Net: *Ich habe mich zum Avatar-Kurs angemeldet, um zu versuchen, die Verhaltensmuster zu ändern, die in Widerspruch zur ordnungsgemäßen Führung meiner Geschäfte standen. Avatar hat mich gelehrt, die Überzeugungen, die für meine Probleme verantwortlich waren, ganz einfach zu identifizieren und mit ihnen fertig zu werden... Die Erfahrungen mit Avatar waren für mich wunderbar und wirklich verblüffend. Mein Leben ist erfüllter, bedeutsamer und angenehmer, seitdem ich zu einem Avatar geworden bin.*[4]

Die Herabkunft des Avatar

Der Gedanke der *Herabkunft* des Avatar von einem nicht näher genannten in einer von vielen möglichen Erscheinungsformen paßt sehr gut zu der umgekehrten Hierarchie, die von der wissenschaftlichen Gemeinschaft ursprünglich mit der Einführung des späteren Internet etabliert wurde – der Client führt *Uploads* und *Downloads* am Server durch.

Die Diskussion der Softwareindustrie über die Avatare dreht sich im Grunde um die in Echtzeit zwischen einer Vielzahl von Servern ablaufenden Interaktionen zwischen Objekten. Wenn man von Avataren spricht, wird die Diskussion persönlicher

would become the Internet – the client *uploads* to and *downloads* from the server that resides above.

The software industry's debate on avatars is really about object interactions passing between a variety of servers in real-time. Talking about avatars personalizes the discussion and brings up issues having to do with the nature of identity, security, interpersonal relations, and societies of the Internet. The concept of an avatar can also be easily transferred to the many variants of computer messages and presentations being transferred from the Web to *client* computer screens. And, finally, all these concepts and hierarchies fit perfectly with financial markets used to trading numbers. The idea of products or services constructing themselves on a computer screen as a result of information *coming down* from the Internet and the World Wide Web is a very attractive prospect for entrepreneurs. There is a sense of power and control the owner of a server has, once removed from the flesh market.

What is particularly fascinating is how many read the mystical concepts of the word avatar into various software applications. For instance, Peter Small writes in the introduction of his online version of a book entitled *Magical Web Avatars:* *The mystical aspect implies that the deity Vishnu has no specific form or shape before manifesting as an avatar on earth. It is implicit that any physical appearance of an avatar is merely a temporary form or phase from an infinite variety of possibilities – transient – form from an indefinite, indefinable number of sources. It is the capturing of this concept, which makes the word avatar ideal for the purpose of describing the Web communication products which will be described in this book.* [Small, 1997] Thus, product promotion is inextricably linked to mysticim and New Age values. This is true for many softwares with mystically encoded connotations, and for the marketing *gurus.*

New Ageism typically encompasses an eclectic mix of different religious elements, claiming no allegiance to nationality or even specific gods. Still, the strong ideological character remains, linked very much to cultural processes and the marketing of products and ideas, and seems pervasive in the structuring of a significant number of new high-tech corporations.

und es werden Themen aufgeworfen, die mit der Natur der Identität, mit der Sicherheit, mit den zwischenmenschlichen Beziehungen und den Internet-Gesellschaften in Zusammenhang stehen. Das Avatar-Konzept läßt sich auch leicht auf die vielen unterschiedlichen Ausprägungen von Computernachrichten und -darstellungen übertragen, die vom Web auf die Monitore der Clients heruntergeladen werden. Und schließlich passen all diese Konzepte und Hierarchien hervorragend zu den Finanzmärkten, die es gewohnt sind, mit Zahlen zu jonglieren. Der Gedanke, daß sich Produkte oder Dienstleistungen als Ergebnis von Informationen, die von Internet und World Wide Web *heruntergeladen werden* auf einem Computerbildschirm selbst *aufbauen*, stellt für Unternehmer eine äußerst attraktive Perspektive dar. Der Besitzer eines Servers empfindet ein Gefühl von Macht und Dominanz, sobald er sich vom herkömmlichen Markt aus Fleisch und Blut distanziert hat.

Ganz besonders faszinierend ist die Art und Weise, in der manche Menschen die mystischen Aspekte des Begriffs Avatar in verschiedene Softwareanwendungen einbringen. So schreibt beispielsweise Peter Small in der Einleitung zu seiner Online-Version eines Buchs mit dem Titel *Magical Web Avatars*: *Der mystische Aspekt impliziert, daß die Gottheit Vishnu über keine spezifische Form oder Gestalt verfügt, bevor er als Avatar auf Erden erscheint. Implizit bedeutet das, daß jegliche physische Erscheinung eines Avatar nicht mehr als ein temporäres Stadium oder eine temporäre Form oder Phase aus einer unendlichen Vielfalt von Möglichkeiten, eine vergängliche Gestalt aus einer nicht definierten und nicht definierbaren Anzahl von Ursprüngen ist. Das Erfassen dieses Begriffs macht den Ausdruck Avatar zum idealen Wort für die Beschreibung der Web-Kommunikationsprodukte in diesem Buch.* [Small, 1997] Die Produktwerbung ist also untrennbar mit Mystizismus und New-Age-Wertvorstellungen verbunden. Dasselbe gilt für viele Software-Produkte mit mystisch codierten Konnotationen und auch für die Marketing-*Gurus*.

Die New-Age-Philosophie umfaßt eine eklektische Mischung unterschiedlicher religiöser Elemente, ohne jedoch die Loyalität gegenüber einer Nationalität oder gar spezifischen Gottheiten für sich in Anspruch zu nehmen. Doch der starke ideologische Charakter, der mit kulturellen Prozessen und der Vermarktung von Produkten und Ideen verbunden ist, bleibt bestehen und scheint im Aufbau zahlreicher neuer High-Tech-Firmen große Bedeutung

Certainly, the very choice of naming an identity in networked spaces an *avatar* indicates this trend. The avatar in cyberspace represents a strange interplay of left-wing utopianism with right-wing entreprenurism, mixed up with esoteric spiritualism. New Age religion operates in tandem with networking technologies and *organic* corporate structures – the new *cool* companies that are emerging all over the high-tech industry map.

James Hillman, a psychologist widely read by the corporate sector's elite, writes in his influential bestseller, *Kinds of Power*: *Economics is the only effective syncretistic cult remaining in the world today, our world's only ecumenical faith. It provides the daily ritual, uniting Christian, Hindu, Mormon, atheist, Buddhist, Sikh, Adventist, animist, evangelist, Muslim, Jew, fundamentalist and New Ager in one common temple, admitting all alike ...* [1995] How perfect the Internet, then, to unite the multinational corporations with their customers regardless of nation, race or creed. The multi-user environment with its dynamic design for instant communication and relations is the ideal space for the creation of communities with their various interests and markets, commercial or otherwise. Hence the World Wide Web, with its friendly graphical user interface. Not like its predecessors, the text-based virtual realities, only accessible by the unix literati. To date, text-based environments are still active with hundreds of thousands of users, and provide useful research data for those planning commercial ventures with graphical multi-user communities on the Web. Naturally, the graphical offspring promise numbers projected into the hundreds of millions. [*Advertising Age*, 1996] There are over 500 MOOs [Turkle, 1995] in existence, with hundreds of thousands of users who might easily make a transition from the text-based environments to more graphically designed spaces.

Hierarchies of Multi-User Environments

Examining the hierarchy of MUDs and MOOs is helpful if we are to begin to understand the evolving social structure of avatars in cyberspace.[5] It is generally acknowledged that the Arch-Wizards are those who *own* the MOO, and that those new to the environment are usually guests who progress in their status as they become more active and experienced.

zu haben. Allein die Entscheidung, eine Identität in vernetzten Räumen als *Avatar* zu bezeichnen, weist bereits auf diesen Trend hin. Im Cyberspace stellt der Avatar ein ungewohntes Zusammenspiel von linken Utopien und rechtem Unternehmertum, gewürzt mit einem Schuß esoterischem Spiritualismus, dar. Die New-Age-Religion operiert Hand in Hand mit Netzwerktechnologien und *organischen* Firmenstrukturen – den neuen *coolen* Gesellschaften, die sich in allen Bereichen der High-Tech-Industrie entwickeln.

Der von der Unternehmerelite hochgeschätzte Psychologe James Hillman schreibt in seinem einflußreichen Bestseller *Kinds of Power*: *Die Wirtschaft ist der einzige effektive synkretistische Kult, der heute in der Welt noch besteht, der einzige ökumenische Glaube unserer Welt. Sie stellt das tägliche Ritual dar, das Christen, Hindus, Mormonen, Atheisten, Buddhisten, Sikhs, Adventisten, Animisten, Protestanten, Moslems, Juden, Fundamentalisten und New Ager in einem gemeinsamen, allen gleichermaßen zugänglichen Heiligtum vereint ...* [1995]. Wie ließe sich dann das Internet vervollkommnen, damit es die multinationalen Gesellschaften mit ihren Kunden ohne Rücksicht auf Nationalität, Rasse oder Glaubensbekenntnis verbindet? Eine Multi-User-Umgebung mit ihrer dynamischen Konzeption, die sofortige Kontaktaufnahme und Kommunikation ermöglicht, ist der ideale Ort für die Schaffung von Gemeinschaften mit unterschiedlichen kommerziellen oder sonstigen Interessen und Märkten. So erklärt sich auch das World Wide Web mit seiner benutzerfreundlichen Graphikschnittstelle – im Gegensatz zu seinen Vorgängern, den textbasierten virtuellen Realitäten, die nur fachkundigen Unix-Anwendern zugänglich waren. Bis zum heutigen Tage sind textbasierte Umgebungen noch immer aktiv. Sie zählen hunderttausende Benutzer und liefern jedem, der wirtschaftliche Projekte mit graphischen Multi-User-Communities im Web plant, nützliche Forschungsdaten. Naturgemäß verspricht der graphische Abkömmling Benutzerzahlen in einer Größenordnung von hunderten Millionen [*Advertising Age*, 1996]. Gegenwärtig gibt es über 500 MOOs [Turkle, 1995] und hunderttausende Anwender, die ohne weiteres von den textbasierten Umgebungen auf stärker graphisch konzipierte Umgebungen umsteigen könnten.

Die Hierarchien von Multi-User-Umgebungen

Eine Analyse der Hierarchie von MUDs und MOOs erweist sich als hilfreich, wenn wir versuchen

Most MUDs and MOOs prefer to allow users to retain anonymity so as not to destroy the online atmosphere by introduction of offline life. An exception to this would be MIT's MediaMOO where each character has a *character name* and a *real name.* [6] Real names don't normally appear, but can be seen with the @whois command. Only janitors [administrators of the MOO] can set or change real names. Because the goal is to enhance community amongst media researchers, you must provide a statement of your research interests in order to be granted a character. Regardless of the specialized purpose of the MOO, whether it is the most down and dirty fantasy dungeon and dragon MOO or a MOO steeped in theory, people in charge of the code reside at the *top.*

For instance, *Avatar III – The Crypt*, is owned and run by a company in the UK that specializes in games.[7] *The Crypt* is a beta site that presumably will become commercial as soon as enough players visit it regularly. When you first enter the site, you will get promotional materials – not at all enshrouded in fantasy – about the company that produces the MOO. The avatar inhabitants are – shopkeepers, moneychangers, pawnbrokers, pedlars, town guardsmen, market traders and citadel traders. The Avatar classes are very different, and guests are allocated to suit the skills of the different classes. The site's narrative and hierarchy uncannily resembles the class system England is so familiar with.

Rose, a user of the five-year-old MOO since day one, has gained the status of a god. She logs on daily to help newbies, and in this way gains points. One needs 1000 experience points to move to the second level, and 1024000 to get to the twelfth and highest level. Gods have the power to move up levels to ensure that the lower level gods can't force higher level gods to do things.[8] Users are encouraged to help those on lower levels, which not only teaches human relations, but ensures a growing community. Thus the ones at the *top* assume a role similar to those held by religious figures of the past. By providing incentives they function as primary agents of socialization, and become more powerful in the process.[9]

Particularly interesting about *Avatar III* is that the role-playing game is housed in a commercial shopping site – Silicon Village. Thus,

wollen, die sich entwickelnde soziale Struktur der Avatare im Cyberspace zu verstehen [5]. Es wird heute allgemein anerkannt, daß die Arch-Wizards die *Besitzer* der MOOs sind und daß Neulinge in der jeweiligen Umgebung im allgemeinen Gäste sind, deren Status sich mit der Zunahme ihrer Aktivitäten und Erfahrungen weiterentwickelt.

Die meisten MUDs und MOOs lassen den Benutzern ihre Anonymität, um die Online-Atmosphäre nicht durch die Einbeziehung des Offline-Lebens zu zerstören. Eine Ausnahme davon bildet das MediaMOO des MIT, wo jeder Benutzer über einen *Aliasnamen* und einen *wirklichen Namen* verfügt [6]. Die wirklichen Namen scheinen üblicherweise nicht auf, können aber mit dem Befehl @whois sichtbar gemacht werden. Nur die Janitors [MOO-Administratoren] können wirkliche Namen eingeben oder ändern. Da das Ziel darin besteht, das Gemeinschaftsgefühl unter den Medienforschern zu stärken, muß jeder, der um die Zuteilung eines Aliasnamens ansucht, seine Forschungsinteressen angeben. Unabhängig von dem besonderen Zweck des jeweiligen MOO, d. h. gleichgültig, ob sich das MOO den niedrigsten, schmutzigsten Phantasien über Burgverliese und Drachen widmet oder hohe theoretische Zielsetzungen verfolgt, sitzen die Verantwortlichen für den Code immer ganz an der *Spitze*.

Avatar III – The Crypt steht beispielsweise im Besitz einer britischen Gesellschaft, die sich auf Spiele spezialisiert hat, und wird von dieser auch betrieben [7]. *The Crypt* ist eine Beta-Adresse, die voraussichtlich kommerziell genutzt werden wird, sobald eine genügend große Anzahl von Spielern sie erst regelmäßig besucht. Beim ersten Besuch dieser Adresse erhält man – ganz und gar nüchtern verpacktes – Werbematerial über die Gesellschaft, die das MOO produziert. Die Avatarbewohner sind Ladenbesitzer, Geldwechsler, Pfandleiher, Hausierer, Stadtwachen, Markt- und Burgfieranten. Die Avatarklassen sind äußerst unterschiedlich, und die Besucher werden so zugeteilt, daß sie den Fähigkeiten der verschiedenen Klassen entsprechen. Die textliche Gestaltung und die Hierarchie dieser Adresse erinnern in unheimlicher Weise an das Klassensystem, mit dem England so vertraut ist.

Rose hat sich als Benutzerin der ersten Stunde in dem mittlerweile fünf Jahre alten MOO in den Rang eines Gottes hochgearbeitet. Sie loggt sich täglich ein, um Neulingen behilflich zu sein, und verdient sich auf diese Weise Punkte. Der Benutzer benötigt 1.000 Erfahrungspunkte, um auf die zweite Ebene vorzurücken, und 1.024.000 Punkte, um die

an entire community is formed around the shopping site, where users have the illusion of anonymity. The Arch-Avatars [owners], on the other hand, can easily track all the personal information they may need on users' likes and dislikes, newsgroup postings, favorite Web sites, and navigational habits. As soon as users enter a site, it becomes possible to learn where they go, what they click on, the domain name, computer type, and general location. Personal information is fast becoming a most precious commodity, and those who are positioned as packagers and resellers of it will profit the most in the Information Age.

Descent of the Graphical Avatar

In is truly awe-inspiring to survey how much progress industry has made in figuring out ways to cash in on the potential markets of the World Wide Web. Star-featured chat rooms sponsored by large companies, soap operas, online trading, and role-playing games seem to be the places where most success is promised, in other words, any space that could potentially form large communities that will regularly log on to communicate, exchange ideas and spend cybercash.

Avatar-filled chat rooms seem to be where most entrepreneurs are placing their bets. By the year 2000, chats are expected to generate 7.9 billion hours of online use, with a resulting $1 billion in advertising revenue [NY Times, 1996]. But, makers of virtual environments predict that scrolling text for chat rooms will soon be replaced with 2-D and 3-D graphical environments, while marketers are busily exploring ways to exploit new technology for advertising.

For example, soap operas on the World Wide Web are seen as ideal environments for marketing strategies involving advertisements built into the narratives.[10] Moreover, in contrast with television, there are virtually no standards regulating Web-based advertising. Currently several cybersoaps allow advertisers the chance to have their products integrated into the story line. [*Advertising Age*, 1996] Meanwhile, Rocket Science Games, a maker of interactive entertainment software, and CyberCash, a company that handles payment transactions on the Internet, are forming a partnership to develop a virtual video game arcade on the World Wide Web. Scheduled for rollout later this year, Virtual

zwölfte und höchste Stufe zu erreichen. Götter können um weitere Stufen nach oben klettern, damit gewährleistet ist, daß Götter einer niedrigeren Ebene Götter einer höheren Ebene zu keinerlei Handlungen zwingen können [8]. Die Benutzer werden dazu ermutigt, Benutzern auf niedrigeren Ebenen behilflich zu sein, was nicht nur eine Lektion in zwischenmenschlichen Beziehungen darstellt, sondern auch das Wachstum der Gemeinschaft sichert. So haben jene, die an der *Spitze* stehen, eine ähnliche Position inne wie religiöse Gestalten der Vergangenheit. Sie bieten Anreize und fungieren dadurch als primäre Agenten der Sozialisierung – und werden bei diesem Prozeß immer mächtiger [9].

Ein besonders interessanter Aspekt in Zusammenhang mit *Avatar III* ist, daß das Rollenspiel in einer kommerziellen Shopping-Site, Silicon Village, angesiedelt ist. So bildet sich um diese Shopping-Site herum eine ganze Gemeinschaft, in der die Benutzer den illusorischen Eindruck haben, anonym zu sein. Die Arch-Avatare, die Eigentümer, können jedoch sämtliche eventuell benötigten persönlichen Informationen über Vorlieben und Abneigungen der Benutzer, die Beteiligung an Newsgroups, bevorzugte Web-Sites und Surfgewohnheiten erhalten. Sobald ein Benutzer sich unter einer Adresse einloggt, besteht die Möglichkeit, Informationen über seine weiteren Bewegungen, die von ihm angeklickten Objekte, den Namen des Bereichs, den Computertyp und die allgemeine Lokalisierung zu erhalten. Persönliche Informationen werden immer rascher zu einer begehrten Ware, und die Verpacker und Wiederverkäufer derartiger Informationen werden in unserem Informationszeitalter am meisten profitieren.

Die Herabkunft des graphischen Avatar

Die Fortschritte, die die Industrie beim Erfinden von Möglichkeiten zum Abkassieren auf den potentiellen Märkten des World Wide Web gemacht hat, sind wirklich beeindruckend. Besonders erfolgversprechend scheinen in diesem Zusammenhang die von großen Gesellschaften gesponserten Chatrooms mit Stars, die Seifenopern, Online-Geschäfte und Rollenspiele zu sein – also Orte, an denen sich potentiell große Gemeinschaften bilden können, die sich regelmäßig einloggen, um miteinander zu kommunizieren, Ideen auszutauschen und Cybercash auszugeben. Die meisten Unternehmer setzen offensichtlich auf Chatrooms, die von jeder Menge Avataren bevölkert sind. Schätzungen zufolge sollen Online-Chats im Jahr 2000 bereits für 7,9 Milliarden Online-Stunden verantwortlich sein – und damit

Arcade will feature interactive versions of classic video games. Users will reportedly be able to modify the environments of the games, and they will pay as little as 25 cents to play each game. Payments will come out of an *electronic wallet* that users could replenish by transferring money from their bank accounts. [San Francisco Chronicle, 1996]

Of course none of these developments would be taking place with this kind of speed if the WWW was a text only environment. Although text-based MOOs and MUDs are still very active communities, and there will probably always be a place for them, the real goldrush has started with the introduction of graphical user interfaces. Graphical Multi-User Konversations [*GMUKs*], are something of a cross between a MOO and a chat room or channel. Rather than limiting users to text-only communications, as in most virtual chat environments, GMUKs add an audio-visual dimension that creates the illusion of movement, and space.

The most popular GMUK, to date, is Time-Warner's *Palace*, a client/server program that creates a visual and spatial chat environment.[11] Currently, there are many *Palace* sites located across the Internet, varying widely in technical and artistic sophistication, as well as graphical themes. Jim Bumgardner and Mark Jeffrey created and designed *The Palace* at Time Warner's Palace Group. The software driving the environment was released in November 1995. More than 300,000 client versions have been downloaded since then, and over 1,000 commercial and private-hosted *Palace* communities have been established. Major investors include Intel, Time Warner, Inc. and Softbank as well as companies like Capitol Records, Twentieth Century Fox, Fox Television, Sony Pictures and MTV.[Suller]

Time/Warner's *avs,* as *Palace* members affectionately call them, fall into two overall categories. The first are the standard set of *smileys* that come with the *Palace* program. These faces are available to all users, including unregistered *guests.* The standard avs are associated with newbies, the unregistered guests who are considered a lower class of the *Palace* population. They have not paid the registration fee, they do not belong to the *Palace* culture, and are limited to wearing only the stan-

auch für Werbeeinnahmen in der Größenordnung von 1 Milliarde Dollar [NY Times, 1996]. Doch die Hersteller von virtuellen Umgebungen prognostizieren, daß schon bald 2D- und 3D-Graphikumgebungen das Scrollen in den Textfenstern der Chatrooms ersetzen werden. Zugleich suchen die Vermarkter eifrig nach Möglichkeiten, die neue Technologie für die Werbung zu nutzen.

Seifenopern im World Wide Web werden beispielsweise als ideale Umgebung für den Einsatz von Marketingstrategien angesehen, die sich auf in den Text integrierte Werbebotschaften konzentrieren[10]. Darüber hinaus gibt es, im Gegensatz zum Fernsehen, praktisch keine Normen für die Werbung im Web. Zur Zeit ermöglichen mehrere Cyberseifenopern Werbefirmen eine Integration ihrer Produkte in die Handlung [*Advertising Age*, 1996]. Rocket Science Games, ein Hersteller interaktiver Unterhaltungssoftware, und CyberCash, eine Gesellschaft, die sich auf Zahlungstransaktionen im Internet spezialisiert hat, sind mittlerweile eine Partnerschaft zur Entwicklung einer virtuellen Videospielhalle im World Wide Web eingegangen. *Virtual Arcade* soll im Laufe dieses Jahres erscheinen und wird interaktive Versionen klassischer Videospiele bieten. Die Benutzer werden – wie verlautet – die Möglichkeit haben, die Spielumgebung zu verändern, und der Preis für jedes Spiel wird nur 25 Cent betragen. Die Zahlungen werden über eine *elektronische Geldbörse* erfolgen, die die Benutzer von ihrem Bankkonto wieder auffüllen können [Francisco Chronicle, 1996].

Natürlich würden all diese Entwicklungen keineswegs so rasch vor sich gehen, wenn das WWW eine reine Textumgebung wäre. Obgleich textbasierte MOOs und MUDs nach wie vor sehr aktive Gemeinschaften sind und es für sie wahrscheinlich immer einen Platz geben wird, hat das wirkliche *Goldfieber* erst mit der Einführung der graphischen Benutzerschnittstellen begonnen. *Graphical Multi-User Konversations* [GMUKs] sind eine Art Mittelding zwischen einem MOO und einem Chatroom oder einem Chatkanal. Die GMUKs bieten den Anwendern nicht nur reine Textkommunikation, wie dies bei den meisten virtuellen Chat-Umgebungen der Fall ist, sondern erweitern diese um eine audiovisuelle Dimension, die die Illusion von Bewegung erzeugt, sowie um eine räumliche Dimension.

Die beliebteste GMUK ist gegenwärtig Time Warners *Palace*, ein Client/Server-Programm, das eine visuelle und räumliche Chat-Umgebung erzeugt[11]. Zur Zeit finden sich im Internet zahlreiche *Palace*-Sites, die stark unterschiedliche technische

dard avs and props. They cannot create their own avatars, and are reduced to wearing a smiley which identifies them as a newbie. Only after paying the registration fee, can the user unlock the prop creating/editing feature of the *Palace* software. At that point they are able to choose from Animal, Cartoon, Celebrity, Evil, Real, Idiosyncratic, Positional, Power, Seductive or *Other* avatars. The Palace is an excellent example of an environment in cyberspace that is a combination of an established entertainment industry's approach to pre-packaged programming for the public, reminiscent of developments such as Disneyland, or any planned community.[8]

Earth to Avatar

The biggest problem that industry developing multi-user environments for avatars faces is the fact that people can assume many identities and are still quite difficult to track down. This is largely due to lack of a universal standard, allowing the avatars to move from one virtual world to another. There are a number of avatars currently on the Web – VRML, 2D, text, Voxel-drawn ones, and Virtual Humans, which refers to the group set up by VR News to exchange information about the development of autonomous agents that look like human beings.

Buying patterns, monetary exchange, security, and authentication must be maintained in the avatar in order for a market to be fully developed. Using standardized avatars can help in using Internet search engines for avatars and avatar properties. Finally, avatar companies have become common – they can price their avatars at a lower cost, make them available to more people and guarantee broader applicability.

In October '96, at the *Earth to Avatar* Conference in San Francisco, architects of 3D graphical interfaces on the web met to discuss the lack of avatar standards. When former Apple Computer Chairman John Sculley gave his analysis of the future of cyberspace at the conference, he said that once the technology is shown to work and standards are agreed, the big league players will move into cyberspace. As avatars become members of self-organizing groups, Sculley sees them as *a driving force shaping the economics of this industry.* [Wilcox] Universal Avatar Standards group

und künstlerische Qualitäten wie auch unterschiedliche graphische Themen aufweisen. The *Palace* wurde von Jim Bumgardner und Mark Jeffrey für Time Warners Palace Group entwickelt und erstellt. Die Software für diese Umgebung wurde im November 1995 freigegeben. Seit damals wurden mehr als 300.000 Client-Versionen heruntergeladen, und mehr als 1.000 kommerzielle und private *Palace*-Gemeinschaften wurden gegründet. Die wichtigsten Investoren sind Intel, Time Warner, Inc. und Softbank sowie Gesellschaften wie Capitol Records, Twentieth Century Fox, Fox Television, Sony Pictures und MTV [Suller].

Time Warners *avs*, wie *Palace*-Mitglieder die Avatare liebevoll nennen, lassen sich in zwei große Kategorien einteilen. Zur ersten dieser Kategorien zählt die Standardgarnitur von *Smileys*, die mit dem *Palace*-Programm geliefert wird. Diese Smileys sind allen Benutzern, auch nicht registrierten *Gästen*, zugänglich. Die Standard-*avs* werden mit Neulingen, den nicht registrierten Gästen, die als niedrigere Klasse der *Palace*-Bevölkerung angesehen werden, assoziiert. Diese Gäste haben die Registrierungsgebühr nicht bezahlt, gehören der *Palace*-Kultur nicht an und müssen sich mit den Standard-*avs* und -*props* begnügen. Sie können keine eigenen Avatare erzeugen und müssen einen Smiley verwenden, der sie als Neuling identifiziert. Erst nachdem er die Registrierungsgebühr bezahlt hat, kann der Benutzer die Funktionen der *Palace*-Software für die Erstellung und Ausgabe von "props" in Verwendung nehmen. An dieser Stelle kann der Benutzer unter folgenden Avataren wählen: Animal, Cartoon, Celebrity, Evil, Real, Idiosyncratic, Positional, Power, Seductive oder *Sonstige*. *Palace* ist ein hervorragendes Beispiel für eine Cyberspace-Umgebung, die den Ansatz einer etablierten Unterhaltungsindustrie in Richtung *pre-packaged programming* [Fertigprogramm] für die Öffentlichkeit darstellt und an Entwicklungen wie Disneyland oder sonst eine geplante Gemeinschaft erinnert[8].

Earth to Avatar

Das größte Problem, mit dem sich die Industrie konfrontiert sieht, die Multi-User-Umgebungen für Avatare herstellt, ist die Tatsache, daß die Menschen viele verschiedene Identitäten annehmen können und noch immer ziemlich schwer rückverfolgbar sind. Dies deswegen, weil es keine universelle Norm gibt, die es den Avataren erlauben würde, sich von einer virtuellen Welt in die andere zu bewegen. Zur Zeit gibt es auf dem Web eine Reihe verschiedener Avatare – VRML-, 2D-, Text- oder Voxel-Avatare

stated that their core aim is to focus on the nature of avatars with regard to such issues as gender representation, ID authentication, personal expression versus social constraints, avatar versus world scale, and the communication of emotion. Maclen Marvit, teleologist of Worlds in San Francisco, provides this overview of UA's approach:

*We are at a point in our industry where lots of companies are doing innovative things, both technically and artistically. The goal of UA is to allow users to move as freely as possible between the technologies and find the best experiences in each, while maintaining a consistent identity. So if Bernie moves from one *world* [developed using] one technology to another *world* in another technology, he can maintain his avatar's representation, his Internet phone number and his proof of identity.*[Wilcox]

The proposal provides an architecture for managing thousands of geographically distant users simultaneously, with interactive behaviors, voice, 3-D graphics and localized audio. It uses a powerful concept known as *regions,* which allows for multiple contiguous worlds, accelerated 3-D graphics, and efficient server/client communications. The avatar standards issue is crucial to the success of VRML as a commercially viable language. Until there is some common definition of an avatar, and universality of movement between spaces on the Internet, it seems unlikely that any VRML company can hope to make serious money.

The proposal discusses creation of a link to a user profile, coded in HTML and containing data the user wishes to be known either about his fantasy identity or a true one, proofs of identity, Vendor-specific extensions and user's history. A history could be with reference to games, for example wizard status in a Role Playing Game [RPG], or it could hold marketing information about purchases made by credit card.

Conclusion

The Internet as it exists today is one large market testing- ground – a living laboartory of sorts. It is clear that the direction most companies are taking is development of multi-user communities with standardized avatars. Thus, users' connection to the physical self and the bank account is direct and clear. Corporate confusion over the concept of the avatar is that

sowie Virtual Humans, die die von VR News geschaffene Gruppe bezeichnet, die dem Austausch von Informationen über die Entwicklung autonomer, Menschen ähnelnder Agenten dient.

Konsummuster, finanzielle Transaktionen, Sicherheit und Identifizierung müssen im Avatar erhalten bleiben, damit sich der Markt voll und ganz entwickeln kann. Die Verwendung genormter Avatare kann bei der Verwendung von Mechanismen für die Suche nach Avataren und deren Eigenschaften im Internet behilflich sein. Schließlich sind heute auch schon Avatarfirmen gang und gäbe – sie können ihre Avatare zu niedrigeren Kosten anbieten, einem größeren Personenkreis zur Verfügung stellen und eine umfassendere Anwendbarkeit garantieren.

Im Oktober 1996 kamen im Rahmen der *Earth-to-Avatar*-Konferenz in San Francisco Architekten von 3D-Graphikschnittstellen im Web zusammen, um über den Mangel an Normen für Avatare zu diskutieren. In seiner Analyse der Zukunft des Cyberspace meinte John Sculley, der frühere Präsident von Apple Computer, sobald erst einmal erwiesen wäre, daß die Technik funktioniert, und Normen vereinbart werden, würden die *Spieler der ersten Liga* im Cyberspace Einzug halten. Sculley sieht die Avatare, die zu Mitgliedern sich selbst organisierender Gruppen werden, als *treibende Wirtschaftskraft für diese Branche* [Wilcox]. Die Universal Avatar Standards Group erklärte, daß ihr wichtigstes Ziel darin bestehe, sich unter Berücksichtigung von Aspekten wie Darstellung des Geschlechts, Nachweis der Identität, persönlicher Ausdruck kontra gesellschaftliche Zwänge, Avatar kontra Weltmaßstab sowie Emotionskommunikation auf die Natur der Avatare zu konzentrieren. Maclen Marvit, Teleologe bei Worlds in San Francisco, liefert den nachfolgenden Überblick über den Ansatz von UA:

*Unsere Branche ist an einem Punkt angelangt, an dem viele Gesellschaften innovativ tätig sind – sowohl in technischer als auch in künstlerischer Hinsicht. Das Ziel von UA besteht darin, den Benutzern die Möglichkeit zu bieten, sich zwischen den verschiedenen Technologien so frei wie nur möglich hin und her zu bewegen und sich dabei aus jeder Technologie das Beste zu holen, während zugleich eine konsistente Identität gewahrt bleibt. Wenn sich also Bernie von einer *Welt*, die unter Verwendung einer Technologie entwickelt wurde, in eine andere *Welt* mit einer anderen Technologie begibt, kann er seine Avatardarstellung, seine Internet-Telefonnummer und seinen Identitätsnachweis mitnehmen.* [Wilcox]

those at the *top* of the hierarchy – the owners of the servers – are bestowing avatar calling on the lowly users. This presumably gives power to the user, who ultimately feels suspicious. Technology becomes *god*, the unnamed avatar, the invisible force. When the Internet2 *descends*, and when avatars are standardized and cybercash perfected, we will be looking out upon a world we can't even imagine.

1 Internet2-also known as I2-is a collaborative effort joining over 100 U.S. universities. <http://www.internet2.edu>
2 <http://www.indonet.com/AnilSrivastava.html>
3 I interviewed Peter Rothman on December 31st, 1996 at MetaTools INC. in Carpinteria. His company, DIVE, was acquired by MetaTools, and he is currently the director of Research & Development.
4 William L. Owens, Wisconsin, USA <http://www.epcnet.com/avatar/ index.html>
5 MOO, technically, means MUD-Object Oriented. And MUD is a Multiple-User Dungeon [or Dimension]. MUDs started as interactive adventure games similar to Dungeons and Dragons for the computer- but a version that participants could play over the Internet. Since those days, the use of MUDs have expanded to other sorts of games and to more social uses. The object-orientation of MOOs puts more of the programming focus on the *objects* that are in the MOO. Some of the most significant research done to date on MUDs and MOOs has taken place at Xerox Parc, University of Virginia and the MIT Media Lab. At Xerox Parc, Curtis Pavel established LambdaMOO and wrote on the social phenomena of Text-Based virtual realities.[1992]
6 MediaMOO <http://asb.www.media.mit.edu/people/asb/MediaMOO> To connect to MediaMOO from a UNIX host: telnet <mediamoo. media.mit.edu 8888>
7 *Avatar III - the Crypt*: <http://www.avatar.co.uk/>
8 I interviewed Rose on May 29, 1997. In RL [real life], she works in a social security office.
9 An example of a code of conduct in a online game can be found at: <http://games.world.co.uk/code_of_conduct.html>
10 Online soaps include:
The Spot: <http://www.thespot.com>
Ferndale: <http://www.ferndale.com>
Techno 3: <http://www.bluepearl.com/bluepearl>
The East Village: <http://www.theeastvillage.co>
11 *The Palace Home Page:* <http://www. thePalace.com>

Dieser Vorschlag bezieht sich auf eine Architektur für die gleichzeitige Verwaltung tausender geographisch voneinander getrennter Benutzer mit interaktivem Verhalten, Stimme, 3D-Graphik und Audiolokalisierung. Er beruht auf einem leistungsfähigen Konzept, das unter dem Begriff *Regionen* bekannt ist und beschleunigte 3D-Graphik sowie effiziente Client/Server-Kommunikation in verschiedenen aneinander angrenzenden Welten ermöglicht. Das Thema der Standardisierung von Avataren ist für den Erfolg von VRML als kommerziell überlebensfähige Sprache von grundlegender Bedeutung. Bis eine gemeinsame Avatar-Definition vorliegt und die Universalität der Bewegung zwischen Räumen im Internet realisiert ist, scheint es für jede VRML-Gesellschaft unrealistisch, sich Hoffnungen auf finanzielle Gewinne zu machen.

Der Vorschlag diskutiert die Einrichtung einer Verbindung zu einem Benutzerprofil, das HTML-codiert ist und Daten enthält, die der Benutzer je nach Wunsch entweder über seine Phantasie- oder über seine wahre Identität bekanntgeben möchte: Identitätsnachweise, verkäuferspezifische Erweiterungen und die Geschichte des Benutzers. Eine Geschichte könnte sich auf Spiele beziehen, z. B. auf den Status eines Wizards in einem Rollenspiel, oder auch Marketinginformation über mittels Kreditkarte getätigte Käufe enthalten.

Schluß

In seiner heutigen Ausprägung ist das Internet ein großes Testgelände für die Auslotung des Markts, ein lebendes Labor sozusagen. Es ist klar, daß der Weg, den die meisten Gesellschaften einschlagen, in der Entwicklung von Multi-User-Communities mit genormten Avataren besteht. So ist die Verbindung zwischen dem Benutzer, dem physischen Selbst und dem Bankkonto direkt und eindeutig. Die von den Firmen gestiftete Verwirrung hinsichtlich der Idee des Avatar besteht darin, daß jene, die an der *Spitze* der Hierarchie stehen – die Besitzer der Server – das Fußvolk der Benutzer zu Avataren beruft. Dies verleiht dem Anwender vermeintliche Macht, und schließlich beginnt er, mißtrauisch zu werden. Die Technologie wird *Gott*, namenloser Avatar, unsichtbare Macht. Wenn Internet2 Realität wird, wenn Avatare genormt werden und Cybercash perfektioniert wird, dann werden wir auf eine Welt blicken, die wir uns heute nicht einmal vorstellen können.

DUNN, A., *Think of Your Soul as a Market Niche*, New York Times Cybertimes September 11, 1996
CLELAND, K., *Chat Gives Marketers Something to Talk About*, Advertising Age, August 5, 1996
CURTIS P. [1992], *Mudding: Social Phenomena in Text-based Virtual Realities*, unpublished, available via anonymous <ftp://parcftp.xerox.com/pub/MOO/papers/DIAC92>
DILLSTONE, F.W., [1951] *The Structure of the Divine Society*, Lutterworth Press
DONOVAN, L., *Secret Identities* [Secure Electronic Signatures Would Aid Internet Commerce], Financial Times 2/6/96
EINSTEIN, D., *Virtual Arcade Games: Play the classics on the Internet*, San Francisco Chronicle, February 13, 1996 p. C3
HENDRICKSON, R. [1987], *Encyclopedia of Word and Phrase Origins*, New York: Facts on File
LEVERE, J., *Advertising: With Soap Operas on Web, What's Next?*, The New York Times March 11, 1996
LONGMAN DICTIONARY, [1985] Harlow [Essex]: Longman
OXFORD DICTIONARY, [1990] New York: Oxford University Press
F. RANDALL F. ET AL., *From Habitat to Global Cyberspace*, unpublished, available via the World Wide Web: <http://www.communities.com/paper/hab2cybr.html>
RANDOM HOUSE DICTIONARY, [1994] New York: Random House
RIEDMAN, P., *Avatars Build Character on 3-D Chat Sites*, Advertising Age, September 1996
SMALL, P., *Magical Web Avatars: The sorcery of biotelemorphic cells*, <http://192.41.36.58/avatars/Index.htm>
STUTLEY, M. [1977], *Dictionary of Hinduism*, London: Routledge & Kegan Paul
STEPHENSON, N. [1992], *Snow Crash*, New York: Bantam Books
SULER, J. [Nov. 1996], *The Psychology of Cyberspace*. World Wide Web, <http://www1.rider.edu/~suler/psycyber>
TURKLE, S. [1984], *The Second Self: Computers and the Human Spirit*, New York: Simon & Schuster
TURKLE, S. [1995], *Life on the Screen*, New York: Simon & Schuster
WEBSTER'S NEW DICTIONARY [1991], Cleveland : Webster's New World
WILOX, S. [1996], *Bringing *behaviors*to VRML: Making sense of the avatar debate*, Netscape World, January 1997<http://www.netscape world. com/netscapeworld/nw-01-1997/nw-01-avatar.html>

1 Internet2 – auch als I2 bekannt – entsteht im Rahmen einer Zusammenarbeit zwischen mehr als 100 Universitäten in den USA <http://www.internet2.edu>

2 <http://www.indonet.com/AnilSrivastava.html>

3 Ich habe Peter Rothman am 31. Dezember 1996 bei MetaTools INC. in Carpinteria interviewt. Seine Gesellschaft DIVE wurde von MetaTools übernommen, wo er gegenwärtig die Forschungs- und Entwicklungsabteilung leitet.

4 WILLIAM L. OWENS, Wisconsin, USA <http://www.epcnet.com/avatar/index.html>

5 MOO ist die Abkürzung für *MUD-Object Oriented*. Und MUD bedeutet *Multiple User Dungeon* [oder Dimension]. Die MUDs begannen als interaktive Adventures, Games ähnlich wie Dungeons and Dragons für den Computer – doch diese Version konnten die Teilnehmer übers Internet spielen. Inzwischen hat sich die Verwendung von MUDs auf andere Arten von Spielen und auch auf eher gesellschaftliche Zwecke ausgeweitet. Die Objektorientierung der MOOs legt den Programmierschwerpunkt verstärkt auf die in den MOOs enthaltenen *Objekte*. Einige der bisher bedeutendsten Forschungsarbeiten über MUDs und MOOs wurden von Xerox Parc, der Universität Virginia und dem MIT Media Lab durchgeführt. Curtis Pavel hat bei Xerox Parc LambdaMOO geschaffen und über die sozialen Phänomene textbasierter virtueller Realitäten geschrieben [1992].

6 MediaMOO <http://asb.www.media.mit.edu/people/asb/MediaMOO> Verbindung mit MediaMOO von einem UNIX-Host aus: telnet <mediamoo.media.mit.edu 8888>

7 *Avatar III – the Crypt*: <http://www.avatar.co.uk/>

8 Ich habe Rose am 29. Mai 1997 interviewt. Im wirklichen Leben arbeitet sie im Büro einer Sozialversicherung.

9 Ein Beispiel für einen Verhaltenscode in einem Online-Spiel läßt sich unter der folgenden Adresse finden: <http://games.world.co.uk/code_of_ conduct.html>

10 Zu den Online-Seifenopern zählen:
The Spot: <http://www.thespot.com>;
Ferndale: <http://www.ferndale.com>;
Techno 3: <http://www.bluepearl.com/bluepearl>;
The East Village: <http://www.theeastvillage.co>

11 Die *Palace*-Homepage: <http://www.thePalace.com>

Daniel Dennett says: We are machines [including our minds]

Tom Sherman interviewed Daniel Dennett by e-mail for FleshFactor

TS: Historically, philosophers have spent a lot of their time explaining how humans are different than animals. For FleshFactor *we, like many others, are currently preoccupied with determining how we differ from machines. You yourself have stated that the brain is a kind of computer. Do you think it is a positive thing to have people think of themselves as [organic] machines?*

DD: I think we philosophers should help people get over their anxiety about being machines, since it is no longer possible to deny it, unless one chooses to be weirdly uninformed. Logically, there are two possibilities: diminish our sense of self-worth because we discover we are machines, or raise our appreciation of the power of machines because we discover we are machines. There is no good reason to slump into the first alternative, and many good reasons for adopting the second.

TS: A lot of contributions to FleshFactor *emphatically state the importance of remembering our species' [animal] relationship within the eco-system. Do you consider your writing on Darwin and natural selection supportive of this need for humans to once again feel they are part of nature?*

Daniel Dennett sagt: Wir sind Maschinen [auch unsere Gehirne]

Tom Sherman führte für FleshFactor ein E-mail-Interview mit Daniel Dennett

TS: Aus historischer Sicht haben die Philosophen einen Gutteil ihrer Zeit damit verbracht, den Unterschied zwischen Mensch und Tier zu begründen. Wie viele andere auch versuchen wir im Rahmen von FleshFactor *gerade festzustellen, inwieweit wir uns von Maschinen unterscheiden. Sie selbst haben erklärt, das Gehirn sei eine Art Computer. Finden Sie es erstrebenswert, daß Menschen sich selbst als [organische] Maschinen sehen?*

DD: Ich denke, unsere Aufgabe als Philosophen ist es, den Leuten über ihre Angst, Maschinen zu sein, hinwegzuhelfen. Diese Tatsache kann ohnehin nicht länger geleugnet werden – es sei denn, man flüchtet sich in komplette Uninformiertheit. Logisch gesehen, gibt es zwei Möglichkeiten: Wir können angesichts der Entdeckung, daß wir Maschinen sind, unser Selbstwertgefühl verlieren oder aber die Leistungsfähigkeit von Maschinen besser schätzen lernen. Es gibt keinen Grund, sich der ersten Alternative zu ergeben, aber viele gute Gründe, sich für die zweite zu entscheiden.

TS: Viele der Beiträge zu FleshFactor *betonen, wie wichtig es ist, die Verwandtschaft unserer Spezies [zu den Tieren] innerhalb des Ökosystems nicht aus den Augen zu verlieren. Glauben Sie, daß Ihre Schriften über Darwin und die natürliche Selektion diesem*

DD: Yes, I do. I realize that many self-appointed guardians of human culture are appalled at the prospect of granting that even human culture – art, ethics, religion, politics, science – is a product of nature, that the cathedral at Chartres is part of the extended human phenotype in exactly the same way a beaver dam is part of the extended phenotype of the beaver. But their hope of *protecting* culture from biology by denying its biological roots is myopic; it could only succeed if culture were some sort of miraculous gift from on high. Manna from heaven. Since that idea is simply preposterous, they should take a deep breath and try to notice a simple fact: art [and culture more generally] is not less wonderful for being a product of nature. Anybody who thinks that evolutionary processes could produce a nightingale but not an ode to a nightingale has an impoverished appreciation of just how wonderful a nightingale is.

TS: You are widely respected by scientists because you go the extra mile to know the science when you write about neuroscience, perceptual psychology or AI. In fact you have stated and largely realized your goal to be a collaborating researcher in these fields, a complementary intellectual force from your position as a contemporary philosopher. Since perception, consciousness and intelligence embody creativity as a kind of 'engine' of change and growth, I'm wondering where artists fit into your thinking on interdisciplinary research, in these fields or others?

DD: Philosophy's primary role, I think, is to open up our imaginations to new prospects, new possibilities. This places philosophy, at its best, about half way between art and science. Without the methods and aspirations of art, philosophy just trudges down well-worn paths, policing the grounds. Without the discipline of scientific inquiry, philosophy is too easy to be worth very much. The point is not just to think new thoughts – anybody who wants to can think new thoughts; the point is to think GOOD new thoughts. As a former [or sometime] sculptor, I have a great sympathy for, and appreciation of, artists – but I have a generally very low opinion of the rest of the art world, and in particular of the pretentious culture of the galleries, critics and collectors. I have a similar attitude towards contemporary *serious* [as op-

Bedürfnis der Menschen entgegenkommen, sich wieder als Teil der Natur zu fühlen?

DD: Ja, ich denke schon. Ich stelle fest, daß viele selbsternannte Wächter der menschlichen Kultur von Entsetzen gepackt werden, wenn sie eingestehen sollen, daß sogar die menschliche Kultur – Kunst, Ethik, Religion, Politik, Wissenschaft – ein Produkt der Natur ist. Daß die Kathedrale von Chartres genauso Teil des erweiterten Phänotyps des Menschen ist wie der Damm eines Bibers Teil des erweiterten Phänotyps des Bibers ist. Aber diese Hoffnung, die Kultur vor der Biologie *schützen* zu können, indem man ihre biologischen Wurzeln leugnet, ist kurzsichtig: Sie könnte sich nur erfüllen, wenn Kultur eine Art wunderbares Geschenk *von oben* wäre, himmlisches Manna. Da das einfach eine groteske Vorstellung ist, sollten diese Menschen einmal tief Luft holen und versuchen, eine simple Tatsache zur Kenntnis zu nehmen: Kunst [und Kultur im allgemeinen] ist nicht weniger wunderbar, nur weil sie ein Produkt der Natur ist. Jeder, der glaubt, Evolution könne zwar eine Nachtigall, nicht aber eine Ode an sie hervorbringen, kann das Wunderbare an einer Nachtigall einfach nicht richtig schätzen.

*TS: Sie genießen durchgehend Respekt unter Wissenschaftlern, weil Sie auch tatsächlich über das jeweilige Sachgebiet Bescheid wissen, wenn Sie über Neurowissenschaft, Wahrnehmungspsychologie oder Künstliche Intelligenz schreiben. In der Tat haben Sie Ihr erklärtes Ziel weitgehend erreicht, mitarbeitender Forscher auf all diesen Gebieten zu sein, eine komplementäre intellektuelle Kraft zu Ihrer Rolle als zeitgenössischer Philosoph. Da Wahrnehmung, Bewußtsein und Intelligenz die Kreativität als eine Art *Motor* für Wachstum und Veränderung brauchen, stellt sich die Frage, welchen Platz Sie den Künstlern in der interdisziplinären Forschung dieser oder anderer Gebiete zuweisen.*

DD: Meiner Meinung nach ist es die Hauptaufgabe der Philosophie, unserer Phantasie neue Aussichten, neue Möglichkeiten zu erschließen. Somit findet sich die Philosophie in ihrer besten Form ungefähr in der Mitte zwischen Kunst und Wissenschaft wieder. Ohne die Ziele und Methoden der Kunst würde die Philosophie ihre ausgetretenen Pfade nie verlassen, sondern nur ihre Position verteidigen. Ohne die Disziplin wissenschaftlicher Forschung bliebe der Philosophie zu wenig Substanz, um von großem Wert zu sein. Es geht nicht nur darum, neue Gedanken zu entwickeln – das kann jeder. Es kommt darauf an, gute neue Gedanken zu entwickeln. Als ehemaliger [oder zeitweiliger] Bildhauer habe ich großes Ver-

posed to popular] music. But these phenomena of high silliness are passing fancies, in my view, and real art will continue to be created, and continue to play its rich, illuminating, insight-provoking roles. We can see the role of art better, I think, if we look back on the art of Galileo's day, or Newton's day, or Darwin's day. The proposal, or hope, that art might play a bigger role today than it has done in the past is unrealistic and unnecessary.

*TS: It seems that your thoughts about the roles of philosophers and artists reveal a belief in a kind of natural selection of ideas or images or melodies; that creative variation or diversity is only one aspect of cultural evolution, but that audiences ultimately decide which ideas, images or melodies are good and worthy of significant replication and dissemination. Surely you must recognize the editorial influence that institutions have on an ecology of ideas, or the control museums or the music industry have on art and music? A good thought, image or song does not often replicate just because it is good. Spielberg's dinosaurs do not outdistance and crush an experimental filmmaker's personal cinema because they are better art. Don't you think it is dangerous to label serious art or music as *high silliness* or *passing fancies*? Isn't variation and diversity essential in a healthy cultural environment?*

DD: Variation and diversity are indeed crucial to a healthy cultural environment. The richer the meme pool, the better. But as a Darwinian I also expect that most artistic ideas, like most organisms, most lineages, will be extinguished after relatively brief trajectories, and that this is nothing to wring our hands about. That's the cost of innovation, and it would be myopic to urge equal support for all ideas. My point is not at all to dismiss serious art, but just to remove it from its presumptuous pedestal. I think that an excellent country & western song can be better art than a second-rate experimental opera – but that's just my personal contribution to cultural selective pressure. Others may counter it with their own, and we'll all be better off if we have a wide variety of different DEMANDING environments.

TS: Following the logic of your writing, it would seem that you would argue that artists are simply genetically hard-wired to be artists. Being a parent, you would have to acknowledge that all children begin their development as

ständnis und große Hochachtung für Künstler. Aber ich habe eine generell schlechte Meinung vom Rest der Kunstwelt und im besonderen von der anmaßenden Kultur der Galerien, Kritiker und Sammler. Eine ganz ähnliche Einstellung habe ich zu zeitgenössischer *ernster* [im Gegensatz zu populärer] Musik. Aber all diese Phänomene von hochtrabender Albernheit sind meiner Meinung nach nur vorübergehende Phantasmen. Wirkliche Kunst wird auch weiterhin geschaffen werden und wird auch weiterhin ihre umfangreiche, erhellende, erkenntnisfördernde Rolle spielen. Wir bekommen vermutlich eine klarere Vorstellung von der Rolle der Kunst, wenn wir einen Blick zurückwerfen auf die Kunst in den Tagen Galileis, Newtons oder Darwins. Der Vorschlag, oder auch die Hoffnung, Kunst möge heute eine größere Rolle spielen als in der Vergangenheit, ist unrealistisch und unangebracht.

*TS: Ihre Gedanken zur Rolle von Philosophen und Künstlern lassen den Glauben an eine Art natürlicher Selektion von Ideen, Bildern oder Melodien erkennen. Es scheint, daß kreative Variation und Diversität nur einen Aspekt der kulturellen Evolution darstellen, daß aber letztendlich das Publikum entscheidet, welche Ideen, Bilder oder Melodien gut und damit wert sind, in nennenswertem Ausmaß vervielfältigt und verbreitet zu werden. Sie können den Einfluß von Verlagen und ähnlichen Institutionen auf die Welt der Ideen, die Kontrolle der Museen und der Musikindustrie über Kunst und Musik doch nicht leugnen? Gute Gedanken, Bilder oder Lieder finden nur selten deswegen Verbreitung, weil sie gut sind. Spielbergs Dinosaurier sind den Filmen eines Experimentalfilmemachers nicht überlegen, weil sie höhere Kunst sind. Halten Sie es nicht für gefährlich, ernste Kunst und Musik als *hochtrabende Albernheit* oder *vorübergehende Phantasmen* zu bezeichnen? Stellen Variation und Diversität nicht die unabdingbaren Voraussetzungen für ein gesundes kulturelles Umfeld dar?*

DD: Variation und Diversität sind in der Tat von entscheidender Bedeutung für ein gesundes kulturelles Umfeld. Je reichhaltiger der Vorrat an Memen, desto besser. Aber als Darwinist gehe ich davon aus, daß der Großteil der künstlerischen Ideen – ebenso wie der Großteil der Organismen und Geschlechter – nach einem relativ kurzen Gastspiel von der Bildfläche verschwinden wird. Es gibt keinen Grund, das zu bedauern. Das ist der Preis der Innovation, es wäre kurzsichtig, alle Ideen im selben Ausmaß fördern zu wollen. Ich bin nicht im entferntesten für die Abschaffung ernster Kunst, ich bin nur der Meinung, wir sollten sie von ihrem anmaßenden Sockel stoßen.

almost infinitely creative individuals, but that for some reasons, exposure to the arts included, only a very small percentage of people manage to stay 'open' as creators. Do you think creativity is constructed genetically? [I am not referring to 'talent' here – the obvious manifestation of hand-eye, hand-ear, or full-body coordination, permitting one to exercise superior drawing, musical or physical skills.]

DD: I have no well-supported conviction about the relative contributions of genetic and environmental factors in *constructing* creativity. I would guess those factors can be extraordinarily varied. I suspect, however, that there are a few simple *tricks* that some people never learn, and that are well-nigh essential for creativity. Chief among them is a taste for making mistakes and then savoring them. People who hate to make mistakes are locking themselves in a closet. The trick is to learn to make mistakes in a fruitful way, so that you and others can gain from them, and so that the damage is minimized. Then making mistakes can be fun, both for you and the onlookers.

TS: There seems to have been a change in the size or scale of the individual person over the past two decades [certainly artists have experienced this...]. Our mediated self presence has expanded with personally, commonly accessible telecommunications technologies, to the point where the individual seems to have attained institutional or corporate influence, without institutional or corporate affiliation. Is this perceived expansion of the self largely illusionary and only temporary [is this just the result of leaving signs here and there in the media environment, or actually communicating frequently with strangers?] Or is the individual and his or her sense of self more or less permanently expanding?

DD: I suppose Alexander the Great and Louis XIV and a few other colossal figures had *selves* that reached as far as everyday human selves can reach today, but not at the speed, or with the efficiency that we all can today. In fact, this unprecedented enlargement of our powers has left us in serious moral confusion. As philosophers so often say, *ought* implies *can* – and a corollary of this is that when new powers become widely available [so that each of us CAN do things our grandfathers couldn't do], we have a harder time deciding what we OUGHT to do. Each one of us, today, CAN make a non-negli-

Ein ausgezeichneter Country&Western-Song ist unter Umständen höhere Kunst als eine zweitklassige Experimentaloper – aber das ist nur mein ganz persönlicher Beitrag zum kulturellen Selektionsdruck. Sollen andere dem ihren eigenen Beitrag entgegensetzen – schließlich sind wir alle mit einer großen Vielfalt an Anforderungen besser bedient.

*TS: Aus der Logik Ihrer Schriften folgt, daß Ihrer Meinung nach die Voraussetzungen dafür, Künstler zu sein, schlicht und einfach genetisch festgelegt sind. Als Vater müssen Sie zugeben, daß alle Kinder zu Beginn ihrer Entwicklung beinahe grenzenlos kreativ sind, daß es aber aus verschiedenen Gründen [wobei auch der Einfluß der Kunst eine Rolle spielt] nur ein geringer Prozentsatz schafft, schöpferisch offen zu bleiben. Glauben Sie, daß Kreativität genetisch vorgegeben ist? [Ich denke dabei nicht an *Talent* – an das sichtbare Ergebnis der Koordination von Hand/Auge, Hand/Ohr sowie des ganzen Körpers als Voraussetzung für überragende zeichnerische, musikalische und sonstige körperliche Fähigkeiten.]*

DD: Ich kann nicht mit einer fundierten Vorstellung davon aufwarten, welche Rolle genetische und umweltbedingte Faktoren bei der *Konstruktion* von Kreativität spielen. Ich vermute, daß es sich um außerordentlich vielfältige Faktoren handelt. Ich habe jedoch den Verdacht, daß es ein paar einfache *Tricks* gibt, die einige Menschen nie erlernen, die aber für Kreativität nahezu unerläßlich sind. Man muß an erster Stelle Gefallen daran finden, Fehler zu machen und sie auszukosten. Menschen mit einer Scheu vor Fehlern bremsen sich sozusagen selbst aus. Der Trick besteht also darin, die Fehler auf eine fruchtbringende Art und Weise zu machen, so daß man selbst und andere davon profitieren können und der Schaden auf ein Minimum reduziert wird. Dann können Fehler Spaß machen, einem selbst und auch den Zusehern.

TS: Die Größe, die Dimension des Individuums scheinen sich in den letzten zwei Jahrzehnten verändert zu haben [zweifellos haben auch Künstler Erfahrungen damit gemacht ...]. Die allgemein verfügbaren Kommunikationstechnologien haben unsere vermittelte Selbstpräsenz erweitert. Mittlerweile sind wir an dem Punkt angelangt, wo Individuen offenbar denselben Einfluß ausüben können wie Institutionen oder Firmen, ohne einer solchen Institution oder Firma anzugehören. Handelt es sich dabei großteils um eine nur temporäre und illusionäre Ausweitung des Selbst [wenn hier und da Zeichen in der Medienlandschaft hinterlassen werden bzw. tatsächlich häufig mit fremden Menschen kommu-

gible difference in, say, the well-being of people starving or enslaved or oppressed in the farthest corners of the earth. With a surfeit of choices, we are embarrassed to discover that our hands are NOT tied, there IS something we can do. What, though, will we choose to do? We can't do everything [and we just don't want to try]. That was not a problem very often faced by our ancestors, even the most virtuous of them. Philosophers have not prepared us well to deal with this problem.

TS: An important aspect of this expansion of choices and potential for acting in the world is an incredible increase in range. Individuals can manage to intervene on a global scale, and they can dramatically increase their volume of information exchange and even the number and nature of their relationships with other people. As the scale and range of personal endeavours increases there can be problems with overcommitment, not to mention psychological and physical exhaustion due to hyper-involvement. Some would say that those who survive this expansion of self have necessarily adapted to a more superficial life, a life lived on the surface. If emotional and intellectual depth is sacrificed for an expansion of range, won't the dilemmas be both about making choices and the degree of commitment to directions chosen?

DD: I think you are right. In fact, I raised just those concerns some years ago, in an essay in *DAEDALUS* entitled *Information, Technology, and the Virtues of Ignorance.* [1986] We have not yet learned how to live good lives in the age of Information, and we philosophers have been particularly backward in our recognition that *classical* perspectives on these problems show signs of obsolescence. Some people may find this shocking, but they would laugh at anybody who thought the art or science of grandfather's day, or Kant's day, or Aristotle's day, defined the field for all time. Why should philosophy – or ethics in particular – be the one area of human culture that cannot tolerate innovation?

TS: One of the main things we are trying to determine through FleshFactor is how much our selfunderstanding of humanness has changed over the past couple of decades, especially in this age of information technologies. The contributors to this net-symposium have been drafting and re-drafting their observations, issuing multiple drafts of a collective self-understanding of

niziert wird]? Oder handelt es sich dabei um eine permanente Ausweitung des Individuums und seines Selbstgefühls?

DD: Alexander der Große, Ludwig XIV. und einige andere bedeutende Persönlichkeiten verfügten vermutlich über ein *Selbst*, dessen Größe an die eines alltäglichen menschlichen Selbst von heute herankommt – nur ohne die heutige Effizienz und Geschwindigkeit. Tatsächlich hat diese noch nie dagewesene Ausweitung unserer Macht eine ernste moralische Konfusion ausgelöst. Wie die Philosophen so gerne sagen, impliziert das *Sollen* auch das *Können*. Daraus folgt, daß uns die Verfügbarkeit neuer Möglichkeiten [jeder von uns kann heute Dinge tun, die unsere Großväter nicht tun konnten] vor die schwierige Entscheidung stellt, was wir tun sollen. Das Verhalten jedes einzelnen kann heutzutage einen nicht unerheblichen Einfluß darauf ausüben, wie es z. B. hungernden, versklavten oder unterdrückten Menschen in den entferntesten Winkeln der Erde ergeht. Angesichts des Übermaßes an Wahlmöglichkeiten stellen wir peinlich berührt fest, daß unsere Hände nicht gebunden sind, daß es etwas gibt, das wir tun können. Wofür sollen wir uns aber entscheiden? Wir können nicht alles tun [und wir haben auch einfach keine Lust zum Ausprobieren]. Mit diesem Problem sahen sich auch die rechtschaffensten unserer Vorfahren nur selten konfrontiert. Die Philosophen haben uns auf den Umgang damit nur schlecht vorbereitet.

TS: Eine bedeutende Rolle bei der Vervielfältigung von Wahlmöglichkeiten und Handlungspotentialen spielt unser unglaublich vergrößerter Aktionsradius. Der einzelne kann auf globaler Ebene Einfluß nehmen, so wie er auch in der Lage ist, den Umfang des Informationsaustausches und sogar die Zahl seiner Beziehungen zu anderen Menschen zu erhöhen. Wenn Ausmaß und Bandbreite persönlicher Bemühungen zunehmen, kann das zum Problem des Überengagements führen – ganz zu schweigen von der psychischen und physischen Erschöpfung als Folge dieses übermäßigen Einsatzes. Man könnte sagen, daß ein Mensch, der diese Ausdehnung des Selbst überlebt, sich automatisch an ein flüchtigeres Leben [an ein Leben an der Oberfläche] anpaßt. Wenn emotionale und intellektuelle Tiefe einem vergrößerten Aktionsradius geopfert werden – besteht das Dilemma dann nicht darin, eine Wahl zu treffen und sich zu entscheiden, in welchem Ausmaß man sich für die einmal gewählte Richtung einsetzen sollte?

DD: Ich denke, Sie haben recht. Tatsächlich habe ich genau diese Bedenken vor einigen Jahren

their humanness. This has served to delineate a line in the sand between people and machines and of course we have found out that increasingly people and machines are on both sides of the line and that those we once thought were people are actually machines and perhaps someday vice versa. In closing, would you offer us what you think is the main way we have changed in our perception of ourselves as humans over the past couple of decades?

DD: In an age of prosthetic body parts and increasingly sophisticated *repairs* of bodily flaws ranging in scale from molecules to limbs, the idea that our bodies are machines has become prosaic, too obvious to warrant comment. The idea that our minds are also machines still encounters enormous resistance, since it seems to imply that we are not free, or responsible. I am optimistic, however, and expect to see this scary illusion evaporate. In twenty years it will not seem paradoxical to declare that we human beings are the only machines [so far] with free will. The major philosophical obstacles to appreciating this have already been cleared away; we just have to keep educating each other and avoiding the overstatements that set the pendulum swinging. In their anxiety, people try to protect what really matters to them by protecting a little too much – as if defending an extra *margin of safety* surrounding the actually defensible visions was the prudent course instead of a recipe for

geäußert, und zwar in einem Aufsatz mit dem Titel *Information, Technology, and the Virtues of Ignorance* in DAEDALUS [1986]. Wir haben noch nicht gelernt, uns im Informationszeitalter zurechtzufinden. Gerade wir Philosophen haben versäumt zu erkennen, daß die *klassischen* Sichtweisen dieses Problems in zunehmendem Maße obsolet werden. Manche finden das vielleicht schockierend, obwohl sie gleichzeitig jeden auslachen würden, der glaubt, daß Kunst und Wissenschaft in den Tagen unserer Großväter oder zu Kants oder Aristoteles' Zeiten ein für alle Mal definiert wurden. Warum sollte ausgerechnet die Philosophie – und speziell die Ethik – als einziger Bereich der menschlichen Kultur Innovationen nicht aufgeschlossen gegenüberstehen?

TS: Eines der Hauptziele von FleshFactor ist es, festzustellen, inwieweit sich das Selbstverständnis unseres Menschseins in den vergangenen Jahrzehnten, besonders im Zeitalter der Informationstechnologien, verändert hat. Die Teilnehmer an diesem Netz-Symposium haben ihre Beobachtungen auf verschiedenste Weise formuliert und so eine Vielzahl von Entwürfen zum kollektiven Selbstverständnis ihres Menschseins hervorgebracht. Damit konnte eine Grenze gezogen werden zwischen Menschen und Maschinen. Und natürlich haben wir feststellen müssen, daß in zunehmendem Maße Menschen und Maschinen auf beiden Seiten dieser Grenze anzutreffen sind, und daß die, die wir einst für Menschen hielten, eigentlich Maschinen sind; und wer weiß, eines Tages vielleicht sogar umgekehrt. Könnten Sie uns abschließend verraten, worin sich Ihrer Meinung nach unsere Selbstwahrnehmung als Menschen in den letzten Jahrzehnten im wesentlichen geändert hat?

DD: Im Zeitalter der künstlichen Körperteile und der zunehmend raffinierten *Reparaturen* von körperlichen Fehlern [von Molekülen bis zu Gliedmaßen], ist die Vorstellung, unsere Körper seien Maschinen, alltäglich geworden – zu prosaisch, um einen Kommentar hervorzurufen. Die Vorstellung, daß auch unsere Gehirne Maschinen sind, stößt hingegen noch auf enormen Widerstand. Denn das scheint doch zu bedeuten, daß wir weder frei noch für unsere Taten verantwortlich sind. Ich bin aber optimistisch und glaube, daß sich diese gruselige Illusion in Luft auflösen wird. In zwanzig Jahren wird es nicht mehr paradox klingen, daß wir Menschen [bis jetzt] die einzigen Maschinen mit freiem Willen sind. Die wichtigsten philosophischen Hindernisse, die dieser Einstellung entgegenstehen, wurden bereits aus dem Weg geräumt. Es genügt, wenn wir uns das einander immer wieder ins Bewußtsein

dogmatic disaster. I can think of no better project for philosophers than showing people – showing them, patiently and calmly – that they can afford to give a little ground and still hang on to everything that really matters.

TS: Thank you, Daniel Dennett.

rufen und alle Übertreibungen vermeiden, die das Pendel in die andere Richtung ausschlagen lassen könnten. In ihrer Angst versuchen die Menschen zu schützen, was ihnen wirklich wichtig ist. Dabei gehen sie ein bißchen zu weit – so als ob eine zusätzliche *Sicherheitszone* rund um die tatsächlich schützenswerten Visionen eine umsichtige Vorsichtsmaßnahme wäre – und nicht das Rezept für ein dogmatisches Desaster. Ich kann mir als Philosoph keine bessere Aufgabe vorstellen, als den Menschen klarzumachen – ihnen ruhig und geduldig klarzumachen –, daß sie sich ruhig ein Stück weit auf die Sache einlassen können, ohne etwas von dem aufgeben zu müssen, was ihnen wichtig ist.

TS: Danke, Daniel Dennett.

MACHINES Я US

Tom Sherman

1 MACHINES Я US ... in machines we trust. We love our machines. They are our friends. We find they are more trustworthy than people. But as we connect our machines with other machines, we find we are connected with people we don't know. We find we are being watched, listened to, observed, monitored by strangers through our machines. We don't like to be observed unless we call the shots. We want to direct every scene we appear in. We want there to be a clear distinction between when we are on the set and when we are off limits. When we are off limits, we are in our zone of privacy. We have a problem. We know that when we use our machines, when our machines are connected to other people's machines, we are vulnerable to unwanted, intrusive observation. We see this as a real, bad problem. We fear the invasion of our privacy. Strangers or even people we know may invade our inner zone. That personal, private zone only we can know. It doesn't really matter whether we know our visitors, or like them, or fear them, or love them – when they are unwelcome, they are intruders. We know these intruders can get to us through our machines. The strange thing is we have become

MACHINES Я US

Tom Sherman

1 MACHINES Я US ... wir vertrauen auf Maschinen. Wir lieben unsere Maschinen. Sie sind unsere Freunde. Wir halten sie für vertrauenswürdiger als Menschen. Aber wenn wir unsere Maschinen an andere Maschinen anschließen, stehen wir plötzlich vor der Tatsache, daß wir mit Menschen verbunden sind, die wir nicht kennen. Wir müssen feststellen, daß wir über unsere Maschinen von Fremden beobachtet, belauscht, überwacht werden. Wir mögen es nicht, beobachtet zu werden, wenn nicht wir selbst den Ton angeben. Wir wollen bei jedem unserer Auftritte Regie führen. Wir wollen einen klaren Unterschied zwischen wann wir im Rampenlicht stehen und wann hinter den Kulissen. Hinter den Kulissen befinden wir uns in unserer privaten Zone. Es gibt da ein Problem. Wir wissen, daß wir uns unerwünschter, lästiger Beobachtung ausliefern, wenn wir unsere Maschinen verwenden, wenn unsere Maschinen an die anderer Menschen angeschlossen werden. Wir empfinden das als echtes Problem. Wir haben Angst vor Eingriffen in unsere Privatsphäre. Fremde, aber auch Bekannte, können in unseren inneren Bereich eindringen – diesen privaten, persönlichen Bereich, der uns allein vorbehalten ist. Dabei macht es keinen wirklichen Unterschied, ob wir unsere Besucher kennen, ob wir sie mögen oder fürchten oder lieben – wenn sie nicht willkommen sind, empfinden wir sie als Eindringlinge. Wir wissen, daß diese Eindringlinge über unsere Maschinen an uns herankommen können. Das Sonderbare daran ist, daß wir beim Wahrnehmen und Verstehen der Welt so von unseren Maschinen abhängig geworden sind, daß wir sie auch brauchen, um uns selbst sehen zu können. Wir brauchen Maschinen, um nach draußen zu sehen, und wir brauchen sie, um nach innen zu sehen. Passen wir also sicherheitshalber darauf auf, daß unsere Maschinen nur mit uns verbunden sind. Stellen wir sicher, daß wir offline sind, wenn wir nach innen schauen, und online nur, wenn wir nach draußen blicken. Versuchen wir sicherzustellen, daß niemand hereinschauen kann, wenn wir gerade einen Blick nach draußen werfen.

so dependent on our machines to help us see and understand the world, that we depend on our machines to help us see ourselves. We depend on machines to look outside and we depend on machines to look inside. So to be on the safe side, let's begin by making sure our machines are linked only with us. Let's make sure we are off-line when we are looking in, on-line only when we are looking out. Let's try to make sure no one can look in when we are looking out.

2 THE MAN WORE DARK GLASSES, chewing gum but saying nothing. Wearing headphones with his music. Just watching. Not interacting, overtly. Hands in his pockets he scans the room. He plays the games at home, where nobody knows the score. He plays with his machines. He never dials out. His machines stand alone. They act like him. They don't have a choice. They are under his control. Machines are great that way. They don't want to make choices. Freedom is just another word for out of control. The nice thing about being alone with a machine is that sense of consistency. When you are looking at yourself through a machine, you're pretty sure you're going to get the same picture, night after night. When you are home alone, inside yourself, consistency is very important. Mental routines are cast in precision steel. Tight circles. Mirror upon mirror. Oh, the range of experience in my apartment. I'm completely free to be who I am. I'll never let you in. My machines are all the company I need. I can relate to them in confidence. They are reliable. No surprises. No intrusions. No others. No regrets.

3 JUST BECAUSE THE THINGS INSIDE CAN'T BE MEASURED, it doesn't mean they're not real. I was asked the other day to tell someone new who I was. I did. It was a primitive description. I remember thinking while I was speaking that I was selling myself short. I know I know myself better than anyone else, but I carry so little of what I know to the surface – to the place where the words are. My self-consciousness. Most of what I'm aware of comes my way when I interact with my machines. Interact isn't exactly the word. I use my machines to find out about myself. Some people like the solitude of Nature – they like to sit on a rock in the middle of nowhere, where it's quiet and still and they can become one with a lake or a sky. You know

2 DER MANN TRUG DUNKLE GLÄSER, kaute Kaugummi, ohne etwas zu sagen. Kopfhörer mit seiner Musik. Schaute bloß zu. Ohne sichtlich zu interagieren. Die Hände in den Hosentaschen, läßt er seinen Blick im Zimmer herumwandern. Er spielt das Spiel zu Hause, wo niemand weiß, wie es steht. Er spielt mit seinen Maschinen. Er nimmt niemals Kontakt mit draußen auf. Seine Maschinen sind für sich allein. Sie verhalten sich wie er. Sie haben keine Wahl. Er hat sie unter Kontrolle. Maschinen sind in dieser Hinsicht großartig. Sie wollen keine Wahl treffen. Freiheit ist nur ein anderes Wort für *außer Kontrolle*. Das Angenehme am Alleinsein mit einer Maschine, ist dieses Gefühl der Beständigkeit. Wenn du dich selbst durch eine Maschine ansiehst, kannst du ziemlich sicher sein, immer dasselbe Bild vorzufinden, Nacht für Nacht. Wenn du allein zu Hause bist, in deinem Inneren, ist Beständigkeit sehr wichtig. Geistige Routinevorgänge, ausgeführt in Edelstahl. Enge Kreise. Spiegel über Spiegel. Ach, die Bandbreite der Erfahrungen in meiner Wohnung. Ich kann ganz der sein, der ich bin. Ich werde dich nie hereinlassen. Meine Maschinen genügen mir als Gesellschaft. Ich kann voll Vertrauen eine Beziehung zu ihnen aufbauen. Sie sind verläßlich. Keine Überraschungen. Keine Störungen. Keine anderen. Keine Reue.

3 DASS DIE DINGE IN UNSEREM INNEREN NICHT GEMESSEN WERDEN KÖNNEN, bedeutet nicht, daß sie nicht wirklich sind. Vor kurzem bat mich ein neuer Bekannter, ihm zu erklären, wer ich sei. Ich kam seinem Wunsch nach. Es war eine primitive Beschreibung. Ich erinnere mich, daß mir während des Sprechens der Gedanke kam, ich betrüge mich selbst. Ich weiß, daß ich mich selbst besser kenne, als irgendjemand sonst, aber ich bringe so wenig von dem, was ich weiß, nach draußen – dorthin, wo die Worte sind. Meine Gehemmtheit. Das meiste, dessen ich mir bewußt bin, wird mir klar, indem ich mit meinen Maschinen interagiere. Interagieren ist nicht ganz das richtige Wort. Ich verwende meine Maschinen, um mehr über mich herauszufinden. Manche Menschen lieben die Einsamkeit der Natur – sie lieben es, auf einem Felsen irgendwo in der Einöde zu sitzen, wo es ruhig und still ist und wo sie eins werden können mit einem See oder mit dem Himmel. Man weiß, in Gedanken sprechen sie mit den Bäumen und den Wolken und irgendwelchen Vögelchen. Ich spreche in meinen Gedanken, mit meiner Stimme, meinen Händen und meinen Fingern zu meinen Maschinen. Ich verwende meine Maschinen gern als Erinnerungshilfe. Ich mag es, Erinnerungen nochmals abzuspielen. Ich mag es, mich an Erinnerungen zu erinnern.

they talk with their minds to trees and clouds and little brown birds. I talk to my machines with my mind, my voice, my hands, my fingers. I like to use my machines to help me remember things. And then I like to play back things I remember. I like to re-remember.

Sometimes my machines capture things I didn't even notice. I forget the details. But my machines help me collect and assemble details and images and music and things that are really important to me. Sometimes I don't know why I collect certain things. I just work with my machines and there's a moment every once in a while... A moment when a machine tells me something about myself. Something I wouldn't want to share right away with someone else.

4 WHEN I GO OUTSIDE I NEVER TRAVEL ALONE. I move with one of my machines and I reach as far and as fast as it will take me. We're tight and we walk in step. When people encounter me, they see us. They get the package. We're inseparable. If they try to pry us apart, we've learned to hold on real tight. Before it gets to the point where my image starts to break up, we'll send out a few adjustments. This is the way I really talk. This is the way I really stalk. I only come out for a fix. I come out to feed. My machines help me find nourishment. We feed together like little brown birds. Foraging in malls. The people without machines are out back, dumpster-diving. We are much more sophisticated. We order frozen meat with remote controls. We watch the meat channel and push the button when we want to make a kill. But that's just my self-image projected into the chill of a freezer compartment. Look out, I'm on a mission to find something to feed on. I've got to find a free port. I've got to dock. I've got to make decisions. I've got to fill the available memory. I've got to release before I'm recognized. And I've got to cover my trail with the moans and groans of machine love, machine hate, machine fear, machine void. Machine love, machine hate, machine fear, machine void. Before you can say interactive carnivore, we're back in the protective shelter of our home.

5 I'M A PERSONAL HUMAN. In this world of machines, where people are one with systems and world-wide-webs and instinctive behavior is valued because it's natural, I'm a personal human. I'm special. Not too unique but

Manchmal fangen meine Maschinen Dinge auf, die ich nicht einmal bemerkt habe. Ich vergesse die Details. Aber meine Maschinen helfen mir dabei, Details und Bilder und Musik und Dinge, die wirklich wichtig für mich sind, zusammenzutragen und zu sammeln. Manchmal weiß ich nicht, wieso ich bestimmte Dinge sammle. Ich arbeite einfach mit meinen Maschinen, und von Zeit zu Zeit gibt es einen Augenblick ... einen Augenblick, in dem mir eine Maschine etwas über mich erzählt. Etwas, das ich nicht an Ort und Stelle mit anderen Menschen teilen möchte.

4 WENN ICH NACH DRAUSSEN GEHE, TUE ICH DAS NIE ALLEIN. Ich bewege mich mit einer meiner Maschinen fort, und sie bestimmt die Geschwindigkeit und die Länge meiner Reise. Wir gehen Hand in Hand im Gleichschritt. Wenn ich auf Menschen stoße, sehen sie uns. Sie bekommen uns im Doppelpack. Wir sind unzertrennlich. Wir haben gelernt, uns fest aneinanderzuklammern, damit uns niemand auseinanderbringen kann. Bevor der Punkt erreicht ist, an dem mein Bild auseinanderzubrechen droht, senden wir ein paar Berichtigungen nach draußen. Das ist meine Art zu sprechen. Das ist meine Art zu gehen. Ich begebe mich nur für Besorgungen nach draußen. Ich begebe mich nur zum Essen nach draußen. Meine Maschinen helfen mir bei der Nahrungssuche. Wir essen gemeinsam wie Spatzen. Futtersuche in Einkaufszentren. Menschen ohne Maschinen stehen vor der Tür, wühlen im Abfall. Wir sind viel raffinierter. Wir bestellen Tiefkühlkost per Fernbedienung. Wir sehen uns den Fleischkanal an und drücken auf den Knopf, wenn wir einen Abschuß machen wollen. Aber das ist nur mein Selbstbild, in die Kälte eines Gefrierfachs projiziert. Aufgepaßt, ich bin auf der Suche nach etwas Eßbarem. Ich muß einen freien Hafen finden. Ich muß irgendwo anlegen. Ich muß Entscheidungen treffen. Ich muß den verfügbaren Speicher füllen. Ich muß aussteigen, ehe ich erkannt werde. Und ich muß meine Spuren mit den Seufzern und dem Stöhnen der Maschinenliebe, des Maschinenhasses, der Maschinenangst, der Maschinenleere verwischen. Maschinenliebe, Maschinenhaß, Maschinenangst, Maschinenleere. Ehe du *interaktiver Fleischfresser* sagen kannst, sind wir wieder in unserem schützenden Zuhause.

5 ICH BIN EIN PERSÖNLICHER MENSCH. In dieser Welt der Maschinen, wo Menschen eins sind mit Systemen und World-Wide-Webs, wird instinktives Verhalten geschätzt, weil es natürlich ist. Ich bin ein persönlicher Mensch. Ich bin etwas Besonderes. Nicht zu einzigartig, aber relativ aufsässig, was die Uhrzeit und vorgegebene Rahmenbedingungen betrifft. Aber dann passe ich auch wieder ins Schema. Ich bin ein

relatively insubordinate when it comes to clock time and anticipatory sets. But then again, I fit the mold. I'm a personal human who stays well within the limits of the systems I play. I act instinctively because logic and reason are best left to the machines – just like I don't try to remember details any longer than I have to. I re-remember a story about spiders weaving their webs in outer space. When they first started doing experiments aboard the Shuttle, scientists sent a couple of Orb Weaver Spiders out into orbit. They wanted to see if these spiders could weave their elaborate webs in zero gravity. The astronauts set up a movie camera to document the spiders weaving their webs. Due to their very busy schedule the astronauts couldn't wait until the spiders started weaving to start filming. They left the camera running for a couple of hours and hoped for the best. When the camera had spent its film, they checked the spiders' compartment, but there were no webs to be found. A few days later, when the Shuttle was back on earth and unloaded, scientists found two finished webs which had apparently been constructed in zero gravity.

They were distorted, but true to their elaborate form. Instinct had prevailed in a strange and hostile environment. The Orb Weavers had managed to act naturally in the most unnatural circumstances. When we forget what it's like to act naturally, it's hard to know when to start the camera rolling.

6 MEMORY HAS REPLACED LOGIC IN TODAY'S WORLD. No one can carry an argument beyond their own position of self-interest. We believe only what we remember to be true. We remember very little on our own. We rely on our machines to substantiate the past. Machines have a facility for memory which is precise and extensive. Machines free us from the responsibility of storing and organizing memories. When we forget – and we forget – we simply have to search our machine memories to re-establish what happened.

With the aid of our machines, we don't just remember, we re-remember. And in partnership with our machines we establish the truth by comparing records, the documentary evidence of the past. We establish our personal perspective by re-remembering. By re-re-remembering... By re-re-re-re-re-re-re-re-

persönlicher Mensch, der innerhalb der Grenzen der Systeme bleibt, die ich spiele. Ich handle instinktiv, weil Logik und Vernunft am besten den Maschinen überlassen werden – so wie ich nicht versuche, mich länger als unbedingt notwendig an Einzelheiten zu erinnern. Ich erinnere mich an eine Geschichte über Spinnen, die ihre Netze im Weltraum spannen. Als mit den Experimenten an Bord des Shuttles begonnen wurde, schickten die Wissenschafter ein paar Orb-Weaver-Spinnen hinaus in die Umlaufbahn. Sie wollten sehen, ob diese Spinnen ihre kunstvollen Netze auch in der Schwerelosigkeit spinnen können. Die Astronauten installierten eine Filmkamera, um die Spinnen beim Netzspinnen aufzunehmen. Aufgrund ihres dichten Programms konnten sie mit dem Filmen nicht warten, bis die Spinnen zu spinnen begannen. Sie ließen die Kamera einige Stunden lang laufen und hofften das Beste. Als der Film voll war, prüften sie den Spinnencontainer, konnten aber keine Netze finden. Einige Tage später, als das Shuttle auf der Erde zurück war und entladen wurde, fanden die Wissenschafter zwei fertige Netze, die offenbar in der Schwerelosigkeit entstanden waren.

Sie waren deformiert, entsprachen aber der üblichen kunstvollen Form. Der Instinkt hatte auch in einer fremden und feindlichen Umgebung gesiegt. Die Orb-Weaver-Spinnen hatten es geschafft, sich unter höchst unnatürlichen Bedingungen natürlich zu verhalten. Wenn wir vergessen, was es heißt, sich natürlich zu verhalten, fällt es uns schwer, die Kamera im rechten Moment einzuschalten.

6 DAS GEDÄCHTNIS HAT IN UNSERER HEUTIGEN WELT DIE LOGIK ERSETZT. Niemand ist in der Lage, ohne Rücksicht auf das eigene Interesse zu argumentieren. Wir glauben nur, was wir als wahr in Erinnerung haben. Wir erinnern uns nur an weniges selbst. Wir vertrauen auf unsere Maschinen, um der Vergangenheit Gestalt zu verleihen. Das Erinnerungsvermögen von Maschinen ist präzis und umfassend. Maschinen befreien uns von der Verantwortung, Erinnerungen zu speichern und zu organisieren. Wenn wir vergessen – und das tun wir – brauchen wir nur den Speicher unserer Maschinen zu durchsuchen, um das Geschehene wiederherzustellen.

Mit Hilfe unserer Maschinen erinnern wir uns nicht bloß, wir erinnern uns an Erinnerungen. Und mit unseren Maschinen als Partner finden wir die Wahrheit, indem wir Aufzeichnungen, das schriftliche Beweismaterial der Vergangenheit, vergleichen. Wir gründen unsere persönliche Perspektive auf Erinnerungen an Erinnerungen. Indem wir uns an Erinnerungen von Erinnerungen erinnern. Indem wir uns

remembering. We stack up the records, the weight of documentary evidence, against the present and we get a sense of our personal perspective. We enjoy the consistency of our perspective. We are anchored by our memory, our machine memory. We depend on our machine memory. We are lost without our machine memory. When our systems crash, destroying all or part of our recorded memories, we have to decide to rebuild or to pull the plug.

7 INTERACTIVITY AND IDENTITY ARE AN INTERESTING COUPLE. After all, everything I'm saying is hinged on relationships, the existence of relationships. Everyone wants to interact, to be a player, to be a player in a game that suits them. When one finds oneself in a relationship with a machine, a machine that he or she controls, interactivity is a given.

Machines that remember well must be driven. They have to be turned on and turned off. They have to be looked at and listened to, touched and spoken to. They have to be fed. They have to be controlled. If they are to be part and parcel of our inner self, they must be secured. We must be able to expand our internal domain without the possibility of a leak. Secrets are hard to keep these days. Information is flying around at light speed. The world outside ourselves is loud with a dense, opaque fog of messages.

Other people's messages. Other people's secrets, amplified and petrified and compressed and homogenized. Other people's secrets become my secrets.

It's hard to recognize my own secrets sometimes. I use my machines to focus my attention. I use my machines to lower the volume, to turn down the intensity, to identify a field of secrets that are mine – or at least I think they're mine – I identify a field of secrets so I can relate, manipulate and operate ... effectively.

8 MY MACHINES ARE PATIENT WITH ME WHEN I'M HAVING TROUBLE FINDING MYSELF. Inhumanly patient. I can take my own sweet time determining who I am. I can build a model of my inner self. I can interact with this model, have a dialogue with my twin, feel progressive as I come into focus. I can feel like I am somebody. I can feel strong enough to go outside. Not as a bundle of everyone else's secrets, but as creature with internal integrity. Once the model self is constructed to a point of satisfac-

an Erinnerungen von Erinnerungen von Erinnerungen erinnern. Wir verschanzen uns vor der Gegenwart hinter den Aufzeichnungen, hinter dem Gewicht des schriftlichen Beweismaterials, und bekommen ein Gefühl der persönlichen Perspektive. Wir genießen die Beständigkeit unserer Perspektive. Die Erinnerungen unserer Maschinen geben uns Halt. Wir sind abhängig von den Erinnerungen unserer Maschinen. Ohne das Gedächtnis unserer Maschinen sind wir verloren. Wenn unsere Systeme zusammenbrechen und dabei die aufgezeichneten Erinnerungen teilweise oder zur Gänze verloren gehen, müssen wir entscheiden, ob wir sie neu errichten wollen oder lieber den Stecken ziehen.

7 INTERAKTIVTÄT UND IDENTITÄT SIND EIN INTERESSANTES PAAR. Letztendlich hat alles, was ich sage, mit Beziehungen zu tun, mit der Existenz von Beziehungen. Jeder Mensch hat den Wunsch zu interagieren, Spieler in einem Spiel zu sein, das ihm entspricht. In Beziehung zu einer Maschine zu stehen, einer Maschine, die er oder sie kontrolliert, hat man zwangsläufig mit Interaktivität zu tun.

Maschinen mit gutem Erinnerungsvermögen müssen bedient werden. Sie müssen ein- und ausgeschaltet werden. Sie müssen angesehen, angehört und berührt werden, du mußt mit ihnen sprechen. Sie müssen gefüttert werden. Sie müssen kontrolliert werden. Wenn sie fester Bestandteil unseres Inneren sein sollen, müssen sie sicher sein. Wir müssen unseren inneren Bereich ausdehnen können ohne das Risiko einer undichten Stelle. Heutzutage ist es schwer, Geheimnisse zu wahren. Informationen fliegen mit Lichtgeschwindigkeit herum. Die Welt außerhalb von uns selbst ist prall gefüllt mit einem dichten, undurchsichtigen Nebel aus Botschaften.

Botschaften anderer Menschen. Geheimnisse anderer Menschen, ausgeschmückt und erstarrt, komprimiert und homogenisiert. Die Geheimnisse anderer Menschen werden zu meinen Geheimnissen.

Manchmal ist es schwierig, meine eigenen Geheimnisse zu erkennen. Ich verwende meine Maschinen, um meine Aufmerksamkeit zu steuern. Ich verwende meine Maschinen, um die Lautstärke leiser zu stellen, um die Intensität zu verringern, um eine Reihe von Geheimnissen zu identifizieren, die meine sind – oder die ich zumindest dafür halte. Ich identifiziere eine Reihe von Geheimnissen, damit ich Beziehungen effizient herstellen, Einfluß nehmen und Dinge ausführen kann.

8 MEINE MASCHINEN HABEN GEDULD MIT MIR, WENN ICH SCHWIERIGKEITEN HABE, MICH SELBST ZU FINDEN. Unmenschliche Geduld. Ich kann

tion, both in complexity and relative clarity, it is time to enjoy my own company. Until I get bored. First there is joy and then there is disappointment. Early recognition and appreciation gives way to predictability and numbing redundancy. Arousal diminishes. Even when the loose ends begin to unravel, there's not enough change to generate surprises. At this point a self-destructive act is prescribed by experience. Erasing memory is one option. Full disclosure is more extreme. The modelled self demands to be jettisoned. Permission is given. You instruct your machine to open its channels to the world outside. You transmit and you submit to intrusion. At the instant of full disclosure there is total silence. Empty wonder. Is anybody out there?

9 WHY DO I CALL MY PERSONAL TECHNOLOGICAL DEVICES, MACHINES? I am interested in the way we create personal identity through the use of objects. When you look around someone's living space and imagine who they are, whether they are neat or messy, nostalgic or romantic, creepy, austere, trendy or basically unconscious, it is easy enough to imagine what goes on inside that particular someone's mind. When someone invites us into their home we learn a lot about them by simply experiencing the ambience of their living space. Domestic architecture is like a machine for reinforcing and transmitting a deeper, hidden interior space. The inside of a home is constructed to permit its owner to feel comfortable and natural and to transmit these feelings to others – one's family, friends and acquaintances. Personal technological devices flesh out one's inner space, whether it's a microwave, a vibrating, reclining chair, a home video theater, a police-band scanner or a personal computer complete with a multilingual voice recognition package. The task of this machine called home is to permit one to be oneself and to reveal what this is to others.

Most interior spaces are neutralized by self-consciousness and strategic efforts at impression management. Superficial as most interiors are, the personal technological devices are the most revealing objects in anyone's home – these machines are loaded with personal information. If we can find out what is in the oven, or what channel the TV is set to, when, or what the computer is used for, we can enter our

mir beliebig Zeit nehmen, um festzustellen, wer ich bin. Ich kann ein Modell meines inneres Selbst herstellen. Ich kann mit diesem Modell interagieren, in einen Dialog treten mit meinem Zwilling, mich fortschrittlich fühlen, wenn ich ins Blickfeld rücke. Ich kann das Gefühl haben, jemand zu sein. Ich kann mich stark genug fühlen, um nach draußen zu gehen. Nicht als ein Bündel von jedermanns Geheimnissen, sondern als ein Wesen mit innerer Integrität. Wenn das Modell selbst erst einmal zufriedenstellend konstruiert wurde, sowohl hinsichtlich Komplexität als auch Klarheit, ist es an der Zeit, meine eigene Gesellschaft zu genießen. Bis mir langweilig wird. Zuerst empfinde ich Freude, dann Enttäuschung. Anfängliche Anerkennung und Wertschätzung machen Vorhersehbarkeit und betäubender Überflüssigkeit Platz. Die Erregung nimmt ab. Auch wenn die losen Enden sich zu entwirren beginnen, entsteht nicht genügend Abwechslung. An diesem Punkt verlangt die Erfahrung eine selbstzerstörerische Handlung. Das Ausradieren der Erinnerung ist eine Möglichkeit. Hundertprozentige Offenbarung eine extremere. Das modellierte Selbst verlangt über Bord geworfen zu werden. Die Erlaubnis wird erteilt. Du weist deine Maschine an, die Kanäle zur Außenwelt zu öffnen. Du sendest und öffnest dich Eindringlingen. Im Augenblick der vollständigen Offenbarung herrscht völlige Stille. Leeres Wunder. Ist irgend jemand da draußen?

9 WARUM NENNE ICH MEINE PERSÖNLICHEN TECHNISCHEN BEHELFE MASCHINEN? Es interessiert mich, wie wir uns durch den Gebrauch von Objekten eine persönliche Identität schaffen. Wenn du dich in der Wohnung eines Menschen umsiehst und dir vorstellst, mit wem du es zu tun hast, ob es ein ordentlicher oder chaotischer, ein nostalgischer oder romantischer, unheimlicher, einfacher, modischer oder ein durch und durch unwissender Mensch ist, fällt es dir nicht schwer, dir vorzustellen, was im Kopf dieses speziellen jemand vor sich geht. Wenn uns jemand zu sich nach Hause einlädt, können wir eine Menge über ihn erfahren, indem wir einfach die Atmosphäre seines Wohnraums erleben. Innenarchitektur ist wie eine Maschine, die die Atmosphäre eines tieferen, versteckten, inneren Raums verstärkt und mitteilt. Das Innere eines Zuhauses wird so gestaltet, daß sich sein Besitzer behaglich und natürlich fühlt und sich diese Gefühle auch auf andere übertragen – auf Familie, Freunde und Bekannte. Persönliche technische Geräte sind das fleischgewordene Abbild dieses Inneren, ob es sich nun um einen Mikrowellenherd, einen Massagestuhl, eine Heimvideoanlage, einen Polizeifunkscanner oder einen PC mit

host's inner sanctum. Getting into the voice diary of someone else's personal computer rivals even the most complete investigation of a stranger's medicine cabinet.

10 WE ARE WHAT WE SEE WHEN WE SEE IT, whenever. A number of people are telling me that perception is everything. Most of them mean they are very concerned with how they are being perceived. A far smaller number are interested in how they perceive others and the world we live in. Machines can play a very important role when it comes to shaping and refining perception. Perception is commonly a half-conscious thing, where you find you are not really paying strict attention and then all of a sudden you find your mind is saturated with your immediate environment. Microseconds later you become aware of your complete immersion. This awareness is what we call experience. As we become conscious of our experience we find the need to describe what we sense. Our machines are very good at description. As we successfully automate the act of description we increase our capacity and thirst for perception. We create an engine for generating experience and storing it and exchanging it and distributing it. We distribute perception and experience through machine-assisted description: You are what you see when you see it, whenever. Again and again and again.

11 I'VE DONE A LOT OF FLYING IN MY LIFETIME. After a relatively slow start, I've spent a ton of time in the air, commuting mostly on domestic flights, choosing between peanuts and cookies, or steak, fish or chicken and trying to cope with the effects of pressurized cabins on my inner ear. I have absolutely no fear of flying. I prefer to sit over the wing in an aisle seat. I disappear into a book or a magazine or a newspaper and I pretend the plane never leaves the ground. I ignore the safety demonstrations. I never use the toilet. I never talk with my fellow-passengers. This morning I had a very strange thing happen. I put my coat and briefcase in the overhead storage compartment and sat down and buckled my seatbelt and put on my stereo headphones and looked around. I knew every single person on the plane. I had met everyone on board at some point or another over the years. Without making eye contact I identified every boarding passenger and then I stood up and fiddled with my briefcase in the overhead

mehrsprachigem Spracherkennungssystem handelt. Diese Maschine, die wir Zuhause nennen, soll uns die Möglichkeit geben, wir selbst zu sein, und gleichzeitig enthüllen, wie dies für andere ist.

Die meisten inneren Räume werden durch Hemmungen und strategische Anstrengungen in Sachen Image-Management unkenntlich gemacht. Oberflächlich, wie Innenräume zumeist sind, stellen technische Behelfe die aufschlußreichsten Gegenstände eines Zuhauses dar – diese Maschinen sind voll mit persönlichen Informationen. Wenn es uns gelingt herauszufinden, was im Ofen ist oder welcher Fernsehkanal eingestellt ist oder wann und wofür der Computer verwendet wird, betreten wir das Allerheiligste unseres Gastgebers. Das Eindringen in die Audionotizen eines fremden Computers kommt einer Durchsuchung der Hausapotheke eines Fremden gleich.

10 WIR SIND, WAS WIR SEHEN, WENN WIR ES SEHEN, jedesmal. Eine Reihe von Leuten sagt mir, Wahrnehmung gehe über alles. Die meisten von ihnen meinen damit, daß sie sich viele Gedanken darüber machen, wie sie von anderen wahrgenommen werden. Eine weitaus kleinere Zahl interessiert sich dafür, wie sie andere und die Welt, in der wir leben, wahrnehmen. Maschinen können beim Gestalten und Verfeinern der Wahrnehmung eine wichtige Rolle spielen. Wahrnehmung ist gemeinhin ein halbbewußter Vorgang. Du bist nicht wirklich aufmerksam, und dann stellst du plötzlich fest, daß du von deiner unmittelbaren Umgebung durchdrungen bist. Mikrosekunden später wirst du deiner vollständigen Immersion gewahr. Dieses Gewahrsein ist es, was wir Erfahrung nennen. Wenn wir uns unserer Erfahrung bewußt werden, empfinden wir das Bedürfnis, das, was wir fühlen, zu beschreiben. Unsere Maschinen sind sehr gut im Beschreiben. Wenn wir den Akt des Beschreibens erfolgreich automatisieren, erhöhen wir unser Wahrnehmungsvermögen und unseren Wahrnehmungshunger. Wir schaffen einen Motor, der Erfahrung generiert, der sie speichert und austauscht und verbreitet. Wir verbreiten Wahrnehmung und Erfahrung mit Hilfe maschinenunterstützter Beschreibungen: Du bist, was du siehst, wenn du es siehst, jedesmal. Wieder und wieder und wieder.

11 ICH BIN IN MEINEM LEBEN SEHR VIEL GEFLOGEN. Nach einem relativ langsamen Start habe ich jede Menge Zeit in der Luft verbracht, meist auf Inlandsflügen, zwischen Erdnüssen und Keksen bzw. Steak, Fisch und Hühnchen wählend, und immer bedacht, Kabinendruck und Innenohr aneinander anzupassen. Ich habe absolut keine Angst vor dem Fliegen. Ich sitze am liebsten im Mittelgang über dem

compartment so I could double check everyone seated behind me.

I knew every single fucking person on the plane, not by name – but I remembered things about all of them. I was afraid I'd be recognized so I hid in my newspaper and thought about how strange it was that I knew everyone on this flight. That's what happens when you fly around a lot, for a number of years. You find you know everyone just a little bit – and in most cases a little bit is more than enough.

12 I USED TO KNOW THIS MAN, he was my friend. I used to love to talk with him. We'd never get tired of talking and laughing. We'd drink and smoke and talk about everything and everyone. We were kind of wild. We'd do stupid things. But time has passed and we've changed and now we act differently when we get together. I guess we've both changed, but I feel like I still want to talk and laugh and be crazy, but there's no room. I feel like my friend doesn't like me anymore and that he is disappointed with the way I've turned out. We've known each other for a long time. We still see the world in a similar way, but he has lost his sense of humor.

He seems to carry a kind of terminal sadness with him. He can no longer experience joy. Everything around him gets flattened by the weight of his attitude. He went through a bad run, where everything went wrong. A whole string of things didn't work out. The disappointments piled up over time to where he couldn't dig himself out. He stopped believing things would get better. Finally he succumbed to the rhythm of falling – of coming up short. Even when there was a clear break in the negative pattern, when the overcast sky opened up to the heavens, he couldn't lift his mood. He was locked into a miserable self-banter. He had lost his sense of humor. I hope I'll never lose mine.

13 A WAY OF BEING ALONE WITHOUT BEING ALONE. I like working with my machines because it's like being alone without being alone. Machines are part of an ecology of human nature. When we are one with a machine we are connected with all machines and everyone else who touches machines. We are one with human nature and it feels comforting to be part of an ecology of people connected by machines and machines connected by people.

Tragflügel. Ich verschwinde hinter einem Buch oder einer Zeitung oder einem Magazin und tue so, als würde die Maschine den Boden nie verlassen. Ich ignoriere die Sicherheitsvorführungen. Ich gehe nie auf die Toilette. Ich spreche nie mit meinen Mitreisenden. Heute morgen hatte ich ein sehr seltsames Erlebnis. Ich verstaute meinen Mantel und meine Aktentasche in der Gepäckablage über mir, setzte mich, schnallte mich an, setzte meine Stereokopfhörer auf und sah mich um. Ich kannte jede einzelne Person in diesem Flugzeug. Ich hatte jeden an Bord im Laufe der Jahre irgendwann einmal getroffen. Direkten Augenkontakt meidend, identifizierte ich alle an Bord kommenden Passagiere. Dann stand ich auf und fingerte an meiner Aktentasche in der Gepäckablage herum, um noch einmal alle überprüfen zu können, die hinter mir saßen. Ich kannte jede verdammte Person im Flugzeug, nicht mit Namen – aber ich hatte Erinnerungen an sie alle. Ich hatte Angst, erkannt zu werden, deshalb versteckte ich mich hinter meiner Zeitung und dachte darüber nach, wie seltsam es war, alle in diesem Flugzeug zu kennen. Das passiert, wenn man jahrelang viel fliegt. Man stellt fest, daß man jeden gerade ein bißchen kennt, und in den meisten Fällen ist ein bißchen auch schon mehr als genug.

12 ICH KANNTE DIESEN MANN, er war mein Freund. Ich liebte es, mich mit ihm zu unterhalten. Wir konnten nie genug davon bekommen, uns zu unterhalten und zu lachen. Wir tranken und rauchten und sprachen über Gott und die Welt. Wir waren irgendwie verrückt. Wir machten dumme Sachen. Aber die Zeit ist vergangen, wir haben uns verändert, und jetzt verhalten wir uns anders, wenn wir einander treffen. Ich vermute, wir haben uns beide verändert, aber ich habe noch immer Lust, mich zu unterhalten und zu lachen und verrückt zu sein. Aber es ist kein Platz dafür. Ich habe das Gefühl, mein Freund mag mich nicht mehr. Ich habe das Gefühl, daß er über meine Entwicklung enttäuscht ist. Wir kennen einander sehr lange. Wir sehen die Welt noch immer auf eine ähnliche Art und Weise, aber er hat seinen Humor verloren.

Er scheint eine Art unheilbare Traurigkeit mit sich herumzutragen. Er kann keine Freude mehr empfinden. Alles in seiner Umgebung wird niedergedrückt durch das Gewicht seiner Haltung. Er hat eine schwierige Zeit durchgemacht, in der ihm alles mißlang. Eine ganze Reihe von Dingen ging schief. Die Enttäuschungen haben sich im Laufe der Zeit angesammelt, bis er sich nicht mehr davon befreien konnte. Er verlor den Glauben daran, daß die Dinge besser werden würden. Schließlich ergab er sich dem

The thing I like about machines is the detached intimacy I can establish and maintain between myself and others. I can be alone with someone else. I can leave my body and be real close without touching flesh. Flesh to flesh is one thing, being alone with someone else without touching is another. Human nature is tied together with machines of all varieties.

It's a world wrapped around a world of other species and other times. It's a point of view that depends on a shared solitude, a pleasure derived from being alone with others.

14 YOU CAN'T TEACH AN OLD MACHINE NEW TRICKS. You can make a new machine do ordinary, dated things, but why bother? Most people in love with machines are just going through the motions. It's not important what they do, it's important how they feel. You can see this with people who love to watch television. People love television because they enjoy being alone with hundreds of thousands and even millions of other people. Simultaneously.

They sit and watch popular programs and they feel part of something bigger than themselves. When the phone rings they expect to receive a personal, exclusive message from another individual. They are not interested in having a television experience when they answer the phone. Of course, video phones will be fair game for advertisers and info-mercials. And in the flip-flop of a machine-identity crisis our television systems will become a new territory for personal, exclusive messages. Video and computers are already being used like telephones, for personal messages, but for a lot of people that's not very useful. These new interactive machines demand our complete attention and direct participation. The problem with interactive technologies is that you can't do anything else at the same time. Parallel activities are ruled out. Listening to the radio or television while reading a book, or watching a movie and daydreaming, or eating and reading a newspaper, or talking and having sex while listening to recorded music, or watching recorded sex while playing live music.....a lot of wonderful parallel activities are being eliminated by interactive technologies. Interactivity, and the exclusionary intimacy it implies, favors memory retrieval in an asynchronous mode. ATM, Asynchronous Transfer Mode is replacing STM,

Rhythmus des Fallens – des Mißlingens. Selbst wenn die Negativserie zu Ende ist, wenn der Himmel aufklart, ändert das nichts an seiner Laune. Er ist in einem unglücklichen Zwist mit sich selbst gefangen. Er hat seinen Humor verloren. Ich hoffe, ich werde meinen nie verlieren.

13 EINE MÖGLICHKEIT ALLEIN ZU SEIN, OHNE ALLEIN ZU SEIN. Ich arbeite gern mit meinen Maschinen, weil ich allein bin, ohne wirklich allein zu sein. Maschinen sind Teil einer Ökologie der menschlichen Natur. Wenn wir mit einer Maschine eins sind, sind wir mit allen Maschinen und mit allen, die Maschinen berühren, verbunden. Wir sind eins mit der menschlichen Natur, und es ist tröstlich, Teil einer Ökologie von Menschen zu sein, die durch Maschinen verbunden sind, und von Maschinen, die durch Menschen verbunden sind. Ich mag an Maschinen die distanzierte Intimität, die ich zwischen mir und anderen herstellen und aufrechterhalten kann. Ich kann mit jemand anderem allein sein. Ich kann meinen Körper verlassen und jemandem wirklich nahe sein, ohne seinen Körper zu berühren. Körper an Körper ist eine Sache, mit jemand anderem allein zu sein, ohne ihn zu berühren, eine andere. Die menschliche Natur wird durch Maschinen aller Art zusammengehalten.

Es ist eine Welt, die eine Welt anderer Spezies und anderer Zeiten umhüllt. Es ist ein Blickwinkel, der auf gemeinsame Einsamkeit angewiesen ist, ein Vergnügen, das daraus entsteht, mit anderen allein zu sein.

14 MAN KANN EINER ALTEN MASCHINE KEINE NEUEN KUNSTSTÜCKE BEIBRINGEN. Du kannst eine neue Maschine dazu bringen, gewöhnliche, altmodische Dinge zu tun, aber wozu? Die meisten in Maschinen verliebte Menschen tun nur so als ob. Es ist nicht wichtig, was sie tun, sondern wie sie sich dabei fühlen. Man kann das bei Menschen beobachten, die gerne fernsehen. Die Menschen lieben das Fernsehen, weil sie es genießen, mit hunderttausenden, ja, sogar Millionen anderen allein zu sein. Gleichzeitig.

Sie sitzen und schauen sich beliebte Sendungen an und fühlen sich als Teil von etwas, das größer ist als sie selbst. Wenn das Telefon läutet, erwarten sie sich eine persönliche, exklusive Nachricht von einer anderen Person. Sie haben kein Interesse am Fernsehen, wenn sie ans Telefon gehen. Sicher, Bildtelefone werden zu einem Spielplatz für Werbung und Verkaufssendungen werden. Und beim Umschalten, das auf eine Maschinenidentitätskrise hinausläuft, werden unsere Fernsehsysteme zu einem neuen Medium für persönliche, exklusive Nachrichten. Video

Synchronous Transfer Mode. STM occurs in shared, real time and ATM is the end of real time as we know it.

15 THERE IS NO LONGER A CENTER FOR SELF-IDENTITY. The body, no matter how firm, is not the permanent address it used to be. We are all homeless in relative terms. Looking back at the body gives us pleasure. But ultimately, it is just another thing in a world of things that gives us feedback and helps us keep our balance. Constructions of external memory replace the body. We deposit external memory wherever we can. We touch, we revisit these memory constructions. We search for familiar territory.

Touching things is good for finding our way.

Establishing form through pattern recognition. Establishing and re-establishing order. Checking our references. Making conversations with ourselves. Forming new relationships. Surrogate relationships. Going through the motions.

Practising, rehearsing for the real thing.

Filling in the details. Embodying stereotypes. Pretending we are sharing secrets. With somebody else. Why is it, when we hold onto our secrets, we feel like outsiders?

Why do we feel so disconnected? It doesn't matter. Our machines are very good listeners. They're the last good listeners ...

und Computer werden bereits jetzt wie Telefone für das Übermitteln persönlicher Botschaften verwendet, was für viele Leute nicht sehr praktisch ist. Diese neuen interaktiven Maschinen verlangen unsere volle Aufmerksamkeit und direkte Beteiligung. Das Problem interaktiver Technologien besteht darin, daß man nichts anderes zur selben Zeit tun kann. Parallele Tätigkeiten sind ausgeschlossen. Radio hören oder fernsehen, während man ein Buch liest, einen Film ansehen und dabei tagträumen, essen und Zeitung lesen, sich unterhalten und miteinander schlafen und gleichzeitig Musik hören oder Sexvideos ansehen und musizieren ... Interaktive Technologien bedeuten das Ende für eine ganze Menge toller Parallelaktivitäten. Interaktivität und die damit einhergehende ausschließende Intimität bevorzugen das Abrufen von Erinnerungen in einem asynchronen Modus. ATM, Asynchronous Transfer Mode, ersetzt STM, Synchronous Transfer Mode. STM findet in Zeitscheiben, geteilter Echtzeit, statt, und ATM ist das Ende der Echtzeit, wie wir sie kennen.

15 ES GIBT KEIN ZENTRUM DER SELBSTIDENTITÄT MEHR. Der Körper, wie beständig er auch sein mag, ist nicht mehr die feste Wohnadresse, die er einmal war. Relativ gesehen, sind wir alle heimatlos. Es bereitet uns Vergnügen, auf unseren Körper zurückzusehen. Aber letztendlich ist er nur ein Ding unter vielen in einer Welt von Dingen, die uns Rückmeldungen geben und uns helfen, im Gleichgewicht zu bleiben. Externe Speicherkonstruktionen ersetzen unseren Körper. Wo immer wir können, deponieren wir externe Erinnerungsspeicher. Wir berühren, wir suchen diese Speicherkonstruktionen auf. Wir suchen nach vertrautem Terrain.

Die Dinge zu berühren, hilft uns, unseren Weg zu finden. Festlegen der Form durch Erkennen von Mustern. Herstellen und Wiederherstellen von Ordnung. Überprüfen unserer Unterlagen. Gespräche mit uns selbst. Knüpfen neuer Beziehungen. Ersatzbeziehungen. So tun als ob. Üben, Proben für das einzig Wahre. Einfügen der Einzelheiten.

Verkörpern von Stereotypen. Vorgeben, Geheimnisse zu teilen. Mit jemand anderem. Warum fühlen wir uns als Außenseiter, wenn wir unsere Geheimnisse nicht preisgeben?

Warum fühlen wir uns so ausgeschlossen? Es spielt keine Rolle. Unsere Maschinen sind sehr gute Zuhörer. Sie sind die letzten guten Zuhörer ...

Blurring the Boundaries between Bodies, Bits & Atoms: From ClearBoard to Tangible Bits

Hiroshi Ishii

At the Seashore

Where the land meets the sea, there is a border. This borderline is constantly moving and changing the shape of the shore. However, it is not only a simple line of a landscape, but also a critical biological locale. Whenever the tides go in and out, the inhabitants in the intertidal zone experience harsh environmental changes. When the tidal animals are exposed, they must withstand the heat and drying. When they are submerged, they must face the constant pounding of waves. Living at this boundary is hard, but it is also a fertile environment for many kinds of life and activity [Ten 87].

Verschwimmende Grenzen zwischen Körpern, Bits und Atomen: von ClearBoard zu Tangible Bits

Hiroshi Ishii

Am Meeresufer

Wo Land und Meer aufeinandertreffen, bilden sie eine Grenze. Es ist eine Grenzlinie, die unentwegt in Bewegung ist und ihre Form verändert. Dabei handelt es sich nicht einfach nur um eine Linie in der Landschaft, sondern auch um eine kritische biologische Zone. Jeder Wechsel der Gezeiten bringt für die Bewohner dieser Zwischenzone tiefgreifende Veränderungen ihrer Umgebung mit sich. Wenn die Tiere dieser Zone vom Wasser freigegeben werden, müssen sie der Hitze und Trockenheit standhalten, wenn sie überflutet werden, dem ununterbrochenen Anrollen der Wellen trotzen. Das Leben an dieser Grenze ist schwierig, zugleich aber ist sie auch ein fruchtbarer Lebensraum für viele Lebens- und Verhaltensformen [Ten 87].

Die digitale Küste

Wo Bits und Atome aufeinandertreffen, entsteht eine andere Art Uferlinie. An dieser Uferlinie zwischen physischem Raum und Cyberspace leben wir heute. Das pausenlose Anrollen von Bitwellen verzerrt unsere Art der Raumwahrnehmung und stellt die Grenzen unseres materiellen Körpers in Frage. Das Leben an dieser Grenze ist schwierig, denn auch wenn wir in die Welt digitaler Informationen ein-

The Digital Seashore

Where bits meet atoms, there is another kind of shoreline. Today, we live on this boundary between physical space and cyberspace. The constant pounding by waves of bits distorts our experience of space, challenging the boundaries of our physical bodies.

Living on this edge is hard because our bodies remain in the physical world, even while we are immersed in digital information. However, this boundary marks a most interesting challenge for designers of media to bridge the gap between the worlds of bits and atoms.

People tend to think of borders as separators, but it is important to understand borders as *interfaces* which actively promote exchange between adjoining worlds. This presentation is about such kinds of interface design. To address the issue of designs which blur the boundary between our bodies, cyberspace, and physical space, I will present two media design projects: *ClearBoard* [1991-94] at NTT Human Interface Laboratories, and *Tangible Bits* [1996-present] at MIT Media Laboratory.

The goal of these projects is to go beyond currently dominant models of *talking head* and *painted bits* by releasing the information out of computers and projecting it into architectural spaces where our bodies reside. I will present our design approaches from the perspective of HCI [Human-Computer Interaction] and CSCW [Computer-Supported Cooperative Work] research.

Distortion of Hybrid Space

Media technology extends the space we inhabit and within which we interact with others, but often in abrupt and arbitrary ways. These *hybrid spaces* can be distorted and discontinuous, with our bodies often losing orientation. These hybrid spaces are no longer seamless.

Video telephony creates interpersonal space that maintains a sense of *telepresence* or *copresence* through the visibility of gestures and facial expressions of remote people. However, the distortions of hybrid space make it difficult to utilize various nonverbal cues to interact smoothly and naturally with remote colleagues.

A limitation of current collaboration media is the ad hoc configuration of shared workspaces, typically consisting of groupware running in a window on a computer screen next to

getaucht sind, bleibt unser Körper in der physischen Welt zurück. Zugleich aber stellt diese Grenze eine überaus interessante Herausforderung für Mediendesigner dar, die Kluft zwischen der Welt der Bits und der Welt der Atome zu überbrücken. Grenzen werden häufig als etwas Trennendes empfunden, man muß sie aber als *Schnittstellen* verstehen, die den Austausch zwischen benachbarten Welten aktiv fördern. Um eben solche Formen des Schnittstellendesigns wird es im folgenden gehen.

Als Beispiel für Entwürfe, die die Grenzen zwischen unseren Körpern, dem Cyberspace und dem physischen Raum verschwimmen lassen, werde ich zwei Mediendesign-Projekte vorstellen: Clearboard [1991-94] an den NTT Human Interface Laboratories und Tangible Bits [1996-jetzt] am MIT Media Laboratory.

Das Ziel dieser Projekte ist es, über die derzeit vorherrschenden *talking head* und *painted bits*-Modelle hinauszugehen, indem die Informationen nicht auf den Computer beschränkt bleiben, sondern in die von unseren Körpern bewohnten Räume projiziert werden. Ich werde unseren Konstruktionsansatz aus der Perspektive der HCI [Human-Computer Interaction]- und CSCW [Computer-Supported Cooperative Work]-Forschung präsentieren.

Verzerrung von Hybridräumen

Die Medientechnologie erweitert den Raum, in dem wir leben und in dem wir mit anderen interagieren – oft jedoch auf abrupte und willkürliche Art und Weise. Diese *Hybridräume* können Verzerrungen und mangelnde Kontinuität aufweisen, so daß unsere Körper häufig die Orientierung verlieren. Es sind keine nahtlosen Räume mehr.

Videotelefone schaffen einen interpersonellen Kommunkationsraum, der durch die Sichtbarkeit von Gestik und Gesichtsausdruck physisch abwesender Personen ein Gefühl der Telepräsenz oder Co-Präsenz bewahrt. Die Verzerrungen des Hybridraumes machen es jedoch schwierig, die verschiedenen nonverbalen Zeichen für eine natürliche und reibungslose Kommunikation mit körperlich nicht anwesenden Kollegen zu verwenden.

Eine Beschränkung gegenwärtiger Medien für die Zusammenarbeit mehrerer Benutzer liegt in der Ad-hoc-Konfiguration des gemeinsamen Arbeitsplatzes. Üblicherweise besteht dieser aus Groupware, die in einem Bildschirmfenster neben einem kleineren zweiten mit einem *talking head* läuft. Das kommt dem Betrachten eines räumlich fragmentierten kubistischen Bildes gleich. Auf diesen gemeinsamen elektronischen Arbeitplätzen sind die klei-

a small *talking head* window. This is like looking at a cubist painting in which space is fragmented. In these electronic shared workspaces, small mouse pointers are completely disembodied, and the discontinuity between the remote person's image and the shared workspace is amplified.

ClearBoard and Seamless Space Design

ClearBoard was designed in collaboration with Minoru Kobayashi at NTT to realize a seamless integration of shared workspace and interpersonal space over a distance [Fig. 1]. A design goal of *ClearBoard* was to allow a pair of users to shift easily between interpersonal space and shared workspace using familiar everyday cues such as a partner's gestures, head movements, eye contact, and gaze direction. The key metaphor of *ClearBoard* design is talking through and drawing on a large transparent glass board [Ishii, Kobayashi, and Grudin 93].

Figure 2 shows ClearBoard-1, the first prototype to support remote collaboration. Two users are discussing a route by drawing a map directly on the screen surface. Both users can share a common map orientation by a mirror reversing the video images. The partners can read all the text and graphics in their correct orientation.

We observed effortless switching of focus between the task and the partner's face. Users could read their partner's facial expression, achieve eye contact, and utilize awareness of the direction of their partner's gaze. We call it *gaze awareness*: the ability to monitor the direction of a partner's gaze and thus his or her focus of attention.

From ClearBoard to Tangible Bits

The *ClearBoard* design not only goes beyond the traditional desktop metaphor and win-

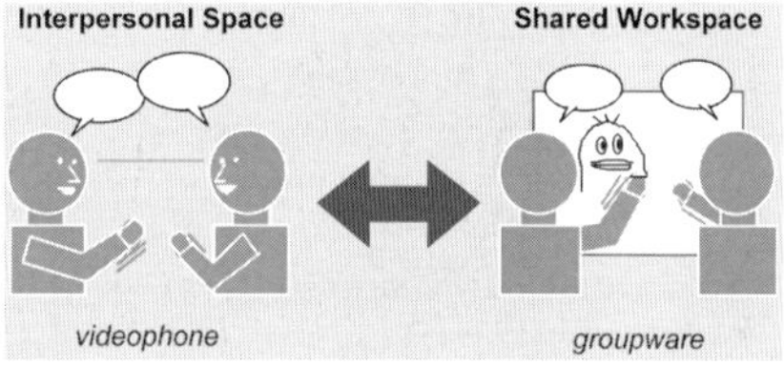

Fig. 1
Seamless integration of interpersonal space and shared workspace/Nahtlose Integration von interpersonellem Kommunikationsraum und gemeinsam genutztem Arbeitsbereich

nen Mauszeiger vollständig vom Körper abgetrennt und die Kontinuität zwischen dem Bild der abwesenden Person und der gemeinsamen Arbeitsfläche ist eingeschränkt.

Clearboard und die Konstruktion von nahtlosen Räumen

Clearboard wurde in Zusammenarbeit mit Minoru Kobayashi am NTT entworfen, um auch auf Distanz eine nahtlose Integration von gemeinsam genutztem Arbeitsbereich und interpersonellem Kommunikationsraum zu verwirklichen [Abb. 1]. Eines der Ziele von *Clearboard* war, zwei Benutzer durch den Einsatz von vertrauten alltäglichen Zeichen wie Gestik, Kopfbewegungen, Augenkontakt und Blickrichtung des Partners problemlos zwischen dem interpersonellen Kommunkationsraum und der gemeinsamen Arbeitsfläche wechseln zu lassen. Als Schlüsselmetapher benutzt *Clearboard* eine große durchsichtige Glasplatte, durch die man hindurchspricht und die auch zum Zeichnen dient [Ishii, Kobayashi und Grudin 93].

Abb. 2 zeigt Clearboard-1, den ersten Prototyp für Fernkooperation. Zwei Benutzer besprechen eine Fahrtroute, indem sie einen Plan direkt auf die Bildschirmoberfläche zeichnen. Durch die spiegelverkehrte Wiedergabe der Videobilder können sich auf dem Plan beide gleich orientieren. Die Partner können jeden Text und jede Graphik in der richtigen Ausrichtung lesen.

Es hat sich gezeigt, daß die Benutzer mit ihrer Aufmerksamkeit mühelos zwischen dieser Aufgabe und dem Gesicht des Partners wechseln konnten. Sie konnten den Gesichtsausdruck ihres Partners lesen, Augenkontakt herstellen und den Umstand nutzen, daß sie die Blickrichtung des Partners mitbekamen. Die Fähigkeit, die Blickrichtung des Partners und damit das Ziel seiner Aufmerksamkeit zu verfolgen, nennen wir *Blickbewußtsein*.

Von Clearboard zu Tangible Bits

Clearboard geht nicht nur über die herkömmliche Schreibtisch-Metapher und die fensterbasierte graphische Benutzeroberfläche hinaus, sondern läßt auch die Imitation physischer Nähe [*Dasein*] hinter sich, die lange Zeit das unumstrittene Ziel der Kommunikationstechnologie war. Mit *Clearboard* bewegen wir uns in Richtung *jenseits des Daseins* [Hollan 92]. Außerdem entwickelt *Clearboard* die Wand von einem passiven Medium der Trennung zu einem dynamischen Medium der Zusammenarbeit weiter, das auseinanderliegende

dows-based GUI, but also goes beyond the imitation of physical proximity [or *being there*] which has long been the unquestioned goal of telecommunication technologies. *ClearBoard* suggests a direction of *beyond being there* [Hollan 92]. Further, *ClearBoard* evolves the concept of the physical wall from a passive partition to a dynamic collaboration medium that integrates distributed real and virtual spaces.

ClearBoard inspired a vision of new architectural spaces where all surfaces including walls, ceilings, desktops, windows, and doors become *interactive surfaces* through which people can interact with other real and virtual environments [Ishii, Kobayashi, and Arita 94].

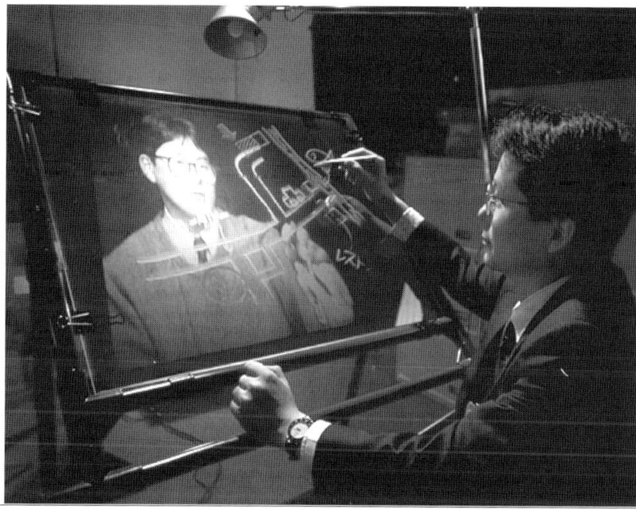

Fig. 2

ClearBoard-1 in use
ClearBoard-1 in Verwendung

reale und virtuelle Räume integriert. Inspiriert durch *Clearboard* entstand die Vision von einem neuen architektonischen Raum, in dem sämtliche Raumelemente wie Wände, Decken, Arbeitsflächen, Fenster und Türen zu *interaktiven Oberflächen* werden, mit deren Hilfe die Menschen mit anderen realen und virtuellen Umgebungen kommunizieren können [Ishii, Kobayashi und Arita 94].

Tangible Bits ist ein Schritt zur Umsetzung dieser Vision, in die gleichzeitig zwei neue Schlüsselideen einfließen. Erstens geht es uns darum, interaktive Oberflächen in Verbindung mit greifbaren physischen Objekten einzusetzen, die zur physischen Darstellung und Manipulation digitaler Informationen dienen. Zweitens möchten wir die interaktiven Oberflächen mit sogenannten Ambient Media koppeln, wobei Licht, Geräusche, Luftströmungen und sogar Wasserbewegungen in der Umgebung Informationen übermittelt werden, die an der Peripherie des menschlichen Bewußtseins liegen.

Derzeit ist die Interaktion zwischen Mensch und Cyberspace größtenteils auf graphische User-Interfaces [GUIs] auf Desktop- oder Laptopgeräten beschränkt. Die Interaktion mit diesen GUIs ist von der gewöhnlichen physischen Umgebung, in der wir leben und kommunizieren, getrennt.

Wir haben eine Reihe von Skills und Arbeitstechniken zur Informationsverabeitung durch haptische Interaktion mit physischen Objekten und mit Hilfe peripherer Sinne entwickelt. Im derzeitigen HCI-Design werden die meisten dieser Techniken aufgrund der mangelnden Vielfalt an Input/Output-Medien und einer übermäßigen Betonung des graphischen Outputs auf Kosten des Inputs aus der realen Welt vernachlässigt.

Die wichtigsten Ideen von Tangible Bits

Der Einsatzbereich von Komputationsprozessen verschiebt sich gegenwärtig in zwei Richtungen weg vom Schreibtisch: auf unsere Haut/unseren Körper und in die physische Umgebung, in der wir leben. Der Wechsel zum Körper wird markiert durch die jüngsten Entwicklungen auf dem neuen Gebiet der *tragbaren Computer* [Mann 96]. Wir konzentrieren uns auf den zweiten Weg: die Integration von Computererweiterungen in unsere materielle Umgebung. Unser Ziel ist, die natürlichen materiellen Gegebenheiten zu nutzen und so zu einer verbesserten Lesbarkeit und Nahtlosigkeit der Interaktion zwischen Mensch und digitaler Information zu gelangen.

Tangible Bits stellt den Versuch dar, die Kluft zwischen Cyberspace und unserer natürlichen Um-

With *Tangible Bits*, we are working towards realizing this vision, coupled simultaneously with two new key ideas. First, we are interested in using interactive surfaces in combination with graspable physical objects used to physically embody and manipulate digital information. Secondly, we wish to couple interactive surfaces with *ambient media,* using ambient light, sound, airflow, and even water movement to communicate information at the periphery of human awareness.

The interactions between people and cyberspace are now largely confined to traditional GUI [Graphical User Interface]-based boxes sitting on desktops or laptops. The interactions with these GUIs are separated from the ordinary physical environment within which we live and interact. Although we have developed various skills and work practices for processing information through haptic interactions with physical objects as well as peripheral senses, most of these practices are neglected in current HCI design because of the lack of diversity of input/output media, and too much bias towards graphical output at the expense of input from the real world.

Key Ideas of Tangible Bits

We see the locus of computation now shifting from the desktop in two major directions: i] onto our skins/bodies, and ii] into the physical environments we inhabit. The transition to our bodies is represented by recent activities in the new field of *wearable computers* [Mann 96]. We are focusing on the second path: integration of computational augmentations into the physical environment. Our intention is to take advantage of natural physical affordances to achieve a heightened legibility and seamlessness of interaction between people and digital information.

Fig. 3

Center and Periphery of User's Attention within Physical Space
Zentrum und Peripherie der Aufmerksamkeit innerhalb des physischen Raumes

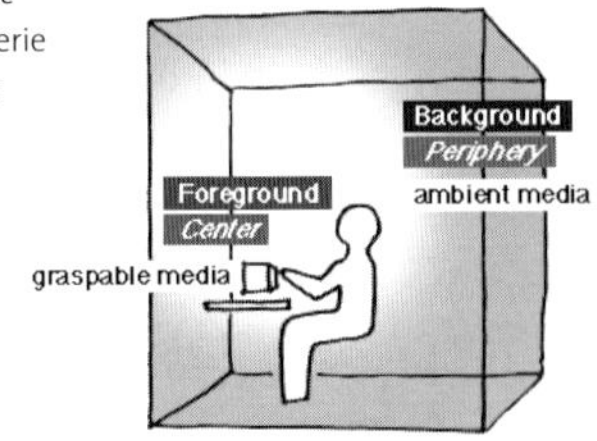

gebung durch das Greifbarmachen digitaler Informationen [Bits] zu überbrücken. Wir beschäftigen uns mit der Entwicklung von Möglichkeiten, Bits von unserer physischen Umgebung aus zugänglich zu machen. Unsere Schlüsselkonzepte sind:

- Interaktive Oberflächen: Transformation aller Oberflächen eines Raumes [Wände, Arbeitsflächen, Decken, Türen, Fenster] in aktive Schnittstellen zwischen materieller und virtueller Welt;
- Koppelung von Bits und Atomen: Alltägliche greifbare Gegenstände [z. B. Karten, Bücher, Modelle] werden nahtlos mit der dazugehörigen digitalen Information gekoppelt;
- Ambient Media: Die Verwendung von Raumzuständen wie Geräusch, Licht, Luftströmungen und Wasserbewegungen als Hintergrundschnittstellen mit dem Cyberspace an der Peripherie der menschlichen Wahrnehmung [Ishii und Ullmer 97].

Letztendlich suchen wir nach Möglichkeiten, jeden Zustand, den Materie in unseren alltäglichen Räumen einnehmen kann – nicht nur feste Materie, sondern auch Flüssigkeiten und Gase – in Schnittstellen zwischen Mensch und digitaler Information zu verwandeln. Wir forschen nach Mitteln, sowohl die Qualität als auch die Bandbreite der Interaktion zwischen Mensch und digitaler Information zu verbessern, indem wir

- die Benutzer durch die Koppelung von Bits mit greifbaren Objekten in die Lage versetzen, Vordergrund-Bits *zu ergreifen und zu manipulieren*;
- den Benutzern mit Hilfe von Ambient Media in einem erweiterten Raum die Möglichkeit geben, sich der Hintergrund-Bits der Peripherie bewußt zu werden.

Die derzeitige HCI-Forschung konzentriert sich in erster Linie auf Vordergrundaktivitäten und vernachlässigt den Hintergrund. Unbewußt nehmen Menschen jedoch vielfältige *Peripherie*-Informationen auf, um die sie sich nicht explizit kümmern. Wird etwas Ungewöhnliches bemerkt, rückt es sofort ins Zentrum ihrer Aufmerksamkeit.

Durch Ambient Media und greifbare Gegenstände den reibungslosen Wechsel der Aufmerksamkeit des Benutzers zwischen Vordergrund und Hintergrund zu ermöglichen, ist eine der größten Herausforderungen für *Tangible Bits* [Abb. 3].

Um die Idee von *Tangible Bits* zu illustrieren und umzusetzen, hat unsere Gruppe verschiedene Plattformen, darunter *metaDESK*, *ambientROOM* [Ishii und Ullmer 97], *inTouch* [Brave und Dahley 97, siehe Seite 282] und *Triangles* [Orth und Gorbet 97, siehe Seite 284] entworfen.

Tangible Bits is an attempt to bridge the gap between cyberspace and the physical environment by making digital information [bits] tangible. We are developing ways to make bits accessible through the physical environment. Our key concepts are:

- Interactive Surfaces: Transformation of each surface within architectural space [e.g., walls, desktops, ceilings, doors, windows] into an active interface between the physical and virtual worlds;
- Coupling of Bits and Atoms: Seamless coupling of everyday graspable objects [e.g., cards, books, models] with the digital information that pertains to them; and
- Ambient Media: Use of ambient media such as sound, light, airflow, and water movement for background interfaces with cyberspace at the periphery of human perception [Ishii and Ullmer 97].

Ultimately, we are seeking ways to turn each state of physical matter – not only solid matter, but also liquids and gases – within everyday architectural spaces into *interfaces* between people and digital information. We are exploring ways of both improving the quality and broadening the bandwidth of interaction between people and digital information by:

- allowing users to *grasp & manipulate* foreground bits by coupling bits with physical objects, and
- enabling users to be aware of background bits at the periphery using ambient media in an augmented space.

Current HCI research is focusing primarily on foreground activity and neglecting the background.

However, subconsciously, people are constantly receiving varied information from the *periphery* without attending to it explicitly. If anything unusual is noticed, it immediately comes to the center of their attention.

The smooth transition of users' focus of attention between background and foreground using ambient media and graspable objects is a key challenge of *Tangible Bits*.

Our group designed several platforms including *metaDESK*, *ambientROOM* [Ishii and Ullmer 97], *inTouch* [Brave and Dahley 97], and *Triangles* [Orth and Gorbet 97] to demonstrate and verify the idea of *Tangible Bits*.

metaDESK [Ishii und Ullmer 97]

Die Oberfläche von *metaDESK* bildet ein Gateway zwischen digitalem und physischem Raum, wobei physische Icons [*phicons*] als Container und Hebel für das physische Manipulieren digitaler Daten dienen. Als physische Schnittstellenelemente verwendet *metaDESK* zudem Vorrichtungen wie die aktive Linse, ein am Arm montiertes LCD-Display, und die passive Linse, eine mobile *Linse* aus Glasfiberbündeln mit Rückprojektion. Die erste Prototypanwendung von *metaDESK* ist *Tangible Geospace*, wo Benutzer physisch mit 2D- und 3D-Bildern vom MIT-Campus interagieren können [Abb. 4].

ambientROOM [Ishii und Ullmer 97]

ambientROOM ist eine Plattform, die die Verwendung von Ambient Media zur Übermittlung von Informationen erkundet, die sich an der Peripherie der menschlichen Wahrnehmung befinden. Durch die Anzeige der Umgebungsfaktoren wie Licht, Schatten, Geräuschkulisse, Luftströmungen und Wasserbewegung vermag der Raum Umweltinformationen über Wetter, Verkehr oder sogar das Treiben Ihres Kindes vermitteln.

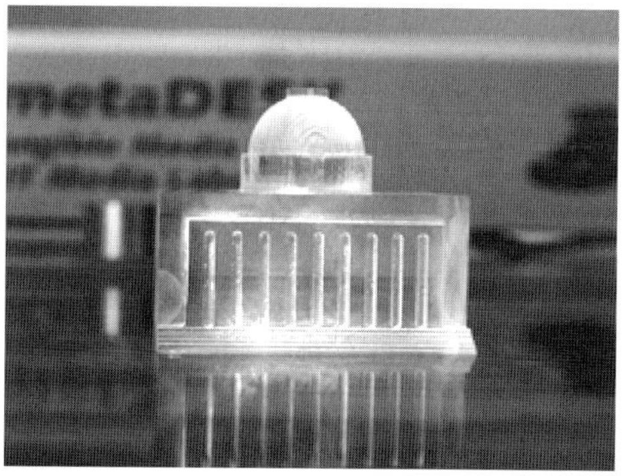

Fig.4 *Phicon [physical icon] of MIT Dome on metaDESK: Container of Bits about MIT/* Phicon [Physisches Icon] der MITKuppel auf dem metaDESK: Bits-Container von MIT

inTouch [Brave und Dahley 97]

inTouch erforscht neue Formen interpersoneller Telekommunikation unter Verwendung des Tastsinns. Der Prototyp besteht aus zwei Vorrichtungen, die jeweils aus drei in eine Unterlage eingebetteten zylindrischen Rollen bestehen [Abb. 4]. Dreht ein Benutzer eine oder alle dieser Rollen, wird diese Bewegung von einer möglicherweise weit entfern-

The surface of the *metaDESK* acts as a gateway between digital and physical space, allowing physical icons [*phicons*] to serve as containers and handles for physically manipulating digital information. The *metaDESK* also makes use of interface devices like the active lens, an arm-mounted LCD display, and the passive lens, a mobile *lens* of back-projected, fiber-cluster glass, as physical interface tools. The first prototype application of *metaDESK* is *Tangible Geospace*, which allows the user to interact physically with 2D and 3D views of the MIT campus [Fig. 4].

ambientROOM [Ishii and Ullmer 97]

The *ambientROOM* is a platform exploring the use of ambient media to communicate information at the periphery of human perception. Ambient displays such as light, shadow, sound, airflow, and water movement enable the room to communicate information about the world, such as weather, traffic, or the even the activities of your child.

inTouch [Brave and Dahley 97]

inTouch explores new forms of interpersonal communication across distance that exploit touch. A prototype is made of two devices, each consisting of three cylindrical rollers embedded in a base [Fig. 5]. When a user rotates any or all of these rollers, the exact movement is mimicked by the partner device, even though it may be located far away. Users can thus feel the distant person's interaction through mutual manipulation of a *shared* physical object.

Triangles [Orth and Gorbet 97]

Triangles is a construction kit of identical, flat, plastic triangles that can be connected to each other both physically and digitally to trigger specific digital events, allowing a simple, but powerful means of physical interacting

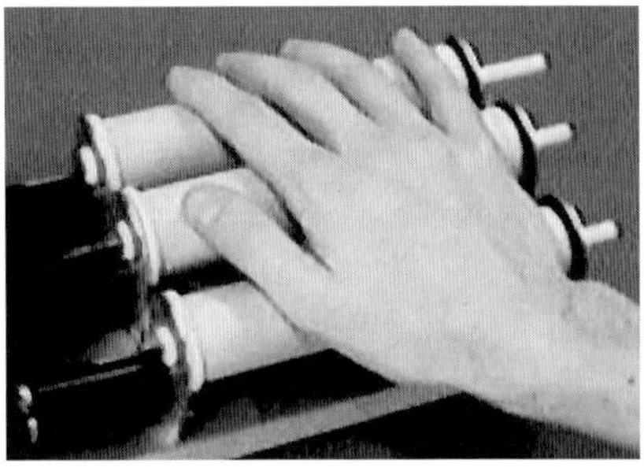

Fig. 5 *inTouch in use/* inTouch in Verwendung

ten Partnervorrichtung exakt nachgeahmt. Durch die beiderseitige Manipulation eines *gemeinsam genutzten* physischen Gegenstandes können die Benutzer also die Interaktion einer abwesenden Person fühlen.

Triangles [Orth und Gorbet 97]

Triangles besteht aus einem Bausatz identischer, flacher, plastischer Dreiecke, die sowohl physisch als auch digital miteinander verbunden werden können, um damit bestimmte digitale Ereignisse auszulösen. Es handelt sich um ein einfaches, aber ausdrucksstarkes Mittel der physischen Interaktion mit digitaler Information [Abb. 6]. Das *Triangle*-Projekt ist ein erster Schritt in Richtung eines umfassenderen Ziels – der Entwicklung von *Objekten mit doppelter Identität*, d. h. von Gegenständen, die durch ihre physische Konstruktion die Struktur und die Beziehungen von digitaler Information greifbar machen können.

Resümee

Wo Land und Meer aufeinandertreffen, haben zahllose Lebewesen verschiedenste kreative Möglichkeiten entwickelt, um inmitten der Turbulenzen und pausenlosen Veränderungen dieser beiden miteinander konkurrierenden Welten gedeihen zu können. An der Grenzlinie zwischen dem Meer aus Bits und dem festen Boden der greifbaren Welt sehen wir uns mit einer ähnlichen Herausforderung konfrontiert: unsere doppelte Staatsbürgerschaft in der digitalen und materiellen Welt, in der Welt der Bits und der Atome, in Einklang zu bringen.

Zur Zeit bilden das Land der Atome und das Meer der Bits zwei getrennte Welten. Die materielle Welt liegt in einem Schlaf, es fehlt ihr großteils an digitalem Inhalt. Unsere Fenster zum Cyberspace bleiben auf *painted bits* beschränkt, die uns aus Myriaden von rechteckigen Bildschirmen zugespielt werden und auf begrenzte Schnittstellen limitiert sind, die unsere Sinne verarmen und unser ästhetisches Empfindungsvermögen unausgeschöpft lassen.

Ich habe hier meine Vision von *ClearBoard* und *Tangible Bits* präsentiert, in der physische Oberflächen, greifbare Objekte und Ambient Media in nahtlose Schnittstellen zwischen Körper, Bits und Atomen umgewandelt werden können. Ich lade Sie ein, gemeinsam mit mir an den Strand zurückzukehren und sich an Meer, Sand, und Luft, an Atomen und Bits, nun vereint zu einem einheitlichen Ganzen, zu erfreuen.

with digital information [Fig. 6]. The *Triangles* project is a first step towards a larger goal of developing 'dual-identity objects' – objects which, by their physical design, are capable of making the structure and relationships of digital information tangible.

Conclusion

Where the land meets the sea, countless creatures have evolved diverse and creative approaches for flourishing among the turbulence and constant change of these competing worlds. On the shoreline between the sea of bits and the firm ground of physicality, we face a similar challenge of reconciling our dual citizenship with the worlds of physicality and digitality, bits and atoms.

The land of atoms and sea of bits are currently worlds divided. The physical world lies sleeping, largely lacking in digital content. Our windows into cyberspace remain limited to *painted bits* leaking out of a myriad of rectangular screens, bound to limited interfaces which impoverish our senses, leaving unsatisfied our aesthetic sensibilities.

Herein, I have presented my visions of the *ClearBoard* and *Tangible Bits*, where the architectural surfaces, graspable objects, and ambient media which surround us may be transformed into seamless interfaces between bodies, bits, and atoms. I invite you to join me in returning to the seashore, and rejoicing in the sea, sand, and air, atoms and bits, joined together as one.

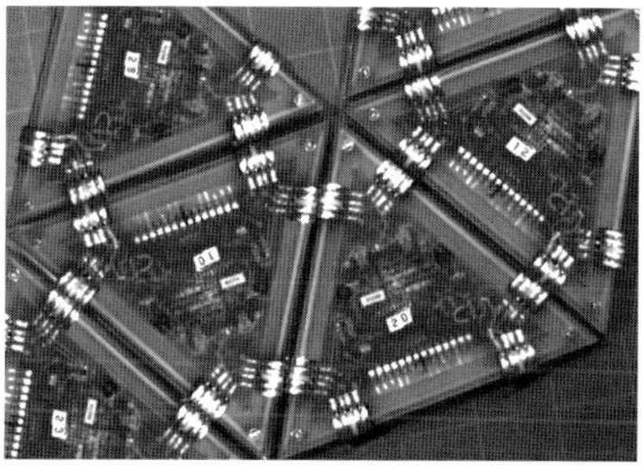

Fig. 6
Triangles connected physically and digitally
Triangles physisch und digital verbunden

BRAVE, S. AND DAHLEY, A., *MiLOs* [Multi-Locational Objects], Ars Electronica Festival 97, Linz 1997

BUXTON, W., *Living in Augmented Reality: Ubiquitous Media and Reactive Environments*, Video-Mediated Communication, Lawrence Erlbaum Associates, 1997, pp. 363-384

HOLLAN, J. and STORNETTA, S., *Beyond Being There*, in: Proceedings of CHI '92, ACM, New York, 1992

ISHII, H. and ULLMER, B., *Tangible Bits: Towards Seamless Interfaces between People, Bits and Atoms*,in: Proceedings of Conference on Human Factors in Computing Systems [CHI '97], ACM, Atlanta, March 1997

ISHII, H., KOBAYASHI, M. and ARITA, K., *Iterative Design of Seamless Collaboration Media*, in: Communications of the ACM [CACM], Special Issue on Internet Technology, ACM, Vol. 37, No. 8, August 1994

ISHII, H., KOBAYASHI, M. and GRUDIN, J., *Integration of Interpersonal Space and Shared Workspace: ClearBoard Design and Experiments*, in: ACM Transactions on Information Systems [TOIS], ACM, Vol. 11, No. 4, October 1993, pp. 349-375

MANN, S. *Smart Clothing: Wearable Multimedia Computing and *Personal Imaging* to Restore the Technological Balance between People and Their Environments*, in: Proceedings of ACM MULTIMEDIA '96, November 1996, 163-174

ORTH, M. and GORBET, M., *Triangles and the Digital Veil*, Ars Electronica Festival 97, Linz 1997

NORMAN TEN, *Living on the Edge*, in: Exploratorium Quarterly, Vol. 11, Issue 3, Fall 1987

WEISER, M., *The Computer for the Twenty-First Century*, in: Scientific American, September 1991, pp. 94-104

I thank Prof. William at the University of Toronto for countless discussions about skill-based design and foreground & background issues, through which many of the ideas in this paper were developed and shaped [Buxton 97]. Thanks are also due to Mark Weiser for his inspiring Ubiquitous Computing work [Weiser 91]. I thank TTT [Things That Think], a new consortium at the MIT Media Lab, for its ongoing support of the Tangible Bits project. I also would like to acknowledge the contribution of many hardworking graduate and undergraduate students at MIT for work on the realization of Tangible Bits ideas. In particular, we thank graduate students Brygg Ullmer, Scott Brave, Andrew Dahley, and Matt Gorbet.

And the Word Was Made Flesh...

Peter Fleissner

Demands on a humane information society

The emotions with which people react to the beginnings of the so-called information society range from euphoria to outrage. As understandable as the individual emotional reaction may be, we should not give credence to its rightness. In this paper I would like to look at the *Informationsmaschine Mensch* and its embeddedness in society, not with uncritical, optimistic exaggeration, nor with an attitude bespeaking a despair of civilization; rather I will avail myself of methods taken from the realm of social and cultural sciences with the aim of evaluating the current trend. What age are we living in? What main trends can we discern? What central problems are emerging? What trends can we expect?

***Valuable* science?**

Such a description, however, obviously cannot be objective, but must always be meshed with one's own wishes and hopes – in my case the wish for peace and co-operative co-existence, for conditions that really deserve to be called *humane*, for living conditions in which

Und das Wort ist Fleisch geworden ...

Peter Fleissner

Anforderungen an eine humane Informationsgesellschaft

Zwischen Euphorie und Entrüstung liegt die Bandbreite der Gefühle, mit denen die Menschen auf die Anfänge der sogenannten Informationsgesellschaft reagieren. So verständlich die jeweilige emotionale Reaktion auch sein mag, so wenig Glauben in ihre Richtigkeit sollte man ihr schenken. Eine adäquatere Beurteilung kann erst aus der Distanz gelingen. In diesem Beitrag möchte ich mich der *Informationsmaschine Mensch* und ihrer gesellschaftlichen Einbettung weder mit unkritisch-optimistischer Übertreibung noch in einer kulturpessimistischen Attitude nähern, sondern Methoden aus dem Bereich der Sozial- und Kulturwissenschaften verwenden, um zu einer Einschätzung der gegenwärtigenTrends zu gelangen. In welcher Zeit leben wir? Welche Haupttrends lassen sich feststellen? Welche zentralen Problemlagen zeichnen sich ab? Welche Tendenzen sind zu erwarten?

***Wertvolle* Wissenschaft?**

Es ist andererseits offensichtlich, daß eine solche Standortbestimmung nicht objektiv sein kann, sondern immer mit den eigenen Wünschen und Hoffnungen verquickt ist, in meinem Fall mit dem

a man does not behave like a wolf to other men. This expression of my personal feelings serves as a compass and a guiding principle for a scientific analysis of the present that is bound by certain methodical standards but from which no particular ethical stance can be derived. That brings us to a core problem of contemporary science that is outwardly unbiased but which, in so being, becomes accessible for all manner of misuse. The first step to be taken by humane science should thus be expressly to disclose its underlying system of values.

So let us take a look at our world with this in mind. Looking to the rich nations of the Earth, the great significance of technological innovations is clearly illustrated. They have advanced to become the key factors of international business competition. No longer are hoards of gold, physical labour or raw materials the foundations of wealth but rather the ability to hold one's own and dominate the world market with new technological means on a global scale. Although the industrial revolution of the previous century represented an unprecedented thrust of virtuoso handling of Nature and natural materials under capitalist conditions, capable of multiplying the productivity of human labour by a factor of between ten and more than one hundred, it not only brought incredible wealth but also undreamt-of poverty upon large sections of the human race, farmers, craftsmen and workers. Personal social predicaments became a breeding-ground for the dissemination of racist anti-Semitic inhuman ideologies, guided by politicians, that were to lead to the great disasters of this century, two world wars and mass murder.

Technology as a bringer of salvation

The ambivalence of technological innovations, amplified by the social order, is not only revealed in 20th-century disaster scenarios but is also expressed in chronic problems of global dimensions. These are not least the result of the sweeping success and fast diffusion of applied natural science on a global scale. Human intervention in natural cycles has caused the greenhouse effect and the hole in the ozone layer, ground-level ozone and radioactive contamination, leading to an imperilment of the fundamental conditions of human life on our

Wunsch nach Frieden und kooperativem Zusammenleben, nach Verhältnissen, die den Namen *menschlich* wirklich verdienen, nach Lebensbedingungen, unter denen der Mensch dem Menschen nicht zum Wolf wird. Diese persönlichen Gefühlsäußerungen dienen als Kompaß und Richtschnur für eine wissenschaftliche Auseinandersetzung mit der Gegenwart, die sich bestimmten methodischen Standards verpflichtet fühlt, aber nicht aus sich heraus eine ethische Position formulieren kann. Damit sprechen wir bereits ein zentrales Problem unserer zeitgenössischen Wissenschaft an, die sich wertfrei gebärdet, gerade dadurch aber für jede mißbräuchliche Verwendung zugänglich wird. Es sollte daher für eine humane Wissenschaft ein erster notwendiger Schritt sein, das ihr zugrundeliegende Wertsystem ausdrücklich auf den Tisch zu legen.

Sehen wir also mit dieser Optik auf unsere Welt. Ein erster Blick in die reichen Länder der Erde macht die große Bedeutung von technischen Innovationen deutlich. Sie sind zum zentralen Faktor der internationalen Wirtschaftskonkurrenz aufgerückt. Nicht mehr Goldschätze, körperliche Arbeit oder Rohstoffe bilden die Grundlage des Reichtums, sondern die Fähigkeit, mit neuen technischen Mitteln in globalem Maßstab auf dem Weltmarkt bestehen und dominant werden zu können. Stellte die industrielle Revolution des vorigen Jahrhunderts unter kapitalistischen Bedingungen einen bisher nie dagewesenen Schub an virtuosem Umgang mit Natur und Naturstoffen dar, geeignet, die Produktivität menschlicher Arbeit um das Zehn- bis mehr als Hundertfache zu verstärken, brachte sie gleichzeitig mit unglaublichem Reichtum auch ungeahntes Elend über weite Teile der Menschen, über Bauern, Handwerker und Arbeiter. Gesellschaftlich erzeugte persönliche Zwangslagen wurden zum fruchtbaren Boden für die Verbreitung rassistischer, antisemitischer, menschenverachtender Ideologien, die, von Politikern organisiert, in die großen Katastrophen dieses Jahrhunderts, in zwei Weltkriege und Massenmord führten.

Technik als Heilsbringer

Die durch die gesellschaftliche Ordnung verstärkte Ambivalenz technischer Innovationen zeigt sich nicht nur in den Katastrophenszenarios des 20. Jahrhunderts, sondern äußert sich auch in den chronischen Problemen globaler Dimension. Sie sind nicht zuletzt Ergebnis des durchschlagenden Erfolgs und der raschen Diffusion angewandter Naturwissenschaft im Weltmaßstab. Der Eingriff der

planet; the promotion of the economic advance of the First World pushed ahead by the new technologies is creating social inequality in the Second and Third Worlds [which are in the process of dissolving into so-called *Reformstaaten* or former Eastern bloc countries]. This inequality is worming its way into the affluent metropolises of the world in the form of slums. Entire societies are endangered by their dependence on the omnipresence of new technology, without which they cannot exist. I do not just mean the atomic bomb or civil nuclear technology, I mean the whole banal dependence of our viability on electricity, telephones, computers and electronic networks.

The most recent progress of technology, the emergence of electronic information and communication technologies, is reflected in statements made by leading politicians and business magnates of the countries of the triad [NAFTA, EU and Japan]. They all stress the necessity of a global, trans-continental or national information infrastructure with the aid of which we could construct a new society, the information society. It would create the necessary jobs that have dwindled in recent decades along with the branches and remnants of industrialized society. All levels of the population would be able to benefit from the information society. The drastically reduced costs of information, communication and organisation would allow us to create a democratic society with little hierarchy in which there would be no room for exclusion. Difference of race, class, social stratum, sex, disability would all be concealed behind the computer screen, and the ideal of human equality and democracy could emerge the world over.

Historically, we can observe an inner kinship with statements made at the beginning of this century in which the Russian revolution evokes the humanizing effect of electrical energy with the slogan *Communism is Soviet power plus the electrification of the whole country* [Lenin 1920: 513]. The aspirations of the French Revolution for the blessings of burgeoning natural science can also be compared to contemporary politico-economic rhetoric. Technology is regarded as being the solver of all societal problems and a carrier of the hopes for paradisiac conditions.

Menschen in die natürlichen Kreisläufe führt über Treibhauseffekt und Ozonloch, über bodennahes Ozon und radioaktive Verseuchung zur Gefährdung der Voraussetzungen menschlichen Lebens auf unserem Planeten; der durch neue Technologien vorangetriebene Ausbau des ökonomischen Vorsprungs in der ersten Welt erzeugt soziale Ungleichheit in der [sich in sogenannte Reformstaaten auflösenden] zweiten und dritten Welt. Letztere schleicht sich im Gegenzug in Form von Slums in die reichen Metropolen der Erde ein. Die Allgegenwart der neuen Technik selbst wird durch die umfassende Abhängigkeit von ihr zur Gefahr für die Gesellschaften, die ohne sie nicht mehr lebensfähig sind. Dabei denke ich nicht nur an die Atombombe oder die zivile Nukleartechnik, sondern ich meine die ganz banale Abhängigkeit unserer Lebensfähigkeit von Stromversorgung, Telefon, Computern und elektronischen Netzen.

Der jüngste Entwicklungsschritt der Technik, die Entfaltung elektronischer Informations- und Kommunikationstechnologien, findet in den Äußerungen führender Politiker und Wirtschaftsbosse der Länder der Triade [NAFTA, EU und Japan] seinen Niederschlag. Sie sprechen alle von der Notwendigkeit einer globalen, kontinentweiten oder nationalen Informationsinfrastruktur, mit deren Hilfe eine neue Gesellschaft, die Informationsgesellschaft, errichtet werden könnte. Sie würde die notwendigen Jobs erzeugen, die in den letzten Jahrzehnten gleichzeitig mit den Ausläufern und fossilen Überbleibsel der Industriegesellschaft vernichtet worden wären. Alle Schichten der Bevölkerung könnten aus der Informationsgesellschaft ihre Vorteile ziehen. Die radikal verringerten Informations-, Kommunikations- und Organisationskosten machten eine hierarchiearme, demokratische Gesellschaft möglich, in der für Ausgrenzungen kein Platz wäre. Unterschiede der Rasse, Klasse, sozialen Schicht, Geschlecht, Behinderung – alles würde hinter den Computerschirmen verborgen bleiben, und die Ideale von menschlicher Gleichheit und Demokratie könnten weltweit hervortreten.

Aus historischer Sicht bemerken wir eine innere Verwandtschaft mit Äußerungen zu Beginn dieses Jahrhunderts, wo die sozialistische Revolution in Rußland auf die humanisierende Wirkung der Elektroenergie mit dem Slogan *Kommunismus – das ist Sowjetmacht plus Elektrifizierung des ganzen Landes* [Lenin 1920: 513] zurückgreift. Auch die Hoffnungen der französischen Revolution auf die Segnungen der beginnenden Naturwissenschaft las-

Current problem areas

No matter how much my personal wishes coincide with the opinions of Euro-politicians, a methodical restriction is called for. As suggested by the above examples, new technologies cannot have a humanizing effect *per se*. They merely offer an extended field of opportunities for social or personal development. Only their embeddedness in society will determine what particular paths will be taken from the range offered. In order to realise a specific potential inherent in a new technology it is first necessary to surmount various obstacles, first and foremost the politico-economic, then the social and the cultural. And that's the crux of the matter.

In the name of deregulation, the state is currently gradually passing on traditional monopolies and substantial former activities to private enterprises, on the one hand for reasons of inefficiency and excessive costs, and on the other because it maintains that public services can no longer be financed. This procedure certainly makes sense in a society in which the wealth of all individuals has greatly increased and in which services can easily be financed from the high incomes of private households. In a society of growing social differences and exclusion, deregulation can also lead to increased disintegration. Although a deregulated economy offers greater scope of action for the individual enterprise, although the strategic scope can be expanded vis-à-vis national and international rivals, and – as is the case with the release of electronic networks and phone services – because we can expect to see Internet charges drop, the national job cutback due to rationalisation and outsourcing bears no balanced relation to the number of jobs that could be created through tele-work and innovative products [under the same economic conditions]. The social decline of large sections of the population in the emerging two thirds society annuls the central precondition for a meaningful strategy of deregulation. Quite the reverse, it necessitates greater commitment by the state to cushion this socially unacceptable situation for a growing minority if society is not to be driven into a decline characterised by desperate individual predicaments, clashes over financial, intellectual and material resources, increased crime, racism, anti-Semitism and anti-women attitudes.

sen sich mit der gegenwärtigen politisch-ökonomischen Rhetorik vergleichen. Technik wird als Löser aller gesellschaftlicher Probleme und als Hoffnungsträger für paradiesische Zustände angesehen.

Gegenwärtige Problemfelder

So sehr meine privaten Wünsche mit der Meinung der Europapolitiker übereinstimmen, so sehr ist eine methodische Einschränkung angebracht: Wie auch die obigen Beispiele andeuten, können neue Technologien nicht per se eine humanisierende Wirkung entfalten. Sie bieten bloß ein erweitertes Feld der Möglichkeiten für soziale oder persönliche Entwicklung. Erst die Einbettung in die Gesellschaft legt fest, welche spezifischen Pfade sich aus den neuen Möglichkeiten realisieren werden. Zur Verwirklichung eines bestimmten Potentials, das in einer neuen Technologie steckt, müssen erst verschiedene Hürden genommen werden, allen voran die politisch-ökonomische, dann die soziale und die kulturelle. Und hier liegt der Hase im Pfeffer.

Im Namen der Deregulierung gibt der Staat derzeit Stück für Stück traditionelle Monopole und wesentliche Aktivitäten früherer Tätigkeit an private Unternehmen ab, einerseits aus Gründen von Ineffizienz und überhöhten Kosten, andererseits aber auch mit der Behauptung der Unfinanzierbarkeit öffentlicher Dienstleistungen. Diese Orientierung macht in einer Gesellschaft durchaus Sinn, wo der Reichtum aller Individuen stark angestiegen ist, wo Leistungen aus dem hohen Einkommen der privaten Haushalte leicht finanziert werden können. In einer Gesellschaft wachsender sozialer Unterschiede und Ausgrenzungen kann Deregulierung auch zu verstärkter Desintegration führen. Obwohl eine deregulierte Wirtschaft für den einzelnen Betrieb einen erhöhten Handlungsspielraum bieten und der Strategieraum gegenüber nationaler und internationaler Konkurrenz erweitert werden kann, und – wie im Falle der Freigabe von elektronischen Netzen und Telefondiensten – auch eine Reduktion der Kosten für das Internet zu erwarten ist, steht der durch Rationalisierung und Auslagerung von Arbeitsplätzen erzeugte Abbau von Jobs im Inland in keinem ausgewogenen Verhältnis zur Erzeugung neuer Arbeitsplätze, die[bei ansonsten gleichen ökonomischen Bedingungen] eventuell durch Telearbeit und innovative Produkte geschaffen werden könnten. Der soziale Abstieg großer Teile der Bevölkerung in der sich abzeichnenden Zweidrittelgesellschaft setzt die zentrale Voraussetzung für eine sinnvolle Deregulierungsstrategie außer Kraft. Im Gegenteil, er macht

Requirements for a humane information society

If real construction of the information society is to succeed, at least three preconditions must be fulfilled. First, the appropriate infrastructure must be created; second, this infrastructure must provide universal access for men and women; third, it must be possible to acquire qualifications allowing us to use the electronic networks. The order of this list of requirements is important. Fulfilling the preceding item is the precondition for being able to fulfil the next. If even just one of these prerequisites is missing, there will be a danger of further division of society already torn by differences of class and stratum.

Is the electronic infrastructure sufficient?

As we know, especially in Austria the infohighway has not yet been built up so adequately as to provide a sufficient communication infrastructure. Essentially, today's users have two grievances: firstly, phone charges are still too high [40 Austrian Schillings per hour] for less wealthy private individuals, above all young or old people, to take advantage of the Internet or other services without it being an excessive financial burden; secondly, the frequency range of existing lines is still fairly low with the effect that graphic images and videos can only be transmitted in poor quality and after prolonged waiting times. However, a development is emerging with regard to the former that is highly likely to bring about a considerable reduction in charges. The Post Office is expected to reduce charges for data transmissions to 10 Austrian Schillings per hour as of Autumn 1997 – in anticipation of future rival services that will be set up according to EU law as of 1st January 1998 when the state monopoly on phone calls ceases to apply.

At the same time, other clusters of companies are waiting to enter the marketplace as network providers. The biggest cable TV company, Telekabel, will provide former TV consumers with a permanent Internet link via its private network with the aid of a few relatively inexpensive addons, at a fraction of previous costs. The Austrian Federal Railways and the electric supply companies [both with nation-wide cable lines] will also take advantage of the needs of the moment and offer their infrastructure on the market. So

ein verstärktes Engagement des Staates zur Abfederung der sozial unzumutbaren Situation für eine wachsende Minderheit nötig, soll die Gesellschaft nicht letztlich in einen Zerfall getrieben werden, der durch verzweifelte individuelle Notlagen, harte Auseinandersetzungen um finanzielle, geistige und stoffliche Ressourcen, erhöhte Kriminalität, Rassismus, Antisemitismus und Frauenfeindlichkeit gekennzeichnet sein wird.

Voraussetzungen für eine humane Informationsgesellschaft

Soll die reale Konstruktion der Informationsgesellschaft gelingen, müssen mindestens drei Voraussetzungen erfüllt werden: Erstens bedarf es einer entsprechenden Infrastruktur, zweitens muß diese Infrastruktur universellen Zugang für jede Frau und jedermann erlauben, drittens muß sichergestellt sein, daß der Erwerb einer entsprechenden Qualifikation die Benützung der elektronischen Netze ermöglicht. Bei der Aufzählung dieser drei Forderungen ist die Reihenfolge wichtig: Die Erfüllung des jeweils vorher angegebenen Punktes ist Voraussetzung für die Möglichkeit der Erfüllung des folgenden. Fehlt nur eine dieser drei Voraussetzungen, droht eine weitere Spaltung der Gesellschaft, die schon bisher durch Klassen- und Schichtengegensätze zerrissen ist.

Ist die elektronische Infrastruktur hinreichend?

Wie wir wissen, ist gerade in Österreich der Datenhighway noch nicht so stark ausgebaut, daß er eine ausreichende Kommunikationsinfrastruktur darstellen würde. Die Klagen der derzeitigen Nutzer gehen in zwei Richtungen: Einerseits sind die Telefongebühren noch viel zu hoch [40 Schilling pro Stunde], daß auch weniger zahlungskräftige private Personen, vor allem Jugendliche oder ältere, ohne übertriebene Belastungen das Internet oder andere Dienste nützen könnten, andererseits ist die Bandbreite der vorhandenen Strecken noch ziemlich niedrig, so daß vor allem Graphiken oder Videos nur in mangelhafter Qualität und nach langem Warten übertragen werden können. Immerhin bahnt sich bezüglich des ersten Punkts eine Entwicklung an, die mit hoher Wahrscheinlichkeit zu einer Reduktion der Gebühren führen wird. Die Post senkt ab Herbst 1997 die Kosten für Datenübertragungen auf voraussichtlich 10 Schilling pro Stunde. Damit beantwortet sie vorauseilend künftige Konkurrenzangebote, die durch den Wegfall des staatlichen Monopols für

we can expect to see electronic network connection charges drop rapidly due to competition and increased demand.

What is more, in a few years' time international syndicates will have low-flying earth satellites [IRIDIUM with 77 satellites, Bill Gates' TELEDISC with allegedly in excess of 800 satellites, INMARSAT with slightly higher-lying 12 satellites, and finally GLOBALSTAR, favoured by the EU, with 48 planned artificial satellites are in planning] [Ege/Fleissner 1995: 27]. Basically, the network of the future should be accessible at reasonable prices and should possess the necessary frequency range. Within its ACTS programme [Advanced Communication Technologies and Services], the EU is planning to create the conditions for an extremely fast electronic infrastructure for the information society, above all on the basis of photon technologies in glass fibre lines [Fabianek et al 1997: 54]. The first field trials are already underway and are planned to venture into frequency ranges of 40 gigabits per second, i.e. roughly 300 times faster than current Post Office lines with 155 megabits or 34 megabits per second [Fleissner et al 1996: 258-259].

It can be safely assumed that the necessary infrastructure will no longer be made available by the state as a monopolist provider – as has been the case in the last one hundred years – but rather by competing private companies. But the state should not withdraw completely. It will still be urgently needed to formulate and monitor technological standards and adequate quality of services; what is more, the state – who else? – must ensure fair access conditions and blanket supply so as to avoid any blank areas on the network map.

Universal access?

In order to obtain a realistic assessment of the extent to which electronic networks are actually used it is helpful to take a look at the empirical structure of the users. In Austria there are no precise data. The number of users will probably be something like 300,000, the vast majority being students and teaching staff at universities, public administration and major software and hardware company employees. So far, proportionately, private households have been of secondary significance. Going by that, around five per cent of the Austrian population ➡

symposium

Telefondienste per 1. Jänner 1998 nach EU-Recht entstehen werden.

Gleichzeitig warten schon andere Unternehmenscluster auf ihren Markteintritt als Netzanbieter. Die größte Kabelfernsehgesellschaft Telekabel wird über ihr privates Netz mittels relativ billiger Zusatzgeräte den bisherigen TV-Konsumenten um einen Bruchteil der bisherigen Kosten eine permanente Verbindung zum Internet ermöglichen können. Die Österreichischen Bundesbahnen und die Elektrizitätsversorgungsunternehmen [beide verfügen über landesweite Kabelstrecken] werden das Gebot der Stunde ebenfalls nützen und ihre Infrastruktur auf dem Markt anbieten. Es ist also zu erwarten, daß durch Konkurrenz und erhöhtes Angebot die Preise für Verbindungen zu elektronischen Netzen rapide fallen werden.

Zusätzlich wird es in einigen Jahren von internationalen Konsortien Systeme tieffliegender Erdsatelliten geben [in Planung sind derzeit IRIDIUM mit 77 Satelliten, TELEDISC von Bill Gates mit angeblich mehr als 800 Satelliten, INMARSAT mit etwas höher positionierten 12 Satelliten, und schließlich GLOBALSTAR, von der EU favorisiert, mit 48 geplanten künstlichen Erdtrabanten], die globale Telefon- und Datenverbindungen erlauben [Ege/ Fleissner 1995: 27]. Insgesamt dürfte das Netz in Zukunft sowohl zu vernünftigen Preisen benützt werden können als auch die nötige Bandbreite vorhanden sein. Die EU plant im Rahmen des ACTS Programms [*Advanced Communication Technologies and Services*] die Voraussetzungen für eine extrem schnelle elektronische Infrastruktur für die Informationsgesellschaft, vor allem auf der Basis von Photonentechnologien in Glasfaserstrecken [Fabianek et al. 1997: 54]. Erste Feldversuche sind bereits implementiert und sollen in Bandbreiten von 40 Gigabit pro Sekunde vorstoßen, also rund 300 mal schneller als die derzeit in Betrieb befindlichen Strecken der Post von 155 Megabit bzw. 34 Megabit pro Sekunde [Fleissner et al. 1996: 258-259].

Es ist als sicher anzunehmen, daß die nötige Infrastruktur nicht mehr – wie in den letzten hundert Jahren – vom Staat als Monopolisten angeboten werden wird, sondern von privaten Unternehmungen, die einander konkurrenzieren. Der Staat sollte sich aber dennoch nicht komplett zurückziehen. Er wird für die Formulierung und Kontrolle der technischen Standards und einer hinreichenden Qualität der Dienstleistungen nach wie vor dringend gebraucht, außerdem muß er – wer sonst? – faire Zugangsbedingungen und eine flächendeckende

is currently on the net [1997]. The trend is rising, and with costs dropping and frequency ranges expanding, private PC owners [supposedly around a quarter of all private Austrian households own a computer] will increasingly start buying modems and net connections.

In the United States, the pioneer in all things connected with electronic networks, this trend towards mass private use can already be evidenced empirically. The dynamism in this case is very much akin to the telephone. Where once the telephone was limited to the world of business, it soon spread as a medium of family communication for gossipmongering between members of local neighbourhoods, above all farmer's wives, in big cities and small towns across America [Flichy 1994: 152]. This, then, was the foundation stone of mass, i.e. profitable, use. It would seem that this story is now being repeated with the Internet in the US. According to an empirical American study by Control Data [1995], the main focus of Internet use, at least in terms of email, was initially in the public sector. 83 per cent of employees of public facilities used email, compared to only 62 per cent of private company employees [CONSUME 1995]. At the beginning of 1996 it was discerned that 63 per cent of all users were using the net for work at home [cf. http://etrg.findsvp.com/internet/demograph.html], and that 69 per cent have an Internet link at home [only 48% at work and 21% at school]. In the US we are hearing reports of a boom among senior citizens. As net connections spread through the general public, the average age is increasing more slowly [26 at the beginning of 1996], a fact corroborated by the higher percentage of women, 35 per cent. The average income of Internet users is $ 61,500, i.e. in the high-income bracket, which is also backed up by the large percentage of white participants, 83 per cent. We can expect to see the average income drop, whereas the percentage of women and the average age will continue to rise.

Various results that correspond to the previous conditions in the US can be found in Germany [see <http://www.w3b.de> for latest survey results]. In 1996 the percentage of schoolgoers [5.8%], students [29.8%], graduate students studying for doctorate [5.1%], and public officials [3.9%] totalled 45 per cent of the overall Internet clientele, while employees made up

Versorgung sicherstellen, sollen nicht weiße Flecken auf der Netzlandkarte entstehen.

Universeller Zugang?

Um eine realistische Einschätzung zu gewinnen, wie weit elektronische Netzwerke tatsächlich genützt werden, ist ein Blick auf die empirische Struktur der NutzerInnen hilfreich. In Österreich existieren keine präzisen Daten. Man wird von rund 300.000 NutzerInnen ausgehen können, wobei der überwiegende Teil durch Studierende und Lehrpersonal an den Universitäten, der öffentlichen Verwaltung und den Beschäftigten großer Unternehmen im Hard- und Softwarebereich repräsentiert wird. Die privaten Haushalte spielen bisher anteilsmäßig eine untergeordnete Rolle. Danach wären derzeit [1997] etwa fünf Prozent der österreichischen Bevölkerung im Netz. Die Tendenz ist steigend, bei sinkenden Kosten und erhöhter Bandbreite werden die privaten PC-Besitzer [angeblich hat hierzulande derzeit rund ein Viertel der Haushalte einen Personalcomputer zur Verfügung] zunehmend ein Modem und einen Netzanschluß erwerben.

In den USA, dem Vorreiter in Sachen elektronischer Vernetzung, läßt sich dieser Trend zur massenhaften privaten Nutzung bereits empirisch nachweisen. Damit zeigt sich eine ähnliche Dynamik wie beim Telefon. War das Telefon zuallererst auf den geschäftlichen Bereich beschränkt, verbreitete es sich rasch als Medium für Familienkommunikation, worüber in den amerikanischen Groß- und Kleinstädten Klatsch und Tratsch zwischen den Mitgliedern lokaler Nachbarschaften, vor allem zwischen Bauersfrauen, ausgetauscht wurden [Flichy 1994: 152]. Damit war der Grundstein für einen massenhaften und damit profitablen Einsatz gelegt. Diese Geschichte scheint sich in den USA jetzt auch für das Internet zu wiederholen: Zunächst lag – trotz deutlich zunehmender kommerzieller Server und wesentlich weiterer Verbreitung – der Schwerpunkt der Nutzung des Internet, zumindest was E-mail betrifft, im öffentlichen Bereich, so eine US-amerikanische empirische Studie von Control Data [1995]. 83 Prozenz der Mitarbeiter von öffentlichen Einrichtungen verwendeten E-mail, bei privaten Unternehmungen waren es demgegenüber nur 62 Prozent [CONSUME 1995]. Anfang 1996 konnte festgestellt werden [siehe <http:// etrg.findsvp.com/internet/demograph.html>], daß bereits 63 Prozent das Netz zur Arbeit in ihren eigenen vier Wänden nützen, 69 Prozent haben einen Zugang zum Netz von daheim [dagegen nur 47 Prozent aus dem Unternehmen und 21 Prozent aus der Schule]. In den

36 per cent. Self-employed persons made up 13 per cent. 45 per cent of all accesses were via university or school, 38 per cent via the employer. At 17 per cent, private access was still fairly low. The usual statement that the Internet is chiefly used by people with a high level of education is also reflected in the German survey: 78.4 per cent of users were high-school graduates [Abitur] in 1996. The relation between the sexes is still distorted in favour of men, although the trend is dropping [FRG: 1995 94%, 1996 91% men]. In Germany, the average age has increased from 29 [1995] to 30 [1996].

So we can hardly speak of universal access to the Internet in Germany and Austria, as is the case with television and, to a great extent, with the telephone.

There are also considerable disparities on a global scale. The main activity of electronic networking is taking place in the major American metropolises, followed by European and Japanese cities and their links. Africa and Latin America are practically blank areas on the global map. So McLuhan's buzzword of the *global village* [McLuhan 1995] will have to wait a while before it becomes reality [only 10 per cent of net users lived in the country in the US at the start of 1996, the majority was located in cities or their immediate surroundings].

Higher education or reduced demands?

Even if costs are reduced and even if user friendliness is considerably enhanced, the education barrier will still be a selection factor favouring the highly-qualified, young and wealthy of this world. There would appear to be two paths to widening net access that are not necessarily mutually exclusive. The first is to reduce the qualifications needed to use net technologies, the second, by reverse, would be to put higher qualifications within the reach of larger sections of the population. Strategies in the vein of the first path would include striving to expand broadband networks in connection with compression technologies or, as an alternative, developing software for easy, safe money transfer in combination with simple searching and ordering facilities on the net. On the one hand, by means of video on demand or interactive virtual reality [electronically mediated encounter between people in virtual space], allowing three-dimensional navigation with

USA wird von einem Boom bei den RentnerInnen berichtet. Mit wachsender Ausdehnung der Netzanschlüsse auf die Gesamtbevölkerung wächst das Durchschnittsalter langsam an [Anfang 1966 36 Jahre], was auch durch den höheren Frauenanteil von 35 Prozent bestätigt wird. Das Durchschnittseinkommen der Internetter liegt mit 61.500 $ bei den gut Verdienenden, worauf auch die hohe Beteiligungsrate von Personen weißer Hautfarbe von 83% hinweist. Es ist zu erwarten, daß in Zukunft das Durchschnittseinkommen fallen, der Frauenanteil und das Durchschnittsalter weiter steigen werden.

Unterschiedliche Resultate, die den früheren Verhältnissen in den USA entsprechen, finden sich in der Bundesrepublik Deutschland [für jeweils neue Umfrageergebnisse siehe <http://www.w3b.de>]. 1996 stellten Schüler [5.8%], Studenten [29.8%], Doktoranden [5.1%] und Beamte [3.9%] in Summe fast 45 Prozent der Internetklientel, die Angestellten machten 36 Prozent aus. Die Selbständigen waren mit 13 Prozent vertreten. Der Zugang erfolgte mit 45 Prozent über die Universität bzw. die Schule, mit 38 Prozent über den Arbeitgeber. Der private Zugang lag mit 17 Prozent noch ziemlich niedrig. Die übliche Aussage, daß das Internet vor allem von Menschen mit hohem Bildungsstand genützt wird, zeigt sich auch in der deutschen Umfrage: 78.4 Prozent der Nutzer besaßen 1996 das Abitur. Die Geschlechterrelation ist immer noch zugunsten der Männer verzerrt, jedoch mit abnehmender Tendenz [BRD: 1995 94%, 1996 91% Männeranteil]. In der BRD stieg das Durchschnittalter erst von 29 Jahren[1995] auf 30 Jahre [1996].

Von einem universellen Zugang, wie er beim Fernsehen und auch weitgehend beim Telefon vorliegt, ist also beim Internet in der BRD und in Österreich noch keine Rede.

Auch im Weltmaßstab zeigen sich beachtliche Disparitäten. Die Hauptaktivität elektronischer Vernetzung findet sich innerhalb der großen amerikanischen Metropolen, gefolgt von den europäischen und japanischen Großstädten und deren Querverbindungen. Afrika und Lateinamerika stellen beinahe weiße Flecken auf der Weltkarte dar. McLuhans Schlagwort vom *Globalen Dorf* [McLuhan 1995] wird daher noch einige Zeit auf seine Realisierung warten müssen [in den USA leben Anfang 1996 nur 10 Prozent der Netznutzer auf dem Lande, die Mehrheit befindet sich in den Städten oder in deren unmittelbarer Umgebung].

the aid of 3D glasses or a head mounted display], the net would be brought into line with television entertainment services, while on the other it would be opened up for mass electronic trade. So the first path could greatly enlarge the demand for net services.

But entertainment and commerce are not the only possible factors for extending use of the net. The second strategy, that proceeds on the basis of increasing the qualifications of the population, would also have the advantage of intensifying the flow of fountains of wealth and culture. There is no limit to the possibilities. I am not just thinking about increasing vocational qualifications [which would above all serve the business world], but also the good old notion of education that was closely linked with humanity. Particularly in an age in which the isolation of the individual is becoming more and more frequent as an empirical phenomenon, in which we hear about increased competition and growing desolidarisation, educational measures would indeed be very important. They could help create a climate characterised by tolerance, co-operation, harmonious and peaceful human relations, in which curiosity and creativity are promoted. On this basis it would be possible to make more humane the new electronic spaces opened up for us by technology, cyberspace and hypertexts, multi-user dungeons and Internet relay chats, the multimedia facilities and video on demand and to fill them with humanity, not least for the commercial benefit of companies and to the advantage of society as a whole on its way towards a sustainable development, without pogroms or wars. Fulfilling the aforementioned demands in terms of infrastructure, accessibility and qualifications is the minimum requirement for a humane information society. However, we must be careful. Even the very best infrastructure setting offers no guarantee that negative traits will not force their way to the fore. Central monitoring, authoritarian governments, racist legislation – essentially, everything is possible with the aid of modern networks. Only humane social policy on as wide an international footing as possible will make it possible to utilise these technological structures in such as way as to contribute to general public welfare.

Höhere Bildung oder Senkung der Anforderungen?

Selbst wenn die Kosten fallen und die Benutzerfreundlichkeit wesentlich verbessert wird, bleibt die Bildungsbarriere immer noch ein Selektionsfaktor, durch den die hochqualifizierten, jungen und begüterten Menschen dieser Erde bevorzugt werden. Für die weitere Ausdehnung der Netznutzung zeichnen sich zwei Wege ab, die einander nicht ausschließen. Der erste besteht in einer Senkung der qualifikatorischen Anforderungen beim Gebrauch der Netztechnologien, der zweite umgekehrt in der Vermittlung höherer Qualifikationen an weite Kreise der Bevölkerung. Auf dem ersten Weg lägen etwa Strategien, die den Ausbau von Breitbandnetzwerken in Verbindung mit Kompressionstechnologien anstreben, oder, als eine weitere Möglichkeit, die Entwicklung einer Software für einfachen und sicheren Geldtransfer in Kombination mit robusten und simplen Such- und Bestellmöglichkeiten im Netz. Einerseits würde das Netz durch das Angebot von Video-on-Demand oder interaktiver Virtueller Realität [die elektronisch vermittelte Begegnung von Menschen in virtuellen Räumen, die dreidimensionale Navigation ermöglichen, etwa mittels einer 3D-Brille oder einem Head Mounted Display] an das Unterhaltungsangebot des Fernsehens angeglichen, andererseits würde es dem massenhaften elektronischen Handel geöffnet. Der erste Weg könnte also die Nachfrage nach Netzdiensten stark ausdehnen.

Unterhaltung und Kommerz sind aber nicht die einzigen möglichen Faktoren zur Ausweitung der Netznutzung. Die zweite Strategie, die von einer Erhöhung der Qualifikation der Bevölkerung ausgeht, hätte den zusätzlichen Vorteil, daß sie die Springquellen des Reichtums und der Kultur zu verstärktem Fließen anregen würde. Der Phantasie sind in dieser Hinsicht keine Grenzen gesetzt. Ich denke dabei nicht nur an die Erhöhung der beruflichen Qualifikation [die vor allem der Wirtschaft dient], sondern an den guten alten Bildungsbegriff, der enge Kontakte zur Humanität unterhielt. Gerade in einer Zeit, wo die Vereinzelung der Individuen verstärkt als empirisches Phänomen auftritt, wo von erhöhter Konkurrenz und von zunehmender Entsolidarisierung die Rede ist, wären Bildungsmaßnahmen von besonderer Bedeutung. Sie könnten mithelfen, ein Klima zu schaffen, das sich durch Toleranz, Kooperation, durch harmonisch und friedlich gestaltete zwischenmenschliche Beziehungen auszeichnet, in der Neugier und Kreativität stimuliert werden. Auf dieser Basis ließen sich die neuen elektronischen Räume,

Where does this fascination come from?

So far, I have opted for a viewpoint that takes into account rational human behaviour. But can such a viewpoint suffice? Doesn't such an approach to the world that is based upon logical human considerations soon lose sight of the world of emotions, yearnings and hopes? Do these sentences, sicklied o'ver with the pale cast of thought', say it all? The media environment says otherwise. Full of euphoria the mass media are picking up on the first steps in the implementation of hyperspace with neologisms such as information superhighway, teleworking, teleshopping and telebanking. The fascination of the mass media and the general public with this subject, I feel, cannot be explained by means of economic or political motives alone. I suspect that this fascination with electronic networks is driven by some historico-cultural force that, despite all modern science, is still fed by the Christian mythical awareness of the developed world in connection with a particular type of personality, the narcissistic personality. This driving force is taking on a more concrete form in an age in which human society on this planet is in an existential crisis and that is thus more susceptible to change [but also to polarization] than ever before. The self-release of the human being from actual and imagined dependencies is reaching a new level. Our survival is not only endangered by the success of traditional industrial mechanical, chemical and electrical technologies. Today man's identity is under debate in two concrete respects, on the one hand as a result of genetic engineering that tamper with the natural biological outfit of the human being and, on the other, due to the new information technologies that are beginning to call into question man's status and self-esteem as the only living being endowed with intelligence and the capacity for thought.

In view of these problems we will see wishes washed up to the surface of society and made practically viable, with all the illusions connected with them, wishes that to date were impossible to fulfil. A process of implementation of religious fantasies in day-to-day human life is being continued, a process that originated in the appearance of markets and money. The Last Judgement is becoming the present in the market, the good are rewarded, the bad punished. In money, the divine power descends to

die uns von der Technik her geöffnet wurden, der Cyberspace und die Hypertexte, die Multi-User-Dungeons und die Internet-Relay-Chats, das Multimediaangebot und Video-on-Demand, human gestalten und mit menschenwürdigen Inhalten füllen, nicht zuletzt auch zum kommerziellen Vorteil der Unternehmen und zum Vorteil der gesamten Gesellschaft in Richtung einer nachhaltigen Entwicklung, ohne Pogrome oder Kriege.

Die Erfüllung der hier genannten Anforderungen an Infrastruktur, Zugänglichkeit und Qualifikation bildet ein Minimalpaket als Voraussetzung für eine humane Informationsgesellschaft. Allerdings ist Vorsicht angebracht. Auch der beste infrastrukturelle Rahmen bietet keine Garantie dafür, daß sich nicht negative Züge in den Vordergrund drängen. Zentrale Überwachung, autoritäre Regierungen, rassistische Gesetzgebung – alles ist auch im Prinzip mit den modernsten Netzen möglich. Erst eine menschenfreundliche Gesellschaftspolitik auf einer möglichst breiten internationalen Basis wird die technischen Strukturen so nutzbar machen, daß sie zum Glück der Menschen positiv beitragen.

Woher kommt die Faszination?

Bisher habe ich eine Sicht gewählt, die vor allem das rationale Verhalten der Menschen berücksichtigt. Reicht aber eine solche Sicht hin? Gerät einer auf logischen Überlegungen der Menschen fußenden Annäherung an die Welt nicht der Bereich der Emotionen, der Sehnsüchte und Hoffnungen, aus dem Blickfeld? Ist mit diesen von des Gedankens Blässe angekränkelten Sätzen schon alles gesagt? Die mediale Umgebung spricht eine andere Sprache: Euphorisch greifen die Massenmedien die ersten Schritte der Realisierung des Hyperspace mit Wortschöpfungen wie Information-Highway, Datenautobahn, Tele-Working, Tele-Shopping oder Tele-Banking auf. Die Faszination der Massenmedien wie des Publikums durch dieses Thema ist meiner Meinung nach nicht allein mit ökonomischen oder politischen Motiven zu erklären. Ich vermute hinter der Faszination an den elektronischen Netzen eine kulturhistorische Triebkraft, die trotz aller modernen Wissenschaft aus dem christlich geprägten mythischen Bewußtsein der entwickelten Welt in Verbindung mit einem Persönlichkeitstypus, der narzistischen Persönlichkeit, gespeist wird. Diese Triebkraft konkretisiert sich in einer Zeit, in der sich die menschliche Gesellschaft auf diesem Planeten in einer bestands-

Earth and lives among us, a power that according to Feuerbach [first edition, quoted from 1957: 371] is a fantastic expression of the human being and, according to Marx and Engels [1845: quoted from 1971: 27], of Man the social being. So anyone can have a bit of divinity in his wallet, i.e. the potential of human activity that can be updated through work. Cyberspace and the electronic networks provide food for other notions of God's attributes – that of omniscience and omnipresence. With that – taking into account all the ambivalence of this comparison – the words of the serpent in the first book of Moses are fulfilled when it promises Man in paradise: *Ye shall be as gods* [Gen. 3:5]. Unfortunately, all of God's attributes have not come down to Earth yet. Wisdom, mercy and love have yet to come.

CONSUME: *Newsletter 3*/1995, vol. 107, Vienna July 1995

EGE, B., and P. FLEISSNER: Gehört die Zukunft den Satelliten?. In: Hernsteiner, Fachzeitschrift für Management, No. 4, 1995: 26-27

FABIANEK, B., K. FITCHEW, ST. MYKEN, A. HOUGHTON: *Optical Network Research and Development in European Community Programs*: From RACE to ACTS. In: IEEE Communications Magazine, April 1997: 50-56

FEUERBACH, L.: *Das Wesen des Christentums*, Reclam, Leipzig 1957

FLEISSNER, P., W. HOFKIRCHNER, H. MÜLLER, M. POHL, CH. STARY: *Der Mensch lebt nicht vom Bit allein*, Peter Lang, Frankfurt am Main etc. 1996

FLICHY, P.: *Tele-Geschichte der modernen Telekommunikation*, Campus Verlag, Frankfurt/New York, Éditions de la Fondation Maison des Sciences de l'Homme, Paris 1996

LENIN, W. I., *Bericht über die Tätigkeit des Rats der Volkskommissare*, 22. Dezember 1920, in: Lenin, W. I., Werke, Band 31, Dietz Verlag, Berlin 1962: 483-515

MCLUHAN, M., B. R. POWERS, *The Global Village: Transformations in World Life and Media in the 21st Century*, Oxford: University Press, 1989

MARX, K., ENGELS, F.: *Selected works*, Progress Verlag, Moscow 1971

gefährdenden Krise befindet und daher für Veränderung [aber auch für Polarisierungen] zugänglicher wird als zuvor. Die Selbstfreisetzung der Menschen aus den tatsächlichen und gedachten Abhängigkeiten erreicht eine neue Stufe. Unser Überleben wird nicht nur durch den Erfolg der traditionellen industriellen mechanischen, chemischen und elektrischen Technologien gefährdet. Heute steht die Identität des Menschen in zweierlei Hinsicht konkret zur Debatte, einerseits durch die Gentechnologie, die an der naturwüchsigen biologischen Ausstattung der Menschen rührt, andererseits durch neue Informationstechnologien, die Stellung und Selbstwertgefühl der Menschen als einzige lebende Wesen mit Intelligenz und Denken zu hinterfragen beginnen.

Angesichts dieser Probleme werden Wünsche, die bisher keine Realisierungschance hatten, mit allen Illusionen, die damit auch hochkommen, an die Oberfläche der Gesellschaft gespült und in der Praxis wirksam. Ein Prozeß der Umsetzung religiöser Phantasie in den menschlichen Alltag setzt sich fort, der mit der Erscheinung des Marktes und des Geldes seinen Ausgang nahm. Das jüngste Gericht wird zur Gegenwart im Markt, die Guten werden belohnt, die Bösen bestraft. Im Geld steigt die göttliche Macht, die laut Feuerbach [Erstausgabe 1841, zitiert aus 1957: 371] das menschliche Wesen, laut Marx und Engels [1845, zitiert aus 1971: 27] das gesellschaftliche Wesen der Menschen in phantastischer Weise zum Ausdruck bringt, auf die Erde herab und wohnt unter uns. Jeder kann daher ein Stückchen Göttlichkeit, sprich, das Potential menschlicher Tätigkeit, über Arbeit aktualisierbar, in der Geldbörse mit sich herumtragen. Der Cyberspace und die elektronischen Netze bedienen weitere Vorstellungen von den Eigenschaften Gottes: Die der Allwissenheit und der Allgegenwart. Damit geht – in aller zu berücksichtigenden Ambivalenz – das Wort der Schlange aus dem Ersten Buch Moses in Erfüllung, die den Menschen im Paradies verheißen hat: *Ihr werdet sein wie Gott!* [1. Mose 3.5]. Leider sind noch immer nicht alle Eigenschaften Gottes auf die Erde herabgefallen. Immer noch fehlen Weisheit, Barmherzigkeit und Liebe.

Humanistic Intelligence

Steve Mann

One of the fundamental contrasts between free democratic societies and totalitarian systems is that the totalitarian government [or other organization] relies on secrecy for the regime but high surveillance and disclosure for all other groups, whereas in the civic culture of liberal democracy, the position is approximately the reverse.

From Simon Davies [pertaining to the massive 1987 Australian campaign against a national ID card]

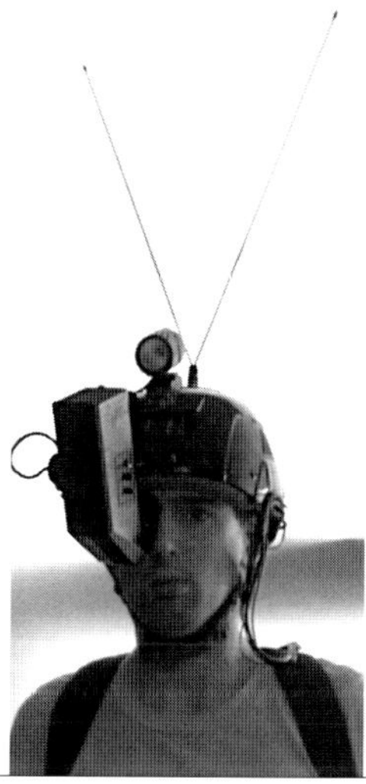

Fig. 1
My 1970s effort at building a personal information space which culminated in this apparatus of 1980.]
Meine in den siebziger Jahren unternommenen Anstrengungen zur Schaffung eines persönlichen Informationsraums fanden ihren Höhepunkt in der Schaffung dieses Geräts aus dem Jahr 1980.

symposium

Humanistic Intelligence

Steve Mann

Einer der grundlegenden Unterschiede zwischen freien demokratischen Gesellschaften und totalitären Systemen liegt in der Tatsache, daß im Falle einer totalitären Regierung [bzw. jeder anderen totalitären Organisation] das Regime für sich Verschwiegenheit und Geheimhaltung in Anspruch nimmt, während alle anderen Gruppen strenger Überwachung und Offenlegung unterworfen sind, wohingegen in der bürgerlichen Kultur einer liberalen Demokratie mehr oder weniger das genaue Gegenteil der Fall ist.

Simon Davies [über die massive Kampagne, die in Australien 1987 gegen die Einführung eines nationalen Personalausweises gestartet wurde]

Einleitung

Als *Lösung* für das Problem der ständig zunehmenden Kriminalität wird uns nur zu oft eine verstärkte Überwachung präsentiert, anstatt das Übel an der Wurzel zu packen, also etwa gegen den Bindungsverlust innerhalb der Gemeinschaft vorzugehen.

Viele Menschen meinen, daß die Gewalt in den Städten – wie auch andere Formen von Verbrechen – dazu geführt hat, daß die Anwendung etwa

Introduction

Increased surveillance is often presented as a *solution* to increased crime, instead of solving the problem at its source, such as by mitigating loss of community connectedness.

Urban violence, and other forms of crime, have made it necessary, in some people's opinion, to dramatically escalate the use of measures, such as surveillance. These measures, which are brought on by large organizations, threaten the existence of a free and democratic society.

Overtly violent crimes in New York city, for example, have appeared to be less frequent, but much of this has been accomplished through the rolling back of civil liberties. Random searches, *no-knock* entry, and, most notably, increased surveillance, have ushered in a new world order of *law and order*.

The recent proliferation of video surveillance cameras, interconnected with high speed computers and central databases is moving us toward a high-speed *surveillance superhighway*. Cameras are used throughout entire cities [such as Liverpool and Baltimore] to monitor citizens in all public areas.

With other forms of one-sided surveillance such as fingerprinting of welfare recipients and see-through-clothing cameras for *securing buildings from employee theft* and *for police to covertly monitor crowds for weapons* [Nowhere to Hide by Joe Constance, <http://www.ingersoll-rand.com/compair/octnov96/radar.htm>], architects of the *surveillance superhighway* promise us a future of reduced crime, while at the same time construct for us a future of reduced accountability for themselves.

The city has become a frightening place, and drastic *solutions* are stepped up to meet in equilibrium with the *drastic problems.* A goal of my work is to challenge both sides of this equilibrium, which appear to feed on one another.

It is arguably true that organizations that use totalitarian video surveillance tend to have fewer overtly violent crimes. What I mean by totalitarian video surveillance is that the video signal is observable by only a select group, and that accountability is denied through restrictions on the collection of video by others.

von Überwachungsmaßnahmen drastisch ausgeweitet werden muß. Derartige Maßnahmen, die von großen Organisationen unterstützt werden, bedrohen jedoch den Fortbestand einer freien und demokratischen Gesellschaft.

So hat sich z. B. herausgestellt, daß die Anzahl der schweren Gewaltverbrechen in New York City zurückgegangen ist. Dieser Rückgang ist allerdings großteils auf die Beschneidung der Freiheiten der Bürger zurückzuführen. Das Recht der Behörden, stichprobenartig Untersuchungen durchzuführen und ohne jegliche Formalitäten in die Wohnungen der Bürger einzudringen, wie auch insbesondere eine verstärkte Überwachung haben eine neue Weltordnung eingeleitet, die auf *Recht und Ordnung* basiert.

Die jüngste Zunahme von Überwachungskameras, die mit Hochgeschwindigkeitscomputern und zentralen Datenbanken verbunden sind, führt uns in Richtung eines Hochgeschwindigkeits-*Überwachungs-Superhighways*.

In manchen Städten [wie Liverpool und Baltimore] werden Kameras im gesamten Stadtgebiet eingesetzt, um die Bürger in allen öffentlichen Räumen zu überwachen.

Die Architekten dieses *Überwachungs-Superhighways* versprechen uns, daß es durch den Einsatz weiterer einseitiger Überwachungsmethoden, wie das Abnehmen der Fingerabdrücke von Sozialhilfeempfängern und den Einsatz von Durchleuchtungsgeräten zum *Schutz von Gebäuden vor Diebstählen durch Angestellte* und zur *verdeckten polizeilichen Durchsuchung von Menschenmassen auf Waffen* dienen [*Nowhere to Hide* von Joe Constance, <http://www.ingersoll-rand.com/compair/octnov96/radar.htm>], künftig weniger Kriminalität geben wird, während sie für uns zugleich eine Zukunft entwerfen, in der sie selbst immer weniger Verantwortung für ihr Tun übernehmen müssen.

Die Stadt ist zu einem angsteinflößenden Ort geworden, und ohnehin bereits drastische *Lösungen* werden noch weiter verschärft, um ein Gleichgewicht mit den *drastischen Problemen* herzustellen. Ein Ziel meiner Arbeit besteht nun darin, beide Seiten dieses Gleichgewichts zu hinterfragen, von denen offensichtlich jede für die Eskalation der jeweils anderen verantwortlich ist.

Es ist möglicherweise wahr, daß es in Organisationen mit totalitärer Videoüberwachung weniger Gewaltverbrechen gibt. Und unter totalitärer Videoüberwachung verstehe ich, daß das Videosignal nur von einer auserwählten Gruppe empfangen werden kann, die anderen den Zugang zu derartigen Video-

A Mafia-run gambling casino might be the most extreme example of a totalitarian video surveillance environment [e.g. that the casino wants to know everything about everyone but reveal nothing about itself]. In such an organization one would not expect to find any overt physical violence but there still might be occasional *disappearances* of those not favorable to the organization.

Many department stores also use video surveillance extensively, yet prohibit others from using cameras in their establishments. A goal of my work is to provide a technological framework to challenge such restrictions. A top-down panopticon-like surveillance hierarchy tends to make Jeremy Bentham's philosophy a self-fulfilling one. The sense of community that once existed, whether in the form of close-knit communities or the more modern *neighbourhood watch* [e.g. trust in other members of the community], has been replaced by absolute trust in governments, large corporations, or other unseen authorities, analogous to the unseen guard in Bentham's watch-tower.

An important goal of my work is to set forth a foundation that I call *Humanistic Intelligence* [H.I.] as a basis for the existential principle of self-determination and mastery over our own destiny, as well as the humanistic notion of self-actualization.

Humanistic Intelligence differs from Artificial Intelligence in the sense that the goal is to *become* intelligent, through prostheses of sorts, rather than be replaced or disenfranchised by intelligent machines. Thus H.I. challenges the notion of environmental intelligence and ubiquitous surveillance. Rather than *smart rooms*, *smart floors*, *smart ceilings*, *smart toilets*, *smart light switches*, etc., H.I. puts forth the notion of *smart people*.

An important goal of H.I. is to take a first step toward a foremost principle of the Enlightenment, that of the dignity of the individual. This is accomplished through a prosthetic transformation of the body into a sovereign space.

Past and present works

With fascism, the trains run on time, crime is low, and morale is high.

I constructed a series of reflectionist and diffusionist [Reflectionism and Diffusionism: new tactics for

überwachungssystemen untersagt und sich dadurch weigert, ihnen gegenüber Rechenschaft abzulegen.

Das extremste Beispiel für eine totalitäre Videoüberwachung ist möglicherweise ein von der Mafia betriebenes Spielcasino [das Casino will alles über jeden einzelnen Spieler wissen, aber keinerlei Einzelheiten über sich selbst preisgeben]. Man würde in einer derartigen Organisation kaum mit unverhohlener physischer Gewalt rechnen, es kann jedoch zum gelegentlichen *Verschwinden* von Personen kommen, die der Organisation nicht zu Gesicht stehen.

Auch viele Kaufhäuser setzen umfangreiche Videoüberwachungssysteme ein, verbieten es aber gleichzeitig anderen, in ihren Räumlichkeiten Kameras zu verwenden. Ich will nun mit meiner Arbeit einen technologischen Rahmen für die Hinterfragung derartiger Beschränkungen schaffen.

In einem faschistischen System kommen die Züge pünktlich an, die Kriminalitätsrate ist niedrig und die Moral hoch.

Eine von oben nach unten strukturierte panoptikonartige Überwachungshierarchie läßt Jeremy Benthams Philosophie wahr werden. Der einstige Gemeinschaftsgeist, der sowohl in den engmaschigen Gemeinschaften als auch in den moderneren *nachbarschaftliche Wachgemeinschaften* bestand [und z. B. durch das Vertrauen in andere Mitglieder der Gemeinschaft zum Ausdruck kam], wurde durch das absolute Vertrauen in die Regierung, große Firmen oder andere – dem unsichtbaren Wächter in Benthams Wachturm vergleichbare – unsichtbare Autoritäten abgelöst.

Ein wichtiges Ziel meiner Arbeit besteht darin, eine Grundlage zu schaffen, die ich *Humanistische Intelligenz* [H. I.] nenne und die als Basis für das existentielle Prinzip der Selbstbestimmung und der Lenkung unseres eigenen Schicksals wie auch des humanistischen Begriffs der Selbstverwirklichung dienen soll.

Die *Humanistische Intelligenz* unterscheidet sich von der Künstlichen Intelligenz dadurch, daß das Ziel eher darin besteht, durch eine Art von Prothesen intelligent zu werden, als durch intelligente Maschinen ersetzt oder seiner Privilegien beraubt zu werden. Damit hinterfragt die H. I. den Begriff der intelligenten Umgebung und der allgegenwärtigen Überwachung. Anstelle von *intelligenten Räumen*, *intelligenten Fußböden*, *intelligenten Plafonds*, *intelligenten Toiletten*, *intelligenten Lichtschaltern* etc. konzentriert sich die H. I. auf den Begriff des *intelligenten Menschen*.

deconstructing the video Surveillance Superhighway [1978-1996], by Steve Mann, 1996] performance pieces in order to challenge the notion of totalitarian surveillance, as well as challenge and appropriate the notion of higher and unquestionable authority.

Here I describe experiments and performances that I have conducted and purposely taken to the extreme in order to [a] illustrate a point and [b] experience reactions and observations first hand. It is not likely that the average reader would go to these extremes but some more subtle variations of these experiments and performances may still be used to provide similar insight or reactions.

My Manager: Externalization of the locus of control

By *externalization of the locus of control*, I am referring to the phenomenon you experience when, for example, you're standing at a department store customer service counter. The clerk has the power of various support media, and might, for example, defer his or her judgment [or pretend to defer his or her judgment] to an external entity such as a telephone [ostensibly that of another entity at the other end of the communications channel], a computer screen, or other form of media to which you do not share the privilege of access. In this sense, the clerk may, if desired, absolve him-self/herself from responsibility for his/her own actions.

Centralized computing, in particular, has ushered in a new era of this form of externalization. A department store clerk may tell us, perhaps untruthfully, that *I cannot process your return; the computer won't let me*. Often the clerk does have the ability to fulfill the request, but chooses voluntarily to be subject to [or to appear to be subject to] a higher and unquestionable authority. Thus the customer is placed in an inferior position of not knowing whether the clerk is acting on his/her own will, or the will of a higher authority that is not subject to question by you, the customer.

This tactic is often the practice of used-car sales representatives who might, for example, say *I'd really like to give you the car for $2000, but let me check with my manager*, and then disappear into a back room for a few minutes, have a cup of coffee, all alone, and then

Ein wichtiges Ziel der H. I. besteht darin, einen ersten Schritt in Richtung des höchsten Prinzips der Aufklärung, dem Grundsatz der Würde des einzelnen, zu unternehmen. Ermöglicht wird dies durch eine prothetische Transformation des Körpers in einen souveränen Raum.

Ältere und neuere Arbeiten

Ich habe eine Reihe von reflektionistischen und diffusionistischen Performances geschaffen, um den Begriff der totalitären Überwachung in Frage zu stellen und den Begriff einer höheren und unanzweifelbaren Autorität zu hinterfragen und zu appropriieren 1978-96, von Steve Mann, 1996].

Im folgenden beschreibe ich Experimente und Performances, die ich realisiert und bewußt bis an die Grenzen getrieben habe, um [a] einen bestimmten Punkt zu illustrieren und [b] Reaktionen und Beobachtungen direkt miterleben zu können. Der durchschnittliche Leser würde wahrscheinlich nicht bis an diese Grenzen gehen wollen, doch auch subtilere Varianten dieser Experimente und Performances können noch dazu dienen, ähnliche Einblicke oder Reaktionen zu erhalten.

My Manager: Externalisierung des Orts der Kontrolle

Mit *Externalisierung des Orts der Kontrolle* spreche ich das Phänomen an, das man erlebt, wenn man z. B. am Kundendienstschalter eines Kaufhauses steht. Der bzw. die Angestellte verfügt zu seiner/ihrer Unterstützung über verschiedene Medien und kann z. B. die Entscheidung [möglicherweise auch nur scheinbar] an eine externe Einheit, wie z. B. ein Telefon [das zu einer anderen Einheit gehört, die sich am anderen Ende des Kommunikationskanals befindet], einen Monitor oder andere Medien delegieren, zu denen wir keinen Zugang haben. In diesem Sinne kann der/die Angestellte, falls er/sie das will, sich der Verantwortung für seine/ihre Handlungen einfach entziehen.

Insbesondere durch den Einsatz zentralisierter Computersysteme wurde eine neue Ära dieser Form der Externalisierung eingeleitet. So könnte uns der/die Angestellte im Kaufhaus – möglicherweise nicht ganz aufrichtig – sagen: *Ich kann Ihre Reklamation nicht bearbeiten, der Computer läßt sie mich nicht eingeben.* Der/die Angestellte hätte oftmals durchaus die Möglichkeit, unserem Wunsch nachzukommen, zieht es aber vor, einer höheren und nicht hinterfragbaren Autorität unterworfen zu sein bzw.

emerge to declare *My manager won't let me sell it to you for that low...*.

One of my performance pieces, entitled *My Manager* was a reflectionist performance piece in which I attempted to provide myself with the same kind of support infrastructure. This was achieved through construction of various forms of a personal information space comprising a computer in a backpack, connected to a display situated over one or both eyes[1] with a radio teletype interface to a remote *manager*.

In this way, I carried with me, in my clothing, a support infrastructure that made it ambiguous as to whether my thoughts and such were my own, or those of a remote entity.

My apparatus differed significantly from a two-way voice radio, where it is clearly apparent to anyone else when the unit is being used. Later, the laptop computers that evolved in the 1980s still failed to provide the ambiguity and uncertainty of my earlier apparatus.

My Manager was my attempt to return to the Enlightenment, and declare the sovereignty of the individual, through the illusion of its subversion. In the spirit of the situationist tradition, I have created a detournement of my own subversion.

Painful Disconnect

In a further embodiment of the *My Manager* performance, a remote agent of my choosing may also provide remote control of my body, in the Stelarc sense, so that I can further subvert myself to an authority that acts in my own interest yet is inaccessible to, and unquestionable by, others.

I may also choose to be given an *electrical corrective signal* [through a high-voltage step-up transformer connected to my garment-based computer] should I become disconnected from the Internet. Thus, if I am asked to step into an elevator or the like, I can honestly reply that this would inflict great pain on me.

In that sense somone who forced me to enter an environment in which I might lose radio contact with potential outside accountability would be committing an act which is equivalent to torture.

As torture is viewed as a human rights violation, the goal of this performance piece is to suggest that disconnectivity, against one's

macht uns das zumindest weis. So wird der Kunde in eine untergebene Position gedrängt und weiß nicht, ob der/die Angestellte nach seinem/ ihrem eigenen Willen oder aber nach dem Willen einer höheren Autorität handelt, die von Ihnen als Kunde nicht zu hinterfragen ist.

Dieselbe Taktik wird oft von Gebrauchtwagenhändlern angewandt, die Ihnen beispielsweise sagen: *Ich würde Ihnen den Wagen wirklich gern für $ 2.000 geben, aber ich muß das mit meinem Chef besprechen*. Daraufhin verschwinden sie für einige Minuten in einem Hinterzimmer, trinken in aller Ruhe eine Tasse Kaffee – allein, wohlgemerkt – und tauchen schließlich auf, um Ihnen zu erklären: *Mein Chef ist leider nicht damit einverstanden, daß ich Ihnen den Wagen zu so einem günstigen Preis überlasse ...*.

Eine meiner Performances mit dem Titel *My Manager* war ein reflektionistisches Werk, in dem ich versucht habe, mir dieselbe Art von unterstützender Infrastruktur zu schaffen. Das erreichte ich durch die Konstruktion verschiedener Formen eines persönlichen Informationsraums, der einen Computer in einem Rucksack umfaßte, der mit einem über einem oder beiden Augen[1] angebrachten Display mit einer Funkfernschreiberschnittstelle verbunden war, welche wiederum die Verbindung zu einem räumlich entfernten *Manager* herstellte.

So trug ich in meiner Kleidung eine unterstützende Infrastruktur mit mir herum, dank derer man nicht mehr eindeutig feststellen konnte, ob meine Gedanken etc. meine eigenen oder die einer räumlich entfernten Einheit waren.

Mein Gerät unterschied sich wesentlich von einem Zweiweg-Funkgerät, bei dem es für jeden Außenstehenden erkennbar ist, wann der Apparat in Verwendung ist. Die Laptops, die sich dann in den achtziger Jahren entwickelten, konnten die Uneindeutigkeit und die Ungewißheit, die mein ursprüngliches Gerät hervorgerufen hatte, noch immer nicht erzielen.

My Manager war mein Versuch, zur Aufklärung zurückzufinden und die Souveränität des Individuums durch die Illusion seiner Subversion zu erklären. Im Geiste der situationistischen Tradition habe ich ein *détournement* meiner eigenen Subversion geschaffen.

Painful Disconnect

In einer weiteren Performance von *My Manager* kann ein räumlich entfernter Agent meiner Wahl

will, should also be viewed as a human rights violation.

Painful Disconnect makes real the notion that denial of the right to self-surveillance by friends and family is equivalent to possible torture or other mistreatment.

Necessification

Because of the long-term adaptation process which I have undergone in the use of this apparatus [e.g. that I have worn it for many years], I have come to rely on it to see properly, and thus in some sense, it has become a visual prosthetic device [*Eudaemonic Eye*, <http://wearcam.org/chi97.html>].

Further toward making it absolutely essential that I wear the device, it also serves as a personal status monitor, e.g. a health monitor of sorts, and therefore, in some sense, asking me to remove it is a first step toward not only placing me in danger of tripping or falling [e.g. injury] but also asking me to put my life in danger through the absence of a health monitor that might otherwise bring medical aid should my heart show early signs of incipient malfunction or the like.

The Personal Safety Device

H.I. provides a further framework for personal safety by acting as a protective and defensive agent. For example, I am able to announce my location to one or more people of my choosing, either automatically through a GPS-ready radioteletype interface, or through a direct input device [e.g. a series of pushbutton switches integrated into my belt or clothing].

Various sensory apparatus I have incorporated into clothing measure both me and my environment. These sensors include a 24.360 GHz radar set, a 10.250GHz radar set, video cameras, microphones, infrared vision system, as well as a variety of sensors that measure quantities upon my own body, such as my heart rate [ECG], footstep rate [transducers in my shoes], etc. Intelligent signal processing may be used to construct an automated personal safety system. The inputs from the various sensors form a feature vector that may be processed by the circuits I've built into my clothing [e.g. 133MHz 586 processor running under the Linux 2.0 operating system, along with various special purpose DSP hardware, TMS320 series processors, etc.].

symposium

im Sinne von Stelarc auch meinen Körper fernsteuern, so daß ich mich weiter einer Autorität unterwerfen kann, die in meinem eigenen Interesse handelt, für andere jedoch weder zugänglich noch hinterfragbar ist.

Ich habe auch die Option, mir bei jeder Trennung vom Internet ein *elektrisches Korrektursignal* [durch einen Hochspannungsaufwärtstransformator, der mit dem in meiner Kleidung montierten Computer verbunden ist] geben zu lassen. Wenn mich jemand auffordern würde, einen Aufzug zu betreten, so könnte ich ehrlich antworten, daß mir das große Schmerzen zufügen würde.

In diesem Sinne würde jemand, der mich dazu zwingt, eine Umgebung zu betreten, in der ich den Funkkontakt mit der potentiellen Außeninstanz verliere, eine Handlung setzen, die einer Folter gleichkommt.

Da die Folter als Menschenrechtsverletzung angesehen wird, besteht das Ziel dieser Performance darin, aufzuzeigen, daß eine Trennung wider Willen ebenfalls als Menschenrechtsverletzung betrachtet werden sollte.

Painful Disconnect realisiert den Gedanken, daß die Verweigerung des Rechts auf Selbstüberwachung durch Freunde und Familienangehörige gleichbedeutend mit möglicher Folter oder anderweitiger Mißhandlung ist.

Necessification

Aufgrund des langfristigen Anpassungsprozesses, den ich in Zusammenhang mit der Verwendung dieses Geräts durchgemacht habe [z. B. durch die Tatsache, daß ich es viele Jahre lang getragen habe], ist es schließlich soweit gekommen, daß ich mich nun auf dieses Gerät verlasse, um richtig zu sehen, und daß es für mich in gewisser Weise eine visuelle Prothese geworden ist [Eudaemonic Eye, <http://wearcam.org/chi97.html>].

Für mich auch deshalb absolut notwendig, daß ich dieses Gerät trage, weil es zusätzlich der Überwachung meiner Gesundheit dient, also sozusagen ein Gesundheitswächter ist. Und deshalb stellt für mich die Aufforderung, es zu entfernen, den ersten Schritt in Richtung Stolper- bzw. Sturzgefahr [d. h. Verletzungsgefahr] dar. Doch ein Entfernen des Gerätes hieße sogar, mein Leben in Gefahr zu bringen, weil dann ein Gesundheitswächter fehlte, der, falls mein Herz Anzeichen vorzeitiger Fehlfunktionen o. ä. zeigt, ärztliche Hilfe rufen könnte.

As an example of how intelligent signal processing can be used as a protective entity, consider what happens when one is approached by an assailant wielding a sawn-off shotgun and demanding cash. In such a situation, the victim's heart rate is apt to increase but with an unexplicable decrease in footstep rate [owing to the assailant's request that the victim stop and hand over a wallet or the like].

Consider a quotient of heart rate divided by footstep rate. One could easily imagine how this quotient, taken over a certain time window, could provide a rough indication of distress. In actual fact, I've been developing more advanced intelligent signal processing algorithms, which include, for example, situational awareness.

Electric Feel Sensing: Synthetic Synesthesia of Sixth and Seventh Senses

Another example of intelligent signal processing comprises a radar system which I have built into my clothing, to provide me with the ability to *feel* if someone sneaks up behind me. The radar system establishes a far-field electromagnetic wave pattern whose demodulated Doppler output is processed and used to drive vibrotactile transducers connected to my body. In this way, when someone sneaks up behind me, I can feel them *pressing* against my body, even though they are still some distance away. The closer they get, the stronger I feel them *pressing* against my body. At 20 or 30 meters, the feeling is very faint, while at 10 meters, the feeling is stronger, and as they approach within stabbing distance, the feeling is much stronger, to the point of being difficult to ignore.

This kind of user-interface is intuitive, because it is mapped in a manner that establishes a one-to-one correspondence with me and my environment. When someone sneaks up behind me from the left, for example, I can feel them *pressing* against the left side of my back, and likewise to the right.

Systems of this nature provide me with additional senses [such as radar, sonar, etc.] beyond the normal five senses. However, to be perceptible, I map the additional senses onto the usual five senses, a mapping that I call *synthetic synesthesia*.

Furthermore, the mapping need not be one-to-one. For example, I often map the radar

The Personal Safety Device / Die persönliche Sicherheitsvorrichtung

Zusätzlich übernimmt die H. I. im Bereich der persönlichen Sicherheit auch eine Schutz- und Verteidigungsfunktion. So kann ich beispielsweise meinen derzeitigen Aufenthaltsort einer oder mehreren Personen meiner Wahl entweder automatisch mittels einer GPS-tauglichen Funkfernschreiberschnittstelle oder über eine direkte Eingabevorrichtung [z. B. eine Reihe von Schaltern, die in meinen Gürtel oder in meine Kleidung integriert sind] mitteilen.

Verschiedene sensorische Geräte, die ich in meine Kleidung integriert habe, führen sowohl an mir als auch an meiner Umgebung Messungen durch. Diese sensorischen Apparate umfassen ein 24.360 GHz-Radargerät, ein 10.250 GHz-Radargerät, Videokameras, Mikrophone, ein Infrarotsichtsystem sowie eine Vielzahl von Sensoren, die Messungen an meinem eigenen Körper durchführen, wie meine Herzfrequenz [EKG], meine Schrittfrequenz [Wandler in meinen Schuhen] etc. messen.

Mit Hilfe intelligenter Signalverarbeitung läßt sich ein automatisiertes persönliches Sicherheitssystem entwickeln. Der Input der verschiedenen Sensoren bildet einen charakteristischen Vektor, der von den in meine Kleidung integrierten Schaltkreisen verarbeitet werden kann [z. B. 133 MHz 586er Prozessor, der unter dem Betriebssystem Linux 2.0 läuft, sowie verschiedene zweckspezifische DSP-Hardware, Prozessoren der Serie TMS320 etc.].

Als Beispiel für die Einsatzmöglichkeiten intelligenter Signalverarbeitung in einer Schutzvorrichtung brauchen Sie sich nur vorzustellen, was passiert, wenn Ihnen ein Angreifer entgegentritt, der in der Hand eine abgesägte Schrotflinte schwingt und Geld von Ihnen verlangt. In einer derartigen Situation steigt die Herzfrequenz des Opfers wahrscheinlich stark an, doch gleichzeitig kommt es zu einem unerklärlichen Rückgang der Schrittfrequenz [der darauf zurückzuführen ist, daß der Angreifer sein Opfer dazu auffordert, stehenzubleiben und eine Brieftasche oder ähnliches herauszugeben].

Nehmen wir nun den Quotienten aus Herzfrequenz und Schrittfrequenz. Man kann sich ohne weiteres vorstellen, daß dieser Quotient – über eine bestimmte Zeitdauer hinweg registriert – grobe Hinweise auf das Vorliegen einer Notsituation liefern könnte. Ich habe tatsächlich höher entwickelte intelligente Signalverarbeitungsalgorithmen erarbeitet, die z. B. Situationsbewußtsein umfassen.

system into more than one of my five senses. One such mapping I tend to favor uses the radar to also switch in a rear-looking video camera.

Intelligent signal processing may, in fact, be used to select the degree to which the rear-looking camera is mixed in, rather than merely switching it in. For example, I designed a radar system having both the in-phase and the quadrature components. Thus the signals may be processed to determine whether objects are moving toward me or away from me. Objects moving toward me from behind are of particular interest, because most objects that are behind me [such as the ground, parked cars, stationary objects] are moving away from me in a relative sense.

The portion of the Doppler spectrum corresponding to objects approaching me may be integrated to arrive at a saliency index. This saliency index is similar to the previosly described heartrate/steprate quotient in the sense that both of these saliency indices attempt to indicate to me or my processing agent the degree of attention that should be paid to some other instrument of situational awareness.

In the case of the radar system, the saliency index may be used to control a video mixer that controls the degree to which my attention is focused on my rear-looking camera. The image from the rear-looking camera is presented to my eye upside-down and backwards [e.g. the camera is mounted upside-down and a circuit is used to flip each raster of video from left to right], so that it appears to me as though the rays of light from behind me are passing through the back of my head, through my retina, and then through the optical center of my eye. This provides a system which obeys the true laws of projective geometry, and re-defines the eye as a device that captures a pencil of light rays from a single point in space, and merely projects this pencil of rays onto a single image plane. I view this image plane upon the miniature computer screen I have built into my eyeglasses.

With the radar's visual saliency index in the control loop, the rays of light from behind me may be modulated in brightness, to correspond with the amount of attention that the processing agent believes that they merit.

Electric Feel Sensing: Die synthetische Synästhesie des sechsten und siebenten Sinnes

Ein weiteres Beispiel für intelligente Signalverarbeitung umfaßt ein Radarsystem, das ich in meine Kleidung integriert habe, um *fühlen* zu können, wenn sich jemand von hinten an mich heranschleicht. Das Radarsystem errichtet ein elektromagnetisches Fernfeld-Wellenmuster, dessen demodulierter Doppler-Output verarbeitet wird und dazu dient, an meinen Körper angeschlossene vibrotaktile Wandler zu betätigen. Wenn also jemand hinter mir herschleicht, kann ich fühlen, wie er sich an meinen Körper *preßt*, obwohl er sich noch in einiger Entfernung befindet. Je näher er kommt, umso stärker fühle ich dieses *Pressen* gegen meinen Körper. Bei einem Abstand von 20 oder 30 Metern ist das Gefühl noch sehr schwach, bei zehn Metern ist es bereits deutlich stärker, und wenn die Person so nahe ist, daß sie mich von hinten erstechen könnte, ist das Gefühl dermaßen stark, daß es schwierig zu ignorieren wäre.

Diese Art von Benutzerschnittstelle ist intuitiv, da sie so konzipiert ist, daß sie zwischen mir und meiner Umwelt ein eins-zu-eins Verhältnis herstellt. Wenn beispielsweise jemand von links hinten auf mich zukommt, kann ich das *Pressen* an der linken Seite meines Rückens spüren, und rechts wäre es genau umgekehrt.

Derartige Systeme verleihen mir zusätzliche Sinne [wie z. B. Radar, Sonar etc.], die über die normalen fünf Sinne hinausgehen. Um diese zusätzlichen Sinne jedoch wahrnehmen zu können, ordne ich sie den normalen fünf Sinnen zu, und diese Zuordnung nenne ich *synthetische Synästhesie*.

Diese Zuordnung braucht allerdings nicht eins-zu-eins zu erfolgen. So ordne ich z. B. das Radarsystem häufig mehr als einem meiner fünf Sinne zu. Bei meiner Lieblingszuordnung wird eine rückwärts blickende Kamera mittels Radar zugeschaltet.

Die intelligente Signalverarbeitung kann nämlich so eingesetzt werden, daß sie auswählt, in welchem Ausmaß die rückwärts blickende Kamera miteinbezogen wird, anstatt sie nur einfach einzuschalten. Ich habe beispielsweise ein Radarsystem konzipiert, das sowohl über phasengleiche als auch über gegenphasige Komponenten verfügt. So können die Signale verarbeitet werden, um festzustellen, ob Objekte sich auf mich zu oder von mir weg bewegen. Von besonderem Interesse sind dabei jene Objekte, die sich mir von hinten nähern, da die meisten Objekte, die sich hinter mir befinden [wie z. B.

SafetyNet

Once a distress signal is detected [by intelligent signal- processing agents or manually by myself], a communications channel may be opened to friends and relatives who have been previously entered on my personal safety list. This communications channel includes live video and other environmental information, which is transmitted and recorded at remote locations in various countries around the world, so that it cannot be destroyed by a potential assailant.

Rather than notify police or other authorities, which could result in a high degree of false alarms, the system notifies members of my *SafetyNet* – a network of friends and relatives looking out for each other's safety. This approach to personal safety may be combined with a high degree of constant connectivity with others such as a radioteletype UNIX *talk* window open at all times, video conferencing from a first-person perspective [e.g. from a wearable video camera] open at all times, etc..

Such a form of personal safety device may also protect one from police brutality and various other forms of human rights violations.

Subversion of Panopticon with Wearable Wireless Webcam

Ordinary cameras have become much smaller now, thanks to the miniaturization afforded by modern technology. However, they still share a common attribute with their predecessors, namely that it is immediately apparent to anyone when the camera is being used, because one must bring it up to one's eye, and look through it, etc., and this usage pattern is likely to put an assailant or the like into an angry mode of thought. For example, in a situation involving police brutality, police may attempt to forbid photography or the like, or may attempt to intimidate those engaged in the practice of documenting an atrocity.

Another weakness of current camera technology is that the storage of images or video is local, so that those committing the atrocity may seize the storage media [film, videocassette, flash memory, floppy disk, or the like], claiming that they need it for *evidence*, when in fact their wish might be that it be destroyed.

I established a *personal imaging* [*Wearable Computing: A First Step Toward Personal Imaging*, IEEE Computer, Vol 30, No. 2, <http://

der Boden, geparkte Fahrzeuge oder unbewegliche Objekte] sich relativ gesehen von mir entfernen.

Jener Anteil des Doppler-Spektrums, der den sich mir nähernden Objekten entspricht, kann zur Erstellung eines Auffälligkeitsindex miteinbezogen werden. Dieser Auffälligkeitsindex ähnelt dem oben beschriebenen Quotienten aus Herzfrequenz und Schrittfrequenz insofern, als diese beiden Auffälligkeitsindizes versuchen, mir oder dem für mich die Verarbeitung übernehmenden Agenten anzuzeigen, welches Maß an Aufmerksamkeit einem anderen Instrument des Situationsbewußtseins zukommen sollte.

Im Falle des Radarsystems kann der Auffälligkeitsindex für die Steuerung eines Videomixers verwendet werden, der wiederum steuert, in welchem Ausmaß sich meine Aufmerksamkeit auf die nach hinten blickende Kamera konzentriert. Das von der rückwärts gerichteten Kamera produzierte Bild wird meinem Auge seitenverkehrt und auf dem Kopf stehend geliefert [d. h. die Kamera ist verkehrt montiert, und jeder Rasterpunkt wird mit Hilfe eines Schaltkreises vertikal gespiegelt], so daß ich den Eindruck habe, die von hinter mir kommenden Lichtstrahlen würden meinen Hinterkopf, meine Netzhaut und dann das Sehzentrum meines Auges durchdringen. So erhält man ein System, das den Gesetzen der projektiven Geometrie folgt und das Auge neu definiert – als Mittel, das ein von einem einzigen Punkt im Raum ausgehendes Bündel von Lichtstrahlen einfängt und dieses Strahlenbündel auf eine einzige Bildebene projiziert. Und diese Bildebene mache ich auf dem Minicomputerbildschirm sichtbar, den ich in meine Brille eingebaut habe.

Mit dem visuellen Auffälligkeitsindex des Radars in der Kontrollschleife kann die Lichtstärke der von hinter mir kommenden Strahlen so moduliert werden, daß es dem Maß an Aufmerksamkeit entspricht, das der verarbeitende Agent für angemessen hält.

SafetyNet

Sobald ein Streßsignal festgestellt wird [entweder durch intelligente Signalverarbeitungseinheiten oder manuell durch mich selbst], kann über einen Kommunikationskanal eine Verbindung mit Freunden und Verwandten, die zuvor in meine persönliche Sicherheitsliste eingegeben wurden, hergestellt werden. Über diesen Kommunikationskanal werden Live-Videoaufnahmen sowie andere Infor-

computer.org/pubs/computer/1997/0297toc.html>] framework for obtaining video from a first-person perspective. This video is part of my personal information space, and therefore accessible to others via a wireless link to the Internet. This means that anyone with access to the Internet can view the images, and thereby take an active role in making sure that there are multiple copies of the images in various countries around the world, so that an assailant, or a violator of human rights, could not destroy the images. Even by placing me under duress, the images could not be destroyed, because I have chosen to not know how many copies of each picture or video sequence there are, or in which countries they are mirrored, archived, and backed up.

A principle of totalitarian video surveillance is that only the guards have access to the privileged vantage point afforded by video cameras. An important goal of my performance piece was to make the situation approximately the reverse, that is, my *personal imaging* system was a first step toward subverting totalitarian surveillance by making some video [at least mine] available to everyone.

I later constructed larger communities of individuals wearing cameras in order to make multiple image streams available to large numbers of individuals.

Recently, with the advent of the World Wide Web, I have simply turned my apparatus into a *WebCam*, resulting in a further simplification of its use, and a further subversion of Panopticon.

My camera [WearCam, short for wearable camera] is situated in such a way that it is not possible for an assailant to determine whether or not an image is being captured at any given time. This is accomplished through - having the camera worn in an always-active mode, so that it in fact functions as a visual prosthetic of sorts.

mationen über meine Umgebung an entfernte Orte in Ländern auf der ganzen Welt übertragen und dort aufgezeichnet, so daß sie von einem potentiellen Angreifer nicht vernichtet werden können.

Um eine große Anzahl möglicher Fehlalarme zu vermeiden, verständigt das System nicht die Polizei oder andere Behörden, sondern Mitglieder meines *SafetyNet* – eines Netzwerks von Freunden und Verwandten, von denen sich jeder um die Sicherheit des anderen kümmert. Dieser Ansatz für die persönliche Sicherheit läßt sich mit einem hohen Grad konstanter Connectivity mit anderen kombinieren, z. B. durch ein ständig offenes UNIX-Funkfernschreiber-*Talk*-Window, ständig zugängliche Videokonferenzen aus der Perspektive der ersten Person [beispielsweise von einer tragbaren Videokamera aus] etc.

Diese Art von persönlicher Sicherheitsvorrichtung kann auch vor Polizeibrutalität und verschiedenen anderen Formen von Menschenrechtsverletzungen schützen.

Die Subversion des Panoptikons mit Hilfe einer tragbaren drahtlosen Webcam

Dank der durch die moderne Technologie möglich gewordenen Miniaturisierung sind gewöhnliche Kameras heute wesentlich kleiner. Doch eines haben sie mit ihren Vorgängern noch immer gemeinsam: Jeder bemerkt sofort, wenn sie verwendet werden, da man die Kamera ja an das Auge führen, durchsehen usw. muß, und dieses Verwendungsmuster wird einen Angreifer wahrscheinlich rot sehen lassen. Im Falle von Polizeibrutalität könnte die Polizei z. B. versuchen, Fotos und ähnliche Aufnahmen zu verbieten bzw. diejenigen einzuschüchtern, die die Übergriffe dokumentieren wollen.

Eine weitere Schwäche der heutigen Kameratechnologie liegt in der lokalen Speicherung von Bildern oder Videoaufnahmen, d. h. diejenigen, die die Übergriffe begehen, können das Speichermedium [also den Film, die Videokassette, die Speicherkarte, die Diskette o. ä.] an sich bringen, indem sie behaupten, daß sie es als *Beweisstück* benötigen, während sie es in Wahrheit vermutlich vernichten wollen.

Ich habe eine *personal imaging*-Anwendung entwickelt, mit deren Hilfe man Videoaufnahmen aus der Perspektive der ersten Person erhalten kann [*Wearable Computing: A First Step Toward Personal Imaging*, IEEE Computer, Vol 30, No. 2, <http://computer.org/pubs/computer/1997/0297toc.html>]. Diese Videoaufnahmen sind Teil meines persönlichen Informationsraums und deshalb anderen über eine drahtlose Internet-Verbindung zugänglich. Das bedeu-

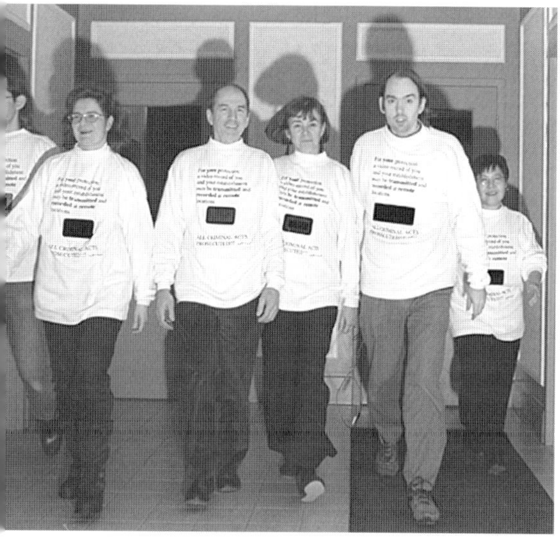

Fig.2
A Firing Squad comprised of various individuals wearing Maybe Cameras. Here, even though I built these units, do not know which ones contain cameras with transmitters, transmitting to the World Wide Web.
*Eine aus mehreren mit *Maybe Cameras* ausgestatteten Personen bestehende Firing Squad. Obgleich ich diese Geräte persönlich gebaut habe, weiß ich selbst nicht, welches der gezeigten Geräte eine Kamera mit Sender enthält, die Bilder an das World Wide Web sendet!*

Maybe Camera

I may also choose that the remote accountability afforded by my SafetyNet be of origin unknown to me, so that if I am asked *Are you recording me?*, I might be able to say that I honestly do not know. This denial of accountability, for taking pictures in establishments where photography is prohibited, was explored through a performance piece called *Firing Squad.*

For *Firing Squad*, I constructed a number of *Maybe Cameras*.

Furthermore, when challenged by representatives of the surveillance superhighway, we simply declared: these are uniforms – standard issue from *Our Manager* – which we are required to wear while running errands on company time.

Second Brain as Personal Diary without Contempt of Court

In many ways, I regard my rig, together with its personal information space, as a second brain – as a true prosthetic device.

Thus, even in situations in which I do make a conscious decision to record an image or

tet also, daß jeder, der Zugang zum Internet hat, diese Bilder sehen und auch eine aktive Rolle in der Verbreitung zahlloser Kopien der Bilder in Ländern auf der ganzen Welt spielen kann, so daß ein Angreifer oder jemand, der sich einer Menschenrechtsverletzung schuldig gemacht hat, diese Bilder nicht vernichten könnte. Sogar wenn man mich unter Druck setzt, könnten die Bilder nicht zerstört werden, da ich nicht weiß, wie viele Kopien jedes Bildes bzw. jeder Videosequenz es gibt und in welchen Ländern diese Aufnahmen angesehen, archiviert und gespeichert werden.

Es ist ein Prinzip der totalitären Videoüberwachung, daß nur die Wächter Zugang zu jenem privilegierten Überblick haben, den Videokameras ermöglichen. Ein wichtiges Ziel meiner Performance bestand nun darin, diese Situation mehr oder weniger umzukehren, d. h. mein *personal imaging*-System war ein erster Schritt zur Unterminierung der totalitären Überwachung, indem Videoaufnahmen [zumindest meine eigenen] jedem einzelnen zugänglich gemacht werden. Später baute ich größere Gemeinschaften von Menschen auf, die Kameras trugen, um einer großen Anzahl von Personen vielfältige Bildströme zugänglich zu machen. In jüngster Zeit habe ich aufgrund der Entwicklung des World Wide Web aus meinem Apparat einfach eine *WebCam* gemacht, so daß er jetzt noch einfacher zu verwenden ist und weiter zur Subversion des Panoptikons beiträgt. Meine Kamera [*WearCam* – die Kurzform für *Wearable Camera*, tragbare Kamera] ist so plaziert, daß es einem Angreifer nicht möglich ist festzustellen, ob gerade Aufnahmen gemacht werden oder nicht. Dies läßt sich dadurch erreichen, daß die Kamera stets eingeschaltet ist, so daß sie in gewisser Weise als eine Art visuelle Prothese fungiert.

Maybe Camera

Ich kann mich auch dafür entscheiden, den Ursprung der von meinem SafetyNet ermöglichten Fern-Verantwortung gar nicht zu kennen. Würde mich also jemand fragen: *Filmen Sie mich gerade?*, könnte ich ihm antworten, daß ich es wirklich nicht weiß. Dieses Ablehnen der Verantwortung für Aufnahmen in Räumlichkeiten, in denen das Fotografieren verboten ist, habe ich in einer Performance mit dem Titel Firing Squad ausgelotet. Für Firing Squad habe ich eine Reihe von *Maybe Cameras* konstruiert. Wenn wir von Vertretern des Überwachungs-Superhighway befragt wurden, erklärten wir einfach: Das sind Uniformen – ein Standardthema aus Our Manager – , die wir tragen müssen, wenn wir während der Arbeitszeit Besorgungen machen.

*A *Maybe Camera* is constructed by first cutting out a number of small [e.g. 8cm by 13cm] pieces of very dark plexiglas [e.g. with transmissivity in the 3% to 15% range], and then placing a miniature camera and transmitter on one or two of these units, and dummy circuitboards and dummy lenses on the others. All units are fitted with leads to a 9 volt battery snap, regardless as to whether they are real units or dummy units. ll units are then sealed in black epoxy, and allowed to set. A series of holes is drilled around the outside of each one, so that it can be sewn onto a shirt, after making a small hole to insert the 9 volt battery snap so that it hangs inside the shirt. Prior to sewing the units onto the shirts, it is preferable to silkscreen the shirts with the words *For YOUR protection, a video record of you and your establishment may be transmitted and recorded at remote locations. ALL CRIMINAL ACTS PROSECUTED!!!*.*

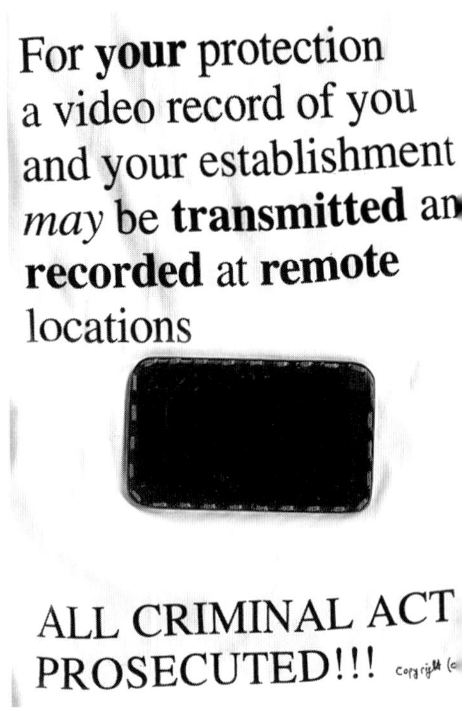

Fig. 3
Close up view of one of the shirt-based realizations of *Maybe Camera*
*Nahaufnahme einer *Maybe Camera* auf einem T-Shirt.*

*Für die Herstellung einer *Maybe Camera* schneidet man zuerst eine Reihe kleiner Stücke [z. B. 8cm x 13cm] aus sehr dunklem Plexiglas aus [z. B. mit einer spezifischen Durchlässigkeit in der Größenordnung von 3% bis 15%]. Dann plaziert man eine Miniaturkamera mit Sender auf ein oder zwei Stücken, während man die anderen mit Platinen- und Linsenattrappen versieht. Jedes Stück wird mit Kabeln an eine 9-Volt-Batterie angeschlossen, unabhängig davon, ob es sich dabei um eine wirkliche Kamera oder um eine Attrappe handelt. Elf dieser Einheiten werden dann in schwarzes Epoxidharz gegossen, das man festwerden läßt. Auf der Außenseite jeder dieser Einheiten bohrt man nun eine Reihe von Löchern, so daß man jedes Exemplar an einem Hemd annähen kann, nachdem man ein kleines Loch für die 9-Volt-Batterie hergestellt hat, die sich innerhalb des Hemds befinden soll. Bevor man die Einheiten nun auf die Hemden näht, empfiehlt es sich, die Hemden mit folgendem Schriftzug zu bedrucken: *Zu IHRER Sicherheit kann eine Videoaufnahme von Ihnen und Ihrer Institution aufgezeichnet und fernübertragen werden. JEDE KRIMINELLE HANDLUNG WIRD STRAFRECHTLICH VERFOLGT!!!*.*

Das zweite Gehirn als persönliches Tagebuch: Keine Mißachtung der Justiz

Ich sehe meine Ausstattung zusammen mit dem persönlichen Informationsraum, den sie schafft, in vielerlei Weise als zweites Gehirn an – als eine wahre Prothese.

So kann ich mir sogar in Situationen, in denen ich mich bewußt dafür entscheide, Foto- oder Videoaufnahmen von einem bestimmten Vorgang zu machen, wünschen, daß diese Aufnahmen in eine Art persönliches Tagebuch aufgenommen werden, das nur *mir* zugänglich ist. [Die Definition dieses *mir* kann jene mit einschließen, die sich innerhalb meiner neu definierten körperlichen Grenze befinden, also beispielsweise andere Mitglieder meines *SafetyNet*.]

Es ist oft vorgekommen, daß sich Menschen sehr unwohl fühlten, wenn sie meinem zweiten Gehirn bestimmte Informationen anvertrauten, da sie befürchteten, trotz all meiner Anstrengungen, diese Informationen geheimzuhalten, könnte diese Geheimhaltung etwa im Falle einer gerichtlichen Vorladung gefährdet sein.

Selbst wenn ich diese Informationen mit einer gewöhnlichen Verschlüsselung schützen sollte,

video of some activity, I may wish that this recording be entered into a personal diary of sorts which is only accessible to *me*. [The definition of *me* may include that which falls within my newly defined corporeal boundary, which might include, for example, other members of my *SafetyNet*.]

People have often felt uneasy entrusting to my second brain certain personal pieces of information, fearing that even if I made my best efforts to keep this information in confidence, it could be compromised through a subpoena.

Even if I were to protect it with ordinary encryption, its security may still be compromised through the process of torture or other forms of duress.

In the same way that our first brain is protected by the Constitution [the Fifth] from contempt of court for refusing to answer [self-incriminate], I desired to establish a means of protecting the *second brain* from self-incrimination.

My solution was to encrypt it with a key that I do not know myself. Thus I may encrypt materials with public keys of other members of my *SafetyNet*. In this way, my *SafetyNet* could recognize when I am under duress, and thus my inability to access my second brain would not be seen in contempt of whatever duress I might be placed under.

Life through the Screen: A Window to the Future

Many important questions were raised by these performance pieces and the new inventions upon which they were realized.

For example, *My Manager* provided a form of personal empowerment brought forth by the ability to take a solid stance and defer any questioning of my will to a [possibly fictitious] higher and unquestionable authority, just as representatives of establishments often do. However, there is also the danger that this could be abused, for example, as a means of controlling or enslaving people.

In particular, the exploration of the remotely controlled body raises not only the question of possible enslavement by a higher authority that is not actually acting in the best interest of the individual wearing the apparatus of control, but also some serious questions about the locus of responsibility for one's acts are raised.

wäre ihre Sicherheit noch immer durch die Anwendung der Folter oder die Ausübung anderer Arten von Druck bedroht. So wie das erste Gehirn von der [mittlerweile fünften] Verfassung vor einer Verurteilung wegen Mißachtung des Gerichts infolge einer Aussageverweigerung [Gefahr der Selbstbelastung] geschützt wird, wollte ich ein Mittel schaffen, um auch das *zweite Gehirn* vor Selbstbelastung zu schützen.

Meine Lösung bestand darin, die Informationen mit einem Schlüssel zu codieren, der mir selbst unbekannt ist. So kann ich Materialien mit öffentlich zugänglichen Schlüsseln anderer Mitglieder meines *SafetyNet* verschlüsseln. Dadurch könnte mein *SafetyNet* erkennen, wann ich unter Druck gesetzt werde, und meine Unfähigkeit, auf mein zweites Gehirn zuzugreifen, würde in diesem Falle nicht als Mißachtung jeglicher Gewalt, der ich unterworfen sein sollte, angesehen werden.

Das Leben durch den Bildschirm: Ein Fenster in die Zukunft

Mit diesen Performances und den neuen Erfindungen, mit deren Hilfe ich sie realisierte, wurden zahlreiche wichtige Fragen angesprochen. So war *My Manager* mit einer Art von persönlichem Machtgewinn verbunden, der dadurch zustande kam, daß ich fähig war, eine starke Haltung einzunehmen und jeglicher Hinterfragung meines Willens durch den Verweis auf eine [möglicherweise fiktive] höhere und nicht hinterfragbare Autorität zu begegnen, wie dies die Vertreter von Institutionen nur allzu oft tun. Doch damit ist auch die Gefahr eines Mißbrauchs, z. B. als Mittel zur Kontrolle oder zur Versklavung von Menschen, verbunden.

Die Erforschung des ferngesteuerten Körpers wirft nicht nur die Frage nach der möglichen Versklavung durch eine höhere Autorität auf, die nicht wirklich im Interesse der mit dem Kontrollgerät ausgestatteten Person tätig ist, sondern auch einige wichtige Fragen über den Sitz der Verantwortung für unsere Handlungen. In einer Zeit, in der wir uns auf eine Zukunft der vernetzten persönlichen Informationsräume zubewegen, müssen wir uns sorgfältig überlegen, wie diese Welten aufgebaut sind.

Das Ziel der Humanistischen Intelligenz, nämlich den einzelnen mit einem höheren Grad an Selbstbestimmung und größerer Fähigkeit zur Lenkung seines eigenen Schicksals auszustatten, wird gegen die Ziele des Utilitarismus und damit auch gegen den Wunsch, lediglich die Produktivität am

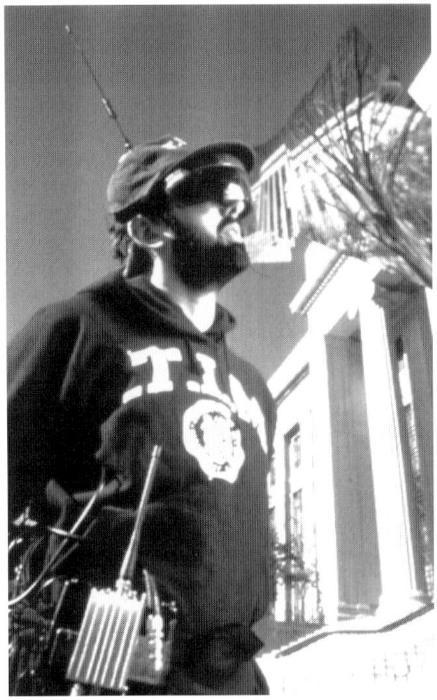

As we move toward a future of networked personal information spaces, we will need to think carefully about how these worlds are constructed.

The goal of humanistic intelligence, that of providing the individual with an increased degree of self-determination and mastery over his or her own destiny, will have to compete against the goals of utilitarianism, and the desire merely to increase workplace productivity and make people more useful to society.

Will we see a future of *cyborgs*, as *puppets* on a virtual string, imprisoned in their workcells, carrying out the orders of an omnipotent boss, or will we see a healthy community of free self-actualized citizens looking out for each other's safety and well-being?

This is the question that we must carefully consider as our *corporeal boundary* will no longer end at the flesh, but, rather, will extend and diffuse into the ether.

Arbeitsplatz und den Nutzens der Menschen für die Gesellschaft zu steigern, ankämpfen müssen.

Werden wir eine Zukunft der *Cyborgs* erleben, die, als *Marionetten* an einem virtuellen Faden in ihren Arbeitszellen eingeschlossen, die Anweisungen eines allmächtigen Vorgesetzten ausführen, oder werden wir eine gesunde Gemeinschaft freier, selbstverwirklichter Bürger erleben, von denen sich jeder um die Sicherheit und das Wohlergehen des anderen kümmert?

Das ist die Frage, mit der wir uns nun sorgfältig beschäftigen müssen, da unsere *körperliche Grenze* nicht mehr mit dem Fleisch endet, sondern sich eher ausweiten und im Äther verbreiten wird.

1 Ich bezeichnete diese Erfindung als *Personal Computer*, obgleich dieser Ausdruck in den letzten Jahren die Bedeutung *Desktop-Computer* angenommen hat. So wurde mein Gerät im Laufe der Jahre als *humanistischer Computer*, *existentieller Computer*, *eudämonischer Computer*, *tragbarer Computer* u. ä. bezeichnet.

Mein Dank gebührt all jenen Menschen in meiner Umgebung, die meine Denkweise beeinflußt haben: Rosalind Picard, Hiroshi Ishii, Krzysztof Wodiczko, William Mitchell, Obed Torres, Thad Starner, Olivier Faugeras, Kent Nickerson, Simon Haykin und viele andere. Ich möchte auch Chris Dodge danken, der diesen Essay vorab gelesen und einige wichtige Verbesserungsvorschläge gemacht hat.

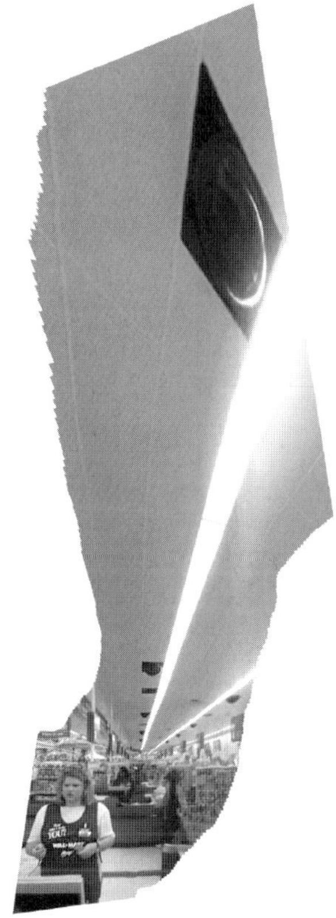

1 I referred to this invention as a *personal computer*, though, in recent years, that term has come to mean a desktop computer. Thus my apparatus has, over the years, been called a *humanistic computer*, *existential computer*, *eudaemonic computer*, *wearable computer*, or the like.

I owe much to those around me, who have influenced my thinking: Rosalind Picard, Hiroshi Ishii, Krzysztof Wodiczko, William Mitchell, Obed Torres, Thad Starner, Olivier Faugeras, Kent Nickerson, Simon Haykin, and many others. I would also like to thank Chris Dodge for reading this essay and making some important suggestions.

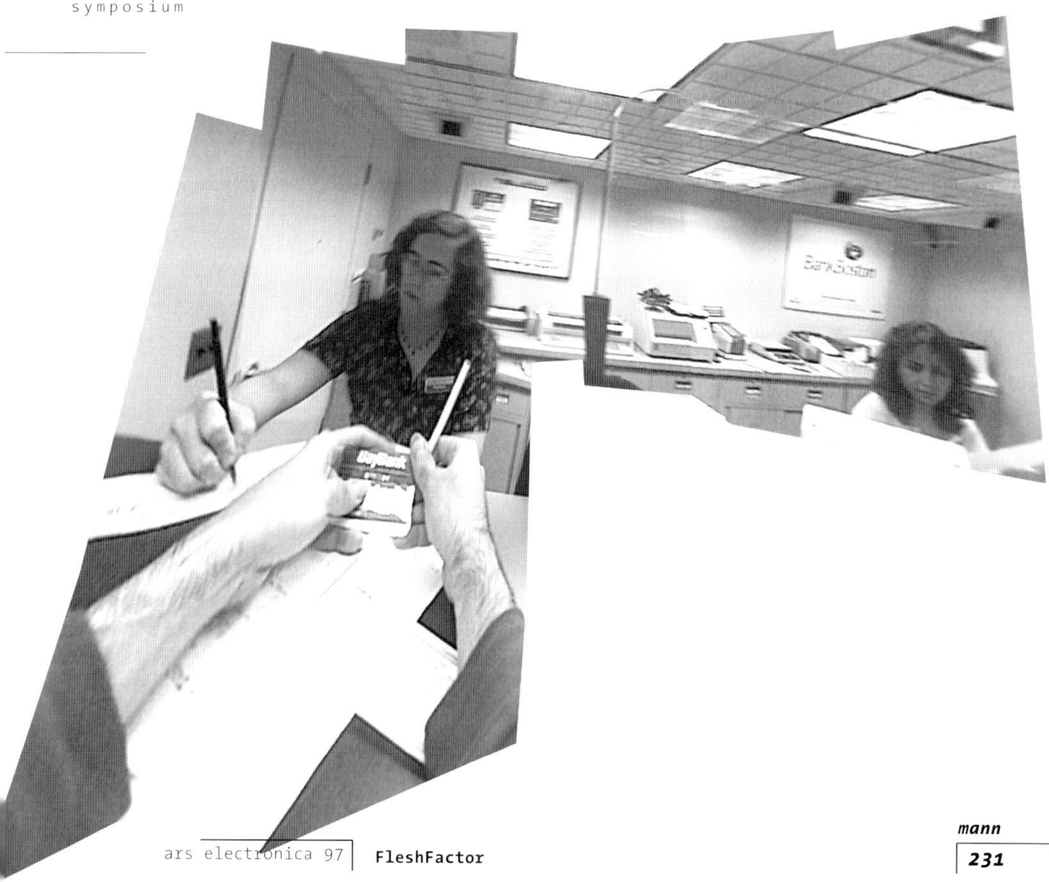

FLORA and FAUNA: Japanese Games and Traditional Culture

Machiko Kusahara

symposium

FLORA und FAUNA: Spiele und traditionelle Kultur in Japan

Machiko Kusahara

In every area of the globe we have flora and fauna. An ecosystem consists of different species that live in networked relationship. Certain species are dominant under certain circumstances. A transition of environment or a sudden change of circumstance would make some species prosper, or become rare. But as a whole it is this inter-related complexity of the flora and fauna that sustains life in the area, making the ecosystem continue through generations.

It is the same with our culture. Now our society is networked. Physical distances are diminishing thanks to the Internet, it is said. We will all live as neighbors sharing the global culture, understanding each other. Some people claim that the global network is destroying cultural tradition. Can this be true?

Certainly our ecosystem is changing. But global communication brings increased awareness of cultural biodiversity as well as similarity. Every culture has its own system in the way of thinking and representing. Each new medium a society develops according to such systems. It is interesting to observe what is going on now in Japanese computer game culture . It is a pursuit of traditional esthetics in digital entertainment. When we see Japanese comics and animations, what we have taken from our tradition is visible.

As in Japanese prints, characters look flat and are rendered in mat colors, with unnaturally deformed faces. The proportions of the faces cannot possibly be derived from any 3-dimensional model. Absence of shading and lack of depth is evident in the landscape.

Even though it may not be generally well-known in the West, the Japanese learned perspective from the West only about 150 years ago. Realism was also brought from the West. Perspective did not originally exist in Asian paintings. Altogether, Japanese perception of 3-dimensional space or body was quite different from that in the West.

One reason why comics and animation have become so successful in Japan might be the fact that they have nothing to do with reality. Flexible use of space in comics coincides with the traditional picture scrolls where events in different time-space can be painted in the same scene. The flat expression of the characters looks more familiar to Japanese eyes than a realistic

Überall auf dieser Erde gibt es Fauna und Flora. Ein Ökosystem besteht aus verschiedenen Arten, die in einem engverflochtenen Beziehungsgefüge miteinander leben. Unter bestimmten Umständen dominieren bestimmte Arten. Ein Umgebungswechsel oder die plötzliche Veränderung lokaler Gegebenheiten könnte bewirken, daß einige Arten gut gedeihen, andere jedoch zurückgehen. Alles in allem sind es aber diese komplexen Zusammenhänge in Fauna und Flora, die das Leben im jeweiligen Gebiet aufrechterhalten und das Fortbestehen des Ökosystems über Generationen sichern. Mit unserer Kultur ist das ebenso. Unsere Gesellschaft ist nun vernetzt. Dank dem Internet verschwinden die Entfernungen zwischen den Dingen, heißt es. Wir leben alle als Nachbarn zusammen, teilen eine globale Kultur, verstehen einander. Manche behaupten, das globale Netz zerstöre kulturelle Traditionen. Kann das stimmen?

Natürlich verändert sich unser Ökosystem. Aber globale Kommunikation bringt ein wachsendes Bewußtsein für kulturelle Artenvielfalt und kulturelle Parallelen mit sich. Jede Kultur hat ihr eigenes Gedanken- und Darstellungssystem. Solche Systeme dienen einer Gesellschaft dazu, für jedes neue Medium passende Anwendungsformen zu entwickeln. Es ist interessant zu beobachten, was momentan in der japanischen Computerspiel-Kultur passiert. Traditionelle Ästhetik findet hier ihre Fortsetzung in digitaler Unterhaltung.

In japanischen Comics und Zeichentrickfilmen wird deutlich, was wir von unserer Tradition übernommen haben. Wie bei japanischen Drucken sind auch hier die Charaktere flach, in matten Farben, mit unnatürlich deformierten Gesichtern. Die Proportion der Gesichter kann unmöglich von einem dreidimensionalen Modell stammen. In der Landschaftsdarstellung fehlen Schattierungen und ein Sinn für räumliche Tiefe. Obwohl diese Tatsache in der westlichen Kultur kaum bekannt ist, haben die Japaner die perspektivische Sichtweise erst vor knapp 150 Jahren vom Westen übernommen. Auch der Realismus kam aus dem Westen nach Japan. Die asiatische Malerei kannte ursprünglich keine Perspektive. Überhaupt nahm man in Japan dreidimensionalen Raum bzw. dreidimensionale Körper völlig anders wahr als im Westen.

Ein Grund, weshalb Comics und Zeichentrickfilme in Japan so erfolgreich sind, könnte darin liegen, daß sie nichts mit der Realität zu tun haben. Der flexible Umgang mit Raum in Comics stimmt mit den traditionellen Bildrollen überein, wo Ereignisse, die zu verschiedenen Zeiten und an verschie-

portrait. When 2-dimensional video games conquered the market it was natural for such characters to populate them. Japanese esthetics in comics and animations seemed to have found its way into digital medium.

Meanwhile, high performance game platforms have arrived. Game designers have had to face a difficult question. More movie, more action, higher interactivity are required, which means the use of 3D computer graphics. Game characters which used to be 2D – often designed according to Japanese comic style – had to be modified into 3D together with their environment. How can flat, non-photorealistic and anti-perspective Japanese traditional taste be transformed into a 3-dimensional world inside a computer, where geometry and optics are the basic rules of visual expression? In addition, it is not only the matter of characters. Animation is another problem.

Virtual Idol Kyoko Date was created last year, based on the know-how of a leading Japanese management company for TV idols known as Hori Pro. The girl character became known as the first *virtual talent* to belong to the company. She had the typical face and body of such an *idol*, rendered in an idealistic style, and natural motion produced by motion capture. But she was a failure. She wasn't charming. Use of motion capture systems is not the right answer, some Japanese animators have started to think. Fuji TV brought up the idea and interface of Bunraku [Japanese puppet] for its TV program, after years of experience in virtual reality and motion capture. We have developed the language of traditional puppetry such as Bunraku. As the language had been refined through history and met our code, it should work with virtual characters better than bringing in the code for human movement.

It is said that motion capturing does not convey emotion. After this experience with *Kyoto Date* Hori Pro is now promoting a virtual doll – a Japanese version of Barbie. The re-discovery of puppets coincides with what is happening in game design. The animator of a successful game that came onto the market recently, *Kowloon's Gate*, says he used the language of Bunraku for its animation while he designed the characters [after many experiments] along the delicate interface between reality and what we know from Japanese comics. Since these

denen Orten stattfinden, in derselben Szene abgebildet sein können. Die flachen Gesichtszüge der Charaktere sehen für japanische Augen vertrauter aus als realistische Porträts. Als zweidimensionale Videospiele den Markt eroberten, war es also nur natürlich, daß sie hauptsächlich von solchen Charakteren bevölkert waren. Die japanische Comic- und Zeichentrick-Ästhetik schien ihren Weg in das digitale Medium gefunden zu haben.

Inzwischen gibt es bereits Hochleistungsplattformen für Spiele, und Spiele-Designer sahen sich mit einer schwierigen Frage konfrontiert. Die Forderung nach mehr Film, mehr Action, größerer Interaktivität führt zwangsweise zur Verwendung von 3D-Computergraphiken. Die Charaktere, früher zweidimensional und häufig dem japanischen Comic-Stil nachempfunden, mußten mitsamt ihrer Umgebung in 3D umgewandelt werden. Wie kann nun die japanische Tradition der flachen, nicht-photorealistischen, anti-perspektivischen Darstellung in die dreidimensionale Computerwelt übernommen werden, wo Geometrie und Optik als Grundregeln des visuellen Ausdrucks gelten? Es geht hier übrigens nicht nur um die Charaktere selbst; ein weiteres Problem ist die Animation.

Virtual Idol Kyoko Date wurde letztes Jahr entwickelt und basiert auf dem Know-how einer führenden japanischen Verwaltungsgesellschaft für TV-*Idols*, bekannt unter dem Namen Hori Pro. Die neuentwickelte Mädchenfigur wurde als erstes *virtuelles Talent* dieser Firma bekannt. Sie hat das typische Gesicht und den typischen Körper eines *Idols*, einen idealistischen Stil und natürliche, durch Motion-Capture erzeugte Bewegungen. Trotzdem war sie ein Flop. Es fehlte ihr das gewisse Etwas. Einige japanische Zeichentrick-Graphiker begannen zu bezweifeln, ob sie mit Motion-Capture-Systemen auf dem richtigen Weg seien. Nach jahrelangen Erfahrungen mit virtueller Realität und Motion-Capture setzt Fuji TV als Idee und Schnittstelle für sein Fernsehprogramm nun auf Bunraku, das japanische Puppenspiel. Die Sprache des traditionellen Puppenspiels Bunraku ist unsere ureigene Entwicklung. Da diese Sprache im Laufe der Geschichte stark verfeinert wurde und unserem Code entspricht, müßte sie auch bei virtuellen Charakteren besser funktionieren als der neueingeführte menschliche Bewegungscode.

Motion-Capture kann Emotionen nicht übertragen, heißt es. Nach der oben erwähnten Lektion wirbt Hori Pro nun für eine virtuelle Puppe – eine japanische Version von Barbie. Die Wiederent-

characters are puppets rather than human beings, they look more natural when properly treated as puppets, he says.

Another interesting feature of *Kowloon's Gate* is the story itself. It is based on Yin-Yang theory which says that the universe is sustained by the balance of these two features. In the game the user is asked to visit virtual Kowloon to adjust the lost balance. Even though a visitor meets many well-designed freaks and monsters and sometimes fights with them, none of them is totally evil or totally good. The game designer [director] tries to establish a new approach to the role-playing game based on the Asian way of thinking. In fact, some Japanese games can be considered as interactive cinema. Because of the Japanese market structure, multimedia works have to take the form of a game to find their place on the market. *Gadget* and *Gadget Trip* by Haruhiko Shono are examples of this. *Kowloon's Gate* can also be considered as such.

The quest for the Japanese style in digital media will continue. It would be interesting, not only for the Japanese, to watch what comes of this. Because, as I stated earlier, it is not just observing a process of media technology penetrating into a culture. It is a phase of biodiversity that will help to enrich our society as it undergoes changes in a media environment.

deckung der Puppen entspricht den Entwicklungen im Spiele-Design. Der Graphikdesigner von *Kowloon's Gate*, einem erfolgreichen Spiel, das kürzlich auf den Markt kam, verwendete laut eigenen Angaben für die Animation den Code des Bunraku und legte die Charaktere [nach zahlreichen Experimenten] an der höchst fragilen Schnittstelle zwischen Realität und den Eigenheiten der japanischen Comics an. Da diese Charaktere eher Puppen als menschliche Wesen sind, sehen sie seiner Meinung nach auch natürlicher aus, wenn man sie wie Puppen behandelt.

Auch die Geschichte von *Kowloon's Gate* ist höchst interessant. Sie basiert auf der Theorie von Yin und Yang, den beiden Elementen, die das Universum im Gleichgewicht halten. Im Spiel wird der Besucher aufgefordert, das virtuelle Kowloon zu besuchen, um das verlorene Gleichgewicht wiederherzustellen. Obwohl der Besucher auf zahlreiche gelungene Monster und Ungeheuer trifft, die er manchmal auch bekämpfen muß, ist keines davon nur gut oder nur böse. Der Designer [Regisseur] des Spiels versucht, auf der Basis asiatischen Denkens einen neuen Ansatz für das Rollenspiel zu finden. Einige japanische Spiele können in der Tat als interaktives Kino gelten. Aufgrund der japanischen Marktstruktur sollten Multimedia-Arbeiten, die auf diesem Markt erfolgreich sein wollen, in Spielform realisiert werden. *Gadget* und *Gadget Trip* von Haruhiko Shono sind – neben *Kowloon's Gate* – Beispiele dafür.

Die Suche nach einem japanischen Stil in den digitalen Medien wird weitergehen. Es wäre nicht nur für Japaner interessant, diese Entwicklungen zu beobachten. Denn, wie ich vorne gesagt habe, sehen wir hier nicht nur, wie die Medientechnologie eine Kultur durchdringt. Wir haben es auch mit einer Steigerung der Artenvielfalt zu tun, die dazu beitragen wird, unsere Gesellschaft in ihrem Anpassungsprozeß an die medial geprägte Umgebung zu bereichern.

Sorry, but Your Soul just Died

Tom Wolfe

Sorry, aber Ihre Seele ist gerade gestorben

Tom Wolfe

Da ich nicht ganz auf dem Laufenden bin, hatte ich gerade erst von der digitalen Revolution gehört, als Louis Rossetto, Mitbegründer der Zeitschrift *Wired*, – ganz der junge kalifornische Visionär, im kragenlosen Hemd, das Haar so lang wie Felix Mendelssohn – letzten Februar in einem Vortrag am Cato Institute den Beginn der digitalen Zivilisation des 21. Jahrhunderts verkündete. Er berief sich dabei auf einen Text des ketzerischen jesuitischen Wissenschaftlers und Philosophen Pierre Teilhard de Chardin, der vor 50 Jahren prophezeit hatte, Radio, Fernsehen und Computer würden eine *Noosphäre* schaffen, eine elektronische Membran, welche die Erde überziehen und die gesamte Menschheit wie ein einziges Nervensystem verbinden würde. Geographische Standorte, Staatsgrenzen, die herkömmlichen Vorstellungen von Märkten und politischen Prozessen – all das würde irrelevant werden. Nun, da sich das Internet in erstaunlichem Tempo über die ganze Welt ausbreitet, meinte Rossetto, stehe dieser wunderbare, modemvermittelte Augenblick unmittelbar bevor.

Mag sein. Aber irgendwie habe ich das Gefühl, in zehn Jahren, im Jahr 2006, wird sich das digitale Universum ziemlich bescheiden ausnehmen neben einer neuen Technologie, die heute noch in den Kinderschuhen steckt und nur in einigen wenigen

Being a bit behind the curve, I had only just heard of the digital revolution last February when Louis Rossetto, co-founder of *Wired* magazine, wearing a shirt with no collar and his hair as long as Felix Mendelssohn's, looking every inch the young California visionary, gave a speech at the Cato Institute announcing the dawn of the twenty-first century's digital civilization. As his text, he chose the maverick Jesuit scientist and philosopher Pierre Teilhard de Chardin, who fifty years ago prophesied that radio, television, and computers would create a *noˆsphere,* an electronic membrane covering the earth and wiring all humanity together in a single nervous system. Geographic locations, national boundaries, the old notions of markets and political processes – all would become irrelevant. With the Internet spreading over the globe at an astonishing pace, said Rossetto, that marvelous modem-driven moment is almost at hand.

Could be. But something tells me that within ten years, by 2006, the entire digital universe is going to seem like pretty mundane stuff compared to a new technology that right now is but a mere glow radiating from a tiny number of American and Cuban [yes, Cuban] hospitals and laboratories. It is called brain imaging, and anyone who cares to get up early and catch a truly blinding twenty-first-century dawn will want to keep an eye on it.

Brain imaging refers to techniques for watching the human brain as it functions, in real time. The most advanced forms currently are three-dimensional electroencephalography using mathematical models; the more familiar PET scan [positron-emission tomography]; the new fMRI [functional magnetic resonance imaging], which shows brain blood-flow patterns, and MRS [magnetic resonance spectroscopy], which measures biochemical changes in the brain; and the even newer PET reporter gene/PET reporter probe, which is, in fact, so new that it still has that length of heavy lumber for a name. Used so far only in animals and a few desperately sick children, the PET reporter gene/PET reporter probe pinpoints and follows the activity of specific genes. On a scanner screen you can actually see the genes light up inside the brain.

amerikanischen und kubanischen [ja, kubanischen] Krankenhäusern und Labors getestet wird. Ich spreche von *Brain Imaging*, und jeder, der gern vorne mit dabei ist und einen wirklich fulminanten Einstieg ins 21. Jahrhundert miterleben möchte, sollte diese Entwicklung im Auge behalten.

Als *Brain Imaging* bezeichnet man bildgebende Verfahren, mit denen man in Echtzeit beobachten kann, wie das menschliche Gehirn arbeitet. Die fortschrittlichsten Methoden sind derzeit die 3D-Elektroenzephalographie auf der Basis mathematischer Modelle, das etwas bekanntere PET-Scanning [Positronenemmissionstomographie], die neuentwickelte funktionelle Magnetresonanztomographie [fMRT], die das Durchblutungsprofil des Gehirns anzeigt, die Magnetresonanzspektroskopie [MRS], die biochemische Veränderungen im Gehirn mißt, und schließlich das Neueste vom Neuen, *PET reporter gene/PET reporter probe*, so brandneu, daß sich bisher für diesen Zungenbrecher von Namen noch keine Abkürzung durchgesetzt hat. PET reporter gene/PET reporter probe fand bislang nur bei Tieren und einigen unheilbar kranken Kindern Anwendung und zeigt bestimmte Gene im Gehirn auf einem Scanner-Schirm als Leuchtpünktchen an.

Für heutige Begriffe sind das alles raffinierte Geräte, aber in zehn Jahren wirken sie wahrscheinlich primitiv im Vergleich zu den bis dahin entwickelten Verfahren, die uns atemberaubende Einblicke in das Gehirn bieten werden.

Brain Imaging wurde zum Zweck der medizinischen Diagnose erfunden; weitaus wichtiger ist jedoch, daß es mit unumstößlicher Präzision gewisse Theorien über *den Geist*, *das Selbst*, *die Seele* und den *freien Willen* bestätigen könnte – Theorien, von denen Wissenschaftler aus dem derzeit aufregendsten Bereich der akademischen Welt, der Neurowissenschaft, bereits felsenfest überzeugt sind. Zugegeben, schon wegen all dieser skeptischen Anführungszeichen wird jeder sofort mißtrauisch werden, aber Ultimative Skepsis macht den versprochenen fulminanten Einstieg ins 21. Jahrhundert erst so richtig perfekt.

Die Neurowissenschaft, die Lehre vom Gehirn und vom Zentralnervensystem, steht kurz vor einer einheitlichen Theorie, die ebenso gewaltige Auswirkungen haben wird wie vor hundert Jahren der Darwinismus. Es gibt auch schon einen neuen Darwin, oder besser ein Up-Date, denn keiner glaubt inbrünstiger an Darwin I. als er. Sein Name ist Edward O. Wilson. Er lehrt Zoologie in Harvard und verfaßte

By 1996 standards, these are sophisticated devices. Ten years from now, however, they may seem primitive compared to the stunning new windows into the brain that will have been developed.

Brain imaging was invented for medical diagnosis. But its far greater importance is that it may very well confirm, in ways too precise to be disputed, certain theories about *the mind,* *the self,* *the soul,* and *free will* that are already devoutly believed in by scholars in what is now the hottest field in the academic world, neuroscience. Granted, all those skeptical quotation marks are enough to put anybody on the qui vive right away, but Ultimate Skepticism is part of the brilliance of the dawn I have promised.

Neuroscience, the science of the brain and the central nervous system, is on the threshold of a unified theory that will have an impact as powerful as that of Darwinism a hundred years ago. Already there is a new Darwin, or perhaps I should say an updated Darwin, since no one ever believed more religiously in Darwin I than he does. His name is Edward O. Wilson. He teaches zoology at Harvard, and he is the author of two books of extraordinary influence, *The Insect Societies and Sociobiology: The New Synthesis.* Not A new synthesis but The new synthesis; in terms of his stature in neuroscience, it is not a mere boast.

Wilson has created and named the new field of sociobiology, and he has compressed its underlying premise into a single sentence. Every human brain, he says, is born not as a blank tablet [a tabula rasa] waiting to be filled in by experience but as *an exposed negative waiting to be slipped into developer fluid.* You can develop the negative well or you can develop it poorly, but either way you are going to get precious little that is not already imprinted on the film. The print is the individual's genetic history, over thousands of years of evolution, and there is not much anybody can do about it. Furthermore, says Wilson, genetics determine not only things such as temperament, role preferences, emotional responses, and levels of aggression, but also many of our most revered moral choices, which are not choices at all in any free-will sense but tendencies imprinted in the hypothalamus and limbic regions of the brain, a con-

u. a. zwei äußerst einflußreiche Bücher, *The Insect Societies* und *Sociobiology: The New Synthesis.* Nicht eine neue Synthese, sondern die neue Synthese – angesichts seiner Position in der Neurowissenschaft wohl mehr als reine Großsprecherei.

Wilson führte eine neue wissenschaftliche Disziplin ein, die er Soziobiologie nennt. Die der Soziobiologie zugrundeliegende Prämisse faßte er in einem einzigen Satz zusammen: Das menschliche Gehirn, so meint er, sei bei der Geburt kein unbeschriebenes Blatt [Tabula rasa], das darauf wartet, mit Erfahrungen vollgeschrieben zu werden, sondern *ein belichtetes Negativ, das nur darauf wartet, in die Entwicklungsflüssigkeit getaucht zu werden*. Man kann das Negativ gut oder schlecht entwickeln, aber in beiden Fällen wird kaum mehr dabei herauskommen, als bereits vorher auf dem Film aufgezeichnet war. Auf dem Abzug ist die genetische Evolutionsgeschichte des Individuums abgebildet, über viele Jahrtausende hinweg; und daran ist kaum zu rütteln. Die Genetik, meint Wilson, bestimmt darüber hinaus nicht nur Dinge wie Temperament, bevorzugtes Rollenverhalten, emotionale Reaktionen und verschiedene Stufen der Aggression, sondern auch viele unserer ehrenhaften moralischen Entscheidungen, die in Wahrheit überhaupt keine Entscheidungen im Sinne eines freien Willens sind, sondern Tendenzen, die im Hypothalamus und in den limbischen Regionen des Gehirns festgelegt sind. Dieser Ansatz wird in einem Buch weiterentwickelt, das 1993 Furore machte: *Das moralische Empfinden* von James Q. Wilson [nicht verwandt mit Edward O.].

Diese neurowissenschaftliche Sicht des Lebens ist mittlerweile in der akademischen Welt zum strategisch umkämpften Gelände avanciert, heiß umkämpft nicht nur unter Wissenschaftlern verschiedenster Disziplinen, sondern durchaus auch in der breiten Öffentlichkeit. Liberale und Konservative, die nicht die leiseste Ahnung von Wissenschaft haben, sind eifrig bemüht, dieses Terrain für sich zu erobern. Das *Gay Rights Movement* z. B. stützt sich auf eine Studie vom Juli 1993, in der der hochrenommierte Wissenschaftler Dean Hamer vom National Institute of Health verkündete, das *Schwulen-Gen* entdeckt zu haben. Ist Homosexualität wie Linkshändigkeit oder haselnußbraune Augen tatsächlich genetisch festgelegt, so sind Gesetze und Sanktionen gegen Homosexuelle ganz offensichtlich wider die Natur. Die Konservativen wiederum setzen auf Studien, die besagen, daß das männliche und das weibliche Gehirn aufgrund unserer langwierigen Evolutionsgeschichte so verschieden gepolt sind, daß sämtli-

cept expanded upon in 1993 in a much-talked-about book, *The Moral Sense*, by James Q. Wilson [no kin to Edward O.].

This, the neuroscientific view of life, has become the strategic high ground in the academic world, and the battle for it has already spread well beyond the scientific disciplines and, for that matter, out into the general public. Both liberals and conservatives without a scientific bone in their bodies are busy trying to seize the terrain. The gay rights movement, for example, has fastened onto a study published in July of 1993 by the highly respected Dean Hamer of the National Institute of Health, announcing the discovery of *the gay gene.* Obviously, if homosexuality is a genetically determined trait, like left-handedness or hazel eyes, then laws and sanctions against it are attempts to legislate against Nature. Conservatives, meantime, have fastened upon studies indicating that men's and women's brains are wired so differently, thanks to the long haul of evolution, that feminist attempts to open up traditionally male roles to women are the same thing: a doomed violation of Nature.

Wilson himself has wound up in deep water on this score; or cold water, if one need edit. In his personal life Wilson is a conventional liberal, PC, as the saying goes – he *is*, after all, a member of the Harvard faculty – concerned about environmental issues and all the usual things. But he has said that *forcing similar role identities* on both men and women *flies in the face of thousands of years in which mammals demonstrated a strong tendency for sexual division of labor. Since this division of labor is persistent from hunter-gatherer through agricultural and industrial societies, it suggests a genetic origin. We do not know when this trait evolved in human evolution or how resistant it is to the continuing and justified pressures for human rights.*

Resistant was Darwin II, the neuroscientist, speaking. *Justified* was the PC Harvard liberal. He was not PC or liberal enough. Feminist protesters invaded a conference where Wilson was appearing, dumped a pitcher of ice water, cubes and all, over his head, and began chanting, *You're all wet! You're all wet!* The most prominent feminist in America, Gloria Steinem,

che feministischen Versuche, in traditionelle Männerdomänen einzudringen, ebenfalls nichts anderes sind als ein zum Scheitern verurteilter Gewaltakt gegen die Natur.

Wilson selbst brachte das Ganze ganz schön in die Klemme – besser gesagt, es ließ ihn als begossener Pudel dastehen. Privat ist er ein konventioneller Liberaler, politisch korrekt, wie es so schön heißt – schließlich ist er Mitglied der Harvard-Fakultät –, interessiert sich für Umweltfragen und derlei Dinge. Und doch sagte er: Männern und Frauen *dieselben Rollenidentitäten aufzuzwingen heißt, sich über Jahrtausende hinwegzusetzen, in denen Säugetiere starke Tendenzen zu geschlechtsspezifischer Arbeitsteilung herausgebildet haben. Da diese Arbeitsteilung – angefangen von den Jägern und Sammlern über die Ackerbauern und Viehzüchter bis herauf zur industriellen Gesellschaft – beibehalten wurde, kann man davon ausgehen, daß sie genetischen Ursprungs ist. Wir wissen nicht, zu welchem Zeitpunkt der menschlichen Evolution sich dieser Charakterzug herausgebildet hat oder wie resistent er gegenüber den kontinuierlichen und gerechtfertigten Bemühungen um die Menschenrechte ist*.

Resistent – da sprach Darwin II, der Neurowissenschaftler; *gerechtfertigt* – das war der politisch korrekte Harvard-Liberale. Er war aber weder politisch korrekt noch liberal genug. Feministische Demonstrantinnen verschafften sich Zutritt zu einer Konferenz, an der Wilson teilnahm, kippten ihm einen Krug Eiswasser samt Eiswürfeln über den Kopf und stimmten einen Sprechchor an: *Du bist am falschen Dampfer! Du bist am falschen Dampfer!* Die prominenteste Feministin Amerikas, Gloria Steinem, forderte in einem Fernsehinterview mit John Stossel von ABC, daß Untersuchungen der genetischen Unterschiede zwischen männlichem und weiblichem Nervensystem in Hinkunft zu unterlassen seien.

Doch all das war noch harmlos im Vergleich zur aktuellen politischen Panikmache in Sachen Neurowissenschaft. Im Februar 1992 hatte Frederick K. Goodwin, angesehener Psychiater, Leiter der Federal Alcohol, Drug Abuse, and Mental Health Administration und amtlich beglaubigter PR-Tolpatsch, den Fehler gemacht, bei einer öffentlichen Versammlung in Washington die zehn Jahre alte *Violence Initiative* des National Institute for Mental Health zu beschreiben. Dabei handelte es sich um ein Experimentalprogramm, das von der Hypothese ausging, ein Großteil der schweren Gewaltverbrechen in den USA ginge wie bei den Affen im Urwald – Goodwin

went on television and, in an interview with John Stossel of ABC, insisted that studies of genetic differences between male and female nervous systems should cease forthwith.

But that turned out to be mild stuff in the current political panic over neuroscience. In February of 1992, Frederick K. Goodwin, a renowned psychiatrist, head of the federal Alcohol, Drug Abuse and Mental Health Administration, and a certified yokel in the field of public relations, made the mistake of describing, at a public meeting in Washington, the National Institute of Mental Health's ten-year-old *Violence Initiative*. This was an experimental program whose hypothesis was that, as among monkeys in the jungle – Goodwin was noted for his monkey studies – much of the criminal mayhem in the United States was caused by a relatively few young males who were genetically predisposed to it; who were hardwired for violent crime, in short. Out in the jungle, among mankind's closest animal relatives, the chimpanzees, it seemed that a handful of genetically twisted young males were the ones who committed practically *all* of the wanton murders of other males and the physical abuse of females. What if the same were true among human beings? What if, in any given community, it turned out to be a handful of young males with toxic DNA who were pushing statistics for violent crime up to such high levels? The Violence Initiative envisioned identifying these individuals in childhood, somehow, some way, someday, and treating them therapeutically with drugs. The notion that crime-ridden urban America was a *jungle,* said Goodwin, was perhaps more than just a tired old metaphor.

That did it. That may have been the stupidest single word uttered by an American public official in the year 1992. The outcry was immediate. Senator Edward Kennedy of Massachusetts and Representative John Dingell of Michigan [who, it became obvious later, suffered from hydrophobia when it came to science projects] not only condemned Goodwin's remarks as racist but also delivered their scientific verdict: Research among primates *is a preposterous basis* for analyzing anything as complex as *the crime and violence that plagues our country today.* [This came as surprising news to NASA scientists who had first trained and sent a chimpanzee called Ham up on

war bekannt für seine Primatenforschung – auf das Konto von verhältnismäßig wenigen jungen Männern, die genetisch dazu prädisponiert waren, die, mit anderen Worten, auf Gewaltverbrechen vorprogrammiert waren. Draußen im Urwald bei den Schimpansen, den uns am nächsten verwandten Primaten, wäre nahezu ausnahmslos eine Handvoll genetisch gestörter junger Männchen dafür verantwortlich, daß andere Männchen getötet und Weibchen mißbraucht werden. Und wenn das nun bei den Menschen genauso wäre? Und wenn es in jeder menschlichen Gemeinschaft diese paar jungen Männchen mit giftiger DNS wären, die die Statistiken für Gewaltverbrechen derart in die Höhe treiben? Die *Violence Initiative* sah vor, diese Individuen schon in der Kindheit irgendwie, irgendwann zu identifizieren und einer medikamentösen Behandlung zu unterziehen. Die Vorstellung, die vom Verbrechen heimgesuchten amerikanischen Städte seien ein *Dschungel*, sagte Goodwin, sei vielleicht doch mehr als nur eine alte, abgegriffene Metapher.

Mehr brauchte es nicht. Das war vielleicht das dümmste Wort, das ein US-Beamter im Jahr 1992 in den Mund nahm. Allgemeine Empörung war die Folge. Der Senator von Massachusetts, Edward Kennedy, und der Abgeordnete von Michigan, John Dingell [der, wie sich später herausstellte, ganz schön wasserscheu war, wenn es um wissenschaftliche Projekte ging], verurteilten Goodwins Bemerkungen nicht nur als rassistisch, sondern gaben auch gleich ihren wissenschaftlichen Senf dazu: Primatenforschung *ist eine widersinnige Basis* für die Analyse derart komplexer Phänomene wie der *Kriminalität und Gewalt, unter denen unser Land heute leidet*. [Diese Neuigkeit überraschte insbesondere jene NASA-Wissenschaftler, die zuerst einen Schimpansen namens Ham abgerichtet und in einer Redstone-Rakete auf einen suborbitalen Raumflug geschickt hatten und dann einen Schimpansen namens Enos – griechisch für *Mann* – abgerichtet und in einer Atlas-Rakete in eine Erdumlaufbahn gebracht hatten. Aufgrund dieser Experimente hatten sie die körperlichen, psychologischen und motorischen Reaktionen der menschlichen Astronauten Alan Shepard und John Glenn, welche die Flüge und Aufgaben der Schimpansen Monate später wiederholten, präzise und umfassend vorhersagen können.] Die *Violence Initiative* wurde mit eugenischen NS-Plänen zur Ausrottung unerwünschter Personen verglichen. Dingells Amtskollege aus Michigan, Abgeordneter John Conyers, damaliger Vorsitzender des Government Operations Committee und leitender Beamter im

top of a Redstone rocket into suborbital space flight and then trained and sent another one, called Enos, which is Greek for *man,* up on an Atlas rocket and around the earth in orbital space flight and had thereby accurately and completely predicted the physical, psychological, and task-motor responses of the human astronauts, Alan Shepard and John Glenn, who repeated the chimpanzees' flights and tasks months later.] The *Violence Initiative* was compared to Nazi eugenic proposals for the extermination of undesirables. Dingell's Michigan colleague, Representative John Conyers, then chairman of the Government Operations Committee and senior member of the Congressional Black Caucus, demanded Goodwin's resignation – and got it two days later, whereupon the government, with the Department of Health and Human Services now doing the talking, denied that the *Violence Initiative* had ever existed. It disappeared down the memory hole, to use Orwell's term.

A conference of criminologists and other academics interested in the neuroscientific studies done so far for the *Violence Initiative* – a conference underwritten in part by a grant from the National Institutes of Health – had been scheduled for May of 1993 at the University of Maryland. Down went the conference, too; the NIH drowned it like a kitten. Last year, a University of Maryland legal scholar named David Wasserman tried to reassemble the troops on the QT, as it were, in a hall all but hidden from human purview in a hamlet called Queenstown in the foggy, boggy boondocks of Queen Annes County on Maryland's Eastern Shore. The NIH, proving it was a hard learner, quietly provided $133,000 for the event but only after Wasserman promised to fireproof the proceedings by also inviting scholars who rejected the notion of a possible genetic genesis of crime and scheduling a cold-shower session dwelling on the evils of the eugenics movement of the early twentieth century. No use, boys! An army of protesters found the poor cringing devils anyway and stormed into the auditorium chanting, *Maryland conference, you can't hide – we know you're pushing genocide!* It took two hours for them to get bored enough to leave, and the conference ended in a complete muddle with the specially recruited fireproofing PC faction issuing a statement that said: *Scientists

Congressional Black Caucus, forderte den Rücktritt Goodwins – welcher nur zwei Tage später erfolgte. Die Regierung, die nun gemeinsam mit dem Department of Health and Human Services das Wort führte, dementierte in der Folge, daß die *Violence Initiative* jemals existiert habe, und diese verschwand, um mit Orwell zu sprechen, im großen Erinnerungsloch.

Für Mai 1993 war an der University of Maryland eine Konferenz für Kriminologen und andere Akademiker geplant gewesen, die sich für die bis dato im Zuge der *Violence Initiative* durchgeführten neurowissenschaftlichen Untersuchungen interessierten – eine Konferenz, welche das National Institute of Health durch einen Zuschuß mitfinanzierten. Daraus wurde nun natürlich nichts; das NIH ließ die Konferenz fallen wie eine heiße Kartoffel. Letztes Jahr versuchte David Wasserman, Rechtswissenschaftler an der University of Maryland, die Truppen – sozusagen still und heimlich – wieder zu versammeln, diesmal vor menschlichen Blicken nahezu völlig abgeschirmt, in einem kleinen Dorf namens Queenstown in der neblig-sumpfigen Pampa von Queen Anne's County an der Ostküste Marylands. Das NIH hatte aus seinen Fehlern nur wenig gelernt und stellte für die Veranstaltung stillschweigend 133.000 Dollar zur Verfügung. Immerhin mußte Wasserman versprechen, zur Sicherheit auch Wissenschaftler einzuladen, die die Vorstellung, Gewalt und Kriminalität könnten genetischen Ursprungs sein, strikt ablehnten, und quasi als *kalte Dusche* eine Sitzung ins Programm aufzunehmen, in der die schändlichen Aktivitäten der Eugenik-Bewegung im frühen 20. Jahrhundert diskutiert werden sollten. Alles vergebens! Ein ganzes Heer von DemonstrantInnen spürte die armen, unterwürfigen Teufel auf und stürmte das Auditorium mit den Rufen: *Hier an dem versteckten Ort unterstützt ihr Völkermord!* Sie schlugen zwei Stunden Radau, bevor sie wieder abzogen, und die Konferenz endete in einem kompletten Durcheinander, in dem die eigens rekrutierten politisch korrekten Alibi-Experten folgende Stellungnahme abgaben: *Weder Wissenschaftler noch Historiker oder Soziologen dürfen zulassen, daß einer rassistischen Pseudowissenschaft akademischer Rückhalt geboten wird.* Heute ist der Begriff *Violence Initiative* im NIH ein Synonym für Tabu. Die momentane Situation gleicht jener Zeit im Mittelalter, als die katholische Kirche das Sezieren menschlicher Leichname untersagte, weil sie fürchtete, die christliche Lehre, daß Gott die Menschen nach seinem Ebenbild erschaffen hat, könne im Licht des Zutagegeförderten zweifelhaft erscheinen.

as well as historians and sociologists must not allow themselves to provide academic respectability for racist pseudoscience.* Today, at the NIH, the term Violence Initiative is a synonym for *taboo*. The present moment resembles that moment in the Middle Ages when the Catholic Church forbade the dissection of human bodies, for fear that what was discovered inside might cast doubt on the Christian doctrine that God created man in his own image.

Even more radio-active is the matter of intelligence, as measured by IQ tests. Privately – not many care to speak out – the vast majority of neuroscientists believe the genetic component of an individual's intelligence is remarkably high. Your intelligence can be improved upon by skilled and devoted mentors or it can be held back by a poor upbringing – i.e., the negative can be well developed or poorly developed – but your genes are what really make the difference. The recent ruckus over Charles Murray and Richard Herrnstein's *The Bell Curve* is probably just the beginning of the bitterness the subject is going to create.

Not long ago, according to two neuroscientists I interviewed, a firm called Neurometrics sought out investors and tried to market an amazing but simple invention known as the IQ Cap. The idea was to provide a way of testing intelligence that would be free of *cultural bias,* one that would not force anyone to deal with words or concepts that might be familiar to people from one culture but not to people from another. The IQ Cap recorded only brain waves; and a computer, not a potentially biased human test-giver, analyzed the results. It was based on the work of neuroscientists such as E. Roy John[1], who is now one of the major pioneers of electroencephalographic brain imaging; Duilio Giannitrapani, author of *The Electrophysiology of Intellectual Functions*; and David Robinson, author of *The Wechsler Adult Intelligence Scale and Personality Assessment: Toward a Biologically Based Theory of Intelligence and Cognition* and many other monographs famous among neuroscientists. I spoke to one researcher who had devised an IQ Cap himself by replicating an experiment described by Giannitrapani in *The Electrophysiology of Intellectual Functions*. It was not a complicated process. You attached sixteen electrodes to the scalp of the person you wanted to test. You had to muss up

Doch das Thema Intelligenz, gemessen durch IQ-Tests, scheint all dies noch zu überstrahlen. Ganz für sich – kaum einer legt Wert darauf, es auszusprechen – sind die meisten Neurowissenschaftler davon überzeugt, daß die menschliche Intelligenz in erstaunlich hohem Maße genetisch bedingt ist. Sie kann durch geschickte und engagierte Mentoren weiterverbessert oder durch schlechte Erziehung unterdrückt werden – d. h. man kann das Negativ gut oder schlecht entwickeln –, aber der entscheidende Unterschied liegt in den Genen. Der Aufruhr, den Charles Murray und Richard Herrnstein vor kurzem mit *The Bell Curve* auslösten, liefert wahrscheinlich nur einen ersten Vorgeschmack auf die Bitterkeit, die dieses Thema noch erzeugen wird.

Vor gar nicht allzu langer Zeit, so erzählten mir zwei Neurowissenschaftler in einem Interview, hatte eine Firma namens Neurometrics Investoren gesucht, um eine simple, aber verblüffende Erfindung namens *IQ Cap* auf den Markt zu bringen. Mit dieser *Kappe* sollte es möglich sein, Intelligenz auf kulturunabhängige Weise zu testen, so daß niemand mehr gezwungen wäre, mit Worten oder Konzepten zu arbeiten, die zwar den Angehörigen einer bestimmten Kultur vertraut, denen anderer Kulturen jedoch völlig fremd sind. Die *IQ Cap* zeichnete nur Gehirnwellen auf, und die Ergebnisse wurden dann von einem Computer, nicht von einem potentiell voreingenommenen menschlichen Versuchsleiter, ausgewertet. Die Idee basierte auf den Arbeiten von Neurowissenschaftlern wie E. Roy John der heute als einer der bedeutendsten Wegbereiter des elektroenzephalographischen Brain Imaging gilt, Duilio Giannitrapani, Autor von *The Electrophysiology of Intellectual Functions*, und David Robinson, Autor von *The Wechsler Adult Intelligence Scale and Personality Assessment: Toward a Biologically Based Theory of Intelligence and Cognition* und zahlreicher weiterer, in neurowissenschaftlichen Kreisen wohlbekannter Monographien. Ich sprach mit einem Forscher, der selbst eine IQ Cap konstruiert hatte, indem er ein Experiment kopierte, das Giannitrapani in *The Electrophysiology of Intellectual Functions* beschreibt. Es war im Prinzip ganz einfach. Man befestigte 16 Elektroden an der Kopfhaut der Versuchsperson. Das Haar geriet dabei etwas durcheinander, aber abschneiden oder gar abrasieren mußte man es nicht. Dann ließ man die Person auf eine Markierung an einer leeren Wand starren. Unser Forscher verwendete einen himbeerroten Reißnagel. Dann legte man einen Kippschalter um. Innerhalb von 16 Sekunden sagte der Cap-Computer präzise [mit einer

his hair a little, but you didn't have to cut it, much less shave it. Then you had him stare at a marker on a blank wall. This particular researcher used a raspberry- red thumbtack. Then you pushed a toggle switch. In sixteen seconds the Cap's computer box gave you an accurate prediction [within one-half of a standard deviation] of what the subject would score on all eleven subtests of the Wechsler Adult Intelligence Scale or, in the case of children, the Wechsler Intelligence Scale for Children – all from sixteen seconds' worth of brain waves. There was nothing culturally biased about the test whatsoever. What could be cultural about staring at a thumbtack on a wall? The savings in time and money were breathtaking. The conventional IQ test took two hours to complete; and the overhead, in terms of paying test-givers, test-scorers, test-preparers, and the rent, was $100 an hour at the very least. The IQ Cap required about fifteen minutes and sixteen seconds – it took about fifteen minutes to put the electrodes on the scalp – and about a tenth of a penny's worth of electricity. Neurometrics's investors were rubbing their hands and licking their chops. They were about to make a killing. In fact – *nobody wanted their damnable IQ Cap!*

It wasn't simply that no one believed you could derive IQ scores from brainwaves – it was that nobody wanted to believe it could be done. Nobody wanted to believe that human brainpower is...*that hardwired*. Nobody wanted to learn in a flash that...*the genetic fix is in*. Nobody wanted to learn that he was... *a hardwired genetic mediocrity* ...and that the best he could hope for in this Trough of Mortal Error was to live out his mediocre life as a stress-free dim bulb. Barry Sterman of UCLA, chief scientist for a firm called Cognitive Neurometrics, who has devised his own brain-wave technology for market research and focus groups, regards brainwave IQ testing as possible – but in the current atmosphere you *wouldn't have a Chinaman's chance of getting a grant* to develop it.

Here we begin to sense the chill that emanates from the hottest field in the academic world. The unspoken and largely unconscious premise of the wrangling over neuroscience's strategic high ground is: We now live in an age in which science is a court from which there is no appeal. And the issue this time around, at the end of the twentieth century, is not the evo-

halben Standardabweichung] voraus, wie die Testperson in allen elf Testbereichen des Hamburg-Wechsler-Intelligenztests für Erwachsene oder, bei Kindern, des Hamburg-Wechsler-Intelligenztests für Kinder abschneiden würde – und das alles nach nur 16 Sekunden Gehirnwellenmessung! Dieser Test war völlig kulturunabhängig. Was könnte schon daran kulturabhängig sein, wenn man auf einen Reißnagel an der Wand starrt? Die Zeit- und Geldersparnis war atemberaubend. Der herkömmliche Intelligenztest dauerte zwei Stunden, und die Unkosten betrugen mindestens 100 Dollar die Stunde, unter Berücksichtigung des Entgelts für Testleiter, Testschreiber, Testvorbereiter sowie der Raummiete. Die IQ Cap brauchte ca. 15 Minuten und 16 Sekunden – ca. 15 Minuten dauerte es, die Elektroden an der Kopfhaut zu befestigen – und kostete ungefähr einen Zehntel-Penny für Strom. Die Investoren von Neurometrics lachten sich schon ins Fäustchen. Das würde der Renner werden. *Aber – niemand wollte ihre gräßliche IQ Cap!*

Das lag nicht etwa daran, daß niemand glaubte, man könne den Intelligenzquotienten aus Gehirnwellen ableiten, sondern vielmehr daran, daß es niemand glauben wollte. Niemand *wollte* glauben, daß die geistige Kapazität des menschlichen Gehirns so ... *fix vorprogrammiert* ist. Niemand wollte in Sekundenschnelle erfahren, daß ... *in den Genen der Wurm drin ist*. Niemand wollte erfahren, daß er ... *genetisch auf Mittelmäßigkeit eingestellt ist* ... und daß er sich in diesem Meer menschlicher Irrungen allerhöchstens erhoffen darf, für den Rest seines mittelmäßiges Leben unbehelligt vor sich hinzudämmern. Barry Sterman von der UCLA, leitender Wissenschaftler der Firma Cognitive Neurometrics, hat eine Gehirnwellen-Technologie für Marktforschungzwecke entwickelt und hält IQ-Tests auf Gehirnwellenbasis für machbar – aber angesichts der momentanen Atmosphäre hätte man *nicht die leiseste Chance, einen Zuschuß für deren Entwicklung zu bekommen*.

Und hier zeigt sich auch schon die Schattenseite dieser funkelnagelneuen akademischen Disziplin, denn die unausgesprochene, ja, meist unbewußte Prämisse dieses Tauziehens um das strategische Terrain der Neurowissenschaft ist: Wir leben heute in einem Zeitalter, in dem Berufung vor dem Gericht der Wissenschaft nicht möglich ist. Was Ende des 20. Jahrhunderts zur Debatte steht, ist nicht die Evolution der Arten – danach kräht kein Hahn mehr –, sondern die Natur unseres eigenen, wertvollen Innenlebens.

lution of the species, which can seem a remote business, but the nature of our own precious inner selves.

The elders of the field, such as Wilson, are well aware of all this and are cautious, or cautious compared to the new generation. Wilson still holds out the possibility – I think he doubts it, but he still holds out the possibility – that at some point in evolutionary history, culture began to influence the development of the human brain in ways that cannot be explained by strict Darwinian theory. But the new generation of neuroscientists are not cautious for a second. In private conversations, the bull sessions, as it were, that create the mental atmosphere of any hot new science – and I love talking to these people – they express an uncompromising determinism.

They start with the most famous statement in all of modern philosophy, Descartes's *Cogito ergo sum,* *I think, therefore I am,* which they regard as the essence of *dualism,* the old-fashioned notion that the mind is something distinct from its mechanism, the brain and the body. [I will get to the second most famous statement in a moment.] This is also known as the *ghost in the machine* fallacy, the quaint belief that there is a ghostly *self* somewhere inside the brain that interprets and directs its operations. Neuroscientists involved in three-dimensional electroencephalography will tell you that there is not even any one place in the brain where consciousness or self-consciousness [*Cogito ergo sum*] is located. This is merely an illusion created by a medley of neurological systems acting in concert. The young generation takes this yet one step further. Since consciousness and thought are entirely physical products of your brain and nervous system – and since your brain arrived fully imprinted at birth – what makes you think you have free will? Where is it going to come from? What *ghost,* what *mind,* what *self,* what *soul,* what anything that will not be immediately grabbed by those scornful quotation marks, is going to bubble up your brain stem to give it to you? I have heard neuroscientists theorize that, given computers of sufficient power and sophistication, it would be possible to predict the course of any human being's life moment by moment, including the fact that the poor devil was about to shake his head over the very idea.

symposium

Die älteren Neurowissenschaftler wie z. B. Wilson sind sich dessen sehr wohl bewußt und dementsprechend vorsichtig, zumindest im Vergleich zur jüngeren Generation. Wilson hat die Hoffnung noch nicht aufgegeben – ich glaube, langsam kommen ihm Zweifel, aber noch hat er die Hoffnung nicht aufgegeben –, daß ab einem gewissen Punkt in der Evolutionsgeschichte die Kultur die Entwicklung des menschlichen Gehirns mitbeeinflußte, und zwar auf eine Art und Weise, die sich nicht durch streng darwinistische Theorien erklären läßt. Aber die neue Generation der Neurowissenschaftler zögert nicht eine Sekunde. In privaten Gesprächsrunden, den sogenannten *Bull Sessions*, in denen die geistige Atmosphäre jeder brandheißen neuen Wissenschaft entsteht – und ich liebe es, mit solchen Menschen zu sprechen –, stellen sie kompromißlose Entschlossenheit zur Schau.

Sie fangen mit dem bekanntesten Satz der gesamten modernen Philosophie an, mit Descartes' *Cogito, ergo sum* – *Ich denke, also bin ich*, ein Satz, der für sie das Wesen des *Dualismus* symbolisiert, die altmodische Vorstellung, der Verstand sei getrennt von seinem Mechanismus, also von Gehirn und Körper, zu betrachten. [Auf den zweitbekanntesten Satz werde ich in Kürze zu sprechen kommen.] Das also wäre der *Geist in der Maschine*-Irrtum, der merkwürdige Glaube, irgendwo im Gehirninneren existiere ein gespenstisches *Selbst*, das die Gehirnarbeit deutet und steuert. Neurowissenschaftler, die sich mit 3D-Elektroenzephalographie befassen, werden Ihnen bestätigen, daß sich Bewußtsein oder Selbst-Bewußtsein [Cogito ergo sum] keineswegs an einem fixen Ort im Gehirn lokalisieren lassen. Ein solcher Ort sei reine Illusion, hervorgerufen durch das Zusammenspiel einer Reihe neurologischer Systeme. Die junge Generation geht sogar noch einen Schritt weiter. Wenn Bewußtsein und Denken rein physikalische Produkte unseres Gehirns und Nervensystems sind – und da unser Gehirn ohnehin schon von Geburt an kein unbeschriebenes Blatt ist –, weshalb sollte man dann glauben, es gäbe einen freien Willen? Woher sollte der wohl stammen? Welcher *Geist*, welcher *Verstand*, welches *Selbst*, welche *Seele*, welches Was-auch-immer, das nicht sofort mit diesen höhnischen Anführungszeichen versehen wird, würde da in kleinen Bläschen den Hirnstamm hochsteigen und ihn uns verleihen? Ich habe selbst zugehört, wie Neurowissenschaftler theoretisierten, daß man mit ausreichend leistungsstarken und komplexen Computern den Lebensweg eines jeden einzelnen Menschen auf die Sekunde genau

I doubt that any Calvinist of the sixteenth century ever believed so completely in predestination as these, the hottest and most intensely rational young scientists in the United States at the end of the twentieth.

Since the late 1970s, in the Age of Wilson, college students have been heading into neuroscience in job lots. The Society for Neuroscience was founded in 1970 with 1,100 members. Today, one generation later, its membership exceeds 26,000. The Society's latest convention, in San Diego, drew 23,052 souls, making it one of the biggest professional conventions in the country. In the venerable field of academic philosophy, young faculty members are jumping ship in embarrassing numbers and shifting into neuroscience. They are heading for the laboratories. Why wrestle with Kant's God, Freedom, and Immortality when it is only a matter of time before neuroscience, probably through brain imaging, reveals the actual physical mechanism that sends these mental constructs, these illusions, synapsing up into the Broca's and Wernicke's areas of the brain?

Which brings us to the second most famous statement in all of modern philosophy: Nietzsche's *God is dead.* The year was 1882. [The book was *Die Fröhliche Wissenschaft* [*The Gay Science*].] Nietzsche said this was not a declaration of atheism, although he was in fact an atheist, but simply the news of an event. He called the death of God a *tremendous event,* the greatest event of modern history. The news was that educated people no longer believed in God, as a result of the rise of rationalism and scientific thought, including Darwinism, over the preceding 250 years. But before you atheists run up your flags of triumph, he said, think of the implications. *The story I have to tell,* wrote Nietzsche, *is the history of the next two centuries.* He predicted [in *Ecce Homo*] that the twentieth century would be a century of *wars such as have never happened on earth,* wars catastrophic beyond all imagining. And why? Because human beings would no longer have a god to turn to, to absolve them of their guilt; but they would still be racked by guilt, since guilt is an impulse instilled in children when they are very young, before the age of reason. As a result, people would loathe not only one another but themselves. The blind and reassuring faith they formerly poured into their belief in God, said

vorhersagen könnte, einschließlich der Tatsache, daß der arme Teufel zu all dem wohl nur noch den Kopf schütteln würde. Ich glaube nicht, daß es im 16. Jahrhundert auch nur einen Calvinisten gegeben hat, der so bedingungslos an die Vorherbestimmung glaubte wie diese enthusiastischen, bis aufs äußerste rationalen jungen US-Wissenschaftler gegen Ende des 20. Jahrhunderts.

Seit den späten 70er Jahren, dem Zeitalter Wilsons, haben sich Unmengen amerikanischer Studenten der Neurowissenschaft verschrieben. 1970 wurde die *Society for Neuroscience* gegründet. Sie zählte zum damaligen Zeitpunkt 1.100 Mitglieder; heute, eine Generation später, hat sie mehr als 26.000 Mitglieder. Am letzten Kongreß der Society in San Diego nahmen 23.052 Personen teil, womit er zu den größten Fachkongressen des Landes zählt. In unerfreulich großen Scharen kehren junge Fakultätsmitglieder der altehrwürdigen akademischen Domäne der Philosophie den Rücken, um zur Neurowissenschaft überzulaufen. Ihr Ziel sind geradewegs die Labors. Wozu sich mit Kants Gott, Freiheit und Unsterblichkeit abplagen, wenn es nur noch eine Frage der Zeit ist, bis die Neurowissenschaft, höchstwahrscheinlich mithilfe des Brain Imaging, den physikalischen Mechanismus aufdeckt, der diese geistigen Konstrukte, diese Illusionen über Synapsen in das Broca'sche und das Wernicke'sche Sprachzentrum des Gehirns hinaufkatapultiert?

Womit wir beim zweitberühmtesten Satz der gesamten modernen Philosophie angelangt wären: Nietzsches *Gott ist tot*. Das war im Jahre 1882. [Das Buch hieß *Die Fröhliche Wissenschaft*]. Das sei kein Bekenntnis zum Atheismus, sagte Nietzsche, der selbst Atheist war, sondern einfach die Nachricht von einem Ereignis. Er bezeichnete den Tod Gottes als *ungeheuerliches Ereignis*, als den größten Augenblick in der Geschichte der Neuzeit. Die Nachricht bestand darin, daß die gebildeten Menschen aufgrund des schon seit 250 Jahren andauernden Siegeszugs des Rationalimus und des wissenschaftlichen Denkens, einschließlich des Darwinismus, nun nicht mehr an Gott glaubten. Aber bevor ihr Atheisten nun eure Triumphbanner hißt, sagte Nietzsche, bedenkt die Konsequenzen. *Die Geschichte, die ich zu erzählen habe,* schrieb er, *ist die Geschichte der kommenden zweihundert Jahre.* Er sagte voraus [in *Ecce Homo*], daß das 20. Jahrhundert ein Jahrhundert der Kriege werden würde, *wie es ihresgleichen bisher auf Erden nicht gegeben hat*, Kriege, die schier unvorstellbare Katastrophen mit sich bringen würden. Und warum? Weil die Menschen keinen Gott

Nietzsche, they would now pour into a belief in barbaric nationalistic brotherhoods: *If the doctrines ... of the lack of any cardinal distinction between man and animal, doctrines I consider true but deadly* – he says in an allusion to Darwinism in *Untimely Meditations* – *are hurled into the people for another generation ... then nobody should be surprised when ... brotherhoods with the aim of the robbery and exploitation of the non-brothers...will appear in the arena of the future.*

Nietzsche's view of guilt, incidentally, is also that of neuro-scientists a century later. They regard guilt as one of those tendencies imprinted in the brain at birth. In some people the genetic work is not complete, and they engage in criminal behavior without a twinge of remorse – thereby intriguing criminologists, who then want to create Violence Initiatives and hold conferences on the subject.

Nietzsche said that mankind would limp on through the twentieth century *on the mere pittance* of the old decaying God-based moral codes. But then, in the twenty-first, would come a period more dreadful than the great wars, a time of *the total eclipse of all values* [in *The Will to Power*]. This would also be a frantic period of *revaluation,* in which people would try to find new systems of values to replace the osteoporotic skeletons of the old. But you will fail, he warned, because you cannot believe in moral codes without simultaneously believing in a god who points at you with his fearsome forefinger and says *Thou shalt* or *Thou shalt not.*

Why should we bother ourselves with a dire prediction that seems so far-fetched as *the total eclipse of all values*? Because of man's track record, I should think. After all, in Europe, in the peaceful decade of the 1880s, it must have seemed even more far-fetched to predict the world wars of the twentieth century and the barbaric brotherhoods of Nazism and Communism. Ecce vates! Ecce vates! Behold the prophet! How much more proof can one demand of a man's powers of prediction?

A hundred years ago those who worried about the death of God could console one another with the fact that they still had their own bright selves and their own inviolable souls for moral ballast and the marvels of modern science to chart the way. But what if, as seems

mehr haben würden, an den sie sich wenden könnten, damit er sie von ihrer Schuld befreie; und von Schuld würden sie geplagt sein, denn Schuld ist ein Impuls, der schon Kleinkindern eingeimpft wird, bevor sie selbständig denken lernen. Die Menschen würden daher nicht nur die anderen, sondern auch sich selbst hassen. Das blinde und beruhigende Vertrauen, das sie zuvor in den Glauben an Gott einbringen konnten, sagte Nietzsche, würde nun in einen Glauben an barbarische nationalistische Bruderschaften fließen: *Wenn die Lehren ... vom Fehlen jeglicher wesentlicher Unterschiede zwischen Mensch und Tier, Doktrinen, die ich für wahr, aber zugleich tödlich halte,* – meint er in den *Unzeitgemäßen Betrachtungen* in Anspielung an den Darwinismus – *noch eine weitere Generation hindurch auf die Menschen losgelassen werden ... so darf sich niemand wundern, wenn ... Bruderschaften, die auf Raub und Ausbeutung der Nicht-Brüder aus sind, ... in Zukunft am Schauplatz der Ereignisse auftauchen.*

Zufällig deckt sich Nietzsches Auffassung von Schuld mit der der Neurowissenschaftler hundert Jahre später. Sie sehen Schuld als eine der Neigungen, die schon von Geburt an im Gehirn angelegt sind. Bei einigen Menschen ist die genetische Vorarbeit mangelhaft, und diese führen dann ohne den geringsten Anflug von Reue kriminelle Handlungen durch – was wiederum die Kriminologen fasziniert, die dann unverzüglich eine *Violence Initiative* initiieren und Konferenzen zu diesem Thema abhalten wollen.

Nietzsche sagte, daß die Menschheit sich *auf den allerletzten Resten* der alten, verfallenden, auf Gott basierenden Moralvorstellungen über das 20. Jahrhundert retten würde. Dann aber, im 21. Jahrhundert, käme eine Zeit, die noch schrecklicher sein würde als die der großen Kriege, eine Zeit des *völligen Wertezusammenbruchs* [in *Der Wille zur Macht*]. Sie wäre auch eine Zeit hektischer *Umwertungen*, in der die Menschen versuchen würden, neue Wertesysteme zu finden, um die porösen Skelette der alten Werte zu ersetzen. Aber ihr werdet versagen, warnte er, weil ihr nicht an einen Sittenkodex glauben könnt, ohne gleichzeitig an einen Gott zu glauben, der mit seinem furchtbaren Zeigefinger auf euch zeigt und sagt *Du sollst* oder *Du sollst nicht*.

Weshalb sollen wir uns überhaupt mit einer so gräßlichen, an den Haaren herbeigezogenen Prophezeiung wie *die völlige Umwertung aller Werte* abgeben? Wegen unserer bisherigen Glanzleistungen, würde ich sagen. Schließlich war es in den friedlichen 80er Jahren des vorigen Jahrhunderts

likely, the greatest marvel of modern science turns out to be brain imaging? And what if, ten years from now, brain imaging has proved, beyond any doubt, that not only Edward O. Wilson but also the young generation are, in fact, correct?

The elders, such as Wilson himself and Daniel C. Dennett, the author of *Darwin's Dangerous Idea: Evolution and the Meaning of Life*, and Richard Dawkins, author of *The Selfish Gene* and *The Blind Watchmaker*, insist that there is nothing to fear from the truth, from the ultimate extension of Darwin's dangerous idea. They present elegant arguments as to why neuroscience should in no way diminish the richness of life, the magic of art, or the righteousness of political causes, including, if one need edit, political correctness at Harvard or Tufts, where Dennett is Director of the Center for Cognitive Studies, or Oxford, where Dawkins is something called Professor of Public Understanding of Science. [Dennett and Dawkins, every bit as much as Wilson, are earnestly, feverishly, politically correct.] Despite their best efforts, however, neuroscience is not rippling out into the public on waves of scholarly reassurance. But rippling out it is, rapidly. The conclusion people out beyond the laboratory walls are drawing is: *The fix is in! We're all hardwired!* That, and: *Don't blame me! I'm wired wrong!*

This sudden switch from a belief in Nurture, in the form of social conditioning, to Nature, in the form of genetics and brain physiology, is the great intellectual event, to borrow Nietzsche's term, of the late twentieth century. Up to now the two most influential ideas of the century have been Marxism and Freudianism. Both were founded upon the premise that human beings and their *ideals* – Marx and Freud knew about quotation marks, too – are completely molded by their environment. To Marx, the crucial environment was one's social class; *ideals* and *faiths* were notions foisted by the upper orders upon the lower as instruments of social control. To Freud, the crucial environment was the Oedipal drama, the unconscious sexual plot that was played out in the family early in a child's existence. The *ideals* and *faiths* you prize so much are merely the parlor furniture you feature for receiving your guests, said Freud; I will show you the cellar, the furnace, the pipes, the sexual steam that

in Europa noch mehr an den Haaren herbeigezogen, die Weltkriege des 20. Jahrhunderts oder die barbarischen Bruderschaften des Nationalsozialismus und Kommunismus vorherzusagen. Ecce vates! Ecce vates! Sehet den Propheten! Wieviele Beweise für die prophetische Begabung eines Mannes kann man noch verlangen?

Vor hundert Jahren konnten sich diejenigen, die der Tod Gottes beunruhigte, gegenseitig mit der Tatsache trösten, daß sie immer noch ihr unvergleichliches Selbst und ihre unverletzliche Seele als moralischen Ballast mit sich führten und die Wunder der modernen Wissenschaft ihnen schon den Weg weisen würden. Aber was, wenn – was recht wahrscheinlich ist – das größte Wunder der modernen Wissenschaft ausgerechnet Brain Imaging hieße? Und was, wenn Brain Imaging heute in zehn Jahren bereits unwiderlegbar bewiesen hätte, daß nicht nur Edward O. Wilson, sondern auch die junge Generation tatsächlich recht hat?

Die älteren, wie Wilson selbst, Daniel C. Dennett, Autor von *Darwins Gefährliches Erbe: Die Evolution und der Sinn des Lebens*, und Richard Dawkins, Autor von *Das egoistische Gen* und *Der blinde Uhrmacher*, bestehen darauf, daß man die Wahrheit nicht zu fürchten braucht und Darwins gefährliches Erbe endgültig antreten sollte. Sie legen elegante Argumente vor, weshalb die Neurowissenschaft den Reichtum des Lebens, die Faszination der Kunst oder die Rechtschaffenheit politischer Anliegen keineswegs vermindern würde, ebensowenig wie wohl die politische Korrektheit in Harvard oder Tufts, wo Dennett dem *Center for Cognitive Studies* vorsteht, oder Oxford, wo Dawkins ein Amt bekleidet, das sich *Professor of Public Understanding of Science* nennt. [Dennett und Dawkins sind ebenso wie Wilson auf durch und durch ernste, ja, fieberhafte Weise politisch korrekt.] Ihren eifrigen Bemühungen zum Trotz erfährt jedoch die Neurowissenschaft auf ihrem Weg an die Öffentlichkeit kaum wissenschaftliche Rückendeckung. Dennoch schreitet sie weiter voran, und sogar schnell. Außerhalb der Labors zieht man aus dieser Entwicklung folgenden Schluß: *Jetzt haben wir den Salat! Wir sind alle vorprogrammiert!* Aber auch: *Ich kann nichts dafür! Ich bin nur falsch verkabelt!*

Dieses plötzliche Umschwenken vom Glauben an die Erziehung, in Gestalt sozialer Konditionierung, zum Glauben an die Natur, in Gestalt der Genetik und der Gehirnphysiologie, ist das intellektuelle Großereignis des ausgehenden 20. Jahrhunderts, um mit Nietzsche zu sprechen. Die bis heute

actually runs the house. By the mid-1950s even anti-Marxists and anti-Freudians had come to assume the centrality of class domination and Oedipally conditioned sexual drives. On top of this came Pavlov, with his *stimulus-response bonds,* and B. F. Skinner, with his *operant conditioning,* turning the supremacy of conditioning into something approaching a precise form of engineering. So how did this brilliant intellectual fashion come to so screeching and ignominious an end?

The demise of Freudianism can be summed up in a single word: lithium. In 1949 an Australian psychiatrist, John Cade, gave five days of lithium therapy – for entirely the wrong reasons – to a fifty-one-year-old mental patient who was so manic-depressive, so hyperactive, unintelligible, and uncontrollable, he had been kept locked up in asylums for twenty years. By the sixth day, thanks to the lithium buildup in his blood, he was a normal human being. Three months later he was released and lived happily ever after in his own home. This was a man who had been locked up and subjected to two decades of Freudian logorrhea to no avail whatsoever. Over the next twenty years antidepressant and tranquilizing drugs completely replaced Freudian talk-talk as treatment for serious mental disturbances. By the mid-1980s, neuroscientists looked upon Freudian psychiatry as a quaint relic based largely upon superstition [such as dream analysis – *dream* analysis!], like phrenology or mesmerism. In fact, among neuroscientists, phrenology now has a higher reputation than Freudian psychiatry, since phrenology was in a certain crude way a precursor of electroencephalography. Freudian psychiatrists are now regarded as old crocks with sham medical degrees, as ears with wire hairs sprouting out of them that people with more money than sense can hire to talk into.

Marxism was finished off even more suddenly – in a single year, 1973 – with the smuggling out of the Soviet Union and the publication in France of the first of the three volumes of Aleksandr Solzhenitsyn's *The Gulag Archipelago*. Other writers, notably the British historian Robert Conquest, had already exposed the Soviet Union's vast network of concentration camps, but their work was based largely on the testimony of refugees, and refugees were routinely discounted as biased and bitter obser-

einflußreichsten Bewegungen dieses Jahrhunderts waren der Marxismus und der Freudianismus. Beide stützten sich auf die Annahme, daß die Menschen und ihre *Ideale* – auch Marx und Freud kannten Anführungszeichen – gänzlich von ihrer Umwelt geformt werden. Für Marx war der wichtigste Umwelteinfluß die soziale Klasse, der man angehörte; *Ideale* und *Glaube* waren Begriffe, welche die oberen den unteren Schichten als soziales Kontrollinstrument aufschwatzten. Für Freud bestand die wichtigste Umgebung im ödipalen Drama, in der unbewußten sexuellen Szenenfolge, die das Kleinkind in der Familie durchlebt. Eure vielgepriesenen *Ideale* und euer *Glaube* sind nur die Einrichtung, die ihr euch für euren Empfangssalon wünscht, sagt Freud; ich werde euch den Keller zeigen, den Heizofen, die Rohrleitungen, den sexuellen Dampf, der das Haus tatsächlich in Schwung hält. Spätestens Mitte der 50er Jahre waren sogar Anti-Marxisten und Anti-Freudianer so weit, daß sie die zentrale Rolle von Klassenherrschaft und ödipal konditioniertem Sexualtrieb anerkannten. Zu guter Letzt kamen auch noch Pawlow mit seinen *Reiz-Reaktions-Verbindungen* und B. F. Skinner mit seiner *operanten Konditionierung* und verliehen der allmächtigen Konditionierung beinah den Status einer exakten Ingenieurswissenschaft. Wie also kam es, daß diese glänzende intellektuelle Mode ein so schmähliches und unwürdiges Ende nahm?

Das Ende des Freudianismus läßt sich mit einem einzigen Wort zusammenfassen: Lithium. Im Jahre 1949 verordnete der australische Psychiater John Cade einem 51jährigen geisteskranken Patienten – aufgrund einer Fehldiagnose – eine fünftägige Lithiumtherapie. Der Patient war hochgradig manisch-depressiv, hyperaktiv, unansprechbar und unberechenbar gewesen und hatte 20 Jahre in verschiedenen geschlossenen Anstalten zugebracht. Am sechsten Tag war er dank der Lithium-Anreicherung in seinem Blut ein ganz normaler Mensch. Drei Monate später wurde er entlassen, und wenn er nicht gestorben ist, so lebt er noch heute glücklich und zufrieden in seinen eigenen vier Wänden. Dieser Mann war 20 lange Jahre als wehrloses Opfer Freud'scher Logorrhoe einfach weggesperrt worden. In den darauffolgenden 20 Jahren sollte nun Freud'sches Gefasel als Behandlungsmethode für ernste Geistesstörungen gänzlich durch die Verabreichung von Antidepressiva und Beruhigungsmitteln ersetzt werden. Spätestens ab Mitte der 80er Jahre sahen Neurowissenschaftler die Freud'sche Psychiatrie nur noch als eigentümliches Relikt, das wie Phrenologie oder

vers. Solzhenitsyn, on the other hand, was a Soviet citizen, still living on Soviet soil, a zek himself for eleven years, zek being Russian slang for concentration camp prisoner. His credibility had been vouched for by none other than Nikita Khrushchev, who in 1962 had permitted the publication of Solzhenitsyn's novella of the gulag, *One Day in the Life of Ivan Denisovich*, as a means of cutting down to size the daunting shadow of his predecessor Stalin. *Yes,* Khrushchev had said in effect, *what this man Solzhenitsyn has to say is true. Such were Stalin's crimes.* Solzhenitsyn's brief fictional description of the Soviet slave labor system was damaging enough. But *The Gulag Archipelago*, a two-thousand-page, densely detailed, nonfiction account of the Soviet Communist Party's systematic extermination of its enemies, real and imagined, of its own countrymen, by the tens *of millions* through an enormous, methodical, bureaucratically controlled *human sewage disposal system,* as Solzhenitsyn called it – The *Gulag Archipelago* was devastating. After all, this was a century in which there was no longer any possible ideological detour around the concentration camp. Among European intellectuals, even French intellectuals, Marxism collapsed as a spiritual force immediately. Ironically, it survived longer in the United States before suffering a final, merciful *coup de grâce* on November 9, 1989, with the breaching of the Berlin Wall, which signaled in an unmistakable fashion what a debacle the Soviets' seventy-two-year field experiment in socialism had been. [Marxism still hangs on, barely, acrobatically, in American universities in a Mannerist form known as Deconstruction, a literary doctrine that depicts language itself as an insidious tool used by The Powers That Be to deceive the proles and peasants.]

Freudianism and Marxism – and with them, the entire belief in social conditioning – were demolished so swiftly, so suddenly, that neuroscience has surged in, as if into an intellectual vacuum. Nor do you have to be a scientist to detect the rush.

Anyone with a child in school knows the signs all too well. I have children in school, and I am intrigued by the faith parents now invest – the craze began about 1990 – in psychologists who diagnose their children as suffering from a defect known as attention deficit

Mesmerismus großteils auf Aberglauben begründet war [wie etwa Traumanalyse – *Traumanalyse*!]. Interessanterweise genießt die Phrenologie heute bei den Neurowissenschaftlern höheres Ansehen als die Freud'sche Psychiatrie, da man sie in gewisser, allerdings stark vereinfachter Weise als Vorläufer des EEG sehen kann. Psychiater im Sinne Freuds gelten heute als alte Wracks mit erschlichenen Doktortiteln, die von Menschen mit mehr Geld als Verstand angeheuert werden, damit sie sich ihre Ohren – aus denen gar drahtige Haare sprießen – vollquatschen lassen.

Mit dem Marxismus ging es sogar noch rascher bergab – in nur einem Jahr, nämlich 1973. In diesem Jahr wurde der erste Band von Alexander Solschenizyns dreibändigem *Archipel Gulag* aus der Sowjetunion herausgeschmuggelt und in Frankreich publiziert. Andere Autoren, insbesondere der britische Historiker Robert Conquest, hatten das dichte Netz sowjetischer Konzentrationslager bereits aufgedeckt, aber ihre Arbeiten stützten sich hauptsächlich auf Zeugenaussagen von Flüchtlingen, und Flüchtlinge galten automatisch als wenig objektive, verbitterte und daher unglaubwürdige Beobachter. Solschenizyn jedoch war Sowjetbürger, lebte noch immer auf sowjetischem Boden und war selbst elf Jahre lang *zek* gewesen – so der russische Slangausdruck für KZ-Häftlinge. Seine Glaubwürdigkeit hatte kein Geringerer als Nikita Chruschtschow bestätigt, der 1962 die Veröffentlichung von Solschenizyns Gulag-Novelle *Ein Tag im Leben des Iwan Denissowitsch* genehmigte, um so aus dem drohenden Schatten seines Vorgängers Stalin zu treten. Chruschtschow selbst hatte also eingestanden: *Ja, was dieser Mann, Solschenizyn, zu sagen hat, stimmt. Solche Verbrechen hat Stalin verübt.* Solschenizyns kurze fiktive Beschreibung des sowjetischen Systems der Zwangsarbeit hatte der UdSSR schon genug geschadet. Aber *Der Archipel Gulag*, ein 2000-seitiger, detailreicher Tatsachenbericht darüber, wie die KPdSU ihre wirklichen und vermeintlichen Feinde, zig Millionen eigener Landsleute durch ein gewaltiges, methodisches, bürokratisch überwachtes *menschliches Abfallentsorgungssystem* – wie Solschenizyn es nannte – systematisch exterminierte, war verheerend. Schließlich konnte man es sich gerade in diesem Jahrhundert nicht mehr erlauben, Konzentrationslager ideologisch irgendwie zu rechtfertigen. Für die europäischen Intellektuellen, sogar für die französischen, stürzte der Marxismus als geistige Großmacht unverzüglich in sich zusammen. Ironischerweise konnte er ausgerechnet in den USA noch eine Zeitlang weitbestehen, bis ihm am 9. November

disorder, or ADD. Of course, I have no way of knowing whether this *disorder* is an actual, physical, neurological condition or not, but neither does anybody else in this early stage of neuroscience. The symptoms of this supposed malady are always the same. The child, or, rather, the boy – forty-nine out of fifty cases are boys –fidgets around in school, slides off his chair, doesn't pay attention, distracts his classmates during class, and performs poorly. In an earlier era he would have been pressured to pay attention, work harder, show some self-discipline. To parents caught up in the new intellectual climate of the 1990s, that approach seems cruel, because my little boy's problem is... *he's wired wrong!* The poor little tyke – *the fix has been in since birth!* Invariably the parents complain, *All he wants to do is sit in front of the television set and watch cartoons and play Sega Genesis.* For how long? *How long? For hours at a time.* Hours at a time; as even any young neuroscientist will tell you, that boy may have a problem, but it is not an attention deficit.

Nevertheless, all across America we have the spectacle of an entire generation of little boys, by the tens of thousands, being dosed up on ADD's magic bullet of choice, Ritalin, the CIBA-Geneva Corporation's brand name for the stimulant methylphenidate. I first encountered Ritalin in 1966 when I was in San Francisco doing research for a book on the psychedelic or hippie movement. A certain species of the genus hippie was known as the Speed Freak, and a certain strain of Speed Freak was known as the Ritalin Head. The Ritalin Heads *loved* Ritalin. You'd see them in the throes of absolute Ritalin raptures ... Not a wiggle, not a peep ... They would sit engrossed in anything at all...a manhole cover, their own palm wrinkles ... indefinitely ... through shoulda-been mealtime after mealtime ... through raging insomnias ... Pure methyl-phenidate nirvana ... From 1990 to 1995, CIBA-Geneva's sales of Ritalin rose 600 percent; and not because of the appetites of subsets of the species Speed Freak in San Francisco, either. It was because an entire generation of American boys, from the best private schools of the Northeast to the worst sludge-trap public schools of Los Angeles and San Diego, was now strung out on methylphenidate, diligently doled out to them every day by their connection, the school nurse. America is a wonderful country! I mean

1989 der Fall der Berliner Mauer – der unmißverständlich demonstrierte, welch ein Debakel das 72 Jahre dauernde Feldexperiment in Sachen Sozialismus gewesen war – den Gnadenstoß versetzte. [Und doch hält er sich, mehr schlecht als recht, mit nahezu akrobatischem Geschick an einigen amerikanischen Universitäten – und zwar in manieristischer Gestalt, als Dekonstruktivismus, jener literarischen Doktrin, derzufolge die jeweiligen Machthaber die Sprache selbst als heimtückisches Werkzeug zur Täuschung des Proletariats und der Bauern benutzen.]

Freudianismus und Marxismus – und mit ihnen der Glaube an soziale Konditionierung – wurden so behende und unvermittelt ausrangiert, daß die Neurowissenschaft ungehindert vorpreschen und dieses intellektuelle Vakuum ausfüllen konnte. Und man muß nicht einmal Wissenschaftler sein, um diese überstürzte Hast zu bemerken.

Die Eltern von Schulkindern kennen die Anzeichen nur allzu gut. Ich habe selbst Kinder in der Schule, und mich fasziniert das Vertrauen, das die Eltern von heute – und diese Mode setzte um 1990 ein – in Psychologen setzen, die diagnostizieren, daß ihre Kinder an einer Störung namens *Attention Deficit Disorder*, kurz ADD, leiden. Natürlich steht es mir nicht zu, zu beurteilen, ob diese *Störung* ein tatsächlicher, körperlicher, neurologischer Zustand ist oder nicht, aber genausowenig steht es in dieser Phase der Neurowissenschaft irgendjemand anderem zu. Das Kind, oder vielmehr der Junge – in 49 von 50 Fällen handelt es sich um Jungen – zappelt im Unterricht herum, rutscht von seinem Sessel, paßt nicht auf, lenkt seine Klassenkameraden ab und erbringt nur schlechte Leistungen. Früher hätte man ihn gezwungen, besser aufzupassen, mehr zu lernen, sich zusammenzureißen. Eltern, die dem neuen intellektuellen Klima der 90er verhaftet sind, finden derartige Methoden grausam, denn mein kleiner Sohn hat ein Problem ... *er ist falsch vorprogrammiert*. Armes Kerlchen – *völlig vermurkst, schon von Geburt an*! Und die Eltern klagen unisono: *Er sitzt die ganze Zeit nur vor dem Fernseher, schaut Zeichentrickfilme an und spielt Sega Mega Drive!* Wie lange? *Stundenlang, ohne Unterbrechung!* Stundenlang! Sogar der unerfahrenste Neurowissenschaftler könnte ihnen sagen, daß dieser Junge ziemlich sicher ein Problem hat, daß es sich aber garantiert nicht um ein Aufmerksamkeitsdefizit handelt!

Nichtsdestotrotz spielt sich momentan amerikaweit folgendes ab: Eine ganze Generation kleiner Jungen, Zehntausende an der Zahl, werden mit dem bevorzugten ADD-Wundermittel Ritalin vollge-

it! No honest writer would challenge that statement! The human comedy never runs out of material! It never lets you down!

Meantime, the notion of a self – a self who exercises self-discipline, postpones gratification, curbs the sexual appetite, stops short of aggression and criminal behavior – a self who can become more intelligent and lift itself to the very peaks of life by its own bootstraps through study, practice, perseverance, and refusal to give up in the face of great odds – this old-fashioned notion [what's a *boot* strap, for God's sake?] of success through enterprise and true grit is already slipping away, slipping away...slipping away...The peculiarly American faith in the power of the individual to transform himself from a helpless cypher into a giant among men, a faith that ran from Emerson [*Self-Reliance*] to Horatio Alger's *Luck and Pluck* stories to Dale Carnegie's *How to Win Friends and Influence People* to Norman Vincent Peale's *The Power of Positive Thinking* to Og Mandino's *The Greatest Salesman in the World* – that faith is now as moribund as the god for whom Nietzsche wrote an obituary in 1882. It lives on today only in the decrepit form of the *motivational talk,* as lecture agents refer to it, given by retired football stars such as Fran Tarkenton to audiences of businessmen, most of them woulda-been athletes [like the author of this article], about how life is like a football game. *It's late in the fourth period and you're down by thirteen points and the Cowboys got you hemmed in on your own one-yard line and it's third and twenty-three. Whaddaya do?...*

Sorry, Fran, but it's third and twenty-three and the genetic fix is in, and the new message is now being pumped out into the popular press and onto television at a stupefying rate. Who are the pumps? They are a new breed who call themselves *evolutionary psychologists.* You can be sure that twenty years ago the same people would have been calling themselves Freudian; but today they are genetic determinists, and the press has a voracious appetite for whatever they come up with.

The most popular study currently – it is *still* being featured on television news shows, months later – is David Lykken and Auke Tellegen's study at the University of Minnesota of two thousand twins that shows, according to these two evolutionary psychologists, that an

pumpt, – so lautet der Markenname der CIBA-Geneva Corporation für das Stimulans Methylphenidat. Ich persönlich machte mit Ritalin erstmals 1966 Bekanntschaft, als ich in San Francisco für ein Buch über die Hippie-Bewegung recherchierte. Eine besondere Spezies der Gattung Hippie waren die *Speed Freaks*, und eine ganz bestimmte Art der Speed Freaks waren die *Ritalin Heads*. Die Ritalin Heads *liebten* Ritalin. Man konnte sie erleben, wie sie in absoluter Ritalin-Verzückung schwelgten ... sich nicht rührten, keinen Mucks machten ... einfach dasaßen, fasziniert von irgendetwas ... einem Kanaldeckel, ihren eigenen Handlinien ... endlos ... von einem versäumten Mittagessen zum nächsten ... ohne ein Auge zuzutun ... ein reines Methylphenidat-Nirwana... Von 1990 bis 1995 stieg CIBA-Genevas Ritalinabsatz um 600%; und nicht, weil eine Unterart der Speed Freaks in San Francisco plötzlich solchen Heißhunger entwickelt hätte, sondern weil eine ganze Generation amerikanischer Jungen, von den besten Privatschulen im Nordosten bis zu den schlimmsten, vergammeltsten öffentlichen Schulen in Los Angeles und San Diego, nun tagtäglich von ihrem Dealer, der Schulkrankenschwester, in aller Sorgfalt mit Methylphenidat abgefüllt wurden. Amerika ist ein wunderbares Land! Wirklich! Kein ehrlicher Schriftsteller würde diese Aussage anfechten! Es liefert immer neuen Stoff für die Komödie des menschlichen Lebens! Es läßt einen nie im Stich!

In der Zwischenzeit glaubt kaum noch jemand an das *Selbst*, das Selbstdisziplin übt, Bedürfnisbefriedigung hintanstellt, den sexuellen Appetit zügelt, vor Aggression und kriminellem Verhalten zurückschreckt, das dazulernen, sich am eigenen Schopf aus dem Sumpf der Mittelmäßigkeit ziehen, durch Lernen, Übung, Ausdauer und Durchhaltevermögen auch große Schwierigkeiten überwinden und Erfolg im Leben haben kann; diese altmodische Vorstellung [was, bitte, ist denn ein Schopf?] von Erfolg durch Eigeninitiative und echten Schneid schwindet immer mehr dahin ... Der typisch amerikanische Glaube an die Fähigkeit des Individuums, durch eigene Kraft von einer hilflosen Null zu einem Giganten unter den Menschen zu werden – ein Glaube, der sich von Emerson [*Selbstvertrauen*] über Horatio Algers *Luck and Pluck*-Erzählungen, Dale Carnegies *Wie man Freunde gewinnt: Die Kunst, beliebt und einflußreich zu werden*, Norman Vincent Peales *Die Kraft positiven Denkens* bis zu Og Mandinos *Der beste Verkäufer der Welt* verfolgen läßt – dieser Glaube ist nun ebenso obsolet wie der Gott, dessen Nachruf Nietzsche 1882 geschrieben hat. Er

individual's happiness is largely genetic. Some people are hardwired to be happy and some are not. Success [or failure] in matters of love, money, reputation, or power is transient stuff; you soon settle back down [or up] to the level of happiness you were born with genetically. Three months ago *Fortune* devoted a long takeout, elaborately illustrated, of a study by evolutionary psychologists at Britain's University of Saint Andrews showing that you judge the facial beauty or handsomeness of people you meet not by any social standards of the age you live in but by criteria hardwired in your brain from the moment you were born. Or, to put it another way, beauty is not in the eye of the beholder but embedded in his genes. In fact, today, in the year 1996, barely three years before the end of the millennium, if your appetite for newspapers, magazines, and television is big enough, you will quickly get the impression that there is nothing in your life, including the fat content of your body, that is not genetically predetermined. If I may mention just a few things the evolutionary psychologists have illuminated for me over the past two months:

The male of the human species is genetically hardwired to be polygamous, i.e., unfaithful to his legal mate. Any magazine-reading male gets the picture soon enough. [Three million years of evolution made me do it!] Women lust after male celebrities, because they are genetically hardwired to sense that alpha males will take better care of their offspring. [I'm just a lifeguard in the gene pool, honey.] Teenage girls are genetically hardwired to be promiscuous and are as helpless to stop themselves as dogs in the park. [The school provides the condoms.] Most murders are the result of genetically hardwired compulsions. [Convicts can read, too, and they report to the prison psychiatrist: "Something came over me ... and then the knife went in." [2]

Where does that leave self-control? Where, indeed, if people believe this ghostly self does not even exist, and brain imaging proves it, once and for all?

So far, neuroscientific theory is based largely on indirect evidence, from studies of animals or of how a normal brain changes when it is invaded [by accidents, disease, radical surgery, or experimental needles]. Darwin II him-

fristet sein Dasein nur noch in Form sogenannter "Anfeuerungsreden", wie sie ausgediente Football-Stars wie Fran Tarkenton vor Geschäftsleuten halten, die selbst [wie der Verfasser dieser Zeilen] gerne Sportler geworden wären; frei nach dem Motto: Das Leben ist ein Football-Spiel. "Also, Jungs, die Spielzeit ist fast um, ihr seid 13 Punkte im Rückstand, die Cowboys haben euch auf eurer eigenen One-Yard-Linie festgenagelt, und ihr habt nur noch einen Versuch, und es fehlen noch 23 Yards. Was also werdet ihr tun?..."

Sorry, Fran, aber ihr habt nur noch einen Versuch, und es fehlen noch 23 Yards, und in den Genen ist der Wurm drin, und diese frohe Botschaft wird gerade in Windeseile der Boulevardpresse und dem Fernsehen aufgetischt. Und von wem? Ah, von einer neuen Gattung, den sogenannten "Evolutionspsychologen". Seien Sie versichert, vor 20 Jahren hätten sich dieselben Leute als Freudianer bezeichnet; aber heute sind sie genetische Deterministen, und die Presse stürzt sich mit Begeisterung auf alles, was ihnen so einfällt.

Die derzeit populärste Studie – sie wird noch heute, Monate nach ihrem Erscheinen, immer wieder in den Nachrichten gebracht – ist die von David Lykken und Auke Tellegen an der University of Minnesota durchgeführte Untersuchung von zweitausend Zwillingspaaren, die zu dem Ergebnis kam, das Glück eines Individuums sei großteils genetisch bedingt. Manche Menschen sind darauf vorprogrammiert, glücklich zu werden, andere nicht. Erfolg [oder Mißerfolg] in der Liebe, in Geldangelegenheiten, in bezug auf Ansehen bzw. Macht sei nur ein vorübergehendes Phänomen; früher oder später lande jeder wieder auf dem hohen bzw. niedrigen Glücksniveau, das schon seit seiner Geburt genetisch festgelegt ist. Vor drei Monaten brachte Fortune eine umfangreiche Sonderbeilage mit ausführlichen Illustrationen zu einer Studie von Evolutionspsychologen an der University of St. Andrews, UK, die zeigte, daß man die Schönheit eines menschlichen Gesichts nicht aufgrund gängiger gesellschaftlicher Standards beurteilt, sondern anhand von Kriterien, die schon seit der Geburt im Gehirn festgeschrieben sind. Oder, mit anderen Worten, schön ist nicht, was gefällt, sondern schön ist, was genetisch vorprogrammiert ist. Und wirklich hat man, wenn man die entsprechenden Meldungen in Zeitungen, Fachmagazinen und Fernsehen aufmerksam verfolgt, heute, 1996, drei Jahre vor der Jahrtausendwende den Eindruck, daß nichts im Leben, nicht einmal der Fettgehalt des eigenen Körpers, *nicht*

self, Edward O. Wilson, has only limited direct knowledge of the human brain. He is a zoologist, not a neurologist, and his theories are extrapolations from the exhaustive work he has done in his specialty, the study of insects. The French surgeon Paul Broca discovered Broca's area, one of the two speech centers of the left hemisphere of the brain, only after one of his patients suffered a stroke. Even the PET scan and the PET reporter gene/PET reporter probe are technically medical invasions, since they require the injection of chemicals or viruses into the body. But they offer glimpses of what the noninvasive imaging of the future will probably look like. A neuroradiologist can read a list of topics out loud to a person being given a PET scan, topics pertaining to sports, music, business, history, whatever, and when he finally hits one the person is interested in, a particular area of the cerebral cortex actually lights up on the screen. Eventually, as brain imaging is refined, the picture may become as clear and complete as those see-through exhibitions, at auto shows, of the inner workings of the internal combustion engine. At that point it may become obvious to everyone that all we are looking at is a piece of machinery, an analog chemical computer, that processes information from the environment. *All,* since you can look and look and you will not find any ghostly self inside, or any mind, or any soul.

Thereupon, in the year 2006 or 2026, some new Nietzsche will step forward to announce: *The self is dead* – except that being prone to the poetic, like Nietzsche I, he will probably say: *The soul is dead.* He will say that he is merely bringing the news, the news of the greatest event of the millennium: *The soul, that last refuge of values, is dead, because educated people no longer believe it exists.* Unless the assurances of the Wilsons and the Dennetts and the Dawkinses also start rippling out, the lurid carnival that will ensue may make the phrase *the total eclipse of all values* seem tame.

If I were a college student today, I don't think I could resist going into neuroscience. Here we have the two most fascinating riddles of the twenty-first century: the riddle of the human mind and the riddle of what happens to the human mind when it comes to know itself absolutely. In any case, we live in an age in which it

genetisch vorbestimmt ist. Ich möchte nur eine kurz Auswahl dessen geben, was ich dank der Evolutionspsychologie in den letzten paar Monaten dazugelernt habe:

Die Männchen der Gattung Mensch sind genetisch darauf vorprogrammiert, polygam, d. h. der angetrauten Partnerin untreu zu sein. Jeder Mann, der Zeitschriften liest, wird sehr bald kapieren, was das heißt. [Drei Millionen Jahre Evolution – dagegen bin ich einfach machtlos!] Frauen stehen auf prominente Männer, weil sie genetisch darauf programmiert sind, Alpha-Männchen aufzuspüren, die den Nachwuchs besser versorgen können. [Ich bin nur Rettungsschwimmer im Gen-Pool, Schatz!] Weibliche Teenager sind genetisch darauf programmiert, häufig ihre Partner zu wechseln, und können sich so wenig zurückhalten wie Hunde im Park. [Die Schule stellt Kondome zur Verfügung.] Die meisten Morde passieren aufgrund genetisch vorprogrammierter Zwänge. [Auch Häftlinge können lesen, und dann erzählen sie dem Gefängnispsychologen: *Irgendwas ist über mich gekommen … und dann war das Messer plötzlich voller Blut …* [2]

Und wo, bitte, bleibt da die Selbstkontrolle? Wo bleibt sie, wenn die Menschen glauben, daß dieses gespenstische Selbst nicht wirklich existiert und wenn Brain Imaging den endgültigen Beweis dafür liefert?

Bislang basiert die neurowissenschaftliche Theorie hauptsächlich auf indirekten Beweisen, die aus Untersuchungen von Tieren stammen oder aus Studien darüber, wie sich ein normales Gehirn verändert, wenn es verletzt wird [durch Unfälle, Krankheit, chirurgische Eingriffe oder Entnahme von Gewebeproben]. Darwin I. selbst, Edward O. Wilson, weiß nur begrenzt über das menschliche Gehirn Bescheid. Er ist Zoologe, nicht Neurologe, und seine Theorien sind Extrapolationen umfassender Studien aus seinem Spezialgebiet Insektenkunde. Auch der französische Chirurg Paul Broca entdeckte das Broca-Sprachzentrum, eines der beiden Sprachzentren in der linken Gehirnhälfte, erst, als einer seiner Patienten einen Schlaganfall erlitt. Sogar PET-Scanning und PET reporter gene/PET reporter probe sind, technisch gesehen, medizinische Eingriffe, da sie die Injektion von Chemikalien oder Viren in den Körper erfordern. Aber sie erlauben schon heute einen Blick darauf, wie die nicht-invasive Bildaufbereitung der Zukunft aussehen wird. Ein Neuroradiologe kann jemandem, der gerade einem PET-Scan unterzogen wird, eine Liste verschiedener Themen, von Sport über Musik, Wirtschaft bis hin zu Geschichte usw. vorlesen, und

is impossible and pointless to avert your eyes from the truth.

Ironically, said Nietzsche, this unflinching eye for truth, this zest for skepticism, is the legacy of Christianity [for complicated reasons that needn't detain us here]. Then he added one final and perhaps ultimate piece of irony in a fragmentary passage in a notebook shortly before he lost his mind [to the late-nineteenth-century's great venereal scourge, syphilis]. He predicted that eventually modern science would turn its juggernaut of skepticism upon itself, question the validity of its own foundations, tear them apart, and self-destruct. I thought about that in the summer of 1994 when a group of mathematicians and computer scientists held a conference at the Santa Fe Institute on *Limits to Scientific Knowledge.* The consensus was that since the human mind is, after all, an entirely physical apparatus, a form of computer, the product of a particular genetic history, it is finite in its capabilities. Being finite, hardwired, it will probably never have the power to comprehend human existence in any complete way. It would be as if a group of dogs were to call a conference to try to understand The Dog. They could try as hard as they wanted, but they wouldn't get very far. Dogs can communicate only about forty notions, all of them primitive, and they can't record anything. The project would be doomed from the start. The human brain is far superior to the dog's, but it is limited nonetheless. So any hope of human beings arriving at some final, complete, self-enclosed theory of human existence is doomed, too.

This, science's Ultimate Skepticism, has been spreading ever since then. Over the past two years even Darwinism, a sacred tenet among American scientists for the past seventy years, has been beset by ... doubts. Scientists – not religiosi – notably the mathematician David Berlinski [*The Deniable Darwin,* *Commentary*, June 1996] and the biochemist Michael Behe [*Darwin's Black Box*, 1996], have begun attacking Darwinism as a mere theory, not a scientific discovery, a theory woefully unsupported by fossil evidence and featuring, at the core of its logic, sheer mush. [Dennett and Dawkins, for whom Darwin is the Only Begotten, the Messiah, are already screaming. They're beside themselves, utterly apoplectic. Wilson, the giant, keeping his cool, has remained above the bat-

symposium

sobald ein Thema dabei ist, für das sich die Testperson interessiert, leuchtet ein bestimmter Bereich der Großhirnrinde am Bildschirm auf. Wenn Brain Imaging erst einmal optimal funktioniert, könnte man das Gehirn genausogut bei der Arbeit beobachten wie den Verbrennungsmotor bei einer Demonstrationsvorführung auf einer Auto-Schau. Wenn wir diesen Punkt erreicht haben, wird jedem klar sein, daß wir hier nichts anders vor uns haben als eine Maschine, einen analogen chemischen Computer, der Informationen aus der Umwelt verarbeitet. Wirklich nichts anders, weil man auch bei ganz genauem Hinsehen weder ein gespenstisches Selbst noch einen Geist oder eine Seele darin entdecken wird.

Und daraufhin wird im Jahr 2006 oder 2026 ein neuer Nietzsche auf den Plan treten und verkünden: *Das Selbst ist tot* – abgesehen davon, daß er, wie Nietzsche I., einen Hang zur Poesie haben und deshalb wahtscheinlich sagen wird: *Die Seele ist tot.* Er wird sagen, er überbringe nur die Nachricht vom größten Ereignis des Jahrtausends: *Die Seele, diese letzte Zufluchtstätte der Werte, ist tot, weil die gebildeten Menschen nicht mehr glauben, daß es sie gibt.* Und wenn die Versicherungen der Wilsons und Dennetts und Dawkinses weiterhin im Sande verlaufen, wird die *völlige Umkehrung aller Werte* ganz schön harmlos aussehen neben der wilden Hysterie, die Nietzsche II auslösen wird.

Wäre ich heute Student, ich könnte der Neurowissenschaft wohl kaum widerstehen, befaßt sie sich doch mit den beiden faszinierendsten Rätseln des 21. Jahrhunderts: dem Rätsel des menschlichen Geistes und dem Rätsel, was mit dem menschlichen Geist passiert, wenn er sich endlich durch und durch kennt. Wir leben in einem Zeitalter, in dem es ohnehin unmöglich und sinnlos ist, den Blick von der Wahrheit abzuwenden.

Ironischerweise, sagt Nietzsche, sind dieser unerschrockene Blick für die Wahrheit, diese Begeisterung für die Skepsis ein Erbe des Christentums [aus komplizierten Gründen, die wir hier nicht näher erläutern wollen]. Dann fügte er, kurz bevor er den Verstand verlor [wegen der Syphilis, dieser großen Geißel des späten 19. Jahrhunderts], in einer fragmentarischen Passage in einem Notizbuch eine letzte und vielleicht endgültige Ironie hinzu. Er sagte voraus, daß die moderne Wissenschaft letztendlich diesen Höllenhund der Skepsis auf sich selbst hetzen würde, die Gültigkeit ihrer eigenen Grundlagen in Frage stellen, diese sodann in der Luft zerfetzen und sich so selbst zerstören würde. Daran mußte ich im

tle.] By 1990 the physicist Petr Beckmann of the University of Colorado had already begun going after Einstein. He greatly admired Einstein for his famous equation of matter and energy, $E=mc^2$, but called his theory of relativity mostly absurd and grotesquely untestable. Beckmann died in 1993. His Fool Killer's cudgel has been taken up by Howard Hayden of the University of Connecticut, who has many admirers among the upcoming generation of Ultimately Skeptical young physicists. The scorn the new breed heaps upon quantum mechanics [*has no real-world applications*...*depends entirely on fairies sprinkling goofball equations in your eyes*], Unified Field Theory [*Nobel worm bait*], and the Big Bang Theory [*creationism for nerds*] has become withering. If only Nietzsche were alive! He would have relished every minute of it!

Recently I happened to be talking to a prominent California geologist, and she told me: *When I first went into geology, we all thought that in science you create a solid layer of findings, through experiment and careful investigation, and then you add a second layer, like a second layer of bricks, all very carefully, and so on. Occasionally some adventurous scientist stacks the bricks up in towers, and these towers turn out to be insubstantial and they get torn down, and you proceed again with the careful layers. But we now realize that the very first layers aren't even resting on solid ground. They are balanced on bubbles, on concepts that are full of air, and those bubbles are being burst today, one after the other.*

I suddenly had a picture of the entire astonishing edifice collapsing and modern man plunging headlong back into the primordial ooze. He's floundering, sloshing about, gulping for air, frantically treading ooze, when he feels something huge and smooth swim beneath him and boost him up, like some almighty dolphin. He can't see it, but he's much impressed. He names it God.

Sommer 1994 denken, als eine Gruppe Mathematiker und Computerwissenschaftler am Santa Fe Institute eine Konferenz zum Thema *Grenzen wissenschaftlicher Erkenntnis* abhielten. Der allgemeine Konsensus war, der menschliche Geist sei ein durch und durch physikalischer Apparat, eine Art Computer, Produkt einer speziellen genetischen Entwicklung, und verfüge daher nur über endliche Fähigkeiten. Ist er endlich und vorprogrammiert, so wird er wohl nie in der Lage sein, menschliches Leben vollständig zu begreifen. Denn das wäre so, als würde ein Rudel Hunde eine Konferenz einberufen, mit dem Ziel, das Wesen des Hundes zu begreifen. Sie könnten sich noch so sehr bemühen, sie würden nicht sehr weit kommen. Hunde können nur ungefähr 40 primitive Begriffe kommunizieren und sie können nichts aufzeichnen. Das Projekt wäre von Anfang an zum Scheitern verurteilt. Das menschliche Gehirn ist dem Hundegehirn bei weitem überlegen, aber es hat trotzdem seine Grenzen. Also ist jegliche Hoffnung, daß die Menschen eine endgültige, komplette, in sich geschlossene Theorie des menschlichen Lebens aufstellen könnten, ebenfalls vergeblich.

Diese Ultimative Skepsis der Wissenschaft findet seitdem starken Anklang. In den letzten beiden Jahren begann man, sogar am Darwinismus – seit 70 Jahren das Allerheiligste der amerikanischen Wissenschaftler – zu zweifeln, ja, tatsächlich zu zweifeln. Nicht Religiosi, sondern Wissenschaftler, insbesondere der Mathematiker David Berlinski [*The Deniable Darwin*, Kommentar, Juni 1996] und der Biochemiker Michael Behe [*Darwin's Black Box*, 1996] begannen damit, den Darwinismus als reine Theorie abzutun und jeglichen Anspruch desselben auf eine wissenschaftliche Entdeckung abzustreiten. Er sei eine Theorie, die nur dürftig durch Fossilienfunde belegt und im Kern ihrer Logik butterweich sei. [Dennett und Dawkins, für die Darwin der Eingeborene Sohn, der Messias ist, schreien schon auf. Sind außer sich, völlig cholerisch. Wilson, der Gigant, macht auf cool und hält sich aus der Schlacht heraus.] Schon 1990 hatte der Physiker Petr Beckmann von der University of Colorado begonnen, sich Einstein vorzuknöpfen. Obwohl er Einstein für seine berühmte Gleichung von Masse und Energie, $E=mc^2$, sehr bewunderte, bezeichnete er dennoch die Relativitätstheorie als großteils absurd und auf groteske Weise unüberprüfbar. Beckmann starb 1993. In seine Fußstapfen trat Howard Hayden von der University of Connecticut, der in der neuen Generation ultimativ skeptischer Jungphysiker viele Bewunderer hat. Der Hohn, mit dem diese junge Generation die Quanten-

1 The term neurometric is closely identified with John, who has devised both the Neurometric Battery, a comprehensive system for analyzing brain functions, and the Neurometric Analyzer, a patented instrument for making use of the Battery; but John had nothing to do with Neurometrics, Inc. He describes the Battery in Neurometric Evaluation of Brain Function in Normal and Learning Disabled Children [ANN ARBOR, University of Michigan Press, 1989].

2 Recounted by the British prison psychiatrist THEODORE DALRYMPLE in the magazine City Journal.

First published in Forbes ASAP
December 2nd, 1996

mechanik [*findet keine Anwendung in der realen Welt*, *dem hat wohl die gute Fee Ködel-Gleichungen in die Augen gestreut*], die Einheitliche Feldtheorie [*Nobelpreis-Wurmköder*], und die Urknall-Theorie [*Kreationismus für Dumpfgummis!*] überhäuft, hat inzwischen völlig vernichtende Ausmaße angenommen. Wäre nur Nietzsche noch am Leben! Er hätte seine helle Freude!

Vor kurzem sprach ich mit einer bekannten kalifornischen Geologin, die meinte: *Als ich anfing, Geologie zu studieren, dachten wir alle, daß man in der Wissenschaft durch Experimente und sorgfältige Untersuchungen eine solide Schicht aus Erkenntnissen aufbaut, und dann sehr, sehr vorsichtig eine zweite Schicht hinzufügt, etwa wie eine zweite Schicht Ziegel, und immer so weiter. Manchmal stapelt ein abenteuerlustiger Wissenschaftler seine Ziegel zu Türmen auf, die sich dann als gegenstandslos herausstellen und wieder eingerissen werden, und dann macht man wieder vorsichtig mit neuen Schichten weiter. Aber wie wir jetzt erkennen, ruhen nicht einmal die ersten Schichten auf festem Untergrund. Sie ruhen auf Seifenblasen, hohlen Konzepten, und diese Seifenblasen fangen jetzt an zu platzen, eine nach der anderen.*

Da hatte ich plötzlich das Bild vor Augen, wie dieses ganze erstaunliche Gebäude in sich zusammenfällt und der moderne Mensch kopfüber wieder zurück in die Ursuppe purzelt. Da strampelt er dann, spritzt um sich, ringt nach Luft, tritt ganz hektisch Ursuppenwasser, und plötzlich spürt er, wie etwas Riesiges, Weiches unter ihm schwimmt und ihn emporhebt wie ein allmächtiger Delphin. Er kann nicht sehen, was es ist, aber er ist total beeindruckt. Er nennt es Gott.

Erstmals erschienen in Forbes ASAP
2. Dezember 1996

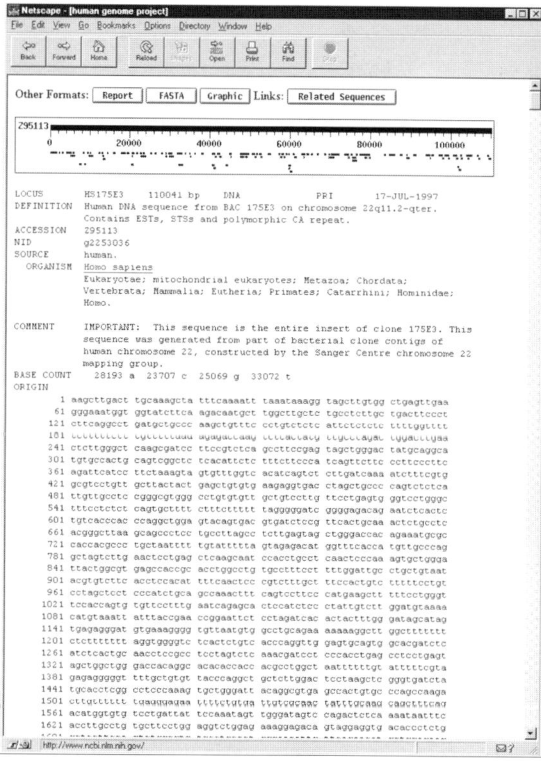

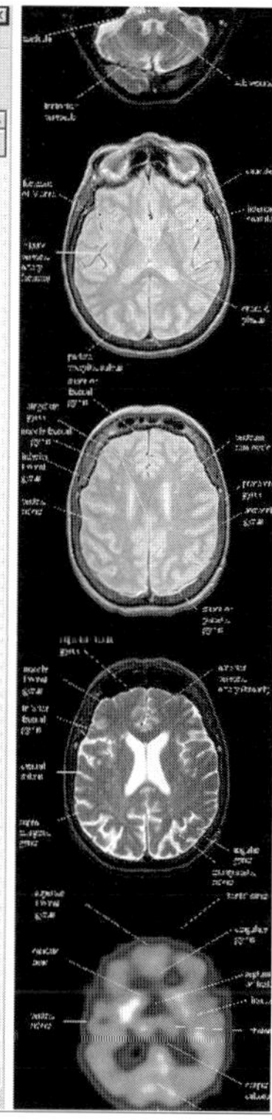

symposium

1 Der Begriff *neurometrisch* wird oft mit E. Roy John assoziiert, dem Erfinder der Neurometrischen Batterie, eines umfassenden Systems zur Analyse von Gehirnfunktionen, und des Neurometrischen Analysators, eines patentierten Instruments zu deren Nutzung. John hat aber nichts mit Neurometrics, Inc. zu tun. Er beschreibt die Batterie in Neurometric Evaluation of Brain Function in Normal and Learning Disabled Children [ANN ARBOR, University of Michigan Press, 1989].

2 LT. THEODORE DALRYMPLE, britischer Gefängnispsychiater, in der Zeitschrift *City Journal*.

Border Patrol ▶

Paul Garrin/David Rokeby

Stationary cameras function as visual sensors to the VNSII interface by David Rokeby that controls the positioning of robotic *snipercams* which lock on to moving targets [the viewer's heads] and *fire shots* [audio of gunshots]. The viewer sees his/her image on video monitors, set into the face of the metal wall, in the crosshairs of the snipercam.

Stationäre Kameras dienen als visuelle Sensoren für das VNSII-Interface von David Rokeby, das die Positionierung von Roboter-*Snipercams* [Heckenschützenkameras] steuert, die sich an beweglichen Zielen *festkrallen* [in diesem Fall an den Köpfen der Besucher] und *Schüsse* abfeuern [entsprechende Schußgeräusche]. Auf Videomonitoren, die in die Metallwand der Installation eingelassen sind, sehen die Besucher ihre eigenen Köpfe im Fadenkreuz.

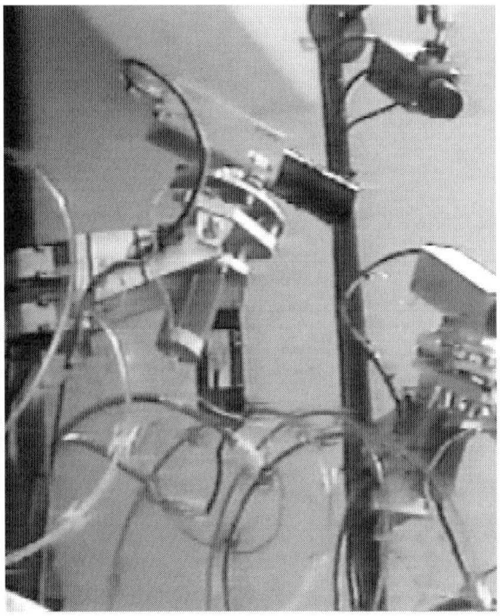

installations

The Invisible Shape of Things Past ▶

Joachim Sauter/Dirk Lüsebrink
[Art+Com]

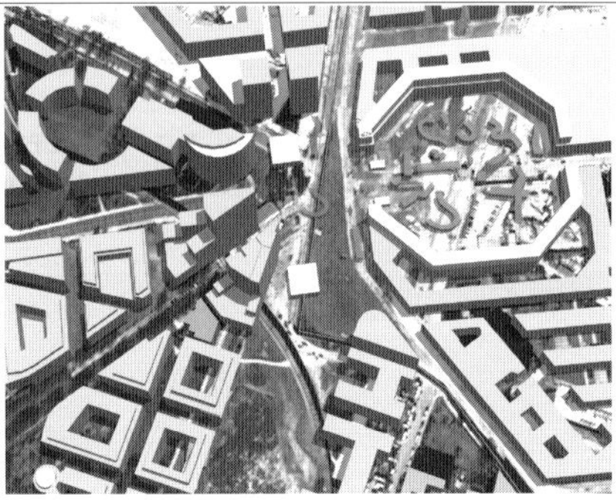

With this Project users are enabled to transform film sequences into interactive virtual objects. This transformation is based on all the camera parameters of a particular film sequence. The angle of the individual frames in relation to the virtual camera path depends on the perspective of the actual camera, the size of the individual frames depends on the focal length used. A virtual architecture of information emerges, which represents the underlying film sequence through its form. This object may be explored interactively, it is the spatial user interface [VRUI] to the information it contains.

Das Projekt ermöglicht es den Nutzern, Filmsequenzen in interaktive virtuelle Objekte umzusetzen. Diese Transformation basiert auf den Kameraparametern der zugrundeliegenden Filmsequenz. Entlang des in den virtuellen Raum übertragenen Kamerapfades werden die Einzelbilder des Filmes aneinandergereiht. Eine virtuelle Informationsarchitektur entsteht, die durch ihre Form die Entstehung der zugrunde liegenden Filmsequenz kommuniziert. Dieses Objekt ist interaktiv erfahrbar, ist räumliches Userinterface [VRUI] zu der in ihm enthaltenen Information.

Moppet ▶

Toshihiro Anzai/Tamio Kihara

Moppet is a new creative system that anyone can use. It is simple, easy and open. A Person can paint and make music at the same time. The system is networked by a telecommunications network. It links many participants and several spaces. The performance may be seen by a large audience.**Moppet* creates CG paintings according to the way the participants move. The movement on *Moppet's* court takes the place of a paintbrush. The painting is projected to a screen over the court.

Moppet ist ein neues kreatives System, das jedermann benutzen kann, es ist einfach und offen. Leute können damit malen und gleichzeitig Musik machen. Das System ist durch ein Telekommunikationsnetzwerk verlinkt und verknüpft viele Mitwirkende und mehrere Räume. Die sich daraus ergebende Performance kann von einem breiten Publikum beobachtet werden. *Moppet* erzeugt computergraphische Gemälde, je nachdem, wie sich die Mitwirkenden bewegen. Die Bewegung auf dem *Moppet-Feld* übernimmt die Rolle des Pinsels, und das Gemälde wird über dem *Spielfeld* auf einen Schirm über dem Feld projiziert.

Timesharing

Mark Madel

▶

You will find a detailed description of the projects in the Prix Ars Electronica 97 book **Cyberarts** *International Compendium Prix Ars Electronica, SpringerWienNewYork 1997.*

Eine ausführliche Beschreibung der Projekte finden Sie im Buch zum Prix Ars Electronica 97 **Cyberarts** *International Compendium Prix Ars Electronica, SpringerWienNewYork 1997.*

Printed circuit- boards, copper, paint, Plexiglas, electronic parts, and software. Mark Madel's electronic objects demand viewer interaction with themselves and,frequently, with other viewers in order for the works to release information of any kind. Madel crafts his sleek works from printed circuit-boards, iced displays, speakers, infrared sensors, and other electronic components and subcomponents; he imbues his objects with complex sets of responses to viewer inputs, addressing the blurred distinctions between interaction and relationship and between coercion and invitation.

Platinen, Kupfer, Farbe, Plexiglas, elektronische Teile und Software: Mark Madels elektronische Objekte verlangen vom Betrachter die Interaktion mit ihnen selbst und oft auch mit anderen Betrachtern, damit die Arbeiten ihre Information preis geben. Madel fertigt seine feine Arbeiten aus Platinen, LCD-Displays, Lautsprechern, Infranetsensoren und anderen elektronischen Komponenten und Subkomponenten. Seine Objekte reagieren mit komplexen Antwortmustern auf die Eingaben des Betrachters und zeigen die verschwommenen Unterscheidungen auf, die zwischen Interaktion und Beziehung, Nötigung und Aufforderung bestehen.

Seeing is Believing

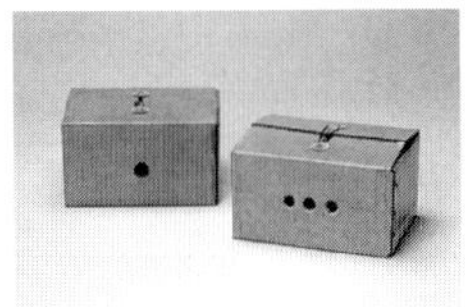

Kazuhiko Hachiya

Seeing Is Believing is an exhibit consisting of several elements. Here I would like to explain what motivated me to create each of these different works and projects.

Mega Diary – Global Diary Project on the Net

One day, I had a dream. I was in a very large library. It was a somewhat peculiar library, because its entire collection consisted of the diaries of all those people who had ever lived. I randomly read through these records of the lives of all mankind. They were written by various types of people of all ages and from all countries, some of them still living and others dead. I read, and I was both moved and impressed. I felt sympathy for the authors, and I laughed and I cried. Two weeks later, I started the *Mega Diary* project, conceived as one hundred people keeping diaries for 100 days and exchanging them with one another on the PC communications net. The diaries would be collected and shown each day through Nifty Serve and the Internet, as well as being broadcast nationwide once a week on FM *visible information radio*. In fact, *Mega Diary* has spurred me to think about how diverse the everyday lives of others are, and how unaware we typically are of this fact, etc. The project has also made me realize that monologue is often a better means of communication than dialogue.

Empty Entity –
The Invisible Electric Light Display

Though we usually tend to forget it, visibility and invisibility are deeply connected with how we humans are structured physical-

Seeing is Believing

Kazuhiko Hachiya

Seeing Is Believing ist ein Ausstellungsobjekt, das aus verschiedenen Elementen besteht, und im folgenden möchte ich erläutern, was mich dazu motiviert hat, jedes dieser Projekte und Werke zu schaffen.

Mega Diary – Ein globales, offenes Tagebuchprojekt im Netz

Eines Tages hatte ich einen Traum. Ich träumte, ich befände mich in einer Bibliothek – einer ganz speziellen Bibliothek, denn sie enthielt nichts anderes als die Tagebücher aller Menschen, die jemals auf dieser Erde gelebt hatten. Ich habe mich – hie und da blätternd – nach und nach durch diese Aufzeichnungen aus dem Leben der Menschheit gelesen. Sie stammten von den unterschiedlichsten Leuten aller Altersstufen und Länder, manche davon noch am Leben, andere schon lange tot. Ich las, und ich war ebenso beeindruckt wie bewegt, ich lachte und weinte. Zwei Wochen später initiierte ich das *Mega Diary*-Projekt, konzipiert für hundert Leute, die hundert Tage lang Tagebücher führen und sie untereinander im Netz austauschen sollten. Die Tagebücher sollten gesammelt und täglich über Nifty Serve und das Internet gezeigt sowie einmal wöchentlich landesweit im *Visible Information Radio* auf UKW ausgestrahlt werden. *Mega Diary* hat mich angespornt, darüber nachzudenken, wie unterschiedlich doch das Alltagsleben der einzelnen Menschen ist und wie wenig uns diese Tatsache normalerweise bewußt ist. Und noch etwas hat mir das Projekt klargemacht: Ein Monolog kann manchmal ein besseres Kommunikationsmittel sein als ein Dialog.

Empty Entity –
Das unsichtbare Lichtdisplay

Obwohl wir normalerweise dazu tendieren, es zu vergessen: Sichtbarkeit und Unsichtbarkeit sind unmittelbar mit der physischen Struktur der Lebewesen verknüpft. Der sichtbare Strahlungsbereich ist von Spezies zu Spezies anders; das menschliche Auge kann elektromagnetische

ly. The range of visible rays differs from species to species. Human eyes can pick up 400 nm [nanometer] to 800 nm electromagnetic waves. Of course, light also exists outside the boundaries of what is visible.

In this piece, each display unit is made up of 8 letters, with 16 x 16 [256] light-emitting diodes [LED] for each letter, and a total of 4 units in the room. Since 15 of 16 of the LEDs are infrared ones, the naked eye sees only flickering lights, produced by the small number of LEDs emitting visible rays. With special eyewear on, however, the viewer can see letters flowing across the units. In this exhibition, the diaries which many people have contributed to *Mega Diary* are displayed. These diaries could be considered as one of the best examples of something which is visible to us, but at the same time is not visible, and is extremely precious nonetheless.

The Sheep: The Tool to See the Invisible

In Exupéry's *The Little Prince*, there is a scene in which the prince begs *me* to draw a picture of a sheep. *I* draw many pictures, but none of them please him. Finally *I* draw a picture of a box, and say, *This is his box. The sheep you asked for is inside!* Then, for the first time, the prince likes *my* picture. In this *box,* which serves as eyewear for the viewer, what is inside, is not a tiny sheep, but a monochrome observation camera and a liquid crystal TV monitor. When you peep through the box, you will surely see a little bit of the invisible. After that, it's a matter of imagination: even if you no longer have the box, or even if the *Mega Diary* project runs to completion, you should still be able to use your imagination to think of those people with whom you have become acquainted. After all, you are no longer a stranger to them, now that you have read their diaries.

In my opinion, though, what one can see constitutes only a fraction of the truth. This is how I felt during the *Mega Diary* project. When I read someone's diary for a long while, I begin to experience emotions toward the author and feel closer to that person, even though I do not know him or her. My *connectedness* or relationship with the person is one of a sort of respect and *belief.*

Wellen zwischen 400 und 800 Nanometer Länge wahrnehmen. Und dennoch existiert Licht auch jenseits dessen, was wir sehen ...

In diesem Stück besteht jedes Display aus acht Buchstaben, die sich jeweils aus 16 x 16 [256] Licht-Emitter-Dioden[LED] zusammensetzen. Vier solcher Displays sind im Raum angebracht. Da 15 der 16 LEDs Infrarotlicht abstrahlen, sieht das unbewaffnete Menschenauge nur ein flackerndes Licht, das die wenigen übrigen LEDs, die im sichtbaren Bereich leuchten, abstrahlen. Mit besonderen Brillen allerdings kann der Betrachter Buchstaben auf den Displays erkennen. In dieser Ausstellung werden die Beiträge, die diese vielen Menschen zum *Mega Diary*-Projekt beigesteuert haben, ausgestellt. Diese Tagebücher sind auch metaphorisch das beste Beispiel für Dinge, die zwar sichtbar, aber gleichzeitig für uns unsichtbar und dennoch von großem Wert sind.

Das Schaf: das Werkzeug zum Sehen des Unsichtbaren

In Antoine de Saint Exupérys *Der Kleine Prinz* gibt es eine Szene, in der der Prinz den Erzähler bittet, doch ein Schaf für ihn zu zeichnen. Der Erzähler zeichnet mehrere Schafe, aber keines gefällt dem Prinzen. So entsteht zuletzt das Bild einer Schachtel, und der Erzähler sagt: *Dies ist seine Schachtel, und das Schaf, das du wolltest, ist drin!* Und da gefällt dem Prinzen erstmals das Bild. In dieser *Schachtel*, die dem Besucher als Sehhilfe dient, ist zwar kein Schaf, wohl aber eine monochrome Beobachtungskamera und ein Flüssigkristall-Monitor. Wenn man durch die Schachtel schaut, sieht man ein Stück des Unsichtbaren. Danach aber ist alles eine Frage der Vorstellungskraft: Selbst wenn man die *Schachtel* nicht mehr auf hat oder wenn das *Mega Diary*-Projekt zu Ende geht, sollte man doch seine Phantasie benutzen und an jene Menschen denken, die man so kennengelernt hat. Schließlich ist man ihnen ja nicht mehr fremd, wenn man ihre Tagebücher gelesen hat.

Meiner Ansicht nach ist das, was man sehen kann, nur ein Bruchteil der Wahrheit. Das jedenfalls fühlte ich während des *Mega Diary*-Projekts. Wenn ich jemandes Tagebuch lese, beginne ich, dem Autor gegenüber eine emotionale Beziehung zu entwickeln und mich ihm näher zu fühlen, auch wenn ich ihn gar nicht kenne. Meine Beziehung, mein Verbundensein mit dieser Person wird getragen von einer Mischung aus Respekt und *Glauben*.

solve et coagula

Stahl Stenslie/Knut Mork/
Karl Anders Oygard

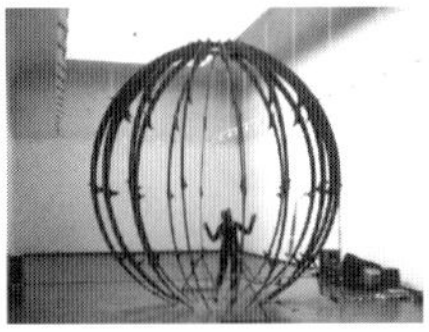

solve et coagula is an attempt to give birth to a new life form: half digital, half organic. Through a multisensorial, full duplex sensory interface, the installation networks the human with an emotional, sensing and artificially intelligent creature; it mates man with a machine turned human and everything that goes with it: ecstatic, monstrous, perverted, craving, seductive, hysterical, violent, beautiful.

solve et coagula is a post-human life form. It presents the emergence of a new species, a bio-cybernetic symbiosis, transforming the conception of being human by networking man with a sensing and emotional machine. Through an intelligent, physical, two-way communication interface, the installation extends the computer's logic and intelligence into a human domain of dark desire.

Through a corporal and sensual symbiosis of an intelligent, interactive three-dimensional creature and a human user[s] *solve et coagula* questions the possibility of a post-human and a post-biological lifeform and the challenge of communication it represents.

solve et coagula

Stahl Stenslie/Knut Mork/
Karl Anders Oygard

solve et coagula stellt den Versuch dar, eine neue – halb digitale, halb organische – Lebensform zu schaffen. Über eine multisensorische Vollduplexschnittstelle vernetzt die Installation den Menschen mit einem fühlenden, empfindsamen, mit künstlicher Intelligenz ausgestatteten Wesen. Sie paart ihn mit einer menschgewordenen Maschine und allem, was dazugehört: Ekstase, Monstrosität, Perversion, Verlangen, Verführung, Hysterie, Brutalität, Schönheit.

solve et coagula ist eine post-humane Lebensform. Es verändert die Vorstellung von Menschsein, indem es den Menschen mit einer empfindsamen und gefühlvollen Maschine vernetzt, und markiert so die Entstehung einer neuen Spezies, einer bio-kybernetischen Symbiose. Mit Hilfe einer intelligenten, physischen, dialogfähigen Schnittstelle werden Intelligenz und Logik des Computers auf die menschliche Domäne des finsteren Begehrens ausgedehnt.

Durch die körperliche und sinnliche Symbiose eines intelligenten, interaktiven, dreidimensionalen Wesens mit einem oder mehreren menschlichen Benutzern prüft *solve et coagula* die Möglichkeit für eine post-humane bzw. post-biologische Lebensform und die damit einhergehenden Anforderungen an die Kommunikation.

Garnet Vision

Hiroo Iwata

Garnet Vision is the first spatial immersive display which covers a full solid angle of the view. The viewer is totally enclosed by twelve rear-projection screens. A rear-projection screen requires a large backyard. We set criteria in order to optimize space utility of the display system: pixel efficiency and space efficiency. Pixel efficiency means how many pixels are displayed on each polygon of a polyhedral screen by a projector. Space efficiency is determined by the ratio of the displayed volume of a polyhedron to the overall dead volume of the backyard of a rear-projection screen. Through examination of these criteria, a rhombic dodecahedron is chosen from various polyhedrons, and it maximizes space utility.

The participant of *Garnet Vision* goes into the dodecahedron screen. S/he can rotate on a transparent floor and sees the full solid angle view. Viewers outside the screen can see half of the rhombic screens so that they can enjoy the image.

Garnet Vision

Hiroo Iwata

Garnet Vision ist das erste immersive Raumdisplay, das eine komplette Rundumperspektive bietet. Der Betrachter steht in einem in sich geschlossenen Gebilde aus zwölf Rückprojektionsflächen. Da Rückprojektionen einen großen Abstand zur Projektionsfläche erfordern, wurden zur optimalen Raumausnutzung die Kriterien Pixeleffizienz und Raumeffizienz festgesetzt. Die Pixeleffizienz bezieht sich auf die Anzahl der pro Projektor auf jedem einzelnen Polygon der vielflächigen Leinwand angezeigten Pixel. Die Raumeffizienz ergibt sich aus dem Verhältnis zwischen dem angezeigten Polyedervolumen und dem gesamten Eigenvolumen des hinter der Leinwand zur Verfügung stehenden Raums. Im Hinblick auf diese Kriterien erwies sich der rhombische Dodekaeder als ideal, da er von allen Polyedern die beste Raumausnutzung gewährleistet.

Die Besucher von *Garnet Vision* begeben sich ins Innere des Leinwand-Dodekaeders, wo sie von einer transparenten Drehbühne aus in das Rundum-Display eintauchen. Die Hälfte der rhombischen Leinwände ist auch für die Besucher außerhalb des Dodekaeders sichtbar, so daß auch sie die Projektion mitverfolgen können.

IPzentrum

TXTD.sign

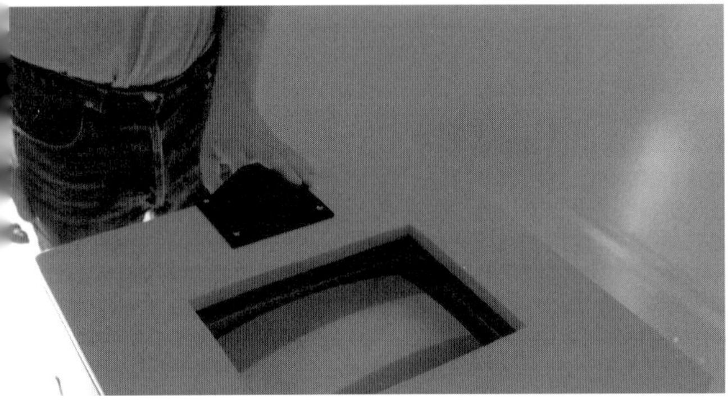

The *IPzentrum* project is based upon considerations concerning the interpretation of earthquakes as one of the elementary forms of expression of our planet. Equally decisive factors were the depiction of the underlying principle of such local events produced by global causes by means of the network of seismographic stations set up to observe them, as well as the intention to enable individual observation within this matrix of events and perceptions.

The internet-based installation consists of a reciprocally generating event system. Event-synchronous data received on earthquakes control the pressure intensity of an sonic field which develops in a [resonation] space. The states of stress experienced by visitors to the installation [resonators] who are being stimulated by this pressure intensity are measured and fed back to the system as additional control data [informational tremor] through a channel of communication [about the events] and the disturbances to it. Communication and its disruption, restoration and severance are likewise data-generated events that influence the process.

installations

IPzentrum

TXTD.sign

As a rule, earthquakes occur as a result of massive subterranean shifts. Most of their energy is released as heat resulting from friction; only a small percentage is transformed into seismic energy and transmitted as wave-like vibrations. Even if earthquakes are local events, the release of kinetic energy nevertheless represents the phenomenology of the planetary body as a whole. On the average, an earthquake with a magnitude of 3 on the 9.0 [basically open-ended] Richter Scale takes place somewhere in the world every ten minutes. Weaker tremors occur even more frequently.

Earthquakes are tremors which originate at an epicenter and radiate through portions of the earth's crust and interior. Earthquakes which spread our across the whole earth are referred to as global quakes.

The internet is a suitable *tool* to carry out the tasks of global seismology. Along with the seismometer and seismograph as their core technology, modern digital seismographic stations consist of a processor dedicated to data collection and feature internet link-up. Although these link-ups are *sub-networks* or *special networks,* the data is available through open channels to the general public in, more or less, real time.

The existence of a worldwide network for the observation of earthquakes is value-generated; it has come about due to and in expectation of catastrophes affecting human life and property. In the face of such a threat, global observation, in as close to real time as possible, is a pressing concern not only from the perspective of civilization; rather, it is also conclusive in the sense of the phenomenology of the event. In this case, the Internet serves to compile and distribute data on a global phenomenon and not the global compilation of a local phenomenon.

The event-generated [since it operates in real time] informational structure thus represents the events about which it provides information. This equation suggests the interpretation of global kinetic energy as informational energy.

The **Ipzentrum** project is based upon this interpretation and its prerequisite assumptions as a treatment of, on one hand, the issue of the subjective preconditions of perception, classification, evaluation and functionalization [use] of various forms of energy, and, on the other, the principle of the mediatized percep-

Dem Projekt *IPzentrum* liegen Überlegungen zur Interpretation von Erdbeben als eine der elementaren Äußerungsformen unseres Planeten zugrunde. Ebenso maßgeblich waren die Abbildung des Prinzips solcher global verursachten lokalen Ereignisse durch das ihrer Beobachtung dienende Netz seismographischer Stationen und die Absicht, individuelle Beobachtung innerhalb dieses Ereignis- und Wahrnehmungszusammenhanges wirksam werden zu lassen.

Die internetbasierte Installation besteht aus einem sich wechselseitig generierenden Ereignissystem. Ereignissynchron empfangene Daten über Erdbeben steuern die Druckintensität eines Schallfeldes, das sich in einem [Resonanz-] Raum entfaltet. Durch die Druckintensität stimulierte Streßzustände von Besuchern [Resonatoren] werden gemessen und über den Weg von Kommunikation [über die Ereignisse] und deren Störung dem System als weitere Steuerungsdaten [informationelle Beben] zugeführt. Kommunikation und deren Störung, Entstörung und Zerstörung sind ebenso datenerzeugende Ereignisse, die den Prozeß beeinflussen.

Erdbeben ereignen sich in der Regel aufgrund unterirdischer Massenverlagerungen. Ein Großteil der Energie wird als Reibungswärme freigesetzt, nur ein kleiner Prozentsatz wird in seismische Energie umgewandelt und als wellenförmige Schwingungen abgestrahlt. Wenn Erdbeben auch lokale Ereignisse sind, so repräsentiert die Freisetzung kinetischer Energie doch die Phänomenolgie des planetaren Körpers als Ganzen. Im Schnitt ereignet sich weltweit alle zehn Minuten ein Erdbeben der Stärke 3 auf der neunteiligen [im Grunde nach oben hin offenen] Richter-Skala. Schwächere Beben erfolgen in geringeren Zeitabständen.

Erdbeben sind von einem Herd ausgehende Erschütterungen, die sich über Teile der Erdoberfläche und des Erdinneren ausbreiten. Erdbeben, die sich über die gesamte Erde erstrecken, werden Weltbeben genannt.

Das Internet ist ein den Aufgaben der globalen Seismologie adäquates *Werkzeug*. Moderne digitale seismographische Stationen bestehen neben Seismometer und Seismograph als Kernstücken aus einem mit der Datenerfassung betreuten Rechner mit Internet-Anbindung. Obwohl es sich dabei um ein Sub- oder Spezialnetz handelt, sind die Daten durch offene Kanäle quasi in Echtzeit für jeden/jede verfügbar.

Seismology is the study of, among other things, the destructive effects of earthquakes and the geological and geotectonic forces at work in the area around the epicenter.

tion of the environment, as a result of which data and information are interpreted as the environment [and its condition with respect to energy].

To hyperbolize to some extent: most fundamental is the assumption that in a culture in which the primary perception of events occurs under conditions of mediatization, events are perceived as not being real [namely, not affecting one's own existence] as long as those media through which the information is disseminated are themselves unaffected by those events. Catastrophes do not exist as long as the reporting about them continues. Therefore, *IPzentrum* can be considered a test installation whose objective is to raise the level of reality of information by means of a linkage to the individual actually perceiving information about events and the triggering possibilities which have thus been opened up to that individual.

The possibilities of communication on various stages with one another which have been implanted here, analogous to extractable principles of natural processes and their subjective evaluation, can be defined as three causal principles:

Störung [disruption]
Ent-Störung [restoration]
Zer-Störung [severance]

The installation consists of three comunicationally linked areas:

1 The area of reception of international earthquake data from the network and its configuration into sonic waves for the purpose of the stimulation of stress on the part of the visitors to the resonation space.

The causal factor here is not the Internet itself [that would be trivial in this case], but rather the network-based structure of seismographic measuring stations distributed throughout the world.

The resonation space is a sensual-psychological interface between both structures of communication [which, in turn, constitute interfaces between the material confrontations of the human body/human property with earthquakes.]

A sub-bass speaker system is set up beneath the resonation space to fill it with low fre-

Die Existenz einer weltweit vernetzten Beobachtung von Erdbeben ist wertgeneriert, sie erfolgt aufgrund von und im Hinblick auf Katastrophen für Körper und Besitz. Globale und möglichst echtzeitige Beobachtung ist nicht nur aus der zivilisatorischen Perspektive auf das Bedrohliche naheliegend, sondern auch schlüssig im Sinne der Phänomenologie des Ereignisses. Das Internet dient in diesem Fall zur Erfassung und Distribution eines globalen Phänomens, nicht zur globalen Erfassung eines lokalen Phänomens.

Die ereignisgenerierte [da echtzeitig betriebene] Informationsstruktur repräsentiert somit die Ereignisse, über die es informiert. Diese Gleichsetzung legt die Interpretation von globaler kinetischer Energie als informationelle Energie nahe. Dem Projekt *IPzentrum* liegen diese Interpretation und ihre Voraussetzungen als Thematisierung von subjektiven Vorbedingungen der Wahrnehmung, Einordnung, Bewertung und Funktionalisierung [Nutzung] verschiedener Formen von Energie einerseits und des Prinzips mediatisierter Wahrnehmung der Umwelt, infolge derer Daten und Informationen als die Umwelt [und ihre energetischen Zustände] interpretiert werden, andererseits zugrunde.

Um es überspitzt zu sagen: Ursächlich ist die Annahme, daß in einer Kultur, in der die primäre Wahrnehmung von Ereignissen in einem Zustand der Mediatisierung erfolgt, Ereignisse solange als nicht real [nämlich die eigene Existenz betreffend] wahrgenommen werden, solange jene Medien, durch welche die Information erfolgt, von den Ereignissen nicht selbst betroffen sind. Katastrophen exisitieren nicht, solange über sie berichtet wird. *IPzentrum* versteht sich mithin als Versuchsanordnung zur Erhöhung des Realitätsgrades von Informationen durch die Einbindung des Informationen über Ereignisse wahrnehmenden Körpers und seiner dabei vorhandenen Triggerungsmöglichlichkeiten.

Die Seismik untersucht u. a. die zerstörenden Wirkungen von Erdbeben und die geologischen und geotektonischen Kräfte im Herdgebiet.

Die dabei implantierten Möglichkeiten der Kommunikation verschiedener Etappen miteinander sind analog zu extrahierbaren Prinzipien natürlicher Vorgänge und ihrer subjektiven Bewertungen als drei kausale Prinzipien definierbar:

quency [sub-bass: 16 to 70 Hertz] sound. The activation of the system takes place by means of the data originating from the respective event areas.

The resonation space is equipped with a biofeedback system, whereby a monitor optically displays the heightened psycho-physical state of individuals [resonators] present in it. Such changes of state are brought about by individuals present in the resonation space or, more precisely, their perception of the body as a resonator and the state in which they find themselves as a result thereof, from which a measurement of the *deformation* of the Web data can ultimately be obtained.

The energy of an earthquake is expressed by the magnitude M. In the case of earthquakes with extremely high levels of energy, M has a value of between 8.5 and 9.

2 The area of configuration as a result of the data gathered on states of stress in informational tremors which has an effect upon the communication [and the communicators] about this effect.

A Web site thematically oriented toward the body and property has been set up as a culmination point and communications interface. Its reception is potentially active – on one hand, by means of informational tremors; on the other hand, through users accessing the web pages, whose textual structure is earthquake-sensitive. Each earthquake server contacted is assigned its own page, whose entropy is dependent upon the reactions of visitors to the resonation space. This means that beyond certain specified data values – for example, the sum of sensual-physical perception and/or Web site activity and/or actual earthquake data – a [temporary] disruption occurs in the accessing user's sphere of activity. Web site user access *hits* function in a way that brings order to the disrupted Web activity. The magnitude of this order-enhancing information, transformed into *anti-earthquakes,* is superimposed with real earthquakes representing disorder – tantamount to a destructive interference.

These Web site activities produce parameters which influence the data on informational tremors and thus have subsequent effects upon the resonance space. In this way, users are capable of minimizing the effects of actual earthquakes upon visitors to the resonance space.

Störung
Ent-Störung
Zer-Störung

Die Installation besteht aus drei miteinander kommunizierenden Bereichen:

1 Bereich der Entnahme von Daten weltweiter Erdbeben aus dem Netz und deren Konfiguration in Schallwellen zur Streßstimulanz der Besucher des Resonanzraumes.

Anlaßfall dabei ist nicht das Internet selbst [das wäre in diesem Fall trivial], sondern die netzbasierte Struktur weltweit verteilter seismographischer Meßstationen.

Der Resonanzraum ist sinnlich-physiologisches Interface zwischen beiden Strukturen der Kommunikation [die ihrerseits Interfaces zwischen den materiellen Konfrontationen von Körper/Besitz mit Erdbeben darstellen].

Unter dem Resonanzraum befindet sich eine Sub-Baß-Anlage zu dessen Beschallung mit niederfrequenten Klängen [Sub-Baß – 16 bis 70 Hertz]. Die Aktivierung der Anlage erfolgt durch den jeweiligen Ereignisbereichen entstammende Daten.

Der Resonanzraum ist mit einem Biofeedbacksystem ausgestattet. Auf einem Monitor erfolgt die optische Wiedergabe der Erhebung des psychophysischen Zustands anwesender Personen [Resonatoren] durch das Biofeedbacksystem. Zustandsveränderungen werden bewirkt von im Raum befindlichen Personen respektive deren Wahrnehmung des Körpers als Resonator und ihrer daraus resultierenden Befindlichkeit, aus denen zuletzt ein Maß für die *Deformation* der Web-Daten gewonnen wird.

2 Bereich der Konfiguration infolge von Streßzuständen erhobener Daten in informationelle Beben mit Wirkung auf die Kommunikation [und Kommunikatoren] über diese Wirkung.

Erdbebenenergie wird durch die Magnitude M ausgedrückt. Bei den energiereichsten Beben hat M Werte zwischen 8,5 und 9.

Eine im World Wide Web als Kulminations- und Kommunikationsknoten eingerichtete Webpage, thematisch an Körper und Besitz orientiert. Ihre Rezeption erfolgt potentiell aktiv, einerseits durch informationelle Beben, andererseits durch

3 The area of configuration as a result of the type of effects upon communication [and communicators] of the data gathered into informational tremors for the purpose of modulation of data having to do with actual earthquakes with effects upon the stress-stimulating sonic waves.

The data collected from the events taking place in the respective areas is transmitted in accordance with real earthquakes to the configuration program in order to control the output level of the sound generator. Due to the fact that sound is produced exclusively in the low frequency range, it is perceived less as a tone audible to the ear than as a pressure felt by the body.

Charles Francis Richter, an American seismologist and professor at the California Institute of Technology, devised the Richter Scale in 1935.

All three areas of the installation are subject to aleatory [contingent] conditions antithetical to mere calculation: in area 1, the unforeseeable occurrence of earthquakes, their duration and intensity; in area 2, the unregulated presence of individuals in the resonation space, their reactions and mental and physical states; in area 3, Web site activities.

Analogous to a *global tremor* – the term used to designate an earthquake registering an intensity of 9 on the Richter Scale – a saturation value has been prescribed for the operation of the system as a whole. The occurrence of this value would mean the destruction of the entire system. It is represented as a quantification of a real event in the sense of danger/threat; formally, it is a virus on the software level as well as technology-destroying intensity on the hardware level and on the level of the body [due to nausea and vomiting as a consequence of the sonic pressure].

Fundamental Technical Structure

Data in ASCII-readable form on actual earthquakes is sent through channels set up in the automated Telnet system to a central server. Following interference with the user-generated data controlling the sub-bass equipment, it is converted into audio data. The process of reading the data into the server also serves the purpose of categorizing it according to location, strength and duration, based upon an earthquake protocol [eq-proto].

Userzugriffe auf Web-Seiten, deren textuelle Struktur erdbebensensitiv ist. Jedem kontaktierten Erbebenserver ist eine eigene Seite zugeordnet, deren Entropie von Reaktionen der Besucher des Resonanzraumes abhängt. Das heißt: Ab bestimmten Datenwerten – beispielsweise der Summe sinnlich-körperlicher Wahrnehmung und/oder den Webpage-Aktivitäten und/oder aktuellen Erdbebendaten – erfolgt eine [vorübergehende] Störung im Wirkungsfeld des Userzugriffs. Userzugriffe erfolgen dadurch, daß Ordnung in das gestörte Webgeschehen gebracht wird. Das Maß der in *Anti-Erdbeben* umgewandelten Ordnungsinformation wird mit den durch Unordnung repräsentierten realen Beben überlagert und kommt einer destruktiven Interferenz gleich. Diese Webpage-Aktivitäten erzeugen Parameter, welche die Daten der informationellen Beben mit Folgewirkung auf den Resonanzraum beinflussen. So vermögen User die Auswirkungen realer Beben auf Besucher des Resonanzraumes zu minimieren

3 Bereich der Konfiguration infolge der Wirkungsweise auf die Kommunikation [und Kommunikatoren] erhobener Daten in informationelle Beben zur reale Beben betreffenden Datenmodulation mit Wirkung auf die streßstimulierenden Schallwellen.

Die aus den Ereignissen in den jeweiligen Bereichen gewonnenen Daten fließen den realen Erdbeben entsprechend ins Konfigurationsprogramm zur Steuerung des Ausgangspegels des Tongenerators. Dadurch daß Schall ausschließlich im tieffrequenten Bereich erzeugt wird, wird er weniger als Lautheit über das Ohr denn als Druck am Körper wahrgenommen.

Alle drei Bereiche der Installation sind aleatorischen Bedingungen unterworfen, die der bloßen Potenzierung entgegenstehen. Bei [1] sind es das unvorhersehbare Auftreten von Erdbeben, ihre Dauer und ihre Stärke; bei [2] sind es die ungeregelte Anwesenheit von Personen im Resonanzraum, deren individuelle Reaktion/Befinden; bei [3] sind es die Webpage-Aktivitäten.

Charles Francis Richter, amerikanischer Seismologe, Professor am California Institute for Technologie, stellte 1935 die Richter-Skala auf.

Dem Betrieb des Gesamtsystems ist – analog der als *Weltbeben* bezeichneten Inten-

The Richter Scale [scale of magnitude] is a modern earthquake scale on an instrumental basis for the purpose of an objective assessment of earthquake strength. The magnitude M – defined, essentially, as the logarithm, to the base 10, of the maximum seismic wave amplitude divided by a reference amplitude of 1 µm – fluctuates between 0 in the case of extremely weak earthquakes and approximately 7.7 to 8.6 for the strongest earthquakes [global tremors]; however, the upper limit is theoretically open-ended.

In this server, various Controlling Client-controlled data streams are established, through which Joined Clients receive information or register with the server.

For the fundamental structure, the significant streams are:

1 the stream of actual earthquake data. The data received from the earthquake server is distributed by means of this stream. Controlling Client is a data evaluator; Joined Clients are sound and biofeedback converters.

2 the biofeedback stream. Controlling Client is the biofeedback converter, Joined Client is the WWW server which receives the biofeedback-generated earthquake data with the accompanying information about the location of an actual earthquake.

3 the repair stream. Controlling Client is the WWW server; Joined Client is the sound converter. The quality of the repair of text pages is exchanged in eq-proto format through this stream.

Controlling Clients are authorized to open a new stream to which Joined Clients are able to dock. The streams are thus dynamic and not static. When a Controlling Client sends data to the stream, this data is also relayed to Joined Clients and, for example, interpreted by the sound converter and sent on through the Midi protocol to the sound system. As Midi velocity data, it in turn controls the output level of the sound generator. The output signal is then transformed by means of eight sub-basses [each with 1200 watt/129 db] with a maximum power of 3000n.

The biofeedback from the individuals exposed to the sonic pressure is quantified and then brought into earthquake-compatible form in the biofeedback converter. The hardware used here is a computer-aided biofeedback system developed by the Viennese firm Insight Instruments, which has been customized for artistic applications by two artists, Sodomka/Breindl, and Norbert Math. The core of this system is an interface [*Medat*] linked to a multisensor which detects skin conductance, tem-

sität eines Erdbebens der Stärke 9 auf der Richterskala – ein Sättigungswert eingeschrieben, der im Falle seines Eintreffens die Zerstörung des Gesamtsystems bedeuten würde. Repräsentiert wird er als realer Ereigniswert im Sinne von Gefahr/Bedrohung, formal als Virus auf Software-Ebene sowie als die Technologie zerstörende Intensität auf Hardware-Ebene und der Ebene des Körpers [durch Übelkeit und Erbrechen infolge des Schalldrucks].

Technische Grundstruktur

Über automatisierte Telnets aufgebaute Verbindungen gelangen die Daten realer Erdbeben in Ascii-lesbarer Form in einen zentralen Server und werden – nach Interferenz mit User-generierten Daten zur Steuerung einer Sub-Baß-Anlage – in ein Klangbild umgewandelt. Die Anlage der Daten im Server erfolgt auch zum Zweck ihrer protokollarisch nach Ort, Stärke und Dauer – dem Erdbeben-Protokoll [*eb-proto*] gemäß – geregelten Verteilung. In diesem Server sind verschiedene vom Controlling Client gesteuerte Daten-Streams etabliert, über die angemeldete Joined Clients Informationen erhalten beziehungsweise am Server anmelden.

Für die Grundstruktur bedeutsame Streams sind:

1 Der Stream realer Erdbebendaten: Vermittels dieses Streams werden die von Erdbebenservern empfangenen Daten verteilt. Controlling Client ist ein Datenauswerter, Joined Clients sind Sound- und Biofeedbackkonverter.

2 Der Biofeedback-Stream: Controlling Client ist der Biofeedbackkonverter, Joined Client ist der WWW-Server, welcher die Biofeedback-generierten Erdbebendaten mit der jeweiligen Information über den Ort eines realen Erdbebens erhält.

3 Der Repair-Stream: Controlling Client ist der WWW-Server, Joined Client der Soundkonverter. Über diesen Stream wird die Qualität der Reparatur der Textseiten in eb-proto-Format ausgetauscht.

Controlling Clients sind befähigt, einen neuen Stream zu öffnen, an den Joined Clients anzudocken vermögen. Die Streams sind also dyna-

Richter-Skala [Magnitudenskala]: moderne Erdbebenskala auf instrumenteller Basis zur objektiven Beurteilung der Erdbebenstärke. Die im wesentlichen als dekadischer Logarithmus der – durch eine Bezugsamplitude von 1 µm dividierten – Maximalamplidude festgelegte Magnitude M schwankt zwischen den Werten 0 bei sehr schwachen Erdbeben und etwa 7,7 bis 8,6 bei stärksten Erdbeben [Weltbeben], ist aber nach oben hin unbegrenzt.

perature and pulse rate. The *Medat* transmits this biofeedback data through a serial interface to a PC where this data is output via MIDI, displayed on a monitor and passed along by means of eq-proto to the server which then makes this data available depending upon queries from various clients or servers – for instance, to the WWW server by means of eq-proto.

The WWW server evaluates the location information and, according to the strength of the earthquake, fractures the text of the Web site corresponding to that location's information. Its repair by the WWW user gets qualified and localized. Location and success of the repair procedure are fed as quake information to the local server which transmits it on to the sound converter. The software was written in C. Four Linux 200 Pentium processors have been placed in service in this installation.

On the average, two earthquakes with magnitudes between 8 and 9, about 800 between 5 and 6 and 50,000 between 3 and 4 occur annually on this planet.

The *IPzentrum* project has been produced in cooperation with the Ars Electronica Center after having won the *stroemung 97* art project competition sponsored by Steweag.

Idea, Concept, Execution and Text:
TXTD.sign Heimo Ranzenbacher, Gerold Muhr
System Programming:
Volker Christian
Biofeedback Adaption:
Norbert Math
Web Site Design:
Norbert Math
Construction and Sound:
Helmut Schäfer, Stefan Ebelsberger

misch und nicht statisch. Sendet ein Controlling Client Daten an den Stream, werden diese Daten auch an die Joined Clients verschickt und beispielsweise vom Soundkonverter interpretiert und über MIDI-Protokoll dem Soundsystem weitergeben. Als MIDI-Velocity-Daten steuern sie wiederum den Ausgangspegel des Soundgenerators. Das Ausgangssignal wird mittels acht Subbässen [à 1200 watt/129 db] in eine Kraft von maximal 3000 n gewandelt.

Das Biofeedback der dem Schalldruck ausgesetzten Personen wird quantifiziert und im Biofeedback-Konverter wieder in erdbebengerechte Form gebracht. Als Hardware findet ein Computer-Aided-Biofeedback-System der Firma Insight Instruments, Wien, Verwendung, das in Zusammenarbeit mit dem Künstlerduo Sodomka/Breindl und Norbert Math für künstlerische Anwendungen weiterentwickelt wurde. Herzstück ist ein Interface [*Medat*], das an einen Multisensor angeschlossen wird. Dieser ermittelt Hautleitwert, Temperatur und Pulsschlag. Über eine serielle Schnittstelle sendet die *Medat* die Biofeedback-Daten an einen PC, wo diese Daten via MIDI ausgegeben, an einem Monitor visualisiert und wieder über eb-proto dem Server zugespielt werden, der nun diese Daten – in Abhängigkeit von Anfragen verschiedener Clients oder Server – etwa dem WWW-Server über eb-proto zur Verfügung stellt.

Der WWW-Server wertet die Ortsinformation aus und zerwürfelt je nach Stärke den mit der Ortsinformation korrespondierenden Text der Webpage, dessen Reparatur durch WWW-User qualifiziert und lokalisiert wird. Ort und Güte der Reparatur werden als Bebeninformation dem lokalen Server zugeführt, der sie wieder dem Soundkonverter vermittelt.

Die Software wurde in C geschrieben. Bei der Installation befinden sich vier Linux 200 Pentium im Einsatz.

Im Jahresdurchschnitt ereignen sich weltweit zwei Beben mit Magnituden zwischen 8 und 9, 800 Beben zwischen 5 und 6 und 50.000 Beben zwischen 3 und 4.

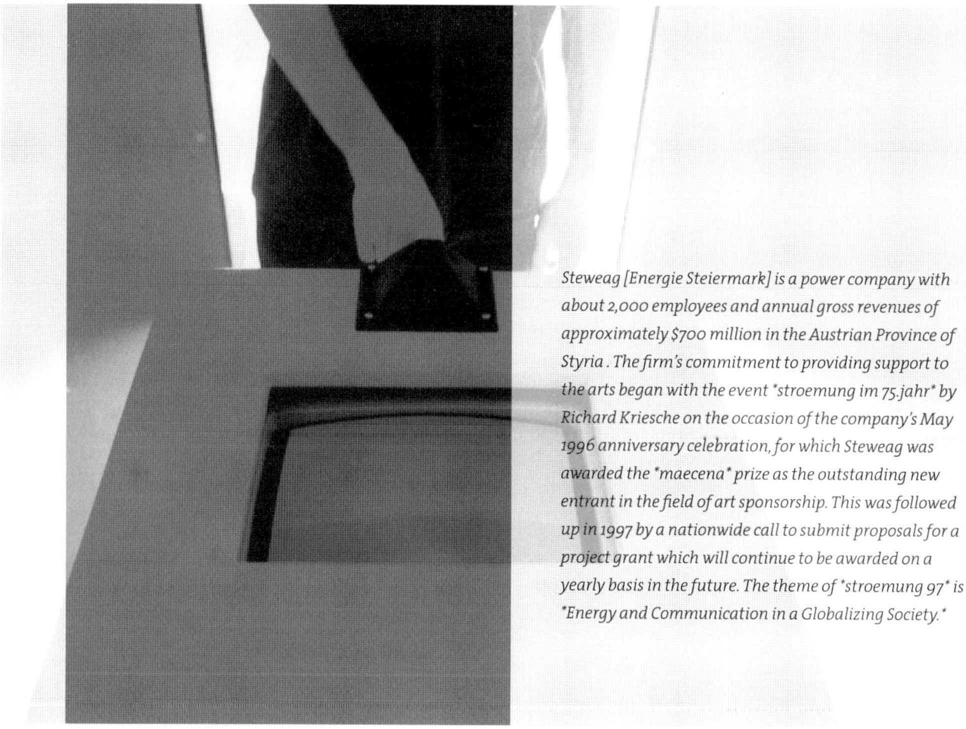

*Steweag [Energie Steiermark] is a power company with about 2,000 employees and annual gross revenues of approximately $700 million in the Austrian Province of Styria . The firm's commitment to providing support to the arts began with the event *stroemung im 75.jahr* by Richard Kriesche on the occasion of the company's May 1996 anniversary celebration, for which Steweag was awarded the *maecena* prize as the outstanding new entrant in the field of art sponsorship. This was followed up in 1997 by a nationwide call to submit proposals for a project grant which will continue to be awarded on a yearly basis in the future. The theme of *stroemung 97* is *Energy and Communication in a Globalizing Society.**

installations

Das Projekt *IPzentrum* wurde als Siegerprojekt des Kunstprojektpreises *stroemung 97* der Steweag in Zusammenarbeit mit dem Ars Electronica Center realisiert.

Idee, Konzept, Durchführung und Text:
TXTD.sign
Heimo Ranzenbacher
Gerold Muhr
Systemprogrammierung:
Volker Christian
Biofeedback-Adaption:
Norbert Math
Webpage-Design:
Norbert Math
Bauten und Ton:
Helmut Schäfer, Stefan Ebelsberger

What Will Remain of These

Chris Dodge

We all lead a life between two poles: the world of motion and the world of stillness. The dialectic between these two extremes creates a tension that is not easily resolved, as there are two distinct representative aesthetics at work. The world of motion is one of self-possession, short-term goals, achievement, and drive. The person that is stuck in the world of motion is unable to view him/herself within a larger group structure, trapped in a merciless temporal now that urges them forward. Likewise, the world of stillness is made out of passivity, narcissism, indecision, uncertainty, and fear. The person that is stuck in this realm is unable to act, trapped in an endless self-reflection. The former is a quality of transience, the latter is a quality of permanence. It is between these two extremes that we, as humans, exist.

In a way, physical and digital architectures are the results of this duality of the human condition. We create large, permanent structures such as buildings and monuments that are expressions of a group identity that endure over time. The static creation out of steel, stone, and bronze is the ultimate form of permanence, something that forms solid foundations on

What Will Remain of These

Chris Dodge

Wir alle führen ein Leben zwischen zwei Polen: der Welt der Bewegung und der Welt der Bewegungslosigkeit. Die Dialektik zwischen diesen beiden Extremen erzeugt eine Spannung, die nicht leicht zu lösen ist, da es sich hierbei um zwei deutlich verschiedene Formen repräsentativer Ästhetik handelt. Die Welt der Bewegung ist gekennzeichnet durch Selbstbeherrschung, kurzfristige Ziele, Leistung und Tatendrang. Wer dieser Welt verhaftet ist, ist unfähig, sich selbst als Teil einer größeren Gruppenstruktur zu sehen. Man ist in einem gnadenlosen zeitlichen Jetzt gefangen, das einen vorwärts treibt. Entsprechend zeichnet sich die Welt der Bewegungslosigkeit durch Passivität, Narzißmus, Unentschlossenheit, Unsicherheit und Angst aus. Wer diesem Reich verhaftet ist, ist unfähig zu handeln und in einer Selbstreflexion ohne Ende gefangen. Ersteres bedeutet Vergänglichkeit, letzteres Dauer. Zwischen diesen beiden Extremen existieren wir Menschen.

In mancher Hinsicht sind physische und digitale Architekturen das Ergebnis dieser für die menschlichen Lebensumstände bezeichnenden Dualität. Die von uns geschaffenen großen, dauerhaften Strukturen – z. B. Gebäude und Denkmäler – sind Ausdrucksformen einer Gruppenidentität, die die Zeit überdauern. Die statische Schöpfung aus Stahl, Stein und Bronze ist die höchste Erscheinungsform der Dauer, sie formt die soliden Grundlagen, auf denen unsere Gesellschaft aufgebaut ist. Diese architektonischen Gebilde – Landstraßen, Bahnhöfe oder Kirchen – bestimmen, wie wir uns in unseren täglichen Rhythmen und unseren Glaubensvorstellungen zurechtfinden. Im Gegensatz dazu stellen Computer und digitale Netze den ultimativen Ausdruck der Vergänglichkeit dar. Mit dem Computer hält ein rasches und hektisches Tempo Einzug, denn der technologische Kontext ist immer in Bewegung. Hier ist

which society is made. These architectural formations – such as highways, train stations, and churches – regulate how we organize ourselves in our daily rhythms and beliefs. In comparison, computers and digital networks form the consummate expression of transience. With computation comes a rapid and hectic pace as the technological context is always in motion. Life here is quick and ephemeral, a brief but brilliant flash. Death in the digital world is obsolescence [a stillness of progress].

My exhibited work, *What Will Remain of These,* couples the bodily motions of people inside an architectural space with graphical activity and data flow over a local-area TCP/IP network. At first appearance, the installation is a large interconnected kinetic visual sculpture that stretches out over several computer stations. This work explores the possibilities of casting the worlds of motion and stillness into metaphors for the struggle between individual and group identities. We are part of a collective being but it is a small contribution, one that evolves over time. The patterns that we make in our daily lives help form the overall appearance of society, but only if we are persistent. One does not have to be conscious of the process or *engaged* in the emergent group identity, as our contributions to this permanence are on a scale that is not visible to us. Likewise, it is only through a commitment of stillness that we can share experiences between each other and discover the richness and similarities between our lives. Thus this work investigates the notion of engagement with an interactive installation: in both cases the audience belongs to one of these two worlds but not necessarily engaged with the interactive environment. This piece allows for both types of contributions: the frantic disengagement of the installation as well as the contemplative acknowledgement of the system.

We all tend to lead similar and overlapping lives, leading to a collective group identity that emerges through these isolated behaviors. Although, at first glance, these group patterns appear to be chaotic and the individuals remain locked within their own identity,if one gets removed enough from the localized context, it becomes clear that we have little control over what emerges as a collective whole. Then what are the qualities of the collective identity? Or,

das Leben schnell und flüchtig, ein kurzes, aber strahlendes Aufblitzen. Tod in der digitalen Welt ist gleichbedeutend mit Obsoleszenz [Stillstand des Fortschritts].

Die von mir gezeigte Arbeit *What will remain of these* verbindet die Körperbewegungen von Menschen in einem architektonischen Raum mit graphischer Aktivität und dem Datenfluß über ein lokales TCP/IP-Netz. Auf den ersten Blick ist die Installation eine große kinetische visuelle Skulptur, die sich über mehrere, miteinander vernetzte Computerstationen erstreckt. Diese Arbeit lotet die Möglichkeiten aus, die Welt der Bewegung und die Welt der Bewegungslosigkeit in Metaphern darzustellen, die für den Kampf zwischen der Identität des einzelnen und der Identität der Gruppe stehen. Wir sind Teil eines kollektiven Ganzen, doch der Beitrag, den wir leisten, ist bescheiden. Er gewinnt erst im Laufe der Zeit an Bedeutung. Die Muster, die wir in unserem täglichen Leben schaffen, tragen zwar dazu bei, die Gesamterscheinung der Gesellschaft zu prägen, doch nur, wenn wir genug Ausdauer an den Tag legen. Dieser Prozeß muß nicht bewußt ablaufen, ebensowenig wie der einzelne an der sich herausbildenden Gruppenidentität *beteiligt* sein muß, denn unser Beitrag zu dieser Dauerhaftigkeit ist für uns nicht sichtbar. Ebenso bedarf es der Bewegungslosigkeit, um Erfahrungen mit anderen teilen und den Reichtum und die Ähnlichkeit in unserem Leben erkennen zu können. Die Arbeit untersucht also den Begriff der Beteiligung an einer interaktiven Installation: In beiden Fällen gehört das Publikum einer dieser Welten an, ist aber nicht unbedingt an der interaktiven Umgebung beteiligt. Die Installation ermöglicht beide Formen der Beteiligung: die entsetzte Abwendung von der Installation ebenso wie die kontemplative Anerkennung des Systems.

Wir alle führen im großen und ganzen sehr ähnliche Leben, was zu einer Gruppenidentität führt, die sich aus diesen einzelnen, isolierten Verhaltensweisen ergibt. Obwohl diese Gruppenmuster auf den ersten Blick chaotisch erscheinen und die Individuen auf ihre eigene Identität begrenzt bleiben, läßt sich aus einer genügend großen Distanz vom lokalen Kontext feststellen, daß wir kaum Einfluß auf das Entstehen des kollektiven Ganzen haben.

as the title intimates, what then remains of all of ourselves over the passage of time?

Adaptive Interfaces and the Uncertainty Principle

What is intriguing about interactive VR computer art, to me, is that there is a resurgence of placing the individual egocentrically in the middle of a constructed world, allowing the user to access the data structures through a one-to-one mapping of stimulus and response. Every *right-turn* command by the user elicits a corresponding turn in the virtual environment. Such a direct cause-and-effect relationship, although well researched and implemented in current computer interface design, ironically does not model a *reality* that I have grown familiar with. In my reality, I am constantly amazed at what I see, tempted by the seemingly endless possibilities, and befuddled by that which I cannot comprehend. VR technologies, to me, would appear to be contrary to the historical growth of the modern arts, bringing us back to the imperatives of Renaissance through the placement of the viewer's eye once again at the perspective center of the universe.[1]

David Rokeby[2] and Perry Hoberman[3] have elegantly addressed the issues of subjectivity and control in interactive computer media art. I would like to add that we need to reconsider the ideas surrounding the role of interactive artists in face of a computational Postmodernism, where absolutes are no longer to be found, being replaced by ever-shifting surfaces that are subjectively interpreted by each of us. Rather than I, as creator of this work, attempting to construct artificial worlds, this installation autonomously uses the real world to build such a shimmering surface that reflects a quality of our daily behaviors back to us. True realty, not a virtual surrogate, reveals itself incarnate. It is not the user who must learn the rules of the digital environment, but rather it is the algorithm that must adapt to that which it sees. Then I consider this work to be an example of human-centric rather than computer-centric interactive art, forming a revisualization of our humanity. What is told is a meta-narrative that is an exposition of process that a large group of people experiences rather than any one specific story.

Was sind nun die Eigenschaften der kollektiven Identität? Oder, wie der Titel nahelegt, was bleibt von uns allen im Laufe der Zeit?

Adaptive Schnittstellen und die Unschärferelation

Das Faszinierende an interaktiver VR-Computerkunst ist für mich, daß das Individuum erneut egozentrisch in den Mittelpunkt einer konstruierten Welt gestellt wird, wobei der Benutzer durch eine Eins-zu-Eins-Abbildung von Reiz und Reaktion Zugriff auf die Datenstrukturen hat. Jeder Befehl des Benutzers, sich *nach rechts zu wenden*, löst in der virtuellen Umgebung eine entsprechende Bewegung aus. Ironischerweise bildet eine derart unmittelbare Beziehung zwischen Ursache und Wirkung, auch wenn sie gut erforscht ist und ihre Umsetzung bei gegenwärtigen Computerschnittstellen gut funktioniert, nicht die *Wirklichkeit* ab, die mir vertraut ist. In meiner Wirklichkeit staune ich immer wieder über das, was ich sehe, ich werde verführt durch die scheinbar endlosen Möglichkeiten und bin verwirrt durch das, was ich nicht verstehen kann. Meiner Meinung nach steht die VR-Technologie im Gegensatz zum historischen Wachstum der modernen Kunst, da sie das Auge des Betrachters erneut in den perspektivischen Mittelpunkt des Universums stellt und uns so zu den Imperativen der Renaissance zurückführt.[1]

David Rokeby[2] und Perry Hoberman[3] haben sich mit dem Thema Subjektivität und Kontrolle in der interaktiven Computermedienkunst auf sehr elegante Art und Weise auseinandergesetzt. Ich möchte hinzufügen, daß wir – angesichts eines Computer-Postmodernismus, in dem das Absolute nicht mehr existiert, sondern von sich ständig ändernden Oberflächen ersetzt wird, die jeder von uns anders interpretiert – unsere Vorstellungen von der Rolle des interaktiven Künstlers neu überdenken müssen. Diese Installation verwendet die wirkliche Welt autonom, um eine glänzende Oberfläche zu erzeugen, die unser tägliches Verhalten an uns zurückspiegelt – und sie tut dies in viel höherem Maße als ich, der Schöpfer dieses Werkes, der versucht, künstliche Welten zu schaffen. Eine unverfälschte, leibhaftige Wirklichkeit enthüllt sich uns, keine virtuelle Ersatzwelt. Nicht der Benutzer muß die Regeln

In this interactive work, the viewer can attain neither absolute knowledge of nor control over the system, as there are no delineated interactive spaces, no direct interfaces, no globally defined rules that govern the cause-and-effect relationships. Interaction is that of the entire population, to which we make a slight contribution. The significance of the individual viewer is minimized, as he/she becomes a mere statistic in the estimation of the intent of the masses. The more determined the individual is to exert control over the environment, the more he/she becomes manipulated by the system, endlessly repeating the physical gestures over-and-over in order to gain a statistical significance.

Rather than using state-machine algorithms that describe he interactions at a global scale, the work uses a continuous temporal-spatial description of the surveillance region to drive a physically based particle system. Such an algorithmically-based work uses approximately 76,000 autonomous entities per computer [the work is highly parallel and distributed], that execute a highly localized set of rules. The rules for each agent are based on mere Newtonian physics of mass, momentum, and forces [friction included]. As the surveillance system watches the architectural space, it derives a 2D matrix of motion estimates[4] that describe how people are moving naturally through that space. At each graphical point in the virtual space, there is a vector that is a weighted summation of estimated motion partial derivatives that forms a *virtual* force. This force matrix is the major interactive parameter of the system. As the system develops over time, the particles are subjected to these forces, putting them into motion, coupling the accumulative flow of the people with the overall movement of the particles. Should the motion of a large massive body of viewers be highly correlated with a minimal amount of variance [i.e. people are moving in a similar manner], its influence over the system would begin to dominate. Through the use of these localized rules, there is a convergence onto a feedback loop, bringing the visual elements as well as the data transmissions between stations into synchronicity with the physical world.

There are no global states in this work, at each instant of the installation it is impos-

der digitalen Umgebung erlernen, sondern der Algorithmus muß sich an das anpassen, was er sieht. So sehe ich diese Arbeit eher als Beispiel für menschzentrierte als für computerzentrierte interaktive Kunst, da sie uns eine neue Vorstellung unseres Menschseins gibt. Es wird weniger eine bestimmte Einzelgeschichte erzählt als vielmehr eine Metageschichte über den Prozeß, den eine große Gruppe von Menschen erlebt.

Diese interaktive Arbeit vermittelt dem Betrachter weder absolute Kenntnis über das System noch läßt sie ihn Kontrolle darüber erlangen, da es keine definierten interaktiven Räume, keine unmittelbaren Schnittstellen, keine umfassend gültigen Regeln gibt, nach denen die Beziehungen von Ursache und Wirkung ablaufen. Die Gruppe als Ganzes, zu der wir einen kleinen Beitrag leisten, bestimmt die Interaktion. Die Bedeutung des einzelnen Betrachters wird auf ein Minimum reduziert, er oder sie wird zu einem rein statistischen Meßwert bei der Einschätzung der Masse. Je mehr das Individuum seine Umgebung kontrollieren will, um durch endloses Wiederholen derselben körperlichen Gesten statistische Bedeutung zu erlangen, desto mehr wird er oder sie vom System manipuliert.

Anstelle von Computeralgorithmen, die die Interaktionen in einem Gesamtzusammenhang beschreiben, verwendet die Installation ein Raum-Zeit-Kontinuum zur Beschreibung des Überwachungsbereichs, um ein auf physikalischen Prinzipien beruhendes Teilchensystem zu steuern. Eine solche auf Algorithmen basierende Arbeit verwendet ungefähr 76.000 autonome Einheiten pro Computer [die Arbeit ist in hohem Maße parallel und verteilt], die einen höchst spezialisierten Befehlssatz ausführen. Die Befehle für jede Einheit basieren ausschließlich auf den Newton'schen Gesetzen für Masse, Impuls und Kräfte [inklusive Reibung]. Das Überwachungssystem leitet von der Beobachtung des architektonischen Raums eine 2D-Matrix der vorausberechneten Bewegung[4] ab, die die natürlichen Bewegungen der Menschen im Raum beschreibt. An jeden graphischen Punkt des virtuellen Raumes wird ein aus der gewichteten Summe aller partiellen Ableitungen der vorausberechneten Bewegung berechneter Vektor angelegt, der eine *virtuelle* Kraft ausmacht. Diese Kräfte-

sible to predict its current appearance, encouraging viewers to visit the work a multiple number of times. It could be argued that this digital world therefore exhibits a quality of emergent behavior, similar to those described by Renick[5] and Louis-Philippe Demers[6]. Although everyone who walks into the surveillance region contributes to the 2D array of accumulated forces, it is impossible to de-correlate each individual's contribution as the system of equations is under-constrained, i.e. there are more unknown variables than known values. There can be no global analytical rule that can account for its current state as both the machine and the individual viewer are eternally locked at a highly localized and subjective understanding of the environment. The longer the installation runs, the more ambiguous the role of each person becomes, as we must fight against the historical records of all those before us. Likewise, any control that we attain through the stubborn insistence of repetitive movements, is washed away over time through the people that pass by in the future. As a subtle reminder, this installation warns us that all efforts of control are ultimately futile.

In addition to the motion estimates, the installation derives a numerical description of estimated stillness. If a person stands quietly long enough, engaging the interactive system in a contemplative passivity, his/her stillness measurement increases. Once this measurement increases past a threshold value, the person's image is gradually faded into the interactive environment. However this is not a static data structure, as the image is made out of particles that are actively moving, hinting at some underlying restlessness. When the viewers disengage themselves from the world of stillness, by moving their bodies in any significant manner,their likeness becomes like colored dust that is blown through the whirlwinds that have been created by all of the other people before and after them. This becomes the interaction between the individual, looking for some unique permanence within the system, and the masses that continually undermine these efforts.

Heisenberg's Uncertainty Principle, which I consider to be one of the basic tenets of Postmoderism, states that it is impossible to understand complex minute systems on a

matrix ist der wichtigste interaktive Parameter des Systems. Wenn sich das System im Laufe der Zeit weiterentwickelt, werden die Teilchen diesen Kräften unterworfen. Sie werden in Bewegung gesetzt, und der akkumulierte Fluß der Menschen wird mit der Gesamtbewegung der Teilchen gekoppelt. Würde die Bewegung einer großen und massiven Menge an Betrachtern mit einer minimalen Anzahl an Abweichungen korrelieren [d. h. würden sich die Menschen alle auf ähnliche Art und Weise bewegen], begänne ihr Einfluß auf das System zu dominieren. Durch den Einsatz dieses spezialisierten Befehlssatzes kommt es zu einer Konvergenz des Systems mit einer Feedback-Schleife, die sowohl die visuellen Elemente als auch die Datenübertragungen zwischen den einzelnen Stationen mit der physikalischen Welt synchronisiert.

Es gibt in dieser Arbeit keine globalen Zustände. In keinem Augenblick ist es möglich, das momentane Aussehen der Installation vorherzusagen, so daß die Betrachter zum mehrmaligen Besuch angeregt werden. Man könnte also sagen, daß diese digitale Welt das emergente Verhalten darstellt, wie es Renick[5] und Louis-Philippe Demers[6] beschreiben. Obwohl jeder, der sich im Überwachungsbereich aufhält, das 2D-Datenfeld der akkumulierten Kräfte beeinflußt, ist es unmöglich, die Beiträge der einzelnen Individuen zu unterscheiden, da das Gleichungssystem unterdeterminiert ist. Mit anderen Worten, es gibt mehr unbekannte Variablen als bekannte. Es kann keine umfassende analytische Regel für die Erklärung des jeweilig aktuellen Zustands geben, da sowohl die Maschine als auch der individuelle Betrachter immer nur auf eine höchst begrenzte und subjektive Vorstellung von der Umgebung zurückgreifen kann. Mit zunehmender Dauer der Installation wird auch die Rolle des einzelnen immer zweideutiger, da er gegen die historischen Aufnahmen aller Betrachter vor ihm ankämpfen muß. So wird auch jeder Einfluß, den er durch das hartnäckige Wiederholen gleichförmiger Bewegungen erlangt, im Laufe der Zeit durch die nach ihm kommenden Menschen verwischt. Diese Installation mahnt uns auf subtile Weise, daß alle Kontrollversuche letztendlich vergeblich sind.

Zusätzlich zur Vorausberechnung der Bewegung gewinnt die Installation eine nu-

global scale because through the process of viewing, the system is fundamentally altered.[7] Likewise, in this installation, there is no objective location from which one can view the work without altering it. Either by walking in the installation space, even oblivious to the interactive exhibit on hand, or pausing for a moment to watch the colorful flow, their presence is constantly leaving a trace within the mathematical algorithm. In a manner, they have attained a dubious immortality, as the colored pixel that was once their image is eternally retained in the system, floating reconfigured in the data network. Thus there is a comforting acquiescence to the physical laws of conservation of mass [our images] and energy [our bodily motions], leaving an eternal marker of our existence.

1 WALICZKY, T., partly taken from a lecture at the *WRO97 Biennial Media Art festival*, Wroclaw, Poland, 1997

2 ROKEBY, D., *Transforming Mirrors, Critical Issues in Electronic Media*, State University of New York Press, 1995

3 HOBERMAN, P., *panel talk*, ACM Multimedia 96, Bosten 1996

4 BERGEN, J., P. BURT, R. HINGORANI, S. PELEG, *Multiple Component Image Motion: Motion Estimation*, David Sarnoff Research Center, January 1990

5 RESNICK, M., *Turtles, Termites, and Traffic Jams: Explorations in Massively Parallel Microworlds*, MIT Press, 1994

6 DEMERS, L.P., B. VORN, *No Man's Land*, Ars Electronica Festival 96, SpringerWienNew York 1996

7 HEISENBERG, W., *Physics and Philosophy: the revolution in modern science*, Harper, New York 1958

merische Beschreibung der vorausberechneten Bewegungslosigkeit. Wenn ein Betrachter lange genug ruhig steht und das interaktive System in kontemplative Passivität versetzt, erhöht dies seinen Meßwert der Bewegungslosigkeit. Überschreitet dieser Meßwert eine bestimmte Schwelle, löst sich das Bild dieser Person langsam in der interaktiven Umgebung auf. Dennoch handelt es sich hierbei nicht um eine Struktur statischer Daten, da sich das Bild aus Teilchen zusammensetzt, die in Bewegung sind und somit eine zugrundeliegende Rastlosigkeit erkennen lassen. Löst sich der Betrachter aus der Welt der Bewegungslosigkeit, indem er seinen Körper hinreichend bewegt, scheint sein Bild zu farbigem Staub zu zerfallen, verweht durch die Wirbelwinde, die die Menschen vor und nach ihm erzeugen. Das ist die Interaktion zwischen dem Individuum auf der Suche nach einer einzigartigen Dauer innerhalb des Systems und der Masse, die diesen Versuch unablässig untergräbt.

Die Unschärferelation von Heisenberg, die ich für einen der bedeutendsten Lehrsätze des Postmodernismus halte, besagt, daß es nicht möglich ist, kleinste komplexe Systeme global zu verstehen, da der Prozeß des Beobachtens das System grundlegend verändert.[7] Folglich gibt es in dieser Installation keine objektive Position, von der aus die Arbeit betrachtet werden könnte, ohne daß etwas verändert würde. Die Anwesenheit der Betrachter hinterläßt pausenlos ihre Spuren im mathematischen Algorithmus, egal, ob sie durch den Installationsraum gehen – vielleicht ohne sich des Ausstellungsstückes überhaupt bewußt zu sein – oder ob sie für einen Moment innehalten, um den farbenfrohen Strom zu betrachten. In gewisser Hinsicht haben sie eine zweifelhafte Unsterblichkeit erlangt, denn der farbige Pixel, einst ihr Bild, bleibt auf ewig im System erhalten und treibt neu konfiguriert im Datennetz. Zu unserer Beruhigung bleibt also, dank der physikalischen Erhaltungsgesetze von Masse [unsere Bilder] und Energie [unsere körperlichen Bewegungen], eine ewige Spur unserer Existenz erhalten.

MiLOs

Scott Brave/Andy Dahley

Too often we allow ourselves to advance technology without reflection on its purpose. We continue the mindless process of making computation faster, more effective, and more efficient so that we can produce more, faster. But instead of taking the time saved to relax or connect with others, we are so romanced by the technology that we use the time to produce even more. In many ways, it seems as if humankind's symbiotic relationship with technology is turning – if it has not already turned – parasitic. We continue to advance technology so that we can only advance it further ... but to what end? Some may argue, from the evolutionary perspective, that technology may some day be responsible for enabling the survival of the human gene pool. But most would agree that there is more to life than the survival of our genes.

MiLOs applies a combination of mature and rising technologies in a way that cannot be mistaken for such self-perpetuating tendencies. Here, we use technology, not to improve the speed or efficiency of any task or process, but simply to bring people closer together in a mechanized world where separation is so easy.

MiLOs

Scott Brave/Andy Dahley

Nur allzu oft huldigen wir dem technischen Fortschritt, ohne uns Gedanken über die Zweckmäßigkeit unseres Tuns zu machen. Sinnlos arbeiten wir daran, Computer schneller, leistungsstärker und effizienter zu machen, um mehr und schneller produzieren zu können. Doch anstatt die Zeit, die wir uns dadurch ersparen, zur Erholung oder zur Pflege zwischenmenschlicher Kontakte zu nützen, sind wir der Technologie derart verfallen, daß wir diese Zeit aufwenden, um noch mehr zu produzieren. In vielerlei Hinsicht scheint es so, als würde die symbiotische Beziehung zwischen Mensch und Technologie sich in Richtung Parasitismus entwickeln – falls wir dieses Stadium nicht ohnehin bereits erreicht haben. Wir arbeiten weiter am technischen Fortschritt, damit wir noch mehr Fortschritt erzielen können ... doch zu welchem Zweck? Aus der Perspektive der Evolution könnte man vielleicht damit argumentieren, daß die Technologie möglicherweise eines Tages für das Überleben des menschlichen Genpools verantwortlich sein könnte. Aber die meisten Menschen werden sich wohl darin einig sein, daß Leben mehr als das bloße Überleben unserer Gene bedeutet.

MiLOs verwendet eine Kombination erprobter und neuer Technologien in einer Art und Weise, die mit einer derartigen Selbsterhaltung nicht das geringste zu tun hat. Wir setzen hier die Technologie nicht dazu ein, um die Geschwindigkeit oder die Effizienz irgendwelcher Aufgaben oder Verfahren zu steigern, sondern ganz einfach, um die Menschen in einer mechanisierten Welt, in der eine Trennung so einfach geworden ist, näher zusammen zu bringen. MiLOs kann mit Hilfe von Silikon, Algorithmen, Metallen und Seltenerdmagneten etwas sehr Einfaches, aber zugleich auch Gewaltiges bewirken, nämlich ein grundlegendes Gesetz der Physik brechen und Magie schaffen. Unter Verwendung haptischer Technologie können wir ein einzelnes physisches Objekt schaffen, das an mehreren Orten zugleich existiert. Dieses multilokalisierte

MiLOs combines silicon, algorithms, metals, and rare-earth magnets to do a very simple but powerful thing: to break a basic law of physics, to create magic. Using haptic technology, we can create a single physical object that exists in multiple places at once. This Multi-Locational Object [MiLO] can be held, felt, and manipulated simultaneously by geographically separated people, thus creating a physical and intimate connection that transcends distance.

Such magic is enabled by the digital ether that is rapidly permeating our world. Our notion of globally accessible information spaces has created a place that is not bounded by the physics of the real world: our own *digital plane*. We currently choose to keep this new plane almost entirely separate from the physical world, allowing ourselves only to peek into it through small windows that sit on our desktops, but we can begin to bridge this unnecessary gap. Now we can begin to create objects that consist of both a real and a virtual self: a body and a spirit. Now we can play God and give multiple physical objects the same soul, so that they think and act in the same way, creatlng the illusion that many objects are one. We can take this a step further and imagine objects all around us which are shared by other distant people or completely link two physical spaces in such a way that everything is shared. The illusion begins to shift from magical objects to spiritual beings, with each person perceiving a spirit of the other person existing in the same space and manipulating the same reality. We can go even further and imagine that the object to be shared is part of the body itself, lungs or a heart, perhaps even a mind, approaching the point where two whole bodies share the same spirit. Here, we stop blindly feeding our technology and master it to mold our own realities.

Objekt [Multi-Locational Object – MILO] kann von mehreren, geographisch voneinander getrennten Menschen gleichzeitig in der Hand gehalten, gefühlt und manipuliert werden, wodurch eine physische und vertrauliche Verbindung entsteht, die Entfernungen überbrückt.

Diese Magie wird durch den digitalen Äther möglich, der unsere Welt unaufhaltsam durchdringt. Unser Konzept von global zugänglichen Informationsräumen hat einen Ort geschaffen, der nicht an die Physik der realen Welt gebunden ist – unsere eigene, digitale Ebene'. Derzeit lassen wir diese neue Ebene beinahe völlig von der physischen Welt getrennt und erlauben uns nur kurze Blicke durch die kleinen Fenster auf unseren Computern, doch wir könnten auch damit beginnen, diesen unnötigen Abgrund zu überbrücken. Wir können jetzt damit beginnen, Objekte zu erschaffen, die sowohl über ein reales als auch über ein virtuelles Selbst, über Körper und Geist verfügen. Wir können nunmehr Gott spielen und verschiedenen physischen Objekten ein und dieselbe Seele geben, damit sie gleich denken und handeln und damit die Illusion entsteht, daß all diese verschiedenen Objekte in Wirklichkeit nur ein einziges wären. Wir können noch einen Schritt weitergehen und uns Objekte in unserer Umgebung vorstellen, die wir mit anderen, geographisch entfernten Menschen teilen, oder zwei physische Räume so vollständig miteinander verbinden, daß alles darin Befindliche geteilt wird. Die Illusion beginnt, sich von magischen Objekten auf geistige Wesen zu verlagern, wobei jede Person den Geist der anderen Person, die im selben Raum existiert und dieselbe Realität manipuliert, spürt. Wir können sogar noch weitergehen und uns vorstellen, daß das zu teilende Objekt ein Teil des Körpers selbst ist, die Lunge oder das Herz, vielleicht auch der Verstand. Und damit nähern wir uns dem Punkt, an dem zwei ganze Körper sich ein und denselben Geist teilen. An diesem Punkt hören wir damit auf, blind der Technologie zu huldigen, sondern unterwerfen sie uns, um unsere eigene Realität zu formen.

Triangles and the Digital Veil

Matt Gorbet/Maggie Orth

**That,* she said...*
*...*is a cyhnk, isn't it?* She nodded toward the carved stone medusoid ...*
When did you learn,* Alsrod asked, *that the meaning of the cyhnk was not the same everywhere in the universe?

Samuel Delaney,
Stars in my Pockets like Grains of Sand

From scattered beliefs and beginnings, each of us brings to every artifact that fills our external world an internal world, filling objects with mutable meaning and function. In their practical use, tools simply have a one-to-one relationship with cause and effect. The hammer drives the nail. Place a computer between the hammer and the nail and the relationship recedes, a software veil is created, and when the hammer strikes, music may play. Yet objects like the hammer also have a symbolic or magical function and meaning. This symbolic meaning already possesses such a veil. Place a symbol before the world and one person feels adoration, another irony. Place a computer between a symbol and the world and what is the role of the layer of software, the digital veil?

Microcontrollers [tiny programmable computer chips] are migrating out of our computers and into thousands of artifacts in our everyday lives, giving them a digital veil. All around us are digitally empowered objects whose function can be changed with a string of bits. Objects like remote controls and pagers possess, like a Byzantine church, a strangely absent exterior, seemingly irrelevant to their

Triangles. Dreiecke und der Digitalschleier

**Das*, sagte sie ...*
... ist ein Cyhnk, oder?* Sie deutete mit dem Kopf in Richtung der aus Stein gemeißelten Qualle ...*
Wann hast du erfahren*, fragte Alsrod, *daß der Cyhnk nicht überall im Universum dieselbe Bedeutung hat?

Samuel Delaney,
Stars in my Pockets like Grains of Sand

Matt Gorbet/Maggie Orth

Aus vereinzelten Überzeugungen und Ansätzen bringt jeder von uns in jedes Artefakt, das Teil unserer äußeren Welt ist, eine innere Welt ein; dadurch werden die Objekte mit veränderlichen Bedeutungen und Funktionen erfüllt. In ihrer praktischen Verwendung zeichnen sich Werkzeuge durch ein einfaches Eins-zu-Eins-Verhältnis von Ursache und Wirkung aus: Der Hammer schlägt den Nagel ein. Aber stellen Sie einen Computer zwischen den Hammer und den Nagel, dann ändert sich diese Beziehung. Es entsteht ein Softwareschleier, und wenn man mit dem Hammer zuschlägt, ertönt möglicherweise Musik. Doch Gegenstände wie unser Hammer haben auch symbolische oder magische Funktionen und Bedeutungen. Diese symbolische Bedeutung besitzt

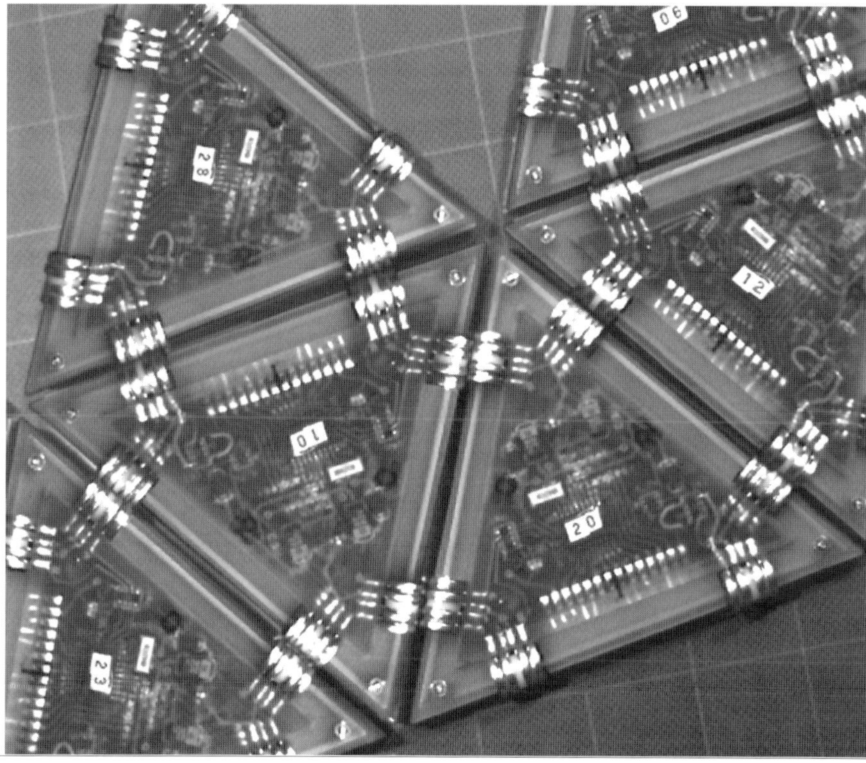

bereits einen derartigen Schleier. Konfrontieren Sie die Welt mit einem Symbol, und der eine wird Bewunderung empfinden, der andere Ironie. Wenn man aber nun einen Computer zwischen das Symbol und die Welt stellt – welche Rolle hat dann die Softwareschicht, der Digitalschleier?

Mikroprozessoren [kleinste programmierbare Computerchips] verlassen unsere Computer und finden Eingang in Tausende Gegenstände unseres täglichen Lebens, die dadurch einen digitalen Schleier erhalten. Wir sind umgeben von digital gesteuerten Objekten, deren Funktion mit einer Bitsequenz verändert werden kann. Objekte wie Fernsteuerungen und Pager haben – wie eine byzantinische Kirche – ein seltsam nichtssagendes Äußeres, das ihrer Aufgabe überhaupt nicht zu entsprechen scheint. Die Hagia Sophia zum Beispiel ist von den Straßen Istanbuls aus praktisch unsichtbar. Um sie den wechselnden Religionen des Reichs anzupassen, wurde ihr durch Änderung ihres internen Codes, ihrer Mosaike, immer wieder eine neue Bedeutung verliehen. Genauso kann auch ein Bitstring die Bedeutung eines Objekts verändern, indem er die Information verändert, die dieses Objekt enthält, kontrolliert oder anzeigt. Diese digitale DNS kann auf ein Individuum oder eine Gruppe reagieren und dieses bzw. diese reflektieren. Sie kann durch materiellen Output, Licht, Klänge und Bewegungen die persönlichen Bedeutungen ändern, die wir Gegenständen zuschreiben. Sie kann auch die magische Funktion eines Gegenstands in Frage stellen und neu definieren.

Unsere Anordnung von Dreiecken ist eine strukturierte Ansammlung programmierbaren Materials mit programmierbarer Bedeutung, die mit einer einzigen Bitsequenz geändert werden kann. Jedes einzelne Dreieck ist mikroprozessorgesteuert und verfügt über eine eigene Identität. Jedes dieser Dreiecke kann mit den anderen kommunizieren, sie erkennen und unterscheiden, es kann auf die Anwesenheit der anderen reagieren und seine eigene zeitliche und räumliche Position in bezug auf die anderen definieren. Ein Computer vermittelt diese Informationen, und wenn das System neu angeordnet wird, wird die genaue Topologie und Geschichte des einzelnen Dreiecks vom Computer erschlossen, gespeichert und upge-

job. Hagia Sophia is nearly invisible from the streets of Istanbul. To suit the changing religions of the empire, it has been given new meaning time and time again by the redesign of its internal code, its mosaics. And so can a string of digital bits change an object's meaning by changing the information the object contains, controls or displays. This digital DNA can react to and reflect an individual or group. It can externalize through material output, light, sound, motion, the personal meaning we all attribute to artifacts. It can also draw into question and redefine an artifact's magical function.

Our array of triangles is a structured mound of programmable matter, with programmable meaning that can be mutated with a single string of bits. Each triangle is a microcontrolled individual, with its own identity. Each can communicate with the others, recognize individuals among them, respond to the presence of the others and place itself in space and time relevant to the others. A computer mediates this information, and as the system is rearranged, its exact topology and history is inferred, stored and updated in the computer. But the mimetic storage of the state of the triangle system is not the goal; rather it is a tool. Because each triangle is a blank sheet, a recipient for images or signs, rearranging the triangles rearranges the meaning of the system. Like a string of hieroglyphics, when the triangles are connected together by a player, the context of each image and its relationship to its neighbors creates new meaning within the system, generating new output. Mimetic knowledge of the system is used by higher level software to interpret arrangements and events within the system.

The triangles depart from our visual history and reflect the possibilities of digital information by departing from the square. Simply understood, three sides imply a branching structure with one output and two inputs, or two outputs and one input. Triangles do not follow gravity; they don't create a simple line of text. Instead they create loops, inverted images and branches. The possible unique configurations of a set of triangles is daunting and demanding. Four triangles can create over 1600 unique states, and six triangles over 500,000 unique states. The connected pieces also create

datet. Doch die mimetische Speicherung des Zustands des Dreiecksystems ist nicht das Ziel, sondern eher ein Werkzeug. Denn jedes Dreieck ist ein unbeschriebenes Blatt, ein Behältnis für Bilder oder Zeichen, und eine Neuanordnung der Dreiecke bedeutet auch eine Neuanordnung der Bedeutung des Systems. Wenn die Dreiecke von einem Spieler zusammengesetzt werden, schafft der Kontext jedes einzelnen Bildes und seine Beziehung zu den Nachbarn wie in einer Abfolge von Hieroglyphen eine neue Bedeutung innerhalb des Systems und generiert einen neuen Output. Die mimetische Kenntnis des Systems wird von höherstufiger Software genutzt, um Anordnungen und Ereignisse im Rahmen des Systems zu interpretieren.

Die Dreiecke verlassen unsere bildbezogene Geschichte und spiegeln die Möglichkeiten der digitalen Information wieder, indem sie vom Quadrat abgehen. Einfach erklärt, bedeuten drei Seiten eine sich verzweigende Struktur mit einem Output und zwei Inputs oder mit zwei Outputs und einem Input. Die Dreiecke unterliegen nicht der Schwerkraft und erzeugen auch keine einfache Textzeile, sondern Schleifen, umgekehrte Bilder und Verzweigungen. Die Anzahl der möglichen eindeutigen Kombinationen eines Satzes von Dreiecken ist sowohl beängstigend als auch eine gewaltige Herausforderung. Vier Dreiecke können mehr als 1.600 eindeutige Zustände einnehmen; bei sechs Dreiecken sind es mehr als 500.000. Die miteinander verbundenen Elemente lassen auch Objekte mit Form und Gestalt – Oberfläche oder Kontext für Bilder und Symbole – entstehen. Die Elemente sind Mosaiksteinchen, die sowohl eine Geschichte erzählen als auch ihren eigenen physischen Kontext konstruieren. Und so wie die Form eines Altarbildes, einer Palette oder eines rechteckigen Gemäldes zur Bedeutung der darauf gemalten Symbole beiträgt, so kann auch die Form der Objekte, die aus den dreieckigen Elementen aufgebaut sind, zur Bedeutung der kombinierten Symbole beitragen.

Man nimmt an, daß die Sumerer die Sprache auf der Grundlage von Verträgen entwickelten, die aus winzigen, die gehandelten Waren darstellenden Tonfiguren bestanden, die in Tonbehältern steckten. Schließlich begannen die Händler, für jede Figur ein

objects with form and shape, the surface or context for the images or symbols. The pieces are tesseri that both depict a story and construct their own physical context. And just as the shape of an altarpiece, a palette or a rectangular painting contributes to the meaning of the symbols on it, so can the shapes of the objects built with the triangular pieces contribute to the meaning of the combined symbols.

It is thought that language developed in Sumeria from clay contracts consisting of tiny clay figures [representing the traded goods] encased in clay wrappers. Eventually, the merchants began pressing a symbol for each figure onto the exterior of the tablet. These signs became letters, and over time, a language. A new language, with new modes of interpretation and syntax is demanded by objects with self-knowledge and programmable meaning. Moreover, the software that can interpret connections or relationships between such objects, and drive content, demands development of mutable content we do not yet possess.

Most technology interface has relied on the past, using familiar models of information organization as metaphors for understanding digital information. Physically, the keyboard and the monitor are vestiges of televisions and typewriters, past technologies. Virtually, the desktop metaphor reflects past information organization systems, files and folders.

These systems help *users* adapt to technology by grounding it in a familiar past. Systems like the triangles are not metaphors of the past, but fantastic propositions for the future. The triangle pieces are deeply embedded in this fantasy – a longing for transcendence through technology – and in the formal abstraction of digital information. Yet at the same time they do not posit an ideal, but a means of exploration. They are a tool for understanding and developing a new language of programmable meaning that is possible in objects that possess the digital veil.

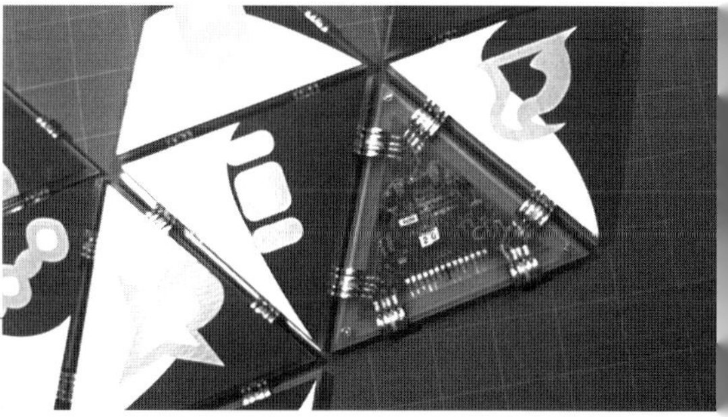

Symbol auf die Außenseite des Behälters zu drücken. Aus diesen Zeichen entwickelten sich dann Buchstaben und im Laufe der Zeit eine Sprache. Objekte mit Selbstkenntnis und programmierbarer Bedeutung fordern eine neue Sprache mit neuen Interpretationsweisen und einer neuen Syntax. Und die Software, die Verbindungen oder Beziehungen zwischen derartigen Objekten interpretieren und deren Inhalt steuern kann, erfordert die Entwicklung eines veränderlichen Inhalts, über den wir derzeit noch nicht verfügen.

Bisher beruhten die meisten technologischen Schnittstellen auf der Vergangenheit und verwendeten uns vertraute Modelle der Informationsorganisation als Metaphern zum Verständnis der digitalen Information. Rein physisch sind Tastatur und Monitor Überbleibsel von Fernsehgeräten und Schreibmaschinen und somit Technologien der Vergangenheit. Die Metapher des Schreibtischs spiegelt eigentlich die vergangenen Systeme der Informationsorganisation mit Akten und Ordnern wieder. Diese Systeme helfen den *Usern*, sich an die Technologie anzupassen, indem diese in einer vertrauten Vergangenheit verankert wird. Systeme wie die Dreiecke sind keine Metaphern der Vergangenheit, sondern phantastische Vorschläge für die Zukunft. Die Dreieckselemente sind zutiefst in diese Phantasie – in einem Streben nach Transzendenz durch Technologie – und in die formale Abstraktion der digitalen Information eingebettet. Doch zugleich postulieren sie kein Ideal, sondern sind ein Forschungsinstrument. Sie sind ein Werkzeug zum Verständnis und zur Entwicklung einer neuen Sprache mit programmierbarer Bedeutung, die überall dort möglich ist, wo ein Objekt über den Digitalschleier verfügt.

AUTODROM**
CRASHCOURSE
Real World/ Virtual World

Stadtwerkstatt

AUTODROM** – a multimedia experimental array and installation, a lot of fun, an entertaining experience. A crash course in the collision of two worlds at the intersection of Reality Road and the Cyberspace Expressway. AUTODROM** – the man-machine interface, a two-way feedback loop interlinking mankind and the virtual world.

The human-controlled machines moving along an actual test track have their equivalent in virtual space in the form of 3-D characters. An additional computer-generated factor has been engineered into the behavior of these figures – the power failure for a specified period resulting from a collision with one of them, analogous to machines in the real world.

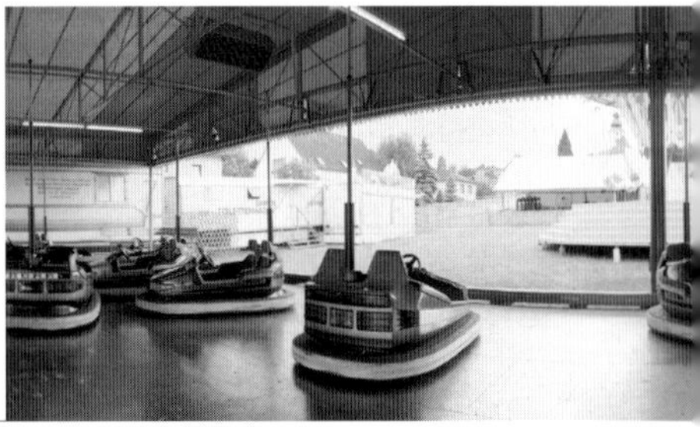

installations

AUTODROM**
CRASHCOURSE
Real World/
Virtual
World

Stadtwerkstatt

Real Space

The Autodrom – referred to as bumper cars in the US or the dodg'ems in Britain – is a familiar sight at amusement parks, carnivals and fairs. It constitutes the point of departure of our experimental array.

The Autodrom consists of a driving surface made of steel panels, the so-called plate, and a steel grid, the current collector lattice, mounted above it. The bumper cars equipped with a steel mast which slides across the lattice constitute the connection between the plate and the grid. DC current flows through the car once the driver has deposited a plastic chip. The electric motor is activated by means of a pedal and the bumper car gets underway.

What is forbidden in traffic on public streets is completely permissible at the Autodrom: unrestrained bumping, ramming, cutting off and crashing into other cars. The Autodrom is a driving school sans fender-benders as well as an electrified dance floor. But the biggest kick has always been the collisions. The Autodrom – driving school and meet-market.

Motion Capturing

The bumper cars are captured optically by video cameras mounted along the length and width of the Autodrom. Each car is identified by a multicolored reflector. Each camera is connected to a processor such as an SGI Indy, so that one Indy takes the x-axis and one the y-axis. Picture recognition software localizes the bumper cars by means of their respective reflectors. Position data on all bumper cars is transmitted 30 times per second [i.e., 30 HZ] to a graphic processor. Thus, the motion of the bumper cars can be ascertained in space and time.

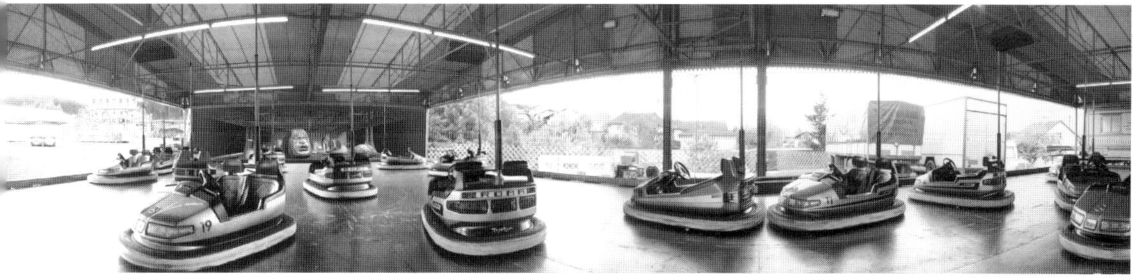

AUTODROM** eine multimediale Versuchsanordnung und Installation zur spielerischen und unterhaltsamen Erfahrung. Ein Crashkurs im Zusammenstoßen zweier Welten, der realen und der der Schnellstraße Cyberspace. AUTODROM** – Interface Mensch Maschine. Eine Rückkoppelung des Menschen mit der virtuellen Welt und umgekehrt.

Die realen Bewegungen von von Menschen gesteuerten Maschinen auf dem Versuchsfeld haben analog im virtuellen Raum ihre Stellvertreter in Form von 3D-Charakteren.

Dort treffen diese Zeichen auf einen zusätzlichen computergenerierten Faktor, der einen Energieausfall der Maschine im Realen auf eine bestimmte Zeit erwirkt, sobald man mit diesem zusammenstößt.

Realer Raum

Das Autodrom, in Deutschland Autoscooter oder Buffauto benannt, findet man in unseren Breiten meist auf Jahrmärkten, Luna Parks, Kirtagen oder Feuerwehrfesten. Es bildet den Ausgangspunkt für unsere Versuchsanordnung.

Das Autodrom besteht aus einer Fahrfläche aus Stahlplatten, der sogenannten Platte, und darüber einem Stahlgitter, dem Stromabnehmernetz. Die Autodromwagen bilden mit dem Schleifbügel die Verbindung zwischen Platte und Stromabnehmernetz. Der Einwurf eines Plastikchips ermöglicht den Durchfluß von Gleichstrom. Mittels des Pedals kann der Elektromotor eingeschaltet werden, und das Fahrzeug setzt sich in Gang.

Das Autodrom läßt das zu, was im Straßenverkehr nicht möglich ist: ungehemmt in ein anderes Auto zu krachen, puffen, stoßen und schneiden. Das Autodrom als Fahrschule, Fahren ohne Kratzer, ist auch elektrifizierter Tanzboden. Die größte Hetz ist und bleibt das Zusammenstoßen. Das Autodrom – Fahrschule und Anmache.

Motion Capturing

Die Abnahme der bewegten Objekte, der Autodromwagen, erfolgt optisch durch Videokameras, die jeweils an der Längsseite und Breitseite des Autodroms postiert sind. Verschiedenfarbige Reflektoren an den Wagen dienen zur Erkennung. Die Kameras sind jeweils mit einem Rechner, z. B. einer SGI Indy, verbunden, das heißt eine Indy übernimmt die

Virtual Space

Analogous to the real space of the Autodrom is a virtual three-dimensional Autodrom. Here, virtual characters move about instead of bumper cars. AUTODROM** users are thus really and virtually present.

The position data from the Indys is fed through a network connection to a graphic processor – either an SGI Onyx or, at least, a Maximum Impact. The network protocol used here is TCP/IP socket-based. By means of its own real-time-capable rendering software, the software running on this processor depicts the characters according to the coordinates transmitted from the Indys. And here is where we have inserted our main character Pac-Head, a computer-generated head behaving according to a separate set of rules.

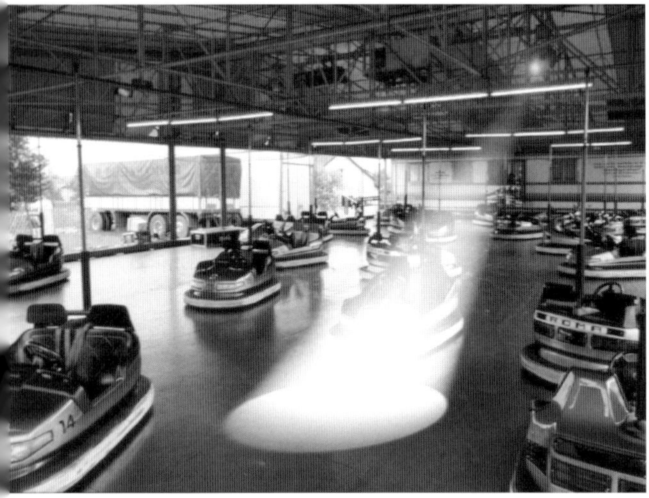

x-Achse und eine die y-Achse. Eine Bilderkennungssoftware lokalisiert die Autos durch ihre unterschiedlichen Reflektoren. Die Positionsdaten werden 30 Mal pro Sekunde von allen Autos, d. h. mit 30 HZ, an den Grafikrechner übermittelt. Dadurch sind die Fahrzeuge zeitlich und örtlich erfaßbar.

Virtueller Raum

Analog zum realen Raum des Autodroms existiert ein virtuelles dreidimensionales Autodrom. In diesem bewegen sich stellvertretend für die Autos virtuelle Charaktere. Die Benutzer des AUTODROM** sind somit real wie auch virtuell präsent.

Ein bilderzeugender Rechner, der entweder eine SGI Onyx oder zumindest eine Maximum Impact ist, bekommt über eine Netzwerkverbindung die Positionsdaten von den Indys. Das hierfür verwendete Netzwerkprotokoll ist TCP/IP Socket-basiert. Die auf diesem Rechner laufende Software stellt über eine eigene echtzeitfähige Rendersoftware die Charaktere entsprechend den von den Indys übermittelten Koordinaten dar. Diesen hinzugefügt ist nun unser Hauptdarsteller, der Pac-Head, ein computergenerierter Kopf, der nach eigenen Gesetzen handelt.

Pac-Head

Er bewegt sich im Gegensatz zu den kurvenden und kreisenden Bewegungen der Autos in Geraden jeweils entlang vor und rückwärts der x- oder y-Achse. Der Pac-Head operiert nach dem Zufallsprinzip und bewegt sich in etwa in der Geschwindigkeit der Autos, also mit ca. 12 km/h. Aber auch das Verhalten der Autos beeinflußt die Steuerung des Kopfes. Sie erfolgt über ein neuronales Netz, das von verschiedenen Faktoren wie der Anzahl der sich bewegenden Fahrzeuge und dem Aggressionspotential, das durch die Kollisionen erkennbar ist, beeinflußt wird. Der Pac-Head, der Hecht im Karpfenteich, jagt die Autos, und sobald er eines erwischt, verschlingt er es.

Rückkoppelungen der Systeme

× **Scanner**

Haben die realen Autos im Virtuellen ihre Stellvertreter, so hat der Pac-Head als virtuelle Existenz einen realen Stellvertreter in Form des Scanners, dessen Lichtkegel die vir-

Pac-Head

In contrast to the curving and circling movements of the bumper cars, Pac-Head moves in a straight line, either forward or backward, along either the x or y axes. The Pac-Head operates according to the principle of randomness, and moves at approximately the same speed as the bumper cars, a little over 7 mph. However, the behavior of the bumper cars also effects the steering of the head. It takes place through a neuronal network which takes into account various factors such as the number of vehicles in motion and the ascertainable potential for aggression in the case of a collision. The Pac-Head – the driving force, the king of the road – chases the bumper cars and, as soon as it catches one, gobbles it up.

The System's Feedback Loops

× **Scanner**

Just as real bumper cars have their symbolic equivalents in virtual reality, the Pac-Head as a virtual existence has an analogous form in the real world – the scanner, whose cone of light reproduces virtual movements in the real space of the driving surface.

× **Sound Transmission – Acoustic Signal**

In order for the AUTODROM** drivers to ascertain the location of the Pac-Head, it is represented acoustically in real space. Speakers are set up at the four corners of the driving space; properly controlled, they can spatially position a sound signal. These signals constitute the acoustic world of the Pac-Head.

× **Crash**

The system responds as soon as there is a collision involving the Pac-Head and a character [the symbolic equivalent of the bumper car] as well as the scanner [the symbolic equivalent of the Pac-Head] and a bumper car. That occurs in the following manner: the scanner's cone of light comes in contact with one of the light cells mounted on the bumper cars, where upon the power supply to the vehicle is cut off and it comes to a halt. The Pac-Head simultaneously devours the character in virtual space, which in turn can be heard at high volume in the Autodrom.

tuellen Bewegungen im realen Raum auf der Fahrfläche nachvollzieht.

× **Beschallung – akustisches Signal**

Zur Lokalisierung des Pac-Heads wird dieser für die AUTODROM** Fahrer akustisch im realen Raum dargestellt. An den vier Ecken der Fahrfläche des Autodroms sind Lautsprecherboxen angebracht, die mit entsprechender Steuerung ein Tonsignal räumlich positionieren können. Diese Signale sind die Geräuschwelt des Pac-Head.

× **Crash**

Sobald der Pac-Head mit dem Stellvertreter des Autos, dem Charakter, sowie der Stellvertreter des Pac-Head, der Scanner, mit dem Auto zusammenstößt, reagiert das System. Das vollzieht sich folgendermaßen: Der Lichtkegel des Scanners trifft auf das mit Lichtzellen präparierte Auto, worauf die Stromzufuhr im Fahrzeug unterbrochen wird – es kommt zum Stehen. Zugleich verschluckt der Pac-Head im virtuellen Raum den Charakter, was wiederum im Autodrom lautstark hören ist.

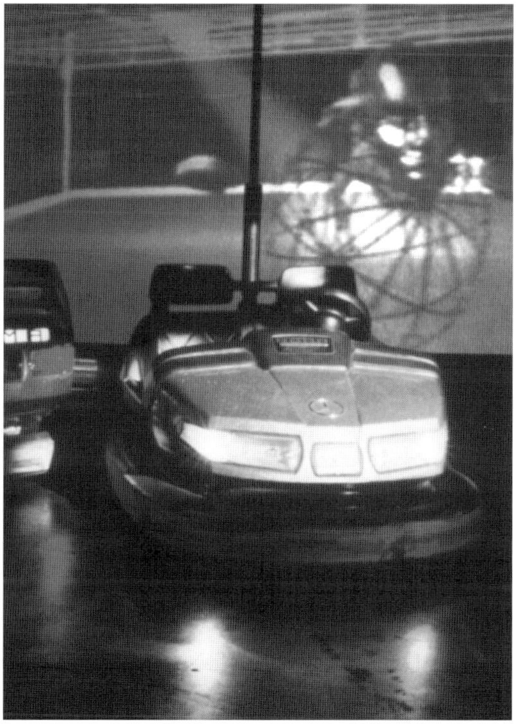

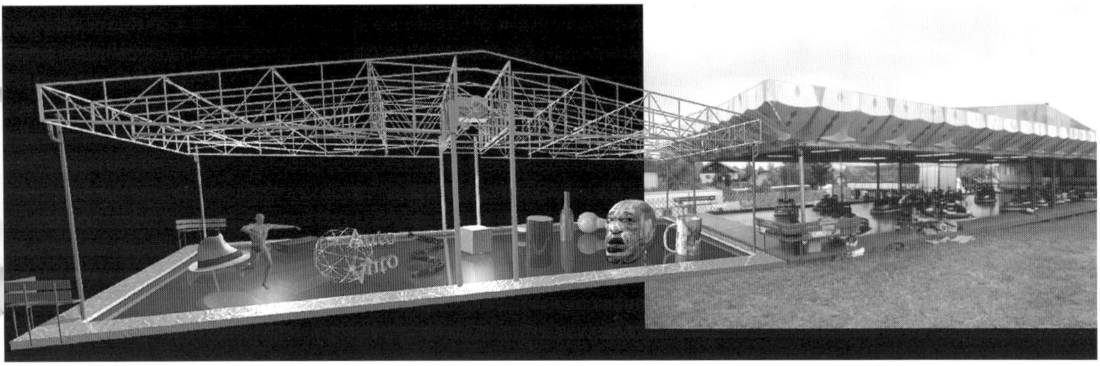

× **Projection**

A rear-projection screen mounted along one end of the Autodrom hall displaying the virtual Autodrom in real-time serves as a control display for the AUTODROM** drivers. This is the optical interface making it possible to follow the course of virtual events – a theatrical performance, in which the Pac-Head and the characters play out their games. This display opens up the interplay between real and virtual events in the AUTODROM**.

× **The Drivers**

They are really and virtually present. The vehicle is the robot in which the human being is the processor. The course of events is the process which is determined by the behavior of individual drivers with respect to one another. The individual does not act in isolation, but rather in conjunction with other individuals – a chaotic process of random and inteded encounters. The human being, in his freedom of movement, is reduced to a single

× **Projektion**

Als Kontrolldisplay für die AUTODROM**-Fahrer dient eine Rückprojektionsleinwand an der Breitseite der Autodromhalle, die in Echtzeit das virtuelle Autodrom spiegelt. Das ist die optische Schnittstelle zur Wahrnehmung der virtuellen Vorgänge. Ein Schauspiel, in dem der Pac-Head und die Charaktere ihre Spiele spielen. Dieses Display eröffnet das Wechselspiel zwischen realen und virtuellen Vorgängen im AUTODROM**.

× **Die Fahrer**

sind real und virtuell präsent. Das Fahrzeug ist der Roboter, in dem der Mensch der Prozessor ist. Das Geschehen ist der Prozeß, welcher durch das Verhalten der einzelnen Fahrer zueinander bestimmt wird. Der Mensch agiert nicht allein, sondern im Verbund mit anderen Menschen – ein chaotischer Prozeß von zufälligen und beabsichtigten Begegnungen. Der Mensch ist in seiner Bewegungsfreiheit auf eine einzelne Zelle reduziert, die sich auf einer vorgegebenen begrenzten Fläche gemeinsam mit anderen gleichgestellten Zellen bewegen kann. Eine Interaktion Mensch/Maschine, Mensch/Virtualität. Die einzelnen Fahrer haben einen virtuellen Stellvertreter, einen Charakter, einen Schauspieler, der eine Rolle gemäß seines Zeichens im virtuellen Raum einnehmen kann.

Durch dieses System können nun weitere Aufgaben impliziert werden, welche den Fahrern eine weitere erzielbare Wirkung im realen wie im virtuellen Raum ermöglichen. Der räumliche Operationsradius des Autodromfahrers in der Matrix des begrenztes Feldes gleicht der Operationsfläche einer Computermaus. In unserer Versuchsanordnung operieren somit zwölf präparierte Autos gleich zwölf Mäusen, die gleichzeitig auf einer Oberfläche agieren und wo jede ihre gleiche Berechtigung hat. Ein Schauspiel, in dem jeder aus dem Publikum eine Rolle spielen kann. Ein weiteres interaktives Gästespiel aus der Rolling™ Art Sektion Stadtwerkstatt/Rivingtonschool.

cell which can maneuver in a range with preset boundaries together with other cells on an equal footing – an interaction of man/machine and of man/virtuality. The individual drivers each have a virtual equivalent, a character, an actor who can adopt a role according to his symbolic equivalent in virtual reality.

Through this system, additional functions can now become implicit which make it possible for drivers to achieve additional effects in reality as well as in virtual reality. The spatial radius of operations of the Autodrom driver in the matrix of a limited area is equivalent to the operative range of a computer mouse. Thus, in our experimental array, 12 bumper cars that have been set up for operation are equivalent to 12 mice simultaneously in action on a single user interface, each operating on the same footing – a theatrical performance in which each member of the audience can play a role. Another interactive game from the Rolling™ Art Section of the Stadtwerkstatt/Rivingtonschool.

Commissioned by Ars Electronica. Realized in part within the Ars Electronica Research & Residence Program.

Auftragsarbeit der Ars Electronica. Teilweise realisiert innerhalb des Ars Electronica Research & Residence Program.

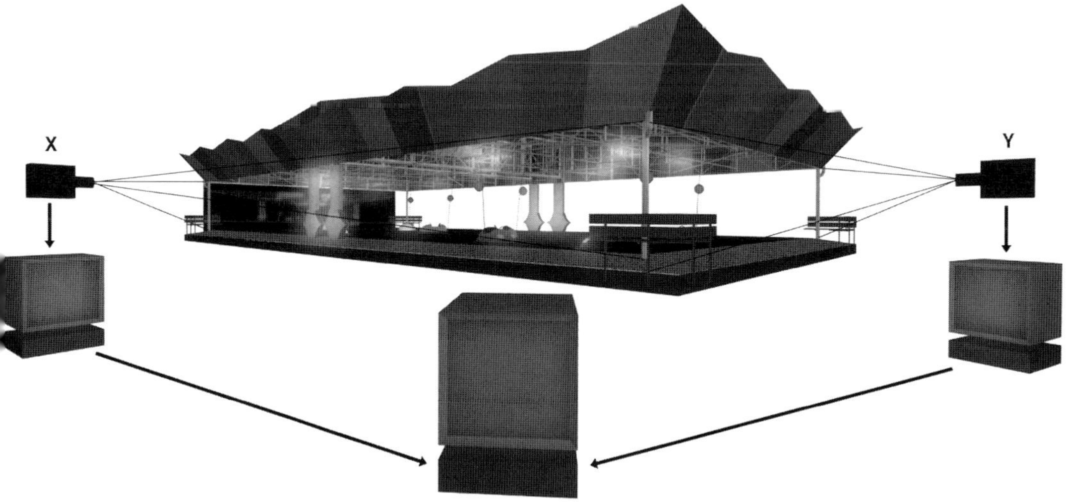

Projekt-Team

Thomas Lehner, Georg Ritter, Peter Hauenschild Erich Berger, Markus Böhler, Vaclav Cizkovsky, Tom Knienieder, Chris Mutter, Matt Smith, Tom Weber Norbert Artner, Christian Eder, Gabriele Kepplinger, Andreas Kozmann, Fritz Kron, Jon Maier, Karl Pitrich, Dejan Radev, Markus Seidl, Johannes Staudinger, Marc Vojka, Alfred Wögerbauer, Franz Xaver, Fischer Film Familie Deisenhammer, KommR Karlheinz Straßmeier

PRoPs: The Avatars Are Loose in the Hauptplatz!

John Canny/Eric Paulos

If Baron Frankenstein had been a little more understanding, he would have foreseen his creation's need to escape the laboratory. As a sentient being, the creature was bound to evolve and discover new environments. It was only doing what it was programmed to do. Not by Frankenstein, but by the much cleverer design of its genetic and memetic raw material.

Avatars are the human life-support system in the world of bits. They also allow us to mediate distance, take on new identities, and do real work in new kinds of social space. In their own environment, they are a highly successful species. They were bound to escape from cyberspace sooner or later. PRoPs are the evolution of avatars into hardware, and they inhabit the platzs and cafes of the real world. A PRoP is a Personal Robotic Presence. It is a telerobot driven by a human pilot over the internet, and it gives them a rudimentary physical body in a distant place. PRoPs are not flesh, but they live in our world. Should we choose, they give us alternative bodies to experience the world through. They support collaboration at a distance in the same way as avatars, and they can be built in the same outrageous shapes and primary color schemes.

PRoPs: Am Hauptplatz sind die Avatare los!

John Canny/Eric Paulos

They can no longer be kept inside the machine. They extend the reach of Internet users back out into the world, but can emerge somewhere far removed from the pilot's computer. They are steerable cameras with wheels, tracks and propellers that will get up and walk out of the computer room as soon as they can.

Telerobotics began because of the limitations of human skin. We moved into the atomic age and then the space age, and realized that armor had its limits, and that remote control is cheaper and safer. The Australian artist Stelarc has exposed the fragility of human skin through his suspension events. Lately he has cracked into the body's control system with his *Ping Body* series. Stelarc sees these kinds of violations as typical of what the body must deal with in the modern age and concludes that it really isn't up to it and is *obsolete*. He has become an early adopter of Cyborg technology [his third arm].

Another branch of telerobotics is a toolmaking craft. Telesurgery and telediagnosis place remarkable instruments in the hands of a surgeon who is nowhere near the patient. Imaging and simulation expose the patient's

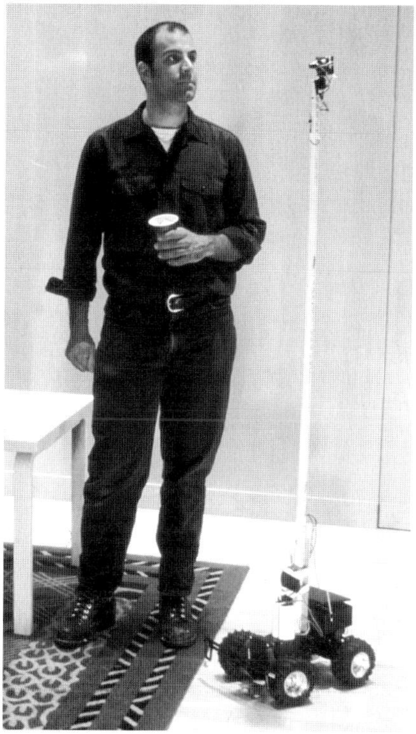

Mit etwas mehr Einfühlungsvermögen hätte Baron Frankenstein ahnen können, daß sein Geschöpf das Bedürfnis haben würde, aus dem Labor zu entkommen. Als fühlendes Wesen mußte es sich zwangsläufig weiterentwickeln und neue Umgebungen entdecken. Es tat also nur, wozu es vorprogrammiert war – allerdings nicht von Frankenstein, sondern durch das weitaus intelligentere Design seines genetischen und memetischen Rohmaterials.

Avatare sind das menschliche Lebenserhaltungssystem in der Welt der Bits. Sie ermöglichen uns, Entfernungen zu überbrücken, neue Identitäten anzunehmen und in verschiedenen Sozialräumen wirkliche Arbeit zu verrichten. In ihrer eigenen Umgebung sind sie eine sehr erfolgreiche Art. Es war klar, daß sie früher oder später aus dem Cyberspace entfliehen würden. PRoPs stellen die Weiterentwicklung der Avatare in Hardware dar, und dergestalt bevölkern Avatare die Plätze und Cafés der realen Welt. Ein PRoP ist eine *Persönliche Robotische Präsenz*, ein Teleroboter, der über das Internet von einem menschlichen Piloten gesteuert wird und diesem an einem externen Ort als rudimentärer materieller Körper dient. PRoPs sind nicht aus Fleisch und Blut, aber sie leben in unserer Welt.

Bei Bedarf bieten sie uns alternative Körper, durch die wir die Welt erleben können. Ebenso wie die Avatare dienen sie der Koordination von Zusammenarbeit über große Entfernungen hinweg. Man kann sie in ebenso gräßlichen Formen und Farbkombinationen produzieren, nur lassen sie sich nicht länger im Inneren von Maschinen festhalten. Sie erweitern den Handlungsradius von Internetbenutzern weit über das Netz in die Welt hinaus und können auch weit weg vom Computer ihres Piloten auftauchen. Sie sind steuerbare Kameras mit Rädern, Schienen und Propellern und werden jede Chance nützen, um aus dem Computerraum zu entwischen.

Ein Hauptgrund für die Entwicklung der Telerobotik lag in den natürlichen Grenzen der menschlichen Haut. Auf unserem Weg vom Atomzeitalter ins Weltraumzeitalter haben wir erkannt, daß der Rüstung Grenzen gesetzt sind und Fernsteuerung billiger und sicherer ist. In seinen *Suspension Events* hat der australische Künstler Stelarc auf die Verletzbarkeit der menschlichen Haut hingewiesen. Vor kurzem

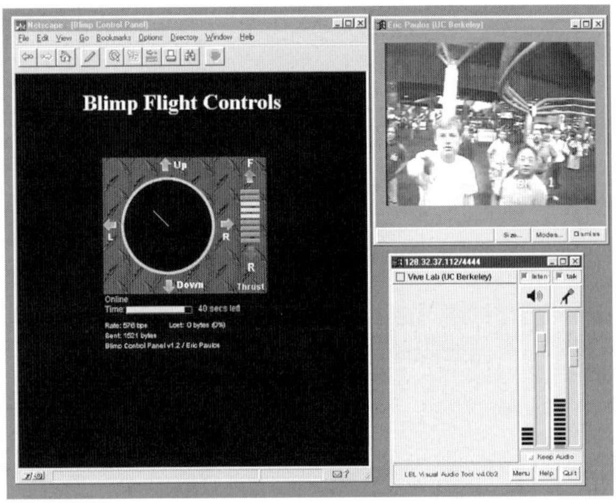

organs instead of a rib-spreader. Projects like the *Telegarden* [Ars Electronica Festival 96] and *Legal Tender* [SIGGRAPH '96] take the tools of gardening and currency testing respectively, and make them available to the Internet community. They also engage the visitor in a dialogue about some real objects in a real but distant place. PRoPs are the application of telerobotics to puppetry. They are specialized for social tasks and provide, in the best case, the dexterity of a puppet hand. But they do provide the pilot/puppeteer with many avenues for self-expression. For telework, this is surely their most important function.

We have been building PRoPs for about three years. A PRoP's pilot sits at a normal PC somewhere on the Internet. The PRoP sends its pilot live video over the Internet, and it has two-way audio that allows the pilot to talk with people around it. Our latest PRoPs have rudimentary vision and gestural capability. They can be described as mobile video-conferencing systems, but that reduction hides most of what is interesting about them. That difference is what our research is about. We are trying to answer the question *what is the difference between communicating and being there?*. The same ques-

ist er mit seiner *Ping Body*-Serie in das Steuerungssystem des Körpers eingedrungen. Für Stelarc ist dieses gewaltsame Eindringen Symbol für das, was dem Körper in unserer modernen Zeit zugemutet wird. Er schließt daraus, daß der Körper diesen Anforderungen nicht wirklich gewachsen und daher *überholt* ist. So wurde Stelarc zu einem der ersten Anwender der Cyborg-Technologie [sein *Dritter Arm*].

Ein anderer Zweig der Telerobotik ist die Kunst des Werkzeugmachens. Mit Tele-Chirurgie und Tele-Diagnose hat ein räumlich von seinem Patienten getrennter Chirurg erstaunliche Instrumente in der Hand. Statt mit Rippenklammern werden die Organe des Patienten durch Bildaufbereitung und Simulation freigelegt. Projekte wie *Telegarden* [Ars Electronica Festival 96] und *Legal Tender* [SIGGRAPH '96] verwenden Gartengeräte bzw. Prüfinstrumente für Währungen und stellen sie der Internet-Gemeinde zur Verfügung. Außerdem verwickeln sie den Besucher in einen Dialog über reale Objekte an realen, aber weiter entfernten Orten. PRoPs stellen eine telerobotische Version des Puppenspiels dar. Sie sind auf soziale Aufgaben spezialisiert und lassen sich bestenfalls so geschickt handhaben wie eine Marionette. Dennoch bieten sie dem Piloten/Puppenspieler zahlreiche Möglichkeiten der Selbstdarstellung. In der Tele-Arbeit ist dies gewiß ihre wichtigste Funktion.

Wir befassen uns nun seit etwa drei Jahren mit der Herstellung von PRoPs. Der Pilot eines PRoP sitzt irgendwo im Netz an einem normalen PC, und der PRoP sendet ihm über das Netz ein Live-Video. Der PRoP ist mit einem Zweiweg-Audio-System ausgestattet, über das der Pilot mit Personen sprechen kann, die sich in der Nähe des PRoP aufhalten. Unsere neuesten PRoPs haben rudimentäre Seh- und Gestikulierfähigkeiten. Man könnte sie als mobile Video-Konferenz-Systeme beschreiben, aber sie darauf zu reduzieren, würde gerade ihre interessantesten Aspekte verhüllen. Und um diesen kleinen Unterschied geht es in unserer Forschung. Wir suchen eine Antwort auf die Frage: *Was ist der Unterschied zwischen bloßer Kommunikation und tatsächlicher Anwesenheit?* Dieselbe Frage stellen sich auch diejenigen, die sich mit dem Studium von Online-Gemeinschaften befassen. Was PRoPs betrifft, so ist der Unterschied besonders kraß, da wir

tion is being asked by people studying online communities. With PRoPs the differences are sharp because, but for the telerobot, we see social interaction between humans in a familiar human environment. In cyberspace, there is the nagging doubt that a subtle aspect of human interaction has already been lost in the choice of digital representation.

When deciding on a body for a PRoP, it's difficult to resist the temptation of flight. Our first PRoPs were all indoor blimps. They were similar in size, but not in posture, to a large human being. They fly without tethers using batteries and radio links, and use small electric motors and propellers for thrust. They now have sonar for height control and an electronic compass for steering, and can be quite easily driven over the mainstream Internet. We called these gadgets *space browsers* because they seemed to have evolved from web and VRML browsers into tools for moving around in physical space. They were good for getting around in galleries and other large spaces, and do give the pilot new perspectives when the ceiling is high enough.

We could have continued endowing PRoPs with super-human skills like flight, but instead our research took a sharp turn in another direction. We discovered that the most interesting things about blimps were their social skills. They allowed roaming, snooping, chance encounters, and they attracted people's attention. Blimps were not ideal for these kinds of things. Superhuman skills are great for superhuman tasks, but if Über-Mensch flies to work, he misses the shared experience and verbal exchange with his colleagues who travel on the ground. Blimps and humans don't even exist in the same medium. By nature, terrestrials are at rest. Blimps by nature are always in motion. A terrestrial PRoP is better when the goal is sharing experiences with humans.

Our current generation of PRoPs are therefore terrestrials. They are best described as stick figures that have a mobile base and a steerable camera at head height. Our first gesturing PRoPs use a small laser pointer which is steerable in two dimensions. The pointer allows the pilot to point at objects in the world and to make gestures that comprise motion only [there are no hands to shape]. We are not interested at this point in building android robots. PRoPs can have many useful social skills

es, abgesehen vom Teleroboter, mit sozialer Interaktion zwischen Menschen in einer vertrauten menschlichen Umgebung zu tun haben. Im Cyberspace quält uns der Zweifel, ob nicht allein schon durch die Wahl der digitalen Darstellungsform ein subtiler Aspekt menschlicher Interaktion verlorengegangen ist.

Wenn man sich für einen geeigneten Körperform für PRoPs entscheiden muß, fällt es schwer, der Versuchung des Fliegens zu widerstehen. Unsere ersten PRoPs waren allesamt kleine Hallen-Luftschiffe, sogenannte Blimps. In der Größe, nicht aber in ihrer Haltung, glichen sie einem großen Menschen. Sie fliegen frei, durch Batterieantrieb und Funksteuerung, und kleine Elektromotoren und Propeller sorgen für die nötige Schubkraft. Inzwischen sind sie auch mit einem Echolot zur Höhenkontrolle und einem elektronischen Kompaß zur Steuerung ausgestattet und relativ einfach über das Mainstream-Internet zu steuern. Wir nannten diese Geräte *Space Browser*, denn offensichtlich stellten sie die Weiterentwicklung von WWW- und VRML-Browsern hin zu Werkzeugen dar, mit denen man sich im physikalischen Raum bewegen kann. Sie eignen sich besonders dazu, sich durch Galerien und andere große Räume zu bewegen, und ist der Raum hoch genug, so können sie dem Piloten in der Tat neue Perspektiven vermitteln.

Wir hätten PRoPs auch weiterhin mit übermenschlichen Fähigkeiten wie der des Fliegens ausstatten können, hätte sich nicht in unserer Forschungsarbeit ein abrupter Richtungswechsel ergeben. Wir entdeckten, daß das Interessanteste an diesen Blimps ihre sozialen Fähigkeiten waren. Sie ermöglichten es einem, umherzustreifen, sich umzusehen, zufällig jemanden zu treffen, und sie zogen Aufmerksamkeit auf sich. Als Flugschiffe waren sie aber für solche Aufgaben nicht wirklich ideal. Übermenschliche Fähigkeiten eignen sich wunderbar für übermenschliche Aufgaben; aber wenn Superman zur Arbeit fliegt, hat er keine Möglichkeit, mit Kollegen, die sich zu Lande fortbewegen, zu kommunizieren oder gemeinsame Erfahrungen zu machen. Blimps und Menschen existieren nicht in ein- und demselben Medium. Erdenbewohner sind von Natur aus im Ruhezustand. Blimps sind von Natur aus ständig in Bewegung. Zum zwischenmenschlichen Erfahrungsaustausch eignet sich ein bodenständiger PRoP besser.

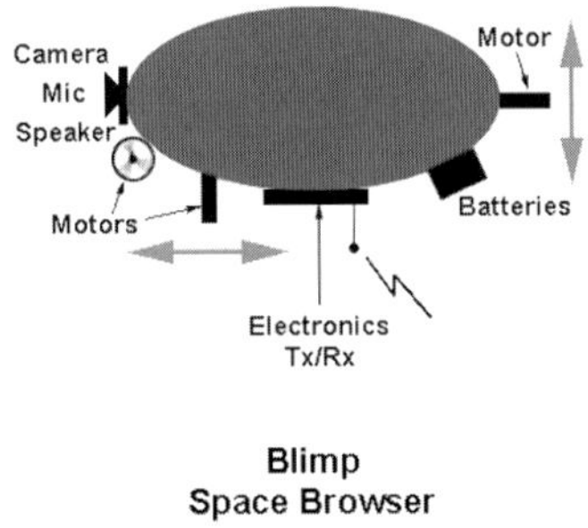

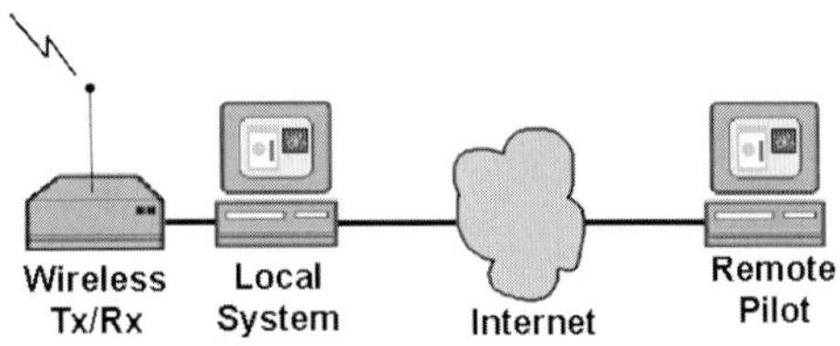

without looking human at all. If we can successfully impart a social skill to a PRoP without copying the human medium, we have learned something important about that skill. Anthropomorphism generates high expectations which these robots often cannot meet. Worse still, an anthropomorphic image conveys emotions and a state of mind which have nothing to do with the pilot's unless they are precisely controlled. Such control is complex and subtle, and well beyond our agenda for now.

Like any projection through a digital medium, PRoPs are impoverished compared to a live human being. When we describe the total experience of being there, we add *in the flesh*. Flesh is our original interface to the world. It is one enormous sensor of warmth, moisture, texture, pressure and shape. There are many barriers to moving from PRoP presence to real presence, and the *flesh barrier* is an impassable one. Our response is to continue anyway. Human beings are master users of media, even impoverished ones.

Unsere neueste PRoP-Generation bewegt sich daher am Boden. Am besten beschreibt man sie als Stangengestalten mit mobiler Basis und einer steuerbaren Kamera in Kopfhöhe. Unsere ersten gestikulierenden PRoPs besitzen einen kleinen, zweidimensional steuerbaren Laser-Zeiger. Mit diesem Zeiger kann der Pilot auf Objekte in der realen Welt zeigen und Gesten vollführen, die ausschließlich auf reiner Bewegung basieren [es gibt keine Hände, die Handzeichen machen könnten]. Derzeit sind wir nicht daran interessiert, androide Roboter zu bauen. PRoPs können viele nützliche soziale Eigenschaften haben, ohne auch nur im entferntesten menschlich auszusehen. Wenn wir einem PRoP erfolgreich eine soziale Fähigkeit einpflanzen können, ohne das Medium Mensch zu kopieren, so haben wir schon etwas Wichtiges über diese Fähigkeit gelernt. Anthropomorphismus erzeugt hohe Erwartungen, die diese Roboter oft nicht erfüllen können. Und was noch schlimmer ist: Eine anthropomorphe Erscheinung vermittelt Gefühle und eine Gemütsverfassung, die mit denen des Piloten nichts zu tun haben, außer, er hat sie perfekt unter Kontrolle. Eine derartige Kontrolle ist äußerst kompliziert und subtil und steht derzeit noch nicht auf unserer Tagesordnung.

Wie jede Projektion auf der Basis digitaler Medien schneiden auch PRoPs im Vergleich zum lebenden Menschen recht armselig ab. Um die Erfahrung körperlicher Präsenz nachdrücklich zu beschreiben, benutzen wir oft die Formulierung *in Fleisch und Blut*. Fleisch ist unsere ursprüngliche Schnittstelle zur Welt. Es dient als gewaltiger Sensor für Wärme, Feuchtigkeit, Oberflächenbeschaffenheit, Druck und Form. Es gibt zahlreiche Barrieren auf dem Weg von der PRoP-Präsenz zur wirklichen Präsenz, und eine der unüberwindbaren Barrieren ist die *Fleisch-Barriere*. Auf dieses Faktum reagieren wir, indem wir trotzdem weitermachen. Menschen sind souveräne Medienbenutzer, auch wenn es sich um *armselige* Medien handelt. Ganz besonders in der elektronischen Kommunikation mit anderen Menschen benutzen wir all unsere kreativen Fähigkeiten, unsere Improvisationsgabe, um uns in den anderen Raum zu projizieren. Das Medium selbst wird dabei zur Nebensache; was wirklich real ist, ist das Zusammentreffen einzelner Individuen.

Especially when we communicate electronically with live human beings, we apply our full creative and improvisational skills to project ourselves into the other space. The medium itself melts away, and what is most real is the meeting of several individuals. Our research agenda is to find out what PRoP users want to do and express, and to capture and transport that action. The challenge for us as scientists is to avoid the instinct to name and circumscribe an action [what does it mean?]. Instead we must look for connotations [what could it mean?], and strive to preserve all of them.

Our PRoP exhibit includes terrestrial and airborne telerobots. The PRoP's designs are representative of just how much [or how little] of their pilot's presence is being projected into the remote space. Computer users within the Design Center, Linz, or from the Internet will drive them and will be able to converse with pedestrian visitors within the center. The blimp PRoPs will be easy to find. The stick figures will prove harder. On the surface, they are conspicuously inorganic, made from polyurethane and other plastics. After all, they have only recently evolved from pixmap values. But in reality they are just other visitors to the Ars Electronica festival. They share with you a fascination for the strange and new, and a craving to explore. You will find you have a lot in common.

Aufgabe unserer Forschungen ist es herauszufinden, was PRoP-Benutzer tun und ausdrücken wollen, und diese Handlungen zu erfassen und zu transportieren. Für uns als Wissenschaftler besteht die Herausforderung darin, dem instinktiven Impuls zum Benennen und Eingrenzen einer Handlung [Was bedeutet sie?] zu widerstehen. Statt dessen müssen wir Konnotationen suchen [Was könnte es bedeuten?] und uns bemühen, jede einzelne davon zu bewahren.

Unsere PRoP-Ausstellungsstücke sind sowohl Flug- als auch Boden-Teleroboter. Das unterschiedliche Design gibt Auskunft darüber, wie viel [oder wie wenig] von der Präsenz ihres Piloten in den fernen Raum projiziert wird. Computerbenutzer im Design Center, Linz, oder direkt im Internet werden sie steuern und sich so mit Besuchern, die zu Fuß im Zentrum unterwegs sind, unterhalten können. Die Blimp PRoPs werden kaum zu übersehen sein, die Stangengestalten schon eher. Ihre Oberfläche ist auffällig unorganisch, denn sie sind aus Polyurethan und anderen Kunststoffen. Schließlich haben sie sich erst vor kurzem aus Pixmap-Werten entwickelt. In Wirklichkeit sind auch sie ganz einfach Besucher des Ars Electronica Festival, ebenso auf Entdeckungsreise wie Sie, ebenso fasziniert von ungewöhnlichen und neuen Perspektiven. Sie werden sehen, Sie haben eine ganze Menge gemeinsam.

Cyborg Detector

Erich Berger/
Patricia Futterer/
Sandy Stone

Technology was once something abjected by the individual; it was clearly outside of the body similar to an object that individuals used. By the turn of this century, the understanding of technology had changed and it was more seen as a tool to extend and perfect the human being. Now more than ever, technology has a very strong status in the West and the interchange of technology and flesh has become characeristic of western culture. At the same time, the question about what is the *FleshFactor* in this technology-informed culture has become a controversial issue.

Technology, the fantasies and dreams about what technology can offer to humans, the history of sense-of-self and the contemporary stratified experiences of reality that we encounter in techno-culture, feed back into the flesh. Through new interfaces/boundaries, the smooth flesh receives more than just an imprint of information. The flesh itself mutates in this ongoing exchanging process.

The identity of humans is no longer based on a body with a carbon substratum alone. By merging flesh that has a carbon substratum, metal and silicon substrated devices like semi-

Cyborg Detector

Erich Berger/
Patricia Futterer/
Sandy Stone

Die Technologie wurde früher von den Menschen gering geschätzt. Sie befand sich eindeutig außerhalb des Körpers – so wie ein Objekt, das der Mensch zu seinen Zwecken verwendet. Um die Jahrhundertwende hatte sich das Verständnis der Technologie geändert, sie wurde nun eher als Werkzeug betrachtet, das der Erweiterung und Vervollkommnung des Menschen dient. Heute ist der Stellenwert der Technologie in der westlichen Welt höher als je zuvor, und der Austausch zwischen Technologie und *Fleisch* wurde zu einem charakteristischen Aspekt der westlichen Kultur. Gleichzeitig wurde die Frage des *FleshFactor* in dieser technologiebewußten Kultur zu einem Streitthema.

Die Technologie, die Vorstellungen und Träume vom Nutzen der Technologie für den Menschen, die geschichtliche Entwicklung des Selbstverständnisses und die zeitgenössischen geschichteten Erfahrungen der Realität, die wir in der Techno-Kultur vorfinden, wirken alle auf das Fleisch zurück. Durch neue Schnittstellen/Grenzen wird das Fleisch nicht mehr bloß durch Information geprägt, sondern mutiert in diesem kontinuierlichen Austauschprozeß selbst.

conductor chips, the human experience of a sense-of-self is expanded by the properties and cultural factors of the components absorbed.

There are many definitions of cyborgs, but basically, anybody could be a cyborg. Cyborgs are ... flesh, hardware, software, culture and imagination.

The cyborg detector is an installation that gives visitors an experience of the interplay of technology and human identity. The boundaries between technology and flesh are not clear-cut. Just as there is no clear definition of the boundaries of identity, there is no clear definition of cyborgs, either.

Cyborgs are prototypes of contemporary cultural identity. We intend to bring people to ask themselves how integrated technology and their sense-of-self in the information-society are in their lives.

The installation: cyborg-detector

We will *evaluate* the cyborg-degree of a person [anyone] by measuring their technological and cultural use and attitude via a metal detector and an interface questionnaire.

This does not mean that someone with a high degree of metal content is necessarily a cyborg, if they don't identify with the cultural implications of cyberculture.

Visitors will walk through a metal detecting system that measures the metal content of their bodies. Then, they will be led to a clinic office where a digitally generated *scientist* skilled in counseling cyborgs will interview them to determine their cultural attitude toward, and use of, technology and cyberculture. However, the scientist seems to lack strength of character, because s/he changes shape in an attempt to track the cyborgness of the interviewee.

Finally a database calculates the cyborg-content and the scientist tells them their cyborg degree.

But technological calculation by a machine or a determination /categorization by humanoids or cyborgs cannot realistically determine the state of a being.

The final question that the individual has to ask her/himself is: *Are you a cyborg?* which is the most important question in determining the degree of cyborg.

Die Identität des Menschen beruht nicht länger allein auf einem hauptsächlich aus Kohlenstoffverbindungen aufgebauten Körper. Durch die Kombination des aus organischen Verbindungen bestehenden Fleisches mit Vorrichtungen aus Metall und Silikon, wie beispielsweise Halbleiterchips, wird die Erfahrung des menschlichen Selbstverständnisses um die Eigenschaften und die kulturellen Faktoren der neu integrierten Komponenten erweitert.

Für Cyborgs gibt es viele verschiedene Definitionen, aber grundsätzlich könnte jeder ein Cyborg sein. Cyborgs sind ... Fleisch, Hardware, Software, Kultur und Imagination.

Der *Cyborg Detector* ist eine Installation, die den Besucher das Zusammenwirken von Technik und menschlicher Identität erleben läßt. Die Grenzen zwischen Technologie und Fleisch sind nicht eindeutig. Und so, wie es keine eindeutige Definition der Grenzen der Identität gibt, gibt es auch keine eindeutige Definition der Cyborgs.Sie sind Prototypen der modernen kulturellen Identität. Wir wollen mit unserer Installation die Menschen dazu anregen, sich selbst zu fragen, wie weit die Technologie und ihr eigenes Selbstverständnis innerhalb der Informationsgesellschaft in ihr Leben integriert sind.

Die Installation: Cyborg Detector

Wir *bestimmen* den Cyborg-Grad einer [beliebigen] Person, indem wir die Gewohnheiten und die Einstellung dieser Person in bezug auf Technologie und Kultur mit Hilfe eines Metalldetektors und eines Schnittstellen-Fragebogens ermitteln. Das bedeutet allerdings nicht, daß Personen mit einem hohen Metallgehalt unbedingt Cyborgs sind, wenn sie sich nicht mit den kulturellen Implikationen der Cyber-Kultur identifizieren. Die Besucher durchqueren ein Metalldetektorsystem, das den Metallgehalt des Körpers mißt. Danach kommen sie in einen Klinikraum, wo sie ein/e auf Cyborg-Beratung spezialisierte/r digital generierte/r *WissenschaftlerIn* über ihre kulturelle Einstellung in bezug auf Technologie und Cyber-Kultur befragt und feststellt, welchen Gebrauch sie davon machen. Dem/der WissenschaftlerIn scheint es jedoch an Charakterstärke zu fehlen, denn er bzw. sie wechselt seine Gestalt, um herauszufinden, ob sein Gegenüber tatsächlich ein Cyborg ist. Schließlich berechnet eine Daten-

The result gives them an indication of their own cyborg-activity at this moment.

If appropriate, the scientist also gives them a cyborg ID badge. This ID is a spool with a specific resonance to a sensor at the Ars Electronica Center Entrance. If the cyborg passes the entrance of the Ars Electronica Center, the sensor detects the cyborg and sets off a visual and acoustic cyborg welcome-signal. The monitor then signals: *cyborg detected*.

Non-cyborgs can go for an upgrade at a special terminal. There they can redesign their identity by downloading information and integrating a piece of hardware into their lives. Afterwards, they can go back and repeat the cyborg-test, and they may find that the virtual scientist has incorporated their hardware into his/her body as well.

The cyborg-activity at Ars Electronica Center is made accessible and visible worldwide via the Web. Tests and upgrades are only possible locally because it involves a living person. The information download for non-cyborgs is also available on the Web.

The determination of cyborg-degrees depends on the sense-of-self of an individual. Technology is so integrated in western culture and practice that it has become a subliminal influence on the reality of individuals. Subconscious immersion and techno-existence have caused the definition of a cyborg to depend on the perception of the self in this environment.

bank den Cyborg-Gehalt, und der/die WissenschaftlerIn teilt dem Untersuchten seinen Cyborg-Grad mit.

Doch technische Berechnungen durch eine Maschine oder die Klassifizierung in Humanoide und Cyborgs können den Status eines Wesens nicht realistisch bestimmen. Die letzte Frage, die der Untersuchte sich selbst stellen muß, lautet: *Bist du ein Cyborg?* Und das ist für die Ermittlung des Cyborg-Grads die wichtigste Frage überhaupt.

Das Ergebnis zeigt dem Untersuchten seine eigene gegenwärtige Cyborg-Aktivität an. Gegebenenfalls übergibt der/die WissenschaftlerIn dem Untersuchten auch eine Cyborg-Plakette. Dabei handelt es sich um eine Spule mit einer spezifischen Resonanz auf einen Sensor, der am Eingang des Ars Electronica Center angebracht ist. Wenn der Cyborg nun den Eingang des Ars Electronica Center passiert, identifiziert der Sensor den Cyborg und löst ein optisches und akustisches Cyborg-Willkommenssignal aus. Der Monitor zeigt in diesem Fall die folgende Message an: *Cyborg detected*.

Nicht-Cyborgs können sich zur Aufwertung ihres Status an ein spezielles Terminal begeben. Dort können sie ihre Identität durch Herunterladen von Informationen und Integration einer Hardwarekomponente in ihr Leben neu entwerfen.Danach können sie sich nochmals dem Cyborg-Test unterziehen. Dabei werden sie vielleicht feststellen, daß der/die virtuelle WissenschaftlerIn ihre Hardware auch in seinen/ihren Körper integriert hat.

Die Cyborg-Aktivitäten im Ars Electronica Center sind über das Web weltweit zugänglich. Tests sind allerdings nur vor Ort möglich, da hierfür die Anwesenheit der lebenden Person erforderlich ist. Die Informationen, die sich Nicht-Cyborgs herunterladen können, stehen auch im Web zur Verfügung.

Die Bestimmung des Cyborg-Grads einer Person hängt von ihrem Selbstverständnis ab. Die Technologie ist heute in einem solchen Ausmaß in die Kultur und das Leben der westlichen Welt integriert, daß sie einen unterschwelligen Einfluß auf die Realität der Menschen ausübt. Durch die unbewußte Immersion und die Techno-Existenz hängt die Definition

Bodyscan

Eva Wohlgemuth

In February 1997 I had a 3D whole-body scan created in Monterrey, California. The smallest text file of me is 1MB, so I fit on a disk; you can just about recognise ME as a wireframe, but when it's rendered there can be no doubt, IT IS ME! [I do resemble myself, but of course I'm not compelled to accept this similarity.]

So, am I more than just my dataset – as we always assumed – or has my dataset become an essential requirement for me to assert my position in cyberspace?

Bodymapping as a conjuration of identity or as a possibility of socially integrated remapping? This is the starting point for my topological experiments.

Bodyscan

Eva Wohlgemuth

Im Februar 1997 habe ich in Monterrey, Kalifornien, einen 3D-Ganzkörper-Body-Scan herstellen lassen. Als kleinstes Textfile habe ich nun 1 MB und passe somit auf eine Diskette, als Wireframe erkennt man MICH, und gerendert gibt's keinen Zweifel mehr, DAS BIN ICH! [Ich sehe mir ähnlich, aber ich bin natürlich nicht gebunden, diese Ähnlichkeit zu akzeptieren.]

Bin ICH – wie wir immer annehmen – noch immer mehr als mein Datenset, oder ist mein Datenset nun eine Grundvoraussetzung geworden, um im Cyberspace einen Platz zu behaupten? Bodymapping als Identitätsbeschwörung oder als Möglichkeit eines sozial integrativen Remapping? Hier liegt der Ausgangspunkt meiner topologischen Experimente.

Las transpiraciones del desgaste o la devaluacion aspirada

César Martínez Silva

Air is life's oldest fuel. It was the first natural source of energy, essential to life for the first aerobic creatures which inhabited Earth amidst the existential loneliness at the inception of all life; the substance of the first breath, out of which ultimately developed that which we are today. But the air is being consumed by, among others, one of the most highly developed species on this planet. And the result is that air – a resource essential to life – is now becoming increasingly scarce and ever more virtual. It almost seems as if virtuality were one of our greatest virtues. This substantial human intrusion upon the Earth in general, and the neo-apocalyptic postmodern contra-civilization of life in particular, are confronting us with enormous dangers in our transition to transmodernity. For this reason, we must develop a new, alternative technology that has fewer destructive consequences. When we travel from one place to another, for example, and if we wish to release thereby a more environmentally-friendly form of energy, the electronic media could well constitute a superior alternative to fossil fuels. Our civilization of excess and its environmental consequences have made

Las transpiraciones del desgaste o la devaluacion aspirada

César Martínez Silva

Die Luft ist der älteste Brennstoff des Lebens. Sie war die erste natürliche Energiequelle, lebensnotwendig für die ersten aeroben Wesen, die auf der Erde inmitten der existentiellen Einsamkeit am Anfang allen Lebens lebten, für die ersten Atemzüge, aus denen sich schließlich entwickelte, was wir heute sind. Doch die Luft wird verbraucht, unter anderem durch eine der am höchsten entwickelten Spezies dieses Planeten. Damit wird die Luft heute als lebensnotwendige Ressource immer knapper und auch immer virtueller. Es scheint beinahe so, als wäre die Virtualität eine unserer größten Tugenden. Diese bedeutenden menschlichen Eingriffe auf der Erde im allgemeinen und die neoapokalyptische postmoderne Kontrazivilisation des Lebens selbst bringen für uns am Übergang zur Transmoderne große Gefahren mit sich, und deshalb müssen wir eine neue, alternative Technik entwickeln, die weniger zerstörerische Auswirkungen hat. Wenn wir uns etwa von einem Ort zum anderen begeben oder eine die Umwelt weniger belastende Energie freisetzen wollen, könnten die elektronischen Medien eine bessere Alternative darstellen als die fossilen Brennstoffe.

smog an executioner which threatens our entire existence by cutting us off from the very air we breathe. We can use the term *intelligence and its deterioration* to characterize this phenomenon. The deterioration of intelligence is not only the result, but also the great paradox, of this not-so-very-farfetched nightmare – a moment in time which constitutes simultaneously a phase within a developmental trend and a climactic high point. Calling this progress is rather less accurate than referring to it as the *expansion and intensification of disorder* which is inherent in the energetic absurdity of creative intelligence plotting a blueprint for destruction and implementing a plan of life like the duration of forgetting. And in spite of our being fully aware that the process of breathing is the way we go about regulating feelings such as fear, emotional harmony and various other emotional states, stress and anxiety, as well as our very mobility, we continue to work tirelessly toward our self-asphyxiation, so that we now stand – on the threshold of a new millennium – on the verge of drawing our last breath. The irritation of the lungs and the asphyxiating air quality now longer display only gradual, long-term affects. They are no longer limited to regulating the quality of our feelings; rather, they have also come to exert control over our emotional coefficients and/or the intellectual-affective complex of life in general, such that life itself now runs the risk of dozing off at any moment and losing its way in the fog of civilization. Smog is the stuff making up an incessantly ongoing moment; it seems as if our respiratory tract would merge with the expressways, as automobile traffic transforms itself into a traffic jam within the obstructed muscles of our heart, into an endless series of micro-infarcts. Without clean air, life itself will cease to be a latent force pinning its ultimate hope on a bioenergetic possibility which offers more than the senseless dependence upon petroleum, an obsession in which life is petrified into an explosive land mine and every living thing is transformed into a living fossil. Fossil fuel will make fossils of us all.

Description

Five to 10 human balloons [i.e., balloons in the shape of human bodies] are arranged in various positions. Some of them are lying on

Unsere maßlose Zivilisation und ihre Folgen haben den Smog zu einem Henker gemacht, der unsere gesamte Existenz bedroht und uns die Luft zum Leben nimmt. Dieses Phänomen könnten wir als *die Intelligenz und ihr Verschleiß* bezeichnen. Der Verschleiß der Intelligenz ist nicht nur das Resultat, sondern auch das große Paradoxon des gar nicht so phantastischen Alptraums dieses zugleich Weiterentwicklung und Höhepunkt darstellenden Augenblicks, den wir weniger als Fortschritt, sondern vielmehr als *Verbreitung oder Ausweitung der Unordnung* bezeichnen könnten und der in dem energetischen Absurdum der kreativen Intelligenz besteht, die Zerstörung zu planen und die Planung des Lebens anzulegen wie die Dauer des Vergessens.

Und obgleich wir wissen, daß wir durch die Atmung Gefühle wie Furcht, Ausgeglichenheit, verschiedene Gemütszustände, Streß und Ängste, aber auch unsere Bewegungsfähigkeit regulieren, arbeiten wir weiter beharrlich darauf hin, uns selbst zu ersticken, und stehen an der Schwelle zu einem neuen Jahrtausend knapp vor unserem letzten Atemzug. Die Reizung der Lunge und die erstickende Luftqualität wirken sich nicht mehr nur langsam aus. Sie beschränken sich nicht mehr darauf, die Qualität unserer Gefühle zu regulieren, sondern sie steuern inzwischen auch unseren emotionalen Koeffizienten bzw. den intellektuell-affektiven Komplex des Lebens im allgemeinen, denn das Leben läuft Gefahr, jeden Augenblick einzuschlafen und sich im Nebel der Zivilisation zu verirren: Der Smog ist Sache eines fortwährenden Augenblicks, und es scheint so, als würden unsere Atemwege mit den Schnellstraßen verschmelzen und der Automobilverkehr sich in ein Stocken der Herzmuskeltätigkeit, in eine endlose Reihe von Mikroinfarkten verwandeln. Ohne saubere Luft wird das Leben aufhören, eine latente Kraft zu sein, die letzten Endes auf eine bioenergetische Möglichkeit hofft, die mehr bietet als den sinnlosen Zusammenhang der Erdölbesessenheit, die das Leben zu einer explosiven Mine versteinert und alles in lebende Fossilien verwandelt: Der fossile Brennstoff wird uns alle zu Fossilien machen.

the ground, others along a wall, others are seated. The natural-looking and life-size human figures are replicas of actual human models, whereby the most minute details – down to the fingerprints, pores, the consistency of the skin, etc. – have been reproduced to the greatest extent possible. The balloons are made of expandable rubber latex; they have been given a wide range of colors and forms, from black surfaces to those treated to resemble clouds. The figures are connected to one another at various parts of the body: the anus, the mouth, the navel or the nose. Plastic tubes such as those used in hospitals for artificial respiration connect the balloons to air pistols or hair dryers which are controlled by electronic timing devices. These timers regulate the injection and ejection of air at intervals of approximately 30 seconds. Through this process of deformation of the human form, these deflated and collapsed sculptures generate a dramatic ongoing discourse. These figurative and highly significant remnants of human forms are meant to urge the viewer to analyze their meaning.

Beschreibung

Fünf bis zehn menschliche Ballons, d. h. Ballons in Form menschlicher Körper, sind in unterschiedlichen Positionen angeordnet. Einige von ihnen liegen auf dem Boden, andere auf einer Mauer, und wieder andere sitzen. Die menschlichen Figuren sind natur- und maßstabsgetreu lebenden Modellen nachgebildet, die bis in die kleinsten Details, bis zu Fingerabdrücken, den Poren, der Struktur der Haut etc. so gut wie möglich wiedergegeben wurden. Die Ballons bestehen aus dehnbarem Kautschuk in den verschiedensten Farben und Formen, von schwarz bis hin zu Oberflächen, die wie Wolken gearbeitet sind. Die Figuren sind teils über den After, teils über den Mund und teils auch über Nabel oder Nase miteinander verbunden. Plastikschläuche der Art, wie sie in Krankenhäusern zur künstlichen Beatmung eingesetzt werden, verbinden die Ballons mit Luftdruckpistolen oder Haarföns, die von elektronischen Zeitschaltern gesteuert werden. Diese Zeitschalter regeln die Luftzufuhr und den Luftausstoß in Intervallen von etwa 30 Sekunden. Durch die Deformierung der menschlichen Gestalt generieren die luftleeren, zusammengesunkenen Skulpturen einen fortlaufenden dramatischen Diskurs. Diese figurativen und bedeutungsschweren Überbleibsel menschlicher Formen sollen den Betrachter dazu auffordern, ihre Bedeutung zu hinterfragen.

Kage

Motoshi Chikamori

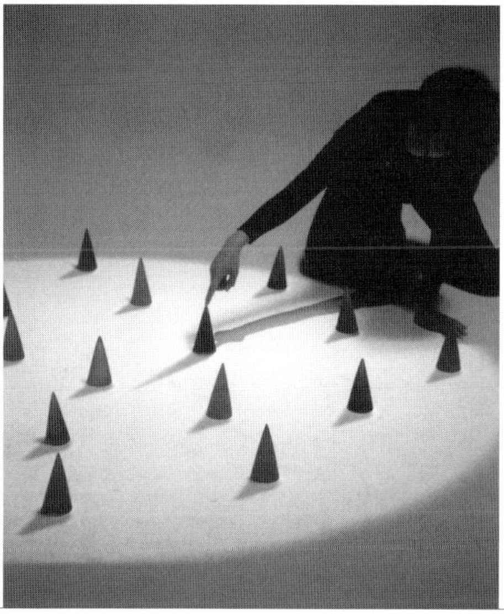

Since older times, shadows have proved existence [a ghost, for example, has no shadow]. However, like the image projected on the TV monitor, the shadow itself doesn't have substance.

In this *Kage* [a Japanese word meaning shadow, silhouette, reflection, shade and image], I took notice of this shadow-substance characteristic and by using a cone-shaped object, I created its shadow with computer graphics.

The computerized shadows projected down toward the floor remain still, like all shadows do, but when some objects which are placed on the floor are directly touched, various kinds of patterns will appear on computerized shadow images. If the viewer touches another object, all the shadows disperse at once, or turn all sorts of colors.

While these things are happening, the viewer is always illuminated by the projector from the ceiling, so that the shadow of the viewer himself is also projected on the floor as well as the computerized shadows. When the false shadow, created by the computer graphics, and his own real shadow are both projected on the same plane picture, the viewer recognizes his shadow and his existence once again.

installations

Kage

Motoshi Chikamori

Seit altersher gilt der Schatten als Beweis für die Existenz [Gespenster haben zum Beispiel keinen Schatten]. Doch ebenso wie das auf den Fernsehschirm projizierte Bild ist auch der Schatten substanzlos.

In *Kage* [ein japanisches Wort mit der Bedeutung Schatten, Silhouette, Spiegelung, Schattierung und Bild] gehe ich auf diese Eigenart des Schattens und seiner Substanz ein, indem ich mittels Computergrafik den Schatten eines kegelförmigen Objektes generiere.

Wie alle Schatten bleiben auch die auf den Boden projizierten Computerschatten unbeweglich. Aber durch direkte Berührung von am Boden verteilten Objekten entstehen auf dem Computerschattenbild verschiedenste Muster. Berührt der Besucher ein anderes Objekt, lösen sich alle Schatten sofort auf oder verwandeln sich in eine Vielzahl verschiedener Farben.

Währenddessen steht der Besucher ständig im Lichtstrahl des Projektors an der Decke, so daß zusätzlich zu den Computerschatten auch der Schatten des Besuchers auf den Boden projiziert wird. Wenn der falsche, computergenerierte Schatten auf derselben Bildfläche mit seinem echten Schatten zusammentrifft, wird der Besucher einmal mehr seines Schattens und damit seiner Existenz gewahr.

Pinocchio – Die virtuelle Marionette

Wolfgang Hilbert

Pinocchio – die virtuelle Marionette is an interactive computer sculpture which enables the user to assume the role of a puppeteer and maneuver a virtual figure. Installation users actually operate a cross-shaped hand piece which controls the strings leading to a virtual figure located in a stage area. Through a process of experimentation, the user can discover how to precisely control the motions of the virtual marionette in real time by manipulating the hand piece. This seemingly absolute human control over a piece of technology, however, soon turns out to be a fallacy. After a certain amount of time has elapsed, the user comes to realize that the marionette has begun to act independently and no longer reacts to user commands. It breaks away from the user and disappears from the monitor screen. The spatial realm of virtual action breaks down to a black screen and thus completely dissolves. All that remains is the user – alone in real space, holding a manipulation device that has become useless. At some randomly-determined point in time, the marionette reappears on the edge of the monitor screen, steps forward and abdicates independent action. The user thus reassumes control over the marionette and the spatial realm of virtual action.

Pinocchio – Die virtuelle Marionette

Wolfgang Hilbert

Pinocchio – Die virtuelle Marionette ist eine interaktive Computerskulptur, bei der der Benutzer in die Rolle eines Puppenspielers schlüpft und eine virtuelle Figur bewegen kann. Von einem realen Marionettenkreuz, das der Benutzer der Installation bedienen kann, führen Schnüre zum Bühnenraum, auf der sich eine virtuelle Figur befindet. Der Akteur der Installation kann experimentell herausfinden, wie er durch Bewegung des Marionettenkreuzes die virtuelle Marionette in Echtzeit präzise in ihren Bewegungen steuern kann. Diese scheinbar absolute Kontrolle über die Technik durch den Menschen stellt sich aber bald als Trugschluß heraus. Nach einer unvorhersehbaren Zeitspanne muß der Benutzer feststellen, daß sich die Marionette selbständig macht und nicht mehr auf seine Befehle reagiert. Sie wendet sich vom Benutzer ab und verschwindet vom Bildschirm. Der virtuelle Aktionsraum verkommt zur schwarzen Mattscheibe und löst sich dadurch auf. Der Benutzer bleibt im realen Raum alleine mit seinem nutzlos gewordenen Steuerungswerkzeug zurück. Erst zu einem vom Zufall bestimmten Zeitpunkt taucht die Marionette am Bildschirmrand wieder auf, wandert nach vorne und legt ihre Eigenständigkeit ab. Der Benutzer erhält somit erneut die Kontrolle über die Marionette und den virtuellen Aktionsraum zurück.

Corps et Graphie

Marie-Hélène Tramus

This installation suggests that the viewer become a choreographer, who creates with several simplified computer-generated dancers a kind of living organism which is able to move around in real time. Actually his creation has to do with an imaginary choreography, which consists of creating a sort of plant-like animated organism. The rounded and flexible moves of the dancers present the imaginary idea of a body which is able to be metamorphosed into a plant-like, tree-like, flower-like body and so on.

The dancers' movements are not realistic since they go beyond the physical possibilities of a real body by performing imaginary movements that cannot be reproduced in the real world. They suggest, just as Oskar Schlemmer wrote in *Mechanisches Ballett,* *carrying out unconstrained imaginary shapes with unlimited variations*.

Software Anyflo by Michel Bret

Corps et Graphie

Marie-Hélène Tramus

Die Installation lädt den Betrachter ein, als Choreograph mit vereinfachten computergenerierten TänzerInnen eine Art lebenden Organismus zu kreieren, der sich in Echtzeit bewegen kann. Eigentlich orientiert sich diese Kreation an einer imaginären Choreographie, in der es um die Erschaffung eines pflanzenähnlichen, belebten Organismus geht. Die abgerundeten, flexiblen Bewegungen der TänzerInnen repräsentieren die imaginäre Vorstellung von einem Körper, der sich in pflanzen-, baum- und blumenähnliche Körper etc. verwandeln kann. Die Bewegungen der TänzerInnen sind nicht realistisch, da sie über die physischen Möglichkeiten echter Körper hinausgehen und imaginäre Bewegungen vollführen, die in der echten Welt nicht reproduziert werden können. Wie schon Oskar Schlemmer in *Mechanisches Ballett* schreibt, vollführen sie *uneingeschränkte imaginäre Formen in unbegrenzten Variationen*.

Software Anyflo von Michael Bret

Der Teddyautomat

Uli Winters/Christoph Ebener

At first glance, the *Teddyautomat*, the teddy bear slot machine, resembles the familiar video games commonly found in arcades and bars. Behind a glass partition, a classic stuffed toy bear sits in a steel chamber with moveable side walls. After depositing a coin, the user has the choice of pushing one of two illuminated buttons – either*Teddy gets squashed* or*Teddy is spared.* The number of the respective choices made thus far is displayed on a counter below each button. A round of voting lasts 10 minutes; the time still remaining until the ballots are counted and the winning result is carried out is displayed on a countdown clock. In addition, one minute before time is up, potential voters are issued a shrill warning to*place your bets* *[Faites vos jeux!]*. If the vote comes out in Teddy's favor, nothing happens; if the majority decides that*Teddy gets squashed,* the toy bear is turned to face the spike-covered walls and is slowly impaled and crushed.

Der Teddyautomat

Uli Winters/Christoph Ebener

Der *Teddyautomat* ähnelt auf dem ersten Blick den bekannten Videospielautomaten, wie sie in Spielhallen oder Kneipen stehen. Hinter der Glasscheibe sitzt ein klassischer Stoffteddy in einer Stahlkammer mit beweglichen Seitenwänden. Der Benutzer hat nach Einwerfen einer Münze die Wahl, auf einen der beiden erleuchteten Knöpfe zu drücken – entweder *Teddy quetschen* oder *Teddy wird verschont*. Die bisher abgegebenen Stimmen werden durch Zählwerke unter den Knöpfen angezeigt. Ein Abstimmungsgang dauert zehn Minuten, die noch verbleibende Zeit bis zur Auswertung und Umsetzung des Abstimmungsergebnisses wird durch die abwärtslaufende Uhr angezeigt, zusätzlich fordert eine Minute vor Abstimmungsende ein schriller Warnton zum **Faites vos jeux** auf. Fällt die Abstimmung zugunsten des Teddys aus, passiert nichts, hat sich die Mehrzahl der Abstimmenden für *Teddy quetschen* entschieden, wird der Teddy mit dem Gesicht zur Wand gedreht und von den mit Nägeln versehenen Wänden langsam gequetscht und durchlöchert.

Kybermax
und Moritz

Markus Brandt

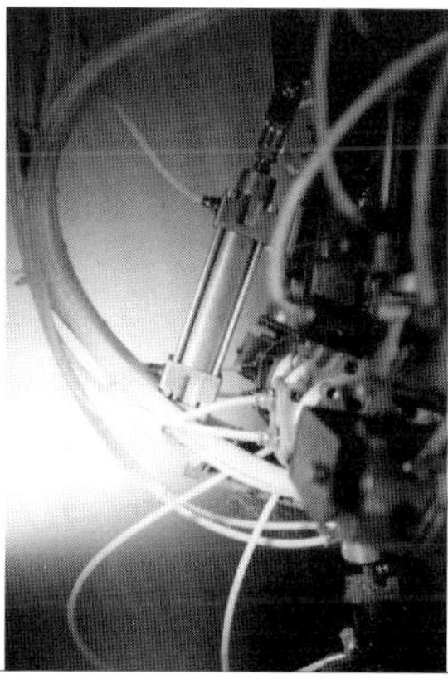

Max and Moritz are two identical human-form cybernetic sculptures built on steel frames. They are 210 cm tall and can move like humans from the hips up. They are driven by compressed-air cylinders and controlled by computers. Three persons control one sculpture through the Internet. Two are responsible for moving the arms and one for the body axis. Provided that communication works, six people can make Max and Moritz act together.

Max is in Vienna while Moritz is travelling through Europe. At the beginning they are both in Berlin, but then move to Vienna where they are separated. In Linz the two of them are starting off as a pair in the net.

The cybernetic situation is transferred to the real-world locations of the sculptures. In addition, Max transmits his impressions of his current surroundings into the net. Moritz waits for invitations from the net so he can send experiences to his stationary brother.

A project by BRANDT
Martin Reiter, tø public netbase
Markus Diess, Michael Wieser
Sponsored by Norgren Pneumatik, Tacheles Berlin, tø Vienna, Wavesound Salzburg, Ars Electronica, EuNet, PING, Office of the Federal Chancellor, Salzburg provincial and municipal authorities, Foreign Office

installations

Kybermax
und Moritz

Markus Brandt

Max und Moritz sind zwei idente, auf Stahlskeletten aufgebaute Bewegungsskulpturen von menschlicher Gestalt, 210 cm groß und ab der Hüfte aufwärts beweglich wie ein Mensch. Sie werden von Druckluftzylindern angetrieben und von Computern kontrolliert.

Drei Personen steuern jeweils über das Internet eine Skulptur. Zwei sind für die Bewegungen der Arme verantwortlich, eine für die Körperachse zuständig. Sechs Personen können – vernünftige Kommunikation vorausgesetzt – Max und Moritz gemeinsam agieren lassen.

Max steht in Wien, während sich Moritz auf einer Reise durch Europa befindet. zuerst sind beide noch in Berlin, ziehen dann nach Wien und werden dann getrennt. In Linz starten sie beide als Paar im Netz.

Die kybernetische Situation wird an die realen Standorte der Skulpturen übertragen. Moritz sendet außerdem seine Eindrücke der jeweiligen Umgebung ins Netz. Moritz wartet auf Einladungen aus dem Netz, um seinem stationären Bruder Erfahrungen zukommen zu lassen.

Ein Projekt von BRANDT
Martin Reiter, tø public netbase
Markus Diess, Michael Wieser
Unterstützt durch Norgren Pneumatik, Tacheles Berlin, tø Wien, Wavesound Salzburg, Ars Electronica, EuNet, PING, Bundeskanzleramt, Land und Stadt Salzburg, Außenministerium

Laterna Magica – Electronic Street Art

Leonid Filatov/Joachim Eckl

The street lamp is a form of technology that – outside, under the stars – sheds light into the darkness of night. Light, in all its qualities, plays an essential role in human life. Here, we are primarily interested in the phenomenon of illumination. At the moment human beings learned to make fire, the era of artificial illumination began. The development of street lighting has brought with it more powerful social side effects than any other technological innovation. It has provided mankind with additional hours for outdoor activities, expanded social life in public spaces into the night, and, thus, changed human behavior.

The discovery of this new level of our physical environment – so familiar to us by day – would have been impossible without the street lamp. The social effects and behavioral changes brought about by the TV set's arrival in the living room have frequently been addressed. Analogies and parallels to the campfire of the cavemen have been drawn, but almost everyone seems to have forgotten about the psychological significance that the street lamp has for us humans.

Laterna Magica – Electronic Street Art

Leonid Filatov/Joachim Eckl

Die Straßenlaterne ist Technologie , die unter freiem Himmel Licht ins Dunkel der Nacht bringt. Licht spielt – in all seinen Qualitäten – eine essentielle Rolle im Leben der Menschen. Wir sind hier vor allem am Phänomen der Beleuchtung interessiert. Ab dem Zeitpunkt, an dem die Menschen gelernt haben, Feuer zu machen, hat die Ära der künstlichen Beleuchtung begonnen. Die Entwicklung der Straßenbeleuchtung hat stärkere soziale Nebeneffekte mit sich gebracht als irgendeine andere technologische Innovation. Sie hat den Menschen zusätzliche Stunden für Aktivitäten

Another factor which has provided us with the inspiration to use the street lamp as a instrument for electronic street art is its inconspicuous appearance. It is a common object of everyday life. The *Laterna Magica* – like every normal street lamp – lights up its surroundings at night. But we have expanded the functional mechanism of this source of illumination by one decisive dimension by building a video projector into it. When a passer-by enters the cone of light given off by the lamp, he/she is picked up by a motion detector and thereby activates the projector. Images are then projected onto the street, with the street lamp continuing to provide illumination. Passers-by now find themselves, as it were, on the inside of a video monitor screen. Upon exiting the motion detector's range, only the projection disappears and the normal street lighting remains on.

The projection itself can be anything: pictures from an exhibition, a film, text messages, and – via computer with Internet access – all images which the Internet makes available. Moreover, the Internet serves as a transmitter for live images originating from anywhere in the world. With *Laterna Magica*, the street lamp becomes a new web interface.

We are interested in two aspects of this process of superimposing disparate strata of reality: the free access for all to information from the Internet, and the possibility of free expression – without intervention and adaptation – in public spaces. Thus, *Laterna Magica* is potentially a tool for those seeking to express themselves via computer in public spaces and all who wish to find a new quality of the imagination.

unter freiem Himmel eröffnet, das soziale Leben im öffentlichen Raum in die Nacht hinein ausgedehnt und so das Verhalten der Menschen verändert. Die Entdeckung dieser neuen Ebene der am Tag vertrauten physischen Umwelt wäre ohne Straßenlaterne nicht möglich. Oft werden die sozialen Effekte und Veränderungen im Verhalten angesprochen, die der Einzug des Fernsehers in die Wohnzimmer bewirkt hat. Analogien und Parallelen zum Lagerfeuer der Höhlenmenschen werden gezogen. Die psychologische Bedeutung, die die Straßenlaterne auf uns Menschen hat, scheint von fast allen vergessen worden zu sein.

Ihre unauffällige Erscheinung hat uns die Verwendung der Straßenlaterne als Werkzeug für elektronische Straßenkunst nahegelegt. Als Objekt ist sie gewohnter Alltag. Die *Laterna Magica* erhellt – wie jede normale Straßenlaterne – bei Nacht ihre Umgebung. Wir erweitern jedoch den Funktionsmechanismus des Beleuchtungskörpers um eine entscheidende Dimension, indem wir ihm einen Video-Projektor einbauen. Betritt ein Passant den Lichtkegel der eingeschalteten Laterne, so aktiviert er/sie mittels Bewegungsmelder den Projektor. Nun werden Bilder auf die Straße projiziert, wobei die Beleuchtungsfunktion der Straßenlaterne gewahrt bleibt. Der Passant befindet sich jetzt quasi auf der Innenseite eines Monitor-Bildschirms. Verläßt er die entsprechende Zone, verschwindet lediglich die Projektion, und die einfache Straßenbeleuchtung bleibt zurück.

Die Projektion selbst kann alles sein. Bilder einer Ausstellung, ein Film, Textbotschaften und – über einen Computer ans Internet angedockt – alle Bildquellen, die das Netz bietet. Das Internet dient darüber hinaus als Transmitter für Live-Bilder, von wo auch immer am Globus. Mit *Laterna Magica* wird die Straßenlaterne zu einem neuen Interface für das Web.

Bei der Überlagerung dieser unterschiedlichen Schichten von Wirklichkeit interessieren uns zwei Aspekte: Der freie Zugang zu Informationen aus dem Internet für alle und die Möglichkeit des freien Ausdrucks – ohne Eingriffe und Bearbeitung – im öffentlichen Raum. Die *Laterna Magica* ist also potentielles Werkzeug für alle, die im öffentlichen Raum via Computer Ausdruck und eine neue Qualität der Imagination finden wollen.

The Levi-Montalcini Variations ▶

Maryanne Amacher

With VR [Virtual Reality], 3D sonic imaging and graphics, telepresence, and cyberspace as a point of departure, the work examines possibilities of individualizing multi-dimensional sonic environments for listeners and for spaces. Immersive *aural architectures* are constructed, addressing new concepts of experience design – an approach to auditory communication with sonic perceptual information being processed by the listener, in addition to acoustically produced sonic information.

Ausgehend von Virtueller Realität [VR], 3D-Klangbildern und -Graphik, Telepräsenz und Cyberspace untersucht das Werk die Möglichkeiten, eine multidimensionale Klangumgebung für Zuhörer und Räume zu individualisieren. Eine alles umhüllende *aurale Architektur* wird konstruiert, die neue Konzepte des Erfahrungsdesigns anspricht, ein Ansatz zur auditorischen Komposition als *Geographie der Wahrnehmung*. Ein intelligentes Interface wird mit der vom Hörer verarbeiteten Klangwahrnehmungsinformation ebenso kommunizieren, sie verstärken und auf sie reagieren wie auf die akustisch produzierte Klanginformation.

Unsound Objects ▶

Jonty Harrison

In *Unsound Objects*, the sounds used are all from the *real world* – recordings of actual sonic events which have undergone varying degrees of computer modification. The work operates on three levels. The first addresses what Denis Smalley has called *spectro-morphology* which is the closest to what we understand in the West as *music*.

The second is related to *soundscape*. The third level of the discourse is precisely the points of interconnection [collision, friction, impact, interpenetration?] of these two apparently contradictory worlds; it is concerned with the recontextualisation of recognisable sounds and the *meanings* released by this process.

In *Unsound Objects* stammen alle verwendeten Klänge aus der *realen Welt* – Aufnahmen von tatsächlichen Klangereignissen, die unterschiedlichen Graden der Bearbeitung mittels Computer unterworfen wurden. Das Werk operiert auf drei Ebenen. Die erste spricht das an, was Denis Smalley die *Spektro-Morphologie* genannt hat, die noch am ehesten das beschreibt, was in der westlichen Kultur als *Musik* verstanden wird. Die zweite Ebene bezieht sich auf den Begriff *Soundscape*. Die dritte Diskursebene umfaßt genau jene Verbindungs-[oder Kollisions-, Reibungs-, Aufschlags-, Durchdringungs-?]-Punkte dieser scheinbar gegensätzlichen Welten, sie beschäftigt sich mit der Re-Kontextualisierung erkennbarer Klänge und mit den *Bedeutungen*, die von diesen ausgelöst werden.

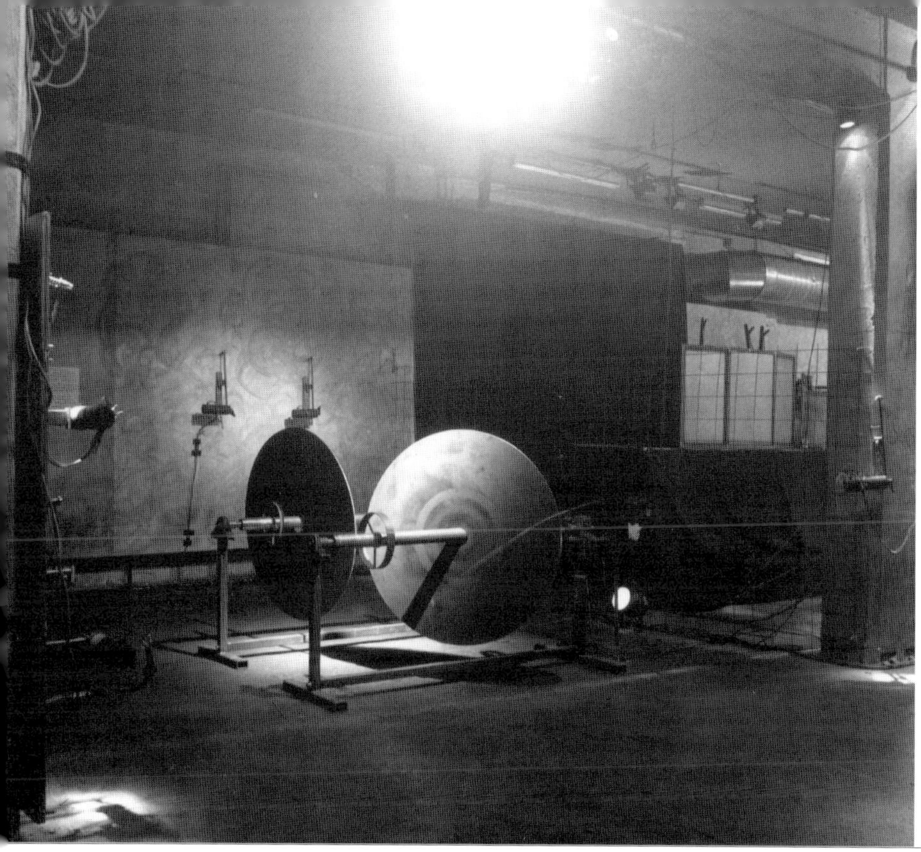

Matt Heckert,
Rings of Saturn

Munich Samba ▶

Matt Heckert

▶

You will find a detailed description of the projects in the Prix Ars Electronica 97 book **Cyberarts** *International Compendium Prix Ars Electronica, SpringerWienNewYork 1997.*

Eine ausführliche Beschreibung der Projekte finden Sie im Buch zum Prix Ars Electronica 97 **Cyberarts** *International Compendium Prix Ars Electronica, SpringerWienNewYork 1997.*

The criterion for this project was to build machines that were *playable*. Continuous controllers are used to vary motor speeds and sound events are used for switching transistors, and it is this information that is recorded by the software. Once recorded and stored as a sequence or sub-sequence, any series of control commands can be used at any time. When called up over the computer keyboard, control information is sent out instantly and the system responds much like any MIDI controlled electronic instrument, but the big difference is the inertial delay encountered when rousing a machine out of its rest ...

Das Kriterium für dieses Projekt war, Maschinen zu erzeugen, die *spielbar* waren. Stufenlose Regler werden zur Einstellung der Motorgeschwindigkeiten verwendet, *Notenereignisse* schalten die Transistoren, und diese Information wird dann von der Software aufgezeichnet. Ist sie einmal als Sequenz oder Sub-Sequenz gespeichert, kann jederzeit jede beliebige Serie von Steuerbefehlen abgerufen werden. Wird sie über die Tastatur aufgerufen, wird diese Steuerinformation sofort abgesandt, und das System regiert darauf [fast] wie jedes andere MIDI-gesteuerte Instrument. Der große Unterschied liegt in der Anfangsträgheit, die merkbar wird, wenn eine Maschine aus ihrer Ruhe gerissen wird ...

World Skin

A Photographic Safari into the Land of War

Maurice Benayoun/
Jean-Baptiste Barrière

Armed with cameras, we are making our way through a three-dimensional space. The landscape before our eyes is scarred by war – demolished buildings, armed men, tanks and artillery, piles of rubble, the wounded and the maimed. This arrangement of photographs and news pictures from different zones and theaters of war depicts a universe filled with mute violence. The audio reproduces the sound of a world in which to breathe is to suffer. Special effects? Hardly. We, the visitors, feel as though our presence could disturb this chaotic equilibrium, but it is precisely our intervention that stirs up the pain. We are taking pictures; and here, photography is a weapon of extinguishment.

The land of war has no borders. Like so many tourists, we are visiting it with camera in hand. Each of us can take pictures, capture a moment of this world wrestling with death. The image thus recorded exists for no one any more. Each photographed fragment disappears from the screen and is replaced by a black silhouette. With each click of the shutter, a part of the world is extinguished. Each exposure is printed out. As soon as an image is printed to

CAVE

World Skin

Eine Fotosafari ins Land des Kriegs

Maurice Benayoun/
Jean-Baptiste Barrière

paper, it is no longer visible on the projection screen. All that remains is its eerie shadow, cast according to the viewer's perspective and concealing fragments of future photographs. The farther we penetrate into this universe, the more strongly aware we become of its infinite nature. And the chaotic elements renew themselves, so that as soon as we recognize them, they recompose themselves once again in a tragedy without end.

I take pictures. Through what I do – first aggression, then feeling the pleasure of sharing – I rip the skin off the body of the world. This skin becomes a trophy, and my fame grows with the disappearance of the world.

Here, being engulfed by war is an immersion into a picture, but it is a theatrical performance as well. In the sequence of events which characterize the story of a single person, war is an exceptional incident which reveals humanity's deepest abyss. It promotes the process of reification of another human being. Taking pictures expropriates the intimacy of the pain while, at the same time, bearing witness to it.

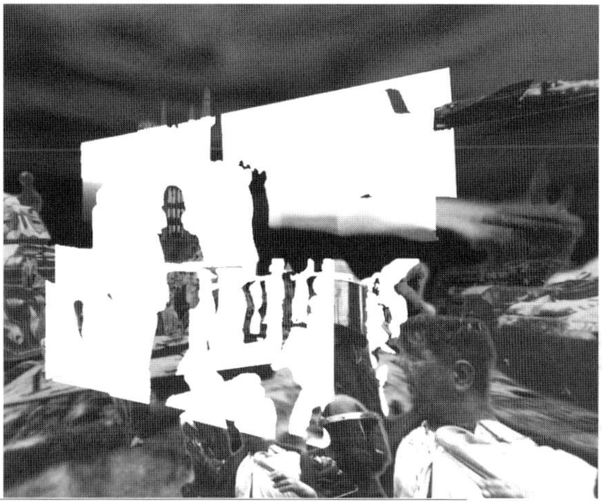

CAVE

Mit Fotoapparaten bewaffnet bewegen wir uns durch einen dreidimensionalen Raum. Die Landschaft vor unseren Augen ist vom Krieg gezeichnet. Zerstörte Gebäude, bewaffnete Männer, Panzer, Kanonen, Trümmerhaufen, Verwundete, Verstümmelte. Diese Zusammenstellung von Fotos und Nachrichtenbildern von verschiedenen Kriegsschauplätzen stellt ein von stummer Gewalt erfülltes Universum dar. Der Sound gibt den Ton einer Welt wieder, in der Atmen gleichbedeutend mit Leiden ist. Kaum Effekte. Man fühlt, daß unsere Anwesenheit als Besucher dieses chaotische Gleichgewicht stören könnte. Doch gerade unser Eingreifen wird den Schmerz wachrütteln. Wir fotografieren, und das Fotografieren ist hier eine Waffe der Auslöschung.

Das Land des Kriegs hat keine Grenzen. Wie so viele Touristen besuchen wir es mit der Kamera in der Hand. Jeder kann Bilder aufnehmen, einen Augenblick dieser mit dem Tode ringenden Welt einfangen. Was er aufnimmt, existiert für niemanden mehr. Jedes fotografierte Fragment verschwindet von der Bildfläche und wird durch eine schwarze Silhouette ersetzt. Mit jeder Aufnahme wird ein Teil der Welt ausgelöscht. Jedes aufgenommene Bild wird ausgedruckt. Sobald ein Bild auf Papier ausgedruckt ist, ist es auf dem Projektionsschirm nicht mehr zu sehen. Zurück bleibt nur sein gespenstischer Schatten, der je nach Blickwinkel verteilt ist und Fragmente zukünftiger Fotografien verdeckt. Je weiter wir in dieses Universum vordringen, umso stärker wird uns sein unendlicher Charakter bewußt, und die chaotischen Elemente erneuern sich, sobald wir sie wiederentdecken, setzen sich in einer Tragödie ohne Ende wieder anders zusammen.

Ich fotografiere. Durch meine Handlung – zuerst Aggression, dann das Vergnügen des Teilens – reiße ich der Welt die Haut vom Leibe. Diese Haut wird zu einer Trophäe, und mein Ruhm wächst mit dem Verschwinden der Welt.

Das Eintauchen in den Krieg ist hier ein Eintauchen in das Bild, aber auch ein Schauspiel. In der Ordnung der Ereignisse, die die persönliche Geschichte charakterisieren, ist der Krieg ein besonderer Vorfall, der die tiefsten Abgründe der Menschheit enthüllt. Er trägt zur Verdinglichung des anderen bei. Das Aufnehmen der Bilder enteignet die Intimität des Schmerzes und legt zugleich Zeugnis von ihm ab.

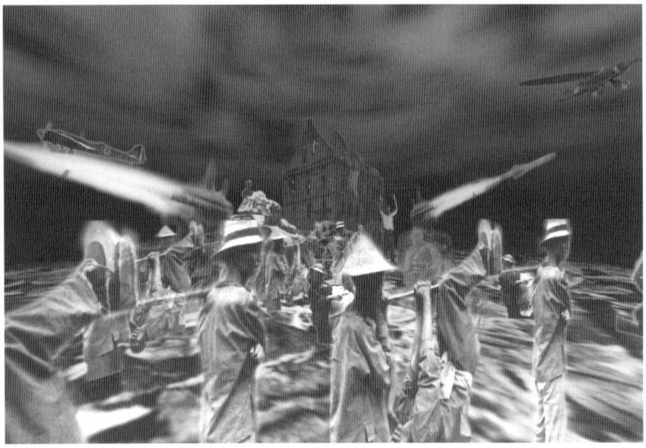

This has to do with the status of the image in our process of getting a grasp on this world. The rawest and most brutal realities are reduced to an emotional superficiality in our perception. Acquisition, evaluation and understanding of the world constitute a process of capturing it. Capturing means making something one's own; and once it is in one's possession, that thing can no longer be taken by another.

In German, one says *schießen,* *nehmen;* in French, *prise de vues.* Shooting, taking. In the case of a material storage medium, *taking* something is the equivalent of taking it with you. Photography captures the light reflected by the world. It constitutes an individual process of capturing and arranging. The image is adapted to the viewfinder.

The picture neutralizes the content. Media bring everything onto one and the same level. Physical memory – paper, for example – is the door that remains open to a certain kind of forgetting. We interpose the lens [Objektiv in German] between ourselves and the world. We safeguard ourselves from the responsibility of acting. One *takes* the picture, and the world *proffers* itself as a theatrical event. The world and the destruction constitute the preferred stage for this drama – tragedy as a play of nature in action.

The living are the tourists of death. If art is a serious game, then so is war. War is a game in which the body is placed at risk as an incessantly, unremittingly posed question of the reduction of existence to its bare remains.

Worum es hier geht, ist der Stellenwert des Bildes bei unserer Inbesitznahme der Welt. Die ungeschminktesten und brutalsten Realitäten werden in unserer Wahrnehmung auf eine emotionale Oberfläche reduziert. Die Aneignung, die Bewertung, das Verständnis der Welt stellen ein Einfangen dar. Einfangen bedeutet, sich etwas zu eigen zu machen, und was einmal in Besitz genommen wurde, kann niemand mehr nehmen.

Im Englischen sagt man: *shot*, *shooting*, im Französischen *prise de vues*. Schießen/Nehmen. Bei einem materiellen Träger kommt das *Nehmen* einem Mitnehmen gleich. Die Fotografie fängt das von der Welt reflektierte Licht ein. Sie stellt ein individuelles Einfangen und Ordnen dar. Das Bild wird dem Sucher angepaßt.

Das Bild neutralisiert den Inhalt. Die Medien bringen alles auf ein und dieselbe Ebene. Das physische Gedächtnis, das Papier [beispielsweise], ist die Tür, die einer gewissen Art von Vergessen offensteht. Wir stellen das *Objektiv* zwischen uns und die Welt. Wir schützen uns vor der Verpflichtung zum Handeln.

Man *nimmt* das Bild auf, und die Welt *bietet* sich als Schauspiel dar. Die Welt und die Zerstörung stellen die bevorzugte Bühne für dieses Theater dar. Die Tragödie als Schauspiel der Natur in Aktion.

Die Lebenden sind die Touristen des Todes.

Wenn die Kunst ein ernstes Spiel ist, so trifft dies auch auf den Krieg zu. Der Krieg ist ein Spiel, das den Körper als unendlich wiederholte Frage nach der Reduktion des Seins auf seine bloße Hülle einsetzt.

Die gedruckte Spur ist das Pendant zum Vergessen. Das *gute Gewissen* steht im Widerspruch zum *guten Gedächtnis*. Man weiß, was man behält, doch man weiß nicht, was man aus seinem Gedächtnis streicht. Der Zuschauer/Tourist trägt hier zu einer Verstärkung der tragischen Dimension des Schauspiels bei. Ohne ihn bliebe diese Welt ihrem Schmerz überlassen. Er rüttelt diesen Schmerz wach, enthüllt ihn. Durch die Medien wird der Krieg zu einer öffentlichen Bühne – in dem Sinne, in dem man von einer *öffentlichen Frau* spricht – und auf dieser obszönen Bühne gibt sich der Schmerz zu erkennen, wird jeder mit Haut und Haar verschlungen.

The printed trace is the counterpart of forgetting. A *good conscience* is a contradiction of a *good memory.* One knows what one has retained, but one does not know what one has stricken from one's memory.

Here, the viewer/tourist contributes to an amplification of the tragic dimension of the drama. Without him, this world is forsaken, left to its pain. He jostles this pain awake, exposes it. Through the media, war becomes a public stage – in the sense in which a whore might be referred to as a *public woman* – and pain reveals its true identity on this obscene stage, and all are completely devoured. The sight of the wounded calls to mind the image of a human being as a construct which can be dismantled. Material, more or less. The logic of the material holds the upper hand over the logic of the spirit, the endangered connective tissue of the social fabric.

War is a dangerous, interactive community undertaking. Interactive creation plays with this chaos, in which placing the body at stake suggests a relative vulnerability. The world falls victim to the viewer's glance, and everyone is involved in its disappearance. The collective unveiling becomes a personal pleasure, the object of fetischistic satisfaction. I keep to myself what I have seen [or rather, the traces of what I have seen]. To possess a printed vestige, to possess the image – inherent in this is the paradox of the virtual, which is better suited to the glorification of the ephemeral. The sound track is there to enable us to go beyond the play of images and to experience this immersion as real participation in the drama. In sharp contrast to the video games that transform us into passionate warriors, here the audio unmasks the true nature of apparently harmless gestures and seeks to provide a form of experience rather than a form of comprehension. Some things cannot be shared. Among them are the pain and the image of our remembrance. The worlds to be explored here can bring these things closer to us – but always simply as metaphors, never as a simulacrum.

Software-Development:
Patrick Bouchand, Tristan Lorach
David Nahon, Z.A Production
Silicon Graphics Europe

Der Anblick des Verwundeten ruft uns das Bild des Menschen als zerlegbares Gebilde ins Gedächtnis. Mehr oder weniger Materie. Die Logik der Materie behält die Oberhand über die Logik des Geistes, das bedrohte Bindemittel der sozialen Gefüge.

Der Krieg ist ein gefährliches interaktives Gemeinschaftswerk. Die interaktive Schöpfung spielt mit diesem Chaos, in dem der Einsatz des Körpers eine relative Verwundbarkeit nahelegt. Die Welt fällt dem Blick zum Opfer, und jeder ist an ihrem Verschwinden beteiligt. Die kollektive Enthüllung wird zum persönlichen Vergnügen, zum Objekt einer fetischistischen Befriedigung. Ich behalte für mich, was ich gesehen habe [bzw. die Spuren dessen, was ich gesehen habe]. Eine gedruckte Spur zu besitzen, das Bild zu besitzen – darin besteht das Paradoxon des Virtuellen, das sich besser an die Glorifizierung des Vergänglichen anpaßt. Das Klangmaterial ist dazu da, um uns dieses Eintauchen über die Bilderspiele hinaus als reale Beteiligung an dem Drama erleben zu lassen. Fernab von den Videospielen, die uns in leidenschaftliche Kämpfer verwandeln, enthüllt hier der Klang die wahre Natur offensichtlich harmloser Gesten und will eher ein Erleben als ein Verständnis vermitteln. Manche Dinge kann man nicht teilen. Dazu gehören der Schmerz und das Bild unserer Erinnerung. Die zu erforschenden Welten können uns diese Dinge näherbringen, aber immer nur als Metaphern und nie als Simulakrum.

Multi Mega Book in the CAVE

Franz Fischnaller/
Yesenia Maharaj Singh

What is the *Multi Mega Book* in the CAVE?

The *Multi Mega Book* in the CAVE [VR application] expands one maxi-page of the ongoing *Multi Mega Book* multi-media installation [an *up-to-date* electronic book sculpture] – the shift from the printed+book to the electronic text+digital skin.

The user experiences, and creatively interacts with, two moments of human history – the Renaissance and the Electronic Age integrated into one unique environment. The application juxtaposes two revolutions which have transformed the history of communication and in consequence human history.

The interactive visitor freely explores the different dimensions of the two key centuries through the use of the CAVE[TM] a Virtual Reality Theater. When the user enters the CAVE, the *Multi Mega Book* is in front of him/her. S/he can turn the pages, and move through them into various parts of the worlds within. One world is an idealized Renaissance city; the user can see famous buildings, walk through Leonardo's *Last Supper*, and visit and use Gutenberg's printing press.

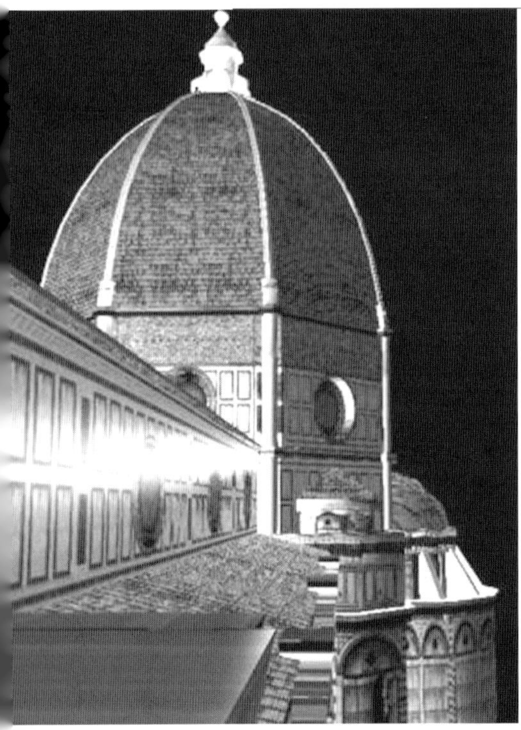

Multi Mega Book im CAVE

Franz Fischnaller/
Yesenia Maharaj Singh

Was ist das Multi Mega Book im CAVE?

Das *Multi Mega Book* im CAVE [VR-Anwendung] eröffnet eine Maxiseite der aktuellen Multimediainstallation *Multi Mega Book* [eine *moderne* elektronische Buchplastik] – der Wechsel vom Gedruckten+Buch zum elektronischen Text+digitaler Haut.

Der Benutzer erlebt zwei Epochen der Menschheitsgeschichte – die Renaissance und das Elektronische Zeitalter, die zu einer einzigartigen Umgebung verschmolzen sind und mit denen er kreativ interagieren kann. Die Anwendung stellt zwei revolutionäre Perioden, die die Geschichte der Kommunikation und in weiterer Folge die Menschheitsgeschichte verändert haben, nebeneinander.

A tunnel leads from here to another city – a *CD-City* which visualizes the movement of digital, networked information, a city in which everything is interactive.

The navigation and the interaction of the *Multi Mega Book* is often surprising, designed to draw the user from the Renaissance to the Information Age, exploring two different modes of communication and showing how both eras combined mathematics, innovation, art and cutting edge technology.

In its entirety the *Multi Mega Book* is a metaphor for means of communication through time. The different pages of the Multi Mega Book-installation give access to different aspects of the history of communication. The *Multi Mega Book* in the CAVE focuses on the specific argument of *The shift from the printed+book to the electronic text+digital skin*.

Nem: The Avatar in the *Multi Mega Book*

Nem is composed using basic geometric forms – circle, triangle, sphere. These shapes shift to create a column or a character. In the Renaissance city he appears first as an *info-point* column. As the visitors approach, he opens up into a *humanoid* figure and establishes an interactive relationship with them as he guides them through the environment.

In the CD-City Nem is a *network agent* – he no longer guides the visitor from place to place but acts as a node for sending and receiving information.

The changes in Nem's shape and behavior are related to the epoch. In the Renaissance, both guide and visitor have to move their bodies to get to the original source of the information. In the CD-City where the information is mainly digitalized, Nem exists as a *high speed carrier*, bringing information to the user who is not required to travel to its physical source. However, as the digital interchange flows around the CD-City, the visitor is encouraged to travel, and to interact with any of several Nem network agents.

Concept

The age of the *scrivener* is transformed by the arrival of the printing industries – the printed book is itself transformed by the arrival of digital *inputs*. There is a change and we are part of this revolution. Instead of fearing that

Der interaktive Besucher kann verschiedene Dimensionen beider Epochen im CAVE™, einer Virtual-Reality-Bühne, nach Belieben erkunden. Beim Betreten des CAVE befindet sich das *Multi Mega Book* vor ihm/ihr. Er/sie kann umblättern und sich in die verschiedenen Teile der darin enthaltenen Welten bewegen. Eine idealisierte Renaissancestadt bildet die eine Welt. Man kann berühmte Bauwerke besichtigen, durch Leonardos *Letztes Abendmahl* spazieren und Gutenbergs Druckerpresse bestaunen und bedienen.

Von hier führt ein Tunnel in eine weitere Stadt – eine *CD-City*, die einen digitalen, vernetzten Informationsaustausch visualisiert – eine Stadt, in der alles interaktiv passiert.

Navigation und Interaktion des *Multi Mega Book* sind oft überraschend, sollen den Besucher aus der Renaissance ins Informationszeitalter zerren, zwei verschiedene Kommunikationsmodi erkunden lassen und zeigen, wie in beiden Epochen Mathematik, Innovation, Kunst und Spitzentechnologie miteinander verknüpft wurden.

In seiner Gesamtheit ist das *Multi Mega Book* eine Metapher für Kommunikationsmittel im Spiegel der Zeit. Die Seiten des *Multi Mega Book* geben Aufschluß über verschiedene Aspekte der Kommunikationsgeschichte. Dabei konzentriert sich das Multi Mega Book im CAVE besonders auf *Den Wechsel vom Gedruckten+Buch zum elektronischen Text +digitaler Schicht.*

Nem: Der Avatar im Multi Mega Book

Nem ist aus den geometrischen Grundformen – Kreis, Dreieck, Kugel – zusammengesetzt. Diese Formen verwandeln sich und werden zur Säule oder Person. In der Renaissancestadt erscheint Nem zuerst als *Info*-Säule. Geht der Besucher auf ihn zu, wird er zu einer *humanoiden* Gestalt, die als Führer durch die Umgebung in Interaktion tritt.

In der CD-City ist Nem ein *Netzwerkagent* – er führt den Besucher nicht mehr von Ort zu Ort, sondern handelt als [Netzwerk]Knoten, der Informationen sendet und empfängt.

Die Veränderungen in Nems Gestalt und Verhalten beziehen sich auf die jeweilige Epoche. In der Renaissance müssen sowohl Führer als auch Besucher sich zu den ursprünglichen Informationsquellen hinbegeben. In der

run-away-technology will create a collective amnesia in culture and in literature, we like to approach and use the media to invent new technological systems, to construct new memories, to develop contemporary forms of communication and to extend the idea and the concept of the communication, the ways you approach the intangibility and versatility of information. Let's deal with content in a much more creative, free and futuristic way, more adapted to the way people communicate today: let's create new information pathways which are interactive, volatile, versatile, radical, but always aesthetically challenging and sublime!!

Mission – Statement

- To explore the technological potential of the CAVE [cave virtual environment]
- To explore and expand the boundaries of traditional artistic media and of visitor participation in an art-work
- To create an application which will be an example of how an immersive, interface technology, such as the CAVE, can be used
- To illustrate and interpret a crucial transformation in the evolution of communication and technology
- To create an emotional, immersive experience for the public of being in different centuries and in different worlds all in one unique container, the *Multi Mega Book* in the CAVE
- To stimulate the visitor, both through audio/visual impact and through the sense of excitement and control that navigating through and interacting with a VR environment brings
- To make the interface with the complex technology invisible and the illusion seamless, so that the visitor is caught up in the spirit of the experience and does not feel threatened by lifeless metallic machinery
- Creating and integrating Avatars, which will be used for CAVE to CAVE interaction over high speed networks, so that users in different geographical locations can share this VR Renaissance city and 21st century city and in the visualization of information

In Co-operation with Dave Pape and Josephine Anstey, EVL [Electronic Visualisation Lab], University of Illinois at Chicago.

CD-City, wo Information in erster Linie digitalisiert vorliegt, ist Nem ein *Hochgeschwindigkeitsträgersignal*, das die Informationen zum Besucher bringt, der nun nicht mehr die Informationsquelle aufsuchen muß. Da der digitale Informationsfluß sich über ganz CD-City erstreckt, sollte sich der Besucher dennoch weiterbewegen und auch mit anderen Nem-Netzwerkagenten interagieren.

Konzept

Das Zeitalter des *Schreibers* wandelte sich mit der Einführung des Buchdrucks; das gedruckte Buch wiederum wandelte sich mit den ersten digitalen *Eingaben*. Veränderungen sind im Gange, und wir sind Teil dieses Umbruchs. Anstatt zu befürchten, diese sich rasant entwickelnde Technologie würde zu kollektiver Amnesie in Kultur und Literatur führen, sollten wir diese Medien dazu nutzen, neue technische Systeme zu erfinden, neue Speichermedien zu schaffen, zeitgemäße Formen der Kommunikation zu entwickeln und den Gedanken der Kommunikation dahingehend weiterzuspinnen, wie man die Immaterialität und Flexibilität von Informationen anspricht. Gehen wir doch kreativer, freier und futuristischer mit Inhalten um, wie es den heutigen Kommunikationsgewohnheiten besser entspäche: Schaffen wird interaktive, veränderliche, flexible, radikale, jedoch immer ästhetisch ansprechende und sublime Informationspfade!

Unsere Zielsetzungen sind:

- Das technische Potential des CAVE [virtuelle Umgebung] auszuloten.
- Die Grenzen traditioneller künstlerischer Medien und der Besucherbeteiligung an einem Kunstwerk zu erkunden und zu erweitern.
- Eine Anwendung zu entwickeln, die die Möglichkeiten von beeinflußbaren VR-Systemen wie dem CAVE aufzeigt.
- Einen Meilenstein in der Evolution von Kommunikation und Technologie darzustellen und zu erläutern.
- Dem Publikum eine emotionale, ganzheitliche Erfahrung zu verschaffen, indem wir es in einem einzigen Raum, nämlich dem *Multi Mega Book* im CAVE,

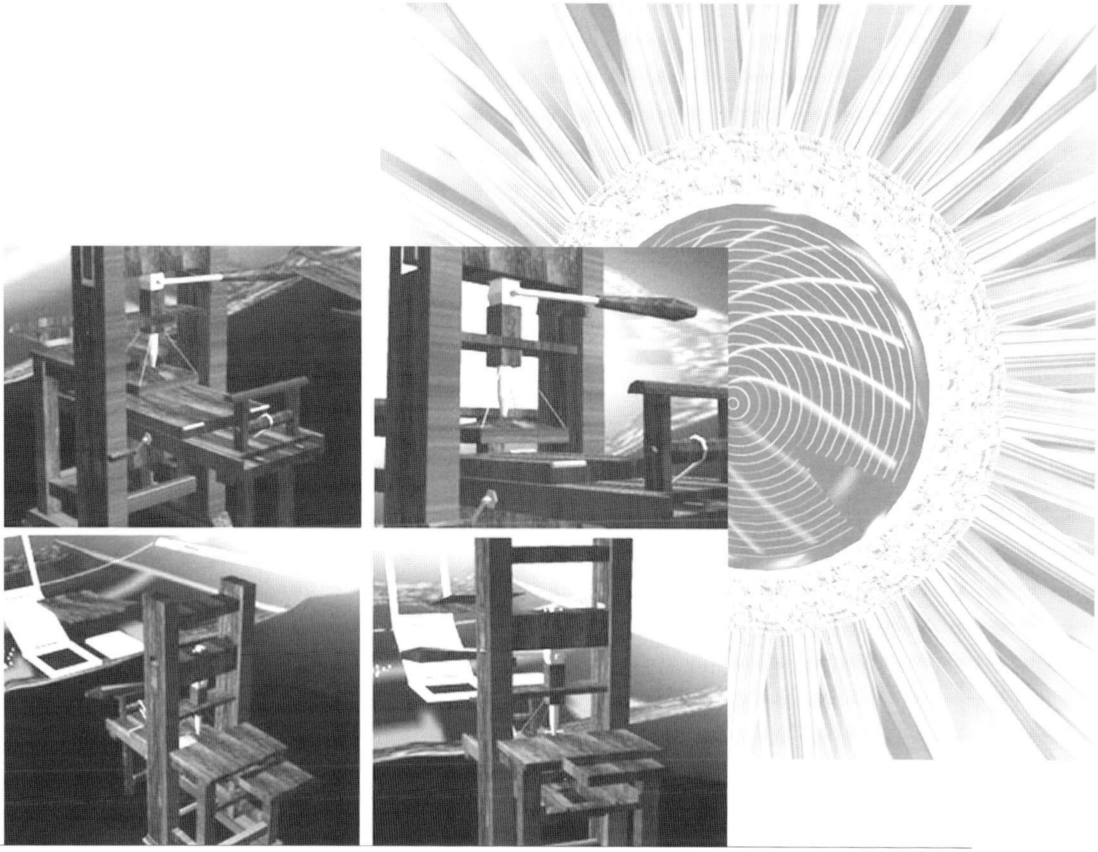

CAVE

in verschiedene Jahrhunderten und verschiedene Welten eintauchen lassen.

- Den Besucher sowohl durch audiovisuelle Einflüsse als auch durch die Erfahrung von Erregung und Kontrolle, die das Navigieren und Interagieren in einer VR-Umgebung mit sich bringen, zu stimulieren.
- Die Schnittstelle mit der komplexen Technologie unsichtbar und die Illusion perfekt zu machen, damit sich der Besucher der Erfahrung hingeben kann und nicht von lebloser, metallischer Maschinerie abgeschreckt wird.
- Avatare zu generieren und zu integrieren, die über Hochgeschwindigkeitsnetzwerke eine CAVE-zu-CAVE-Interaktion ermöglichen, damit Besucher an verschiedenen geographischen Orten an diesen VR-Städten der Renaissance und des 21. Jahrhunderts teilhaben können.
- Eine wesentlich ästhetischere Interpretation von Bildern und visuellem Design in einer Virtual-Reality-Umgebung zu entwickeln. VR und den CAVE als schlüssiges Beispiel für die Schaffung einer neuen Ausdrucksform in Design und Visualisierung von Informationen zu nutzen.

In Zusammenarbeit mit Dave Pape und Josephine Anstey, EVL [Electronic Visualisation Lab], University of Illinois at Chicago.

Teilweise realisiert innerhalb des Ars Electronica Research & Residence Program.
Realized in part within the Ars Electronica Research & Residence Program.

City of News

Flavia Sparacino/Alex Pentland/
Glorianna Davenport/
Michal Hlavac/Mary Obelnicki

Is there a way for us to define ourselves and the space in which we dwell, when the city is increasingly referenced as a space of disappearance, a space of the future but not of the present, a space of anxiety and loss ?

M. Christine Boyer

In a 1995 article, which appeared in *Le Monde Diplomatique*, the French theorist of technology, Paul Virilio, describes the phenomenon of the *loss of orientation* experienced by the exponentially increasing crowd which is relentlessly enthralled in cyberspace. Virilio observes that the construction of information superhighways, which are globalized and instantaneously updated, presents us with a threat, a menace to our perception of what reality is, of what it means for us to exist, as individuals, here and now. Induced by the splitting of the sensible world into real and virtual parallel with the *invention of the perspective of real-time*, this threat causes a shock, a *mental concussion*, that hooks the happenings of events to a globalized monorail track. We have extended Virilio's concern to the varied world of the Net, we have lost our bearings in the flatland of data offered by our *regular* browser, and experienced information anxiety as a shock caused by the vast unstructured landscape under the infinite horizon of the World Wide Web. As *spacemakers* [Walser, 1990], we have therefore undertaken the task to *escape flatland* [Tufte, 1990], to design an information browser that organizes

CAVE

City of News

Flavia Sparacino/Alex Pentland/
Glorianna Davenport/Michal
Hlavac/Mary Obelnicki

Haben wir eine Möglichkeit, uns selbst und den Raum, den wir bewohnen, zu definieren, während die Stadt zunehmend als Raum des Verschwindens, als Raum der Zukunft, nicht aber der Gegenwart, als Raum von Angst und Verlust definiert wird?

M. Christine Boyer

"The Metropolis would arrive like the circus, set up shop, operate for a period of time, and then move on".
Ron Herron

information as it fetches it, in real-time, in a virtual three-dimensional space which anchors our perceptual flow of data to a cognitive map of a [virtual] place. This place is a city.

CITY OF NEWS

Since William Gibson, in his visionary science-fiction novel called *Neuromancer*, described "the Matrix", i.e. the new informational network, as Los Angeles seen from five thousand feet up in the air, the idea of mapping the informational wasteland of the web to a metroscape has become an urge more than an invention. *City of News* is a dynamically growing urban landscape of information. It is an immersive, interactive, web browser that takes advantage of people's strength remembering the surrounding three-dimensional spatial layout. Starting from a chosen "home page", where home is finally associated with a physical space, our browser fetches and displays URLs so as to form skyscrapers and alleys of text and images through which the user can "fly".

The City is organized in urban quarters [districts] that provide territorial regrouping of urban activities. Similarly to some major contemporary cities there is a financial district, an entertainment district, and a shopping district. In addition to these areas we have created other functional groupings by creating a mapping between modern newspaper layout and city planning. Hence the name *City of News* for this designwork. There are therefore sports, books, advertising, science, and opinion districts.

One could think of these districts as urban quarters associated to the different conceptual areas of one of the many currently available search engines on the WWW. According to the architectural suggestions of the Krier brothers [Krier, 1984], zoning does not fragment the virtual city in huge sections where a citizen can only accomplish a single task. *City of News* is federation of autonomous quarters, which are "cities within the city" [ibid], and that are distinguished mainly by the people who inhabit them [students or artists, for example] and their common tastes or preferences [like Paris]. The City evolves and grows organically through exploration: following a link causes a

In einem Artikel, der 1995 in *Le Monde Diplomatique* veröffentlicht wurde, beschreibt der französische Technologietheoretiker Paul Virilio das Phänomen des "Orientierungsverlusts", das die exponentiell wachsende Bevölkerungsgruppe, die der Faszination des Cyberspace erlegen ist, erlebt. Virilio stellt fest, daß die Konstruktion globalisierter, unmittelbar aktualisierter Informations-Superhighways eine Bedrohung für uns darstellt, eine Gefährdung unserer Wahrnehmung dessen, was Realität ist, was es für uns bedeutet, als Individuen hier und jetzt zu existieren. Diese Bedrohung, die auf die Spaltung der sinnlich wahrnehmbaren Welt in eine reale und eine virtuelle und auf die gleichzeitige "Erfindung der Perspektive der Echtzeit" zurückzuführen ist, verursacht einen Schock, eine "mentale Gehirnerschütterung", die das Erleben von Ereignissen auf eine globalisierte, eingleisige Schiene verlegt. Wir haben Virilios Besorgnis auf die vielfältige Welt des Net ausgedehnt, haben die Orientierung in dem von unserem "normalen" Browser angebotenen riesigen Datenflachland verloren und die Informationsangst als einen von der grenzenlosen, unstrukturierten Landschaft unter dem unendlichen Horizont des World Wide Web verursachten Schock erlebt. Als "Spacemakers" [Walser, 1990] haben wir uns deshalb das Ziel gesetzt, ein "Entrinnen aus diesem Flachland" [Tufte, 1990] zu suchen, einen Browser zu erstellen, der die Informationen, während er sie abruft, in Echtzeit in einem virtuellen dreidimensionalen Raum organisiert, der den Fluß der von uns wahrgenommenen Daten in einer kognitiven Karte eines [virtuellen] Orts verankert. Dieser Ort ist eine Stadt.

"Die Metropolis kam an wie der Zirkus, schlug ihre Zelte auf, blieb eine Zeit lang in Betrieb und zog dann weiter."
Ron Herron

City of News

Seit William Gibson in seinem visionären Science-Fiction-Roman *Neuromancer* "die Matrix", d. h. das neue Informationsnetz, mit der Ansicht von Los Angeles aus fünfzehnhundert Metern Höhe verglichen hat, ist der Gedanke an eine Strukturierung der Informationswüste des Web als urbane Landschaft mehr ein Drang als eine Erfindung. Die *City of News* ist eine dynamisch wachsende, urbane Informationslandschaft. Es handelt sich dabei

"Places are spaces that you can remember, that you can care about and make part of your life ... The world should be filled with places so vivid and distinct that they can carry significance... Places could bring emotions, recollections, people and even ideas to mind."
Donlyn Lyndon

new building to be raised in the district to which it belongs, conceptually, by the content it carries.

So far we have implemented a navigational interface based on speech and gesture recognition [Wren, 1997]. We are currently considering using a wireless digital baton and a *space-ship console* to drive our three-dimensional browser. This work was inspired by Jeffrey Shaw's *Legible City* [1989] and finds a precursor in Apple's eWorld [1994].

The Memory City

In the late 70s, a group of researchers at MIT, who gathered under the name of Arch-Mac [Architecture Machine Group], created an immersive, video-based simulated space, called the *Aspen Movie Map*. This interactive system, which offered a faithful digital reproduction of the city of Aspen, became a platform to investigate spatial learning in virtual environments [Mohl, 1981]. Although the *Movie Map* required a detailed recording of the place to explore beforehand, it constitutes an important predecessor to *City of News* for its attention in providing the user with a cognitive map of the virtual surroundings.

Kevin Lynch [Lynch, 1960] has done a remarkable study in identifying the elements that make of a city a legible, memorable and coherent place. The elements according to which an image of the city is constructed are: paths, edges, districts, nodes, and landmarks. While we have organized *City of News* around districts, added memorable landmarks, as organic constructions or as virtual sculpures, and aligned typographic buildings along paths, we have also designed *City of News* to serve as a Memory Theatre.

The *Classical Art of Memory* depended on the mental construction of complex architectures composed by places inhabited by vivid images. These images would provide associational hooks to the material to be recollected.

Inspired by Yates' description of Camillo's Memory Theatre we have endowed *City of News* with salient images extracted from webnewspapers' front pages. These act as architectural landmarks and memory cues in the different districts. They appear attached to huge

um einen vom Benutzer betretbaren, interaktiven Web-Browser, der sich die Stärke der Menschen, sich das sie umgebende dreidimensionale räumliche Layout zu merken, zunutze macht. Unser Browser geht von einer gewählten *Homepage* aus, wo das *Home* letztendlich mit einem physischen Raum assoziiert ist, und holt URLs, die er anzeigt, indem er Wolkenkratzer und Straßen aus Text und Bildern entstehen läßt, die der Benutzer *durchfliegen* kann.

Die Stadt ist in Stadtviertel [Bezirke] gegliedert, die eine territoriale Gruppierung der verschiedenen urbanen Aktivitäten darstellen. Analog zu einigen der größten zeitgenössischen Städte gibt es einen Finanzdistrikt, ein Unterhaltungsviertel und ein Einkaufsviertel. Zusätzlich zu dieser Gliederung in Stadtviertel haben wir noch eine zusätzliche funktionelle Gruppierung vorgenommen, indem wir unsere Stadtplanung am Layout einer modernen Zeitung orientierten, wovon sich übrigens auch die Bezeichnung *City of News* ableitet. Deshalb gibt es Sport-, Bücher-, Werbe-, Wissenschafts- und Meinungsbezirke.

Man könnte nun meinen, diese Bezirke wären nichts weiter als Stadtviertel, die den verschiedenen Begriffsgebieten einer der unzähligen Web-Suchmaschinen entsprechen. Den architektonischen Überlegungen der Brüder Krier [Krier, 1984] zufolge fragmentiert eine Zonengliederung die virtuelle Stadt nicht in riesige Bereiche, in denen ein Bürger jeweils nur eine einzelne Aufgabe ausführen kann. *City of News* ist ein Verbund autonomer Viertel, die jeweils *eine Stadt innerhalb der Stadt* [ibid] sind und sich hauptsächlich durch ihre Bewohner [z. B. Studenten oder Künstler] sowie ihre gemeinsamen Vorlieben oder Präferenzen [wie Paris] voneinander unterscheiden. Die Stadt entwickelt sich und wächst organisch durch ihre Erforschung. Folgt man einem Link, entsteht ein neues Gebäude in genau dem Bezirk, dem es aufgrund seines Inhalts begrifflich zuzuordnen ist.

"Orte sind Räume, an die man sich erinnern kann, um die man sich sorgen kann und die man zu einem Teil seines Lebens machen kann ... Die Welt sollte voll von Orten sein, die so lebendig und einzigartig sind, daß sie Bedeutungen tragen können ... Orte könnten Emotionen, Erinnerungen, Menschen und sogar Ideen ins Gedächtnis rufen."
Donlyn Lyndon

"Architects aspiring to place their constructs within the non-space of cyberspace will have to learn to think in terms of genetic engines of artificial life"
Marcos Novak

and tall billboards, like those that animate the city of Tokyo with glooming publicity. Yates also describes a lesser known Art of Memory, developed by Raymond Lull. This was an abstract art of memory based on concepts associated with letters. The art of recalling would then become a combinatorics exercise rather than a promenade through a virtual path.

A similar abstract model for organizing news data [not in real-time] was adopted by Earl Rennison in his *Galaxy of News*, at the MIT Media Lab's Visible Language Workshop. The main difference between this last design work and *City of News* consists in the spatial, urban-like, organization of data, together with the real-time construction and evolution of the landscape of the latter.

Organic Architecture

City of News is an *architecture machine* which gives *the physical environment the ability to design itself* [Negroponte, 1975]. However, this machine operates according to the organic laws of the garden. As the user follows a link on the World Wide Web, [s]he creates new city-elements that are added according to an algorithm which simulates artificial growth and evolution. Following a link becomes equivalent to a pursuit of possibility which determines a change in the environment: the consequence of every choice is amplified, causing a building to be raised or a path to be followed. In the previous age of the machine, city planners would design cities according to the rigid discipline of the workchain and plan traffic flow to the rhythm of clockwork.

In our contemporary time, global networks of computers, time-shared activities, Internet life and usenet groups define a life-like skin or membrane of virtual places and activities. Hence we have found that an organic pattern of development of the city would be best suited to represent life-on-the-web i.e. *the Net*. From William Mitchell's mathematical formalism of The Logic of Architecture to Marcos Novak's genetics-based Liquid Architecture; from Christopher Alexander's rational design of Notes on the Synthesis of Form to his later nature-inspired *Pattern Language*, we witness a trend towards finding biologically-dri-

Bisher haben wir eine Navigationsschnittstelle eingerichtet, die auf Sprach- und Gestenerkennung [Wren, 1997] beruht. Gegenwärtig denken wir daran, einen drahtlosen digitalen Steuerknüppel und eine *Raumschiffkonsole* zu verwenden, um unseren dreidimensionalen Browser zu steuern. Diese Arbeit, die in Apples *e-World* [1994] einen Vorläufer besitzt, wurde von Jeffrey Shaws *Legible City* [1989] inspiriert.

Die Stadt der Erinnerung

In den späten siebziger Jahren schuf eine Gruppe von Forschern am MIT, die sich unter der Bezeichnung Arch-Mac [Architecture Machine Group] zusammengetan hatten, einen vom Benutzer betretbaren, videobasierten, simulierten Raum, dem sie den Namen *Aspen Movie Map* gaben. Dieses interaktive System, das eine getreue digitale Reproduktion der Stadt Aspen darstellt, wurde zu einer Plattform für die Erforschung des räumlichen Lernens in virtuellen Umgebungen [Mohl, 1981]. Obwohl die *Movie Map* im vorhinein detaillierte Informationen über den zu erforschenden Ort erforderte, stellt sie einen wichtigen Vorläufer der *City of News* dar, da sie dem Benutzer eine kognitive Karte der virtuellen Umgebung liefert. Kevin Lynch [Lynch, 1960] hat eine bemerkenswerte Studie durchgeführt, in deren Verlauf er jene Elemente identifizierte, die eine Stadt zu einem lesbaren, einprägsamen und kohärenten Ort machen: Wege, Ränder, Bezirke, Knoten und Erkennungszeichen. Während wir die *City of News* in Form von Bezirken organisiert und dabei einprägsame Erkennungszeichen wie organische Strukturen oder virtuelle Skulpturen hinzugefügt und typographische Gebäude entlang der Wege angeordnet haben, konstruierten wir unsere *City of News* gleichzeitig so, daß sie als Schauplatz der Erinnerung dienen kann.

Die *klassische Erinnerungsweise* war von der mentalen Konstruktion komplexer architektonischer Strukturen abhängig, die sich aus von lebendigen Bildern bevölkerten Orten zusammensetzen. Diese Bilder lieferten die Assoziationsverbindungen zu dem Material, das es sich einzuprägen galt.

Inspiriert durch Yates Beschreibung von Camillos *Memory Theatre* statteten wir *City of News* mit einprägsamen Bildern aus, die wir

"Could not this ideal city, at one and the same time, behave, quite explicitly, as both a theatre of prophecy AND a theatre of memory ? ... For, if without prophecy there is no hope, then, without memory there can be no communication."

Colin Rowe

ven or simu-life solutions to complex problems of design and organization. In parallel to this phenomenon, an increasing number of individuals, communities and social groups wish to plan their own worlds, under the techno-promise of personalized news and entertainement services. A new utopian movement seems to animate the view of the city as a *theatre of prophecy* [Rowe, 1978] overlapping the theatre of memory previously described.

Postmodern Utopia

The fantasy of a comprehensive city of deliverance, which dates back to early Modern Architecture, invests also the collective imagination of cyberspace. Howard's smokeless *Garden City*, Wright's decentralized *Broadacre City*, Le Corbusier's enthusiastic *Radiant City*, and Sant'Elia's dynamic *New City* are just a few among the many historical examples of visionary architectures for future cities. More recently an English group of architects that calls itself *Archigram* [Architectural Telegram] has designed fantastic spaces like: Walking Cities, Plug-in Cities, Instant Cities, and Inflatable Cities, which respond to our contemporary transformed imaginary view of the urban space.

The new city is seen as *an immense node of communication, a messy nexus of messages, storage and transportation facilities, a massive education machine of its own complexity, involving equally all media, including buildings* [Benedikt, 1991]. *City of News* certainly participates in the utopian dimension of this historical line of thought as it carries within itself a hope for an ideal space of information sharing and consumption. At the same time it does not pretend to offer all information available on the Web in a fully rationalized and nonpolluted way.

As many architectural theorists have observed, there are some similarities between the virtual space of computer networks and posturban spaces of disorder and decay. *City of News* reflects this view of the city from *the Periphery of the Empire*, as a science-fiction narrative à la Hugh Ferris. It is a gleaming metro-

den Titelseiten von Web-Zeitungen entnommen hatten. Diese fungieren in den verschiedenen Bezirken als architektonische Erkennungszeichen und Gedächtnisstichworte. Sie sind auf großen, hohen Plakatwänden angebracht, die jenen ähneln, die die Stadt Tokio mit düsterer Publicity beleben. Darüber hinaus beschreibt Yates auch eine weniger bekannte Erinnerungsmethode, die von Raymond Lull entwickelt wurde. Dabei handelte es sich um eine abstrakte Erinnerungsweise, die auf mit Buchstaben assoziierten Begriffen beruht. Das Erinnern wurde dabei eher zu einer Übung in Kombinationsfähigkeit als zu einem Spaziergang auf einem virtuellen Weg. Ein ähnliches abstraktes Modell für die Organisation von Nachrichtendaten [nicht in Echtzeit] wurde von Earl Rennison in seiner *Galaxy of News* im Visible Language Workshop des MIT Media Lab verwendet. Der Hauptunterschied zwischen dieser letzten Arbeit und *City of News* besteht in der räumlichen, stadtartigen Organisation der Daten sowie in der Echtzeitkonstruktion und -evolution der Landschaft in *City of News*.

Organische Architektur

City of News ist eine *Architekturmaschine*, die *der physischen Umgebung die Möglichkeit gibt, sich selbst zu gestalten* [Negroponte, 1975]. Diese Maschine funktioniert nach den organischen Gesetzen eines Gartens. Während der Benutzer innerhalb des World Wide Web einem Link folgt, erzeugt er neue Stadtelemente, die einem künstliches Wachstum und Evolution simulierenden Algorithmus entsprechend der bestehenden Struktur hinzugefügt werden. Das Verfolgen eines Links wird damit gleichbedeutend mit der Verfolgung einer Möglichkeit, die eine Veränderung der Umwelt bewirkt: Die Konsequenz jeder getroffenen Wahl wird intensiviert und führt dazu, daß ein Gebäude hochwächst oder ein Weg weiterverfolgt wird. Im vorangegangenen Maschinenzeitalter folgten die Stadtplaner bei ihrer Planungstätigkeit der strengen Disziplin der Arbeitskette und planten den Verkehrsfluß zum Rhythmus des Uhrwerks.

"Architekten, die danach streben, ihre Konstrukte innerhalb des Unraums des Cyperspace zu plazieren, werden lernen müssen, die genetischen Motoren des künstlichen Lebens in ihr Denken miteinzubeziehen."

Marcos Novak

Places that are memorable are necessary. We need to think about where we are and what is unique and special about our surroundings so that we can better understand ourselves and how we relate to others.

Donlyn Lyndon

polis, a tempting city, a glorious slum of information that hosts the Internet addicts as well as the hyper-efficient businessmen that surf the wave of real-time, a city that welcomes, excites, and consumes people. It is a city imbued with a post-modern nostalgia for the future and that ambitiously wishes to compare itself to the film architectures of *Blade Runner, Brazil,* and *Batman.*

Conclusions

City of News was first completed in May 1996 and it is since a work in progress. As it progresses, we feel that this project raises more questions than the ones it provides answers to. As we push along the city metaphor, we ask ourselves: *What does it mean to have an Information Hospital or an Information Cemetery ?* *What are the criteria for the livability of this cybercity ?* Because, although we make cities, they also make us. We have built a virtual environment under the natural law of the **creatio mundi** rather than by following the compulsion to the **fuga mundi**. It is an environment where to organize is to construct, and to build an informational structure that facilitates the recollection of memories. At the same time, we hope that our audiences become aware of how information affects who they are, and how the urban layout of their surroundings has an influence in making them the way they are. In a near future, as we find ourselves tied together under the new perspective of a globalized real-time, we are not likely to ask each other any more, *Do you have the time ?* but instead, *Do you have the place ?*

In unserer gegenwärtigen Zeit definieren die globalen Computernetze, die Time-Sharing-Aktivitäten, das Leben im Internet und die Usenet-Gruppen eine lebensähnliche Haut bzw. Membran virtueller Orte und Aktivitäten. Daher sind wir zu dem Schluß gelangt, daß ein organisches Stadtentwicklungsmuster am besten geeignet wäre, um das Leben im Web, d. h. *das Net* abzubilden. Von William Mitchells mathematischem Formalismus in *The Logic of Architecture* bis hin zu Marcos Novaks genetikbasierter *Liquid Architecture*, von Christopher Alexanders rationalen *Notes on the Synthesis of Form* bis hin zu seiner späteren, von der Natur inspirierten *Pattern Language* erleben wir einen Trend hin zu biologisch gesteuerten oder das Leben simulierenden Lösungen für komplexe Konstruktions- und Organisationsprobleme. Parallel zu diesem Phänomen möchten immer mehr Einzelpersonen, Gemeinschaften und soziale Gruppen ihre eigenen Welten planen und dadurch das Techno-Versprechen personalisierter Nachrichten- und Unterhaltungsdienste in Anspruch nehmen. Eine neue utopische Bewegung scheint die Auffassung der Stadt als einen *Schauplatz der Prophezeiung* [Rowe, 1978] zu beleben, der sich mit dem vorne beschriebenen *Schauplatz der Erinnerung* überschneidet.

Postmoderne Utopie

Der Traum von einer umfassenden Stadt der Erlösung, der auf die frühe moderne Architektur zurückgeht, findet sich auch in der kollektiven Vorstellung vom Cyberspace wieder. Howards rauchfreie *Garden City*, Wrights dezentralisierte *Broadacre-City*, Le Corbusiers enthusiastische *Cité Radieuse* und Sant'Elias dynamische *New City* sind nur einige unter den vielen historischen Beispielen für visionäre Architekturen für zukünftige Städte. In jüngerer Zeit hat eine englische Gruppe von Architekten, die unter dem Namen *Archigram* [Architectural Telegram] arbeiten, phantastische Räume wie gehende Städte, ansteckbare Städte, Instantstädte und aufblasbare Städte erfun-

Könnte nicht diese ideale Stadt zu ein und derselben Zeit explizit als Schauplatz der Prophezeiung UND als Schauplatz der Erinnerung fungieren? ... Denn so, wie es ohne Prophezeiung keine Hoffnung gibt, kann es ohne Erinnerung keine Kommunikation geben.

Colin Rowe

Banham, Reyner, *The Visions of Ron Herron*, New York, Academy Editions, 1994, pg 45
Benedikt, Michael ed., *Cyberspace: first steps*, Cambridge, Mass., MIT Press, 1991. In: Introduction, by Michael Benedikt, pg 16
Boyer, M. Christine, *CyberCities: visual perception in the age of electronic communication*, New York, Princeton Architectural Press, 1996, pg 242
Krier, Leon, *Houses, palaces, cities*, New York, Architectural Design AD Editions, 1984
Lynch, Kevin, *The image of the city*, Cambridge Mass., The Technology Press & Harvard University Press, 1960
Lyndon, Donlyn and Moore, Charles W., *Chambers for a memory palace*, Cambridge, Mass., MIT Press, 1994, pg xii
Mohl, Robert, *Cognitive space in the interactive movie map : an investigation of spatial learning in virtual environments*, Thesis Arch Ph.D, 1981
Negroponte, Nicholas, *Soft Architecture Machines*, Cambridge Mass., MIT Press, 1975
Novak Marcos, *Transmitting Architecture. Architects in Cyberspace*, in: Architectural Design vol. 65, no. 11/12, Cambridge, VCH Publishers, 1995, pg 46
Rowe, Colin and Koetter, Fred, *Collage city*, Cambridge, Mass., MIT Press, 1978, pg 49
Tufte, Edward R., *Envisioning Information*, Cheshire, Conn., Graphic Press, 1990
Walser, Randall, *Elements of a Cyberspace Playhouse*, Proceedings of the National Computer Graphics Association, Anaheim, CA, March 1990
Wren, Christopher, Sparacino, Flavia et al., *Perceptive Spaces for Peformance and Entertainment: Untethered Interaction using Computer Vision and Audition*, in: Applied Artificial Intelligence, vol. 11, no. 4, June 1997

den, die unserer zeitgenössischen transformierten imaginären Auffassung vom urbanen Raum entsprechen.

Die neue Stadt wird aufgefaßt als *ein immenser Kommunikationsknoten, ein wirrer Nexus von Botschaften, Speicher- und Transportmedien, eine massive Bildungsmaschine ihrer eigenen Komplexität, die alle Medien einschließlich der Gebäude gleichermaßen umschließt* [Benedikt, 1991]. Die *City of News* hat sicherlich Anteil an der utopischen Dimension dieses historischen Gedankens, da sie die Hoffnung auf einen idealen Raum in sich trägt, in dem Information geteilt und konsumiert werden kann. Gleichzeitig nimmt das Projekt nicht für sich in Anspruch, die gesamte im Web verfügbare Information auf absolut rationale, nicht kontaminierte Art und Weise anzubieten.

Wie viele Architekturtheoretiker beobachtet haben, gibt es einige Gemeinsamkeiten zwischen dem virtuellen Raum der Computernetze und den posturbanen Räumen von Unordnung und Verfall. Die *City of News* spiegelt diese Auffassung der Stadt von *der Peripherie des Reichs* als Science-Fiction-Erzählung à la Hugh Ferris wieder. Sie ist eine glitzernde Metropole, eine verführerische Stadt, ein glorreicher Informationsslum, der sowohl dem Internet-Süchtigen als auch dem hypereffizienten Geschäftsmann, die beide auf der Welle der Echtzeit surfen, ein Zuhause bietet, eine Stadt, die die Menschen willkommen heißt, erregt und verschlingt. Sie ist eine Stadt, die durchdrungen ist von einem postmodernen nostalgischen Sehnen nach der Zukunft, die sich selbst ehrgeizig mit den Filmarchitekturen aus *Blade Runner, Brazil* und *Batman* zu vergleichen sucht.

Einprägsame Orte sind notwendig. Wir müssen darüber nachdenken, wo wir sind und was an unserer Umgebung einzigartig und besonders ist, damit wir uns selbst und unser Verhältnis zu anderen besser verstehen können.
Donlyn Lyndon

Schlußfolgerungen

Die *City of News* wurde im Mai 1996 fertiggestellt und befindet sich seither in einem laufenden Prozeß der Weiterentwicklung. Während unser Projekt gedeiht, haben wir das Gefühl, daß es mehr Fragen aufwirft als beantwortet. Während wir uns weiter mit der Metapher der Stadt beschäftigen, fragen wir

uns: *Was bedeutet es, ein Informationskrankenhaus oder einen Informationsfriedhof zu haben?* *Welche Kriterien bestimmen den Lebenswert dieser Cyberstadt?* Denn obwohl wir Städte schaffen, schaffen sie gleichzeitig uns. Wir haben eine virtuelle Umgebung geschaffen, indem wir dem Naturgesetz der *creatio mundi* anstatt dem Drang zur *fuga mundi* folgten. Es handelt sich dabei um eine Umgebung, in der Organisation gleichbedeutend mit Konstruktion ist und den Aufbau einer Informationsstruktur bedeutet, die das Abrufen von Erinnerungen erleichtert. Gleichzeitig hoffen wir, daß unsere Besucher erkennen, wie Information das beeinflußt, was sie sind, und wie das urbane Layout ihrer Umgebung sie beeinflußt, indem es sie zu dem macht, was sie sind. In der nahen Zukunft, während wir uns unter der neuen Perspektive einer globalisierten Echtzeit aneinandergefesselt finden, werden wir uns wahrscheinlich nicht mehr fragen: *Wie spät ist es?*, sondern *Wo sind wir?*

Teilweise realisiert innerhalb des/
Realized in part within the Ars Electronica Research & Residence Program.

Liquid Meditation

Margaret H. Watson

From the banks of a small pond in Chicago, I discovered a myriad of beautiful reflections. Liquid abstractions of nature as diverse and exceptional as the ceaseless palette of perpetual sunsets flow unnoticed beneath the shade. Through their simple, mesmerizing movements, the beholder is transformed into something beyond external. Immersion through imagination and an internal connection create a bond between nature and human. Truth reveals itself in such moments of clarity.

Liquid Meditation began with the dual goal of sharing these moments and creating a physical immersion within them. In virtual reality, the water reflections could be introduced in a new way, as images within a strange architectural structure. Within the space, the images are the reality and the world is the art. But, visitors to the space are uncertain. The abstraction of the images convince us that they are not real.

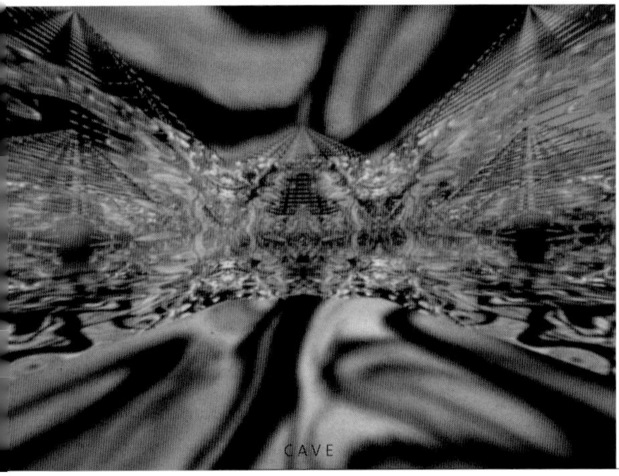

CAVE

Liquid Meditation

Margaret H. Watson

Vom Ufer eines kleinen Sees in Chicago aus beobachtete ich Myriaden herrlicher Lichtreflexe. Flüssige Abstraktionen der Natur, so verschiedenartig und außergewöhnlich wie eine endlose Palette aufeinanderfolgender Sonnenuntergänge, treiben unbemerkt im Schatten der Bäume. Ihre einfachen, mesmerisierenden Bewegungen versetzen den Betrachter in einen Zustand, der über Äußerlichkeiten hinausgeht. Indem er in die Phantasie eintaucht und eine inneren Bezug herstellt, entsteht eine innere Verbindung zwischen Natur und Mensch. In solchen Momenten der Klarheit offenbart sich die Wahrheit.

In addition, the abstraction within the work allows an individual to examine a real moment in time in a new and exciting way. Beautiful reflective surfaces transform into worlds that encompass the user. Liquid photographs flow in pieces through reprocessing within a virtual fountain or come to life through mathematical animation. Water video pulses and flows infinitely in a world where moments can continue for an eternity.

Conceptual goals of the project included embedding philosophies of life and reflection within the architecture and the work as a whole. Through individual discovery within the world, participants can hopefully examine life with new insight.

Liquid Meditation was created for the CAVE™ VR System at the Electronic Visualization Laboratory at the University of Illinois at Chicago. Sound was created by Eric Butkus.

CAVE

Liquid Meditation ging von einer zweifachen Zielsetzung aus: diese Momente zu teilen und ein physisches Eintauchen in sie zu ermöglichen. In der virtuellen Realität konnten die Reflexe auf dem Wasser auf neue Weise eingeführt werden: als Bilder innerhalb einer fremden architektonischen Struktur. Im Raum sind diese Bilder Realität und die Welt Kunst. Aber die Besucher dieses Raumes sind noch unsicher. Die Abstraktion der Bilder überzeugt uns davon, daß sie nicht echt sind.

Durch die Abstraktion innerhalb des Werkes kann der einzelne Besucher außerdem einen realen Moment in der Zeit auf neue, aufregende Weise erleben. Schöne reflektierende Oberflächen verwandeln sich in Welten, die den Benutzer einschließen. Bruchstücke flüssiger Fotografien wirbeln durch einen virtuellen Springbrunnen und werden wiederverarbeitet oder durch mathematische Animation zum Leben erweckt. In einer Welt, in der Augenblicke eine Ewigkeit dauern können, pulst und fließt unaufhörlich Video-Wasser.

Die konzeptuellen Ziele des Projekts umfaßten die Einbettung von Lebensphilosophie und Reflexionen in die Architektur und in das Werk insgesamt. Durch individuelle Entdeckungen in dieser Welt werden die Teilnehmer hoffentlich in der Lage sein, neue Einsichten in die Fragen des Lebens zu gewinnen.

Liquid Meditation wurde für das VR-System CAVE™ im Electronic Visualization Laboratory an der University of Illinois, Chicago, erstellt. Der Sound stammt von Eric Butkus.

remote sensations

In Co-operation with the
In Kooperation mit dem

OFFENES KULTURHAUS

Installations and Processes in the Urban Public Space

Remote Sensations is a cooperative project of the Offenes Kulturhaus Linz and the Ars Electronica Center. It is a compilation of artists' positions on, experiences with, and sensory perception of a culture undergoing a process of telematic self-organization. *Remote Sensations* was designed to focus primarily upon the highly charged interplay of forces between the urban lebensraum as a system of commercial activity and human behavior interlinked by a network of rules and conditions, an interface in the sense of a factor of perception of telepresent things or events, and the technological nature of that interface, upon which telepresence and network-linkage [globally speaking] is based.

Telepresence is a consequence of *remoteness* in space – also in the sense of obliteration – and of time which has been compressed down to the point of zero. Telematic technology is the means of achieving this. On one hand, these delineation's of individual positions are presented here in order to establish a model, as it were, of perception [online, on-the-air and by means of the senses] which is characterized by the technological structure which produces *remoteness* and/or the technological structure of that *remote* space itself, and – in contrast to the experience of telepresence – the experience, among others, of being telepresent oneself. On the other hand, urban spaces function simultaneously as projection surfaces; due to the fact that they are the object of images projected upon the public realm of the city, they ought to be recognized as a construction which has long been subject to the process of cultural reorganization.

Installationen und Prozesse im öffentlichen Stadtraum

Remote Sensations ist ein Kooperations-Projekt des Offenen Kulturhauses Linz und des Ars Electronica Center. Es versammelt Positionen von KunstlerInnen zu einer sich telematisch organisierenden Kultur, deren Erfahrung und sinnlichen Wahrnehmung.

Konzipiert wurde *Remote Sensations* vor allem im Hinblick auf das Spannungsfeld zwischen dem Lebensraum Stadt als ein durch Regeln und Bedingungen vernetztes Betriebs- und Handlungssystem, Interface im Sinne eines Wahrnehmungsfaktors von telepräsenten Dingen oder Ereignissen und der technologischen Natur des Interface, auf der Telepräsenz und Vernetzung, global gesprochen, beruht.

Telepräsenz ist eine Folge der *Entfernung* – auch im Sinne von Auslöschung – des Raumes und der auf Null hin komprimierten Zeit. Telematik [bzw. Technologie] ist das Mittel dazu. Durch die Beiträge soll einerseits die von der technologischen Struktur zur *Entfernung* bzw. des *entfernten* Raumes geprägte Wahrnehmung [online, on-air und vermittels der Sinne] gleichsam modellhaft etabliert und – im Unterschied zur Erfahrung der Telepräsenz – unter anderem die Erfahrung selbst telepräsent werden. Andererseits fungiert der urbane Raum zugleich als Projektionsfläche und soll dadurch, daß er auch Gegenstand von Projektionen in die urbane Öffentlichkeit hinein ist, als vom Prozeß der kulturellen Neuorganisation längst erfaßtes Gefüge erkannt werden können.

Architettura della Separazione

Interactive Sound/ Video Installation & Theater Performance *Scanning Bacchae*

Isabella Bordoni,
Roberto Paci Dalò/
Giardini Pensili

"Now, as for these actual heterotopias: how can they be described, what sense do they make? One might posit a science – but no, let us eschew this heavily depreciated term, and let us say: a descriptive system whose task, in a certain society, would be the study, the analysis, the description, the "reading" [as one is inclined to say nowadays] of these various spaces, these other places; to a certain extent, a simultaneously mythic and real disputation of the space in which we live. This description could be called heterotopiology."

Michel Foucault

The Installation

Architettura della Separazione is an interactive sound and light installation in the Linz shipyard. Computer- and sensor-controlled audio and video equipment has been installed in this space; performances of the theatrical work *Scanning Bacchae*, based upon Euripides' play *The Bacchae*, will also take place in this same venue. In addition, a web site will be set up on the Ars Electronica Server and radio broadcasts are being planned to run parallel to these events. *Architettura della Separazione* was designed especially for the Ars Electronica Festival.

Architettura della Separazione

Interaktive Klang- und Videoinstallation & Theaterperformance *Scanning Bacchae*

Isabella Bordoni,
Roberto Paci Dalò/
Giardini Pensili

Die Installation

Architettura della Separazione ist eine interaktive Klang- und Lichtinstallation in der Linzer Schiffswerft. Computer- und sensorgesteuerte Klang- und Lichtanlagen werden im Raum installiert, und im selben Ambiente finden auch Aufführungen der auf Euripides' *Bakchen* basierenden Theaterperformance *Scanning Bacchae* statt.

"Was nun die eigentlichen Heterotopien anlangt: Wie kann man sie beschreiben, welchen Sinn haben sie? Man könnte eine Wissenschaft annehmen – nein, lassen wir das heruntergekommene Wort, sagen wir: eine systematische Beschreibung, deren Aufgabe in einer bestimmten Gesellschaft das Studium, die Analyse, die Beschreibung, die "Lektüre" [wie man jetzt gern sagt] dieser verschiedenen Räume, dieser anderen Orte wäre: gewissermaßen eine zugleich mythische und reale Bestreitung des Raumes, in dem wir leben; diese Beschreibung könnte Heterotopologie heißen."

Michel Foucault

The project has been specifically designed as a contribution to the theme of this year's festival, since it deals with the creation of ambiences in the physical world and in electronic space, to which the *Human Interface* can also be linked up. All of these environments serve as a laboratory and, following the festival, the web site will remain on-line as an ongoing project.

The following list of key words establishes the realm under investigation within the framework of this project: heterotopy, city, body, scanning, sampling, broadcasting, border. *Architettura della Separazione* is an environment oriented toward the practice of hearing. The focal point of the project is the city itself, which is analyzed in an interplay of acoustic, spatial, historical, geographic, political and urban architectural studies. The grounds of the VOEST-Alpine Works have been chosen as the symbolic space in which to conduct this exploration. As a city within a city, as a unique example of an autonomous conurbation within a place historically defined as *Linz*: the VOEST-Alpine Works constitute an extreme variant. The theory of the project is also directly related to the work of the Italian philosopher Giorgio Agamben who – particularly in *Homo sacer* – investigated the concepts of sovereignty and deviation. A consummate heterotopia and one which is, moreover, still in operation, and thus unique in Europe; a part of the dream of industrial culture, at present, dynamically interrelated with the digital Linz.

Architettura della Separazione is thus the result of a series of scanning and sampling activities which have been carried out in Linz. It ought to be regarded as a next-generation developmental phase advancing upon earlier large-scale interactive installations such as *Locus* [1994] and *Teatro dell'ascolto* [Theater of Hearing, 1995]. In these projects, dramaturgical and narrative performances have taken applied technologies on a journey into the depths of remembrance of lived spaces, into the interplay between remembering and forgetting, and into the consciousness of those empty and uncertain spaces which exist between the actual, the presumptive and the possible.

Bodies are becoming like cities, their temporal coordinates transformed into spatial ones. In a poetic condensation, history has been replaced by geographies, stories by maps, memories by scenarios. We no longer perceive ourselves as continuity but as location.
D. Gregory

Parallel dazu wird auf dem Ars-Electronica-Server eine Web-Site erstellt, Rundfunkübertragungen sind geplant. *Architettura della Separazione* wurde speziell für das Ars Electronica Festival entworfen.

Das Projekt versteht sich als themenspezifischer Beitrag zum diesjährigen Festival, da es mit der Erzeugung von Ambienten in der physikalischen Welt und im elektronischen Raum befaßt ist, in die sich auch die *Schnittstelle Mensch* einschalten kann. All diese Umgebungen dienen als Laboratorium, und die Web-Site wird nach dem Festival als On-going-Project weitergeführt.

Der im Rahmen des Projekts erforschte Bereich läßt sich an folgenden Schlüsselwörten festmachen: *heterotopy, city, body, scanning, sampling, broadcasting, border. Architettura della Separazione* ist eine Umgebung, die auf die Praxis des Hörens ausgerichtet ist. Im Mittelpunkt des Projekts steht die Stadt selbst, die in einem Zusammenspiel akustischer, räumlicher, historischer, geographischer, politischer und städtebaulicher Studien analysiert wird.

Als sinnbildlicher Raum für diese Erforschung wurde das Areal der VOEST-Alpine gewählt. Als Stadt innerhalb der Stadt, als einzigartiges Beispiel für einen autonomen Ballungsraum innerhalb eines historisch als *Linz* definierten Ortes stellt die VOEST-Alpine als Raum eine Abweichung dar. Die Theorie des Projekts steht denn auch in direkter Beziehung zu den Werken des italienischen Philosophen Giorgio Agamben, der – insbesondere in *Homo sacer* – die Begriffe Souveränität und Abweichung untersucht. Eine perfekt realisierte und noch in Betrieb befindliche Heterotopie [einzigartig in Europa], Teil des Traumes von der industriellen Kultur, derzeit in dynamischer Beziehung zum digitalen Linz.

Architettura della Separazione resultiert also aus einer Reihe von in Linz durchgeführten Scan- und Sampling-Aktivitäten und ist als Weiterentwicklung früherer interaktiver Großinstallationen wie *Locus* [1994] und *Teatro dell'ascolto* [Theater des Hörens, 1995] zu verstehen. In diesen Projekten führten dramaturgische und narrative Vorstellungen die verwendeten Technologien auf eine Reise in

Here, the city is that complex machine that accommodates as well as modifies the flow of information, a machine which houses a corpus whose subcomponents are put under surveillance and pressure. Here, the cityscape is simultaneously a homeland and a foreign place, a border town which reveals itself incessantly, whereby it most often has at its disposal geographical and political codices which are both provisional and biased. If one regards the city as a symbol of the process of becoming, then residing would be the original form of staying at a place. On the other hand, that would imply that the subdivision of a place is to be interpreted as a minimal transference of a body to another body.

"The heterotopia is capable of merging together at a single location multiple spaces and multiple placements which are inherently incompatible. In this way, the theater makes it possible for a whole series of mutually irreconcilable places to succeed one another onto the rectangle of the stage. Similarly, the cinema is a remarkable rectangular room, in whose background one sees a three-dimensional space projected onto a two-dimensional screen. But perhaps the garden is the oldest of these heterotopias containing highly contradictory positionings."
Michel Foucault

Architettura della Separazione penetrates everything that bodies penetrate, and shares with them their transitoriness and, at the same time, their diversity of perspectives and visions. It demands, produces and glorifies a body which becomes a space, so that the space becomes flesh. The body as an entity is a standard of measurement and a magnitude, a track and a border. These are tracks and borders upon which identity in transition is based.

Therefore, this is a matter of *inhabiting* the geography, the politics, the history and – not least of all – the emotionality of this neighborhood. This takes place both through the staging of a performance which is based, in particular, on the theory and practice of scanning – thus, on the original text, on a space created primarily by means of digital technologies, on sound, and on relationship between places and bodies.

Performance

Scanning Bacchae is being staged in the ambiance of *Linz,* and the city itself provides the infrastructure for the dramaturgy. At times, the installation thus becomes the digital set of the performance. Both of these circumstances can be experienced by the audience in completely different ways. Sometimes,

die Tiefen der Erinnerung an gelebte Räume, im Wechselspiel zwischen Erinnerung und Vergessen und im Bewußtsein jener leeren und diskutierbaren Räume, die zwischen dem Wirklichen, dem Mutmaßlichen und dem Möglichen existieren.

Hier ist die Stadt jene komplexe Maschine, die den Informationsfluß beherbergt und verändert, die einen Korpus beherbergt, dessen Teilkörper bedrängt und überwacht werden. Die Stadtlandschaft ist hier zugleich Ort der Heimat und der Fremde, ein Grenzort, der sich unablässig offenbart und dabei – in der Regel – über geographische und politische Kodizes verfügt, welche provisorisch und parteiisch sind. Sieht man die Stadt als Symbol des Werdens, so wäre das Wohnen die ursprüngliche Form des Aufenthalts an einem Ort. Das wiederum hieße, die Gliederung eines Gebietes als minimale Übertragung eines Körpers auf einen anderen Körper aufzufassen.

Architettura della Separazione durchdringt alles, was auch Körper durchdringen, und teilt mit diesen die Unbeständigkeit und zugleich Vielfalt der Perspektiven und Visionen. Sie fordert, erzeugt und verherrlicht einen Körper, der zu Raum wird, auf daß der Raum Fleisch wird. Die Einheit Körper ist Maßstab und Größe, Fährte und Grenze. Es sind Fährten und Grenzen, die Identität in Bewegung begründen.

Es geht also darum, die Geographie, Politik, Geschichte und nicht zuletzt die Emotionalität dieser Umgebung zu *bewohnen*. Dies geschieht zugleich durch die Aufführung einer Performance, die insbesondere auf Theorie und Praxis des Scanning aufbaut, also auf dem Originaltext, auf einem vornehmlich durch digitale Technologien geschaffenen Raum, auf Klang und auf der Beziehung zwischen Orten und Körpern.

Performance

Scanning Bacchae wird im Ambiente *Linz* aufgeführt, und die Stadt selbst liefert die Infrastruktur für die Dramaturgie. Die Installation wird also zuweilen zum digitalen Set der Performance. Für das Publikum sind diese beiden Umstände in völlig unterschiedlicher Weise erfahrbar. Einmal wird von Zeiten und Strecken ausgegangen, die der Besucher fest-

the point of temporal and spatial departure is one which the visitor can precisely ascertain; at other times, events proceed from a given space at a given time. From the standpoint of perception, this is a matter of two different modalities from which a third is derived – one which brings about the emergence of a force field from the hybridization of the first two.

The text which serves as the source of inspiration and point of orientation for *Scanning Bacchae* is Euripides' *The Bacchae* – a natural focus for the effort to reconcile pleasure and discipline. The original, contemporary text follows the traces of a tragedy which is based upon the pressing need for identity – whether it be individual, national or territorial – and is, in this sense, thoroughly modern. Euripides' *Bacchae* thus seem to be the origin of a non-moral point of view. This work provides a glimpse of a ritual which is neither purely private nor totally collective, but rather micro-communal – the ritual of a geometry of feelings, of liberation, of ecstasy and hysteria, of forgetting. Force field, battle field, playing field, ritual of the body and glorification of one's own psychic and physical mechanism, the competitive drive as mental conditioning analogous to physical training.

In Co-operation with Radio FRO – Freier Rundfunk Oberösterreich, Stadtwerkstatt Linz, RADIO LADA, ORF Kunstradio, RAI Audiobox, STEIM Amsterdam, Università di Siena / Multimedia Communication Laboratory del Corso in Scienze della Comunicazione, INU Istituto Nazionale di Urbanistica, Roma
Collaborating Consultants: Robert Adrian X, Giorgio Conti [Archivi della Modernità Venezia], Guido Guidi
Prodution Team: Isabella Bordoni, Roberto Paci Dalò, Tom Demeyer [STEIM], Norbert Math

AGAMBEN, GIORGIO *Homo sacer*, Torino 1995
AGAMBEN, GIORGIO *Mezzi senza fine*, Torino 1996
EURIPIDES, *The Bacchae and other Plays*, Harmondsworth 1973
FOUCAULT, MICHEL, *Eterotopia. Luoghi e non luoghi metropolitani*, Milano 1994 [dt.: *Andere Räume*. in: BARCK, KARLHEINZ/GENTE, PETER/Paris, HEIDI/ RICHTER STEFAN [HRSG.], *Aisthesis, Wahrnehmung heute oder Perspektiven einer anderen Ästhetik*, Leipzig 1990]

Die Heterotopie vermag an einen einzigen Ort mehrere Räume, mehrere Plazierungen zusammenzulegen, die an sich unvereinbar sind. So läßt das Theater auf dem Viereck der Bühne eine ganze Reihe von einander fremden Orten aufeinander folgen; so ist das Kino ein merkwürdiger viereckiger Saal, in dessen Hintergrund man einen zweidimensionalen Schirm einen dreidimensionalen Raum sich projizieren sieht. Aber vielleicht ist die älteste dieser Heterotopien mit widersprüchlichen Plazierungen der Garten.

Michel Foucault

legt, dann wiederum von einem gegebenen Raum und einer gegebenen Zeit. Vom Standpunkt der Wahrnehmung aus handelt es sich um zwei verschiedene Modalitäten, aus denen sich eine dritte ableitet, die aus der Hybridisierung der beiden ersteren ein eigenes Kräftefeld entstehen läßt.

Der Text, der *Scanning Bacchae* als Quelle der Inspiration und Orientierung zugrundeliegt, sind die Bakchen von Euripides – natürlicher Ort der Bemühung, Genuß und Disziplin zu vereinbaren. Der zeitgenössische Originaltext folgt den Spuren einer Tragödie, die aufgrund des dringenden Bedürfnisses nach Identität – sei diese nun individuell, national oder territorial – durchaus modern ist. Euripides' *Bakchen* scheinen also Ursprung einer nicht moralischen Sichtweise, sie gewähren einen Blick auf ein Ritual, das weder rein privat noch gänzlich kollektiv ist, sondern eher mikrogemeinschaftlich – Ritual einer Geometrie der Gefühle, der Befreiung, der Unsinnigkeit, der Vergeßlichkeit.

Kräftefeld, Schlachtfeld, Sportplatz, Ritual der Körper und Verherrlichung des eigenen psychischen und physischen Mechanismus, der Wettbewerbsfähigkeitstick als geistige Dressur analog zum körperlichen Training.

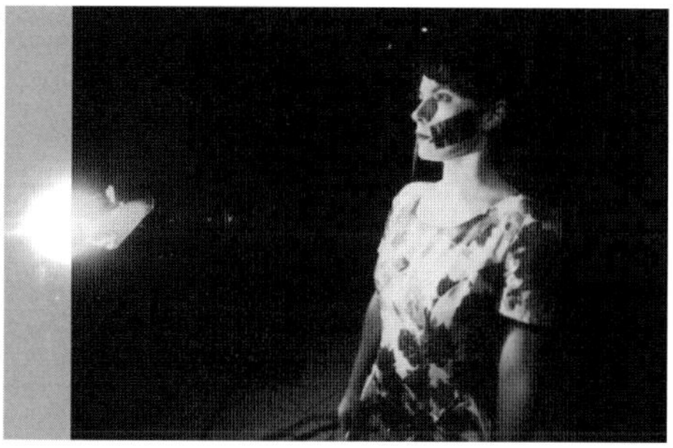

Relational Architecture #2 Displaced Emperors

Rafael Lozano-Hemmer

Relational architecture *general concept*

Relational architecture can be defined as the technological actualisation of buildings and public spaces with alien memory. Relational architecture transforms the master-narratives of a specific building by adding and subtracting audiovisual elements to affect it, effect it and re-contextualize it. Relational buildings have audience-activated hyperlinks to predetermined spatiotemporal settings that may include other buildings, other political or aesthetic contexts, other histories, or other physics.

Virtual architecture could be differentiated from relational architecture in that the former is based on simulation while the latter is based on dissimulation. Virtual buildings are data constructs that strive for realism, asking the participant to *suspend disbelief* and *play along* with the environment; relational buildings, on the other hand, are real buildings pretending to be something other than themselves, masquerading as that which they might become, asking participants to *suspend belief* and probe, interact and experiment with the false construct. Virtual architecture tends to miniaturize buildings to the participant's scale,

Relationale Architektur #2 Displaced Emperors

Rafael Lozano-Hemmer

for example through VR peripherals such as HMDs or CAVEs, while relational architecture amplifies the participant to the building's scale, or emphasizes the relationship between urban and personal scale. In this sense, virtual architecture dematerializes the body, while relational architecture dematerializes the environment.

Virtual and relational architectures are not opposing practices, nor are they mutually exclusive. They are similar in that both are largely participant-centered, computer-generated, and less permanent, expensive, sheltering and territorial than physical architecture.

Relational architecture need not be inscribed within postmodern parasitic or symbiotic practice nor post-structural self-referentiality: it is not necessarily engaged in deconstruction, nor does it need to use the language or structure of the building itself. Instead, relational architecture events could be considered *buildings with subtitles*, where the translators may or may not speak the building's language: the subtitles need not be causal, referential, or even contextual. Relational architecture pieces vindicate their synthetic, artificial qualities, and reserve the right to be effectist, improvisational and useless.

The real motivation behind relational architecture is the modification of behaviour: the artist creates a situation where the building, the urban context and the participants relate in new, *alien* ways. The piece can be considered successful if the artist's intervention modifies the point of equilibrium between the public's actions and the building's reactions, and vice versa. There can be a variety of causal, chaotic, telepresent, or emergent behaviours programmed into the piece but the uncertainty of the outcome is one of the main motivations for doing such a piece.

Although relational architecture is a relatively new field within media arts, precedents date back to ancient Greece [Simonides' discovery of mnemonics], and to the use of the Art of Memory in Chinese and Hermetic rhetoric traditions. Contemporary practices of site-specific installation, street performance and public art have been of paramount importance in the development of the field. A significant number of artists have been, and continue to be, influential in the practice, among them Krzysztof Wodiczko, Archigram, Toyo Ito, Gordon Matta-Clark, Jenny Holzer, the Situationists,

Relationale Architektur

Relationale Architektur kann man als die technologische Aktualisierung von Gebäuden und öffentlichen Räumen durch ein Fremdgedächtnis definieren. Relationale Architektur besetzt die Meta-Narrative eines bestimmten Gebäudes durch die Hinzufügung oder Wegnahme audiovisueller Elemente, um so auf sie einzuwirken, sie zur Wirkung zu bringen, zu rekontextualisieren. Relationale Gebäude weisen publikumsaktivierte Hyperlinks zu vorbestimmten raumzeitlichen Situationen auf, die aus anderen Gebäuden, anderen politischen oder ästhetischen Kontexten, anderen historischen Erzählungen oder einer anderen Physis bestehen können.

Virtuelle und relationale Architektur sind vielleicht darin unterschieden, daß erstere vor allem auf Simulation, letztere dagegen auf Dissimulation beruht. Virtuelle Gebäude sind Datenkonstrukte, die auf Realismus aus sind, die die Teilnehmer auffordern, ihre Zweifel auszublenden und mit der Umgebung mitzuspielen; relationale Gebäude hingegen sind wirkliche Gebäude, die sich als etwas anderes ausgeben als sie sind, die sich als etwas maskieren, das sie sein könnten, und die Teilnehmer auffordern, ihren Glauben auszublenden und die Verkleidung zu erproben, mit ihr zu interagieren und zu experimentieren. Die beiden Ansätze bedienen sich auch unterschiedlicher Vorgangsweisen in bezug auf den Maßstab: Die virtuelle Architektur miniaturisiert Gebäude gerne auf die Größe des Teilnehmers, etwa mittels VR-Peripheriegeräten wie Datenhelmen, CAVEs oder Pods, wogegen die relationale Architektur den Teilnehmer mit technischen Mitteln auf den Maßstab des Gebäudes vergrößert oder das Verhältnis zwischen urbanem und persönlichem Maßstab unterstreicht. In diesem Sinne dematerialisiert die virtuelle Architektur den Körper, während die relationale die Umwelt dematerialisiert.

Virtuelle und relationale Architektur sind keine gegensätzlichen Praxen und schließen einander auch nicht aus. Sie sind einander insofern ähnlich, als beide computergeneriert und stark teilnehmerbezogen sind, und daß sie weniger kostspielig, dauerhaft, schutzbietend und territorial als physische Architektur sind.

Relationale Architektur braucht sich weder in die parasitäre oder symbiotische Praxis

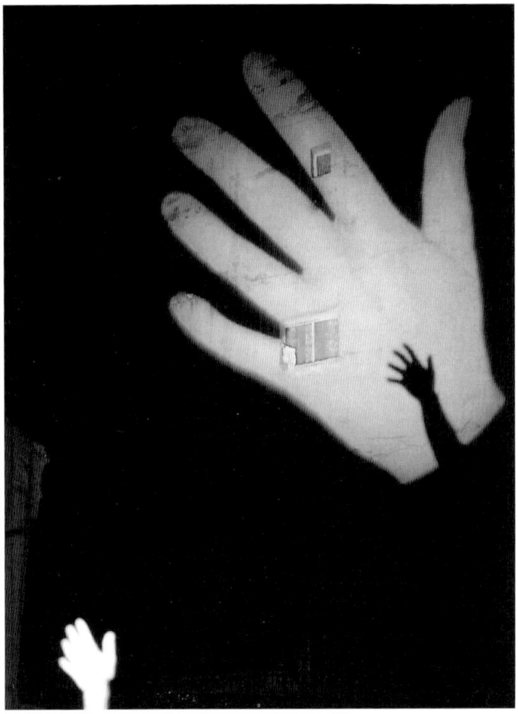

Fig. 1 Architakt interface/*Architakt-Interface*

Christian Möller, Christo, Peter Greenaway, Vito Acconci, Dennis Adams, Knowbotic Research, Dan Graham, and Rachel Whiteread.

Rafael Lozano-Hemmer and Will Bauer are collaborating in the development of a series of relational architecture pieces to be presented over the next few years. The pieces entail the development of novel architectural interfaces using real-time computer graphics, 3D sensors, electro-acoustic music and robotic lights. The events, which will take place after dusk, will be presented in half a dozen cities including Barcelona, Graz, Madrid and Mexico City.

Displaced Emperors

Displaced Emperors is a relational architecture piece designed to transform the emblematic Linz Castle high above the bank of the Danube. The piece constructs a vector between two apparently unrelated historical oddities that link Mexico and Austria: the Mexican empire of Maximilian of Habsburg [1864-1867] and the *Penacho de Montezuma*, the Quetzal-feather crown of one of the last Aztec Emperors, currently housed in the Ethnological Museum in Vienna. This juxtaposition seeks to involve

der Postmoderne noch in die poststrukturalistische Selbstrefentialität einzuschreiben: Sie betreibt nicht unbedingt Dekonstruktion und muß sich auch nicht der Sprache oder Struktur des Gebäudes selbst bedienen. Eher könnte man relationale Architekturereignisse als *Gebäude mit interaktiven Untertiteln* betrachten, deren Übersetzer die Sprache des Gebäudes zwar sprechen können, aber nicht müssen: Die Untertitel müssen nicht kausal, referentiell und nicht einmal kontextuell sein. Relationale Architekturarbeiten erheben Anspruch auf ihre synthetischen, artifiziellen Eigenschaften und nehmen sich das Recht heraus, effektvoll, improvisatorisch und nutzlos zu sein.

Doch die eigentliche Motivation der relationalen Architektur besteht in der Modifikation von Verhaltensweisen: Der Künstler stellt eine Situation her, in der Gebäude, urbaner Kontext und Teilnehmer in einen neuen und *fremdartigen* Bezug zueinander treten. Die Arbeit kann als gelungen betrachtet werden, wenn die Intervention des Künstlers das dynamische Gleichgewicht zwischen Publikumsaktion und Gebäudereaktion – und vice versa – verändert. Eine Vielzahl kausaler, chaotischer, telepräsenter prädeterminierter oder emergenter Verhaltensweisen können in die Arbeit einprogrammiert werden, doch die Ungewißheit des Ausgangs ist eines der Hauptmotive für die Durchführung einer solchen Arbeit.

Wiewohl die relationale Architektur ein relativ neues Feld auf dem Gebiet der Medienkunst darstellt, reichen die Vorläufer bis in die Antike [Simonides' Entdeckung der Mnemotechnik] und zum Gebrauch der Gedächtniskunst in der chinesischen und der hermetischen Rhetoriktradition zurück. Zeitgenössische Praktiken der ortsspezifischen Installation, der Straßenperformance und der Kunst im öffentlichen Raum waren für die Entwicklung des Gebietes von wesentlicher Bedeutung. Eine beträchtliche Anzahl von Künstlern haben in Vergangenheit oder Gegenwart diese Praxis beeinflußt, darunter Kristoff Wodiczko, Archigram, Toyo Ito, Gordon Matta-Clark, Jenny Holzer, die Situationisten, Christian Möller, Christo, Peter Greenaway, Vito Acconci, Dennis Adams, Knowbotic Research, Dan Graham, Richard Serra and Rachel Whiteread.

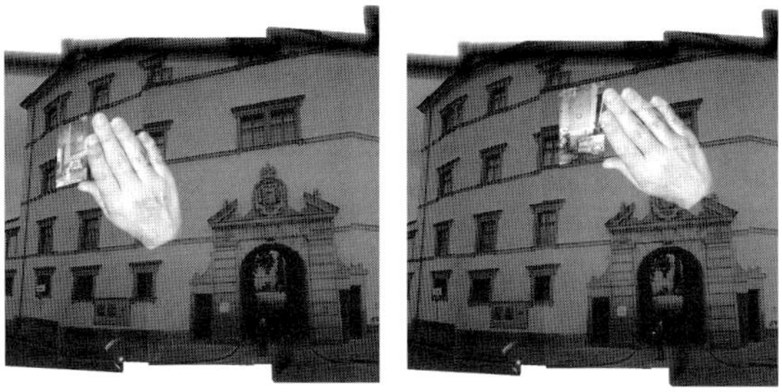

Fig. 2
Revealing palaces within palaces/*Das Aufdecken von Schlössern in Schlössern*

the public in a web of power relations in which history is seen as a virtual environment and identity is a performance sponsored by the myth of cultural property.

1 Architact

Participants standing in the plaza situated between the Castle's Rudolfstor gate and Hofberg street interact with the Castle by pointing at it with their hand. A wireless 3D tracker calculates the direction of the participant's arm and a large, animated projection of a human hand appears wherever he or she is pointing [figure 1]. When the participant moves his or her arm, the telematic hand follows, sliding over the Castle's facade, creating the effect of an amplified caress. Depending on where and how the participant *touches* the Castle, it transforms itself into Chapultepec Palace, Borda Gardens, or other residences of the Habsburg Emperors in Mexico. The telematic hand *reveals* the Mexican palaces as though they were inside the Linz Castle: the exterior becomes the interior [figure 2]. As the hand activates certain windows, other audiovisual events relating to relevant architectural references are triggered and controlled. Fleshfactor: the *architact* interface allows participants to read the building's media layer – a telematic braille that makes perception a highly physical act.

Maximilian and his wife Carlota were elected Emperor and Empress of Mexico by a small group of conservative notables who wanted to protect their interests against the national liberal policies proposed by Benito Juarez [figure 3]. With the help of Napoleon III's army, Maximilian, himself a liberal, took over the country in 1864 having been deceived over the amount of popular support that his regime

remote sensations

Rafael Lozano-Hemmer und Will Bauer arbeiten gemeinsam an der Entwicklung einer Reihe von relationalen Architekurarbeiten, die im Lauf der nächsten Jahre präsentiert werden. Die Arbeiten umfassen die Entwicklung neuer Architekturschnittstellen, die mit Echtzeitcomputergraphik, 3D-Sensoren, elektroakustischer Musik und besonders Robotic Lighting arbeiten. Die Events, die nach Einbruch der Dämmerung stattfinden, werden in einem halben Dutzend Städten präsentiert, darunter Barcelona, Graz, Madrid und Mexico City.

Displaced Emperors

Für die Ars Electronica wurde eine relationale Architekturarbeit entwickelt, die das hoch über dem Donauufer liegende emblematische Linzer Schloß transformiert. Die Arbeit stellt einen Vektor zwischen zwei scheinbar unzusammenhängenden historischen Eigentümlichkeiten her, die Mexiko und Österreich miteinander verbinden: das mexikanische Kaiserreich des Maximilian von Habsburg [1864-1867] und der *Penacho de Montezuma*, die Quetzalfedernkrone eines der letzten Aztekenherrscher, die im Besitz des Wiener Völkerkundemuseums ist. Die Arbeit möchte das Publikum in ein Gewebe von Machtbeziehungen verwickeln, in dem Geschichte als virtuelle Umwelt und Identität als eine vom Mythos des Kulturbesitzes getragene Performance gesehen wird.

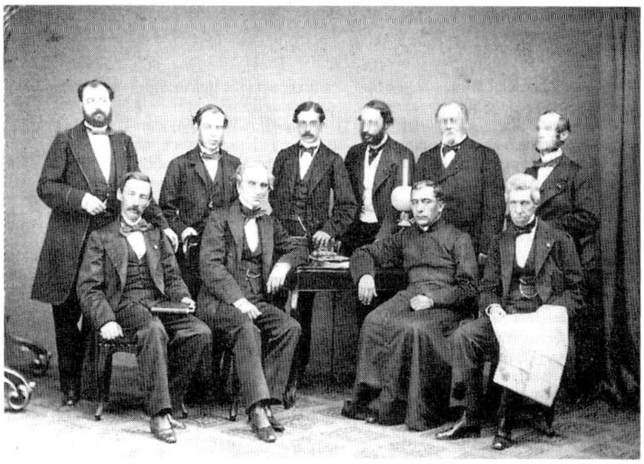

Fig. 3
The notables who elected Maximilian/ *Die Notabeln, die Maximilian gewählt haben*

1 Architact

Die auf dem kleinen Platz zwischen Rudolfstor und Hofbergstraße stehenden Teilnehmer interagieren mit dem Schloß, indem sie

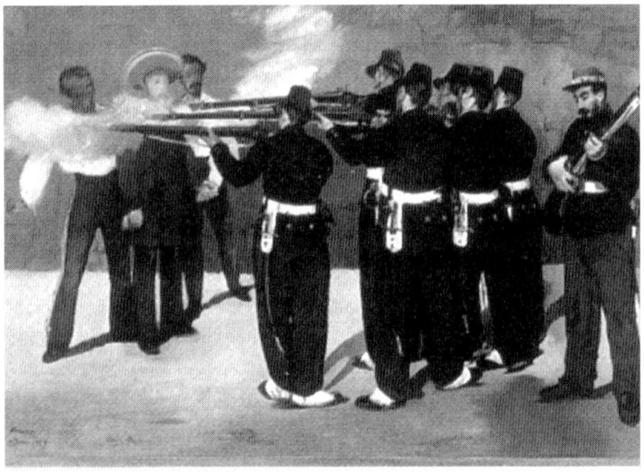

Fig. 4
The execution of Emperor Maximilian, by Manet/
Die Hinrichtung Kaiser Maximilians, von Manet

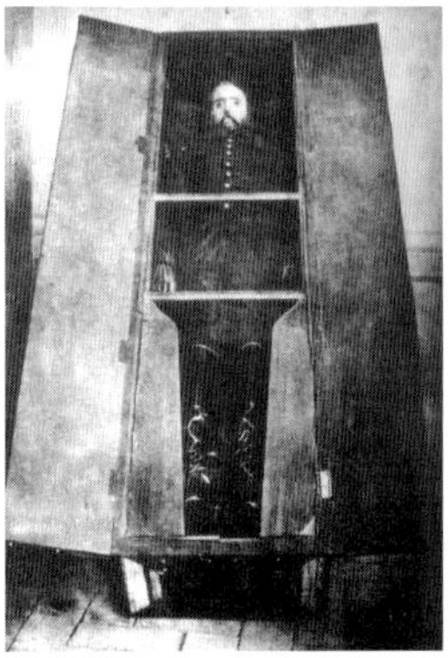

Fig. 5
Maximilian shipped back to Austria/
Maximilian wird nach Österreich überführt

would have. The story ends in tragedy with the withdrawal of the French troops and Maximilian's capture and execution in 1867, an event portrayed by Manet in a painting that Bataille called the beginning of the modern movement [figure 4]. Maximilian's body was embalmed and shipped back to Austria in the Novara: it now rests in the imperial crypt of the Church of the Capuchins in Vienna [figure 5].

During their *his* reign, Maximilian and Carlota lived in Chapultepec Palace, which they transformed so that it was reminiscent of their palace at Miramar in Trieste. This Italian palace, in turn, had several references to prior Habsburg palaces in Austria including the Schönbrunn. The Austrian palaces were themselves an expression of a variety of classical stylistic archetypes. This **mise-en-abime** formed by palaces within palaces will be exploited in **Displaced Emperors** as a source of architectural samples to be mixed and remixed by the participant, who becomes a kind of deterritorial, detemporalized *architecture jockey* [figure 6].

remote sensations

mit der Hand darauf zeigen. Ein drahtloser 3D-Tracker errechnet die Richtung des TeilnehmerInnenarms, worauf eine große animierte Menschenhand dort projiziert wird, wohin er/sie zeigt [Abb. 1]. Bewegt der/die TeilnehmerIn seinen/ihren Arm, so bewegt sich auch die telematische Hand; sie gleitet über die Schloßfassade und erzeugt den Eindruck einer verstärkten Liebkosung. Je nachdem wo und wie der/die TeilnehmerIn das Schloß *berührt*, verwandelt sich dieses in das Schloß Chapultepec, in die Borda-Park-Residenz oder andere Wohnsitze der Habsburgerkaiser in Mexiko. Die telematische Hand *enthüllt* die mexikanischen Schlösser, als befänden sie sich innerhalb des Linzer Schlosses: Das Außen wird zum Innen [Abb. 2]. Wenn die Hand bestimmte Fenster aktiviert, werden andere mit einschlägigen architektonischen Bezügen gekoppelte audiovisuelle Ereignisse ausgelöst und gesteuert. FleshFactor: Durch die Architact-Schnittstelle können die Teilnehmer die Medienschicht des Gebäudes wie eine telematische Blindenschrift lesen, die die Wahrnehmung zu einem hochgradig körperlichen Akt macht.

Die Wahl Maximilians und seiner Frau Carlota zum Kaiser von Mexiko wurde durch eine kleine Gruppe konservativer Notabeln betrieben, die ihre Interessen gegen die von Benito Juarez propagierte national-liberale Politik schützen wollten [Abb. 3]. Getäuscht über den Rückhalt seines Regimes im Volk übernahm Maximilian, der selbst ein Liberaler war, im Jahr 1864 mit Hilfe der Armee Napoleons III. das Land. Die Geschichte endet tragisch mit dem Rückzug der französischen Truppen und der Gefangennahme und Hinrichtung Maximilians im Jahr 1867, ein Ereignis, das Manet in einem von Bataille als Beginn der Moderne bezeichneten Gemälde dargestellt hat [Abb. 4]. Der Leichnam Maximilians wurde einbalsamiert und auf der Novara nach Europa zurückgebracht: Er befindet sich heute in der Kaisergruft der Kapuzinerkirche in Wien [Abb. 5].

Während seiner Herrschaft residierte Maximilian mit seiner Frau im Schloß Chapultepec, das sie sich ähnlich ihrem Schloß Miramar in Triest umbauen ließen. Dieses italienische Schloß wies seinerseits zahlreiche Bezüge zu Habsburgerschlössern in Österreich, darunter auch Schönbrunn, auf. Die österreichi-

2 Push Button Override

At a makeshift souvenir shop near the Castle there is a computer monitor that shows the location of the architact participants with Orwellian precision [figure 7]. The monitor is beside a big bright red button clearly labeled *Montezuma*. Pressing the Montezuma button will do three things: a] turn off all the lights except a searchlight with the cultural property symbol which will automatically follow the participant who has the tracker; b] turn on a very large projection of the *Penacho de Montezuma* on the fasade of the Castle; and c]trigger distorted Mariachi music [figure 8]. As soon as the button is released, the participants at the Castle can resume their interaction.

ig. 6
absburg Palaces/
e Paläste der
absburger

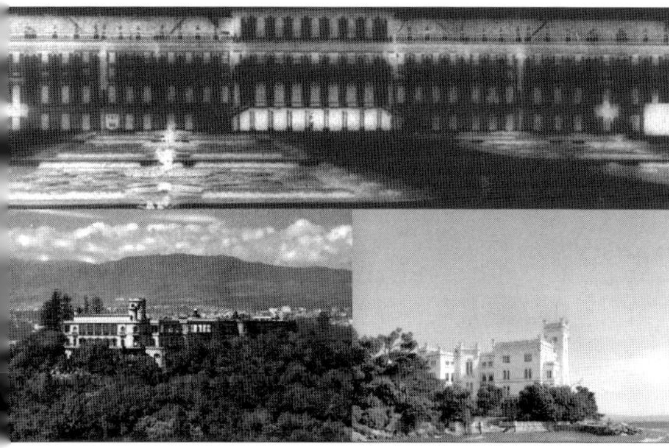

The *Penacho de Montezuma* is an Aztec headdress made out of the green tail feathers of the extinct Quetzal bird. Although there is no hard evidence that the Penacho was Emperor Montezuma II's *crown,* it is well known that it was the symbol of the most outstanding political and religious power in Pre-Columbian Mexico. According to one version of its history, the Penacho was given by Montezuma to Spanish conqueror Hernán Cortès, who in turn gave it as a gift to Emperor Carlos I of Spain in 1519. In that same year Cortès captured and imprisoned the Aztec Emperor, who died shortly after under mysterious circumstances: according to Indian witnesses he was murdered by the Spaniards. The Penacho was passed from Carlos I to his brother Fernando who kept it in his art collection in the Ambras Castle. The Penacho was sent to Vienna and in 1878 it was taken out of the closet where it had been kept, folded and motheaten, for decades. The piece is now on display at the Ethnological Museum in Vienna.

schen Schlösser wiederum zitierten eine Vielfalt klassischer stilistischer Archetypen. Dieses aus Schlössern in Schlössern bestehende *Mise-en-âbime* wird in *Displaced Emperors* als Quelle von Architektursamples ausgebeutet, die vom Teilnehmer immer wieder neu abgemischt werden können, wodurch dieser zu einer Art deterritorialem, detemporalem *architecture jockey* wird [Abb. 6].

2 Push Button Override [Abschaltung per Knopfdruck]

In einem improvisierten Andenkenstand ist ein Computermonitor aufgestellt, der den Schauplatz der Architact-Teilnehmern mit Orwellscher Präzision wiedergibt [Abb. 7]. Neben dem Monitor befindet sich ein großer knallroter Druckknopf, der deutlich mit *Montezuma* gekennzeichnet ist. Das Drücken des Montezuma-Knopfs hat drei Dinge zur Folge: a] Es schalten sich bis auf einen Suchscheinwerfer mit dem Kulturbesitzsymbol, der automatisch den Teilnehmer mit dem Tracker ins Visier nimmt, sämtliche Lichter aus; b] eine übergroße Projektion des *Penacho de Montezuma* wird auf die Schloßfassade geworfen;

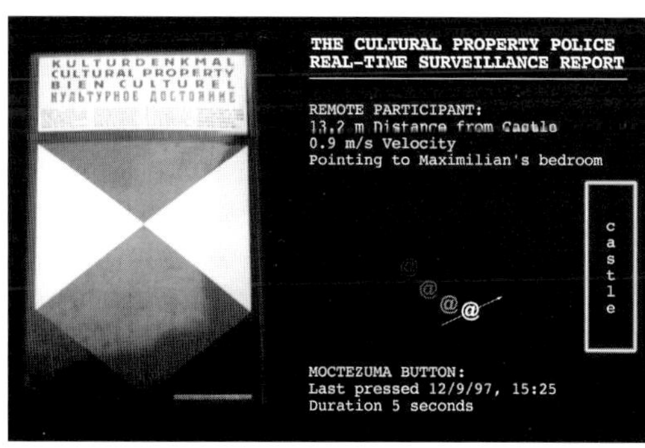

Fig. 7
Surveillance monitor at souvenir shop/
Überwachungsmonitor am Andenkenstand

c] verzerrte mexikanische Straßenmusik setzt ein [Abb. 8]. Sobald der Knopf wieder losgelassen wird, können die Teilnehmer am Schloß ihre Interaktion fortsetzen.

Der *Penacho de Montezuma* ist ein aztekischer Kopfschmuck aus den grünen Schwanzfedern des ausgestorbenen Quetzal. Wiewohl es keinen sicheren Beweis dafür gibt, daß der Penacho die *Krone* Montezumas II. war, stellt er bekanntermaßen das Symbol der höchsten politischen und religiösen Macht des präkolumbischen Mexiko dar. Einer Geschichtsversion gemäß überreichte Montezuma den

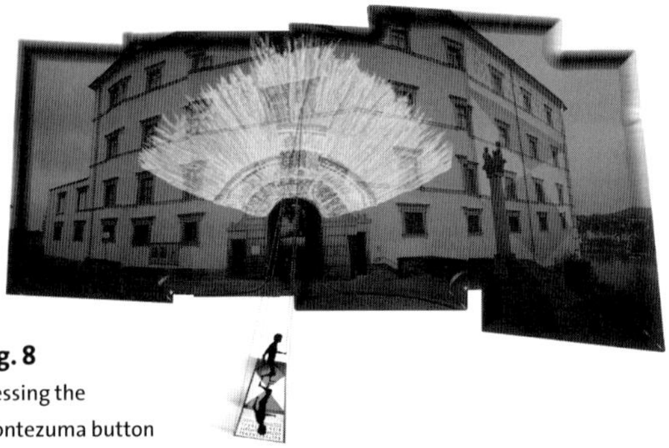

Fig. 8
Pressing the Montezuma button
Das Drücken des Montezuma-Knopfes

Mexicans believe that the Penacho is a very important part of their national identity, a piece with extraordinary emotional, cultural and symbolic value. Indeed, Aztecs assigned considerably more significance to objects made with feathers than with gold and silver. Many notable Austrians have expressed their desire to see the Penacho return to Mexico, among them Rudolf Burger, Carl Pruscha, and Peter Noever. These Austrians believe that the Penacho should be given as a gift to Mexicans as a symbolic gesture, among other reasons, to thank them for their protest in the League of Nations during the German annexation of Austria in 1938.

The Montezuma button is a causal, irritating 1-bit intervention which serves as a metaphor for the simplistic, executive override features found in all complex control systems. The button is surrounded by copious information [posters, leaflets, etc.] on the political and legal situation of the Penacho, and whether it should be returned to Mexico, kept in Vienna, burnt, digitized, or otherwise preserved or destroyed. The Montezuma button is a parody of the currency of cultural exchange and a probe into the arbitrariness of the concept of *heritage*.

Rafael Lozano-Hemmer: concept, direction, visuals, text
Will Bauer: audio, programming, custom hardware
Susie Ramsay: production coordinator
Daniel Rivera: research correspondent
Sponsors:
Martin Professional A/S and M TEC Vertriebsgesellschaft m.b.H.: robotic lighting
Pigi ETC Audiovisuel: high power projection with interactive control

Penacho dem spanischen Eroberer Hernán Cortèz, der ihn 1519 seinerseits dem König von Spanien, Carlos I., zum Geschenk machte. Im selben Jahr nahm Cortèz den Aztekenherrscher gefangen, und ein Jahr später starb dieser unter mysteriösen Umständen: Nach indianischen Zeugenberichten wurde er von den Spaniern ermordet. Carlos I. gab den Penacho an seinen Bruder Fernando weiter, der ihn in seiner Kunstsammlung in Schloß Ambras aufbewahrte. Von dort gelangte er nach Wien, wo man ihn 1878 schließlich aus dem Schrank hervorholte, in dem er jahrzehntelang zusammengefaltet und mottenzerfressen gelagert hatte. Das Objekt ist heute im Wiener Völkerkundemuseum ausgestellt.

Für Mexikaner ist der Penacho ein äußerst wichtiger Bestandteil ihrer nationalen Identität, ein Objekt von außerordentlichem emotionalem, kulturellem und symbolischem Wert. Überdies maßen Azteken Objekten aus Federn wesentlich größere Bedeutung bei als solchen aus Gold oder Silber. Viele angesehene Österreicher – darunter Rudolf Burger, Carl Pruscha und Peter Noever – haben erklärt, daß sie den Penacho gerne an Mexiko zurückgegeben sähen. Diese Österreicher sind der Meinung, man sollte den Penacho den Mexikanern zum Geschenk machen, um ihnen unter anderem dafür zu danken, daß sie 1938 beim Anschluß Österreichs an Deutschland beim Völkerbund Protest eingelegt haben.

Der Montezuma-Knopf ist eine kausale, irritierende 1-Bit-Intervention, die als Metapher für die einfachen, in allen komplexen Kontrollsystemen zu findenden Automatikabschaltfunktionen dient. Der Knopf ist von einer Unmenge Informationsmaterial [Poster, Handzettel usw.] über die politische und rechtliche Lage des Penacho umgeben: ob er an Mexiko zurückgegeben, in Wien behalten, verbrannt, digitalisiert oder auf andere Weise erhalten oder zerstört werden soll. Der Montezuma-Knopf ist eine Parodie auf die Währung des kulturellen Austausches und eine Hinterfragung der Willkür des Begriffs *Kulturerbe*.

Polyphemus' Eye

Concha Jerez/José Iges

The giant with a single eye is, in fact, just a poetic reference that takes us from those times of Ulysses to our day. Certainly, many things have changed since then. One of them has been the state of sophistication of that giant, in other words the sociopolitical and economic system in which we are immersed, as he observes us, his eye constantly on the watch. His is an electronic impersonal eye that is the one of the systems of surveillance.

When we talk about an eye, we would do better to speak simply of *just* a vivisectionate brain fed on its decision-taking by thousands of tiny eyes and ears. On the one hand there are the almost omnipresent surveillance cameras; on the other hand, the systems of telephonic listening, right down to the tiny microphones that pick up all kind of conversations. And, further than that, with the development of the informatics networks, our body and, with it, our public and private activity appear permanently deconstructed and regenerated, like a digital Frankenstein made of small fragments, of indications that, of course, can be used against us.

Das Auge des Polyphem

Concha Jerez/José Iges

Der einäugige Riese – hier dient er nur als poetisches Gedankenspiel, das uns aus den Tagen des Odysseus in unsere Zeit führt. Seit jenen Tagen hat sich freilich viel verändert. So auch der Entwicklungsgrad des Riesen oder, mit anderen Worten, das soziopolitische und wirtschaftliche System, in das wir eingebunden sind, während sein Auge mit nie nachlassender Aufmerksamkeit auf uns gerichtet ist und uns beobachtet. Das Auge des Polyphem ist ein unpersönliches, elektronisches; es ist das Auge der Überwachungssysteme.

Es wäre treffender, statt von einem Auge von einem vivisezierenden Gehirn zu sprechen, das Entscheidungen trifft und dabei von tausenden winzigen Augen und Ohren mit Informationen gefüttert wird. Zum einen sind wir von omnipräsenten Überwachungskameras umgeben, zum anderen von Telefonabhörsystemen, von winzigen Mikrophonen, die jedes Gespräch auffangen. Es scheint zudem, als würde durch die Entwicklung der Informationsnetze unser Körper und mit ihm unser privates und öffentliches Leben unentwegt seziert und wieder neu zusammengesetzt – als wäre der Mensch ein digitaler Frankenstein, aufgebaut aus Informationsbruchstücken, die selbstverständlich auch zu unserem Nachteil verwendet werden können.

Was diese Sicherheitssysteme betrifft, so wird behauptet, daß der Unterschied zwischen einem demokratischen und einem diktatorischen System darin bestehe, daß in ersterem die Repression mit viel subtileren, beinahe unmerklichen Methoden geschehe. Diese Behauptung ruft uns die Grenzen der Freiheit in einem demokratischen System in Erinnerung. Überwachung vermittelt uns das Gefühl

It has been said that, on matters of security, what differentiates between a democratic system and a dictatorial system is that repression is exercised with much subtler, almost imperceptible methods. This statement immediately makes us reflect on the limitations of freedom in a democratic system. Surveillance gives us security within the system, but at the same time supervises – potentially all the time – social and intimate activity that ought to be presided over by the assumption of innocence. The systems of surveillance would, according to these reasonings, be the practical limits of the system of freedom. The impunity of the *voyeur* would be confronted in them with the one eye thatin its turn scrutinizes him.

But while the *voyeur* is a private eye that looks at the potentially forbidden and is, therefore, dangerous, the systems of security are the public eye that spies as continually as it does indifferently. It doesn't select the individual: everything comes under its lens quite indiscriminately. The impersonality that the system tries then to mix for its own profit with objectivity, is its distinctive feature. In the same way, the microphone or the ear-piece of the bugged telephone accept all kinds of messages and, as we know, there are technological tools that allow conversations to be intercepted and a great number of them to be simultaneously recorded. They are deterrent weapons that protect certain interests, as opposed to other weapons that are there -in the best of cases- for accumulating evidence on how a crime against property or against physical integrity was committed.

While the crime is committed, the electronic eye or ear capture it, but the human eye and ear are the ones to interpret the facts. But here we are no longer talking about the gaze of the *voyeur*. It's a purely professional gaze – or listening-in. People are more and more afraid of meeting someone's eye, but they accept without question being submitted to the scrutiny of the surveillance professionals. And when they decide themselves to scrutinize the movements or actions of others, they prefer to do so from a technological watch-tower, as do the professionals. This is then from the anonymity of the Internet, from the TV *reality shows*, from the ever-open *hot* lines with the news of radio stations. The *voyeur* can be arrested *in fla-*

der Sicherheit innerhalb eines Systems, doch gleichzeitig durchdringt sie auch – unter Umständen sogar pausenlos – unser gesellschaftliches und privates Leben, in dem eigentlich das Prinzip der Unschuldsvermutung gelten sollte. Spinnt man diesen Gedanken weiter, so stellt das Überwachungssystem die Grenzen des Systems der Freiheit dar. Der Ungestraftheit des *Voyeurs* steht dann jenes Auge gegenüber, das ihn seinerseits einer genauen Prüfung unterzieht.

Doch während der *Voyeur* den Privatdetektiv darstellt, der etwas potentiell Verbotenes und daher Gefährliches betrachtet, repräsentieren die Sicherheitssysteme die unablässig und ungerührt herumspionierende öffentliche Wachsamkeit. Sie ist nicht an einem bestimmten Individuum interessiert; alles und jedes wird wahllos und willkürlich von ihr aufgezeichnet. Diese Unpersönlichkeit, der das System dann aus Gründen der Vorteilhaftigkeit den Anschein der Objektivität zu geben trachtet, ist ihr unverwechselbares Kennzeichen. Wie Hörer und Sprechmuschel des angezapften Telefons alle möglichen Nachrichten aufnehmen, fangen verschiedenste technische Gerätschaften diese Unterhaltungen ab und halten sie auf Band fest. Sie sind Abschrekkungswaffen zum Schutz bestimmter Interessen. Ihnen stehen Waffen gegenüber, die im Idealfall dazu dienen, Beweise über den Hergang eines Eigentumsdelikts oder einer Körperverletzung zu sammeln. Das elektronische Auge fängt den Moment des Verbrechens ein, doch die Interpretation dieser Fakten obliegt dem menschlichen Auge und Ohr. Hier jedoch sprechen wir nicht länger über den Blick des *Voyeurs*. Hier handelt es sich um einen ganz und gar professionellen Blick oder um professionelles Lauschen. Die Menschen haben in zunehmendem Maße Angst, dem Blick eines Mitmenschen zu begegnen, doch gleichzeitig nehmen sie es unwidersprochen hin, dem prüfenden Blick der Überwachungsprofis ausgesetzt zu sein. Und wenn sie selbst Lust verspüren, die Aktivitäten und Bewegungen anderer Menschen zu beobachten, so tun sie es den Profis gleich und wählen hierfür einen elektronischen Wachturm: die Anonymität des Internet, *Reality Shows* im Fernsehen oder die stets verfügbaren *Hotlines* mit den Nachrichten der Radiostationen. Der *Voyeur* kann

*granti**, but not the televiewer, for whom the system extends security status that, like a protective cloak, has to take in all social groups, whether or not they wish to be protected.

So interactivity is the calculated risk of a fairground chamber of horrors. True interactivity is linked to the risks of horizontal dialogue. On the interactivity of the technological systems there is previous decision-taking that refers to vertical design, hierarchicized. It's another track of the systems of security, a *ludic* corollary of the technology that serves them. To put it another way: the electronic technology serves as a tool of control and as a space of evasion. Thc convictcd individual is escaped at the same time that he or she is controlled, the mor they are controlled, the more they escape.

Space of evasion and space of invasion. If the cultural industry has provided us with appropriate products for invading more spaces for evasion each time, while our living space finds itself more and more invaded by the systems of surveillance, what can art do? How should it respond? Polyphemus met Ulysses, and the giant Goliath the far smaller David. Should it be the task of the artist of our days to generate what some call *a context and a content that would displace the strategies of the technoculture of reduction of knowledge and of communication to the information transmitted by the media*? If this is so, art should be able to clean up with the prejudices and bad habits of the eyes and the ears of the people. We all could be like Ulysses, in that case, because our contemporary Polyphemus will end by noticing that we are all conscious of his look, when we look at him consciously, when he looks at us and through his look discovers the falseness of the answer.

in flagranti erwischt werden, nicht aber der von ferne Zusehende, den das System in Schutz nimmt; einen Schutz, den es wie einen Mantel über alle sozialen Gruppen breiten muß, ob sie diesen Schutz nun wünschen oder nicht.

Interaktivität ist also dem kalkulierbaren Risiko einer Geisterbahn vergleichbar. Wahre Interaktivität ist immer mit den Risiken des horizontalen Dialogs verbunden. Die Interaktivität technischer Systeme ist in ihrem Aufbau durch vertikale, hierarchische Strukturen bestimmt. Sie ist die andere Seite der Sicherheitssysteme, eine *spielerische* Version der sie stützenden Technologie. Oder anders ausgedrückt: Elektronische Hilfsmittel sind Kontrollwerkzeug und Fluchtmöglichkeit in einem. Der Verurteilte entflieht in dem Augenblick, in dem er kontrolliert wird; je mehr Kontrolle es gibt, desto stärker ist die Flucht.

Fluchtmittel und Zugriffsmittel. Wenn die Kulturindustrie uns die Möglichkeiten geliefert hat, uns immer mehr Fluchträume zu erobern, während unser Lebensraum in zunehmendem Maße dem Zugriff der Überwachungssysteme ausgesetzt ist – was kann Kunst bewirken? Wie soll sie reagieren? Polyphem traf auf Odysseus und der Riese Goliath auf den viel kleineren David. Gehört es heute, wie einige meinen, zu den Aufgaben des Künstlers, *Kontext und Inhalt zu schaffen, die Ersatz sein können für die Strategie der Technokultur, Wissen und Kommunikation auf die durch Medien bereitgestellten Informationen zu reduzieren*? Wenn dies der Fall ist, so sollte die Kunst in der Lage sein, mit den Vorurteilen und schlechten Angewohnheiten der Augen und Ohren der Menschen aufzuräumen. Dann könnten wir alle wie Odysseus sein, denn wenn wir ihn bewußt ansehen, wird unser moderner Polyphem letztendlich bemerken, daß wir alle um seinen Blick wissen und durch seinen Blick die Falschheit der Antwort erkennen.

Le triangle d'incertitude – The Triangle of Uncertainty

Suite for maritime landscapes

Cécile Le Prado

Concept

Sailors and seafarers find their bearings at sea by means of natural points of reference located along the coast. These points, for example church spires, hills, water-towers or lighthouses that generally stand out from the rest of the coastline, are called amers [seamarks or landmarks]. All you have to do is identify three such landmarks in complementary directions so as to be able to construct a triangle which inevitably contains your ship. This triangle drawn on the navigation map is called the *triangle of uncertainty.*

The sound installation principle *Le triangle d'incertitude* takes up the principle of triangular navigation substituting these visual seamarks with acoustic *landmarks* – also information elements used in navigation – that can be recognised by listening carefully. Lighthouses, buoys, ship's radio and many other technical facilities warn the sailor of hazards or obstacles.

This installation project is concerned with constructing a triangle of uncertainty on the ground of a fictive, virtual space on the basis of sound recordings made at the following locations: the southern tip of Ireland [Fastnet Rock], the western edge of France [Brittany], and the westernmost point of Spain [Cap Finisterre].

In essence, the installation refers to the position of sounds in space, constantly chopping and changing between orientation and uncertainty.

Realisation

The recordings play an important role for the conception of the work and are made by Cécile Le Prado. Both pre-selected sounds are recorded, such as a lighthouse foghorn or the whistle of a buoy out at sea, as well as sounds

Le triangle d'incertitude – Das Dreieck der Ungewißheit

Suite für Meereslandschaften

Cécile Le Prado

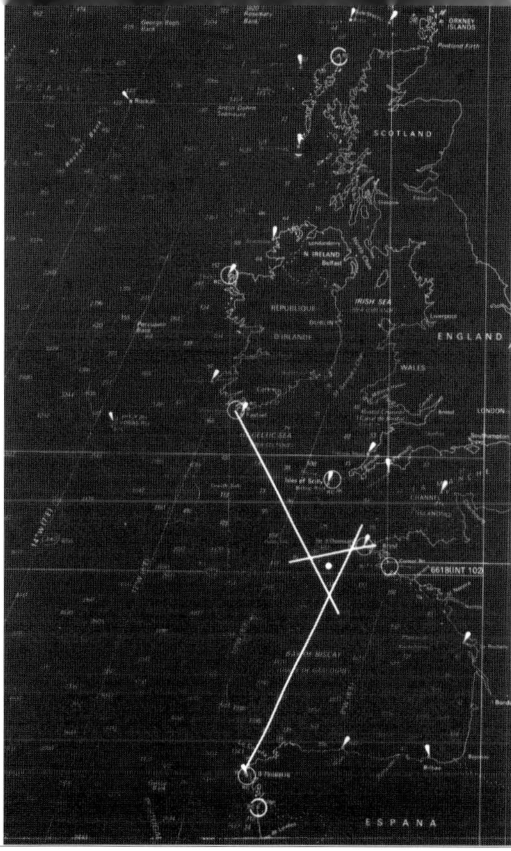

discovered coincidentally during recording. The sounds are recorded because of their extraordinary, innate acoustic and musical qualities which gives the recording a very specific, irreversible three-dimensional image. One example is water gushing through a hole in the pier in the port of Malpica in Spain. Owing to its musical aspect, this sound resembles a reworked studio sound, albeit maintaining its typical harbour quality. The history of the recording also plays an essential role during composition work in the studio, for although the ear is indeed stimulated at this particular moment, certain recollections of the circumstances, visual and other impressions will actually decide on what nature the installation will assume at a later point.

In the studio the recorded sounds are digitally sorted and cut, and some of them are reworked before taking their place in a kind of storyboard. This reworking is often triggered by a harmonic or temporal quality [to widen the concept of rhythm], a quality that already existed when the original recording was made. By simulating an acoustic space in real time and by selecting the paths these sound sources take

Konzept

Auf dem Meer orientieren sich Matrosen und Seefahrer anhand von natürlichen, an der Küste gelegenen Anhaltspunkten wie z. B. an Kirchtürmen, Hügeln, Wassertürmen oder Leuchttürmen, die sich meist vom übrigen Küstenprofil abheben und *Seezeichen* genannt werden. Es genügt, drei davon in komplementären Richtungen zu identifizieren, um ein Dreieck ziehen zu können, in dem sich das Schiff unweigerlich befindet. Dieses auf der Navigationskarte eingezeichnete Dreieck wird als *Dreieck der Ungewißheit* bezeichnet.

Das Soundinstallationsprojekt *Le triangle d'incertitude* greift das Prinzip der Dreiecksnavigation auf und ersetzt dabei diese visuellen Seezeichen durch akustische Marksteine – ebenfalls Informationselemente für die Seefahrer –, die durch aufmerksames Horchen erkannt werden. Leuchttürme, Bojen, Funkanlagen an Bord und etliche andere technische Einrichtungen warnen den Seefahrer vor Gefahren oder Hindernissen.

Bei dem Installationsprojekt geht es darum, auf dem Boden eines fiktiven und virtuellen Raums ein Dreieck der Ungewißheit zu ziehen, und zwar ausgehend von Tonaufnahmen, die an folgenden Punkten durchgeführt werden: an der südlichen Spitze Irlands [Fastnet], am westlichsten Ende von Frankreich [Bretagne] sowie am westlichsten Punkt Spaniens [Cap Finisterre].

Aufgrund ihres Wesens verweist die Installation also auf eine Positionierung der Töne im Raum, wobei ständig zwischen Orientierung und Ungewißheit hin und her gewechselt wird.

Realisierung

Die Tonaufnahmen spielen für die Konzeption eine wichtige Rolle und werden von Cécile Le Prado durchgeführt. Dabei werden sowohl vorher ausgewählte Töne wie das Nebelhorn eines Leuchtturms oder das Heulen einer Boje draußen auf dem Meer als auch zufällig bei den Aufnahmen entdeckte Töne aufgenommen. Sie werden wegen ihrer außergewöhnlichen, ureigenen akustischen und musikalischen Eigenschaften aufgenommen, was einer Aufnahme ein ganz spezifisches und irreversibles räumliches Bild verleiht. Ein Beispiel dafür wäre das Loch in einem Pier im

in this space, what is created is an *écriture de la spatialisation,* writing for spatial recording, as an element of composition. It is gradually refined by repeated listening and modification.

This work was created with the aid of the Spat® spatialisator. This newly developed software by IRCAM and the Atelier Espaces is a virtual acoustic processor that is essentially based on a perceptive analysis of space. With the aid of the Spat®, this construction simulated in the studio can be adapted to meet the requirements of various playback sites.

The final stage of realisation consists in integrating the installation implemented in the studio into an outdoor or interior setting. The interplay between the composition, the *natural* acoustic environment and the acoustics of the installation site is always very interesting. Certain aspects of the studio composition vanish, while others become more important. The site develops and gradually takes on the form of the suggestion made in the studio, particularly depending on the time of day, weather conditions, etc. The interaction of a given site and installation determines a specific combination of restrictions and options. In this sense, the *triangle of uncertainty* is extremely constraining. It is heard under very precise conditions. The loudspeakers have to be equidistant to each other and set up in a circle. The ideal space of perception, in which the spatial effects can actually be perceived, is limited to a relatively small area within this circle.

Credits
Musical arrangement: Cécile Le Prado in the IRCAM studios [Institut de recherche et de Coordination Acoustique Musique]
Scientific adviser [Spat®]: Jean-Marc Jot
Master mixing adviser: Frédéric Prin
Sound men: Mar Pazos Oviedo, Christian Dubet
*The sound installation *Le triangle d'incertitude* is a production of Clameurs, realised and transmitted by *l'autre rive*.*
Co-production: Centre National Dramatique et Chorégraphique Le Quartz de Brest, Etablissement Public du Parc et de la Grande Halle de la Villette.
Sponsored by AFAA [Association française d'action artistique], Audio 33 – Amadeus Concept.

Hafen von Malpica in Spanien, in das Meerwasser strömte. Dieser Laut ähnelt von vornherein aufgrund seines musikalischen Aspekts einem im Studio nachbearbeiteten Ton, wobei er aber seinen typischen Hafencharakter beibehält. Die Geschichte der Tonaufnahme spielt auch zum Zeitpunkt der Komposition im Studio eine wesentliche Rolle, denn auch wenn das Ohr zwar in diesem Moment tatsächlich stimuliert wird, so sind doch gewisse Erinnerungen an die Umstände, an visuelle und andere Impressionen ausschlaggebend dafür, welchen Charakter die Installation später annehmen wird.

Im Studio werden die aufgezeichneten Töne digital aussortiert, geschnitten und manche von ihnen nachbearbeitet, bevor sie in eine Art *Story Board* aufgenommen werden. Die Bearbeitung wird oft durch eine harmonische oder zeitliche Eigenschaft [um den Begriff des Rhythmus zu erweitern] ausgelöst, die bereits zum Zeitpunkt der ursprünglichen Tonaufnahme vorhanden war.

Durch die Echtzeit-Simulation eines akustischen Raums und durch die Auswahl der Wege der Tonquellen in diesem Raum entsteht als Element der Komposition eine *écriture de la spatialisation*, eine Schrift für die räumliche Aufzeichnung. Durch mehrmaliges Abhören und Modifizieren wird sie nach und nach verfeinert.

Für diese Arbeit wurde Spatialisators Spat, benutzt. Diese vom IRCAM und dem Atelier Espaces nouveaux entwickelte Software ist ein virtueller Akustikprozessor, der im wesentlichen auf einer Analyse der Raumwahrnehmung beruht. Mit Hilfe des Spat kann dieser im Studio simulierte Aufbau später an die Erfordernisse verschiedener Wiedergabeorte adaptiert werden.

Die letzte Stufe der Realisierung besteht darin, die in einem Studio implementierte Installation in eine Umgebung im Freien oder in einen Raum zu integrieren. Die Wechselwirkungen zwischen Komposition, *natürlicher* akustischer Umgebung und der Akustik des Installationsortes sind immer sehr interessant. Bestimmte Aspekte der Studiokomposition verschwinden, während andere wichtiger werden. Der Standort entwickelt sich und nimmt nach und nach die Form des im Studio erarbeiteten Vorschlags an, insbesondere in

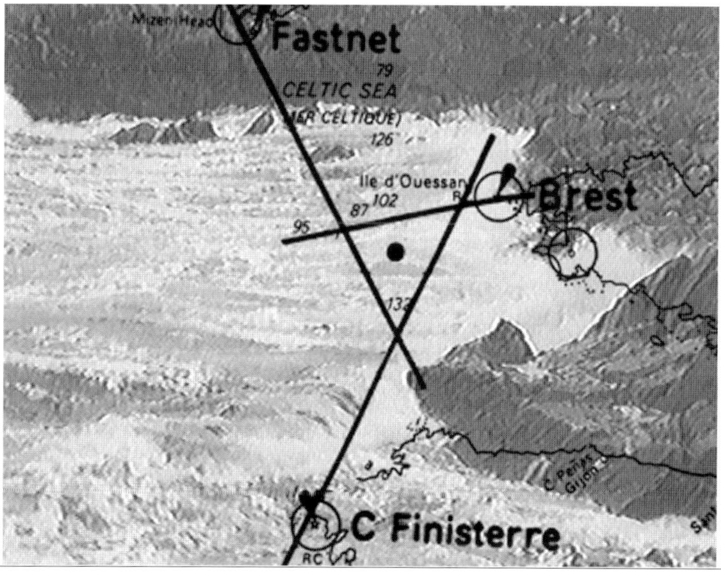

remote sensations

Abhängigkeit von Tageszeit, Witterungsverhältnissen etc. Das Zusammenwirken von Standort und Installation bedingt eine für die Anpassung spezifische Kombination von Zwängen und Wahlmöglichkeiten. In diesem Sinn ist das *Dreieck der Ungewißheit* sehr einschränkend. Es wird unter sehr präzisen Bedingungen gehört. Dabei müssen auch die Lautsprecher in gleichem Abstand zueinander in einem Kreis aufgestellt werden. Der ideale Wahrnehmungsraum, in dem die Raumeffekte auch tatsächlich wahrgenommen werden können, ist auf einen relativ kleinen Raum innerhalb dieses Kreises beschränkt.

Mitarbeit:
Musikalische Bearbeitung:
Cécile Le Prado in den Studios von IRCAM [Institut de Recherche et de Coordination Acoustique Musique]
Wissenschaftliche Beratung [Spat]: Jean-Marc Jot
Musikalische Assistenz: Gilbert Nouno
Beratung Abmischung/Überspielung: Frédéric Prin
Tonassistenten: Mar Pazos Oviedo, Christian Dubet
*Die Soundinstallation *Le Triangle d'incertitude* ist eine Produktion von Clameurs, durchgeführt und übertragen von *l'autre rive* [das andere Ufer].*
Koproduktion: Centre National Dramatique et Choréographique Le Quartz de Brest, Etablissement Public du Parc et de la Grande Halle de la Villette. Mit Unterstützung der AFAA [Association française d'action artistique] de Audio 33 – Amadeus Concept.

Aus dem Französischen von Christine Plunger

Globe Theater A Robotic Pageant

Act, II Scene 2: Machine Nostalgia

Adrianne Wortzel

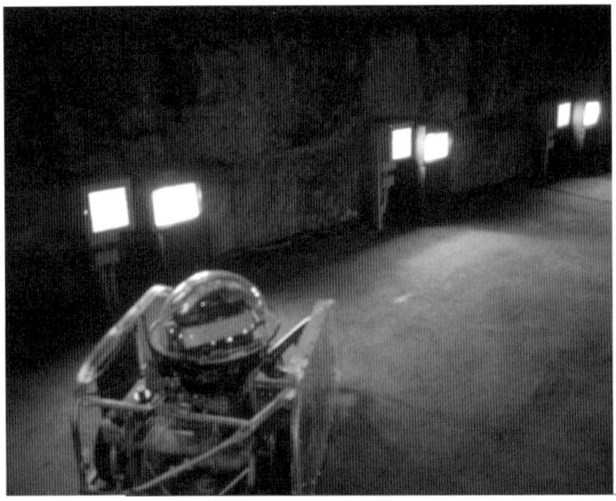

Step by step we have mapped our world empirically by instrument and by the movement of our physical selves across, above and within it. We live now in a world where technology allows each individual's exact location to be transparent. Where we are is suddenly everybody's business. The world is now indeed a stage, an amphitheater, a world of worlds, a theater in the round, a pluralistic armature lending itself simultaneously to both the portrayal and enactment of theatrical events.

It would seem then that our only chance to enjoy anonymity and solitude is to keep on the move, to travel too quickly to be registered by instruments of our own making. The shortest distance between two points may now be a straight line traveled at extreme speed. Thus, a return to nomadic life may provide our only opportunity to be heard and not seen.

Like other natural creatures in the world, we move in clusters and carry on our activities in an organized urban frenzy. Each of us has our own particular agenda and, as the robots do, play our role as archivist, librarian, detective, provider, spy and/or archaeologist.

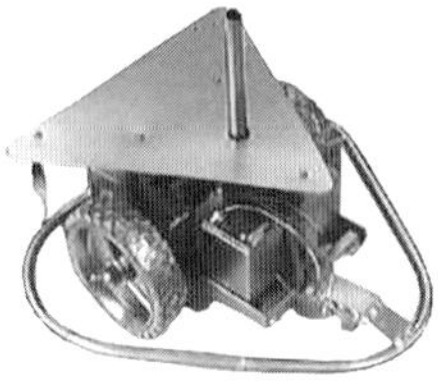

Globe Theater Ein Historienspiel für Roboter

II. Akt, 2. Szene: Nostalgie der Maschinen

Adrianne Wortzel

Schritt für Schritt haben wir nun unsere Welt empirisch kartographiert, mit Hilfe von Instrumenten und indem wir unsere Körper auf und in ihr umherbewegten. Wir leben jetzt in einer Welt, in der Technologie den exakten Standort einzelner Individuen trans-

In *Globe Theater*, a panoply of robots appear and disappear, moving along a map of their own making while writing down the world. The robots as creatures create their own diagrammatic scripting, coding and mapping. Scurrying along, they carry nostalgia high in their ranks like a banner, conjuring up not only territory as it was and is, but anticipating new territory: the mysterious part of the road about to be underfoot but yet unknown, which could be the stuff of fire, water, air or earth.

By the gatherings of information and imagery and interpretations of their findings, the locale in which these robotic actors spring up becomes a series of stage-sets through which they move as a form of projection. The clusters they form in the physical world exhibit some of our best qualities: curiosity and a passion for study, interpretation and display of human history. Like a false door in an Ancient Egyptian tomb, the frenzy of these idiosyncratic characters and their dramatic adventures masks and protects their subtext: a political devotion to keeping imagination alive.

These intrepid characters explore and remap the world ideologically again, retaining all its diversity, and even deepening it. They are not limited to either a medieval flat, circular disc or a round sphere. To these curiosity machines, the world is chameleon-like, and can change shape, color and scope at will.

The stories emerging from the efforts of these robotic creatures are expressed in their own form of theatrical play, emulating medieval pageantry and the genres of detective and mystery stories, science fiction, fables, scholarly and scientific reporting and journalism. As artists, we are now inventors, archaeologists, and detectives. Like the robots, our studies tend to bridge things, to discard arbitrary borders between things isolated and juxtaposed. Robots and computers liberate us from the prospect of being overwhelmed by all the information in the world. It is their turn now to handle the storage and organization of as well as the access to information, leaving us, hopefully, free for the breaking of new artistic and philosophical ground.

parent machen kann. Wo wir sind, geht plötzlich jeden etwas an. Die Welt ist nun tatsächlich eine Bühne, ein Amphitheater, eine Welt der Welten, ein Arenatheater, eine pluralistische Armatur, die sich selbst gleichzeitig zur Schilderung und Aufführung schauspielerischer Ereignisse zur Verfügung stellt.

Unsere einzige Chance auf Anonymität und Einsamkeit besteht also scheinbar darin, uns fortwährend zu bewegen, und zwar so schnell, daß keines der von uns geschaffenen Instrumente uns registrieren kann. Der kürzeste Abstand zwischen zwei Punkten könnte heute eine gerade Linie sein, die man in Höchstgeschwindigkeit zurücklegt, und unsere einzige Möglichkeit, zwar gehört, nicht aber gesehen zu werden, die Rückkehr zum Nomadendasein.

Wie andere natürliche Wesen auf dieser Welt bewegen wir uns in dichten Gruppen fort und gehen unseren Aktivitäten in urban organisierter Betriebsamkeit nach. Jeder von uns hat seine persönliche Tagesordnung und spielt, wie Roboter es eben tun, seine Rolle als Archivist, Bibliothekar, Detektiv, Lieferant, Spion und/oder Archäologe.

In *Globe Theater* zieht ein ganzes Spektrum von Robotern an uns vorbei, sie tasten sich eine Karte entlang, die sie selbst erstellten, und beschreiben die Welt. Als Kreaturen erschaffen die Roboter so ihre eigene diagrammatische Niederschrift, Kodierung, Zuordnung. Die Nostalgie stolz vor sich hertragend wie ein Banner, eilen sie dahin und beschwören nicht nur das Territorium selbst herauf, wie es war und ist, sondern antizipieren ein neues: jenen geheimnisvollen Teil des Weges, der bald beschritten wird, jetzt aber noch unbekannt ist und sowohl Feuer, Wasser, Luft oder Erde sein könnte.

Indem sie Informationen und Metaphern sammeln und ihre Funde interpretieren, wird der Schauplatz, an dem diese robotischen Akteure auftauchen, zu einer Reihe von Bühnenszenen, durch die sie sich als eine Art von Projektion bewegen. Die Gruppen, die sie in der physischen Welt bilden, stellen einige unserer besten Eigenschaften zur Schau: die Neugierde und die Leidenschaft für Studium, Interpretation und Darstellung der menschlichen Geschichte. Wie die Attrappe einer Tür in einem alten ägyptischen Grabmal verdeckt und schützt die hek-

Cast of Characters:
Monastic robots as follows:

The Ship's Deputy Detective:
The Intrepid Detective of
The Good Ship Beagle
She: A recasting of H. Rider Haggard's
Fictive Character
Visconde de Santarem [1791-1856]:
map historian, inventor of the word
cartographie
Libra: Keeper of the Peace,
Conductor of Jurisprudence
Kiru: Librarian of Juxtapositions
In All Their Degrees
Callimachus: Poet, Librarian,
the Alexandrian Library, 260 BC
Four projector towers:
north, south, east and west

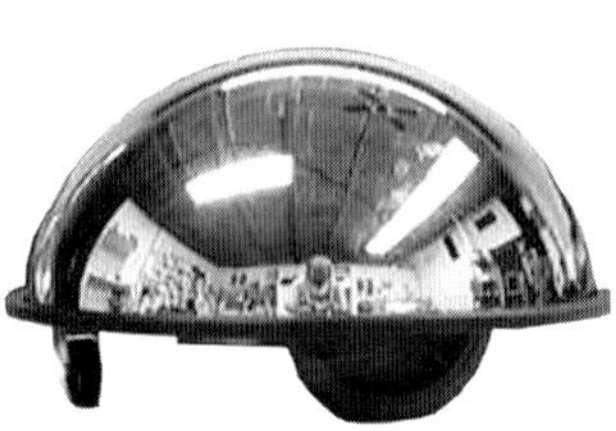

Act II, Scene 2:

CALLIMACHUS: A magic carpet flies and is so incredible that it is in fact difficult to believe.

KIRU: Camouflage Town has an exact duplicate. During periods when the tribe feels invincible, Camouflage Town serves as a decoy battlefield; it is there they lure greedy enemies to war with rumors of treasures and tools.

Because of my ability to withstand the stress of contradictions I am responsible for the recording of archaic extremes. Relentlessly, I solicit contributions from everyone I meet. hot/cold, joy/grief, benign/lethal, up/down, inside/outside. Our Tribe's reverence for words affects every aspect of our culture. Indeed, troubled by the fact that words can be false, our judicial procedures are conducted entirely in mime. This includes the reenactment of crimes for judge and jury. Use of the spoken word for conducting jurisprudence is unthinkable.

tische Betriebsamkeit dieser eigenwilligen Charaktere und ihrer dramatischen Abenteuer einen Subtext: die politische Hingabe, mit der sie die Phantasie am Leben erhalten.

Diese kühnen Charaktere widmen sich der ideologischen Neuerkundung und Neuabbildung der Welt und bewahren, ja, vertiefen dabei all ihre Vielfalt. Sie beschränken sich dabei weder auf die flache, kreisförmige Scheibe des Mittelalters noch auf die Kugelform. Die Welt erscheint diesen Neugierdemaschinen vielmehr als Chamäleon, denn sie kann Form, Farbe und Umfang nach eigenem Willen verändern.

Die aus den Bemühungen der robotischen Wesen resultierenden Geschichten werden in der ihnen eigenen Form des Schauspiels zum Ausdruck gebracht – einer Nachahmung des mittelalterlichen Historienspiels und der Genres Detektiv- und Kriminalgeschichte, Science-Fiction, Fabel, hochgeistig-wissenschaftliche Reportage und Journalismus. Als Künstler sind nun wir die Erfinder, Archäologen und Detektive. Wie Roboter schlagen unsere Studien oft Brücken zwischen den Dingen, entfernen willkürliche Grenzen zwischen Isoliertem und Nebeneinandergestelltem. Roboter und Computer befreien uns von der Aussicht darauf, die ganze Informationslast der Welt könne uns erdrücken. Nun sind sie an der Reihe, Informationsspeicherung, -organisation und -zugriff handzuhaben, was uns hoffentlich die Freiheit läßt, neue künstlerische und philosophische Räume zu erschließen.

Die handelnden Personen:
Die Ordensroboter

Der Stellvertretende Detektiv des Schiffes: Der Kühne Detektiv des Guten Schiffes Beagle
Sie: Eine Neubesetzung der Fiktiven Person von H. Rider Haggard
Visconde de Santarem (1791–1856) Kartenhistoriker, Erfinder des Begriffs »Cartographie«
Libra: Bewahrer des Friedens, Vollstrecker der Jurisprudenz
Kiru: Bibliothekar der Nebeneinanderstellung Auf Allen Ebenen
Callimachus: Dichter, Bibliothekar, Alexandrinische Bibliothek, 260 v.Chr.
Vier Projektor-Türme:
Nord, Süd, Ost, West

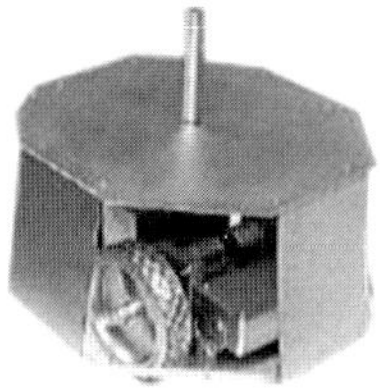

LIBRA: Bi-polarity told the story of imagination for centuries; there was no way for human beings to know their bearings unless they considered them in relationship to something else.

KIRU: There are also many written laws about the word as spoken: one such law, roughly translated, says that *trouble begins when a quality is applied to the name of a color.* It must be ascertained whether the characteristic is a true qualifier of the color, or a separate quality deserving of its own name as a color.* In rulings on these distinctions, we are fierce.

SHE: Everyone cheered like mad when women's veils became old hat. Emancipated, we all went home carrying the burden of fashion.

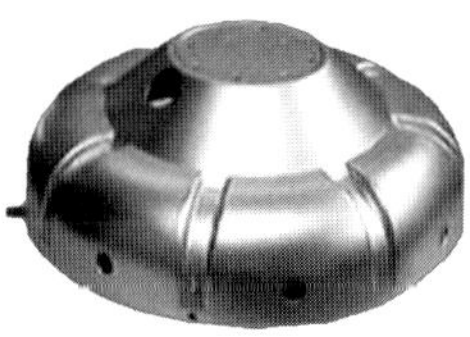

2. Akt, II. Szene:

CALLIMACHIUS: Ein fliegender Teppich fliegt und ist so unglaublich, daß es in der Tat schwerfällt, es zu glauben.

KIRU: Camouflage Town hat ein exaktes Duplikat. In Zeiten, in denen sich der Stamm unbesiegbar fühlt, dient Camouflage Town als Köder-Schlachtfeld; beutehungrige Feinde locken sie mit Gerüchten über Schätze und Gerätschaften dorthin in den Krieg. Aufgrund meiner Fähigkeit, der Belastung der Gegensätze zu widerstehen, bin ich verantwortlich für die Aufzeichnung archaischer Extreme. Unermüdlich erbitte ich Beiträge von jedem, der mir begegnet. Heiß/kalt, Freude/Trauer, gutartig/tödlich, auf/ab, innen/außen. Die Ehrfurcht unseres Stammes vor Worten beeinflußt jeden Aspekt unserer Kultur. Beunruhigt durch die Tatsache, daß Worte falsch sein könnten, werden sogar gerichtliche Verfahren gänzlich in Pantomime abgewickelt. Dies gilt auch für die Nachstellung von Verbrechen für Richter und Geschworene. Die Verwendung des gesprochenen Wortes in der Rechtspraxis ist undenkbar.

LIBRA: Seit Jahrhunderten ist die Geschichte der Phantasie von Bipolarität geprägt; die Menschen hatten keine andere Möglichkeit, ihre Position zu kennen, als sie zu etwas anderem in Bezug zu setzen.

KIRU: Es gibt auch zahlreiche geschriebene Gesetze über das gesprochene Wort; ein solches Gesetz lautet, grob übersetzt, *Schwierigkeiten beginnen dann, wenn man dem Namen einer Farbe eine Eigenschaft zuspricht*. Es muß festgestellt werden, ob die Eigenschaft ein wahrer Gradmesser der Farbe ist oder eine separate Qualität, die ihren eigenen Namen als Farbe verdient.In Entscheidungen über derartige Unterschiede sind wir unerbittlich.

SIE: Alle jubelten wie verrückt, als die Schleier der Frauen altmodisch wurden. Emanzipiert gingen wir alle heim und trugen die Bürde der Mode.

3D-Audio-Düker

Horst Zachmann

A space not normally accessible to the public – the Donau-Düker, a tunnel under the Danube – is being acoustically *reproduced* in three-dimensional audio [also known as virtual acoustic or binaural acoustic] to enable listeners to experience via headphone the unique tonal qualities of this place.

The configuration of a virtual acoustic space is done in a manner similar to that of 3-D visual animation. Recordings of actual sounds occurring in the Düker [acoustic objects such as the noise made by the propeller of a passing ship or the steps of someone walking through the tunnel] are animated by means of a three-dimensional path [3-D spline] recreating the original movement of the sound, and are spatially projected via headphone. *Observers* assume the same position as the microphone during the recording process, such that the *line of vision* runs along the length of the tunnel [in the direction of Urfahr on the north bank of the Danube]. Thus, a ship sailing downriver [from west to east] approaches from the upper left, proceeds overhead and withdraws to the upper right; someone walking through the Düker [from Linz in the direction of Urfahr]

3D-Audio-Düker

Horst Zachmann

Ein normalerweise für die Öffentlichkeit nicht zugänglicher Raum, der Donau-Düker [ein Tunnel unter der Donau], wird mittles 3D-Audio [auch Virtual Acoustic oder Binaural Acoustic genannt] akustisch dreidimensional *abgebildet* und via Kopfhörer in seiner ortsspezifischen Klanggestalt wiedererlebbar gemacht.

Die Gestaltung des virtuellen akustischen Raumes erfolgt in ähnlicher Weise wie die einer visuellen 3D-Animation. Im Düker aufgenommene konkrete Klangereignisse bzw. Klangbilder [akustische Objekte wie Schraubgeräusche von Schiffen, Schritte einer durch den Tunnel gehenden Person ...] werden mittels einem der ursprünglichen Bewegung der Klangobjekte nachempfundenen dreidimen-

approaches from the rear and proceeds past on either the left or right.

In the case of the scenario described above – as with every other – individual listeners experience various different distortions of perception with respect to the position and the movement of the sound source within the virtual acoustic space. The degree of [spatial] distortion is determined by several individual factors. The simulation of a three-dimensional acoustic space projected through two loudspeakers is accomplished by means of spectral modification [convolution] of the sound. In addition, there is the application of transfer functions, generally referred to as *head-related transfer functions* [HRTFs] or *free-field-to-ear transfer functions.* These transfer functions must be individually derived in an extremely time-consuming procedure – what actually takes place is the transformation of the physiological preconditions for the reception of acoustic signals into mathematical functions, and this is done for every point within a spherically shaped raster. For this reason, recourse is usually taken to previously existing HRTFs, as has also been the case with this installation. Of prime concern is the fact that these transformations contain functions of the position – as well as the thoroughly individual functions of the auditory characteristics – of the individual from whom the HRTF was derived. Decisive factors determining individual auditory characteristics are head shape and size, as well as the formation of the outer and inner ear. The degree to which the above-listed individual auditory factors inherent in the HRTFs coincide with those of the listener constitutes the limiting quantity with respect to distortion in the perception of sound direction.

Düker [German]: A pipeline running beneath a river, canal or tunnel; based on the [physics] principle of communicating tubes.

sionalen Pfades [3D-spline] animiert und via Kopfhörer räumlich projiziert. Die *BetrachterInnen* nehmen dieselbe Position wie das Mikrofon während der Aufnahme ein, wobei die Blickrichtung entlang des Tunnels verläuft [in Richtung Urfahr]. Ein flußabwärts fahrendes Schiff nähert sich somit von links oben und entfernt sich wieder über den Kopf hinweg nach rechts, eine den Düker durchschreitende Person [von Linz in Richtung Urfahr] nähert sich sich von hinten und geht dann dann links oder rechts vorbei ...

Bei dem soeben geschilderten Szenario [wie auch bei jedem anderen] entstehen für die HörerInnen individuell verschiedene Wahrnehmungsverzerrungen in bezug auf die Position und Bewegung der Klangquellen innerhalb des virtuellen akustischen Raumes. Der Grad der [räumlichen] Verzerrung ist durch mehrere individuelle Faktoren bestimmt. Die Simulation eines dreidimensionalen akustischen Raumes, projiziert über zwei Lautsprecher, erfolgt durch spektrale Modifikationen [convolution] des Klangobjektes. Dazu kommen Übertragungsfunktionen zur Anwendung, allgemein bekannt als *head-related transfer functions* [HRTFs] oder auch *free-field-to-ear transfer functions*.

Diese Übertragungsfunktionen müssen von einer Person abgeleitet werden, wobei das Verfahren äußerst zeitraubend ist [es erfolgt eine Transformation der physiologischen Voraussetzungen für die Wahrnehmung akustischer Signale in mathematische Funktionen und dies für jeden Punkt innerhalb eines kugelförmigen Rasters]. Aus diesem Grund wird meist auf bereits existierende HRTFs zurückgegriffen, wie auch bei dieser Installation. In erster Linie beinhalten diese Transformationen Funktionen der Position, aber auch stets individuelle Funktionen der Höreigenschaften jener Person, von welcher die HRTFs abgeleitet wurden. Maßgebliche Faktoren für die individuelle Höreigenschaft sind die Form bzw. die Größe des Kopfes sowie die Beschaffenheit des Außen- und Innenohrs. Die Übereinstimmung der soeben aufgezählten in den HRTFs eingebundenen Faktoren der individuellen Höreigenschaft mit denen des/der HörerIn stellt die Einflußgröße für die Verzerrung der Richtungswahrnehmung dar.

Düker: Auf dem Prinzip der kommunizierenden Röhren beruhende Führung von Rohrleitungen unter Flüssen, Kanälen oder Tunneln.

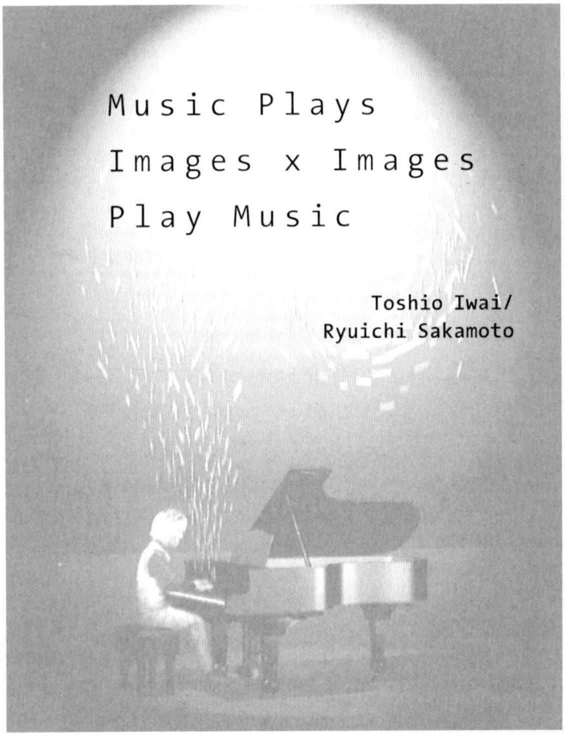

The idea for this collaborative performance has its origins in Toshio Iwai's installation *Piano – as image media* created at the ZKM, Karlsruhe, Germany in 1995. Conceived upon Iwai's return to Japan when he met Ryuichi Sakamoto, *Music Plays Images x Images Play Music* is a multi-media concert that uses the system of Iwai's piano piece and visualizes in real time a musical performance by Sakamoto. Over the course of a year, Iwai, who lives in Tokyo, often corresponded by e-mail with Sakamoto, who lives in New York. During their correspondence, the concept for the collaboration expanded rapidly, developing from the simple idea of *Sakamoto playing Iwai's 'Piano – as image media,'* to a performance that links, in various ways, musical sounds with visual images. The result of the collaboration was more than a *novel combination of music and image.* Many elements including the actual presence of Sakamoto/Iwai, the machinery that is called the piano, the acoustic sounds produced by the piano, and the virtual images generated from computers were linked and developed in various ways. From the feedback produced, a radically new space of musicality-visuality was created.

events

Music Plays Images x Images Play Music

Toshio Iwai/Ryuichi Sakamoto

Die Idee für diese gemeinsame Performance entstand in Zusammenhang mit Toshio Iwais Installation *Piano – as image media* am ZKM, Karlsruhe 1995. Das nach Iwais Rückkehr nach Japan und bei einer Begegnung mit Ryuichi Sakamoto konzipierte *Music Plays Images x Images Play Music* ist ein multimediales Konzert, das das System von Iwais Klavierstück verwendet und Sakamotos musikalische Performance in Echtzeit visualisiert. Während eines Jahres stand Iwai, der in Tokio lebt, in E-mail-Kontakt mit dem in New York ansässigen Sakamoto. Im Zuge dieser Korrespondenz erweiterte sich ihr Konzept beträchtlich – aus der anfänglichen Idee *Sakamoto spielt Iwais Klavier als Bildmedium* wurde eine Performance, die musikalische Klänge auf verschiedenste Art mit visuellen Bildern verknüpft. Das Ergebnis dieser Zusammenarbeit war weit mehr als eine neuartige Kombination aus Musik und Bild. Viele Elemente – die tatsächliche Präsenz von Sakamoto und Iwai; jene Maschine, die man landläufig Klavier nennt; die akustischen Klänge, die damit erzeugt wurden; und die virtuellen Bilder, die aus dem Computer stammten – wurden auf mannigfaltige Weise verbunden und entwickelt. Aus dem dabei entstehenden Feedback entstand ein völ-

In addition, the performance was transmitted over the Internet and relayed world-wide. This experiment, the first of its kind, was an attempt to utilize the interactive medium of the Internet. People on the other side of the Internet were able to play the piano by remote control and in turn Sakamoto had a session with their playing.

The Set-Up of the Stage

Two concert grand pianos are placed on the stage. A semi-transparent screen 8 meters in height and 10 meters in width is suspended above them. The lids of both pianos are removed and their interiors and keyboards clearly illuminated. The screen is irradiated with a beautiful shade of blue. A black and white video camera is placed on each of the pianos in order to film the movements of the performer's fingers and the piano keys. The video cameras project enlarged images of each piano keyboard onto the screen on either side of the pianos. Several computers are set up on a long narrow table placed on the right side of the stage.

The Content of the Performance

1 Sakamoto does not initially appear on the stage. Amidst the silence, the piano begins to play on its own without a player. An image of Sakamoto playing the piano gradually comes into view on the screen to the side of the piano. Sakamoto's image slowly disappears as the music ends.

2 Sakamoto appears on the left side of the stage. He begins to play the small keyboard placed there. As he plays this keyboard, the piano starts to play. A faint light gradually emanates from the piano. At a certain point, Sakamoto stops playing. However, the last musical phrase repeats itself automatically, slowly fading out.

3 Sakamoto plays the piano directly. The light-images that visually represent each note of the musical piece begin to rise from within the piano. The images capture not only the timing of the notes, but every aspect of the music, including the length of the notes and their volume. They are represented in a way that the eye can recognize.

4 During Sakamoto's performance, Iwai gradually modifies the image. The lights, which correspond to each note of the piece, are trans-

lig neuartiger Raum der Musikalität und Visualität. Darüber hinaus wurde dieses Experiment über das Internet weltweit übertragen – der erste Versuch dieser Art, das interaktive Medium Internet in eine solche Aufführung einzubeziehen. Internet-User auf der ganzen Welt konnten via Remote-Control auf dem Flügel spielen, während Sakamoto mit ihrem Spiel interagieren konnte.

Die Bühne

Zwei Konzertflügel stehen auf der Bühne, eine semitransparente Projektionsfläche von zehn Metern Breite und acht Metern Höhe hängt über ihnen. Die Deckel der beiden Klaviere sind entfernt, ihr Inneres und die Tastaturen sind hell ausgeleuchtet. Die Projektionsfläche wird mit einem schönen Blauton angestrahlt. Auf jedem Klavier ist eine Schwarz-Weiß-Videokamera montiert, die die Bewegungen der Finger und Tasten aufnimmt. Diese Kameras projizieren vergrößerte Abbildungen der Tastaturen auf Projektionsflächen beidseits der Klaviere. Mehrere Computer sind auf einem schmalen, langen Tisch auf der rechten Seite der Bühne aufgestellt.

Die Performance

1 Am Anfang erscheint Sakamoto nicht auf der Bühne. In der Stille beginnt das Klavier von selbst, ohne Pianisten, zu spielen. Ein Bild des klavierspielenden Sakamoto erscheint langsam auf der Projektionsfläche seitlich des Klaviers und verschwindet wieder, wenn die Musik endet.

2 Sakamoto tritt auf der linken Seite der Bühne auf. Er spielt dort ein kleines Keyboard, und währenddessen beginnt auch das Klavier zu spielen. Ein schwaches Leuchten geht vom Klavier aus. An einem bestimmten Punkt hört Sakamoto zu spielen auf. Dennoch wird die letzte musikalische Phrase vom Flügel automatisch weitergespielt, bis sie langsam ausblendet.

3 Sakamoto spielt nun direkt auf dem Flügel. Lichtpunkte, die die einzelnen gespielten Note darstellen, steigen aus dem Inneren des Klaviers auf. Das Bild der Note gibt nicht nur ihr Timing wieder, sondern jeden Aspekt der Musik, die Länge des Tons, den Anschlag. Die Darstellung erfolgt so, daß sie für das Auge nachvollziehbar ist.

formed over time in various ways. They do not merely rise from within the piano and fade into thin air. They radiate from the center of the screen out in all directions or revolve in a whirling pattern, eventually disappearing into a vortex. The metamorphoses of the projected images influence Sakamoto's playing as he watches the various transformations.

5 The image-objects, composed of 88 elements – the same number as the number of keys on a piano – appear on the center of the screen. Each of the elements coincides with the keys of the piano and the objects are continually transformed according to Sakamoto's piano performance.

6 Clicking a computer mouse, Iwai places dots of light onto the screen. Whenever the dots of light fall on the piano, the piano begins to play. The dots of light then rebound to their original position, striking the keyboard at fixed intervals. Depending on where the dots of light are placed, the pitch of the notes and the patterns of repetition change. The number of dots of light are increased. The dots of light bouncing from the piano are all shifted back and forth from left to right. The whole musical scale changes according to how the dots of light are moved. The dots of light are transformed into rays and then polygonal figures.

7 The video camera films Sakamoto's entire body. The computer captures the image in real time. Sakamoto's silhouette is pixelized and then projected onto the screen above the piano. When Sakamoto moves and the image of his body overlaps with the piano, the piano plays. When Sakamoto moves toward or away from the camera, or when a close-up image of his hands is projected, the sound is changed dynamically. The images of Sakamoto's hands and body are what plays the machine called the piano. Iwai implements further modifications by zooming in on and rotating Sakamoto's image on the screen, thereby slowly modifying the sound. Sakamoto continues to move his body while looking on.

8 A chessboard-like grid appears on the screen and begins to rotate. Sakamoto and Iwai take turns placing glowing dots of light onto the grid, thereby creating a repetition of short melodic patterns. As the music is created through this collaboration, Iwai transposes the musical pattern, changing the octave and alter-

4 Während Sakamotos Spiel verändert Iwai nach und nach das Bild. Die Lichter, die jeweils einer Note des Stücks entsprechen, werden im Lauf der Zeit auf unterschiedliche Weise verwandelt. Sie steigen auch nicht mehr nur aus dem Klavier auf, sondern verbreiten sich aus der Mitte der Leinwand in alle Richtungen, sie drehen sich in einem Wirbel, um schließlich in einem Strudel zu verschwinden. Die Metamorphose der projizierten Bilder beeinflußt Sakamotos Spiel, der die verschiedenen Transformationen beobachtet.

5 Bildobjekte, bestehend aus 88 Elementen –ebensovielen, wie ein Klavier Tasten hat–, erscheinen in der Mitte der Projektionsfläche. Jedes Element entspricht einer Taste, und die Objekte verändern ihre Form je nach Sakamotos Spiel.

6 Mit einem Mausklick positioniert Iwai Lichtpunkte auf die Projektionswand. Wann immer solche Lichtpunkte auf die Tastatur fallen, spielt der Flügel. Dann springen die Lichtpunkte in ihre Ausgangsposition zurück, von wo sie in fixen Intervallen neuerlich auf die Tastatur *purzeln*. Je nachdem, wo die Lichtpunkte postiert sind, ändern sich die Höhe des angeschlagenen Tons und das repetitive Muster. Die Anzahl der Lichtpunkte wird vergrößert, die zurückspringenden Punkte werden nach links und rechts verschoben. Je nachdem wie die Lichtpunkte bewegt werden, verändert sich auch die gesamte musikalische Skala. Aus den Lichtpunkten werden Strahlen und später Polygone.

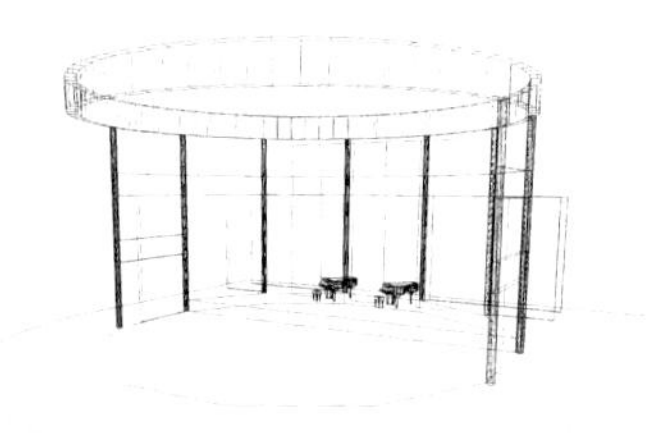

7 Die Videokamera filmt Sakamotos ganzen Körper. Der Computer setzt das Bild in Echtzeit um, die Silhouette wird in Pixel umgerechnet und auf die Leinwand über dem Klavier projiziert. Wenn Sakamoto sich bewegt und das Abbild seines Körpers sich mit dem Klavier über-

ing the sounds and the images. Sakamoto continues to create new patterns. Finally, with the completed musical phrases as a backdrop, Sakamoto improvises on the piano. Iwai continues to modify the performance piece.

9 The music played by Sakamoto is turned into an image. The image that springs from the first piano and lands on the second piano creates a parabola in its fall. The second piano plays according to this image. The figure of Sakamoto performing on the first piano is projected next to the second piano with a delay that coincides with the imaged music arriving at the second piano. It appears as if there are two Sakamotos playing the two different pianos.

10 The short musical phrase performed by Sakamoto and the resulting image loop between the two pianos, repeating again and again. Sakamoto continues to add more sounds to the loop. The repeating images and sounds, flowing forth like a waterfall between the two pianos, grow in layered richness and complexity.

translated from the Japanese by Dano O'Neill

Original performance:
Planning by Shin-ichiro Ikebe
Produced by Art Tower Mito, Mito-city, Japan
*Sound Engineering by Akira Shimura [Star*Tech Inc.]*
Supported by IAMAS, NTT InterCommunication Center, Yamaha co.ltd., JVC Inc., Human Media Inc., Kab Inc.
Documented by TV-MAN UNION Inc.
Internet broadcasting by Naozumi Takenaka, Kouichiro Eto, Internet 1996 World Exposition Japan

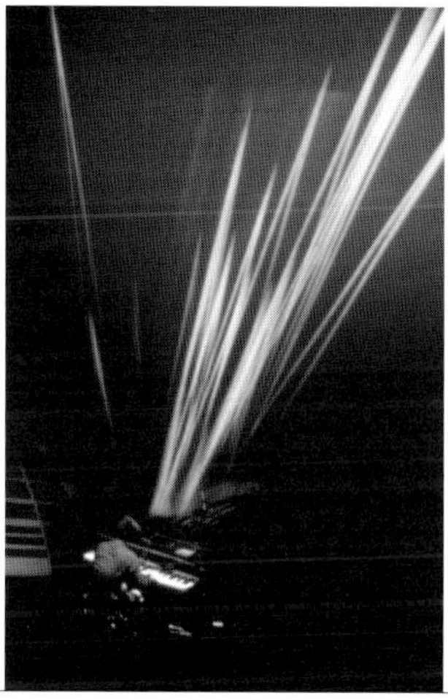

lappt, beginnt das Klavier zu spielen. Wenn sich Sakamoto zur Kamera hin oder von ihr weg bewegt oder wenn eine Nahaufnahme seiner Hand projiziert wird, ändert sich die Dynamik des Klangs: Das Abbild von Sakamoto und seinen Händen spielt jene Maschine, die man Klavier nennt. Iwai bringt weitere Veränderungen ein, indem er Sakamotos Bild auf der Projektionsfläche dreht, hineinzoomt und so fort. Mit der Änderung des Abbilds ändert sich auch der Klang. Sakamoto beobachtet die Veränderungen und bewegt sich weiter vor der Kamera.

8 Ein schachbrettähnliches Muster erscheint auf der Projektionsfläche und beginnt sich zu drehen. Sakamoto und Iwai setzen abwechselnd Lichtpunkte auf dieses Gitter, worauf sich ein kurzes musikalisches Muster ständig wiederholt. Während aus dieser Zusammenarbeit eine Musik entsteht, transponiert Iwai das musikalische Muster, indem er die Oktav wechselt und sowohl Klänge als auch Bilder verändert. Sakamoto seinerseits erzeugt weiter neue Muster. Wenn schließlich genug Klangmaterial als Hintergrund vorhanden ist, improvisiert Sakamoto auf dem Klavier, während Iwai weiter die Hintergrundmusik verändert.

9 Die von Sakamoto gespielte Musik wird in ein Bild umgesetzt, das vom ersten Flügel wegspringt und in einer Parabel auf den zweiten niederfällt. Der zweite Flügel spielt je nachdem, wie dieses Bild auf ihm auftrifft. Das Bild von Sakamoto, der den ersten Flügel spielt, wird mit derselben Zeitverzögerung neben das zweite Klavier projiziert, die durch den Flug der *Ton-Bilder* entsteht. Es sieht so aus, als würden zwei Sakamotos jetzt die zwei Klaviere spielen.

10 Die von Sakamoto gespielte kurze musikalische Phrase und Sakamotos Bild kreisen zwischen den beiden Klavieren hin und her und wiederholen ihre Musik. Sakamoto fügt dieser Schleife immer neue Klänge hinzu. Die sich wiederholenden Bilder und Klänge, die wie ein Wasserfall zwischen den beiden Klavieren hin- und herfließen, überlagern sich langsam und gewinnen so an Komplexität.

Aus dem Englischen von Helmut P. Einfalt

Music Plays Images x Images Play Music,
European Premiere/Europapremiere, Ars Electronica 97
In co-operation with/In Kooperation mit Posthof, Linz.

OR

Dumb Type

Dumb Type's new production, in both performance and installation, is a *grey humour* reflection on the zone[s] between life and death.
OR – binary system
OR – Alternative A or B
OR – o[zero] radius – invisible circle – point/dot
OR – operation room

It is about the state of *white out* like in a blizzard, where you are deprived of the ability to see, where you can't recognize anything, where you don't know whether you are alive OR dead.
But what distinguishes one from the other?
Where is the border?
What is death?
What is it?

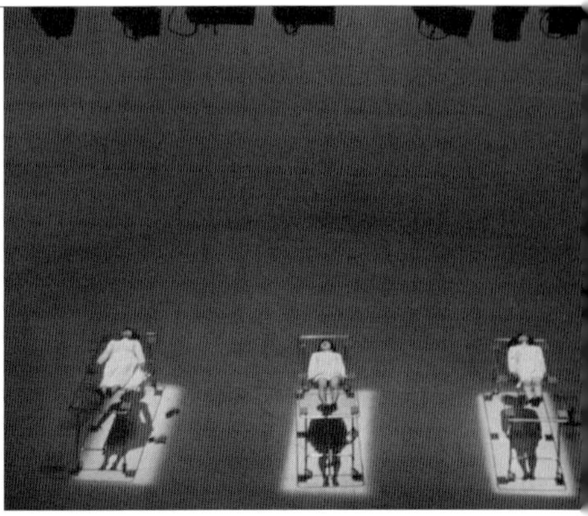

OR

Dumb Type

Images of death, looked at from various viewpoints, be it religious, philosophical, medical, cultural or emotional, are projected on a white semicircle screen and a white, open stage, flooded in flickering light. An advanced technique of combining electrical images, sounds, lighting and performers, which is Dumb Type's specialty, aims at switching off any intentions of grasping this mortal phenomenon, and bringing you into the white out.

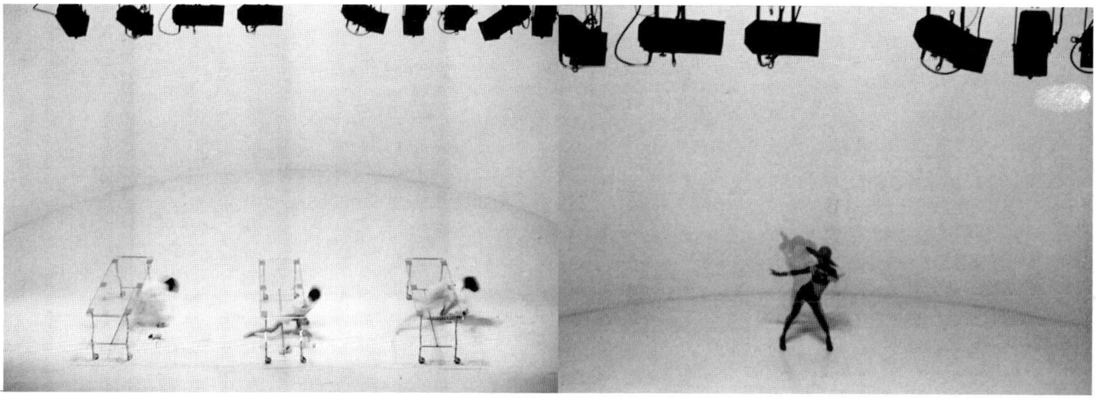

Mit *grauem Humor* reflektiert Dumb Type in seiner neuen Produktion, sowohl in der Performance als auch in der Installation, über die Zone[n] zwischen Leben und Tod.
OR – binäres System
OR – Alternative A oder B
OR – O[Null]-Radius – unsichtbarer Kreis – Punkt
OR – Kontrollraum

Im Zentrum steht der Zustand des *white-out*, eines starken Schneegestöbers etwa während eines Blizzards, wo du vollkommen der Sicht beraubt wirst, wo du nichts erkennen kannst, wo du nicht weißt, ob du tot bist OdeR lebendig.
Aber was unterscheidet eins vom anderen?
Wo ist die Grenze?
Was ist der Tod?
Was ist er?

Bilder des Todes, von unterschiedlichen Standpunkten – vom religiösen, philosophischen, medizinischen, kulturellen und vom emotionalen aus betrachtet – werden auf eine weiße, halbkreisförmige Leinwand projiziert. Diese umrahmt eine gleichfalls weiße, in flimmerndes Licht getauchte, offene Bühne. Die kunstvolle Kombination von elektrischen Bildern, Tönen, Beleuchtung und Darstellern [übrigens Dumb Types Spezialität] stellt den Versuch dar, alle Bemühungen zum Verständnis dieses tödlichen Phänomens zu vereiteln und den Besucher in den Zustand des *white out* zu versetzen.

An Evening Spent in a Hypercompetitive State of Mind

Time's up

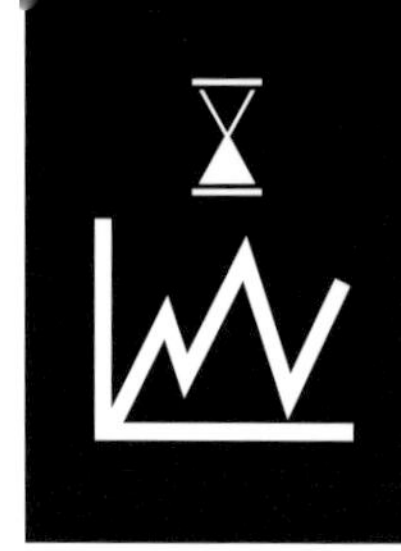

... I like you, 'cause you tell it how it is. If you don't tell it how it is, you're telling it the way it isn't and the way it isn't is never gonna be the way it is.

Listener on FANNET, sports talk show

Bits of wisdom like this continually surprise us when we excitedly listen in on the discussions of sports fans. As a rule, this language seems to be much too arcane for us to give more than the slightest idea of what is actually meant to be communicated to us by these codes.

Sure, we understand that we have to lend our support to Arnold Schwarzenegger's national fitness program, but that doesn't mean we want to look like him. The spectrum extending from National Walk-to-Work Day to the daily training regimen of a medal-hopeful in Olympic weightlifting [including nutrition program and dress regulations] is simply too wide for us to be able to find our own individual form of fitness simply defined within it.

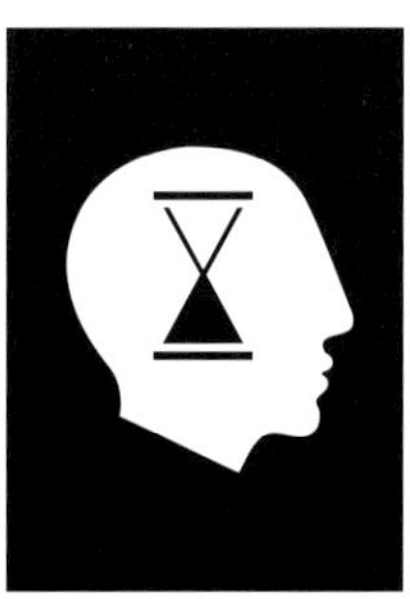

An Evening Spent in a Hypercompetitive State of Mind

Time's up

... I like you, cause you tell it how it is. If you don't tell it how it is, you're telling it the way it isn't and the way it isn't is never gonna be the way it is.

Hörer auf FANNET, sports talkshow

Time's up understands this problematic issue and attempts to break the codes. The very latest electronic technology is being deployed to investigate, above all, the fundamental rules of biomechanical behavioral patterns' applicability to the field of sport. These are, seemingly, the primal rootsF from which they emerged, and are thus being implemented as the initial key to the primary codex of human drives.

Radical and new training methods have been developed on the basis of T.H.H. Boykett's *Theory of Hypercompetition* and are now being made available to the general public.

In a kind of biomechanical game show, members of the audience are urged to check, and to playfully rediscover, their own state of fitness on the level of individual perception and control behavior.

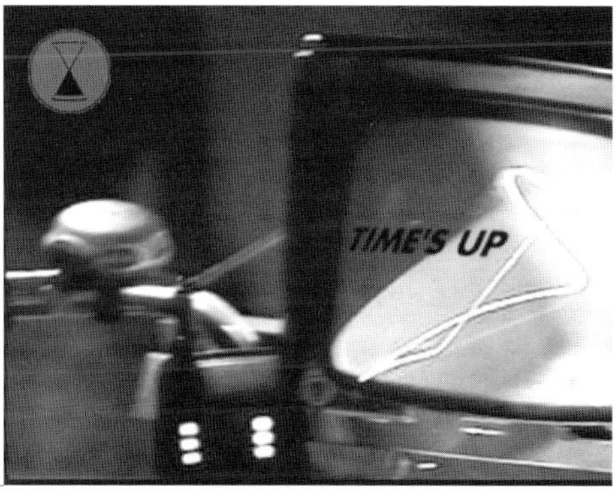

Solche und ähnliche Weisheiten überraschen uns immer wieder, wenn wir aufgeregt sportbegeisterten Diskussionen lauschen. Im Regelfall erscheint uns diese Sprache zu verschlüsselt, als daß wir auch nur ansatzweise erahnen könnten, was uns in diesen Codes eigentlich mitgeteilt werden soll.

Wir verstehen zwar noch, daß wir Arnold Schwarzeneggers nationales Fitnessprogramm mittragen müssen, jedoch wollen wir nicht so aussehen wie er. Das Spektrum zwischen Nationalwandertag und täglichem Schweißtrieb als olympische Medaillenhoffnung der Stemmer, inklusive Ernährungsprogramme und Kleidungsvorschriften, ist einfach zu breit, als daß wir unsere eigene individuelle Form der Fitness hier einfach definiert vorfinden könnten.

Time's up versteht diese Problematik und versucht die Codes zu entschlüsseln. Vor allem die Grundregeln biomechanischer Verhaltensmuster werden unter Einsatz modernster elektronischer Hilfsmittel auf ihre Anwendbarkeit in sportlichem Gelände, der scheinbar ureigensten Wurzel ihres Entstehens, überprüft und somit als erster Schlüssel zum primären Kodex menschlicher Antriebe eingesetzt. Radikal neue Trainingsmethoden wurden entwickelt, basierend auf T.H.H.Boyketts *Theory of Hypercompetition* und nun der breiteren Öffentlichkeit zugeführt.

In einer Art biomechanischer Gameshow wird das Publikum dazu angehalten, seine eigene Fitness auf den Ebenen des individuellen Wahrnehmungs- und Kontrollverhaltens zu überprüfen und spielerisch wiederzuentdecken.

Auftragsarbeit der Ars Electronica/
Commissioned by Ars Electronica

Koproduktion/Co-production:
Spiel.Art, Marstall, Richard Castelli

*Sponsoren/Sponsors: Baltic Engineering, Catasonic Records, *Literatur die leuchtet – Lichtzeile ™*, Opcode, *Let's make things better – Philips, VA Stahl*

So we do move, after all

A polemic on establishing mechanical mundanity

Time's up/
Johannes Domsich

Und wir bewegen uns doch

Eine Polemik zur Etablierung der mechanischen Alltäglichkeit

Time's up/
Johannes Domsich

Die Unendlichkeit der Welt in ihren Möglichkeiten, die sie uns zur Verfügung stellt, zeigt sich gleichwohl in den hämischen Tellerwäscher-Karriere-Phantasien des Kommerzes als in Sätzen wie *jedem Tierchen sein Plaisierchen* – nur: Ist uns diese Chance zur Individualität gegeben, haben wir Wissen, Zeit oder Geld, so saloppe Individualitäten zu leben, sie durchzuhalten und zu ertragen? Wenig ist so klischeehaft umwuchert wie die Freiheit des Menschen, zu tun und zu lassen was ihm beliebt. Wenig so emotional, ja, beinahe mythologisch verklärt wie die Gängelung, die er in seinem Leben erfährt. Leben, so scheint es, bestimmt sich aus den Extremen einer Balance zwischen Wollen und Können, einem Kampf zwischen Ich und der Öffentlichkeit, der nur im Reden oder im Schweigen zu führen ist.

Individualität ist der Imperativ der beginnenden zweiten Hälfte des 20. Jahrhunderts. Eine Bürde, an der wir fortan schwer zu tragen haben, die uns quält durch die permanente Evaluation unser selbst und der Bilder der anderen. Verwechselbar und unverwechselbar ist die Borderline der Kultur, ein Stakkato aus Ja oder Nein, das uns zwischen den Extremen der Liebe und der Ablehnung hin und hertorkeln läßt. Nun ist aber Individualität der dornige Weg des Ich mit all seinen Konzepten, seinem Willen, den Wünschen und Träumen in den Raum der Gesellschaft nicht länger ein Scheideweg zwischen dem richtigen und dem falschen Leben, wie der Mythos der Antike ihn zeigt. Wir stehen nicht wie Herakles grübelnd an Weggabelung, versunken in Gedanken, wohin wir uns wenden

The infinite possibilities the world offers us are manifested in the sardonic rags to riches fantasies of the dream factory and in adages such as *each to his own,* and yet: do we really have this opportunity of being individual, do we possess the knowledge, time or money to live, survive and endure such casual individualities?

Few things are as cliché-ridden as the human freedom to do as one pleases. Few things are as emotionally, almost mythologically, transfigured as the leading strings we are subjected to in our lifetime. Life, it would seem, is a balance between the extremes of wanting and being able to do something, a permanent battle between the ego and the public that can only be waged in words or in silence.

Individuality is the imperative of the beginning latter half of the 20th century. A burden that henceforth will be a heavy cross for us to bear and that will torment us by the permanent compulsion to evaluate ourselves and the images of others. The borderline of culture is undistinctive and distinctive, a staccato of yes and no that makes us reel between the extremes of love and rejection. But individuality, the thorny road of the ego with all its concepts, its will, wishes and dreams, into the social sphere is no longer a cross-roads between right and wrong living as described by the myths of the ancient world. We are not brooding at the fork in the road like Heracles, lost in thought, wondering which way to turn. And there is no mentor arguing the consequences of the decision, thus taking us by the hand with divine prejudice. No, we are racing forward in slow motion on an individualisation highway – prematurely senescent and yet apparently stuck fast in adolescence - side by side but without any real chance of ever meeting, restoring our strength, if we are lucky, in the cool, inhospitable resting places of hedonism. We no longer compare, we no longer vary the lives of our predecessors, their knowledge is but a childlike concept of a long-forgotten time. Time is what we would need to shape a life of ramifications and to embark on the meandering path of possibilities.

Who controls our destinations, who determines the vehicles between the treadmill of day-to-day life and the jungle of therapeutic aberrations? Coincidence and not hesitant brooding. Is it the last religion left to us, the administrator of the estate of spirituality that

sollen. Und kein Mentor argumentiert uns die Folgen der Entscheidung, um uns letztendlich mit göttlicher Voreingenommenheit an der Hand zu nehmen. Nein, wir rasen im Zeitlupentempo – früh vergreist und doch ohne erkennbares Ende der Pubertät – auf einem Individualisation-Highway voran, parallel, ohne rechte Chance auf Begegnung, und laben uns bestenfalls in den ungemütlichen Raststätten der Hedonie. Wir vergleichen nicht, variieren nicht mehr die Leben unserer Ahnen, ihr Wissen ist uns nur kindliches Konzept einer überkommenen Zeit. Zeit – sie bräuchten wir, um ein Leben der Verästelungen zu entwerfen, den geschlungenen Pfad der Möglichkeiten beschreiten zu können.

Wer beherrscht unsere Ziele, wer bestimmt die Gefährte zwischen den Mühlen des Alltags und dem Dschungel therapeutischer Verirrungen? Der Zufall und kein innehaltendes Grübeln. Er ist die letzte Religion, die uns geblieben ist, als Nachlaßverweser der Spiritualität, die uns die Religionen dieser Welt gestohlen haben? Alltäglichkeit bildet die Demarkation unseres Lebens, ersetzt Tag und Nacht, Schlaf und Wachsein, die Grauzone zwischen den bedeutungsvollen und den unwichtigen Dingen, die wir als unser Leben akzeptieren müssen.

Nichts ist uns selbstverständlich, denn nichts ist in Wahrheit noch vergleichbar. Aus den Massen der Mediation sind massenhafte Medien [Einzelkämpfer] geworden. So viele Menschen es gibt, so viele Meinungen sind zu hören und Empfindungen zu ahnen. Wir ähneln dem Gedankenexperiment, eine spiegelnde Kugel in einer verspiegelten Hohlkugel zu sein – aber woher käme das Licht unserer Selbstspiegelung, wenn nicht durch den Blick des anderen, des Fremden?

Diese fröstelnde Individualität läßt uns nicht mehr schlafen, sie fordert permanente Kreation des Ich, unentwegte Fixierung der Ziele und die Musealisierung, die Verklärung unserer Vergangenheit. Wir definieren uns [im Partygeplänkel] nicht durch das, was wir tun, sondern durch das, was wir uns erträumen. Der Entwurf unseres Lebens ist mehr Roman als Realität. Nichts darf bedeutungslos sein, kein Lebensrest, der nicht der Analyse würdig wäre. Vielleicht hat der Mensch um den Preis seiner Kultivierung ein Ende in der Extase der Selbst-

has robbed us of the religions of this world? Ordinariness is the demarcation of our lives, it replaces day and night, sleep and waking, the grey areas between the essentialities and trifles that we must accept as being our life.

Nothing is a matter of course, for nothing is truly comparable. The masses of mediation have become mass media [solo fighters]. There are as many opinions and sentiments as there are people. We resemble the thought experiment of being a reflective sphere in a reflected hollow sphere – but where would the light of our self-reflection come from if not from the view of the other, the stranger?

This chilly individuality keeps us awake, it demands permanent creation of the ego, incessant establishment of objectives and musealization, the transfiguration of our past. We define ourselves [in party squabbling] not by what we do, but rather by what we dream of. The blueprint of our lives is more a novel than reality. Nothing may be insignificant, no remnant of life is unworthy of analysis. Perhaps mankind has found his end in the ecstasy of self-realization at the cost of cultivation. It is no longer the products or, before them, the creativity of the tools that determine our nature. Gone is the equality of movement from experience, the security and knowledge of what we do. [Correctness produces frustration in its authority and tempts us with the ornament – the painted face that cannot only be a Loosean crime.] Work and art, Meyerhold maintains, bear no resemblance to one another any more. Gone is the knowledge that what is right requires, indeed possesses, no justification.

Man as a creator has become the creature of his self – be it as a result of hubris or indolence. He is the product that is assessed merely according to how sought-after it is, how long it can preserve its youth, how well it is suited as an archive of culture [B. Groys], as a place within the mechanised, medialised memory of anonymous masses that can only be bought with power. We produce ourselves, with machines of vanity in the magazines and fitness centres of the civilised world. We toughen up for a project that is again but an I and not a We, and we live solitude in the schizophrenic state of being commodity and buyer at once. And it is precisely this solitude – often interpreted as a self-elected or much longed-for hermitage – that hurls us into

verwirklichung gefunden. Nicht mehr die Produkte oder zuvor noch die Kreativität der Werkzeuge sind es, die uns bestimmen. Verschwunden ist die Gleichheit der Bewegung aus Erfahrung, Sicherheit und dem Wissen um das, was wir tun. [Richtiges produziert auch Frustration in seiner Autorität und verführt uns zum Ornament – dem geschminkten Gesicht, das auch nicht nur Loos'sches Verbrechen sein kann.] Arbeit und Kunst besitzen, wie Meyerhold meint, keine Ähnlichkeit mehr. Verloren ist das Wissen, daß das Richtige keiner Erklärung bedarf, ja, keine besitzt.

Der Mensch als Kreator ist – aus Hybris oder aus Faulheit – zur Kreatur seiner selbst geworden. Er ist das Produkt, das nur danach bewertet wird, wie sehr es begehrt wird, wie lange es sich Jugend zu erhalten vermag, wie gut es sich für ein Archiv der Kultur eignet [B.Groys], ein Platz in der mechanisierten, medialisierten Erinnerung anonymer Massen, den man sich nur mir Macht erkaufen kann. Wir produzieren uns selbst, mit Maschinen der Eitelkeit in den Gazetten und den Fitneßstudios der Zivilisation. Wir ertüchtigen uns für ein Projekt, das wieder nur ein Ich ist und kein Wir, und wir leben die Einsamkeit in der Schizophrenie, zugleich Ware und Käufer zu sein. Und eben diese Einsamkeit – oft noch wird sie als selbst gewählte oder ersehnte Eremitage interpretiert – stürzt uns in eine Ahnung von Verlorenheit. Beziehungslosigkeit zerrt an unseren Nerven und läßt uns von der Wiege der wilden Großfamilie schwärmen. Doch in der Segmentiertheit unserer Leben haben wir nur die Kraft für *Lebensabschnitt-Partnerschaften*, denn Treue, die Verantwortlichkeit bedeutet, ist uns im Kollaps der Wegwerfgesellschaft abhanden gekommen.

Der Mensch scheint in einer Hysterie, in einer flirrenden Nervosität sich dem Zustand völliger Erschöpfung zu nähern [G. Steiner]. Er kann nicht schlafen, denn der Schlaf ist der Automatismus des Alltags, in dem die Sozialisierung und nicht der *Regisseurschauspieler Ich* bestimmt. Wir können nicht in die Kultur zurücksinken, nur reagieren, nur treiben, da wir uns nur noch selbst Kultur sind – einer für einen, jeder ist sein Künstler, jeder ein Medium seiner selbst. Und unser Bild findet

a premonition of forlornness. Our lack of relationships is nerve racking and makes us yearn for the cradle of the wild extended family. But in the segmentation of our lives we only have the strength for *life-period partnerships,* for we have lost fidelity, that means responsibility, in the demise of the throwaway society.

Mankind would seem to be nearing a state of complete exhaustion in his hysteria and whirring nervousness [G. Steiner]. He cannot sleep for sleep is the automatism of everyday life in which socialization and not the *director-actor ego* calls the tune. We cannot sink back into culture but only react and drift along, for we are all the culture that is left to us – one for one, everyone is his own artist, everyone a medium of his self. And our image is only found in the prejudices that are the last wretched remnants of societies, a parody of cultural identity.

We want to and yet we don't want to, we can and yet we cannot. Delegation [capitulation] guides the creativity of mankind with the aid of which he wished to create for himself a snugness of inactivity – a [digital] land of milk and honey in which his will commands and not, as in the paradise of happiness [bliss), the consequence of suffering [good behaviour]. He who is alone can of course call the shots [and moan about his own orders]. Machines are designed to be servants both taking on responsibility and doing work. We have *excarnated* everything [A. Assmann] by having others rule, think and work ... Nothing is left, we have nothing more to do other than devote our attention cosmetically, as it were, to ourselves. And so we play at working, with loosened tie knots and red ears that come from drugs and not diligence – that is also but a kind of narcotic. The reassuring (albeit transfigured) gesture of work has become a gesture of self-gratification.

But when the cat's away, the mice will play.

What is happening in the world we [the pearl of Creation as men of private means] have retired from? Can we be sure of the automatons, the stewards of our materialism? This is why we distrust machines or glorify them, which, in the end, amounts to the same thing. We are incapable of using them merely due to the fact that we cannot devote our attention [quietly] to ourselves. In this way we humanize them into being virtual colleagues, agents, secretaries, dialogue or sex partners, we who have come to be virtual

sich nur in den Vorurteilen, die der letzte kümmerliche Reste der Sozietäten sind, als Parodie kultureller Identität.

Wir wollen und wir wollen nicht, wir können und wir können nicht. So leitet Delegation [Kapitulation] die Kreativität des Menschen, mit deren Hilfe er sich eine Gemütlichkeit des Nichtstuns erschaffen wollte – ein [digitales] Schlaraffenland, in dem sein Wille befiehlt und nicht wie im Paradies Glück [-seligkeit] die Folge des Leidens [Bravseins] ist. Wer allein ist, kann wohl auch allein bestimmen [und über seine eigenen Befehle murren]. Maschinen sind gedacht wie Knechte, die gleichermaßen Verantwortung und Arbeit übernehmen. Alles ist von uns *exkarniert* [A. Assmann], indem wir regieren lassen, denken lassen, arbeiten lassen ... Nichts ist geblieben, wir haben nichts mehr zu tun, als uns uns selber, quasi kosmetisch, zu widmen. So spielt man Arbeit mit gelockerten Kravattenknöpfen und roten Ohren, die uns die Droge macht und nicht der Fleiß, der wiewohl auch nur eine Narkotikum ist. Aus der beruhigenden [wenngleich verklärten] Geste der Arbeit ist die der Selbstbefriedigung geworden.

Doch ist die Katze aus dem Haus, tanzen die Mäuse. Was geschieht in der Welt, aus der wir uns [die Perle der Schöpfung als Privatier] zurückgezogen haben? Können wir uns der Automaten, der Gutsverwalter unseres Materialismus sicher sein? Darum mißtrauen wir den Maschinen oder verherrlichen sie, was eigentlich das selbe ist. Wir sind unfähig uns ihrer zu bedienen nur aus der Tatsache heraus, daß wir uns nicht mit uns [still] beschäftigen können. So vermenschlichen wir, die wir eigentlich selbst virtuelle Weltendörfler geworden sind, sie zu virtuellen Kollegen, Agenten, Sekretären, Dialog- und Sexualpartnern und verpassen ihnen den Irrgarten Digitalität.

Maschinen sind zu mehr nutze. Im eitelsten und gleichzeitig feigsten Fall erträumen wir uns ein Vehikel unseres Geistes durch die Zeit. Unsterblichkeit erfeilscht durch den Verzicht auf Körper. Doch ohne den Körper würde sich unser Denken und unser Wollen mit einem Schlag verändern. Wunderbarerweise hat Hollywood recht: Der Tod steht uns gut! Wer möchte endlos leben, ohne die Be-

global villagers ourselves, and hurl them into the labyrinth of digitization.

Machines can be of more use than this. In the most conceited and, at the same time, cowardly case we dream of inventing a vehicle for our mind to travel through time. Immortality bought at the cost of incorporeality. But without a body our minds and desires would be completely transformed. Miraculously enough, Hollywood is right: Death does become us! Who wants to liver forever without the conditions of the body? We would have no language, for nothing could be *grasped,* *handed down* or *touched upon,* the appeal of second chances [M. Frisch] is gone, adrenaline is an ineffective drug, and sex is too lonely as a monologue to give any pleasure. Ergo, there's just no doing without a body, and the next fantasy has to do with the stage: no more ageing, but rather unending adolescence.

Everything that has to be done from now on has time, although time [visualized as a grinning Reaper] really no longer exists. The enactment of decline can now commence for we no longer sense it in ourselves but rather in actors, delighting in the effect of time [J. Tinguely]. Romanticism has found its place in a patina free of humans – the Earth is wearing out, not Man [M. Jackson]. For if the human body and its movements are the last product of the ego, that only maximises nightmarish mortal agony. Decline proves the impossibility of continuity, and our yearning for standstill grows after a life without patina. But patina cannot be digitized, rather digitization cancels time as the function of representation. This is why the land of milk and honey is the site of absolute immobility, the human will directs at a standstill. With the magic of genetics we have machines live and die for us. Why are robots [that's why robots are] so reluctant to learn to walk?

Make sure you get somewhere in life! How I used to [and still do] hate this phrase wielded by those who have nothing left before them in life. We cannot detach ourselves from the parable of flowing [*the river flows, the wise man knows,* M. Gore], it gives us solace like the rain that excuses us when we do not wish to leave our caves. The synonym of getting somewhere in life is an endless source of luxury, the dream of being moved, just as we are *moved* by what is beautiful and by what is right. Yet

dingungen des Körpers? Wir hätten keine Sprache mehr, denn nichts ist mehr zu *begreifen*, zu *vertreten*, zu *begehen*, der Reiz zweiter Chancen [M. Frisch] ist vorüber, Adrenalin als Droge wirkungslos und Sex als Monolog zu einsam, um zu gefallen. Ergo, ohne Körper geht es nicht, und die nächste Phantasie betritt die Bühne: kein Altern mehr, sondern die unendliche Pubertät. Alles, was hinfort getan werden muß, hat Zeit, die es damit eigentlich [visualisiert als grinsender Sensenmann] nicht mehr gibt. Die Inszenierung des Verfalls kann nun beginnen, denn wir spüren ihn nicht mehr an uns selbst, sondern an Akteuren, um uns an der Wirkung der Zeit zu delektieren [J. Tinguely]. Romantik hat ihren Platz in einer menschenfreien Patina gefunden – die Erde nutzt sich ab, nicht der Mensch [M. Jackson]. Denn ist der menschliche Körper und seine Bewegungen das letzte Produkt des Ich, maximiert das nur die schaurige Todesangst. Der Verfall beweist uns die Unmöglichkeit von Kontinuität, und die Sehnsucht nach Stillstand, nach einem Leben ohne Patina steigt. Patina aber ist nicht digitalisierbar, vielmehr löst Digitalität die Zeit als die Funktion der Abbildung auf. Darum ist das Schlaraffenland der Ort der absoluten Bewegungslosigkeit, der menschliche Wille dirigiert im Stillstand. Mit der Magie der Genetik lassen wir Maschine für uns leben und sterben. Warum [darum] lernen Roboter so widerwillig gehen?

Schau, daß etwas aus dir wird! Wie habe ich sie gehaßt, diese Phrase derer, die nichts mehr vor sich haben. Wir können uns von der Parabel des Fließens [*the river flows, the wise man knows*, M. Gore] nicht trennen, sie ist tröstlich wie der Regen, der uns entschuldigt, wenn wir unsere Höhlen nicht verlassen wollen. Das Synonym des Weiterkommens im Leben ist eine endlose Quelle des Luxus, der Traum vom Bewegtwerden, eben so wie uns das Schöne, das Richtige *bewegt*. Doch wir sind zu träge geworden, den Bildern der Welt zu vertrauen, uns ihnen hinzugeben und uns in unseren Köpfen zu bewegen. Wieder diese zermürbende Delegation. Die Essenz des Erfolges ist nicht mehr Glück, denn jetzt *läuft es wie am Schnürchen*, und wir haben Spaß *am laufenden Band*. Das erklärt wohl unter ande-

we have become too inert to trust the images of the world, to abandon ourselves to them and to move in our minds. It's that agonizing delegation again. The essence of success is no longer happiness for now everything's going *like clockwork,* and we're having fun non-stop. This probably explains our fascination with the weather channels and media sport. The success of the weather and all manner of Olympic games is due to their independence of human will. Perhaps it is too banal: Man conceives what he needs, his thinking is binary and banal in terms of what he has and what he has not. If he is trapped like an unprotected worm in the vale of tears between original sin and purgatory, he just dreams up a golem, Avalon and flying, roast doves. But if he is hanging on the umbilical cord, isolated like a deep-sea diver, he is delirious at the mercy of a menacing Nature of Kantian dimensions. There's no pleasing human beings [nor their God] which is why we find so many starving managers in the *wild* and workaholics in the free marketplace of the free world.

Modern lifestyle - which has substituted the concepts of modernism and perhaps of all times – can be described in two determinants: Permanent existence with selective presence. There's no other explanation for the manipulability of mankind, there's no other way I can imagine the vast amount of energy applied to create systems of absence. It would seem that we are quite happy on our puppet strings, simplifying the world to the essence of a PR manual: Is our product [am I] right, do we [I] communicate correctly, do the customers like it [me] – do they love each other?

Everything we have devised with the aim of experiencing more, knowing more, and better recognising, has also achieved the exact opposite. For the enhancement of perception also entails a weakening or eradication of the other. Keen hearing, far-sightedness, sensitivity and eloquence equally imply deafness, blindness, superficiality and speechlessness. In truth, this intensification conceals, and the world is verily intensive enough as it is. It is alien to us and yet it haunts our fears. Take time for everyday life! Sleep does not breed monsters, it prevents nonsense and crime. Stay in the downy feathers of unreflectedness, you won't miss much because:

When the cat's away, clever mice will sleep.

rem auch die Faszination der *weather channels* und des medialen Sports. Der Erfolg des Wetters und der Olympiaden jeder Art liegt in ihrer Unbedingtheit vom menschlichen Willen. Vielleicht ist es so banal: Der Mensch konzipiert das, was ihm gerade fehlt, denkt binär banal in Haben und Nicht-Haben. Ist er schutzlos wie ein Wurm im Jammertal zwischen Erbsünde und Fegefeuer eingekeilt, erträumt er Golem, Avalon und fliegende, gebratene Täubchen. Hängt er hingegen an der Nabelschnur, abgeschottet wie ein Tiefseetaucher, deliriert er von Ausgeliefertheit in einer drohenden Natur von kantschem Format. Dem Menschen kann es nicht recht gemacht werden [genau wie seinem Gott], darum findet man so viele hungernde Manager in der *freien* Natur und Workaholics im freien Wettbewerb der freien Welt.

Lifestyle der Gegenwart – er hat die Konzepte der Modernen, vielleicht aller Zeiten, ersetzt – kann man in zwei Determinanten beschreiben: Permanente Existenz bei punktueller Anwesenheit. Anders ist diese Manipulierbarkeit der Menschheit nicht zu erklären, anders kann ich mir die Energie nicht vorstellen, die aufgewandt wird, um Systeme der Abwesenheit zu erschaffen. Wir gehen, scheint's, gerne an den Marionettenfäden, vereinfachen die Welt bis zur Essenz eines PR-Handbuchs: Ist unser Produkt [ich] richtig, kommunizieren wir [ich] es richtig, wird es [ich] vom Kunden [ich] angenommen – lieben Sie sich?

Alles, was wir uns zurechtgebastelt haben, um mehr zu erleben, mehr zu wisssen und genauer zu erkennen, hat auch das Gegenteil erreicht. Denn die Verstärkung einer Wahrnehmung führt gleichwohl zur Schwächung oder Auslöschung der anderen. Hellhörigkeit, Weitsichtigkeit, Sensibilität und Eloquenz bedeuten zugleich Taubheit, Blindheit, Oberflächlichkeit und Sprachlosigkeit. Intensivierung überdeckt in Wahrheit, und die Welt ist wahrlich intensiv genug. Sie ist uns fern und rumort doch in unseren Ängsten. Nehmen Sie sich Zeit für den Alltag! Der Schlaf gebiert nicht Ungeheuer, er verhindert Unfug und Verbrechen. Bleiben Sie in den Daunen der Unreflektiertheit, Sie versäumen nicht allzuviel, denn: Wenn die Katze aus dem Haus ist, schlafen die klugen Mäuse.

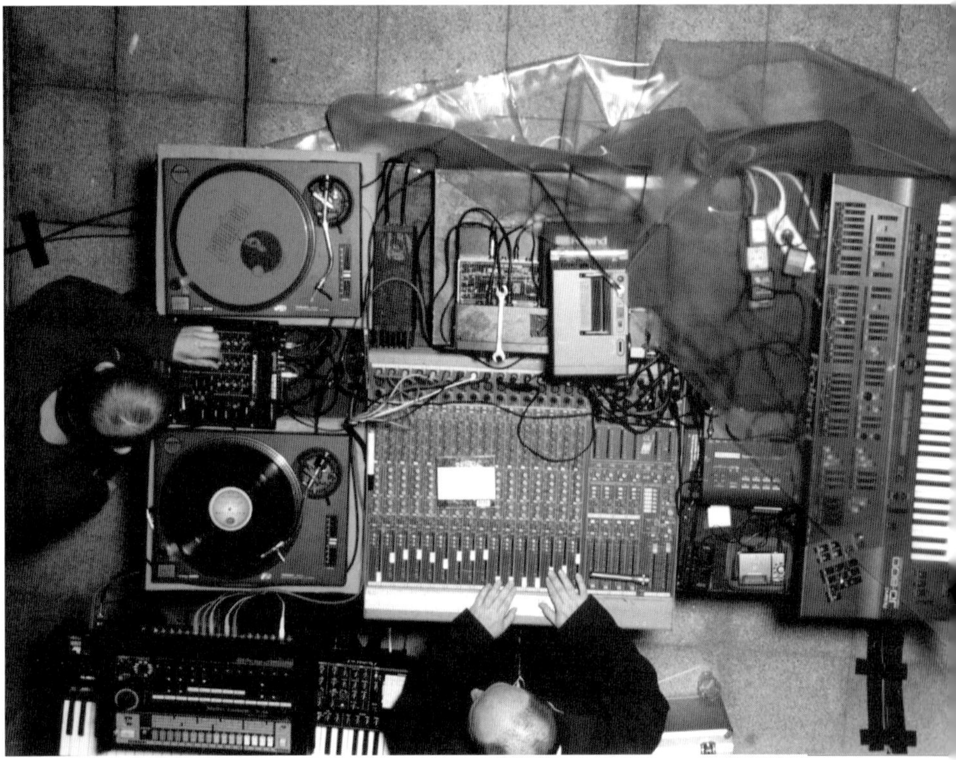

Sub'tronic

Didi Neidhart im Gespräch mit
Wolfgang Dorninger

Sub'tronic

Didi Neidhart
in Conversation with
Wolfgang Dorninger

Sub'tronic is a slogan referring to events with music as their medium. *Sub* stands for the dominant frequency in the sub-bass range, *'tronic* for the electronic orientation of the performance styles. Sub'tronic also stands for nightlife in public spaces – which are, generally speaking, used in a way other than the one for which they were designed, reconfigured with transient media, and frequented by highly unusual people.

DN: This year, Sub'tronic's entertainment space features a bar, a "dancecube," a relaxation area, and something that you've named Pulse. Tell us a little more about what each has to offer.

WD: *Sub'tronic* is setting up a bar and a dancecube in the Concert Hall of the Stadtwerkstatt. The bar and the dancecube are approximately 70% visually and acoustically insulated from each other. Partitions limit the bar guests' view of the dancers, audio volume is acoustically reduced to conversation level, and events taking place in the dancecube are being displayed by means of time-delayed video. Pulse is a small, dramatically lit space, a transit corridor leading to the relaxation area. Both Pulse and the relaxation area can be reached only through the dancecube. In the relaxation area, guests (who have prereserved) can kick back, wind down from the festival stress, and enjoy fruit juices, a little peace and quiet, and a massage.

DN: According to the press release, the soundscapes in the relaxation area have been designed to enhance human qualities in the areas of sexuality or management. What kind of sound mix can we expect from the DJs this year?

Sub'tronic ist ein Slogan für Events mit Musik als Träger. *Sub* steht für die dominierenden Frequenzen im Tieftonbereich und *'tronic* für die elektronische Ausrichtung der dargebotenen Stile. *Sub'tronic* steht auch für Nachtaktivität in öffentlichen Räumen, die zumeist zweckentfremdet benützt, mit flüchtigen Medien umgestaltet und von sonderbaren Menschen frequentiert werden.

DN: Im Entertainment-Raumangebot von Sub'tronic *gibt es heuer eine Bar, einen *dancecube,* einen Entspannungsraum und etwas, was Ihr Puls nennt. Was hat man darunter zu verstehen?*

WD: Im Konzertsaal der Stadtwerkstatt gestaltet *Sub'tronic* eine Bar und einen *dancecube*. Bar und Dancecube sind optisch und akustisch zu 70 Prozent getrennt. Der Blick der Barbesucher auf die Tänzer wird unterbunden, die Akustik auf Gesprächslautstärke reduziert, wobei die Geschehnisse des Dancecube zeitverschoben durch Videoaufzeichnungen eingeblendet werden. *Puls* ist ein kleiner Lichtraum, eine Schleuse auf dem Weg zum Entspannungsraum. Wobei Puls und Entspannungsraum nur durch den Dancecube betreten werden können. Im Entspannungsraum können sich Menschen gegen Voranmeldung von den Plagen eines Festivals heilen lassen und bei Fruchtsäften, Ruhe und Massage wegdriften.

DN: Die Soundscapes im Ruheraum sollen laut Beipackzettel menschliche Qualitäten im Bereich Sexualität oder Management steigern. Welche DJ-Sounds können wir heuer erwarten?

WD: Vor allem Bhangra, Latin-House, Electro, Jungle, Drum & Bass. Also Musikstile, deren Ursprünge vielfach in einem Import und Re-Import verschiedener Kulturen zu finden sind. Kurz gesagt, geht es um kulturelle Äußerungen von Emigranten und modernen Nomaden, die in der Fremde so etwas wie *Heimat* und kulturelles [Selbst-]Bewußtsein etablieren wollten. Damit wurden auch Datenbanken für spätere Generationen angelegt, die vor allem den verschiedenen Minoritäten, z. B. Afro-Amerikanern, Latinos, Schwulen oder indischen und pakistanischen Jugendlichen in England, erstmals eine öffentliche Stimme und ein Bewußtsein über die eigene Geschichte sowie den eigenen gesellschaftlichen und kul-

WD: Primarily Bhangra, Latin House, Electro, Jungle, Drum & Bass. In general, music styles whose roots are to be found in the import or re-import of various different cultures. Essentially, this has to do with the cultural expressions of émigrés and modern nomads seeking to establish something like a *homeland* and cultural [self]confidence in a foreign country. In the same vein, data banks are also being set up, primarily to provide future generation of different minority groups such as Afro-Americans, Latinos, Gays, or Indian and Pakistani young people in England with a public voice for the first time, as well as a consciousness of their own history and their own social and cultural status. The best example of this is HipHop. But here, we have to keep in mind that these cultures regard themselves as *displaced.* They do not think in terms of territories – either real or virtual – defined by fixed borders; rather, they feel committed to sort of a partisan mentality. That means that the styles and sounds actually tend to sneak up and grab you, so that when someone who has been brought up in the tradition of Western Culture thinks he's finally figured them out, they've either already disappeared or they pop up in a totally different place. In this way, the fusion of the various traditionalistic styles of imported [youth] culture with the new technologies [the sampler as digital historical library of minority groups]has led to de- and re-contextualizations and the emergence of new forms – as well as the re-animation of old forms – of tribalistic youth cultures.

Musical styles like House came into existence in small, relatively compact urban spaces [houses]. Chicago House, from which Techno is ultimately derived, oriented itself stylistically on the Munich Sound [Giorgio Moroder] and employed the reduced pattern of this music as a soundtrack for *vouge'ing.* House originated in the competition between the *houses.* Coming out of the Black transgender and Gay movements, this sound became world music through the transculturally operating music industry. It goes without saying, of course, that practically all innovations in Pop music stem from groups on the margins of society who have been ethnically, socially and culturally oppressed. Being Black, Hispanic and Gay in America means being subject to multiple forms of oppression and leading an existence on the edge of oblivion.

turellen Status gegeben haben. Das beste Beipiel dafür ist HipHop. Dabei darf man aber nicht außer acht lassen, daß sich diese Kulturen als *displaced* verstehen, nicht in fix umgrenzten, realen wie virtuellen, Territorien denken und sich eher einer Partisanenmentalität verpflichtet fühlen. Das heißt, die Styles und Sounds erwischen dich eigentlich immer aus dem Hinterhalt, und wenn du dir mit deiner abendländischen Bildung endlich einen Reim darauf gemacht hast, sind sie entweder schon verschwunden oder tauchen ganz woanders auf. Somit führte das Aufeinanderprallen der Traditionalismen importierter [Jugend-]Kulturen und neuer Technologien [der Sampler als digitale Geschichts-Bibliothek minoritärer Gruppen] zu De- und Re-Kontextualisierungen, die neue Formen, aber auch Re-Animationen alter Formen tribalistischer Jugendkulturen entstehen ließen.

Musikstile wie House sind in kleinen überschaubaren urbanen Räumen [*Häusern*] entstanden. Chicago-House, der Ursprung von Techno im weitläufigen Sinn, orientierte sich stilistisch am Munich-Sound [Giorgio Moroder] und benützte reduzierte Muster dieser Musik als Soundtrack zum *vouge'ing*. Im Wettstreit der *Häuser* entstand also House. Dieser Sound wurde – von der schwarzen Transgender- und Gay-Bewegung ausgehend – zur Weltmusik, zum Beitrag einer transkulturell operierenden Musikindustrie. Müßig anzumerken, daß nahezu alle Innovationen der Popmusik von Randgruppen, die ethnisch, sozial und kulturell unterdrückt wurden, entstanden sind. Schwarz, hispanic und schwul sein in Amerika bedeutet: doppelte Unterdrückung und eine Existenz am Rande von nirgendwo.

Die Frage ist: Wie kann eine Struktur, die sehr klein ist, eine Mikrostruktur, kulturell so lange überleben, bevor sie zu einem Objekt der Begierde von Konzernen wird? Und wie verändert sich das Leben jener Menschen, die einfach nur Spaß haben wollten, weil sie mit ihren Freunden neue und alte Codes mischten und dabei etwas Neues kreierten, das auf einmal so interessant wird, daß es Menschen ganz woanders teilen wollen?

Eine anderes Beispiel ist *Bhangra,* wo die in England geborenen Kinder von pakista-

The question is: how can a structure that is so very small – a microstructure – culturally survive for very long, before it becomes an object of desire on the part of major corporations? And what changes are brought about in the lives of those people who just wanted to have fun, because they and their friends liked mixing new and old codes and created something new in the process that suddenly became so interesting that other people in completely different places wanted to share it?Another example is *Bhangra,* the mixture of Indian folkloric and film music with Reggae, Techno and HipHop created by the English-born children of Pakistani and Indian immigrants. This music is the music of a certain neighborhood and a specific milieu; certainly, it can be exported but, at the same time, it requires roots. It's not postmodern fusion music; it's a form of crossover that has really been lived, that has actually already taken place in the lives of these human beings. All that they have done is to interweave those strands that were essential to the fabric of their lives. And this is how you hear history happening.

DN: In addition, Sub'tronic *is also putting on live concerts. What's the concept behind these events?*

WD: All of the concerts are taking place outdoors, each one at a different architecturally appealing venue – in a tunnel, under an arch, in channels, on the docks, under bridges... Sub'tronic needs spaces like these – the stuff of which festivals are made – in order for the transient media to be able to diffuse and to provide the electronic music with a resonating body and a means to escape the space of the apparatus-world.

Parallel to the commercialization of Techno that has been going on since 1992, there has developed an intensified awareness of experimental action. Rebelliousness and conscious refusal to accept the status quo created new forms and scenes which also provides, paradoxically, the very potential – both aesthetically and with respect to content – which commercial Techo so desperately needs as an infusion to enable it to survive. The acceleration of this process of accumulation has created new markets and opportunities for everyone involved. Experimental electronic music, administered in

nischen und indischen Einwanderern indische Folklore, indische Filmmusiken mit Reaggae, Techno und HipHop mischen. Diese Musiken sind Viertel-Musiken, die sich zwar exportieren lassen, aber Wurzeln brauchen. Es ist keine postmoderne Fusion-Musik, es ist einfach gelebter Crossover, der eigentlich schon vorher im Leben dieser Menschen stattgefunden hat. Sie haben nur das weitergesponnen, was in ihrem Leben Sache war. Somit hört man die Geschichte mit.

DN: Daneben bietet Sub'tronic *aber auch noch Live-Konzerte. Welches Konzept steckt hinter diesen Events?*

WD: Sämtliche Livekonzerte spielen im Freien, respektive an architektonisch reizvollen Plätzen. In einem Tunnel, unter einem Tor, in Schleusen, in Hafenbecken, unter Brücken ... *Sub'tronic* benötigt diese Räume, diese Feststoffe, damit die flüchtigen Medien sich ausbreiten können und die elektronische Musik einen Klangkörper bekommt, den Raum der Apparatewelt verlassen kann.

Mit der Kommerzialisierung von Techno ab 1992 entwickelte sich parallel dazu ein verstärktes Bewußtsein für experimentelles Wirken. Die bewußte Verweigerung und Widerborstigkeit schuf neue Formen und Szenen, die paradoxerweise auch jenes ästhetische und inhaltliche Potential lieferten, das der Kommerz-Techno als Auffrischung zum Überleben dringend benötigt. Die Beschleunigung dieses Akkumulationsprozesses schuf für alle Beteiligten neue Märkte und Möglichkeiten. Experimentelle elektronische Musik, als Wurmfortsatz der Neuen Klassik elitär und universitär verwaltet, erhielt somit einen gewieften Spielpartner, der, ausgestattet mit der Leichtigkeit des Pop, diese Formen auch dementsprechend vermarktet. Dementsprechend hat sich auch die Oberfläche des Auftretens verändert.

DN: Wie wird das bei Sub'tronic dargestellt und vermittelt?

WD: Bei *Sub'tronic* suchen wir jene Orte auf, die akustisch verführerisch, optisch interessant und nur mit speziellen Fortbewegungsmitteln zu erreichen sind. An einem Abend [Mitwoch, 10. September, 23 Uhr-4 Uhr] mittels Schiff. Wir fahren mit dem Schiff an das Ende der Scheibe, hängen uns dann weit hinaus und

elitist and academic fashion as an appendix of the New Classicism, is thus being confronted by a wily new contender outfitted with the lightness of Pop, which can also market these forms accordingly. The outward appearance of this scene has also changed correspondingly.

DN: How is that being portrayed and communicated at Sub'tronic?

WD: For *Sub'tronic*, we're seeking venues that are acoustically seductive, visually interesting, and can be reached only with special modes of transportation. On one evening [Wednesday, September 10th, 11 p.m. to 4 a.m.], this will be by ship. We're sailing out to the edge of the known world, where we're going to hang overboard as far as we can and try to look all the way down. This cruise will be navigated by the head honchos of Mego Records in Vienna. There's going to be concerts taking place under bridges, at the harbor, in a channel and on the Danube – space as an improvisational partner. Any visitor who gets on board will not be able to leave the ship in the usual way. What that means is that individuals who have a problem with the extreme positions that are being presented cannot simply go home. Okay, there's a soundproof room for anybody who gets really stressed out – we don't want anyone jumping overboard. But there's not going to be any half in, half out; no more voyeurism.

DN: Last year, there was a live music performance aboard a panorama [observation car] train rolling through the nighttime ambiance of the VOEST Steel Works. Will you be doing something similar this year?

WD: Last year, the audio mix on the train was provided by two men who got into issues dealing with work, a world dominated by men. And Aural Screenshots & James Plotkin constructed a trap which everyone promptly fell into: the world of industrial and mechanical romanticism. This year, it's time for two women to take their stand. Ikue Mori and Tenko will be conducting the panorama train through the VOEST plant grounds. The other concerts are taking place in the vicinity of the Ars Electronica Center – under the Donautor, on the banks of the Danube, and in the tunnel under the Nibelungenbrücke.

DN: What technologies are being employed, and how are different artists showcasing their individual talents with them?

versuchen darunter zu schauen. Navigiert wird diese Fahrt von den Protagonisten von *Mego-Records* aus Wien. Es werden Konzerte unter Brücken stattfinden, im Hafen, in einer Schleuse und auf der Donau. Der Raum als Improvisationspartner. Jeder Besucher, der an Bord geht, kann das Schiff nicht auf dem üblichen Weg verlassen. Das heißt also, daß Menschen, die mit den gebotenen Extrempositionen Probleme bekommen, nicht einfach nach Hause gehen können. Gut, es gibt für all jene, die sehr gestreßt sind, einen schalltoten Raum, damit keiner über Bord springt. Es gibt keine halben Sachen, keinen Voyeurismus mehr.

DN: Im Vorjahr gab es Livemusik in einem Panorama-Zug, der durch das nächtliche Ambiente eines Stahlwerkes [VOEST] fuhr. Wird es heuer etwas Ähnliches geben?

WD: Im Vorjahr wurde der Zug von drei Männern beschallt, die auf eine Arbeitswelt, dominiert von Männern, einzugehen hatten. Im Vorjahr bauten Aural Screenshots & James Plotkin eine Falle auf, in die auch alle promt hineingetappt sind: In die Welt der Industrie- und Maschinenromantik. Heuer werden zwei Frauen Position beziehen. Ikue Mori und Tenko werden den Panoramazug durch das Werksgelände der VOEST steuern.

Die anderen Konzerte finden im AEC-Quarter statt. Unter dem Donautor, an der Donau und im Tunnel unter der Nibelungenbrücke.

DN: Welche Technologien werden eingesetzt, und wie positionieren sich die diversen Künstler dadurch?

WD: Es werden selbstgebaute Analogsynthesizer, Sampler und Computer verwendet, es wird mit Film, Video und Licht gearbeitet. Wobei anzumerken ist, daß die Performer die Räume zwar *neu vermessen,* aber nicht neu bauen. Es sind Musiker, die ihre Arbeitsweise nicht ausschließlich für Festivals ausrichten, sondern eher für den Musikbetrieb. Die sehen sich als Teil einer Popbewegung. Und das gefällt mir, weil es mehr Pop für die Avantgarde und mehr Avantgarde für den Pop bedarf.

WD: Home-made analog synthesizers, samplers and computers are being used. Artists will be working with film, video, and light. Here, I ought to mention that the performers will indeed be *reconfiguring* the space, but not reconstructing it. There will be musicians whose mode of playing is not oriented exclusively toward festivals, but rather more toward the music business. They see themselves as part of the Pop mainstream. And I like that, because we need more Pop in the avant-garde and more avant-garde in Pop.

Program

Live PA:
Mego Night feat.
General Magic,
Farmers Manual,
Fennesz, Pita [all A],
Hecker [G], Haswell [UK]
and Bruce Gilbert [UK);

others:
Ikue Mori [J],
Tenko [USA], Plotkin [USA]/
Linschinger [A],
Leo Anibaldi [UK],
Lilith [USA].

DJs:
Charlie Cabrañez [USA]
BMG [USA]
Martha Hurry [A]

remote sensations

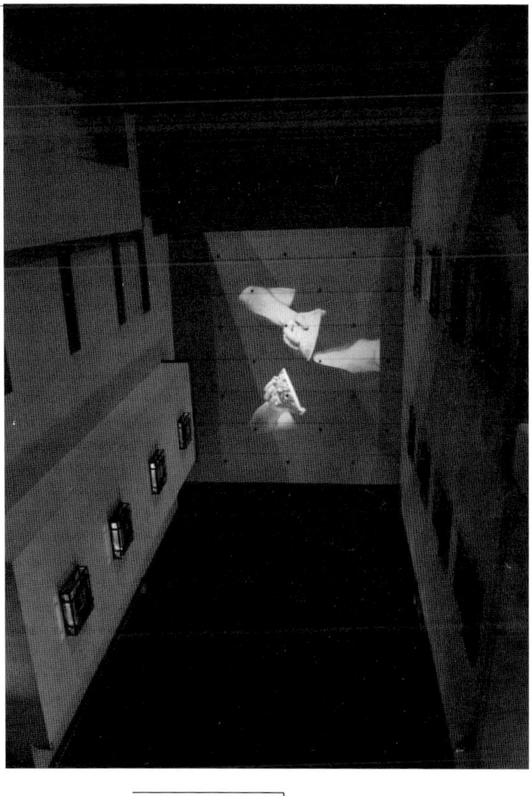

Networking

Heimo Ranzenbacher

Observers of the art world are fond of overusing the term "revolution," nevertheless, one can scarcely help but identifying new trends which truly are revolutionary. They find expression in practice, and in the discussions surrounding the tendencies toward dissipation exhibited by both the concept of a work of art and the idea of authorship, as well as in the consequences for the context of aesthetic activity implicit in these developments.

According to Thomas Kuhn, a scientist constructs his conception of reality with reference to certain "paradigms." A paradigm is not a separate theory, but rather a conceptual framework within which data gathered by means of experiment and observation is formulated. It is neither true nor false; instead, it merely reflects a perspective, an aspect of reality. In a certain sense, this also applies to art. From time to time, the history of ideas undergoes a paradigm shift which, along with world views, encompasses aesthetic theories as well. Such a shift has already gotten underway. In science, this has manifested itself in the rejection of the mechanistic-materialistic world view. In art – and particularly in new art, in the art of elec-

openX

Networking

Heimo Ranzenbacher

tronic space and postulated connectivity – immaterialities are taking on decisive significance, whereby a wide range of artistic criteria are also in transition. The new cannot be grasped with the old; the new is unsuited to be applied to the old. Each is relevant only in relation to its respective referential system, and it thus makes no sense to attempt to pit one against the other. In this way, cultural or paradigmatic relevance is becoming a definitive characteristic – if not the central aesthetic determinant – of new art.

"The term 'immaterial' is a rather risky neologism. All that is meant thereby is the fact that nowadays [...] that which is material can no longer be regarded as something in an oppositional duality such as that of a subject and an object. The consciousness of immaterialities permits us to comprehend the worldwide process of mediatization."
[Jean François Lyotard, immaterialität und postmoderne, merve 1985]

The cultural encyclopedia of our age and the novel conditions of a network-linked existence recorded in its pages make it also seem advisable for art to take its leave of Schopenhauer's *Principium individuationis*. Where the fate of individuals is a consequence of dependencies and systematic interrelationships, it becomes virtually impossible to attribute all forms of interconnectedness in life to the fate of individuals. The capacity which has been conferred upon the artist to properly act as an interpreter is affected by this. The fact that we are also confronting the immanent departure of an art, from which we demand more than sheer entertainment value [contemplation, or the stimulation of our interest disciplined along lines of tradition], has begun to radically change the way in which an artist works. The rejection of the work of art in favor of the process, and the relinquishment of the creator's authority over a creation based upon the possibility of processing creations – have themselves turned attention to these possibilities, with technology as their motive force. The way in which these artists go about their work will be radicalized to the same degree as their conception of themselves

openX

Der Begriff "Revolution" wird in der Kunst gern überstrapaziert; und doch kommt man nicht umhin, in der Tat revolutionäre Veränderungen auszumachen. Sie finden ihren Ausdruck in der Praxis und im einschlägigen Diskurs der Auflösungstendenzen sowohl des Werk- als auch des Autorenbegriffs und der damit verbundenen Konsequenzen für ästhetische Handlungszusammenhänge.

Nach Thomas Kuhn konstruiert der Wissenschaftler seine Vorstellung von der Wirklichkeit in bezug auf bestimmte "Paradigmen". Ein Paradigma ist keine eigenständige Theorie, sondern ein Denkschema, um das herum die durch Experiment und Beobachtung erworbenen Daten angeordnet werden. Es ist weder richtig noch falsch, sondern spiegelt lediglich eine Perspektive, einen Wirklichkeitsaspekt wider. Das gilt in einem gewissen Sinn auch für die Kunst. Von Zeit zu Zeit unterliegt die Geistesgeschichte einem Paradigmenwechsel, der mit den Weltbildern auch ästhetische Theorien erfaßt. Ein solcher Wandel hat bereits eingesetzt. In der Wissenschaft vollzieht er sich in der Abkehr von dem mechanistischen-materialistischen Weltbild; in der Kunst, speziell der neuen, der Kunst des elektronischen Raumes und der postulierten Konnektivität, erlangen die Immaterialien maßgebliche Bedeutung. Damit verändern sich auch etwaige disziplinäre Kriterien. Mit den alten ist das Neue nicht zu erfassen; die neuen eignen sich nicht, auf das Alte angewendet zu werden. Sie sind nur im Verhältnis zum jeweiligen Bezugssystem relevant und können daher nicht sinnvoll gegeneinander ins Treffen geführt werden. Kulturelle bzw. paradigmatische Relevanz wird solcherart zu einer, wenn nicht zur zentralen ästhetischen Bestimmungsgröße der neuen Kunst.

"Beim Begriff 'Immaterial' handelt es sich um einen etwas gewagten Neologismus. Damit ist lediglich ausgedrückt, daß heute [...] das Material nicht mehr als etwas angesehen werden kann, das sich wie ein Objekt einem Subjekt entgegensetzt. Das Bewußtsein von den Immaterialien gestattet uns, den weltweiten Prozeß der Mediatisierung zu begreifen."
Jean François Lyotard, immaterialität und postmoderne, merve 1985

as creators of *net-works,* a selection of which openX has collected.

It might be said that telematic or network-supported art organizes itself as an experimental arrangement for a telematic society. Interactivity expands the rigid borders of works of art into flowing peripheries and introduces into the discourse the concept of form as a participatory magnitude – or leads directly into the process which reaches its consummation in the acceptance or infiltration of its systematic conditions. The artist, in the form of an emphatic abnegation of his status as author, holds up a mirror of understanding in front of the individual's conception of himself as a sovereign being – understanding induced by a totally interconnected world. The art which is constituted in this way is one that emerges out of particularistic experience and acts within a context which its own emergence has helped to bring about.

Radical constructivism and the theory of autopoiesis teach us that we ourselves consist of individual points, becoming a unified entity which, in turn, exists as an individual point in the inconceivable totality of the universe. Life can only be experienced particularistically, so that every insight is verifiable only in relation to something.
[Gerhard Johann Lischka, kunstforum international, vol. 103]

In science, the consequences of constitutive paradigms are rather more of a theoretical nature [having to do with the theoretical knowledge that forms our view of the world], whereas in art, it is practice itself which is affected – due, namely, to the paradigm shift that has taken place, for which social reality has prepared the way. Taken as a whole, the forms assumed by art seem like those of a project aimed at designing experimental configurations of possible utopias. Outlined experimentally by projects such as openX, they are already taking shape [*as a future which is collapsing upon us* – Gerfried Stocker] in the form of an acknowledgment of technological designs. What seems to be taking place with this acknowledgment is the phenomenon of a self-fulfilling prophecy, meaning that in the process of technology assimilating culture, technology establishes its informational *nature* – expressed through connectivity, immateriality, interactivity and reversibility – as a cultural one.

Analogous to the functionalism inherent in the question of the relationship among mind, brain and world – of such enormous

Die kulturelle Enzyklopädie unserer Zeit und die neuen Bedingungen einer vernetzten Existenz, die sie erfaßt, lassen es angeraten erscheinen, daß sich auch die Kunst von dem Schopenhauer'schen Principium individuationis verabschiedet. Wo das Geschick von Individuen eine Folge von Abhängigkeiten, systemischen Verstrickungen ist, werden schwerlich noch alle Verbindlichkeiten des Lebens am Los von Individuen auszulegen sein. Die Befähigung zur Auslegung selbst, die dem Künstler zugesprochen wurde, ist davon betroffen. Daß uns auch der Abschied von einer Kunst bevorsteht, der wir mehr als schieren Unterhaltungwert [Kontemplation oder die Erregung unseres an Traditionslinien disziplinierten Interesses] abverlangen, hat die Arbeitsweise des Künstlers radikal zu verändern begonnen. Die Abkehr vom Werk zugunsten des Prozesses, der in der Möglichkeit, Kreationen zu prozessieren, begründete Verzicht auf die Autorität als Kreator über die Kreation etc. hat den Blick auf diese Möglichkeiten mit Technologie als ihren Träger selbst gelenkt. Radikalisiert wird diese Arbeitsweise ebenso wie das Selbstverständnis als Künstler von *Netz-Werkern*, die *openX* exemplarisch versammelt.

Telematische bzw. netzwerkgestützte Kunst organisiert sich, so könnte man sagen, als Versuchsanordnung für die telematische Gesellschaft; Interaktivität erweitert die starren Grenzen der Werke in fließende und führt die Gestalt als partizipatorische Größe in den Diskurs ein – oder direkt in den Prozeß über, der sich in Anerkennung oder Unterwanderung seiner systemischen Bedingungen vollzieht. Dem Selbstverständnis des Bürgers als Souverän hält der Künstler in Form der betonten Auflösung seines Autorenstatus den Spiegel des Verständnisses vor, das man sich von einer in allem zusammenhängenden Welt zu machen angehalten ist. Es konstituiert sich eine Kunst, die aus der partikularen Erfahrung heraus lebt und im Kontext agiert, dem sie dadurch zur Erscheinung verhilft.

Der radikale Konstruktivismus und die Theorie der Autopoiesis lehren uns, daß wir, selber aus Punkten bestehend, zu einer Ganzheit werden, die wiederum als Punkt in einer unvorstellbaren Ganzheit des Universums lebt. Das Leben ist nur partikular erfahrbar, somit jede Erkenntnis nur an etwas verifizierbar.
[Gerhard Johann Lischka, kunstforum international, Bd. 103]

importance in research on artificial intelligence – which no longer poses the question of the composition of mind, brain and atom, rather asks how they are organized with respect to their function, art which organizes itself out of particularistic experience and dispenses with the sovereign author likewise has to do with functional organization which evokes events [processes] and is no longer a matter of the internal and formal organization of works of art [projects]. This seems to be like wetness, which is indeed a real characteristic of water, but which we would never attribute to an individual molecule of water; the phenomenon of wetness occurs only when an adequate number of molecules have been brought together or a sufficient degree of complexity has been achieved in the system *water.* Staying with this image – traditional art can be described, more or less, as molecularly oriented [namely, upon the symbolic/iconographic representation of specific conditions]; new art, on the other hand, emerges as a manifestation of the complexity of the system itself. Observation oriented toward the work of art is unsuited to this complexity.

Among the phenomenological characteristics of a work of art is that it permits to being described [and justified] monetarily. It ultimately distinguishes itself through the fact that it specifically legitimizes this through the utilization of a specially designed and managed, monetarily-describable infrastructure set up for this purpose: namely, the entire administrative hierarchy of the art establishment's operational system, from the galleries to the middle-men [both bureaucratic and *freelance*] to the academies and the purveyors of art history as an academic discipline. Art institutes, museums, galleries, archives, as well as traditional systems and methods of preserving and brokering art can all be named as components integrated into this operating system, a catalog simultaneously articulating the spaces of traditional art as well as the sphere of hegemony over it. Art history and art administration have their own methods of grasp, judgment and attribution of art; by concentrating on the object of art and not on its structure [its structural organization], art objects are generated which are appropriate to these methods.

Während in der Wissenschaft die Konsequenzen der konstitutiven Paradigmen mehr theoretischer Natur sind [das theoretische Wissen betreffen, das unser Weltbild prägt], so ist die Kunst in ihrer Praxis betroffen. Nämlich durch ihren Vollzug des Paradigmenwechsels, den die gesellschaftliche Realität sich erst zu vollziehen anschickt. Insgesamt muten die Ausformungen der Kunst wie die eines Projekts von Versuchsanordnungen für mögliche Utopien an. Experimentell skizziert durch Projekte in der Art von *openX*, treten sie bereits in Form einer Anerkennung technologischer Entwürfe in Erscheinung. Es scheint sich mit dieser Anerkennung das Phänomen der Selbsterfüllenden Prophezeiung einzustellen, die besagt, daß im Zuge der Assimilierung der Kultur von Technologie, diese ihre [durch Konnektivität, Immaterialität, Interaktivität und Reversibilität bekundete] informatische *Natur* als eine kulturelle etabliert.

Analog zum Funktionalismus in der für die KI-Forschung bedeutsamen Frage der Geist-Hirn-Welt-Beziehung, der nicht mehr die Frage nach der Beschaffenheit von Geist, Gehirn und Atom stellt, sondern wie sie bezüglich ihrer Funktion organisiert sind, geht es bei einer Kunst, die sich aus partikulärer Erfahrung heraus und ohne souveränen Autor organisiert, ebenfalls um die funktionelle Organisation, die Ereignisse [Prozesse] hervorruft – nicht mehr um die innere und formale Organisation von Werken [Projekten]. Sie erscheint wie Nässe, die zwar eine reale Eigenschaft von Wasser ist, die wir jedoch niemals einem einzelnen Wassermolekül zusprechen würden, und die als Phänomen erst dann auftritt, wenn sich genug Moleküle zusammenfinden oder ein ausreichender Grad von Komplexität im System *Wasser* erreicht wird. Bei diesem Bild bleibend, ist traditionelle Kunst quasi als molekular orientiert [nämlich an der symbolischen/ ikonografischen Repräsentanz von spezifischen Zuständen] zu beschreiben; die neue Kunst hingegen tritt als Erscheinung der Komplexität im System selbst zutage. Die werkorientierte Betrachtung ist dieser Komplexität nicht adäquat.

Zur Phänomenologie des Werkes zählt, daß es sich monetär beschreiben [und rechtfertigen] läßt. Es zeichnet sich zuletzt dadurch aus, daß es durch die Inanspruchnahme einer auf es abgestimmten, verwalteten, monetär

The artist positions himself within this [structural] hegemony. Highly significant is the process of development from liberation to institutionalized freedom, which will be broadly outlined here. In the Romanticism movement that followed in the wake of the Enlightenment, artists developed a new conception of themselves which culminated in the liberation from prescription and constraint to be found in the exclusive dedication to one's own creative gifts. The artist is understood to be the proclaimer of a truth accessible to him alone; originality becomes the core of the concept of genius. This thinking which conceptualized artists as an intellectual elite corresponded to their increasing social isolation. And it is this very cliché which continued to determine their position, despite the picture beginning to emerge that had its historical equivalent in the Renaissance artist. After all, the engineer-artist has not yet gone beyond society's perceptual horizon.

An additional line of tradition extends from the loss of the client who commissioned works of art, a development which came about as a result of political and social upheavals in the wake of the French Revolution. The political restoration, furthermore, was directed against progressive artists [such as Millet and Daumier], this time as a result of their political involvement on behalf of democratic or socialist ideas.

The relationship of art to dominant segments of society has ultimately continued to be characterized by cleavage and contradiction. Since Antiquity, these powers have made use of art for the purpose of representation, glorification and propaganda. It has only been since the 19th century, after artists severed connections to their traditional clients [who were only partially replaced by the bourgeoisie and private patrons], that they have been able to more effectively counter this process of domination. [To be sure, artists had to play the fool, as well as stand in bread lines, in return for this freedom.] Recognition was ultimately achieved through educational institutions, the art trade and art criticism – not only a relatively inadequate means to further art, but also an instrument of [conceptual] command over it. The so-called bourgeois concept of art basically refers only to the *recognition of the instruments of implementation of judgmental criteria.* That

beschreibbaren Infrastruktur diese speziell legitimiert. Nämlich die gesamte Repräsentanz des Betriebssystems Kunst, von den Galerien über die beamteten und *freien* Vermittler bis zu den Akademien und der Kunstgeschichte als wissenschaftliche Disziplin. Als dem Betriebssystem Kunst eingegliedert werden Kunsthochschulen, Museen, Galerien, die Archive, traditionelle Aufzeichnungs- und Vermittlungssysteme und -methoden nominiert. Darin beschreiben sich zugleich die Räume der traditionellen Kunst als Sphäre der Hegemonie über Kunst: Die der Kunstgeschichte und -verwaltung eigene Methode der Kunsterfassung generiert [durch Konzentration auf den Gegenstand der Kunst und nicht ihre Struktur, ihre strukturelle Organisation] Kunstgegenstände, die der Methode adäquat sind.

Der Künstler positionierte sich innerhalb dieser [strukturellen] Hegemonie. Bezeichnend ist ihre Entwicklung – von der Befreiung zur institutionalisierten Freiheit ...

In der Romantik bildete sich – im Gefolge der Aufklärung – ein neues Selbstverständnis des Künstlers heraus, das in der Befreiung von Vorschrift und Zwang in der alleinigen Verpflichtung dem eigenen Ingenium gegenüber mündete. Der Künstler als Künder einer nur ihm zugänglichen Wahrheit; die Originalität wird Mittelpunkt des Geniebegriffs. Diesem geistigen Elitedenken entsprach eine zunehmende gesellschaftliche Isolation des Künstlers. Deren Klischee bestimmt seine Stellung ungeachtet des sich abzeichnenden Bildes, das sein historisches Äquivalent im Renaissance-Künstler hat, nach wie vor. Denn der Ingenieur-Künstler hat den gesellschaftlichen Wahrnehmungshorizont noch nicht überschritten.

Eine weitere Traditionslinie leitet sich vom Verlust der Auftraggeber her, der sich durch politische und gesellschaftliche Veränderungen als Folge der Französischen Revolution ergab. Die politische Restauration richtete sich wiederum gegen fortschrittliche Künstler [wie Millet oder Daumier], diesmal gegen sein politisches Engagement für demokratische oder sozialistische Ideen.

Das Verhältnis der Kunst zu den gesellschaftlich herrschenden Kräften ist letztlich zwiespältig geblieben. Seit der Antike bedienten sich diese der Kunst zur Repräsentation,

is its formal description. Stylistic and thematic innovations against which this concept puts up superficial resistance have nothing to do with its formal definition.

We see ourselves confronted nowadays with a similar development. The ruling powers are proceeding in this matter rather more subtly – they are demanding the confirmation of their unbroken capacity to prevail in the form of organizational correspondences. The operational system of the art establishment is to be interpreted as one of these correspondences. The course of events following the French Revolution ,which meant the loss of clients who commissioned works of art, is repeating itself today in the form of the abandonment of an operational system which is to a certain extent assured, in favor of the sphere of a general cultural technology. The political-social restoration which comes about with the recognition of this change is now aimed only indirectly at *progressive artists,* as the forces arrayed behind them ultimately share the loss of monetary and infrastructural descriptive models, the instruments of acceptance. But this restorative force also confers something in return upon informational art in the form of the resistance on the part of those forces against the looming loss of effectiveness of their instruments. The mobilization of this restorative force reveals itself most conspicuously when one recognizes the methodology employed by institutions in viewing art [and even in determining what is art] as a process of establishing a fixed place for the institutional structure itself. The difference from the past is that they can, indeed, ignore the new art, but not the change, because if they did, they would relegate their own instrumentarium to ineffectuality and insignificance and, with it, a not inconsiderable segment of their organizational conception of self. And that would ultimately mean that they themselves had torpedoed the bourgeois conception of art [its formal concept], the very one for which they stand.

The cleavage and contradiction which has characterized the relationship of art and power since time immemorial has turned virulent in a completely new way. At the same time, this situation can be considered as an indicator for the problems generally facing our culture as a result of the Information Revolution. Art

Glorifizierung und Propaganda. Erst seit dem 19. Jahrhundert, nachdem sich der Künstler von seinen traditionellen Auftraggebern [die nur zum geringen Teil durch das Bürgertum und private Mäzäne ersetzt wurden] gelöst hatte, konnte er der Vereinnahmung wirksamer begegnen. [Gewiß, die Freiheit war mit Narrenkappe und Hungertuch bekleidet.] Anerkennung erfuhr er letzten Endes durch die institutionalisierten Ausbildungsstätten, den Kunsthandel und die Kunstkritik – ein nicht nur relativ unzureichendes Instrumentarium der Förderung, sondern zugleich auch ein Instrumentarium der [begrifflichen] Vereinnahmung. Der sogenannte bürgerliche Kunstbegriff rekurriert im Grunde nur auf die *Anerkennung der Instrumente der Erfassung*. Das ist seine formale Beschreibung. Stilistische und thematische Innovationen, gegen die er sich oberflächlich stemmt, tangieren sein formales Konzept in keiner Weise.

Indes walten die herrschenden Kräfte subtiler, sie fordern die Bestätigung ihrer ungebrochenen Kraft zu herrschen durch organisatorische Entsprechungen. Das Betriebssystem Kunst ist als eine dieser Entsprechungen zu interpretieren. Was für die Kunst im Gefolge der Französischen Revolution der Verlust der Auftraggeber bedeutete, wiederholt sich heute in Form der Preisgabe eines einigermaßen gesicherten Betriebssystems zugunsten der Sphäre einer allgemeinen Kulturtechnologie. Die politisch-gesellschaftliche Restauration, die in Anerkennung des Wandels erfolgt, richtet sich nunmehr nur indirekt gegen den *fortschrittlichen Künstler*, als die hinter ihr stehenden Kräfte seinen Verlust der monetären und infrastrukturellen Beschreibungsmodelle, die Instrumente der Akzeptanz, zuletzt teilen. Dafür teilt sich die restaurative Kraft der informatischen Kunst in Form des Widerstands der Kräfte gegen den drohenden Wirksamkeitsverlust ihrer Instrumente mit. Die Mobilisierung der restaurativen Kraft erklärt sich speziell dann, wenn man die Methodik der Institutionen zur Kunstbetrachtung [-erfassung] als Festschreibung der institutionellen Struktur erkennt. Der Unterschied zu früher ist: sie können zwar die neue Kunst ignorieren, aber nicht den Wandel. Sie würden nämlich das ihnen eigene Instrumentarium und damit ein nicht unbeträchtliches Segment ihres organisatorischen Selbst-

history as a scholarly discipline [and its allied fields such as art criticism] are very directly affected by this.

In its new form of organization, art seems, in a certain respect, to have continued to follow criteria of the art historical view which, since *Kant's critique of judgment* [1790], have been considered fundamental methodological principles of art history [as a scholarly discipline] and its affiliated instruments of artistic attribution, such as art criticism and brokerage. But the consequences are totally different.

The advent of Kant's [and Hegel's] philosophical aesthetics established a systematic way of looking at things which took as its measure the concept of the truth of the mind in history. The convergence of aesthetic systems and cultural-historical processes introduced in this way formed the basis of a system of judgment with regard to the aesthetic meaning of art [the character of truth]. In the process of acceptance of this principle, the development of the arts took place more or less through their works. The system of judgment basically became a matter of the organization of the object of judgment, the work of art. The development of art formerly met with resistance motivated by the convention which it negated, whereas now that the *character of truth* is realized organizationally, it withdraws from the range of grasp of potential resistance in the process of judgment itself. The principle of the dualistic judgmental system – view and examination – and aesthetic meaning converge. This has consequences particularly for the status of the observer.

Just as chaos research, cosmology, computer science, the chemistry of self-organizing systems and the rather troublesome findings of quantum mechanics have provided support for the paradigm shift in the scientific world view, the foundation of the view of art has likewise been shaken for a number of reasons, not the least of which is the fact that, here as well, the observer is entangled in a most fundamental way within the observed world. This entanglement is even clearer in art than it is in physics, since this observation is subject to the conditions of the appearance of the observed object [i.e, a process]. This paradigm shift is incisively manifested for the observer precisely as a result of traditional methods of observation

verständnisses in die Bedeutungs- und Wirkungslosigkeit entlassen. Das hieße zuletzt den bürgerlichen Kunstbegriff [sein formales Konzept], für den sie stehen, selbst zu torpetieren.

Die seit jeher existierende Zwiespältigkeit im Verhältnis von Kunst und Macht wird auf völlig neue Weise virulent. Sie kann zugleich als Indiz für die Probleme erkannt werden, die unserer Kultur allgemein durch die informationelle Revolution bevorstehen. Die Kunstgeschichte als wissenschaftliche Disziplin [und ihr anverwandte Bereiche wie die Kunstkritik] ist davon sehr direkt betroffen.

In ihrer Neuorganisation scheint die Kunst in gewisser Hinsicht noch Kriterien der kunsthistorischen Anschauung zu folgen, die seit Kants *Kritik der Urteilskraft* [1790] als ein grundlegendes Prinzip der Methodik der Kunstgeschichte [als wissenschaftliche Disziplin] und der ihr anverwandten Instrumente der Kunst-Erfassung gilt, der Kunstkritik, -vermittlung usw. Aber die Konsequenzen sind völlig andere.

Mit Kants [und Hegels] philosophischer Ästhetik etablierte sich eine systematische Anschauungsweise, die den Begriff der Wahrheit des Geistes in der Geschichte zum Maß nahm. Die so eingeführte Konvergenz ästhetischer Systeme und kulturhistorischer Prozesse begründete ein Beurteilungssystem im Hinblick auf die ästhetische Bedeutung [den Wahrheits-Charakter] der Kunst. In der Anerkennung dieses Prinzips fand mehr oder weniger die Entwicklung der Künste durch ihre Werke statt. Das Beurteilungssystem ging im Grunde in der Organisation des Gegenstands der Beurteilung, des Werkes, auf. Doch stieß Kunst in ihrer Entwicklung ehedem auf den Widerstand, der durch Konvention motiviert war, die sie negierte, so entzieht sie sich nunmehr, da sie den *Wahrheits-Charakter* organisatorisch realisiert, selbst dem Erfassungsradius des möglichen Widerstands in der Beurteilung. Die Prinzipien des Dualismus Beurteilungssystem [Anschauung und Betrachtung] und ästhetische Bedeutung konvergieren. Das hat insbesonders für den Status des Beobachters Folgen.

Wie Chaosforschung, Kosmologie, Informatik, die Chemie selbstorganisierender Systeme und die unbequemen Erkenntnisse der Quantenmechanik den Paradigmenwechsel im wissenschaftlichen Weltbild untermauern,

becoming successively less suitable. In new art, the fields of production, presentation and distribution are collapsing into one another; its appearance is based within the sphere of connectivity in which observation mutates into a processual act.

And as if it were not enough that art history thereby helps bring about the disappearance of its instrumental competence, it is also no longer even capable of corresponding to its own program as a discipline which is, in principle, objectively positioned to the phenomena of art – a claim which raises quite enough contradictions on its own. It had to open up its methods to, and adjust them towards, the conditions of the spatial context of the manifestation and organization of informational art.

Informational art [which can be singled out for its freedom to organize itself and to bring its forms of organization to its forms of representation and thus, as aesthetically recognizable processes] stands outside the formal bourgeois concept of art, which defines itself by means of particular instrumental competence and effectiveness. Informational art carries out the paradigm shift which society implicitly recognizes through its [necessary] resistance – namely, to the solution to the organizational problems with which it has been confronted. The instruments of artistic recognition are poorly suited to the task of comprehending such a paradigm shift. Art history, which not only holds the mandate for the determination of and the judgment upon art, but which also provides the socioeconomic descriptive model of the entire artistic undertaking, is a part of this project as well as an expression of historical consciousness. As such, it is incumbent upon it to create the preconditions for a social and cultural truth alongside that of the mind in history. This task is a prospective one, since social truth as a standard of measurement in the system of judging art and determining what constitutes art appears to be the truth of the mind in the future.

gerät auch das Kunstbild nicht zuletzt durch die Einsicht ins Wanken, daß auch in diesem Bereich der Beobachter auf äußerst fundamentale Weise in die beobachtete Welt verstrickt ist. Diese Verstrickung ist in der Kunst noch einleuchtender als in der Physik, zumal die Beobachtung den Bedingungen des Erscheinens des beobachteten Gegenstands [eines Prozesses] unterworfen ist. Der Wandel [Paradigmenwechsel] manifestiert sich für den Beobachtbar nachvollziehbar gerade durch die sukzessive untauglicher werdenden traditionellen Methoden der Beobachtung. In der neuen Kunst fallen Produktion, Präsentation und Distribution ineinander; ihr Erscheinen begründet sich in der Sphäre der Konnektivität, darin Beobachtung zum prozessualen Akt mutiert.

Nicht genug, daß für die Kunstgeschichte damit das Schwinden ihrer instrumentellen Kompetenz einhergeht, sie vermag auch als im Prinzip zu den Phänomenen der Kunst objektiv positionierte Disziplin [ein Anspruch, der ohnehin genug Widerspruch auslöst] ihrem Programm gar nicht mehr zu entsprechen. Sie müßte ihre Methoden den Bedingungen des Erscheinungs- und Organisationsraumes der informatischen Kunst gegenüber öffnen und darauf eichen.

Informatische Kunst steht außerhalb des formalen bürgerlichen Kunstbegriffes, der sich durch einschlägige instrumentelle Kompetenz und Wirksamkeit definiert. Informatische Kunst exekutiert den Paradigmenwechsel, den die Gesellschaft implizite durch [notwendigen] Widerstand – nämlich zur Lösung der organisatorischen Probleme, vor der er sie stellt – anerkennt. Die Instrumente der Anerkennung von Kunst sind indes wenig geeignet, deren Paradigmenwechsel nachzuvollziehen. Kunstgeschichte, die nicht nur das Mandat des Erfassens und Beurteilens von Kunst hat, sondern damit sozioökonomische Beschreibungsmodelle des Projekts Kunst liefert, ist als Teil dieses Projekts und als Ausdruck des historischen Bewußtseins angehalten, Voraussetzungen für eine soziale und kulturelle Wahrheit neben der des Geistes in der Geschichte zu schaffen. Dieser Auftrag ist prospektiv: Denn soziale Wahrheit als Maß im Beurteilungs- und Erfassungssystem erscheint als die Wahrheit des Geistes in der Zukunft.

openX

is an attempt to present the methods of various artists specialized in working within networked systems. It is the installation of a temporary open-plan studio in which their current artistic activities are presented.

openX

is a *walk-in* network and hence an experiment in itself, designed to develop different forms of presentation for those fields of artistic activities which are manifest in a process marginal to the object or the event.

You will find detailed information and links to the openX projects at: http:\\www.aec.at/fleshfactor

openX

openX

ist der Versuch, durch die Einrichtung eines temporären Großraumateliers die Aktivitäten von Protagonisten der aktuellen künstlerischen Arbeit in und mit vernetzten Systemen exemplarisch vorzustellen.

openX

ein begehbares Netzwerk, ist seinerseits ein Experiment zur Entwicklung von Präsentationsformen für künstlerische Aktions- und Handlungsfelder, die sich abseits von Objekt oder Event im Prozeß erschließen.

Ausführliche Informationen und Links zu den Projekten von openX unter: http:\\www.aec.at/fleshfactor

Ausländer und Staatenlose

http://www:.toysatellite.com.au/agarton/auslander

In 1914, Elena Garton fled St. Petersburg and a revolution that was to change her country forever. Throughout the 1930's and 40's, Elena wrote plays and short stories, many of which she completed when finally settling in Australia. Providing an insight into more than three decades of life on the road in war-torn Europe, Elena's work underpins the journey that is, *Ausländer und Staatenlose*, an interactive online opera by composer, performer and Internet artist, Andrew Garton.

Translated as *foreigners and stateless persons*, *Ausländer und Staatenlose* explores cultural dislocation in the 20th Century. The opera intertwines the phenomenon of refugee culture and transmigration with that of the composer's own direct experiences and stories authored by Elena, his grandmother.

Ausländer is conceived in the tradition of such experimental works as Robert Wilson's play, *Black Rider*, the multimedia opera by Wilson and Philip Glass, *Einstein* on the Beach, and the radio-phonic composition, *Radio Inferno*, by German composers Andreas Ammer and FM Einheit. *Ausländer und Staatenlose*, as a work-in-progress, will be launched at Ars Electronica along with mirror sites in Russia, the Czech Republic, the United Kingdom and Australia.

Andrew Garton

Ausländer und Staatenlose *is being realized with generous support from the Centre for Animation and Interactive Media [Royal Melbourne Institute of Technology], Pegasus Networks, WiredAudio, SSEYO Pty Ltd, Creative Labs, Ars Electronica, Econnect, GreenNet und GlusNet.*

Ausländer und Staatenlose

Im Jahr 1914 verließ Elena Garton St. Petersburg auf der Flucht vor einer Revolution, die ihr Land für immer verändern sollte. In den 30er und 40er Jahren begann Elena, Theaterstücke und Kurzgeschichten zu schreiben, von denen sie einen Großteil in Australien fertigstellte, wo sie sich schließlich niederließ.

Elenas Werk bietet einen Einblick in mehr als drei Jahrzehnte des Lebens auf der Straße in einem von Kriegen zerrissenen Europa und diente als Grundlage für die interaktive Online-Oper *Ausländer und Staatenlose* des Komponisten, Künstlers und Internetakteurs Andrew Garton.

Ausländer und Staatenlose beschäftigt sich mit der kulturellen Entwurzelung im 20. Jahrhundert. Diese Oper verknüpft das Phänomen der Flüchtlingskultur und der Transmigration mit eigenen unmittelbaren Erfahrungen des Autors und den Geschichten seiner Großmutter Elena. *Ausländer* entstand in der Tradition experimenteller Werke wie Robert Wilsons Stück *Black Rider*, der von Wilson und Philip Glass geschaffenen Multimedia-Oper *Einstein on the Beach* und der radiophonischen Komposition *Radio Inferno* der deutschen Komponisten Andreas Ammer und FM Einheit.

Ausländer und Staatenlose *wird als Work-in-Progress auf der Ars Electronica und mit Mirror-Sites in Rußland, der Tschechischen Republik, Großbritannien und Australien gestartet.*

Andrew Garton

Ausländer und Staatenlose *wird realisiert mit der großzügigen Unterstützung des Centre for Animation and Interactive Media [Royal Melbourne Institute of Technology], sowie von Pegasus Networks, WiredAudio, SSEYO Pty Ltd, Creative Labs, Ars Electronica, Econnect, GreenNet und GlasNet.*

Terminal Bar

http://www.terminal.cz

Terminal Bar sees itself as a living, dynamic system which is part of a larger, evolving cyber-culture in the Czech Republic, cultivated on such open systems as BBS, information databases, interactive VRML installations and in spaces dedicated to internet access, i.e. the concept of the cyberbar or electronic cafe. The *Terminal Bar* as a network presence has fashioned itself as an interface mechanism between the digital networks and live cultural events in Prague and the Czech Republic. We started our process of documentation with a web-based database of our films and books, which quickly extended to a larger database of related materials. The emphasis was not on creating an exhaustive database, but a well thought-out relational database of interesting and unusual information, an open-ended resource for our own use. As the *Terminal Bar* began to be invited to different actions, festivals and conferences, we began to compile more varied types of data and take advantage of the multimedia capabilities available in digital data transfer to aid in our documentation projects. Our primary emphasis is on a practical and flexible means to store and transmit the content utilizing the advantages of intuitive web documents with the power of a relational database in creating an expanding interactive archive.

Bradley Kirkpatrick

Terminal Bar

Terminal Bar versteht sich als lebendes, dynamisches System, das Teil der sich in der Tschechischen Republik entwickelnden Cyberkultur ist. Seine Wurzeln liegen in offenen Systemen wie BBS, Informationsdatenbanken, interaktiven VRML-Installationen und in Räumen, die Internetzugang anbieten, wie Cyberbar und Electronic Cafe. Als Netzwerkpräsenz hat sich *Terminal Bar* zu einem Schnittstellenmechanismus zwischen den digitalen Netzwerken und aktuellen kulturellen Veranstaltungen in Prag und in der Tschechischen Republik entwickelt.

Zu Beginn unseres Dokumentationsverfahrens stand eine Web-basierte Datenbank für unsere Filme und Bücher, die sich sehr schnell zu einer umfassenderen Datenbank für ähnliches Material entwickelte. Es ging uns nicht so sehr darum, ein lückenloses System zur Speicherung von Informationen zu schaffen, als vielmehr eine gut durchdachte, relationale Datenbank mit interessanten und außergewöhnlichen Informationen, ein unbegrenztes Hilfsmittel für den Eigengebrauch. Als *Terminal Bar* zunehmend zu verschiedenen Aktionen, Festivals und Konferenzen eingeladen wurde, erweiterten wir das Spektrum der gesammelten Daten und begannen, das mittels digitalem Datentransfer verfügbare Multimediapotential für unsere Dokumentationsprojekte zu nutzen. Unser Hauptaugenmerk liegt darauf, ein praktisches und flexibles Mittel zum Speichern und Übertragen von Inhalten zu schaffen, wobei wir die Vorteile intuitiver Webdokumente mit den Möglichkeiten einer relationalen Datenbank für ein expandierendes interaktives Archiv nutzen.

Bradley Kirkpatrick

Face Settings and Kunstradio

http://www.thing.at/face/

As I see it, work in the Internet is work in the global public space. But this public space is also the most lonely, intimate place, moving timelessly around the Earth ... that's what makes Internet work so immeasurable and exciting for me. I like it as a concept that can no longer be found and certainly not brought to a close.

In the project *Face Settings*, this mental concept may be a hybrid between a dining table and a computer display that, as a platform for communication and experience for women, describes their presence in the networks.

For KUNSTRADIO it implies developing surfaces in collaboration with sound artists, authors and visual artists, surfaces that are constantly redescribing their work in the global, public space.

Eva Wohlgemuth

Face Settings

http://www.thing.at/face

Internet allows a multifaceted existence – from various places in the world, I am able to work, play and interact with friends, lovers and colleagues. Face Settings offers possibilities to organize effective communication events-activities. For me, past networking and curatorial experience is useful for this life, and is a natural outgrowth of my art & design education. I strive to bring my knowledge of TV and media art production, museum practice and media theory to the Net workplace. I seek fresh responses, and expanded audiences for the Net projects I am involved in.

Kathy Rae Huffman

openX

Face Settings und Kunstradio

Arbeit im Internet ist für mich gefühlsmäßig Arbeit im globalen öffentlichen Raum. Aber dieser öffentliche Raum ist zu gleich auch der einsamste und intimste, und er bewegt sich zeitlos um die Erde ... das macht die Internetarbeit für mich maßlos und aufregend. Ich mag sie als Konzept, das nicht länger gefunden und schon gar nicht zu einem Ende gebracht werden kann. Im Projekt *Face Settings* mag dieses mentale Konzept ein Hybrid aus Eßtisch und Computerbildschirm sein, das als Kommunikations- und Erfahrungsplattform für Frauen deren Präsenz in den Netzwerken beschreibt. Für KUNSTRADIO bedeutet es, in Zusammenarbeit mit SoundkünstlerInnen, LiteratInnen und Visual Artists jene Oberflächen zu entwickeln, die deren Arbeiten immer aufs neue im globalen, öffentlichen Raum beschreiben.

Eva Wohlgemuth

Face Settings

Das Internet ermöglicht eine vielschichtige Existenz- von verschiedenen Plätzen auf der Welt kann ich arbeiten, spielen und mit Freunden, Geliebten und Kollegen interagieren. *Face Settings* erlaubt es uns , Kommunikationsaktivitäten und -events effizient zu organisieren. Für mich sind alle früheren Erfahrungen mit meiner Arbeit mit Netzwerken und als Kuratorin nützlich für dieses Leben, sie sind eine natürliche Fortsetzung meiner Kunst- und Designausbildung. Mir geht es darum, mein Wissen im Bereich der TV- und Medienkunstproduktion und meine Museumserfahrung in die Arbeit mit dem *Netz* einzubringen. Ich suche nach neuen Antworten und einem erweiterten Publikum für die Netz-Projekte, in die ich involviert bin.

Kathy Rae Huffman

AntiLoop

and as I breathe in fresh air with every breath
I take and therefore constantly breathe
my whole life long;
how could it be that not everything
possible can happen at any time
except by my own intention;
[Loop is the function of a machine
which simulates
that anything can stay as it is]
Darb-i Fetih, Rupert Huber

RealRadio

The difference to classical broadcasting lies in the globe-embracing range and the possibility of direct contact with the transmitter. Anyone with the technical possibilities of receiving RealAudio radio is also capable of transmitting. As opposed to classical radio, the Internet is not [yet] a one-way medium. One possibility is to offer a discussion on an IRC channel in addition to the transmission, so as to allow direct feedback. Another component is the fact that transmissions can be produced with a minimum of technological requirements due to the inferior quality of transmissions that is possible – Desktop Radio: with the aid of recording equipment and a home PC with audio facilities anyone can make radio. Anyone with access to the international data networks can operate as a transmitter/receiver.

Radio is broadcast through the net by means of streaming. The most popular form is probably RealAudio. The audio files are optimised with quality loss as the Internet's frequency range is insufficient for normal quality transmissions. This is the reason for the inferior quality that is nevertheless perfectly adequate for voice reproduction. Music has to be specially filtered so as to achieve an acceptable quality of sound.

Markus Seidl

openX

AntiLoop

und nachdem ich mit jedem Atemzug neue
Luft mir hole
und ständig, mein ganzes Leben lang, atme;
wie könnte es sein, daß nicht jederzeit alles
geschehen kann, was nur möglich ist,
außer durch meine Absicht ...
[Loop ist die Funktion einer Maschine, die
vortäuscht, daß irgendetwas so bleiben
kann, wie es ist.]
Darb-i Fetih, Rupert Huber

RealRadio

Der Unterschied zum klassischen Broadcasting liegt in der globusumspannenden Reichweite und in der unmittelbaren Kontaktmöglichkeit zum Sender. Jede/r, der/die über die technischen Möglichkeiten zum Empfang von RealAudio-Radio verfügt, verfügt auch über die Möglichkeit, selbst zu senden. Das Internet ist im Gegensatz zum klassischen Radio [noch] kein Einwegmedium. Eine Möglichkeit ist, zusätzlich zur Sendung noch eine Diskussion auf einem IRC-Channel anzubieten und so direktes Feedback zu ermöglichen.

Eine weitere Komponente besteht darin, daß Sendungen aufgrund der ohnehin nur geringen Übertragungsqualität mit geringstem technischen Aufwand produziert werden können. DesktopRadio: Mit einem Aufnahmegerät und einem audiofähigen Home-PC kann jede/r Radio machen. Mit einem Zugang zu den weltweiten Datennetzen kann jede/r als Sender/Empfänger agieren.

Radio wird übers Netz im Streaming-Verfahren gesendet. Das wohl populärste ist RealAudio. Die Audiodaten werden verlustbehaftet komprimiert, da für eine Übertragung in normaler Qualität die Bandbreite des Internet nicht ausreicht. Anders als bei Stimmen muß man bei Musikbeiträgen speziell filtern, um eine annehmbare Tonqualität zu erreichen.

Markus Seidl

Remote Viewing

http://remote.tø.or.at

Spraying the walls through a real-time-interaction push-media application located on the WWW. Invited participants [and anybody with access to the password] can contribute to the show with text and image via the Internet and thus actively work with the environment from anywhere in the world. Slogans, images and other visual signals are transmitted and will be beamed into the exhibition. The basic display unit for the *Remote Viewing* installation consists of a PC with soundcard and 32MB RAM or more with a direct connection to the Internet. Using Netscape 3.0 or higher connected to one or more databeamer [VGA] 640x480 it projects the selfrefreshing screen/image. *Remote Viewing* uses a 24hour RealAudio Channel.

Konrad Becker

Last Entry: Bombay, 1st of July ...

http://www.aec.at/residence/lastentry/index.html

Last Entry: Bombay, 1st of July ... is a collaborative documentary about a person – about you or him or her ? Identity, sex and places are unknown and they will vary. Inspired by Virginia Woolf's *Orlando*, a figure travelling through time and space, this net story mirrors the virtual as a stage and residence by slipping into identities and virtual profiles in a networked community of realities and fictions. Driven only by the users' input, it forms a dynamic network of personal experiences, memories and interventions. As an unpredictable web of individual episodes, it reflects on 'digital storytelling' as a cross between anecdote and archetype, diary and legend.

Andrea Zapp

Remote Viewing

Spraying the walls – Wände besprühen mit einer interaktiven Echtzeit-Push-Media-Applikation im WWW. Geladene Teilnehmer [und jeder, der Zugang zum Paßwort hat] können via Internet mi t Text- und Bildbeiträgen an der Show mitwirken und so von überall in der Welt aktiv mit dieser Umgebung arbeiten. Slogans, Bilder und andere visuelle Signale werden übertragen und in die Ausstellung eingeblendet. Als Grundsichtgerät für die *Remote Viewing*-Installation dient ein PC mit Soundkarte, mindestens 32 MB RAM und direktem Internetanschluß. Die selbstauffrischende Bildanzeige wird unter der Verwendung von Netscape 3.0 oder höher über einen oder mehrere Datenprojektoren [VGA 640x480] projiziert. *Remote Viewing* läuft über einen 24-Stunden-RealAudio-Kanal.

Konrad Becker

Last Entry: Bombay, 1st of July ...

Last Entry: Bombay, 1st of July ... ist eine in Zusammenarbeit entstehende Dokumentation über eine Person – über Sie oder ihn oder sie? Identität, Geschlecht und Ort sind unbekannt und werden wechseln. Diese von Virginia Woolfs Orlando, einer Figur, die durch Raum und Zeit reist, inspirierte Net-Geschichte spiegelt das Virtuelle als Übergangsstadium und temporären Aufenthaltsort, indem sie in einer vernetzten Gemeinschaft von Realitäten und Fiktionen zwischen verschiedenen Identitäten und virtuellen Profilen wechselt. Sie entwickelt sich, nur durch den Input des Benutzers gesteuert, zu einem dynamischen Netz aus persönlichen Erfahrungen, Erinnerungen und Eingriffen. Als unvorhersagbares Gespinst aus lauter Einzelepisoden beschäftigt sie sich mir der *digitalen Erzählkunst* als Kreuzung zwischen Anekdote und Archetyp, Tagebuch und Legende.

Andrea Zapp

Conversation with Angels

http://ampcom.kaapeli.fi

Conversation with Angels is a multi-user VRML 2.0 world created by Ampcom [Andy Best & Merja Puustinen]. Using the latest possibilites for interactive communication on the Internet, Ampcom are creating a series of 3D spaces inhabited by robots, whose characters are based on actual real people and experiences. Visitors to the site can choose an avatar with which to enter the worlds, and via a text interface can chat with the robot personalities. There is a serial killer, a middle-aged single mother, a redneck survivalist, and a lesbian princess, amongst others, all types that the average net surfer doesn't bump into too often! By providing politically and socially provoking content, Ampcom aim to steer debate away from cyber hype and actually challenge real world prejudices. As visitors can also chat to each other, the hope is that a sense of community and place will build up, that it will become a part of life, in the same way that we now talk of MTV or soap operas.

Artistic design & creation: Ampcom [Andy Best & Merja Puustinen], Producer: Outi Rousu, Co-production: The Banff Centre for the Arts

Virtual Feedback

Virtual Feedback is a structure for spatial environments which are controlled from the Internet – thus, they exist simultaneously on two levels: in a real space and as a client in the computers of network users. Control of the spatial installation [for example, its video and audio projections] is by means of a program which automatically downloads and runs itself on the computers of network users. By means of a graphic user interface which displays the spatial environment as a wiring diagram, users can – if it is in their interest to do so – intervene in

Conversation with Angels

Conversation with Angels ist eine von Ampcom [Andy Best & Merja Puustinen] entwickelte Multi-User-VRML-2.0-Welt. Unter Verwendung der neuesten Mittel interaktiver Kommunikation im Internet schafft Ampcom eine Reihe von 3D-Räumen, bewohnt von Robotern, deren Persönlichkeit auf realen Personen und Erlebnissen beruht. Besucher der Site können die Welten mittels eines Avatars betreten oder über ein Textinterface mit den Roboterpersönlichkeiten chatten. Darunter befinden sich u.a. ein Serienmörder, eine alleinerziehende Mutter mittleren Alters, ein kommunistenfressender Überlebensfreak und eine lesbische Prinzessin, lauter Typen, denen durchschnittliche Netzsurfer nicht alle Tage begegnen! Mit dem Angebot eines politisch und sozial herausfordernden Inhalts versucht Ampcom die Diskussion vom Cyberhype wegzubringen und Vorurteile der wirklichen Welt zu thematisieren. Da Besucher auch die Möglichkeit haben, miteinander zu chatten, hoffen wir, daß sich ein gewisses Gemeinschafts- und Ortsgefühl entwickelt, und daß dieses zu einem Teil des Lebens wird, wie das heute MTV oder Seifenopern sind.

Künstlerische Gestaltung & Konzeption: Ampcom (Andy Best & Merja Puustinen), Produzent: Outi Rousu Koproduktion: The Banff Centre for the Arts

Virtual Feedback

Virtual Feedback ist eine Struktur für Raum-Environments, die vom Internet aus gesteuert werden, also gleichzeitig auf zwei Ebenen existieren: In einem realen Raum und als Client in den Computern der Netz-User. Die Steuerung der Raum-Installation [etwa deren Bild- und Klangprojektionen] erfolgt durch ein Programm, das sich selbsttätig auf die Computer der Netz-User lädt und ausführt. Über eine graphische Oberfläche, die das Raum-Environment als Schaltplan darstellt, können die User, soweit es in ihrem Interesse liegt, in die Abläufe am realen Ort eingreifen und über Quasi-Echtzeit-Rückkopplungen [z. B. RealAudio Live Stream, Live Camera] ihre Interaktionen mitverfolgen.

a course of events taking place at some real location and follow their interaction through quasi-real-time feedback [e.g. RealAudio live stream, live camera]. The intelligence in the spatial installation's control process thus develops exclusively within users' computers and depends upon users' readiness to make processing capability available as well as themselves to intervene in the course of events. In principle, users are also in a position to develop the system further. In other words, interaction is not restricted to a predetermined scheme; rather, it can also lead to a modification/expansion of the entire system. In this way, *Virtual Feedback* becomes a system of interactive environment tools that can be developed and used within a community of artists.

Norbert Math/Andrea Sodomka/
Martin Breindl

Net Sauna

http://muu.autono.net/

Net Sauna is a space for genuine dialogue.

As a metaphor it is a culturally specific yet inclusive space that contrasts globalized constructions such as museums, theaters, and broadcast media. Body and politics intertwined are rescued from the mere field of rhetoric and brought into a small warm quiet place.

Four members of MUU Artist Association in Helsinki – John Hopkins, Tapio Mäkelä, Terhi Penttilä and Liisa Vähäkylä – have developed this communication-based net project.

Tapio Mäkelä

Die Intelligenz in der Steuerung der Raum-Installation entwickelt sich damit ausschließlich an den Computern der User und ist von ihrer Bereitschaft abhängig, deren Rechenleistung zur Verfügung zu stellen und auch selbst in die Abläufe einzugreifen. Die User sind prinzipiell auch in der Lage, selbst das System weiterzuentwickeln, d. h. Interaktion beschränkt sich nicht auf vorherbestimmte Schemata, sondern kann auch zu einer Modifikation/ Erweiterung des gesamten Systemes führen. Auf diese Weise entwickelt sich *Virtual Feedback* zu einem System von Werkzeugen [interactive environment tools], das in einer Gemeinschaft von KünstlerInnen entwickelt und verwendet werden kann.

Norbert Math/Andrea Sodomka/
Martin Breindl

Net Sauna

Net Sauna ist ein Raum für echten Dialog,

eine Metapher für einen kulturspezifischen und doch inklusiven Raum, der im Kontrast zu globalisierten Konstruktionen wie Museen, Theatern und Rundfunkmedien steht. Körper und Politik werden in ihrer Verschränkung aus dem bloßen Bereich der Rhetorik errettet und in einen kleinen, warmen, ruhigen Raum gebracht.

Dieses kommunikationsbasierte Netz-

Projekt wurde von John Hopkins, Tapio Mäkelä, Terhi Penttilä und Liisa Vähäkylä, Mitgliedern der MUU Artist Association in Helsinki, entwickelt.

Tapio Mäkelä

Remote C

Obliterate coherent presence with
disturbances in space and time
disguised as 'communication'
to facilitate the extraction
of vital energies.

http://remote.aec.at

Remote C is a collaborative project comprised of the individual works of several net.artists working remotely from various locations throughout Europe within the common frame of the WWW. While the participating artists don't constitute an *Art Group*, this temporary grouping is an attempt to map out some of the possibilities offered through communications technologies for cultural production. The project is the result of an ongoing dialog that has grown up around the art works emerging in the context of communication technologies, with each of the artists pursuing very different modes of realization and representation, yet mutually respecting one another in their attempts to test the boundaries of art and technology.

Each of the projects within *Remote C* is realized over time with remote access to the Ars Electronica Center server while at the same time responding to the other works through links and various pages. The overall frame of Remote C is built up over time as the project becomes more complex and creates a Web-based environment that extends into realspace via radio, telephony, and a CD-ROM.

Diana McCarty/Andreas Broeckmann

Das Spiel

The aim is to create a very concentrated form of info-stream, where the data themselves are either not the most important thing or lose their previous sense, combining to become infotainment.

Das Net.spiel Website consists of already existing data on the Net – sounds, texts, images, making it possible for users to create their own *info-stories*. The information stream can be left without a particular location, as data can be found in different places, at the same time it becomes clear for each local community where those or other data come from.

Remote C

Verdeckte kohärente Präsenz mit
Störungen in Raum und Zeit
Getarnt als 'Kommunikation'
Zur Erleichterung der Extraktion
Lebensnotwendiger Energien.

Remote C ist ein Gemeinschaftsprojekt aus Werken einzelner Net.künstler, die von verschiedenen Orten Europas aus im Rahmen des WWW zusammenarbeiten. Die Teilnehmer bilden jedoch selbst keine *Kunstgruppe*, sondern versuchen vielmehr, in dieser temporären Gruppierung einige Möglichkeiten abzustecken, die die Kommunikationstechnologie für die Kulturproduktion eröffnet. Das Projekt ergibt sich aus dem andauernden Dialog über die in diesem Kontext entstehenden Kunstwerke, wobei jeder Künstler unterschiedliche Realisations- und Repräsentationsformen wählt und gleichzeitig die anderen Teilnehmer in ihren Versuchen, die Grenzen von Kunst und Technologie auszuloten, respektiert.

Jedes Einzelprojekt zu *Remote C* wird durch Fernzugriff auf dem Server des Ars Electronica Center realisiert und verweist zugleich durch Links und diverse Seiten auf die übrigen Arbeiten. Der Gesamtrahmen von *Remote C* ergibt sich im Laufe der Zeit dadurch, daß das Projekt immer komplexer wird und eine WWW-basierte Umgebung erzeugt, die sich via Radio, Telephon und CD-ROM in den realen Raum erstreckt.

Diana McCarty/Andreas Broeckmann

Das Spiel

Ziel ist es, eine sehr konzentrierte Form eines Informationsflusses zu erzeugen, in dem Daten selbst nicht vorrangig sind oder zumindest ihre vormalige Bedeutung verlieren und zu Infotainment werden.

Die Web-Site *Das Net.spiel* besteht aus bereits im Netz existierenden Daten – Klängen, Texten, Bildern –, mit denen die Benutzer eigene *Info-Stories* erzeugen können. Der Informationsfluß kommt ohne bestimmten Standort aus, da die Daten selbst an unterschiedlichen Stellen anzutreffen sind. Zugleich wird für jede lokale Gruppe ersichtlich, woher diese oder andere Daten kommen.

AIZEJ TUR NEZIN KUR, ATNES TO NEZIN KO [saying of Latvian folk tale] Go anywhere, bring anything
First level
Next level
Next level
Next level
Next level
Next level
...

Rasa Smite & Raitis Smits

Form Art Competition

This is an international competition of *Form Art*, which is a new form of art, based on the Internet technology. This form of art was first proposed and developed by Alexei Shulgin [http://www.c3/hyper3/form].

This new art form implies a use of executable form elements such as buttons, checkboxes, text fields, text areas and select/option form elements primarily for the creation of graphics and artistic interactive interfaces. The advantage of this language is that Form Art files are text files and are very small in size and therefore can be downloaded very fast. Also they are platform-independent.

The domain name [www.form.org or www.form.ru] will be set up.

The competition for Form Art works will be widely announced.

The winner will get a cash prize.

The competition will end up with an online competition of submitted Form Art works.

Alexei Shulgin

The Enjoyable Internet Digester

Entering the site, to the spectator is offered a blend futuristic web TV console and modern web search engine. It is the Interface of *The Enjoyable Internet Digester* – which allows the user to experience the range between the efficiency of up-to-date Information simplification [due to the acute Information overload] and entertainment. The user can choose from a wide range of approaches to *surfing* – from an entirely self-running kaleidoscopic *multi-media* show to entirely controlled, personalized preference hierarchy visualization. By entering any URL or just writing in any search

AIZEJ TUR NEZIN KUR, ATNES TO NEZIN KO [Spruch aus einem lettischen Volksmärchen] Geh' wohin du willst, bring' was du willst
Erste Ebene
Nächste Ebene
Nächste Ebene
Nächste Ebene
Nächste Ebene
Nächste Ebene
...

Rasa Smite & Raitis Smits

Form Art Competition

Es handelt sich hier um einen internationalen Wettbewerb für *Form Art*, eine neue Kunstform auf der Basis der Internet-Technologie. Diese Kunstform wurde erstmals von Alexei Shulgin [http://www.c3/ hyper3/ form] propagiert und entwickelt.

Sie basiert auf der Verwendung ausführbarer Dialogelemente wie Schaltflächen, Markierungsfelder, Textfelder, Textbereiche und Optionsschaltflächen, wie sie primär zur Erstellung von Graphiken und interaktiven künstlerischen Schnittstellen verwendet werden. Der Vorteil dieser Sprache ist, daß Form-Art-Dateien relativ kleine Textdateien sind, die sehr schnell heruntergeladen werden können. Außerdem sind sie plattformunabhängig.

Die Bezeichnung der Domain [www.form.org oder www.form.ru] wird eingerichtet.

Es erfolgt eine umfassende Ankündigung des Wettbewerbs für Form-Art-Werke.

Der Gewinner bekommt einen Geldpreis.

Am Ende des Wettbewerbs nehmen die eingereichten Form-Art-Werke an einem Online-Wettbewerb teil.

Alexei Shulgin

The Enjoyable Internet Digester

Beim Einstieg auf die WWW-Site bietet sich dem Betrachter eine futuristische Kombination aus einer WWW-TV-Konsole und einer modernen WWW-Suchmaschine. Es handelt sich um die Schnittstelle für *The Enjoyable Internet Digester*, mit der der Benutzer das weite Spektrum zwischen der Effizienz moderner Informations-Simplifizierung [aufgrund aku-

word or phrase the user will launch an agent-software that will try to present the most desirable result. If the result is still not satisfactory the interface would offer either options to specify the target or make it possible to take shortcuts to alternative, associative actions. The performance of the device would be tuneable depending on the bandwidth availability or the user, too, would be able playfully to adjust the reduction of text information, for instance, to image patterns or spatial sound landscapes.

Jaanis Garancs

<NO SUBJECT> MU

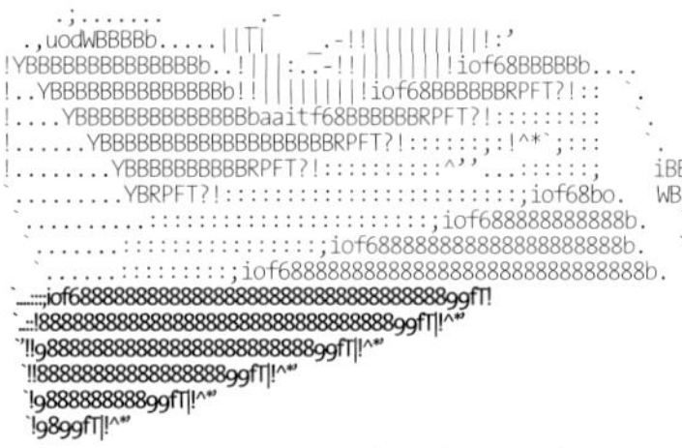

Joan Heemskerk/Dirk Paesmans
http://www.jodi.org/mu

The Great Gatsby

The *Great Gatsby* is not a net version of the famous American novel, but a net interpretation of the Great American Dream, an attempt to identify the Great Net Dream and its main heroes. At the same time *The Great Gatsby* is a story exploring the possibilities of narrative web structures. The work consists of original graphics, pages, scripts and *found page* materials as well.

Olia Lialina

Access Denied Don't Enter Go Away

Access Denied Don't Enter Go Away is a node in the Internet that tries to protect the personal data it contains from unauthorized access. The protection installed is not perfectly safe or reliable and as such provides the owner and the audience with a platform for exploring the mechanisms of secrets, cracking, data leaks and social engineering for computer networks.

Luka Frelih

ter Informations-Überladung] und Unterhaltung erkunden kann. Man wählt aus einem weiten Bereich möglicher *Surf*-Ansätze – von der vollautomatisch ablaufenden, kaleidoskopischen Multi-Media-Show zur steuerbaren, personalisierten Visualisierung von Präferenzhierarchien. Durch Eingabe einer beliebigen URL oder eines beliebigen Suchbegriffes aktiviert der Benutzer einen Agenten, der ein möglichst entsprechendes Ergebnis präsentieren wird. Ist das Resultat unzufriedenstellend, wird die Schnittstelle entweder Optionen für eine genauere Zielvorgabe anbieten oder es ermöglichen, Abkürzungen zu alternativen, assoziativen Handlungen zu wählen. Die Geräteleistung wäre je nach verfügbarer Bandbreite abstimmbar, bzw. der Benutzer könnte die Text-Information spielerisch reduzieren, um z. B. Muster oder räumliche Klanglandschaften darzustellen.

Jaanis Garancs

The Great Gatsby

The Great Gatsby ist nicht die Netz-Version des bekannten amerikanischen Romans, sondern eine Interpretation des Großen Amerikanischen Traums im Netz, ein Versuch, den Großen Netz-Traum und seine wichtigsten Helden zu identifizieren. Zugleich ist *The Great Gatsby* eine Geschichte, die die Möglichkeiten narrativer WWW-Strukturen erkundet. Die Arbeit besteht aus Originalgraphiken, WWW-Seiten, Skripts und *found page*-Material.

Olia Lialina

<NO SUBJECT> MU

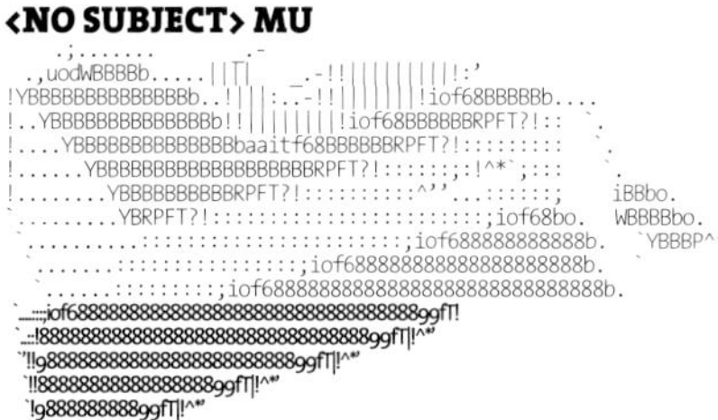

Joan Heemskerk/Dirk Paesmans
http://www.jodi.org/mu

Remote-cdrom
description:
an instant offline mirror server of some of the data of the *Remote C* project
media:
mini cdrom 3.5 inch
content:
linux operating system, reduced set of commands, webserver, webbrowser, webprojects submitted by the *Remote C* participants in their own directories
concept:
in their own backup directory each of the participants can upload any content they want
context:
the speed of change of Internet technology and the question of inscription, conservation and distribution and selection of digital art on the net.
participants:
participants of *Remote C*
print run: 1000

Pit Schultz

openX

Access Denied Don't Enter Go Away

Access denied don't enter go away ist ein Knoten im Internet, der dazu dient, im Netz enthaltene persönliche Daten vor unerlaubtem Zugriff zu schützen. Der installierte Schutz ist nicht hundertprozentig sicher bzw. zuverlässig und bietet so Dateneigentümern und Publikum eine Plattform zur Erforschung von Verschlüsselungsmechanismen, Knacktechniken, Datenlecks und sozialer Technologie für Computernetzwerke.

Luka Frelih

Remote-cdrom
Offline Mirror-Server ausgewählter Daten des *Remote C*-Projekts
Medien:
Mini CD-ROM, 3,5 Zoll
Inhalt:
Linux-Betriebssystem, reduzierter Befehlssatz, Web-Server, Web-Browser, von den Teilnehmern an *Remote C* in ihre Verzeichnisse eingebrachte Web-Projekte
Konzept:
Jeder Teilnehmer kann gewünschte Inhalte in die Sicherungskopie seines eigenen Verzeichnisses laden
Kontext:
Die Geschwindigkeit, mit der sich Internet-Technologien ändern, und die Frage der Einbringung, Konservierung, Distribution und Selektion digitaler Kunst im Netz
Teilnehmer:
Remote C-Teilnehmer
Auflage: 1000

Pit Schultz

Clone the Party!

An e-mail exchange between
Beusch/Cassani and
Heimo Ranzenbacher
on the subject of the TNC Network

HR: Our perception of western culture is increasingly characterized by the terms intangible, processual, systemic and unconfined to a specific locality; art which strives in its conceptualization to be culturally relevant is subject to this perception. New Art has become, to a certain extent, a form of organization on the basis of this cultural perception and whose central concepts it radicalizes. How do you describe your attitude as artists faced with this new set of cultural conditions?

B/C: Our answer to the current cultural environment has been to set up and expand the TNC Network. The booming cyberradio Radio TNC has emerged out of the media-fiction *Great Web Crash* which we launched online almost two years ago. In the meantime, this, in turn, has generated largely autonomous spin-offs such as the *CyberMemorial* or the *Headcheese Affair*. Right now, the TNC Connection is active as initiator of Web Shows and global network events [*Crash Party, Clone Party*]. At the same time, we have taken advantage of opportunities to function as consultants – for example, setting up a cyberchannel in a Paris suburb's cable network – and we have also carried out

Clone the Party!

Ein E-mail-Wechsel zwischen
Beusch/Cassani und
Heimo Ranzenbacher
über das TNC-Network

What the people of Linz still refer to as the heavens is what we in TNC circles call the Skypage.

Was die Linzer noch Himmel nennen, nennen wir in TNC-Kreisen die Sky-Page.

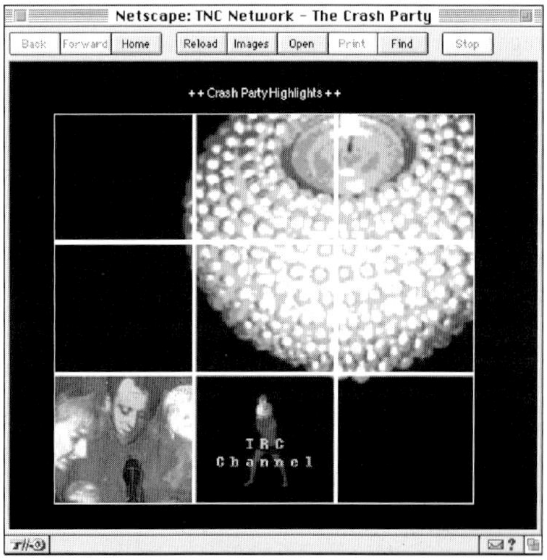

production assignments in Europe and the US.

HR: Could this field of activity with which you as artists are involved perhaps be described as *configuration art* – by which I mean to distinguish it from *communication art* which, roughly speaking, addresses the telematic environment in order to treat it as its subject, positioning itself outside of this environment – namely, in the traditional field of art identified by art projects and works of art? Your work, on the other hand, seems rather to be based upon the fundamental process of its implementation into the telematic environment – with, necessarily, systemic mutual interaction – and ultimately results in the configuration of additional, new possibilities which have been opened up in this way. Art itself seems to be the project; and, derived from this *project: Art,* art projects emerge in a new environment, the formation of which they have helped to bring about.

B/C: We much prefer the term *networking,* understood in its most comprehensive sense as a configuring activity in the telematic environment. A highly dynamic network like the TNC Connection does not come about on its own. Once cultural phenomena have condensed into a setting charged with tension [the *Web Crash*], what subsequently occurs is a link-up of the know-how and infrastructure made available by a wide array of individuals and sub-networks – from the internationally recruited guest crew; to the French news channel France Info, the trend-conscious Berlin station Radio Fritz, the Ars Electronica Center, and the Paris

Clone Party [September 11, 1997]

*To celebrate the upcoming cloning of a human being, partygoers from throughout the world are squeezing into their blue-genes and linking up in a global network to dance the Body Sampling Step. At the same time, the network/radio event *between the laughter and the tears* initiated by Beusch/Cassani is becoming a high-profile presence at numerous network-linked public and private online and real-world venues. Hybridized digital doubles of the party crew [TNC guest hosts, guest DJs, etc.] are actively involved as party agents throughout the network, scanning the various party floors, engaging the circulating data streams and mixing the TNC party channel out of what they encounter. Together with live reports and party news flashes, this is fed on into the flow of the worldwide party loop via Internet, satellite and radio.*

http://radiotnc.aec.at/cloneparty/

openX

HR: Das Verständnis unserer westlichen Kultur wird zunehmend geprägt durch die Begriffe immateriell, prozeßhaft, systemisch und ortlos: Kunst, will sie kulturell relevant sein, unterliegt in ihrer Begrifflichkeit diesem Verständnis. Die Neue Kunst ist gewissermaßen zu einer Organisationsform auf der Basis des kulturellen Verständnisses geworden, die dessen zentrale Begriffe radikalisiert. Wie stellt sich Eure Haltung als Künstler gegenüber diesem neuen kulturellen Bedingungsfeld dar?

B/C: Unsere Antwort auf das aktuelle kulturelle Bedingungsfeld ist der Auf- und Ausbau des TNC-Networks. Aus der vor bald zwei Jahren im Netz lancierten Media-Fiction vom *Great Web Crash* entstand das boomende Cyberradio Radio TNC. Dieses generierte seinerseits mittlerweile weitgehend autonomisierte Side-Projects wie das *CyberMemorial* oder die *Headcheese-Affäre*. Heute agiert die TNC-Connection als Initiatorin von Web-Shows und globalen Netzwerk-Events [*Crash Party, Clone Party*]. Gleichzeitig werden Consulting-Funktionen wahrgenommen, beispielsweise für den Aufbau eines Cyberchannels im Kabelnetz eines Pariser Vororts, und Produktionsaufträge in Europa und den USA ausgeführt.

HR: Wäre dieses Leistungsfeld, mit dem ihr als Künstler befaßt seid, eventuell mit *Konfigurationskunst* zu beschreiben – erläutert am Unterschied zur Kommunikationskunst, die sich grob gesagt dadurch, daß sie das telematische Environment beansprucht, um es zu thematisieren, außerhalb dieses – nämlich im herkömmlichen, durch Kunstprojekte

Clone Party [11. September 1997]

*Zur Feier des bevorstehenden Menschen-Clonings zwängen sich Partygoer aus aller Welt in ihre Blue-Genes und tanzen global vernetzt den Body-Sampling-Step. Das von Beusch/Cassani initiierte Netzwerk/Radio-Event *between the laugther and the tears* steigt simultan an zahlreichen miteinander vernetzten öffentlichen und privaten Online- und Real-World-Venues. Hybridisierte digitale Doubles der Party-Crew [TNC-Guest-Animatoren, Guest-DJ's etc.] agieren im vernetzten Raum als Party-Agents, scannen die verschiedenen Partyfloors ab, klinken sich ein in die zirkulierenden Datastreams und mischen daraus den TNC-Party-Channel. Dieser wird zusammen mit Live-Reports und Party-News-Flashes via Internet, über Satellit und Radio wieder in die weltweite Party-Schlaufe eingeschleust.*

http://radiotnc.aec.at/cloneparty/

Technology Museum, to name just a few; all the way to HotWired. Depending upon the nature of each TNC event, sectors of this core-network are activated and new elements are added. For example, the link-up of the various user sub-networks is what provided the decisive kick for the *Crash Party* and enabled it to go beyond the level of hip online spectacle to become a culturally relevant event. Now, we are fulfilling our responsibility within the TNC production and communications network by making sure that the process which has been unleashed develops further as quickly as the Headcheese Sample gets moldy. ... We continue to coordinate most of these activities: functioning as catalysts and hosts providing stimulus for events like the *Clone Party*, and, outfitted with a data-snorkel, still taking the plunge into the whirlpool of intangible production – the Shift-key fully depressed. Multitasking is a matter of course in a network-linked production process.

HR: Does your understanding of your role correspond at all with the generally held image of the artistic profession?

B/C: **Vous n'êtes pas des organisateurs, vous êtes des artistes, merde alors!** [*You're not organizers, damn it, you're artists.*] This was one curator's commentary in 1992 on our activities, which thus did not conform at all to the usual preconceptions. It is clear that the projects and events which we have initiated and which are based upon the radical new structures of power and responsibility inherent in network-linked systems can no longer be subsumed by traditional conceptions of a work of art and its author. This is just as discernible in our goal [the set-up and expansion of the TNC Connection] as it is in the various functions that we are carrying out thereby. In place of the authority of an author over a work, there emerges what we often describe with the term *shared process and data management.*

HR: You can be counted among the handful of individuals who are employing radio as a prestructured – and, as a consequence, structuring – network. What does radio mean for you in general and in connection with strategies specific to TNC.

B/C: In the last 10 years, during which we have produced channels disseminating music, culture and information, radio, like all conventional media, has been subjected to a gigantic pro-

und -werke identifizierbaren Bereich der Kunst – positioniert? Eure Arbeit hingegen gründet eher auf dem basalen Prozeß ihrer Implementierung in das telematische Environment – mit notwendigerweise systemischen Wechselwirkungen – und mündet in die Konfiguration so auch neu eröffneter Möglichkeiten. Die Kunst selbst erscheint als Projekt; und aus diesem Projekt Kunst leiten sich Kunstprojekte in einem durch es mitgestalteten neuen Umfeld ab.

B/C: Der Begriff *Networking*, als eine im umfassendsten Sinn konfigurierende Aktivität im telematischen Environment, gefällt uns besser. Ein solch dynamisches Netzwerk wie die TNC-Connection entsteht nicht von alleine. Auf die Verdichtung kultureller Phänomene zu einem spannungsgeladenen Setting [der Web-Crash] folgte die Verlinkung des Know-how bzw. der Infrastruktur verschiedenster Einzelpersonen und Sub-Netze, von der international rekrutierten Guest-Crew über u. a. den französischen News-Channel France Info, den Berliner Trendsender Radio Fritz, das Ars Electronica Center, das Pariser Technologiemuseum bis hin zu HotWired. Je nach TNC-Event werden Teile dieses Basis-Networks aktiviert, neue kommen hinzu. Die Verkoppelung der verschiedenen User-Subnetze hat beispielsweise der *Crash Party* den entscheidenden Kick gegeben und dafür gesorgt, daß sie weit über das hippe Online-Spektakel zum kulturell relevanten Event wurde. Heute nehmen wir unsere Verantwortung im TNC-Produktions- und Kommunikationsnetz wahr, indem wir dafür sorgen, daß der eingeleitete Prozeß sich so beschleunigt weiterentwickelt, wie das Headcheese-Sample vor sich hinfault ... Wir koordinieren weiterhin einen großen Teil der Aktivitäten, wirken als Katalysatoren und Animatoren für Events wie die *Clone Party* und tauchen wei-

Headcheese-Affäre: *Im TNC-Online-Studio der Ars Electronica '96 brachte ein italienischer Besucher ein Stück formaggio di porco [Headcheese] in Umlauf. Das beschleunigt vor sich hinfaulende Fleischkäse-Sample hat seither eine Odyssee angetreten, tiefsinnige Debatten über digitalen Kannibalismus und Cyber-Reinkarnation ausgelöst und während einer TNC/HotWired-Liveshow die Net-Comunity in der ersten globalen *ecstatic headcheese eating union* versammelt ...*

http://radiotnc.aec.at/headcheese/
http://www.hotwired.-com/talk/poptalk/96/49/index4b.html

cess of change. While we were completing the first fully digital production for Radio France in 1989, one of the technicians showed up with an impressive set of sunglasses, which he proceeded to successively don in an effort to protect his eyes from the pernicious effects of the flickering video monitor. During the coffee breaks, we discussed the subject of his red, watery eyes at epic length, and hardly said a word about the newly-acquired state-of-the-art hard-disk recording system. Although the video screen quality was really rather primitive, this theatrical performance with sunglasses sent a signal which said, above all: *What can I possibly do to avoid seeing things change?* At this time, we were playing the uncomfortable role of the iconoclasts, attacking the status quo and confronting radio – that is to say, our production partner – with the pattern of change going on before its very eyes. And we took advantage of this situation to propagate forms of work which were appropriate to changed conditions of production, meaning that we did away with the rigid partitions separating technician, author, director and producer which had been based upon top-down media-thinking. Nor were we faced by no resistance when we first went on the air in the Austrian Broadcasting Corporation channel with our Macintosh that we brought from Paris, or integrated public broadcasting stations into network events and introduced them to the concepts of network-linked production processes. The fact that this was first time that their programs were being presented live on the Internet – through the cyberradio channels of Radio TNC – most pointedly brought these new realities into confrontation with their conception of themselves which was a relic left over from another age. Of course, for a long time, Radio

The Headcheese Affair

*In the TNC online studio at Ars Electronica 96, an Italian visitor began passing around a piece of formaggio di porco [headcheese]. The rapidly rotting headcheese sample then set out on a round-the-world odyssey, triggering profound debates on digital cannibalism and cyberreincarnation and, during a TNC/HotWired live show, gathering the net community together into the first global *ecstatic headcheese eating union*...*

http://radiotnc.aec.at/headcheese/
http://www.hotwired.com/talk/poptalk/96/49/index4b.html

openX

terhin mit einem Data-Schnorchel ausgerüstet – die Shift-Taste gedrückt – in den Whirl-Pool der immateriellen Produktion ein. In einem vernetzten Produktionsprozeß ist Multi-Tasking selbstverständlich.

HR: Entspricht Euer Selbstverständnis überhaupt noch dem üblichen Bild von der Profession des Künstlers?

B/C: *Vous n'êtes pas des organisateurs, vous êtes des artistes, merde alors!* – *Ihr habt nicht Organisatoren zu sein, sondern Künstler, verdammt nochmal!* Mit diesen Worten kommentierte 1992 ein Kurator unsere Tätigkeit, die so überhaupt nicht den gängigen Vorstellungen entsprach. Es ist klar, daß die von uns initiierten Projekte und Events, denen die radikal neuen Macht- und Verantwortungsstrukturen vernetzter Systeme zugrunde liegen, nicht mehr mit dem herkömmlichen Werk/Autor-Begriff erfaßt werden können. Im Ziel [Auf- und Ausbau der TNC-Connection] klingt das genauso an wie in den verschiedenen Funktionen, die wir dabei erfüllen. An die Stelle der Autorität des Autors über ein Werk tritt das, was wir oft mit dem Begriff *gemeinsames Prozeß- und Data-Management* umschreiben.

HR. Ihr gehört zu den ganz wenigen, die Radio als vorstrukturiertes und in der Folge strukturierendes Netz verwenden. Was bedeutet Radio für Euch allgemein und im Zusammenhang mit den TNC-spezifischen Strategien?

B/C: In den vergangenen zehn Jahren, in denen wir mit Music-, Kultur- und Infochannels produziert haben, war das Radio – wie alle herkömmlichen Medien – einem gigantischen Wandel ausgesetzt. Als wir bei Radio France 1989 die erste volldigitale Produktion realisiert haben, erschien einer der Techniker mit einem beeindruckenden Set von Sonnenbrillen, die er sich eine nach der anderen aufsetzte, um seine Augen vor dem verderblichen Bildschirmflimmern zu schützen. In den Kaffeepausen haben wir uns denn auch episch lang über seine brennenden Augen unterhalten, kaum je aber über das neu angeschaffte State-of-the-Art Harddisk-Recordingsystem. Selbst wenn die Bildschirmqualität wirklich etwas rudimentär war, signalisierte die Sonnenbrillen-Performance vor allem dies: *Was-könnte-ich-tun-damit-ich-gar-nicht-sehe-was-sich-verändert?* Wir haben in dieser Zeit die unbequeme Rolle der Ikonoklasten gespielt, den Status quo

TNC was one of the very few platforms on which radio – with its techno-aesthetic possibilities, its historically relative nature, its material constraints and limitations – was linked up to the Internet in a consistent fashion and in all conceivable combinations. The experience we gained during this process has been made available to others in a study commissioned by the French Ministry of Communications which we completed in late 1996.

HR: Your strategies have the effect of opening up or dissolving the unidirectional relationship between the transmitter and the receiver, in favor of a dynamic process which basically does away with controlling intervention. Is radio becoming archaic as an information-generating medium as a result of this linkage to technologies which permit it to process information?

B/C: *How come my Fiat doesn't have an Internet link-up!?* was what one desperate listener quite properly asked during the *Crash Party*. Luckily, the radio was there to make up for Fiat's regrettable technological deficiency. The TNC Party Channel, which will once again perform an important function in the *Clone Party*, was broadcast during the *Crash Party* via Internet and satellite as well as standard radio wave transmission [on the frequencies of Radio Fritz]. The link-up of this existing, *pre-structured* sub-network to the TNC network – for example, at the *Crash Party* – had the quite tangible effect of keeping the Fiat driver posted during his trip about the latest developments on the various online party floors and providing him with a feed via cellular phone into the global party loop. In other words, the link-up of radio and Internet in an appropriately configured setting offers a high innovation potential in the sphere of interplay known as a Fiat – push and pull.

HR: The latest project to come out of TNC networking is the *Clone Party*, which you have announced as a refinement of and an expansion upon the production pattern developed in the *Crash Party*. Why *clone*? After all, doesn't cloning refer to the production of an heir, in the vocabulary of information, a next-generation spin-off. *Crash Party* was based upon a fiction, both in the sense of a story as well as of an assumption, of a cognitive model which, during the course of its design for the purpose of exploration of possibilities, simultaneously

angegriffen und das Radio, d. h. unsere Produktionspartner, mit den Pattern des vor sich gehenden Wandels konfrontiert. Und wir haben die Situation genutzt, um Arbeitsformen zu propagieren, die den veränderten Produktionsbedingungen gerecht wurden, d. h. die starre, im top-down Media-Denken verankerte Trennung zwischen Techniker, Autor, Realisator, Producer etc. auflösten. Genausowenig ging es ohne Widerstand, als wir im ORF erstmals ab unserem aus Paris angeschleppten Mac Live-Sendungen fuhren oder öffentlich-rechtliche Anstalten in Netz-Events eingebunden und mit den Konzepten von vernetzten Produktionsprozessen vertraut gemacht haben. Die Tatsache, daß ihre Programme dabei erstmals live auf Internet gesendet wurden, und zwar auf den Kanälen des CyberRadios Radio TNC, hat das aus einer anderen Zeit herübergerettete Selbstverständnis in wirksamster Weise mit den neuen Realitäten konfrontiert. Radio TNC war denn auch lange eine der ganz wenigen Plattformen, auf welchen Radio mit seinen techno-ästhetischen Möglichkeiten, historischen Bedingtheiten, seinen Sachzwängen und Begrenzungen konsequent und in allen erdenklichen Kombinationen mit dem Internet gekoppelt wurde. Die dabei gesammelten Erfahrungen haben wir Ende 1996 in einer vom französischen Kommunikationsministerium in Auftrag gegebenen Studie weitergegeben.

HR: Eure Strategien bewirken die Öffnung/Auflösung des unidirektionalen Verhältnisses zwischen Sender und Empfänger zugunsten einer Dynamik, die sich im Grunde des lenkenden Zugriffs entzieht. Wird Radio als informationsgenerierendes Medium durch die Anbindung an Technologien, die es erlauben, Informationen zu prozessieren, hinfällig?

B/C: *Warum hat mein Fiat keinen Internetanschluss!?* fragte ein verzweifelter Hörer während der *Crash Party* völlig zu recht. Zum Glück war das Radio da, um das bedauernswerte Fiat-Tech-Defizit aufzufangen. Der TNC-Party-Channel, der auch in der *Clone Party* wieder eine wichtige Funktion spielen wird, wurde während der *Crash Party* über Internet, über Satellit und via Äther [auf den Frequenzen von Radio Fritz] verbreitet. Die Anbindung dieses bestehenden, *vorstrukturierten*Sub-Netzes

generated its own form of practice. The crash of a web site with direct consequences for its users [by means of the dissolution of the borders between man and machine] and a rescue effort assuming multimedia proportions with derivative effects in *real life* ... You have, as it were, given practical application to the principle upon which Umberto Eco's novel *Foucault's Pendulum* was based: the successive implementation of the real by the fictive. The Clone Party, on the other hand, seems to manage without fiction.

B/C: The setting for the *Crash Party* was a mix of carefully measured dosages of cyberclichés, techno-catastrophism and TNC goodies. The storyline of the Great Web Crash and its victims disappearing into virtual oblivion had tremendous appeal both to an 11-year-old nerd as well as to a media activist of a more mature age, triggered inputs and turned the *Crash Party* into an immersive-participatory network event. The setting of the *Clone Party*, on the other hand, proceeds from a *cognitive model which, during the course of its design for the purpose of exploration of [genetic engineering] possibilities, generates its own form of practice*: Ian Wilmuts epochmaking success with Dolly ... On September 11, 1997, when we will squeeze into our blue-genes and link up in a global network to dance the Body Sampling Step in celebration of the upcoming cloning of a human being, the interpenetration of fiction and reality will have already brewed up such a high-proof cocktail that we random-generated beings will have our heads spinning long before the hangover sets in ...

The Great Web Crash

On February 4, 1996, the first Web Crash plunged the Internet community into a state of panic. The Internet stayed down for hours; throughout the world, data was being lost by the gigabyte; a flesh-and-blood cyberhost vanished without a trace in the virtual great beyond. Crashologists from around the world have advanced the most audacious theories, but the riddle of this newfangled technological catastrophe remains unsolved...The Great Web Crash, an interactive media fiction launched in the Internet by Beusch/Cassani in 1995, is the initial setting on which the TNC Connection is based [see the Ars Electronica Festival 96 catalog, pp. 366-375].

http://radiotnc.aec.at/webcrash/

openX

an das TNC-Netz hatte in der *Crash Party* zum Beispiel den ganz konkreten Effekt, den Fiat-Fahrer während seiner Fahrt über die Entwicklung auf den verschiedenen Online-Party-Floors auf dem laufenden zu halten und ihn via Funktelefon in die globale Party-Schlaufe einzuschleusen. Mit anderen Worten: Die Verbindung von Radio und Internet bietet in einem entsprechend konfigurierten Setting ein hohes Innovationspotential im Spannungsfeld von ... Fiat, Push und Pull.

HR: Das aktuelle, dem TNC-Networking entstammende Projekt ist die *Clone Party*, von Euch als Verfeinerung und Ausbau der in der *Crash Party* entwickelten Produktionsmuster angekündigt. Warum *Clone*? Bezeichnet doch Cloning das Erzeugen einer erb-, sprich an Information gleichen Nachkommenschaft. *Crash Party* beruhte auf einer Fiktion, sowohl im Sinne einer Geschichte als auch einer Annahme, eines Denkmodells, das im Zuge seines Entwurfs zur Erforschung von Möglichkeiten zugleich seine eigene Praxis generierte. Der Crash einer Web-Site mit unmittelbaren Konsequenzen für ihre Betreiber [durch die Auflösung der Grenzen zwischen Mensch und Maschine] und eine Rettungsaktion von multimedialen Ausmaßen mit Ausformungen im *wirklichen Leben*... Ihr habt gleichsam in die Praxis überführt, was Umberto Ecos Roman *Das Foucault'sche Pendel* zugrunde liegt: die sukzessive Durchsetzung des Realen vom Fiktiven. Die *Clone Party* hingegen scheint ohne Fiktion auszukommen.

B/C: Das Setting für die *Crash Party* war ein sorgfältig dosierter Mix aus Cyber-Klischees, Techno-Katastrophismus und TNC-Goodies. Das Storyboard vom *Great Web Crash* und seinen im virtuellen Nichts verschollenen Opfern hat den elfjährigen Nerdster ebenso wie den Media-

Great Web Crash

Am 4. Februar 1996 versetzte der erste Web Crash die Internet-Community in Panik. Das Netz brach für Stunden zusammen, rund um die Welt gingen gigabyteweise Daten verloren, ein Cyber-Animator aus Fleisch und Blut verschwand spurlos im virtuellen Nichts. Crashologen aus aller Welt haben die kühnsten Theorien geoutet, aber das Rätsel der neuartigen Technologiekatastrophe bleibt weiterhin ungelöst ... Die 1995 von Beusch/Cassani im Netz lancierte interaktive Media-Fiction vom Great Web Crash liegt der TNC-Connection als Initial-Setting zugrunde. [vgl. Katalog Ars Electronica Festival 96, S. 366 – 375].

http://radiotnc.aec.at/webcrash/

HR: The buzz as indication of cybergenesis kicking in among the sons of man ...

B/C: It must have been precisely this feeling of giddiness that overcame Gerfried Stocker as he opened the first CyberMemorial at the Ars Electronica Festival 96. In a solemn ceremony in the Radio TNC online studio, he was to have cut the virtual ribbon with a crisp click of the mouse while pronouncing those words which have long since become legendary: *Love, Peace and Radio TNC – Cyberimmortality for Everybody!* Indeed, in the face of this uplifting perspective which has proved so intoxicating for us sons of man, Gerfried Stocker inadvertently sliced through the ceremonial ribbon during the trial run ...

CyberMemorial

*For over a year, users have been chiseling their inscriptions into the silicon of the virtual monument commemorating the victims of the Great Web Crash and spreading their message of good news throughout the Internet: *Cyberimmortality for everybody!**

http://radiotnc.aec.at /cybermemorial/

HR: The Clone Party is being announced by online flyer; it will feature live videos and tele-DJs; the TNC Wavemaster will provide for plenty of offbeat cybertainment, etc. What significance does dealing with elements of popular culture have for you?

B/C: In the Internet, with its pronounced hyper-transcultural nature, it is senseless to purvey highly concentrated images of identity evoking strictly demarcated cultural sectors. For us, the prime consideration as far as this is concerned is not dealing with elements, but rather the issue of presence in culturally relevant spaces, in which eclectic, complex code-ensembles design their identities themselves and are undergoing permanent change.

HR: In what way do you see an analogy between Dolly, the product of the genetic engineer's art, the projected successful cloning of a human being, and network-linked existences? In the cyborg? I'm not referring here to the fictional being; but rather to one that is closer to our reality – that is a hybrid of human being and machine, but only insofar as it is represented by the increasing obsolescence of certain dichotomies such as man/woman, nature/culture owing to its special technological nature. A phenomenological being.

B/C: *What the people of Linz still refer to as the heavens is what we in TNC circles call the Skypage. And the Linz Skypage is blue again

Activist reiferen Alters animiert, Inputs getriggert und die *Crash Party* zum immersiv-partizipativen Netzevent gemacht. Das Setting der *Clone Party* geht seinerseits aus von einem *Denkmodell, das im Zuge seines Entwurfs zur Erforschung von [gentechnologischen] Möglichkeiten seine eigene Praxis generiert*: Ian Wilmuts epochale Reussite mit Dolly ... Wenn wir uns am 11. September 1997 zur Feier des bevorstehenden Menschen-Clonings in unsere Blue-Genes zwängen und global vernetzt den Body-Sampling-Step tanzen, ist die Interpenetration von Fiktion und Realität schon derart hochprozentig, daß sich uns random-generierten Wesen lange vor dem Hangover der Kopf dreht ...

HR: Das Schwindelgefühl als Indiz für die Erfaßtheit der Menschenkinder von der Cyber-Genese ...

B/C: Es muß genau dieses Schwindelgefühl gewesen sein, das Gerfried Stocker erfaßte, als er am Ars Electronica Festival 96 das erste *CyberMemorial* eröffnete. Im Online-Studio von Radio TNC sollte er mit einem scharfen Mausklick in einem feierlichen Akt die virtuelle Samtschleife durchschneiden und die mittlerweile längst legendären Worte aussprechen: *Love, peace & Radio TNC – Cyberimmortality for everybody!* Angesichts der für uns Menschenkinder schwindelerregend erhebenden Perspektive hat Gerfried Stocker die Samtschleife allerdings versehentlich schon beim Probelauf hochgefahren ...

HR: Die *Clone Party* wird per Online-Flyer angesagt, es gibt Live-Videos, Tele-DJing, TNC-Wavemaster sorgen für Offbeat-Cybertainment etc. Welche Bedeutung hat für Euch der Umgang mit Elementen der Popularkultur?

B/C: Im Netz mit seiner hyper-transkulturellen Ausprägung sind kompakte Identitätsangebote scharf abgegrenzter Kultursektoren sinnlos. Für uns stellt sich insofern nicht in erster Linie die Frage nach dem Umgang mit Elementen, sondern jene der Präsenz in kulturell relevanten Räumen, in denen eklektizistische, komplexe Code-Ensembles ihre Identitäten selbst entwerfen und permanent verändern.

CyberMemorial

*Seit über einem Jahr meißeln UserInnen ihre Inschriften ins Silizium des virtuellen Monuments zum Gedenken an die Opfer des Great Web Crash und verbreiten im Netz die frohe Botschaft: *Cyberimmortality for everybody!**

http://radiotnc.aec.at/ cybermemorial/

today for the first time in ages; and the sun that is projected upon it is shining again ...* The lines of tension which we are building into the *Clone Party* setting [also] converge in the cyborg. A conceptual pairing of burning interest to us in this regard is jest/seriousness. This is suitable, for instance, in order to determine the human portion of the hybrid we've just referred to. Illustrated in the exclusive TNC Cyborg Test: If the above statement can still make you laugh, you're not a cyborg yet ...

HR: The sensation surrounding Dolly is not only a scientifically but also a culturally determined one. In Japan, for example, experimentation with genetic engineering has far fewer ethical implications than, say, a heart transplant. What is your position on the issue of genetic engineering and the culture-specific views expressed pro and con, or of ambivalent attitudes in such questions, in light of all globalizing trends? Have your views been taken into account in the *Clone Party*?

B/C: The *Clone Party* is a distributed, global event. Each participant represents his or her own culture-specific point of view – there will be ample access possibilities and channels of communication [the TNC party studio at the Ars Electronica Festival, the long online lead-in, the *private* party floors, etc.]. At the *Crash Party* in London, the anniversary of the *Great Web Crash* was celebrated, as expected, by imbibing liquid refreshment in pubs, whereas the partygoers in Osaka – as is apparently customary at Japanese birthday parties – served up red-colored Sekihan rice which they sent out to the party community in the form of steaming GIFs ...

HR: You have announced in the Internet that *Interface* will be the *Clone Party's* theme. Interface is being addressed as a possibility/form of organization of the sensory perception of a process which has been initiated and takes place unconfined to a specific locality, and reaches its culmination on the spot. Could this be a way of describing the *FleshFactor*

Radio TNC

Radio TNC evolved out of the media fiction of the Great Web Crash. Since February 1996, an international guest crew has taken turns hosting the legendary online microphone of the booming cyberradio. The program has included live DJ mixes, talk shows, straight news flashes, cyberserials and TNC specials [live online and on-the-air at, among other locations, the Ars Electronica Festival 96 and 97 as well as Isea '97 in Chicago].

http://radiotnc.aec.at

openX

HR: Worin besteht für Euch die Analogie zwischen dem Produkt der Gen-Ingenieurskunst, Dolly, projektiertem Menschen-Cloning und den vernetzten Existenzen? Im Cyborg? Ich meine damit nicht das fiktionale Wesen, sondern das unserer Realität nähere, das ein Hybrid aus Mensch und Maschine nur insofern ist, als es die zunehmende Obsoleszenz bestimmter Dichotomien – Mann/Frau, Natur/Kultur etc. – aufgrund apparativer Seinsweisen repräsentiert. Ein phänomenologisches Wesen.

B/C: *Was die Linzer noch Himmel nennen, nennen wir in TNC-Kreisen die Skypage. Und die Linzer Skypage ist heute erstmals seit langem wieder blau, und auch die Sonne, die darauf projiziert wird, scheint wieder ...* Die Spannungslinien, die wir im Clone Party-Setting anlegen, schneiden sich natürlich [auch] im Cyborg. Ein Begriffspaar, das uns dabei brennnend interessiert, ist Witz/Ernst. Es eignet sich beispielsweise zur Bestimmung des Human-Anteils des angesprochenen Hybrids. Veranschaulicht im exklusiven TNC-Cyborg-Test: Wenn Dich das obige Statement noch zum Lachen bringt, bist Du noch kein Cyborg ...

HR: Die mit Dolly verbundene Sensation ist nicht nur eine wissenschaftliche, sondern auch kulturell bestimmt. In Japan z. B. hat das Gen-Ingenieurswesen weit weniger ethische Implikationen als etwa eine Herzverpflanzung. Wie haltet Ihr es mit der Sache des Gen-Ingenieurswesens und der kulturspezifischen Bekundung des Pro, Kontra oder Ambivalenten in solchen Fragen angesichts aller Globalisierung? Findet Eure Haltung in der *Clone Party* Berücksichtigung?

B/C: Die *Clone Party* ist ein distribuiertes, globales Ereignis. Jeder Akteur vertritt seine/ihre kulturspezifische Sicht – es gibt Einstiegsmöglichkeiten und Kommunikationskanäle genug [das TNC-Party-Studio beim Ars Electronica Festival, der lange Online-Vorlauf, die *privaten* Party-Floors etc]. In der *Crash Party* wurde der Jahrestag des *Great Web Crash* in London wie erwartet trinkenderweise in Pubs gefeiert, während die Partygoer in Osaka – wie in Japan an Geburtstagen offenbar üblich – rot gefärbten Sekihan-Reis auftischten und in Form von dampfenden GIFs an die Party-Community verschickten ...

which the Ars Electronica Festival 97 has taken as its theme – in the sense of the experience of the individual as the interface in the relationship of technology and its cultural manifestations? This would also imply that on-the-spot experiences become the essential factor in the subsequent process – the *global party loop* ... and bring about online experiences.

B/C: Each partygoer is a junction and an interface in a highly complex techno-social event and mediates his or her subjective experiences to others as an individual in a network-linked experiential sphere. The perception of the event as a whole – splintered and, of necessity, never more than a partial impression – immediately encouraged the Crash partygoers to make use of all available interconnected channels in order to exchange information and impressions. Whether you were at HotWired in San Francisco dancing to Beta Lounge's DJ kicks, or alone in your apartment with a six-pack of beer taking part in a CU-SeeMe-Chat, or in the Berlin real-world venue sitting with others in front of a terminal uploading video files to the FTP server – there were as many ways to party in this network-linked format as there were participants. Or, as an inveterate IRC user formulated it: *The entire evening, I did exactly what I do every other evening: chatting. But during the *Crash Party*, for the first time in my life, I felt in the tips of my fingers what it means to be an active part of a global Internet event.*

HR: What kind of refinements and expanded features have you worked in since the *Crash Party*?

B/C: The long online lead-in of the *Clone Party* is being used to generally refine the interface design, so that each partygoer can become aware of and take advantage of the interface function previously mentioned. There is also the increased sensitization of the TNC guest hosts and DJs to the network-linked space in which they are active. They appear as party agents, as digital doubles, and stimulate the interaction of others. Users have the opportunity to operate and promote their own homepages, so-called *private* online partyfloors [and thus party sub-networks]. Of course, there is also the on-the-spot TNC party channel broadcast via radio and Internet. It functions as an indicator of complexity, scanning the party floors in the Internet and in the real world,

HR: Der Schwerpunkt der *Clone Party*, habt Ihr im Netz angekündigt, liege beim Interface. Interface wird als eine Möglichkeit/Organisationsform des sinnlichen Nachvollzugs eines Prozesses, der im Ortlosen initiiert wurde und erfolgt, und seiner Kulmination vor Ort angesprochen. Könnte damit der *FleshFactor* beschrieben werden, den das Ars Electronica Festival 97 im Sinne der Erfahrung des Individuums als Schnittstelle im Verhältnis von Technologie und ihren kulturellen Prägungen thematisiert? Dies würde auch bedeuten, daß Erfahrungen vor Ort zum prägenden Faktor des nachfolgenden Prozesses, der *globalen Party-Schlaufe*, werden ... und Online-Erfahrungen bewirken?

B/C: Jeder Partygoer ist Knoten und Schnittstelle in einem hochkomplexen techno-sozialen Event und vermittelt den anderen seine/ihre subjektiven Erlebnisse als Individuum in vernetzten Erfahrungsräumen. Die aufgesplittete, zwangsläufig immer nur partielle Wahrnehmung des gesamten Events hat die Crash Partygoer sofort dazu bewegt, alle verfügbaren, zusammengeschalteten Kanäle zum Austausch von Informationen und Eindrücken zu nutzen. Ob man bei HotWired in San Francisco zu Beta Lounge's DJ-Kicks getanzt hat, ob man alleine in seiner Wohnung mit einem Bier-Sixpack an einem CU-SeeMe-Chat teilnahm oder in der Berliner Real-World-Venue mit anderen vor dem Terminal saß und Bilddateien auf den FTP-Server uploadete: Es gab so viele Arten, diese vernetzte Form von Party zu feiern, wie es Teilnehmer gab. Oder wie ein eingefleischter IRC-User es formuliert hat: *Ich habe den ganzen Abend über das gleiche getan wie an jedem anderen Abend: chatten. Aber während der *Crash Party* spürte ich zum ersten Mal in meinen Fingerspitzen, was es heißt, aktiver Teil in einem globalen Net-Event zu sein.*

Radio TNC

Radio TNC ist aus der Media-Fiction vom Great Web Crash hervorgegangen. Seit Februar 1996 löst sich eine internationale Guest-Crew am legendären Online-Mikrofon des boomenden CyberRadios ab. Auf dem Programm: Live-DJ-Mixes, Talkshows, straighte News-Flashes, CyberSerials und TNC-Specials [live online und on air u.a. an der Ars Electronica Festival 96 und '97 sowie an der Isea '97 in Chicago].

http://radiotnc.aec.at

engaging the circulating data streams and inputting the live statements of partygoers and party floor operators into the global party loop.

HR: What is emerging is a quasi-fractal picture of a potentially global *Clone Party* – by means of a core idea out of which a setting forms as a type of branching arrangement, the structure of which reflects the idea and its subsequent processes, at least in their potentiality. Can it be said that the principle of cloning – with all due apologies for the rather audacious mixture of fractals with cloning – has thus also been realized as, so to speak, project- and/or process-immanent and is not simply a mere afterthought?

B/C: Precisely. The slogan *Clone the party!* is, of course, programmatic. If we replace the term *branches* with *sub-networks,* then we are describing the very process that we are trying to achieve, for example, with the various online party floors: a series of cloned clone-parties which duplicate the initial setting in its potentiality – but which subsequently diverge from it according to the nature of their contextual character. With each newly linked up *private* online party floor, with each spontaneously launched home party, the network event reproduces itself horizontally.

HR: The party concept – it carries with it something easy-going, a sense of casualness in the form of a social get-together ...

B/C: A very *heavy* occasion in rather *light* surroundings. For the duration of one long night, the setting of the *Clone Party* is the scene of a test-run of new perspectives of human existence, and whose objective is to make new network-linked spaces capable of being experienced.

HR: Lately, the voices heard in the discourse surrounding these *new perspectives of human existence* have sounded more like Cassandra's cries prophesying misfortune. Stanislaw Lem, for instance, has spoken of *exformation*; in Fluchtgeschwindigkeit, Paul Virilio has postulated the indivisibility of the aesthetics of perception from the ethics of perception. Are network projects such as Clone Party – particularly on account of their emphasis upon playfulness – celebrations as apologia of the conditions of network-linked existence?

B/C: Since the historic web crash of February 4, 1996, the crashed homepage of cyberradio Radio TNC has become a favorite destination

HR: Welcher Art sind Verfeinerung und Ausbau der Features gegenüber der *Crash Party?*

B/C: Der lange Online-Vorlauf der *Clone Party* wird zur allgemeinen Verfeinerung des Interface-Design genutzt, damit jeder Partygoer die erwähnte Schnittstellenfunktion wahrnehmen [im doppelten Wortsinn] kann. Dazu gehört die verstärkte Sensibilisierung der TNC-Guest-Animatoren und DJs für den vernetzten Raum, in dem sie agieren. Sie tauchen auf als Party-Agents, als digitale Doubles, und stimulieren die Interaktion. UserInnen haben die Möglichkeit, eigene Homepages, sogenannte *private* Online-Partyfloors [und damit Sub-Party-Netzwerke] zu betreiben und zu promoten. Dazu gehört natürlich auch der vor Ort, über Radio und Internet verbreitete TNC-Party-Channel. Er funktioniert als Komplexitätsindikator, scannt die Partyfloors auf dem Netz und in der Real World ab, klinkt sich ein in die verschiedenen Datastreams und gibt die Live-Statements von Partygoern und Betreibern von Party-Floors in die globale Party-Schlaufe ein.

HR: Es entsteht das quasi-fraktale Bild einer potentiell globalen *Clone Party* – durch eine Kernidee, aus der sich das Setting in der Art von Zweigen herausbildet, die in ihrer Struktur die Idee und ihr folgenden Prozesse zumindest in ihrer Potentialität abbilden. Das Prinzip des Cloning wird – bei Nachsicht mit der etwas gewagten Vermischung des Fraktalen mit Cloning – sozusagen auch projekt-bzw. prozeßimmanent verwirklicht und ist nicht nur ein Aufhänger?

B/C: Genau. Der Slogan *Clone the party!* ist natürlich Programm. Ersetzen wir den Begriff *Zweige* durch *Sub-Netze*, und wir sind beim Prozeß, den wir beispielsweise mit den verschiedenen Online-Partyfloors anstreben: eine Reihe geklonter Clone-Parties, die das Initial-Setting in seiner Potentialität abbilden – sich aber in der Folge je nach kontextueller Prägung ausdifferenzieren. Mit jedem neu aufgeschalteten *privaten* Online-Partyfloor, jeder spontan lancierten Heim-Party, pflanzt sich das Netzwerk-Event in horizontaler Richtung fort.

HR: Der Party-Begriff – er transportiert etwas Leichtes, Leicht-Sinniges in Form eines sozialen Verbundes ...

for a great many net-trotters. What better place to contemplate the joys and sorrows of one's own existence in the Internet than amid the pitiful ruins of the most up-to-date communications technology? Where the *Clone Party* is taking this was announced in the online flyer – an ambiance between *the laughter and the tears* ...

HR: The setting in which the *Clone Party* takes place is simultaneously the field than [co]determines the course of events. It is the public space of radio and the Internet, the urban as well as the [presumably] private space; spaces permeated by one another and having in common the fact that they can be said to be politicized spaces. They are public in the sense that they are public access places enabling information to be made public, discursive in the sense of the acceptance of authority. At present, we are just as far removed from the utopia of a dialogue-based democracy – as represented by the processual aspect of the *Clone Party* – as we are from a form of art which asserts [or engenders] its freedom in the sphere of information. Nevertheless, the *Clone Party* is, in my opinion, a model – freedom attained by means of a setting featuring a dialogic structure within a discursive one. What is your view on this?

B/C: One of the most interesting moments of the *Crash Party* occurred immediately after a restaging of the web crash, when users were called upon to restore the crashed homepages of our participating partners by uploading Image files from a cache to an FTP directory which had been set up for this purpose. Within minutes, the server was hopelessly overloaded. Of course, the users were not the least bit interested in a reconstruction of the original, rather prefer-

The TNC Network

The TNC Connection founded by Beusch/Cassani operates cyber-radio Radio TNC, produces offbeat cybertainment [Great Web Crash, Headcheese Affair], global network events [Crash Party, Clone Party] and carries out consulting and production assignments in Europe and the US. Depending upon the demands of each respective TNC event, the core network establishes link-ups with the know-how and/or infrastructure of various available sub-networks [including the Ars Electronica Center; Beta Lounge, San Francisco; Radio Fritz, Berlin; the BBC; music channel Couleur 3; the Technology Museum, Paris; France Info; and HotWired].

http://radiotnc.aec.at

openX

B/C: Ein *tief-sinniger* Anlaß in einem *leicht-sinnigen* Rahmen: Für die Dauer einer langen Nacht ist das Setting der *Clone Party* Schauplatz für einen Test-Run angesichts der neuen Perspektiven menschlicher Existenz, mit dem Ziel, neue vernetzte Erlebnisräume erfahrbar zu machen.

HR: In jüngster Zeit werden die Stimmen im Diskurs der *neuen Perspektiven menschlicher Existenz* als Kassandrarufe laut. Man spricht, mit Stanislaw Lem, von *Exformation*; Paul Virilio hat in *Fluchtgeschwindigkeit* die Untrennbarkeit der Ästhetik der Wahrnehmung von einer Ethik der Wahrnehmung postuliert. Sind Netzwerk-Projekte in der Art – und, ob der Lustbetontheit, speziell – von *Clone Party* apologetische Feiern der Bedingungen vernetzter Existenz?

B/C: Seit dem historischen Web-Crash vom 4. Februar 1996 ist die gecrashte Homepage des CyberRadios Radio TNC beliebtes Ausflugsziel zahlreicher Net-Trotter geworden. Wo läßt sich besser über Freud und Leid der eigenen vernetzten Existenz nachdenken, als in den jämmerlichen Trümmern modernster Kommunikationstechnologie? Was die *Clone Party* angeht: Der Online-Flyer kündigt eine Ambiance zwischen *the laugther and the tears* an ...

HR: Das Umfeld, das Setting, in dem sich *Clone Party* ereignet, ist zugleich das Feld, das die Ereignisse [mit-]bestimmt. Es ist der öffentliche Raum des Radios und der Netzwerke, der urbane ebenso wie der [vermeintlich] private Raum. Räume, die voneinander durchdrungen und, vereinheitlicht, politisierte Räume zu nennen sind. Sie sind öffentlich im Sinne veröffentlichter-veröffentlichender Räume, diskursiv im Sinne der Akzeptanz von Autorität. Von der Utopie einer dialogischen Demokratie, wie sie der prozessuale Aspekt von *Clone Party* dar-

TNC-Network

Die von Beusch/Cassani gegründete TNC-Connection betreibt das CyberRadio Radio TNC, produziert Offbeat-Cybertainment [Great Web Crash, Headcheese-Affäre], globale Netzwerk-Events [Crash Party, Clone Party] und führt Consulting- und Produktionsaufträge in Europa und den USA aus. Je nach TNC-Event wird das Basis-Network verlinkt mit dem Know-how bzw. der Infrastruktur von bestehenden Sub-Netzen [u. a. Ars Electronica Center; Beta Lounge, San Francisco; Radio Fritz, Berlin; BBC; Music-Channel Couleur 3; Technologiemuseum, Paris; France Info; HotWired].

http://radiotnc.aec.at

ring free-style repair. And they began to totally revamp the designs of the homepages – including those of public broadcasting stations.

HR: This also describes something totally different than is the case with framework- [or matrix-] oriented interactive works of art featuring merely inverse dynamics. With inverse-dynamics systems, all the talk about doing away with the authority of the author over his work is purely rhetorical. The open, offensive dynamics which are initiated here, however, do indeed blur the borders between the creators – and the framework they have set up – and those who have been activated by them.

B/C: When the DJ in San Francisco samples a Wilmut statement, when we in Linz mix the RealAudio stream from Paris into the *Party Channel*, when a user in Holland leaves the chat room – these are all events, each, needless to say, of a completely different nature, but each effecting the course of events in its respective sub-network. However, *toutes proportions gardées*, due to their link-up to the global party loop, all have consequences upon the course which the event as a whole takes. The question of who where how when what has played a role in the *Clone Party* setting becoming the *Clone Party* or the *Clone Party* network is no longer determinable in a process such as this one characterized by *offensive dynamics.* On the other hand, what can be determined – and directly experienced – is the massive parallelism and complexity of a pulsing, network-linked process.

HR: The announced goal of the *Clone Party* is to make new network-linked spaces capable of being experienced and you have described

Crash Party [February 4, 1997]

To celebrate the birthday of cyberradio Radio TNC, the international Internet community sets off virtual fireworks and recalls with horror the Great Web Crash of February 4, 1997. At the invitation of Beusch/Cassani, an international crew mobilizes its action-tested party know-how and mixes the datastreams of anniversary gigs in San Francisco, Osaka, Berlin, London, Munich, New York, Paris, Amsterdam and Vienna into a five-hour live event: a party channel broadcast via Internet and satellite as well as standard radio wave transmission, featuring multiple RealAudio channels, CU-SeeMe sessions, tele-DJing, action video imaging of man and machine, an IRC channel for chat-lag addicts...

http://radiotnc.aec.at/crashparty/

openX

stellt, sind wir gegenwärtig ebenso weit entfernt wie von einer Kunst, die in der Informationssphäre ihre Freiheit durchsetzt [bzw. prozessiert]. Die *Clone Party* ist jedoch meines Erachtens ein Modell – der Freiheit durch das Setting einer dialogischen Struktur innerhalb einer diskursiven. Wie seht Ihr das?

B/C: Einer der interessantesten Momente der *Crash Party* war jener, als nach einem neuerlichen inszenierten Web-Crash UserInnen aufgefordert wurden, die zerstörten Homepages der beteiligten Partner wiederherzustellen, indem Image-Files, die sich noch im Cache befanden, auf ein extra aufgeschaltetes FTP-Verzeichnis geladen werden konnten. Innerhalb von Minuten waren die Server hoffnungslos überlastet. Den UserInnen ging es dabei natürlich keineswegs um Original-Rekonstruktion, sondern um Freestyle-Reparatur. Sie begannen, das Erscheinungsbild der Homepages [darunter jenes eines öffentlich-rechtlichen Senders] nach ihren eigenen Vorstellungen zu redesignen ...

HR: Dadurch beschreibt sich auch etwas grundsätzlich anderes als bei rahmen- [bzw. matrix-]orientierten interaktiven Kunstwerken mit bloß inversiver Dynamik. Bei inversiv-dynamischen Systemen ist die Rede von der Preisgabe der Autorität des Autors über sein Werk lediglich rhetorisch. Die offene, offensive Dynamik hingegen, die hier eröffnet wird, verwischt jedoch die Grenzen zwischen den Gestaltern – auch des Rahmens – und den von ihnen Aktivierten.

B/C: Wenn der DJ in San Francisco ein Wilmut-Statement samplet, wenn wir in Linz den RealAudio-Stream aus Paris in den Party-Channel einmischen, wenn ein User in Holland den Chat verläßt – dann sind das, freilich in unterschiedlicher Ausprägung, alles Ereignisse, die den Ablauf des Events im jeweiligen Sub-Netz betreffen, aber, toutes proportions gardées, durch ihre Einbindung in die globale Party-Schlaufe, auch Auswirkungen auf den Ablauf des Gesamtevents haben. Die Frage, wer wo wie wann was dazu beigetragen hat, damit aus dem Clone Party-Setting die *Clone Party* bzw. das Clone Party-Netz wird, ist in einem solchen durch *offensive Dynamik* geprägten Prozeß nicht mehr nachvollziehbar.

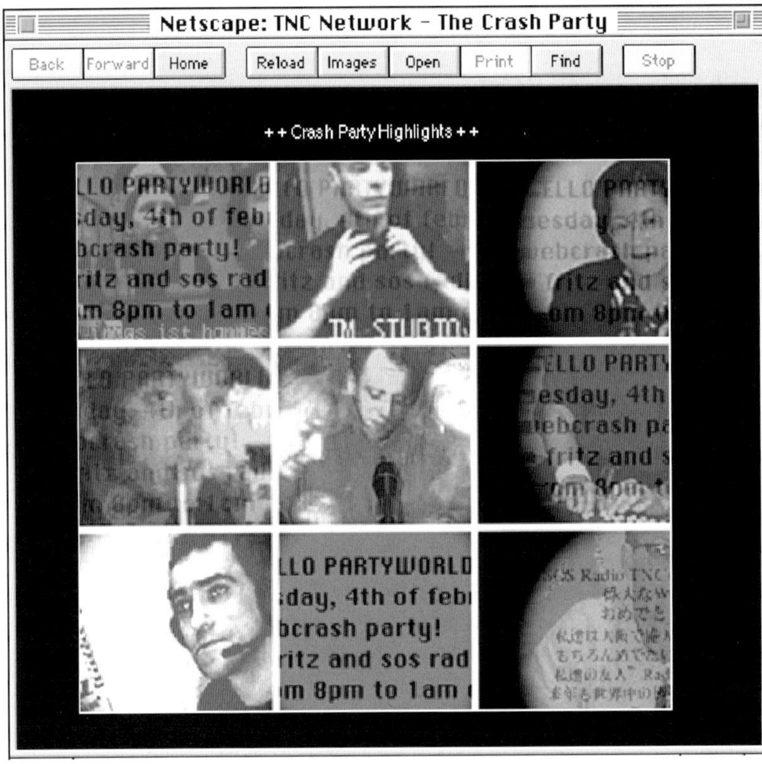

How come my Fiat doesn't have an Internet link-up!?
Warum hat mein Fiat keinen Internetanschluß!?

Nachvollziehbar – und direkt erfahrbar – ist hingegen die massive Parallelität und Komplexität eines pulsierenden, vernetzten Prozesses.

HR: Ihr habt die Erfahrbarkeit der neuen vernetzten Erlebnisräume als Ziel von *Clone Party* angegeben und die *Clone Party* als eine Art Verdichtung eines laufenden Prozesses – des vorhin *Projekt Kunst* genannten. Welcher Art ist Eure Erfahrung kunstprojektorientierten vernetzten Agierens?

B/C: Events wie die *Crash Party* treffen in der Koppelung von Online- und Real-World-Erfahrung das Lebensgefühl einer sich per Mausklick vermehrenden Spezies, für die vernetztes Agieren nichts mit dem Bestellen einer Pizza via Internet zu tun hat. Es ist die Spezies der êtres interconnectés.

Crash Party [4. Februar 1997]

Zum Geburtstag des CyberRadios Radio TNC zündet die Net-Community rund um die Welt ein virtuelles Feuerwerk und erinnert sich mit Schaudern an den Großen Web Crash vom 4. Februar 1996. Auf Einladung von Beusch/Cassani mobilisiert eine internationale Crew ihr aktionsgeprüftes Party-Know-how und mischt die Datastreams der Anniversary-Gigs in San Francisco, Osaka, Berlin, London, München, New York, Paris, Amsterdam und Wien zu einem fünfstündigen Live-Event: Ein über Äther, Satellit und Netz verbreiteter Party-Channel, multiple RealAudio-Kanäle, CU-SeeMe-Sessions, Tele-Djing, Aktions-Bilder von Mensch & Maschine und ein IRC-Kanal für Chat-Lag-Addicts...

http://radiotnc.aec.at/crashparty/

the *Clone Party* as a type of intensification of an on-going process – which we previously referred to as *project: Art.* How would you characterize your experience in your art project-oriented network-linked activities?

B/C: Events like the *Crash Party* – occurring at the nexus of online and real-world experiences – impact the awareness of life as lived by a species whose numbers increase by the click of a mouse, for whom network-linked activity has absolutely nothing to do with ordering a pizza by Internet. It is the species of the *êtres interconnectés*.

During the Crash Party, for the first time in my life, I felt in the tips of my fingers what it means to be an active part of a global Internet event.
Während der Crash Party spürte ich zum ersten Mal in meinen Fingerspitzen, was es heißt, aktiver Teil in einem globalen Net-Event zu sein.

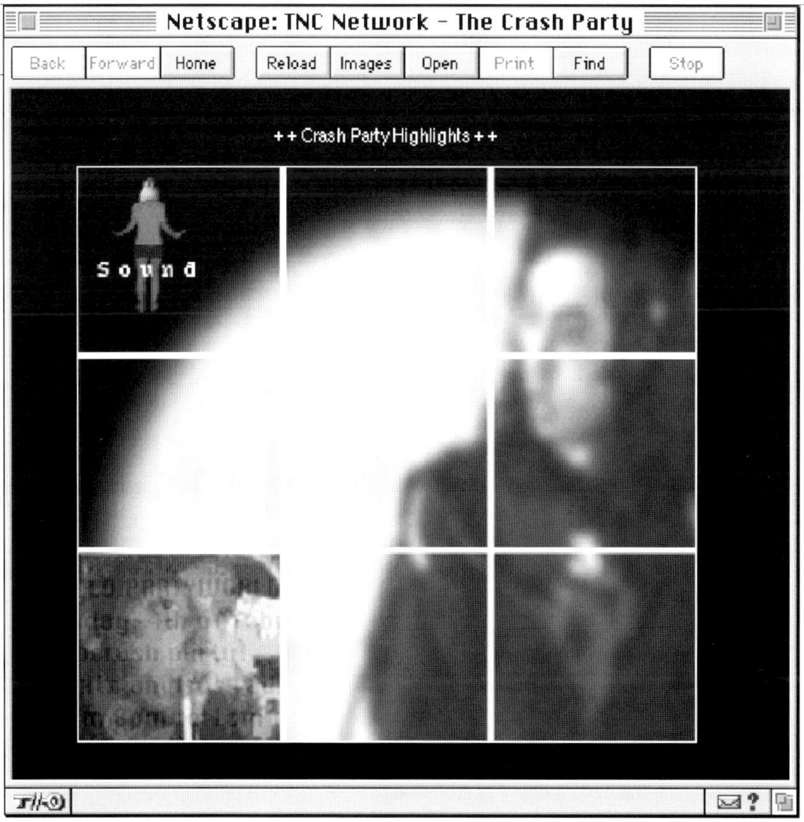

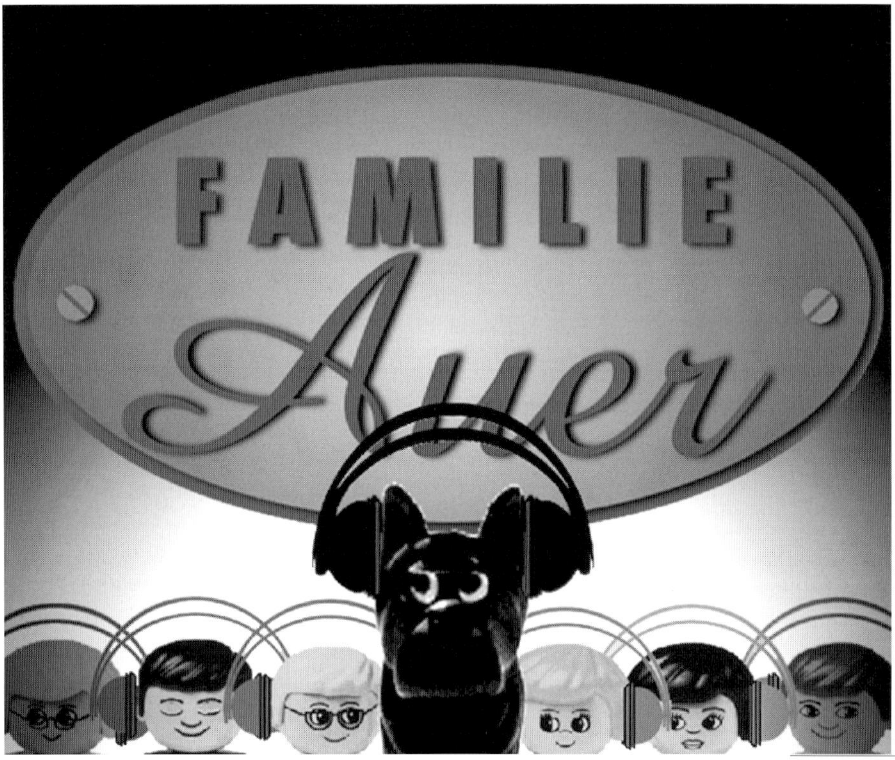

Die Familie Auer

Ein KUNSTRADIO Projekt von vielen

Heidi Grundmann

The Familie Auer

A KUNSTRADIO Project. A Collaborative Effort.

Heidi Grundmann

*Ö 1 KUNSTRADIO will celebrate its 10th anniversary in December 1997. Originally conceived as a weekly program featuring radio art on Österreich 1, the Austrian National Broadcasting Company's [ORF] cultural channel, the focus of KUNSTRADIO's activities quickly expanded to include conducting symposia as well as producing installations in public spaces linked by radio, multimedia and simultaneous telematic projects, international live radio and Internet projects, etc. KUNSTRADIO has been online since April 1995 at http://thing.at/orfkunstradio/. During the second half of 1997, all of KUNSTRADIO's projects and activities are being devoted to the theme *Recycling the Future*[1], including its contribution to the Ars Electronica Festival 1997, at which FAMILIE AUER will be one of the projects presented.*

Over the 10 years since KUNSTRADIO began producing and broadcasting radio art, both art and radio have undergone fundamental changes in response to the pressure exerted by new digital communications technologies. But even 10 years ago, the days when families gathered in front of the receiver to listen together to a radio play or a football game were long gone. In the field of art, a new, radio-specific form of art had just received full official recognition: an audiotheque was set up for visitors to Documenta 8, in which Klaus Schöning [founder and head of the acoustic arts studio at the German broadcasting company WDR] presented the work of Ars Acustica in a comprehensive historical retrospective. It was not long before Ars Acustica was garnering such high praise even among previously skeptical radio drama directors representing the public broadcasting stations associated together in the European Broadcasting Union that the editors responsible for it were granted permission to form their own work group. It was precisely this long-overdue step which made it clear that Ars Acustica – like the traditional radio plays it was deconstructing, the so-called *new radio

In den zehn Jahren seit das KUNSTRADIO begonnen hat, Radiokunst zu produzieren und zu senden, haben sich sowohl *Radio* wie auch *Kunst* unter dem Druck der neuen digi talen Kommunikationstechnologien grundlegend verändert. Doch selbst vor zehn Jahren waren jene Zeiten längst vorbei, in denen sich Familien vor dem Radio-Apparat versammelten, um sich gemeinsam ein Hörspiel oder eine Fußballübertragung anzuhören. Im Kunstbereich hatte gerade eine neue radiospezifische Kunstform ganz offiziell Anerkennung gefunden: die Documenta 8 enthielt eine eigene Audiothek, in der Klaus Schöning [Gründer und Leiter des Studio Akustische Kunst beim WDR] die Ars Acustica samt ihren historischen Wurzeln darstellte. Wenig später fand die Ars Acustica selbst bei den ihr gegenüber mißtrauischen Hörspielleitern der in der EBU [Europäischen Rundfunkunion] zusammengeschlossenen öffentlich rechtlichen Anstalten immerhin so viel Anerkennung, daß man ihr zugestand, eine eigene Gruppierung der für sie zuständigen Redakteure zu formieren. Gerade dieser längst überfällige Schritt machte deutlich, daß die Ars Acustica wie das von ihr – im sogenannten Neuen Hörspiel der 60er Jahre – dekonstruierte traditionelle Hörspiel nur im System des europäischen öffentlich rechtlichen [und osteuropäischen Staats-] Rundfunks bzw. in den ähnlich strukturierten Anstalten in Kanada und Australien überhaupt zu Sichtbarkeit und Anerkennung hatte reifen können. Als *vom Radio initiierte und verwaltete Kunst* konnte Klaus Schöning die Ars Acustica bezeichnen und darauf hinweisen, daß die für die Geschichte und Definition der Ars Acustica entscheidenden Radiowerke eines John Cage in Europa [beim WDR]und nicht in den USA mit ihrem ganz anderen medienpolitischen System realisiert worden waren. In großen Installationen, z. B. des

*Im Dezember 1997 wird das Ö1 KUNSTRADIO zehn Jahre alt. Ursprünglich als wöchentliche Sendung für Radiokunst im [Kultur-]Kanal Österreich 1 des ORF konzipiert, weiteten sich die Aktivitäten des KUNSTRADIOs schnell auf die Veranstaltung von Symposien und die Realisierung von Installationen im mit dem Radio verknüpften öffentlichen Raum, von multimedialen Projekte, telematischen Simultanprojekten und internationalen Live Radio und Internetprojekten etc. aus. Seit April 1995 ist das KUNSTRADIO ON LINE. [http://thing.at/orfkunstradio/]. Im zweiten Halbjahr 1997 hat das KUNSTRADIO alle seine Projekte und Aktivitäten unter das Motto *Recycling the Future*[1] gestellt – darunter auch seinen Beitrag zum Ars Electronica Festival 97, bei dem u. a. das Projekt Familie Auer vorgestellt wird.*

dramas of the 1960s – could only have matured to a state of high visibility and recognition within the framework of the European public [and Eastern European state] broadcasting systems or in similarly structured institutions in Canada and Australia. Klaus Schöning characterizes Ars Acustica as *art initiated and administered by radio* and points to the fact that works of radio art of such enormous significance for the history and definition of Ars Acustica by important artists such as John Cage were produced in Europe [at WDR] and not in the US with its totally different set of media policies. In large-scale installations, such as one by the American, Bill Fontana, this European *art initiated and administered by radio* repeatedly brought *the apparatus of radio into the public sphere* [Manfred Mixner], where it also listened in as well to the phenomenon of simultaneity. But radio art also had still other roots, most notably in the *impoverished* college and coop radio stations in Canada, the US and Australia, which lacked the means to put on highly complex studio productions à la Ars Acustica or to finance cable hook-ups and satellites for intercontinental sculptures. Performances employing [existing] forms taken from popular radio and film [Hank Bull/Patrick Ready, Vancouver; ts-ts-ts, Melbourne[2]], the hissing noise of the channel itself [G.X.Jupitter Larsen, Vancouver], unmanipulated natural sounds as the material of conceptual radio compositions [Terry Fox, San Francisco], language and music as sculptural material [Lawrence Weiner, New York] and so forth, were presented at these stations even without access to major studios – and, it should be noted, without the specific context of programs with a national broadcast range and international remote feeds.

Several of the artists who got actively involved with the medium of radio were among those pioneers of telecommunications art who were granted an official imprimatur by the system of *graphic art* at the 1986 Venice Biennial. Since the 1970s, this art, which, has been calling into question concepts such as the traditional idea of authorship or the self-contained work of art as practiced by international network projects [telephone, slow scan TV, computer communication, fax] while, at the same time, taking as its subject aspects of media policy related to these new technologies [such

Amerikaners Bill Fontana, hatte diese europäische *vom Radio initiierte und verwaltete Kunst* auch immer wieder *den Apparat des Radios in den öffentlichen Raum* getragen [Manfred Mixner] und dort u. a. dem Phänomen der Simultaneität nachgehört.

Radiokunst aber hatte auch noch andere Wurzeln – vor allem in den *armen* Collegeradios und Coop Radios Kanadas, der USA und Australiens z. B., denen die Mittel zu den komplexen Studioproduktionen der Ars Acustica genauso fehlten wie jene für Leitungen und Satelliten für interkontinentale Skulpturen: das Spiel mit [vorgefundenen] Formen aus dem Populärradio und -Film [Hank Bull/Patrick Ready, Vancouver; ts-ts-ts, Melbourne[2]], mit dem Rauschen der Kanäle selbst [G.X. Jupitter Larsen, Vancouver], mit unmanipulierten Naturgeräuschen als Material konzeptueller Radiokompositionen [Terry Fox, San Francisco], mit Sprache und Musik als skulpturalem Material [Lawrence Weiner, New York] usw. fand dort auch ohne Zugang zu großen Studios etc. statt – allerdings auch ohne den spezifischen Kontext von Programmen mit nationaler Reichweite und internationalen Leitungen.

Einige von jenen KünstlerInnen, die sich mit dem Medium Radio auseinandersetzten, zählten zu jenen Pionieren einer Telekommunikationskunst, die im Jahre 1986 bei der Biennale von Venedig die offiziellen Weihen durch das System *bildende Kunst* gefunden hat. Diese Kunst, die seit den 70er Jahren den traditionellen Begriff der Autorenschaft oder den des in sich abgeschlossenen Werkes in der Praxis von weltweiten Netzprojekten [Telefon, Slow Scan TV, Computer Communication, Fax] in Frage stellte und zugleich medienpolitische Aspekte der Neuen Technologien, z. B. den des Zugangs zu den Kommunikationsmedien, thematisierte, wurde Ende der 80er/ Anfang der 90er Jahre auch im Radio virulent. In Liveprojekten wurden unterschiedliche Räume und Situationen verknüpft und uferten aus dem Kunstkontext in den Kontext des Alltagsradios aus, wo sowohl Redakteure wie auch Hörer die Kunstherkunft des Materials und damit ihre *Schwellenangst* vergaßen [Bill Fontana], oder die Hörer selbst zu AutorInnen wurden, die z. T. keine Ahnung hatten, daß sie an einem Kunstprojekt teilnahmen [Chris Mann, Wolfgang Temmel[3]].

as access to new communications media], became a virulent force in radio as well during the late 1980s and early 1990s. Highly diverse spaces and situations were linked up in live-projects that went beyond the contextual boundaries of art and into the context of everyday radio, in which not only the editors disregarded the artistic origins of their material and thereby overcame their *fear of entering uncharted territory* [Bill Fontana], but the audience did so as well. Or the listeners themselves became authors, many not having had the slightest idea that they were even taking part in an art project [Chris Mann, Wolfgang Temmel[3]].

The *collage-ification* of a wide range of spheres – public and institutional, real and in the media – with the help of communication and broadcasting technologies made possible the testing of a *distributive* concept of a work of art which had the overall effect of withdrawing not only the control previously exerted by the author who had now assumed the role of initiator, but also the overall view formerly enjoyed by the audience which had become co-author. The influence exerted upon interlinked live broadcasts – for example, by users surfing

*No author/creator in our media society, still has control over how, in what context, and in which form his/her – probably fragmented and recycled – *work* will ultimately be received. Because, consciously and/or unconsciously, each of us has long since become a crystallization point within an ongoing, highly personal collage process. Whether we are channel-surfing on TV, watching the tube while talking on the phone, or simultaneously listening to music and editing a document displayed on a computer screen – we exist in a multimedia environment which we ourselves are constantly reassembling on various different levels of perception out of a stream of possible set pieces and fragments.**[4]

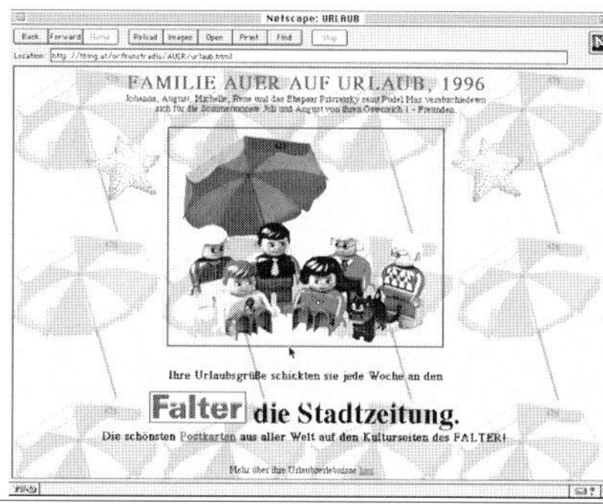

openX

Die Collagierung von unterschiedlichen öffentlichen und institutionalisierten, medialen und realen Räumen mit Hilfe von Übertragungs- und Sendetechnologien ermöglichte die Erprobung eines *verteilten* Werkbegriffes, der sich in seiner Gesamtheit nicht nur der Kontrolle der sich auf die Rolle von InitiatorInnen zurückziehenden AutorInnen, sondern auch des Gesamteinblicks durch die zu Ko-Autoren gewordenen RezipientInnen entzog. Die Beeinflussung von miteinander verknüpften Live-Sendungen z. B. durch UserInnen, die in vorgefundenen mit dem Radionetz verbundenen Homepages des WWW surften, war nur eine von vielen Möglichkeiten einer *remoten/verteilten* künstlerischen und nicht-künstlerischen Produktion in einem Gewebe von weltweit verstreuten miteinander vernetzten, sich gegenseitig beeinflussenden Produktionsräumen, -Paradigmen und Materialien der unterschiedlichsten Art, wie sie in einem vereinbarten Zeitraum etwa von 24 oder 18 Stunden live – zum Leben erweckt – wurden [Horizontal Radio, 1995[5]; Rivers & Bridges, 1996[6]].

*Kein Autor/Macher aber hat in unserer Mediengesellschaft noch Kontrolle darüber, wie, in welchem Kontext und welchen Ausschnitten sein/ihr wohl portioniertes *Werk* letztlich rezipiert wird. Denn jede/r von uns ist längst bewußt und/oder unbewußt zu einem Kristallisationspunkt eines ständigen höchst persönlichen Collageprozesses geworden. Ob wir durch das TV Programm zappen, während des Telefonierens weiter fernsehen, gleichzeitig Musik hören und Korrekturen an einem auf dem Bildschirm gezeigten Text anbringen usw. – wir befinden uns in einem multimedialen Environment, das wir uns aus einem Strom von möglichen Versatzstücken und Fragmenten selbst auf unterschiedlichen Wahrnehmungsebenen immer wieder anders zusammenstellen.*[4]

Ein Projekt, das verschiedene Aspekte der aktuellen Radiokunst [als Teil der Kommunikationskunst] und ihrer Geschichte auf sehr unspektakuläre Weise beleuchtet – und zwar über einen längeren Zeitraum und unter Einbeziehung neuer technischer Entwicklungen – , ist das Radio- und Internet-Projekt *Familie Auer*, das sich auf ein massenmediales Populärgenre bezieht:

Es begann als Kantinengespräch mit einem Autor [Lucas Cejpek] – irgendwann im Jahre 1995 – für das KUNSTRADIO vor allem das Jahr von *Horizontal Radio* und des Starts von

onto the Web site which had been set up in conjunction with the radio network – was only one of a variety of possibilities by which *remote/distributive* artistic and non-artistic productions could be called into existence in an international matrix of interlinked and mutually influencing production spaces, paradigms and materials of the most diverse sort, and how such a network could be operated live during a pre-established time frame of, say, 24 or 18 hours [Horizontal Radio, 1995[5]; Rivers & Bridges, 1996[6]].

*Thus, in communications art, context is a cultural fact. A playground is not specially created for the occasion; rather, a game is set in motion on the basis of the conditions of the public space. This framework of cultural interaction is modified by the active user – at least in the form in which it is perceived. Along with the artistic performance itself comes the *Art* of its usage, whereby *Art,* of course, is meant in both senses of the word. [Translator's Note: Besides the English cognate, the German word Art here means manner, style or way.] Until now, the production of [aesthetic] information has usually been a private matter. The sphere of information, though, makes not only the data itself but also the process of producing data/information a public affair.*[*7]

One project which, in a quite unspectacular way, sheds light upon various aspects of the current state of radio art [as a part of communications art] and its history – indeed, over a rather lengthy period of time and by taking into account modern technical developments – is the radio and Internet project *Familie Auer*, based upon a popular mass media genre. It began as a lunchroom chat with author Lucas Cejpek sometime in 1995 – for KUNSTRADIO, a year highlighted by *Horizontal Radio* and the launch of KUNSTRADIO *online*. The idea was to develop a family situation series on radio and Internet. Al Bundy – a radio genre archetype who had made it on TV – surfaced as a potential model: parents, two teenage kids, neighbors, a pet – a Viennese *Married With Children.* In the fall of 1995, a group of four writers[8] came up with names for the family members and sketched the lead characters with four traits each. Enthusiastic as a result of this initial meeting, they drew up a catalog of rules, including copyright conditions, for all writers and composers who might collaborate on the project in the future. At the first full staff meeting of all KUNSTRADIO writers who were interested in getting on board the *Familie Auer* project – as

KUNSTRADIO ON LINE. Es ging um die Idee einer Familienserie im Radio und im Internet: Al Bundy – ein TV gewordenes Radiogenre – tauchte als ein mögliches Modell auf: Eltern, zwei Teenager-Kinder, Nachbarn, ein Tier. Eine wienerische Familie sollte es werden. Im Herbst 1995 erfand eine Gruppe von vier LiteratInnen[8] die Namen der Familienmitglieder und beschrieb die Charaktere mit je vier Eigenschaften. Im Überschwang ihrer Zusammenkunft entstand auch ein Katalog von Regeln für alle anderen in Zukunft vielleicht mitwirkenden AutorInnen und KomponistInnen samt Copyright-Bestimmungen. Bei einem ersten größeren Treffen all jener KUNSTRADIO-AutorInnen [wie immer mit unterschiedlichstem Background und unterschiedlichen Alters], die am Projekt *Familie Auer* interessiert waren, wurde dieser Regelkatalog samt allen Copyright-Überlegungen sofort ad acta gelegt und beschlossen, daß man sich für die verschiedenen sich abzeichnenden Aufgaben im Radio und Internet zu wechselnden Teams zusammenschließen würde. Als einzige Vorgaben für die Radioepisoden wurden akzeptiert: eine eigene Kennmelodie ohne erklärende Einführung

*In der Kommunikationskunst ist der Kontext also ein kulturelles Faktum. Es wird nicht extra ein Spielplatz geschaffen, sondern es wird ein Spiel im und auf der Basis der Bedingungen des öffentlichen Raumes in Gang gesetzt. Dieser kulturelle Interaktionsrahmen wird durch offensive Benutzer verändert – zumindest in seiner Wahrnehmungsgestalt. Zur Darstellung kommt die Art der Benutzung, und dabei ist *Art* natürlich doppeldeutig gemeint. Bislang war die Erzeugung von [ästhetischer] Information gewöhnlich Privatsache. Der Datenraum macht indes nicht nur die Daten selbst, sondern auch die Erzeugung von Daten/Information zu einer öffentlichen Angelegenheit.*[*7]

und mit einem Hinweis auf die Internetadresse am Ende jeder Episode, ein gleichbleibendes SchauspielerInnenteam, die Erstellung einer *Datenbank* von Standardsätzen, Geräuschen, musikalischen Versatzstücken, Gelächter usw. Eine zunächst zur Diskussion gestellte Arbeitsteilung nach Art des traditionellen Hörspieles [von einem Regisseur inszeniertes Manuskript, illustrative Geräusche etc.]wurde von einer Mehrheit der am Projekt *Familie Auer* Beteiligten umgehend abgelehnt. Bereits mit den im Laufe der Zeit immer selbständiger agierenden SchauspielerInnen aufgenommene Texte wur-

usual, with extremely diverse backgrounds and highly divergent ages – this catalog of rules including copyright provisions was immediately adopted ad acta and it was decided that teams would be formed on a rotating basis to deal with all the tasks which began to emerge in conjunction with a radio and Internet production. A single set of guidelines was established for the radio episodes: a theme melody unique to the show, no explanatory preface, a reference to the Internet address at the end of each episode, a cast consisting of a group of regulars, the creation of a *data bank* containing standard lines, sound effects, musical excerpts, laughter, etc. Within a short time, the cast became increasingly comfortable with improvisation, so that scripts which had already been finalized instead became – fragmented – clips for the *data bank,* which the writing teams, working closely with the sound engineers in the studio, used as material for the *composition* of the initial episodes and which, in ever-changing and expanded form, remained available for future segments. In the very first month, the sound engineers already began to get involved as [co]authors.

*The so-called *new radio drama* began (in the 1960s) with the process of *getting the author into the studio*[9] and with the technical feasibility of stereophonic sound ... In a collaborative effort, as it were, involving writers, dramatists, theater directors, composers, filmmakers and graphic artists, a new aesthetic concept began to emerge ... The dominant position of a verbally signifying language gave way to a balanced blend of language, music and sound, and led to the coining of an *acoustic language,* articulating itself in a variety of idioms in order to harmonize heterogeneous acoustical material.*[10]

Once a week from January 4, 1996 until the middle of February 1997, a *Familie Auer* episode averaging approximately five minutes in length was broadcast on Österreich 1, ORF's cultural channel. Each episode was produced by a team of writers, composers, artists and technicians. These teams were continually regrouping among a staff whose number grew in time to over 70. The *initiative and management originating from radio* was limited to organizational matters; no influence was exerted upon the development of the project itself – except that KUNSTRADIO made it clear from the outset that it was not interested in a traditional series of radio plays with no Internet component.

openX

den stattdessen – fragmentiert – zu Teilen der *Datenbank*, die den aufs engste mit den Tonmeistern zusammenarbeitenden Teams im Studio als Material für die *Komposition* der ersten Folgen diente und in ständig sich erweiternder Form auch für spätere Folgen zur Verfügung stand. Schon im ersten Monat betätigten sich auch die Tonmeister als [Ko-] Autoren.

Vom 4. Januar 1996 bis Mitte Februar 1997 wurde im Kulturkanal Österreich 1 allwöchentlich eine durchnittlich ca. fünf Minuten lange Episode aus dem Leben der *Familie Auer* ausgestrahlt. Jede Folge wurde von einem Team aus LiteratInnen, KomponistInnen, KünstlerInnen, TechnikerInnen produziert. Diese Teams formierten sich immer wieder neu aus einer im Laufe der Zeit auf über 70 Mitwirkende anwachsenden Gruppe. Die vom Radio ausgehende Initiative und Verwaltung beschränkte sich auf Organisatorisches, auf die Entwicklung des Projektes selbst wurde kein Einfluß genommen – außer daß von Anfang an klargestellt wurde, daß für das KUNSTRADIO eine traditionelle Hörspielserie ohne Internet nicht von Interesse sei.

*Mit dem *Schritt des Autors vom Schreibtisch ins Studio*[9] und mit der technischen Ermöglichung der Stereophonie begann [in den 60er Jahren] das sogenannte *Neue Hörspiel* [...] Quasi in Zusammenarbeit von Schriftstellern, Dramaturgen, Theaterregisseuren, Komponisten, Filmemachern und bildenden Künstlern fand man zu einem neuen ästethischen Selbstverständnis [...] Die Vormachtstellung einer verbalen bedeutenden Sprache wich einer gleichberechtigten Zusammenführung von Sprache, Musik und Geräusch und führte zu der Ausprägung einer *akustischen Sprache*, die sich in verschiedenen Spielarten, heterogene akustische Materialien miteinander in Beziehung zu setzen, artikuliert.*[10]

Die Selbstdefinition von KünstlerInnen, LiteratInnen, KomponistInnen, MedienkünstlerInnen sowie TechnikerInnen und OrganisatorInnen gerät in einem Projekt wie *Familie Auer* in geradezu turbulente Bewegung. Kooperation, Teamwork, Interdisziplinarität, Verzicht auf das Copyright für eingebrachte Ideen oder auf die Kontrolle nicht nur über die Weiterentwicklung des Projektes, sondern auch über einzelne Bausteine, all dies ist etwas, das erst erlernt/erprobt werden muß. Doch den wenigen *Auer*-AutorInnen, die sich – bewußt auf ihren traditionellen Rollen beharrend –

The self-definition of artists, writers, composers, media artists as well as technicians and producers involved in a project like *Familie Auer* goes through an almost turbulent process of transition. Co-operation, teamwork, interdisciplinary skills, relinquishment not only of copyright to the ideas one has contributed but also artistic control over the subsequent development of the project including all of its individual components – all of this had to be learned or tested. Nevertheless, the few *Auer* writers who adamantly refused to give up their traditional roles and resigned from the project because the loss of their accustomed control had become a problem for them can be compared to the much larger number of those who, for example, in accordance with the intention of the project as a whole, consented to waive direct credit even in the case of radio or Internet episodes to which they had made major contributions ... One of the preconditions accepted by these writers was that each episode and every other step in the production process was only a partial aspect of a much larger entity composed entirely of fragments. This was not a matter of imposing a personal agenda or implementing specialized standards; rather, the point was to explore the possibilities in the media for interdisciplinary collaboration on the part of a coalition which was transforming itself and acquiring new facets with dizzying speed and which increasingly resolutely forswore more than token intervention by its individual members.

Familie Auer's homepage – a separate Web site within KUNSTRADIO *online* – was set up at the same time the first radio episodes aired in early January 1996 and was likewise designed by teams of artists, including some who worked on the episodes themselves. The site is still up and running[11]; it features *picture stories* [including Real Audio files], games, a *Familie Auer* Fan Club as well as sound files from the radio episodes, etc. A few writers with no previous Web experience worked closely with artists familiar with the Web to provide their own input into the site design. There were segments in which the outcome of the radio episodes could be influenced by online users.

In the world of contemporary radio, it is a borderline absurd undertaking to expect potentially interested listeners to consistently

zurückgezogen haben, weil der Verlust der gewohnten Kontrolle ihnen zum Problem wurde, steht die sehr viel größere Anzahl jener gegenüber, die im Einklang mit den Intentionen des Gesamtprojektes z. B. auf die Nennung ihrer Namen selbst bei jenen Radio-oder Internet-Episoden verzichteten, an denen sie extensiv mitgearbeitet haben ... Diese AutorInnen waren sich u. a. darüber im klaren, daß jede Episode und jeder andere Schritt in der Projekt-Realisierung jeweils nur Teilaspekt eines größeren, aus Fragmenten zusammengesetzten Ganzen war. Es ging nicht um die Verwirklichung eigener spezialisierter Ansprüche und Standards, sondern um die kollaborative interdisziplinäre Erkundung eines medialen Verbundes, der sich mit rasender Geschwindigkeit wandelt und differenziert und sich einer mehr als alibihaften Intervention einzelner immer deutlicher entzieht.

Als Sub-Homepage bei KUNSTRADIO - ONLINE entstand gleichzeitig mit der ersten Radioepisode Anfang Jänner 96 die – immer noch existierende[11] – ebenfalls von KünstlerInnenteams, die sich zum Teil mit den Teams der Radioepisoden überschnitten, gestaltete Homepage der *Familie Auer*: sie enthält *Bildgeschichten* [unter Einschluß von RealAudio Files], Spiele, einen *Familie Auer*-Fan-Club sowie Sound-Files der Radio-Episoden usw. Einige AutorInnen, die selbst nicht für das WWW arbeiten, setzten in enger Zusammenarbeit mit KünstlerInnen, die mit der Arbeit im Web vertraut sind, eigene Ideen um. Es gab Projektteile, in denen der Ausgang der Radioepisoden von den Usern im Netz beeinflußt werden konnte.

Im Radio von heute ist eine wöchentliche Serie in der Länge von etwas weniger als zwei Popmusik-Titeln in bezug auf ihre Auffindbarkeit durch potentiell interessierte HörerInnen ein geradezu absurdes Unterfangen – noch dazu, wenn die Beginnzeit 22 Uhr 17 lautet, gewohnheitsmäß einen *Kunst*-Kontext signalisiert, keinerlei Erklärung und Einführung geboten wird und narrative Elemente nur als Zitate auftreten. Im Medienverbund von Ankündigungen in den Radioprogrammbeilagen der Printmedien, Hinweisen im Hörfunk, im Internet, auf Public Voice etc. wurde die *Familie Auer* aber selbst bei jenen *Kulturinteressierten* bekannt, die

tune in to a weekly series whose episodes are slightly shorter than two pop music songs – and, as if this weren't enough, one with a starting time of 10:17 p.m. which normally indicates an *art* orientation, offers absolutely no explanation or lead-in, and in which narrative elements occur only in the form of quotations. However, using a media package including listings in print media radio program supplements, plus advertising on-the-air in radio, online on the Internet, and in public voice etc., *Familie Auer* achieved recognition even among those *culture-vultures* who had never heard a single radio episode or never happened upon *Familie Auer's* Web site.

Whereas the radio episodes vanished into the fleetingness of the ether every Thursday evening at 10:17 sharp, the Web episodes of *Familie Auer* can still be found at any time, the Real Audio files can be called up at any time, site visitors can take part in the games and send e-mail at any time. [Indeed, answering all the e-mail frequently proved to be too much for the *Familie Auer* team to handle, particularly since only a few of the artists involved had their own means of accessing the Internet.]

The *Familie Auer* project explores a wide segment of the spectrum ranging from *unprogrammed* to *programmed* communications media – from chat rooms to e-mail, call-ins to a live radio show, the voice box, game playing in the WWW, the pre-produced radio episode all the way to newspapers and the CD.

By late spring 1996, the *Familie Auer* staff – who had themselves developed into a kind of family – decided to install a *Familie Auer* public voice box, for which, once again, separate teams had to be established. It was also decided to produce and mail out a postcard containing the various addresses to get in touch with the *Familie Auer*.

A 43-minute-long live broadcast[13] at the end of June marked the half year anniversary of the *Familie Auer*. It had several levels: for a time

The telephone was, and still is, the only generally available, unprogrammed, participatory, personal and interactive communications medium – aside from face to face contact. Programmed broadcasting media like radio and television are universally available...but they are one-way systems in which a commodity – information, entertainment, services – is distributed to a consuming, or potentially consuming, public. ...With the telephone on the other hand, it is the service itself which is the commodity and the user supplies his or her own content..[12]

nie eine der Hörfunkfolgen gehört haben bzw. im WWW nie auf die *Familie Auer* gestoßen sind.

Während die Radioepisoden also pünktlich jeden Donnerstag um 22 Uhr 17 in die Flüchtigkeit des Äthers entschwanden, lassen sich die Web-Episoden der *Familie Auer* jederzeit und immer noch aufsuchen, die RealAudio-Files können jederzeit abgerufen werden, an den Spielen kann man sich jederzeit beteiligen, seine E-mails jederzeit abschicken [mit der Beantwortung aller E-mails war das *Familie Auer* Team allerdings häufig überfordert, besonders, weil erst wenige der beteiligten KünstlerInnen über einen eigenen Zugang zum Netz verfügten].

Das Projekt *Familie Auer* exploriert ein breites Spektrum auf der Skala vom *unprogrammierten* bis zum *programmierten* Kommunikationsmedium – vom Chat über die E-mail, den Anruf bei einer Live-Radiosendung, die Voice Box, das Spiel im WWW, die vorproduzierte Radioepisode bis hin zur Zeitung und CD.

Im späten Frühjahr 1996 wurde auf Beschluß der bereits zu einer Art von Familie gewordenen ProduzentInnen der *Familie Auer* eine *Familie Auer* Public Voice Box installiert, für die wieder eigene Teams tätig werden mußten. Es kam auch zur Produktion und Aussendung einer Karte mit den unterschiedlichen Adressen, an denen die *Familie Auer* anzutreffen war.

Eine 43 Minuten lange Live-Sendung[13] markierte Ende Juni ein halbes Jahr *Familie Auer* und hatte verschiedene Ebenen: Im WWW und bei der *Auer* Hotline [Public Voice] wurden die UserInnen schon eine Zeitlang vor dem Sendungsdatum aufgefordert, Texte einzuschicken, nach denen die SchauspielerInnen sich kurz vor und in der Live-Sendung in neue

Das Telefon war und ist immer noch das einzige allgemein verfügbare, nicht programmierte, allen Teilnehmern offenstehende, persönliche, interaktive Medium zur Kommunikation – abgesehen vom unmittelbaren persönlichen Kontakt. Programmorientierte Rundfunkmedien wie Radio und Fernsehen sind überall verfügbar, aber sie sind Einbahn-Systeme, in denen eine Ware – Information, Unterhaltung, Dienstleistungen – an eine breite Schicht von zumindest potentiellen Verbrauchern vertrieben wird. [...] Beim Telefon dagegen ist die Dienstleistung selbst die Ware, die erst der Benutzer, die Benutzerin mit Inhalt füllt.[12]

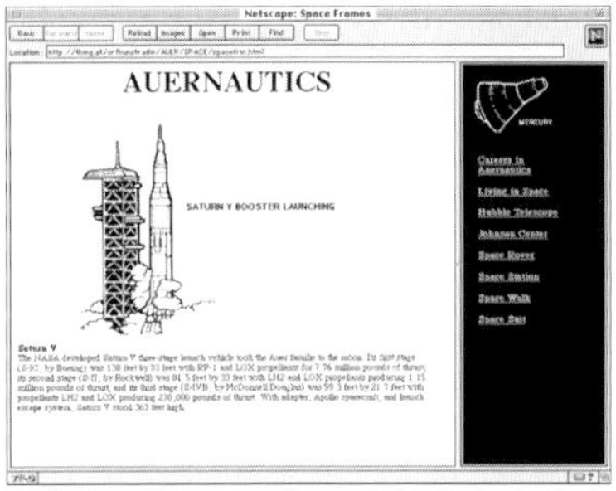

prior to the broadcast date, Web users and *Auer* public voice hotline callers were requested to send in texts from which the actors could develop new *Familie Auer* situations for the live broadcast and the episodes leading up to it. The material for the live broadcast was collected on two CDs [one of which features random mode playback] containing short segments from the previously produced radio episodes together with other brief sequences [e.g., laughter, musical accents] which can be accessed on a sampler, as well as the scenes played according to user texts which were stored in the studio's computer shortly before and during the live broadcast. During the show, the actors – ad-libbing in character – took listener calls to the accompaniment of live accordion flourishes. The unique aspect of these listener calls during the live broadcast was that the callers played roles as well and thus became co-authors.

A second live broadcast at the end of January 1997[14] featured even more levels: there was a small live studio audience which provided laughter and applause, both spontaneously and on demand; Internet users once again had the opportunity to submit texts for the actors to work into the show; the listener telephone hotline was also active, and, in addition, fans could check out the *Familie Auer* live chat room. The live radio mix [augmented by samples from previously produced episodes, *data bank* material as well as Internet sound files] could be accessed in Internet in Real Audio live mode [worldwide] and was complemented by video from a live Web camera.

A little over six months separated the two *Familie Auer* live broadcasts. During this time, technology[15] for the WWW underwent

Familie Auer Situationen begeben konnten. Zwei CDs [eine davon im Zufallsmodus abgespielt] mit kurzen Modulen aus bisher produzierten Radioepisoden bildeten zusammen mit anderen von einem Sampler abrufbaren Kurzsequenzen [z. B. Gelächter, Musikakzente] und den im Computer des Hörspielstudios gespeicherten, kurz vor und während der Sendung nach den Usertexten gespielten Szenen das Material zur Live-Sendung. Während dieser beantworteten die SchauspielerInnen – in ihre Rollen schlüpfend – zudem spontan Höreranrufe und wurden dabei von einem Live-Akkordeon akzentuiert. Die Besonderheit der Höreranrufe bei der Live *Familie Auer*: Auch die HörerInnen spielten bei ihren Anrufen Rollen und wurden zu Co-Autoren.

Eine zweite Live-Sendung Ende Jänner 1997[14] hatte noch mehr Ebenen: Es gab ein kleines Live-Publikum im Studio, das auf Aufforderung und spontan Gelächter und Applaus spendete, es gab für UserInnen wiederum die Möglichkeit ihre im Internet deponierten Texte von den SchauspielerInnen umsetzen zu lassen, auch das Hörertelefon war wieder aktiv, dazu konnte man noch mit der *Familie Auer* live chatten. Die Live-Radio-Mischung [zu der wiederum Samples aus bisher produzierten Folgen, aus der *Datenbank* sowie Sound Files aus dem Netz kamen] konnte im RealAudio Live Modus [weltweit] im Netz verfolgt werden und wurde von Bildern aus einer Live-Web-Kamera ergänzt.

Zwischen den beiden *Familie Auer* Live-Sendungen lag ein gutes halbes Jahr – in diesem halben Jahr hat sich die Technologie[15] für das WWW rasch weiterentwickelt – eine Diskussion um Push- und Pull Media entstand; der Begriff Internet-Radio bürgert sich immer mehr ein, die Möglichkeiten und Definitionen von Net.Radio und Net.Art werden diskutiert. Das KUNSTRADIO selbst begann im September 1996 immer häufiger Live-Webcasts zu veranstalten, die nur zum Teil mit den KUNSTRADIO Sendungen auf Österreich 1 zu tun haben, und zur Definition dessen, was Net.Radio sein könnte, beitragen ...[16]

Die Präsenz der Familie Auer beim Ars Electronica Festival 97 manifestiert sich on line, on site und on air: Wiederum ist das *Spielfeld* Familie Auer Rahmen für eine durchaus ernsthafte Auseinandersetzung mit unter-

rapid development; a discussion arose over the issue of push media and pull media; Internet Radio became a well-established concept; the potentialities and definitions of Net.Radio and Net.Art were discussed. Beginning in September 1996, KUNSTRADIO itself staged more and more live webcasts – many of which had no connection to KUNSTRADIO programming on Österreich 1 – and which contributed to the definition of what Net.Radio could be...[16]

The *Familie Auer* is present online, on site and on-the-air at the *Ars Electronica Festival* 97. The *Familie Auer* *playground,* however, is the setting for a thoroughly serious confrontation with a wide variety of issues in the fields of production and distribution.

To quote a publicity release:The focus of KUNSTRADIO's project office at *Ars Electronica* 97 is on the interdisciplinary development of projects and working methods suitable to the – until now, barely explored – context which emerges from the online, on-the-air and on-site link-ups of media spheres and physical spaces. For an entire week, on-site in the Design Center in Linz as well as at remote locations linked online with Linz and in radio broadcasts, an international team working under the motto *Recycling the Future* will take up the challenges posed by simultaneous, in some cases interactive, production in and for diverse, online-linked spatial and temporal situations.[17] In having developed new production strategies befitting the diverse aspects of the new media mix, in which traditional radio – transformed almost beyond recognition – has been establishing itself ever more solidly, the background of the *Familie Auer* project thus raises some serious issues. [Incidentally, this media mix is usually interpreted as a *new sector in which to do business* and not as a cultural-artistic field – a view generally uncontested even in public broadcasting circles.] The production process in a sphere of activity characterized by an interlinked network of diverse media leads to a revised view of the telephone, radio, live broadcast, print media, CDs, the answering machine, etc., and to the discovery that transmission, communication, distribution and storage media that have heretofore been considered as independent can be regarded as diverse aspects of one mega-network, in which the computer becomes the Primary Medium

schiedlichen Produktions- und Distributionsräumen. Aus einem Ankündigungstext: *Gegenstand des KUNSTRADIO-Projektbüros bei der Ars Electronica 97 ist die interdisziplinäre Entwicklung von Projekten und entsprechenden Arbeitsmethoden für den bisher kaum erforschten Kontext, der aus der Verknüpfung verschiedener medialer und realer Räume on line, on air und on site entsteht. eine Woche lang wird sich – unter dem Motto Recycling the Future – ein internationales Team vor Ort im Designcenter in Linz sowie an mit Linz vernetzten Außenstellen sowie in Radiosendungen der Herausforderung des simultanen, z. T. interaktiven Produzierens in und für miteinander vernetzte unterschiedliche raumzeitliche Situationen stellen.[17]

In der Entwicklung neuer Produktionsstrategien für die unterschiedlichen Aspekte des neuen Medienverbundes, in den das traditionelle Radio – sich dabei bis zur Unkenntlichkeit verändernd – immer stärker eingebunden wird, hat die *Familie Auer* also einen durchaus ernsthaften Hintergrund. [Dieser Medienverbund wird übrigens – unwidersprochen – selbst vom öffentlich-rechtlichen Rundfunk meist im Sinne von *neuen Geschäftsfeldern* und nicht als kulturell-künstlerisches Feld interpretiert]. Die Produktion in der Vernetzung unterschiedlicher medialer Aktionsräume führt zu einem neuen Blick auf das Telefon, das Radio, die Live-Übertragung, Printmedien, CDs, den Anrufbeantworter usw. und zu der Entdeckung, daß die bisher als eigenständig empfundenen Übertragungs-, Kommunikations-, Distributions- und Speichermedien als unterschiedliche Aspekte eines Megaverbundes betrachtet werden können, in dem der Computer zum Primary Medium wird [Wolfgang Hagen], durch den alle diese Aspekte angesteuert werden können.

Radio hört sich immer noch an wie das alte programmierte Medium voller Inhalte, nach deren Ablauf man seine Uhr stellen könnte, wenn das noch notwendig wäre ... Und tatsächlich gehen Radiomacher vielerorten immer noch von der Prämisse des von Anfang bis Ende angehörten Werkes aus, von der Fiktion eines der genau abgemessenen Sendung inständig Beiwohnens der HörerInnen ...

In der immer größer werdenden Vielzahl *programmierter* Kanäle jedoch wird Radio

[Wolfgang Hagen] through which all of these aspects can be orchestrated.

Radio still sounds like the old programmed medium, chock full of content presented in a sequence so tightly scheduled that you could set your watch by it, if that were still necessary ... And many radio programmers actually still do proceed according to the premise of works heard from beginning to end, upon the fiction of a program proceeding in precisely measured fashion and being received by constantly tuned-in listeners ... Among the ever-growing number of programmed channels, however, radio is becoming undifferentiated noise from which a periodic ID signal streams forth announcing traffic reports and news; or *Radio on Demand,* as fragments frozen in time which must first be collected together by listeners who have become users in order to be fit into that collage which is the everyday media environment each of us patch together for ourselves.Even the World Wide Web in Internet – its communications-enhancing elements having lagged far behind early utopian expectations – is already becoming, with its long downloading times, a background medium as well, and thus only one among many media asserting a merely sporadic/isolated claim upon our attention and making up a segment of our environmental collage. But regardless of how we interpret our side of the *coalition of technology and physiology* [F.A. Kittler] in order to somehow bring it into conformity with our image of ourselves, so that the other side of the coalition does not come to display what we will have become – we are registered solely as statistics, numbers on the *hit* counter, creditworthy or not.

1 The theme *Recycling the Future* refers to, among other things, artistic forms developed by the futuristic turn-of-the-century avant-garde, such as the collage, the *ready-made,* etc., which have assumed decisive importance in the whole *Recombinant Culture* of the century now approaching its end, and which are also continuing to be used and adapted precisely by those artists (in a wide range of disciplines) whose work combines new and traditional communications media.

2 All the artists mentioned here may be considered as proxies representing many others.

3 Also see *Im Netz der Systeme*, Kunstforum, Ars Electronica catalog, 1989

4 H. Grundmann, *Horizontal Radio*, in: *Neue Zeitschrift für Musik*, Mainz, 1996

openX

zum Rauschen, aus dem mit Sondersignal Verkehrsmeldungen oder Nachrichten herausschnellen; oder aus dem vom zum User gewordenen Hörer als Radio on Demand in der Zeit eingefrorene Bruchstücke erst aufgesammelt werden müssen, um in jene Collage eingepaßt zu werden, aus der jeder von uns sich sein alltägliches mediales Environment bastelt.

Selbst das World Wide Web im Internet, dessen kommunikative Elemente weit hinter den Erwartungen der frühen Netz-Utopisten zurückbleiben, wird mit seinen langen Downloading-Zeiten bereits zum Hintergrundmedium und damit zu einem der vielen, die Aufmerksamkeit nur sporadisch/punktuell beanspruchenden Medien, die wir laufend als unser Environment collagieren. Oder wie immer wir unsere Seite des *Verbundes aus Technologie und Physiologie* [F.A. Kittler] interpretieren, um sie irgendwie mit unserem Selbst-Bild in Einklang zu bringen , das uns die andere Seite des Verbundes – spiegellos – nicht einmal zurückwirft. Registriert werden wir nur als Statistik, Quote, Hit – als kreditwürdig oder nicht.

1 Das Motto *Recycling the Future* verweist u. a. auf jene von den zukunftsfrohen Avantgarden zu Beginn unseres Jahrhunderts entwickelten künstlerischen Verfahren wie die Collage, das Ready Made etc., die für die gesamte 'Recombinant Culture' des zu Ende gehenden Jahrhunderts bestimmend geworden sind, und gerade auch von jenen KünstlerInnen (aller Sparten) weiterverwendet und -verwertet werden, denen es um die Kombination neuer und traditioneller Kommunikations-Medien geht.

2 Alle hier genannten KünstlerInnen stehen stellvertretend für viele andere

3 s. a. *Im Netz der Systeme*, Kunstforum, Katalog Ars Electronica, 1989

4 H.Grundmann *Horizontal Radio*, Neue Zeitschrift für Musik, Mainz, 1996

5 s. *Katalog Ars Electronica 1995* sowie http://thing.at/orfkunstradio/HORRAD/horrad.html

6 s. Katalog Ars Electronica 1996 sowie http://thing.at/orfkunstradio/RIV_BRI/

7 Heimo Ranzenbacher in: *Ars Electronica Festival 96 – Memesis*, Springer Verlag, Wien, New York 1996, S. 434

8 Lucas Cejpek, Ilse Kilic, Margret Kreidl, Fritz Widhalm.

5 See the *Ars Electronica 1995 catalog* as well as visiting http://thing.at/orfkunstradio/HORRAD/horrad.html

6 See the *Ars Electronica 1996 catalog* as well as visiting http://thing.at/orfkunstradio/RIV_BRI/

7 Heimo Ranzenbacher in: *Ars Electronica Festival 96* – Memesis, Springer, Wien/New York 1996, p. 434

8 Lucas Cejpek, Ilse Kilic, Margret Kreidl and Fritz Widhalm.

9 Aside from a few isolated cases, this process of *getting the author into the studio* was instituted programmatically for the first time in Austria in 1990 by the KUNSTRADIO project RP4, in which participants were invited to a workshop in digital radio Studio 4 where each was able to produce an individual project. Also see RP4, five CDs in a box by Helmut Mark.

10 Petra Maria Meyer: *Die Stimme und ihre Schrift: die Graphophonie der akustischen Kunst*, Passagen Verlag, Vienna, 1993

11 http://thing.at/orfkunstradio/auer/

12 Robert Adrian, *Infobahn Blues*, in: *Medien und Öffentlichkeit*, Rudolf Maresch ed., Boer Verlag, Munich, 1995 and Digital Delirium, A. & M. Kroker ed., New World Perspectives, Montreal, 1997

13 June 27, 1996, Österreich 1, 10:20 to 11:00 p.m.

14 January 30, 1997, Österreich 1, 10:17 to 11:00 p.m.

15 The roll played by artists – of which an ever-increasing number can be assigned to a new category: artist-technician – in the creative testing and exploration of the potential offered by the latest technologies has received virtually no official recognition, but has had considerable effects, for example, upon the development of know-how on the part of individual engineers who have collaborated on radio art projects and then gone on to apply the capabilities gained thereby in other phases of their broadcasting activities.

16 Visit http://thing.at/orfkunstradio/EVENTS/event_frame.html

17 From this text, released several months prior to the Ars Electronica Festival 1997, it is impossible to tell exactly what form the KUNSTRADIO presence at the festival will actually take. Further details are available at KUNSTRADIO ON LINE at http://thing.at/orfkunstradio/; e-mail queries can be addressed to kunstradio@thing.at

openX

9 In Österreich wurde dieser *Schritt des Autors ins Studio* - abgesehen von Einzelfällen programmatisch erst 1990 in dem KUNSTRADIO Projekt RP4 vollzogen, bei dem die Teilnehmer eines Workshops im digitalen Hörspielstudio 4 eingeladen waren, jeweils ein eigenes Projekt in diesem Studio zu realisieren. S.a.: RP4, 5 CDs in einer Box von Helmut Mark.

10 Petra Maria Meyer: *Die Stimme und ihre Schrift: die Graphophonie der akustischen Kunst*. Passagen Verlag, Wien, 1993.

11 http://thing.at/orfkunstradio/auer/

12 Robert Adrian *Infobahn Blues*, in: 'Medien und Öffentlichkeit', Rudolf Maresch Hgr, Boer Verlag, München 1995 und 'Digital Delirium', A. & M. Kroker ed., New World Perspectives, Montréal 1997.(The telephone was, and still is, the only generally available, unprogrammed, participatory, personal and interactive communications medium - aside from face to face contact. Programmed broadcasting media like radio and television are universally available ... but they are one-way systems in which a commodity – information, entertainment, services – is distributed to a consuming, or potentially consuming, public. ...With the telephone on the other hand, it is the service itself which is the commodity and the user supplies his or her own content....)

13 27.6.1996, Österreich 1, 22 Uhr 20 bis 23 Uhr

14 30.1.1997, Österreich 1, 22 Uhr 17 bis 23 Uhr

15 Die Rolle, die KünstlerInnen – von denen eine immer größere Anzahl einem neuen Typ des Künstler-Technikers zuzuzählen ist –, bei der kreativen Erprobung und Erforschung neuester Technologien spielen, findet zwar offiziell kaum Beachtung, hat aber z.B., was die Entwicklung des Know Hows einzelner Ingenieure, die an Radiokunstprojekten mitarbeiten und das in diesen Projekten erworbene Wissen dann in ihren Rundfunk-Alltag tragen, beträchtliche Auswirkungen.

16 s. http://thing.at/orfkunstradio/EVENTS/event_frame.html

17 Aus diesem einige Monate vor dem Ars Electronica Festival 1997 abzuschließenden Text kann nicht abgelesen werden, wie das KUNSTRADIO tatsächlich bei diesem Festival präsent sein wird. Eine Dokumentation wird bei KUNSTRADIO ON LINE zu finden oder zumindest via e-mail zu erfragen sein: http://thing.at/orfkunstradio/e-mail: kunstradio@thing.at

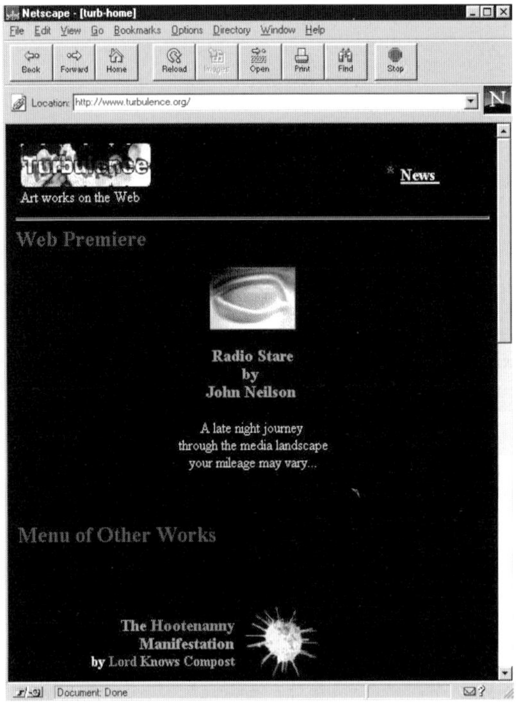

Turbulence

http://www.turbulence.org

Helen Thorington

Now in its second year, *Turbulence* is both an art site on the World Wide Web and an enlarging group of artists who have created for it and who meet regularly to discuss their work, contribute to the overall development of the online site, develop new, collaborative projects, and assist one another with the sometimes awesome task of keeping up with web developments.

openX

Turbulence

http://www.turbulence.org

Helen Thorington

Turbulence, ein mittlerweile seit zwei Jahren bestehendes Projekt, umfaßt einerseits eine Kunst-Site im World Wide Web, andererseits eine wachsende Gruppe von Künstlern, die für das Projekt gearbeitet haben und einander regelmäßig treffen, um sich über ihre Arbeiten auszutauschen, zur allgemeinen Entwicklung der Web-Site beizutragen, neue Projekte zur Zusammenarbeit auszuarbeiten und einander bei der manchmal übergroßen Aufgabe zu unterstützen, mit den Entwicklungen des Web Schritt zu halten.

The *Turbulence* project has two main goals. The first is to provide artists, from all disciplines and with varying degrees of online experience with the opportunity to explore the specific characteristics of the web medium, and make use of the multimedia and online technologies. The second is to provide substantive new work that will improve the quality of the Internet environment and enhance the experience, skills and understanding of users through example, online discussion and collaborative efforts.

Turbulence commissions a wide variety of artists. Their backgrounds may be in literature, music, the visual, performing and/or media arts. They may be known artists who have no experience with multimedia technologies or artists already engaged in expanding the technologies of multimedia.

In general, *Turbulence* looks for works that allow users to interact with the content, add to it and feed the results back to the Internet site. It launched launched on April 1, 1996 with a narrative work, North Country by Helen Thorington with Eric Schefter. North Country, which centers around an unidentified skeleton found in the woods of upstate New York, makes extensive use of RealAudio and it offers its users the opportunity to help determine the direction of the story.

North Country was followed in 1996 by five additional works: Harris Skibell's *Snuff*, a Java-based work that sniffs out, retrieves and collates *competing* media on the Web, and visibly and perceptibly filters their text, graphic and audio content, leaving the remains on the snuff site; Jonathan Giles' *MRT*, which presents an elaborate symphony of small machines, and makes extensive use of QuickTime movies and sound; Marianne Petit's *The Grimm Tale*, an interactive narrative based on one of the Grimm brothers' fairy tales; *notwalls*, a virtual reality construction by architect Laurel Wilson that poses 3-D space against the flat space of the browser page; and *Vocabulary*, an interactive musical work by composer Christine Baczewska, where users can recompose Baczewska's vocal composition.

These works were followed in 1997 by John Hudak's *Artifacts*, which is built around the RealAudio sounds [or artifacts] you hate to hear when you listen to sound on the web; Benton

Turbulence verfolgt vorrangig zwei Ziele. Das erste besteht darin, Künstlern aller Richtungen mit unterschiedlichem Ausmaß an Online-Erfahrungen die Möglichkeit zu bieten, die charakteristischen Eigenheiten des Web zu erforschen und von verschiedenen Multimedia- und Online-Techniken Gebrauch zu machen. Das zweite Ziel des Projektes ist, überzeugende neue Arbeiten vorzulegen, die zur Verbesserung des Internet beitragen und die Erfahrungen, die Geschicklichkeit und das Verständnis der Benutzer durch Beispiele, Online-Diskussionen und gemeinsames Arbeiten erhöhen.

Eine ganze Reihe verschiedener Künstler mit unterschiedlichem Background arbeitet für *Turbulence*. Sie kommen aus dem Gebiet der Literatur, der Musik, der visuellen, darstellenden und/oder Medienkunst. Darunter finden sich namhafte Künstler ohne Multimedia-Erfahrungen ebenso wie Künstler, die bereits an der Weiterentwicklung von Multimedia-Technologien mitarbeiten.

Ganz allgemein sucht *Turbulence* nach Arbeiten, die es dem Benutzer ermöglichen, sich mit dem Inhalt der Web-Site aktiv auseinanderzusetzen, Neues hinzuzufügen und die Ergebnisse wieder einzuspeisen. Die Premiere fand am 1. April 1996 mit der Erzählung *North Country* von Helen Thorington [in Zusammenarbeit mit Eric Schefter] statt. Diese Geschichte, in der es um einen nicht identifizierbaren Skelettfund in den nördlichen Wäldern des Bundesstaates New York geht, macht umfangreichen Gebrauch von RealAudio und bietet seinen Benutzern die Möglichkeit, selbst die Entwicklung der Erzählung mitzubestimmen.

Auf *North Country* folgten im Jahre 1996 fünf weitere Arbeiten: Harris Skibells *Snuff*, ein Java-basiertes Projekt, das *konkurrierende* Medien im Web aufspürt, herunterlädt und vergleicht, Text, Graphik und akustischen Inhalt dieser Medien sicht- und hörbar filtert, und die Reste auf der Snuff-Site ablegt; Jonathan Giles *MRT*, eine kunstvolle Symphonie kleiner Maschinen, die ausgiebig von Ton und QuickTime-Clips Gebrauch macht; Marianne Petits *The Grimm Tale*, eine interaktive, auf einem der Märchen der Gebrüder Grimm aufbauende Erzählung; *notwalls*, eine Virtual-Reality-Konstruktion des Architekten Laurel Wilson, die der flachen Seite im Browser einen 3D-Raum

Bainbridge's *Hootenany Manifestation*, which likens the Internet to the early American frontier where the huckster operated freely; and John Nielson's *Radio Stare* which combines Nielson's own rhythms with uncontrolled feeds from a scanner, making it a voyeuristic work, in a way, and a unique-to-the-web kind of project.

While most of *Turbulence's* works have been the creations of individual artists, the group has also taken part in networked activities. These include an 8-week experimental exhibition of networked digital worlds on the Internet organized for the MIT List Visual Arts Center. Over an eight week period, from January 25-March 29, 1997, *Turbulence* artists Helen Thorington, Nick Didkovsky and others, created and delivered simultaneously to the Internet and to the List Center by RealAudio a live improvisational sound composition known as *Turbulence*.

Jonathan Giles whose work *MRT* can be seen on the *Turbulence* site, has also given a series of Internet performances that make use of CU-SeeMe technology. For these he has made materials – principally sound and background graphics – available to users in advance so that they can contribute to and enhance their own version of the CU-See Me performance. There are plans for the development of a group performance series, to take place locally, in New York City, and simultaneously on the web.

Turbulence has also developed an interactive drama project for the web. Called *Nine Points of Entry*, the initial contributions were made by three Russian artists; three Belgian artists; and three American artists. Users are invited to use these contributions as points of entry into a work they will write.

Plans for the future include the development of an additional *Turbulence* site that makes use of an object-oriented relational database and a set of specially developed procedures and tools that make complex interactions possible, both between the materials in the database, and between them and data stored in other available databases.

Behind the Turbulence site and the artists, and responsible for the administration and the continuance of the project is the not-for-profit organization, New Radio and Performing Arts [NRPA] and its Executive Director, Helen Thorington.

openX

gegenüberstellt; sowie *Vocabulary*, eine interaktive musikalische Arbeit der Komponistin Christine Baczewska, bei der der Benutzer Baczewskas vokale Komposition umkomponieren kann.

Im Jahre 1997 folgten dann John Hudaks Arbeit mit dem Titel *Artifact*, die sich mit den RealAudio-Störgeräuschen [Artefakten] des Web beschäftigt; Benton Bainbridge mit *Hootenany Manifestation*, der das Internet mit der amerikanischen Grenze zur Wildnis vergleicht, wo Geschäftemacher ohne Schranken agierten; sowie John Nielsons *Radio Stare*, die Nielsons eigene Rhythmen mit nicht kontrolliert zugeführten Scannerdaten verbindet und so in gewisser Hinsicht zu einem voyeuristischen Werk macht, zu einem Projekt, das nur im Web möglich ist. Für 1997 sind vier weitere Arbeiten geplant.

Obwohl der Großteil der Arbeiten für *Turbulence* die Werke einzelner Künstler waren, hat sich die Gruppe auch an vernetzten Aktivitäten beteiligt. Dazu gehört eine achtwöchige experimentelle Ausstellung vernetzter digitaler Welten im Internet, die für das List Visual Arts Center des MIT organisiert wurde. Vom 25. Jänner bis 29. März 1997 schufen die *Turbulence*-Künstler Helen Thorington, Nick Didkovsky und andere mittels RealAudio eine live improvisierte Klangkomposition mit dem Titel *Turbulence*, die gleichzeitig im Internet und am List Center aufgeführt wurde.

Jonathan Giles, dessen Arbeit *MRT* auf dem *Turbulence*-Site zu finden ist, hat eine Reihe von Internetaktionen veranstaltet, die CU-SeeMe-Techniken verwenden. Zu diesem Zweck ließ er den Benutzern das Material – in der Hauptsache Ton und Hintergrundgraphiken – bereits im voraus zukommen, sodaß sie zu einer eigenen Version der CU-SeeMe-Aktion beitragen und diese verbessern konnten.

Es gibt Pläne für eine Serie von Gruppenperformances, die sowohl in New York City als auch im Web stattfinden sollen.

Turbulence hat auch ein interaktives Dramaprojekt mit dem Namen *Nine Points of Entry* für das Web entwickelt. Die ersten Beiträge dafür wurden von drei russischen, drei belgischen und drei amerikanischen Künstlern geliefert. Die Benutzer sind dazu eingeladen, diese Beiträge als Einstiegspunkte in ein von ihnen zu schreibendes Werk zu verwenden.

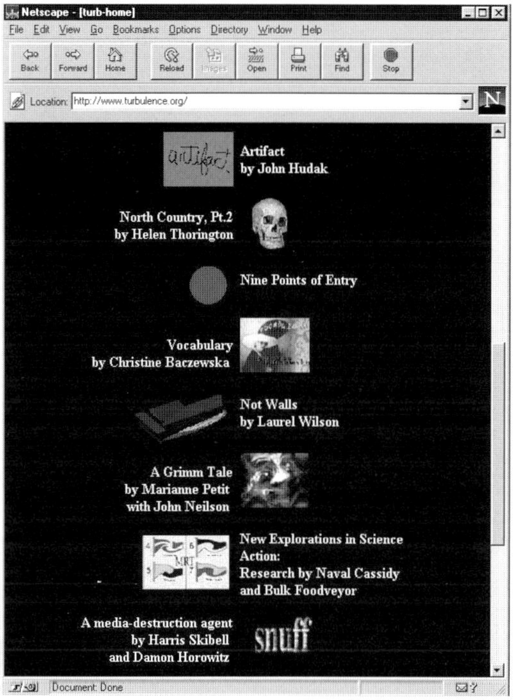

openX

Künftige Pläne konzentrieren sich auf die Entwicklung einer weiteren *Turbulence*-Site, das sich einer objektorientierten, relationalen Datenbank bedient, sowie einer Reihe von eigens entwickelten Verfahren und Instrumenten, die komplexe Interaktionen ermöglichen – sowohl zwischen dem Material in der Datenbank als auch zwischen diesem und in anderen Datenbanken gespeicherten Informationen.

Hinter der *Turbulence*-Site mit ihren Künstlern steht die für die Verwaltung und Fortsetzung des Projektes verantwortliche Non-Profit-Organisation New Radio and Performing Arts [NRPA] mit ihrer Leiterin Helen Thorington.

Station Rose in the Social Web

Station Rose/*John Coate*

workshops

Station Rose in the Social Web

Station Rose/*John Coate*

Nach zahlreichen Performances, Symposien, Ausstellungen & Clubbings sowie dem täglichen Stationsbetrieb stand 1991 eines der einschneidendsten Ereignisse in den Aktivitäten von Station Rose an: der Weggang von der Heimat.

Auf dem Festival Cyberthon, einem Marathon in Sachen Cyberspace und Virtual Reality, das 1990 in San Francisco stattfand, trat Station Rose mit *Public Brain Session* auf. Als einzige europäische Künstler performten wir um 2 a.m., rund um die Uhr gab es aufregende Demos, Shows, Performances, VR-Applikationen, Vorträge, sowie den *WELL*-Infostand.

Gleich nach der Übersiedelung nach Frankfurt führten wir für das Österreichische Ministerium für Wissenschaft und Forschung den Forschungsauftrag *Virtuelle Realität als Neuer Grenzbereich* durch, dessen Resultate 1992 in Form einer der ersten Kunst-CD-ROMs im deutschsprachigen Raum veröffentlicht wurden. Das brachte uns zurück nach San Francisco. Neben Howard Rheingold, Timothy Leary und der Gang von *Mondo 2000* trafen wir John Coate, den wir kurz vorher bei Cyberthon kennengelernt hatten. Als damaliger Managing

After numerous performances, symposia, exhibitions, clubbings and day-to-day station work, 1991 saw one of the most momentous events in the activities of Station Rose: Migration. At the Cyberthon festival, a cyberspace and virtual reality marathon, Station Rose appeared in San Francisco in 1990 with their Public Brain Session. We were the only European artists to perform at the 2 a.m. part of the programme; there were demos, shows, performances, VR applications, lectures and the WELL info stand round the clock.

Soon after moving to Frankfurt we conducted the research assignment *virtual reality as a new borderline area* for the Austrian Ministry of Science and Research; the results of this study in 1992 were among the first art CD-ROM to be published in the German-speaking world.

That took us back to San Francisco. In addition to Howard Rheingold, Timothy Leary, and the gang at Mondo 2000, we also met John Coate whom we had got to know a short time previously at the Cyberthon. As the then Managing Director of The WELL, he explained to us the philosophy and the laws of the virtual community of The WELL.

Back home in Frankfurt we experienced for ourselves what it means to be part of a virtual community. The day-to-day exchange of thoughts with people in cyberspace gave us just as much a feeling of being at home as did personal contacts with people in Frankfurt. In 1991 Frankfurt was just as new to Station Rose as the Net. Only two months had passed since our move to RL and our net hook-up.

John Coate I first met Station Rose in September 1990 a few days before the Cyberthon event in San Francisco.
That year was my fifth as Conference Manager for The WELL in Sausalito, California. Cyberthon was the legendary 24-hour continuous demo/presentation/networking festival held in an industrial warehouse down by the dock of San Francisco Bay. Station Rose *had travelled from Vienna to perform one of their Public Brain Sessions of light, sound and consciousness in the 2 a.m. part of the program.*
But they didn't have a place to stay. So the event sponsors arranged for them to stay at my girlfriend Calliope's house. Calliope and I went to pick up Gary and Elisa at the airport with no real

Director von *The WELL* erklärte er uns die Philosophie und die Gesetze der Virtual Community von *The WELL*.Wieder zu Hause in Frankfurt, erfuhren wir am eigenen Leibe, was es heißt, Teil einer Virtual Community zu sein. Der tägliche Gedankenaustausch mit Personen im Cyberspace erzeugte ein mindestens ebenso starkes Heimatgefühl wie die persönlichen Kontakte in Frankfurt.

1991 war Frankfurt für Station Rose genauso neu wie das Netz. Nur zwei Monate lagen zwischen dem Umzug nach RL und unserem Netzzugang.

Ich lernte Station Rose im September 1990 kennen, nur wenige Tage vor dem Cyberthon Festival in San Francisco.Das war damals mein fünftes Jahr als Conference Manager für The WELL *in Sausalito, Kalifornien. Cyberthon war jenes legendäre 24-stündige Nonstop-Demo-/Präsentations-/Networking-Festival in einem Industrielagerhaus unten an den Docks der San Francisco Bay. Station Rose war aus Wien angereist, um im 2:00-Morgen-Programm* Public Brain Sessions, *eine Licht-, Klang- und Bewußtseinsperformance aufzuführen. Da sie nicht wußten, wo sie übernachten sollten, arrangierten die Sponsoren des Festivals eine Übernachtungsmöglichkeit im Haus meiner Freundin Calliope. Calliope und ich holten Gary und Elisa vom Flughafen ab, ohne überhaupt zu wissen, wie die beiden aussehen. Also gingen wir zum Förderband und beobachteten das Gepäck, denn wir wußten, daß sie irgendwelche robusten Gerätekisten dabeihaben mußten. Und tatsächlich: Dieses flippige, absolut gutaussehende Pärchen in den schrillen Klamotten schnappte sich das Zeug. Wir gingen zu ihnen rüber und sagten: *Station Rose?* Sie antworteten: *Yah ... yah!*, und das war der Beginn einer großartigen Dauerfreundschaft, die in shiftenden Räumen wuchs und gedieh, im realen Raum ebenso wie im Cyberspace. Im Laufe der Jahre haben die beiden uns dreimal besucht, als sie Feldforschungen für ihre Projekte durchführten. Wir verschafften ihnen [Station Rose] Anschluß an die Cyber-Gemeinde von San Francisco, die zu einem wesentlichen Bestandteil ihrer globalen Netz-Matrix geworden ist. Sie kamen genau zu dem Zeitpunkt an, als The WELL seine Glanzzeit erlebte.*

*idea of what they looked like. So we went to the luggage carousel and looked at the luggage as it came out knowing that it would be some sort of heavy-duty equipment cases. Sure enough, this hip couple with bright-colored clothing and outrageous good looks picked up the stuff. We went over to them and said, *Station Rose?* They said, *yah ... yah!* and thus began a great and lasting friendship that grew and matured through shifting space, both real and cyber. Over the years they have visited us three times while doing field research for their projects.*
We connected them [Station Rose] to the San Francisco cyber-community which became an intrinsic part of their world-wide network matrix. They arrived right when The WELL was in its heyday.

The *virtual home* grew alongside our *analogue* home. We talked about The WELL in the clubs and restaurants of our exile home. A basic need for social contact was satisfied in cyberspace, a powerful feeling of belonging evolved, an attachment – in a word, a virtual community.

After 5 years on the net, Howard Rheingold invited us to host the Frankfurt Conference in his online project *Electric Minds* <www.minds.com> in autumn 1996. We had already worked together on *Brainstorms* where we had devised a kind of *editorial jam session*, supplying multimedia contributions in HTML to his online project though the Net that were then edited by Rheingold.

Electric Minds offered us the opportunity to put to the test the multimedia skills of Internet communication we had learned. In addition to monthly text contributions to the World Wide Jam in which we report on interesting facts from the close global setting, Station Rose's task consists in keeping the *Frankfurt Conference* going.

At that time we had about five thousand paying subscribers, we were recently profitable as a small business and we had a core of many hundreds who all knew, each in their way, that they were involved in something exciting and meaningful. Here were a whole bunch of smart interesting people using computers to meet and converse and it was revolutionizing their lives. We

Die *virtuelle Heimat* wuchs parallel zur *analogen*. Gespräche wurden über *The WELL* geführt und in den Clubs und Restaurants in der Exilheimat. Ein Grundbedürfnis nach sozialem Kontakt wurde im Cyberspace gestillt, es entstand ein starkes Zugehörigkeitsgefühl, ein Verbundensein, eine virtuelle Gemeinschaft eben.

Damals hatten wir ungefähr 5000 zahlende Abonnenten und machten als Kleinunternehmen seit neuestem Profit. Wir hatten ein Stammpublikum von mehreren Hundert, die alle, jeder auf seine Weise, wußten, daß sie in etwas Aufregendes und Bedeutendes verwickelt waren. Da war also ein ganzer Haufen intelligenter, interessanter Menschen, die Computer benutzten, um sich zu treffen und zu unterhalten, und das war etwas Revolutionäres in ihrem Leben. Wir waren untereinander verbunden, wir waren mit dem frühen Internet verbunden, und diese globale Konversation machte uns richtig high. Und wir beschränkten unsere Interaktion auch nicht auf Online-Konversation allein. Wir veranstalteten jeden Monat Parties und manchmal Happenings mit unseren eigenen Rock'n' Roll-Bands und Revue-Vorstellungen. Wir hatten Picknicks, Hochzeiten und Begräbnisse. Wir halfen einander bei der Jobsuche. Es war klar, daß unsere Beziehungen die Quelle dieser Faszination waren, und die Technologie ihr Nährboden.

Nach fünf Jahren im Netz wurden wir von Howard Rheingold im Herbst 1996 eingeladen, Hosts der *Frankfurt Conference* bei seinem Online-Projekt *Electric Minds* <www.minds.com> zu sein. Schon vorher hatten wir im Rahmen von Brainstorms zusammengearbeitet und eine Art *editorial jam session* erfunden, bei der wir über das Netz Multimedia-Beiträge in HTML zu seinem Online-Projekt lieferten, die von Rheingold editiert wurden.

Electric Minds bot die Möglichkeit, unsere dort erworbenen Kenntnisse in Multimedia und Internetkommunikation unter Beweis zu stellen. Neben monatlichen Textbeiträgen für World Wide Jam, bei der wir über Interessantes aus der näheren globalen Umgebung berich-

were connected to each other and we were connected to the early Internet and we were high on the global conversation. We didn't confine our interaction to just online conversation, either. We had parties every month and sometimes we had wild happenings with our own rock and roll bands and floor shows. We had picnics and weddings and funerals. We helped each other find work. It was clear that the relationships were the source of the magic and the technology nurtured it.

Special software developed by The WELL [Well Engaged] not only allows visitors to contribute text. Rather, the make-up of Well Engaged allows the user to integrate HTML commands. This is why almost every topic of our *Frankfurt Conference* is a multimedia blend of images, sounds, animations and text.

At this point we would like to detail the outstanding feature of Well Engaged, that is the possibility of social interaction. Well Engaged lifts *Electric Minds* to the next level of communication within the World Wide Web, the level of the Social Web. Chatting is taking a step forward, is being augmented by intensifying personal, social interaction within the virtual community – as we have seen in conference systems à la Well and chat forums – but with the additional feature of publishing in real time. Here, sitting down together and telling each other stories round the campfire means *telling* stories in images, sounds, gif-anis, text and links which does better justice to the high demands of the World Wide Web, i.e. the claim to being a multimedia structure.

Just to remind you – homepages are multimedia showcases that offer information to look at and listen to, to download, but not the possibility of interaction. Homepage updates need off-line support; a conference in *Electric Minds*, on the other hand, needs online support.

*Soon we blurred the border between a *virtual* community and an actual community. Our new society seemed to have an amphibious quality, a bilingual nature. You could interact virtually or actually ... and you got to decide for yourself how much or how little of each one you wanted to do. I had sort of stumbled into the online business. I was hired in 1986 when The WELL was*

ten, ist es Aufgabe der Station Rose, die *Frankfurt Conference* in Gang zu halten.

Eine von *The WELL* entwickelte Software [Well Engaged] ermöglicht es den Besuchern, nicht nur Text beizutragen, sondern auch HTML-Befehle einzubinden. Daher ist beinahe jeder Topic unserer *Frankfurt Conference* eine multimediale Mischung aus Bildern, Tönen, Animationen und Text.

Die Besonderheit von Well Engaged, nämlich die Möglichkeit zu einer sozialen Interaktion, wollen wir hier genau erläutern. Well Engaged hebt *Electric Minds* innerhalb des World Wide Web auf ein höheres Level der Kommunikation, eben auf das des *Social Web*. Chats machen einen Schritt vorwärts, sie werden erweitert, indem die persönlichen, sozialen Interaktionen in der Virtual Community verstärkt werden, so wie man es schon von Conference-Systemen à la *WELL* und Chat-Foren generell kennt. Was dazukommt, ist Publishing in Echtzeit. Sich-Zusammensetzen und Geschichten-am-Lagerfeuer-Erzählen heißt hier, Geschichten in Bildern, Soundz, Gif-Anis, Text und Links zu *erzählen*, was dem hohen Anspruch des World Wide Web, nämlich multimedial zu sein, gerecht wird.

Zur Erinnerung: Homepages sind multimediale Auslageflächen, die Informationen anbieten, zum Ansehen & -hören, Downloaden einladen, jedoch nicht zum Interagieren. Updates von Homepages brauchen Offline -Betreuung; eine Conference in *Electric Minds* braucht hingegen Online-Betreuung. Das Conference-System von *Electric Minds* hat das Versprechen der *Echtzeit* eingelöst, indem es die Möglichkeit bietet, multimediale Daten sofort zu posten. Verglichen mit *klassischem* Online-Publishing ist die Ästhethik, die daraus resultierende Kunstform, ist eine andere, neue. Sie ist außerdem noch sehr jung und ungezähmt und kann im Zusammenspiel mit anderen neuen Möglichkeiten wie Webcasting bislang ungeahnte Wege beschreiten.

*Bald schon verwischten sich die Grenzen zwischen der *virtuellen* und der realen Gemeinde. Unsere neue Gesellschaft schien amphibische Qualität zu haben, schien bilingualer Natur zu sein. Man konnte virtuell oder wirklich inter-*

*a one-person business and very few people knew that computers had anything at all to do with communication. I didn't know anything about computers when I started, but I did know some things about how people in groups can get along with each other better. This came from having lived in communal situations, both rural and urban, from the time I was nineteen until I was thirty-two. During that time I had lived on buses with as many as ten people, large army tents with up to twenty, urban households with more than thirty, and big ramshackle country hippie houses with over forty people, adults and kids. I had been a farmer, a mechanic, an interstate truck driver and a carpenter. Most of this was down at the Farm in Tennessee, which was the largest single intentional community in America during the Seventies, and up in Washington DC and New York City. Along with all the people I lived with, we were always providing lodging to guests who wanted to visit us and talk about what we were doing. After thirteen years of living wired-up to hundreds of other peoples' lives and minds, I came to The WELL and felt amazingly at home. My job put me in the middle of this new *virtual town square* that was forming. Mainly I helped introduce people to one another and encourage the positive care and feeding of the relationships.*

The conference system of *Electric Minds* has realised the idea of real time by making it possible to post multimedia data immediately. The aesthetics, the art form, that this produces is different and new when compared to *classical* online publishing. This form is also still very young and could embark on completely new, undreamt-of paths thanks to its untamedness, in an interplay with other new possibilities such as webcasting.

Formation of your own virtual community, as is the case with our *Frankfurt Conference,* is a far-reaching fact and most definitely has consequences, seeing that it makes social behaviour transparent. At the beginning of *Electric Minds*, a lot of users had come so as to have been in on it from the start. Some of them only came once, some came several times, and others still keep coming. This last group feels a need for global communication, together practising human, digital behaviour, experiencing that tingling online feeling.

agieren ... und man konnte selbst entscheiden, in welchem Ausmaß. Ich war irgendwie ins Online-Geschäft hineingestolpert. Ich wurde 1986 angestellt, als The WELL *ein Ein-Personen-Betrieb war und nur sehr wenige Menschen wußten, daß Computer überhaupt irgendwas mit Kommunikation zu tun hatten. Am Anfang verstand ich überhaupt nichts von Computern, aber ich wußte einiges darüber, wie Menschen in Gruppen besser miteinander auskommen können. Das kam daher, daß ich zwischen meinem 19. und 32. Lebensjahr sowohl auf dem Land als auch in der Stadt in kommunalen Situationen gelebt hatte. Ich hatte in dieser Zeit z. B. mit gut und gern zehn Personen in einem Bus gelebt, in großen Armee-Zelten mit bis zu 20 Personen, in städtischen Haushalten mit mehr als 30 und in großen baufälligen Hippie-Landhäusern mit mehr als 40 Erwachsenen und Kindern. Ich hatte als Farmer, Mechaniker, Fernfahrer und Tischler gearbeitet, zumeist unten auf der Farm in Tennessee – in den 70er Jahren die größte einzelne intentionale Gemeinde Amerikas – oder oben in Washington DC und New York City. Gemeinsam mit all den Leuten, mit denen ich zusammenwohnte, haben wir Besucher beherbergt, die etwas über unsere Aktivitäten erfahren wollten. Nach dreizehn Jahren, in denen ich in Leben und Vorstellungen hunderter anderer Menschen verwickelt war, kam ich zu* The WELL *und fühlte mich überraschenderweise gleich zuhause. Durch meinen Job stand ich im Mittelpunkt dieses neu entstehenden *virtuellen Marktplatzes*. Meine Hauptaufgabe bestand darin, Menschen einander vorzustellen und sie dazu zu ermuntern, ihre Beziehungen zu pflegen und zu erweitern.*

Die Bildung der eigenen Virtual Community, wie sie in unserem Fall die *Frankfurt Conference* darstellt, ist ein einschneidender Fact und hat definitiv Folgen, macht sie doch soziales Verhalten transparent. So waren zum Start von *Electric Minds* viele User gekommen, um von Anfang an dabei gewesen zu sein. Einige kamen nur einmal, einige mehrere Male, und einige kommen immer wieder. Diese letzte Gruppe agiert aus demselben Bedürfnis nach globaler Kommunikation, und gemeinsam wird eine menschliche, digitale Umgangsform

*So naturally, when I, along with Calliope [who is now my wife] met them and we saw how well we understood and liked each other, we introduced them into our circle of friends and companions including Howard Rheingold, Freddy *Are We Really?* Hahne and Mark *Spoonman* Petrakis. We were all pretty much children of the Sixties with a love of group consciousness, positive energy and psychic adventure. Our interest in boundaries and limits was to go beyond them. So we had a common frame of reference that was exactly attenuated to the benefits that communication in cyberspace could bestow. And we have gone on to start other online projects such as Electric Minds and the SF Gate that derive their philosophies directly from what we had learned together. We learned it, it worked, we know it's real and we still act according to it. It lives at the essence of how we function as social, artistic and economic beings. What could be better?*

For Station Rose, the *Frankfurt Conference* is the next step towards responsible handling of the Net, active integration of the Net into daily life, far removed from the homepage consumer society of criticising web-potatoes bemoaning the lack of speed or other sporting shortcomings.

For Station Rose, the *Frankfurt Conference* is the next step towards an online home after having been part of the online community The WELL for 6 years now. The conference is a day-to-day obligation. A conference needs to be taken care of. This obligation only makes itself felt over the months. People cultivating online friendships across the globe.

Circumstances led us to turn our back on our home country in 1991 so as to offer ourselves new homes. The online home provides space for existing & new relationships and parallel to that a suitable setting for producing and showing art. Together with *webcasting*, which Station Rose is in the process of launching right now, the social web offers undreamt-of possibilities of multimedia interaction, new languages and new relationships. It all depends on how we behave towards each other and how we wish to interact in real-time. Bad times could be on the way for web-potatoes.

miteinander geübt, ein prickelndes Online-Gefühl erlebt.

Die *Frankfurt Conference* ist für Station Rose der nächste Schritt zu einem verantwortungsvollen Umgang mit dem Netz geworden, zur aktiven Integration des Netzes in das tägliche Leben, weit entfernt von einer Homepage-Konsumgesellschaft kritisierender Web-Potatoes, die über fehlende Geschwindigkeit oder ähnliche Sportdefizite jammern.

*Als ich die beiden also gemeinsam mit Calliope [die inzwischen meine Frau ist] traf und wir sahen, wie gut wir uns verstanden und wie sympathisch wir einander waren, stellten wir sie natürlich unseren Freunden und Geschäftspartnern vor: Howard Rheingold, Freddy *Are We Really?* Hahne und Mark *Spoonman* Petrakis. Wir alle waren echte Kinder der 60er, mit einem Faible für Gruppenbewußtsein, positive Energie und psychische Abenteuer. Das Interessante an Grenzen und Schranken war für uns, sie zu überschreiten. So hatten wir einen gemeinsamen Bezugsrahmen, der haargenau auf die Vorteile der Kommunikation im Cyberspace abgestimmt war. Und so starteten wir auch andere Online-Projekte, wie z. B.* Electric Minds *und* SF Gate, *die ihre Philosphie direkt von dem ableiten, was wir gemeinsam gelernt hatten. Wir hatten es gelernt, es funktionierte, wir wissen, daß es echt ist, und wir leben noch heute danach. Es basiert auf unseren essentiellen Funktionen als soziale, künstlerische und wirtschaftliche Wesen. Gibt es etwas besseres?*

Die *Frankfurt Conference* ist für Station Rose the next step zu einer Online-Heimat, nachdem wir selbst seit sechs Jahren Teil der Online-Community *The WELL* sind. Die Conference ist eine Verpflichtung auf täglicher Basis. Um eine Conference hat man sich zu kümmern. Diese Verpflichtung macht sich erst im Laufe der Monate bemerkbar. Verteilt über den Globus, pflegen Menschen ihre Online-Freundschaften.

Die Umstände haben uns 1991 der Heimat den Rücken zukehren lassen, um uns daraufhin neue Heimaten anzubieten. Die Online-Heimat bietet Platz für bereits existierende & neue Beziehungen, parallel dazu bietet sie das

But the great event that has happened since the explosion of the Internet in the 90s is that these networking tools are increasingly available to everyone and people are more able than ever to turn them to their own advantage. Email, chat, conferencing, voice, video, and personal home pages are now seen by millions as a way to meet new people and connect to those we already know. Cyberspace has no flavor and no energy of its own. It is only as good or bad as the people who inhabit it. Problems abound, and anytime you get a public gathering that develops some good social energy, people come along who are so starved for attention or so in need of being the lone dissenter or defender of their principle that it becomes argumentative. And the online world is a place where even the simplest conflicts can seem impossible to resolve because it is so easy to misunderstand. But, over time, with patience and perseverance, people can find their commonalities by discovering and discussing their differences. And relationships of all kinds can be developed, strengthened and nurtured. Real life and real magic, in the virtual world, is now easy and available to anyone who wants to take the journey.

passende Feld, um Kunst zu produzieren & zu zeigen. Zusammen mit Webcasting, das Station Rose gerade startet, bietet das Social Web ungeahnte Möglichkeiten zur multimedialen Interaktion, zu neuen Sprachen, zu neuen Beziehungen. Es kommt nur darauf an, wie man miteinander umgehen und in Echtzeit interagieren will. Es könnten schlechte Zeiten für Webpotaoes anbrechen. ;-)

Seit der Explosion des Internet in den 90ern ist etwas Großartiges passiert: Diese Networking-Instrumente stehen immer mehr Leuten zur Verfügung, und diese können sie mehr denn je zu ihrem eigenen Vorteil nützen. E-mail, Chatting, Diskussionsforen, Sprache, Video und persönliche Homepages bieten heute Millionen von Menschen die Möglichkeit, neue Bekanntschaften zu schließen und mit den Menschen verbunden zu bleiben, die man schon kennt. Der Cyberspace hat keinen eigenen Geschmack und keine eigene Energie. Er ist genau so gut oder schlecht wie die Leute, die ihn bewohnen. Es gibt zahlreiche Probleme, und bei jeder öffentlichen Versammlung, die wirklich gute gesellschaftliche Energien entwickelt, kommen Leute daher, die so ausgehungert sind nach Aufmerksamkeit oder es so nötig haben, der einzige Gegner oder Verteidiger eines Prinzips zu sein, daß es zu einer Streiterei kommt. Und die Online-Welt ist ein Ort, wo selbst der kleinste Konflikt unlösbar erscheinen kann, weil es so einfach ist, sich mißzuverstehen. Aber im Laufe der Zeit, mit viel Geduld und Ausdauer, können die Menschen ihre Gemeinsamkeiten dadurch entdecken, daß sie sich ihrer unterschiedlichen Auffassungen bewußt werden und sie diskutieren. Und so kann man alle möglichen Beziehungen entwickeln, vertiefen und stärken. Wirkliches Leben und wirkliche Faszination stehen nun in der virtuellen Welt jedem zur Verfügung, der die Reise wagen möchte.

ou∂eis – a world wide odyssey

kis.production

Genesis

It all began with a meeting of artists, various people connected with the arts and university professors where possibilities of reducing youth unemployment in Austria were discussed. This was followed by a large family birthday party and dinner at an open air restaurant which brought together people involved in theater, either professionally or as theater-goers, as well as computer freaks.

Tradition

The experimental and anti-mainstream theater of the 20th century demanded a break with tradition as regards stage construction, texts and performance. Even in the 1920s Italian futurist Enrico Prampolini suggested eliminating the proscenium stage because it reduces the dramatic action.

In the 1960s Fringe theater began to forsake conventional playhouses, to find new settings to perform in and involve the audience. Experimenting with new techniques and ways of production became the distinguished element of all groups in the Fringe Theater Movement, as Pip Simmons emphasizes in the

ou∂eis – a world wide odyssey

kis.production

Genesis

Es begann mit einer Besprechung zwischen Künstlern, Kunstvermittlern und Universitätsprofessoren. Man unterhielt sich über Möglichkeiten, die Jugendarbeitslosigkeit in Österreich zu bekämpfen. Darauf folgte ein Geburtstagsfest im Kreise einer Großfamilie und ein Abendessen in einem Gastgarten, bei dem Theaterschaffende und -rezipienten, Theater- und Computerfreaks aufeinandertrafen.

'The theatre is changing. Not before our eyes, but in our perception of its traditional physical space.' Andrew Garton

program for the Theater of Nations in 1979. In order to promote the development of modern theater art, new media like film, photography, video or television were soon incorporated into Fringe theater production and new creative processes where sought after. Visual aspects predominate in the *performance art* branch of the English Fringe Theater movement. In the *actor- and writer-based companies*, collective work and experimenting with dramatic means of expression are employed.

The new venues are many and various: former movie theaters, factories and tram depots, and the street is also used as a performing space. These public locations have recently been enlarged through the exploration of electronic space.

Internet

The theater scene in the Internet evolved from meeting places in the Net set up by theater theoreticians and artists for exchanging information and experience, and for the development of new projects. These are centered around several discussion lists and the communication environment of ATHEMOO. The virtual space of ATHEMOO was designed by Dr Juli Burk, Associate Professor of Theater at the University of Hawaii, in June 1995. It provides theater people with the possibility of synchronous meetings.

A play can be performed using the Internet in various ways. It is not absolutely necessary to create a whole new space in the Internet to perform a play. A stage can be situated in some ot the already existing rooms, the online meeting places. Performances took place as early as 1993 in the text-based environments IRC and later in the MOO (Multi User Dimension Object Oriented). Furthermore there are experiments with the more colorful surroundings of the two-dimensional chat place *Palace,* and with the use CU-SeeMe videoconferencing software, which includes real-time video and audio.

Collective Collaboration

In the theatrical production of oudeis – a world wide odyssey the collaborative creative work, the traditional working method of the Fringe, was enlarged to the level of a world-

Tradition

Das experimentelle und alternative Theater des 20. Jahrhunderts fordert in Bau, Textwahl und Aufführungspraxis einen Bruch mit den Theatertraditionen. Weil die dramatische Handlung in den traditionellen Bühnen *zum Sklaven des Bühnenrahmens und des prospektivischen Blickwinkels gemacht wird*, muß jene Art von Bühnenbau aufgehoben werden, schreibt Enrico Prampolini schon 1924 in *Die futuristische Bühnenatmosphäre*.

In den 60er Jahren beginnen die Künstler des *freien Theaters* die Theaterhäuser zu verlassen, neue Schauplätze zu suchen und das Publikum verstärkt in das Geschehen einzubeziehen. Vor allem um *das Ausprobieren neuer Techniken, neuer Produktionsweisen – darum geht es allen Gruppen, die zum 'Fringe Theatre' gehören*, betont der Londoner Regisseur und Schauspieler Pip Simmons im Programmheft Theater der Nationen, 1979. In der Forderung, den Entwicklungen einer modernen Theaterkunst gerecht zu werden, wurden so abseits der etablierten Bühnen bereits früh neue Medien wie Film, Photographie, Video oder Fernsehen in das Bühnengeschehen einbezogen und nach neuen kreativen Prozessen gesucht. Besonders im *performance art*-Bereich der englischen Fringe-Theater-Bewegung dominieren die visuellen Eindrücke, in den *actor and writer based companies* bedient man sich kollektiver Arbeitsformen und Experimenten mit theatralischen Ausdrucksmitteln.

'The effective combination of live theatre and the Internet is very tricky!' Dan Zellner

Neugefundene Orte und Mittel sind weitgestreut, je nach Inszenierungskonzept werden sowohl ehemalige Kinos, Fabrikshallen und Straßenbahnremisen, aber auch Straßenecken zu einem Platz für Theater umgestaltet. Im Sinne eines offenen Spielraums und der Inkludierung der Neuen Medien ist in den 90er Jahren eine neue Komponente dazugekommen: der elektronische Raum.

Internet

Die Theaterszene im Internet entwickelte sich aus Treffpunkten im Netz, die sich Theatertheoretiker und -künstler geschaffen haben, um Erfahrungen auszutauschen und Projekte zu entwickeln. Zentrum dieser Treffpunkte bilden verschiedene Diskussionslisten

"Here we are, all participating in the gestation of this giant beast known as The Oudeis Project."
L.H. Grant

wide collaboration. Via the medium Internet people from various continents and cultural environments have been drawn together. Starting from a small local group in Vienna, there are now a number of people involved who communicate via e-mail and in online meetings.

Communication has been established via three mailing lists convering the organization, the dramaturgy and the technical aspects. By means of these Listserv mailing lists, information can be exchanged easily among this group of people. In addition to that a synchronous form of communication is necessary for the creativity as well. Regular meetings of the worldwide team take place in the environment of ATHEMOO.

Odyssey

Over 2600 years ago, Homer told the famous story of the wanderings of Odysseus. Many theories have dealt with the metaphor of the places that Odysseus visited before he returned to Ithaca after ten years. As described by Christine Pellech in *Die Odyssey. Eine antike Weltumsegelung* (Reimer, Berlin 1983), his wanderings lead him all across the Seven Seas. Using the description given by Homer (directions, ocean currents, prevailing winds, the time taken) she finds a possible route for this voyage around the world.

Odysseus wants to go home!
Monika Wunderer

Several works now reinterpret Odysseus' journey and its stages in a contemporary way. Artists of our century were also inspired by thoughts of changing distances an the significance of locations, an outstanding example being Walter Grond in his Absolut Home [Droschl, 1996].

Odysseus' journey constitutes an excellent metaphor for illustrating the theory of acceleration, the shrinking of the world to a global village. Instead of traveling along the sea-routes, Odysseus will journey along the lines of the Internet.

ouðeis

The structure of the play is influenced by the form of ancient Greek tragedies. The seven epeisodia, i.e. scenes, are framed by stasima,

und die Kommunikationsumgebung des ATHEMOO. Der virtuelle Raum des ATHEMOO wurde an der Universität von Hawaii in Manoa im Juni 1995 von Dr. Juli Burk erstellt und bietet seitdem Theaterschaffenden die Möglichkeit zu synchronen Treffen.

Ein Stück kann unter Verwendung des Internet auf verschiedenste Arten und Weisen aufgeführt werden. Es ist nicht zwingend notwendig, dafür einen vollkommen neuen Ort im Internet zu schaffen. Bühnen können in schon bestehenden Räumen, den Online-Meeting-Places, errichtet werden. Vorstellungen fanden bereits 1993 in den text-basierten Umgebungen IRC [Internet Relay Chat] und später in MOOs [Multi User Dimension Object Oriented] statt. Des weiteren gab es Experimente mit der etwas *bunteren* Umgebung *Palace*, einem zweidimensionalen Chat-Place, und unter Verwendung von CU-SeeMe-Videoconferencing-Software, die Video und Audio in Echtzeit bietet.

Kollektive Kollaboration

In der Produktion von *oudeis – a world wide odyssey* wurde die kreative Zusammenarbeit, eine in der Fringe-Tradition stehende Arbeitsweise, zu einer weltweiten Kollaboration erweitert. Mitarbeiter von verschiedensten Kontinenten und kulturellen Umfeldern fanden sich mittels des Mediums Internet zusammen. Ausgehend von einer lokalen Gruppe in Wien vergrößerte sich das Team zu einer stattlichen Anzahl von Partnern in der ganzen Welt, die über E-mail und Online-Treffen kommunizieren.

"Big tnx for these amazing thoughts. From the technical point of view: Everything is possible, it's just a question of money, time and bandwidth."
Rainer Fügenstein

Die Kommunikation wird über drei Mailinglisten, die sich mit der Organisation, der Dramaturgie und der technischen Seite befassen, geführt. Diese Listserv-Mailinglisten ermöglichen selbst in einer so großen Gruppe einen zielgerechten Informationsfluß. Als Zusatz hierzu wird jedoch auch eine synchrone Kommunikationsform für die kreative Arbeit benötigt. Im erwähnten ATHEMOO finden regelmäßige Treffen des weltweiten Teams statt.

Odyssee

Vor mehr als 2600 Jahren verfaßte Homer das Epos über die Irrfahrten des Odysseus.

the songs of the choros. Each epeisodion stages one of the ordeals Odysseus has to undergo on the different stages of his journey. Odysseus travels to the island of the Cyclops where he meets the cruel Polyphemus, the island of Aeolus, lord of the winds, the island of Aeaea, home of beautiful Circe, and even arrives in Hades, staying for some years on Ortygia, the island of Calypso, before he returns to his faithful Penelope in Ithaca.

Each actor will speak in his mother tongue.

The interaction between the stages in different parts of the world will take place in multilingual dialogues. The stasima between the scenes are sung in Greek. Odysseus is traveling virtually from stage to stage, from city to city, from venue to venue. In each epeisodion another audience in another country can see a real actor playing Odysseus. This actor is represented by a light cone on the other stages.

the world does NOT speak in English ... I think there are more than a hundred live languages in it ... that's what 'world-wide' would mean to me!
Santiago Pereson

People on every stage, on every location, will be able to watch the performance at the same time. They will see real actors interact with virtual ones, hearing the words of Homer.

Choros

being physically present at one of the theaters it will be possible to access the performance via Internet. This gives the opportunity not only to see the action on stage but also take an active part in the performance.

Stasima, parts sung by the choros, will be seen and heard between the epeisodia. The choros in the tragedy represented the people. In oudeis the choros will represent the audience which follows the play on their computer screens, a special opportunity for this audience to interact and comment on the play

**music is dressed s*
Santiago Pereson

Sounds of voices singing a capella in Greek, composed by an international ensemble led by Santiago Pereson, will be produced by instructions sent by the virtual audience during the play. A loudspeaker system will broadcast this sound on every stage. The sum of these voices will sound like a chorus, each voice being triggered by someone over the net.

Viele Theoretiker beschäftigten sich mit den Metaphern der Orte, die Odysseus in den zehn Jahren vor seiner Rückkehr nach Ithaka besuchte. Christine Pellech beschrieb in *Die Odyssey. Eine antike Weltumsegelung* [Reimer, Berlin 1983], daß ihn seine Wanderungen über die sieben Weltmeere führten. Unter der Verwendung der von Homer verfertigten Beschreibungen [Himmelsrichtungen, See- und Windströmungen, Reisedauer ...] skizziert sie eine mögliche Route seiner Weltumsegelung.

Odysseus' Reise und ihre Stationen werden in verschiedensten Werken auf eine zeitgenössische Art interpretiert. Künstler unseres Jahrhunderts wurden auch vom Gedanken der sich ändernden Distanzen und Bedeutsamkeit der Orte beeinflußt. Ein uns inspirierendes Beispiel dafür ist Walter Grond und sein *Absolut Homer* [Droschl, 1996].

Die Reise des Odysseus bietet eine exzellente Metapher, um die Theorie der Beschleunigung und die Enträumlichung der Welt zu einem globalen Dorf zu beleuchten. Anstatt entlang der Seewege wird Odysseus entlang der Leitungen des Internet reisen.

oudeis

Die Struktur des Stücks ist von der Form der antiken griechischen Tragödie beeinflußt. Die sieben Epeisodia, i. e. die Szenen, sind von den Stasima umgeben, den Gesängen des Choros. Jedes Epeisodion bringt eines der Ereignisse, die Odysseus an den verschiedenen Stationen seiner Reise zu durchleben hat, auf die Bühne. Nach Homer besucht Odysseus die Insel der Kyklopen, wo er auf den grausamen Polyphem trifft, die Insel von Aiolos, dem Gott der Winde, die Insel Aiaia, die Heimat der schönen Kirke, selbst in den Hades steigt er hinab, bevor er einige Jahre auf Ogyia bei Kalypso ruht, um dann nach Ithaka zu Penelope heimkehren zu können.

Jeder Schauspieler wird seine Muttersprache verwenden. Die Interaktion zwischen den Bühnen an den verschiedenen Orten der Welt wird in multilingualen Dialogen stattfinden. Die Stasima zwischen den Szenen werden in Griechisch gesungen. Odysseus reist virtuell von Bühne zu Bühne, von Stadt zu Stadt, von Aufführungsort zu Aufführungsort. In jedem

I would worry if there is no concentration on the audience, for without an audience is there really a performance?
Nina LeNoir

"how do you show a real actor making love with a virtual actor or even more problematic, a virtual actor making love with another virtual actor?"
L.H. Grant

Prototype

The worldwide opening of the global theater performance of oudeis – a worldwide odyssey will take place in 1998. The complex idea and its realization leave a number of questions unanswered. A prototype of the stage and performing concept is intended to answer some of these and pose others. Furthermore the different levels of development of the worldwide partners will be aligned. In a real-life meeting of the participants, some of whom only know each other virtually, at this year's Ars Electronica, further perspectives of the project will be worked out.

The worldWorking arrangements on two scenes, which will be shown as open rehearsals on two stages, will examine and explore the interaction between real and virtual actors. The transmission setups and the inclusion of active participation via the World Wide Web will also be tested.

One hour

Theater is created in the temporal and spatial unity of a role being acted out and the observance of this performance. It is oudeis' aim to reach this oneness by transcending geographical frontiers.

The interaction between the stages and its visualization will take place in real-time, the late night show on one continent will therefore be seen as a matinee on another. Time zones and the duration and rapidity of transmission are included as additional elements in the direction.

Progress

The lightcones will be animated by an idea revolutionary to theater. It will be one of the first times that what an actor really feels while performing is shown. Acting never shows the real emotions of an actor but the emotions of the character he or she is playing. Assuming that the actors playing Odysseus and his companions do not really fear for their lives while together with cruel Polyphemus on stage, the audience are never able to see what the actors are really concentratiing on at any one particular moment.

The use of special sensor devices that the actors are carrying will show these normally hidden emotions. The data gathered from

Epeisodion kann ein anderes Publikum eines anderen Landes einen Schauspieler des Odysseus sehen. Dieser Schauspieler wird auf den anderen Bühnen als Lichtkegel repräsentiert.

Choros

Zusätzlich zur körperlichen Anwesenheit in einem der Theaterhäuser wird es die Möglichkeit geben, die Aufführung im World Wide Web zu verfolgen. Das wiederum ermöglicht eine aktivere Teilnahme am Bühnengeschehen. Zwischen den Epeisodia werden die Stasima, die Gesänge des Choros, zu sehen und zu hören sein. In der Tragödie stand der Choros für das Volk. In *oudeis* wird er die Stimmung des Cyberpublikums wiedergeben. Das auf diese Weise mit dem Stück interaktiv verbundene Publikum hat die Möglichkeit, die Handlung zu kommentieren.

Der Klang von griechischen A-cappella-Gesängen, die von einer internationalen Gruppe um Santiago Pereson komponiert werden, wird durch Anweisungen ausgelöst werden, die die virtuellen Zuschauer während des Stückes senden. Eine Lautsprecheranlage wird diese Musik auf allen Bühnen reproduzieren. Die Summe dieser Stimmen wird den Chor bilden, und jede Stimme wird von jemandem aus dem Netz hervorgerufen werden.

Prototyp

TwylaM-S says, "I really think that it is. It's slated for next spring, I think." SantiagoP says "autumn here..." Talk at ATHEMOO

Die weltweite Premiere der globalen Theateraufführung von *oudeis – a world wide odyssey* wird 1998 stattfinden. Die Komplexität der Idee und ihrer Realisierung läßt im Diskurs viele Fragen unbeantwortet. Ein Prototyp des Bühnen- und Aufführungskonzepts soll einige dieser Fragen beantworten – und neue stellen. Weiters werden die unterschiedlichen Entwicklungsstufen der weltweiten Partner auf einen gemeinsamen Stand gebracht. Im Zuge eines realen Treffens beim diesjährigen Ars Electronica Festival werden die Teilnehmer, die sich zum Teil nur virtuell kennen, die weiteren Perspektiven des Projekts erarbeiten.

Die Arbeit an zwei Szenen, die in öffentlichen Proben auf zwei Bühnen dargestellt werden, untersucht die Möglichkeiten der Interaktion zwischen realen und virtuellen

"i think virtual actors should not be light cones but virtual actors. more than a beam of light should be within them."
Santiago Pereson

these sensors is transformed into light data pertaining to the color and intensity of light. The positions of the actors are scanned via the lighting system of the stages. All this information is transported via the Internet to the other stages and produces the virtual actors there. Of course the performance will look different each evening, because the virtual actors, as a visualization of the real actors, are real living and feeling human beings, and not previously programmed light variations.

Documentation

To document the ongoing process in the collaborative work of the oudeis team, in addition to the information contained in the hypermail archives of the discussion lists, a monthly newspaper called Status Quo was established in summer 1996. It is available via World Wide Weg where it can also be downloaded as a printable version. Since its first edition it has been growing steadily and now documents not only the development of the oudeis project but also presents other projects currently being staged with the use of the Internet all around the world.

Routing

In 1998 the map of Odysseus' world voyage will be redrawn to a world tour appropriate for the 20th century, following possible routes of a data packet through the Net. From Europe Odysseus goes to Illinois, south to Argentina and Brazil, around the globe to Australia and north again to Asia. The eighth stage is the stage found in the World Wide Web, accessible by every computer all around the world that is hooked up to the Internet.

ouðeis – a worldwide odyssey will be seen on seven stages all around the world. On every stage a real actor will not only perform but will interact with his virtual counterparts on the stages that are combined by the lines of the Internet. Besides watching this performance in one of the theaters worldwide it will be possible to access the performance via Internet and take an active part in the performance.

"Long live Oudeis!"
L.H. Grant

Darstellern. Geprüft werden auch die Übertragungsmöglichkeiten sowie die Inkludierung der aktiven Teilnahme im World Wide Web.

One hour

In der zeit-räumlichen Einheit von Rollenspiel und Zuschauen entsteht Theater. Oudeis hat sich zum Ziel gesetzt, diese Einheit durch die Aufhebung der geographischen Grenzen zu erreichen.

Die Interaktion zwischen den Bühnen und die Visualisierung wird in Echtzeit stattfinden, die Abendvorstellung des einen Kontinents wird als Matinee des anderen zu sehen sein. Zeitzonen, Übertragungsdauer und Schnelligkeit werden als zusätzliche Parameter in das Inszenierungskonzept einbezogen.

Progreß

Die Lichtkegel werden von einer für das Theater revolutionären Idee belebt. Es wird eines der ersten Male sein, daß gezeigt wird, was ein Schauspieler wirklich fühlt, während er oder sie spielt. Das Schauspiel zeigt niemals die wirklichen Emotionen des Darstellers, sondern die Gefühle des dargestellten Charakters. Unter der Annahme, daß die Darsteller des Odysseus und seiner Gefährten nicht wirklich um ihr Leben bangen, während sie sich mit dem grausamen Polyphem gemeinsam auf der Bühne befinden, kann der Zuseher niemals erkennen, worauf sich die Schauspieler in diesem Moment tatsächlich konzentrieren.

Dank einer speziellen Sensortechnik, die an den Schauspielern verwendet wird, können diese normalerweise versteckten Emotionen gezeigt werden. Die von diesen Sensoren aufgenommenen Daten werden in Information über Farbe und Intensität des Lichtkegels umgewandelt. Die Positionen der Schauspieler werden von den Lichtsystemen der Bühnen erfaßt. Diese Information wird in ihrer Gesamtheit über das Internet zu den anderen Bühnen transportiert und produziert dort die virtuellen Schauspieler. Dadurch ist gesichert, daß jede Aufführung einzigartig ist, denn die virtuellen Schauspieler als Visualisierung der realen Schauspieler werden echte, lebende und fühlende Menschen und nicht vorprogrammierte Lichtvariationen sein.

"Die Odyssey ist episch angelegt, dehnt sich über Jahre aus und wird beschleunigt zu einer Stunde."
Gernot Lechner

Dokumentation

Als Work-in-Progress existiert dieses Projekt bereits in der laufenden Diskussion, in der Arbeit an seiner Entwicklung und der Reflektion der Kunst- und Theaterszene.

Um diesen Entwicklungsprozeß in der kollektiven Arbeit des oudeis-Teams über den Inhalt der Hypermail-Archive der Diskussionslisten hinausgehend zu dokumentieren, wurde im Sommer 1996 die monatliche Zeitschrift *Status Quo* gegründet, die über das World Wide Web abrufbar und dort auch als druckbare Version verfügbar ist. Seit ihrer ersten Ausgabe war sie in ständigem Wachsen begriffen und dokumentiert mittlerweile nicht nur die Weiterentwicklung des ouδeis-Projektes, sondern präsentiert auch andere Projekte, die zur Zeit im Internet aufgeführt werden.

Routing

Im Jahr 1998 wird die Karte von Odysseus' Weltreise neu gezeichnet werden, um eine für das 20. Jahrhundert passende Reiseroute zu zeigen, den möglichen Routen des Datenpakets durch das Netz folgend.

Von Europa reist Odysseus nach Illinois, südwärts nach Argentinien und Brasilien, um die Südhalbkugel nach Australien, und von dort wieder nordwärts nach Asien. Die achte Bühne ist im World Wide Web zu finden, wo sie über jeden Computer, der Zugang zum Internet hat, erreichbar ist.

"The need of having an interaction between the stages is that we should think of the world as one big stage."
Monika Wunderer

ouδeis – a world wide odyssey wird auf sieben über die ganze Welt verteilten Bühnen zu sehen sein. Auf jeder Bühne wird ein realer Schauspieler nicht nur spielen, sondern mit seinen virtuellen Gegenspielern, den realen Schauspielern der anderen Bühnen, über die Leitungen des Internet interagieren. Über die Teilnahme an der Aufführung in einem der Theater hinaus wird es die Möglichkeit geben, ihr über das Internet beizuwohnen und so darin eine aktive Rolle zu übernehmen.

Biographies/Biografien

Ampcom [Merja Puustinen & Andy Best, SF], has realized several environmental art projects such as *Suburbarama Honeymoon*, interactive installations such as *DAD@Destroy All Dreams*, and telematic performances.

Konrad Becker [A] is hyperreality researcher/developer and interdisciplinary event designer. He is chairman of the tø/Institute for New Culture-Technologies [Public Netbase; Brain. Vader], the Institut für Wissenschaftliche Sensation and Public Tranceport Systems.
He is a founding member of Monoton and other groups, provider of electronic underground music and psycho-acoustics since 1979. Presentations and publications include text, video, music, installations and environments focussing on subjective science and cultural synthesis.

Maurice Benayoun [F] 1957, research projects in the fields of multimedia, special effects, the contribution of new technologies to audio-visual production and interactivity. Since 1987 he has been the artistic director of Z.A. Production. Since 1984, he is Professor at the University of Paris 1 [Panthéon-Sorbonne] et *Artiste Invité* at the École Nationale Supérieure des Beaux Arts de Paris.

Erich Berger [A] technician, musician, artist

Beusch/Cassani, 1963/66, have lived in Paris sind 1991. They are responsible for a few of the most remarkable multimedia projects of recent years. What emerged from this collaboration with European radio stations, museums and festivals has been interpreted by some as a refreshing parallel narrative to the communications-media, while others have seen it as off-beat mediatainment or the playful re-encoding of the clichés of video culture. This inherent dynamism generated by means of a media fiction, the mixture of sound, text and image, and the central position occupied by interaction with users are also in evidence in the Internetproject SOS RADIO TNC.
Beusch/Cassani see themselves as two pixels whose power of illumination is constantly infolding in new constellations.

The BILWET Agency [NL] founded in 1983 in Amsterdam, is engaged in promoting Illegal Science through travels, lectures and taking walks. It is currently involved in Dutch landscape painting, work simulation, *The Family of Man, Insanity of Cities, the Question of Confusion, IKEA for All.* Publications in German: *Bewegungslehre* [1991], *Medien-Archiv* [1993], *Datendandy* [1994] and *Elektronische Einsamkeit* [1997].[i.e. *Theory of Movement*, *Media Archive*, *Data Dandy*, and *Electronic Solitude*].

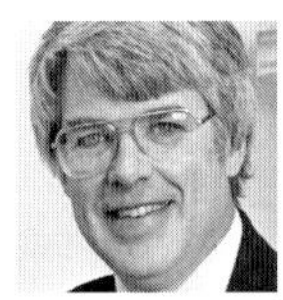

Robert R. Birge [USA] is professor of chemistry and director of the W.M. Keck Center for Molecular Electronics, and research director of the New York State Center for Advanced Technology in Computer Applications and Software Engineering at Syracuse University. He also holds joint appointments in the departments of Biology, Physics and Electrical Engineering. His research interests include the application of nonlinear laser spectroscopy and quantum theory to the study of light-transducing proteins as well as the development of protein based molecular electronic devices and hybrid computers. He is associate editor of *Bio-Spectroscopy* and has co-chaired advisory panels for the National Institutes of Health and the National Academy of Sciences.

Isabella Bordoni [I], 1962, Poet, theatre director, performer. Co-founder in 1985 of Giardini Pensili [theatre company and media lab]. She presents her texts [poetry and fiction] in theatre pieces, concerts and in telematic and network projects. She wrote several hoerspiele – mostly performed live – produced by SFB, YLE, RNE, ORF and RAI and she made the media radio a powerful and flexible total machine. In 1987 she was Artist-in-Residence at the Djerassi Foundation, San Francisco.

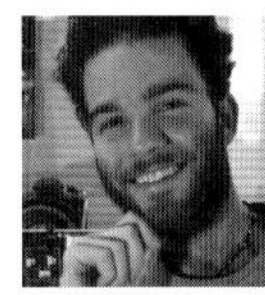

Scott Brave [USA] graduated from Stanford University in 1995 with a BS in Computer Systems Engineering. Over the past two years, Scott has also worked extensively with Immersion Corporation to develop new applications for haptics technology, including a system to allow people with neuromotor disabilities to interface with computers.
He is currently working with Prof. Hiroshi Ishii in the Tangible Media Group at the MIT Media Lab and is focusing on the application of haptics to interpersonal communication.

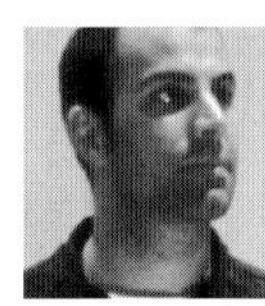

John Canny [USA] is a Professor in the Computer Science Division at the University of California, Berkeley, which he joined in August 1987. He received the ACM Doctoral Dissertation Award [best thesis in computer science] in 1987. His thesis dealt with robotic motion planning and described a universal and optimal algorithm for a large class of planning problems. He shared the Machtey award in 1987 for best student paper at the IEEE FOCS [Foundations of Computer Science] conference. He was one of the first 20 recipients of a Packard Foundation Fellowship in 1988. In 1989 he became an NSF Presidential Young Investigator.

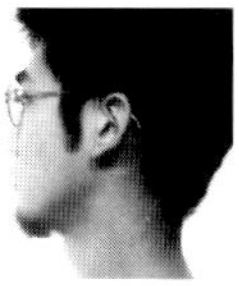

Motoshi Chikamori [J], 1971, Tokyo. 1991-95 study of Environmental Information at Keio University. 1995 study at University of Tsukuba, Plastic Arts and Mixed Media Dept.

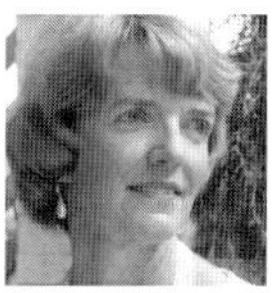

Patricia Smith Churchland [USA] is a Professor of Philosophy at the University of California, San Diego [1984-]. She is also an Adjunct Professor, The Salk Institute for Biological Studies [1989-]. Churchland has been the recipient of a MacArthur Foundation Research Fellow [1991] and National Science Foundation Research Grant [1987-89]; she was the President of the American Philosophical Association [Pacific/1992-93] and President of the Society for Philosophy and Psychology [1984-85]; and on the board of governors of the Philosophy of Science Association [1985-87]. Churchland is the author of three books, including *The Computational Brain* [MIT Press, 1992] and *Neuroscience: Toward a Unified Science of the Mind-Brain* [MIT Press, 1986].

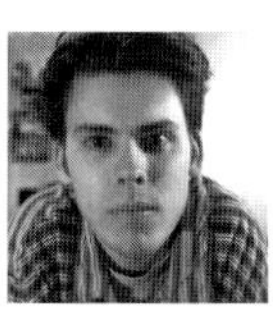

Andrew Dahley [USA]is a product designer in Professor Hiroshi Ishii's Tangible Media Group at the MIT Media Laboratory. He designed a furniture system for cooperative learning classrooms, which won the Design Distinction award in the annual design review of *I.D. magazine*, July 1995. At the MIT Media Lab, he has been exploring ways to manipulate and interact with bits by coupling them with objects and environments of the physical world.

John Coate [USA] has been in the online networking business for more than eleven years. He is now the General Manager of the SF Gate [www.sfgate.com], the most popular regional news website in America. For six years he was Conferencing Manager for *The WELL* where he helped establish the concept of the "virtual community," as depicted in the May 1997 cover story of *WIRED* Magazine. He is the author of the seminal essay *Cyberspace Innkeeping: Building Online Community* and has lectured at Stanford, MIT and at numerous events relating to multimedia and the Internet.

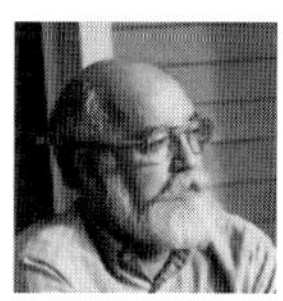

Daniel C. Dennett [USA] is Distinguished Arts and Sciences Professor, Professor of Philosophy, and Director of the Center for Cognitive Studies at Tufts University. His first book, *Content and Consciousness*, appeared in 1969, followed by *Brainstorms* [1978], *Elbow Room* [1984], *The Intentional Stance* [1987], *Consciousness Explained* [1991], *Darwin's Dangerous Idea* [1995], and *Kinds of Minds* [1996]. He co-edited *The Mind's I* with Douglas Hofstadter in 1981. His next book, *Brainchildren: A Collection of Essays 1984-1996* [MIT Press], is forthcoming in 1997.

Chris Dodge [USA], 1969, graduated with honors from New York University, 1991, BA Film/Video, Music Composition, and Computer Science. Master of Science candidate and researcher of Media Art and Technology, Media Lab, MIT, 1995-97. Artist-in-Residence at Zentrum für Kunst und Medientechnologie [ZKM], Karlsruhe, Germany, 1995-1997. Exhibitor in the MultiMediale 4 festival at the ZKM, May 1995. Interactive Computer Graphics designer for the *Brain Opera*, created by Tod Machover of the Media Laboratory, 1996-97. Invited exhibitor and speaker at the WRO97 Biennial Media Art Festival, May 1997. Finalist exhibitor at the ARTEC97 Biennial Media Art Festival, May 1997.

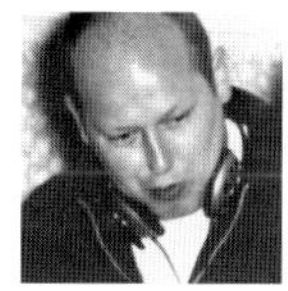

Wolfgang Dorninger [A], 1960, attended the Institute for Applied Arts in Vienna where he completed the Master Program for Visual Media Design. He is also a musician, playing in the groups Monochrome Bleu, Josef K. Noyce and Wipe Out. Dorninger has composed numerous musical works for film, theater and dance. He operates the Sonic Sound Studio in Linz.

Dumb Type, founded by graduates of the Kyoto City Art College in Japan in 1984, is a pluridisciplinary collective of architects, sound engineers, video artists, dancers, musicians and computer scientists. Their projects defy any categorization and break open the bounds of theatre, video installation and graphic art.

Christoph Ebener [D], 1967, objects and installations: *security technologies, repair systems, products for a better world, blond girls, no fear.*

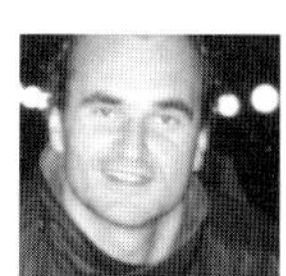

Joachim Eckl [A] 1962, 1981/88 Studies of psychology at Salzburg University. 1988/89 Center for Child Development Research/N.Y. Image maker, performance and installation projects: *Brecht/Clay/Freud, Dear Me, Homo Erectus, Bodies and Brains* ... Foundation of the artist group "The Only One". 1992 foundation of the production unit MAKE for develop-

ment and implementation of projects in the public space. 1997 Artist-in-Residence project at the Ars Electronica Center.

Arthur Elsenaar [NL] spent most of his youth building ultra-high frequency radio and television transmitters that were used illegally by several hundred pirate stations throughout the Netherlands. In the early nineties he studied Cultural Engineering at the Fine Art Academy Minerva in Groningen.

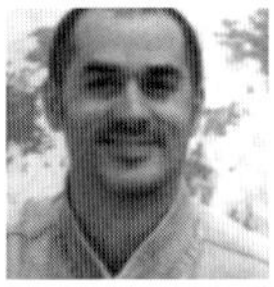

Leonid Filatov [USA], 1958. At the beginning I learned to understand how the things that surround me work. He completed a masters degree in interactive telecommunications at Tish School of Arts. In 1996 I founded *Interuptive Media* [IM] production and developed *Electronic Street Art*. *Laterna Magica 96* started the series of projects that explore this concept.

Franz Fischnaller [I] studied art and design in Germany, Italy and USA. He works in the art and design fields and parallel to it he has undertaken the development of design+art+technology, that will permit new possibilities for the integration of art and technology and confront the reality of *Man&art-Machine&art-interface&art*. He has been involved in art+design+technology, in both theory and practice.

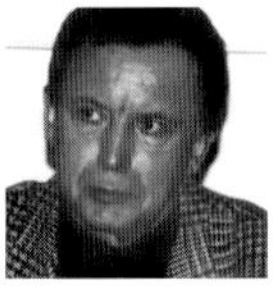

Peter Fleissner, 1944. Studied telecommunications, economics, econometrics, social cybernetics, philosophy; 1971 doctorate in mathematics; 1973-1990 Institute of Socio-Economic Development Research and Technology Evaluation of the Austrian Academy of Sciences; 1974-1982 International Institute for Applied Systems Analysis; 1981 postdoctoral thesis in econometric social cybernetics; 1987 Scholar at MIT under Jay Forrester; research projects in Austria, USA, FRG, GDR, Slovakia, Bulgaria, Poland and Vietnam; 1990-1997 o. Univ.-Prof. for representation and effect research, information technology at Vienna University of Technology; from August 1997 head of the department *Technology, employment and competition* of the EU Institute for Technological Future Research [IPTS] in Seville.

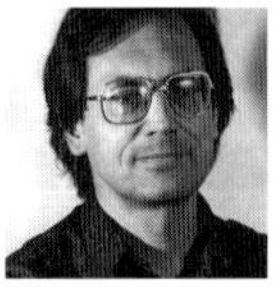

Peter Fromherz [D] 1942, 1969 Dr.rer.nat. [physical chemistry], University of Marburg, 1981, Professor of experimental physics [biophysics], University of Ulm, 1994 Director of Max-Planck-Institut of biochemistry [section membrane and neuro-physics].

Patricia Futterer [A], media theorist and artist.

Paul Garrin [USA] works as a media artist and has been collaborating with Nam June Paik for a long time. His documentation of the *Tompkins Square Riot* 1988 in New York City is known as the spark which ignited the *camcorder revolution*. He has been Artist-in-Residence at the Berlin Videofest in 1990 and has been awarded several highly recognized prizes.

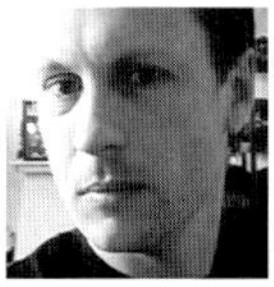

Andrew Garton [AUS] composer, performer, Internet artist. He has an extensive background in experimental electronic composition, the performing and digital arts. He has a strong interest in public communications, spending a considerable portion of the past seven years working on public access computer network projects in Australia, Southeast Asia and Indochina. His current work explores the reclamation of public space via generative sound-scapes and the Internet as theatre of suspended space.

Guillermo Gòmez-Peña [MEX], is an interdisciplinary artist and writer known for his innovative use of performance, journalism, video, radio and installation art to explore cross-cultural issues. He draws on his Latino background to brigde cultural borders with the use of high technology.

Thyrza Nichols Goodeve [USA], is Senior Instructor at the Whitney Museum Independent Study Program in New York City. Her interviews and essays have appeared in *Artforum*, *Parkett*, and *Art in America*.

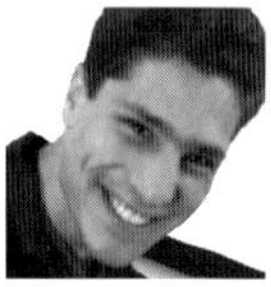

Matt Gorbet [USA], 1973, is a graduate student at the MIT Media Laboratory. In his research with Professor Hiroshi Ishii's Tangible Media Group, he is developing dual-identity objects – physical objects capable of embodying and manipulating data. Before joining Ishii's group, he collaborated on many other Media Lab projects, including an instant holographic portrait system and Tod Machover's 1996 *Brain Opera* project, for which he created a 3D music game called *Harmonic Driving*. He has also been involved in hardware and software projects for NYNEX and SGI, and has a diverse background in interactive art, graphic design, video and sculpture.

Heidi Grundmann [A]
In 1987, after working for many years as a cultural journalist, critic, editor and producer at the ORF [Austrian Broadcasting Corporation], she founded the weekly radio program KUNST-RADIO-RADIOKUNST. It consists of original works for radio by artists of all disciplines. Heidi Grundmann also lectures and writes on art and new media and has organized and curated many symposia and exhibitions related to art practice in the electronic media, especially around radio and TV. She is chairperson of Ars Acustica International, the EBU experts group of radio art, and founding member and president of TRANSIT – a non-for-profit association for the production fo cultural projects in the public space of the electronic media.

Kazuhiko Hachiya [J], 1966 graduated from Kyushu Institute of Design [Visual Communication Design].
He has had several exhibitions in Japan. Lives and works in Tokyo.

Donna Haraway [USA], is the author of *Primate Visions: Gender, Race and Nature in the World of Modern Science; Simians, Cyborgs and Women: The Reinvention of Nature,* and *Crystals, Fabrics and Fields: Metaphors of Organicism in 20th-Century Developmental Biology.* She teaches science studies, feminist theory, and woman's studies at the University of California, Santa Cruz.

Huge Harry [01] is a commercially available voice synthesis machine, designed at the MIT Speech Laboratory. Currently, he works as a researcher and a spokes-machine at the Institute of Artificial Art in Amsterdam. He has also performed as a singer. Recently, Huge Harry has also started to work as a political activist, trying to achieve equal rights for computers.

Wolfgang Hilbert [A] 1969, graduate of the Department for Advanced Studies in Electronic Data Processing and Organization, Vienna. Since 1992, student at the Institute of Applied Arts in Vienna, design of visual media, Prof. Peter Weibel.

Rupert Huber [A], 1967, composer, musician. Collaboration with Sam Auinger [*Berliner Theorie*, 1997], Richard Dorfmeister [*Tosca*, 1994-97], Giardini Pensili [*Trance Bakxai*, 1997]. Compositions for radio, stage, Internet [*Darb-i Fetih*,1996], Guest of DAAD artist programme 1997 [*Berliner Theorie*]. In many years of collaboration with ORF KUNSTRADIO he created the documentary CDs *Zeitgleich* and *Horizontal Radio* and works for KUNSTRADIO ONLINE [*Familie Auer, applause*].

Kathy Rae Huffman [USA] is a freelance curator, writer and networker. Since 1991 Huffman has been based in Europe, where she lectures extensively on Internet art, art video, interactive TV, and the history of artists and TV. She is a correspondent for *Telepolis* online magazine [Heise Verlag], for the column *pop~TARTS*, and contributes to *Rhizome*, the journal for net culture. Together with Eva Wohlgemuth, Huffman realizes Internet communication works.

José Iges [E], 1951, is an Industrial Engineer, musical composer and performer in "live electronic". He starts on the electroacoustic music at the ALEA Laboratory in Madrid. He has been member of the Art and Computer Science Seminary and of the Madrid's group ELENFANTE. Within 1988 and 1989 he has made several "Sound Spaces", integrated with "Visual Installations" of the artist Concha Jerez. With the co-authorship of Concha Jerez, he has been making a series of projects called "Media Interferences".

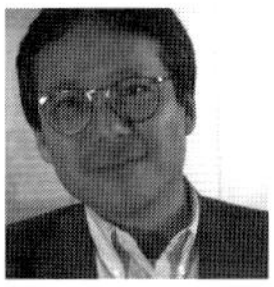

Hiroshi Ishii [J]
His focus is on media design to augment interactions between humans, computers, and the physical environment. He has done extensive research on Computer-Supported Co-operative Work [CSCW] and Human-Computer Interaction [HCI]. His team at NTT Human Interface Laboratories invented TeamWorkStation and *ClearBoard*. He has been active in the ACM SIGCHI community. At the MIT Media Lab, he directs the Tangible Media Group.

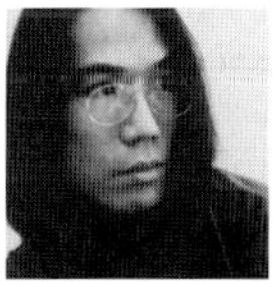

Toshio Iwai [J], 1962, is an interactive artist and graduated from the Tsukuba University. He has had several solo exhibitions worldwide and two of his pieces are permanently displayed at the San Francisco Exploratorium. He has been Artist-in-Residence at ZKM/Karlsruhe and is currently Artist-in Residence at IAMAS.

Hiroo Iwata [J], 1957, MS and PhD in engineering from the University of Tokyo. He is an Associate Professor at the Institute of Engineering Mechanics at the University of Tsukuba where he teaches human interface and conducts research projects on Virtual Reality. He is active in research on haptic interface in virtual environments. He has developed various force displays and applied them to 3D shape modelling and scientific visualization.

Concha Jerez [E], 1941, is an intermedia artist. She has made individual works in a continuous way since 1973 till now in Spain, Germany, France, Italy, Austria, England etc. Since 1976, her art work centers on the

development of the concept of installation, as an in situ work, on large concrete spaces. During 1988 and 1989 she has made several *Visual Installations* integrated with the *Sound Spaces* of the musical composer José Iges. With the co-authorship of José Iges, she has been making a series of projects called *Media Interferences*. Since 1991 she is Associated Professor of the Facultad de Bellas Artes of the University of Salamanca.

Hari Kunzru [USA] is associate editor of *Wired* UK.

Machiko Kusahara [J] studied mathematics and history of science at Tokyo's International Christian University and is an Associate Professor of Media Art at the Faculty of Arts, Tokyo Institute of Polytechnics. She has been teaching computer graphics theory and media since 1986 and has published several books on computer graphics and A-Life. She is a member of the ACM/SIGGRAPH, Information Processing Society of Japan, Japan Society of Image Arts and Science, NICOGRAPH, 3D FORUM and A-Life Network of Japan. Her recent research has been centered around the transition of the nature of artistic creativity in interactive art, specially in relation to the concept of networking and A-Life.

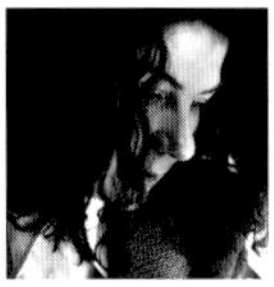

Cécile Le Prado [F], 1956. Composer. Le Prado studied music and electroacoustic composition at the Nantes Conservatory. She has collaborated with various research centers, including particularly INA-GRM and IRCAM, Paris, CICV, Montbéliard, and CIRM, Nice. Her work has focussed especially on the realization of sound installations and compositions for image and choreography.

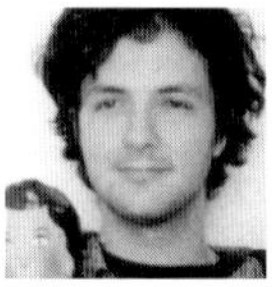

Rafael Lozano-Hemmer is a Mexican-Canadian media artist. Works with teleabsence, installation and performance art. Rather than returning the *Penacho de Montezuma* to Mexico, he would prefer if Austria sent some Habsburg jewels as a romantic cultural exchange and for the Penacho to become an integral part of Austrian identity.

Steve Mann [USA] is a doctoral student at the MIT Media Laboratory where he co-founded the MIT wearable computing project. He currently holds degrees in Physics and Electrical Engineering. Steve is known to many as inventor of the so-called *wearable computer* and *WearCam* [personal imaging system]. His present research includes photometric image-based modeling, pencigraphic imaging, and wearable, tetherless computer-mediated reality. He is also an accomplished artist, having received numerous awards for his work in the interrogative, situationist, and visual arts. Steve currently holds degrees in physics and electrical engineering.

Max More [USA] is editor and co-founder of *Extropy* and President of the Extropy Institute which aims to guide humanity into an unbounded future by encouraging the use of emerging and future technologies to overcome historically unchallenged limits to full human flourishing. He holds a BA in Philosophy, Politics and Economics from Oxford University, an MA in Philosophy from USC and is now writing his PhD in Philosophy at USC.

Knut Mork [N] is an artist and software engineer. His previous works [*sense:less* and *A Single Drop of Blood*] experiment with the construction of synaesthetic experiences.

MUU Artist Association [SF] John Hopkins, Tapio Mäkelä, Terhi Penttilä and Liisa Vähäkylä.

Lars Nilsson [N] is a mathematician and programmer at TeleVR, Norwegian Telecom R&D.

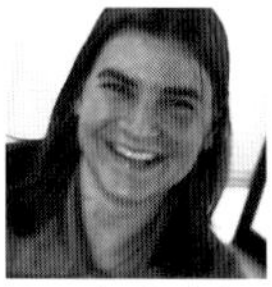

Maggie Orth [USA] is a PhD candidate in technology design at the MIT Media Lab. She began her work there as the Production Director and Designer of Tod Machover's *Brain Opera*. Her research in the design of technology devices integrates the vocabularies of *smart* materials, electronics, and conceptual and formal visual design. Current device design projects include a *magic phone* for Motorola, technology design for the Meteor project, and the Triangles. Other projects include her women's, technology, and fantasy column for *Jane*, magazine, and her *Techne* web-site. She received a MSVis from the Center for Advanced Visual Studies, MIT, in 1993 and a BFA from the Rhode Island School of Design in 1986.

Ouðeis found his companions as early as October 1995 in Vienna. There are now a number of international people involved, communicating and collaborating via email, telephone, in online meetings, Viennese cafes and bureaus. The way things were in May 1997: Director: Gernot Lechner; Production Dramaturgy and Communications: Monika Wunderer; Composition: Santiago Pereson; Adaptation: L. H. Grant and G. Lechner, U. Noe, M.Wunderer, S. Pereson; Costumes: Ulli Noe, Tech-Crew [:] net:lab [Zyka/Bauer/Koger]; Network: Rainer Fügenstein; Logistics: Mayer/Rosenburg / Zellner; Documentation: Georg Leyrer.

Karl Anders Øygard [N] is a programmer at TeleVR, Norwegian Telecom R&D, and leading the 3D development of MPEG 4.

Roberto Paci Dalò [I], 1962, composer/theatre/director/media wizard. Most of his work – under the concept of *dramaturgy of media* – is dedicated to the new communications technologies creating performing arts and telematic live projects produced by European radio stations, museums, festivals. In 1985 he co-founded Giardini Pensili. In 1995 he created RADIO LADA, the online cult web art radio. In 1993-94 he was guest of the Berliner Künstlerprogramm des DAAD. He was also Associate professor at the Department of Scienze della Comunicazione, University of Siena and trustee of the Mediterranean network of the telematic project *Horizontal Radio* [1995]. Since 1991 he has been the artistic director of the radio and media festival LADA/L' Arte dell'Ascolto.

Heimo Ranzenbacher [A], 1958, lives in Graz as journalist, art critic, theorist and artist. Various publications in catalogues and specialized journals; diverse addresses at symposia; diverse art projects, including: *Klang Figur*, interactive sound performance [in collaboration with Werner Jauk], steirischer herbst, Graz 1991; founded TXTD.sign – a studio for aesthetic services, 1993; *Lichtzeichen, Utopie-Kunststraße* installation, Innsbruck 1994; *Sonderartikel Esc*, Graz 1995.

REMOTE C
Rachel Baker [rachel@irational.org] is an artist, secretary and socialite. She is currently in residence as 'Trina Mould' at the Institution Of Rot. Sep 97 [sep97@irational.org] and is a liberator of opposites and embracer of contradiction.
Andreas Broeckmann [abroeck@v2.nl] lives and works in Berlin and Rotterdam. He is a project manager at V2_Organisation.
Vuk Cosic [vuk@ljudmila. org] is an archaeologist, writer, cook, net.artist, and smooth talker. He can be found in Ljubljana, Triest, and many other places when he can get a visa.
Luka Frelih [luka@ljudmila.org] lives in Ljubljana and likes talking to computers. He also likes talking to people, computer networks, microphones, cameras, broadcasting equipment, receivers, recorders, backpacks, mirrors, portable data carriers, the sun and probably to a few other things, too.
Jaanis Garancs [janis@ kkh.se] is a programmer, artist and one of the founders of E-L@b in Riga. He resides in Stockholm.
Joan Heemskerk [jodi@ jodi.org]
Olia Lialina [olia@glasnet.ru] is an experimental film and video critic and curator, director of the Moscow CINE FANTOM film club and a Net artist.
Eric Kluitnberg [eric@media - gn.nl] is a teacher and freelance curator based in Amsterdam.
Diana McCarty [diana@dial. isys.hu] lives and works in Budapest. She is the project coordinator of the Media Research Foundation.
Dirk Paesmans [jodi@jodi.org]
Pit Schultz [pit@icf.de] is a net critic and artist, and the owner of the nettime mailing list. He lives in Berlin and Budapest.
Alexei Shulgin [easylife@ glasnet.ru] is a photographer and net.artist. He lives in Moscow and is the inventor of FORM art.
Rasa Smite [rasa@parks.lv] is an artist and founder of E-L@b in Riga.
Raitis Smits [raitis@parks.lv] is an artist and founder of E-L@b in Riga.

Markus Seidl [A], 1973
Music since 1992. Context/theory since 1994. Lives/works in Linz and surroundings.

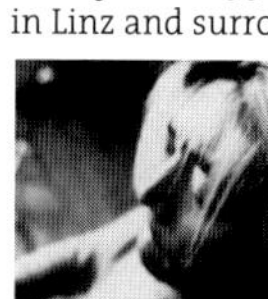

Ruyichi Sakamoto [J] 1952, MFA from the Tokyo National University of Fine Arts. He is an internationally recognized composer, performer and media artist. His musical works for films [Bernardo Bertolucci: *The Last Emperor, The Sheltering Sky, Little Buddha*] have received Grammy, Academy and Golden Globe Awards.

Remko Scha [NL] was trained as a physicist and has worked on Natural Language Processing at Philips Research Labs [Eindhoven, the Netherlands] and BBN Labs [Cambridge, Mass., USA]. Currently, he is head of the Computational Linguistics Department at the University of Amsterdam.

Tom Sherman [CDN] is an artist and theorist. He is best known for his video art and writing about person/machine relationship. In 1981, with his video *Transvideo*, he described and critiqued the *information superhighway* in considerable detail. In 1983 he published *Cultural Engineering*, a comprehensive examination of the conflicts between the individual and state in a democracy held together by electronic media. The same year he founded the Media Arts Section of the Canada Council, Canada's federal agency for support of the arts. Throughout the 90s, Sherman has continued his experiments with voice and image recognition systems.

Roberto Sifuentes [USA] is an interdisciplinary artist whose work examines the perceptions of Chicano and Mexican cultures. He performs his work internationally and collaborates frequently with Guillermo Gòmez-Peña, with whom he created an interactive television special *El Naftazteca: Cyber-Aztec TV for 2000 AD*, which was broadcast in November 1994 to over 6 million homes. His collaborative work with Gòmez-Peña has also yielded the performance art pieces *Borderama* and the *Dangerous Border Game*, as well as the performance/installation *The Temple of Confessions* and *The Mexterminator*.

Flavia Sparacino [I/USA] is a graduate student at the MIT Media Lab. Her main research interest is in combining computer graphics endowed with perceptual intelligence (media creatures), with film/photography, for storytelling in inter-

active performance spaces, web-based worlds, advertisement, and news presentation. Her other interests include sensors, story interfaces, and computer generated music. She received a BS in Electrical Engineering from Politecnico di Milano, a BS in Robotics from Ecole Centrale Paris and an MS in Cognitive Sciences at the Ecole Pratique des Hautes Etudes, Paris, France.

Stadtwerkstatt [A], Linz, an independent cultural society founded in 1979, dedicated to promoting and furthering initiative in the arts. Since its inception, numerous activities in the area of art and culture, with particular concentration upon "art as a public affair," projects and campaigns focused on art in urban spaces. Since 1986, employment of the medium of television as an "artistic tool" and production of STWST-TV live programming. During the last few years, commitment to encouraging public access to electronic media: operation of the Province of Upper Austria's art and culture Internet server [servus.at] and the experimental independent station Radio FRO available in Cable Urfahr.

Station Rose [A/D] was founded in 1988 as an open public multimedia-lab in Vienna, Austria, by visual artist Elisa Rose and composer Gary Danner. Both have performed, have done art shows, fashion shows and concerts since the late seventies, and had obtained their diplomas at "Hochschule für Angewandte Kunst" in 1987. In 1991 they moved to Frankfurt, Germany, where they live a Digital Bohemian Lifestyle ever since. Station Rose sees the roots of their multimedia language in classic culture as well as in pop culture.

Stahl Stenslie [N] is working on cognition and perception manipulative projects within the fields of art, media and network-research. He graduated from the University of Oslo, the Art Academies of Oslo and Duesseldorf, and has a masters degree from the Media Academy of Cologne, Germany.

Stelarc [AUS] has used medical instruments, prosthetics, Virtual Reality systems and the Internet to explore, extend and enhance the body's operational parameters. He has interactively performed with a Third Hand, Robot Manipulaters, a Virtual Arm, a Virtual Body, and a Stomach Sculpture. He has recently developed a touch-screen interfaced Multiple Muscle Stimulation system, enabling remote access, actuation and choreography of the body. Performances such as *Ping Body* and *Parasite* probe notions of telematic scaling and the engineering of extended, external and virtual nervous systems for the body using the Internet.

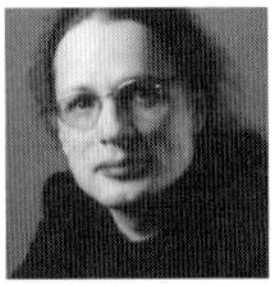

Gerfried Stocker [A] 1964. He is graduate of the Institute for Telecommunication Engineering and Electronics in Graz. Since 1990, he has been working as an independent artist. In 1991, he founded x-space, a team for the realization of interdisciplinary projects. In this framework numerous installations and performance projects have been carried out in the field of interaction, robotics and telecommunications. Stocker was also responsible for the concept of various radio and network projects and the organization of the worldwide radio- and network project *Horizontal Radio*. Since 1995, Gerfried Stocker has been the artistic director of the Ars Electronica Festival and the managing director of the Ars Electronica Center.

Sandy Stone [USA], Assistant Professor in the Radio-TV-Film Department, the University of Texas at Austin; cultural theorist; performance artist; director of the ACTLab; and spiritual leader of the cadre of mad, brilliant cybercrazies who inhabit it. She is teaching film and video production, gender and sexuality; interface and interaction theory. Her research interests is the traffic in the boundaries between art and technology.

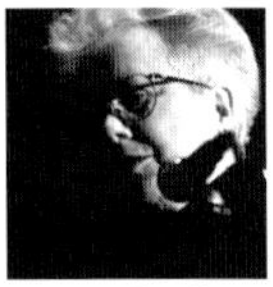

Helen Thorington [USA] is a writer, tape composer and new media artist. Thorington has created numerous soundscores for film and installation. Thorington is the founder and Executive Director of New Radio and Performing Arts, Inc. She is also the originator and producer of the national weekly radio series, "New American Radio" and of the "somewhere" and "Turbulence" websites.

Time's Up [A] founded by Tim Boykett [Australia] and Just Merit [Austria], has its principal locus in the Linz harbour of Austria. Pop science will never satisfactorily explain the reactions of the individual to their dependence upon biomechanics, control, perception and their resulting chain reactions. Together with international specialists [artists, researchers, biomechanics, etc.] Time's Up produces situations that investigate the impact of these three factors upon the individual, choosing a form of situationist research towards artistic ends.

Victoria Vesna [USA] is an installation and performance artist working with electronic technology. Her work has moved from performance and video installations to experimental research that connects networked environments to physical public spaces. Victoria is an Associate Professor at UC Santa Barbara teaching Electronic Intermedia and Computer Image and has been instrumental in fostering an interdisciplinary collaboration between the College of Engineering and Art Studio. Currently, she is one of five

artist fellows in an online PhD program at CAIIA Centre for Advanced Inquiry in Interactive Arts at the University of Wales.

Margaret H. Watson [USA] 1967, Master of Fine Arts degree in Electronic Visualization. She has primarily worked with the CAVE VR system. Working as a Virtual Reality artist, she has exhibited her applications in a number of computer graphics festivals including SIGGRAPH, ISEA and the Ars Electronica Festival.

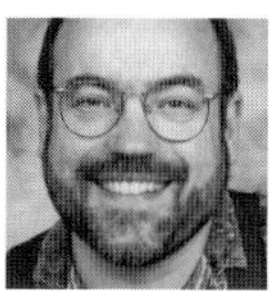

Mark Weiser [USA] is the Chief Technologist at the Xerox Palo Alto Research Center [PARC]. PhD in Computer and Communications Sciences from the University of Michigan [1979]. In 1987 he joined Xerox PARC as member of the technical staff, then heading the Computer Science Laboratory for seven years. His over 75 technical publications are on such areas as the psychology of programming, program slicing, operating systems, programming environments, garbage collection, and technological ethics. Weiser's work since 1988 has been focused on Ubiquitous Computing, a program he initiated that envisions PC's being replaced with invisible computers imbedded in everyday objects. Weiser is the drummer with rock band Severe Tire Damage, the first live band on the Internet.

Eva Wohlgemuth [A], born 1955 studied at the Academy of the Fine Arts in Vienna.

Marie-Hélène Tramus [F] Assistant Professor in Arts and Technologies of Image of the University of Paris 8, and Doctor in Aesthetics, Sciences and Technologies of Arts, has participated in the making of computer generated films and interactive installations.

Uli Winters [D], 1965, Arts degree from the Institute for Visual Arts in Hamburg. Constructs machines: dran denken maschine, sprengkasten, zeitkonserve, zumsel-trilogie, love-reminder® ...

Tom Wolfe [USA] has chronicled American popular culture for more than three decades. His best-selling books include *The Electric Kool-Aid Acid Test, The Right Stuff,* and *The Bonfire of the Vanities*. His new novel, due 1998, is set in Georgia.

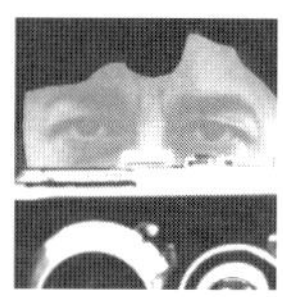

Adrianne Wortzel [USA] holds an MFA from the School of Visual Arts, New York. She is currently Adjunct Professor of Mechanical Engineering, Inventing the Inventor teaching at the Cooper Union for the Advancement of Science and Art.

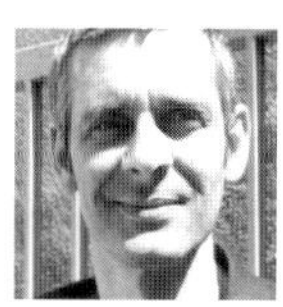

Horst Zachmann [A], 1958, currently an associate staff member of the Department of Electroacoustics at Vienna's Institute of Music, working on the research project "The Influence of Movement on the Design of Virtual Spaces." Extensive work in the field of electroacoustic music, sound sculptures and sound installations.

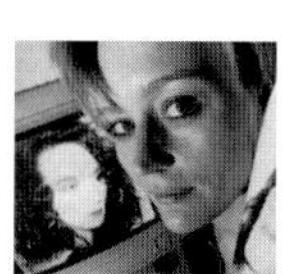

Andrea Zapp [D], 1964, she studied film theory, russian language and literature at the universities in Marburg and Moscow. After working at the Institute for Film and Image in Munich, she was programme director of the "Interactiva Festival" in Cologne in 1992 and 1993. Since 1995 she is lecturing at the Academy for Film and Television [HFF] in Potsdam-Babelsberg. She is focussing on the topic of narratives and storytelling, reflecting the transformation of traditional media elements into networked digital models of navigation and communicative environments.

BILDNACHWEIS/PHOTO CREDITS:
S. 48, 63
Lynn Randolph, Houston, Texas
S. 70
Dr. Hanna Damasio, Iowa
S. 84, 86, 89, 90, 93
Robert R. Birge, New York
S. 96
Paul Garrin
S. 109
x-space
S. 148, 149, 150, 153
Tony Figallo
S. 156
S. Hunter
S. 158, 161
Peter Fromherz
S. 200 - 205
Hiroshi Ishii, Boston, Mass.
S. 217, 226 - 228, 230 - 231
Steve Mann, Boston, Mass.
S. 311
Daniel Gerber
S. 335
x-space
S. 338
Daniel Canogar
S. 350
Jose A. Betancourt
S. 356
Art Tower Mito, Mito
S. 360, 361
E. Valette, Paris
S. 363
Tina Auer
S. 370, 375
Felix Nöbauer, Linz
S. 441/2: Becky Cohen, Encinitas, CA
S. 441/5: Felix Nöbauer, Linz
S. 443/2: ORF
S. 445/1: ORF
S. 446/1: Ars Electronica Center, Linz
S. 447/4: Rolf Schulten, Berlin